Dear West Customer:

West Academic Publishing has changed the look of its American Casebook Series®.

In keeping with our efforts to promote sustainability, we have replaced our former covers with book covers that are more environmentally friendly. Our casebooks will now be covered in a 100% renewable natural fiber. In addition, we have migrated to an ink supplier that favors vegetable-based materials, such as soy.

Using soy inks and natural fibers to print our textbooks reduces VOC emissions. Moreover, our primary paper supplier is certified by the Forest Stewardship Council, which is testament to our commitment to conservation and responsible business management.

The new cover design has migrated from the long-standing brown cover to a contemporary charcoal fabric cover with silver-stamped lettering and black accents. Please know that inside the cover, our books continue to provide the same trusted content that you've come to expect from West.

We've retained the ample margins that you have told us you appreciate in our texts while moving to a new, larger font, improving readability. We hope that you will find these books a pleasing addition to your bookshelf.

Another visible change is that you will no longer see the brand name Thomson West on our print products. With the recent merger of Thomson and Reuters, I am pleased to announce that books published under the West Academic Publishing imprint will once again display the West brand.

It will likely be several years before all of our casebooks are published with the new cover and interior design. We ask for your patience as the new covers are rolled out on new and revised books knowing that behind both the new and old covers, you will find the finest in legal education materials for teaching and learning.

Thank you for your continued patronage of the West brand, which is both rooted in history and forward looking towards future innovations in legal education. We invite you to be a part of our next evolution.

Best regards,

Louis H. Higgins
Editor in Chief, West Academic Publishing

CLIMATE CHANGE LAW
MITIGATION AND ADAPTATION

■ ■ ■

By

Richard G. Hildreth
Professor of Law and Director of the Ocean & Coastal
Law Center
Dean's Distinguished Faculty Fellow
University of Oregon School of Law

David R. Hodas
Professor of Law
Widener University School of Law

Nicholas A. Robinson
University Professor,
Gilbert & Sarah Kerlin Distinguished Professor
of Environmental Law
Pace University

James Gustave Speth
Carl W. Knobloch, Jr. Dean Emeritus,
Sara Shallenberger Brown Professor in the
Practice of Environmental Policy
School of Forestry & Environmental Studies,
Yale University

AMERICAN CASEBOOK SERIES®

WEST®

A Thomson Reuters business

Mat #40775873

© 2009 Thomson Reuters
  610 Opperman Drive
  St. Paul, MN 55123
  1–800–313–9378
Printed in the United States of America

ISBN: 978–0–314–19938–6

DEDICATIONS

Dick Hildreth dedicates his contributions to this book with love to Bob, Sue, Mary Jane, Mary Lou, Caroline, Ian, Emily, Martina, and Judy.

David Hodas dedicates this book to the next generation–Nathan, Jenn, Sam, Maria, and Libby, and all others who join the chain, and to Judy.

Nick Robinson dedicates this book's vision of a sustainable climate future to Cynthia, Tom, Julia, Eliza, Lucy, Andy, Justin, Quinn, Troy, and Shelley.

Gus Speth dedicates this book to the grandchildren, now Cameron, Rodgers and Lilla.

PREFACE

"But just as we've led the global economy in developing new sources of energy, we've also led in consuming energy. While we make up less than 5 percent of the world's population, we produce roughly a quarter of the world's demand for oil.

"And this appetite comes now at a tremendous cost to our economy. It's the cost measured by our trade deficit; 20 percent of what we spend on imports is the price of our oil imports. We send billions of dollars overseas to oil-exporting nations, and I think all of you know many of them are not our friends. It's the same costs attributable to our vulnerability to the volatility of oil markets. Every time the world oil market goes up, you're getting stuck at the pump. It's the cost we feel in shifting weather patterns that are already causing record-breaking droughts, unprecedented wildfires, more intense storms.

* * * "Now, the choice we face is not between saving our environment and saving our economy. The choice we face is between prosperity and decline. We can remain the world's leading importer of oil, or we can become the world's leading exporter of clean energy. We can allow climate change to wreak unnatural havoc across the landscape, or we can create jobs working to prevent its worst effects. We can hand over the jobs of the 21st century to our competitors, or we can confront what countries in Europe and Asia have already recognized as both a challenge and an opportunity: The nation that leads the world in creating new energy sources will be the nation that leads the 21st-century global economy."

President Barack H. Obama
Earth Day, April 22, 2009
Newton, Iowa

* * * * *

Humans have been altering the Earth since the dawn of the agricultural revolution. We accelerated the process with the industrial revolution. Our modern era has produce extraordinary technological innovations, such as in medicine, telecommunications, cybernetics, or ecological and Earth science. Our post-modern period brings us starkly to confront the issues that we only tangentially addressed while our human population grew rapidly.

Coping with the causes and effects of climate change requires every dimension of human endeavor to be rethought. Earth's climate envelops the web of life, and the law must facilitate and prod a searching reexamination of the technologies and behaviors now threatening it.

The study of the law of climate change also necessitates a new, and on-going, synthesis of legal experience. Just as all scientific disciplines have been called to contribute to the analysis and reports of the U.N. Intergovernmental Panel on Climate Change, so also every subject taught in law school will need to begin to incorporate a component of climate change law. President Obama's 2009 Earth Day address is an understatement. Our challenges are vast.

Climate change law is a new synthesis of several fields. Like *environmental law*, it is the result of painstaking scientific analysis about Earth's biosphere, including its climate. Like *law of securities and commodities*, it depends upon rigorous financial disclosures and verification systems, as a global market in trading carbon credits grows. Unlike traditional *energy law*, it eschews continued use of coal and other fossil fuels, and looks to maximize renewable energy systems; as wind, solar, kinetic, biologic and hydrologic energy regimes expand, new legal challenges will supplant the familiar energy law issues associated with carbon fuels. Sustainable energy law is a core theme in climate change law. Moreover, the fields of *international law* and *municipal law* alike are key to climate change law. Climate change presents issues both world-wide and local, and the solutions to reducing greenhouse gas emissions must be implemented locally as part of a global legal system of comparable efforts to stabilize climatic conditions.

Just as the field of *administrative law* underpins or affects almost every field of law practiced and taught, and yet retains its own core doctrines, so climate change law is today permeating all legal subjects.

In the chapters that follow, we have drawn on elements of energy law, environmental law, corporate law, the law of finance, taxation, property law, natural resources law, tort law, land use and zoning law, comparative and international law, administrative law and the law of individual human rights and evolving law of community environmental rights. These elements need to be aligned to advance the shared objectives to mitigate greenhouse gas emissions and to adapt to the changing conditions like sea level rise, migration of species or new risks to public health.

This book represents a new synthesis of these fields of law. **Chapter 1** examines the nature of the climate change phenomena and why society's "business as usual" attitudes will change, or be changed by, the effects of the altered climate. **Chapter 2** sets forth the scientific assessment of the scope and scale of the emerging climate crisis. **Chapter 3** presents the world-wide effort, through international law, to coordinate and harmonize the responses within all nations to protect the climate and biosphere, amidst change unprecedented in human existence. **Chapter 4** reviews the basic economics of climate change.

Chapter 5 focuses on the emerging law of sustainable energy regimes, a field that will mature and grow quickly. With **Chapter 6**, we arrive at the first core approach of climate change law: *mitigation*. Which legal tools can best be deployed world-wide to combat greenhouse gas emissions and eliminate or off-set them? **Chapter 7** examines the second core climate change element: *adaptation*. How can law be revised to encourage societies to try to adapt to the often radical impacts of new climactic conditions? In **Chapter 8** we return to applied economic considerations, deploying market regulation, securities law, insurance law and other economic legal tools to move socio-economic activity toward becoming carbon neutral. The question posed is whether these tools are adequate, or whether governments should revise the ground rules for corporate charters. **Chapter 9** points to future legal developments, some of them imminent. Delaware has a plan to become carbon neutral; how would you scale it up for a larger state or a nation? Congressional action on climate change legislation has begun and will continue energetically in the coming decade. China, the European Union, and others are enacting major reforms. The parties to the UN Framework Convention on Climate Change will be negotiating further ways to harmonize the laws of all nations to prevent deepening climate change.

We invite your critique of our new synthesis. Together, lawyers in every country are beginning to define the doctrines that will come to characterize Climate Change Law. Trade lawyers across the world know the rules of the game and follow a tradition that has evolved over scores of centuries. They constitute an *epistemic community*: experts who share common values and information and labor together as facilitate commerce across and within nations. The global medical profession is another epistemic community. The world's earth scientists have formed an epistemic community in the Intergovernmental Panel on Climate Change (IPCC), featured in Chapter 2. As a field, environmental law, hardly one generation old, still strives to become an epistemic community. Each of our schools is a member of the IUCN Academy of Environmental Law, a consortium of law schools and faculties world-wide (www.iucnael.org). The Academy is leading a global effort to build the capacity for climate change legal education around the world.

In order to address Earth's needs for climate change mitigation and adaptation, the law must be congruent and work in tandem across all legal systems and nations. Climate Change law cannot succeed until there are comparable epistemic communities in sustainable energy systems, carbon neutral economic tools, and environmental impact assessment and public participation procedures world-wide. This book modestly seeks to strengthen a global legal perspective on Earth's changing climate and biosphere.

As students and teachers and lawyers, we find it both challenging and exciting to offer an early synthesis of the law of climate change. As you practice law, you can advance the rapidly evolving synthesis of climate change law. You will need to engage with scientists, engineers and others as professional partners. The next IPPC review launched in 2009 raises questions of social science: how can legal regimes become congruent and equally strive to protect Earth's climate? Lawyers will adapt our legal systems to reflect what we learn from the ever more refined studies of the IPCC and others, and to incorporate engineering innovations and discoveries of "green" technologies.

We accepted West Publishing's invitation to prepare this casebook recognizing that the international and domestic legal regimes for mitigating climate change will be evolving for some time. The treatment throughout is both multi-disciplinary and scalar from the law applied in a village, to the state, national, regional and international levels. We are grateful to the scholars whose works we excerpt here, and we regret that space limitations precluded us from reprinting many equally important legal works. We shall reference and link to these on the Internet companion webpage accompanying this book.

The readings are provided as a platform for class discussion and each chapter's **Problem Exercises** are provided to facilitate further exploration. How quickly can the remedial objectives of climate change law be realized? You can answer the questions posed in each chapter about the "**carbon neutral law school**" to fashion your own answer to that question. Will this be fast enough to avert some of climate change's predicted "worst case" scenarios?

In addition to specific thanks and acknowledgements set forth below, we express our gratitude *Prof. Richard L. Ottinger,* who has laid a prodigious intellectual and legal foundation for building the new field of climate change law, both as a member of Congress and as a leader in sustainable energy law initiatives internationally through the International Union for the Conservation of Nature and Natural Resources (IUCN). In our two-year effort to develop this book, our Colleagues at the University of Oregon, Pace University School of Law, Widener University School of Law, and the Yale University School of Forestry and Environmental Studies, have been superb in their support of our editorial efforts. At **Oregon**, Dick Hildreth wishes to thank the School of Law for its long-standing support of his work in environmental and natural resources law, and now climate change law, in particular, administrative assistant Debby Warren, law librarian Andrea Coffman, and research assistant Alison Torbitt. At **Pace**, Nick Robinson echoes these thanks and commends the work of his staff assistant Karen Ferro, Leslie Crincoli, and Law Library Director Marie Newman and Associate Director Jack McNeil, Pace Environmental Law Program Director Alexandra Dunn, and among his research assistants especially thanks Sean Dixon and Jill Richardson for their sustained support. David Hodas wishes to thank at **Widener**, Dean Linda Ammons, Vice Dean R. Patrick Kelly, and Dean of Faculty Erin Daly for their support and encouragement of this project and environmental law (in its broadest sense) at the Law School, Associate Dean Michael Singer for providing the resources in support of the books webpage, webmaster Cassandra King, law librarian Janet Lindenmuth and research assistants Jonathan Spadea and Jennifer Weiler. Gus Speth at **Yale** is grateful for the support of his executive staff, and colleagues on the faculty, and especially for all who helped design and construct Kroon Hall at Yale, a model for the new generation of "green" academic buildings that minimize all their environmental impacts. Finally, we thank the staff of West Publishing for their patience and support throughout the preparation of this book.

As we prepared this book, we have come to appreciate the enormity of the global tasks ahead. Left to "normal" functioning of Earth's systems, it would take 1,000 years to reabsorb all carbon dioxide we have pumped into the atmosphere in the past 150 years. World-wide, we probably have only the time of *your generation* to re-engineer the energy systems around the planet, cease new emissions of greenhouse gases, and scrub "legacy" carbon dioxide out of the atmosphere. The less societies do to prevent climate disruption, the more they must retreat from coasts as sea levels rise and otherwise cope with the myriad of other climate change impacts.

Whatever fields of law students pursue after graduating from law school, you will inevitably practice and develop climate change law. We hope that this book may provide some initial legal foundation for these endeavors.

Dick Hildreth, David Hodas, Nick Robinson, Gus Speth

La Jolla, California, 2009

EDITOR'S NOTE

Most footnotes, references and citations are omitted from edited materials without indication. Back to back deletions from different paragraphs are shown with only one set of three (***) asterisks. Full texts may be accessed on our companion web site for this book.

CASEBOOK AND TEACHER'S MANUAL WEB SITES

The authors, in cooperation with Widener University School of Law, are pleased to maintain a website facilitating further research into the issues set forth in Climate Change Law: Mitigation & Adaptation. You will find hyperlinks to the source materials excerpted in the book, links to related sites, links to recent legal developments (such as new legislation, regulations, innovative local laws, and treaty decisions) and references for further study. Web links will be updated as required to facilitate efficient study associated with this book.

For professors, the Teacher's Manual is available from West in the traditional soft-cover form and on a password protected basis at http://exchange.westlaw.com/.

The   address   for   the   casebook   website   is: **http://blogs.law.widener.edu/climatechangelaw**

COPYRIGHT ACKNOWLEDGEMENTS

The authors gratefully acknowledge the individuals and institutions that each has granted permission to reprint excerpts from the following publications for which each holds a copyright, with all their rights reserved:

American Council for an Energy-Efficient Economy (ACEEE), et al, Reducing the Cost of Addressing Climate Change Through Energy Efficiency, (February 2009), //aceee.org/energy/climate/Reducing%20the%20Cost%20of%20Addressing%20Cl imate%20Change.pdf, Copyright by American Council for an Energy-Efficient Economy (ACEEE), et al 2009.

Agardy Ph.D., Tundi, An Ocean of Energy There for the Taking, World Ocean Observer Newsletter editor, September 12, 2008, Copyright by Tundi Agardy, Ph.D. 2008.

Avi-Yonah, Reuven S. and Uhlmann, David M., Combating Global Climate Change: Why A Carbon Tax Is A Better Response to Global Warming Than Cap and Trade, 28 Stanford Envtl. L. J. 3 (2009), Copyright by Reuven S. Avi-Yonah and David M. Uhlmann 2009.
Cleveland, Cutler (Lead Author); Robert Costanza (Topic Editor). 2007.
"Boulding, Kenneth Ewart." In: Encyclopedia of Earth. Eds. Cutler J.

Cleveland (Washington, D.C.: Environmental Information Coalition, National Council for Science and the Environment). [First published in the Encyclopedia of Earth June 16, 2006; Last revised July 24, 2007; Retrieved July 31, 2009]. http://www.eoearth.org/article/Boulding,_Kenneth_Ewart

Brawer, Judi and Vespa, Matthew, Thinking Globally, Acting Locally: The Role of Local Government in Minimizing Greenhouse Gas Emissions From New Development, 44 Idaho L. Rev. 589 (2008), Copyright by Idaho L. Rev., Judi Brawer and Matthew Vespa 2008.

Chu, Dr. Steven and Goldemberg, José, Lighting the Way: Toward A Sustainable Energy Future, www.interacademycouncil.net/cms/reports/11840.aspx (2007), Copyright by Dr. Steven Chu and José Goldemberg, Ph.D. 2007.

Congressional Budget Office, The Congress of the United States, The Economics of Climate Change: A Primer, April 2003, http://www.cbo.gov/doc.cfm?index=4171&type=0

Congressional Budget Office, The Congress of the United States, Potential Impacts of Climate Change in the United States, (May 2009), http://www.cbo.gov/ftpdocs/101xx/doc10107/05-04-ClimateChange_forWeb.pdf

Craig, David J., The Deep Sleep, Columbia, 14 (Fall 2008), Copyright by Columbia magazine 2008.

Craig, Robin K., Climate Change, Regulatory Fragmentation, and Water Triage, 79 U. Colo. L. Rev. (2008), Copyright by Robin Kundis Craig 2008 and reprinted with permission of the University of Colorado Law Review 2008.

Doelle, Meinhard, Climate Change and the Use of the Dispute Settlement Regime of the Law of the Sea Convention, 37 Ocean Devel. & Intl. L. 319 (2006), Copyright Meinhard Doelle 2006.

European Space Agency, Computer Generated Image of trackable objects in orbit around Earth, ESA Portal Multimedia Gallery, reproduced with permission.

Furrey, Laura, Nadel, Steven and Laitner, John A. "Skip", Laying the Foundation for Implementing a Federal Energy Efficiency Resource Standard, ACEEE Report Number E091, http://aceee.org (March 2009), Copyright by American Council for an Energy-Efficient Economy 2009.

Gerrard, Michael B., What the Law and Lawyers Can and Cannot Do About Global Warming, 16 Southeastern Envtl. L.J. 1 (2007), Copyright by Michael B. Gerrard 2007.

Glaser, P., et al., Global Warming Solutions Regulatory Challenges and Common Law Liabilities Associated with the Geologic Sequestration of Carbon Dioxide, 6 Geo. J. L. & Pub. Policy 429, 430-431, 437-446 (2008), Copyright by

Hodas, David R, State Law Responses to Global Warming: Is it Constitutional to Think Globally and Act Locally? 21 Pace Environmental Law Review 53 (2003), Copyright by David R. Hodas 2003.

Holdren, John P., Meeting the Climate-Change Challenge, Eight Annual John H. Chafee Memorial Lecture on Science and the Environment. Washington, D.C.: National Council for Science and the Environment, www.ncseonline.org/conference/chafee08final.pdf (2008), Copyright by National Council for Science & the Environment 2008.

Hoppock, David, Monast, Jonas, and Williams, Eric, Transforming Utility and Ratepayer Support for Electrical Energy Efficiency Nationwide, Climate Change Policy Partnership, Duke University (2008), http://www.nicholas.duke.edu/ccpp/ccpp_pdfs/ee%20web.pdf, Copyright by David Hoppock, Jonas Monast and Eric Williams of the Climate Change Policy Partnership at Duke University 2008.

IPCC, 2007: Summary for Policymakers. In: Climate Change 2007: The Physical Science Basis. Contribution of Working Group I to the Fourth Assessment Report of the Intergovernmental Panel on Climate Change [Solomon, S., D. Qin, M. Manning, Z. Chen, M. Marquis, K.B. Averyt, M.Tignor and H.L. Miller (eds.)]. Cambridge University Press, Cambridge, United Kingdom and New York, NY, USA.

Jones, Robert E. and Kim, Margret J., China: Climate Change Superpower and the Clean Technology Revolution, published in Natural Resources & Environment, Volume 22, Number 3, Winter 2008. © 2008 by the American Bar Association. Reproduced with permission. All rights reserved. This information or any portion thereof may not be copied or disseminated in any form or by any means or stored in an electronic database or retrieval system without the express written consent of the American Bar Association.

Kostyack, John and Rohlf, Daniel, Conserving Endangered Species in an Era of Global Warming, 38 Environmental Law Reporter 10203 (2008), Copyright by John Kostyack and Daniel Rohlf 2008 and The Environmental Law Reporter 2008.

Kuhn, Thomas S., The Structure of Scientific Revolutions, The University of Chicago Press (1996), Copyright by the University of Chicago Press 1996, Reproduced with permission.

Kurukulasuriya, L. and Robinson, N.A. (eds.), Training Manual on International Environmental Law (2006), Copyright United Nations Environment Programme, 2006, Reproduced with permission.

Lee, Henry, Clark, William C. and Devereaux, Charan. 2008. Biofuels and Sustainable Development: Report of An Executive Session on the Grand Challenges of a Sustainability Transition, San Servolo Island, Venice, Italy: May 19-20, 2008. (Sustainability Science Program, Center for International Development, Harvard University). www.cid.harvard.edu/sustsci, reproduced with permission.

Lewis, Nathan S., Powering the Planet, 11 Engineering & Science 2 (2007), Copyright by Nathan S. Lewis 2007.

Mann, Roberta F., To Tax or Not to Tax Carbon—Is That the Question? Natural Resources & Environment 44 (Summer 2009), Copyright by Roberta Mann 2009.

McFarland, Jeffrey M., Warming Up to Climate Change Risk Disclosure, 14 Fordham J. of Corp. & Fin. L. 281 (2009), Copyright by Jeffrey M. McFarland 2008.

Narain, Sunita, Down to Earth – Editorial: Who's Afraid of 2 degrees Centigrade?, Centre for Science and Environment, India, CSE's Fortnightly Bulletin (August 24, 2009), www.cseindia.org.

National Aeronautics and Space Administration (NASA), Photographs "Earth," "Sun light reflected from Earth", and computer generated image of "Earth At Night" (C. Mayhew and R. Simmon, NASA/GSFC. DMSP)

Nolon, John R., Shifting Ground to Address Climate Change: The Land Use Law Solution, 10 Gov't., L. and Policy J. 23 (2008), Reprinted with permission from: Government, Law and Policy Journal, Summer 2008, Vol. 10, No. 1, published by the New York State Bar Association, One Elk Street, Albany, NY 12207.

Nordhaus, William D., Keynote Address at Climate Change: Global Risks, Challenges, and Decisions, Copenhagen, Denmark, (March 10-12, 2009), http://climatecongress.ku.dk/speakers/professorwilliamnordhaus-plenaryspeaker-11march2009.pdf/, Copyright by William D. Nordhaus 2009

Ottinger, Richard L., UNEP Handbook on Drafting Laws on Energy Efficiency and Renewable Energy Resources 1-14 (2007), Copyright by Richard L. Ottinger 2007.

Pacala, Steven and Socolow, Robert, Stabilization Wedges: Solving the Climate Problem for the Next 50 Years with Current Technologies, 305 Science 968 (2004). Copyright 2004.

Peterson, Thomas D., McKinstry Jr., Robert B., Dernbach, John C., Developing A Comprehensive Approach to Climate Change Policy in the United States that Fully Integrates Levels of Government and Economic Sectors, 26 U. Virginia Envtl. L. Rev. 227 (2008), Copyright by John C. Dernbach 2008, Copyright by Virginia Environmental Law Journal 2008.

Repetto, Robert, The Climate Crisis and the Adaptation Myth, www.yale.edu/environmment/publications (2008)

Robinson, Nicholas A., Energy Law and Sustainable Development, (IUCN 2003), Nicholas A. Robinson, Foreword to Bradbrook and Ottinger, Copyright by Nicholas A. Robinson 2003.

CLIMATE CHANGE LAW: MITIGATION AND ADAPTATION
Hildreth, Hodas, Robinson, Speth

SUMMARY OF CONTENTS

TABLE OF CONTENTS

CHAPTER 1. INTRODUCING CLIMATE CHANGE

CHAPTER 6. MITIGATING CLIMATE CHANGE

TABLE OF CASES

CLIMATE CHANGE LAW
MITIGATION AND ADAPTATION

*

CHAPTER 1. INTRODUCING CLIMATE CHANGE

Climatescape: **A Climate for Change?**

Setting the stage for studying the myriad of legal issues of climate change, Chapter 1 proposes that the climate cannot be disaggregated from the rest of Earth's Biosphere. Scientists have long known that the human economy was loading the atmosphere with new volumes of carbon dioxide and other greenhouse gases. How did society's reliance on a "business as usual" approach to industrialization blind policy makers to the growing impacts of climate disruption? Will our global society accommodate and adjust to the effects of an altered climate as we are to pollution, urbanization, or other aspects of economic growth? As John Holdren, or Dr. Steven Chu and José Goldemberg make plain, our current laws and technological innovations are inadequate to cope with what is now understood about the scale and scope of anthropogenic changes to Earth's climate. The U.S. House of Representatives has reported major climate impacts for the USA; what type of legislation should Congress enact? Why is the U.S. or other governments not deploying the available technologies to abate climate change, as Steven Pacala and Robert Socolow have shown can be done? Even if greenhouse gas emissions are controlled, as Gus Speth and Peter Haas explain, will such controls be enough? Why has environmental law failed to align human conduct with "the laws of nature"? Can litigation in the courts of one nation, or legislation within a single nation, provide the means to restore stability to Earth's climate? If climate disruption raises new questions of security, will the defense budgets be aligned behind climate change mitigation, or be spent on military responses to crises? Are we all at the cusp of a new world view, a revolution in scientific understanding of conditions on Earth that all humans will come to recognize? If so, what changes in each country will be required? To pursue a global approach, nations have adopted **"The Bali Action Plan"** to guide *mitigation* of all greenhouse gases, and *adaptation* to the new conditions that climate change is producing on Earth. The question: will this be enough to sustain the biosphere? Do you, and your law school, have a stake in this?

A. ENVISIONING THE BIOSPHERE AND ITS CLIMATE

All the systems that sustain life on Earth constitute the "biosphere." Humans have called this realm "nature," our natural home, our source of food and fuel. The sun provides the energy for Earth's living systems. Life evolved on Earth drawing upon the sun's energy, storing it in plants, minerals and animals. The ozone molecules of the stratosphere protect life from the extreme ultraviolet rays of the sun, and the concentration of carbon dioxide, and other "greenhouse gases," in the atmosphere absorb solar energy to warm the climate to levels within which life can thrive. As humans learned to draw

upon Earth's natural endowments they produced the rich array of civilizations and cultures that we know today and historically.

Recent advances in science and technology allow humans to craft models
of the Earth's workings and how its natural cycles function. The study of
Earth's climate relies in part on satellites and the data they produce for scientific analysis. However, humans are slower to reshape their behavioral
patterns in light of what the sciences describe. We use space to study Earth,
but we also misuse space. Humans have learned to penetrate beyond the biosphere, littering orbital space with 3,270 satellites, only 950 of which function
today. Humans are imposing their social order on the orbital space near the
Earth. P. Dickens & J. Ormrod, Cosmic Society, Towards a Sociology of the
Universe (2008). On February 10, 2009, an obsolete Russian Kosmos 2251
military satellite collided with Iridium 33, a commercial US communications
satellite, producing 600 pieces of debris. Orbital junk from this collision and
other can threaten the satellite sensing which is needed in order to gather
data to evaluate climate change.

Astronauts' photographs make plain the beauty and singularity of the
biosphere and its source of energy, the sun. Oceans and clouds dominate the
view of Earth from space. The hydrologic cycle is driven by solar energy, distributing water across the planet, and contributing to Earth's "climate." With
the assistance of computer generated images, humans can envision their impacts on the planet as they consume the energy stored in fossil fuels.

Satellites make possible analysis and visioning how oceans absorb and release heat from solar radiation, or the decline of glaciers and polar ice cover,
or the extent of deforestation. The appetite of the growing human population
for energy is illustrated by the image of Earth's cities at night without clouds.
Our uncoordinated littering and consumption of orbital space is plain in the
European Space Agency's computer-generated image of trackable objects in
orbit (the deserts of the Arabian Peninsula appear in the upper left of Earth's
image).

These photographs set the stage for exploring the policy, legal, scientific
and technical decision-making about climate change. Human societies are
grounded in different geographies and settings, but Earth's atmosphere is a
"commons." How can humans safeguard Earth's climate? What would be the
implications for international cooperation and economic and social development, if the law mandated that "Nature shall be respected and its essential
processes shall not be impaired." World Charter for Nature, Para 1, UNGA
Res. 37/7 (1982). Since all life depends on Earth's natural cycles, how might
law effectively advance this norm?

These photographs do not show the borders of any political subdivisions
that humans have established on the surface of the Earth, or whose energy

fingerprints appear on any object in orbital space. As you study these images, what do **you** envision? What measures must village councils, national parliaments, administrative agencies, commercial enterprises, farmers, builders of housing and urban planners, lawyers, bankers, or human families and individuals undertake in order to stabilize "greenhouse gas concentrations in the atmosphere at a level that would prevent dangerous anthropogenic interference with the climate system." How can formal legislation and legal custom ensure that greenhouse gases will be scrubbed out of the atmosphere fast enough to prevent dangerous climatic disruptions, "within a timeframe sufficient to allow ecosystems to adapt naturally to climate change, to ensure that food production is not threatened and to enable economic development to proceed in a sustainable manner." Article 2, "Objective," 1992 United Nations Framework Convention on Climate Change (UNFCCC), excerpted in Chapter 3.

Earth (NASA photograph)
The Biosphere

Within Earth's biosphere, the atmosphere occupies a relatively small space. In proportion to the scale of the photograph above, the atmosphere has less width than does this page on which this photograph of the Earth is printed. The climate is the complex system that distributes the heat from the sun, and water vapor and gases, throughout the atmosphere, interacting with the oceans and the lands. In old geography, the "climate" was deemed to be one of 30 zones into which the surface of the Earth was divided from the equator to each pole. Today with the benefit of monitoring by satellites and modeling by computers, scientists study Earth's global climate. Humans "see" the Earth's biosphere as was never possible in the past. At the same time, humans have begun to fill orbital space with a volume of waste and space junk threatening both satellites and the space station with collisions, as the computer generated image on the next page indicates. We depend on these satellites to monitor climate change.

Solar energy and the sun reflected from Earth

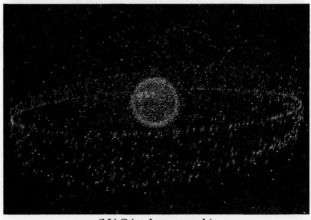

(NASA photograph)

Computer-generated image of trackable objects in orbit around Earth (The Middle East can just be made out in the top left of the globe) European Space Agency Image

Earth at Night
Credit: C. Mayhew & R. Simmon (NASA/GSFC), NOAA/NGDC, DMSP Digital Archive

B. THE PROBLEM OF CLIMATE DISRUPTION

MEETING THE CLIMATE-CHANGE CHALLENGE
John P. Holdren
www.ncseonline.org/conference/chafee08final.pdf (2008)

"The Main Messages"

* * * The first of these messages is that I think we in the scientific community have made a mistake by allowing the term "global warming" to capture the podium, the platform, the title of this problem. Global warming is a misnomer, because it implies something that is gradual, something that is uniform, something that is quite possibly benign. What we are experiencing with climate change is none of those things. It is certainly not uniform. It is rapid compared to the pace at which social systems and environmental systems can adjust. It is certainly not benign. We should be calling it "global climatic disruption" rather than "global warming."

The second key point is that the disruption and its impacts are now growing much more rapidly than almost anybody expected even a few years ago. The result of that, in my view, is that the world is already experiencing "dangerous anthropogenic interference in the climate system." Many of you will recognize that term in quotes as part of the text of the United Nations Framework Convention on Climate Change, which was signed by the senior President Bush in 1992 and subsequently ratified by the United States and 190 other nations. That Convention embodies the goal of avoiding dangerous anthropogenic interference in the climate system, and it is my contention that that goal is already out of reach. We are experiencing dangerous anthropogenic interference by any reasonable definition today. The question now is whether we can avoid catastrophic human interference in the climate system.

Our options in this domain are three. They are mitigation, adaptation, and suffering. Basically, if we do less mitigation and adaptation, we're going to do a lot more suffering.

In mitigation and adaptation, there's a lot of low-hanging fruit— measures that are inexpensive, measures that offer substantial co-benefits, measures that would be worth taking even if we were weren't worried about climate change—but it's not enough. We need a price on greenhouse gas emissions in order to motivate reaching higher into the tree, and we need research and development to bring more fruit into reach. * * *

Mitigation means measures taken to reduce the pace and the magnitude of the changes in global climate we're causing. Adaptation means measures taken to reduce the adverse impacts on well-being that result from the changes that do occur. And suffering, of course, is the third option—suffering the adverse impacts that we fail to avoid by either mitigation or adaptation.

It's crucial to understand that we're already doing some of each. We're doing some mitigation, we're doing some adaptation, we're doing some suffering. What's up for grabs, depending on what steps we take, is the future mix of those three. And minimizing the amount of suffering in that mix can only be achieved by doing a lot of mitigation *and* a lot of adaptation. Mitigation alone won't work, because climate change is already occurring, and nothing we can do can stop it quickly.

But adaptation alone won't work, because adaptation gets costlier and less effective as the climatic changes to which one is trying to adapt get bigger. We need enough mitigation to avoid unmanageable climate change, and enough adaptation to manage the climate change that is unavoidable. * * *

* * * The question now is can we avoid climate catastrophe? In that connection we need to understand that the average global surface temperature— that sensitive index of the state of the climate that's gone up about 0.8°C since the beginning of the last century—would rise something like 0.5°C more (reaching 1.3° or 1.4°C above the 1900 level) even if the concentrations could be stabilized instantaneously where they are today. The reason for that is the thermal lag of the oceans. The oceans have a huge heat capacity, and it takes them a long time to catch up with changes you've imposed on the radiation balance of the atmosphere.

The chance of crossing a tipping point into truly catastrophic climatic change appears to grow rapidly, moreover, for increases in the average surface temperature of more than about 2°C above the 1900 level. This, combined with studies of the magnitude of the effort required to stabilize the climate, suggests that limiting the increase to less than 2°C is the most prudent target that might still be attainable. One can name more prudent targets, but most analysts think it unlikely that we can attain a target more demanding than this. And if we miss 2°C but manage to stop at 2.5°C, that at least would give better odds of avoiding catastrophe than 3°C, which a few years ago many people were saying might be an acceptable target. It doesn't look very good given what we know now.

Some key realities about mitigation tell us how big the challenge really is. *First*, the human caused carbon dioxide emissions are the biggest piece of the problem. They're about half of it, and their share is growing. About three-quarters of that carbon dioxide comes from burning oil, coal, and natural gas, and those energy sources are 80 percent of the energy supply of the world today. The remaining quarter comes from deforestation and burning in the tropics. And while 60 percent of the fossil CO_2 came from industrialized countries in 2006, the developing countries are going to dominate within a few years. Thus mitigation has to happen everywhere.

The global energy system unfortunately cannot be changed quickly. We've invested about $15 trillion in the energy-supply system we've got. That's the replacement cost of all the power plants, refineries, transmission lines, drilling rigs, and other energy-supply infrastructure in the world. That investment ordinarily turns over in about 40 years. If you want the energy system in 2050 to look a lot different than the way it looks today, you have to start changing it now. And deforestation—the other fourth of the CO_2 problem—is also not easy to change. The forces driving deforestation in the tropics are deeply embedded in the economics of food, fuel, timber, trade, and development. We can stop it, but it won't be easy. * * *

There are some more realities about mitigation that need to be faced. First, in applying the more costly solutions, the industrialized nations are going to have to go first. We're going to have to pay more of the upfront costs, offering assistance in this to developing countries. That's a matter of historical responsibility. It's a matter of capacity. It's a matter of equity. And it's a matter of international law under the Framework Convention on Climate Change.

Second, developing countries are going to have to be compensated for reducing and avoiding deforestation. Without additional incentives not to cut down tropical forests, essentially all of them will disappear in this century. The impact of that on atmospheric CO_2 would put stabilizing at 450 parts per million or even 550 parts per million out of reach. (It would also have a staggering impact on global biodiversity.)

The *third* reality is that, without a formal and binding global agreement on the allocation of emissions after 2012, the needed degree of reductions will not be achieved. The job is just not going to get done by the actions of individual countries in the absence of a global agreement. I believe the best basis for such an agreement in the short term is probably reduction in emissions intensity—that is, countries agree to reduce the ratio of greenhouse gas emissions to gross domestic product at a particular rate. In the longer run, I believe the only politically acceptable basis for a global agreement will be equal per-capita emissions rights, which means people who are emitting above the allowable global average will have to pay people who are emitting below the allowable global average for their emissions permits.

REPORT, AMERICAN CLEAN ENERGY AND SECURITY ACT OF 2009 [H.R. 2454]
Committee on Energy and Commerce, U.S. House of Representatives, 111TH Cong. Rept. No. 111–137 (June 5, 2009)

THE IMPACTS OF CLIMATE CHANGE

The current and anticipated impacts of climate change have been increasingly well documented in the scientific literature. These impacts include effects on water scarcity and quality, the Arctic and Antarctic, warming and acidification of the world's oceans, sea level rise and coastal impacts, extreme weather events, public health, forests and wildfires, wildlife and endangered species, and national security.

INCREASING WATER SCARCITY AND DECLINING WATER QUALITY

One of the most dramatic impacts of global warming in the 21st century will be the exacerbation of already severe water scarcity—both in the United States and abroad. Freshwater scarcity and threats to water quality are increasing dramatically both in the United States and across the world. More than a billion people currently lack access to safe drinking water. By 2025, 1.8 billion people are expected to be living in regions experiencing water scarcity and "two-thirds of the world's population could be living under water stressed conditions." Climate change will greatly exacerbate current and future water stress. For example, the IPCC projects that by 2020, between 75 and 250 million people in Africa alone will experience an increase of water stress due to climate change. For Asia, the number is between 120 million and 1.2 billion people, and for Latin American it is 12 to 81 million.

Global warming is leading to rapid melting of land ice, glaciers, ice caps, and snow fields which over time will exacerbate water scarcity in many regions of the globe. One-sixth of the world population currently relies on meltwater from glaciers and snow cover for drinking water and irrigation for agriculture. The IPCC's 2008 Climate Change and Water report projects widespread reductions in snow cover throughout the 21st Century, and a 60 percent volume loss in glaciers in various regions. The melting of these ice reservoirs, which store 75 percent of the world's freshwater, will exacerbate water scarcity conditions. While melting will temporarily increase freshwater supply, more winter precipitation falling as rain rather than snow, and an earlier snowmelt season will deplete frozen freshwater reserves.

Increased water stress due to climate change will disproportionately affect the dry tropics and dry regions at lower mid-latitudes—notably Southeast Asia, southern Africa, Brazil, and the American Southwest. According to the 2008 IPCC Climate Change and Water Report, semi-arid and arid areas in Southeast Asia, Southern Africa, Brazil, and the western United States are "projected to suffer a decrease of water resources due to climate change." In Asia, decreasing precipitation and rising temperatures result in increasing frequency and intensity of droughts. In northwestern China and Mongolia, snow and glacier melt will cause floods in the spring in the near term but result in freshwater shortages by the end of the century. Global warming of 5.4 °F to 7.2 °F may result in more persistent El Niño conditions that would shift the Amazon rainforest from "tropical forest to dry savannah"—imperiling an ecosystem that sustains thousands of people and is one of the greatest concentrations of biodiversity on Earth.

The United States is already experiencing water stress, which will worsen severely in the coming decades due to climate change. In the American West, the Sierra Nevada snowpack is at its lowest level in 20 years and threatens most of the water supply to Northern California. Experts warn that "even the most optimistic climate models for the second half of this century suggest that 30 to 70 percent of this snowpack will disappear." The Southwest is already experiencing a severely reduced flow in the Colorado River—upon which 30 million people depend for water—as a consequence to decreasing snowmelt from the Rocky Mountains. The Midwest is expected to experience "drought-like conditions resulting from elevated temperatures, which increases levels of evaporation, contributing to decreases in soil moisture and reductions in lake and river beds" as a result of climate change. In addition to a range of other costs, agriculture in the Great Plains and the Southwest is likely to suffer massive economic losses due to increasing water scarcity. A recent study led by NOAA [National Oceanic and Atmospheric Administration] found that if CO_2 is allowed to peak above 450 parts per million, the impacts would include "irreversible dry season rainfall reductions . . . comparable to those of the 'dust bowl' era" in the southwestern U.S.

Climate change will also negatively impact the quality of freshwater resources. For example, reduced flows will reduce rivers' ability to dilute effluent, leading to increased pathogen or chemical loading. In addition, increased heavy precipitation events due to climate change—discussed below—

"may increase the total microbial load in watercourses and drinking-water reservoirs." And warmer water temperature combined with higher phosphorus concentrations will increase the occurrence of freshwater algal blooms, with adverse impacts on freshwater ecosystems and fisheries. Fish habitat may also be compromised because altered water chemistry will promote the intrusion of invasive species. These impacts will exacerbate the precarious state of freshwater fish species in North America, nearly 40 percent of which are already at risk.

IMPACTS ON THE ARCTIC AND ANTARCTIC

The Arctic is one of the hotspots of global warming. Over the past 50 years average temperatures in the Arctic have increased as much as 7 °F, five times the global average. In the next 100 years, some areas in the Arctic may see an increase in average temperatures as high as 13 °F.

As temperatures rise in the Arctic, sea ice and glaciers are melting at an unprecedented and alarming rate. In 2007, a record 386,000 square miles of Arctic sea ice melted away, an area larger than Texas and Arizona combined and as big a decline in one year as has occurred over the last decade. In 2008, the sea ice extent was only slightly greater than in 2007, but the sea ice volume is likely the lowest on record due to the decline in multiyear old ice and the thinness of the remaining ice. Recent observations suggest that Arctic sea ice could completely disappear during the summer as early as 2020.

The Greenland ice sheet is melting at an alarming rate. Between 1979 and 2002, the extent of melting in Greenland has increased on average by 16 percent—an area roughly the size of Sweden. In the record-breaking year of 2005, parts of Greenland melted that have never melted during the 27-year-long satellite record.

A complete melting of Greenland would result in a rise in global sea level of more than 20 feet, with catastrophic consequences for coastal regions around the world. Furthermore, melting Arctic glaciers would contribute large amounts of fresh water into the ocean, potentially changing oceanic currents, damaging eco-systems and altering current weather conditions.

At the opposite end of world, massive amounts of water are stored in the two ice sheets of Antarctica. The larger East Antarctic ice sheet covers the majority of the continent, while the West Antarctic ice sheet has significant ice shelves partially floating in the ocean. In the spring of 2002, scientists were shocked to discover that an ice shelf the size of Rhode Island had disintegrated from the West Antarctica ice sheet in just over a month, rather than the millennium previously assumed. Until recently, it was believed that only coastal areas of the West Antarctic were vulnerable to melting. Satellite analysis has now revealed that large inland regions are also showing signs of the impacts of warming. NASA and university researchers have found clear evidence that an area the size of California melted in January 2005 in response to warm temperatures.

WARMING AND ACIDIFICATION OF THE WORLD'S OCEANS

The world's oceans will suffer devastating impacts as a result of global climate change. The oceans are already warming due to climate change. The oceans cover 70 percent of the Earth's surface and are critical components of the climate system for redistributing heat around the world and absorbing CO_2 from the atmosphere. According to the IPCC, global ocean temperature has risen by 0.18° F from 1961 to 2003. Since the ocean has a heat capacity 1,000 times greater than that of the atmosphere, it has taken up 20 times more heat than the atmosphere during this same period. As a result of the ocean's relatively large heat capacity, it has a great effect on the Earth's heat balance and how energy from solar radiation is distributed throughout the global environment.

Increasing atmospheric CO_2 concentrations are causing acidification of the oceans. Elevated atmospheric CO_2 concentrations lead to higher absorption of CO_2 into the upper ocean, which makes the surface waters more acidic and reduces the concentration of carbonate ions. According to the National Oceanic and Atmospheric Administration (NOAA), ocean chemistry currently is changing at least 100 times more rapidly than it has changed during the 650,000 years preceding our industrial era. If current emission trends continue, the ocean will experience acidification to an extent and at rates that have not occurred for tens of millions of years. Ocean acidification has serious implications for the calcification rates of organisms living at all levels within the global ocean, from corals to zooplankton that serve as the foundation of many ocean food chains. According to NOAA, when dissolved carbon dioxide was increased to two times pre-industrial levels, a decrease in the calcification rate by 5 to 50 percent was observed.

Warming and acidification of ocean waters due to climate change are contributing to the collapse of coral reefs around the globe. Coral reefs are habitat for about a quarter of marine species, are the most diverse among marine ecosystems, and are already in a state of decline. Recent studies indicate that more than a third of all coral species are already endangered. When key temperature thresholds are exceeded, mass bleaching and complete coral mortality often result. By mid-century, these temperature thresholds are expected to be exceeded on an annual or bi-annual basis for the majority of reefs worldwide. After bleaching, algae quickly colonize dead corals and may make future coral growth and restoration more difficult. Other factors that influence the health of reefs are impacted by climate change, including sea level rise, storm severity and dust and mineral aerosols. These, together with non-climate factors such as over-fishing, invasion of non-native species, pollution, and increased nutrient and sediment loads, add multiple stresses, increasing coral reefs' vulnerability to climate change. Corals could become rare on tropical and subtropical reefs by 2050 due to the combined effects of acidification and increasing frequency of extreme temperature events that cause bleaching. * * *

Climate change threatens global fisheries. Warmer water and acidification not only harm coral reefs that function as fish hatcheries, but could also change the circulation of the world's ocean currents. Most fish species have a fairly narrow range of optimum temperatures due to temperature effects on their basic metabolism and the availability of food sources that have their own optimum temperature ranges. A given species' geographic range may expand, shrink, or be relocated with changes in ocean conditions caused by climate change. The United Nations Environment Programme found that "climate change may slow down ocean thermohaline circulation crucial to coastal water quality and nutrient cycling in more than 75 percent of the world's fishing grounds." Less hospitable waters would have a significant effect on the global fishing industry. In the United States alone, commercial and recreational fisheries contribute $60 billion to the economy each year and employ more than 500,000 people.

SEA LEVEL RISE AND COASTAL IMPACTS

Sea levels are already rising, and are predicted to rise by at least 1–2 feet by 2100—with the potential for a nearly 40-foot rise in sea level if the Greenland and West Antarctica ice sheets were to melt completely. The IPCC predicts that sea levels will rise by 8 to 24 inches above current levels by 2100, primarily due to thermal expansion from rising ocean temperatures 166—with current emissions trends more consistent with the higher end of this range. However, how much and how quickly the polar ice sheets will melt in response to global warming is a critical question. Many scientists are increasingly concerned that the Greenland and West Antarctic ice sheets are melting at a greater rate than previously predicted. Because scientists do not fully understand the dynamics of ice sheet melting, the IPCC found that larger values of sea level rise could not be excluded. A complete melting of the Greenland ice sheet alone would cause a 20-foot rise in sea level, and complete melting of the West Antarctic ice sheet would cause a 16-foot sea level rise.

Sea level rise will have severe impacts on the world's coastal populations, including in the United States. Rising sea levels are already causing inundation of low-lying lands, erosion of wetlands and beaches, exacerbation of storm surges and flooding, and increases in the salinity of coastal estuaries and aquifers. The most dramatic near-term effects of sea level rise are being felt by inhabitants of small island states, the very existence of which is now endangered. Further, about one billion people live in areas within feet elevation of today's sea level, including many U.S. cities on the East Coast and Gulf of Mexico, almost all of Bangladesh, and areas occupied by more than 250 million people in China. In total, more than 70 percent of the world's population lives on coastal plains, and 11 of the world's 15 largest cities are on the coast.

In addition, rising sea level due to climate change will threaten drinking water supplies in coastal areas—causing intrusion of saltwater into both surface water and ground water. If sea level rise pushes salty water further upstream, existing water intakes might draw on salty water during dry periods. The freshwater Everglades currently recharge Florida's Biscayne aquifer, the primary water supply to the most populous counties in South Florida, including the cities of Miami and Fort Lauderdale. As rising water levels submerge low-lying portions of the Everglades, portions of the aquifer would become saline. Aquifers in New Jersey east of Philadelphia are recharged by the Delaware River which also may become saline in parts in the future, leading to a degradation of drinking water quality.

EXTREME WEATHER EVENTS

Global warming has already changed the intensity, duration, frequency, and geographic range of a variety of weather patterns and will continue to do so—with potentially severe impacts on the United States and the world. There is a broad scientific consensus that the United States is vulnerable to weather hazards that will be exacerbated by climate change. The cost of damages from weather disasters has increased markedly from the 1980s, rising to more than 100 billion dollars in 2007. In addition to a rise in total cost, the frequency of weather disasters costing more than one billion dollars has increased.

Global warming will lead to more extreme precipitation events and flooding. The IPCC has found that "[t]he frequency of heavy precipitation events has increased over most land areas, consistent with warming and observed increases of atmospheric water vapor." The U.S. Climate Change Science Program has concluded that heavy precipitation events averaged over North America have increased over the past 50 years. * * *

Severe thunderstorms, hail, tornados, and winter storms may also increase. The current observational record for these smaller scale storms is insufficient to determine whether there are trends correlated to warming temperatures. However, these phenomena are often associated with heavy precipitation events and hurricanes; as the latter storms become more frequent and possibly increase in intensity, then the probability of thunderstorms, hail, and tornadoes should also increase. Warming temperatures may also expand the range over which tornados occur. Over the last few years, tornados have occurred earlier in the year and further north than what is typically thought of as "tornado alley." Finally, strong cold season storms are also likely to become more frequent, with stronger winds and more extreme wave heights.

PUBLIC HEALTH

There is a broad consensus among experts within the worldwide public health community that climate change poses a serious risk to public health. The IPCC's Fourth Assessment report concluded that climate change's likely impacts on public health include:

- More frequent and more intense heat waves, leading to marked short-term increases in mortality.
- Increased numbers of people suffering from death, disease, and injury from floods, storms, fires and droughts.
- Increased cardio-respiratory morbidity and mortality associated with ground-level ozone pollution.
- Changes in the range of some infectious disease vectors.
- Increased malnutrition and consequent disorders, including those relating to child growth and development. * * *

There is consensus that heat waves "have become more frequent over most land areas" and there is confidence that climate change will result in the "very likely increase in frequency of hot extremes." There is evidence that present day heat waves over Europe and North America "coincide with a specific atmospheric circulation pattern that is intensified by ongoing increases in greenhouse gasses." The intensity, duration and frequency of heat waves will increase in western and southern regions of the United States and in the Mediterranean region. Other areas not currently as susceptible, such as northwest North America, France, Germany, and the Balkans will also experience "increased heat wave severity in the 21st century." With continued warming by 2100, Washington, D.C. will experience the temperatures that Houston does today, Denver will be as warm as Memphis is today, and Anchorage will be as warm as New York City is today. The populations most at risk of dying in a heat wave are the elderly and people in underserved communities, and as growth in the U.S. population over the age of 65 coincides with warmer temperatures, more deaths can be anticipated.

Global warming will exacerbate ground-level ozone pollution, leading to substantial increases in deaths and respiratory illness. The ozone forming reaction occurs at a higher rate with more intense sunlight and higher temperatures. Thus, as temperatures rise from global warming, ground level ozone is expected to increase. Ozone is a known public health threat that can damage lung tissue causing respiratory illness, and exacerbate pre-existing respiratory conditions. The IPCC predicts increased levels of ozone across the eastern United States, "with the cities most polluted today experiencing the greatest increase in ozone pollution." The increase in temperature in urban areas specifically and increases in ozone can increase rates of cardiovascular and pulmonary illnesses as well as temperature-related morbidity and mortality for children and the elderly. Similar impacts will be felt in urban areas around the globe. By mid-century, ozone related deaths from climate change are predicted to increase by approximately 4.5 percent from the 1990s levels. Even modest exposure to ozone may encourage the development of asthma in children. Recently, an analysis linking CO_2 emissions to mortality revealed that for each increase of 1.8 °F caused by CO_2, the resulting air pollution would lead annually to about a thousand additional deaths and many more cases of respiratory illness and asthma in the United States. * * *

FORESTS AND WILDFIRES

The clearing and degradation of tropical forests is a major driver of global climate change. Forests cover about 30 percent of the Earth's land surface and hold almost half of the world's terrestrial carbon. They can act both as a source of carbon emissions to the atmosphere when cut, burned, or otherwise degraded and as a sink when they grow, removing carbon dioxide from the air through photosynthesis.

Since the 1950s, greenhouse gas emissions from land use change, including deforestation and degradation, have been significant, on the order of 20 to 50 percent of fossil fuel emissions. Deforestation and degradation currently account for 20 to 25 percent of global anthropogenic greenhouse gas emissions, roughly equivalent to the total fossil fuel emissions from the United States. These emissions come predominantly from deforestation of tropical rainforests.

Tropical forests play an especially crucial role. When forests are destroyed by fire, much of the carbon they store returns to the atmosphere, enhancing global warming. When a forest is cleared for crop or grazing land, the soils can become a large source of global warming emissions, depending on how farmers and ranchers manage the land. In places such as Indonesia, the soils of swampy lowland forests are rich in partially decayed organic matter, known as peat. During extended droughts, such as during El Niño events, the forests and the peat become flammable, especially if they have been degraded by logging or accidental fire. When they burn, they release huge volumes of CO_2 and other greenhouse gases. * * *

Global warming is also exacerbating insect infestations (most notably bark beetles), which in turn make forests more susceptible to wildfire. Drought stress makes trees and vegetation more susceptible to attack by insects, and warmer winter temperatures allow a higher number of insects to survive and increase their populations. Warmer temperatures can also increase reproductive rates of insects, resulting in two generations in a single year. Finally, warmer temperatures allow insects to invade areas previously outside their natural range, as has happened with the mountain pine beetle in the western United States. Research has also demonstrated links between warmer temperatures and drought on extensive insect outbreaks in southwestern forests and Alaska.

WILDLIFE AND ENDANGERED SPECIES

If climate change goes unchecked, it could lead to the extinction of up to 40 percent of the world's species by the latter half of this century. The International Union for the Conservation of Nature's [IUCN] 2008 annual report lists 38 percent of catalogued species as already threatened with extinction—including nearly 25 percent of all mammals. According to the IPCC's Fourth Assessment Report, "the resilience of many ecosystems is likely to be exceeded this century by an unprecedented combination of climate change, associated disturbances, (e.g. flooding, drought, wildfire, insects, ocean acidification), and other global change drivers." * * *

The species most vulnerable to climate change have a specialized habitat, a narrow environmental tolerance that is likely to be exceeded due to climate change, and dependence on specific environmental triggers or interactions that are likely to be disrupted by climate change. The IPCC identifies "coral reefs, the sea-ice biome, and other high-latitude ecosystems (e.g. boreal forests), mountain ecosystems and mediterranean-climate ecosystems" as the systems most vulnerable to the impacts of climate change. One tragic and iconic example is the polar bear. Polar bear populations are expected to decline by 30 percent in the next 35 to 50 years—and to disappear from Alaska altogether—due to disappearing habitat resulting from global warming.

NATIONAL SECURITY IMPACTS

The current and projected impacts of global warming have serious national security consequences for the United States and our allies, in many cases acting as "threat multipliers." The security issues raised by global warming have received increasing scrutiny in the last few years both in Congress and in international venues, including a debate at the UN Security Council in April 2007. The first-ever U.S. government analysis of the security threats posed by global climate change was issued in June 2008 as the National Intelligence Assessment (NIA), *National Security Implications of Global Climate Change to 2030.* * * * In addition, U.S. and European military and security policy analysts have issued a number of public reports exploring the security consequences of global warming and potential responses. All of these reports emphasize concerns over a few key security impacts, including migration, water scarcity, infrastructure at risk from extreme weather, and new economic routes and access to new energy resources. In most cases, global warming is not creating "new" security threats, but rather is acting as a "threat multiplier."

Numerous impacts of global warming could ultimately increase both the temporary and permanent migration of people inside and across existing national borders—increasing risks of geopolitical instability. Nations dealing with an influx may have neither the resources nor the desire to support climate migrants. As in the past, movement of people into new territory can increase the likelihood of conflict and the potential need for intervention from U.S. and allied military forces.

Rising sea levels threaten low-lying island nations and populous coastal areas. Even if not totally inundated, rising sea levels can render these areas uninhabitable due to sea water incursion into fresh water resources and increased exposure to storms. For example, the risk of coastal flooding in Bangladesh is growing and could force 30 million people to search for higher ground in a country already known for political violence. India is already building a wall along its border with Bangladesh. The densely-populated and oil-rich Niger Delta is already the scene of conflict over the sharing of oil revenues. Land loss and increased risk of storms will exacerbate these tensions as well as the challenge of maintaining the existing oil infrastructure. Other important economic and agricultural coastal areas, like Egypt's Nile Delta and China's southeast coast, are also threatened from rising sea-levels and severe storms. Similar impacts in Central America and the Caribbean could add pressure to pre-existing migration patterns from those areas to the United States.

Increased water scarcity due to climate change exacerbates the risk of conflict over water resources. * * * [C]hanging precipitation patterns and increasing temperatures are likely to increase the risk of water scarcity and degraded water quality in many areas. Security experts have long been concerned about the prospects for conflict over water resources in many regions of the developing world, which will be exacerbated by climate change. Water scarcity will also increase the pressure on groups to migrate to areas perceived to have more resources.

Global warming is predicted to directly impact U.S. military infrastructure at risk of damage from extreme weather and melting permafrost. Infrastructure upgrades, repair and replacement to increase resilience to global warming impacts, and rebuilding after extreme weather events will be costly. For example, the East and Gulf Coasts will be at increased risk from storm surge, and U.S. naval shipbuilding facilities have already been damaged by Hurricanes Katrina and Rita. Many active U.S. coastal military installations around the world are at a significant and increasing risk of damage from storm surges and associated flooding and damages. For example, the U.S. airbase at Diego Garcia in the Indian Ocean, which is critical to operations in Iraq and the surrounding region, is an average of four feet above sea level and is threatened by sea level rise and storm surges.

Changes in severe weather can also threaten energy supplies, as demonstrated in the devastating hurricane season in 2005. The paths of Hurricane Katrina and Hurricane Rita passed through three-quarters of the oil platforms and two-thirds of the natural gas platforms in the Gulf of Mexico and a major concentration of refining capacity on land. Together they destroyed more than a hundred offshore platforms and damaged 183 pipelines. More than 1.5 million barrels of oil and 10 billion cubic feet of natural gas production per day were taken off-line for both hurricanes. Katrina also significantly affected electricity supply with 2.7 million customers and other critical infrastructure losing power. * * *

Finally, accelerating melting of Arctic sea ice is impacting the United States' strategic interests in the region. Russia has moved to stake claim to more than 460,000 square miles of territory, including areas with potential oil and natural gas resources. With the opening of the Northwest Passage for the first time in recorded history, the Prime Minister of Canada announced his intention to increase his country's military presence in the Arctic. Other circumpolar nations, including the United States, have begun to examine their potential claims on Arctic territory and identify necessary preparations for increased maritime traffic in the area.

THE ECONOMIC COSTS OF CLIMATE CHANGE

Climate change impacts of the types described above will have staggering economic impacts in the United States and the rest of the world in the coming decades. Measuring these impacts in dollars is a unique challenge, requiring analysis of local and global impacts, long time horizons, quantification of risk and uncertainty, and capturing the possibility of tipping points that induce major, catastrophic change. While the variables are many and complex, estimates of potential economic impacts are massive. The Stern Review excerpted in Chapter 4—one of the most in-depth and respected economic impact analyses on climate change conducted thus far—used formal economic models to estimate that unabated climate change will cost at least 5 percent of global gross domestic product (GDP) each year. This amounts to around $3.3 trillion per year at the current value of the global economy. If a wider range of risks and impacts is taken into account, the damages could rise to 20 percent of GDP or more annually over the next two centuries.

In the United States, the economic impacts of climate change are predicted to be felt throughout the country and within all sectors of the economy. The greatest economic impacts are predicted to stem from stress to fresh water supply networks, changes to the agricultural sector, threats to coastal infrastructure from storms and sea level rise, effects on energy supply and demand, increased risk to human health, and more frequent and extensive forest fires. Tourism and other weather-dependent industries may be hit especially hard. Modeling results from a recent Tufts University and Natural Resources Defense Council study show that if present trends continue, the total cost of four global warming impacts alone—hurricane damage, real estate losses, energy costs, and water costs—could cost the United States nearly $1.9 trillion annually by 2100 (in constant 2008 dollars), or 1.8 percent of U.S. GDP. Factoring in a wider range of harms such as health impacts and wildlife damages, these costs could reach 3.6 percent of GDP annually in the United States by 2100.

IMPACTS ON VULNERABLE COMMUNITIES

Climate change is predicted to have devastating impacts on the developing world, reversing gains in poverty reduction, food security and nutrition, health, and basic services and putting millions of lives at risk. Poor communities are especially vulnerable because they have less capacity to adapt to changes in climate and are more dependent on climate-sensitive resources such as local water and food supplies. Increased exposure to drought and water scarcity, more intense storms, floods, and other environmental pressures are projected to reverse many of the recent gains in poverty alleviation around the world, adding to the total of 2.6 billion people now living on $2 a day or less. By the end of the century, an additional 145–220 million people in South Asia and Sub Saharan Africa could fall below the $2 per day poverty level as a result of climate change impacts.

Poor communities and communities of color within the United States are vulnerable to climate change impacts as well, and suffer disproportionately from illnesses due to the social determinants of health. As Hurricane Katrina demonstrated, poorer communities are especially vulnerable to extreme weather events. Poorer communities and communities of color are also more vulnerable to public health impacts of climate change. Today, more than 70 percent of African Americans live in counties in violation of federal air pollution standards. As a result, African Americans are nearly three times as likely to be hospitalized or killed by asthma. In Harlem, New York, 25 percent of children now have asthma. Latinos—66 percent of whom live in areas that violate federal air quality standards—face disproportionate health impacts as well. These impacts are exacerbated by their disproportionate lack of health insurance and lower utilization of health services compared with both non-Hispanic whites and African Americans.

Vulnerable Alaskans are already dealing with the harsh reality of global warming. According to the U.S. Army Corps of Engineers, at least three Alaskan villages—Shishmaref, Kivalina, and Newtok—will be lost to coastal erosion due to rising sea levels in the next 8 to 13 years. With flooding and erosion currently affecting 184 out of 213, or 86 percent, of Alaska Native villages to some extent, the number of villages needing major assistance is likely to increase. The cost of saving these villages through either man-made erosion protection or total community relocation could be up to $200 million or more per village. [Litigation concerning the flooding in Kivalina is discussed in Chapter 7.]

* * * * *

For a through analysis of climate change impacts in the U.S., see T. Karl et al., Global Climate Change Impacts in the United States (2009), a synthesis of research performed by the U.S. Global Change Research Program.

C. OPPORTUNITIES FOR AN ENERGY TRANSFORMATION

LIGHTING THE WAY: TOWARD A SUSTAINABLE
ENERGY FUTURE
Dr. Steven Chu and José Goldemberg
www.interacademycouncil.net/cms/reports/11840.aspx (2007)

Human prosperity has been intimately tied to our ability to capture, collect, and harness energy. The control of fire and the domestication of plants and animals were two of the essential factors that allowed our ancestors to transition from a harsh, nomadic existence into stable, rooted societies that could generate the collective wealth needed to spawn civilizations. For millennia, energy in the form of biomass and fossilized biomass was used for cooking and heating, and for the creation of materials that ranged from bricks to bronze. Despite these developments, relative wealth in virtually all civilizations was fundamentally defined by access to and control over energy, as measured by the number of animal and humans that served at the beck and call of a particular individual. * * *

While the current energy outlook is very sobering, we believe that there are sustainable solutions to the energy problem. A combination of local, national, and international fiscal and regulatory policies can greatly accelerate efficiency improvements, which remain in many cases the most cost-effective and readily implemented part of the solution. Significant efficiency gains were achieved in recent years and more can be obtained with policy changes that encourage the development and deployment of better technologies. For developing countries with rapidly growing energy consumption, 'leapfrogging' past the wasteful energy trajectory historically followed by today's industrialized countries is in their best economic and societal interests. Providing assistance to these countries aimed at promoting the introduction of efficient and environmentally friendly energy technologies as early as possible should therefore be an urgent priority for the international community.

A timely transition to sustainable energy systems also requires policies that drive toward optimal societal choices, taking into account both the short-

and long-term consequences of energy use. Discharging raw sewage into a river will always be less expensive at a micro-economic level than first treating the waste, especially for 'up-stream' polluters. At a macro scale, however, where the long-term costs to human health, quality of life, and the environment are folded into the calculation, sewage treatment clearly becomes the low-cost option for society as a whole.

Thus, it becomes critical to consider the additional costs of mitigating these impacts when attempting to assess the true low-cost option in any long-term, macro-economic analysis of energy use and production. The cost of carbon emissions and other adverse impacts of current modes of energy use must be factored into market and policy decisions.

In addition to extensive energy efficiency enhancements and rapid deployment of low-carbon technologies, including advanced fossil-fuel systems with carbon capture and sequestration and nuclear energy, a sustainable energy future will be more readily attainable if renewable energy sources become a significant part of the energy supply portfolio. Science and technology are again essential to delivering this part of the solution. Significant improvements in our ability to convert solar energy into electricity are needed, as are economical, large scale technologies for storing energy and transmitting it across long distances. Improved storage and transmission technologies would allow intermittent renewable sources to play a greater role in supplying the world's electricity needs. At the same time, efficient methods of converting cellulosic biomass into high-quality liquid fuels could greatly reduce the carbon footprint of the world's rapidly growing transportation sector and relieve current supply pressures on increasingly precious petroleum fuels. * * *

STABILIZATION WEDGES: SOLVING THE CLIMATE PROBLEM FOR THE NEXT 50 YEARS WITH CURRENT TECHNOLOGIES
Steven Pacala and Robert Socolow
305 Science 968 (2004)

Humanity already possesses the fundamental scientific, technical, and industrial know-how to solve the carbon and climate problem for the next half-century. A portfolio of technologies now exists to meet the world's energy needs over the next 50 years and limit atmospheric CO_2 to a trajectory that avoids a doubling of the preindustrial concentration. Every element in this portfolio has passed beyond the laboratory bench and demonstration project; many are already implemented somewhere at full industrial scale. Although no element is a credible candidate for doing the entire job (or even half the job) by itself, the portfolio as a whole is large enough that not every element has to be used. * * *

What Do We Mean by "Solving the Carbon and Climate Problem for the Next Half-Century"?

Proposals to limit atmospheric CO_2 to a concentration that would prevent most damaging climate change have focused on a goal of 500 ± 50 parts per million (ppm), or less than double the preindustrial concentration of 280 ppm. The current [2004] concentration is ~375 ppm. The CO_2 emissions reductions necessary to achieve any such target depend on the emissions judged likely to occur in the absence of a focus on carbon [called a business-as-usual (BAU) trajectory], the quantitative details of the stabilization target, and the future behavior of natural sinks for atmospheric CO_2 (i.e., the oceans and terrestrial biosphere). We focus exclusively on CO_2, because it is the dominant anthropogenic greenhouse gas; industrial-scale mitigation options also exist for subordinate gases, such as methane and N_2O.

Very roughly, stabilization at 500 ppm requires that emissions be held near the present level of 7 billion tons of carbon per year (GtC/year) for the next 50 years, even though they are currently on course to more than double. * * * The next 50 years is a sensible horizon from several perspectives. It is the length of a career, the life-time of a power plant, and an interval for which the technology is close enough to envision. * * *

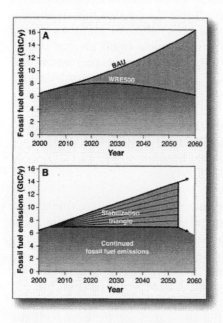

Fig. 1. (A) The top curve is a representative BAU emissions path for global carbon emissions as CO_2 from fossil fuel combustion and cement manufacture: 1.5% per year growth starting from 7.0 GtC/year in 2004. The bottom curve is a CO_2 emissions path consistent with atmospheric CO_2 stabilization at 500 ppm by 2125 akin to the Wigley, Richels, and Edmonds (WRE) family of stabilization curves described in (11), modified as described in Section 1 of the SOM text. The bottom curve assumes an ocean uptake calculated with the High-Latitude Exchange Interior Diffusion Advection (HILDA) ocean model (12) and a constant net land uptake of 0.5 GtC/year (Section 1 of the SOM text). The area between the two curves represents the avoided carbon emissions required for stabilization. **Fig. 1. (B)** Idealization of (A): A stabilization triangle of avoided emissions (green) and allowed emissions (blue). The allowed emissions are fixed at 7 GtC/year beginning in 2004. The stabilization triangle is divided into seven wedges, each of which reaches 1 GtC/year

in 2054. With linear growth, the total avoided emissions per wedge is 25 GtC, and the total area of the stabilization triangle is 175 GtC. The arrow at the bottom right of the stabilization triangle points downward to emphasize that fossil fuel emissions must decline substantially below 7 GtC/year after 2054 to achieve stabilization at 500 ppm.

The Stabilization Triangle

We idealize the 50-year emissions reductions as a perfect triangle in Fig. 1B. Stabilization is represented by a "flat" trajectory of fossil fuel emissions at 7 GtC/year, and BAU is represented by a straight-line "ramp" trajectory rising to 14 GtC/year in 2054. The "stabilization triangle," located between the flat trajectory and BAU, removes exactly one-third of BAU emissions.

To keep the focus on technologies that have the potential to produce a material difference by 2054, we divide the stabilization triangle into seven equal "wedges." A wedge represents an activity that reduces emissions to the atmosphere that starts at zero today and increases linearly until it accounts for 1 GtC/year of reduced carbon emissions in 50 years. It thus represents a cumulative total of 25 GtC of reduced emissions over 50 years. In this paper, to "solve the carbon and climate problem over the next half-century" means to deploy the technologies and/or lifestyle changes necessary to fill all seven wedges of the stabilization triangle.

Stabilization at any level requires that net emissions do not simply remain constant, but eventually drop to zero. For example, in one simple model that begins with the stabilization triangle but looks beyond 2054, 500-ppm stabilization is achieved by 50 years of flat emissions, followed by a linear decline of about two-thirds in the following 50 years, and a very slow decline thereafter that matches the declining ocean sink. To develop the revolutionary technologies required for such large emissions reductions in the second half of the century, enhanced research and development would have to begin immediately.

Policies designed to stabilize at 500 ppm would inevitably be renegotiated periodically to take into account the results of research and development, experience with specific wedges, and revised estimates of the size of the stabilization triangle. But not filling the stabilization triangle will put 500-ppm stabilization out of reach. In that same simple model, 50 years of BAU emissions followed by 50 years of a flat trajectory at 14 GtC/year leads to more than a tripling of the preindustrial concentration.

It is important to understand that each of the seven wedges represents an effort beyond what would occur under BAU. Our BAU simply continues the 1.5% annual carbon emissions growth of the past 30 years. This historic trend in emissions has been accompanied by 2% growth in primary energy consumption and 3% growth in gross world product (GWP) * * *. If carbon emissions were to grow 2% per year, then ~10 wedges would be needed instead of 7, and if carbon emissions were to grow at 3% per year, then ~18 wedges would be required * * *. Thus, a continuation of the historical rate of decarbonization of the fuel mix prevents the need for three additional wedges, and ongoing improvements in energy efficiency prevent the need for eight additional wedges. Most readers will reject at least one of the wedges listed here, believing that the corresponding deployment is certain to occur in BAU, but readers will disagree about which to reject on such grounds. On the other hand, our list of mitigation options is not exhaustive.

What Current Options Could Be Scaled Up to Produce at Least One Wedge?

Wedges can be achieved from energy efficiency, from the decarbonization of the supply of electricity and fuels (by means of fuel shifting, carbon capture and storage, nuclear energy, and renewable energy), and from biological storage in forests and agricultural soils. * * * Although several options could be scaled up to two or more wedges, we doubt that any could fill the stabilization triangle, or even half of it, alone. * * *

Because the same BAU carbon emissions cannot be displaced twice, achieving one wedge often interacts with achieving another. The more the electricity system becomes decarbonized, for example, the less the available savings from greater efficiency of electricity use, and vice versa. Interactions among wedges are discussed in the SOM text. Also, our focus is not on costs. In general, the achievement of a wedge will require some price trajectory for carbon, the details of which depend on many assumptions, including future fuels prices, public acceptance, and cost reductions by means of learning. Instead, our analysis is intended to complement the comprehensive but complex "integrated assessments" of carbon mitigation by letting the full-scale examples that are already in the marketplace make a simple case for technological readiness.

Category I: Efficiency and Conservation

Improvements in efficiency and conservation probably offer the greatest potential to provide wedges. For example, in 2002, the United States announced the goal of decreasing its carbon intensity (carbon emissions per unit GDP) by 18% over the next decade, a decrease of 1.96% per year. An entire wedge would be created if the United States were to reset its carbon intensity goal to a decrease of 2.11% per year and extend it to 50 years, and if every country were to follow suit by adding the same 0.15% per year increment to its own carbon intensity goal. However, efficiency and conservation options are less tangible than those from the other categories. Improvements in energy efficiency will come from literally hundreds of innovations that range from new catalysts and chemical processes, to more efficient lighting and insulation for buildings, to the growth of the service economy and telecommuting. Here, we provide four of many possible comparisons of greater and less efficiency in 2054 * * *.

Option 1: Improved fuel economy. Suppose that in 2054, 2 billion cars (roughly four times as many as today) average 10,000 miles per year (as they do today). One wedge would be achieved if, instead of averaging 30 miles per gallon (mpg) on conventional fuel, cars in 2054 averaged 60 mpg, with fuel type and distance traveled unchanged.

Option 2: Reduced reliance on cars. A wedge would also be achieved if the average fuel economy of the 2 billion 2054 cars were 30 mpg, but the annual distance traveled were 5000 miles instead of 10,000 miles.

Option 3: More efficient buildings. According to a 1996 study by the IPCC, a wedge is the difference between pursuing and not pursuing "known and established approaches" to energy-efficient space heating and cooling, water heating, lighting, and refrigeration in residential and commercial buildings. These approaches reduce mid-century emissions from buildings by about one-fourth. About half of potential savings are in the buildings in developing countries.

Option 4: Improved power plant efficiency. In 2000, coal power plants, operating on average at 32% efficiency, produced about one-fourth of all carbon emissions: 1.7 GtC/year out of 6.2 GtC/year. A wedge would be created if twice today's quantity of coal-based electricity in 2054 were produced at 60% instead of 40% efficiency.

*Category II: Decarbonization of Electricity and Fuels * * **

Option 5: Substituting natural gas for coal. Carbon emissions per unit of electricity are about half as large from natural gas power plants as from coal plants. Assume that the capacity factor of the average baseload coal plant in 2054 has increased to 90% and that its efficiency has improved to 50%. Because 700 GW of such plants emit carbon at a rate of 1 GtC/year, a wedge would be achieved by displacing 1400 GW of baseload coal with baseload gas by 2054. The power shifted to gas for this wedge is four times as large as the total current gas-based power.

Option 6: Storage of carbon captured in power plants. Carbon capture and storage (CCS) technology prevents about 90% of the fossil carbon from reaching the atmosphere, so a wedge would be provided by the installation of CCS at 800 GW of baseload coal plants by 2054 or 1600 GW of baseload natural gas plants. The most likely approach has two steps: (i) precombustion capture of CO_2, in which hydrogen and CO_2 are produced and the hydrogen is then burned to produce electricity, followed by (ii) geologic storage, in which the waste CO_2 is injected into subsurface geologic reservoirs. Hydrogen production from fossil fuels is already a very large business. Globally, hydrogen plants consume about 2% of primary energy and emit 0.1 GtC/year of CO_2. The capture part of a wedge of CCS electricity would thus require only a tenfold expansion of plants resembling today's large hydrogen plants over the next 50 years.

The scale of the storage part of this wedge can be expressed as a multiple of the scale of current enhanced oil recovery, or current seasonal storage of natural gas, or the first geological storage demonstration project. Today, about 0.01 GtC/year of carbon as CO_2 is injected into geologic reservoirs to spur enhanced oil recovery, so a wedge of geologic storage requires that CO_2 injection be scaled up by a factor of 100 over the next 50 years. To smooth out seasonal demand in the United States, the natural gas industry annually draws roughly 4000 billion standard cubic feet (Bscf) into and out of geologic storage, and a carbon flow of 1 GtC/year (whether as methane or CO_2) is a flow of 69,000 Bscf/year (190 Bscf per day), so a wedge would be a flow to storage 15 and 20 times as large as the current flow. Norway's Sleipner project in the North Sea strips CO_2 from natural gas offshore and reinjects 0.3 million tons of carbon a year (MtC/year) into a non–fossil-fuel–bearing formation, so a wedge would be 3500 Sleipner-sized projects (or fewer, larger projects) over the next 50 years.

A worldwide effort is under way to assess the capacity available for multi-century storage and to assess risks of leaks large enough to endanger human or environmental health.

Option 7: Storage of carbon captured in hydrogen plants. The hydrogen resulting from precombustion capture of CO_2 can be sent off-site to displace the consumption of conventional fuels rather than being consumed onsite to produce electricity. The capture part of a wedge would require the installation of CCS, by 2054, at coal plants producing 250 MtH_2/year, or at natural gas plants producing 500 MtH_2/year. The former is six times the current rate of hydrogen production. The storage part of this option is the same as in Option 6.

Option 8: Storage of carbon captured in synfuels plants. Looming over carbon management in 2054 is the possibility of large-scale production of synthetic fuel (synfuel) from coal. Carbon emissions, however, need not exceed those associated with fuel refined from crude oil if synfuels production is accompanied by CCS. Assuming that half of the carbon entering a 2054 synfuels plant leaves as fuel but the other half can be captured as CO_2, the capture part of a wedge in 2054 would be the difference between capturing and venting the CO_2 from coal synfuels plants producing 30 million barrels of synfuels per day. (The flow of carbon in 24 million barrels per day of crude oil is 1 GtC/year; we assume the same value for the flow in synfuels and allow for imperfect capture.) Currently, the Sasol plants in South Africa, the world's largest synfuels facility, produce 165,000 barrels per day from coal. Thus, a wedge requires 200 Sasol-scale coal-to-synfuels facilities with CCS in 2054. The storage part of this option is again the same as in Option 6.

Option 9: Nuclear fission. On the basis of the Option 5 estimates, a wedge of nuclear electricity would displace 700 GW of efficient baseload coal capacity in 2054. This would require 700 GW of nuclear power with the same 90% capacity factor assumed for the coal plants, or about twice the nuclear capacity currently deployed. The global pace of nuclear power plant construction from 1975 to 1990 would yield a wedge, if it continued for 50 years. Substantial expansion in nuclear power requires restoration of public confidence in safety and waste disposal, and international security agreements governing uranium enrichment and plutonium recycling.

Option 10: Wind electricity. We account for the intermittent output of windmills by equating 3 GW of nominal peak capacity (3 GW_p) with 1 GW of baseload capacity. Thus, a wedge of wind electricity would require the deployment of 2000 GW_p that displaces coal electricity in 2054 (or 2 million 1-MW_p wind turbines). Installed wind capacity has been growing at about 30% per year for more than 10 years and is currently about 40 GW_p. A wedge of wind electricity would thus require 50 times today's deployment. The wind turbines would "occupy" about 30 million hectares (about 3% of the area of the United States), some on land and some offshore. Because windmills are widely spaced, land with windmills can have multiple uses.

Option 11: Photovoltaic electricity. Similar to a wedge of wind electricity, a wedge from photovoltaic (PV) electricity would require 2000 GW_p of installed capacity that displaces coal electricity in 2054. Although only 3 GW_p of PV are currently installed, PV electricity has been growing at a rate of 30% per year. A wedge of PV electricity would require 700 times today's deployment, and about 2 million hectares of land in 2054, or 2 to 3 m^2 per person.

Option 12: Renewable hydrogen. Renewable electricity can produce carbon-free hydrogen for vehicle fuel by the electrolysis of water. The hydrogen produced by 4 million 1-MW_p windmills in 2054, if used in high-efficiency fuel-cell cars, would achieve a wedge of displaced gasoline or diesel fuel. Compared with Option 10, this is twice as many 1-MW_p windmills as would be required to produce the electricity that achieves a wedge by displacing high-efficiency baseload coal. This interesting factor-of-two carbon-saving advantage of wind-electricity over wind-hydrogen is still larger if the coal plant is less efficient or the fuel-cell vehicle is less spectacular.

Option 13: Biofuels. Fossil-carbon fuels can also be replaced by biofuels such as ethanol. A wedge of biofuel would be achieved by the production of about 34 million barrels per day of ethanol in 2054 that could displace gasoline, provided the ethanol itself were fossil-carbon free. This ethanol production rate would be about 50 times larger than today's global production rate, almost all of which can be attributed to Brazilian sugarcane and United States corn. An ethanol wedge would require 250 million hectares committed to high-yield (15 dry tons/hectare) plantations by 2054, an area equal to about one-sixth of the world's cropland. An even larger area would be required to the extent that the biofuels require fossil-carbon inputs. Because land suitable for annually harvested biofuels crops is also often suitable for conventional agriculture, biofuels production could compromise agricultural productivity.

Category III: Natural Sinks

Although the literature on biological sequestration includes a diverse array of options and some very large estimates of the global potential, here we restrict our attention to the pair of options that are already implemented at large scale and that could be scaled up to a wedge or more without a lot of new research. * * *

Option 14: Forest management. Conservative assumptions lead to the conclusion that at least one wedge would be available from reduced tropical deforestation and the management of temperate and tropical forests. At least one half-wedge would be created if the current rate of clear-cutting of primary tropical forest were reduced to zero over 50 years instead of being halved. A second half-wedge would be created by reforesting or afforesting approximately 250 million hectares in the tropics or 400 million hectares in the temperate zone (current areas of tropical and temperate forests are 1500 and 700 million hectares, respectively). A third half-wedge would be created by establishing approximately 300 million hectares of plantations on nonforested land.

Option 15: Agricultural soils management. When forest or natural grassland is converted to cropland, up to one-half of the soil carbon is lost, primarily because annual tilling increases the rate of decomposition by aerating undecomposed organic matter. About 55 GtC, or two wedges' worth, has been lost historically in this way. Practices such as conservation tillage (e.g., seeds are drilled into the soil without plowing), the use of cover crops, and erosion control can reverse the losses. By 1995, conservation tillage practices had been adopted on 110 million hectares of the world's 1600 million hectares of cropland. If conservation tillage could be extended to all cropland, accompanied by a verification program that enforces the adoption of soil conservation practices that actually work as advertised, a good case could be made for the IPCC's estimate that an additional half to one wedge could be stored in this way.

Conclusions

In confronting the problem of greenhouse warming, the choice today is between action and delay. Here, we presented a part of the case for action by identifying a set of options that have the capacity to provide the seven stabilization wedges and solve the climate problem for the next half-century. None of the options is a pipe dream or an unproven idea. Today, one can buy electricity from a wind turbine, PV array, gas turbine, or nuclear power plant. One can buy hydrogen produced with the chemistry of carbon capture, biofuel to power one's car, and hundreds of devices that improve energy efficiency. One can visit tropical forests where clear-cutting has ceased, farms practicing conservation tillage, and facilities that inject carbon into geologic reservoirs. Every one of these options is already implemented at an industrial scale and could be scaled up further over 50 years to provide at least one wedge.

D. IMPLICATIONS OF "BUSINESS AS USUAL"

GLOBAL ENVIRONMENTAL GOVERNANCE
James Gustave Speth and Peter M. Haas (2006)

There are more people and economic activity on the planet than ever before, and the environmental consequences of actions large and small are now more widely felt than ever before. A house constructed in the United States often contains wood imported from fragile tropical ecosystems; the transportation of materials required consumption of polluting fossil fuels; many of the building supplies used in construction release gases that can be toxic to construction workers and to the occupants of the house. Small-scale decisions combine to have larger consequences, in terms of both public health and the broader health of the global environment on which human societies and their economies depend. As the number of people on the planet grows, and their consumer aspirations grow even faster, the collective human footprint on the planet is becoming increasingly heavy and global in scope.

How can we address these global environmental threats? * * *

These threats can be examined from global, national, and local perspectives. Each perspective has value, and each receives attention here. Through the global perspective, we can gauge the health of the planet and examine how human societies are interacting with the natural world. At the national level, where territory is controlled by sovereign nations, the most important political decisions are actually made in today's world. At the local level, individuals and communities make choices about what products to buy and what kinds of lives to live, at least those of us fortunate enough to live where such choices are possible. We know the local environmental quality because we see it, breathe it, work and play in it. There is tremendous power in this concreteness but also the potential for confusion if the threats are global—such as climate change—seemingly remote and certainly hard to perceive.

Few people deliberately set out to destroy the environment, although in war and on other occasions such intentional destruction has occurred. Corporate executives, government officials, and citizens don't begin each day with the intent to do environmental damage. People act to reap rewards, and most often the benefits of economic decisions are immediate and gratifying while the costs of these decisions are often borne broadly by others, sometimes others in far parts of the world who have no way of expressing their displeasure, or those in the future who are not yet even born. So we continue to drive inefficient vehicles and keep our houses overly warm in the winter and chillingly cold in the summer and companies continue to produce gas-guzzling SUV's and generate electricity in outmoded coal-fired power plants—all despite strong warnings that our reliance on fossil fuels—coal, oil, and natural gas—is warming the earth.

These problems are not solved simply by decree; steps must be taken to provide a powerful new set of incentives and disincentives to institutions and individuals whose behavior affects the environment. Creating these incentives is conventionally the realm of government, acting at all three levels and wielding powers to tax, spend, and regulate. But funds can also be raised privately without taxation, consumers spend far more than governments, and various means exist to accomplish *de facto* regulation even without governmental authority to coerce. So governance can sometimes be accomplished, up to a point, without governments. * * *

The Real World: Only One Earth

As the 1987 World Commission on Environment and Development (the Brundtland Commission) wrote, "the Earth is one but the world is not." How do we achieve environmental sustainability in our world today? The real world's 6.5 billion people are already spread across six continents, settle in geographic patterns that have been determined historically over thousands of years. They work in a $55 trillion world economy (in 2003 U.S. dollars) made possible by technologies designed when the environment was not a concern and obeying price and other market signals that do not take environmental protection into account. They live in nation-states claiming sovereignty within their geographic borders, including the sovereign right to develop the natural resources within those borders as they see fit. These nation-states are divided by race, religion, ethnicity, language, history and natural resources.

The Globalization of Environmental Threats

It took all of human history up until 1900 for global population to grow to 1.5 billion. But during the twentieth century, 1.5 billion people were added, on average, every 33 years. Over the last 25 years between 1979 and 2004, global population increased by another 2 billion, from, 4.4 billion to 6.4 billion. Virtually all of this growth occurred in the developing world.

Population increased fourfold in the last century, but world economic output increased 20-fold, five times faster than population due to increasing affluence. It took all of history to grow the world economy to $7 trillion by 1950 (in 2003 U.S. dollars). Amazingly, it now grows by this amount every 5 to 10 years. In the 40 years between 1965 and 2005, the size of the world economy doubled–and then doubled again. Most of this growth has occurred in the richer industrial countries.

As a result of this phenomenal expansion, especially the growth of economic activity and rising human consumption, environmental costs have mounted exponentially. Simultaneously, concerns that were once strictly local, such as clearing of forests and pollution from burning fuels, have become global challenges. As early as 1957 Roger Revelle, a famous oceanographer, observed that human societies are conducting a large-scale geophysical experiment of a kind that could not have happened in the past nor be reproduced in the future. In 1989, the environmental writer Bill McKibben declared "the end of nature," by which he meant the end of our thinking about nature as an entity or force independent of *Homo sapiens*. Although previously we might have conserved the "forces of nature" as largely free of human influence, the twentieth century brought us a new condition. Human influences on the environment are now everywhere, affecting all natural systems and cycles, all the oceans, and every continent.

Recently, scientists have been sounding alarms with greater frequency and urgency. Ecologist Jane Lubchenco, in her 1998 address as president of the American Association for the Advancement of Science, made the following call from the rostrum: "The conclusions...are inescapable: during the last few decades, humans have emerged as a new force of nature. We are modifying physical, chemical, and biological systems in new ways, at faster rates, and over larger spatial scales than ever recorded on Earth. Humans have unwittingly embarked upon a grand experiment with our planet. The outcome of this experiment is unknown, but has profound implications for all of life on Earth." * * *

Ten Major Global Environmental Challenges

Accompanying the twentieth century's vast economic expansion have been two categories of change of enormous consequence for the natural environment. First is the dramatic increase in the consumption of the earth's natural resources, principally the so-called renewable resources—the forests, the air, the soils, the fish and animal life, the freshwater. Renewable resources have been appropriated by humans at rates far is excess of sustainable yields. (In an ironic twist, the supply of the earth's nonrenewable resources—principally the fossil fuels and the nonfuel minerals—originally thought to be most subject to scarcities, have thus far been regularly available.)

The second development has been the exponential growth of what we have come to call pollution. Pollution is a case of too much of something in the wrong place. In appropriate quantities, many potential pollutants are beneficial. For example, phosphates and nitrates are plant nutrients essential to life. Too much of these nutrients in aquatic systems, however, and plant growth and decay sap the water of vital oxygen needed by fish and other organisms in the water. Eutrophication is the result. Or take the case of carbon dioxide (CO_2). If it were not for this compound occurring naturally in the atmosphere, our planet would be a frozen wasteland. The CO_2 creates a greenhouse blanket, keeping heat in to warm our atmosphere. Yet, the buildup of too much CO_2 from fossil fuel burning and other sources now threatens to alter the planet's climate and disrupt both ecosystems and human communities.

Today, pollution is occurring on an unprecedented scale worldwide. It is pervasive, affecting in some way virtually everyone and everything on the globe, from CO_2 in our atmosphere, to polychlorinated biphenyl (PCB) in our bodies, to acid rain on our land.

It is the combination of these developments—high demands on renewable resources and large-scale pollution—that has given rise to the major global threats we now face. * * * We will focus on what we see as the 10 principal threats:

- Acid rain and regional-scale air pollution
- Ozone depletion by chlorofluorocarbons and other industrial and agricultural chemicals
- Global warming and climate change due to the increase in "greenhouse gases" in the atmosphere
- Deforestation, especially in the tropics
- Land degradation due to desertification, erosion, compaction, salinization, and other factors
- Freshwater pollution and scarcities

- Marine threats, including overfishing, habitat destruction, acidification, and pollution
- Threats to human health from persistent organic pollutants and heavy metals
- Declines in biodiversity and ecosystem service through loss of species and ecosystems
- Excessive nitrogen production and overfertilization

We can frame these 10 threats in terms of our two previously identified overall trends: overuse and misuse of renewable resources and the increase in pollution, as is presented in the table above.

Collectively, these 10 concerns are seriously threatening Earth's natural endowment, productivity, and habitability, including the services natural ecosystems provide to human societies. The following sections of this chapter describe these threats and indicate their scope and significance. * * *

Many of the examples cited in this chapter involve the United States. The United States exemplifies much of the environmental neglect that characterizes today's times. The United States is not alone in neglecting the environmental effects of its activities, but as the world's largest economy and major superpower, the United States is a country to which many others turn for leadership and a role model and, due to its size, the effects of U.S. decisions often have international impacts. The Environmental Sustainability index, following, provides a snapshot of the United States' performance in a comparative perspective.

Acid Rain and Regional Air Pollution

Before acid rain, most people viewed air pollution as primarily a local, urban event. In fact, the atmosphere can transport many air pollutants hundreds of miles before returning them to Earth's surface. While these pollutants are being picked up and moved, the atmosphere acts as a chemical laboratory, transforming the pollutants as they interact with other substances, moisture, and solar energy. Emissions of sulfur and nitrogen oxides, primarily from fossil fuel combustion such as coal-fired power plants, can be transformed chemically in the atmosphere into sulfuric and nitric acids. These acids then come back to Earth's surface through deposition, primarily through rain, giving us the popular term *acid rain*.

Acid rain can cause damage to buildings and exposed metals, eating through surfaces over time, but its impacts on the natural environment have attracted by far the most concern. When these acids come down in wet or dry deposition and pollute lakes and rivers, they change these water bodies' pH balances. Increasing acidity has enormous ramifications for fish and aquatic plants, and thousands of lakes in the United States and Europe have essentially "died" from excessive acid (low pH). Acidity can also affect some forests and soils adversely.

Despite three decades of efforts to reduce sulfur and nitrogen oxide pollution, data from the United States indicate little actual recovery of lakes and soils. It has become clear to many that further cuts in pollutants will be needed for full ecological recovery of these ecosystems.

Although acid deposition is still seen as the primary atmospheric agent damaging aquatic ecosystems, other air pollutants, including smog, can join in contributing to crop damage and forest problems. Smog is formed when nitrogen oxides and volatile hydrocarbons react in the presence of sunlight to produce ozone and other photochemical oxidants. For example, air pollution has been implicated in large-scale forest die-offs in southwestern China, and the World Bank estimates that the cost of air pollution in China's forests and crops exceeds $5 billion annually. Japan, India, the Republic of Korea, and Thailand also have regions with serious pollution damage to crops and forests.

Acid rain is also a classic transborder pollution problem. Examples of regions with transboundary acidification include the United States-Canada, Europe, and China-Japan.

Ozone Depletion

As noted at the outset of this chapter, the Molina-Rowland research sparked an international response. The United States, Canada, and Sweden first banned inessential uses of CFC propellants, and several other countries followed suit. World production of the two major CFCs decreased in the late 1970's, but then increased again due to nonaerosol uses. Nations acted in concert in 1985 when they adopted a landmark treaty, the Vienna Convention for the Protection of the Ozone Layer. This convention and its better-known progeny, the 1987 Montreal Protocol, have now required the virtual elimination of CFCs and other ozone-destroying chemicals in the industrial countries, and the process is now moving to focus primarily on the developing countries, with an ultimate goal of eliminating the remaining emissions. Scientists estimate that the ozone layer could recover by midcentury if necessary actions are taken, but the recovery process has hardly begun today.

Climate Disruption

Global climate change is the most threatening of the major global change issues. It is also the most complex and controversial. We know that the "greenhouse effect" works: without the naturally occurring heat-trapping gases in Earth's atmosphere, the planet would be about 30°C cooler on average—an iceball rather than a life-support system. The problem arises because human activities have now sharply increased the presence of greenhouse gases in the atmosphere. These gases prevent the escape of Earth's infrared radiation into space. In general, the more gases, the greater the atmosphere's heat-trapping capacity.

The atmospheric concentration of carbon dioxide, the principal greenhouse gas, has increased by a third over the preindustrial level due principally to the use of fossil fuels (coal, oil, natural gas) and to large-scale deforestation. Carbon dioxide in the atmosphere is now at its highest level in over 420,000 years. The concentration of methane (CH_4), another greenhouse gas, is about 150 percent above preindustrial levels. Methane accumulates from the use of fossil fuels, cattle raising, rice growing, and landfill emissions. Atmospheric nitrous oxide (N_2O) concentrations are also up due to fertilizer use, cattle feed lots, and the chemical industry, and it is also an infrared-trapping gas. A number of specialty chemicals in the halocarbon family, including the CFCs of ozone-depletion fame, are also potent greenhouse gases.

What are the consequences of the buildup of these gases? One authoritative report on the subject was issued in 2002 by the U.S. National Academy of Sciences (NAS), responding to a request of the Bush administration. The NAS report reached the conclusion that, indeed, greenhouse gases are accumulating in Earth's atmosphere as a result of human activities. These gases are contributing to rising temperatures, about 1°F global average rise in the twentieth century, and these warming trends could increase by 2.5F to 10.5F in this century. The NAS report went on to note that global temperature would continue to rise well into the next century even if the levels of greenhouse gases in the atmosphere were stabilized much earlier. These conclusions broadly conform to the current scientific consensus reflected in the work of the Intergovernmental Panel on Climate Change, the international scientific body responsible for providing authoritative policy relevant advice on climate change.

The likely direct consequences of this phenomenon include a warmer and wetter planet (with greater warming toward the poles), changes in precipitation patterns leading to more floods and droughts, more severe hurricanes and cyclones, and significant sea level rise. * * *

There is little doubt that the process of human-induced global warming has begun. Ice is melting at the poles and glaciers are retreating; spring is arriving earlier; and ranges of various species are shifting. Meanwhile, the process of reducing greenhouse gas emissions has hardly started. Global carbon dioxide emission climbed by 22 percent between 1980 and 2000.

One of the most comprehensive studies of the regional impact of climate change is the 2004 Arctic Climate Impact Assessment, a joint effort of the eight Arctic nations, including the United States. It concluded that the Arctic is warming much more rapidly than previously known, at nearly twice the rate as the rest of the globe, and increasing greenhouse gases from human activities will likely make it warmer still. In Alaska, western Canada, and eastern Russia, average winter temperatures have increased as much as 3 to 4°C in the past 50 years and are projected to rise 4 to 7°C over the next 100 years. Warming over Greenland could melt the Greenland ice sheet, gradually contributing to global sea-level rise. Over the long term, Greenland contains enough melt water to eventually rise sea level by about 23 feet. The report makes clear that Arctic developments could affect societies far away from the region by contributing to a rise in sea level, adding positive feedback that accelerates warming, and disrupting ocean currents, including the Gulf Stream. Projections see the Arctic icecap continuing to diminish and eventually disappear in the summer. Governments of the circumpolar north have begun positioning themselves strategically to claim sovereign control over new shipping lanes opened up by the disappearing ice. In an ironic twist, a Reuters news story in 2004 headlined as follows: "Denmark Seeks to Claim North Pole, Hopes to Strike Oil."

Another area of ongoing climate change impact is in the north American West, where tens of millions of acres of forest are being devastated by bark beetles and other infestations. The pests, which have attacked pine, fir, and spruce trees in the U.S. West, British Columbia, and Alaska, are normally contained by severe winters. The warming and mild winters in the region have increased their reproduction, abundance, and geographic range.

Hurricane Katrina, which led to the devastating flooding of New Orleans in 2005, was fueled by the warm waters of the Gulf of Mexico. Global warming has contributed to the warming of the tropical Atlantic, and the number of category 4 and 5 hurricanes—the most severe—has increased sharply in recent decades. One cannot associate a particular hurricane with global warming, but scientists are now reasonably confident that global warming is increasing the odds of intense, high-energy hurricanes.

To date, the industrial countries have contributed far more to the buildup of greenhouse gases than the developing countries—the United States alone is responsible for 30 percent—and they have reaped huge economic benefits in the process. The United States emits roughly the same amount of greenhouse gases as 2.6 billion people living in 150 developing nations. Industrial countries account for about 70 percent of carbon dioxide emissions, about 3.3 tons per capita. By contrast, the developing countries emit the rest at only half a ton per capita. Although developing country emissions of greenhouse gases are increasing rapidly, especially in China and elsewhere in Asia, it is doubtful that the developing nations will act to curb their emissions unless the industrial nations—both richer and the source of most of the climate problems we face—validate the seriousness of the issue and demonstrate their commitment to action by taking the first steps.

At the same time, the developing world is more vulnerable to climate change. Its people are more directly dependent on the natural resource base, more exposed to extreme weather events, and less capable economically and technologically to make needed adaptations. The disruption of water supplies or agriculture, the loss of glacial melt water in spring and summer, as well as rising sea levels and other impacts, could easily contribute to social tensions, violent conflicts, humanitarian emergencies, and the creation of ecological refugees. If these North-South differences are not addressed with great care, they could easily emerge as an increasing source of international tension.

Deforestation

It is estimated that about half of the world's temperate and tropical forests have been cleared, mostly for agriculture. A recent study of deforestation indicates that only about 20 percent of Earth's original forests remain in a wild, unmanaged state, and these areas are decreasing. Forest loss has been particularly serious in the tropics, which are home to about two-thirds of our planet's plant and animal species. The tropical forests encompass almost a billion acres of forested land in the area between the Tropics of Cancer and Capricorn. Brazil, Indonesia, and the Democratic Republic of Congo alone contain half of the world's tropical forests, and the rest are scattered throughout Latin America, Africa, and Asia. In recent decades, the rate of tropical forest loss has been about an acre a second. In terms of total forest area globally, these large losses are only very partially offset by increases in forest area in the United States and some other countries.

Tropical forests are particularly sensitive to disturbances. Although they are among the most productive ecosystems in terms of biological productivity, this productivity is deceptive. Most nutrients are in the plant matter itself, not in the soil. Soils in the tropics are notoriously poor. Furthermore, the sheer diversity of species that makes tropical forests so valuable also diminishes their ability to regenerate. In a 1 acre area of forest, one could find literally hundreds of species of plants, but perhaps only a few specimens per species. After deforestation, often the only plants that can survive in the open, nutrient-poor soil are fire-resistant grasses like *Imperata,* which chokes off the growth of the original species and prevents regeneration of a forest canopy.

Today, central governments own almost 80 percent of the remaining intact forests in developing countries. Forest ownership and management by central governments have sometimes resulted in mismanagement, heavy political and economic pressures to allow cutting and immigration, and widespread corruption, cronyism, and illegal logging. For example, in Vietnam the government nationalized the entire country's forest estate in the 1960s, leading eventually to a rapid increase in forest destruction nationwide as previous local controls and regulations were superceded by state-owned logging companies.

Many countries with high deforestation rates rank high in the international corruption index. Timber concessions in Indonesia, for example, have been awarded to loyal military officers for political reasons, and they have in turn forged partnerships with business groups to exploit their concessions. Around the world, corruption and mismanagement of forests have often gone together. It has been estimated that about three-fourths of Indonesia's timber trade and half of Vietnam's timber cut is illegally felled.

Timber concessions—the right to take trees—have been granted at below market rates and without safeguards or requirements for good management. Government subsidization of projects like road building has further fueled both timber booms and large-scale settlement. Another favorite policy of forest-rich countries is to promote agricultural development and ranching in previously forested areas, sometimes with government subsidies so deep that the enterprises would be essentially uneconomical without them. Cattle ranching in the Amazon is the most well known example in this regard.

These pressures for forest destruction have been both worsened and ameliorated by international factors. International development agencies like the World Bank, though much better today than in 1980, have poured many millions into dams, highways, power development, and transmigration schemes, often to the detriment of forest areas. Critics of globalization charge that economic globalization and the World Trade Organization are magnifying the trend toward expanded logging by encouraging high levels of foreign investment, weaker domestic regulation in the face of international competition, and loss of local community controls. On the other hand, international aid agencies (including the World Bank), conservation groups, and local authorities have cooperated in protecting many areas of unprecedented size and importance.

Land Degradation and Desertification

Today, about a fourth of Earth's terrestrial surface is devoted to crops, orchards, and rangelands for livestock. Arid and semiarid zones constitute large share of this area. These drylands are a critical source of food and account for about a fifth of the world's food production. About a fourth of the developing world's people—some 1.3 billion in all—live on these dry and other fragile lands. They are not naturally the most productive of agricultural lands, though irrigation can make a remarkable difference, and they are among the most ecologically vulnerable.

Land degradation when most serious is often called desertification. Dessertification is sometimes thought of as spreading sand dunes, and though that is a modest part of the problem, the concept of desertification in use today is much broader. It refers to the impoverishment of ecosystems and productive capacity in drylands and has many symptoms:

- Desolation of native vegetation and landscape devegetation
- Salinization of topsoil and water
- Reduction of surface waters and declining groundwater tables
- Unnaturally high soil erosion

An estimated 80 percent of agricultural land in dry regions suffers from moderate to severe desertification. Africa, which is 70 percent dryland areas, is particularly affected, but so are large areas in India and elsewhere in Asia, as well as major regions of the Western Hemisphere, including the southwestern United States and northern Mexico. Among desertification's many consequences are huge losses in food production, greater vulnerability to drought and famine, ecological refugees, loss of biodiversity, and social unrest. * * *

Freshwater Degradation and Shortages

It is doubtful that any natural areas have been as degraded by human activities as freshwater systems. Natural water courses and the vibrant life associated with them have been extensively affected by dams, dikes, diversions, stream channelization, wetland filling, and other modifications, not to mention pollution. Sixty percent of the world's major river basins have been severely or moderately fragmented by dams or other construction. Much of this activity is done to secure access to the water, but power production, flood control, navigation, and land reclamation have also been important factors. As freshwater is diverted away from natural sources, other ecosystems dependent on that water, suffer such as aquatic systems, wetlands, and forests. Human demand for water climbed ninefold in the twentieth century, much faster than population growth, and the trend continues today. It has been estimated that demands for irrigation and other water needs now claim 20 percent of the world's river supply and that the portion will grow to 40 percent by 2020.

Yet water shortages are already apparent in many countries. Rising demands for water have meant that many rivers no longer reach the sea in the dry season, such as the Colorado, Yellow, Ganges, and Nile, and the Syr Darya and Amu Darya rivers in central Asia. Adding insult to injury, natural watercourses have been the recipients of truly enormous volumes of pollutants around the world, from raw sewage to manufacturing effluents to agricultural and urban runoff to waste heat.

Meeting the world's demands for freshwater is proving problematic. About a third of the world's people already live in countries that are classified as "water stressed," meaning that already 20 to 40 percent of the available freshwater is being used by human societies. Projections indicate that the number of such people could rise from about 40 percent to 65 percent by 2025. About a billion people, a fifth of the world's population, lack clean drinking water; 40 percent lack sanitary services. According to WHO calculations, each year about 5 million people die from diseases caused by unsafe drinking water and lack of water for sanitation and hygiene. In the poorest countries dehydration and diarrhea are among the most common causes of infant mortality.

The most serious consequences of these freshwater problems are widespread poor health, constrained development of industry and agriculture, loss of services provided by natural aquatic ecosystems (including freshwater fisheries and natural flood control and water purification), species loss, and pollution of coastal areas. Absent a major response, these problems are only expected to increase in coming years. * * *

Marine Fisheries Decline

It is difficult to exaggerate the negative impact that human societies are having on the health of marine fisheries. In 1960, 5 percent of marine fisheries were fished to capacity or overfished. Today that number is 75 percent. The global catch of fish has gone down steadily since 1988 (once the highly volatile Peruvian anchoveta catch is out of the calculation). In 2003, scientists reported that populations of large predator fish—including popularly consumed varieties such as swordfish, marlin, and tuna- - are down 90 percent over original stocks; only 10 percent remain. Over 300,000 whales, dolphins, and other cetaceans die each year from entanglement in nets and other fishing gear. Each year 44 billion pounds of fish about a quarter of the total landed weight—is discarded as unwanted bycatch.

Overfishing is the key culprit here, but the marine environment is also being affected by destruction of mangroves and coastal wetlands, about half of which have been lost, and by pollution and silt from runoff. Particularly hard hit have been the coral reefs. About 20 percent of coral reefs worldwide have been lost, and a further 20 percent are severely threatened.

Beyond biodiversity loss, there are major consequences for human societies stemming from the depletion of the oceans. In Asia, fish are the principal protein source for about half the population. A fifth of the world's people get a fifth or more of their protein from fish. Fishery exports are an important economic asset for developing countries; they are responsible for half the world's export of fish. Indirectly fish products serve as a major source of fertilizer and nutrient for commercial livestock.

Many factors contribute to overfishing. A major cause has been the efforts of some maritime countries, including the United States and Japan, to subsidize their fishing industries. In addition, many migratory species of fish are caught in the open oceans—outside the national sovereignty of any particular country. In such areas no country is able to enforce limits on fisheries takings, nor do many countries feel the responsibility for formulating policies for such areas beyond national control.

Toxic Pollutants

Among the most serious environmental threats to human health and to ecosystems are chemicals known as persistent organic pollutants, or POPs. Rachel Carson's book *Silent Spring*, published in 1962, highlighted for a wide audience the dangers of these new manufactured chemical compounds, such as the then commonly used pesticide DDT. "For the first time in the history of the world, every human being is now subjected to contact with dangerous chemicals, from the moment of conception until death. In the less than two decades of their use, the synthetic pesticides have been so thoroughly distributed throughout the animate and inanimate world that they occur virtually everywhere. * * *

Child health experts at Mount Sinai School of medicine in New York report that today virtually every person on Earth can be shown to harbor detectible levels of dozens of POPs. It has been known for a long time that POPs were showing up all over the globe, even far outside the range of where the POPs were originally used. For example, Inuit mothers in the Arctic have been measured to have levels of POPs in their breast milk five times greater than found in industrial countries. * * *

But the POP issue is only one of many toxic and hazardous substance problems to attract international attention. Inorganic chemicals, notably the heavy metals like mercury, are also receiving international attention as pollutants. An assessment by the U.N. Environment Programme on mercury's threat to humans and wildlife has led to an international plan to help reduce mercury releases, much of which comes from coal-burning power plants. Mercury is a potent neurotoxin, and perhaps a third of mercury deposition in the United States comes from sources outside the country. Though legislation is before the U.S. Congress to reduce mercury emissions, it is doubtful that anything short of international action will suffice. Beyond mercury, a wide range of toxic substances continue to pose environmental threats—hazardous and radioactive wastes and other heavy metals including lead and arsenic among them.

Loss of Biological Diversity

While attention has typically focused on endangered species and their possible extinction, the broader concept of biological diversity, or biodiversity, is more fundamental. Biodiversity is defined as having three dimensions: the genetic variety within a given species; the millions of individual species of plants, animals, and microorganisms; and the diversity of different types of ecosystems such as alpine tundra, southern hardwood bottomlands, or tropical rainforests.

The focus on biodiversity as opposed to individual species was warmly embraced by many in the 1980s and 1990s, and it soon became a dominant paradigm in the biological sciences. New journals, such as *Conservation Biology* and *Biodiversity and Conservation,* sprang up. In the process, the idea of biodiversity has sometimes come to represent the field of conservation and the science of ecology writ large. As E. O. Wilson asserted in his popular book *The Diversity of Life,* "Biological diversity—'biodiversity' in the new parlance—is the key to the maintenance of the world as we know it." * * *

The cumulative effect of all the factors is that species loss today is estimated to be perhaps 1,000 times the natural or normal rate species go extinct. Many scientists believe we are on the brink of the sixth great wave of species loss on Earth, and the only one caused by the human species.

There are many reasons for the world community to be concerned about the loss of biodiversity. One was well stated in the preamble to the 1982 *World Charter for Nature:* "Every form of life is unique, warranting respect regardless of its worth to man, and to accord other organisms such recognition, man must be guided by a moral code of conduct." In addition to ethical considerations, biodiversity is the source of the ecosystem services that make life possible—ecosystem services such as nutrient cycling, pollination, air and water purification, climate regulation, drought and flood control, not to mention the commercial products of field, forest, and stream. Consider that many oils, chemicals, rubber, spices, nuts, honey, and fruits were first harvested in the wild; moreover, a third of all prescription drugs were originally harvested as substances found in nature. Many nongovernmental organizations (NGOs) have made protection of biodiversity a centerpiece of their land conservation strategies and now often include attention to the economic benefits of biodiversity as a factor in protected area plans.

Excess Nitrogen

The nine global challenges just discussed were all identified as early as 1980 as major threats meriting international action. The problem of excess nitrogen in ecosystems has not received similar recognition, but it deserves to be on this list of serious threats.

Earth's atmosphere is mostly nitrogen, bound together as N_2 and not re-active. Bacteria such as those associated with legumes "fix" nitrogen, chang-ing it to a biologically active form that plants can use. But here is the prob-lem: we humans have started fixing nitrogen too, industrially. Today hu-mans are fixing as much nitrogen as nature does. Once fixed, nitrogen re-mains active for a very long time, cascading through the biosphere.

Today, the anthropogenic nitrogen is coming primarily from two sources: about 75 percent from fertilizers and 25 percent from fossil fuel combustion. Nitrogen fertilizers are often ammonia based; their use is a huge global en-terprise. Ninety percent of this fertilizer is wasted, though, ending up in wa-terways and in the air and soil. High-temperature combustion in power plants oxidized the nitrogen to produce a variety of nitrogen oxides.

Nitrogen in waterways leads to overfertilization and, when heavy, to al-gal blooms and eutrophication—aquatic life simply dies from lack of oxygen. There are now over 150 dead zones in the ocean, mostly due to excess fertili-zation. Nitrate in ground and surface waters is also a threat to human health. And there is another pathway. Forty percent of the world's grain goes to feed livestock, which produce vast volumes of nitrogen-rich manure, much of which ends up in the water. All this extra nitrogen is also having effects on biodiversity and natural systems—shifting the species composition of ecosystems by favoring those that respond most to nitrogen. Absent cor-rective action, nitrogen added to waterways is projected to increase 25 per-cent in the Organization for Economic Cooperation and Development (OECD) countries and 100 percent in the developing world between 1995 and 2020.

In the air, nitrogen oxide from fossil fuel combustion reacts with volatile hydrocarbons and sunlight to produce smog, a nasty mix of photochemical oxidants, one of which is ozone. It can also become nitric acid and contribute to acid deposition. Ozone (from smog) and nitrous oxide (from fertilized soils) are greenhouse gases, so nitrogen fixation also contributes to global warming. As the 2001 Summary Statement from the Second International Nitrogen Conference notes, biologically active nitrogen can "contribute to smog, fine particle formation, visibility impairment, acid deposition, excess nutrient in-puts to estuaries and near-coastal waters, global warming, and stratospheric ozone depletion." Essential to life and necessary in our gardens and agricul-tural fields, nitrogen is the classic case of too much of a good thing.

The problem is global. Asia now contributes 35 percent of the world's synthetic nitrogen. Serious though this problem is, it has yet to attract the attention that CFCs or carbon dioxide have received.

Some Connections among the Issues

An important observation about the global environmental challenges is that there are complex linkages among them. The previous discussions of biodiversity and excess nitrogen dramatize this point. Because of such connections and interactions, these problems are especially difficult to manage effectively. The interconnections among the issues also bring to the fore a key feature of global policymaking—the management of uncertainty and risk.

Fossil fuel use—the burning of coal, oil, and natural gas—provides one type of linkage. Fossil fuels are responsible for acid rain and most of the human-induced climate change. They also cause the buildup of tropospheric ozone (smog occurring at Earth's surface), which itself is a greenhouse gas in addition to being a health hazard and destroyer of crops and forests, where it often acts in concert with acid rain.

Another set of considerations link climate change and stratospheric ozone depletion. CFCs and certain other gases that deplete the ozone layer are also greenhouse gases, contributing to global warming. (There are also CFC substitutes that are greenhouse gases.) Global warming can actually cool the stratosphere and that in turn can worsen ozone depletion. And the increase in UVB radiation due to the thinner ozone layer can alter Earth's ecosystems and interact with the terrestrial and aquatic effects of climate change.

Deforestation contributes to biodiversity loss, climate change, and desertification. Climate change, acid rain, ozone depletion, toxic chemicals, and water reductions can in turn adversely affect world forests.

Because climate provides the setting or envelope for life, changing climate will affect everything. Among other things, it is likely to worsen desertification, lead to both additional flooding and increased droughts, impact fresh water supplies, adversely affect biodiversity and forests, and further degrade aquatic ecosystems.

It is impossible to isolate environmental issues from economic ones. For instance, industrialization and the growth of world trade have contributed directly to the widespread use of fossil fuels, the global transport of oil by ships, and the broader transportation of goods by ship worldwide. The increased reliance on imported oil increases the likelihood of oil spills. Marine commerce provides the vectors by which alien species invasions occur, as foreign species hitch rides on ships and then enter new ecosystems where there are no natural predators. * * *

Underlying Drivers of Deterioration

The 10 major global environmental challenges can be thought of as the end result of an interacting set of underlying causes, or drivers of deterioration. Understanding these drivers is important for the simple reason that, in the end, societies will have to come to grips with them to forestall an appalling deterioration of our natural assets.

Three of the more obvious root causes of these problems are conveniently described in what is called the "IPAT equation," which sees environmental impact (I) as the product of population (P), affluence (A), and technology (T). *
* * Consider, for example, carbon dioxide emissions as a measure of environmental impact. If population doubles in a given period of time and per capita income go up threefold, and nothing else changes, we would expect CO_2 emission to go up sixfold. If they actually went up by only fourfold, it would be because technological change had made it possible to produce each dollar of GDP with less CO_2 emissions. The society in question would be decreasing what is called the carbon intensity of production. Carbon intensity, which has in fact been decreasing in the United States, can be cut by increasing energy efficiency, by shifting to nonfossil energy (renewable and nuclear power), and by shifting to the lighter hydrocarbons—oil and natural gas—within the fossil fuel family. These are all different types of technological change within the framework of the IPAT equation.

The fourfold expansion in human numbers in the twentieth century, from 1.5 billion to over 6 billion, has been a huge driver of environmental decline. And the story is far from over. Global population is projected to go up another 25 percent in the next 20 years. Virtually all of the current growth is in the developing world, but this has not always been the case. The billion or so souls in the rich countries had their population explosion earlier, and these countries have now largely completed what is called the demographic transition. The transition begins when improvements in health and nutrition lead to reduced infant mortality and longer lives. Fertility rates do not immediately decline, so population grows rapidly. Later, fertility rates decline and population size tends again toward stability. The transition is thus one from high births and high deaths to low births and low deaths. Indeed, in some industrial countries birth rates are now well below replacement levels.

It is possible that the demographic transition will be completed in the developing world around midcentury and that global population growth may level off at about 9 billion and then perhaps begin to decline. These numbers may be optimistic and depend importantly on continuation of national and international population programs.

The IPAT equation also helps us see a key fact about population growth. In highly affluent societies, a given increase in population numbers will have a disproportionately large environmental impact, based on today's patterns of resource consumption and pollution. As immigration accounted for about a third of U.S. population growth during the 1990's and U.s. population growth is one of the highest in the world in numbers of people added per year, this consideration has led a few environmentalists to question U.S. immigration policy—a thorny issue, to be sure—and to call for a U.S. population growth policy.

In the developing world today, high fertility rates are often driven by a set of reinforcing factors: the status of women, lack of employment opportunities for women and educational opportunities for girls, lack of maternal and child health care and family planning services, as well as poverty and deprivation generally. Addressing these issues together can lead to dramatic declines in fertility rates. * * *

The consumption habits of the affluent have been repeatedly cited both for their environmental impacts and for their assault on equity: "We are all consuming more on a per capita basis in the U.S., Europe, and Asia, resulting in accelerated use of natural resources and associated environmental impacts both at home and abroad. Indeed, more goods and services have been consumed since 1950 than by all previous generations combined. From 1950 to 1990, per capita consumption of plastic increased five-fold and aluminum by seven-fold. While America has the highest per capita consumption levels in the world, the resource consumption in Western Europe and Japan is only slightly less. * * *

The third IPAT factor, technology, is at least as important as the other two. Indeed if one assumes that population and affluence will generally increase for the foreseeable future, only rapid changes in technology—the greening of technology—offers hope within IPAT for reducing environmental impacts. Of the three, it's the only term that promises movement in the "right" direction. We saw this important reality in the IPAT example involving CO_2 emissions and carbon intensity.

The core problem in this context is that most of the technologies (including techniques) that today dominate agriculture, energy, manufacturing, transportation, and the build environment were developed in an era when environmental considerations, far from being dominant ones, were hardly considerations at all.

The situation regarding technology is thus much like that on consumption. Public attitudes toward new technology have generally been supportive, welcoming, and trustful. * * * The control of technologies has been largely in the hands of large corporations that benefit from their deployment and are clearly in no position to be impartial judges of the public's best interests. The unaided market fails to guide technology toward good environmental choices;

governments have failed to correct poor market signals. And once a technology has reached a certain level of deployment, it gains an often unwelcome lifespan.

At a deeper level, beyond the immediate drivers reflected in the IPAT equation, we find a variety of other drivers at work. Several involve the nature of our economic system: a deep commitment to continuing high rates of economic growth—what has been called 'growthmania" or "the growth fetish"; the concentration of power in a relatively small number of large corporations and the narrow imperatives of profitability that impel their operations; a market economy guided by prices and other market signals that are environmentally misleading because they do not incorporate the full environmental costs of doing business (an example of "market failure"); and an ongoing economic globalization that is largely unregulated for environmental and social ends and thus is an accelerator of all these forces because it speeds patterns of growth and development that remain unsustainable environmentally.

An additional driver, the opposite of affluence, is world poverty and the extreme gaps in incomes between poor and rich countries. The conventional observation that the poor are often forced to degrade their own environments because no alternatives are open to them is still valid in a world where at least a billion people live in conditions of abject poverty and extreme deprivation and where close to half the world's people survive on less than $2 per day. The search for land pushes them into forest; the need for fuelwood and structural material leads to denuding the landscape; the imperative of supplying food leads to excessive cropping and grazing. Meanwhile, the absolute and the relative poverty of the majority of nations creates a powerful push for economic growth at all costs, including environmental ones. Per capita GDP of the United States in 2002 was $36,000; in Europe, $22,900; in China, $980; in India, $490; and in Nigeria, $360 or about $1 per day per person.

Beyond all these factors, at the deepest level there are systems of values and habits of thought that conspire against environmental protection. Two ingrained ones in our society go by the awkward words *anthropocentrism* and *contempocentrism*. The former puts humans at the center of the world often at the expense of other life on Earth. In the process it ignores one of the two guiding principles of environmental ethics: our duty to the community of life that evolved here with us. The latter—contempocentrism—discounts the future in favor of the present and thus violates the other key principle of environmental ethics—our duty to future generations. * * *

Notes and Questions

1. Each of the ten environmental problems sketched by Speth and Haas is addressed by different international, regional and national environmental

laws. What overarching framework is needed to facilitate their integration? How can synergies among the ten legal frameworks be marshaled to enhance the likelihood that the problems of each sector can be addressed more effectively? Climate change is part of this larger picture. See J. Wiener, Responding to the Global Warming Problem: Something Borrowed for Something Blue: Legal Transplants and the Evolution of Global Environmental Law, 27 Ecology L. Q. 1295 (2001). Up to 2009, nations have demonstrated no consensus to design a new multilateral environmental agency. N. Robinson, Befogged Vision: International Environmental Governance a Decade After Rio, 27 William & Mary   Envtl. L. & Policy Rev. 299 (2002).

2. Of the ten environmental trends, only the stratospheric ozone, climate change (global warming), biodiversity, desertification and marine environment are addressed by global treaties. Relatively few nations participate in the desertification agreement. Northern Europe and North American have stabilized, but not eliminated acid rain, while acid rain in Asia has grown enormously. No international laws govern deforestation. A handful of regional river basin agreements address allocation of freshwater resources among nations, and an international agreement for wetlands encourages protecting this biome. Treaties to protect the Earth's Nitrogen cycle do not exist. Even where treaties do exist, it is up to nations to enact national environmental laws to implement their objectives. What changes in policy and perspective will be required before foreign ministries and national executive authorities understand that each of the ten problem areas require global cooperation and local action? René Dubos counseled those at the 1972 UN Stockholm Conference on the Human Environment to "think globally, act locally." Is this admonition sufficient? How do governments decide to make environmental issues a priority? See the discussion on the stages of public environmental awareness in N. Robinson, Legal Systems, Decisionmaking, and the Science of Earth's Systems: Procedural Missing Links, 27 Ecology L. Q. 1077, 1097-1116 (2001).

3. Is the "IPAT" equation sufficient? Should there not be another factor added, like the temporal dimension? If a problem is allowed to foster over a long time, it can produce a crescendo of ever-greater impacts; if a technology is used beyond its expected life, the impacts accumulate and there is no incentive to apply technological innovations. The global impact of most environmental problems was understood in Agenda 21 as of 1992, but "business as usual" precludes or retards implementing Agenda 21. It takes time to restore damaged ecosystems, or benefit from planting trees to sequester carbon dioxide. As Nicholas Stern points out in his Chapter 1 excerpt, governments and their taxpayers will pay more to resolve environmental crisis in the future than they would if they attended to them today. N. Stern, The Economics of Climate Change (2007). How would you restate the IPAT equation to deal with time and delay?

A BRIDGE AT THE EDGE OF THE WORLD: CAPITALISM, THE ENVIRONMENT, AND CROSSING FROM CRISIS TO SUSTAINABILITY
James Gustave Speth (2008)

* * * Promoting growth—achieving ever-greater economic wealth and prosperity—may be the most widely shared and robust cause in the world today. Economic growth has been called "the secular religion of the advancing industrial societies." Leading macroeconomists declare it the summum bonum of their craft. * * *

Growth is traditionally measured as an increase in Gross Domestic Product, and GDP growth is what is meant here by growth. It has given much of the world remarkable material progress—progress in the things that economies can produce and money can buy—but this prosperity has been and is being purchased at a huge environmental cost. McNeill reports the following increases over the century from the 1890s to the 1990s:

World economy	up	14 fold
World population	up	4 fold
Water use	up	9 fold
Sulfur dioxide emissions	up	13 fold
Energy use	up	16 fold
Carbon dioxide emissions	up	17 fold
Marine fish catch	up	35 fold

Such trends continue into the present. Over the past quarter century—a period during which major environmental programs were in place and operational in many countries—the following increases occurred globally on average each decade from 1980 to 2005:

Gross world product	46 percent
Paper and paper products	41 percent
Fish harvest	41 percent
Meat consumption	37 percent
Passenger cars	30 percent
Energy use	23 percent
Fossil fuel use	20 percent
World population	18 percent
Grain harvest	18 percent
Nitrogen oxide emissions	18 percent
Water withdrawals	16 percent
Carbon dioxide emissions	16 percent
Fertilizer use	10 percent
Sulfur dioxide emissions	9 percent

Each of these indicators measures environmental impact in some way, and each show that impacts are increasing, not declining. It is significant that these rates of resource consumption and pollution are lower that the growth of the world economy. The eco-efficiency of the economy is improving through "dematerialization," the increased productivity of resource inputs, and the reduction of wastes discharged per unit of output. However, eco-efficiency is not improving fast enough to prevent impacts from rising. Donella Meadows summed it up nicely: things are getting worse at a slower rate. * * *

What, then, is the operating system at work here? It is a complex of political, economic, and social arrangements that can be accurately described as features of modern-day capitalism. Immediately one says: but communism was worse for the environment, and that's true. Its authoritarian political system and highly centralized economic planning produced one environmental disaster for another. But this argument is largely irrelevant since communism is largely irrelevant. We live in a world dominated by a variety of capitalisms. In the end, no form of economy does well on the environment unless forced to by vigorously enforced rules and powerful incentives and penalties created by government and consumers. * * *

* * * [We] see why the economy and environment are constantly colliding. First, the capitalist economy, to the degree it is successful, is inherently an exponential growth economy. A leading economist, William Baumol, summed up the relationship nicely: "Under capitalism, innovative activity—which in other types of economy is fortuitous and optional—becomes mandatory, a life-and-death matter for the firm. And the spread of new technology, which in other economies has proceeded at a stately pace, often requiring decades or even centuries, under capitalism is speeded up remarkably because, quite simply, time is money. That, in short is the * * * explanation of the incredible growth of the free-market economies. The capitalist economy can usefully be viewed as a machine whose primary product is economic growth. Indeed, its effectiveness in this role is unparalleled.

Second, the profit motive powerfully affects the capitalist's behavior. Surplus product—profit—can be increased by preserving and perpetuating the market failures Oates described. Surplus product can also be increased through environmentally perverse subsidies and other advantages. Today's corporations have been called "externalizing machines," so committed are they to finding subsidies, tax breaks, and regulatory loopholes from government. The environment, of course, suffers as a result.

Third, as Karl Polanyi described long ago in *The Great Transformation,* the spread of the market into new areas, with its emphasis on efficiency and ever-expanding commodification, can be very costly environmentally and socially. It is a pleasure to read Polanyi. He saw so clearly in 1944 the costs of unbridled capitalism, yet he believed this "19th century system," as he called it, was collapsing. He saw the self-adjusting market as a stark utopia. "Such an institution could not exist for any length of time without annihilating the human and natural substance of society; it would have physically destroyed man and transformed his surroundings into a wilderness." * * *

* * * Last, there are fundamental biases in capitalism that favor the present over the future and the private over the public. Future generations cannot participate in capitalism's markets. From an environmental perspective, that is a huge flaw because the essence of sustainable development is equity toward future generations. Regarding the bias toward the private over the public (private spending versus public spending, private property versus public property, and so on), economists have even had to invent theories of government spending and public goods to justify the public sector's existence. Greater emphasis on the public side would serve our environment better. In America, for example, large public investments are overdue in land conservation; in environmental education, research, and development; and in incentives to spur new ecologically sophisticated technologies.

But the system that drives today's unsustainable growth includes other powerful elements beyond these. First, there is what the modern corporation has become. The corporation, the most important institution and agent of modern capitalism, has become both huge and hugely powerful. There are today more than sixty-three thousand multinational corporations. As recently as 1990, there were fewer than half that. Of the one hundred largest economies in the world, fifty-three are corporations. Exxon Mobil is larger than 180 nations. Corporations are required by law and driven by self-interest to increase their monetary value of the benefit of their owners, the shareholders, and pressures to show quick results in this regard have grown steadily. The corporate sector wields great political and economic power and has routinely used that power to restrain ameliorative governmental action. And it has driven the rise of transnational capital as the basis for economic globalization. The international system of investing, buying and selling is becoming a single global economy. Unfortunately, what we have today is the globalization of market failure.

Second, there is what society has become. Values today are strongly materialistic, anthropocentric, and contempocentric. Today's consumerism places high priority on meeting human needs through ever-increasing purchase of material goods and services. We may say "the best things in life are free," but not many of us act that way. The anthropocentric view that nature belongs to us rather than we to nature eases the exploitation of the natural world. The habit of focusing on the present and discounting the future leads away from a thoughtful appraisal of long-term consequences and the world we are making. * * *

These features, presented starkly without caveats and qualifications that could be added, aptly characterize key dimensions of today's world operating system. They are all features of contemporary capitalism. They are linked, mutually supportive, indeed mutually reinforcing. Taken together, they have given rise to an economic reality that is both enormously large and, from an environment perspective, largely out of control and therefore very destructive. Capitalism as we know it today is incapable of sustaining the environment. * * *

* * * One thing that will become clear in this search is that many of the solutions will be found outside the environmental sector in alliance with communities of concern that are not in the first instance environmental. And the question will arise: is the operating system just described delivering the goods for these other communities? If today's growth and capitalism are delivering high levels of life satisfaction, genuine well-being, and true happiness to societies broadly, then there may be scant chance for real change. But if what we actually have is "spiritual hunger in an age of plenty," there is a large space for hope. A system that cannot deliver the well-being of people and nature is in deep trouble. It invites ideas and actions that are transformative.

E. THE QUEST FOR EFFECTIVE ENVIRONMENTAL LAWS

Since at least the 1972 United Nations Stockholm Conference on the Human Environment, all nations have sought to fashion laws to harmonize human behavior with the scientifically described "laws of nature." Such laws have ancient roots. The oldest written symbol for law is the ancient Chinese pictogram, *FA*. The three parts of the pictogram show, on the upper left side, a human being with water running down hill below. The legendary animal Zhi is serving as the judge, with his horn aimed at the human to determine his dishonesty or guilt. The water symbolizes the even-handed quality of Zhi's judgments, always balanced and fair, like water that follows gravity to find its own level and balance.

The ancient pictograph reminds us that humans have been reflecting on their relations with nature for eons. As legislatures begin to reshape the law to provide management of the atmosphere, it is useful to reflect on the history of environmental law. It is rather brief, but its emergence coincides with the measurable impact of humans as a force shaping life on Earth.

Contemporary environmental law has its roots in the laws for the "conservation" of nature enacted beginning in the late 19th century. These laws, many of which are still in force today, reflected a human aversion to destruction of nature at the time, the praise of natural beauty by painters and writers of that period, and the emergence of a humane attitude toward animals. Natural resource laws proliferated in the early 20th century, seeking the rational use of renewable resources and the careful exploitation of non-renewable resources. With the intense pollution following the Second World War, the field of environmental law was born. The International Union for the Conservation of Nature and Natural Resources (IUCN), established in 1948, began its environmental law program in 1963. A decade later, the 1972 UN Stockholm Conference inaugurated a new era of international cooperation and national environmental law-making. But such laws had not turned back the tide of environmental destruction across the Earth, and this led to the focus on "sustainable development," and the policy prescriptions of the 1992 UN Conference on Environment and Development in Rio de Janeiro.

As governments confront the challenges of climate change, it will be useful to assess what aspects of environmental law worked well and which did not. Some historical perspective is needed. The practice of law today in bound up in an uncertain, historic and problematic transformation of life on Earth. How humans respond to "climate change" will determine the fate of natural communities of life, including humankind. How did human society reach this "tipping point?"

Humans conceived the science of ecology just as the Industrial Revolution was taking hold. D. Wooster, The Economy of Nature: a History of Ecological Ideas (1994). The perceptions of a Vermont lawyer, diplomat, and fish conservation commissioner, George Perkins Marsh chronicled how humans were transforming the planet as early as 1864, in his seminal study entitled Man and Nature; or Physical Geography as Modified by Human Action (1864). As William F. Ruddiman has observed, "Well before the industrial era began in the late 1700s, humans had come a very long way from those first sporadic attempts to plant a few grains of wheat and barley some 12,000 years earlier. Within the last several thousand years, we had become a force capable of transforming the very look of the landscape and also become a factor in the operation of the climate system." W. Ruddiman, Plows, Plagues & Petroleum: How Humans Took Control of Climate (2005). In 1896, the Swedish chemist, Svante Arrhenius, posited the theory that the carbon dioxide released from the combustion of coal would result in global warming. Arrhenius postulated the consequences. E. Crawford, Arrhenius: From Ionic Theory to the Greenhouse Effect (2009).

The Progressive Era in the United States saw the enactment of the first generation of natural resource stewardship laws, to curb the excessive exploitation of shared resources such as the water ways or forests or soils. During and after the Second World War, vast new sources of air and water pollution were unleashed on North America, and in the rebuilding of Europe and Asia, further substantial increased in air and water and solid waste pollution began to afflict much of the rest of the world. Environmental laws were enacted to abate this pollution in the 1970-1980 period. See R. Lazarus, The Making of Environmental Law (2004).

Much of that legislation has been inadequately enforced in developed regions and remains to be implemented in the developing regions. For example, "acid rain" continues to afflict North American and Europe, although reduced in volume and perpetuated in a kind of "defeasible license to pollute" by the U.S. Clean Air Act's cap and trade system. In Asia, "atmospheric brown cloud" gathers over the Indian Ocean from South China and South East Asia, and is dispersed through the Monsoon's "acid rains" over the Indian subcontinent.

The ravishing of the global commons produced tepid responses from an international community of nations that was still preoccupied with the aftermath of the Cold War. Following the United Nations Conference on the Human Environment in Stockholm (1972), nations negotiated a set of multilateral environmental agreements (MEAs) and began to enact the national legislation to implement them. Barbara Lausche, Weaving a Web of Environmental Law (2008). In 1987, the United Nations World Commission on Environment and Development published its report, entitled Our Common Future (1987) and disseminated massively and globally by Oxford University Press. Known also as the "Bruntlund Report" after the Commission's Chairwoman, Gro Harlem Bruntland, then the Prime Minister of Norway, Our Common Future noted:

> There are thresholds that cannot be crossed without endangering the basic integrity of the system. Today, we are close to many of these thresholds; we must be ever mindful of the risk of endangering the survival of life on Earth. Moreover, the speed with which changes in resource use are taking place gives little time in which to anticipate and prevent unexpected effects.

> The "greenhouse effect," one threat to life support systems, springs directly from increased resource use. The burning of fossil fuels and the cutting and burning of forests release carbon dioxide (CO_2). The accumulation in the atmosphere of CO_2 and certain other gases traps solar radiation near the Earth's surface, causing global warming. This could cause sea-level rises over the next 45 years large enough to inundate many low-lying coastal cities and river deltas. It could also drastically upset national and international agricultural production and trade systems.

In 1992 nations negotiated and opened for signature at the Rio Earth Summit the foundational MEA within which protection of the Earth's atmosphere proceeds, the United Nations Framework Convention on Climate Change (1992) ("UNFCCC"). Nations ratifying this treaty, including the United States, agreed to work toward the "ultimate objective" of achieving "stabilization of greenhouse gas concentrations in the atmosphere at a level that would prevent dangerous anthropogenic interference with the climate system. Such a level should be achieved within a timeframe sufficient to allow ecosystems to adapt naturally to climate change, to ensure that food production is not threatened and to enable economic development to proceed in a sustainable fashion." (Article 4, UNFCCC).

From 1992 to 2008, nations made halting progress toward implementing the UNFCCC. The "climate skeptics" and advocates of "business as usual" opposed measures at elaborating or implementing this MEA. The Administration of President George W. Bush and Vice President Cheney actively opposed measures to implement environmental legislation and meet treaty obligations. Concerned that the time within which to prevent irreversible change was eroding, the States Party to the UNFCCC met at their 13th session of the Conference of the Parties ("COP") in Bali, in December of 2007, and adopted the "Bali Action Plan," UNFCCC COP Decision 1/CP.13 (FCCC/CP/2007/6/Add. 1). Under the terms of the UNFCCC, this decision could be taken by majority vote, and the United States had no veto to prevent it. Negotiations took place at the 14th COP in Poznan, Poland in December of 2009, with an expectation that there will be further concrete agreements to achieve the UNFCCC objective in December of 2009 at the 15th COP meeting in Denmark.

The challenges of integrating management of the human impact on the atmosphere into environmental law are profound and complex. No sector of human endeavor is outside the impact of climate change or immune from its effects. The very complexity and enormity of the challenges of responding to climate change, in both scope and scale, render the problems difficult to discern across all sectors, as noted by Stephen Pacala and Robert Socolow in their seminal article, "Stabilization Wedges: Solving the Climate Problem for the Next 50 Years with Current Technologies," *Science*, vol. 305 (Aug. 13, 2004).

Our Common Future noted that "the Earth is one but the world is not." We confront the challenge to think in the idiom that Rene Dubos presented to the 1972 UN Stockholm Conference on the Human Environment: "think globally and act locally." Should we also think across generations? See M. Wood, Law and Climate Change: Government's Atmospheric Trust Responsibility, 38 ELR 10652 (2009).

F. DISREGARDING THE GATHERING STORM

As early as 1981, President Carter's Council on Environmental Quality (CEQ) issued a report that "addressed the problem of carbon dioxide pollution" and cited the "major long-term climatic and economic problems" that would ensure if emissions were not averted. P. Shabecoff, U.S. Study Warms of Extensive Problems From Carbon Dioxide Pollution, N.Y. Times (Jan. 13, 1981). The Chair of the Council was James Gustave Speth. Speth notes that the CEQ report recommended capping carbon dioxide levels at 50% above the pre-industrial level, and observes "Because the United States and others failed to act on early warnings like ours, the prospects of halting the buildup of greenhouse gases at safe levels are now fast slipping away." J. Speth, "Dean's Message: Time for Civic Unreasonableness," Environment: Yale at 2 (School of Forestry & Environmental Studies, Spring 2008). Speth continues:

A number of factors probably combined to produce this unfortunate result. The climate issue is technically complex and not easy to master. * * * Its most serious consequences stretch into the distant future, presenting the type of long-term problem with which our political system has great difficulty. * * * The combination of energy industry opposition and consumer concern plus higher energy prices has proved fatal.

Journalist Ross Gelbspan and others have pointed to the shortcomings of the media and other instruments of public information, which did not keep the climate issue on the front burner * * * In his book, The Boiling Point, Gelbspan notes two other important and related patterns: One is that the desire of American journalists to seek balance by presenting two sides to even one-sided issues can actually introduce bias. The other pattern Gelbspan sees stems from the acquisition of most news outlets by a small group of conglomerates. With this change, Gelbspan believes that "the directions of the business have been determined by the profit-driven demands of Wall Street."

More significant than the shortcomings of the media * * * has been the rise of the modern right in recent American politics. * * * Frederick Buell, in his valuable and undernoticed book, From Apocalypse to Way of Life: Environmental Crisis in the American Century has chronicled what happened: "Something happened to strip the environmental cause of what seemed to be its self-evident inevitability. * * * The most important explanation for these events isn't hard to find. In reaction to the decade of crisis, a string and enormously successful anti-environmental disinformation industry sprang up. * * * The public drive for environmental change has been "neutralized" by the 1980s, blocked by an increasingly organized and elaborate corporate and conservative opposition. * * *

Finally, I would argue that the failure to rise to the climate-change challenge is part of a larger failure to treat as priorities a number of major environmental threats and that we all complicit in that failure. * * * After a quarter century of neglect, societies now risk ruining the planet. * * * Our values are too materialistic, too anthropocentric and too contempocentric, with the result that we have hardly begun what Thomas Berry has said must be our Great Work–"moving the human project from its devastating exploitation to a benign presence."

George Bernard Shaw famously remarked that all progress depends on being unreasonable. It's time for a large amount of civic unreasonableness. It is time for the environmental community—indeed all of us—to step back from the day-to-day and develop a deeper critique of what is on.

Many of theologian Thomas Berry's views are embraced in the Earth Charter, www.earthcharter.org. Is the popular neglect of the Earth Charter, or of environmental ethics generally, caused by the same forces that relegated the science of climate change to the sidelines? Do you agree with Speth's assessment? Were not the corporate or conservative forces sincere in their advocacy in support of business as usual and against calls for environmental reforms? Which side was choosing to ignore "sound" science? Is the political context ripe in the USA, or in any other country (China? the EU?), for a new environmental rights movement, akin to the US civil rights movement of the 1960s? Or are the transformations required to deal with climate change as much about technological choice and international cooperation as they are about "rights"?

See also D. Craig, The Deep Sleep, Columbia (2008).

G. EASY ADAPTATION: "IRRATIONAL EXUBERANCE?"

The "business as usual" bias encourages many initially to adopt an optimism that they somehow have a singular advantage that will permit them to weather climate change and adapt. Others hope for a gradual adjustment without economic dislocation, wishing for a "silver bullet" solution to curb greenhouse gas emissions such as a "cap and trade" system with tradable emission allowances or some amazing new technology. But according to President Obama on Earth Day 2009: "There aren't any silver bullets."

THE CLIMATE CRISIS AND THE ADAPTATION MYTH
Robert Repetto
www.yale.edu/environment/publications (2008)

Influential studies have predicted that moderate climate change, up to 3 or 4 degrees Fahrenheit, will not be very damaging to the United States as a whole and will bring some benefits. Underlying the argument that climate change will not be very damaging to the U.S. economy is the contention that vulnerable organizations, firms and households will take steps to adapt. This assumption is based partly on the fact that the United States is rich in technology, economic resources, competent organizations and educated people, all of which combine to create a high capacity to adapt. More fundamentally, the contention rests on the observation that the United States spans a wide variety of climatic conditions to which households and enterprises have adapted successfully in the past. According to a recent review, "The literature indicates that U.S. society can on the whole adapt with either net gains or some costs if warming occurs at the lower end of the projected range of magnitude, assuming no change in climate variability and generally making optimistic assumptions about adaptation." * * *

* * * However, saying that the U.S. *can* adapt does not imply that it *will* adapt, at least not in the efficient and timely way needed if major damages are to be avoided. The question is whether it is likely that such steps will actually be taken and whether they will be taken in sufficient time to limit damages. If not, damages from climate change will be considerably higher than has been estimated. There is an important distinction between *anticipatory or preventive adaptation* that predicts and responds to vulnerabilities before damages are incurred and *reactive adaptation* that gears up to limit the recurrence of damage only after effects of climate change have been felt and damage done, in order to limit recurrence of the damage. If adaptation is mainly reactive, then damages will be much greater. Unfortunately, experience shows that, in the United States, responses to disaster are mainly reactive, often characterized by inattention beforehand and over-response afterwards. In the case of climate change, reactive adaptation will be especially costly because, decade by decade, the severity of climate change impacts is likely to increase as greenhouse gas concentrations in the atmosphere rise. Reactive adaptation would be likely to lag persistently behind the emerging risks. The more rapid the rise in atmospheric concentrations, the faster the rate of climate change and the less effective reactive adaptation is likely to be. * * *

Climate uncertainty

* * * There are many reasons to doubt whether adaptation steps will be timely and efficient, even in the U.S. where the capabilities exist. Some of these doubts arise from the characteristics of the climate problem. Others

arise from the tendency, exposed by behavioral economists, for inefficiencies in human and organizational behaviors. One of the most significant obstacles arises from the fact that most damages are incurred as the result of extreme weather events: unusual heat waves, droughts, floods, hurricanes and storm surges. These damages occur because most human and natural systems can tolerate climatic fluctuations within ranges, but tend to fail when conditions move outside those ranges. If a roof is built to withstand wind speeds of one hundred miles per hour, speeds below that rate may blow off a few shingles, but if speeds exceed one hundred miles per hour, the roof might well blow off, causing catastrophic damage to the structure. If a flood levee is designed to stop the flood likely to occur once in a hundred years, a flood greater than that will probably overtop the levee, causing severe flooding behind it. For such reasons, studies such as the Stern review and work by economist William Nordhaus have found that climate damages rise very non-linearly with changes in weather variables. * * *

Moral hazard

Adaptation, in some instances, is inhibited by moral hazard issues. For example, governmental crop insurance and disaster relief programs have *reduced* the incentives for farmers, households, and businesses to take action to avoid weather damages. Between 1989 and 2007 indemnified losses insured by the Federal Crop Insurance Program increased from $1.2 to $3.8 billion, an average annual rate of increase of 6 percent per year. This insurance against crop loss is subsidized from the federal budget. During that period, the premium subsidy rose from $0.2 billion to $3.8 billion, an average annual rate of 17.6 percent per year. This subsidized insurance program provided strong incentives for farmers to take actions that increased their exposure to weather-related risks, which account for almost all losses. The incentives were further expanded by farm subsidies that raised farmers' returns from agricultural operations whether or not crop damages occurred. * * *

Behavioral economics has illuminated other characteristics of human decision-making under uncertainty that are likely to inhibit adaptation. Humans are myopic decision-makers, sharply discounting events in the farther future or past. In particular, people assign a relatively low priority to climate change because its effects are perceived to occur in the future, not the present:

- People tend to underestimate cumulative probabilities when the probability of an event in a single period is low (i.e., the probability that the event will happen within x years is surprisingly high to most people). For example, people build or buy houses in fire-prone, flood and earthquake zones, even though the probability that an event will occur within their lifetimes is quite high;

- Humans exhibit strong "anchoring" to the status quo, tending to make only small adjustments away from it. Many people, for example, even refuse orders to evacuate when under immediate threat from natural disasters;
- People tend to resist and deny information that contradicts their value or ideological beliefs. An identifiable minority of "climate skeptics" continues to deny the scientific evidence and the conclusions of scientists regarding climate change.

In the following review of experience to date with adaptation to climate change, it will be seen that all these obstacles have played their roles. * * *

In New York City, municipal authorities began just in the past two years to plan for an adaptation strategy, based on recognition of more severe vulnerabilities to flooding and hurricane damages as a result of sea level increase. Sea level rise and surges associated with severe storms would be likely to inundate Kennedy Airport and lower Manhattan, including the subway entrances and tunnels into Manhattan. "New York City has been working toward the establishment of a New York City Climate Change Adaptation Task Force, which will be convened this year. To advise this and other efforts, the City will convene a group of scientists and insurance experts as a technical committee, which will develop scenarios on which Task Force members will base their adaptation strategies."

New York City building codes are 40 years old. With respect to wind damages, they require only protection up to 110mph winds, though more intense hurricanes could result in wind speeds up to 135 mph. With respect to flooding, they rely on 1983 flood maps corresponding to a Category I hurricane and are based on historical data. Even the newer replacement maps adopted in late 2007, with enlarged flood zones, are still based only on historical data, and not on climate change modeling data.

In the Gulf of Mexico, Hurricane Katrina resulted in an exceptional storm surge that overwhelmed the levees protecting New Orleans, resulting in catastrophic flooding. In reviewing the Katrina disaster, Berkeley engineer Robert Bea discovered that the Corps of Engineers had applied a safety factor of 1.3 to the benchmark hundred-year flood height, estimated from historical data, in designing the height of levees (contrasted with a factor of 4-6 used in offshore oil platforms, which withstood the hurricane). It emerged that this factor of 1.3 was carried over from the 1940s, when the Corps used it in protecting agricultural land and pasture in the South from flooding. The levees the Corps had built and rebuilt were designed to allow up to 2 feet of water to overtop the barrier in a hundred-year flood, as estimated with data decades old. Bea also found that the Corps was rebuilding levees to the same standard—an earth mound without concrete sheathing—that had failed in the face of Katrina. * * *

* * * The U.S. Climate Change Science Program recently initiated an assessment study of potential impacts, vulnerabilities and adaptation responses of the nation's transportation infrastructure to climate change, using the central Gulf Coast as a case study. It found substantial vulnerabilities. For example, storm surges associated with hurricanes could easily reach 7 meters in height. With storm surge at 7 m (23 ft), more than half of the area's major highways (64 percent of interstates; 57 percent of arterials), almost half of the rail miles, 29 airports, and virtually all of the ports are subject to flooding. * * *

* * * Many private business sectors are exposed to significant risks from climate change, along with opportunities. Government policies to mitigate greenhouse gas emissions will create financial and regulatory risks for many industries, along with new opportunities for companies to expand in providing solutions to climate problems. However, the private sector is also exposed to the same physical risks that public agencies must contend with, not only risks to their own facilities, infrastructure and staff, but also to those of their suppliers and customers. The presumption has been that the private sector will adapt efficiently and briskly to those risks, even if government agencies lag. According to Mendelsohn and Neuman, "Efficient private adaptation is likely to occur, even if there is no official (government) response to global warming." * * *

Insurance companies are concerned about increasing storm losses, especially from hurricane damages. The empirical record over the past 30-35 years indicates an increase in hurricane intensity. Some companies have reduced coverage in vulnerable areas. Many are re-examining their actuarial estimates and/or have markedly increased premium rates. Yet, according to one observer, "Although insurers first expressed concern about climate change more than three decades ago, fewer than one in a hundred appear to have seriously examined the business implications." Efforts by the insurance companies to project future hurricane losses through quantitative risk modeling have been obstructed in some states, including Texas and Florida, by insurance regulatory commissions that have recommended against the use of such models in rate-making. * * *

H. CLIMATE CHANGE AND NATIONAL SECURITY

GLOBAL CLIMATE CHANGE AND NATIONAL SECURITY
James Stuhltrager
22 ABA Natural Resources & Environment 36 (2008)

Depending on the audience, global climate change has many different meanings. For environmentalists, global climate change may be the number one threat facing the world. Many argue that humans are the sole cause of the problem and that it is incumbent on us to take steps to reverse course. Some in that community go so far as to see mitigating global climate change as a chance to reverse the course of modernity. For many business leaders, doing so presents a serious challenge to some traditional industries, threatening the basic building blocks, such as petroleum and coal, upon which Western nations have built their economies. They argue that science has yet to determine the exact causes of climate change, and it is premature to disrupt the economy to address a threat that man may not cause. However, others in the business community view climate change as a tremendous opportunity to develop and sell cutting-edge technologies to reduce the impact of man-made greenhouse gases.

For the military, global climate change represents considerable uncertainty and risk. *See* CAN, NATIONAL SECURITY AND THE THREAT OF CLIMATE CHANGE (2007), prepared under direction of an Advisory Board comprised of three-star and four-star Flag Officers from the Army, Navy, Air Force and Marine Corps, www.SecurityAndClimate.cna.org. There are numerous reports detailing the potential causes of global climate change, including the November 18, 2007, *4th Assessment Report of the Intergovernmental Panel on Climate Change,* which reports that "the warming of the climate system is unequivocal." www.IPCC.ch. For the military cannot wait for the science to be perfected to begin planning for the potential effects of global climate change. Likewise, the military cannot morally judge the causes of global climate change. What matters is that it is occurring and the results will have impacts on military operations.

Instead of focusing on the causes of climate change, or even how to prevent it, the military must plan for the risks posed by global climate change. Risk is defined as the chances that an event will occur multiplied by the magnitude of its occurrence. Viewed through that lens, the effects and potential outcomes of global climate change—whether it is manmade or naturally occurring—are disastrous.

In terms of risk and military strategy, the disastrous effects of global climate change can best be described as a low probability/high consequence event. The low probability is due to science still being unsettled about the actual magnitude and timing of the potential impacts of global climate change and the chances of halting or reversing its causes. Perhaps the apocalyptic scenarios envisioned by some will never come to fruition. However, the potential high consequences of a worst-case scenario, such as droughts, famines, and floods, are disastrous, so the U.S. military has no choice but to consider the effects of global climate change. * * *

Stability is the heart of our national security policy. Our Cold War strategy centered on maintaining the balance of power with the Soviet Union. The United States sought alliances that maintained stability, even when such actions may have been counter to other compelling interests or may have produced long-term negative consequences.   Other such examples abound, including our aid to Iraq during the Iran-Iraq war, aid to the Mujahideen in Afghanistan, and support for undemocratic regimes in Southeast Asia and Latin America. Although there may have been downsides to these actions, in the strategic picture, maintenance of a bipolar balance of power and the stability it produced was paramount.

The loss of stability is the primary threat of global climate change.   Climate change does not create new enemies for the United States or empower our existing foes. It is not a weapon that enemies can harness directly. Instead, climate change is an engine of destabilization, resulting in long-term shifts in weather, precipitation, sea level, food supplies, and population. Our enemies, both current and future, may exploit these shifts for their own gain. Climate change is a threat multiplier. The range of troubling national security risks were recently summarized by General Gordon R. Sullivan, USA (Ret.) in his September 27, 2007, testimony before the U.S. House of Representatives Subcommittee on Investigations and Oversight, Committee on Science and Technology. * * *

The Effects of Global Climate Change on National Security

To begin the planning for global climate change, the military must first understand the potential effects to which it may be required to adapt. Some of the effects to which it may be required to adapt. Some of the effects are direct, such as changes in precipitation that restrict access to potable water. Others are indirect, such as the mass movement of populations in response to drought induced by climate change. Ultimately, the most serious effects these occurrences may have on national security will be the effect on already weakened and failing governments.

Perhaps the immediate potential consequence of global climate change will be the impact resulting from changes in precipitation. Adequate quantities of freshwater for irrigation, drinking, and sanitation are essential to human existence. Changes in the amounts or patterns of precipitation, especially droughts, can produce disastrous results. The potential loss of drinking water may occur from both drought conditions and the reduction of mountain glaciers.   According to the International Water Management Institute (IWMI), many countries in the world's most troubled regions, such as North Africa and the Middle East, already are considered "water scarce." These countries soon will be joined by Pakistan, South Africa, and large parts of India and China. Indeed, by 2025, the IWMI estimates that 1.8 billion people will live in countries or regions with absolute water scarcity, due to both increases in population and decreased water supply. The Intergovernmental Panel on Climate Change notes that although total precipitation amounts may not change much because of global climate change, the variability in precipitation patterns likely will result in more frequent droughts in water-scarce countries. * * *

On the other side of the equation, there are potential security implications of too much precipitation. As this article is being written, England is experiencing floods such as it has not seen in years. The devastating effects of Hurricane Katrina are still fresh in the minds of local, state, and federal governments. These events stretched the capabilities of even the most developed countries to respond. The potential for larger storm events caused by climate change would easily overwhelm the capability of many third-world governments to respond.

Related to precipitation changes is the effect of drought on food production. Perhaps the best example of this is occurring today in Africa. The continent has experienced major droughts during the last thirty years. The severe droughts of the 1980s in Ethiopia and the associated pictures of starving women and children have been replaced most recently by those in Darfur. In each case, long-term drought had a severe impact on food production, affecting crops in Ethiopia and grazing lands in Darfur. Climate change will continue to exacerbate these types of problems. Scientist estimate that for every 1.8°F rise in temperature, grain production in these regions will be reduced by 10 percent.

These changes in precipitation patterns, availability of potable water, and food production may have indirect impacts on security, mainly taking the form of mass migrations due to both resource scarcity and the resulting political instability. There are three main types of migration, and each has its attendant problems. Internal migration – migration within a country's borders – may cause short-term economic and political consequences. These consequences may be quite severe, such as the estimated 4.5 million people displaced in Ethiopia, or relatively benign, such as the diaspora that resulted from Hurricane Katrina. However, if even a developed nation struggles to accommodate the estimated 300,000 people displaced by Katrina, the prospects are far worse for developing nations.

Cross-border migration, migration that crosses international borders, can fuel ethnic tensions in receiving nations and possibly lead to international conflict. Although there are many causes of cross-border migration, such as the difference in economic opportunities between Mexico and the United States, environmental factors may cause mass migrations over relatively short time periods; the sudden influx of people may overwhelm host nations.

The final type of migration is international migration that crosses regions. The best example is the flow of immigrants from Asia and Africa to Europe. Although not as dramatic as cross-border migration, this type of migration may cause long-term impacts on the receiving region. For example, the influx of people from Islamic countries has, in part, increased religious tensions in Western Europe and resulted in incidents such as the 2005 riots in France. * * *

The Arctic region presents a fascinating study of how global climate change already is affecting national security. For untold centuries, the Arctic ice cap has prevented that region from becoming a battleground. During the height of the Cold War, the skies above were monitored for ballistic missile and strategic bomber attacks, but the seas and lands below went untouched. However, with the end of the Cold War, many nations lost interest in the region. Canada disbanded the remainder of an already meager naval force in the region, the United States deleted future icebreaker procurement, and the Russians lost interest.

However, in the last few years many nations have taken a renewed interest in the region. The thinning of the polar ice cap has spurred a sudden emphasis on the Arctic. For years, scientists have known that its ice cap is thinning. Satellite imagery has shown that the Arctic ice cap is already nearly 30 percent smaller than it was twenty-five years ago. This thinning has caused the Arctic region to be more accessible to surface navigation. The number of ships transiting the Northwest passage has increased steadily over the last decade as well as the number of vessels navigating in the Canadian Arctic provinces. * * *

This rush to claim the Arctic is reminiscent of early efforts to conquer Antarctica. At the beginning of the twentieth century, many countries were eager to claim at least a portion of Antarctica. However, the 1959 Antarctic Treaty (12 U.S.T, 794, 402 U.N.T.S. 71, signed Dec. 1, 1959, entered into force June 23, 1961) suspended all claims to the continent and prohibited all military activity. There is no such protection for the Arctic region, and without one, military operations in the area increasingly are more likely to occur. For example, throughout the summer of 2007, Russian Bear bombers conducted at least seven exercises in the Arctic. This level of activity has not occurred since the Cold War and may be related in part to the increased accessibility to the Arctic Ocean. * * *

I. PRACTICING CLIMATE CHANGE LAW

WHAT THE LAW AND LAWYERS CAN AND CANNOT DO ABOUT GLOBAL WARMING
Michael B. Gerrard
16 Southeastern Envtl. L. J. 1 (2007)

II. Typology of Climate Change Litigation

By my count, as of December 2007 forty-seven lawsuits have been filed in the United States concerning global climate change.[4] These lawsuits are joined by several administrative proceedings and officially–threatened actions. About half of the lawsuits have led to judicial decisions. Several of them are under appeal and more decisions are pending. Lately, much attention has deservedly gone to the United States Supreme Court's April 2, 2007 decision in *Massachusetts v. EPA.* However, this case is only the tip of the figurative iceberg, and unlike most actual icebergs it is growing rather than melting.

Climate-related lawsuits can be broadly divided among those that raise statutory claims, common law claims, and public international law claims. The vast majority of these lawsuits raise statutory claims.

A. Statutory Claims

The statutory claims can be divided into four kinds of efforts: (1) by states and environmental groups to force the government to act on climate change; (2) by states and environmental groups to stop government actions believed to have a negative climate impact; (3) by industrial companies to block government action; and (4) by environmental groups to regulate private conduct.

Some statutory claims in the first group aim to force the government to take affirmative steps toward change. Examples include *Massachusetts v. EPA* and *Coke Oven Environmental Task Force v. EPA,* which both involved alleged violations of the Clean Air Act. The Endangered Species Act is cited as authority in *Natural Resources Defense Council v. Kempthorne,* as well as in numerous petitions from the Center for Biological Diversity ("CBD") to the Secretary of the Interior, the Secretary of Commerce, and the National Oceanic and Atmospheric Administration requesting they list various species as endangered or threatened. CBD also filed petitions in 2007 based on the Clean Water Act, asking nine states to declare their coastal waters "impaired" by carbon dioxide emissions, and to revise the water quality criteria for pH because of ocean acidification influenced by climate change. * * *

Other statutory claims aim to stop the government from undertaking or approving actions that may contribute to global warming. Environmentalists brought lawsuits citing the National Environmental Policy Act ("NEPA"), calling, with some success, for consideration of climate change in environmental impact statements. Environmental groups also brought lawsuits seeking to use the state equivalents of NEPA to compel assessment of the climate impacts of proposed projects and plans. In *State v. County of San Bernardino,*

---

[4] *See* Michael B. Gerrard & J. Cullen Howe, *Climate Change Litigation in the U.S., available* at http://www.climatecasechart.com (providing a list of environmental lawsuits organized according to the nature of the claim, with links to the decisions or, for undecided cases, the complaints). [The first page of this chart is included below.] * * *

California sued the county claiming their growth plan did not adequately address environmental concerns, particularly the green house gas emissions that would result. This led to a settlement agreement under which the county agreed to conduct such a study and to undertake substantive mitigation measures.

The automobile industry has brought lawsuits in several states challenging the states ability to regulate greenhouse gas emissions from new automobiles. Two of these cases were fully litigated, leading to decisions in both upholding the states' authority provided that the U.S. Environmental Protection Agency ("EPA") granted the requisite waiver. However, on December 19, 2007, EPA Administrator Stephen L. Johnson denied the California waiver request. Several states promptly brought suit challenging this denial. [EPA subsequently approved California's waiver request as discussed in Chapter 6.]

Another focus of activity has been the disclosure of climate issues in statements filed by public corporations with the Securities and Exchange Commission ("SEC"). A coalition of groups, led by Environmental Defense, petitioned the SEC on September 18, 2007, asking the SEC to issue guidance on such disclosures. A few days earlier, the Attorney General of New York, Andrew Cuomo, issued subpoenas to five electric utility companies seeking documents on the climate aspects of their securities disclosures.

Public international law claims also have been brought alleging that global climate change violates human rights and destroys cultural and national landmarks. In December 2005, a group of Inuit from Alaska and northern Canada filed a petition with the Inter-American Commission on Human Rights alleging greenhouse gas emissions from the United States have so severely affected their lives that the action amounts to a violation of the 1948 American Declaration of the Rights and Duties of Man and other international laws. Two months later, the International Environmental Law Project at Lewis and Clark Law School petitioned the United Nations World Heritage Committee to list Waterton-Glacier International Peace Park as a World Heritage Site in Danger. The petition asserts that the flora, fauna, and glaciers at the Park—the characteristics that make it worthy of World Heritage Site designation—are being destroyed by U.S. greenhouse gas emissions.

B. Common Law Claims

Lawsuits have also been filed based on common law claims. These cases can be divided into those that seek injunctive relief and those that seek monetary damages. The plaintiffs in both *Korsinsky v. EPA* and *Connecticut v. American Electric Power Co.* sought injunctive relief. In each of these cases, the courts ruled for the defendants. In *Korsinsky,* a pro se case, the Second Circuit held that the plaintiffs claim that global warming and carbon dioxide emissions may potentially cause him future harm was too speculative to establish standing. In *American Electric* the district court held that suing electric utilities for their contribution to global warming under nuisance theories and asking the court to create a cap on emissions raises "non-justiciable political questions that are consigned to the political branches, not the Judiciary." The Second Circuit heard an appeal from the plaintiff in *American Electric* in June 2006 but has not yet ruled.

Meanwhile, in both *Comer v. Nationwide Mutual Ins. Co.* and *People ex rel. Brown v. General Motors Corp.,* plaintiffs sought monetary damages related to climate change. In *Comer,* the plaintiffs, Mississippi property owners, sought redress for the damage caused by Hurricane Katrina. They sued numerous companies in the coal, chemical, oil, and other industries alleging they contributed to global warming, which in turn, they said, worsened the magnitude of Hurricane Katrina. The court dismissed the suit, finding that it raised non-justiciable political questions.

A similar result occurred in *General Motors.* California claimed emissions from vehicles manufactured by the automakers were worsening climate change. The district court here, too, found that the complaint raised non-justiciable political questions. Both of these decisions are being appealed.

III. The Limitations of Tort Law

Based on the results to date, it does not appear that tort litigation is a fruitful legal avenue for addressing climate change. The district courts in *Connecticut, Comer,* and *General Motors* all expressed a strong reluctance to forge a judicial solution to what they considered a political problem, especially when difficult technical questions were involved. While the United States Supreme Court in *Massachusetts v. EPA* afforded broad standing to *states* to challenge *administrative action,* that is a far cry from entertaining what could well become the largest mass tort in the history of the world.

But, just for the sake of argument, if this kind of common law litigation were to gain traction in the courts, where would it take us? The United States legal community has extensive experience with massive litigation over environmental liability from navigating the Comprehensive Environmental Response, Compensation, and Liability Act ("CERCLA"). Many aspects of current and possible climate change tort litigation resemble CERCLA cases. Examining these similarities and their differences may help illuminate the shape that tort litigation over climate change might take were the courts or Congress to allow it.

CERCLA demonstrated the importance of due diligence and detailed, focused study of particular sites and facilities in the context of transactions. When a problem is identified in the course of a large transaction, there are often the incentives and the resources to fix it. The knowledge that a problem could get in the way of a future transaction is a powerful inducement to take care of it in advance and, if possible, to avoid it altogether.

Generally, the business community is more receptive toward information-driven regulations than command-and-control regulations, and these regulations have also proven more acceptable to the public than taxes. Therefore, Congress may be more likely to enact information-driven regulation. Two examples of such programs that Congress has already enacted are NEPA and the toxic release inventory program under Emergency Planning & Community Right-to-Know Act ("EPCRA").

The disclosure obligations imposed by the SEC have not come close to fulfilling their potential in the environmental arena. This failure can be attributed, in part, to the "materiality" standard that shields many potential liabilities from disclosure. As noted above, in September 2007, a coalition of environmental and investors' groups petitioned the SEC to issue guidance on disclosures of climate-related liabilities.

It is possible to envision a scheme for greenhouse gases that would realize the benefits of CERCLA without the downsides discussed above. A statute would be needed that would apply to a broad array of entities, including private companies, nonprofit institutions, and federal, state and local governments. It would require entities that are subject to the law to do three things: *analyze; disclose;* and, ideally, *mitigate.* These entities would analyze their emissions of greenhouse gases, a process that would require roughly the same amount of work as completing Phase I and Phase II studies for hazardous waste contamination. It is not conceptually difficult to disclose emissions once they are quantified. The process of mitigation is far trickier, but a menu of numerical performance guidelines and recommended best practices could be provided. * * *

As previously stated, I am skeptical that tort litigation will be an effective way to combat climate change. Where *should* litigation efforts focus to have the maximum impact on climate change? Many lawyers for environmental groups have concluded that the most productive course is to litigate against proposed coal-fired power plants.

Though the media have paid a great deal of attention to new plants being built in China, much current activity exists in the United States. In October 2007, the National Energy Technology Laboratory tallied 45 new coal-fired power plants that were progressing toward completion, and another 76 that had been announced and were in the early stages of development, for a total of 121 plants with a total capacity of 71,680 MW. While not all plants will be completed, if even half of the proposed plants are built, their carbon dioxide emissions would be substantial. Since carbon dioxide persists in the atmosphere for many decades, these plants would have real cumulative impacts. If the plants are built or retrofitted with carbon capture and sequestration or with some other technology that emerges during the plants' lifetime in order to reduce their carbon dioxide emissions, their impact would be correspondingly lower. However, at this point, no one can predict with any confidence that this will happen.

If past is prologue, plants permitted before a new regulatory scheme comes into force will be grandfathered unless they are significantly modified, and once they are operating, they will be next to impossible to shut down before they are retired. Thus, in the view of the environmental groups that are fighting these plants, a defeat of any of them will achieve a real contribution in the fight against climate change. Administrative proceedings before state environmental agencies and state public utility commissions serve as the most active arena for such litigation at present.

Of course, not all environmental lawyers are litigators and, due to conflicts, time availability, geographic location, and other factors, not all of the litigators are in position to get involved in fighting coal plants. It is also possible that carbon capture and sequestration or other clean coal technologies will emerge and reduce the impetus for such fights.

There are many other roles for lawyers in the fight against climate change. Lawyers can, for example, help design and implement programs like the Regional Greenhouse Gas Initiative and the state programs such as those recently adopted by the legislatures of California and New Jersey. Lawyers can facilitate the construction of renewable energy plants, district energy systems, and other facilities to generate energy with lower greenhouse gas emissions or to reduce the need for energy; these facilities involve considerable work for lawyers in a myriad of practice areas: environmental, financing, tax, real estate, contracting, zoning, and insurance, to name a few. Lawyers may also find legal work in putting up green buildings, retrofitting old buildings to consume less energy, helping companies in the industrial, transportation, agricultural, utilities, and other sectors understand and meet their emerging legal obligations, and developing and carrying out disclosure obligations in real estate transactions.

Adaptation mechanisms deserve considerably more legal attention than they have received. The Intergovernmental Panel on Climate Change projects that, even if major efforts are undertaken to reduce greenhouse gas emissions worldwide, sea levels and temperatures will continue to rise through the balance of the 21st Century with parallel variations in climactic condition. This will create changes in the availability of water, agricultural land, and the underlying environmental systems upon which society relies. Possible legal reactions to these anticipated impacts include flood protection, flood hazard mapping, protecting buildings and infrastructure from rising water tables, sizing of storm water facilities, sizing of wastewater treatment plants, strengthening structures to withstand higher wind loads, and modifying heating, ventilation, and air conditioning systems to withstand worse heat waves.

Lawyers can also act to reduce the climate change impact of their own law offices. The American Bar Association and the EPA have adopted the "ABA-EPA Law Office Climate Challenge" enumerating numerous energy saving actions. * * *

In some ways, today feels like the summer of 1914. Today, as then, the nations of the world know that something catastrophic may be about to happen. Today, as then, the nations also know that they might be able to prevent further negative effects, and efforts are underway to stop it. However, in 1914, those efforts failed and the leaders who could have made a difference were unwilling to make the compromises and sacrifices that would be required. Thus, an unnecessary catastrophe did happen. We may be at another such historical moment right now. The decisions that are being made this year, and the decisions that will be made next year, will have lasting consequences for the globe. The importance of concerted effort and wise choices by the legal profession cannot be overstated.

Notes and Questions

For additional reading on the U.S. climate change practice topics discussed in the Gerrard article excerpted above, see the chart from the Gerrard article following this note and D. Antolini & C. Rachtschaffen, Common Law Remedies: A Refresher, 38 ELR 10114 (2008); L. Baker, Global Warming: Attorneys General Declare Public Nuisance 27 U. Haw. L. Rev. 525 (2006); W. Burns & H. Osofsky, Adjudicating Climate Change: State, National, and International Approaches (2009); A. Burtka, Representing Mother Earth, Trial 28 (April 2008); J. Dernbach & S. Kakade, Climate Change Law: An Introduction, 29 Energy L.J. 1 (2008); J. Donald & C. Davis, Carbon Dioxide: Harmless, Ubiquitous, and Certainly Not a "Pollutant" Under a Liability Policy's Absolute Pollution Exclusion, 39 Seton Hall L. Rev. 107 (2009); D. Farber, Apportioning Climate Change Costs, 26 UCLA J. Envtl. L. & Pol'y 21 (2007-08); D. Farber, Modeling Climate Change and Its Impacts: Law, Policy, and Science, 86 Texas L. Rev. 1655 (2008); J. Gitzlaf, Getting Back to Basics: Why Nuisance Claims Are of Limited Value in Shifting the Costs of Climate Change, 39 ELR 10218 (2009); D. Grimm, Global Warming and Market Share Liability: A Proposed Model for Allocating Tort Damages Among CO_2 Producers, 32 Colum. J. Envtl. L. 209 (2007); S. Hecht, Climate Change and Transformation of Risk: Insurance Matters, 55 UCLA L. Rev. 1559 (2008); E. Malone & M. Strong, When 2 + 2 = 5 (or Zero): Emission Reporting Risks of Facilities with Complex Ownership Structures in Emerging Issues in Environmental Law & Climate Change (2008); E. Michaut & R. Watson, The

Green(er) Law Practice, Trial 38 (April 2008); S. Morath, The Endangered Species Act: A New Avenue for Climate Change Litigation?, 29 Pub. Land & Resources L. Rev. 23 (2008); G. Morse & A. Dowling, Federal and State Tax Incentives for Renewable Energy in Emerging Issues in Environmental Law & Climate Change (2008); M. Pawa, Global Warming Litigation Heats Up, Trial 18 (April 2008); M. Pawa, Global Warming: The Ultimate Public Nuisance, 39 ELR 10230 (2009); C. Rechtschaffen & D. Antolini, Creative Common Law Strategies for Protecting the Environment (2008); W. Rodgers & A. Mortiz, The Worst Case and the Worst Example: An Agenda for Any Young Lawyer Who Wants to Save the World from Climate Chaos, S.E. Envtl. L.J. (forthcoming 2009); A. Strauss, Suing the United States in International Forums for Global Warming Emissions, 38 Envtl. L. Rep. 10185 (2003); S. Tomkins, L. Stone, & M. Onken, Litigating Global Warming: Likely Legal Challenges to Emerging Greenhouse Cap-and-Trade Programs in the United States, 39 Envtl. L. Rep. 10389 (2009); L. Wasden & B. Kane, Massachusetts v. EPA: A Strategic and Jurisdictional Recipe for State Attorneys General in the Context of Emission Accelerated Global Warming Solutions, 44 Idaho L. Rev. 704 (2008); J. Zasloff, The Judicial Carbon Tax: Reconstructing Public Nuisance and Climate Change, 55 UCLA L. Rev. 1827 (2008).

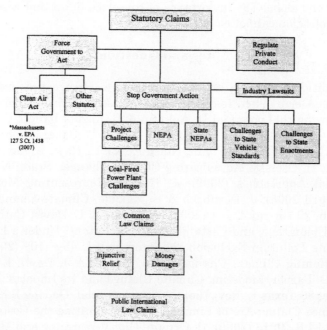

J. PARADIGM SHIFTS: SUSTAINING EARTH'S BIOSPHERE

Will human societies perceive the need to change their laws in anticipation of experiencing the effects of climate change, or will change be forced upon them? Do the impacts that climate change is producing throughout

Earth's biosphere require a fundamentally new understanding of how humans can or should behave? How long will it take for this new world-view to become accepted? Does it constitute a new kind of "scientific revolution," accepted by the natural and physical sciences, but resisted by economists and some or other social sciences? What does the new paradigms of climate, altered by humans, imply for when and how humans will revise their legal systems to accommodate climate change mitigation and adaptation?

THE STRUCTURE OF SCIENTIFIC REVOLUTIONS
Thomas S. Kuhn
The University of Chicago Press (1996)

Within the new paradigm, old terms, concepts, and experiments fall into new relationships one with the other. The inevitable result is what we must call, though the term is not quite right, a misunderstanding between the two competing schools. The laymen who scoffed at Einstein's general theory of relativity because space could not be "curved"–it was not that sort of thing– were not simply wrong or mistaken. Nor were the mathematicians, physicists, and philosophers who tried to develop a Euclidean version of Einstein's theory. What had previously been meant by space was necessarily flat, homogeneous, isotropic, and unaffected by the presence of matter. If it had not been, Newtonian physics would not have worked. To make the transition to Einstein's universe, the whole conceptual web whose strands are space, time, matter, force, and so on, had to be shifted and laid down again on nature whole. Only men who had together undergone or failed to undergo that transformation would be able to discover precisely what they agreed or disagreed about. Communication across the revolutionary divide is inevitably partial. Consider, for another example, the men who called Copernicus mad because he proclaimed that the earth moved. They were not either just wrong or quite wrong. Part of what they meant by 'earth' was fixed position. Their earth, at least could not be moved. Correspondingly, Copernicus' innovation was not simply to move the earth. Rather, it was a whole new way of regarding the problems of physics and astronomy, one that necessarily changed the meaning of both 'earth' and 'motion.' Without those changes the concept of a moving earth was mad. On the other hand, once they had been made and understood, both Descartes and Huyghens could realize that the earth's motion was a question with no content for science.

These examples point to the third and most fundamental aspect of the incommensurability of competing paradigms. In a sense that I am unable to explicate further, the proponents of competing paradigms practice their trades in different worlds. One contains constrained bodies that fall slowly, the other pendulums that repeat their motions again and again. In one, solutions are compounds, in the other mixtures. One is embedded in a flat, the other in a curved, matrix of space. Practicing in different worlds, the two groups of scientists see different things when they look from the same point in the same direction. Again, that is not to say that they can see anything they please. Both are looking at the world, and what they look at has not changed. But in some areas they see different things, and they see them in different relations one to the other. That is why a law that cannot even be demonstrated to one group of scientists may occasionally seem intuitively obvious to another. Equally, it is why, before they can hope to communicate fully, one group or the other must experience the conversion that we have been calling a paradigm shift. Just because it is a transition between incommensurables, the transition between competing paradigms cannot be made a step at a time, forced by logic and neutral experience. Like the gestalt switch, it must occur all at once (though not necessarily in an instant) or not at all.

How, then, are scientists brought to make this transposition? Part of the answer is that they are very often not. Copernicanism made few converts for almost a century after Copernicus' death. Newton's work was not generally accepted, particularly on the Continent, for more than half a century after the *Principia* appeared. Preistley never accepted the oxygen theory, nor Lord Kelvin the electromagnetic theory, and so on. The difficulties of conversion have often been noted by scientists themselves. Darwin, in a particularly perceptive passage at the end of his *Origin of Species,* wrote: "Although I am fully convinced of the truth of the views given in this volume . . . , I by no means expect to convince experienced naturalists whose minds are stocked with a multitude of facts all viewed, during a long course of years, from a point of view directly opposite to mine.

* * * [B]ut I look with confidence to the future,—to young and rising naturalists, who will be able to view both sides of the question with impartiality." And Max Planck, surveying his own career in his *Scientific Autobiography*, sadly remarked that "a new scientific truth does not triumph by convincing its opponents and making them see the light, but rather because its opponents eventually die, and a new generation grows up that is familiar with it."

These facts and others like them are too commonly known to need further emphasis. But they do need re-evaluation. In the past they have most often been taken to indicate that scientists, being only human, cannot always admit their errors, even when confronted with strict proof. I would argue, rather, that in these matters neither proof nor error is at issue. The transfer of allegiance from paradigm to paradigm is a conversion experience that cannot be forced. Lifelong resistance, particularly from those whose productive careers have committed them to an older tradition of normal science, is not a violation of scientific standards but an index to the nature of scientific research itself. The source of resistance is the assurance that the older paradigm will ultimately solve all its problems, that nature can be shoved into the box the paradigm may emerge.

Still, to say that resistance is inevitable and legitimate, that paradigm change cannot be justified by proof, is not to say that no arguments are relevant or that scientists cannot be persuaded to change their minds. Though a generation is sometimes required to effect the change, scientific communities have again and again been converted to new paradigms. Furthermore, these conversions occur not despite the fact that scientists are human but because they are. Though some scientists, particularly the older and more experienced ones, may resist indefinitely, most of them can be reached in one way or another. Conversions will occur a few at a time until, after the last hold-outs have died, the whole profession will again be practicing under a single, but now a different, paradigm. We must therefore ask how conversion is induced and how resisted.

What sort of answer to that question may we expect? Just because it is asked about techniques of persuasion, or about argument and counterargument in a situation in which there can be no proof, our question is a new one, demanding a sort of study that has not previously been undertaken. We shall have to settle for a very partial and impressionistic survey. In addition, what has already been said combines with the result of that survey to suggest that, when asked about persuasion rather than proof, the question of the nature of scientific argument has no single or uniform answer. Individual scientists embrace a new paradigm for all sorts of reasons and usually for several at once. Some of these reasons—for example, the sun worship that helped make Kepler a Copernican—lie outside the apparent sphere of science entirely. Others must depend upon idiosyncrasies of autobiography and personality. Even the nationality or the prior reputation of the innovator and his teachers can sometimes play a significant role. Ultimately, therefore, we must learn to ask this question differently. Our concern will not then be with the arguments that in fact convert one or another individual, but rather with the sort of community that always sooner or later re-forms as a single group.

Notes and Questions

1. Technology assessment was once a hallmark of Congressional decision-making. The Office of Technology Assessment helped Congress anticipate the strengths and weaknesses of pending legislation in light of possible unanticipated consequences of supporting one type of technology or another. Is it time to re-establish this Office?

2. Once legislators, locally or nationally, acknowledged that a new climate change paradigm exists, what law reforms are required? Should attention be given to identifying irreversible change, that must be accommodated, and changes that can be averted? In this article, Turning Back From the Brink: Detecting an Impending Regime Shift in Time to Avert It (Proceedings of the National Academy of Sciences, 2009), Reinette Biggs, Stephen R. Carpenter

and William A. Brock examine steps that governments in the Anthropocene era may take to stabilize Earth's climate and ecosystems:

Ecological regime shifts are large, abrupt, long-lasting changes in ecosystems that often have considerable impacts on human economies and societies. Avoiding unintentional regime shifts is widely regarded as desirable, but prediction of ecological regime shifts is notoriously difficult. Recent research indicates that changes in ecological time series (e.g., increased variability and autocorrelation) could potentially serve as early warning indicators of impending shifts. A critical question, however, is whether such indicators provide sufficient warning to adapt management to avert regime shifts. * * * We find that if drivers can only be manipulated gradually management action is needed substantially before a regime shift to avert it; if drivers can be rapidly altered aversive action may be delayed until a shift is underway. Large increases in the indicators only occur once a regime shift is initiated, often too late for management to avert a shift. To improve usefulness in averting regime shifts, we suggest that research focus on defining critical indicator levels rather than detecting change in the indicators. * * * Averting ecological regime shifts is also dependent on developing policy processes that enable society to respond more rapidly to information about impending regime shifts. * * *

Averting Regime Shifts. Our findings emphasize the need for monitoring and proactive intervention in averting ecological regime shifts, especially in cases where underlying drivers cannot be rapidly manipulated. * * * However, bureaucratic inertia, policy compromise, and the risk of unforeseen environmental shocks, make delaying action until a regime shift is underway a dangerous strategy even where it is theoretically feasible. If the variable driving a regime shift can only be manipulated gradually (as in the case of shoreline development), our results indicate that taking action substantially before the onset of a regime shift is crucial if a shift is to be averted. Proactive intervention is also desirable from the standpoint of cost, because the closer the system has moved to a regime shift, the stronger (and generally more costly and socially disruptive) the action needed to prevent a regime shift. * * *

Our results highlight that in systems subject to regime shifts there is often a discrete window for policy action, after which it becomes impossible to avert a shift. The existence of such window, where the same action in 2 adjacent years could differ radically in its effectiveness, is seldom considered in environmental decision-making processes. * * * Atmospheric carbon dioxide (CO_2) levels are a variable that cannot be rapidly and drastically reduced. As highlighted by other authors, timely action to avert potential CO_2-induced regime shifts is therefore likely to be critical. * * *

K. A NEW INTERNATIONAL CLIMATE LAW BY 2012: THE ROAD FROM BALI

Coping with climate change will require changes in agriculture, silvaculture, coastal and estuarine land uses, transportation systems, housing, urban management and design, electrical energy generating and use, changes in moot industrial and commercial sectors of our economy, and changes in individual behavior. The change must push against the weight of economic lobbying from natural resources exploiters, such as fossil fuel extractors, or the transportation sector, where wealth is already accumulated and invested. These sectors resist change in order to avoid disruption and ensure short-term profit. Although many do not yet recognize it, across all these sectors, the Bali Action Plan spreads its all-encompassing framework.

Climate change law, if it is to succeed in realizing the objective of the United Nations Framework Convention on Climate Change (UNFCCC) to stabilize the Earth's climate, will require that both national and local initiatives embrace the same international scientific knowledge, follow the same norms, and move to attain measurable benchmarks collectively. The first step in outlining the concrete negotiating positions was taken in Bali, at the 13th Conference of the Parties (COP) of the UNFCCC in December 2007. The "Bali Action Plan" offers international guidance, but requires congruent national measures to realize the plan. A kind of "Earth Law" is being cobbled together, an amalgam of elements from international public law and national law, both public administrative law, and private law. The Bali Action Plan aims for of "a shared vision for long-term cooperative action, including a long-term global goal for emission reductions, to achieve the ultimate objective of the Convention."

In forging this vision, States must agree on the equitable measures that permit binding together the "common but differentiated responsibilities and respective capabilities" of all nations, in light of their different social and economic conditions and other relevant factors. Principle 7 of the 1992 Rio Declaration on Environment and Development contains the policy framework for this principle of common but differentiated responsibilities:

State shall cooperate in a spirit of global partnership to conceive, protect and restore the health and integrity of the Earth's ecosystem. In view of the different contributions to global environmental degradation, States have common but differentiated responsibilities. The developed countries acknowledge the responsibility that they bear in the international pursuit of sustainable development in view of the pressures their societies place on the global environment and of the technologies and financial resources they command.

The framework for the Bali Action Plan has four elements: (1) mitigating the emission of greenhouse gases; (2) adjusting policies and actions to adapt to those effects of climate change that are not avoidable by mitigation; (3) providing the financing to allow all nations to undertake these measures; and (4) stimulating innovations in technology and the transfer of appropriate technologies so that all nations can share their benefits.

As you address each of the chapters in the casebook, measure what they describe against the common framework of the Bali Action Plan. How can individual national or local measures to cope with climate change fit into the framework? What steps would be needed to universalize their application? How can any cap-and-trade system produce revenues to help finance adaptation, on behalf of developing nations, communities in need whether in developed or developing regions, and ecosystems and the community of life outside the human socio-economic realms?

Through the Bali Action Plan, nations expect to agree on enhanced "national/international" actions including, but not limited to the following elements (UNFCCC COP 13, DOC. 1/CP. 13 (DEC. 2007):

1) **Mitigation**
    (i)   Measurable, reportable and verifiable nationally appropriate mitigation commitments or actions, including quantified emission limitation and reduction objectives, by all developed country Parties, while ensuring the comparability of efforts among them, taking into account differences in their national circumstances;
    (ii)   Nationally appropriate mitigation actions by developing country Parties in the context of sustainable development, supported and enabled by technology, financing and capacity-building, in a measurable, reportable and verifiable manner;
    (iii) Policy approaches and positive incentives on issues relating to reducing emissions from deforestation in developing countries; and the role of conservation, sustainable management of forests and enhancement of forest carbon stocks in developing countries;
    (iv)   Cooperative sectoral approaches and sector-specific actions, in order to enhance implementation of Article 4, paragraph 1(c), of the Convention;
    (v)   Various approaches, including opportunities for using markets, to enhance the cost-effectiveness of, and to promote, mitigation actions, bearing in mind different circumstances of developed and developing countries;
    (vi)   Economic and social consequences of response measures;

(vii)   Ways to strengthen the catalytic role of the Convention in encouraging multilateral bodies, the public and private sectors and civil society, building on synergies among activities and processes, as a means to support mitigation in a coherent and integrated manner;

2) **Adaptation**

(i)   International cooperation to support implementation of adaptation actions, including through vulnerability assessments, prioritization of actions, financial needs assessments, capacity-building and response strategies, integration of adaptation actions into sectoral and national planning, specific projects and programmes, means to incentivize the implementation of adaptation actions, and other ways to enable climate-resilient development and reduce vulnerability of all Parties, taking into account the urgent and immediate needs of developing States, and further taking into account the needs of countries in Africa affected by drought, desertification and floods;

(ii)   Risk management and risk reduction strategies, including risk sharing and transfer mechanisms such as insurance;

(iii) Disaster reduction strategies and means to address loss and damage associated with climate change impacts in developing countries that are particularly vulnerable to the adverse effects of climate change;

(iv) Economic diversification to build resilience;

(v)   Ways to strengthen the catalytic role of the convention in encouraging multilateral bodies, the public and private sectors and civil society, building on synergies among activities and processes, as a means to support adaptation in a coherent and integrated manner;

3) **Technological development and dissemination**

(i)   Effective mechanisms and enhanced means for the removal of obstacles to, and provision of financial and other incentives for, scaling up of the development and transfer of technology to developing country Parties in order to promote access to affordable environmentally sound technologies;

(ii)   Ways to accelerate deployment, diffusion and transfer of affordable environmentally sound technologies;

(iii) Cooperation on research and development of current, new and innovative technology, including win-win solutions;

(iv) The effectiveness of mechanisms and tools for technology cooperation in specific sectors;

4) **Financial resources and investment**

(i)   Improved access to adequate, predictable and sustainable financial resources and financial and technical support, and the provision of new and additional resources, including official and concessional funding for developing country Parties;

(ii)   Positive incentives for developing country Parties for the enhanced implementation of national mitigation strategies and adaptation action;

(iii)   Innovative means of funding to assist developing county Parties that are particularly vulnerable to the adverse impacts of climate change in meeting the cost of adaptation;

(iv)   Means to incentivize the implementation of adaptation actions on the basis of sustainable development policies;

(v)   Mobilization of public and private-sector funding and investment, including facilitation of climate-friendly investment choices;

(vi)   Financial and technical support for capacity-building in the assessment of the costs of adaptation in developing countries, in particular the most vulnerable ones, to aid in determining their financial needs;

Notes and Questions

1. Many further proposals were added to the negotiating text for the draft agreement under the Bali Action Plan at the working group meeting in Bonn, Germany, in August 2009. See the Environmental Negotiations Bulletin, www.iisd.ca/climate/ccwgi.

2. Whither the United States under President Obama? President Barak Obama appointed two of the scientists whose works are excepted above to his Administration. John P. Holdren is his Science Advisor and Physics Nobel Laureate Steven Chu is his Secretary of Energy. How might the President turn their scientific assessments into policy and law?

Al Gore and UN Secretary-General Ban Ki-moon have called for the US and the other 34 nations that have launched public spending for stimulating their recessionary economy, to invest the new $2,250 billion in converting to non-carbon based systems. "This stimulus * * * must help catapult the world economy into the 21st century, not perpetuate the dying industries and bad habits of yesteryear." "Green Growth is Essential to any stimulus," Financial Times (London), p. 13 (Feb. 17, 2009). How can this vision be realized?

3. Does the Bali Action Plan take into account the policy tensions in debates over the economy vs. environment? How might the major groups of nations—the Small Island States, the European Union, NAFTA, the Russian Federation, The People's Republic of China, the Arab League, South American States, or the African Union – approach the question of "their" impact on the shared commons of the climate? Are the realities of national sovereignty such that no common ground can be found, and all States are victims of the "prisoner's dilemma"? In negotiating the new post-Kyoto agreement at Poznan, Poland in December of 2008, nations had articulated their strong national interests, rather than finding ways to share responsibility for the

common atmosphere. Yvo de Boer, Executive Secretary of the UN Framework Convention on Climate Change, observed that "It's a worrying sign that people are taking up positions for a hard negotiation.... What we need to achieve in Copenhagen is clarity on key political issues so that everything after that is filling in the details." F. Harvey, "A Night from Day," Financial Times (London) p. 5, col. 1 (Jan. 2, 2009).

How can nations agree to cuts of greenhouse gases to levels that might be 25-40% below the 1990 levels by 2020, as Senator John Kerry informally proposed at the 14th Conference of the Parties of the UNFCCC in Poznan, Poland, in 2008? Why does the diplomatic debate focus on targets for cuts of greenhouse gas emissions when nations face immediate adaptation problems associated with sea level rise and intense storms? Should not assistance for adaptation be an immediate priority? What neutral principles should guide decision-making among the competing priorities of the Bali Action Plan?

4. Scientists, such as James Hansen at the NASA/Goddard Institute for Space Studies in New York, estimate that CO_2 levels must return to levels below 350 ppm, from the current levels of 385 ppm. See J. Hansen, et al., Target Atmospheric CO_2: Where Should Humanity Aim? 2 Open Atmospheric Science Journal 217 (2008). The Administration of President Bush and Vice President Cheney rejected Hansen's views and sought to suppress his reports. President Bush was criticized in the EU and elsewhere for his unilateral foreign policies and for by-passing the UN system. The Bali Action Plan makes clear that the Conference of the Parties of the UNFCCC is the primary forum for all international climate change decision-making. However, just as there remain skeptics about whether climate change poses all the threats predicted, so there are skeptics about the efficacy of multilateral and UN-based diplomacy.

What is your opinion of the following recommendations of a bipartisan Task Force of the Council on Foreign Relations, which called for a cut of greenhouse gas emissions from between 60% and 80% from 1990 levels by 2050. "The Task Force recommends that the United States, in concert with the other major advanced industrial and emerging economies, create a standing process that would bring together the world's largest emitters to implement aggressive emission reductions." This would be a core element of a new strategy that would complement and strengthen ongoing UN efforts. The 'Partnership for Climate Cooperation' would be different from the valuable Major Economies Meetings that the Bush Administration and several other governments have advanced, as it would be rooted in an aggressive effort to cut U.S. emissions and would focus on practical actions and implementation of specific strategies. The partnership would seek practical strategies to move away from traditional fuels, technologies and behaviors that cause most emissions of greenhouse gases. Exploring opportunities to link emissions trading systems 'from the bottom up' would be an important element. It would also address agricultural and land management practices, such as those that lead to deforestation. Confronting Climate Change: A Strategy for U.S. Foreign Policy (Independent Task Force Report No. 61, June 2008).

One Task Force member, Lawrence Summers, while not a climate skeptic, presents another view. He dissented from the Council Task Force report in part, noting that "The Task Force rightly notes that the costs of addressing climate change are highly uncertain, but I remain concerned that many policy-makers do not sufficiently appreciate how large these uncertainties are or the consequences of paying them insufficient attention. Environmental certainty enjoys much attention while uncertainty over the cost of curbing emissions receives too little. The balance is wrong, particularly in the short term, since emissions in any given year matter little, while high costs, even for a short period, can cause substantial economic harm, particularly to the most vulnerable. * * * Ultimately, however, there will be substantial risk—economic and environmental—in any choices we make. I concur in this report not because I share all its tactical judgments but because I share the animating strategic judgment that there is far more danger of the United States doing too little rather than too much to address climate change." Id. at 94.

5. Bottom Up? Top Down? Subsidiarity?: We think that we know how law functions in a vertical approach, as a "command and control" system. How does law function across many jurisdictions, in a bottom up approach, accumulating many congruent but independent decisions?

For example, New York City aims to reduce greenhouse gas emissions by 30% below 1990 levels by the year 2030. See PLANYC at http://www.nyc.gov/html/planyc2030/html/plan/plan.shtml. New York joins Buenos Aires, Paris, and cities from New Zealand to Ukraine in making such commitments. On February 10, 2009, 350 cities across Europe signed a climate change agreement to reduce CO_2 emission by 20% by the year 2020. The cities are located in 23 European Union nations. Many cities will often exceed national goals (Paris 25% by 2020; Hamburg 40% by 2020). See http://www.eumayors.eu. Does this constitute customary law? Is it subsidiarity in action?

The European Union promotes the "subsidiarity principle," where decisions are taken at the lowest level of government, or social unit, which can most effectively address a question. M. Bothe, The Subsidiarity Principle, in E. Dommen, ed., Four Principles For Sustainable Development (1993). What level can best cope with which aspects of climate change?

6. *Carbon Neutral Law Schools*: Colleges and Universities are doing their part for mitigation and adaptation to climate change, beyond teaching classes. Does your contract to study law give you a stake or legal interest or

claim to ask what your own law school is doing? 284 institutions launched the American College and University Presidents' Climate Commitment in 2007. "They promised to eliminate or offset every iota of greenhouse gases resulting from light bulbs in their buildings, from flights and car trips by their faculty, even from the transportation of food to their dining halls." C. Deutsch, "College Presidents Lead The Fight for Carbon Neutrality," New York Times, p. B7 (June 13, 2007). Do you know the carbon footprint of your law school? Isn't this as important as its bar passage rate? Do you know how quickly your school could become carbon neutral, and be part of the solution to climate change? Prof. William Moomaw at the Fletcher School of Law and Diplomacy in Tufts University, and one of his graduate students, Kelly Sims, back in 1998 launched the "Tufts Climate Initiative," a program making Tufts a leader and role model for all universities. www.tufts.edu/tci. What can universities do? See A. Rappaport & S. Creighton, Degrees That Matter—Climate Change and the University (2007).

CHAPTER 2. CLIMATE SCIENCE

Climatescape: **Re-conceiving Life on Earth?**

Through a global network of scientists, employing the new capacity for study afforded by satellite remote sensing, computer modeling, and cross-disciplinary collaboration, the Intergovernmental Panel on Climate Change (IPPC) has described the characteristics of the Anthropocene era, our time in which humans have irrevocably altered the Earth. The era of easy access to fossil fuels, and rapid releases of carbon dioxide to the atmosphere, has brought prosperity to many, but is unsustainable because of its effects on the atmosphere of the planet. Manufactured "greenhouse gases" (GHGs) also have added to the problem of retaining solar heat in Earth's natural systems. Human degradation of biological systems produces feed-back loops, which exacerbate climate change. The degradation of forests and biological systems deprives the atmosphere of the benefits of photosynthesis and degrades eco-system services which support life on Earth. As the atmosphere warms, it holds more water vapor, rain fall intensifies and the hydrologic cycle changes, producing new areas for droughts and floods. In Chapter 2, introducing the science of climate change provides the basic knowledge needed to assess why there is enormous investment in new energy systems and technologies to move the economy away from its dependency on oil, coal and other fossil fuels. How fast does this need to be achieved in order to stabilize climatic conditions suitable for sustaining human society? Science issues reappear throughout the coming chapters. How does a lawyer keep abreast of the rapidly evolving scientific analysis? The IPPC's scoping agenda for its study in 2009-2014 will cover legal issues. Does the proposed climate change endangerment finding by the Administrator of the U.S. Environmental Protection Agency under the Clean Air Act constitute a turning point in governmental acceptance of the new world-view about Earth's climate? On what basis should nations set a "cap" on human GHG emissions into the atmosphere?

A. INTRODUCTION

Beginning with the discovery of fire, the history of the improvement of human welfare is the story of the human ability to harness energy. Yet there is compelling evidence that the current rate of consumption of fossil-fuels, e.g., coal, oil, natural gas (methane)—sources of energy derived from natural processes of decay and compression of once living plants and animals—while improving the quality of life, is causing a significant warming of the surface of the earth, which itself is causing a significant and potentially disastrous change in the planet's climate.

This chapter will outline the scientific understanding of the relationship between human activity and climate change and the range of consequences climate change threatens to impose on human society and the world's ecosystems. Understanding the science of global warming is essential because laws crafted to mitigate and adapt to global warming must be congruent with the scientific processes or the laws will be ineffective, or even detrimental. Human laws must conform to the laws of nature.

The essence of the global warming problem is that the current rate of burning fossil fuels releases into the atmosphere with relative suddenness carbon the earth removed from the atmosphere over millions of years and stored underground. The remains of ancient plants and animals were buried under conditions of enormous pressure over such long periods that the carbon comprising their structures was converted into coal, oil, or natural gas. Why do we use so much fossil fuel? The beneficial effects gained by exploiting the earth's storehouses of fossil fuel have been dramatic: Simply harnessing oxen, for example, multiplied the power available to a human being by a factor of 10. The invention of the vertical water wheel increased productivity by a factor of 6; the steam engine increased it by another order of magnitude. The use of motor vehicles greatly reduced journey times and expanded human ability to transport goods to markets.

Today the ready availability of plentiful, affordable energy allows many people to enjoy unprecedented comfort, mobility, and productivity. In industrialized countries, people use more than 100 times as much energy, on a per capita basis, than humans did before they learned to exploit the energy potential of fire.

Although, this consumption of our energy capital (fossil fuels) has allowed society to prosper, burning fossil fuels is not a harmless, cost-free activity. Some of the pollutants created by burning fossil fuels are inherently harmful and impose external costs on society. Other emissions from fossil fuel combustion, such as carbon dioxide (CO_2), are themselves benign (unless present in a high enough concentration to cause asphyxiation.) However, CO_2, together with water vapor, methane, nitrous oxide and other trace gases, have the ability to trap heat in the atmosphere. For over a century scientists have known that the gases that trap infrared radiation (heat) in the atmosphere make life on earth possible. Without these greenhouse gases, the earth would be a frigid rock, much like the moon or Mars; with excessive amounts of heat-trapping gases in the atmosphere, the earth would be an inferno, like Venus. The greater the concentration of greenhouse gases in the atmosphere, the more heat is trapped, and the warmer the earth becomes.

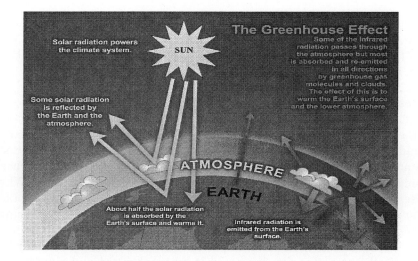

IPCC Fourth Assessment Report (FAR) FAQ Fig. 1.3

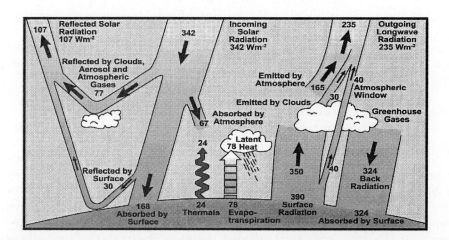

IPCC FAR FAQ 1.1, Figure 1. Estimate of the Earth's annual and global mean energy balance. Over the long term, the amount of incoming solar radiation absorbed by the Earth and atmosphere is balanced by the Earth and Atmosphere releasing the same amount of outgoing longwave radiation. About half of the incoming solar radiation is absorbed by the Earth's surface. This energy is transferred to the atmosphere by warming the air in contact with the surface (thermals), by evapotranspiration and by longwave radiation that is absorbed by clouds and greenhouse gases. The atmosphere in turn radiates longwave energy back to Earth as well as out to space.

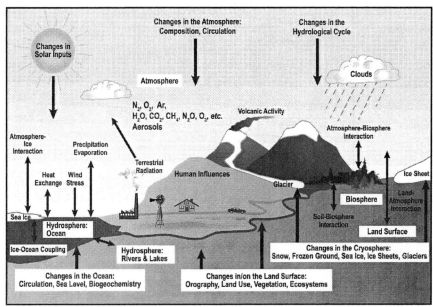

IPCC FAR FAQ Fig. 1.2

* * * * *

OUT OF GAS: THE END OF THE AGE OF OIL
David Goodstein (2004)

THE FUTURE

For hundreds of millions of years, animal, vegetable, and mineral matter drifted downward through the waters to settle on the floors of ancient seas. In a few privileged places on Earth, strata of porous rock formed that were particularly rich in organic inclusions. With time, these strata were buried deep beneath the seabed. The interior of Earth is hot, heated by the decay of natural radioactive elements. If the porous source rock sank just deep enough, it reached the proper temperature for the organic matter to be transformed into oil. Then the weight of the rock above it could squeeze the oil out of the source rock like water out of a sponge, into layers above and below, where it could be trapped. * * *

Oil consists of long-chain hydrocarbon molecules. If the source rock sank too deep, the excessive heat at greater depths * * * broke these long molecules into the shorter hydrocarbon molecules we call natural gas. Meanwhile, in certain swampy places, the decay of dead plant matter created peat bogs. In the course of the eons, buried under sediments and heated by Earth's interior, the peat was transformed into coal, a substance that consists mostly of elemental carbon. Coal, oil, and natural gas are the primary fossil fuels. They are energy from the Sun, stored within the earth.

Until only two hundred years ago * * * the human race was able to live almost entirely on light as it arrived from the Sun. The Sun nourished plants, which provided food and warmth for us and our animals. * * * At the end of the eighteenth century, no more than a few hundred million people populated the planet. A bit of coal was burned, especially since trees had started becoming scarce in Europe * * * and small amounts of oil that seeped to the surface found some application, but by and large Earth's legacy of fossil fuels was left untouched.

Today we who live in the developed world expect illumination at night and air conditioning in summer. We * * * [drive] vehicles * * * on roads paved with asphalt (another by-product of the age of oil). * * * Amenities that were once reserved for the rich are available to most people, refrigeration rather than spices preserves food, and machines do much of our hard labor. Ships, planes, trains, and trucks transport goods of every description all around the world. Earth's population exceeds six billion people. * * *

[W]e no longer live on light as it arrives from the Sun. Instead we are using up the fuels made from sunlight that Earth stored up for us over those many hundreds of millions of years. * * *

ENERGY MYTHS AND A BRIEF HISTORY OF ENERGY

A body that has radiant energy falling on it warms up until it is sending energy away at the same rate it receives it. Only then is it in a kind of equilibrium, neither warming nor cooling. * * * That is the primary fact governing the temperature at the surface of our planet.

* * * Earth has a gaseous atmosphere, largely transparent to sunlight but nearly opaque to the planet's infrared radiation. The blanket of atmosphere traps and re-radiates part of the heat that Earth is trying to radiate away. The books remain balanced, with the atmosphere radiating into space the same amount of energy Earth receives but also radiating energy back to Earth's surface, warming it to a comfortable average temperature of 57° F. That is what's known as the greenhouse effect. Without the greenhouse effect and the global warming that results, we probably would not be alive.

There is a tiny but vital exception to the perfect energy balance of the Earth-Sun system. Of the light that falls on Earth, an almost imperceptible fraction gets used up nourishing life. Through photosynthesis, plants make use of the Sun's rays to grow. Animals eat some of the plants. Eventually, animals and plants die. Natural geological processes bury some of that organic matter deep in the earth. As we have seen, that is how the fossil fuels are produced. So a tiny fraction of the distilled essence of sunlight is stored in the form of fossil fuels. Though the process of accumulation is slow and inefficient, it has been going on for hundreds of millions of years and the Earth has built up a substantial supply. * * *

[O]il companies refer to * * * [their activities] as "production," but no oil company produces a drop of oil—that's one reason it's so cheap. Of course, poking a hole in the ground and figuring out where to poke it does cost something. But can it really be true that this precious fluid that has taken the earth hundreds of millions of years to accumulate is worth nothing more than the cost of pumping it out of the ground? Or have conventional economics, property rights, and the rest somehow broken down here? * * *

Surprisingly, however, it is not energy that we have to conserve. One of the most fundamental laws of physics says that energy is always conserved. Energy can change from one form to another, or it can flow from one body to another, but it can never be created or destroyed. We don't have to conserve energy, because nature does it for us. * * * There is something that we are using up and that we need to learn to conserve. It's called fuel. * * *

ELECTRICITY AND RADIANT ENERGY

* * * [T]here are two kinds of electricity, called *positive* and *negative* *charge*. There is a force of attraction between positive and negative charges and a force of repulsion between like charges (either positive-positive or negative-negative). The strength of the force diminishes with distance from the charge, just as the intensity of light from the Sun diminishes with distance from the Sun. At the most fundamental level, that is all that can be said about electricity. We don't know why any of those statements are true; we just know that they are. * * *

[In 1820 H. C. Oersted discovered that an electric current produces a magntic field. In 1831] Michael Faraday discovered that if a magnet was moved through a copper coil, it would induce a surge of electric current. This phenomenon is called electromagnetic induction, and it is the basic means by which most electricity is generated today. A turbine is used to rotate a coil of wire in a magnetic field. An oscillating current is induced that can be sent far away to light our lamps, run our refrigerators, and power our computers. * * *

[The relationship between electricity and magnetism are described by what] we today call Maxwell's equations * * * one of the most perfect scientific theories ever devised. * * * Among other things, it predicts that whenever electric charges jiggle around, they radiate energy that travels away at the speed of light. * * *

If they jiggle at just the right frequency, what they radiate is visible light. But energy is also radiated at higher or lower frequencies, which we can't see;

for example, gentle oscillations produce long waves that we call radio waves. * * * At higher frequencies, but frequencies still too low for our eyes to see, the radiant energy is called infrared radiation. Moving up in frequency, there is a narrow band that we can see, called visible light, * * *; beyond what we can see, lie ultraviolet rays, X rays, and finally gamma rays. * * *

* * * We use electricity to transfer energy from one place to another, and to do almost anything you can think of once it gets there. It most often comes from a power plant that burns fossil fuel to power a turbine generator—although sometimes the turbine is powered by heat from a nuclear reactor or by water under the pressure of a reservoir (hydroelectric power). The turbine performs work to turn the coil that induces electric current * * *. The current is sent a long distance over transmission lines, to where it can be turned into more work by an electric motor, or into light by an electric lamp, or used in * * * other ways.

When electricity flows through a wire, it encounters resistance. * * * [A]ny moving thing in the real world encounters resistance, in the form of friction, viscosity, and so on. Electrical resistance is of the same nature. Just as friction turns mechanical kinetic energy into heat, electrical resistance turns some of the flowing electrical energy into heat. * * * Because of this and related phenomena, only about 75 percent of the electrical energy generated in American stationary power plants actually gets to the end user.

* * * One of the problems of the electric power grid is that electrical energy is very hard to store in large quantities. * * * There has to be enough generating capacity to meet the highest demand—for example, on the hottest summer day, when all the air conditioners are running—even though some of those generators will not be needed most * * * of the time. For all practical purposes, electricity * * * is always consumed at the same rate it is generated. * * *

RADIANT ENERGY AND EARTH'S CLIMATE

Svante August Arrhenius, * * * in a paper published in 1896, first put forth the hypothesis that carbon dioxide resulting from the burning of fossil fuel could lead to global warming. * * * To understand how that might happen, we have to consider the relationship between radiant energy and temperature.

We already know that all matter is made up of electrically charged electrons and nuclei that are jiggling around with random thermal energy at all times. * * * [J]iggling electric charges radiate energy away at the speed of light, * * * at all frequencies at all times. Radiation from other bodies is also falling on all bodies all the time. If the rate at which a body is radiating is not equal to the rate at which it is absorbing radiant energy, it either warms up or cools down until the two rates are equal.

* * *[In 1900 Max Planck estimated] the amount of radiation at each frequency that might be expected * * * from bodies at various temperatures. At the lowest temperature, the intensity of the radiation reaches a maximum somewhere deep in the infrared and then falls back down to zero, never reaching the visible. * * * You are radiating electromagnetic radiation at all times, but * * * [y]ou don't glow in the dark, because you're just too cool. * * * At the temperature of the surface of the Sun, the maximum radiation occurs near the visible. We see all colors simultaneously, and the result looks white. * * *

* * * Nuclear reactions inside the Sun heat its surface white hot, to a temperature of nearly 6,000 kelvins, or about 11,000°F. From the surface of the Sun, radiant energy streams outward in all directions at the speed of light. * * * Ninety-three million miles away, Earth in its orbit intercepts a tiny fraction of this solar radiation.

Earth, like any other body, radiates energy at all times. If it radiates less energy than it receives, it must be warming up. If it radiates more than it receives, then unless it has its own internal energy source, it must be cooling down. (Actually, Earth does have an internal source: Natural radioactivity * * *, the gradual decay of naturally occurring heavy unstable nuclei keeps the planet's interior hot but has little effect on its surface temperature * * *)

The intensity of the Sun's radiation at the orbit of Earth is 1,372 watts per square meter. In this bath of radiant energy, Earth turns on its axis like a chicken roasting on a spit, and the energy from the Sun spreads over its spherical surface. The net result, averaged over the surface of the planet and over an entire year, is a flux of 343 watts of solar energy per square meter at the top of the atmosphere. * * * 30 percent of that flux of energy is reflected directly back out into space * * *. The rest is absorbed and eventually reradiated as invisible infrared radiation. In order to radiate, on the average, 70 percent of 343 watts per square meter back out into space, Earth's surface would have to have a temperature of 255 kelvins, which corresponds to -18°C, or 0° F. * * * But that is not the whole story.

Aside from the fundamental inalterable fact that Earth is 93 million miles from the Sun, a number of other factors influence the climate of our planet. Among these are its tilted axis, the El Nino cycle, the jet stream and various currents in the oceans, and the greenhouse effect. * * *

Of all the factors that affect our climate, by far the most important is the greenhouse effect. Think of three separate systems—Earth, the atmosphere, and space * * *. Each system must remain in balance, losing and gaining energy at the same rate. This balance is automatic and self-correcting. If the atmosphere or the earth gets out of balance, each will warm or cool until balance is restored. From space, 343 watts per square meter arrive; part is reflected back and the remainder is ultimately re-radiated as infrared radiation. The atmosphere, which is composed mostly of nitrogen and oxygen, is largely transparent to sunlight, so most of the radiation that is not reflected by the clouds falls directly on Earth, warming it and causing it to radiate in the infrared. The nitrogen and oxygen in the atmosphere are also transparent to infrared radiation, but the atmosphere contains traces of other gases that are *not* transparent to infrared. The most abundant of those gases is water vapor, but they also include methane, carbon dioxide, ozone, nitrous oxides, and chlorofluorocarbons. These are the so called greenhouse gases. They absorb the infrared radiation from Earth's surface and re-radiate it, both up toward space and down toward Earth, warming our planet to an average temperature higher than it would otherwise have. * * *

The atmospheric increase in carbon dioxide is part of a complex carbon cycle that is only partly understood. Carbon dioxide is removed from the atmosphere by dissolving in the oceans, where it may be taken out of circulation for a long time, if the water that absorbs it sinks to the bottom—for example, in the Atlantic Thermohaline flow. The dissolved carbon may also be incorporated into mineral matter that sinks to the bottom of the sea. In most places, however, surface water tends to absorb all the carbon dioxide it can and only very slowly exchanges with deeper waters capable of absorbing more.

Carbon dioxide is also absorbed by plant life, which, through photosynthesis, incorporates the carbon into organic matter. All organic molecules contain carbon. However, the carbon absorbed by plant life soon finds its way back into the atmosphere as carbon dioxide. If the plants are agricultural, some of it will be eaten. In the course of digestion and respiration, the potential energy stored in the food molecules is released by turning the carbon atoms back into carbon dioxide. If it goes into forests, the carbon dioxide is restored to the atmosphere when the wood burns or rots.

And, of course, some plant and animal matter turns into fossil fuel, from which we liberate carbon dioxide when we burn up the fuel. It turns out that a little more than half the carbon dioxide we liberate from fossil fuels lingers in the atmosphere, instead of being removed by the natural carbon cycle. Since the beginning of the Industrial Age, we have increased the amount of carbon dioxide in the atmosphere * * *.

* * * Increasing the amount of carbon dioxide increases the amount of infrared radiation intercepted by the atmosphere and radiated back to Earth. That warms the planet slightly, causing more water to evaporate. Water vapor is a powerful greenhouse gas, so the effect of the carbon dioxide is ampli-

fied. The warming also causes the polar ice caps to shrink, reducing the amount of sunlight reflected directly back to space, which leads to even further warming. On the other hand, the extra moisture in the air tends to condense into more clouds, and clouds reflect sunlight, decreasing the warming. With the present composition of the atmosphere but no clouds, Earth would be warmer by about 7° F; thus the clouds have a huge cooling effect. * * *

* * * [If] there were no greenhouse gases * * * [t]he temperature would immediately drop to 255 kelvins [-18°C, or 0° F] * * * [W]ater everywhere would freeze, reflecting more sunlight and further cooling the planet. * * *

We don't know how big a perturbation it would take to tip Earth's atmosphere into an entirely different state, one that might make it uninhabitable. However, even the relatively small perturbations we've already made can have dramatic effects. * * *

B. CLIMATE CHANGE SCIENCE—THE BASICS

Analysis of the climate change problem requires consideration of several threshold questions: Are atmospheric greenhouse gas (GHG) concentrations increasing? Is this increase in GHG concentrations warming the earth? If so, what portion of the GHG increase and warming due to human activities and how much is due to natural causes beyond human control? If human activity is warming the earth, what level of GHG concentration by what year will cause "dangerous * * * interference with the climate system?" How much will human society need to reduce its GHG emissions to mitigate or avoid the danger? Finally, what will be the consequences of the warming we will cause and how will society adapt to these new climate conditions? See B. Bolin, A History of Science and Politics of Climate Change: The Role of the Intergovernmental Panel on Climate Change (2007).

INTERGOVERNMENTAL PANEL ON CLIMATE CHANGE, CLIMATE CHANGE 2007: THE PHYSICAL SCIENCE BASIS: SUMMARY FOR POLICYMAKERS

HUMAN AND NATURAL DRIVERS OF CLIMATE CHANGE

Changes in the atmospheric abundance of greenhouse gases and aerosols, in solar radiation and in land surface properties alter the energy balance of the climate system. These changes are expressed in terms of radiative forcing[1], which is used to compare how a range of human and natural factors

---

[1] *Radiative forcing* is a measure of the influence that a factor has in altering the balance of incoming and outgoing energy in the Earth-atmosphere system and is an index of the importance of the factor as a potential climate change mechanism. Positive forcing tends to warm the surface while negative forcing tends to cool it. In this report radiative forcing values are for 2005 relative to pre-industrial conditions defined at

drive warming or cooling influences on global climate. * * * Global atmospheric concentrations of carbon dioxide, methane and nitrous oxide have increased markedly as a result of human activities since 1750 and now far exceed pre-industrial values determined from ice cores spanning many thousands of years (see Figure SPM-1). The global increases in carbon dioxide concentration are due primarily to fossil fuel use and land-use change, while those of methane and nitrous oxide are primarily due to agriculture.

• Carbon dioxide is the most important anthropogenic greenhouse gas (see Figure SPM-2). The global atmospheric concentration of carbon dioxide has increased from a pre-industrial value of about 280 ppm to 379 ppm[2] in 2005. The atmospheric concentration of carbon dioxide in 2005 exceeds by far the natural range over the last 650,000 years (180 to 300 ppm) as determined from ice cores. The annual carbon dioxide concentration growth-rate was larger during the last 10 years (1995–2005 average: 1.9 ppm per year), than it has been since the beginning of continuous direct atmospheric measurements (1960–2005 average: 1.4 ppm per year) although there is year-to-year variability in growth rates.

• The primary source of the increased atmospheric concentration of carbon dioxide since the pre-industrial period results from fossil fuel use, with land use change providing another significant but smaller contribution. Annual fossil carbon dioxide emissions increased from an average of 6.4 [6.0 to 6.8] GtC* (23.5 [22.0 to 25.0] GtCO2) per year in the 1990s, to 7.2 [6.9 to 7.5] GtC (26.4 [25.3 to 27.5] GtCO2) per year in 2000–2005 (2004 and 2005 data are interim estimates). Carbon dioxide emissions associated with land-use change are estimated to be 1.6 [0.5 to 2.7] GtC (5.9 [1.8 to 9.9] GtCO2) per year over the 1990s, although these estimates have a large uncertainty.

• The global atmospheric concentration of methane has increased from a pre-industrial value of about 715 ppb to 1732 ppb in the early 1990s, and is 1774 ppb in 2005. The atmospheric concentration of methane in 2005 exceeds by far the natural range of the last 650,000 years (320 to 790 ppb) as determined from ice cores. Growth rates have declined since the early 1990s, consistent with total emissions (sum of anthropogenic and natural sources) being nearly constant during this period. It is *very likely*[6]

1750 and are expressed in watts per square metre (W m-2).

[2] ppm (parts per million) or ppb (parts per billion, 1 billion = 1,000 million) is the ratio of the number of greenhouse gas molecules to the total number of molecules of dry air. For example: 300 ppm means 300 molecules of a greenhouse gas per million molecules of dry air.

* GtC is a gigaton of carbon. A gigaton is one billion tons. An emission of 1 GtC corresponds to 3.67 GtCO2.

[6] In this Summary for Policymakers, the following terms have been used to indicate the assessed likelihood, using expert judgment, of an outcome or a result: Virtually

that the observed increase in methane concentration is due to anthropogenic activities, predominantly agriculture and fossil fuel use, but relative contributions from different source types are not well determined.

- The global atmospheric nitrous oxide concentration increased from a preindustrial value of about 270 ppb to 319 ppb in 2005. The growth rate has been approximately constant since 1980. More than a third of all nitrous oxide emissions are anthropogenic and are primarily due to agriculture.

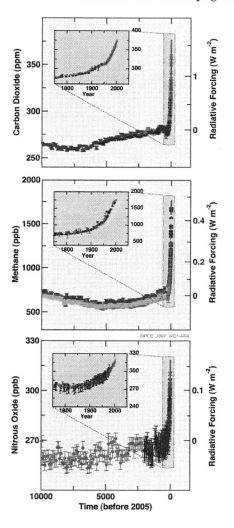

Figure SPM.1. Atmospheric concentrations of carbon dioxide, methane and nitrous oxide over the last 10,000 years (large panels) and since 1750 (inset panels). Measurements are shown from ice cores (symbols with different colours for different studies) and atmospheric samples (red lines). The corresponding radiative forcings are shown on the right hand axes of the large panels.

The understanding of anthropogenic warming and cooling influences on climate has improved since the Third Assessment Report (TAR), leading to *very*

---

certain > 99% probability of occurrence, Extremely likely > 95%, Very likely > 90%, Likely > 66%, More likely than not > 50%, Unlikely < 33%, Very unlikely < 10%, Extremely unlikely < 5%.

high confidence[7] that the globally averaged net effect of human activities since 1750 has been one of warming, with a radiative forcing of +1.6 [+0.6 to +2.4] W m-2. (see Figure SPM-2).

- The combined radiative forcing due to increases in carbon dioxide, methane, and nitrous oxide is +2.30 [+2.07 to +2.53] W m-2, and its rate of increase during the industrial era is *very likely* to have been unprecedented in more than 10,000 years. The carbon dioxide radiative forcing increased by 20% from 1995 to 2005, the largest change for any decade in at least the last 200 years.

- Anthropogenic contributions to aerosols (primarily sulphate, organic carbon, black carbon, nitrate and dust) together produce a cooling effect, with a total direct radiative forcing of -0.5 [-0.9 to -0.1] W m-2 and an indirect cloud albedo forcing of -0.7 [-1.8 to -0.3] W m-2. These forcings are now better understood than at the time of the TAR due to improved *in situ*, satellite and ground-based measurements and more comprehensive modelling, but remain the dominant uncertainty in radiative forcing. Aerosols also influence cloud lifetime and precipitation.

- Significant anthropogenic contributions to radiative forcing come from several other sources. Tropospheric ozone changes due to emissions of ozone-forming chemicals (nitrogen oxides, carbon monoxide, and hydrocarbons) contribute +0.35 [+0.25 to +0.65] W m-2. The direct radiative forcing due to changes in halocarbons is +0.34 [+0.31 to +0.37] W m-2. Changes in surface albedo, due to land-cover changes and deposition of black carbon aerosols on snow, exert respective forcings of -0.2 [-0.4 to 0.0] and +0.1 [0.0 to +0.2] W m-2. Additional terms smaller than +0.1 W m-2 are shown in Figure SPM-2.

- Changes in solar irradiance since 1750 are estimated to cause a radiative forcing of +0.12 [+0.06 to +0.30] W m-2, which is less than half the estimate given in the TAR.

---

[7] In this Summary for Policymakers the following levels of confidence have been used to express expert judgments on the correctness of the underlying science: *very high confidence* at least a 9 out of 10 chance of being correct; *high confidence* about an 8 out of 10 chance of being correct.

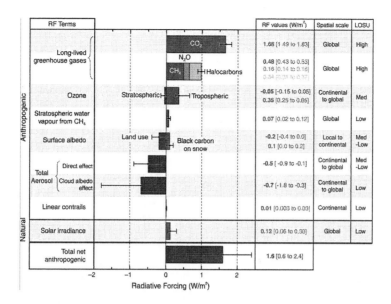

RADIATIVE FORCING COMPONENTS

Figure SPM.2. *Global average radiative forcing (RF) estimates and ranges in 2005 for anthropogenic carbon dioxide (CO2), methane (CH4), nitrous oxide (N2O) and other important agents and mechanisms, together with the typical geographical extent (spatial scale) of the forcing and the assessed level of scientific understanding (LOSU). The net anthropogenic radiative forcing and its range are also shown. These require summing asymmetric uncertainty estimates from the component terms, and cannot be obtained by simple addition. Additional forcing factors not included here are considered to have a very low LOSU. Volcanic aerosols contribute an additional natural forcing but are not included in this figure due to their episodic nature. The range for linear contrails does not include other possible effects of aviation on cloudiness.* }

DIRECT OBSERVATIONS OF RECENT CLIMATE CHANGE

* * *

Warming of the climate system is unequivocal, as is now evident from observations of increases in global average air and ocean temperatures, widespread melting of snow and ice, and rising global mean sea level.

• Eleven of the last twelve years (1995 -2006) rank among the 12 warmest years in the instrumental record of global surface temperature (since 1850). The updated 100-year linear trend (1906–2005) of 0.74 [0.56 to 0.92]°C is therefore larger than the corresponding trend for 1901-2000 given in the TAR of 0.6 [0.4 to 0.8]°C. The linear warming trend over the last 50 years (0.13 [0.10 to 0.16]°C per decade) is nearly twice that for the last 100 years. The total temperature increase from 1850 – 1899 to 2001 – 2005 is 0.76 [0.57 to 0.95]°C. Urban heat island effects are real but local, and have a negligible influence (less than 0.006°C per decade over land and zero over the oceans) on these values.

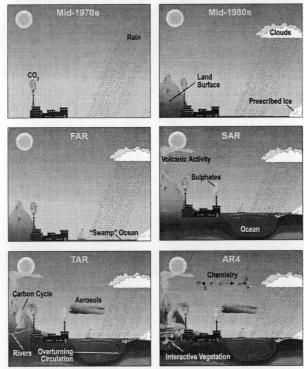

Chapter 1 Historical Overview of Climate Change Science
Figure 1.2. *The complexity of climate models has increased over the last few decades. The additional physics incorporated in the models are shown pictorially by the different features of the modelled world.*

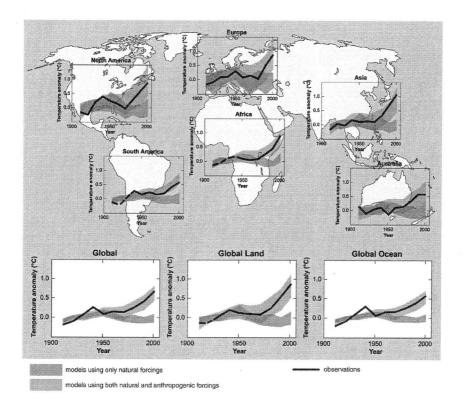

GLOBAL AND CONTINENTAL TEMPERATURE CHANGE

Figure SPM.4. *Comparison of observed continental- and global-scale changes in surface temperature with results simulated by climate models using natural and anthropogenic forcings. Decadal averages of observations are shown for the period 1906 to 2005 (black line) plotted against the centre of the decade and relative to the corresponding average for 1901–1950. Lines are dashed where spatial coverage is less than 50%. Blue shaded bands show the 5–95% range for 19 simulations from five climate models using only the natural forcings due to solar activity and volcanoes. Red shaded bands show the 5–95% range for 58 simulations*

- New analyses of balloon-borne and satellite measurements of lower- and mid-tropospheric temperature show warming rates that are similar to those of the surface temperature record and are consistent within their respective uncertainties, largely reconciling a discrepancy noted in the TAR.

- The average atmospheric water vapour content has increased since at least the 1980s over land and ocean as well as in the upper troposphere.

The increase is broadly consistent with the extra water vapour that warmer air can hold.

• Observations since 1961 show that the average temperature of the global ocean has increased to depths of at least 3000 m and that the ocean has been absorbing more than 80% of the heat added to the climate system. Such warming causes seawater to expand, contributing to sea level rise.

• Mountain glaciers and snow cover have declined on average in both hemispheres. Widespread decreases in glaciers and ice caps have contributed to sea level rise (ice caps do not include contributions from the Greenland and Antarctic ice sheets).

• New data * * * now shows that losses from the ice sheets of Greenland and Antarctica have very likely contributed to sea level rise over 1993 to 2003. Flow speed has increased for some Greenland and Antarctic outlet glaciers, which drain ice from the interior of the ice sheets. The corresponding increased ice sheet mass loss has often followed thinning, reduction or loss of ice shelves or loss of floating glacier tongues. Such dynamical ice loss is sufficient to explain most of the Antarctic net mass loss and approximately half of the Greenland net mass loss. The remainder of the ice loss from Greenland has occurred because losses due to melting have exceeded accumulation due to snowfall.

• Global average sea level rose at an average rate of 1.8 [1.3 to 2.3] mm per year over 1961 to 2003. The rate was faster over 1993 to 2003, about 3.1 [2.4 to 3.8] mm per year. Whether the faster rate for 1993 to 2003 reflects decadal variability or an increase in the longer-term trend is unclear. There is *high confidence* that the rate of observed sea level rise increased from the 19th to the 20th century. The total 20th century rise is estimated to be 0.17 [0.12 to 0.22] m. * * *

At continental, regional, and ocean basin scales, numerous long-term changes in climate have been observed. These include changes in Arctic temperatures and ice, widespread changes in precipitation amounts, ocean salinity, wind patterns and aspects of extreme weather including droughts, heavy precipitation, heat waves and the intensity of tropical cyclones [which include hurricanes and typhoons].

• Average Arctic temperatures increased at almost twice the global average rate in the past 100 years. Arctic temperatures have high decadal variability, and a warm period was also observed from 1925 to 1945.

• Satellite data since 1978 show that annual average Arctic sea ice extent has shrunk by 2.7 [2.1 to 3.3]% per decade, with larger decreases in summer of 7.4 [5.0 to 9.8]% per decade. These values are consistent with those reported in the TAR.

- Temperatures at the top of the permafrost layer have generally increased since the 1980s in the Arctic (by up to 3°C). The maximum area covered by seasonally frozen ground has decreased by about 7% in the Northern Hemisphere since 1900, with a decrease in spring of up to 15%.

- Long-term trends from 1900 to 2005 have been observed in precipitation amount over many large regions. Significantly increased precipitation has been observed in eastern parts of North and South America, northern Europe and northern and central Asia. Drying has been observed in the Sahel, the Mediterranean, southern Africa and parts of southern Asia. Precipitation is highly variable spatially and temporally, and data are limited in some regions. Long-term trends have not been observed for the other large regions assessed.

- Changes in precipitation and evaporation over the oceans are suggested by freshening of mid and high latitude waters together with increased salinity in low latitude waters.

- Mid-latitude westerly winds have strengthened in both hemispheres since the 1960s.

- More intense and longer droughts have been observed over wider areas since the 1970s, particularly in the tropics and subtropics. Increased drying linked with higher temperatures and decreased precipitation have contributed to changes in drought. Changes in sea surface temperatures (SST), wind patterns, and decreased snowpack and snow cover have also been linked to droughts.

- The frequency of heavy precipitation events has increased over most land areas, consistent with warming and observed increases of atmospheric water vapour.

- Widespread changes in extreme temperatures have been observed over the last 50 years. Cold days, cold nights and frost have become less frequent, while hot days, hot nights, and heat waves have become more frequent.

- There is observational evidence for an increase of intense tropical cyclone activity in the North Atlantic since about 1970, correlated with increases of tropical sea surface temperatures. There are also suggestions of increased intense tropical cyclone activity in some other regions where concerns over data quality are greater. Multi-decadal variability and the quality of the tropical cyclone records prior to routine satellite observations in about 1970 complicate the detection of long-term trends in tropical cyclone activity. There is no clear trend in the annual numbers of tropical cyclones.

CHANGES IN TEMPERATURE, SEA LEVEL AND NORTHERN HEMISPHERE SNOW COVER

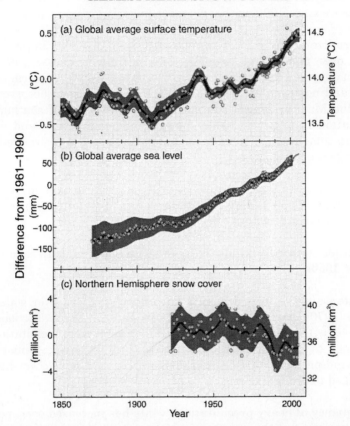

Figure SPM.3. Observed changes in (a) global average surface temperature, (b) global average sea level from tide gauge (blue) and satellite (red) data and (c) Northern Hemisphere snow cover for March-April. All changes are relative to corresponding averages for the period 1961–1990. Smoothed curves represent decadal average values while circles show yearly values. The shaded areas are the uncertainty intervals estimated from a comprehensive analysis of known uncertainties (a and b) and from the time series (c).

Some aspects of climate have not been observed to change.

- A decrease in diurnal temperature range (DTR) was reported in the TAR, but the data available then extended only from 1950 to 1993. Updated observations reveal that DTR has not changed from 1979 to 2004 as both day- and night-time temperature have risen at about the same rate. The trends are highly variable from one region to another.

- Antarctic sea ice extent continues to show inter-annual variability and localized changes but no statistically significant average trends, consistent with the lack of warming reflected in atmospheric temperatures averaged across the region.

- There is insufficient evidence to determine whether trends exist in the meridional overturning circulation of the global ocean or in small scale phenomena such as tornadoes, hail, lightning and dust-storms.

A PALEOCLIMATIC PERSPECTIVE

* * *

Paleoclimate information supports the interpretation that the warmth of the last half century is unusual in at least the previous 1300 years. The last time the polar regions were significantly warmer than present for an extended period (about 125,000 years ago), reductions in polar ice volume led to 4 to 6 meters of sea level rise.

- Average Northern Hemisphere temperatures during the second half of the 20th century were *very likely* higher than during any other 50-year period in the last 500 years and *likely* the highest in at least the past 1300 years. Some recent studies indicate greater variability in Northern Hemisphere temperatures than suggested in the TAR, particularly finding that cooler periods existed in the 12 to 14th, 17th, and 19th centuries. Warmer periods prior to the 20th century are within the uncertainty range given in the TAR.

- Global average sea level in the last interglacial period (about 125,000 years ago) was *likely* 4 to 6 m higher than during the 20th century, mainly due to the retreat of polar ice. Ice core data indicate that average polar temperatures at that time were 3 to 5°C higher than present, because of differences in the Earth's orbit. The Greenland ice sheet and other Arctic ice fields *likely* contributed no more than 4 m of the observed sea level rise. There may also have been a contribution from Antarctica.

UNDERSTANDING AND ATTRIBUTING CLIMATE CHANGE

* * *

Most of the observed increase in globally averaged temperatures since the mid-20th century is *very likely* due to the observed increase in anthropogenic greenhouse gas concentrations. This is an advance since the TAR's conclusion that "most of the observed warming over the last 50 years is *likely* to have been due to the increase in greenhouse gas concentrations". Discernible human influences now extend to other aspects of climate, including ocean warming, continental-average temperatures, temperature extremes and wind patterns.

- It is *likely* that increases in greenhouse gas concentrations alone would have caused more warming than observed because volcanic and anthropogenic aerosols have offset some warming that would otherwise have taken place.

- The observed widespread warming of the atmosphere and ocean, together with ice mass loss, support the conclusion that it is *extremely unlikely* that global climate change of the past fifty years can be explained without external forcing, and very likely that it is not due to known natural causes alone.

- Warming of the climate system has been detected in changes of surface and atmospheric temperatures, temperatures in the upper several hundred meters of the ocean and in contributions to sea level rise. Attribution studies have established anthropogenic contributions to all of these changes. The observed pattern of tropospheric warming and stratospheric cooling is *very likely* due to the combined influences of greenhouse gas increases and stratospheric ozone depletion.

- It is *likely* that there has been significant anthropogenic warming over the past 50 years averaged over each continent except Antarctica. The observed patterns of warming, including greater warming over land than over the ocean, and their changes over time, are only simulated by models that include anthropogenic forcing. The ability of coupled climate models to simulate the observed temperature evolution on each of six continents provides stronger evidence of human influence on climate than was available in the TAR.

- Difficulties remain in reliably simulating and attributing observed temperature changes at smaller scales. On these scales, natural climate variability is relatively larger making it harder to distinguish changes expected due to external forcings. Uncertainties in local forcings and feedbacks also make it difficult to estimate the contribution of greenhouse gas increases to observed small-scale temperature changes.

- Anthropogenic forcing is *likely* to have contributed to changes in wind patterns, affecting extra-tropical storm tracks and temperature patterns in both hemispheres. However, the observed changes in the Northern Hemisphere circulation are larger than simulated in response to 20th century forcing change.

- Temperatures of the most extreme hot nights, cold nights and cold days are *likely* to have increased due to anthropogenic forcing. It is *more likely*

than not that anthropogenic forcing has increased the risk of heat waves.
* * *

- It is *very unlikely* that climate changes of at least the seven centuries prior to 1950 were due to variability generated within the climate system alone. A significant fraction of the reconstructed Northern Hemisphere interdecadal temperature variability over those centuries is very likely attributable to volcanic eruptions and changes in solar irradiance, and it is likely that anthropogenic forcing contributed to the early 20th century warming evident in these records.

C. HOW WARM WILL THE EARTH BECOME BECAUSE OF HUMAN EMISSIONS OF GREENHOUSE GASES?

INTERGOVERNMENTAL PANEL ON CLIMATE CHANGE, CLIMATE CHANGE 2007: THE PHYSICAL SCIENCE BASIS: SUMMARY FOR POLICYMAKERS

PROJECTIONS OF FUTURE CHANGES IN CLIMATE

* * *

For the next two decades a warming of about 0.2°C per decade is projected for a range of * * * emission scenarios. Even if the concentrations of all greenhouse gases and aerosols had been kept constant at year 2000 levels, a further warming of about 0.1°C per decade would be expected.

- Since IPCC's first report in 1990, assessed projections have suggested global averaged temperature increases between about 0.15 and 0.3°C per decade for 1990 to 2005. This can now be compared with observed values of about 0.2°C per decade, strengthening confidence in near-term projections.

- Model experiments show that even if all radiative forcing agents are held constant at year 2000 levels, a further warming trend would occur in the next two decades at a rate of about 0.1°C per decade, due mainly to the slow response of the oceans. About twice as much warming (0.2°C per decade) would be expected if emissions are within the range of the SRES scenarios. Best-estimate projections from models indicate that decadal-average warming over each inhabited continent by 2030 is insensitive to the choice among SRES scenarios and is *very likely* to be at least twice as large as the corresponding model-estimated natural variability during the 20th century.

Continued greenhouse gas emissions at or above current rates would cause further warming and induce many changes in the global climate system during the 21st century that would *very likely* be larger than those observed during the 20th century.

- Advances in climate change modelling now enable best estimates and *likely* assessed uncertainty ranges to be given for projected warming for different emission scenarios. * * *

- [T]he best estimate [for globally average surface air warming] for the low scenario (B1) is 1.8°C (likely range is 1.1°C to 2.9°C), and the best estimate for the high scenario (A1FI) is 4.0°C (likely range is 2.4°C to 6.4°C). * * * The new assessment of the likely ranges now relies on a larger number of climate models of increasing complexity and realism, as well as new information regarding the nature of feedbacks from the carbon cycle and constraints on climate response from observations.

- Warming tends to reduce land and ocean uptake of atmospheric carbon dioxide, increasing the fraction of anthropogenic emissions that remains in the atmosphere. For the A2 scenario, for example, the climate carbon cycle feedback increases the corresponding global average warming at 2100 by more than 1°C. Assessed upper ranges for temperature projections are larger than in the TAR mainly because the broader range of models now available suggests stronger climate-carbon cycle feed backs. * * *

- Models used to date do not include uncertainties in climate-carbon cycle feedback nor do they include the full effects of changes in ice sheet flow, because a basis in published literature is lacking. The projections include a contribution due to increased ice flow from Greenland and Antarctica at the rates observed for 1993-2003, but these flow rates could increase or decrease in the future. For example, if this contribution were to grow linearly with global average temperature change, the upper ranges of sea level rise * * * would increase by 0.1 m to 0.2 m. Larger values cannot be excluded, but understanding of these effects is too limited to assess their likelihood or provide a best estimate or an upper bound for sea level rise.

- Increasing atmospheric carbon dioxide concentrations lead to increasing acidification of the ocean. Projections * * * give reductions in average global surface ocean pH of between 0.14 and 0.35 units over the 21st century, adding to the present decrease of 0.1 units since pre-industrial times. * * *

Anthropogenic warming and sea level rise would continue for centuries due to the timescales associated with climate processes and feedbacks, even if greenhouse gas concentrations were to be stabilized. * * *

- Contraction of the Greenland ice sheet is projected to continue to contribute to sea level rise after 2100. Current models suggest ice mass losses increase with temperature more rapidly than gains due to precipitation and that the surface mass balance becomes negative at a global average warming (relative to pre-industrial values) in excess of 1.9 to 4.6°C. If a negative surface mass balance were sustained for millennia, that would lead to virtually complete elimination of the Greenland ice sheet and a resulting contribution to sea level rise of about 7 m. The corresponding future temperatures in Greenland are comparable to those inferred for the last interglacial period 125,000 years ago, when paleoclimatic information suggests reductions of polar land ice extent and 4 to 6 m of sea level rise.

• Dynamical processes related to ice flow not included in current models but suggested by recent observations could increase the vulnerability of the ice sheets to warming, increasing future sea level rise. * * *

• Current global model studies project that the Antarctic ice sheet will remain too cold for widespread surface melting and is expected to gain in mass due to increased snowfall. However, net loss of ice mass could occur if dynamical ice discharge dominates the ice sheet mass balance.

• Both past and future anthropogenic carbon dioxide emissions will continue to contribute to warming and sea level rise for more than a millennium, due to the timescales required for removal of this gas from the atmosphere.

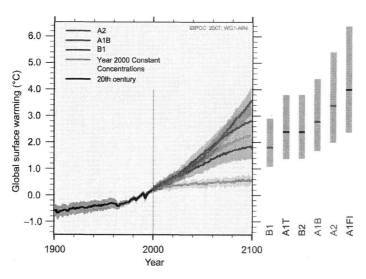

Figure SPM.5. *Solid lines are multi-model global averages of surface warming (relative to 1980–1999) for the scenarios A2, A1B and B1, shown as continuations of the 20th century simulations. Shading denotes the ±1 standard deviation range of individual model annual averages. The orange line is for*

*the experiment where concentrations were held constant at year 2000 values. The grey bars at right indicate the best estimate (solid line within each bar) and the **likely** range assessed for the six SRES marker scenarios. The assessment of the best estimate and **likely** ranges in the grey bars includes the AOGCMs in the left part of the figure, as well as results from a hierarchy of independent models and observational constraints.*

D. WHAT GHG CONCENTRATION IN THE ATMOSPHERE WOULD CAUSE "DANGEROUS ANTHROPOGENIC INTERFERENCE WITH THE CLIMATE SYSTEM"?

TARGET ATMOSPHERIC CO_2: WHERE SHOULD HUMANITY AIM?
James Hansen et al.
2 The Open Atmospheric Science Journal 217 (2008)

1. INTRODUCTION

Human activities are altering Earth's atmospheric composition. Concern about global warming due to long-lived human-made greenhouse gases (GHGs) led to the United Nations Framework Convention on Climate Change with the objective of stabilizing GHGs in the atmosphere at a level preventing "dangerous anthropogenic interference with the climate system."

The Intergovernmental Panel on Climate Change [IPCC, and others used several "reasons for concern" to estimate that global warming of more than 2-3°C may be dangerous. The European Union adopted 2°C above preindustrial global temperature as a goal to limit human-made warming. Hansen *et al.* argued for a limit of 1°C global warming (relative to 2000, 1.7°C relative to preindustrial time), aiming to avoid practically irreversible ice sheet and species loss. This 1°C limit, with nominal climate sensitivity of °C per W/m2 and plausible control of other GHGs [6], implies maximum CO_2 ~ 450 ppm.

Our current analysis suggests that humanity must aim for an even lower level of GHGs. Paleoclimate data and ongoing global changes indicate that 'slow' climate feedback processes not included in most climate models, such as ice sheet disintegration, vegetation migration, and GHG release from soils, tundra or ocean sediments, may begin to come into play on time scales as short as centuries or less. Rapid on-going climate changes and realization that Earth is out of energy balance, implying that more warming is 'in the pipeline', add urgency to investigation of the dangerous level of GHGs. * * *

We use paleoclimate data to show that long-term climate has high sensitivity to climate forcings and that the present global mean CO_2, 385 ppm, is already in the dangerous zone. Despite rapid current CO_2 growth, ~2 ppm/year, we show that it is conceivable to reduce CO_2 this century to less than the current amount, but only *via* prompt policy changes.

1.1. Climate Sensitivity

A global climate forcing, measured in W/m2 averaged over the planet, is an imposed perturbation of the planet's energy balance. Increase of solar irradiance (So) by 2% and doubling of atmospheric CO_2 are each forcings of about 4 W/m2.

[Fast feedbacks in the climate system can be analyzed by] asking how much global surface temperature would increase if atmospheric CO_2 were instantly doubled, assuming that slowly-changing planetary surface conditions, such as ice sheets and forest cover, were fixed. Long-lived GHGs, except for the specified CO_2 change, were also fixed, not responding to climate change. The * * * problem thus provides a measure of climate sensitivity including only the effect of 'fast' feedback processes, such as changes of water vapor, clouds and sea ice. Classification of climate change mechanisms into fast and slow feedbacks is useful, even though time scales of these changes may overlap. We include as fast feedbacks aerosol changes, e.g., of desert dust and marine dimethylsulfide, that occur in response to climate change.

[In 1979] Charney [reported how he] used climate models to estimate fast feedback doubled CO_2 sensitivity of $3 \pm 1.5°C$. Water vapor increase and sea ice decrease in response to global warming were both found to be strong positive feedbacks, amplifying the surface temperature response. Climate models in the current IPCC assessment still agree with Charney's estimate.

Climate models alone are unable to define climate sensitivity more precisely, because it is difficult to prove that models realistically incorporate all feedback processes. The Earth's history, however, allows empirical inference of both fast feedback climate sensitivity and long-term sensitivity to specified GHG change including the slow ice sheet feedback. * * *

The implication is that global climate sensitivity of 3°C for doubled CO_2, although valid for the idealized Charney definition of climate sensitivity, is a considerable understatement of expected equilibrium global warming in response to imposed doubled CO_2. Additional warming, due to slow climate feedbacks including loss of ice and spread of flora over the vast high-latitude land area in the Northern Hemisphere, approximately doubles equilibrium climate sensitivity. Equilibrium sensitivity 6°C for doubled CO_2 is relevant to the case in which GHG changes are specified. That is appropriate to the anthropogenic case, provided the GHG amounts are estimated from carbon cycle models including climate feedbacks such as methane release from tundra and ocean sediments. The equilibrium sensitivity is even higher if the GHG feedback is included as part of the climate response, as is appropriate for analysis of the climate response to Earth orbital perturbations. The very high sensitivity with both albedo and GHG slow feedbacks included accounts for the huge magnitude of glacial-interglacial fluctuations in the Pleistocene in response to small forcings.

Equilibrium climate response would not be reached in decades or even in a century, because surface warming is slowed by the inertia of the ocean and ice sheets. However, Earth's history suggests that positive feedbacks, especially surface albedo changes, can spur rapid global warmings, including sea level rise as fast as several meters per century. Thus if humans push the climate system sufficiently far into disequilibrium, positive climate feedbacks may set in motion dramatic climate change and climate impacts that cannot be controlled.

4. ANTHROPOCENE ERA

Human-made global climate forcings now prevail over natural forcings **Fig. (2)**. Earth may have entered the Anthropocene era 6-8 ky ago, but the net human-made forcing was small, perhaps slightly negative, prior to the industrial era. GHG forcing overwhelmed natural and negative human-made forcings only in the past quarter century **Fig. (2)**.

Human-made climate change is delayed by ocean and ice sheet response times. Warming 'in the pipeline', mostly attributable to slow feedbacks, is now about 2°C **Fig. (2)**. No additional forcing is required to raise global temperature to at least the level of the Pliocene, 2-3 million years ago, a degree of warming that would surely yield 'dangerous' climate impacts.

4.1. Tipping Points

Realization that today's climate is far out of equilibrium with current climate forcings raises the specter of 'tipping points', the concept that climate can reach a point where, without additional forcing, rapid changes proceed practically out of our control. Arctic sea ice and the West Antarctic Ice Sheet are examples of potential tipping points. Arctic sea ice loss is magnified by the positive feedback of increased absorption of sunlight as global warming initiates sea ice retreat. West Antarctic ice loss can be accelerated by several feedbacks, once ice loss is substantial.

We define: (1) the *tipping level*, the global climate forcing that, if long maintained, gives rise to a specific consequence, and (2) the *point of no return*, a climate state beyond which the consequence is inevitable, even if climate forcings are reduced. A point of no return can be avoided, even if the tipping level is temporarily exceeded. Ocean and ice sheet inertia permit overshoot, provided the climate forcing is returned below the tipping level before initiating irreversible dynamic change.

Points of no return are inherently difficult to define, because the dynamical problems are nonlinear. Existing models are more lethargic than the real world for phenomena now unfolding, including changes of sea ice, ice streams, ice shelves, and expansion of the subtropics.

The tipping level is easier to assess, because the paleoclimate quasi-equilibrium response to known climate forcing is relevant. The tipping level is a measure of the long-term climate forcing that humanity must aim to stay beneath to avoid large climate impacts. The tipping level does not define the magnitude or period of tolerable overshoot. However, if overshoot is in place for centuries, the thermal perturbation will so penetrate the ocean that recovery without dramatic effects, such as ice sheet disintegration, becomes unlikely.

4.2. Target CO_2

Combined, GHGs other than CO_2 cause climate forcing comparable to that of CO_2 , but growth of non-CO_2 GHGs is falling below IPCC scenarios. Thus total GHG climate forcing change is now determined mainly by CO_2. Coincidentally, CO_2 forcing is similar to the net human-made forcing, because non-CO_2 GHGs tend to offset negative aerosol forcing.

Thus we take future CO_2 change as approximating the net human-made forcing change, with two caveats. First, special effort to reduce non-CO_2 GHGs could alleviate the CO_2 requirement, allowing up to about +25 ppm CO_2 for the same climate effect, while resurgent growth of non-CO_2 GHGs could reduce allowed CO_2 a similar amount. Second, reduction of human-made aerosols, which have a net cooling effect, could force stricter GHG requirements. However, an emphasis on reducing black soot could largely offset reductions of high albedo aerosols.

Our estimated history of CO_2 through the Cenozoic Era provides a sobering perspective for assessing an appropriate target for future CO_2 levels. A CO_2 amount of order 450 ppm or larger, if long maintained, would push Earth toward the ice-free state. Although ocean and ice sheet inertia limit the rate of climate change, such a CO_2 level likely would cause the passing of climate tipping points and initiate dynamic responses that could be out of humanity's control.

The climate system, because of its inertia, has not yet fully responded to the recent increase of human-made climate forcings. Yet climate impacts are already occurring that allow us to make an initial estimate for a target atmospheric CO_2 level. No doubt the target will need to be adjusted as climate data and knowledge improve, but the urgency and difficulty of reducing the human-made forcing will be less, and more likely manageable, if excess forcing is limited soon.

Civilization is adapted to climate zones of the Holocene. Theory and models indicate that subtropical regions expand poleward with global warming. Data reveal a 4-degree latitudinal shift already, larger than model predictions, yielding increased aridity in southern United States, the Mediterranean region, Australia and parts of Africa. Impacts of this climate shift support the conclusion that 385 ppm CO_2 is already deleterious.

Alpine glaciers are in near-global retreat. After a one-time added flush of fresh water, glacier demise will yield summers and autumns of frequently dry rivers, including rivers originating in the Himalayas, Andes and Rocky Mountains that now supply water to hundreds of millions of people. Present glacier retreat, and warming in the pipeline, indicate that 385 ppm CO_2 is already a threat.

Equilibrium sea level rise for today's 385 ppm CO_2 is at least several meters, judging from Paleoclimate history. Accelerating mass losses from Greenland and West Antarctica heighten concerns about ice sheet stability. An initial CO_2 target of 350 ppm, to be reassessed as effects on ice sheet mass balance are observed, is suggested.

Stabilization of Arctic sea ice cover requires, to first approximation, restoration of planetary energy balance. Climate models driven by known forcings yield a present planetary energy imbalance of +0.5-1 W/m2. Observed heat increase in the upper 700 m of the ocean confirms the planetary energy imbalance, but observations of the entire ocean are needed for quantification. CO_2 amount must be reduced to 325-355 ppm to increase outgoing flux 0.5-1 W/m2, if other forcings are unchanged. A further imbalance reduction, and thus CO_2 ~300-325 ppm, may be needed to restore sea ice to its area of 25 years ago.

Coral reefs are suffering from multiple stresses, with ocean acidification and ocean warming principal among them. Given additional warming 'in-the-pipeline', 385 ppm CO_2 is already deleterious. A 300-350 ppm CO_2 target would significantly relieve both of these stresses.

4.3. CO_2 Scenarios

A large fraction of fossil fuel CO_2 emissions stays in the air a long time, one-quarter remaining airborne for several centuries. Thus moderate delay of fossil fuel use will not appreciably reduce long-term human-made climate change. Preservation of a climate resembling that to which humanity is accustomed, the climate of the Holocene, requires that most remaining fossil fuel carbon is never emitted to the atmosphere.

Coal is the largest reservoir of conventional fossil fuels, exceeding combined reserves of oil and gas. The only realistic way to sharply curtail CO_2 emissions is to phase out coal use except where CO_2 is captured and sequestered.

Phase-out of coal emissions by 2030 keeps maximum CO_2 close to 400 ppm, depending on oil and gas reserves and reserve growth. IPCC reserves assume that half of readily extractable oil has already been used. EIA estimates have larger reserves and reserve growth. Even if EIA estimates are accurate, the IPCC case remains valid if the most difficult to extract oil and gas is left in the ground, *via* a rising price on carbon emissions that discourages remote exploration and environmental regulations that place some areas off-limit. If IPCC gas reserves are underestimated, the IPCC case * * * remains valid if the additional gas reserves are used at facilities where CO_2 is captured.

However, even with phase-out of coal emissions and assuming IPCC oil and gas reserves, CO_2 would remain above 350 ppm for more than two centuries. Ongoing Arctic and ice sheet changes, examples of rapid paleoclimate change, and other criteria cited above all drive us to consider scenarios that bring CO_2 more rapidly back to 350 ppm or less.

4.4. Policy Relevance

Desire to reduce airborne CO_2 raises the question of whether CO_2 could be drawn from the air artificially. There are no large-scale technologies for CO_2 air capture now, but with strong research and development support and industrial scale pilot projects sustained over decades it may be possible to achieve costs ~$200/tC or perhaps less. At $200/tC, the cost of removing 50 ppm of CO_2 is ~$20 trillion.

Improved agricultural and forestry practices offer a more natural way to draw down CO_2. Deforestation contributed a net emission of 60±30 ppm over the past few hundred years, of which ~20 ppm CO_2 remains in the air today. Reforestation could absorb a substantial fraction of the 60±30 ppm net deforestation emission.

Carbon sequestration in soil also has significant potential. Biochar, produced in pyrolysis of residues from crops, forestry, and animal wastes, can be used to restore soil fertility while storing carbon for centuries to millennia. Biochar helps soil retain nutrients and fertilizers, reducing emissions of GHGs such as N_2O. Replacing slash-and-burn agriculture with slash-and-char and use of agricultural and forestry wastes for biochar production could provide a CO_2 drawdown of ~8 ppm or more in half a century.

A rising price on carbon emissions and payment for carbon sequestration is surely needed to make drawdown of airborne CO_2 a reality. A 50 ppm drawdown *via* agricultural and forestry practices seems plausible. But if most of the CO_2 in coal is put into the air, no such "natural" drawdown of CO_2 to 350 ppm is feasible. Indeed, if the world continues on a business-as-usual path for even another decade without initiating phase-out of unconstrained coal use, prospects for avoiding a dangerously large, extended overshoot of the 350 ppm level will be dim.

4.5. Caveats: Climate Variability, Climate Models, and Uncertainties

Climate has great variability, much of which is unforced and unpredictable. This fact raises a practical issue: what is the chance that climate variations, e.g., a temporary cooling trend, will affect public recognition of climate change, making it difficult to implement mitigation policies? Also what are the greatest uncertainties in the expectation of a continued global warming trend? And what are the impacts of climate model limitations, given the inability of models to realistically simulate many aspects of climate change and climate processes?

The atmosphere and ocean exhibit coupled nonlinear chaotic variability that cascades to all time scales. Variability is so large that the significance of recent decadal global temperature change would be very limited, if the data were considered simply as a time series, without further information. However, other knowledge includes information on the causes of some of the temperature variability, the planet's energy imbalance, and global climate forcings.

The El Nino Southern Oscillation (ENSO) accounts for most low latitude temperature variability and much of the global variability. The global impact of ENSO is coherent from month to month, as shown by the global-ocean-mean SST, for which the ocean's thermal inertia minimizes the effect of weather noise. The cool anomaly of 2008 coincides with an ENSO minimum and does not imply a change of decadal temperature trend.

Decadal time scale variability, such as predicted weakening of the Atlantic overturning circulation, could interrupt global warming... But the impact of regional dynamical effects on global temperature is opposed by the planet's energy imbalance, a product of the climate system's thermal inertia, which is confirmed by increasing ocean heat storage. This energy imbalance makes decadal interruption of global warming, in the absence of a negative climate forcing, improbable.

Volcanoes and the sun can cause significant negative forcings. However, even if the solar irradiance remained at its value in the current solar minimum, this reduced forcing would be offset by increasing CO_2 within seven years. Human-made aerosols cause a greater negative forcing, both directly and through their effects on clouds. The first satellite observations of aerosols and clouds with accuracy sufficient to quantify this forcing are planned to begin in 2009, but most analysts anticipate that human-made aerosols will decrease in the future, rather than increase further.

Climate models have many deficiencies in their abilities to simulate climate change. However, model uncertainties cut both ways: it is at least as likely that models underestimate effects of human-made GHGs as overestimate them. Model deficiencies in evaluating tipping points, the possibility that rapid changes can occur without additional climate forcing, are of special concern. Loss of Arctic sea ice, for example, has proceeded more rapidly than predicted by climate models. There are reasons to expect that other nonlinear problems, such as ice sheet disintegration and extinction of interdependent species and ecosystems, also have the potential for rapid change.

We suggest an initial objective of reducing atmospheric CO_2 to 350 ppm, with the target to be adjusted as scientific understanding and empirical evidence of climate effects accumulate. Although a case already could be made that the eventual target probably needs to be lower, the 350 ppm target is sufficient to qualitatively change the discussion and drive fundamental changes in energy policy. Limited opportunities for reduction of non-CO_2 human-caused forcings are important to pursue but do not alter the initial 350 ppm CO_2 target. This target must be pursued on a timescale of decades, as paleoclimate and on going changes, and the ocean response time, suggest that it would be foolhardy to allow CO_2 to stay in the dangerous zone for centuries.

A practical global strategy almost surely requires a rising global price on CO_2 emissions and phase-out of coal use except for cases where the CO_2 is captured and sequestered. The carbon price should eliminate use of unconventional fossil fuels, unless, as is unlikely, the CO_2 can be captured. A reward system for improved agricultural and forestry practices that sequester carbon could remove the current CO_2 overshoot. With simultaneous policies to reduce non-CO_2 greenhouse gases, it appears still feasible to avert catastrophic climate change.

POTENTIAL IMPACTS OF CLIMATE CHANGE IN THE UNITED STATES
Congressional Budget Office (May 2009)

The Current State of the Art in Climate Modeling

Climate models have gradually but steadily improved in detail, in the range of phenomena that they include, and in their ability to replicate characteristics of the Earth's climate system. Studies that measure and compare the ability of the current generation of models to simulate recent climate conditions—such as the extensive comparison of 23 of the most complex models in the Fourth Assessment Report of the Intergovernmental Panel on Climate Change—show that nearly all of them have improved in most respects. The most advanced models typically include linked representations of the atmosphere, oceans, sea ice, and land surface; most types of greenhouse gases and other relevant components of atmospheric chemistry; and characteristics of the carbon cycle. The models replicate seasonal and large-scale regional variations in temperature and, to a lesser extent, precipitation; they also replicate large-scale ocean currents, large-scale ocean and climate oscillations, and storms and jet streams in the middle latitudes. However, for some phenomena, such as the dynamics of glaciers, the models remain in early stages of development. Moreover, because the global models have relatively coarse spatial resolutions, regional models of higher resolution are used to "downscale" the results of large models to analyze smaller-scale phenomena. The quality of such downscaling exercises is constrained by the limitations of and uncertainties in the global models.

The models plausibly replicate 20th-century climate trends when they are run with historical emissions of greenhouse gases, other types of emissions, and variations in natural forces, such as volcanic eruptions and fluctuations in solar energy. No model replicates those climate trends through variations in natural forces alone.

Because research groups vary in the way they represent uncertain aspects of the Earth's climate system, the models produce a range of results for many important climate indicators. Studies comparing the models find that the average of the models' simulations (referred to as the "ensemble-mean model") generally replicates features of the system better than does any single model. As a result, researchers have focused on ensemble-mean projections of climate change under various scenarios as being a type of "best guess" of likely changes, taking the range of model results as representing, to an extent, the uncertainty in researchers' current understanding of likely developments.

However, that approach understates uncertainty because it overlooks the fact that each model incorporates its builders' best guesses for uncertain parameters (guesses that do not reflect the full range of uncertainty about them) and that no model includes all human influences on regional climates. To better analyze the full extent of uncertainty, researchers turn to simpler models that can be "tuned" to replicate the results of larger models but that can also be systematically varied to simulate other possible combinations of parameters.

PROPOSED ENDANGERMENT AND CAUSE OR CONTRIBUTE FINDINGS FOR GREENHOUSE GASES UNDER SECTION 202 (a) OF THE CLEAN AIR ACT
U.S. Environmental Protection Agency
74 Fed. Reg 18886 (April 24, 2009)

SUMMARY: Today the Administrator is proposing to find that greenhouse gases in the atmosphere endanger the public health and welfare of current and future generations. Concentrations of greenhouse gases are at unprecedented levels compared to the recent and distant past. These high atmospheric levels are the unambiguous result of human emissions, and are very likely the cause of the observed increase in average temperatures and other climatic changes. The effects of climate change observed to date and projected to occur in the future-including but not limited to the increased likelihood of more frequent and intense heat waves, more wildfires, degraded air quality, more heavy downpours and flooding, increased drought, greater sea level rise, more intense storms, harm to water resources, harm to agriculture, and harm to wildlife and ecosystems-are effects on public health and welfare within the meaning of the Clean Air Act. In light of the likelihood that greenhouse gases cause these effects, and the magnitude of the effects that are occurring and are very likely to occur in the future, the Administrator proposes to find that. atmospheric concentrations of greenhouse gases endanger public health and welfare within the meaning of Section 202(a) of the Clean Air Act. She proposes to make this finding specifically with respect to six greenhouse gases that together constitute the root of the climate change problem: carbon dioxide, methane, nitrous oxide, hydrofluorocarbons, perfluorocarbons, and sulfur hexafluoride. * * *

A. Approach in Utilizing the Best Available Scientific Information

EPA has developed a technical support document (TSD) which synthesizes major findings from the best available scientific assessments that have gone through rigorous and transparent peer review. The TSD therefore relies most heavily on the major assessment reports of both the Intergovernmental Panel on Climate Change (IPCC) and the U.S. Climate Change Science Program (CCSP). EPA took this approach rather than conducting a new assessment of the scientific literature. The IPCC and CCSP assessments base their findings on the large body of many individual, peer reviewed studies in the literature, and then the IPCC and CCSP assessments themselves go through a transparent peer-review process. The TSD was in turn reviewed by a dozen federal government scientists, who have contributed. significantly to the body of climate change literature, and indeed. to our common understanding of this problem. The information in the TSD has therefore been developed and prepared. in a manner that is consistent with EPA's Guidelines for Ensuring and Maximizing the Quality, Objectivity, Utility and Integrity of Information Disseminated by the Environmental Protection Agency. Furthermore, relying most heavily on the assessment reports that reflect the scientific literature more broadly guards against an over reliance on and narrow consideration of individual studies. * * *

Regarding the scope of the relevant scientific findings, EPA took the approach that the timeframe under consideration should be consistent with the timeframe over which greenhouse gases may influence the climate (i.e., observed effects and projected effects over the next several decades and indeed at least for the remainder of this century). Moreover, the analysis was not restricted to only those climate and public health or welfare effects which may be attributable solely to greenhouse gas emissions from section 202(a) sources under the Act. In addition, although the primary focus for evaluation of risks and impacts to public health or welfare was on the U.S., careful consideration was also given to the global context.

Finally, climate policy or societal responses to any known or perceived risks and impacts to public health or welfare, which may or may not be implemented in the future -- whether through planned adaptation or greenhouse gas mitigation measures were not explicitly assessed in the endangerment analysis. Some observed and projected effects or risks due to climate change reported in the TSD and summarized below do have embedded within them assumptions about autonomous behavioral or management changes to cope with climate change. We have noted these situations in the TSD. However, it is the Administrator's position that the purpose of the endangerment analysis is to assess the risks posed to public health and welfare, rather than to estimate how various adaptation and greenhouse gas mitigation policies may ameliorate or exacerbate any endangerment that exists. Indeed, the presumed need for adaptation and greenhouse gas mitigation to occur to avoid, lessen or delay the risks and impacts associated with human-induced climate change presupposes that there is endangerment to public health or welfare. * * *

B. The Air Pollution

In applying the endangerment test to greenhouse gases under section 202(a), the Administrator must define the scope and nature of the relevant air pollution that must be evaluated. For this action, the Administrator is proposing that the air pollution be defined as the combined mix of six key directly-emitted and long-lived greenhouse gases which together constitute the root cause of human-induced climate change: carbon dioxide (CO_2), methane, nitrous oxide, hrydrofluorocarbons, perfluorocarbons, and sulfur hexafluoride. The Administrator acknowledges that there are other anthropogenic climate forcers which play a role in climate change (discussed below), but that for today's action these other climate forcers are not the priority and may need to be evaluated further. What follows is a summary of key scientific findings from the TSD and the Administrator's rationale for the proposed definition of air pollution.

1. Common Features of the Six Key Greenhouse Gases

There are a number of scientific and policy reasons why the Administrator is proposing that the air pollution for this endangerment finding be defined as the combination of the six greenhouse gases. These six greenhouse gases are well studied by and have been the primary focus of climate change research, and are therefore the Administrator's first priority in addressing endangerment for greenhouse gases. These six greenhouse gases share common physical properties relevant to the climate change problem: all are long-lived [3]in the atmosphere; all become globally well mixed in the atmosphere regardless of where the emissions occur; all trap outgoing heat that would otherwise escape to space; and all are directly emitted as greenhouse gases rather than forming as a greenhouse gas in the atmosphere after emission of a precursor gas. Because of these properties, the climate effects of these greenhouse gases are generally better understood than the climate effects associated with most other climate-forcing agents (described in more detail in subsection 4 below). * * *

Because these six greenhouse gases share common properties and are the key driver of human-induced climate change, they have been the common focus of climate change science and policy to date. The United Nations Framework Convention on Climate Change (UNFCCC) addresses these six long-lived. well-mixed greenhouse gases not controlled by the Montreal Protocol on Substances that Deplete the Ozone Layer. The IPCC scientific assessments focus primarily on these six greenhouse gases and their effects on climate.

Treating the air pollution as the mix of the six greenhouse gases is consistent with other provisions of the Act and previous EPA practice under the Act, where separate air pollutants from different sources but with common properties may be treated as a class (e.g. Class I and Class II substances under Title VI). This approach addresses the cumulative effect that the elevated concentrations of the six greenhouse gases have on climate, and thus on different elements of health, society and the environment.[4]

The scientific literature that assesses the potential risks and end-point impacts of human-induced climate change does not typically assess these impacts on a gas-by-gas basis. It is true that estimates are available for how

---

[11] We use "long-lived" here to mean that the gas has a lifetime in the atmosphere sufficient to become globally well mixed throughout the entire atmosphere, which requires a minimum atmospheric lifetime of about one year. IPCC also refers to these six greenhouse gases as long-lived. Methane has an atmospheric lifetime of roughly a decade. One of the most commonly used hydrofluorocarbons (HFC-134a) has a lifetime of 14 years. Nitrous oxide has a lifetime of 114 years; sulfur hexafluoride over 3,000 years; and some PFCs up to 10.000 to 50,000 years. Carbon dioxide is generally thought to have a lifetime of roughly 100 years, but for a given amount of carbon dioxide emitted some fraction is quickly absorbed by the oceans and terrestrial vegetation and the remainder will only slowly decay in the atmosphere after several years, and indeed some portion will remain in the atmosphere for many centuries.

[13] Due to the cumulative purpose of the statutory language, even if the Administrator were to look at the atmospheric concentration of each greenhouse gas individually, she would still consider the impact of the concentration of a single greenhouse gas in combination with that caused by the other greenhouse gases.

individual greenhouse gases and other climate-forcing agents are contributing to the anthropogenic heating (or cooling) effect being exerted on the global climate. However, as one moves farther down the causal chain towards endpoint risks and impacts to human health, society and the environment, such impacts, whether observed or projected, are typically not attributed to the temperature increase or other climatic change due to the elevated atmospheric concentration of just one of the greenhouse gases.

2. Evidence That the Six Greenhouse Gases Are at Unprecedented Levels in the Atmosphere

Given the long atmospheric lifetime and global mixing of greenhouse gases, global average atmospheric concentrations are an important metric by which to measure changes in atmospheric composition. Current atmospheric greenhouse gas concentrations are now at elevated levels as a result of both historic and current. anthropogenic emissions. The global atmospheric carbon dioxide concentration has increased about 38 percent from pre-industrial levels to 2009, and almost all of the increase is due to anthropogenic emissions. The current (year 2009) carbon dioxide concentration is 386 parts per million (ppm) and has recently been increasing by about 2.0 ppm per year. The global atmospheric concentration of methane has increased by 149 percent since preindustrial levels (through 2007), and the nitrous oxide concentration has increased 23 percent (through 2007). The observed concentration increase in these gases can also be attributed primarily to anthropogenic emissions. The industrial fluorinated gases, hydrofluorocarbons, perfluorocarbons, and sulfur hexafluoride, are almost entirely anthropogenic in origin, and have relatively low atmospheric concentrations but are increasing rapidly; concentrations of many of these gases have increased by large factors (between 4.3 and 1.3) between 1998 and 2005.

Historic data that go back many thousands of years show that current atmospheric concentrations of the two most important directly emitted, long lived greenhouse gases (carbon dioxide and methane) are well above the natural range of atmospheric concentrations compared to the last 650,000 years.

Atmospheric greenhouse gas concentrations have been increasing because human emissions have been outpacing the ability of the natural environment to remove greenhouse gases from the atmosphere over timescales of decades to centuries.

The Administrator recognizes these scientific findings that the current global atmospheric concentrations of the six greenhouse gases are now at unprecedented and record-high levels compared to both the recent and distant past. It is also unambiguous that the current elevated greenhouse gas concentrations are the primary result of human activities.

Total concentrations of these greenhouse gases are projected to continue climbing, and thus to continue pushing unprecedented levels upwards for the foreseeable future under different plausible assumptions of U.S. and global greenhouse gas-emitting activities. Given the long atmospheric lifetime of the six greenhouse gases, significant changes in total greenhouse gas global atmospheric concentrations do not come about quickly (i.e. within a few years). Future atmospheric greenhouse gas concentrations -- not only for the remainder of the current century but indeed for decades and in some cases centuries well beyond 2100-will be influenced by our present and near-term greenhouse gas emissions. Consideration of future plausible scenarios, and how our current greenhouse gas emissions essentially commit present and future generations to cope with an altered atmosphere and climate, reinforces the Administrator's judgment that it is appropriate to define the combination of the six key greenhouse gases as the air pollution. * * *

4. Other Climate Forcers

There are other greenhouse gases and aerosols that have warming (and cooling) effects but are not being included in the proposed definition of air pollution. These include water vapor, chlorofluorocarbons (CFCs), hydrochlorofluorocarbons (HCFCs), halons, tropospheric ozone (O_3), black carbon, and other short-lived precursor gases. For each of these substances, there are different scientific and policy reasons why these substances are not being included in the proposed definition of air pollution for purposes of section 202(a). * * *

C. The Administrator's Proposed Finding That the Air Pollution Endangers Public Health and Welfare

The scientific evidence clearly indicates that atmospheric levels of the six greenhouse gases are at unprecedented elevated levels due to human activities, and that most of the observed global and continental warming can be attributed to this anthropogenic rise in greenhouse gases. The information presented here builds on these facts that support the proposed definition of air pollution. * * *

1. Evidence of Currently Observed Climatic and Related Effects
There is compelling evidence that a number of climate and physical changes are occurring now that can be attributed to the anthropogenic rise in atmospheric greenhouse gases, and other changes that are consistent with the direction of change expected from warming and human-induced climate change. These observed changes described below can adversely affect and pose risks to both public health and welfare.

The global indicators of change go beyond the well-established surface air temperature rise discussed above. Observational evidence from all continents and most oceans shows that many natural systems are being affected by regional climate changes, particularly temperature increases. Observations show that changes are occurring in the amount, intensity, frequency, and type of precipitation. There is strong evidence that global sea level gradually rose in the 20th century and is currently rising at an increased rate. Widespread changes in extreme temperatures have been observed in the last 50 years. Globally, cold days, cold nights, and frost have become less frequent, while hot days, hot nights, and heat waves have become more frequent.

Satellite data since 1978 show that annual average Arctic sea ice extent has shrunk by 2.7 ± 0.6 percent per decade, with larger decreases in summer of 7.4 ± 2.4 percent per decade. The latest data from NASA indicate Arctic sea ice set a record low in September 2007, 38 percent below the 1979-2007 average. In September 2008, Arctic sea ice reached its second lowest extent on record.

Like global mean temperatures, U.S.air temperatures have warmed during. the 20th and into the 21st century. * * *

• 2005-2007 · were exceptionally warm years (among the top 10 warmest on record), while 2008 was slightly warmer than average (the 39th warmest year on record), 0.2 °F (0.1 °C) above the 20th century (1901-2000) mean.

• The last ten 5-year periods (2004-2008, 2003-2007, 2002-2006, 2001-2005, 2000-2004, 1999-2003, 1998-2002, 1997-2001, 1996-2000,and 1995-1999), were the warmest 5-year periods in the 114 years of national records, demonstrating the anomalous warmth of the last 15 years.

Over the contiguous U.S., total annual precipitation increased at an average rate of 6.5 percent over the period 1901-2006. It is likely that there have been increases in the number of heavy precipitation events within many land regions, even in those where there has been a reduction in total precipitation amount, consistent with a warming climate.

Sea level has been rising along most of the U.S. Atlantic and Gulf coasts. In the mid-Atlantic region from New York to North Carolina, tide-gauge observations indicate that relative sea-level rise (the combination of global sea-level rise and land subsidence) rates were higher than the global mean and generally ranged between 2.4 and 4.4 millimeters per year, or about 0.3 meters (1 foot) over the twentieth century.

Climate changes are very likely already affecting U.S. water resources, agriculture, land resources, and biodiversity as a result of climate variability and change. A 2008 CCSP report that examined these observed changes concluded, "[t]he number and frequency of forest fires and insect outbreaks are increasing in the interior West, the Southwest, and Alaska. Precipitation, stream flow, and stream, temperatures are increasing in most of the continental U.S. The western U.S. is experiencing reduced snowpack and earlier peaks in spring runoff. The growth of many crops and weeds is being stimulated. Migration of plant and animal species is changing the composition and structure of arid, polar, aquatic, coastal, and other ecosystems." * * *

2. Future Projected Climatic and Related Effects

Because atmospheric greenhouse gas concentrations are expected to climb for the foreseeable future, temperatures will continue to rise and the overall rate and magnitude of human-induced climate change will likely increase, such that risks to public health and welfare will likewise grow over time so that future generations will be especially vulnerable; their vulnerability will include potentially catastrophic harms. Projected effects here focus on the next several decades and the timeframe out to 2100.

The majority of future reference-case scenarios (assuming no explicit greenhouse gas mitigation actions beyond those already enacted) project an increase of global greenhouse gas emissions over the century, with climbing greenhouse gas concentrations. Long-lived gas concentrations increase even for those scenarios where annual emissions toward the end of the century are assumed to be lower than current annual emissions. Indeed, for a given amount of CO_2 released today, about half will be taken up by the oceans and terrestrial vegetation over the next 30 years, a further 30 percent will be removed over a few centuries, and the remaining 20 percent will only slowly decay over time such that it will take many thousands of years to remove from the atmosphere. Carbon dioxide is expected to remain the dominant anthropogenic driver of climate change over the course of the 21st century. The heating effect associated with the non-CO_2 greenhouse gases is still significant and growing over time.

Future warming over the course of the 21st century, even under scenarios of low emissions growth, is very likely to be greater than observed warming over the past century. * * *

All of the U.S. is very likely to warm during this century, and most areas of the U,S, are expected to warm by more than the global average. The largest warming through 2100 is projected to occur in winter over northern parts of Alaska. In western, central and eastern regions of North America, the projected warming has less seasonal variation and is not as large, especially near the coast, consistent with less warming over the oceans.

The U.S. is projected to see an overall average increase in the intensity of precipitation events, which is likely to increase the risk of flood events, though projections for specific regions are very uncertain.

As the climate warms, glaciers will lose mass owing to dominance of summer melting over winter precipitation increases, contributing to sea level rise.

For North American coasts, sea level rise may be similar to the global mean, with slightly higher rates in western Alaska. The projected rate of sea level rise off the low-lying U.S. South Atlantic and Gulf coasts is also higher than the global average.

Based on a range of models, it is likely that tropical cyclones (tropical storms and hurricanes) will become more intense, with stronger peak winds and more heavy precipitation associated with ongoing increases of tropical sea surface temperatures. Storm surge levels are likely to increase due to projected sea level rise. Frequency changes in hurricanes are currently too uncertain for confident projections.

3. Impacts on Public Health

Many of the observed and projected changes in climate and climate-sensitive systems discussed above pose serious risks to public health. The following discussion outlines specific public health concerns raised by observations and plausible future outcomes, recognizing the statutory requirement that the Administrator consider how sensitive or susceptible populations may be particularly at risk. As our discussion of increasing temperatures suggests, the adverse effects of greenhouse gas emissions are expected to mount over time. The findings of the IPCC, and of many others, indicate that risks to public health will be more severe in 20 years than in ten years, more severe in 30 years than in 20 years, more severe in 40 years than in 30 years, and so forth. There is disagreement about whether and when increases in adverse effects will be linear or nonlinear; on some projections, nonlinear increases in such effects can reasonably be expected at some future point. We believe that existing evidence supports a finding that there are current adverse effects. This evidence also supports a finding that these effects will become more serious over the next several decades, in some cases out to 2100.

To be clear, ambient concentrations of carbon dioxide and the other greenhouse gases, whether at current levels or at projected ambient levels under scenarios of high emissions growth over time, do not cause direct adverse health effects such as respiratory or toxic effects. All public health risks and impacts described here as a result of elevated atmospheric concentrations of greenhouse gases occur via climate change. The pathway or mechanism occurs through changes in climate, but the end result is an adverse effect on the health of the population. Thus these effects from climate change are appropriately denoted public health effects. It is important to acknowledge that effects on "welfare" do not always entail effects on "public health," and the Administrator does not mean to interpret "public health" to include "welfare" effects as such. Today's interpretation does not collapse the two categories-many "welfare" effects do not and cannot involve public health. The Administrator simply means to recognize, with the scientific community, that concentrations of greenhouse gases endanger public health through a wide range of pathways.

As described above, there is evidence that unusually hot days and nights and heat waves have become more frequent in the U.S. Severe heat waves are projected to intensify in magnitude and duration over the portions of the U.S. where these events already occur, with likely increases in mortality and morbidity. The populations most sensitive to hot temperatures are older adults, the chronically sick, the very young, city-dwellers, those taking medications that disrupt thermoregulation, the mentally ill, those lacking access to air conditioning, those working or playing outdoors, and the socially isolated.

The Administrator also acknowledges that warming temperatures may bring about some health benefits. Both extremely cold days and extremely hot days are dangerous to human health. But at least in the short run, modest temperature increases may produce health benefits in the U.S. (and elsewhere). Although the IPCC projects reduced human mortality from cold exposure through 2100, it is currently difficult to ascertain the balance between increased heat-related mortality and decreased cold-related mortality. With respect to health, different regions will be affected in different ways. The Administrator does not believe that it is now possible to quantify the various effects. Because the risks from unusually hot days and nights, and from heat waves, are very serious, it is reasonable to find on balance that these risks support a finding that public health is endangered even if it is also possible that modest temperature increases will have some beneficial health effects.

Increases in regional ozone pollution in the U.S. relative to ozone levels without climate change are expected due to higher temperatures and a modification of meteorological factors. Increases in regional ozone pollution increase the risks of respiratory infection, aggravation of asthma, and premature death. EPA does have in place National Ambient Air Quality Standards (NAAQS) for ozone, which are premised on the harmfulness of ozone to public health and welfare. These standards and their accompanying regulatory regime have helped to reduce the dangers from ozone in the U.S. Substantial challenges remain with respect to achieving the air quality protection promised by the NAAQS for ozone. These challenges will be exacerbated by climate change.

There will likely be an increase in the spread of several food and water-borne pathogens (e.g.. Salmonella, Vibrio) among susceptible populations depending on the pathogens' survival, persistence, habitat range and transmission under changing climate and environmental conditions. The primary climate-related factors that affect these pathogens include temperature, precipitation, extreme weather events, and shifts in their ecological regimes.

Climate change, including the direct changes in carbon dioxide concentrations themselves, could impact the production, distribution, dispersion and allergenicity of aeroallergens and the growth and distribution of weeds, grasses and trees that produce them. These changes in aeroallergens and subsequent human exposures could affect the prevalence and severity of allergy symptoms. However, the scientific literature does not provide definitive data or conclusions on how climate change might impact aeroallergens and subsequently the prevalence of allergenic illnesses in the U.S.

The IPCC reports with very high confidence that climate change impacts on human health in U.S. cities will be compounded by population growth and an aging population. The CCSP reports that climate change has the potential to accentuate the disparities already evident in the American health care systems as many of the expected health effects are likely to fall disproportionately on the poor, the elderly. the disabled, and the uninsured.

Within settlements experiencing climate change stressors, certain parts of the population may be especially vulnerable based on their circumstances. These include the poor, the elderly, the very young, those already in poor health, the disabled, those living alone, those with limited rights and power (such as recent immigrants with limited English skills), and/or indigenous populations dependent on one or a few resources.

These potential impacts of climate change have taken on added meaning in light of the risk that hurricanes are likely to become more severe with climate change, and in light of our heightened awareness about how vulnerable the U.S. Gulf Coast can be. * * *

4. Impacts on Public Welfare
The Act defines "effects on welfare" as including, but not limited to, "effects on soils, water, crops, vegetation, manmade materials. animals, wildlife, weather, visibility, and climate, damage to and deterioration of property, and hazards to transportation, as well as effects on economic values and on personal comfort and well-being * * *." CAA Section 302(h). It is clear that current and projected levels of greenhouse gases and resultant climate change are already adversely affecting, and will continue to adversely affect, public welfare within the meaning of the Act. As noted, the adverse effects of greenhouse gases are expected to increase over time with growing temperatures. This point holds for welfare as it does for health. In the future, the adverse effects will increase and perhaps accelerate; projected risks focus on the next several decades and out to 2100. * * *

Higher temperatures will very likely reduce livestock production during the summer season, but these losses will very likely he partially offset by warmer temperatures during the winter season.

Climate change has very likely increased the size and number of forest fires, insect outbreaks, and tree mortality in the interior west, the Southwest, and Alaska, and will continue to do so. An increased frequency of disturbance is at least as important to ecosystem function as incremental changes in temperature, precipitation, atmospheric CO_2, nitrogen deposition, and ozone pollution. IPCC reported that overall forest growth for North America as a whole will likely increase modestly (10-20 percent) as a result of extended growing seasons and elevated CO2 over the next century, but with important spatial and temporal variation.

In addition to human health effects, tropospheric ozone increases as a result of temperature increases and other climatic changes can have significant adverse effects on crop yields, pasture and forest growth and species composition.

Coastal communities and habitats will be increasingly stressed by climate change impacts interacting with development and pollution. Sea level is rising along much of the U.S. coast, and the rate of change will increase in the future, exacerbating the impacts of progressive inundation, storm-surge flooding, and shoreline erosion. Coastal aquifers and estuaries are vulnerable to salt water intrusion due to rising sea levels, which could compromise water sources used for municipal drinking water, agricultural crops, and other human uses. Storm impacts are likely to be more severe, especially along the Gulf and Atlantic coasts. Salt marshes, other coastal habitats, and dependent species are threatened by sea-level rise, fixed structures blocking landward migration, and changes in vegetation. Population growth and rising value of infrastructure in coastal areas increases vulnerability to climate variability and future climate change.

Water infrastructure, including drinking water and wastewater treatment plants, and sewer and stormwater management systems, may be at greater risk of flooding, sea level rise and storm surge, low flows, and other factors that could impair functioning. For example, some of these impacts are already being experienced in Alaska, where rapidly melting permafrost has damaged and disrupted drinking water distribution systems and wastewater infrastructure.

Ocean acidification is projected to continue, resulting in the reduced biological production of marine calcifiers, including corals.

Climate change is likely to affect U.S. energy use (e.g., heating and cooling requirements), and energy production (e.g., effects on hydropower), physical infrastructures and institutional infrastructures. Climate change will likely interact with and possibly exacerbate ongoing environmental change and environmental pressures in settlements, particularly in Alaska where indigenous communities are facing major environmental changes from sea ice loss and coastal erosion that threaten traditional ways of life.

Over the 21st century, changes in climate will cause some species to shift north and to higher elevations and fundamentally rearrange U.S. ecosystems. Differential capacities to adapt to range shifts and constraints from development, habitat fragmentation, invasive species. And broken ecological connections will alter ecosystem structure, composition, function, and services.

The Administrator acknowledges that as for human health, so too for welfare: moderate temperature increases may have some benefits, particularly for agriculture and forestry over the short term * * *. This possibility is not inconsistent with a judgment that greenhouse gases in the atmosphere endanger welfare. Beneficial effects can coexist with harmful effects, and it is not necessary to reach a firm conclusion, for particular domains and sectors, about the net result in order to reach an overall conclusion in favor of endangerment.

5. The Administrator's Consideration of International Effects

The Administrator judges that the impacts to public health and welfare occurring within the U.S. alone warrant her proposed endangerment finding. In addition, the Administrator believes that consideration of climate change effects in other world regions adds support for today's proposal, but that consideration of international impacts is not necessary in order to reach a judgment that there is endangerment to public health and welfare. Thus, the Administrator does not now take a position on the legal question whether international effects, on their own, would be sufficient to support an endangerment finding. Some of the world's regions are expected to face greater impacts due to climate change because they are more vulnerable. Even apart from the effects of climate change on other world regions-effects which are considerable-the Administrator also believes many of these impacts could raise economic, trade, humanitarian and even national security issues for the U.S.

The IPCC identifies the most vulnerable world regions as the Arctic, because of high rates of projected warming on natural systems; Africa, especially the sub-Saharan region, because of current low adaptive capacity (e.g.. lack of infrastructure and resources) as well as climate change; small islands, due to high exposure of population and infrastructure to risk of sea-level rise and increased storm surge; and Asian mega deltas, due to large populations and high exposure to sea level rise, storm surge and river flooding.

6. The Administrator's Consideration of Key Uncertainties

There are many inherent uncertainties associated with characterizing both the observed and projected risks and impacts to public health and welfare due to current and projected greenhouse gas concentrations. Both probability and severity are not easy to specify. It is difficult to attribute any single past event (hurricane, flood, drought, or heat wave) to elevated greenhouse gas concentrations even if it is understood that anthropogenic climate change has already made such events more likely or more extreme. The precise rate and magnitude of future climate change, for both the globe and for the U.S., remain uncertain, even in the hypothetical case where current greenhouse gas concentrations would remain constant over the next several decades. Projecting the exact magnitude of a particular impact due to climate change is difficult due to what are often long time frames to consider, the uncertain nature of how the system or sector will be affected by climate change, and uncertainties about how other factors (e.g., income levels, technologies, demographics) will change over time which can in turn affect the vulnerability of the system or sector to climate change.

Many uncertainties could push in the direction of either greater or lesser risks as they become better understood. EPA has acknowledged the possibility of beneficial effects on both health and welfare. Other possibilities include catastrophic events. Examples of such key uncertainties involve how the frequency of hurricanes and other extreme weather events may change in a changing climate, the potential to trigger thresholds for abrupt climate change (e.g. disintegration of the Greenland Ice Sheet or collapse of the West Antarctic Ice Sheet), and how responsive the climate ultimately will be to the heating effect being caused by anthropogenic greenhouse gases. Even if the probability of extremely high-impact events may be small, the existence of such high impact events, and the potential for other currently unknown catastrophic impacts that could plausibly result from record-high atmospheric greenhouse gas levels, substantially bolsters the case for an endangerment finding with respect to greenhouse gases.[5] These uncertainties will be with us for the foreseeable future. However, Congress expected the Administrator to consider uncertainties and extrapolate from limited data. It also recognized that there are inherent limitations and difficulties in information on public health and welfare, but nonetheless expected the Administrator to exercise her judgment based on the information available.

At the same time, there is a broad base of scientific evidence that has been reviewed extensively by the scientific community, which supports the findings discussed about how anthropogenic increases in greenhouse gases

---

[5] A recent economic study that has received considerable attention in the climate change research community (Weitzman, The Review of Economics and Statistics, 2009) has determined that if the probability distribution of the magnitude of possible impacts has a "fat tail", then the expected utility of reducing the probability of that tail becomes astronomical. The study determined that anthropogenic climate change is a plausible candidate for such a "fat tailed" damage function.

are affecting the climate and the key risks to public health and welfare that human-induced climate change pose. The Administrator believes that the scientific findings in totality provide compelling evidence of human-induced climate change, and that serious risks and potential impacts to public health and welfare have been clearly identified, even if they cannot always be quantified with confidence. The Administrator's proposed endangerment finding is based on weighing the scientific evidence, considering the uncertainties, and balancing any benefits to human health, society and the environment that may also occur. Given the evolution of climate change science over the past 15 years or more, the Administrator believes the evidence of discernible human influence on the global climate, and the risks that such climate change poses, has become more compelling, and therefore believes the evidence that there is endangerment to the public health and welfare of current and future generations has likewise become more compelling in step with our increasing understanding of the climate change problem.   * * *

[The Administrator's proposed legal conclusions based on the above scientific analysis are excerpted in Chapter 6.]

Notes and Questions

1.   The U.S. Environmental Protection Agency's endangerment finding confirms, and is based upon much of the same science as the Intergovernmental Panel on Climate Change. In light of this scientific consensus, what weight should be given to the "climate skeptics" and their analysis that suggests climate change is not the severe and looming crisis that the EPA has determine it to be? On the other hand, what about those who see no hope for human society mitigating or adapting to the potentially ravaging effects of climate change before the tipping point is reached. See S. Dujack, A Last Change to Save the Planet, 26 The Environmental Forum 22 (2009); J. Lovelock, Gaia's Revenge (2007).

2.   *Carbon Neutral Law Schools*: Do you know where and how the electricity in your law school is generated? How much fossilized solar energy does your law school consume in heating, cafeteria cooking and transportation? What indirect greenhouse gas emissions occur as a result of your law school activities, from commuting students, staff and faculty port the deliveries of goods and services to the law school? If you use the 1990 base year, adopted as the reference year by the USA and other nations in the UN Framework Convention on Climate Change, how large has been your law school's contribution to climate change since then? In order for your law school to know what steps are needed to become carbon neutral, you will need to design and compile an emissions inventory as a baseline. See "Elements of an Emission Inventory" (Appendix C) in A. Rappaport & S. Creighton, Degrees that Matter – Climate Change and the University 327-330 (2007). Will your mitigation plan be an incremental approach to *ad hoc* changes, or be one that plans and make capi-

tal investments to permanently avert the need for fossil fuels, or be a systems approach that reinvents a carbon-free law school and off-sets past emissions since 1990? See the tools for your campus developed by the National Wildlife Federation at www.nwf.org/campusecology/.

E. THE NEXT STEP: ISSUES THAT MUST BE ADDRESSED

SCOPING MEETING FOR THE IPCC FIFTH ASSESSMENT REPORT (AR5): IPCC CHAIRMAN'S VISION PAPER
IPCC Secretariat, AR5-SCOP/Doc. 2 (2009) http://www.ipcc.ch/workshops-experts-meetings-ar5-scoping.htm

Background

* * * The [4th IPCC Assessment Report] AR4 identified a number of areas where additional knowledge is needed. Among these areas are extremes, including hurricanes; sea-level rise; impacts of interacting stresses; limits to adaptation; and the economics of a range of mitigation options at different points in the future. * * *

New Information and Knowledge

* * * Another issue * * * concerns instabilities and irreversibilities of climate change, often called "tipping points", and questions on when we might reach these, based on realistic projections. These represent another dimension of the concept of dangerous anthropogenic interference with the climate system, the subject of Article 2 of the UN Framework Convention on Climate Change (UNFCCC). As previous assessments have, however, clearly established, because the notion "dangerous" involves value judgements, the scientific assessments of the IPCC address some but not all components of defining dangerous anthropogenic interference with the climate system. An important issue, therefore, is whether the AR5 can provide enough knowledge and information by which the work of the negotiators can be facilitated in defining what would be "dangerous".

* * * [I]ssues that would need to be kept in focus in * * * AR5 [:]

Radiative forcing
· Gases/forcings not covered by the Kyoto Protocol
· Alternative metrics
· Air pollution, ozone precursors, sulphate aerosols, black carbon and other precursors of climate change
· Chemical and biological feedbacks
· Stratospheric processes, recovery of the ozone hole
· Full impacts of aviation
· Interchangability of baskets of emissions within a climate change context

Regional modelling, clouds aerosols, uncertainties etc.

- Long term modelling
- Regional modelling
- Ice related issues in the context of land and sea.
- Irreversible and abrupt changes and feedbacks related to them.

Food, managed forests, biomass
- Disaggregation of agricultural production modes by region, size of land holdings and technology used
- Specific consideration of current and projected sources/sinks and their potential, implications of climate change impacts
- Human dimensions, including employment, gender, dependence on ecosystem services
- Food-biofuel competition based on technology and type of biofuel
- Long term changes in carbon stocks

Biodiversity, ecosphere (feedbacks)
- Observations and projections
- Paleo data analysis
- Species at risk of extinction or migration
- Resilience of specific ecosystems

Oceans
- Carbon-uptake
- Acidification, biosphere, coastal protection
- Other biotic stresses for different levels of climate change
- Changes in circulation

Water, hydrology
- Changing needs of human populations, demographic changes, agriculture, industry and commerce
- Changes in availability & flow due to climate change
- Hydropower and implications of climate change.

Settlements, infrastructure
- Cities, rural settlements and implications of mix
- Present level and projections of infrastructure, transport and mobility
- Integration of adaptation and mitigation in planning
- Coastal zones and vulnerability of ports and coastal infrastructure

Vulnerable regions, sectors, systems and hot spots
- Small islands developing states
- Least-developed countries
- Drylands, deserts, and desert like regions
- Mountain ecosystems
- Mediterranean region
- Boreal, Arctic, Antarctic, Greenland

Human security
- Food, water, shelter, health, and impacts of climate change
- Migration and immigration – legal, equity, and security issues
- Employment and impacts of climate change as well as opportunities in different regions

• Gender aspects, children, elderly, and climate change impacts, adaptation & mitigation
• Potential conflicts and climate change
• Regional disaggregation & differences
• Equity issues related to historical responsibility, differential impacts, and vulnerability
• MDGs, energy access, poverty, and climate change

Feedbacks related to C/N/P cycles
• Chemical and biological changes
• Carbon-fertilization
• Methane
• Oceans
• Forests and soils

Scenarios, storylines, second best scenarios
•Investigation of the links between storylines (population, society, development, economy, etc.) and costs (mitigation and adaptation with the associated non-climate effects, and damages)
• Upper limits for different temperature changes
• Feasibility of low levels of emissions and concentrations
• Inevitable climate change and inertia
• Implications of peaking time of GHG emissions
• Disaggregation of emissions pathways according to regions
• Interchangability of baskets of emissions
• Discount rates and their effect on viability of adaptation and mitigation measures
• Accelerated technological change
• Lifestyle changes, including dietary changes, habitat and consumption patterns

Mitigation
• Assessment according to needs, not just sectors (food, transport etc.), disaggregated for regions
• Detailed technology assessment
• Transition paths of low carbon society
• Geo-engineering, nuclear (fusion, fission) options
• R&D, technology transfer and institutional structures
• Distribution patterns of low carbon technology (past, current, future)
• Life cycle analysis of all options
• Assumptions for fossil fuel availability and production in the future
• Assessment of past and current practice, culture and development pathways
• Lifestyles, social acceptability of different options and public awareness
• Integration with adaptation and linkage with sustainable development

Adaptation
• Assessment of current and past practice
• Autonomous adaptation and implications
• Limits of adaptive capacity and systemic capability
• Adaptation to unavoidable climate change under different conditions
• Extreme events and disasters
• Link with mitigation and sustainable development

Economics and costs

- Non monetary and humanitarian impacts
- Definition of economic concepts and their applicability under different conditions
- Discount rates and implications for adaptation & mitigation
- Cost of inaction in humanitarian and monetized terms
- Cost-benefit analysis of adaptation and mitigation measures (including co-benefits, equity issues and implications for sustainable development)
- Cost-effectiveness of measures, evaluation of past practice and trends
- Use of market instruments for mitigation and adaptation
- Insurance and compensation

Education, communication, social science
- Analysis of barriers to disseminating knowledge
- Acceptability of change and attitudinal barriers and inertia
- Risk perception and psychology of risk

Synergies and tradeoffs with other Multilateral Environmental Agreement
- Biodiversity
- Desertification
- Forests
- Air pollution
- Ozone depletion

* * *

Emerging Topics:

Detection and attribution of regional climate change is the natural extension of the physical science basis that so far was limited to large-scale quantities such as global mean temperature change. Extension is made possible by a naturally increasing signal-to-noise ratio in observations associated with progressing climate change, as well as better resolved global climate models, and improved process understanding. Post-AR4 research has reported successful detection and attribution of changes in polar ice coverage, zonal mean precipitation, and others. One focus in the assessment performed by WGI would be the detection and attribution of changes on regional scales, as well as changes in climate modes (e.g., El Niño - Southern Oscillation (ENSO) or North Atlantic Oscillation (NAO)) and extreme events. * * *

Climate projections have been a cornerstone of all previous IPCC Assessment Reports and this will continue to be the case in the AR5. Recent advances in climate modelling could provide the basis to focus on both (i) short-term climate predictions (to 2030) using the most complex coupled climate models available, and (ii), long-term climate projections extending beyond 2100 using climate models of different complexities. * * *

Long-term climate projections, extending beyond 2100, need to be highlighted further, as the definition of dangerous climate change cannot solely be based on short-term changes but also needs to consider the slower timescales inherent in the climate system, as expressed in lagged sea-level rise, for example. * * * Topics that will require further attention are (i) the quantification of allowable emissions for stabilisation of atmospheric greenhouse gases and/or climate, including considerations of geo-engineering and other mitigation options, (ii) the quantification of long-term climate and ecosystem commitments as well as (iii) the concerns about potentially irreversible climate change on human timescales.

Sea level rise is caused by a number of processes with contributions from: (i) thermal expansion of the ocean, (ii) melting of glaciers and small ice caps, (iii) melting of Greenland and Antarctica, (iv) changes in circulation, and (v) changes in land storage. Both the size and the uncertainty of each of these contributions need to be quantified for a useful projection of sea level rise and its regional expression. Major uncertainties associated with the response of the two large ice sheets, Antarctica and Greenland, to the direct effects of warming and changes in accumulation (snow fall) as well as to the indirect effects (ocean warming, sea level rise feedback) have so far remained the primary source of uncertainty for comprehensive sea level projections. This is compounded by the possibility of ice stream and whole ice sheet instabilities that may be triggered by slow changes. In particular, renewed discussion of instabilities of the West Antarctic Ice Sheet and of thresholds for a Greenland ice sheet meltdown requires extensive assessment. * * *

Carbon cycle–climate feedbacks have already been identified in the IPCC AR4 as significant. At that time, only a few comprehensive climate models had explicitly taken an interactive carbon cycle into account. For the AR5, it is expected that a larger number of such comprehensive models will be available. However, the uncertainties associated with, for example, the response of soils and vegetation to increased warming and changes in the hydrological cycle, or changes in the physical and biogeochemical status of the ocean due to ocean acidification and climate change increase the uncertainties of climate projections for the next century. In addition, recent studies have highlighted the importance of combining carbon and other elemental cycles (such as nitrogen, iron, sulphur) interactively in order to capture the full dynamics of global biogeochemical cycles and their feedbacks on climate. In particular, joint assessment of the carbon and nitrogen cycles is expected to improve the mechanistic understanding of feedback processes and their strength. * * *

Regional climate change can now be addressed on the basis of high-resolution global climate models that provide a globally consistent basis for projections. * * * A particular focus in assessing regional climate change will be changes in the hydrological cycle, which could be addressed as a cross-cutting issue. One specific, related question is how the behaviour of monsoon circulations may change in future. A further important issue is the possibility of improving projections of possible changes in the frequency and intensity of climate extremes. * * *

Irreversibility of climate change has generated renewed interest as models indicate the very long residence time of climate changes in the Earth system. This is associated with the slow-responding components such as the ocean, the terrestrial ice sheets, and the fact that a fraction of the emitted atmospheric CO2 has an infinite lifetime in the atmosphere. Abrupt, irreversible climate change has been linked to the melting of permafrost, to changes in vegetation, and to changes in oceanic and atmospheric circulation. Most of the information regarding irreversible and abrupt climate change comes from recent paleoclimatic studies of marine, terrestrial and cryospheric proxy data. This can now be assessed in combination with model simulations and projections.

The IPCC AR4 derived the combined radiative forcing of all anthropogenic forcing agents, the drivers of climate change, including CO2, non-CO2 greenhouse gases, and aerosols. Despite this substantial progress, uncertainties remain. A particularly large uncertainty in radiative forcing is due to the response of clouds, the interaction of aerosols with clouds, and cloud-chemistry interactions. * * * This assessment will address the extent to which this influences climate sensitivity, the response of cloud cover, and the hydrological cycle * * * [and] the links between air pollution or air quality and climate as well as interactions between stratospheric ozone and climate. * * *

In the AR5, new knowledge and new demands from stakeholders will set the stage for increased emphasis on a number of key topics and cross-cuts. These include:

• Framing the assessment of impacts in the context of risk management, where risk integrates consequence and probability.
• Assessing impacts of climate change in the context of other stresses, including stresses related to development status, economic base, infrastructure, geopolitical setting, land use, and ecological resources.
• Expanding the coverage of adaptation to include more information on consequences, experiences with mainstreaming, and decision support for adaptation strategies.
• Integrating impacts, adaptation, and mitigation with common currencies and common frameworks.
• Broadening the range of assessed impacts, with increasing coverage of oceans, security, indirect impacts, interactive impacts, and impacts related to extremes and disasters.
• Exploring the interaction of climate change with development.
• Better integrating climate science with climate impacts, especially in areas where the impacts can provide strong feedbacks to the climate system, including land and ocean carbon cycles, exchanges of other greenhouse gases, and ice.
• Assessing new impact studies based on AR5 climate, including multi-

model comparisons and validation against observations.

· Improving the treatment of regional aspects of climate change, reducing redundancy with sectoral chapters and increasing integration of climate science, impacts, adaptation, and vulnerability. * * *

Managing the risks of climate change

The AR4 Synthesis Report concluded that responding to climate change involves an iterative risk management process that includes both mitigation and adaptation, taking into account actual and avoided climate change damages, co-benefits, sustainability, equity, and attitudes to risk. Decision-makers need an assessment of current practice at local, national, regional, and international scales to identify best practices, opportunities to increase climate resilience, and approaches to overcome barriers to implementation.

Effective support for good decisions depends on extracting information from the full range of possible outcomes, weighted by probability. Taking advantage of the information content across the entire probability distribution of possible outcomes presents great challenges, but the scientific community is increasingly capable of presenting this kind of information, and the stakeholder community is increasingly ready to act on it. All of the components of risk management need to be assessed and communicated, if stakeholders are to obtain the maximum possible value from this approach. * * *

Adaptation

* * * Further understanding is needed about opportunities to address the barriers and limits of adaptation, partly because effective adaptation measures are highly dependent on specific geographical and climate risk factors as well as institutional, political, and financial constraints.

Integrating impacts, adaptation and mitigation

The global experience with a changing climate is rapidly cementing the realization that response strategies will need to include both mitigation and adaptation, in a setting where not all impacts are avoided. In this kind of environment, it is important to create a uniform context for considering investments in and consequences of investments in both adaptation and mitigation. * * * It is increasingly clear, however, that this kind of analysis can be greatly enriched with more knowledge on the costs and benefits of adaptation, and on the costs of the impacts. * * * Part of the problem is that non-market resources are difficult to monetize. This does not mean, however, that they cannot be evaluated. One of the challenges for the AR5 will be building on the existing valuations in a way that allows for the emergence of common metrics and support for multi-sector analyses.

The impacts of climate change will vary regionally. Aggregate costs can hide disparate impacts. * * * Better understanding is needed of not only the aggregate costs, but also regional and sectoral specification of costs and how they might vary across temporal scales. There also is interest in better understanding how to incorporate non-market impacts when calculating the costs of climate change.

Reducing current and projected impacts of climate change requires effective climate policy that involves a portfolio of adaptation and mitigation actions, with the decisions taken at different governance levels. Better understanding is needed of how creating synergies between adaptation and mitigation can increase the cost-effectiveness of actions. * * *

Broadening the range of assessed impacts

* * * For the AR5, the scientific literature on a range of impacts, not covered in detail in the AR4, should be ripe for a careful assessment. One area is impacts of extreme events and weather-related disasters. * * * Another area with abundant new science is the oceans. New science on acidification, thermal tolerance of fish and other ocean organisms, food webs, and nutrients is advancing rapidly, and the opportunity for assessment is solid. A third area with rapidly developing science involves climate and security. Climate-security issues range from disputes over resources to population migration to rapid distribution of emerging disease. * * *

Understanding the interactions between climate change and development

The AR4 concluded that climate change will affect the ability of many nations to achieve sustainable development pathways. Enhancing society's response capacity through the pursuit of sustainable development is therefore one way of promoting both adaptation and mitigation.

Understanding of how development planners incorporate information about climate variability and change into their decisions is limited, thus limiting the integrated assessment of vulnerability. Adapting to climate change and promoting sustainable development share common goals and determinants including access to resources (including information and technology), equity in the distribution of resources, stocks of human and social capital, access to risk sharing mechanisms, and abilities of decision-support mechanisms to cope with uncertainty. Despite this, some development activities exacerbate climate-related vulnerabilities. * * *

Integrating climate science and climate impacts

The distinction between impacts of climate change and drivers of future climate change is frequently blurry. An increase in wildfires might be attributed to climate change, but an important consequence of the increase could be the release of CO2 and other GHGs to the atmosphere, amplifying the global warming. Similarly, the disappearance of sea ice has important consequences both for shipping and for reflecting shortwave radiation from the surface. * * *

Regional aspects of climate change

Regional aspects are fundamental to a useful assessment of climate science, impacts, adaptation, and vulnerability. Regions vary in important determinants of vulnerability, and they often (but not always) share constraints and opportunities from climate similarities, socioeconomic status, infrastructure, etc. In addition, regions may choose to develop coordinated policies. * * *

Stabilization Targets and Costs: The costs of mitigation targets and related adaptation needs have to be assessed in an integrated manner despite the fact that mitigation and adaptation options are uncertain. We do not know when and where particular impacts, technologies or institutions will occur–especially local impacts–and which technologies or institutions will develop. These uncertainties have a crucial effect on the design of mitigation and adaptation strategies. The portfolio of mitigation options has to be tailored to sectors and regions. An assessment of sector-specific costs is crucial for a better understanding of the barriers of implementation. In addition, the transformation towards a low-emission economy is to be specific for different regional aspects taking into account international trade and development patterns.

Sectors, Infrastructure and Land-use: The creation of an appropriate infrastructure is at the heart of sustainable development as most infrastructures are not exclusively dedicated to mitigation of or adaptation to climate change. Instead, they are built to serve human needs such as housing, energy, water, transport, communication etc.

Equity, Fairness, Sustainable Development and Life Style Changes: Problems of collective action, or public good problems that may overlap with various parallel challenges, can only be solved if the solution is considered to be fair and based on adequate equity principles. In general, the equity principle has to be applied to inter- and intra-generational justice as a prerequisite for sustainable development as well as lifestyle changes.

International Cooperation and Global Finance: The management of mitigation and adaptation options has to deal with a multitude of collective action problems. The climate challenge consists of many of these problems. Up to now, climate economics and policy analyses have had a strong emphasis on policy design. However, institutional aspects and capital market issues deserve equal attendance. * * *

2.3 Equity, Fairness, Regional Sustainable Development and Life Style Changes

Both inter- and intra-generational justice have strong links to sustainable development. * * * The debate on time preferences and on investments in mitigation and adaptation can only be understood in the context of intergenerational justice. However, assessing the distribution of mitigation costs and impacts for the poor requires a careful discussion of intragenerational justice. This requires a stronger participation of developing country economists and development economists, who have hardly participated * * * to date. * * *

Significant emission reductions will also require changes in lifestyle. This may include a change in valuation of the kind and level of consumption considered necessary for wellbeing (e.g. car size). The ability to make changes in lifestyle also interacts with infrastructure policies. The ability to use public transport instead of cars, for instance, depends on the very existence of the related infrastructure.

2.4 International Cooperation and Global Finance
2.4.1 Collective Action Problems
The cost estimates of the IPCC depend on the crucial assumption of an existing global carbon market or a global carbon tax. Both assumptions define a benchmark for a first-best optimum but are politically unrealistic. There is broad agreement that a sound climate policy can avoid dangerous climate change without prohibitive economic costs; that is, *if* it can resolve the public good problem. However, with good reason it is often emphasised that the climate problem is the greatest public good problem of humankind, the correction of which will cause considerable institutional costs. It is increasingly doubted that an international agreement to reduce worldwide emissions can be reached in a timely fashion.

The international discussion of global climate-policy options has furthermore revealed that the climate problem does not consist of a single public good problem but of a multitude of collective action problems: An extensive use of biomass would for instance require additional international agreements, e.g. on forest protection or food supply, and an extensive use of nuclear energy based on fast breeder reactors would demand international agreements on proliferation control. Cap and trade systems could be complemented by international technology cooperation, which has additional cobenefits for other sectors. Additional adaptation measures of developing countries also call for collective action that cannot be performed by the markets alone and that is closely related to the topic of development. These overlapping public good problems make the management of climate change more complex to analyse, but also give rise to enhanced enforceability of effective climate change policies through linking issues. As recent studies have shown, issue linking might increase the probability that free rider behaviour can be limited to an acceptable extent. An assessment of how these links have to be designed to manage the climate public good problem should be on top of the research agenda.

Competitiveness, Energy Security, Growth and Climate Policy

Politicians and other stakeholders are confronted with competitiveness effects of emission-intensive industries, the security of energy supply, and the economic consequences of climate policy for growth and employment. * * * However, a methodologically convincing analysis of the impacts of mitigation strategies for different sectors (transport, electricity, industry, heat market, housing, agriculture, health) within the different temporal timeframes still needs to be accomplished. The effect on employment and the sectoral winners and losers is decisive for the success of any climate policy. Moreover, energy security has become a prime concern of foreign policy and geopolitical strategies in China, the USA and Europe. Many decision makers see energy security as a more important challenge than climate change. A realistic assessment is needed to explore the trade-offs, but also the potential synergies and side-benefits. * * *

Technological Change and Technology Transfer

Inducing innovation is a long-term challenge. Unfortunately, the literature is quite inconclusive regarding what kind of policy instruments should be applied in the area of climate and energy policy. This discussion must go beyond comparing taxes and quantities. It seems much more promising to think about hybrid solutions, combining taxes, quantity instruments, subsidies and standards in an innovative way. * * * However, the theoretical basis for this application has to be strengthened.

Technology transfer remains a challenge. The Clean Development Mechanisms (CDM) is regarded as an important vehicle, but so far it has not performed satisfactorily and a general revision of this instrument is under discussion. In recent years most of the multilateral development finance institutions (World Bank Group, Regional Development Banks) have introduced some financing and technical assistance facilities for renewable energy, energy efficiency, and carbon trade. These instruments need to be evaluated and enhanced. Intellectual property rights (IP) as private rights promote innovation and the dissemination of knowledge on the one hand, but make access to knowledge more difficult or costly on the other hand. In any policy context, including climate change, a balance between the protection if IP rights and the promotion of public objectives, such as the transfer of technology, is necessary. Therefore, AR5 needs an assessment on how to improve technology cooperation and technology transfer between Annex I and Non Annex I countries.

2.4.2 Climate Policy Instruments, Global Finance, and Risk Management

For policymakers, the short-term distribution of costs is much more important than the long-term reduction of average mitigation costs. Therefore, policymakers would like to be informed about the short-term implications of long-term policies. In addition, the private sector is interested in the long-term implications of short-term policy instruments. Long-term investments in new technologies will only be feasible for the private sector if it can rely on credible long-term targets. As is well known from macro-economic policy, a sequence of short-term policy targets can be time-inconsistent in the sense that policymakers may have an incentive to change their targets over time, which will prevent firms from making the necessary innovations for successful and efficient transformation of the energy system. It is an unresolved question of what kind of policy instruments are needed to encourage long-term and risky investments like in CCS or renewable energies.

Sources of Finance and Capital Market

Large parts of the additional investments will have to take place in non-OECD countries. Developing countries, however, will not be able to bear all the financial needs. New sources of finance need to be explored. One possibility would be to auction part of the international emission permits. * * *

Climate change effects directly impact several branches of the insurance sector; some are in danger of facing extraordinary losses. A trend towards more risk-averse policies already exists, e.g. insurance is limited or unavailable in areas where large floods have occurred in recent decades, affecting industry, households, and governments. Higher risk premiums increase expenses for local economies. In developing countries the use of insurance is far lower than in developed regions due to a lack of financial assets. Thus, developing this sector in those regions can provide a suitable adaptation strategy. * * *

In order to trigger such a behavioural shift in the private sectors, which are to bear large fractions of the transition, effective political incentives will be inevitable, leading to the issue of investment climate and risks from regulation. * * *

Carbon Pricing

Carbon pricing will be among the most important measures to mainstream emission mitigation in the rest of the economy. Therefore, instruments that attach a price to carbon will be of particular relevance. * * *

2.4.3 Key Elements of an International Regime

By the time of the WG III's contribution to AR5, the agreements coming out of Copenhagen will have been negotiated and will need to be assessed. * * * This becomes particularly apparent in the design of an adequate international climate policy and sound energy security approach. As a consequence, the *architecture* of a future *climate regime* needs to integrate the following components:

• Equity, poverty reduction, and sustainable development considerations;
• Pricing of GHG emissions through emissions trade and possible links to energy security and competitiveness require a careful analysis;
• Implementation of a technology policy including provisions to pool innovations and to encourage first-movers;
• Fair distribution of emission rights among the participating countries as well as compensation of climate damages by the polluter;
• Provision of an infrastructure to finance investments in climate protection, mostly for developing countries;
• Establishment of political instruments in mega cities and developing young cities, for instance congestion charges or incentives for low-emission housing;
• Control of global land use, especially implementation of incentives to avoid tropical deforestation taking into account possible links to biodiversity and food security;
• Assessment of geo-engineering as a public good: Some scientists argue that geo-engineering options which directly control the radiation budget of the earth could be agreed upon by a smaller number of countries and would thus involve considerably lower institutional costs than an agreement on a world-wide reduction of CO2 emissions;
• Adaptation fund: The design of an adaptation fund will be crucial for the involvement of developing countries. International regime architecture needs to take into account the uncertainties of the climate and economic systems when structuring its policy instruments. These instruments should serve to catalyze climate protection paths that are robust against uncertainties of the climate system (e.g. climate sensitivity) as well as the socio-technical system (e.g. technical progress in renewable energy sources). * * *

Depending on their structure, climate-policy agreements could have considerable geopolitical implications that require thorough analyses. If such analyses are not carried out, an international agreement for climate protection will not be implemented because it might not be in accordance with the interests of nations pursuing economic growth and energy security. The increasing utilisation of brown and hard coal in the USA and China is attributable to the desire to reduce dependence on oil and gas imports. The question on how an ambitious climate policy will change international labour division by shifting the importance from oil and gas producers to those of coal (China, India), biomass (Russia) and solar energy (North Africa, South America) has not yet been closely examined.

Furthermore, the emergence of numerous climate change initiatives by non-nation state actors in cities and regions (as well as other stakeholders at civil and/or corporate levels) seeking to reduce emissions of greenhouse gasses may have significant implications for climate change governance. * * * A thorough understanding of these initiatives would establish a local basis for assigning responsibilities, coordinating efforts, and promoting equity, accountability, and qualitative participation in the global management of climate change.

Notes and Questions

1. The AR5 Scoping Vision Paper identifies a broad scope of scientific, social, policy, legal, and economic uncertainties that the IPCC needs to address. How might these uncertainties affect the development of national and international responses to climate change.

2. The Scoping Vision Paper states that "climate problem is the greatest public good problem of humankind, the correction of which will cause considerable institutional costs." Is that so? What might be some of the "institutional costs"?

3. Should lawyers be part of the IPCC AR5 process? Which of the issues would benefit from being analyzed from a legal, regulatory or law-making perspective? What value added can thoughtful, well-trained lawyers add? Or, is the world facing a zero-sum game where lawyers, if acting as effective advocates, will obstruct possibilities of achieving collective action? What about the role of lawyers as effective counselors? What about lawyers as effective negotiators in a setting where a stable long-run global partnership must be established? What about the role of lawyers in helping to craft, implement and enforce an effective, workable climate change legal regime—internationally, nationally, and locally?

4. The IPCC in AR5 will be developing alternative scenarios for what might happen to the climate depending on how much nations are able to mitigate and adapt to climate change. What might these look like? Consider the four scenarios prepared for the Millennium Ecosystem Assessment in 2005. Ecosystems and Our Human Planet: Summary for Decision-makers, Millennium Ecosystem Assessment (2005) 41-51. This was a review by panels of scientists world-wide, akin to the IPCC process, to assess the impacts of the loss of biodiversity. Since sequestering carbon dioxide is a key component of adaptation, along with sustaining ecosystem services upon which humans depend, these scenarios are important in identifying possible future conditions, so that governments can learn adaptively to cope with a range of alternative situations that can arise in the future. Are these four scenarios credible surrogates for climate change as well as biodiversity?

PROBLEM EXERCISE ON CLIMATE SCIENCE

Scientific analysis of climate change involves using computer models, and there is a fair amount of debate about the models and their assumptions, and the data they rely upon (inputs) and the projections they yield (outputs). Does this debate obscure issues that already exist with respect to equity among rich and poor communities, or sustainable development objectives? Can studies, such as AR5 of the IPCC, indicate what measures can be taken now, such as acting upon the recommendations in Agenda 21 (1992), to accomplish sustainable development objectives, already accepted internationally, that coincidently mitigate or adopt the effects of climate change? What specific topics would lawyers identify for the scientists working on AR5?

CHAPTER 3. INTERNATIONAL CLIMATE CHANGE LAW

Climatescape: Forging Elements for an Earth Law?

Nations have been negotiating international laws to address environmental for decades. Since 1972, The UN Environment Programme, and other international organizations, have agreed on many "multilateral environmental agreements" (MEAs). Understanding how international law functions is key to building further climate change law. Some MEAs, such as the Montreal Protocol for protection of Earth's stratospheric ozone layer, have built effective world-wide governance systems that also effectively mitigate potent greenhouse gas emissions. The same cannot yet be said of the MEAs for sustaining biological diversity or the marine environment, both of which are crucial in their interactions with the climate. Ocean law is covered in the context of Adaptation in Chapter 6. Little effective treaty law exists for forest stewardship, a topic which is also discussed with respect to biologic sequestration in Chapter 6 on Adaptation. The international regime for the Polar Regions make scant provision for the impacts on and from climate change. As small island states and low lying coastal regions contemplate inundation and forced migrations, what scope is there for human rights, or humanitarian laws on disaster relief? Only since 2002 have nations agreed to negotiate international cooperation for sustainable energy law. Can the UN Framework Convention on Climate Change, through negotiations such as those in Copenhagen in December 2009, implement that Bali Action Plan by agreeing on the many new protocols and programs that will be needed to cope with all the aspects of climate change? Experience with the economic tools designed under the Kyoto Protocol raises questions of effectiveness and equity that a wider use of such techniques will require. The pattern of MEA negotiation requires gradual and re-iterative sets of agreements and implementation measures. How can a climate regime be agreed upon in the time frames suggest by the scientists in Chapter 2, to avert more significant anthropogenic disruption of the Earth's climate?

A. MULTILATERAL ENVIRONMENTAL DIPLOMACY

The Bali Action Plan covered in Chapter 1 is the blueprint guiding the international decision-making on climate change. This chapter on international law provides the background and related context for the Bali Action Plan, and explores its ramifications for related bodies of law as nations negotiate and agree upon the international law of climate change.

Earth's climate, and Earth's carbon and hydrologic cycles, exist quite apart from the rules of international law agreed upon by sovereign states.

International Law assumed that Earth's natural environment was a given; as the Intergovernmental Panel on Climate Change has explained, the time has come for international law to reflect what scientists have discovered about the Earth's environment and its climate.

Nations first formally recognized that environmental problems transcended their territorial limits of power at the United Nations Stockholm Conference on the Human Environment in 1972. At that time they agreed to establish the United Nations Environment Programme (UNEP), with a narrow mandate: to study and report on trends in environmental degradation and to assist developing nations in building their capacity to cope with environmental challenges.

At Stockholm the nations agreed upon "Principle 21" of the Stockholm Declaration on the Human Environment, which codified a general principle of international law, that "States have * * * the sovereign right to exploit their own resources pursuance to their own environmental policies, and the responsibility to ensure that the activities within their jurisdiction or control do not Cause damage to the environment of other States or of areas beyond the limits of national jurisdiction." At Stockholm, nations acknowledged their international duty to protect the Earth's shared environment and their transnational duty not to harm the environment of other nations.

Since 1972, Multilateral Environmental Agreements (MEAs) have become the means by which nations reconciled their right to exploit nature within their jurisdiction while protecting areas outside their jurisdiction. MEAs are a type of treaty, by which states align their national laws to achieve agreed upon international goals. International agencies have facilitated the negotiation and implementation of these agreements:

(a) The UN Educational, Scientific and Cultural Organization (UNESCO) sponsored the Convention on the Protection of the World Cultural and Natural Heritage.

(b) The UN Economic Commission for Europe (UNECE), which includes Canada, the USA and the States of the former USSR as well as Europe, has facilitated negotiation of the Geneva Convention on Long-Range Transboundary Air Pollution (1979), the Espoo Convention on Environmental Impact Assessment in a Transboundary Context (1997) with its Protocol on Strategic Environmental Assessment (2003), and the Aarhus Agreement on Access to Information, Public Participation in Decision-making and Access to Justice in Environmental Matters (1998).

(c) The International Union for the Conservation of Nature and Natural Resources (IUCN), organized in 1948, spear-headed the 1973 Convention on the International Trade in Endangered Species, the Ramsar Convention on

Wetlands of International Importance, the Bonn Convention on the Conservation of Migratory Species of Wild Animals, the African Convention on Conservation of Nature and Natural Resources, and the articulation of environmental rules for the UN Convention on the Law of the Sea (1985), and together with UNEP, the Convention on Biological Diversity (1992). See N. Robinson, IUCN As Catalyst for a Law of the Biosphere: Acting Globally and Locally, 35 Envtl. L. 249 (2005).

(d) The UN Environment Programme (UNEP) has played a major role as a catalyst in developing MEAs. Among the many MEAs it advanced, UNEP facilitated the Vienna Convention on the Protection of the Stratospheric Ozone Layer (1985) and subsequent Montreal Protocol (1987), the Basel Convention on Control of Transboundary Movements of Hazardous Wastes and their Disposal, the Rotterdam Convention on Prior Informed Consent (1998), the Convention to Combat Desertification (1994), and the UN Framework Convention on Climate Change (1992).

While each MEA is a discrete treaty with its own governing organs and secretariat, and each addresses a separate aspect of national impacts on the global or transnational environment, taken as a whole the MEAs constitute the framework of international law that governs the Earth's natural systems. Earth's climate is affected, to greater or lesser degrees, by actions taken under each of these MEAs. However, there is as yet little effective coordination among the MEAs. Each has a separate secretariat. UNEP has been criticized for not building robust cooperation among the MEA secretariats (some of which are provided by UNEP). There are many possible synergies that could be realized among the MEAs as they are implemented. At the same time, although nation states adhere to many MEAs, individual nations do not coordinate their policies across their many national agencies that are assigned to handle the implementation of each MEA. In the USA, for instance, the President's Council on Environmental Quality has not used most of its regulatory authority provided to it since 1970 pursuant to the National Environmental Policy Act (NEPA), Section 102(2)(A), (B), (E), (F), and (H). Like the USA, most nations fail to coordinate their implementation systems under the many MEAs, even when managing the same natural environmental systems. N. Robinson, NEPA at 40: International Dimensions, 39 ELR 10674 (2009).

The international law of the climate, then, is more than just the obligations agreed to in 1992 at the Rio de Janeiro Conference on Environment and Development, when States signed the United Nations Framework Convention on Climate Change (UNFCCC). See D. Bodansky, The United Nations Framework Convention on Climate Change: A Commentary, 8 Yale J. Int'l L. 451 (1993). The UNFCCC Secretariat (http://unfccc.int/), located in Bonn, Germany, like the secretariats of other MEAs, is thinly staffed and has little capacity to coordinate with the secretariats of other MEAs. The Conferences of the Parties (COP) of each MEA similarly are not structured to interact with each other, although the COP for the Convention on Biological Diversity did hold a meeting in Bonn to facilitate cooperation on matters of mutual interest, such as deforestation.

The system of global environmental governance that emerged after the agreements at Stockholm in 1972 reached its widest scope with the adoption of Agenda 21, the action plan agreed to at the UN Conference on Environment and Development in Rio de Janeiro. A/CONF.151/26 (1992), www.un.org/esa/sustdev/documents/agenda21/index.htm; see the *traveaux préparatoires* for Agenda 21 in N. Robinson, et al., eds, Agenda 21 and the UNCED Proceedings (1993). Agenda 21 includes Chapter 9 on "Protection of the Atmosphere," and sought to integrate human activities affecting the environment by embracing the concept of "sustainable development." First broached by IUCN in its program "Caring for the Earth," see M. Holdgate, The Green Web–A Union for the Conservation of Nature (1999), this idea was popularized by the UN World Commission on Environment and Development in its report Our Common Future (1987): "Development that meets the needs and aspirations of the present without compromising the ability to meet those of the future."

Understanding and applying the international law of the atmosphere, or climate, requires an understanding of the rules of international law, as stated under the UN Vienna Convention on the Law of Treaties (1969). See the UN Treaty   Handbook, http://untreaty.un.org/English/TreatyHandbook/hbframeset.htm. The environmental norms must also be evaluated in terms of the general principles of international law (such as Stockholm Principle 21). See P. Sands, Principles of International Environmental Law (2d ed. 2003). The obligations in each MEA are also construed in light of the subsidiary decisions adopted by the Conference of the Parties to each MEA about how nations agree to implement the MEA.

As you read the selections in this chapter, ask yourself how can the UNFCCC be effective if it is seen primarily as a self-contained treaty system? How might the climate regime be understood and implemented within the broader framework of MEAs? What do the scientific reports on the Earth's environment, such as those of the IPCC, suggest about how nations should guide the UNFCCC regime and the MEAs more widely? How might the negotiations under the Bali Action Plan bring about a better integration of the MEAs to help with climate change mitigation and adaptation?

* * * * *

One way to evaluate the type of international cooperation, or governance, needed to cope with climate change and other environmental problems, is to imagine an ideal world order. We can then more clearly see the gap between what is and what it needs to be, and we can address the step-by-step measures to move toward global environmental stewardship.

Nations reinvented the norms for world order in the 1940s with the establishment of the United Nations in New York and the financial institutions conceived at Bretton Woods, New Hampshire. They neglected the environmental aspects of world order. In 2009, nations again face the need to invent international law to cope with climate change and environmental degradation.

The ten escalating environmental degradation trends outlined by Speth and Haas in Chapter 1 are both causes and consequences of climate change. Nations have acknowledged that measures must be taken to reverse these trends. In Agenda 21, the 1992 UN Conference on Environment and Development produced an action plan to do so, which opens with this acknowledgement: "Humanity stands at a defining moment in its history." (Para. 1.1). Thereafter, in 2000, the UN General Assembly adopted the Millennium Development Goals, in order to address the basic needs of the 2 billion poorest people on the Earth and raise their standard of living. Nations launched a UN program to attain concrete objectives by 2015. In 2002, the UN World Summit on Sustainable Development adopted the Johannesburg Plan of Implementation, including the first globally agreed policies for energy reforms. www.johannesburgsummit.org. Albeit slowly, nations have agreed to realign their development programs to fulfill these obligations, which in turn drives demand for natural resources and public funds. In 2007, the world economy began its deepest recession in 80 years, and the inadequacy of the world's financial institutions became evident. The "Bretton Woods" institutions were created before 1945, when the number of sovereign states and the size of the world's population and economy were vastly smaller than today.

In 2009, reform of the world's economic order became the subject of negotiations in The Group of 20, or G-20 nations (Argentina, Australia, Brazil, Canada, China, France, Germany, India, Indonesia, Italy, Japan, South Korea, Mexico, Russia, Saudi Arabia, South Africa, Turkey, United Kingdom, and the USA, plus the European Union). Parallel in time are the negotiations under the UN Framework Convention on Climate Change (UNFCCC) to negotiate new climate regime under the Bali Action Plan. How should nations integrate these two tracks of negotiations? Are not the economy of nature and the economy of commerce in truth one? As Italy's Finance Minister, Tomas Padoa-Schioppa, told the International Monetary Fund, "We know how the world economy can function, how things go, with 7 billion humans and with 15% of them with high living standards, but we don't know how it will function when that 15% rises towards 50%." C. Giles and K. Guha, Subprime 'Just One of Many Problems' Padoa-Schioppa Warns IMF Meeting—Global Growth is Unsustainable, Financial Times, p. 2, col., 1 (April 14, 2008).

What elements would you include in an ideal environmental stewardship regime for the Earth? Speth and Haas were prescient in preparing the following hypothetical exercise contained in Global Environmental Governance (2006):

> *What legal and policies initiatives and reforms will be required to transition from the norms and regimes of today's world to realize the ideal elements you have outlined? What concrete steps must be fashioned to get there?*

STEWARDSHIP ASSIGNMENTS: A THOUGHT EXPERIMENT
J.G. Speth and P.M. Haas
Global Environmental Governance (2006)

Let us begin with a very global perspective. Can you imagine Earth without people, not today's Earth but an Earth that evolved to the present without us? If you can contemplate such a world with satisfaction rather than sadness—a world with forests of majestic old-growth trees, with oceans brimming over with fish, with clear skies literally darkened by passing flocks of birds, thriving with an awe-inspiring diversity of life and landscape but without people—then you not only have a vivid environmental imagination but, more to the point, you are ready for your first assignment as an environmental steward.

Imagine further that you live on a different planet that also circles Earth's sun. Though your world has become depleted and polluted, you and your people have decided to leave Earth alone—to protect it and all its beauty and let it evolve in its own uninterrupted way. It is enough to know that it is there in all its richness, protected for all time, wild whole, and beautiful.

Your assignment of protecting the pristine Earth is almost entirely far-fetched, but not completely. Consider that on Sunday, September 21, 2003, the space probe *Galileo,* having provided scientists extraordinary amounts of new information about Jupiter's moons, where life might already exist waiting to be discovered, a decision had been made to leave Jupiter's moons intact and unpolluted. And in the United States today an area the size of California has been set aside as "forever wild" in a magnificent system of national wilderness areas.

But now imagine that another decision has been made. Your world has just learned that it is going to be demolished to make room for an intergalactic hyper-spatial express route. When your people complained to the Hyperspace Planning Council about this planned destruction, you were told that the proposed expressway plan had been duly posted in the local planning department in Alpha Centauri and that the time for public comment had long since expired! (With apologies to *The Hitchhikers Guide to the Galaxy.*)

As a result of these unfortunate developments, your people—all 6.5 billion of you—have now decided to colonize the pristine Earth. Our new assignment as environmental steward is to settle Earth in a way that allows all of you to enjoy a decent standard of living while having the smallest possible impact on Earth's environment.

In contemplating this difficult assignment, two things occur to you right away. First, if you are going to sustain Earth's environment, you had better understand how Earth works: how Earth's abundant species interact among themselves and with the landscape; how Earth's great natural cycles of water, oxygen, carbon, nitrogen, and others work together to sustain life; where the areas of greatest species richness and diversity and also the zones of greatest fragility are located. If you hope to disturb Earth minimally, then you have first to understand it. So there is first and foremost a huge science project to be undertaken—the science of environmental sustainability.

Second, you see right away that all the nation-states fleeing your planet together must agree at the outset on a set of principles to guide your settlement of Earth, to do so in such a way that the planet will provide a lasting home for you and your people. You're not going to want to undertake such a task more than once! Where do you begin?

One recent effort on the part of international lawyers to elaborate sustainable development principles for nation-states to consider was the New Delhi Declaration of Principles of International Law Relating to Sustainable Development, developed in 2002 by the International Law Association. It provides the following:

- "States are under a duty to manage natural resources, including natural resources within their own territory or jurisdiction, in a rational, sustainable and safe way so as to contribute to the development of their peoples ... and to the conservation and sustainable use of natural resources and the protection of the environment, including ecosystems. States must take into account the needs of future generations in determining the rate of use of natural resources. All relevant actors (including States, industrial concerns and other components of civil society) are under a duty to avoid wasteful use of natural resources and promote waste minimization policies."

- "The protection, preservation and enhancement of the natural environment, particularly the proper management of the climate system, biological diversity and fauna and flora of the Earth, are the common concern of humankind. The resources of outer space and celestial bodies and of the sea-bed, ocean floor and subsoil thereof beyond the limits of national jurisdiction are the common heritage of humankind."

• But are these proposed principles of international law sufficiently ambitious and unambiguous to guide the contemplated settlement of Earth? Perhaps, but you may want to consider more demanding requirements. And in any event, such broad principles must be supplemented with specific policies and programs that address such fundamental issues as the growth of human populations, the choice of technologies to be used on Earth, the pattern of human settlements to be allowed, the permitted means of transportation and communication, and so on. Moreover, to deal with the problem of the sovereign nations of your planet cooperating in the settlement of Earth, you may wish to consider far-reaching provisions such as these:

• "The Earth shall be used by all States Parties exclusively for peaceful purposes."

• "In exploring and using the Earth, States Parties shall take measures to prevent the disruption of the existing balance of its environment whether by introducing adverse changes in that environment, by its harmful contamination through the introduction of extra-environmental matter or otherwise."

• The Earth and its natural resource are the common heritage of mankind ..."

• "The Earth is not subject to national appropriation by any claim of sovereignty, by means of use or occupation, or by any other means."

• "Neither the surface nor the subsurface of the Earth, nor any part thereof of natural resources in place, shall become property of any State, international intergovernmental or non-governmental entity or of any natural person."

These are in fact actual provisions of the Moon Treaty, the 1979 Agreement Governing the Activities of States on the Moon and Other Celestial Bodies, with *Earth* substituted for moon in the text. As of 2005, only 13 countries had ratified the 1979 Moon Treaty. No country with a significant space program, including the United States, had ratified it.

In the end there is the question whether it will be possible for 6.5 billion of you to settle Earth and build a world economy that can provide everyone a prosperous standard of living, all the while protecting the treasured natural beauty and bounty of the planet. Whatever the odds of achieving this truly sustainable development on Earth, they are improved if the people and nations undertaking the colonization are at peace not at war, if they are democracies not dictatorships, if their people are well-informed about science and policy choices, if they share deeply the values of social justice and environmental protection and care about the future as well as themselves, if they have a tradition of working together cooperatively to forge common goals and solve mutual problems, and if they enjoy a level of economic development that enables them to spend resources on environmental protection. Do the nations of your world meet these tests? If they cannot agree on fundamental goals and how to realize them, and cooperate successfully among themselves, then their experiment in global governance on the new planet will likely fail.

B. THE FUNDAMENTALS OF INTERNATIONAL LAW

The international law for climate change is grounded in the well settled framework of public international law. The UN Environment Programme (UNEP) has restated the accepted law of MEAs, and summarized the basic norms of international environmental law, in its Training Manual on International Environmental law. Excerpted here is a restatement of the basic provisions of public international law which govern the operations of the UN Framework Convention on Climate Change and the related MEAs.

As you read the following materials, consider how a lawyer or civil servant from a developing nation would regard these norms of international law. How much of a universal foundation do they provide upon which to ground the emerging law of the climate?

MULTILATERAL ENVIRONMENTAL AGREEMENTS
Lal Kurukulasuriya and Nicholas A. Robinson
UNEP Training Manual on International Environmental Law (2006)

I. Introduction

* * * In order to understand international environmental law, it is necessary to have a basic grasp of general international law. International environmental law is a subset of international law; and international law has been developing over a long period of time. Since a significant part of international environmental law is incorporated in Multilateral Environmental Agreements ("MEAs"), an introduction to treaty law is essential for understanding the contents of this Manual. In addition to exploring the basic principles relating to treaty law, this chapter will also discuss certain aspects of the negotiation of MEAs.

II. Sources of International Law

The principal judicial organ of the United Nations ("UN") is the International Court of Justice ("ICJ"). The jurisdiction of the ICJ, specified in article

36 (1) of its Statute, "comprises all cases which the parties refer to it and all matters specially provided for in the Charter of the United Nations or in treaties and conventions in force..." The United Nations' Charter further stipulates that all members of the United Nations are *ipso facto* parties to the ICJ Statute (article 93). Besides decisions, the ICJ is authorized to render advisory opinions on any legal question, when requested by the General Assembly or the Security Council. Other organs of the United Nations and specialized agencies may also request advisory opinions of the ICJ on legal questions arising within the scope of their activities, when authorized by the United Nations General Assembly ("UNGA") (article 96). The ICJ, by the very nature of its functions, plays an important role in the development of international law. Accordingly, the sources of law relied upon by the ICJ are pertinent when examining the sources of international law and, consequently, international environmental law.

Article 38 (1) of this Statute lists the four sources that the ICJ may rely upon to determine the law applicable to a case brought to its attention. The sources listed in article 38(1) are regarded as the authoritative sources of international law, and thus also of international environmental law.

**Statute of the International Court of Justice
(Article 38)**

"1. The Court, whose function is to decide in accordance with international law such disputes as are submitted to it, shall apply:
a. International conventions, whether general or particular, establishing rules expressly recognized by the contesting states;
b. International custom, as evidence of a general practice accepted as law;
c. The general principles of law recognized by civilized nations;
d. Subject to the provisions of Article 59, judicial decisions and the teachings of the most highly qualified publicists of the various nations, as subsidiary means for the determination of rules of law."

Article 38 establishes a practical hierarchy of sources of international law in settling of disputes. First, relevant treaty provisions applicable between the parties to the dispute must be employed. In the event that there are no applicable treaty provisions, rules of "customary international law" should be applied. If neither a treaty provision nor a customary rule of international law can be identified, then reliance should be place on the general principles of law recognized by civilized nations. Finally, judicial decisions and writings of highly qualified jurists may be utilized as a subsidiary means of determining the dispute. It is important to remember that in many cases, due to the absence of any unambiguous rules, the ICJ has had to rely on multiple sources.

Article 38(1)(a), (b) and (c) are the main sources of international law and international environmental law. However, given the uncertainties that prevail, article 38(1)(d) also becomes a significant source in this area of law.

1. Law of Treaties

Today, treaties are the major mechanism employed by states in the conduct of their relations with each other. They provide the framework for modern international relations and the main source of international law. The starting point for determining what constitutes a treaty is to be found in a treaty itself, the Vienna Convention on the Law of Treaties, a treaty on treaty law. It was concluded in 1969 and entered into force in 1980 ("1969 Vienna Convention"). Whilst the United Nations has 191 Member States, the 1969 Vienna convention has only 105 parties (as of September 2005). A treaty is binding only among its parties. Although the 1969 Vienna convention is not a treaty with global participation, it is widely acknowledged that many of its provisions have codified existing customary international law. Other provisions may have acquired customary international law status. Since customary international law and treaty law have the same status at international law, many provisions of the 1969 Vienna Convention are considered to be binding on all states. * * *

Article 2(1)(a) of the 1969 Vienna Convention defines a treaty as "international agreement concluded between states in written form and governed by international law, whether embodied in a single instrument or in two or more related instruments and whatever its particular designation." Accordingly, the designation employed in a document does not determine whether it is a treaty. Regardless of the designation, an international agreement falling under the above definition is considered to be a treaty. The term "treaty" is the generic name. The term "treaty" encompasses, among others, the terms convention, agreement, pact, protocol, charter, statute, convenant, engagement, accord, exchange of notes, *modus Vivendi,* and Memorandum of Understanding. As long as an instrument falls under the above definition, it would be considered to be a treaty and, therefore, binding under international law. International organizations are also recognized as capable of concluding treaties, depending on their constituent instruments. * * *

The term "protocol" is used for agreements less formal than those entitled "treaty" or "convention", but they also possess the same legal force. A protocol signifies an instrument that creates legally binding obligations at international law. In most cases this term encompasses an instrument which is subsidiary to a treaty. The term is used to cover, among others, the following instruments:

- An optional protocol to a treaty is an instrument that establishes additional rights and obligations with regard to a treaty. Parties to the main treaty are not obliged to become party to an optional protocol. An optional protocol is sometimes adopted on the same day as the main treaty, but is of independent signature and ratification. Such protocols enable certain parties of the treaty to establish among themselves a framework of obligations which reach further than the main treaty and to which not all parties of the main treaty consent, creating a "two-tier system." An example is found in the optional protocol of which deals with direct access for individuals to the committee established under it.

- A protocol can be a supplementary treaty, in this case it is an instrument which contains supplementary provisions to a previous treaty (e.g., the 1966 Protocol relating to the Status of Refugees to the 1951 Convention relating to the Status of Refugees).

- A protocol can be based on and further elaborate a framework convention. The framework "umbrella convention," which sets general objectives, contains the most fundamental rules of a more general character, both procedural and substantive. These objectives are subsequently elaborated by a protocol, with specific substantive obligations, consistent with the rules agreed upon in the framework treaty. This structure is known as the so-called "framework-protocol approach." Examples include the 1985 Vienna Convention for the Protection of the Ozone Layer and its 1987 Montreal Protocol on Substances that deplete the Ozone Layer with its subsequent amendments, the 1992 United Nations Framework Convention on Climate Change with its 1997 Kyoto protocol, and the 1992 Convention on the Protection and Use of Transboundary Watercourses and International Lakes with its 1999 Protocol on Water and health and its 2003 (Kiev) Protocol on Civil Liability and compensation for Damage caused by the Transboundary Effects of Industrial Accidents on Transboundary Water. (See chapters 9 and 10 of this Manual).

- A protocol of signature is another instrument subsidiary to a main treaty, and is drawn up by the same parties. Such a protocol deals with additional matters such as the interpretation of particular clauses of the treaty. Ratification of the treaty will normally also involve ratification of such a protocol. The Protocol of Provisional Application of the General Agreement on Tariffs and Trade ("GATT") was concluded to bring the 1947 GATT quickly into force in view of the difficulties facing the ratification of the International Trade Organization.

The term "declaration" is used to describe various international instruments. However, in most cases declarations are not legally binding. The term is often deliberately chosen to indicate that the parties do not intend to create binding obligations but merely seek to declare certain aspirations. Examples include the 1992 Rio Declaration on Environment and Development, the 2000 United Nations Millennium Declaration and the 2002 Johannesburg Declaration on Sustainable Development. Exceptionally, declarations may sometimes be treaties in the generic sense intended to be binding at international law. An example is the 1984 Joint Declaration of the government of the United Kingdom of Great Britain and Northern Ireland and the Government of the People's Republic of China on the Question of Hong Kong, which was registered as a treaty by both parties with the United Nations Secretariat, pursuant to article 102 of the United Nations Charter. It is therefore necessary to establish in each individual case whether the parties intended to create binding obligations, often a difficult task. Some instruments entitled "declarations" were not originally intended to have binding force but their provisions may have reflected customary international law or may have gained binding character as customary international law at a later stage, as is the case with the 1948 Universal Declaration of Human Rights.

Once the text of a treaty is agreed upon, states indicate their intention to undertake measures to express their consent to be bound by the treaty. Signing the treaty usually achieves this purpose; and a state that signs a treaty is a signatory to the treaty. Signature also authenticates the text and is a voluntary act. Often major treatises are opened for signature amidst much pomp and ceremony. * * * Once a treaty is signed, customary law, as well as the 1969 Vienna Convention, provides that a state must not act contrary to the object and purpose of the particular treaty, even if it has not entered into force yet.

1969 Vienna Convention on the Law of Treaties
(Article 18)

"A State is obliged to refrain from acts which would defeat the object and purpose of a treaty when: (a) it has signed the treaty or has exchanged instruments constituting the treaty subject to ratification, acceptance or approval, until it shall have made its intention clear not to become a party to the treaty; or (b) it has expressed its consent to be bound by the treaty, pending the entry into force of the treaty and provided that such entry into force is not unduly delayed."

The next step is the ratification of the treaty. Bilateral treaties, often dealing with more routine and less politicized matters, do not normally require ratification and are brought into force by definitive signature, without recourse to the additional procedure of ratification.

In the first instance, the signatory state is required to comply with its constitutional and other domestic legal requirements in order to ratify the treaty. This act of ratification, depending on domestic legal provisions, may have to be approved by the legislature, parliament, the head of State, or similar entity. It is important to distinguish between the act of domestic ratification and the act of international ratification. Once the domestic legal requirements are satisfied, in order to undertake the international act of ratification the state concerned must formally inform the other parties to the treaty of its commitment to undertake the binding obligations under the treaty. In the case of a multilateral treaty, this constitutes submitting a formal instrument signed by the head of State or Government or the Minister of Foreign Affairs to the depositary who, in turn, informs the other parties. With ratification, a signatory state expresses its consent to be bound by the treaty. Instead of ratification, it can also use the mechanism of acceptance or approval, depending on its domestic legal or policy requirements. A nonsignatory state, which wishes to join the treaty after its entry into force, usually does so by lodging an instrument of accession. * * *

Accordingly, the adoption of the treaty text does not, by itself, create any international obligations. Similarly, in the case of multilateral treaties, signature by a state normally does not create legally binding obligations. A state usually signs a treaty stipulating that it is subject to ratification, acceptance or approval. It is the action of ratification, accession, acceptance, approval, *et cetera*, which creates legally binding rights and obligations. However, the creation of binding rights and obligations is subject to the treaty's entry into force. A treaty does not enter into force and create legally binding rights and obligations until the necessary conditions stipulated by it are satisfied. For example, the expression of the parties' consent to be bound by a specified number of states. Sometimes, depending on the treaty provisions, it is possible for treaty parties to agree to apply a treaty provisionally until its entry into force.

One of the mechanisms used in treaty law to facilitate agreement on the text is to leave the possibility open for a state to make a reservation on becoming a party. A reservation modifies or excludes the application of a treaty provision. A state may use this option for joining a treaty even though it is concerned about certain provisions. A reservation must be lodged at the time of signature, or ratification, or acceptance, or approval, or accession. * * * In general, reservations are permissible except when they are prohibited by the treaty, they are not expressly authorized reservations if the treaty provides only specified reservations, or they are otherwise incompatible with the object and purpose of the treaty. * * *

An important issue is how to make changes to an already agreed treaty text. The treaty itself normally provides for a procedure to change its provisions, usually by amending the specific provision. Depending on the provisions of the treaty, amendment of a treaty usually needs the consensus of all parties or a specified majority such as two-thirds of the parties, who must be present and voting. Besides amending, there is also the possibility of revising a treaty. The term "revision" is typically reserved for a more profound change of text. * * *

In most cases, the treaty enters into force when a specified number of states have ratified it. A provision in the treaty that governs its entry into force will stipulate that entry into force will occur after a certain time period has elapsed (such as 90 days) after the tenth (i.e., 1973 Convention on International Trade in Endangered Species of Wild Fauna and Flora), fifteenth (i.e., 1979 Convention on the Conservation of Migratory Species of Wild Animals), twentieth (i.e., 1985 Vienna convention for the Protection of the Ozone Layer), thirtieth (1992 convention on Biological Diversity) or fiftieth (i.e., 1992 United Nations Framework Convention on Climate Change, 1994 Desertification Convention after ratification, accession, approval, acceptance, etc. A treaty enters into force only for the states that have ratified it. * * *

A treaty can also specify certain additional conditions regarding the states that have to ratify the treaty before it can enter into force. For example, the 1987 Montreal Protocol to the Vienna Convention [for the Protection of the Ozone Layer] includes the provision that it would enter into force on 1 January 1989, provided that there were at least eleven ratifications of states which were responsible in 1986 for at least two-thirds of the estimated global consumption of the substances the protocol is covering (article 16). The entry into force of the 1997 Kyoto protocol is also subjected to strict conditions—it will enter into force "on the ninetieth day after the date on which not less than fifty-five parties to the Convention, incorporating parties included in Annex I which accounted in total for at least 55% of the total carbon dioxide emissions for 1990 of the parties included in Annex I, have deposited their instruments of ratification, acceptance, approval or accession" (article 24).

2. Customary International Law

The second most important source of international law, and thus of international environmental law, is customary international law. Before treaties became as important as they are today, customary international law was the leading source of international law: the way things have always been done becomes the way things must be done.

Once a rule of customary law is recognized, it is binding on all states, because it is then assumed to be a binding rule of conduct. Initially, customary international law as we know it today developed in the context of the evolving interaction among European states. However, there is an increasingly prominent group of writers who suggest that other regions of the world also contributed to the evolution of customary international law.

There are two criteria for determining if a rule of international customary law exists: (1) the state practice should be consistent with the "rule of constant and uniform usage" (*inveterate consuetudo*) and (2) the state practice exists because of the belief that such practice is required by law *(opinion juris)*. Both elements are complementary and compulsory for the creation of customary international law. Since customary law requires this rather heavy burden of proof and its existence is often surrounded by uncertainties, treaties have become increasingly important to regulate international relations among states.

Customary law was mentioned in relation to the 1948 Universal Declaration of Human Rights. Namely, the provisions of the declaration, although not specifically intended to be legally binding, are now generally accepted as constituting customary international law. Customary international law is as legally binding as treaty law. It can be argued that customary international law has a wider scope: a treaty is applicable only to its parties and it does not create either rights or obligations for a third state without its consent, but customary law is applicable to *all* states (unless it constitutes regional custom).

Two specific terms related to the concept of customary international law require further attention. The first one is "soft law." This term does not have a fixed legal meaning, but it usually refers to any international instrument, other than a treaty, containing principles, norms, standards or other statements of expected behavior. Often, the term soft law is used as synonymous with non-legally binding. A treaty that is legally binding can be considered to represent hard law; however, a non-legally binding instrument does not necessarily constitute soft law. The consequences of a non-legally binding instrument are not clear. Sometimes it is said that they contain political or moral obligations, but this is not the same as soft law. Non-legally binding agreements emerge when states agree on a specific issue, but they do not, or do not yet, wish to bind themselves legally; nevertheless they wish to adopt certain non-binding rules and principles before they become law. This approach often facilitates consensus, which is more difficult to achieve on binding instruments. There could also be an expectation that a rule or principle adopted by consensus, although not legally binding, will nevertheless be complied with. Often the existence of non-legally binding norms will fuel civil society activism to compel compliance. The Non-Legally Binding Authoritative Statement of Principles for a Global Consensus on the Management, Conservation and Sustainable Development of all Type of Forests ("Forest Principles"), for example, is an illustration of this phenomenon. The relationship between the Forest Principles and a binding forest regime is that they are shaping or will shape consensus for a future multilateral convention, or are building upon a common legal position that will possibly come to constitute customary international law.

The second term is "peremptory norm" *(jus cogens)*. This concept refers to norms in international law that cannot be overruled other than by a subsequent peremptory norm. They are of the highest order. *Jus cogens* has precedence over treaty law. Exactly which norms can be designated as *jus cogens* is still subject to some controversy. Examples are the ban on slavery, the prohibition of genocide or torture, or the prohibition on the use of force.

3. General Principles of Law

The third source of international law [is general principles of law]. * * * There is no universally agreed upon set of general principles and concepts. They usually include both principles of the international legal system as well as those common to the major national legal systems of the world. The ICJ will sometimes analyse principles of domestic law in order to develop an appropriate rule of international law.

The ICJ, in its 1996 Advisory Opinion on Legality of the Threat or Use of Nuclear Weapons, points to the Martens Clause as an affirmation that the principles and rules of humanitarian law apply to nuclear weapons. In his dissenting opinion, Judge Shahabuddeen cites the Martens Clause: "the inhabitants and the belligerents remain under the protection and the rule of the principles of the law of nations, as they result from the usages established among civilized peoples, from the laws of humanity, and the dictates of the public conscience". Judge Shahabuddeen states that the Martens Clause provided its own self-sufficient and conclusive authority for the proposition that there were already in existence principles of international law under which considerations of humanity could themselves exert legal force to govern military conduct in cases in which no relevant rule was provided by conventional law. It can be construed that some treaties reflect, codify or create general principles of law.

4. Judicial Decisions and Qualified Teachings

The fourth source enumerated in article 38(1)(d) of the Statute of the International Court of Justice, judicial decisions and the teachings of the most highly qualified publicists of the various nations, is qualified as an additional means for the determination of rules of law. Decisions of the ICJ itself or of other international tribunals, and writings of publicists are considered if: there is no treaty on a particular contentious issue in international law, no customary rule of international law and no applicable general principles of international law. Many international law journals publish articles by eminent lawyers addressing a great variety of issues pertaining to all aspects of international law. * * *

Article 38 is not intended to provide an exhaustive list of sources of international law. There are other possible sources which the ICJ might rely on to assist in its deliberations, such as acts of international or regional organizations, Resolutions of the United Nations Security Council and the United Nations General Assembly, and Regulations, Decisions and Directives of the European Union, among others.

Also, decisions of the Conference of the Parties to a MEA, and conference declarations or statements, may contribute to the development of international law.

There is no definite procedure established on how to negotiate a Multilateral Environmental Agreement. Some common elements, however, may be derived from the practice of states over the last few decades.

III. Negotiating Multilateral Environmental Agreements

* * * The first step in the negotiation process is for an adequate number of countries to show interest in regulating a particular issue through a multilateral mechanism. The existence of a common challenge and the need for a solution is necessary. In certain cases, the number of acutely interested parties may be as few as two. For example, the draft convention on Cloning was tabled in the Sixth Committee of the General Assembly by Germany and France. A counter proposal was advanced by the United States of America. In other cases, a larger number of countries need to demonstrate a clear desire for a new instrument. Once this stage of establishing a common interest in addressing a global problem is established, states need to agree on a forum for the negotiation of a multilateral instrument. Usually an existing international organization such as the United Nations or an entity such as the United Nations Environment Programme ("UNEP") will provide this forum. The United Nations has frequently established special fora for the negotiation of MEA through General Assembly resolutions. The 1992 United Nations Framework Convention on Climate Change ("UNFCCC') was negotiated by a specially established body—the Intergovernmental Negotiating Committee ("INC"). It is also possible to conduct the negotiations in a subsidiary body of the General Assembly such as the Sixth Committee, which is the Legal Committee. Treaty bodies could also provide the fora for such negotiations. For example, pursuant to article 19(3) of the 1992 Convention on Biological Diversity, the Conference of the Parties, by its decision II/5, established an Open-Ended Ad Hoc Working Group on Biosafety to develop the draft protocol on biosafety, which later resulted in an agreed text and subsequent adoption of the 2000 Cartagena Protocol on Biosafety.

The negotiating forum will start the negotiating process by establishing a committee or convening an international conference to consider the particular issue. This could take many forms, from an informal ad hoc group of governmental experts to a formal institutional structure as in the case of the INC for the negotiation of the 1992 UNFCCC. It is also possible for an international organization to establish a subsidiary body to prepare a text for consideration and adoption by an Intergovernmental Diplomatic Conference. Certain treaties were first proposed by the International Law Commission and subsequently negotiated and adopted by intergovernmental bodies. Governments also often draft negotiating texts. During the negotiations, delegates generally remain in close contact with their governments; they have preliminary instructions that are usually not communicated to other parties. At any stage they may consult their governments and, if necessary, obtain fresh instructions. Governments could also change their positions depending on developments. Depending on the importance of the treaty under negotiation, governments may expend considerable resources in order to safeguard and advance their own national interests in the context of arriving at a global standard. In many cases this may require building numerous alliances and interest groups in order to advance national positions. The European Union usually operates as a block in MEAS negotiations but often formed alliances with other like-minded countries. The host organization will organize preparatory committees, working groups of technical and legal experts, scientific symposia and preliminary conferences. The host body will also provide technical back-up to the negotiators.

Increasingly, the need for universal participation in the negotiation of MEA has been acknowledged. Consequently, developing countries are often provided financial assistance to participate in environmental negotiations. Given this opportunity and the widely acknowledged need for developing countries to be closely engaged in these negotiations in view of the global nature of environmental challenges, they have the possibility to exert a greater influence on the future development of legal principles in the environmental field than was available to them in other treaty negotiating fora.

In the negotiating forum, states are the most important actors, since most treaties only carry direct obligations for states. However, the proper implementation of and compliance with a treaty cannot be achieved without involving a whole range of non-state actors, including civil society groups, Non-Governmental Organizations ("NGOs"), scientific groups, and business and industry, among others. Therefore the participation of these groups in the negotiating processes that lead to an MEA is now more readily facilitated. Some national delegations to intergovernmental negotiations now contain NGO representatives while some smaller states might even rely on NGOs to represent them at such negotiations. In such situations, NGOs may have a notable influence on the outcomes of the negotiations. * * *

As mentioned above, international environmental treaty making may involve a two-step approach, the "Framework Convention-Protocol" style. In this event, the treaty itself contains only general requirements, directions

and obligations. Subsequently the specific measures and details will be negotiated, as happened with the 2000 Cartagena Protocol on Biosafety with the
1992 Convention on Biological Diversity. Or, additional non-legally binding
instruments can elaborate on these measures to be taken by the parties, as
was the case with the 2002 Bonn guidelines on Access to Genetic Resources
and Fair and Equitable Sharing of the Benefits Arising out of their Utilization, with the same convention. The convention-protocol approach allows
countries to "sign on" at the outset to an agreement even if there is no agreement on the specific actions that need to be taken under it subsequently.
Among the major shortcomings of the convention-protocol approach is that it
encourages a process that is often long and drawn out.

IV. Administering Treaties

Treaties do not only create rights and obligations for state parties, they
often also create their own administrative structure to assist parties to comply with their provisions and to provide a forum for continued governance.

Environmental treaties usually rely on voluntary compliance with their
obligations, rather than on coerced compliance. Accordingly, there is a tendency to develop non-compliance mechanisms designed to secure compliance
by the parties with the terms of a treaty or decisions of the Conference of the
Parties ('COP') through voluntary means. The emphasis in these noncompli-
ance mechanisms is to assist parties to meet their obligations rather than
identify guilt in non-compliers and impose punitive sanctions. Even in the
absence of a formal procedure, non-compliance problems are likely to be handled in a similar way in many environmental regimes. Non-compliance procedures are best understood as a form of dispute avoidance or alternative
dispute resolution, in the sense that resort to binding third party procedures
is avoided. The treaty parties will instead seek to obtain compliance through
voluntary means and in the process reinforce the stability of the regime as a
whole.

An example is the non-compliance procedure adopted by the parties to
the 1987 Montreal Protocol on Substances that Deplete the Ozone Layer.
Whenever there are compliance problems, the matter is referred to an implementation committee consisting of ten parties, whose main task is to consider and examine the problem and then find an amicable solution based on
the 1987 Montreal Protocol. It is possible for a party itself to draw the attention of the implementing committee to its inability to comply with the Protocol with a view to obtaining assistance with compliance measures.

Breach of an environmental treaty is unlikely to justify punitive action.
Punitive action is generally avoided by states in favour of softer non-
compliance procedures that rely on international supervisory institutions to
bring about compliance through consultation and practical assistance. Effec-

tive supervision of the operation and implementation of treaty regimes often depends on the availability of adequate information.

Most environmental treaties establish a Conference of the Parties, a Secretariat, and subsidiary bodies.

The COP forms the primary policy-making organ of the treaty. All parties to a treaty meet, usually annually or biannually, and survey the progress achieved by the treaty regime, the status of implementation, possibilities for amendments, revisions, and additional protocols. * * *

The Secretariat of a convention is responsible for the daily operations. In general, it provides for communication among parties, organizes meetings and meeting documents in support of the COP, assists in implementation and it may assist in activities such as capacity building. The Secretariat gathers and distributes information and it increasingly coordinates with other legal environmental regimes and secretariats. * * *

Many environmental regimes provide for a scientific commission or other technical committee, comprised of experts. In most cases, they include members designated by governments or by the COP, although they generally function independently. They can be included in the treaty or by a decision of the COP. For example, the 1992 Convention and Biological Diversity has a Subsidiary Body on Scientific, Technical and Technological Advice, the 1998 PIC Convention provides for a Chemical Review Committee, and the Committee for Environmental Protection was established by the 1991 Protocol on Environmental Protection to the Antarctic Treaty. They can address recommendations or proposals to the COP or to other treaty bodies. They usually provide informative reports in the area of their specialization related to the convention and its implementation.

Notes and Questions

1. The Law of treaties is silent about collaboration among MEAs. While each MEA establishes a Secretariat, whose expenses are met by contributions of the States Party to each agreement, these treaties do not provide for how the MEAS should cooperate among themselves. How should the law of treaties by revised to provide for collaboration among MEA Secretariats? How should the nations organize their participation in each MEA to accomplish such collaboration among the MEAs?

For example the UNFCCC Secretariat in Bonn, Germany, could collaborate with the Convention on Biological Diversity, whose Secretariat is in Montreal, on deforestation issue. The UNEP provides the Secretariat that supports the MEA Vienna Convention and Montreal Protocol to protect the Stratospheric Ozone, which treaty reduces potent greenhouse gas emissions but does entirely so apart from the UNFCCC. UNEP's headquarters are in Nairobi, Kenya. A proposal to co-locate all MEAs in Geneva, Switzerland, was rejected by nations who sought the prestige of hosting an MEA within their territory. Currently UNEP is administering secretariat functions to the following MEAs: (A) *Biodiversity Cluster* [1992 Convention on Biological Diversity; 2000 Cartagena Protocol on Biosafety; 1979 (Bonn) Convention on the Conservation of Migratory Species of Wild Animals, Related Agreements and Memoranda of Understanding Concerning Specific Species concluded under the Auspices of CMS; and 1973 Convention on International Trade in Endangered Species.] and (B) the *Chemicals and Hazardous Wastes Cluster* [1989 Basel Convention on the Control of Transboundary Movements of Hazardous Wastes and their Disposal; 1999 Protocol on Liability and Compensation to the Basel Convention; 2001 (Stockholm) Convention on Persistent Organic Pollutants; 1998 (Rotterdam) Convention on the Prior Informed Consent Procedure for Certain Hazardous Chemicals and Pesticides in International Trade; 1985 Vienna Convention for the Protection of the Ozone Layer; 1987 Montreal Protocol on Substances that Deplete the Ozone Layer].

In addition, UNEP has supported the negotiations of twelve conventions and action plans for the protection of the various regional seas. There are also stand-alone secretariats of MEAs under the United Nations umbrella such as the Desertification Convention Secretariat, and secretariats of regional agreements with regional organizations.

2. Are the ground rules for establishing treaties alone sufficient to ensure their implementation, or does the degree of implementation depend on the measures taken by each COP? In turn, what national leadership is needed to sustain the work over time of both an MEA's COP and its Secretariat? What is required nationally for a State to be consistent in its support of the personnel and financing of an MEA? Consider the success of the Stratospheric Ozone regime in this regard. See D. Zaelke, D. Kaniaru & E. Kruzikova, Making Law Work for Environmental Compliance and Sustainable Development (2005).

PROBLEM EXERCISE ON TRANSBOUNDARY ENERGY FACILITIES

Assume that the California Power Company (CPC) recently received the necessary Canadian national and British Columbia provincial government approvals to construct and operate a very large coal-fired electricity generating plant in Trail, British Columbia just north of the U.S.-Canada border and Washington state. CPC's plant would be located next door to the infamous Trail Smelter, see Trail Smelter Arbitral Tribunal: Decision, 35 Am. J. Intl. L. 684 (1941). CPC is a California corporation headquartered in Los Angeles which sells electricity throughout southern California from its coal, oil, natural gas, hydroelectric, solar and wind powered generating plants located throughout California. CPC also operates a very profitable energy conservation program which sells and installs energy efficient lights and appliances and weatherizes its electricity customers' commercial facilities and homes.

Coal to fuel CPC's new Trail plant would come from nearby high sulfur content coal deposits which CPC would mine using a strip mining technique which would remove the forest covered lands above the coal deposits. To encourage CPC to locate its plant in Trail and provide mining and other jobs to replace jobs lost in the forestry sector, the Canadian national and British Columbia provincial legislatures recently enacted statutes specifically exempting CPC's mining operations from the normally applicable stringent national and provincial reforestation and land reclamation requirements. Electricity generated by CPC's new plant would be transmitted to California on a new high voltage transmission line that CPC would construct from Trail south across Washington and Oregon to link up with CPC's existing transmission lines in northern California.

Strong winds from the north blow from Trail across the U.S. border most of the year. Potential adverse impacts from the CPC plant's burning of high sulfur content coal include the regional transboundary and global impacts of sulfur dioxide (SO_2) and carbon dioxide (CO_2) emissions.

Concerns about the CPC plant's projected SO_2 and CO_2 emissions and the environmental impacts from CPC's British Columbia coal strip mining and high voltage transmission line construction and operation have been raised by: the United States government through its Secretary of State and Environmental Protection Agency Administrator, the heads of the Washington State Department of Ecology and Oregon Department of Environmental Quality; British Columbian and Washington state agribusinesses and small farm fruit growers whose SO_2 sensitive orchards are located south of Trail; and several international and Canadian and U.S. west coast environmental NGOs.

Ratified treaties and other international agreements in force and potentially relevant to the above facts include:

(A) the 1991 U.S.-Canada Bilateral Air Quality Agreement (30 I.L.M. 676);
(B) the North American Free Trade Agreement (NAFTA) (32 I.L.M. 289);
(C) the North American Agreement on Environmental Cooperation (NAAEC) (32 I.L.M. 1480);
(D) the United Nations Framework Convention on Climate Change (FCCC) (31 I.L.M. 849) excerpted in section D of this chapter, infra; and
(E) 1997 Kyoto Protocol (37 I.L.M. 32) to the FCCC also excerpted below.

Part 1: Analyze <u>specifically</u> how these treaties and agreements could <u>apply</u> (or <u>not</u> apply) to the above facts.

Part 2: Are there any <u>customary</u> rules of international environmental law potentially applicable to the problem? If so, specifically <u>identify</u> them and <u>explain</u> how they might apply to the facts.

Part 3: Are there any well established or emerging <u>general principles</u> of international environmental law potentially applicable to the facts? If so, specifically <u>identify</u> them and <u>explain</u> how they might apply to the facts.

Part 4: Assume all the governments, CPC, and the other interested parties have selected you as an <u>impartial</u> climate change law expert to recommend a resolution. Based on your analyses in parts 1, 2, and 3 above, and your knowledge of relevant international and domestic courts, environmental agencies, financial institutions, and corporate and non-governmental organizations, describe and explain your resolution, including any roles relevant courts, agencies, institutions, and organizations might play in your resolution. With regard to courts, consider the decisions in Massachusetts v. EPA, 127 S.Ct. 1438 (2007) excerpted in chapter 6, North Carolina v. TVA, 38 ELR 20037 (4th Cir. Jan. 31, 2008), Pakootas v. Teck Cominco Metals, 452 F. 3d 1066 (9th Cir. 2006), affirming, 2004 WL 2578982 (E.D. Wash 2004), cert. denied, 128 S.Ct. 858 (2008) and NEDC v. Owens Corning, 434 F. Supp. 2d 957 (D. Or. 2006) noted in chapter 6. Also in your response to Part 4, <u>briefly</u> discuss any less environmentally damaging, more sustainable ways that CPC could meet the needs of its California electricity customers without mining and burning coal in its proposed Trail plant and building the new high voltage transmission line.

C . INTERNATIONAL PROTECTION OF THE STRATOSPHERIC OZONE LAYER

1. Introduction to the Vienna Convention

Nations employed the rules of public international law to fashion one MEA that has successfully united virtually all nations in a global program to eliminate one of the most potent family of green house gases, those related to chlorofluorocarbons (CFCs). More than 95% of these GHGs have been eliminated from production and use. The Vienna Convention (1985) and its dynamic Montreal Protocol (1987) are a model of how progressively to shape an international environmental law regime. See The Art of Diplomacy: Celebrating 20 Years of the Montreal Protocol, Our Planet (UNEP, September 2007) at www.unep.org/ourplanet). At the 20th anniversary of the Montreal Protocol in 2007, States reflected on their success. For a synopsis of the historic steps taken between 1987 and 2007, see 19 Earth Negotiations Bulletin, no. 60, (Sept. 24, 2007).

Each CFC molecule is 20,000 times more powerful as a GHG than is a single CO_2 molecule. Eliminating these chemicals is an enormous contribution to mitigating GHG emissions. The current phase out of hydrofluorochlorocarbons (HCFCs) will avoid the equivalent of 22 billion metric tons of CO_2. By comparison, had the Kyoto Protocol under the UN Framework Convention on Climate Change been fully effective, it would have avoided 1 billion metric tons of carbon-dioxide equivalence by 2012.

How did this enormous step to protect the climate and atmosphere come about?

In 1975, the World Meteorological Organization published analysis based on scientific reports by Mario Molina and F.S. Rowland (1974 Formed some 400 million years ago, the stratospheric ozone layer was discovered by French physicists Charles Fabry and Henri Buisson in 1913. It exists in the upper atmosphere, ten kilometers above the Earth, and is being depleted by the release of various combinations of chemical elements associated with chlorofluorcarbons (CFCs). CFCs had been synthesized in 1929, for use initially a coolant in refrigerators. Many other uses emerged for this class of man-made gases. The ozone layer protects Earth from strong ultraviolet rays (UV-B) from the sun. As chlorine molecules reached the stratospheric layer, one chlorine atom could destroy 100,000 ozone molecules. The ozone layer protects humans from skin cancers and cataracts, and protects plants and animals in a variety of ways. The WMO reports led UNEP to convene negotiations in 1981 to prepare a global framework convention to protect the ozone layer. In the interim, nations enacted inconsistent national legislation, ranging from a ban on the use of CFCs as a propellant for spray cans in the USA in 1978, to adding warning labels to the use of such cans in certain European nations. Other uses of CFCs went on in business as usual.

The negotiations produced the Vienna Convention for the Protection of the Ozone Layer (1983). Since scientists did not yet have confirmed evidence that the CFCs produced as gases for air conditioning and as solvents to clean electrical and computer circuitry, the initial obligations in the MEA were modest: to cooperate to study the potential problem and act is there was a need. Based on the United Nations' Charter obligation of States to cooperate together to peacefully resolve international issues, this MEA has emerged as a model for how nations can collaborate and harmonize their national regulatory systems to protect a shared global resource. Since each CFC molecule, once released, resides in the atmosphere for a decade before reaching the stratosphere, the international collaboration to remove CFCs has contributed enormously to mitigate releases of a greenhouse gas.

Consider the core obligations of this MEA, and how they might be replicated in new climate change agreements under the UNFCCC and the Bali Action Plan. One builds international law gradually and progressively. Would a skeptic in 1985 have believed that these provisions from the Vienna Convention could have successfully shaped a universal regulatory regime to protect of global commons?

2. Vienna Convention for the Protection of the Ozone Layer
26 I.L.M. 1529 (1985)

Article 2
General Obligations

1.   The Parties shall take appropriate measures in accordance with the provisions of this Convention and of those protocols in force to which they are party to protect human health and the environment against adverse effects resulting or likely to result from human activities which modify or are likely to modify the ozone layer.

2.   To this end, the Parties shall in accordance with the means at their disposal and their capabilities;

(a) Co-operate by means of systematic observations, research and information exchange in order to better understand and assess the effects of human activities on the ozone layer and the effects on human health and the environment from modification of the ozone layer;

(b) Adopt appropriate legislative or administrative measures and co-operate in harmonizing appropriate policies to control, limit, reduce or prevent human activities under their jurisdiction or control should it be found that these activities have or are likely to have adverse effects resulting from modification or likely modification of the ozone layer;

(c) Co-operate in the formulation of agreed measures, procedures and standards for the implementation of this Convention, with a view to the adoption of protocols and annexes;

3.   The provisions of this Convention shall in no way affect the right of Parties to adopt, in accordance with international law, domestic measures additional domestic measures already taken by a Party, provided that these measures are domestic measures already taken by a party, provided that these measures ar not incompatible with their obligations under this Convention.

4.   The application of this article shall be based on relevant scientific and technical considerations.

Article 3
Research and Systematic Observations

1.The Parties undertake, as appropriate, to initiate and co-operate in, directly or through competent international bodies, the conduct of research and scientific assessments on:

(a) The physical and chemical processes that may affect the ozone layer;

(b) The human health and other biological effects deriving from any modifications of the ozone layer, particularly those resulting from changes in ultraviolet solar radiation having biological effects. * * *

(c) Climatic effects deriving from any modifications of the ozone layer;

(d) Effects deriving from any modifications of the ozone layer and any consequent change in UV-B radiation on natural and synthetic materials useful to mankind;

(e) Substances, practices, processes and activities that may affect the ozone layer, and their cumulative effects;

(f) Alternative substances and technologies; * * *

1. The Parties undertake to promote or establish, as appropriate, directly or through competent international bodies * * * joint or complementary programmes for systematic observation of the state of the ozone layer and other relevant parameters. * * *

2. The Parties undertake to co-operate, directly or through competent international bodies, in ensuring the collection, validation and transmission of research and observational data through appropriate world data centres in a regular and timely fashion.

Article 4
Co-operation in the Legal Scientific and Technical Fields

1. The Parties shall facilitate and encourage the exchange of scientific, technical, socio-economic, commercial and legal information relevant to this Convention as further elaborated in annex II. Such information shall be supplied to bodies agreed upon by the Parties. Any such body receiving information regarded as confidential by the supplying Party shall ensure that such information is not disclosed and shall aggregate it to protect its confidentiality before it is made available to all Parties.

2. The Parties shall co-operate, consistent with their national laws, regulations and practices and taking into account in particular the needs of the developing countries, in promoting, directly or through competent international bodies, the development and transfer of technology and knowledge. Such cooperation shall be carried out particularly through:

(a) Facilitation of the acquisition of alternative technologies by other Parties;

(b) Provision of information on alternative technologies and equipment * * *.

(c) The supply of necessary equipment and facilities for research and systematic observations;

(d) Appropriate training of scientific and technical personnel. * * *

Article 8
Adoption of Protocols

1. Any Party may propose amendments to this Convention or to any protocol. Such amendments shall take due account, inter alia, of relevant scientific and technical considerations.

2. Amendments to this Convention shall be adopted at a meeting of the Conference of the Parties. Amendments to any protocol shall be adopted at a meeting of the Parties to the protocol in question. The text of any proposed amendment of this Convention or to any protocol, except as may otherwise be provided in such protocol, shall be communicated to the Parties by the secretariat at least six months before the meeting at which it is proposed for adoption. The secretariat shall also communicate proposed amendments to the signatories to this Convention for information.

3. The Parties shall make every effort to reach agreement on any proposed amendment to this Convention by consensus. If all efforts at consensus have been exhausted, and no agreement reached, the amendment shall as a last resort be adopted by a three-fourth majority vote of the Parties present and voting at the meeting, and shall be submitted by the Depositary to all Parties for ratification, approval or acceptance.

4. The procedure mentioned in paragraph 3 above shall apply to amendments to any protocol, except that a two-thirds majority of the parties to that protocol present and voting at the meeting shall suffice for their adoption.

Article 10
Adoption and Amendment of Annexes

1. The annexes to this Convention or to any protocol shall form an integral part of this Convention or of such protocol, as the case may be, and, unless expressly provided otherwise, a reference to this Convention or its protocols constitutes at the same time a reference to any annexes thereto. Such annexes shall be restricted to scientific, technical and administrative matters.

2. Except as may be otherwise provided in any protocol with respect to its annexes, the following procedure shall apply to the proposal, adoption and entry into force of additional annexes to this Convention or of annexes to a protocol;

(a) Annexes to this Convention shall be proposed and adopted according to the procedure laid down in article 9, paragraphs 2 and 3, while annexes to any protocol shall be proposed and adopted according to the procedure laid down in article 9, paragraphs 2 and 4;

(b) Any party that is unable to approve an additional annex to this Convention or an annex to any protocol to which it is party shall so notify the Depositary, in writing, within six months from date of the communication of the adoption by the Depositary. The Depositary shall without delay notify all Parties of any such notification received. A party may at any time substitute an acceptance for a previous declaration of objection and the annexes shall thereupon enter into force for that Party;

(c) On the expiry of six months from the date of the circulation of the communication by the Depositary, the annex shall become effective for all Parties to this convention or to any protocol concerned which have not submitted a notification in accordance with the provision of subparagraph (b) above.

3. Introduction to the Montreal Protocol

This framework for the Vienna Convention was elaborated soon after its negotiation. Scientists discovered a "hole" in the Stratospheric Ozone layer over Antarctic. Then confirmation that CFCs were depleting Ozone Layer protection for Earth accelerated international scientific research, and led to the negotiation of the Montreal Protocol on Substances that Deplete the Ozone Layer (1987).   See Richard Benedict, Ozone Diplomacy (1991). Benedict was instrumental in securing the US government's support for the negotiation and implementation of the Montreal Protocol. The European Union, and its CFC manufacturers, initially had been reluctant to support a strong Protocol. As his book demonstrates, U.S. leadership played a major role in securing international consensus for the Protocol.

Under the terms of the Montreal Protocol, the Parties agreed to firm targets for reducing production and use of CFCs and other ozone depleting substance, and a process to continue advancing and refining the global work to eliminate ozone depleting substances (ODS). States undertook studies to determine what additional chemical substances needed to be banned, and then amended the annexes to the Protocol to provide for phase-outs and bans. At the second Meeting of the Parties (MOP) to the Montreal Protocol in London in 1990, restrictions were significantly tighten on CFCs and Halons and two new substances were included. Throughout the 1990s, new chemical substances were added to the regulatory regime, and by 1997 each nation agreed to implement a system, for licensing the import or export of the regulated Ozone Depleting Substances. The Montreal Protocol has a "Phase-Out" timetable for ODS.[6]

At the 12th Meeting of the Parties in Beijing, in 1999, the Parties agreed to control the production of hydrochlorfluorocarbons (HCFCs). In September of 2007, at the 19th Meeting of the Parties in Montreal, agreement was reached to accelerate the phase-out of HCFCs and to substantially reduce the "critical use exemptions" by which states had sought to continue their use of HCFCs (MOP-19, Decision XIX/6). The use of exemptions and special circumstances has built flexibility into the implementation of the MEA and helped it win political acceptance. Measures to help laggard states do not retard progress by all other states, and eventually the laggard states are brought into the advanced ODS phase outs.

One of the important international law provisions of the Montreal Protocol is the capacity states have entrusted to the MOP to amend the Annexes and revise both the regulated substances and the process for their elimina-

---

[6] Chemicals regulated include CFCs, Halons, Carbon tetrachloride, 1,1,1,-trichloroethan, HBFCs, HCFCs, Methyl bromide, and Bromochloromethane. Other candidate gases are under study.

tion. This routine amendment process is critical to the success of the Montreal Protocol. The international decisions are then incorporated into national regulatory systems by each nation.

Throughout, the Parties also campaigned to make adherence to the Convention as universal as possible, pledging to eliminate all trade relations with nations that did not ratify the Convention. Thereafter, in 1991 to assist nations to implement the Convention, a Multilateral Fund was created to pay for establishing and training key agencies in every nations as focal points for overseeing the implementation of the ban on production and trade and use of Ozone Depleting Substances. The Multilateral Fund operates with transparency and routinely reports to the MOP for the Montreal Protocol (see www.multilateralfund.org and Fund's report to the 19th MOP, UN DOC. UNEP/OzL.Pro.19/4), which assessed the incremental costs that states would have to bear in an accelerated phase-out of HCFCs. The UN Development Programme, UN Environment Programme, UN Industrial Development Organization (UNIDO) and the World Bank have contracted with the Fund to undertake training and capacity building to assist developing nations and the economies in transition for implementation of the obligations. States replenish the fund with new contributions at regular intervals. Congress has appropriated significant contributions from the USA for this Multilateral Fund consistently over the years, including under the Administration of President George W. Bush.

Part of the implementation and capacity building included the transfer of new technology to nations as they phased out their use of Ozone Depleting Substances. The introduction of new chemical substances and new technological alternatives was a key part of shifting the international economic system away from the use of ODS, even after the manufacturing of the ODS had been largely discontinued.

At a subsequent meeting in Copenhagen, the Parties agreed to establish a non-compliance system, by which states having difficulties in implementing the international legal obligations would have to account for their shortcomings and develop means to come into compliance. The compliance committee of the MOP for the Montreal Protocol has been effective. At the MOP 19, for instance, the Committee noted that Greece and Iran has returned to a state of compliance but that Saudi Arabia risked falling into non-compliance. Peer pressure and the adverse publicity associated with compliance reviews is a powerful force in producing support within a non-compliance nations to give renewed priority to implementation of their MEA obligations.

Within each nation, a focal point has been established to guide the implementation of the convention. This process has created world-wide a set of national specialists who share a common mission. They collaborate together and have become a single epistemic community around the Earth. The Multilateral Fund for implementing the Montreal Protocol has helped finance efforts to build a common regulatory approach to managing the reductions in ODS. See, for instance, the Regulations to Control Ozone Depleting Substances: A Guide Book (2000), prepared by the Stockholm Environment Institute (www.sei.se), The governments of States Parties and the Secretariat serviced by UNEP in Nairobi, have given equal weight to capacity building and confidence building among the Parties. A continuous improvement process has been undertaken. See www.unep/org/tools for implementation materials for national ozone focal point agencies, for customs officers and commercial uses such as farmers and small businesses. The ongoing work is directed at reclaiming the CFCs and other Ozone Depleting Substances still in use, and restricting or eliminating the trade in Ozone Depleting Substances. Many nations, such as the USA under the Clean Air Act, 42 USC § 7671, make the release of CFCs a crime, and there is an active international effort to use each nation's criminal laws to combat the black market trade of smuggling of banned Ozone Depleting Substances. The MOP for the Montreal Protocol oversees efforts to prevent the illegal trade is ODS. See e.g., UN DOC. UNEP/OzL.Preo. 19/L.2, Decision XIX/I (2007).

Throughout the negotiations and implementation phases, non-governmental organizations (NGOs), such as the Natural Resources Defense Council, have consistently and actively inter-acted with States Parties and the Secretariat, as well an engaging with representatives of industry. Law students, alumni and faculty at American University Washington College of Law, led by Prof. Durwood Zaelke and Prof. Perry Wallace, actively participated in the negotiations in 2007 to accelerate the phase out of HCFCs at MOP 19. See "How A Coalition of Alumni Achieved Five Times the Impact of the Kyoto Protocol," Global Network at 6-7 (American University, Spring 2008). From time to time, some industrial interests have lobbied against measures to strengthen the MEA, (see, e.g., the now defunct effort by an "Alliance for Responsible Atmospheric Policy" to avert tough curbs on HCFCs, www.arap.org/pr/hfes-eu.html). Both NGOs and industry groups are accredited to attend the MOP meetings and make their views know to the governmental delegates. Before decisions are taken, "contact groups" of key delegates are convened to work out proposed decisions, and selected private and public sector representatives inter-act with these negotiating teams.

The Vienna Convention and Montreal Protocol have been progressively elaborated and strengthened at global, regional and national levels. Industry has been engaged to find alternatives to the substances being banned and phased out. A regime that did not exist before 1985 has since become as professional as that of the cooperation of public health officials under the aegis of the World Health Organization.

The ozone protection regime is an exemplar of the successful MEA. The UNEP Training Manual on International Environmental Law (Chapter 9, para. 37) concludes that: "The international ozone regime has been successful in several ways. The Vienna Convention has currently (September 2005) 190 parties and the Montreal Protocol has 189 parties, including Brazil, China the European Community India, Russia and the United States. The amendments to the Protocol, together with the availability of financial mans, have helped in a dynamic and flexible way. Controls on ozone depleting substances were strengthened in 1990, 1992, 1997, and 1999 [and 2007], and new substances have been added. Third, since the formal non-compliance procedure has been successful, compliance in developed countries has been very high. Most importantly, the flexible compliance mechanism of the Montreal Protocol is often considered to be a role model in environmental agreements."

The prospects are that Ozone Depleting Substances will be phased out entirely and eventually will be removed from the atmosphere by interaction with the Stratospheric Ozone Layer. Assuming that the Earth's atmospheric systems will function as they have in the past, the expectation is that the stratospheric ozone layer will have recovered by 2045. Simultaneously a class of potent greenhouse gases will have been eliminated from the atmosphere.

As you consider how the following provisions of the Montreal Protocol supported this record of successful harmonization of environmental law world-wide, ask yourself what provisions could be adapted or embraced by the negotiators of the new agreement under the UNFCCC pursuant to the Bali Action Plan noted in Chapter 1.

4. Montreal Protocol on Substances That Deplete the Ozone Layer
26 I.L.M. 1550 (1987)

Article 2
Control Measures

1.   Each Party shall ensure that [each year] its calculated level of consumption of the controlled substances in Group I or annex A does not exceed its calculated level of consumption in 1986. By the end of the same period, each Party producing one or more of these substances shall ensure that its calculated level of production of the substances does not exceed its calculated level of production in 1986, except that such level may have increased by no more than ten per cent based on the 1986 level. Such increase shall be permitted only so as to satisfy the basic domestic needs of the Parties operating under Article 5 and for the purposes of industrial rationalization between Parties. * * *

3.   Each Party shall ensure that for the period 1 July 1993 to 30 June 1994 and in each twelve-month period thereafter, its calculated level of consumption of the controlled substances in Group I of Annex A does not exceed, annually, eighty per cent of its calculated level of consumption in 1986. * * *

4.   Each Party shall ensure that for the period 1 July 1998 to 20 June 1999, and in each twelve-month period thereafter, its calculated level of consumption of the con-

trolled substances in Group I of Annex A does not exceed, annually, fifty percent of its calculated level of consumption in 1986. * * *

9.   (a) Based on the assessments made pursuant to Article 6, the Parties may decide whether:

i.   Adjustments to the ozone depleting potentials specified in Annex A should be made and, if so, what the adjustments should be; and

ii.   Further adjustments and reductions of production or consumption of the controlled substances from 1986 levels should be undertaken and, if so, what the scope, amount and timing of any such reductions and adjustments should be.

(b)   Proposals for such adjustments shall be communicated to the Parties by the secretariat at least six months before the meeting of the Parties at which they are proposed for adoption.

(c)   In taking such decisions, the Parties shall make every effort to reach agreement by consensus. If all efforts at consensus have been exhausted, and no agreement reached, such decisions shall, as a last resort, be adopted by a two-thirds majority vote of the parties present and voting representing at least fifty per cent of the total consumption of the controlled substances of the Parties. * * *

11. Notwithstanding the provisions contained in this Article, Parties may take more stringent measures than those required by this Article.

Article 3
Calculation of Control Levels

For the purposes of Articles 2 and 5, each Party shall, for each Group of substances in Annex A, determine its calculated levels of:

(a)   Production by:

(i)   Multiplying its annual production of each controlled substance by the ozone depleting potential specified in respect of it in Annex A; and

(ii)   Adding together, for each such Group, the resulting figures;

(b)   imports and exports, respectively, by following * * * the procedure set out in subparagraph (a); and

(c)   consumption by adding together its calculated levels of production and imports and subtracting its calculated level of exports as determined in accordance with subparagraphs (a) and (b). However, beginning on 1 January 1993, any export of controlled substances to non-Parties shall not be subtracted in calculating the consumption level of the exporting Party.

Article 4
Control of Trade with Non-Parties

1.   Within one year of the entry into force of this Protocol, each Party shall ban the import of controlled substances from any State not party to this Protocol.

2.   Beginning on 1 January 1993, no Party operating under paragraph 1 of Article 5 may export any controlled substance to any State not party to this Protocol.

3.   Within three years of the date of the entry into force of this Protocol, the Parties shall * * * elaborate in an annex a list of products containing controlled substances. Parties that have not objected to the annex in accordance with those procedures shall ban, within one year of the annex having become effective, the import of those products from any State not party to this Protocol.

4.   Within five years of the entry into force of this Protocol, the Parties shall determine the feasibility of banning or restricting, from States not party to this Protocol, the import of products produced with, but not containing, controlled substances. If determined feasible, the Parties shall * * * elaborate in an annex a list of such products. * * *

5.   Each Party shall discourage the export, to any State not party to this Protocol, of technology for producing and for utilizing controlled substances.

6.   Each Party shall refrain from providing new subsidies, aid, credits guarantees or insurance programmes for the export to States not party to this Protocol of products, equipment, plants or technology that would facilitate the production of controlled substances.

Article 5
Special Situation of Developing Countries

1.   Any Party that is a developing country and whose annual calculated level of consumption of the controlled substances is less than 0.3 kilograms per capita on the date of the entry into force of the Protocol for it, or anytime thereafter within ten years of the date of entry into force of the Protocol shall, in order to meet its basic domestic needs, be entitled to delay its compliance with the control * * * ten years after that specified in those paragraphs

2.   The Parties undertake to facilitate access to environmentally safe alternative substances and technology for Parties that are developing countries and assist them to make expeditious use of such alternatives.

3.   The Parties undertake to facilitate access to environmentally safe alternative substances and technology for Parties that are developing countries and assist them to make expeditious use of such alternatives.

Article 6
Assessment and Review of Control Measures

Beginning in 1990, and at least every four years thereafter, the Parties shall assess the control measures provided for in Article 2 on the basis of available scientific, environmental, technical and economic information. At least one year before each assessment, the Parties shall convene appropriate panels of experts qualified in the fields mentioned and determine the composition and terms of reference of any such panels. Within one year of being convened, the panels will report their conclusions, through the secretariat, to the Parties. * * *

ANNEX A

CONTROLLED SUBSTANCES

Substance	Ozone Depleting Potential*
Group I	
$CFCl_3$ (CFC-11)	1.0
CF_2Cl_2 (CFC-12)	1.0
$C_2F_3Cl_3$ (CFC-113)	0.8
$C_2F_4Cl_2$ (CFC-114)	1.0
C_2F_5Cl (CFC-115)	0.6
Group 11	
CF_2BrCl (halon-1211)	3.0
CF_3Br (halon-1301)	10.0
$C_2F_4Br_2$ (halon-2402)	(to be determined)

*These ozone depleting potentials are estimates based on existing knowledge and will be reviewed and revised periodically.

* * * * *

5. Copenhagen Amendments to the Montreal Protocol
32 I.L.M. 874 (1992)

Annex IV: Non-Compliance Procedure

The following procedure has been formulated pursuant to Article 8 of the Montreal Protocol. It shall apply without prejudice to the operation of the settlement of disputes procedure laid down in Article 11 of the Vienna Convention.

1. If one or more Parties have reservations regarding another Party's implementation of its obligations under the Protocol, those concerns may be addressed in writing to the Secretariat. Such a submission shall be supported by corroborating information.

2. The Secretariat shall, within two weeks of its receiving a submission, send a copy of that submission to the Party whose implementation of a particular provision of the Protocol is at issue. Any reply and information in support thereof are to be submitted to the Secretariat and to the Parties involved within three months of the date of the dispatch or such longer period as the circumstances of any particular case may require. The Secretariat shall then transmit the submission, the reply and the information provided by the Parties to the Implementation Committee referred to in paragraph 5, which shall consider the matter as soon as possible.

3. Where the Secretariat, during the course of preparing its report, becomes aware of possible non-compliance by any Party with its obligations under the Protocol, it may request the Party concerned to furnish necessary information about the matter. If there is no response from the Party concerned within three months or such longer period as the circumstances of the matter may require or the matter is not resolved through administrative action or through diplomatic contacts, the Secretariat shall include the matter in its report to the Meeting of the Parties, pursuant to Article 12(c) of the Protocol and inform the Implementation Committee accordingly.

4. Where a party concludes that, despite having made its best, bona fide efforts, it is unable to comply fully with its obligations under the Protocol, it may address to the Secretariat a submission in writing, explaining, in particular, the specific circumstances that it considers to be the cause of its non-compliance. The Secretariat shall transmit such submission to the Implementation Committee which shall consider it as soon as practicable.

5. An Implementation Committee is hereby established. It shall consist of 10 Parties elected by the meeting of the Parties for two years, based on equitable geographical distribution. Outgoing Parties may be re-elected for one immediate consecutive term. The Committee shall elect its own President and vice-President. Each shall serve for one year at a time. The Vice-President shall, in addition, serve as the rapporteur of the committee.

6. The Implementation committee shall, unless it decides otherwise, meet twice a year. The Secretariat shall arrange for and service its meetings.

7. The functions of the Implementation Committee shall be:

(a) To receive, consider and report on any submission in accordance with paragraphs 1, 2, and 4;

(b) To receive, consider and report on any information or observations forwarded by the Secretariat in connection with the preparation of the reports referred to in Article 12(c) of the Protocol and on any other information received and forwarded by the Secretariat concerning compliance with the provisions of the Protocol.

(c) To request, where it considers necessary, through the Secretariat, further information on matters under its consideration;

(d) To undertake, upon the invitation of the Party concerned, information-gathering in the territory of the Party for fulfilling the functions of the Committee;

(e) To maintain, in particular for the purposes of drawing up its recommendations, an exchange of information with the Executive Committee of the Multilateral Fund related to the provision of financial and technical cooperation, including the transfer of technologies to Parties operating under Article 5, paragraph 1, of the Protocol.

8. The Implementation Committee shall consider the submissions, information and observations referred to in paragraph 7 with a view to securing an amicable solution of the matter on the basis of respect for the provisions of the Protocol.

9. The Implementation committee shall report to the Meeting of the Parties, including any recommendations it considers appropriate. The report shall be made available to the Parties not later than six weeks before their meeting. After receiving a report by the Committee the Parties may, taking into consideration the circumstances of the matter, decide upon and call for steps to bring about full compliance with the Protocol, and to further the Protocol's objectives.

10. Where a Party that is not a member of the Implementation Committee is identified in a submission under paragraph 1, or itself makes such a submission, it shall be entitled to participate in the consideration by the Committee of that submission.

11. No Party, whether or not a member of the Implementation Committee involved in a matter under consideration by the Implementation Committee, shall take part in the elaboration and adoption of recommendations on that matter to be included in the report of the Committee.

14. The Meeting of the Parties may request the Implementation Committee to make recommendations to assist the Meeting's consideration of matters of possible non-compliance.

15. The members of the Implementation Committee and any Party involved in its deliberations shall protect the confidentiality of information they receive in confidence.

16. The report, which shall not contain any information received in confidence, shall be made available to any person upon request. All information exchanged by or with the committee that is related to any recommendation by the Committee to the Meeting of the Parties shall be made available by the Secretariat to any Party upon its request; that Party shall ensure the confidentiality of the information it has received in confidence.

Notes and Questions

1. Nations report on their measures to implement their obligations under the Montreal Protocol. A comparative law analysis of the national implementation regimes offer insights into how to harmonize the civil law, common law, socialist law and Islamic legal regimes into one, coherent international undertaking. The common tools are administrative law, regulation of trade relations, harmonization of customs inspections, and use of criminal law systems as needed. See the compilation of these reports assembled by UNEP's Division of Technology, Industry and Economics (www.uneptie.org/ozoneaction.html). For examples, see Canada (www.ec.gc.ca/ozone/EN/index.cfm) or South Africa (www.environment.goc.za/). China's National Accelerated Phase Out Plan is removing CFCs and halons, and will remove HCFCs from the largest producer and consumer of these gases among developing nations. Because of regulating the ODS under the Clean Air Act Amendments of 1990, the USA met its obligations sooner and at less cost than anticipated. "By 1996, our phase outs were occurring four years faster and covering 13 more chemicals than planned, while estimated costs dropped from $3.55 to $2.45 per kilogram." The Office of Management and Budget reports indicate "we are getting more health benefits through protecting the ozone than from almost any other CAA program. Ending damage to the ozone layer is expected to prevent 6.3 million future U.S. deaths from skin cancer: benefits exceeding costs twenty fold." D. Huffor "USA," Our Planet at 10 (September 2007).

2. The website for the Ozone Secretariat is at www.unep.org/ozone. Why is the success story of this MEA so little understood by those who debate what do to about other greenhouse gases?

3. National efforts to fashion the Ozone Protection MEA have taken over 4 decades to become a nearly universal and effective world-wide legal regime. While removing the ODS chemicals have and will mitigate emissions of a potent greenhouse gas in the meantime, it will take another 4 decades to learn whether the Stratospheric Ozone is restored. What can we learn from the Ozone Protection regime to guide the Bali Action Plan under the UNFCCC? How can the successful elements of the Ozone regime be adapted or replicated to deal with mitigation of other greenhouse gases? For an update abut the Ozone Layer, see <www.nasa.gov/vision/earth/environment/ozone_resource_page.html>

4. Could a phase-out and ban on the release of CO_2 from specified activities, or a ban on burning fossil fuels in order to avert release of CO_s, be analogous to the ban on CFCs and other ODS?

5. The Vienna Convention is cited as an example of the Precautionary Principle in action. Principle 15 of the Rio Declaration on Environment and development states that "In order to protect the environment, the precautionary approach shall be widely applied by States according to their capabilities. Where there are threats of serious or irreversible damage, lack of full scientific certainty shall not be used as a reason for postponing cost-effective measures to prevent environmental degradation." Should this principle be widely applied to the as yet unrealized effects of climate change. See D. Freestone & E. Hay, eds., The Precautionary Principle and International Law: The Challenge of Implementation (1996); A. Trouwborst, Evolution and Status of the Precautionary Principle in International Law (2002). Since the United States has supported the Ozone regime, why has the Department of State consistently opposed use of the Precautionary Principle in negotiating other MEAs? Should Congress require use of the Precautionary Principle, as for instance in strengthening the National Environmental Policy Act, 42 USC 4321, and the use of environmental impact statements, 40 CFR Pt. 1500?

6. The Ozone regime also offers an illustration of "technology forcing," and correlating the technology to the state of scientific knowledge and the economic conditions. By banning the use of CFCs and the widely accepted chemical compounds, industry was obliged to seek alternatives. In 1987, DuPont took the position that it could produce substitutes for CFCs within five years, if the regulatory ban was put in place so that there would be market for their alternative products. S. Anderson and K. Sarma, Protecting the Ozone Layer: The United Nations History (2002). Technology forcing issues continues with the current phase out of the HCFCs. See S. Anderson & D. Zaelke, Industry Genius: People and Inventions Protecting Climate and the Fragile Industry Genius: People and Inventions Protecting Climate and Ozone Layer (2003). The MOP and Secretariat have been advised by the MEA's Technology and Economic Assessment Panel (TEAP), which builds common knowledge and understanding of what is realistic and possible in the phase out of old technology and the use of new alternatives. The MOP established a quadrennial system of assessments by the TEAP, and its Scientific Assessment Panel (SAP) and Environmental Effects Assessment Panel (EEAP).

7. Should the success of the Montreal Protocol make it a candidate MEA to take on an expanded mandate, and work to eliminate other GHGs? See S. Anderson, K. Sarma, & K. Taddonio, Technology Transfer for the Ozone Layer: Lessons for Climate Change (2007). As Mohamed T. El-Ashry observes, "The convergence of science and diplomacy in developing ozone policy–and the social response that followed–represents an unprecedented compact between scientists, governments, industry, and civil society. * * * It is said that reaching agreement on the Montreal Protocol was helped by the political leadership exercised by the United States, which (as with greenhouse gases now) was the largest emitted of ozone-depleting chemicals. Will

history repeat itself?" M. El-Ashry, "A New Compact?" Our Planet at 15 (September 2007). See also W. Lang, Is the Ozone Depletion Regime A Model for an Emerging Regime on Global Warming? 9 U.C.L.A. J. Envtl. L. & Policy 161 (1991).

8.   As the gases that function in refrigeration, air conditioning and insulating foams, have been phased out because they destroy the stratospheric ozone layer, use of alternative substitute gases has become widespread. The Hydrofluorocarbons (HCFs). Scientists now question whether HCFs can be the safe long-term solution sought. While HCFs do not destroy the Ozone Layer, they are thousands of times more potent than carbon dioxide as greenhouse gases. HFCs are listed as a gas to be regulated under the Kyoto Protocol. See G. Velders, et al., The Large Contribution of Projected HFC Emissions to Future Climate Forcing, Proceedings of the National Academy of Sciences (June 22, 2009).   What formal technological collaboration is needed to meet society's needs for air conditioning and refrigeration while also eliminating GHGs? How can the member states of both the Montreal Protocol and the Kyoto Protocol shape collaborative systems to address ssuch a priority?

PROBLEM EXERCISE ON THE NITROGEN CYCLE

The global legal and administrative network to eliminate Ozone Depleting Substances regulates an important, but discrete number of manufactured chemical compounds. Carbon dioxide (at its highest level in the atmosphere since 500,000 years ago) and methane (150 % above pre industrial levels) exist widely in natural settings, and the human activities that produce the gases in excess of natural background levels are diverse. Which other greenhouse gases have their origin in manufactured industrial settings, and thus could be regulated in ways analogous to the system in place to remove ODS?

The political consensus in the European Union and among the States supporting the Bali Action Plan is to concentrate all international negotiations on climate change under the rubric of the UNFCCC. This is supposed to focus attention and produce a more focused response to climate change mitigation and adaptation. However, since there are many drivers of climate change, one may question whether it is possible and desirable to concentrate the climate change focus in one forum. Could more progress be made by allocating certain topics to other specialized MEAs? Consider nitrogen.

The Nitrogen Cycle is being altered by humans much as the Carbon Cycle and the Hydrologic Cycle have been and are being changed by human actions. As much as 75% of the atmospheric nitrous oxides (NO_x), as well as the dead estuarine marine zones produced by the Nitrogen Cascade, derive from the use of manufactured fertilizers. Some 25% results from burning fossil fuels. Atmospheric Nitrogen has a lifetime of 114 years, and the increasing levels will remain as GHGs during this time. Although the atmospheric nitrogen comes through two distinct pathways, is not each pathway amenable to a different regulatory approach?

While fertilizers are valuable enhancements to agricultural production, excess applications end up altering the Nitrogen Cycle. Reactive nitrogen was only invented in the 19th century, and the inadvertent human manipulation of the carbon cycle is a product of the Industrial Revolution as much as current agricultural practices. Since the are a finite number of fertilizer manufacturers in the world, in a finite number of nations, the manufacturing setting is analogous to the situation of the ODS. To date local laws in some state governments and in some Member States of the European Union regulate the application of fertilizers to reduce excessive, but there is no universal approach to managing nitrogen added to the environment. Asian agriculture now contributes 35% of the synthetic nitrogen added to the environment.

Little international attention has been paid to the 1992 recommendations of Agenda 21 that governments should "determine plant nutrient requirements and supply strategies and optimize the use of both organic and inorganic sources, as appropriate, to increase farming, efficiency and production." (Para. 14.87c).

How should nations regulate the production and use of nitrogen? Nitrous oxides are already listed in Annex A of the Kyoto Protocol. Is this the best place to develop a regulatory program for nitrogen? Should the pattern of management pioneered by the Montreal Protocol be replicated? Unlike ODS, which nations seem to eliminate altogether, some use of nitrogen for fertilizer is desired? How should dosage be measured? Should dosages and allowable uses be different for farmers versus golf courses? What is the responsibility of the manufacturers of reactive nitrogen fertilizers for the misuse of their product?

NGOs, such as the Natural Resources Defense Council, and scientific bodies such as the Woods Hole Center, have urged UNEP to convene diplomatic meetings to address the gathering crisis of the Nitrogen Cycle. Were you to advise the UNEP Executive Director in response to this urging, what would you recommend?

If N_2O is a candidate for a new MEA, rather than using the model of the Montreal Protocol, what about these other manufactured GHGs:

Perfluorocarbons (PFCs) and sulfur hexafluoride (SF_6), two substances also currently included in Annex A to the Kyoto Protocol? If these GHGs remain under the umbrella of the UNFCCC, should they be subject to new and distinct Protocols like the Montreal Protocol, or be left to the MOP of the Kyoto Protocol to address? Why is there so little priority given to these greenhouse gases within the Kyoto Protocol's negotiations? Should the control of these manufactured gases be transferred to the systematic controls in place under the Montreal Protocol?

D. THE 1992 UN FRAMEWORK CONVENTION ON CLIMATE CHANGE

1. Introduction

The success of the Ozone Protection regime in abating releases of potent Greenhouse gases (GHG) invites comparison to the broader approach of the UN Framework Convention on Climate Change (UNFCCC). As Our Common Future emphasized in 1987, followed by two World Climate Conferences (1979 and 1990) and the creation by the World Meteorological Organization (WMO) and UNEP of the Intergovernmental Panel on Climate Change IPPC) in 1988. The scientific warnings about global warming changing the climate were serious enough to warrant action. The UN General Assembly declared that "climate change is a common concern of mankind" in 1988 and then convened an international negotiating committee (INC), with a target to conclude negotiation of a treaty on climate change by the time of the UN Conference on Environment and Development in 1992 in Rio de Janeiro. UNGA Res. 45/212 (Dec. 21, 1990). D. Goldberg, As The World Burns: Negotiating the Framework Convention on Climate Change, 5 Geo. Int'l Envtl. L. Rev. 239 (1993). While all climate change implications were not yet certain, the precautionary approach was used in the design of the UNFCCC.

In 1992, 154 nations signed the UNFCCC and the treaty entered into force in 1994. The Senate ratified the treaty and President George H.W. Bush's Secretary of State James Baker, announced the US 'no-regrets" policy. The US would begin to reduce GHG emissions whenever it made economic and policy sense to do so for other reasons, such as to improve fuel efficiency. That gradual policy approach was laid aside by President William J. Clinton, who sought to promote a more aggressive international approach toward climate change. This led to the negotiation of the Kyoto Protocol, with the strong intervention of Vice President Albert Gore to consummate the negotiation of the agreement at UNFCCC COP-3 in Kyoto, Japan in 1997. Thereafter, the US Senate refused to support the treaty, and President George W. Bush in March of 2001 announced that the USA would not become a party to the Kyoto Protocol. When the Kyoto Protocol entered into force in 2004, the US remained outside the Members of the Parties for the Protocol. For example at COP-4 in Buenos Aires, a Plan of Action was adopted to define the Kyoto Protocol's operational rules and implementation. The USA continued as a State Party to the UNFCCC and participant in the UNFCCC Conference of the Parties.

The COP for the UNFCCC has made gradual progress in implementations of the agreement. The work of each session is reported in the documents for each COP on the UNFCCC web site, http://unfccc.int/ and in the detail daily reports on the negotiations which are available from Earth Negotiations Bulletin published by the International Institute for Sustainable Development at www.iisd.ca. Given weak participation by the USA, and little leadership from many other sectors, there was little progress in establishing a work plan for shaping international action on climate change. The First COP in Berlin in 1995 adopted the Berlin Mandate, which was further clarified in COP-2. The USA's resistance to moving quickly on climate change produced a stalemate at COP-6 in The Hague in 2000, but at a resumed session the COP-6 Parties did adopt the Bonn Agreement on the rules of the Kyoto Protocol. COP-8 in New Delhi and COP-9 in Milan and COP-10 in Buenos Aires clarified the operation rules for the UNFCCC, but these negotiations had little effect on the constantly increasing volume of GHG is the atmosphere; indeed, the travel to the meetings made incremental additions to that volume. Since 2005, the UNFCCC COP and the Kyoto MOP have been meeting at the same time.

A decision of the COP in 1995, known as the "Berlin Mandate," (UN Doc FCCC/CP/1995/L.4) set the stage for the often contentious negotiations leading to the Kyoto Protocol. At the same time, the focus of attention was away from other options, such as building agreements on the other commitments in Article 4 (c) on other relevant sectors "including energy, transport, industry, agriculture, forestry, and waste management." Little effort was made to launch contact groups or deliberations to arrive at action plans for these sectors, since all the focus was on targets and timetables.

Notwithstanding the active multilateral negotiations leading to the Kyoto Protocol, and the meetings to organize work under the UNFCCC, in many nations, particularly the USA, little domestic action on climate change was undertaken and that often locally or regionally (see, e.g. the Regional Greenhouse Gas Initiative of the Northeastern States and eastern Canadian Provinces, www.rggi.org), while GHG emissions continued to rise. See, the reports of the Tyndall Centre for Climate Change, www.tyndall.ac.uk. At the federal level, little was accomplished as the US Senate adopted a Resolution rejected the formulas of the Kyoto Protocol. Senate Res. 98, Report No. 105-54 105th Cong. (July 25, 1997), and the Bush Administration favored only voluntary measures to deal with climate change issues. Meanwhile, China adopted its first national law mandating the use and expansion of renewable energy sources in 2003, discussed in A. Bradbrook, R. Lyster & R. Ottinger, The Law of Energy for Sustainable Development (2005). The European Union began its Emission Trading System (ETS) to begin an economic cap-and-trade system to mitigation GHG emissions. See http://europe.eu.int/comm./environment/climat/home_en.htm These sorts of reforms, however, while consistent with the UNFCCC obligations, were not part of a global approach to climate change mitigation and adaptation.

In adhering to the UNFCCC, nations agreed to establish national inventories of GHG emissions and sinks, to promote cooperation in scientific studies and technological innovation, to advance sustainable management of forest, oceans and ecosystems, and to integrate climate change factors into national social, economic and environmental policies. Article 4 provides the basis for elaborating a number of further agreements, protocols or programs and projects. Most of what is promised in Article 4 remains to be acted upon. The industrialized nations are listed in Annex I, and arguably they committed to return their anthropogenic emissions of GHG to 1990 levels by 2000; the UNFCCC text in Article 4(2), however, can be read to suggest that States did not make such an explicitly binding obligation.

The COP receives reports from the Subsidiary Body for Scientific and Technical Advise (SBSAT) and from the Supplementary Body for Implementation (SBI). The States Parties are to report to the COP their progress in meeting their obligations under Article 12(1), and a review of the commitments is to be made at regular intervals under Article 4(2)d.

Article 4 also provides for building the capacity of developing countries that are State Parties to the UNFCCC. Developed States are "to promote, facilitate and finance, transfer technology and know-how to developing countries. The UNFCCC financial mechanism in Article 11 has been delegated to the Global Environmental Facility (GEF) to handle. As recommended in Agenda 21 (Chapter 33), the GEF is an international financing facility with funds contributed by donor States, serving also other MEAs, primarily the Convention on Biological Diversity and Convention to Combat Desertification Stockholm Convention on Persistent Organic Pollutants. GEF also makes grants to developing countries to build their capacity to address environmental issues. www.gefweb.org. The GEF's Scientific and Technical Advisory Committee is at http://stapgef.unep.org. The UNFCCC COP has created three specific funds to assist developing nations: under the UNFCCC, the Special Climate Change Fund ("SCCF") and the Least Developed Countries Fund ("LDCF"), and under the Kyoto Protocol the Adaptation Fund.

The relationship between forests as sinks for sequestering carbon dioxide through photosynthesis has proven difficult for the Parties. The Bali Action Plan, UN Doc. UNFCCC COP 13, 1/CP.13 (Dec. 2007), gives priority to developing policies and positive incentives for "reducing emissions from deforestation" and from degradation of lands, known as "Reduced Emissions from Deforestation and Degradation, or "REDD". REDD, with an addition element of forest conservation, has become focus for sequestration of carbon via photosynthesis. While an obvious sink for CO_2, forest management has a controversial history in international policy, and finding consensus for REDD remains a challenge for negotiators.

Article 3.3 of the Kyoto Protocol would allow States to meet their allocated reduction targets by including an assessment of the climate impacts of anthropogenic "afforestation, reforestation, and deforestation." Since there is no international regime on forest stewardship, and timber is regarded as a traditional commodity, as reflected in the International Tropical Timber Agreement (1985), there has been substantial disagreement among States regarding conservation, forest management and conservation. Only China has long-standing accomplishments in and a significant commitment to afforestation. Despite the annual UN Forum on Forest debates in the General Assembly, there is not agreement on a new international law for forest management. In 1992, the UN Conference on Environment and Development failed to endorse a new MEA for forests and adopted a declaration "Non-Legally Binding Authoritative Statement of Principles for a Global Consensus on the Management, Conservation and Sustainable Development of all Types of Forests" (UN Doc. A/Conf. 151/26). Chapter 11 of Agenda 21 made recommendations to curb deforestation, but little has been done to end deforestation. It is no wonder, then, that the references to managing forests as a sink for sequestering carbon dioxide through photosynthesis has not been central to the UNFCCC negotiations.

While the UN Food and Agricultural Organization has the longest experience with silvaculture, forests are a concern of the Convention on Biological Diversity, the Ramsar Convention on Wetlands of International Importance (mangroves) the Desertification Convention and other intergovernmental organizations. The decisions of the UNFCCC COP should viewed within this wider context of other MEAs.

In 2001 the COP for the UNFCCC adopted the Bonn Agreement on "Land-Use, Land-Use Change and Forestry" (LULUCF). This policy determination set the stage for nations to claim forestry impacts as a credit toward meeting a state's assigned emission reduction targets. The focus was not on the how to measure the effectiveness of the sequestration in forests, or measuring the biodiversity value of forests as a component of healthy forests. The focus was not on the effect that climate change will have in damaging forest health. The UNFCCC Subsidiary Body for Scientific and Technological Advise (SBSTA) provided the COP with procedures for including planting forests within the Clean Development Mechanism, which the COP accepted. UN Doc. FCCC/SBSTA/2003/L.27, Annex (2003). The narrow focus on forests credits as trading "chips" in emission accounting has been criticized. A. Gillespie, Sinks and the Climate Change Regime: The State of Play, 13 Duke Envtl. L. & Policy Forum 279 (2003). The forest issues have come to be termed "Reducing Emissions from Deforestation and Degradation" or "REDD". Because well being of forests and their ecosystems depend increasingly on proactive nature conservation practices and laws, the UNFCC negotiations have come to refer to REDD-plus, meaning building nature conservation in to the programs that will reduce emissions attributable to deforestation and degradation.

In addition to a lack of forest stewardship, there is no agreed international regime for land use planning. Many nations lack any land registration system or cadastres to document land ownership, and in turn have no town and country planning or zoning systems. Incremental urban sprawl and converting vegetative cover to uses without vegetation, impacts upon carbon dioxide sequestration. The UNFCCC equations do not yet examine this aspect. The United Nations HABITAT Programme, which coordinates assistance to urban conurbations around the world, is so minimally staffed that it cannot effectively provide climate change information for local authorities.

In light of the world-wide pattern of neglect of land use and forest issues by the international community of nations, it is not surprising that the UNFCCC polices on REDD are so narrowly framed. As you study the Bonn LULUCF decisions, consider what would be needed to make this sector of climate change mitigation and adaptation more effective.

Bonn Agreement, Part VII:
Land-Use, Land-Use Change and Forestry (2001)

1.   The Conference of the Parties:
Affirms that the following principles govern the treatment of land-use, land-use change and forestry (LULUCF) activities:

(a)   That the treatment of these activities be based on sound science,

(b)   Consistent methodologies be used over time for the estimation and reporting of these activities,

(c)   The aim stated in Article 3, paragraph 1, of the Kyoto Protocol not be changed by accounting for LULUCF activities,

(d)   That the mere presence of carbon stocks be excluded from accounting

(e)   That the implementation of LULUCF activities contributes to the conservation of biodiversity and sustainable use of natural resources,

(f)   That accounting for LULUCF does not imply a transfer of commitments to a future commitment period,

(g)   That reversal of any removal due to LULUCF activities be accounted for at the appropriate point in time,

(h)   That accounting excludes removals resulting from (a) elevated carbon dioxide concentrations above their pre-industrial level; (b) indirect nitrogen deposition and (c) the dynamic effects of age structure resulting from activities and practices before the reference year.

2.   The Conference of the Parties agrees:
On a definition of "forest" and on definitions of the activities "afforestation", "reforestation" and "deforestation" for the purpose of implementing Article 3.3. These activities shall be defined on the basis of a change in land use.

3. That debits from harvesting during the first commitment period following afforestation and reforestation since 1990 shall not be greater than credits earned on that unit of land.

4. That "forest management", "cropland management", "grazing land management" and "revegetation" are eligible land-use, land-use change and forestry activities under Article 3, paragraph 4, of the Kyoto Protocol. A Party may choose to apply any or all of these activities during the first commitment period. A Party shall fix its choice of eligible activities prior to the start of the first commitment period.

5. That, during the first commitment period, a Party that selects any or all of the activities mentioned in paragraph 4 above shall demonstrate that such activities have occurred since 1990, and are human-induced. Such activities should not account for emissions and removals resulting from afforestation, reforestation and deforestation as determined under Article 3, paragraph 3.

6. That the following accounting rules are applicable in the first commitment period. They aim to pragmatically implement the guiding principles in the preamble:

(a) Application of net-net accounting (net emissions or removals over the commitment period less net removals in the base year, times five) for agricultural activities (cropland management, grazing land management and revegetation);

(b) Accounting for forest management up to the level of any possible Article 3.3 debits, if the total carbon stock change in the managed forests since 1990 is equal to or larger than this Article 3.3 debit (up to 8.2 megatons of carbon per Party per year; no discounting);

(c) Additions to and subtractions from the assigned amount of a Party, resulting from forest management under Article 3.4 after the application of the Article 3.3 debit compensation described in subparagraph (b) above, and resulting from forest management undertaken under Article 6, shall not exceed the value inscribed in Appendix Z to this decision.

7. That the eligibility of LULUCF activities under Article 12 [addressing the Clean Development Mechanism] is limited to afforestation and reforestation."

Since the UNFCCC in Article 4(1)(d) expressly obliges States Parties to "promote and cooperate in the conservation and enhancement, as appropriate, of sinks and reservoirs of all greenhouse gases * * * including * * * forests * * *," it is evident that much of the COP's work on forests remains to be addressed.

The COP has worked to advance other aspects of the Climate regime. In working toward agreeing on the content of what was to become the Kyoto Protocol, at COP-7 in Marrakesh the Parties adopted a compliance procedure. The Compliance Committee has two branch: a "Facilitative branch" to give advice and encouragement in implementing the Kyoto Protocol and an "Enforcement Branch" to determine if the Annex I Parties have met their emission targets. Appeals from the enforcement procedure go to the COP/MOP. If an Annex I nations fails to meet its obligations, there are three consequences: 1) for everyone ton of emissions by which the target is not met, 1.3 tons can be deducted from its emission allocation for the subsequent compliance period; 2) a detailed plan must be prepared setting forth how the State will met its reduced the next compliance period; 3) the State Party is barred from selling any of its international emission trading allowances until it demonstrates it is in compliance.

As you study these excerpts from the UNFCCC, consider what actions a nation should undertake (a) nationally, in designing a national action plan for climate change mitigation and adaptation, in and for technology innovation and use how developed States should facilitate rapid diffusion of appropriate technologies and in the case of developing States how they should prepare to implement and apply such technologies; and (b) what specific further protocols and programs should be proposed to implement the international obligations of Article 4.

2. Text of the UNFCCC
31 I.L.M. 849 (1992)

The Parties to this Convention,

Acknowledging that change in the Earth's climate and its adverse effects are a common concern of humankind,* * *

Noting that the largest share of historical and current global emissions of greenhouse gases has originated in developed countries, that per capita emissions in developing countries are still relatively low and that the share of global emissions originating in developing countries will grow to meet their social and development needs, * * *

Have agreed as follows:

ARTICLE 1: DEFINITIONS

For the purposes of this Convention: * * *

5. "Emissions" means the release of greenhouse gases and/or their precursors into the atmosphere over a specified area and period of time.

6. "Greenhouse gases" means those gaseous constituents of the atmosphere, both natural and anthropogenic, that absorb and re-emit infrared radiation. * * *

7. "Reservoir" means a component or components of the climate system where a greenhouse gas or a precursor of a greenhouse gas is stored.

8. "Sink" means any process, activity or mechanism which removes a greenhouse gas, an aerosol or a precursor of a greenhouse gas from the atmosphere.

9. "Source" means any process or activity which releases a greenhouse gas, an aerosol or a precursor of a greenhouse gas into the atmosphere.

ARTICLE 2: OBJECTIVE

The ultimate objective of this Convention and any related legal instruments that the Conference of the Parties may adopt is to achieve, in accordance with the relevant provisions of the Convention, stabilization of greenhouse gas concentrations in the atmosphere at a level that would prevent dangerous anthropogenic interference with the climate system. Such a level should be achieved within a time frame sufficient to allow ecosystems to adapt naturally to climate change, to ensure that food production is not threatened and to enable economic development to proceed in a sustainable manner.

ARTICLE 3: PRINCIPLES

In their actions to achieve the objective of the convention and to implement its provisions, the Parties shall be guided, inter alia, by the following:

1. The Parties should protect the climate system for the benefit of present and future generations of humankind, on the basis of equity and in accordance with their common but differentiated responsibilities and respective capabilities. According, the developed country Parties should take the lead in combating climate change and the adverse effects thereof. * * *

2. The Parties should take precautionary measures to anticipate, prevent or minimize the causes of climate change and mitigate its adverse effects. Where there are threats of serious or irreversible damage, lack of full scientific certainty should not be used as a reason for postponing such measures, taking into account that policies and measures to deal with climate change should be cost-effective so as to ensure global benefits at the lowest possible cost. To achieve this, such policies and measures should take into account different socio-economic contexts, be comprehensive, cover all relevant sources, sinks and reservoirs of greenhouse gases and adaptation, and comprise all economic sectors. Efforts to address climate change may be carried out cooperatively by interested Parties. * * *

ARTICLE 4: COMMITMENTS

1. All Parties, taking into account their common but differentiated responsibilities and their specific national and regional development priorities, objectives and circumstances, shall:

(a) Develop, periodically update, publish and make available to the Conference of the Parties, in accordance with Article 12, national inventories of anthropogenic emissions by sources and removals by sinks of all greenhouse gases not controlled by the Montreal Protocol, using comparable methodologies to be agreed upon by the Conference of the Parties;

(b) Formulate, implement, publish and regularly update national and where appropriate, regional programmes containing measures to mitigate climate change by addressing anthropogenic emissions by sources and removals by sinks of all greenhouse gases not controlled by the Montreal Protocol, and measures to facilitate adequate adaptation to climate change;

(c) Promote and cooperate in the development, application and diffusion, including transfer, of technologies, practices that control, reduce or prevent anthropogenic emissions of greenhouse gases not controlled by the Montreal Protocol in all relevant sectors, including the energy, transport, industry, agriculture, forestry and waste management sectors;

(d) Promote sustainable management, and promote and cooperate in the conservation and enhancement, as appropriate, or sinks and reservoirs of all greenhouse gases not controlled by the Montreal Protocol, including biomass, forests and oceans as well as other terrestrial, coastal and marine ecosystems;

(e) Cooperate in preparing for adaptation to the impacts of climate change; develop and elaborate appropriate and integrated plans for coastal zone management, water resources and agriculture, and for the protection and rehabilitation of areas, particularly in Africa, affected by drought and desertification, as well as floods;

(f) Take climate change considerations into account, to the extent feasible, in their relevant social, economic and environmental policies and actions, and employ appropriate methods, for example impact assessments, formulated and determined nationally, with a view to minimizing adverse effects on the economy, on public health and on the quality of the environment, of projects or measures undertaken by them to mitigate or adapt to climat change;

(g) Promote and cooperate in scientific, technological, technical, socio-economic and other research, systematic observation and development of data archives related to the climate system and intended to further the understanding and to reduce or eliminate the remaining uncertainties regarding the causes, effects, magnitude and timing of climate change and the economic and social consequences of various response strategies;

(h) Promote and cooperate in the full, open and prompt exchange of relevant scientific, technological, technical, socio-economic and legal information related to the climate system and climate change, and to the economic and social consequences of various response strategies;

(i) Promote and cooperate in education, training and public awareness related to climate change and encourage the widest participation in this process, including that of non-governmental organizations; and

(j) Communicate to the Conference of the Parties information related to implementation, in accordance with Article 12.

2.   The developed country Parties and other Parties included in annex I commit themselves specifically as provided for in the following:

(a) Each of these Parties shall adopt national policies and take corresponding measures on the mitigation of climate change, by limiting its anthropogenic emissions of greenhouse gases and protecting and enhancing its greenhouse gas sinks and reservoirs. These policies and measures will demonstrate that developed countries are taking the lead in modifying longer-term trends in anthropogenic emissions consistent with the objective of the convention, recognizing that the return by the end of the present decade to earlier levels of anthropogenic emissions of carbon dioxide and other greenhouse gases not controlled by the Montreal Protocol would contribute to such modification, and taking into account the differences in these Parties' starting points and approaches, economic structure and resource bases, the need to maintain strong and sustainable economic growth, available technologies and other individual circumstances, as well as the need for equitable and appropriate contributions by each of these Parties to the global effort regarding that objective. These Parties may implement such policies and measures jointly with other Parties and may assist other Parties in contributing to the achievement of the objective of the Convention and, in particular, that of this subparagraph;

(b) In order to promote progress to this end, each of these Parties shall communicate, within six months of the entry into force of the Convention for it and periodically thereafter, and in accordance with Article 12, detailed information on its resulting projected anthropogenic emissions by sources and removals by sinks of greenhouse gases not controlled by the Montreal Protocol for the period referred to in subparagraph 9a), with the aim of returning individually or jointly to their 1990 levels of these anthropogenic emissions of carbon dioxide and other greenhouse gases not controlled by the Montreal Protocol. This information will be reviewed by the Conference of the Parties, at its first session and periodically thereafter, in accordance with Article 7; * * *

(c) The Conference of the Parties shall, at its first session, review the adequacy of subparagraphs (a) and (b) above. Such review shall be carried out in the light of the best available scientific information and assessment on climate change and its impacts, as well as relevant technical, social and economic information. Based on this review, the Conference of the Parties shall take appropriate action, which may include the adoption of amendments to the commitments in subparagraphs (a) and (b) above. Such review shall be carried out in the light of the best available scientific information and assessment on climate change and its impacts, as well as relevant technical, social and economic information. Based on this review, the Conference of the Parties shall take appropriate action, which may include the adoption of amendments to the commitments in subparagraphs (a) and (b) above. The Conference of the Parties, at its first session, shall also take decisions regarding criteria for joint implementation as indicated in subparagraph (a) above. A second review of subparagraphs (a) and (b) shall take place not later than 31 December 1998, and thereafter at regular intervals determined by the Conference of the Parties, until the objective of the Convention is met; * * *

3.   The developed country Parties and other developed Parties included in Annex II shall provide new and additional financial resources to meet the agreed full costs incurred by developing country Parties in complying with their obligations under Article 12, paragraph 1. They shall also provide such financial resources, including for the transfer of technology, needed by the developing country Parties to meet the agreed full incremental costs of implementing measures that are covered by paragraph 1 of this Article and that are agreed between a developing country Party and the international entity or entities referred to in Article 11, in accordance with that Article. The implementation of these commitments shall take into account the need for adequacy and predictability in the flow of funds and the importance of appropriate burden sharing among the developed country Parties.

4.   The developed country Parties and other developed Parties included in annex II shall also assist the developing country Parties that are particularly vulnerable to the adverse effects of climate change in meeting costs of adaptation those adverse effects.

5.   The developed country Parties and other developed Parties included in annex II shall take all practicable steps to promote, facilitate and finance, as appropriate, the transfer of, or access to environmentally sound technologies and know-how to other Parties, particularly developing country Parties, to enable them to implement the provisions of the Convention. In this process, the developed country parties shall support the development and enhancement of endogenous capacities and technologies of developing country parties. Other Parties and organizations in a position to do so may also assist in facilitating the transfer of such technologies.

6.   In the implementation of their commitments under paragraph 2 above, a certain degree of flexibility shall be allowed by the Conference of the Parties of the Parties included in annex I undergoing the process of transition to a market economy, in order to enhance the ability of these Parties to address climate change, including with regard to the historical level of anthropogenic emissions of greenhouse gases not controlled by the Montreal Protocol chosen as a reference.

7.   The extent to which developing country Parties will effectively implement their commitments under the Convention will depend on the effective implementation by developed country Parties of their commitments under the Convention related to financial resources and transfer of technology and will take fully into account that economic and social development and poverty eradication are the first and overriding priorities of the developing country Parties. * * *

3. Introduction to the Kyoto Protocol

Enormous political attention has been given to the Kyoto Protocol, because of the "flip/flop" between the Clinton-Gore and Bush-Cheney Presidencies in the USA. The reluctance of the USA to engage in serious negotiations retarded all collaborative activity under the UNFCCC. Ultimately, the lack of implementation for much of the Kyoto Protocol's provisions, and the fact that the Kyoto Protocol was to end on 2012, militated in favor of a new approach. The European Union, in concert with many developing nations, proposed a tight two-year negotiating time-table to supplant the stalemate of the Kyoto Protocol and launch a new round of negotiations in 2007-2009 designed to attain a new agreement in December 2009 when the COP/MOP meets in Copenhagen, Denmark.

Since the Kyoto Protocol remains in force, and has been ratified by a large number of States, one of the key open questions for on-going negotiations is how to build an international regime on climate change mitigation and adaptation that will mesh the obligations set forth in the Kyoto Protocol, or how to agree to change the Kyoto Protocol.

Many provisions of the Kyoto Protocol are distinct from the provisions on targets and timetables, and have not been the focus of objections by the USA or others. Thus much of the agreed institutional framework in the Protocol may be continued in force after 2012.

The Kyoto Protocol in Article 17 obliges the States Parties to define the rules and procedures for emission trading, including "in particular for verification, reporting and accountability." Trading is intended to be supplemental to national domestic actions by which States meet their emission reduction allocations. Given the lack of transparency and the speculative trading by banks and financial institutions in collateralized debt obligations that triggered the 2007 global Recession, there is much that the UNFCCC and Kyoto Protocol Parties must do to ensure that an emission trading system is effective and follows the rule of law, both within nations and transnationally. See N. Robinson, Hedging Against Wider Collapse: Lessons From the Melt Downs, in Dekeletere, Lye, et al., eds., Critical Issues in Environmental Taxation (2009).

Three Kyoto Protocol provisions that provide for flexibility in meeting GHG reduction targets may need to be refined and extended before that can be more widely put into practice. (1) Some provisions, such as "Joint Implementation" under Article 6 and the emission trading contemplated in Article 17 of the Kyoto Protocol, involve the sale of "emission reduction units" ("ERUs") from an Annex I Party or a private enterprise to another Annex I Party, or another private entity. Specific projects or activities give rise to the ERUs. Much remains to be done to provide integrity and accountability to ensure that JI does reduce in fact GHG emissions. (2) The provision for "Bubbles" allow two or more State Parties to combine their reduction obligations by creating a bubble by which the Parties achieve a joint fulfillment of their Article 4 obligations for the cluster of Parties; thus when one Party is very successful and another much less so, their combined performance in attaining emission reductions can be combined to the target and timetable. (3) Another provision, that for the Clean Development Mechanism under Article 12 of the Kyoto Protocol allows for certifying emission reductions ("CERs") from a project activity in developing countries to be used by a developed Annex I country, or its private entities, to meet their targets and timetables. One problem with CDM is "leakage," a phenomenon when reducing or sequestering GHG emissions in one Party shifts the emission activity to another Party. Each of these three practices is pioneering and limited in scope and scale. Practice under each of these three approaches has been criticized as flawed, and much practical work is needed to make the systems reliable, transparent, efficient and effective. The World Bank has developed a Prototype Carbon Fund since 1999 to demonstrate that JI and CDM can function efficiently. It remains to be seen how to ramp up small scale activity into a global, worldwide activity.

More contentious issues in the reconsideration of the Kyoto Protocol inevitably focus on modifying the targets and timetables, and the events that meeting or avoiding them may in turn trigger, and providing additional funding for developing nations to design and implement climate change mitigation and adaptation programs, and to ensure rapid transfer of appropriate technology. Some of these issues were evident as soon as the Kyoto Protocol was agreed. C. Breidenrich, et al., The Kyoto Protocol to the UN Framework Convention on Climate Change, 92 Am. J. Int'l L. 315 (1998).

In studying these excerpts from the Kyoto Protocol, consider how a nation would establish a national implementation action plan to accord with the Protocol. What could the COP/MOP for the UNFCCC and the Kyoto Protocol do to facilitate use of the provisions within different nations?

4. Text of the Kyoto Protocol to the UNFCCC
37 I.L.M. 32 (1997)

Article 2

1.   Each Party included in Annex I in achieving its quantified emission limitation and reduction commitments under Article 3, in order to promote sustainable development, shall:

(a) Implement and/or further elaborate policies and measures in accordance with its national circumstances, such as:

(i)   Enhancement of energy efficiency in relevant sectors of the national economy;

(ii)   Protection and enhancement of sinks and reservoirs of greenhouse gases not controlled by the Montreal Protocol, taking into account its commitments under relevant international environmental agreements; promotion of sustainable forest management practices, afforestation and reforestation;

(iii)   Promotion of sustainable forms of agriculture in light of climate change considerations;

(iv)   Promotion, research development and increased use of new and renewable forms of energy, of carbon dioxide sequestration technologies and of advanced and innovative environmentally sound technologies;

(v)   Progressive reduction or phasing out of market imperfections, fiscal incentives, tax and duty exemptions and subsidies in all greenhouse gas emitting sectors that run counter to the objective of the Convention and application of market instruments

(vi)   Encouragement of appropriate reforms in relevant sectors aimed at promoting policies and measures which limit or reduce emissions of greenhouse gases not controlled by the Montreal Protocol;

(vii)   Measures to limit and/or reduce emissions of greenhouse gases not controlled by the Montreal Protocol in the transport sector;

(viii)   Limitation and/or reduction of methane through recovery and use in waste management, as well as in the production, transport and distribution of energy;

(b) Cooperate with other such Parties to enhance the individual and combined effectiveness of their policies and measures adopted under this Article, pursuant to Article 4, paragraph 2(e)(i), of the Convention. To this end, these Parties shall take steps to share their experience and exchange information on such policies and measures, including developing ways of improving their comparability, transparency and effectiveness. * * *

Article 3

1.   The Parties included in Annex I shall, individually or jointly, ensure that their aggregate anthropogenic carbon dioxide equivalent emissions of the greenhouse gases listed in Annex A do not exceed their assigned amounts, calculated pursuant to their quantified emission limitation and reduction commitments inscribed in Annex B and in accordance with the provisions of this Article, with a view to reducing their overall emissions of such gases by at least 5 per cent below 1990 levels in the commitment period 2008 to 2012.

2. Each Party included in Annex I shall, by 2005, have made demonstrable progress in achieving its commitments under this Protocol. * * *

Article 12

1.   A clean development mechanism is hereby defined.

2.   The purpose of the clean development mechanism shall be to assist Parties not included in Annex I in achieving sustainable development and in contributing to the ultimate objective of the Convention, and to assist Parties included in Annex I in achieving compliance with their quantified emission limitation and reduction commitments under Article 3.

3.   Under the clean development mechanism:

(a)   Parties not included in Annex I will benefit from project activities resulting in certified emission reductions; and

(b)   Parties included in Annex I may use the certified emission reductions accruing from such project activities to contribute to compliance with part of their quantified emission limitation and reduction commitments under Article 3, as determined by the Conference of the Parties serving as the meeting of the Parties to this Protocol.

4.   The clean development mechanism shall be subject to the authority and guidance of the Conference of the Parties serving as the meeting of the Parties to this Protocol and be supervised by an executive board of the clean development mechanism.

5.   Emission reductions resulting from each project activity shall be certified by operational entities to be designated by the Conference of the Parties serving as the meeting of the Parties to this Protocol, on the basis of:

(a)   Voluntary participation approved by each Party involved;

(b)   Real, measurable, and long-term benefits related to the mitigation of climate change; and

(c) Reductions in emissions that are additional to any that would occur in the absence of the certified project activity.

6.   The clean development mechanism shall assist in arranging funding of certified project activities as necessary. * * *

8.   The Conference of the Parties serving as the meeting of the Parties to this Protocol shall ensure that a share of the proceeds from certified project activities is used to cover administrative expenses as well as to assist developing country Parties that are particularly vulnerable to the adverse effects of climate change to meet the costs of adaptation.

9.   Participation under the clean development mechanism, including in activities mentioned in paragraph 3(a) above and acquisition of certified emission reductions, may involve private and/or public entities, and is to be subject to whatever guidance may be provided by the executive board of the clean development mechanism.

10.   Certified emission reductions obtained during the period from the year 2000 up to the beginning of the first commitment period can be used to assist in achieving compliance in the first commitment period. * * *

Article 17

The Conference of the Parties shall define the relevant principles, modalities, rules and guidelines, in particular for verification, reporting and accountability for emissions trading. The Parties included in Annex B may participate in emissions trading for the purposes of fulfilling their commitments under Article 3 of this Protocol. Any such trading shall be supplemental to domestic actions.

MEASURING THE CLEAN DEVELOPMENT MECHANISM'S PERFORMANCE AND POTENTIAL
Michael Wara
55 UCLA L. Rev. 1759 (2008)

The Clean Development Mechanism (CDM), a market-based emissions trading mechanism created under the auspices of the Protocol, certifies GHG emission-reduction credits generated by projects in the developing world that can be sold to emitting developed countries facing compliance obligations under the treaty. Payment for the credit is intended to fund the cost of reducing GHG emissions, thereby facilitating developing-country participation in the international climate regime and assisting in the achievement of sustainable development. All emissions reductions certified under the CDM are supposed to be voluntary, real, and additional to any that would occur in the absence of the credit system. * * *

The CDM was designed around the insight that the marginal cost of emissions reductions in developing, and especially rapidly developing, countries would be less than those faced by developed nations. The basis for this insight was that the cost of building more efficient, lower-GHG-emitting industrial and energy facilities in the developing world would be far lower than the cost of prematurely retiring or retrofitting existing developed-world capital stock. By means of the CDM, GHG emissions reductions could occur in the developing world that would otherwise have occurred in the developed world at far higher cost. The expectation was that by putting a price on GHG emissions in the developing world and by linking that price to developed-world cap-and-trade markets for CO_2, costs of compliance with the Protocol in the developed world could be significantly reduced. * * *

The CDM in its current form is, from an environmental perspective, highly imperfect. It is nonetheless creating both powerful political institutions and stakeholders interested in maintaining the current system or something similar. * * * The CDM is failing as a market because its rules, rather than producing real reductions, have accounting loopholes that allow participants to manufacture GHG credits at little or no cost beyond the payment of consultants necessary to surmount the necessary regulatory hurdles. Further, although it is supplying credits to developed signatories of the Protocol at prices less than they would otherwise be, the CDM is an excessive subsidy that represents a massive waste of developed-world resources. It is too late to change the structure of the CDM to address its shortcomings prior to the end of the first commitment period. * * * [A]fter 2012, both the financial resources devoted to the current CDM architecture and the additional resources likely to be added as developed-world commitments to cut GHGs deepen, might be far more efficaciously allocated in the international effort to stem global warming. * * *

B. Clean Development Mechanism

1. Structure of the CDM

The CDM is a market-based approach to the problem of global warming. It allows buyers, who may be Annex B parties or firms within Annex B nations, to purchase credits from emission reduction projects carried out in non-Annex B nations. The CDM builds on experience derived from various regional markets for atmospheric pollutants, most notably the United States' experience with emissions trading under the Clean Air Act. The developing country (non-Annex B) firms that are sellers of Certified Emission Reductions (CERs), the currency of the CDM system, have no limit to the mass of GHGs that they may emit under the Protocol. This absence of a cap on emissions for designated parties necessitates a far more complex design than had been attempted for most previous pollution markets. Adding further complexity to the program is the fact that the CDM is the first atmospheric pollutant trading program that covers multiple gases and allows conversion between them through the medium of its common currency, CERs.

Further, the CDM is a project-based system. It accomplishes its objectives at the microlevel of individual emission reduction projects that are each validated by designated third party verifiers and then registered by the mechanism's governing body, the CDM Executive Board (CDM EB), as eligible for crediting. Each project wishing to participate in the CDM must prepare a Project Design Document (PDD) that explains in detail how its future emissions reductions will be voluntary, real, additional, and will not induce leakage. It must also either utilize a previously approved monitoring methodology that explains in detail how it will monitor emissions reductions made by the project or propose a new methodology. Voluntary emissions reductions are not compelled by national or provincial law or regulation. Real emissions reductions are monitored with sufficient care to ensure that they actually occur. Additional emissions reductions are those that are in addition to any that would have occurred absent the CDM subsidy. Leakage of emissions occurs when emissions reductions that would have occurred from a CDM project absent the CDM subsidy are displaced to another location because of the subsidy.

All four of these concepts require that a hypothetical baseline of emissions be defined for each project, and in the case of leakage, the world outside the project. This baseline represents the timeline of emissions that would have occurred absent the subsidy provided by the CDM (and thus absent the emission reduction project). It is an attempt to estimate the counterfactual of typical levels of emissions in a world without CDM. The CDM project baseline is described in terms that vary by project type. Nevertheless, several common variables can be seen in most PDDs. Project proponents often describe the regulatory baseline, that is, the emissions permitted by local law and regulation. They also often describe the financial baseline, which is the lack of an adequate return on investment without the benefit of the CDM subsidy. They often describe typical technologies applied by the type of project in the PDD and how the CDM-subsidized project exceeds these local standards. Finally, they sometimes must describe a sectoral or national baseline for installations of the project type. Ultimately, the CDM project proponents must quantify, third party verifiers must check, and the CDM EB must certify the hypothetical emissions that would have occurred in the future without the CDM project subsidy.

Project proponents and environmental regulators do not live in a world without CDM. As will be shown below, they have acted strategically in order to maximize many projects' baselines and so maximize the potential for the generation of CER revenues. The fact that most industries involved in CDM projects are already highly regulated makes this strategy attractive and easy to implement. An environmental regulator faced with the choice of preventing an emission with a costly domestic regulation or by means of the CDM will have obvious political incentives for selecting the international program over new domestic regulation.

The end product of the CDM process is the issuance by the CDM EB of an emission offset to the project participants. This offset can then be sold to an Annex B nation or a party within one that has obligations under the Protocol. The offset, called a certified emission reduction or CER, assuming that certain CDM facilities are established, may be used by Annex B countries in lieu of emissions reductions within their territories in order to meet their targets under the Protocol. Private parties that are assigned emissions allowances by their governments may also purchase CERs and use them as permits to emit in excess of their assigned allocations, or as an alternative to purchasing allocations from other participants in their domestic market. * * *

2. Goals of the CDM

The CDM was created for three reasons. First, it aims to accomplish the overarching goals of the Framework Convention. Second, it aims to encourage sustainable development in non-Annex B nations. Third, the CDM is intended to reduce the cost of compliance with the Protocol for Annex B nations. * * *

The CDM is intended, according to the Protocol, to help in accomplishing the Convention's goal of "prevent[ing] dangerous interference" with the climate system. It aims to do this by assisting developing countries to reduce their emissions of GHGs. * * * [B]y providing non-Annex B nations with financial incentives for low-carbon intensity development, they might be nudged, however slightly, onto more climate-friendly trajectories.

The second CDM objective--sustainable development--is left largely undefined by the Protocol or the implementing directives of later conferences of the parties. To the extent that the provision has teeth, it is given them by the requirement under the CDM that the host country DNA of a project must certify that the project meets the DNA's standards of sustainability. * * *

The third CDM goal--lowering the cost of compliance for Annex B parties--was thought possible for two reasons. First, the majority of new energy capacity to be built up during the First Compliance Period will be located in the developing world where rates of economic growth are highest and energy infrastructure is least developed. Also, the relative cost of prematurely retiring high-carbon-emission intensity power plants is significantly higher than building new low- or zero-carbon emission energy capacity. Thus, if the CDM could be used to subsidize the substitution of new, clean power capacity in the developing world for the premature retirement of old, dirty power capacity in the developed world, it could substantially lower the cost of treaty compliance. * * * However, * * * a substantial proportion of the emissions reductions generated by the CDM are not of this type and are in reality extremely inefficient in terms of the cost of the subsidy compared to the cost of environmental benefits obtained. * * * [I]t is increasingly difficult to tell which

CDM projects are producing emissions reductions additional to those that would have occurred in the baseline, and which are claiming credit for non-additional, anyway credits.

II. Rapid Development of the Clean Development Mechanism Since 2004

The CDM project pipeline began operation in December of 2003, when the first project was accepted for public comment and validation. In November of 2004, the first project was registered by the CDM EB. Finally, in October 2005, the first CERs were issued to a project participant's account. Since then, there has been extremely rapid growth in the number, type, and total volume of emissions reductions in the CDM pipeline. * * *

From the last quarter of 2005 to the present, the potential CDM supply has grown at a breakneck pace. By January 1, 2008, more than 1150 million tons (Mt) CO_2 equivalent (CO_2e) had been registered for delivery via the CDM by the end of the first compliance period. Another pattern emerging from the project registrations that have occurred is the dominance of large projects in the CDM. * * * [A] small number of very large projects dominate the supply of CERs from registered projects. In fact, the 45 largest projects (5 percent of the total number) represent 64 percent of the total supply to the end of the First Commitment Period. * * *

As of this writing, there are more than 2800 projects in the CDM pipeline that will eventually, if all are registered and deliver reductions as promised in their PDDs, supply more than 2600 Mt CO_2e to the market for Protocol compliance instruments. This amount represents approximately 2.8 percent of Annex B 1990 GHG emissions for each year of the First Commitment Period. * * *

III. Current Supply of CERs in the CDM Pipeline by Project Type

The original intent of the CDM was to spur development of low-carbon energy infrastructure in the developing world both through achievement of sustainable development goals and substitution for early retirement of expensive, high-carbon energy infrastructure in the developed world. It comes as a surprise, then, to find then that the CDM pipeline bears only a partial relationship to this vision. Instead, the subsidy provided by purchase of CERs to date will largely ensure that high GWP industrial gases such as trifluoromethane (HFC-23) and N_2O as well as CH_4 emitted by landfills and confined-animal-feeding operations (CAFOs) in non-Annex B nations are captured and destroyed. The very large projects dominating the supply of CERs are confined primarily to two relatively obscure industries--adipic acid and chlorodifluoromethane (HCFC-22) production. Adipic acid is the feedstock for the production of nylon-66 and releases abundant N_2O as a production by-product. HCFC-22 has two major applications. It is one of two major refrigerants that was phased in to replace the CFC's under the auspices of the Montreal Protocol to Protect on Substances that Deplete the Ozone Layer. HCFC-22 is also the primary feedstock in the production of PTFE, more commonly known by its Dupont brand name, Teflon. HCFC-22 production inevitably produces HFC-23 as an unwanted byproduct. These two relatively small industries represent nearly 55 percent of the supply of issued CERs in the CDM to date.

Contrary to ex-ante predictions, CO_2-based projects, including renewable energy, fuel switching from coal to gas, demand side energy efficiency, waste heat capture, and cement process modification account for less than half of the CER supply to 2012. Renewable energy projects alone account for 28 percent. Nineteen HFC-23 capture projects at HCFC-22 production facilities and three projects that capture the N_2O made as a byproduct of adipic acid or nitric acid production account for the third of the pipeline composed of high GWP industrial gas reduction projects. Finally, CH_4-capture and flaring projects, mostly located at large landfills, coal mines, and CAFOs, account for another 19 percent. Moreover, because the HFC-23, N_2O, and to a lesser extent, CH_4, projects are typically of larger size than the renewable energy projects, they are more likely to overcome the transaction costs associated with registration and production of CERs than the smaller * * * projects that compose the CDM's renewable portfolio. * * *

Contrary to theory and expectation, the CDM market is not a subsidy implemented by means of a market mechanism by which CO_2 reductions that would have taken place in the developed world take place in the developing world. Rather, most CDM funds are paying for the substitution of CO_2 reductions in the developed world for emissions reductions in the developing world of industrial gases and methane. Indeed, the industrial gas emissions that account for one third of CDM reductions do not even occur in the developed world, not because of an absence of adipic acid or HCFC-22 manufacture, but because Annex B industries, after recognizing the threat posed by these emissions and the low cost of abating them, have opted to voluntarily capture and destroy them.

While renewable energy projects do make up 1600 out of 2647 (60 percent) projects in the CDM project pipeline, they account for only 28 percent of the emissions reductions produced. It is important to note that a significant proportion of the CERs generated by biomass power projects are from the CH_4 emissions that are avoided because biomass is burned rather than allowed to biodegrade. Much of the publicity surrounding the CDM has emphasized the number of renewable energy projects sponsored by the CDM while neglecting the relative volume of emissions, hence CERs produced and the relative scale of subsidy provided to various sectors. This emphasis provides a false picture of the true subsidy flows being generated by the international market for carbon. * * *

IV. Strategic Manipulation of Baselines: The Case of HFC-23 Abatement Projects in the CDM

A. HFC-23 is a High GWP By product of HCFC-22 Manufacture

Our first story concerns both the strategic behavior on the part of proponents of HFC-23 capture projects, an important class of large projects within the CDM, and the responses of the CDM EB to these attempts to inflate credit issuance. These emission reduction projects are an important component of the emissions market's initial rapid growth. There are nineteen HFC-23 capture projects currently participating in the CDM. These projects consist of the capture and destruction of HFC-23 produced as a byproduct of HCFC-22 manufacture. The primary use of HCFC-22 is as a refrigerant, although its use as a feedstock for fluoroplastics such as PTFE is also significant and growing. For every 100 tons of HCFC-22 produced, between 1.5 and 4 tons of HFC-23 are produced. This group of emission reduction projects have played an important role in shaping the early CDM emissions market and, because of their substantial market share, in determining its environmental performance.

An understanding of the incentives faced by creators of HFC-23 abatement projects must begin with an understanding of the atmospheric chemistry of HFC-23, because this chemistry lies at the heart of what makes them successful CDM projects. HFC-23 is an extremely potent and long-lived greenhouse gas. Its one-hundred-year GWP is 11,700. As a consequence of this high GWP and the rules of the CDM, which convert the other six Protocol gases to CO_2e and hence CERs using their GWPs, 1 ton of HFC-23 abated is considered equivalent to 11700 tons of CO_2. In other words, for every kilogram of HCFC-22 produced, between 15 and 30 g of HFC-23 is produced, and potentially captured and destroyed. This 15 to 30 g of HFC-23 is equivalent to 175 to 350 kg of CO_2, or 0.175 to 0.350 CERs.

Although approximately half of HCFC-22 production occurs in the developed world, there are essentially no byproduct emissions of HFC-23 there because major producers have voluntarily adopted measures to capture and destroy it. Participation in voluntary abatement programs was substantial but not universal by 2005. The situation in the developing world was, prior to CDM, quite different. There, HCFC-22 manufacturers vented all HFC-23 produced to the atmosphere. One market analyst predicts that global HCFC-22 production will grow by 6 to 7 percent per year until 2020 and by 16 percent per year in the developing world. Thus, reducing non-Annex B emissions of HFC-23 should be a goal of any treaty aimed at curbing GHG emissions.

Non-Annex B manufacturers of HCFC-22 have, to a remarkable extent, become participants in the CDM. Developing world production of HCFC-22 in 2005 was approximately 237,000 metric tons. Assuming a 3 percent

HFC-23 production rate, which has been fairly typical for the 19 HCFC-22 plants participating in the CDM, this equates to a production of 83 million CERs per year. Taken together, the PDDs of the nineteen HCFC-22 plants estimate that they will produce 81.8 million CERs per year. Using these estimates, it would appear that essentially all developing world HCFC-22 production, as of 2005, is currently participating in the CDM. This is a remarkable achievement for the CDM and begs the question of how a financial mechanism was able to achieve near total market penetration in an industry so quickly. An examination of the economics of HCFC-22 abatement and HFC-23 capture explains that the reasons may have as much to do with the perverse incentives created by the carbon market as with an ability to identify low cost emissions reduction opportunities.

B. The Perverse Incentives of HFC-23 Abatement as a CDM Project

The economics of HFC-23 projects create incentives for strategic behavior that, if left unchecked, would undermine the environmental efficacy of the CDM. Consider the 1 kg of HCFC-22 produced by a CDM project that the calculation above showed to be equivalent to 0.35 t CO_2 or 0.35 CERs. At * * * market prices of €10/CER, the production of 1 kg of HCFC-22 will produce a subsidy of €3.51. The cost of HFC-23 abatement is estimated to be on the order of €0.09/kg HCFC-22. Thus, the net from subsidy minus abatement costs to an HCFC-22 producer is approximately €3.41/kg HCFC-22. This subsidy compares quite favorably with the wholesale price for HCFC-22, which as of the fourth quarter of 2005 was approximately €1.60/kg. A developing world producer of HCFC-22 can earn more than twice as much from its CDM subsidy as it can gross from the sale of its primary product. Even when CER prices were only half of their current value, HCFC-22 manufacturers found these calculations to be a compelling incentive to enter the CDM process. Given these incentives, it is perhaps not a tremendous surprise that participation in the CDM by the non-Annex B based HCFC-22 industry is nearly universal.

The perverse incentives created by the economics of HFC-23 capture CDM projects were, from a very early stage, a point of controversy. The CDM methodology, without which HFC-23 projects could not advance to registration, went through several rounds of revision because of fears that HCFC-22 manufacturers would produce gas simply to generate CERs, thereby diluting the CDM's currency, at least in terms of its environmental effectiveness. Recall that a key requirement of CERs is that they be "additional to any that would have occurred in the absence of the project activity." The economics of HFC-23 projects are a reductio ad absurdum of this requirement. It is quite likely that no capture of HFC-23 would occur without the CDM. On the other hand, with the CDM, HCFC-22 factories have very strong incentives to create extra HFC-23 specifically to capture and destroy it. Indeed, merely by capturing what they would have made anyway, a manufacturer can triple revenues and, based on the cost estimates presented above, more than triple profits.

C. Imperfect Regulatory Compromise for HFC-23 Plants in the CDM

To deal with the perverse incentives to overproduce HCFC-22 in order to capture and destroy HFC-23, the CDM EB decided to approve only those projects involving previously existing HCFC-22 production capacity. New plants or added capacity are not currently allowed into the CDM. * * *

Even with these relatively restrictive rules on eligibility, there is circumstantial evidence and very good reason to suspect that HCFC-22 manufacturers participating in the CDM have behaved strategically to direct a greater share of the subsidy to themselves by artificially inflating their base-year production in two ways. First, the fraction of HFC-23 produced by the production of HCFC-22 can be reduced by modification of the conditions under which chemical synthesis occurs. Dupont has consistently produced, in its United States HCFC-22 plant, HFC-23 byproduct percentages as low as 1.3 percent. Developing-country manufacturers have not been able to achieve such rates of HFC-23 production, with reported rates between 2 and 4 percent. The economics of HCFC-22 production in the absence of a CDM subsidy dictate that HFC-23 production should be minimized because it is a waste product costing both energy and materials. For this reason, almost all plants have historically monitored their HFC-23/HCFC-22 ratio in order to optimize productivity of HCFC-22.

Dupont argued in comments presented to the CDM EB that the crediting methodology for HFC-23 projects should be limited to crediting global best practice--the Dupont value. CDM project proponents responded that their plants lacked necessary capacity and could not be expected to perform with the same efficiency as those in the developed world. Presented with these conflicting arguments, the CDM EB forged a crude compromise. The CDM methodology eventually approved for HFC-23 abatement set 3 percent as the maximum percentage of HFC-23 byproduct allowable in the baseline data of a participating plant, a rough average of reported developing world values. The average of all reported baseline data from the nineteen participating plants is 2.99 percent--very close to the maximum allowable value. * * * Furthermore, the presence of the CDM and the prospect that crediting may ultimately be allowed for new plants removes any incentive to improve capital stock or process at existing plants, or to invest extra capital in state of the art facilities. Rather, it encourages construction of inefficient plants in order to create a high baseline and maximize potential for future CDM revenues.

Second, at least some of the HCFC-22 plants participating in the CDM appear to have ramped up production during the baseline period (2000-2004) far beyond expected growth in the sector (15 percent per annum). * * * Most plants exceeded the growth rates predicted for the developing-world industry as a whole. The increases in HCFC-22 production among the developing-world manufacturers led to a CDM participant production growth rate of 50 percent rather than 33 percent, as had been predicted ex-ante by market analysts. Whether these plants increased production because of demand for HCFC-22 or in anticipation of higher CER revenue is impossible to say given existing publicly available information. Nevertheless, circumstantial evidence suggests that, rather than building new plants, HCFC-22 manufacturers elected to add capacity at existing plants during the CDM baseline period in order to take advantage of the CDM subsidy.

In response to the windfall profits enjoyed by their domestic HCFC-22 producers as a result of the CDM, China has imposed a 65 percent tax on CER revenue generated by HFC-23 projects. Revenues from this fund, currently in excess of $2 billion, are to be devoted to sustainable development, although none have yet been dispersed. In this way, as had been predicted by the critics of the CDM's baseline concept, Chinese environmental regulators, rather than create regulations that would eliminate a CDM project's eligibility, have acted to extract a substantial portion of the subsidy-derived rent. This tax reduces the CERs income to only 60 percent of that derived from the sale of HCFC-22. However, at prices greater than €15, even with a 65 percent tax, it will again make sense to produce gas solely for CER revenue.

The CDM provides perverse economic incentives to HCFC-22 producers that have led to a large fraction of the CER supply being produced by HFC-23 abatement. Even if some fraction of these reductions are voluntary, real, and additional, they still may not be the best use of Annex B resources for addressing non-Annex B GHG emissions. To abate all developing-world HFC-23 emissions would cost approximately $31 million per year. Instead, by means of a CDM subsidy, the Annex B nations will likely pay between €250 and €750 million to abate 2005 non-Annex B HFC-23 emissions. This is a remarkably inefficient path to an environmental goal. * * *

The case of HFC-23 capture projects, which currently account for nearly 22 percent of the CERs expected for delivery by 2012, illustrates both the success and some fairly significant problems with the CDM market. On one hand, the CDM was successful in identifying a class of emitters with very low marginal abatement costs and inducing near total sectoral abatement. On the other hand, it appears quite likely that the sector is also gaming the system by modifying its behavior in order to generate extra credits that can then be sold to developed countries with compliance obligations. Because of the inherent information asymmetries, the regulator has had a very difficult time, and indeed has not genuinely tried, dealing with these problems. It is not clear under the current system how it could. At the same time, because of the limitation on eligibility for old plants, the problems associated with

HFC-23 for the CDM are to some extent limited. It is worth noting, however, that what saves the CDM from being awash in CDM credits does not help the environment. Recent press reports indicate incredibly high rates of growth in the HCFC-22 market, including the construction of new plants. Until these plants are included in the CDM or some other climate regime, they will emit their HFC-23 byproducts into the atmosphere. * * *

VI. Reform of the Post-2012 Regime

The parties to both the Kyoto Protocol and the UNFCCC are now considering what to do to accomplish the goal of the UNFCCC after the first compliance period ends in 2012. Global carbon trading is likely to play a role in any future architecture. At the same time, the U.S. Senate is considering proposals for an economy-wide cap-and-trade program for GHGs that would allow extensive utilization of international carbon credits. Thus, consideration of how to improve the performance of the CDM is critical from both a domestic and an international perspective.

This description of the current and likely future state of the CDM is meant to point out that, before we assume that expansion of the current offset trading market is the appropriate route for engaging with developing countries, it is worth looking at the empirical evidence from the trading program as it exists now. That evidence, as detailed in the two examples above, suggests that the CDM is leading to widespread strategic behavior. In the case of the HFC-23 projects, the incentives created by the CDM are leading to undesirable behavior in the name of claiming credit. HFC-23 projects appear to be creating extra GHGs in order to claim credit for their capture and destruction even as they do capture and destroy some emissions that would have contributed to climate change. In the case of the CCGT projects, the incentives created by the CDM are likely leading to no change in behavior except for widespread claims for credits. Furthermore, procedures for project regulation likely limit the CDM EB from examining the issues most central to whether the projects are producing additional emissions reductions.

In addition, both cases present severe information challenges for the regulator. The rules of the game in the CDM systematically create incentives for project proponents to manipulate the transfer of information to the CDM EB while providing it with essentially no other information-gathering resources. In the case of HFC-23, the CDM creates strong incentives for project proponents to conceal the extent to which process efficiencies might lower their GHG production rate. In the case of the CCGTs, the system creates strong incentives for project proponents to misrepresent the motivations for their choice of power plant technology. Unlike in a natural market, buyers of CDM credits have no incentive to disclose information they have regarding projects. Their incentive, just like the generators of credits, is to facilitate the approval of projects and the issuance of credits. This informational problem is particularly acute because the CDM EB is called upon to make decisions requiring technical expertise across a wide array of both countries and industries.

Notes and Questions

1. In the above article Michael Wara finds that the evidence from CDM trading "suggests that the CDM is leading to widespread strategic behavior. In the case of HFC-23 projects, the incentives created by CDM are leading to undesirable behavior in the name of claiming credit. * * * In the case of CCGT[combined cycle gas turbines], the incentives are likely leading to no change in behavior except for widespread claims of credits. * * * In addition, both cases present severe information challenges for the regulator. The rules of the game in the CDM systematically create incentives for project proponents to manipulate the transfer of information to the CDM EB [Executive Board] while providing it essentially no other information-gathering resources."

2. Critiques of the Kyoto Protocol suggest that alternative approaches could address the emission reduction obligations of newly industrialized developing nations, such as China, Brazil, Mexico and South Africa, in ways to accommodate their socio-economic needs, while maintaining strong reduction obligations for the developed states and relieving the less developed states of obligations which would be hard to meet and contribute little to reducing GHG emission. The CDM projects are claimed by this middle group of States, and do not benefit the non-industrialized developing states. See A. Mumma and D. Hodas, Designing A Global Post-Kyoto Climate Change Protocol that Advances Human Development, 20 Geo. Int'l Envtl. L. Rev. 619 (2008).

3. China and the USA together account for about half of the GHG emissions that cause climate change. Each has begun considering establishing a national emission cap and trade regime. The EU, with Norway, Switzerland and Lichtenstein also participating, in 2003 established an emission trading system for carbon dioxide emission from energy sectors, ferrous metal production the mineral industry (cement, glass, ceramics, etc)., and the paper, pulp and board production. Each EU State also has a National Allocation Plan on how meet emission reduction targets. EU Directive 2003/87/EC.

Should the EU link its ETS to the trading system in another region, such as the USA or China, consistent with Article 17 of the Kyoto Protocol.? Should these major powers at the same time, or though the UNFCCC financial mechanisms, assist other nations to build their trading capacity to participate in the new markets, thereby expanding the cap and trade to a global market? How is this best done, by leading markets working together or by a fully multilateral approach under the UNFCCC and Kyoto Protocol?

4.   When President George W. Bush reversed a campaign pledge and decided not to support cooperating with the UNFCCC COP and the Kyoto Protocol MOP on the implementation of the emissions limitations in the Protocol, he frustrated the objective of the UNFCCC, which the USA had ratified, and of the Protocol, which the USA had negotiated in good faith and signed. He later "unsigned" the Convention on Biological Diversity, which the USA had negotiated in good faith and signed, but not ratified. These acts are inconsistent with the Vienna Convention on the Law of Treaties. Should the State Department review the legality of these actions, and renounce them in order to re-establish respect for the rule of law under the Vienna Convention on the Law of Treaties? Would such an action have substantive legal importance?

5.   Is the negotiation of a new post-Kyoto agreement under the Bali Action Plan practical? No significant agreement was reached at the COP in Poznan, Poland, and much more needs to be decided than can be in the few months that the Obama Administration had to negotiate with other nations before the December 2009 COP in Copenhagen, Denmark. How can 190 delegations arrive at a meaningful consensus? Most MEA COPs assign the negotiation of decisions or amendments to "contact groups," in which a small number of States represent the interest of all. The Protocol agreed to in Kyoto was achieved in the last two days of conference, before thousands of delegates and participants, under the glare of global media focus and with intense political pressure riding on the outcome. The Protocol did not reflect strong support in the capitals of the world's nations. The UNFCCC and Convention on Biological Diversity were negotiated by a relatively small number of nations and submitted to the 1992 Rio Earth Summit for signature. Should the UNFCCC COP consider dividing the tasks of preparing subsidiary agreements under Article 4 to small negotiating teams?

6.   As discussed in Chapters 4 and 6, many economists feel that the most efficient way to reduce dependency on fossil fuels is to adopt a tax, and let the economy shift to alternative energy systems. Should the elaboration of the UNFCCC in the future include an obligation to set a tax on the use of fossil fuels?

DESIGNING A GLOBAL POST-KYOTO CLIMATE CHANGE PROTOCOL THAT ADVANCES HUMAN DEVELOPMENT
Albert Mumma and David Hodas
20 Geo. Int'l Envtl. L. Rev. 619 (2008)

* * * Under the Kyoto Protocol, only Annex I countries assumed emission reduction obligations. Of particular significance is the fact that, as a corollary, only Annex I countries were assigned allowable GHG emissions under the Kyoto Protocol. In this lies the key design flaw of the Kyoto Protocol. * * *

III. THE OBLIGATION TO REDUCE GHG EMISSIONS

* * *

The obligation assumed by Annex I country parties is to ensure that their emissions "do not exceed their assigned amounts." The pillar on which the reduction commitment stands, therefore, is the assigned amounts. The aim which the Protocol seeks to achieve in limiting countries' GHG emissions is to reduce their overall emissions by at least 5 per cent below 1990 levels in the commitment period 2008 to 2012. Additionally the commitments assumed by countries in the commitment period 2008 to 2012 are but one step in achieving the ultimate objective of the UNFCCC, which is "the stabilization of greenhouse gas concentrations in the atmosphere at a level that would prevent dangerous anthropogenic interference with the climate system."

The question that must be answered is this: can the methodology of assigning certain countries—but not others—amounts of greenhouse gases combined with their commitment to not exceed the assigned amounts lead to the achievement of the ultimate objective of the UNFCCC? This article argues that it cannot.

The Kyoto Protocol obligations are premised on an allocation of emission entitlements to Annex I countries—developed countries but not to non-Annex I countries. African countries are all non-Annex I countries, along with a whole host of other non-industrialized and newly industrializing countries. A number of the present non-Annex I countries (such as China, India, Brazil, Mexico, Indonesia and South Africa) have sizeable economies and potentially will become large emitters in the near future, in several cases even outstripping the emissions by some countries appearing on the list of Annex I countries. In fact, China is now the world's largest CO_2 emitter, and if China achieves its goal of quadrupling its gross domestic product by 2020 following a business as usual path, its GHG emissions could double and drown the world's mitigation efforts.

The decision to not impose reduction obligations on countries with the capacity and potential to emit large quantities of GHG in the future means that, regardless of whether Annex I countries comply with their obligations, overall GHG emissions worldwide may continue to rise on account of the emissions from those potentially future large emitters who are presently not placed under reduction obligations. If this happens, the achievement of the ultimate objective of the UNFCCC would be defeated. This point has been cited by the United States in refusing to ratify the Kyoto Protocol.

Secondly, the Kyoto Protocol allows countries to take advantage of flexible mechanisms based on the market principle. But, to the extent that some countries are under an obligation to reduce emissions while others are not, the flexible mechanisms become incapable of achieving the ultimate objective of the UNFCC on account of serious leakage problems, i.e., the displacement of emissions where only project-based considerations are factored into the calculations of the emissions avoided or reduced as a result of a project undertaken in a non-Annex I country.

That the Kyoto Protocol, as presently designed, is incapable of facilitating the achievement of the ultimate objective of the UNFCCC is, in our view, beyond dispute. That having been said, understanding what led to its design is important in charting the strategy for the negotiations on a post-Kyoto protocol. If state parties are to be persuaded to depart form the Kyoto Protocol architecture in favor of another one, they—state parties—must appreciate the fallacy in the assumptions that dictated the adoption of the Kyoto Protocol architecture.

IV. THE PRINCIPLE OF COMMON BUT DIFFERENTIATED RESPONSIBILITIES

The design of the Kyoto Protocol reflects the generally held view that by excluding developing nations from any obligations, it was operationalizing the UNFCCC principle of "common but differentiated responsibilities." Most negotiators—perhaps with the exception of the U.S. negotiators—accepted as a matter of course that the principle of common but differentiated responsibilities meant that only industrialized countries would assume reduction obligations under the UNFCCC and subsequent protocols. The rationale appears to have been that GHG reduction obligations would undermine the economic development of non-Annex I countries, which would be unacceptable because it would undermine the global effort towards the eradication of poverty.

A. THE ROLE OF THE PRINCIPLE OF COMMON BUT DIFFERENTIATED RESPONSIBILITIES IN THE UNFCCC REGIME

The obligations of the UNFCCC are premised on the principle of common but differentiated responsibility. Article 3 (Principles) establishes the obligation that "Parties should protect the climate system for the benefit of present and future generations of humankind, on the basis of equity and in accordance with their common but differentiated responsibilities and respective capabilities." Article 4 (Commitments) subjects all of its requirements to the specific condition that "[a]ll Parties ... tak[e] into account their common but differentiated responsibilities."

The obligations of the Kyoto Protocol are similarly premised on the UNFCCC principle of common but differentiated responsibility. Kyoto Protocol Article 10, which imposes obligations on all Parties with respect to the formulation of GHG management programmes among other measures, qualifies these obligations on the basis of "common but differentiated responsibilities."

Equally significant are the provisions that stipulate that the consequence of the adoption of the principle of common but differentiated responsibility is that developed country parties must take the lead in tackling the global problem of climate change. This is premised on the "historical" responsibility of developed country parties for the present level of GHG emissions in the atmosphere as well as the sustainable development needs of the developing countries, which, it is argued, can only be met by increasing their "per capita" emissions of GHGs. Similarly, Article 4(1) of the UNFCCC, which stipulates the principles by which the Parties shall be guided (the first of which is the principle of common but differentiated responsibilities) argues that "accordingly, the developed country Parties should take the lead in combating climate change and the adverse effects thereof."

On the basis of the assumption that reduction commitments would only be imposed on developed country parties, and in keeping with the principle of common but differentiated responsibilities, the Kyoto Protocol does not impose any such obligations on non-Annex I Parties. Indeed, Article 10, which imposes obligations on "All Parties," is at pains to stress that these obligations are imposed "without introducing any new commitments for Parties not included in Annex I, but reaffirming existing commitments under Article 4, paragraph 1 of the Convention."

The developing country view would appear to be that the principle of common but differentiated responsibilities implies that developing countries must not assume emissions reduction commitments under even a post Kyoto climate change regime. This is shown by the following quote attributed to Yvo de Boer, the Executive Secretary of the UNFCCC Secretariat. Describing it as the "consensus of the international community," the quote goes on to state that:

> Developing countries ... have unshirkable responsibilities for climate change and should fulfill their major obligations. They should fully meet their emission reduction targets set by the Kyoto Protocol and continue to take the lead in cutting emissions after 2012, when the Protocol expires. For developing countries, as their accumulative emissions in the past and per capita emissions are low, their primary task at present remains economic growth and poverty eradication. To this end developing countries will have a growing demand for energy, a basic prerequisite for their development. At current stage it is inappropriate to impose compulsory emissions reductions targets on developing countries. These countries, should nevertheless take actions in line with their specific conditions, to tackle climate change. They need to pay special attention to introducing advanced clean technologies and adapting them to their own conditions so as to contribute within their power, to this global endeavor.

The view that developing country parties should not assume emissions reduction obligations even under a post-Kyoto Protocol climate change regime puts developing countries at odds with the United States, which refuses to participate in the Kyoto Protocol or any other international legal regime unless the major emitters among the developing countries assume reduction obligations. A GHG control regime that does not impose binding responsibilities on all countries has no chance of succeeding in achieving its ultimate objective. The prevailing developing country view opposing any new developing country obligations jeopardizes the chances of successfully negotiating a post-Kyoto Protocol regime, or, even if one is adopted, of getting the required ratifications to bring it into effect. * * *

Whereas we share the view that developed country Parties should take the lead in tackling the global problem of climate change, our view is that the principle of common but differentiated responsibilities does not necessarily exempt developing country Parties from all emissions reduction obligations, more so the major economies among the developing countries. We argue that this is borne out by an examination of the concept, history and rationale of the principle of common but differentiated responsibilities.

B. ROBUST COMMON BUT DIFFERENTIATED RESPONSIBILITIES— CONCEPT, HISTORY AND RATIONALE

The principle known as "common but differentiated responsibilities" is relatively new to international law. It addresses the perennial challenge of how nations should share the global commons. It recognizes that there are global resources, such as the atmosphere, which human society has common interest in protecting, but which the obligation to protect will vary in accordance with a nation's level of development, resources, and institutional capabilities.

Although the history of the principle is murky, it certainly has its conceptual roots in the ideas expressed in the Stockholm Declaration, such as Principle 1: "Man has the fundamental right to freedom, equality and adequate conditions of life, in an environment of a quality that permits a life of dignity and well-being, and he bears a solemn responsibility to protect and improve the environment for present and future generations." Rights and duties must be inexorably linked: States have "the sovereign right to exploit their own resources according to their own environmental policies and the responsibility to ensure that activities within their jurisdiction or control do not cause damage to the environment of other States or of areas beyond the limits of national jurisdictions." However, while all States and people must accept the duty to protect the environment, ecosystems, and natural resources for present and future generations, the efforts to fulfill this duty must be "shar[ed] equitably."

How, and why, did the world accept the notion that developing nations should be excluded from the fundamental obligation to participate in emissions reduction and/or avoidance within the overall framework of a global cap on GHG concentrations? The exemption of developing nations from any cap in the Kyoto Protocol was based on this notion. What arguments were advanced to support that outcome? It is unclear, but fundamentally, the world acted on the premise that economic development is (and always will be) directly and inherently correlated with the use of fossil fuel, which emits CO_2. It is based on a model of development that can only see business as usual--development based on low-cost fossil fuel. * * * The idea that the efficient use of energy, particularly renewable energy, by adopting innovative policies that promote efficient technology within a reordered market framework whose price signals include the externality of global warming could create a new low-carbon development paradigm was unimaginable or implicitly rejected as simply impossible. Possibilities other than business-as-usual were completely absent from this thinking.

The era of development based on low-cost oil is over, so we must reconceive how we will get and use the energy necessary for our economic and social lives. As we argue later in this article, by using energy efficiently and harnessing renewable energy (which we will use efficiently) we can supply the energy services society needs, but with significantly lower emissions. Common but differentiated responsibilities can mean that developing countries have a cap, one that they can grow into and will be adequate for their sustainable development—if they are efficient and focused on renewable sources of energy. They must commit to moving to a new, low-carbon, energy future that bypasses the old low-cost fossil fuel paradigm. They are entitled to insist on substantial financial, technological, and institutional assistance in making this transition—which the developed nations must provide—but developing countries must commit to thinking and acting in new ways to fulfill their common but differentiated responsibilities.

Unfortunately, one victim of this business-as-usual mindset was the principle of "common but differentiated responsibility," which was used in the Kyoto Protocol to justify continued reliance by the developing countries on the old fossil fuel intensive development paradigm. Thus, in the Kyoto Protocol "common but differentiated responsibilities" lost its original meaning that all nations have a duty to protect common resources, but the nature and extent of each nation's obligations will be equitably allocated, duty being the common denominator. Instead, the concept has come to be understood as excluding developing nations from climate change obligations. The adjectives remain-- common and differentiated, but the noun—responsibility—they modify has been removed from the term. There is no necessary reason why common but differentiated responsibility should mean no responsibility. Thus, Kyoto is flawed for the reasons described above and because it is a false articulation of common but differentiated responsibilities.

In saying this, we have not lost sight of the fact that the UNFCCC imposed on all countries, including developing countries, obligations relating, inter alia, to the creation of national inventories of GHG emissions, the implementation of national programmes to mitigate climate change, and the inclusion of climate change issues in national policies. But it is our view that the lynchpin of the UNFCCC climate change mitigation regime is the GHG reduction and/or avoidance commitments, which, under the Kyoto Protocol, are assumed only by Annex 1 countries. The decision not to subject the developing countries to this fundamental obligation renders the other largely supportive obligations of the Convention, for practical purposes, hortatory. * * *

Unfortunately, the abandonment of the principle of common but differentiated responsibilities triggered the demise of the Kyoto Protocol in the United States, first in the U.S. Senate in the form of the Byrd-Hagel Resolution, and ultimately by the Bush Administration. The Bush Administration, which appeared to consider energy efficiency investments to be little more than "demand destruction," was looking for a reason to reject any U.S. obligation to reduce its CO_2 emissions, and the abandonment of common but differentiated responsibility was a handy excuse. It is a principle that must be rehabilitated in the negotiations for a post-Kyoto Protocol climate change mitigation regime.

Sustainable Development does depend on the utilization of fossil fuels, and the emission of GHGs. To that extent, clearly developing countries must be allowed to continue to emit GHG at levels above those which they emit presently. Our argument however, is that this should be premised on the principle that all countries must be placed under an obligation to take action to achieve the ultimate objective of the UNFCCC. The ultimate objective of the UNFCCC simply cannot be achieved under a business as usual scenario for the non-Annex I countries, particularly for major economies among them, some of whom are bigger emitters overall than the smaller economies within the Annex I group. Therefore, future emissions must be taken into account notwithstanding the imperative not to jeopardize the sustainable development prospects of the developing countries. This can be achieved by placing Annex I countries under emissions reduction obligations while placing non-Annex I countries under emissions avoidance obligations. * * *

Evidence is growing that emissions avoidance through the introduction of energy efficiency throughout the world (developed and developing countries alike) can stabilize GHG emissions at levels that would avoid damaging climate change. * * *

Notes and Questions

1. Prof. Jonathan B. Weiner argues, "Subglobal action ... to reduce GHGs has several disadvantages ... perhaps most important, it suffers from cross-

border 'leakage' of emissions: subglobal regulatory coverage encourages source activities to shift or 'leak' to unregulated areas over time .... The total amount of leakage depends on the force of these three levers [a price effect, a 'slack off' effect, and a capital relocation effect] and on a fourth variable: the relative emissions per unit of economic activity in the regulated and unregulated places." Think Globally, Act Globally: The Limits of Local Climate Change Policies, 155 U. Pa. L. Rev. 1961, 1967-69 (2007).

PROBLEM EXERCISE ON CARBON TRADING

Ambiguity over how to measure greenhouse gases, or take credit for their abatement has produced an initial distrust about how the climate change regime will work. Weaknesses in the initial designs of the procedures for the Clean Development Mechanisms and Joint Implementation have necessitated a thorough and slow verification and registration process, and this has resulted in the relatively small scale of such undertakings. "Guidelines for the Implementation of Article 6 of the Kyoto Protocol," UN Doc. FCCC Decision 9/CMP.1, Appendix B (2005) and "Modalities and procedures for a Clean Development Mechanisms as Defined in Article 12 of the Kyoto Protocol, UN Doc. FCCC Decision 3/CMP.1, Annex, paragraphs 44-52 (2005). See M. Nigoff, The Clean Development Mechanism: Does the Current Structure Facilitate Kyoto Protocol Compliance? 18 Geo. Int'l Envtl. L. Rev. 249 (2006). The UNFCCC Methodologies Panel seeks to apply and refine new methodologies for CDM. See, e.g., the Report of the 39th Meeting of the Methodologies Panel   to   the   Executive   Board,   UNFCCC. http://cdm.unfccc.int/goto/MPpropmeth/ (June 22-26, 2009).

While carbon off-sets traded by entities structuring voluntary deals outside the Kyoto Protocol are often more efficient, that in turn have been criticized for a lack of transparency and inability ot secure verification that they work as intended. The World Wide Fund for Nature (WWF) has established a "Gold Standard" to ensure that CDM projects function as they should. The Gold Standard: Manual for Project Developers, Version 3 (May 2006), www.wwf.org. "While carbon trading is now a permanent feature of the global economy, uncertainty over the shape that future carbon markets will take means that there remains considerable risk in long-term credit delivery arrangements. In this environment of uncertainty, the use of standardized commodity or derivative trading contracts carries with it a considerable degree of risk." A. Beatty & E. Williams, Trends in Carbon Trading: Practical Lessons–Crucial Issues in Climate Change and the Kyoto Mechanisms in Asia, (Conference of the Asia Pacific Center for Environmental Law, National University of Singapore 2007).

Economic interests in some nations have also exploited "loop holes." Much of the concern for a universal and transparent accounting system for emissions and off-sets derives from the lack of clear rules for measuring GHG and setting the baselines. As Michael Wara noted above, in the case of the Kyoto Protocol, in February of 2007, several Chinese refrigerant manufacturers had made significant profits by exploiting the Protocol's regulations for HFC-23 by installing an inexpensive scrubber at their factories, thereby removing the HFC-23 exhausts, and gaining "carbon credits" which they could then sell to developed country buyers who needed off-sets for their GHG emissions, making a handsome profit. F. Harvey, Billions Lost In Kyoto Carbon Trade Loophole, Financial Times, p. 5, col. 1 (February 8, 2007). One ton of HFC-23 is the equivalent of 11,700 tons of CO_2, and the value of the carbon credits far exceeded the cost of the scrubbers.

In the economies in transition, Russia and other former USSR States, the great energy waste and inefficiency of infrastructure still in use from the Soviet Union mean that Joint Implementation (JI) projects for modernization that uses energy efficiently can produce a very large volume of emission reduction units (ERUs). The region also has a potentially substantial excess of certified emission reductions under Clean Development Mechanism (CDM). This could depress the market price for these carbon credits and undermine the utility of these flexibility mechanisms. Current trade in CDM credits favors Asia (China and India primarily) and Latin American (Brazil and Mexico and Africa as of 2009 had only 29 project (mostly South Africa). This inequitable distribution of the CDMs causes further criticism about the process. See CDM Registration, UNFCCC Secretariat, http://cdm.ungccc.int/Statistics/Registration/NumOfRegisteredProjByHoistPartiesPieChart.html.

JI, CDM, and emission trading under Article 17 are open to parties to the Kyoto Protocol. Private enterprises may undertake JI and CDM projects. See Modalities, Rules and Guidelines for Emission Trading Under Art. 17 of the Kyoto Protocol, UN Doc. FCCC Decision 11/CMP/.1, Annex, para. 5 (2005). U.S. companies today would have to do so through off-shore entitles, since the USA is not a party to the Kyoto Protocol. Since the proposed USA-wide market in carbon credits is considered as one part eventually of a global market, and the financing markets are global and multinational companies have global operations, the question arises will the USA ratify an amended Kyoto Protocol, or will the new post-Kyoto agreement open carbon trading to all UNFCCC Member States? One foundation for such a global market will be the verification and integrity of the system being negotiated.

Since the cap on emissions that obliges economic interests to deal in carbon credits, it is important to ensure that the process of setting the cap, and ensuring its observation, is realistic. Because of the EU cap, European interests have bought most of the ERUs and CERs since they began. Many of the proposals for the Copenhagen COP in 2009 addresses these issues. Does this mean the EU is attaining its emission reductions?

Skepticism about claims for caps is strong. The Worldwide Fund for Nature (WWF) has charged that the European Union is manipulating its record, and is not in fact achieving the GHG reductions promised. WWF's Stefan Singer compared the EU's plan to achieve at 20% emissions reduction by 2020 on 1990 levels "means no more than 4-5% emissions reductions domestically" from 2009 onwards. He explained that the EU already had achieved an 8% cut, mainly due to de-industrialization in former communist Eastern European states since 1990, and of the 12% left the EU plans to achieve 60% of that via off-sets, using CDM. Singer observes that "This in principle is not a problem if there were a strong domestic target as well, and if the clean development mechanism would have been shown to be truly additional. But that is not the case." He suggests that off-sets projects in developing countries would have probably occurred anyway due to pollution control laws (as in the Chinese HFC-23 case). As a result, the EU 20% reduction is more like a 4-5% reduction between 2009 and 2020. Singer contends that the Kyoto Protocol's flexibility off-set mechanisms are "a trick on the atmosphere." See "EU 'cheating' the world on climate, says WWF," Euractiv (April 14, 2009).

These sorts of uncertainties about any future emission trading system, and the JI and CDM flexibility mechanisms, have made the negotiation and agreement of standards and integrity of procedures a major theme of the Bali Action Plan negotiations.

What measures should states undertake in order to provide a clear, equitable, verifiable and transparent set of rules that ensure that emission mitigation actions will in fact take place, while generating the funds to invest in adaptation? Should the states commission preparation of a framework a set of over-all rules, and then delegate the preparation of specific rules appropriate for each sector (as in the case of bunker oils for air or ship transport)? Should standards be set for national markets and allow trading or JI and CDM projects only after an international authority has certified that the given nation's domestic market meets rigorous standards?

5. Fulfilling the Bali Action Plan

a. The Challenges Embraced in the Bali Action Plan

The UNFCCC COP meeting for the 13th time in Bali in December 2007, coinciding with the 3rd MOP of the Kyoto Protocol Parties, launched a two year process to negotiate a new agreement for the period commencing in 2012 when the Kyoto Protocol's commitments expire. The COP created a subsidiary body, the Ad Hoc Working Group on Long-Term Cooperative Action under the Convention ("AWLCA"). The COP agreed to hold its 14th meeting in Poznan, Poland, in December of 2008, and its 15th COP in Copenhagen, Denmark in December of 2009. The COP at Poznan considered many proposals for a Post-Kyoto agreement, e.g. the Ad Hoc Working Group on Long-

Term Cooperative Action's Note by the Chair on Ideas and Proposals on Paragraph 1 of the Bali Action Plan, UN Doc. FCCC/AWGLCA/2008/16 (November 20, 2008), but deferred most decision-making for the post-2012 framework regime to the COP at Copenhagen.

Given the extensive number of climate change issues that remain to be addressed and determined under the UNFCCC, subsequent deliberations will necessarily produce a further action plan for follow-up negotiations, not unlike the Bali Action Plan itself, but with more substantive guidance. See D. Bodansky, International Climate Change Efforts Beyond 2012: A Survey of Approaches, Pew Center on Climate Change (2004), at www.pewclimate.org. States will continue some of the momentum already underway: (a) the expert Group on Technology Transfer should be extended for another five years and report to the Subsidiary Body for Scientific and Technical Advise (SBSTA) and the Subsidiary Body for Implementation (SBI); (b) the management of the Kyoto Protocol's Adaptation Fund needs to be decided; (c) agreement to transfer "green" technology and facilitate its implementation by developing countries; (d) some agreement on additional and new financing to assist developing countries to prepare for climate change mitigation and adaptation. See E. Burleson, Climate Change Consensus: Emerging International Law, 34 William & Mary Envtl. L. & Policy Rev. (2009).

The issue of caps for the reductions in emissions of GHGs from developed and developing countries has generated a range of competing proposals, but no matter what cap is initially selected, based on competing formulae for the computations, it is likely that further emission reductions will be required over time and more sequestration needed in order to reach an atmospheric level that minimizes adverse changes. James Hansen of NASA has posited that nations need to scrub carbon dioxide from the atmosphere's current, rising levels back to the level of 350 ppm to avoid irreversible, damaging climate change. J. Hansen, Tipping Point: Perspective of a Climatologist, in E. Fearn & K. Redford, eds., The State of the Wild: A Global Portrait of Wildlife, Wild Lands and Oceans (2007). Moreover, the experience with the targets and timetables under the experience of the Stratospheric Ozone regime under the Montreal Protocol demonstrates that they necessarily evolve as the science and technology improves, and political confidence builds in the capacity to meet the targets, and as a result they gradually become more stringent and effective. And as excerpted in Chapter 2, the Chairman of the IPCC has outlined the scope of the IPCC's 5th Assessment and once these issues are evaluated by governments, further changes to implementing and refining the UNFCCC obligations will inevitably emerge. See www.ipcc.ch/scoping%20meeting%20AR5/documents/doc02.pdf

The UN Secretary-General, Ban Ki-moon, made it a priority to lend the support of the UN Secretariat to the UNFCCC negotiations for a new climate change agreement, and some agreement will emerge even if it leaves much still to be decided in the future. UN News (Fed. 5, 2009), www.un.org/apps/news/story.asp?NewsID=29780&Cr=Climate.

Resolving issues of regulating emissions by aircraft and ships, from consuming bunker fuel oil, illustrates the complex character of climate change mitigation decision-making under the UNFCCC. Nations will need to consider allocating resources to facilitate the cooperation and coordination among many international organizations, including the MEAs, and the UNFCCC.

Climate effects of consuming bunker fuels has been studied by the IPCC. IPCC Special Report, Aviation and the Global Atmosphere, How Do Aircraft Effect Climate and Ozone (1999). The International Civil Aviation Organization (Montreal) ("ICAO") is responsible for aircraft operations under the Chicago Convention on International Civil Aviation (1944). www.icao.int. The European Union has been urging action by the ICAO. In 2007, ICAO's 36th Assembly urged its Member States not to implement emission trading until all agreed to do so. Res. A36-22, Appendix L. Notwithstanding this decision by ICAO, the EU Directive on emission trading was amended to include CO_2 from civil aviation. EU Directive 2008/101/EC, amending Directive 2003/87/EC so as to include aviation activities in the scheme for greenhouse gas emission allowance trading within the Community, para. (9), L. 8/4, 13.1.2009 Official Journal of the EU (2009). The European Civil Aviation Conference (ECAC), www.ecac-ceac.org/index.php, has urged that a uniform world-wide cap and procedure be adopted at COP-15, and apply to all ICAO States. ICAO submitted its proposals to COP 14 as "Shared Vision on International Aviation and Climate Change" (Submission of the ICAO to the Workshop on Shared Vision for Cooperative Action, Poznan, December 1-10, 2008). The airlines and aircrfaft industry has been concerned about their emissions for some time. See www.icao.int/icao/eb/env/aee.htm

Similar problems exist with the shipping industry, whose operations are under the jurisdiction of the International Maritime Organization (London), ("IMO") www.imo.org. W. Hardy, EU Commission Wants ICAO, IMO to do More on Climate, Reuters (November 19, 2007). www.reuters.com/articlePrint?articleid=USL1923336020. The EU has positioned the "Single European Sky" of the ECAC against the ICAO in order to position the UNFCCC COP 15 to take action. As this example suggests, comparable measures to force a global position, sector by sector, could be launched in the MEAs, or in other bodies such as the IMO. The IMO's Marine Environment Protection Committee has initiated short-term onshore power supplies) and long-term measures (redesign of ships, alternative fuels, and emission trading) to deal with CO_2 emissions from ships. UN Doc. MEPC/57, 57th Session (March 31-April 4, 2008), under the 1973 International Convention for the Prevention of Pollution from Ships ("MARPOL"). IMO and ICAO have different environmental capacities under different treaties, and are arriving at different approaches to their bunker fuel issues. How should nations deploy their international law to reconcile these differences? Should the EU have sought agreement from China or the USA or other nations with significant shipping and aviation sectors before forcing the issue of bunker fuel?

As political will is generated, agreement on mitigation measures across a number of sectors will be realized, especially where the technology already exists (e.g. IUCN Statement by Narindar Kakar to the UNGA Thematic Dialogue on "Energy Efficiency, Energy Conservation and New and Renewable Sources of Energy," June 18, 2009 www.iucn.org/energy, on appliance standards, building codes, lighting standards, combined heat, power, and district energy systems, as available technologies for reducing emissions through energy efficiency). Until recently, the UNFCCC COP debates focused on rhetorical arguments about what historic responsibility the developed nations had for climate change and what payments they should make to developed nations in order to help them deal with climate change, above and beyond the contributions for advancing sustainable development. As national delegates to the COP, and its subsidiary bodies and working groups, become better informed about actual technologies that can be deployed at once, cooperative decision-making will become easier. As the experience of the Stratospheric Ozone regime illustrates, in each sector an epistemic community of like-minded experts must be deployed to harmonize national conduct and implement mitigation and adaptation measures.

The debates within the UNFCCC COP since 1997 have reflected a lack of consensus among the Member States regarding how to proceed. While divisive approach by the Bush-Cheney Administration in the USA exacerbated negotiations both developed States in the European Union and developing States alike, there were also divisions within Europe between the EU and Russia, and among the developing States. Brazil and India and China developed positions independent of the "Group of 77," the negotiation forum of developing nations. The Group of 77 failed to support the urgent needs of the small island states, who in turn created the Association of Small Island States (AOSIS) to press their case. The G-77 has also not pressed the urgency the case of the most vulnerable of the least developed States. Uncertainty about how to handle climate change has split up the United Nations members into a shifting group of interests, which in turn has precluded agreement on consensus. Facile East-West and North-South political divisions are an artifact of the past.

With the appointment of the USA negotiators from the Barack Obama Administration in March of 2009, a new round of negotiations began to fulfill the objectives of the Bali Action Plan. The documents from the on-going negotiations are being disseminated widely. The UNFCCC released the negotiating documents for the UNFCCC Ad Hoc Working Group On Further Commitments for Annex I Parties Under the Kyoto Protocol on July 2, 2009 (UN Doc. UNFCCC/KP/AWG/2009/10 (July 1, 2009). Further documentation is being disseminated by a project known as "Climate-L.org", a knowledge management project of the International Institute for Sustainable Development (IISD) in cooperation with the UN Systems Chief Executives Board for Coordination (CEB), funded by the Swiss and British governments. Of course, the bilateral and contact group negotiations are not made public until some consensus on a proposal is attained, and therefore access to the documents is inevitably out of step with the actual state of multilateral climate change decision-making.

One of the benefits of the focused negotiation timetable launched by the Bali Action Plan is that many states have advanced proposals for elaborating the climate change regime to be considered over the coming years as states try to shape national and regional and international climate change agreements and action plans. The proposals for action have been summarized and organized into the format of a draft negotiating text by the Chair of the AWG on Further Commitments for Annex I Parties Under the Kyoto Protocol, as "Documentation to facilitate negotiations among Parties," UN Doc. FCCC/KP/AWG/2009/10 (July 1, 2009).

b. The Negotiation Proposals Based on the Four Pillars of the Bali Action Plan

In advance of Copenhagen, virtually all nations have advanced coherent proposals for international action. Many have been advanced based upon active national efforts. For instance, China has a National Climate Change Program, issued on June 4, 2008 by the National Development and Reform Commission (NDRC). www.china.org.cn/english/environment/213624.htm. Part 5 outlines China's position on the key climate change issues and the need for international cooperation. India is examining reforms to its energy sector, with significant reform proposals made by the Energy and Resources Institute of India, the World Bank and others. See Indian Ministry of Environment and Forests/UK Dep't. of Environment, Food and Rural Affairs, www.defra.gov.uk (2007). The European Union has several years of careful work to shape and agree to its climate change programs, and begin implementation in the EU Member States. The EU issued its paper, "Towards A Comprehensive Climate Change Agreement in Copenhagen," Commission of the European Communities, Communication from the Commission to the European Parliament, the Council, the European Economic and Social Committee and the Committee of the Regions, COM (2009) 39 (January 28, 2009). Within the EU, in 2007 France promulgated a major reform on climate change, the "Grenelle de l'Environnement," *Journal Officiel,* http://www.assemblee-nationale.fr/13/pdf/projects/pl1442.pdf. Germany has adopted a Strategy for Adaptation to Climate Change, to coordinate work of the Lander with the federal government.

www.bmu.de/english/climate/downloads/doc/42841.phb. Nations in other regions are active as well. The Association of Small Island States (AOSIS), has advanced focused recommendations to deal with the threats that sea level and climate change pose to their national existence.

Until the summer of 2009, the USA has had no comparable national climate change policy. This has retarded the capacity of the USA to submit proposals to the UNFCCC COP negotiations under the Bali Action Plan. In other specialized multilateral negotiations involving conference diplomacy, the State Department has the benefit of experts assigned from agencies such as Energy, EPA, Interior, NOAA, or NASS, to advise on issues of US foreign policy. The Bush/Cheney Administration policies precluded such government-wide collaboration. Equally limiting is the fact that the State Department has too few experts on staff capable of understanding the many legal, technological, economic and other undertakings of U.S. state governments to address climate change mitigation and adaptation. See The State Response To Climate Change: 50 State Survey, in M. Gerrard, ed., Global Climate Change and the Law (2007), updated annually at www.law.pace.edu.

The Note by the Chair, entitled "Documentation to facilitate negotiations among Parties," UN Doc. FCCC/KP/AWG/20009/10 (July 1, 2009) excerpted below and other UNFCCC texts reflecting drafting of proposals for implementing the Bali Action Plan are a distillation of the national positions that states have advanced in the negotiations. They cover the four themes, or pillars, of the Bali Action Plan: Mitigation, Adaptation, Technology and Finance, plus they add a preliminary text that all states will need to embrace to align behind a global international action to address the challenges of climate change. See also the proposals in UN Doc. FCCC/KP/AWG/2008/8.

As you study these proposals, consider how they may evolve as the USA formulates its various negotiating positions in the coming months and years. What measures would be needed to build the confidence of different states to the point of joining a consensus behind a given set of recommendations?

Documentation to facilitate negotiations among Parties
Note by the Chair (1 July 2009)

A shared vision for long-term cooperative action

Note: This section of the [Copenhagen] negotiating text (paras. 1-9 below) illustrates how elements from Parties' proposals could be woven into an introductory statement on a shared vision.

1. Warming of the climate system, as a consequence of human activity, is unequivocal. As assessed by the Intergovernmental Panel for Climate Change (IPCC) in its Fourth Assessment Report, the serious adverse effects of climate change, notably those on crop production and food security, water

resources and human health, as well as on housing and infrastructure, are becoming a major obstacle to efforts to promote sustainable economic and social development and to reduce poverty, which are the first and overriding priorities of developing countries.

2. The adverse effects of climate change will be felt most acutely by those segments of the population who are already in vulnerable situations owing to factors such as geography, poverty, gender, age, indigenous or minority status and disability. These adverse effects also undermine the equitable development needs of present and future generations.

3. Deep cuts in global emissions will be required to prevent dangerous interference with the climate system and achieve the ultimate objective of the Convention. Early and urgent action to this end is necessary. A delay in reducing emissions will significantly constrain opportunities to achieve lower stabilization levels of greenhouse gases (GHGs) and increase the risk of more severe climate change impacts.

4. An economic transition is needed that shifts global economic growth patterns towards a low emission economy based on more sustainable production and consumption, promoting sustainable lifestyles and climate-resilient development while ensuring a just transition of the workforce. The active participation of all stakeholders in this transition should be sought, be they governmental, private business or civil society, including the youth and addressing the need for gender equity.

5. Developed country Parties must show leadership in mitigation commitments or actions, in supporting developing country Parties in undertaking adaptation measures and nationally appropriate mitigation actions (NAMAs), and in assisting them through the transfer of technology and financial resources to move towards a low-emission development path.

6. Urgent and immediate adaptation needs of developing countries that are particularly vulnerable to the adverse effects of climate change require special attention. Countries lacking sufficient capacity to respond to the challenges of climate change require access to opportunities to obtain this capacity in a timely manner.

7. The urgent need to confront dangerous climate change requires political determination to continue building an inclusive, fair and effective climate regime, one that takes into account the need of developing countries' need for development space, and is based on a new and equitable global partnership that drives cooperative action to enable the full, effective and sustained implementation of the Convention.

8. The shared vision for long-term cooperative action shall be guided by the ultimate objective of the Convention and its principles, in particular the principles of equity and of common but differentiated responsibilities and respective capabilities, as well as the precautionary principle, that are enshrined in the Convention to guide the international community in addressing climate change. It also takes into account social and economic conditions and other relevant factors.

9. The shared vision for long-term cooperative action aims to achieve sustainable and climate resilient development and to enhance action on adaptation, mitigation, technology, finance and capacity building, integrating the means of implementation needed to support action on adaptation and mitigation, in order to achieve the ultimate objective of the Convention. * * *

This transparent form of conference diplomacy makes the texts available to all interested parties. The negotiating texts so disclosed are a good reflection of the gaps in positions, between industrialized nations and developing nations, between small island states and other countries most vulnerable to climate change and other developing states, and between economies in transition or states whose economies depend on production of fossil fuels.

It is likely that the many alternatives will form the basis for on-going negotiations which will continue well beyond the Copenhagen COP. As such, you should study the negotiating texts. Can we see trends in their progression over time? Do you see emerging elements of consensus? Is the "shared vision" a serious statement of principles, or a provisional text intended as a place marker, to let a clearer statement of "vision" emerge?

The key elements of the negotiating text as nations approached the Copenhagen COP set the stage for this on-going attempt to design the essential elements fulfilling the Bali Action Plan:

1) Enhanced action on Adaptation – Developing nations are at risk, and have advanced adaptation ahead of mitigation. Priority is sought for the least developed countries and the small island states expressly.

2) Enhanced action on mitigation – Developed countries are to agree on a cap on emissions, and competing concepts of how to express this cap remain to be decided. The criteria for how deeply an industrialized state should curb emissions are spelled out in negotiating paragraph 56. An objective and thorough and transparent analysis of the technical capacities to make these reductions is to be undertaken.

3) Measurement, reporting and verification–Procedures for close inspection of the mitigation commitments are to be required.

4) Mitigation by developing countries – There are a set of five or more alternative negotiating positions on what mitigation measures to require of which classes of developing counties, and national action plans (NAMAs) will be adopted and implemented.

5) Reducing Emissions from Deforestation and forest degradation (REDD) – A set of guiding principles and objectives is set forth in paragraphs 106-112, and up to five different competing alternative texts are proposed for how to implement REDD.

6) Economic and social consequences of response measures – As the States act to adapt and mitigate, they are to avoid adverse effects on international trans and socio-economic and environmental conditions, especially

those that affect developing nations. Insurance and risk management provisions are to be adopted.

7)Enhanced action for financing, technology and capacity-building – Several competing negotiation texts exist for these provisions. The texts anticipate that several funds will be established to pay for these costs. Paragraphs 180-198 present competing negotiating options for how to advance enhanced technological development and transfer, and address issues of intellectual property rights.

8)Institutional arrangements at the national level – Provisions are largely agreed for each country to establish coordinating bodies for all stakeholders and for compliance.

9)Capacity Building – The negotiating text provides a broad mandate for training and education and other elements of capacity building to enable countries to implement the climate change mitigation and adaptation obligations

Notes and Questions

1. Why does the negotiating text released in July 2009 contain an elaborate focus on alternative possible procedural aspects of the new agreement derive from? Is the climate change scope so vast that states cannot prioritize concrete measures to address? Is the discussion of topics bunker fuels best left to subsidiary decision-making?

2. When the COP-15 decides on an accord that can be approved for submission to the States Parties of the UNFCCC COP for ratification, the choices reflected in the options outlined above will be significant parts of the *traveaux préparatoires*, or the "legislative history" used to interpret the agreement and define the next phase of decision-making to elaborate or implement it. What "common vision" can or should inform the choices made? Should general principles of law be used to define the "vision"? Should the UNFCCC parties adopt an ethical framework such as the Earth Charter (www.earthcharter.org) to guide the vision?

3. If the objective is to build an efficient and effective governance system for climate change decision-making, which of the several alternatives options are best framed to do so? Which options reflect a narrow focus, protecting the interests of certain governments?

4. The lack of political consensus prior to the COP-15 at Copenhagen has generated the range of proposals in 201 separate articles of the chair's negotiating text (July 1, 2009), with many more yet to be negotiated. Since this is a multilateral negotiation, involving all nations, provisions for different groups of nations are being negotiated. If mitigation of GHGs is urgent, will such a process to accommodate every sovereign state burden and slow down progress toward agreeing on the means to make deep emission cuts?

Consider in your response the proposal advanced by Prof. Robert Socolow of Princeton University in the lead-up to the agreement on the Bali Action Plan itself. What combination of nations would be likely to endorse his proposal which is summarized next?

At a thematic debate convened by the President of the UN General Assembly in July of 2007 on "Climate Change As A Global Challenge" in the 61st Session of the UN General Assembly leading up to the adoption of the Bali Action Plan, Robert Socolow addressed an informal meeting of the Assembly at the outset of the Thematic Debate. See www.un.org/ga/president/61/followup/climatechange/programme:shtml.
Building upon his reports demonstrating mitigation could be achieved, Stabilization Wedges: Solving the Climate Problem for the Next 50 Years with Current Technologies in *Science* with Pacala excerpted in Chapter 1 and A Plan to Keep Carbon in Check in *Scientific American*, he posited a new formulation for "equitable" climate change mitigation by which the developed states in the Organization of Economic Development and Cooperation (OECD) would cut their emissions in order to allow developing nations to continue to sustainably develop their countries to accommodate their growing populations and abate poverty. Assuming the need to cut GHG emissions from 14 GtC/y in 2004 to 7 GtC/y in 2054, he posited that using existing technology and best management practices in the seven "wedges" (energy efficiency, decarbonized electricity generation, decarbonized fuels, fuel displacement by low-carbon electricity, forest and soils stewardship, and methane management), OECD nations could realistically cut carbon emissions from 6 billion tons/year to 2 billion tons/year, while developing nation would emit less, from over 8 billion tons a year to under 6 billion tons per year. He would require nothing of the least developed nations (some 5 billion people) until after 2030, as their reductions would not affect global GHG trends significantly, and their socio-economic development needs are urgent.

5. If Article 4 of the UNFCCC can address specific sectors, why did the Copenhagen draft negotiating text only mention agriculture (draft Article 134) and some aspects of transportation (draft Article 135)?

6. Since the UNFCCC COP can examine cooperation with the ICAO and IMO on bunker fuels, why did the negotiating text not mention cooperation or interaction with other competent treaty organizations, such as with the CBD on REDD and REDD-plus conservation (draft Article 102)? Is the brief mention of ecosystem management (draft Article 32) sufficient to provide integration with the Convention on Biological Diversity, which has adopted the ecosystem approach?

7. Is not politics, and a political consensus, the art of the possible? Political leaders and experts all advanced many theoretically possible and competing proposals, many as logical and sound as Socolow's. Good ideas are not in

short supply. But do good ideas win the day? Multilateral conference diplomacy is a political forum, not unlike a legislature. How are treaties, like statutes, negotiated? Is not the forum's choice of a chairperson essential to the process? Diplomatic leadership is essential and is not the same as legislative leadership in a national parliament or Congress. Even if nations support a negotiation, leaders experienced in conference diplomacy are needed.

　　Analogous challenges have arisen before. When the daunting task of preparing for the 1992 "Earth Summit" was begun, nations turned to the law professor and diplomat who had led much of the negotiations for the UN Conference on the Law of the Sea, which produced the UN Convention on the Law of the Sea (1982). Ambassador Tommy Koh of Singapore devoted two years to chairing the preparatory committee for the UN Conference on Environment and developed the extraordinary consensus that ultimately adopted Agenda 21 at the largest Summit meeting ever convened, and then in the UN General Assembly. He published his reflections on how to build the sort of consensus needed now for climate change in T. Koh, The Earth Summit's Negotiating Process: Some Reflections on the Art and Science of Negotiating, in N. Robinson, ed., Agenda 21: Earth's Action Plan (1993). Another extraordinary diplomat who has reflected on his art is Richard Benedict in his book Ozone Diplomacy (1998). He played a major role in the negotiation of the Montreal Protocol discussed and excerpted above.

8.　Although not an MEA, the UN Convention in The Law of the Sea (1982) 1833 U.N.T.S. 397, contains in Part XII The Environmental Framework Law of the Sea. UNCLOS rules will need to be coordinated with the new rules for climate stewardship. International ocean law is discussed in Chapter 6, Section D, and Chapter 7, Section D.

9.　As discussed further below, another body of treaty law, as well as general principles of international law, underpins the climate change negotiations: the law of human rights. The Maldive Islands, whose very existence is threatened by sea level rise, has pressed the human rights of its citizens, and the responsibilities of the rest of the world to ensure observance of those rights. Other developing nations have stressed their economic and social rights to sustainable development. In the contest of energy and climate change, the breach of basic human rights is stark: 1.6 billion people lack access to any electricity and more than 2 billion depend on biomass fuels for cooking and heating. The wealthiest billion people consume more than 50% of the global distribution of energy resources, and the poorest billion consume less than 4%. Most nations, including the USA, have ratified the UN Covenants both on Social and Economic Rights, and on Civil and Political Rights. Is not the disproportionate consumption of energy by the rich denying basic rights to the poor? See Report on Human Rights and the Environment: Final Report of the Special Rapporteur [Fatma Zohra Ksentini] UN Doc. E/CN.4/Sub.2/1994/9 (Annex III), and UNGA Res. 45/94, UN Doc. A/45/94 (1991). See also C. Crawford, Our Bandit Future? Cities, Shanty Towns and

Climate Change Governance, 36 Fordham Urb. L. J. 211 (2009). If the considerations of equity within global sustainable development were not sufficient a motivation, the fact that small island developing states, such as The Maldives or Tuvolu, will become largely uninhabitable as sea levels rise, is a stark reminder of each State's duty (Principle 21 of the Stockholm Declaration on the Human Environment, 1972) not to harm the environment of another state, as well as to respect the basic human rights of individuals in those states. G. Handl et al., eds., Human Rights and Protection of the Environment: Economic, Social and Cultural Rights (2001).

10. The United Nations General Assembly has adopted the soft law Declaration on the Rights of Indigenous People. Many regions of the Earth are governed by Indigenous People, whose contributions of knowledge and stewardship will be important to realizing climate change mitigation and adaptation objectives. In Chapter 26, Agenda 21 recognized the role of indigenous people and their communities. Denmark as the host to COP-15 is also the state within which the Greenland Home Rule government of the Inuit is situated. How should the UNFCCC be restructured to involve the indigenous nations of the world? They are integral to the governance of the Arctic. They are key to maintaining the forest regions of the Amazon in Brazil. What seat at the table should they have in the climate change regime?

PROBLEM EXERCISE ON ADDITIONAL UNFCCC PROTOCOLS

Evaluating Article 4(d) of the UNFCCC in light of the accord reached at COP 15 in Copenhagen in December of 2009, what decisions would be needed to launch negotiations for a series of subsidiary protocols or programs on the specific topics agreed to in 1992: (a) energy, (b) transport, (c) industry, (d) agriculture, (e) forestry, and (f) waste management? For instance, in the case of the transportation sector, there are a finite number of manufacturing enterprises that make motor vehicles, and their "host" governments could agree on mandates to phase out the internal combustion engine and fossil fuels, and produce vehicles with alternative engines. Similarly, there is a trade in selling obsolete cars second hand from Europe into African and eastern or central Europe, and from Japan to SE Asia or Russia, and from North America to Mexico and Latin America. These exporting States could agree to ban exports of second hand cars, and facilitate import of appropriate new vehicles into these developing nations. The older cars pollute and perpetuate GHG emission. How could the UNFCCC COP convene a contact group of nations, with participation from both motor vehicle manufacturers and civil society (environmental non-governmental organizations and consumer groups and public health advocates) to negotiate such transport reforms? What would a "Protocol on Motor Vehicle Manufacturing and Trade" encompass?

E. CLIMATE CHANGE SYNERGIES AMONG MEAS

1. Introduction

As the excerpt on Global Environmental Governance by Speth and Haas explains, from a scientific perspective managing human impacts on Earth's climate cannot be divorced from managing other anthropogenic impacts on the Earth's environment. Tools do exist to evaluate impacts across all scientific disciplines and types of human activities, as in environmental impact assessment (EIA) laws, which have spread globally from their origins in the National Environmental Policy Act of 1969 in the USA. UNFCCC Article 4(1)(f) explicitly obligates States Parties to "take climate change considerations into account, to the extent feasible, in their relevant social, economic and environmental policies and actions, and employ appropriate methods, for example environmental impact statements, formulated and determined nationally, with a view toward minimizing adverse effects on the economy, on public health and on the quality of the environment, of projects or measures undertaken by them to mitigate or adapt to climate change." EIA techniques nationally are well developed in many nations, but under- utilized by all. See L. Kurukulasuriya & N. Robinson, UNEP Training Manual on International Environmental Law (2006).

EIA methodology requires integration of all environmental impacts associated with an activity, and these in turn require assessment of the level of protection of the environment required by law. Under the provisions, for instance of NEPA, impacts are both direct and indirect, and include cumulative impacts "which results from the incremental impact of the action when added to other past, present and reasonably foreseeable future actions regardless of what agency * * * or person undertake such actions." 40 C.F.R. Section 1508.7. The scope of the EIA is to include connected actions and cumulative actions and the actions being taken by other governmental entities. Id. at Section 1508.25 "Mitigation" is clearly defined. Id. at Section 1508.21,

EIA could be employed by nations to integrate their obligations under the various MEAs. Under Section 106 of the UN Convention on the Law of the Sea, states are obliged to use EIA for impacts on the marine environment. Since EIA legislation already exists in many states, the COP for the UNFCCC could launch an international EIA methodology for climate change mitigation and adaptation under Article 4 of the UNFCCC.

The need to integrate MEA obligations is especially clear in the context of forest stewardship for climate mitigation and adaptation. With the focus on REDD in the Bali Action Plan, the status of forest law must be carefully evaluated. Hans Hoogeveen has summed up the need for developing coordinated forest laws and practice in From Complex Problem to Integrated Solution, UN Chronicle (No. 2 2007):

* * * In dealing with climate change and forests, the following issues call for immediate and medium-term attention, in order to make a positive contribution of forests to mitigate climate change, adapt forest management to the changing climatic condition, and safeguard the benefits and interest of stakeholders. Sustainable development of society and conservation of the biological diversity of forests, habitat for wildlife and the overall environment must be safeguarded in the equation of climate change mitigation.

Work synergistically and collaboratively. UNFCCC and [UN Forum on Forests] UNFF should work collaboratively on forest-related climate change issues, as both cannot achieve their objectives on their own. The Collaborative Partnership on Forests (CPF), formed to support the work of UNFF, provides a pathway for such collaboration. Both UNFCCC and UNFF Secretariats, together with 12 other forest-related international organizations, instrument secretariat and institutions, should join forces to seek linkages reaching beyond traditionally demarcated competences and lines of operation.

More coherence within the UN system. Member States operating within the different governing bodies on international forest policies and climate change should convey consistent messages to relevant bodies. Time and again, lack of internal coordination at the country level results in incoherent, and sometimes conflicting, political signals. Robust and forward-looking decisions can be made in shaping the future agenda, only when Member States speak with one voice.

See the bigger picture. Looking at forests for climate change mitigation must take into consideration sustainable development, poverty eradication, rights of indigenous and local communities to forest resources, conservation of biodiversity and other environmental benefits of forests, such as air and water.

Prevent deforestation. Avoid perverse incentives to deforest and provide economic incentives to prevent deforestation, as well as establish afforestation and reforestation projects.

Carbon accounting. Methodological issues related to carbon accounting, including the development of criteria and indicators, and the inherent problems of additionality, leakage and permanence, should be addressed as early as possible.

Strengthen legal instruments. In response to the issues identified above, take advantage of the recently adopted non-legally binding instrument on all types of forests and the UNFF multi-year programme of work to develop and implement a common policy base on the issue of forests, focusing action on the ground.

Well-managed forests can provide practical and affordable solutions to the climate change problem. * * *

Hoogeveen's analysis also needs to integrate the silvaculture work of the UN Food & Agricultural Organization, and make linkages to the many national forest services. EIA methodology applied consistently across regions or among all nations could make these links operationally at the point of assessing governmental actions, but as Hoogeveen observes, a more systematic approach is needed across all international agencies that address for policy. Eventually, a climate change protocol on forests may be needed. See R. Tarasofsky, Assessing the International Forest Regime (IUCN ELP Paper 37, 1999) at www.iucn.org/themes/law. The gap in international public law on forest stewardship will either be addressed by negotiating new treaty instruments, or by decisions taken under the existing umbrella framework Convention on Biological Diversity. The CBD in Article 22 expressly provides that it " shall not affect the rights and obligations of any Contracting Party deriving from any existing international agreement, except where the exercise of those rights and obligations would cause a serious damage or threat to biological diversity." The CBD's COP could build on this provision to coordinate with other MEAs. The USA has not yet ratified this Convention and is not a Member of its COP.

Even without employing an analytic process for linking the roles that each MEA can serve to bolster the UNFCCC objective, it is evident that each MEA can do much to address climate change mitigation and adaptation. The States Party to all these MEAs could require climate change to become a priority objective of each MEA.

There are overlapping aspects among work under various of the MEAs, and collaborative approaches to that work could maximize the synergies among the MEAs. The UN has tried to coordinate among its specialized agencies and programs and the related independent treaty organizations for many years. Each MEA is a separate treaty organization, and largely autonomous, and each MEA has scarcely adequate resources for its core mission. Even if the tools and methods existed to facilitate inter-agency cooperation (and few do locally, nationally or internationally), it would be most difficult to build collaboration among the MEAs.

Given the pervasive scope of climate change, and the urgent need to advance both mitigation and adaptation, should not States advance a common set of decisions through each MEA COP to give priority to climate change issues? In addition, should not the States Party to the UNFCCC give priority to "out-sourcing" as much of their work as possible to other MEAs, rather than duplicating the efforts or further delaying consideration or action by the UNFCCC COP? It will be up to the Member States of each MEA to agree to such a process, but since these States Parties comprise largely the same governments that comprise the UNFCCC and the other MEAs, this could be done. Why has it not been done?

Should not climate negotiators consider biodiversity for its own sake? "For example, we should discourage carbon sequestration projects that reduce biodiversity ad social well-being, such as monoculture afforestation. Instead, we should seek win-win sustainable development solutions that reduces GHGs while protecting and enhancing biodiversity." D. Hodas, Biodiversity and Climate Change Laws: A Failure to Communicate? in M. Jeffery et al., Biodiversity Law (2006).

The competencies of several of the MEAs are outlined here to suggest the benefits for climate change mitigation and adaptation. Even without coordination fails, the law of climate change can draw on the legal competencies and programs of these MEAs. As you study these treaty provisions, reflect on how each could be aligned to further the objectives of the UNFCCC.

2. The 1992 UN Convention on Biological Diversity
31 I.L.M. 818 (1992)

Preamble
The Parties to the Convention:

Conscious of the intrinsic value of biological diversity and of the ecological, genetic, social, economic, scientific, educational, cultural, recreational and aesthetic values of biological diversity and its components, * * *

Affirming that the conservation of biological diversity is a common concern of humankind,

Reaffirming that States have sovereign rights over their own biological resources,

Reaffirming also that States are responsible for conserving their biological diversity and for using their biological resources in a sustainable manner, * * *

Noting that it is vital to anticipate, prevent and attack the causes of significant reduction or loss of biological diversity of source,

Noting also that where there is a threat of significant reduction or loss of biological diversity, lack of full scientific certainty should not be used as a reason for postponing measures to avoid or minimize such a threat, * * *

Aware that conservation and sustainable use of biological diversity is of critical importance for meeting the food, health and other needs of the growing world population, for which purpose access to and sharing of both genetic resources and technologies are essential, * * *

Determined to conserve and sustainably use biological diversity for the benefit of present and future generations,

Article 1

The objectives of this Convention, to be pursued in accordance with its relevant provisions, are the conservation of biological diversity, the sustainable use of its components and the far and equitable sharing of the benefits arising out of the utilization of genetic resources, including by appropriate access to genetic resources and by appropriate transfer of relevant technologies, taking into account all rights over those resources and to technologies, and by appropriate funding.

* * * * *

Decisions By the CBD COP: The Ecosystem Approach

(a) Ecosystem Management

Under the Convention, the COP has adopted the methodology of the "Ecosystem Approach," which is defined "as a strategy for the integrated management of land, water and living resources that promotes conservation and sustainable use in an equitable way." The ecosystem management approach requires "adaptive management to deal with the complex and dynamic levels of biological organization, which encompasses the essential structure, processes, functions and interactions among organisms and their environment. It recognized humans, with their cultural diversity, are an integral component of many ecosystems." Para. A.4, UN Doc. CBD Decisions V/6: Ecosystem Approach, Annex (2003). In that decision in 2003, the COP for the Convention on Biological Diversity has adopted 12 complementary and interlinked principles to guide application of the ecosystem approach. See also UN Doc. CBD Decisions VII/11 (2005).

(b) Indigenous Management and Forests

Implementation of Forest-Related Decisions of the UNCED at the National and International Levels, Including an Examination of Sectoral and Cross-Sectoral Linkages, Programme Element I.3: Traditional Forest-related Knowledge, UN Doc. CSD, E/CN.17/IF1996/9, paras 16-19 (Feb. 1, 1996).

Until the beginning of the 1990s, very few [forest] planning processes promoted the participation of indigenous people in policy programmes and projects formulation. These people felt marginalized and ignored because their political institutions were not recognized, and they suffered from development directed from above. During the last five years, some progress has been observed, in particular due to the creation and action of national and international alliances of indigenous people. * * *

Advances in technological, technical and scientific studies on the nature and substance of indigenous and traditional knowledge and forest management practices underlines the necessity for a broad, coordinated approach. Among the advances already made in this direction is the emergence of scientific evidence to the effect that:

(a) The language, culture and knowledge of indigenous and local communities are disappearing at alarming rates;

(b) Many presumed "natural" ecosystems or "wilderness" areas are in fact "human or cultural landscapes" resulting from millennial interactions with forest-dwellers;

(c) Traditional ecological knowledge is complex, sophisticated and critically relevant to understanding how to conserve forest ecosystems and to utilize them sustainably.

(d) Indigenous and traditional forest management systems are likely to focus on the conservation of non- or semi-domesticated, non-timber species because these provide the majority of food supplies, medicines, oils, essences, dyes, colours, repellents, insecticides, building materials, clothing, etc;

(e) Most species associated with forests possess existence values for local communities which are often ignored, obscured or even cancelled out by imposed conservation, development and market schemes; [and]

(f)As indigenous and local communities frequently integrate forest and agricultural management system, "foresters" and "farmers" can be seen as forming part of the same continuum. * * *

3. The "Soft Law" UN Policies on Forests

NON-LEGALLY BINDING AUTHORITATIVE STATEMENT OF PRINCIPLES FOR A GLOBAL CONSENSUS ON THE MANAGEMENT, CONSERVATION AND SUSTAINABLE DEVELOPMENT OF ALL TYPES OF FORESTS

A/CONF.151/26 (Vol. III) 14 Aug. 1992, Report of the United Nations Conference on Environment and Development, annex III 1992)

PREAMBLE

* * * The guiding objective of these principles is to contribute to the management, conservation and sustainable development of forests and to provide for their multiple and complementary functions and uses.

(a) Forestry issues and opportunities should be examined in a holistic and balanced manner within the overall context of environment and development, taking into consideration the multiple functions and uses of forests, including traditional uses, and the likely economic and social stress when these uses are constrained or restricted, as well as the potential for development that sustainable forest management can offer. * * *

(b) These principles should apply to all types of forests, both natural and planted, in all geographic regions and climatic zones, including austral, boreal, sub-temperate, temperate, subtropical and tropical.

(c) All types of forests embody complex and unique ecological processes which are the basis for their present and potential capacity to provide resources to satisfy human needs as well as environmental values, and as such their sound management and conservation is of concern to the Governments of the countries to which they belong and are of value to local communities and to the environment as a whole. * * *

PRINCIPLES/ELEMENTS

1.(a) States have, in accordance with the Charter of the United Nations and the principles of international law, the sovereign right to exploit their own resources pursuant to their own environmental policies and have the responsibility to ensure that activities within their jurisdiction or control do not cause damage to the environment of other States or areas beyond the limits of national jurisdiction.

(b) The agreed full incremental cost of achieving benefits associated with forest conservation and sustainable development requires increased international cooperation and should be equitably shared by the international community.

2.(a) States have the sovereign and inalienable right to utilize, manage and develop their forests in accordance with their development needs and level of socioeconomic development and on the basis of national policies consistent with sustainable development and legislation, including the conversion of such areas for other uses within the overall socio-economic development plan and based on rational land-use policies.

(b) Forest resources and forest lands should be sustainably managed to meet the social, economic, ecological, cultural and spiritual needs of present and future generations. These needs are for forest products and services, such as wood and wood products, water, food, fodder, medicine, fuel, shelter, employment, recreation, habitats for wildlife, landscape diversity, carbon sinks and reservoirs, and for other forest products. Appropriate measures should be taken to protect forests against harmful effects of pollution, including air-borne pollution, fires, pests and diseases, in order to maintain their full multiple value. * * *

(d) Governments should promote and provide opportunities for the participation of interested parties, including local communities and indigenous people, industries, labour, non-governmental organizations and individuals, forest dwellers and women, in the development, implementation and planning of national forest policies. * * *

4. The vital role of all types of forests in maintaining the ecological processes and balance at the local, national, regional and global levels through, *inter alia,* their role in protecting fragile ecosystems, watersheds and freshwater resources and as rich storehouses of biodiversity and biological resources and sources of genetic material for biotechnology products, as well as photosynthesis, should be recognized. * * *

5.(a) National forest policies should recognize and duly support the identity, culture and the rights of indigenous people, their communities and other communities and forest dwellers. Appropriate conditions should be promoted for these groups to enable them to have an economic stake in forest use, perform economic activities, and achieve and maintain cultural identity and social organization, as well as adequate levels of livelihood and well-being, through, *inter alia,* those land tenure arrangements which serve as incentives for the sustainable management of forests.

(b) The full participation of women in all aspects of the management, conservation and sustainable development of forests should be actively promoted.

1.(a) All types of forests play an important role in meeting energy requirements through the provision of a renewable source of bio-energy, particularly in developing countries, and the demands for fuelwood for household and industrial needs should be met through sustainable forest management, afforestation and reforestation. To this end, the potential contribution of plantations of both indigenous and introduced species for the provision of both fuel and industrial wood should be recognized. * * *

2. * * * (b) Specific financial resources should be provided to developing countries with significant forest areas which establish programmes for the conservation of forests including protected natural forest areas. These resources should be directed notably to economic sectors which would stimulate economic and social substitution activities.

3. * * * (f) National policies and/or legislation aimed at management, conservation and sustainable development of forests should include the protection of ecologically viable representative or unique examples of forests, including primary/old-growth forests, cultural, spiritual, historical, religious and other unique and valued forests of national importance.

(g) Access to biological resources, including genetic material, shall be with due regard to the sovereign rights of the countries where the forests are located and to the sharing on mutually agreed terms of technology and profits from biotechnology products that are derived from these resources.

(h) National policies should ensure that environmental impact assessments should be carried out where actions are likely to have significant adverse impacts on important forest resources, and where such actions are subject to a decision of a competent national authority.

9.(a) The efforts of developing countries to strengthen the management, conservation and sustainable development of their forest resources should be supported by the international community, taking into account the importance of redressing external indebtedness, particularly where aggravated by the net transfer of resources to developed countries, as well as the problem of achieving at least the replacement value of forests through improved market access for forest products, especially processed products. In this respect, special attention should also be given to the counties undergoing the process of transition to market economies. * * *

10. New and additional financial resources should be provided to developing countries to enable them to sustainably manage, conserve and develop their forest resources, including through afforestation, reforestation and combating deforestation and forest and land degradation.

11. In order to enable, in particular, developing countries to enhance their endogenous capacity and to better manage, conserve and develop their forest resources, the access to and transfer of environmentally sound technologies and corresponding know-how on favourable terms, including on concessional and preferential terms, as mutually agreed, in accordance with the relevant provisions of Agenda 21, should be promoted, facilitated and financed, as appropriate.

12. * * * (d) Appropriate indigenous capacity and local knowledge regarding the conservation and sustainable development of forests should, through institutional and financial support and in collaboration with the people in local communities concerned, be recognized, respected, recorded, developed and, as appropriate, introduced in the implementation of programmes. Benefits arising from the utilization of indigenous knowledge should therefore be equitably shared with such people. * * *

13.(a) Trade in forest products should be based on non-discriminatory and multilaterally agreed rules and procedures consistent with international trade law and practices. In this context, open and free international trade in forest products should be facilitated.

(b) Reduction or removal of tariff barriers and impediments to the provision of better market access and better prices for higher value-added forest products and their local processing should be encouraged to enable producer countries to better conserve and manage their renewable forest resources.

14. Unilateral measures, incompatible with international obligations or agreements, to restrict and/or ban international trade in timber or other forest products should be removed or avoided, in order to attain long-term sustainable forest management.

4. Wetlands

1971 Convention on Wetlands of International Importance
1976 U.N.T.S. 246

Article 1

1. For the purpose of this Convention wetlands are areas of marsh, fen, peatland or water, whether natural or artificial, permanent or temporary, with water that is static or flowing, fresh, brackish or salt, including areas of marine water the depth of which at low tide does not exceed six metres.

2. Wetlands should be selected for the List on account of their international significance in terms of ecology, botany, zoology, limnology or hydrology. In the first instance wetlands of international importance to waterfowl at any season should be included. * * *

5. Any Contracting Party shall have the right to add to the list further wetlands situated within its territory, to extend the boundaries of those wetlands already included by it in the List and shall, at the earliest possible time, inform the organization or government responsible for the continuing bureau duties specified in Article of any such changes. * * *

Article 2

* * *

5. Any contracting Party shall have * * * duties specified in Article 8 for any such changes. * * *

Article 4

1. Each Contracting Party shall promote the conservation of wetlands and waterfowl by establishing nature reserves on wetlands, whether they are included in the List or not, and provide adequately for their wardening.

2. Where a Contracting Party in its urgent national interest deletes or restricts the boundaries of a wetland included in the List, it should as far possible compensate for any loss of wetland resources, and in particular should create additional nature reserves for waterfowl and for the protection either in the same area or elsewhere, of an adequate portion of the original habitat. * * *

Article 5

The Contracting Parties shall consult with each other about implementing obligations arising from the Convention, especially in the case of a wetland extending over the territories of more than one Contracting Party or where water system is shared by

Contracting Parties. They shall at the same time endeavour to co-ordinate and support present and future policies and regulations concerning the conservation of wetlands and their flora and fauna.

Notes and Questions

1. The UN and its member states have made several attempts to integrate the work of the MEAs to achieve greater coordination for effectiveness and efficiency. Over the past two decades, these have each been inconclusive. The UN Environment Programme has been criticized for not developing the concrete modalities for synergies to enhance performance across the MEAs. See T. Inomata, Management Review of Environmental Governance Within the United Nations System, UN Doc. JIU/REP/2008/3 (2008). This UN Joint Inspection Unit report, issued at the UN Offices in Geneva, Switzerland, provides nations with the basis for aligning their financial contributions to the MEAs in ways that can provide the coordination needed to support climate change mitigation and adaptation objectives. It notes that creation of existing financial mechanisms for the MEAs had not resulted in providing stable and predictable funding to implement the MEAs. It finds that information is not efficiently shared across the MEAs, and management coordination is rudimentary. How can the UNFCCC negotiations under the Bali Action Plan help build such synergies, or will the conclusion of a new post-Kyoto agreement simply complicate or fracture the inter-MEA cooperation process further?

2. Each MEA has a role to play in responding to environmental disaster. The UN General Assembly began to provide for assistance in cases of natural disaster with UNGA Resolution 2816 (1971), creating the UN Disaster Relief Coordinator (UNDRO). Since then, UN agencies have made significant strides in developing coordinated systems for an international strategy for disaster reduction. The Hyogo Framework for Action 2005-2015 provides for building resilience at the national and community levels to disasters. See Acting With Common Purpose, Proceedings of the First Session of the Global Platform for Disaster Risk Reduction (Geneva, 2007), UN Doc. ISDR/GP/2007/7 (Geneva 2007); www.preventionweb.net/globalplatform/Index.html. How should the MEAs contribute to the Hyogo Framework, and *vice versa*? Can disaster risk reduction negotiations under the UNFCCC build cooperation among the MEAs? Which nations will pay for such preventative adaptation?

3. The Copenhagen negotiating text has proposals that climate change mitigation and adaptation should not adversely affect international trade. Is this a chimera? The text also provides for mitigation of GHG emissions internationally from civil aviation and shipping. Most countries anticipate that GHG mitigation will change manufacture and trade. See the World Bank report, International Trade and Climate Change: Economic, Legal and Institutional Perspectives (2007). Since climate change mitigation and adaptation are essentially environmental protection measures, will the measures adopted for

climate change be exempt from World Trade Organization's rules, in accordance with the General Agreement on Tariffs and Trade (GATT) Article XX? How should the world's trade minister collaborate with the UNFCCC, or are they to be disconnected from the global regime to reduced GHG emissions? The WTO's Committee on Trade and Environment has been charged with negotiating ways to clarify "the relationship between existing WTO rules and specific trade obligations" in the MEAs. WTO Ministerial Conference, 4th Session, Doha (2001), UN Doc. WTO WT/MIN(01)/DEC/W/1 (2001). Is this charge too narrow? Will the UNFCCC decisions restrict the WTO to a subsidiary role?

PROBLEM EXERCISE ON GEOENGINEERING

Alarmed at the "worst case" prospects of global climate change, a wide range of often fanciful proposals for "geo-engineering" have emerged. These tend to focus closely on a single technological "fix" to sequester carbon dioxide. Some have already raised intergovernmental concerns, such as by the International Maritime Organization. See Statement of Concern Regarding Iron Fertilization of the Oceans to Sequester Carbon Dioxide, UN Doc. IMO LC-LP.1/Circ14 (2007). Technological measures on a global scale would be launched to shield the Earth from solar radiation or maximize the marine uptake of carbon dioxide by changing ocean chemistry. These measures could be launched by one nation, or several nations, but would affect the entire biosphere. How would such measures be considered under Principle 21 of the Stockholm Conference on the Human Environment, as a general principle of international law? How would such measures be considered under the UNFCCC or the CBD or the UNCLOS? Few, if any, of the proponents of geo-engineering consider whether their proposals would be lawful under international law; what does this failure to consider the role (or rule) of law suggest about the political recognition accorded to environmental law as a platform for the emerging law of climate change?

Consider, for example, the analysis by D. Victor et al., The Geoegineering Option: A Last Resort Against Global Warming, Foreign Affairs (March/April 2009):

> * * * Governments should immediately begin to undertake serious research on geoengineering and help create international norms governing its use. * * *

> Today, the term "geoengineering" refers to a variety of strategies designed to cool the climate. Some, for example, would slowly remove carbon dioxide from the atmosphere, either by manipulating the biosphere (such as by fertilizing the ocean with nutrients that would allow plankton to grow faster and thus absorb more carbon) or by directly scrubbing the air with devices that resemble big cooling towers.

However, from what is known today, increasing the earth's albedo offers the most promising method for rapidly cooling the planet.

Most schemes that would alter the earth's albedo envision putting reflective particles into the upper atmosphere, much as volcanoes do already. Such schemes offer quick impacts with relatively little effort. For example, just one kilogram of sulfur well placed in the stratosphere would roughly offset the warming effect of several hundred thousand kilograms of carbon dioxide. Other schemes include seeding bright reflective clouds by blowing seawater or other substances into the lower atmosphere. Substantial reductions of global warming are also possible to achieve by converting dark places that absorb lots of sunlight to lighter shades—for example, by replacing dark forest with more reflective grasslands. (Engineered plants might be designed for the task.)

More ambitious projects could include launching a huge cloud of thin refracting discs into a special space orbit that parks the discs between the sun and the earth in order to bend just a bit of sunlight away before it hits the planet. * * *

At some point in the near future, it is conceivable that a nation that has not done enough to confront climate change will conclude that global warming has become so harmful to its interests that it should unilaterally engage in geoengineering. Although it is hardly wise to mess with a poorly understood global climate system using instruments whose effects are also unknown, politicians must take geoengineering seriously because it is cheap, easy, and takes only one government with sufficient hubris or desperation to set it in motion. Except in the most dire climatic emergency, universal agreement on the best approach is highly unlikely. Unilateral action would create a crisis of legitimacy that could make it especially difficult to manage geoengineering schemes once they are under way. * * *

How should international law address geo-engineering actions?

F. EARTH'S POLAR REGIONS

1. Introduction

The effects of climate change are readily apparent at the Earth's North and South Poles. These changes affect regions with vastly different legal regimes. The Antarctic continent (14 million square kilometers located around the South Pole and 60 degrees of latitude south) and adjacent seas are wholly governed by international public law treaties, principles and customs. The Arctic (14,056 million square kilometers located between the North Pole and

60 degrees latitude north) has no comparable land at the pole itself, and the adjacent circumpolar lands are governed by the nations whose sovereign territory was acquired and recognized over time: The Russian Federation, the U.S. (Alaska), Canada, Iceland, Denmark (The Greenland Home rule Inuit government), Norway, Sweden and Finland. The UN Convention on the Law of the Sea (UNCLOS) governs in the marine areas of both Poles, including the rights of free navigation through the polar waters.

The 1959 Antarctic Treaty, 19 I.L.M. 860, promoted by the U.S. under President Dwight Eisenhower, suspended the territorial claims of sovereignty over Antarctica made by various nations, and launched the era of scientific study. Article IX(1)(f) of the Treaty provides that the parties may make recommendations on measures regarding the "preservation and conservation of living resources of Antarctica." Scientific study in Antarctica permitted the first discovery of the "hole" in the stratospheric ozone layer over that continent; eroding ozone was later discovered over the North Pole. See C. Joyner, Governing the Frozen Commons: The Antarctic Regime and Environmental Protection (1989).

The 1980 Convention on the Conservation of Antarctic Marine Living Resources (CCAMLR), 19 I.L.M. 837 (1980), is akin to a regional MEA, for the Southern Oceans. It includes both the precautionary approach and the ecosystem management approach. It creates a Commission on the Conservation of Antarctic Marine Living Resources to coordinate the cooperation among nations and perform several conservation functions. It also establishes a Scientific Committee. The States Party to the Convention negotiated the Madrid Protocol on Environmental Protection in 1991, designating Antarctica as a nature reserve "devoted to peace and science", governing tourism in Antarctica and in Article 7 banning mining of the continent's abundant reserves of coal and other minerals (subject to a review of the ban in 50 years from the effective date of the Protocol). Article 11 established a Committee for Environmental Protection made up of the Parties and their experts.

The inter-governmental international systems exist to structure a regime for climate change mitigation and adaptation in Antarctica.

In contrast to this international regime, the Arctic environment is managed by the nations whose territories converge at the North Pole. In 1991, these States adopted a soft law Declaration on the Protection of the Arctic Environment, and began a cooperative Arctic Environmental Protection Strategy (AEPS), 30 I.L.M. 624 (1991). The nations agreed to do environmental impact assessments of all development activities in the Arctic and to respect the traditional and cultural needs of the Inuit and other indigenous peoples of the region. Through the Circumpolar Inuit Conference, the Inuit living in all polar nations have established a voluntary network for regional cooperation among their nations. In 1996, through the Ottawa Declaration, the Arctic nations established an Arctic Council to maintain the AEPS and extend cooperation for environmental protection in the region. See www.arctic-council.org/. In 1998 the Arctic Council adopted a soft-law Regional Programme of action for the Protection of the Arctic Marine Environment from Land-Based Activities.

As sea ice in the Arctic melts, it is blown onto the land and coastal erosion increases. The warmer Arctic also melts the top layer of permafrost. Human settlements have had to be relocated away from the coasts. The Arctic is in the midst of adaptation to climate change, and yet few formal governmental programs for adaptation exist. Nations outside the Arctic express concern that the atmosphere of the Arctic is a common concern of mankind, but that the Arctic nations are not organized to provide protection for this resource. See T. Koivurova, E. Keskitalo, & N. Bankes, eds., Climate Governance in the Arctic (2009). Significant pollution of the Arctic region, and much of the climate change, comes from human activity outside of the region, but there is no alignment of national domestic laws with international regimes to enhance protection of the region. The lack of stewardship is complicated by the fact that several States have unresolved boundary disputes between themselves. See Durham University's maps, BBC NEWS, Science/Nature, "Arctic Map Shows Dispute Hotspots," (August 5, 2008) at http://news.bbc.co.uk/1/hi/staging_site/in_depth/the_green_room/7543837.stm . New claims have been pressed; the Members of the Duma in the Russian Federation are asserting Russian sovereignty over a wider area of the North Pole's sea in order to access minerals once frozen under ice, but now accessible. Climate adaptation is difficult to establish where national borders are disputed.

While the Antarctic depends on international law to shape its climate change mitigation and adaptation regimes, the Arctic depends entirely on the national domestic laws in each Circumpolar nation, along with a weak and voluntary cooperative framework. As the Inuit assert their national rights in the region, and pressed by experiencing the effects of climate change, the governments of the region will need to develop new legal institutions or agreements to address the ongoing climate change adaptation needs. See M. Verhaag, It Is Not Too Late: The Need for a Comprehensive International Treaty To Protect The Arctic Environment, 15 Geo. Int'l Envtl. L. Rev. 555 (2003), and E. Bloom, The Polar Regions and the Development of International Law, 92 Am. J. Int'l L. 593 (1998).

As you study these provisions of the Antarctic regime, consider what international treaty might be negotiated for the Arctic. Could such a regime build capacity for more effective national environmental stewardship around the Arctic Circle?

2. Antarctica

PROTOCOL ON ENVIRONMENTAL PROTECTION TO THE ANTARCTIC TREATY
30 I.L.M. 1461 (1991)

Article 2
Objective and Designation

The Parties commit themselves to the comprehensive protection of the Antarctic environment and dependent and associated ecosystems and hereby designate Antarctica as a natural reserve, devoted to peace and science.

Article 3
Environmental Principles

1. The protection of the Antarctic environment and dependent and associated ecosystems and the intrinsic value of Antarctica, including its wilderness and aesthetic values and its value as an area for the conduct of scientific research, in particular research essential to understanding the global environment, shall be fundamental considerations in the planning and conduct of all activities in the Antarctic Treaty area.

2. To this end:

(a) activities in the Antarctic Treaty area shall be planned and conducted so as to limit adverse impacts on the Antarctic environment and dependent and associated ecosystems;

(b) activities in the Antarctic Treaty area shall be planned and conducted so as to avoid:

(i)Adverse effects on climate or weather patterns;

(ii)Significant adverse effects on air or water quality;

(iii)Significant changes in the atmospheric, terrestrial (including aquatic), glacial or marine environments;

(iv)Detrimental changes in the distribution, abundance or productivity of species or populations of species of fauna and flora;

(v)Whether there exists the capacity to monitor key environmental parameters and ecosystem components so as to identify and provide early warning of any adverse effects of the activity and to provide for such modification of operating procedures as may be necessary in the light of the results of monitoring or increased knowledge of the Antarctic environment and dependent and associated ecosystems; and

(vi)Whether there exists the capacity to respond promptly and effectively to accidents, particularly those with potential environmental effects;

(d) regular and effective monitoring shall take place to allow assessment of the impacts of ongoing activities, including the verification of predicted impacts; * * *

Article 7
Prohibition of Mineral Resource Activities

Any activity relating to mineral resources, other than scientific research, shall be prohibited.

Article 8
Environmental Impact Assessment

1.   Proposed activities referred to in paragraph 2 below shall be subject to the procedures set out in Annex I for prior assessment of the impacts of those activities on the Antarctic environment or on dependent or associated ecosystems according to whether those activities are identified as having:

(a) less than a minor or transitory impact;

(b) a minor or transitory impact; or

(c) more than a minor or transitory impact.

2.   Each Party shall ensure that the assessment procedures set out in annex I are applied in the planning processes leading to decisions about any activities undertaken in the Antarctic Treaty area pursuant to scientific research programmes, tourism and all other governmental and non-governmental activities in the Antarctic Treaty area for which advance notice is required under Article VII (5) of the Antarctic Treaty, including associated logistic support activities. * * *

6.   The assessment procedures set out in Annex I shall apply to any change in an activity whether the change arises from an increase or decrease in the intensity of an existing activity, from the addition of an activity, the decommissioning of a facility, or otherwise.

7.   Where activities are planned jointly by more than one Party, the Parties involved shall nominate one of their number to coordinate the implementation of the environmental impact assessment procedures set out in Annex I. * * *

Article 11
Committee for Environmental Protection

1.   There is hereby established the Committee for Environmental Protection.

2.   Each Party shall be entitled to be a member of the Committee and to appoint a representative who may be accompanied by experts and advisers.

3.   Observer status in the Committee shall be open to any Contracting Party to the Antarctic Treaty which is not a Party to this Protocol. * * *

Article 12
Functions of the Committee

1.   The functions of the Committee shall be to provide advice and formulate recommendations to the Parties in connection with the implementation of this Protocol, in-

cluding the operation of its Annexes, for consideration at Antarctic Treaty Consultative Meetings, and to perform such other functions as may be referred to it by the Antarctic Treaty Consultative Meetings. In particular, it shall provide advice on:

(a) the effectiveness of measures taken pursuant to this Protocol;

(b) the need to update, strengthen or otherwise improve such measures;

(c) the need for additional measures, including the need for additional Annexes, where appropriate;

(d) the application and implementation of the environmental impact assessment procedures set out in Article 8 and Annex I;

(e) means of minimizing or mitigating environmental impacts of activities in the Antarctic Treaty area;

(f)procedures for situations requiring urgent action, including response action in environmental emergencies;

(g) the operation and further elaboration of the Antarctic Protected Area system;

(h) inspection procedures, including formats for inspection reports and checklists for the conduct of inspections;

(i)the collection, archiving, exchange and evaluation of information related to environmental protection;

(j)the state of the Antarctic environment; and

(k) the need for scientific research, including environmental monitoring, related to the implementation of this Protocol. * * *

Article 16
Liability

Consistent with the objectives of this Protocol for the comprehensive protection of the Antarctic environment and dependent and associated ecosystems, the Parties undertake to elaborate rules and procedures relating to liability for damage arising from activities taking place in the Antarctic Treaty area and covered by this Protocol. * * *

Article 25
Modification or Amendment

1.   Without prejudice to the provisions of Article 9 [amendment of annexes], this Protocol may be modified or amended at any time in accordance with the procedures set forth in Article XII (1) (a) and (b) of the Antarctic Treaty.

2.   If, after the expiration of 50 years from the date of entry into force of this Protocol, any of the Antarctic Treaty Consultative Parties so requests by a communication addressed to the Depositary, a conference shall be held as soon as practicable to review the operation of this Protocol. * * *

5. (a) With respect to Article 7, the prohibition on Antarctic mineral resource activities contained therein shall continue unless there is in force a binding legal regime on Antarctic mineral resource activities that includes an agreed means for determining whether, and, if so, under which conditions, any such activities would be acceptable. This regime shall fully safeguard the interests of all States referred to in Article IV of the Antarctic Treaty and apply the principles thereof. Therefore, if a modification or amendment to Article 7 is proposed at a Review Conference referred to in paragraph 2 above, it shall include such a binding legal regime. * * *

3. The Arctic

1991 Declaration on the Protection of the Arctic Environment

We commit ourselves to a joint Action Plan of the Arctic Environmental Protection Strategy which includes:

- Cooperation in scientific research to specify sources, pathways, sinks effects of pollution, in particular, oil, acidification, persistent organic contaminants, radioactivity, noise and heavy metals as well as sharing these data;

- Assessment of potential environmental impacts of development activities;

- Full implementation and consideration of further measures to contain pollutants and reduce their adverse effects to the Arctic environment.

We intend to assess on a continuing basis the threats to the Arctic environment through the preparation and updating of reports on the state of the Arctic environment, in order to propose further cooperative action.

We also commit ourselves to implement the following measures of Strategy:

• Arctic Monitoring and Assessment Programme (AMAP) to monitor levels of, and assess the effects of, anthropogenic pollutants in components of the Arctic environment. To this end, an Arctic Monitoring and Assessment Task Force will be established. Norway will provide for an AMAP secretariat.

• Protection of the Marine Environment in the Arctic, to take preventive and other measures directly or through competent international organizations regarding marine pollution in the Arctic irrespective of origin.

• Emergency Prevention, Preparedness and Response in the Arctic, provide a framework for future cooperation in responding to the threat of environmental emergencies;

• Conservation of the Arctic Flora and Fauna, to facilitate the exchange of information and coordination of research on species and habitats of flora and fauna.

We agree to hold regular meetings to assess the progress made and coordinate actions which will implement and further develop the Arctic Environmental Protection Strategy.

We agree to continue to promote cooperation with the Arctic indigenous peoples and to invite their organizations to future meetings as observers.

G. HUMAN AND ENVIRONMENTAL RIGHTS

There is little in the Bali Action Plan that addresses human rights. While the atmosphere is a "common concern of humankind," recognizing this community right is awkward. The human rights regime focuses on the individual human being. The UNFCCC in Article 2 is aspirational, States "should protect the climate system for the benefit of present ands future generations of humankind." If sustaining Earth's biosphere is the fundamental objective, and the MEAs need to be read *in pari materia* with the UNFCCC regime, what should the relationship be to human rights law?

In like vein, human rights law has tended to the needs of individuals, while leaving to one side the legal interests of the community. Community environmental rights remain weekly acknowledged. In the UN Declaration on the Rights of Indigenous Peoples, the UN General Assembly recognized a community right among the indigenous. Should there not be a comparable universal right to life, as expressed in the 1992 UN World Charter for Nature (UNGA Res. 37/7)? See S. Kravchenko & J. Bonine, Human Rights and the Environment (2008).

Is human rights inevitably to become of feature of climate change law, or will it remain largely tangential? Small island states face an existential crisis due to sea level rise. States with territorial elevations only slightly more than a meter above sea level may wonder how human rights law protects their population. So far, human rights principles have not guided the negotiations for a post-Kyoto regime under the UNFCCC. These nations have a vote in the United Nations, and the COPs for MEAs. The Association of Small Island States (AOSIS) seeks to align these votes, but voting as bloc is difficult. Many small island states receive major foreign aid from China, for instance, and short term needs may trump long term human rights perspectives. But they have few natural resources or little geo-political power. They rely on the duty that other States owe them under Stockholm Principle 21 not to harm their territory with GHG emissions, or the duty nations have under Part XII of the UN Convention on the Law of the Sea to protect the oceans. International law, however, provides these states with few means to enforce these acknowledged international obligations. Are these international norms then illusory?

What human rights do citizens of places being threatened by sea level rise have that they can individually assert? Do they also have collective environmental rights under the principles of the 1992 Rio Declaration on Environment and Development, or the 1982 UN World Charter for Nature, UN GA Res. 37/7, or increasingly accepted new instruments such as the Earth Charter (ww.earthcharter.org)? For instance, if present and future generations of persons living in low lying coastal areas will become refugees, is the principle of intergenerational equity violated? The celebrated decision of the Supreme Court of the Philippines, per Chief Justice Hilario Davide, Jr., in Oposa v. Factoran, reprinted at 33 I.L.M. 168 (1994), afforded a national remedy for the interests of future generation in the wake of the destruction of national forests and biodiversity, but when the entire nation is at risk, what national remedy could be effective? Before what court or council can a citizen assert her or his right to life? In 2005, the Inuit Circumpolar Conference petitioned the Inter-American Commission on Human Rights for the failure of the USA to protect them from the effects of climate change. The Commission found it could not entertain the Petition. Alaskan-based Inuit suits in U.S. courts have not been based on human rights claims.

Tuvalu has secured an agreement with New Zealand to allow its people to relocate to New Zealand. Australia has declined Tuvalu's request. See S. Kravchenko, Right to Carbon or Right to Life: Human Rights Approaches to Climate Change, 9 Vermont J. Envtl. L. 514 (2008).

The Maldives have been especially active in asserting the human rights of their citizens before international bodies. At the request of the Maldives, the UN Human Rights Council asked the UN High Commissioner for Human Rights to advise on how international law of Human Rights should be considered by states and organizations addressing climate change impacts on individuals. UN Doc. A/HRC/7/L.21/Rev.1 (2008). The High Commissioner reported "The physical impacts of global warming cannot easily be classified as human rights violations, not least because climate change-related harm often cannot clearly be attributed to acts or omissions of specific States." Report of the Office of the High Commissioner for Human Rights on the Relationship Between Climate Change and Human Rights, para. 96, UN Doc. A/HRC/10/61 (2009). The High Commissioner observed that relief for human rights violations associated with climate change impacts should be obtained at the national level. See J. Knox, Linking Human Rights and Climate Change at the United Nations, 33 Harvard Envtl. L. Rev. 477 (2009). How effective will national recourse be for climate change victims?

More questions exist than answers as nations consider how a "rights based regime" should apply to climate change. Should ombundsmen be required in each nation to assert the need for national actions to protect citizens located in places where they are predictably at risk to harmful climatic effects? Should such ombundsmen be authorized to see to compel protection of environmental community rights, such as ecosystem services? The *Ministerio Publico* in Brazil performs some of these functions already. Should all nations have such a ministry? Should the UNFCCC or another UN body make new provisions to establish a forum and remedies for the victims of climate change? Would a case before the European Court of Human Rights or the Intern-American Court of Human Rights be likely to win an ecological refugee from climate change the right of sanctuary? If millions will need a new home, can or will nations open their doors to receive them even if they have such a right? Is there a role for a new international agreement on ecological refuses? See B. Docherty & T. Giannini, Confronting A Rising Tide: A Proposal for a Convention on Climate Change Refugees, 33 Harvard Envtl. L. Rev. 349 (2009). Is S. Kravchenko right when she concludes that "The accelerating pace of climate change puts the lives of current and future generations in danger...Attempts to use international human rights bodies, regional human rights court, or national courts, to combat climate change have met mixed results so far. However, they do start to reframe the debate, which might be their greatest contribution." Kravchencko supra, at 547.

In the short term, will appeals grounded on agreed humans rights be persuasive in accelerating the mitigation of GHG emissions? Will nations alter their immigration laws as an adaptation to the effect of human rights, and receive refugees in large numbers? Will the "laws of humanity and the dictates of public conscience" give rise to a new universal obligation to afford protection for the victims of climate change? In the longer term, it is clear that issues of environmental justice, fairness and equity will play a role in how climate change laws are being administered. See Symposium on Climate Change and Global Justice: Crafting Fair Solutions for Nations and Peoples, 33 Harvard Envtl. L. Rev. 297 (2009).

Notes and Questions

1. *Carbon Neutral Law Schools*: Does your law school have exchange agreements with law schools in another country, or teach a summer school abroad? How should you team up with your partner law school to mitigate your GHG emissions and adapt to the effects of climate change? Should you reach out to one or more law schools in developing countries and design and implement a joint implementation (JI) project, whether *ad hoc* or under the Kyoto Protocol format? Has your law school joined the IUCN Academy of Environmental Law (www.iucnael.org), a consortium of law schools across the world that advances environmental law for climate change mitigation and adaptation and other aspects of sustainable development? As a matter of equity, can a law school in a developed nation do its part to become carbon neutral without also assisting counterpart law schools in developing nations?

2. Is the right to energy so fundamental that it should rank as a human right, or be part of the right to development? Compare the several resolutions of the UN General Assembly, on "the Declaration on the Right to Development," UN Doc. UNGA A/Res/41/128 (1986), and A/Res/56/180 (2002), and consider Ian Brownlie, The Human Right to Development (1989). How does a right to energy rank with the responsibility to protect Earth's natural systems, as enshrined in the UN World Charter for Nature, Res 37/7, or the duty on states not to harm the territory or people of other states under Principle 21 of the Stockholm Declaration? Do these rights need a procedure in order that they be observed and attained? None of the MEAs, and few other international agreements, address energy as such. The Organization of Oil Exporting Parties (OPEC) draws its parties from oil exporting nations, other than the U.S. The International Energy Agency is established under the umbrella of the Organization for Economic Cooperation and Development (OECD), originally to encourage cooperation on fossil fuel supplies. The U.N. World Summit on Sustainable Development (WSSD) in 2002 adopted the first fully multilateral objectives for renewable energy. The gradual history of UN efforts to embrace renewable energy is summarized at N. Robinson, "Foreword" to A. Bradbrook & R. Ottinger, Energy Law & Sustainable Development (2003). The WSSD's Johannesburg Plan of Implementation adopted 6 goals for providing environmentally sound energy services and resources, including modern biomass technologies, furthering the transition to cleaner use of natural gas and liquid fossil fuels, and enhancing the institutional and regulatory framework and policies for a shift to sustainable energy systems. Report of the World Summit on Sustainable Development, Johannesburg August 26-Sept. 4, 2002, UN doc., A/CONF.199/20. Since then, 130 nations have established and become Members of the International Renewable Energy Agency (IRENA), which was established in Germany last January 2009. At the end of June, 2009, IRENA accepted the invitation of the United Arab Emirates to provide the headquarters for the new agency in Masdar City, Abu Dhabi. This city aims to be the Earth's first carbon-neutral, zero-waste city completely powered by renewable energy. IRENA's first Director General hails from France. The USA is a member, along with the small island states, and many developing nations. Germany will host the organization's "Innovations Branch," and Vienna will host a liaison office for the agency to work with other international energy and UN bodies, via the UN's regional office in Vienna. Abbas Al Lawati, UAE to Host IRENA HQ, The   Nation,   June   29,   2009,   at www.gulfnews.com/nation/Environmental/10327093.html.

CHAPTER 4. ECONOMIC FUNDAMENTALS

> *Climatescape:* **How Does The Economy Price Climate?**
>
> Nicholas Stern's analysis in 2007 of how the United Kingdom can make the economic transition to a carbon-neutral economy poses a challenge to legislators world-wide. What laws and policies must be changed to cope with climate change? How much more costly will the changes that are forced by climate disruption onto countries in the near future be over changes that countries voluntarily make in the near term? If most economists globally ignore the climate, and treat impacts on it as externalities, how can economic systems begin to price what climate or other ecosystem contribute to economic wealth, or price the losses of those benefits? As a commons, not yet effectively governed by international law, what legal tools should be designed to ensure that economic systems reflect climate disruption cost? This theme is revisited in Chapter 6 on Mitigation when the choices of a climate taxation verses climate cap-and-trade regimes are examined, and also in Chapter 8, in the context of applying different legal instruments, such as insurance, or of designing law reform initiatives.

A. INTRODUCTION

The former Chief Economist of the World Bank, Lord Nicholas Stern, believes that nations can contain greenhouse gas emissions within the existing economic order. In A Blueprint for a Safer World (2009), he examines how to manage climate change and create a new era of economic wellbeing as the world's population grows, through innovations in technology and a more carefully managed economic order. As he sees it, "At the heart of economic policy must be the recognition that the emission of greenhouse gases is a market failure. When we emit greenhouse gases we damage the prospects for others and, unless appropriate policy is in place, we do not bear the costs of the damage. Markets then fail in the sense that their main coordinating mechanism–prices–gives the wrong signals. * * * The appropriate response to a substantial market failure is not to abandon markets but to act directly to fix it, through taxes, or other forms of price correction, or regulation. Acting in this way on climate change, with complementary policies on technology and deforestation, will allow continued and substantial growth and poverty reduction. Allowing market failure to continue will damage the environment, curtail growth and lead to dislocation and conflict." Id. at 11.

What mix for reforms should be used to eliminate greenhouse gas emissions? Will economic instruments, such as taxes or a cap and trade system, be sufficient? Will traditional regulation of companies and their public offerings of securities provide the transparency and integrity to let investors in the markets make informed choices about their carbon footprints and climate change risks? Can insurance instruments be crafted to cover the entire range of climate change economic risks?

Adam Smith is often cited for his articulation of economic markets in An Inquiry Into the Nature and Causes of the Wealth of Nations (1776). Enthusiasts for free markets rarely go on to cite Adam Smith's support for government regulation. Government has the duty to protect "every member of society against injustice or oppression of every other member of it, or the duty of establishing an exact administration of justice." Id. John Stuart Mill believed that freedom depended on the existence of competitive markets. He cautioned, however, that free markets should not be used to destroy biodiversity or to convert all natural capital into human-made capital. Free markets, he argued, must be built on property laws and social mores that favor the common good. R. Costanza, et al, An Introduction to Ecological Economics (1997) 32.

In the context of climate change, the market failures associated with greenhouse gas emissions are causing growing harm to many. Is this inevitable? Is it the tragedy of the commons envisioned by Garrett Hardin in the first excerpt below? Do we correct the problem simply by adopting mix of regulations and economic instruments addressed to making emitters of greenhouse gases responsible for the full costs of their acts, or must we examine the deeper causes of climate disruption?

The Bali Action Plan was agreed upon just as the world entered the deepest global recession in 80 years. Regulatory systems for economic markets are not functioning efficiently or even in accordance with the laws that govern them. R. Posner, A Failure of Capitalism (2009). The collapse of traditional markets mechanisms calls into question whether governments can make corrections for greenhouse gas externalities before they reestablish order in the markets. Can a cap and trade system be engrafted onto existing, broken market systems, or must a parallel, new market be fabricated? Do we have time to sequentially mend the collapse of financial markets and then design a new carbon cycle market, or must governments address both concerns at once?

Analysis of these questions invariably renews the debate about how nations can add 2 billion more inhabitants to the Earth and meet their basic human needs, while consuming natural resources. As set forth in Chapter 3, the UN World Commission on Environment and Development in Our Common Future (1987) outlines the deterioration or collapse of many environment systems in all nations. In response, the UN's Rio de Janeiro Earth Summit of 1992 adopted Agenda 21, with 40 chapters of recommendations on how governments and markets should arrest degradation and build patterns of sustainable development. Chapter 3 addressed combating poverty, while

Chapter 4 focused on changing the consumption patterns of the rich around the world. Most of the recommendations in both chapters remain to be implemented. Why?

Perhaps more fundamental reform of the economic order is required. Do the directors of corporations have duties to society as well as to their stockholders? If companies persist in practices that deplete natural resources unsustainably, and maximize short term profits without regard for the externalities of their greenhouse gases, or their waste of water or electricity, or their failures to reuse and recycle materials, then perhaps the very model of the modern corporation needs to be reconsidered. World free trade agreements all assume that the market will not destroy the environment, and yet despite the analysis of Our Common Future, Agenda 21, or the reports of the Intergovernmental Panel on Climate Change, corporate economic behavior, combined with ineffective government regulation, has impaired most of the natural systems upon which all life depends.

Essentially, the time may have come to change the very definition of a business corporation, to redesign its mandate and mission, to include affirmative duties to protect the environment as a precondition of doing business. Governments in fact have done this when they created the international financial institution to assist former communist nations, with centrally planned economies, to transition to the market economy. The European Bank for Reconstruction & Development (EBRD) now has 20 years of building environmental protection into its investment decision-making. See www.ebrd.com. The EBRD's experience with facilitating a transition in economic life may also help guide economies from a fossil fuel energy regime to carbon neutral energy systems. Should governments reform the World Bank to give it an explicitly environmental mission co-equal to its current economic mission?

As you read the following excerpts, ask yourself what economic measures governments should undertake to stabilize the Earth's carbon cycle and manage greenhouse gas emissions. Can traditional economic measures do the job, or are more fundamental reforms required?

Notes and Questions

1. Is climate change a "tragedy of the commons" as portrayed by Garrett Hardin in 162 Science 1243 (1968)? What is the "commons" or ecosystem service that is free to all users? Who "owns" the atmosphere?

2. Should people be required to pay to use the atmosphere to dispose of byproducts of economic activities? Or should people be paid not to use it for greenhouse gas disposal? Consider these questions in connection with the following excerpts.

THE ROLE OF LAW IN DEFINING SUSTAINABLE DEVELOPMENT: NEPA RECONSIDERED

David R. Hodas

3 Widener L. Symp. J. 1 (1998)

* * * [T]he * * * fundamental question of how law can link environmental values with economic development needs to be addressed. Ad hoc, problem by problem international agreements, as important as they are, create a patchwork-like legal regime that is merely reactive to emerging environmental crises. * * * [D]omestic and international laws are not created in any systematic form, a framework within which environmentally sound, sustainable development decisions can be an integral part of day-to-day activities. * * * [T]he law has yet to be reformulated to reflect equally both the laws of ecology and of economics in effectuating the declaratory principle that each state has a sovereign right to exploit resources and act within its borders, but must be responsible for effects caused outside its borders. The economics side of the balance is embodied in the almost inviolate doctrine of sovereignty, which allows each state to maximize its own welfare as an actor in the world's market. Domestically, the economics side of the equation is represented in the laws of property and contract. Domestic regulation represents our ad hoc and piecemeal response to market failures. What is missing from the international law, and the domestic laws of the sovereign nations of the world, is a requirement of an accounting for the extraterritorial or external effects of purely domestic activities. * * * In economic terms, the environmental damages, if fully borne by the polluter or resource depleter, must be internalized into the decision-making, or else these "external' costs will not, in general, be taken fully into account by [polluters]."

The problem of uninternalized externalities and why law is a necessary internalizing force has been described most eloquently by Garrett Hardin in The Tragedy of the Commons. To each "rational" person, the cost of disposing of wastes in a common resource is less than the cost of purifying wastes before releasing them and "[s]ince this is true for everyone, we are locked into a system of fouling our own nest,' so long as we behave only as independent, rational, free-enterprisers." At every level of activity, private or local actions maximize immediate private or local benefit but have larger regional or global impacts, the costs of which are distributed to others. For instance, in the case of chlorofluorocarbons (CFC), which deplete stratospheric ozone, a single user of CFC enjoys the full benefit of its refrigerating capability, but when the CFCs are released into the atmosphere, their ozone depletion effects on human health and the environment are dispersed throughout the entire world. * * * Even though the entire world would benefit from emission reductions, each country and each person lacks any market-based, "rational" incentive to reduce emissions. Thus, although each country or individual views the use of the environment as a cost-free activity, their use imposes real and significant costs on ecosystem capacity, on society as a whole, and on future generations. * * *

Presently, the cost of emissions and the resultant ecosystem consequences are included in decisions precisely at $0.00.[82] Theoretically, if the price of every resource included the cost to the environment of using that resource,[83] then the market would encourage the efficient use of each resource, reducing total environmental costs to society. * * *

The values that shape our legal system are rooted in the seventeenth century philosophy of people such as John Locke, who lived in a low-population, predominantly rural society in which all actions and effects remained local. Common law doctrines that inform our thinking today date as far back as 1536, when the doctrine of public nuisance and its special injury rule first appeared. The tort law that evolved was based on concepts of specific harms caused by specific actions that were identifiable and localized in space and time. The justifications for strict causation and standing requirements associated with this tort law "made sense in an era when misuse of existing technology affected only people in the immediate vicinity of the activity and caused only limited harm. The concerns of 1536—a horse falling into a ditch along the side of a road—pale in comparison to "modern global climate change, loss of species diversity, chemical plant accidents, supertanker oil spills, contamination of air, land and water, and the like worries about."

The global climate change example illustrates the need to rethink legal relationships. Arguably, under existing law, states and individuals are liable for their wrongful conduct that proximately results in harm to another person or state. Global warming, however, driven by greenhouse gas emissions, results from the lawful and rightful acts of individuals, such as driving cars,

---

[82] F. Paul Bland, Problems of Price and Transportation: Two Proposals to Encourage Competition from Alternative Energy Resources, 10 Harv. Envtl. L. Rev. 345, 386 (1986) ("A decision not to consider external costs in itself quantifies them by setting their value at zero.").

[83] The question of how a particular environmental damage should be valued and what that value should be is beyond the scope of this article. However, considerable energy is going into answering this question. See, e.g., John A. Dixon et al, Economic Analysis of Environmental Impacts 42 (1996); External Environmental Costs of Electric Power: Analysis and Internalization (Olav Hohmeyer & Richard L. Ottinger eds., 1991); Richard L. Ottinger et al., Environmental Costs of Electricity (1990); Social Costs and Sustainability: Valuation and Implementation in the Energy and Transport Sector (Olav Hohmeyer et al. eds, 1997); Social Costs of Energy: Present Status and Future Trends (Olav Hohmeyer & Richard L. Ottinger eds., 1994); United Nations Indicators of Sustainable Development Framework and Methodologies (1996); Partha Dasgupta, Optimal Versus Sustainable Development, in The World Bank, Valuing the Environment 35 (Ismail Serageldin & Andrew Steer eds., 1995); and David W. Pearce, Valuing the Environment: Past Practice, Future Prospect, in The World Bank, Valuing the Environment 47 (Ismail Serageldin & Andrew Steer eds., 1995).

using electricity, raising livestock, growing rice, etc. Any warming will be the result of cumulative emissions scattered in space and time, without identifiable connection to any specific event, with effects that may be complex, diffuse and non-linear in space and time. Thus, even though human actions will cause global warming, the current legal system cannot assign any liability or blame. To make matters worse, the present legal and economic systems provide no incentive to minimize CO_2 emissions. On the contrary, for each person the benefit of present emissions exceeds the costs of emission reductions and the harms to that person in the future, even though the cumulative effect on the world of rapid climate change could be catastrophic. Thus, the legal and economic infrastructure rewards emissions, and each individual producer of CO_2 is acting perfectly rationally under existing systems.

The progressive role of law in ordering relationships to reflect revised visions of the world is frequently overlooked by scientists, policy-makers, government officials, and business persons, all of whom wish to avoid law's intricate rules. Law's potential as a force in molding conduct, however, should not be discounted. For the law to reflect the values of sustainable development, it must reflect the underlying paradigm of the interconnectedness of life on a densely populated, technologically intense world. By ordering a society's social and economic relationships, law serves policies that either shape new enterprises, or preserve established interests.[114]

Current law mirrors the view of most economists that environmental externalities are an inconvenient theoretical contaminant in an otherwise elegant market system. Externalities are only an afterthought in a legal system driven by an individual/market oriented paradigm. * * * There is now a need, indeed a mandate, for a law of environmentally-costed decision-making. * * *

THE ECONOMICS OF CLIMATE CHANGE: A PRIMER
Congressional Budget Office (April 2003)

The Earth's atmosphere and climate are part of the stock of natural resources that are available to people to satisfy their needs and wants over time. From an economic point of view, climate policy involves measuring and comparing people's valuations of climate resources, across alternative uses and at different points in time, and applying the results to choose a best course of action. Effective climate policy would balance the benefits and costs of using the atmosphere and climate and would distribute them among people in an acceptable way.

Common Resources and Property Rights
Prosperity depends not only on technological advances but also on developing legal, political, and economic institutions—such as private property,

---

[114] See Nicholas A. Robinson, A Legal Perspective on Sustainable Development, in The Legal Challenge of Sustainable Development 19, (J. Saunders ed. 1990).

markets, contracts, and courts—that encourage people to use resources to create wealth without fighting over or, in the case of renewable resources, significantly degrading them. The effectiveness of those institutions depends in part on characteristics of the resources. Market institutions do not work well when resources have the characteristics of public goods—that is, when it is difficult to prevent people from using the resources without paying for them (consumption is "non excludable") and when the incremental cost of allowing more users is near zero (consumption is "nonrival"). Market failures also arise when the many people using a resource affect each others' use—for instance, when rush hour drivers create congestion and air pollution. (In that case, consumption is nonexcludable but rival.) Those characteristics make property rights for public goods difficult to create and enforce. Private industry finds it relatively unprofitable to produce such goods, and consumers have relatively little incentive to maintain them. * * *

In the case of climate, people want to use the atmosphere to absorb greenhouse gases so that they may benefit from cheap food and timber and from plentiful fossil energy. In the long run, however, that use may significantly degrade the climate. * * *

Those complexities make it very difficult to determine the costs and benefits of reducing air pollution and to balance or distribute them in a politically acceptable way. Nor is it easy to develop standard property rights for air resources. As a result, people find it extremely challenging to use private markets to resolve conflicts over the use of air resources. The fundamental problem is transaction costs—the costs of motivating and coordinating exchanges; too many parties are involved in too many interactions to negotiate agreement in private markets. High transaction costs force governments to come up with other approaches to managing air pollution.

The Atmosphere and Climate

The problem of climate change involves very large transaction costs. Emissions come from the land and energy using activities of practically everyone in the world, and the potential burden of their effects will be borne through out the world by generations of people who are not even born. Moreover, many of the potential impacts of climate change—the disruption of ecosystems and extinction of species, for instance—are themselves public in nature.

Those factors make it very hard—if not impossible—to clearly define individual rights and responsibilities for many of the activities that may contribute to climate change and the effects that may come from it. Certain types of rights, such as rights to emit greenhouse gases by burning fossil fuels, could be delineated without great difficulty. Other rights, such as credits for carbon stored in the soil and trees of a forest stand or in the ocean, would be more complicated to define. Still others—such as the right to enjoy a particular type of climate in a particular part of the world at a particular time—would be impossible. Without clearly delineated, enforceable rights, individuals cannot easily bargain with one another in markets to resolve their conflicting claims. * * * [S]cientific and economic uncertainty involved makes climate tradeoffs extremely difficult to evaluate. * * *

Reaching collective agreement on a policy involving use of the atmosphere and climate change is an immense challenge because everyone has an incentive to "free ride." A successful agreement need not require equal action by all parties, but an agreement of any kind will break down if some parties sacrifice to meet an overall goal and other parties cheat, increasing their emissions in violation of the goal. Moreover, without a clear sense of whether, when, and by how much emissions should be constrained, nations will find it very hard to agree on the appropriate level of action. Equally important, nations have very different historical and economic circumstances; they vary widely in their ability and willingness to bear the cost of reducing emissions—or the possible costs of climate change. These factors help explain the great difficulty nations are experiencing in trying to reach agreement on a distribution of rights and responsibilities. * * *

Put another way, effective climate policy involves making investments today to yield future returns in the form of a beneficial climate—with due regard for the scientific and economic uncertainty involved. Those investments could take several forms, such as restrictions on emissions levels and research to improve understanding of the physical processes of climate change and to develop alternatives to fossil fuels.

Climate policy thus involves balancing investments that may yield future climate related benefits against other, nonclimaterelated investments—such as education, the development of new technologies, and increases in the stock of physical capital—that are also beneficial. If climate change turned out to be relatively benign, a policy that restricted emissions at very high expense might divert funds from other investments that could have yielded higher returns. Conversely, if climate change proved to be a very serious problem, the same policy could yield a much higher return.

Since resources devoted to climate policy would be diverted from other uses, the total benefit from all types of investment would be greatest if the rates of return were the same "at the margin"—that is, for the last dollar of each type of investment. However, efforts to ensure equal rates of return become extremely complicated in the case of long term issues such as climate change. Few other investments compare with climate policy in yielding an enormous variety of returns on a global scale and over such long periods, or in having returns that are as uncertain.

Furthermore, very long time horizons render the results of cost benefit analyses extremely sensitive to the rate of return that is assumed for the analysis. The appropriate course of action—and the appropriate level of climate related investment—depends on how one balances the competing interests of present and future generations and how one accounts for the existing scientific and economic uncertainty. Those choices, in turn, are expressed in the desired rate of return on that investment—that is, the chosen discount rate. While analysts have reached no consensus on what discount rate should be applied, several of them have argued that it should be lower than the rates assumed in typical cost benefit analyses, for several reasons:

• Society's investment opportunities over the long term are uncertain;
• There are no centuries long financial markets in which to invest risk free or from which to determine very long term rates of return; and
• People's attitudes toward the distant future may not be correctly reflected in the assumption of a constant discount rate based on historical market returns. * * *

If lower discount rates are deemed appropriate for evaluating very long term costs and benefits, they justify taking measures to increase society's rate of investment not only in preserving a benign climate but in expanding the stock of all types of long lasting capital. By increasing investment to the point at which the last investments all earn rates of return that are consistent with the lower discount rate, such measures would tend to reduce current generations' consumption in order to provide more wealth for generations in the future. * * *

Coping with Uncertainty

[S]cientific and economic uncertainty * * * complicates assessment of the costs and benefits of averting climate change. No one wishes to undertake extensive, expensive actions to solve a problem that turns out to be relatively mild—or to take no action to solve a problem that later proves catastrophic. Policymakers are thus forced to hedge their bets and pre pare for more than one possible outcome, with the additional complication that whatever outcome occurs is likely to be largely irreversible.

In general, uncertainty about a problem may indicate the need for more, or less, action to address it, depending on the nature of the unknowns. The amount of appropriate action also depends on how risk averse people are—that is, how much they are willing to pay to avoid an uncertain but costly outcome. The greater their degree of risk aversion, the more people will be willing to sacrifice today to reduce the likelihood of adverse changes in climate.

Studies that explicitly account for uncertainty generally recommend greater effort to avert climate change than do analyses that do not account for it—mainly because the studies include the long term discount rate as an uncertain variable. However, the way those studies treat uncertainty about the discount rate in effect simply applies greater weight to future generations and therefore recommends more action. Because the issue of discounting is mainly a distributional one, many analysts question whether it should be treated as a matter of uncertainty in the same sense that, say, the sensitivity of the climate to carbon dioxide concentrations is uncertain. * * *

Distributional Issues

Crafting climate policy involves not only balancing costs and benefits but also distributing them—within and among countries, regions, and generations. Policies that balance overall costs and benefits do not necessarily balance them for every person, and policies that maximize the net benefits to society do not necessarily provide benefits to each individual. A policy may yield positive net benefits by causing both very large aggregate losses and only slightly larger aggregate gains.[9]

Distributional concerns are at the heart of much of the controversy about climate policy. For example, imposing controls on emissions today would cut coal mining companies' profits but would benefit manufacturers of solar energy equipment. * * * Similarly, emissions control policies would impose costs on people today and yield benefits to people in the future.

Issues Among Generations

Acting to prevent climate change today would place a burden on people now alive and would probably leave coming generations with a climate more similar to today's—but with somewhat less wealth—than they would have had otherwise. In contrast, not acting would benefit people today and probably yield somewhat more wealth in the future—but it might also leave the world with a different and possibly worse climate for many generations to come.

Choosing among policies is not purely a matter of balancing costs and

---

[9] In studying economic problems, economists seek policies that will improve economic efficiency—that will make at least one person better off without making anyone worse off. Such policies are termed *Pareto improvements*. However, many policy proposals whose net benefits exceed their net costs also have substantial distributional effects. That is, the improvements are worth more than the losses, all told, but some people are made worse off even while others are made better off. Economists refer to such policies as *potential Pareto improvements*: in principle, the winners could compensate the losers for their losses and still be better off. Such a policy passes a standard cost benefit test but could still make many people worse off unless it also provided for their compensation.

benefits but also a question of how to distribute the benefits of energy consumption, land use, and climate among generations. Policy recommendations from the integrated assessments described earlier are very sensitive to such intergenerational choices. Instead of restricting emissions, current generations could address these distributional concerns by making additional capital investments to benefit future generations, with the intention of offsetting potential future damages from climate change or of compensating future generations for those damages. However, because of uncertainty about the kind of damages climate change would cause, it is unclear whether (or how much) more capital would be necessary—or useful—to offset them. Also uncertain is whether intervening generations would pass the additional resources on to subsequent generations or consume the resources themselves.

Concerns Within and Among Countries

Dealing with the issue of climate change is likely to involve difficult decisions about distributing costs and burdens within countries. Some workers and industries—coal producers, electric utilities, and others—would probably bear a disproportionate share of the burden of restrictions on domestic emissions, as would the regions of a country that produced fossil energy. Distributional concerns also dominate discussions of international climate policy and are likely to play at least as important a role in its development as the balancing of costs and benefits will. Policymakers in many developing countries emphasize that developed countries are responsible for the bulk of historical emissions and that many developing countries are apparently more vulnerable to—and less able to cope with—the more damaging effects of climate change. Such leaders tend to argue that developed countries should not only shoulder any near term burden of reducing emissions but also compensate developing countries for climate related damages. They also tend to be skeptical of arguments that favor balancing net economic costs and benefits, recognizing that such reasoning may be used to gloss over both distributional issues and disparities in impacts.

In contrast, other policymakers in both developed and developing countries tend to be less concerned about climate related issues because they believe that their nations are not particularly vulnerable to potential changes in climate or will be able to adapt to whatever changes may occur.

4. Trade-Offs Among Policy Options

* * * [P]olicymakers * * * can choose from among a wide variety of approaches * * * .

Governments could control greenhouse gas emissions in a variety of ways. Under direct command and control regulation, the government could specify the types of equipment and technology that may be used, or it could specify energy efficiency or emissions standards for buildings, vehicles, and equipment. Alternatively, the government could impose emissions taxes or fees, which would discourage emissions by increasing their cost. It could also directly control emissions through a system of emissions permits, or allowances, that would strictly limit the total quantity of emissions.

Another option combining elements of taxes and permits would be a hybrid permit system under which the government allocated a fixed quantity of permits but sold an unlimited number of additional permits at a set "trigger" price. In such a system, if the cost of reducing emissions rose above the trigger price, emitters would simply buy additional permits rather than reduce emissions further. The system would thus cap the incremental cost of emissions at the trigger price—acting, in effect, like a tax.

* * * In contrast to direct controls, market based systems give firms and households stronger incentives to find low cost ways to reduce emissions through behavioral changes and innovative technologies.

In the case of carbon dioxide emissions from the burning of fossil fuels, the most direct approaches would involve taxes or permits based on the carbon content of fossil fuels.[1] Under either system, fossil fuel suppliers— producers and importers of coal, oil, and natural gas—would have to pay taxes or acquire permits in proportion to the carbon content of the fuel they sold. Such systems would be relatively simple to administer, monitor, and enforce if they were applied at the point of import or first sale because relatively few companies actually import or produce fossil fuels. The system would impose price increases or restrictions on output that would filter down the distribution chain, but it would avoid the administrative difficulties of a system that directly taxed "down stream" retailers and consumers.

The relative ease of regulating energy related emissions contrasts with the difficulties of regulating emissions from most other sources, particularly the substantial fraction that originates from forestry and farming. Because those other emissions come from many different kinds of mainly small sources under highly variable conditions, they tend to be much more difficult

---

[1] The quantity of carbon dioxide emitted is directly proportionate to the carbon content of fuels and is therefore easy to measure. Carbon taxes fall most heavily on coal, which is composed almost entirely of carbon; they fall somewhat less heavily on petroleum products and least heavily on natural gas because those fuels also contain hydrogen. An emissions tax of $100 per metric ton of carbon equivalent translates to roughly $50 per short ton of coal, 25 cents per gallon of gasoline, and $1.50 per thousand cubic feet of natural gas. Other taxes on fuels—for instance, ad valorem (or value added) taxes in proportion to sales prices or energy taxes in proportion to the energy content of fuels—would not be targeted specifically toward the carbon content and would therefore be somewhat less cost effective in discouraging carbon emissions.

to track and measure. * * * For instance, carbon emissions from fossil fuels could be partly offset by paying landowners to plant trees to absorb and sequester carbon, thus reducing net emissions. Some tree planting is already supported for other purposes, such as soil conservation, and expanding those policies would be relatively straightforward. However, for the purposes of carbon sequestration, such policies are complicated by issues that do not arise in regulating fossil fuels. They include the costs of monitoring tree growth to determine how much carbon is absorbed and the difficulty of determining whether landowners would have grown the trees anyway. Another complicating factor is how sequestration activities might ripple through markets and affect carbon flows on agricultural and forest land not dedicated to sequestration. For instance, a decision to set aside a certain amount of forest for sequestration might lead to another area of forest being cleared that otherwise would have remained untouched. In that case, the carbon sequestered in the set aside area would simply be offset by clearing elsewhere.

Taxes and Permits: Similarities and Differences

Taxes and permits affect a regulated activity in similar ways as long as people can buy and sell the permits on open markets. A tax on the carbon content of fuels directly raises the price of those fuels for the end user; a strict permit system indirectly raises the price by reducing the quantity of fuel that suppliers can sell. Either way, higher prices lead people to reduce their fuel consumption and thus their emissions. So for any level of emissions restrictions in a permit system, there is a corresponding tax level that will achieve the same purpose. In principle, both approaches should lead to identical levels and prices of emissions.

In practice, however, uncertainty about the costs and benefits of restricting emissions can greatly influence the relative cost effectiveness of the two approaches. The government could impose a tax, expecting some level of reduced emissions; but emissions could end up higher or lower than it expected. Likewise, the government could impose a permit system with a cap on emissions and expect a given cost for meeting the cap; but that cost could end up being much higher or lower. And in either case, the price might not be consistent with the uncertain benefits of mitigating climate change. Which system is preferable depends on which type of uncertainty is the greatest and how rapidly costs rise—and benefits fall—as the government tightens restrictions on emissions. * * *

The Distributional Effects of Regulation

Regulatory systems generally create winners and losers, even when the benefits of less pollution are ignored. Balancing the distributional effects of such systems can be more complicated and controversial than balancing their costs and benefits. Economic analysis provides several useful insights about the distributional issues involved in regulating greenhouse gas emissions. * * *

Some analysts have argued that the regulation of energy markets might not be costly because energy conservation pays for itself. According to that point of view, people fail to use energy efficiently, either because they do not make sensible decisions about energy use or because they are poorly informed, or because they face a variety of market failures or barriers that deter them from making more sensible decisions or becoming better informed. Proponents of that view believe that the government may be able to regulate energy use and emissions at a net savings to the economy by providing information, overcoming market barriers, and correcting market failures—for example, by including energy efficiency requirements in standards governing buildings and appliances—and that the resulting energy savings may more than pay for the additional costs of more efficient equipment. * * *

Regulations and Taxes Have Substantial Distributional Effects

A third important insight is that the distributional consequences of pricing and permit systems can be very large compared with their costs and benefits. Whenever the government restricts something of value, people will bid up the market price in trying to obtain it. The difference between the supply, or production, price and the higher market price is known as a scarcity rent.

If the government restricts emissions by imposing a tax, it will receive the scarcity rent as tax revenues. By contrast, if it imposes a permit system and gives the permits away, the permits' recipients will receive the scarcity rents as higher profits—because they can either charge higher prices for the fuel they sell or sell the permit. The income received as tax revenue or scarcity rents can be many times larger than the net efficiency loss. One important consequence of that fact is that efforts to restrict emissions may encourage the affected parties to seek regulatory provisions that provide them with tax exemptions or access to permits—that is, they may engage in rent seeking behavior. For example, fossil fuel suppliers might advocate a system in which they were given emissions permits free of charge—so that they would receive the entire scarcity rent resulting from the emissions limits.

Distributional Effects Depend on How the
Government Regulates Emissions

Under a system of taxes or auctioned permits, the government would receive revenues, and it could redistribute some of them in various ways—by cutting other taxes, reducing government debt, or funding new programs. Each method of "recycling," or returning revenues to the economy, would benefit different groups of consumers and suppliers in different ways. Some of those approaches could offset some of the costs of regulation but probably not all of them.

The case of permits is more complicated than that of taxes because permits can be distributed in different ways: the government could auction them and receive revenues, it could give the permits away, or it could use a combination of the two approaches. Auctioned permits are similar to emissions taxes in their distributional effects. In contrast, freely allocated emissions permits would greatly benefit their recipients, who could reap profits from the now scarce right to sell fossil fuels (while passing on most of the costs to fuel consuming businesses and households) or from the sale of permits to a fuel supplier. One possible approach to a permit system, known as grandfathering, would be to give all the permits to fossil fuel suppliers in proportion to their historical sales. Another method would be to distribute permits free to households and require that fuel suppliers buy them. Suppliers would then include the cost of the permits in the price of fuel. That approach would spread regulatory costs more evenly across the population but would also involve high transaction costs. * * *

TO TAX OR NOT TO TAX CARBON—IS THAT THE QUESTION?
Roberta Mann
ABA Natural Resources & Environment (Summer 2009)

Glaciers are melting, sea levels are rising, and the United States still can't decide on its carbon mitigation strategy. On the bright side, the United States has decided it should have a carbon mitigation strategy. * * * An increasing number of scholars favor the carbon tax choice. Admittedly, many of them are tax professors or economists. One could dismiss these voices under the theory that to a hammer, every problem looks like a nail. On the other hand, if a carbon tax provides benefits, it would be irresponsible to dismiss the option based on a semantic distaste for the term tax.

A cap-and-trade system and carbon taxes are both market mechanisms that reduce demand for carbon-intensive goods by increasing their cost. A classic cap-and-trade system imposes a marketwide quantity restriction while allowing emitters to choose between reducing their own output and purchasing allowances to emit. A classic carbon tax is a cost restriction: emitters will pay a fixed amount for emissions and may choose between reducing emissions or paying a price. In a theoretically perfectly economically efficient market, a carbon tax and a cap-and-trade regime would have the same outcome because one could predict the cost of cap-and-trade and the emissions reductions of a carbon tax. In the real world, a carbon tax would create a stable price and fluctuating emissions. A cap-and-trade system would create stable emissions and fluctuating costs.

Congress could implement a carbon tax in three steps: (1) determine the level of tax; (2) determine where to impose the tax (upstream or downstream) and what to tax (carbon or a more complete list of greenhouse gases (GHGs)); and (3) determine how to apply the tax revenue. Congress could also implement a cap-and-trade system in three steps: (1) set the emissions cap (on carbon or a more complete list of GHGs); (2) determine who receives allowances (upstream or downstream); and (3) distribute (or auction) allowances. If allowances are auctioned, then Congress would also need to decide how to use the auction revenue.

British Columbia and Boulder, Colorado, have implemented a downstream carbon tax, an upstream tax would be more administrable on a national basis as there are many fewer upstream sources of carbon emissions. Congress could address 82 percent of U.S. GHG emissions by levying an upstream carbon tax on fewer than 2,500 upstream or midstream entities, versus millions of downstream end users of energy. Jonathan L. Ramseur & Larry Parker, Carbon Tax and Greenhouse Gas Control: Options and Considerations for Congress, Cong. Res. Serv. R40242 (Feb. 23, 2009). Similarly, carbon dioxide (CO_2) could be used as a proxy for GHG emissions, as CO_2 constitutes the vast majority of GHGs emitted. Because a unit of fossil fuel emits the same amount of carbon regardless of when or where it is burned, measuring tax is as simple as measuring the amount of the particular fossil fuel used.

In a cap-and-trade system, the problems may just be beginning when the allowances have been distributed. Carbon allowances will become the basis for a flurry of new financial derivatives, spurring speculation. The potential dangers of such new derivatives form a more persuasive argument against cap-and-trade in light of recent financial crises, as many have grown more concerned about complex financial instruments. Ultimately, industry concern about excessive costs will drive modifications of any cap-and-trade system. A carbon tax system might also be subject to a drive for modifications for a variety of reasons, but it doesn't need a cost cap. By design, it is a cost restriction. In contrast, the cost of a cap-and-trade system is theoretically unlimited—the market, not the system designers, will decide the cost. A classic cap-and-trade system allocates allowances each year on a use-it-or-lose-it principle. The market decides the cost of the allowances as they trade throughout the year. One likely modification to contain costs is a "safety valve." When costs of carbon allowances exceed a certain amount, the government will release additional allowances at a specified safety valve price. A safety valve sets a ceiling on carbon emission prices, just like a carbon tax. A safety valve also allows additional carbon emissions over the cap, just like a carbon tax. Opponents to safety valves argue that they would provide an "easy out" from the pressure to innovate and reduce the incentive to rapidly reduce emissions.

The availability of banking, borrowing, offsets, and international credits can further complicate a cap-and-trade system. Banking provides timing flexibility by allowing an allowance holder to save its allowances to use in future years. Borrowing entails emitting now and "paying back" later, at a specified "interest rate." Borrowing acts like a safety valve, except that at some point the emitter is supposed to pay back the extra emissions. Offsets can be investments in projects that absorb GHGs, such as forest conservation. Offsets represent projects that absorb carbon, so for cap-and-trade purposes, the offset acts as a negative emission. It can be challenging to accurately measure the amount of carbon absorbed by an offset project, and the projects must be monitored. International credits extend the cap-and-trade system beyond the sovereign boundaries of the United States. In particular, offsets and international credits pose significant compliance issues.

President Obama's budget counts on revenue from carbon allowance auctions to fund tax cuts and health care reform. The two carbon tax bills introduced last year would raise between $70 and $126 billion per year. Thus, revenue could be raised using either carbon mitigation strategy. Costs will increase for consumers under either strategy.

A carbon tax has two main disadvantages: (1) it does not provide a set amount of carbon reduction and, therefore, would yield uncertain emissions, and (2) it is called a tax. However, a cap-and-trade program, particularly if it includes measures to reduce price volatility, may also include a risk of uncertain emissions. And while there is no doubt that the word "tax" strikes terror in the hearts of politicians, opponents of carbon mitigation have argued that a cap-and-trade approach should be labeled "cap-and-tax" because it would effectively act as a tax. If a cap-and-trade is called a tax, why not have a direct, simple tax?

A carbon tax has several advantages over a cap-and-trade program. First, a carbon tax is easier to explain and understand than a cap-and-trade program. A cap-and-trade system may have more moving parts, which may be challenging to follow, particularly the emission allowance allocation scheme. * * * Moreover, if a classic cap-and-trade system is modified to control price volatility, it increases in complexity and becomes less transparent. A carbon tax would not add to the volatility of energy prices, such as electricity and household fuels, unlike a cap-and- trade program. A carbon tax would provide industry with better information to guide investment decisions (e.g., energy-efficiency improvements and/ or equipment upgrades). A carbon tax may provide implementation advantages, including greater transparency, reduced administrative burden, and relative ease of modification.

Of course, although a carbon tax is arguably a simpler approach, it must be conceded that the U.S. tax code is complex. Congress could establish a carbon tax framework that rivals the complexity of a cap-and-trade program.

Congress could also provide subsidies or exemptions to the fossil fuel industry that would run counter to a carbon tax. Further, policymakers could allow for tax credits for carbon sequestration projects, similar to carbon offsets in a cap-and-trade regime. As with carbon offsets in a cap-and-trade program, this would require a further level of administrative responsibilities, potentially weakening the program if the sequestration projects lack credibility.

Perhaps the most significant difference between a carbon tax and a cap-and-trade system is that the legislation would fall into different committee jurisdictions within Congress. Indeed, the committee jurisdiction factor may play the deciding role in the debate. The committees developing the GHG emission legislation may have varying views about the relative values of uncertain costs versus uncertain emission reductions. Ultimately, questions of design may cloud the real issue. The United States, the historical worldwide leader in carbon emissions, needs to control those emissions before it is too late for the planet. Whether the control occurs via a carbon tax, a cap-and-trade system, or the regulatory efforts of the Environmental Protection Agency is a minor point. The entire U.S. economy is free-riding when it comes to carbon emissions. Sooner rather than later, we'll pay the price. One thing is certain: the longer we wait, the higher the price will be.

Notes and Questions

1. Carbon taxes and cap-and-trade programs are discussed further in Chapter 6.

2. Environmental externalities eventually are noticed, as environmental degradation. How should Congress legislate to identify and anticipate externalities? Economists struggle with this challenge. Consider the following excerpt from D.R. Hodas, The Role of Law in Defining Sustainable Development: NEPA Reconsidered, 3 Widener L. Symp. 1, 25 (1998):

> The stubborn tendency of economists to ignore messy, but crucial, reality is behind much of the failure to include externalities (a variety of what economists call transaction costs) in legal doctrine.

On a theoretical level, the consistent tendency to assume away inconvenient facts is traceable to a misuse of the "Coase Theorem" in law and economics. Although the "Coase Theorem" is one of the most famous results in law and economics, it is clear from "The Problem of Social Cost" itself that Coase regarded the zero-transaction-cost assumption as unrealistic. Indeed, his previous work made it clear that he regarded transaction costs as not only widespread but essential to understanding the structure of the economy. More recently, he has explained his view of the Coase Theorem more fully. In discussing what would happen in a world of zero transaction costs, he explains, his aim:

was not to describe what life would be like in such a world but to provide a simple setting in which to develop the analysis and, what was even more important, to make clear the fundamental role which transaction costs do, and should, play in the fashioning of the institutions that make up the economic system. R. Coase, The Firm, the Market, and the Law 13 (1988).

He goes on to point out that a world without transaction costs "has very peculiar properties." Id. at 14. For example, monopolies would act like competitors, insurance companies would not exist, and there would be no economic basis for the existence of firms. Indeed, he points out that since transactions are costless, it would also cost nothing to speed them up, "so that eternity can be experienced in a split second." Id. at 15. "It would not seem worthwhile," he concludes, "to spend much time investigating the properties of such a world."

Little wonder that Coase was dismayed to find the world of zero transaction costs described as a Coasian world. Id. at 174. Instead, he says, "[i]t is the world of modern economic theory, one which I was hoping to persuade economists to leave." The failure of economists to consider transaction costs is, he believes, the major reason for their inability to account for the operation of the economy in the real world. As a result, their policy proposals are the "stuff that dreams are made of." Id. at 185. Given his actual views, the fame and impact of the Coase Theorem are at least a bit ironic. Indeed, in certain respects Coase has more in common with some of his critics that with many of his supporters. See R. Findley & D. Farber, 1997 Supplement to Cases and Materials on Environmental Law 35-36 (4th ed. 1997); D. Farber, Parody Lost, Pragmatism Regained: The Ironic History of the Coase Theorem, 83 Va. L. Rev. 397, 398 (1997).

3. Our evaluation of events is shaped by the data we use to measure those events. To accurately evaluate phenomena our measurement data must be both valid and reliable. To be valid it must be congruent with the phenomena purported to be measured. To be reliable, data generated by consistent measurement techniques must be consistent over time. Because understanding complicated phenomena is both enabled and limited by the measurements we make, what we decide to measure and the measurement criteria we use can dramatically alter how conduct is perceived and evaluated, and affect the reliability and validity of the data.

The accounting standards we apply to business data can have dramatic effects. For instance, an analysis of the 1993 six-month results of a major German manufacturer demonstrated that if the company applied German accounting standards to its data, it earned a profit of about DM 168 million but if American generally accepted standards were used, the company would have suffered a DM 949 million loss— a swing of over DM 1.1 billion (about $660 million in 1993). See K. Meuller, A Financial Analyst's Perspective II, in J. Leggett, ed., Climate Change and the Financial Sector (1996). Did the company make a profit or did it lose money?

The measurements we use to evaluate conduct define how people will act. How would company management react? Investors? How should bonuses be calculate? What incentives or disincentives do the metrics we choose create?

The scientific, economic and social metrics we use to measure climate change impacts, mitigation, compliance and success must be chosen carefully: "what gets measured gets done." Consider what metrics underlie the thinking in the materials you read throughout this book. How are they defined? What conduct will they promote and/or inhibit? What role should lawyers play in articulating the metrics that will be foundational for climate change law internationally, nationally, and locally?

THE ECONOMICS OF CLIMATE CHANGE
Nicholas Stern
(Crown Copyright Reserved 2007)

INTRODUCTION

The economics of climate change is shaped by the science. * * *

Economics has much to say about assessing and managing the risks of climate change, and about how to design national and international responses for both the reduction of emissions and adaptation to the impacts that we can no longer avoid. If economics is used to design cost-effective policies, then taking action to tackle climate change will enable societies' potential for well-being to increase much faster in the long run than without action; we can be 'green' and grow. Indeed, if we are not 'green', we will eventually undermine growth, however measured.

This Review takes an international perspective on the economics of climate change. Climate change is a global issue that requires a global response. The science tells us that emissions have the same effects from wherever they arise. The implication for the economics is that this is clearly and unambiguously an international collective action problem with all the attendant difficulties of generating coherent action and of avoiding free riding. It is a problem requiring international cooperation and leadership. * * *

Economists describe human-induced climate change as an 'externality' and the global climate as a 'public good'. Those who create greenhouse gas emissions as they generate electricity, power their factories, flare off gases, cut down forests, fly in planes, heat their homes or drive their cars do not have to pay for the costs of the climate change that results from their contribution to the accumulation of those gases in the atmosphere. * * *

SUMMARY OF CONCLUSIONS

There is still time to avoid the worst impacts of climate change, if we take strong action now. * * *

Climate change will affect the basic elements of life for people around the world—access to water, food production, health, and the environment. Hundreds of millions of people could suffer hunger, water shortages and coastal flooding as the world warms.

Using the results from formal economic models, the Review estimates that if we don't act, the overall costs and risks of climate change will be equivalent to losing at least 5% of global GDP each year, now and forever. If a wider range of risks and impacts is taken into account, the estimates of damage could rise to 20% of GDP or more.

In contrast, the costs of action—reducing greenhouse gas emissions to avoid the worst impacts of climate change—can be limited to around1 % of global GDP each year.

The investment that takes place in the next 10-20 years will have a profound effect on the climate in the second half of this century and in the next. Our actions now and over the coming decades could create risks of major disruption to economic and social activity, on a scale similar to those associated with the great wars and the economic depression of the first half of the 20th century. And it will be difficult or impossible to reverse these changes.

So prompt and strong action is clearly warranted. Because climate change is a global problem, the response to it must be international. It must be based on a shared vision of long-term goals and agreement on frameworks that will accelerate action over the next decade, and it must build on mutually reinforcing approaches at national, regional and international level. * * *

Even at more moderate levels of warming, all the evidence—from detailed studies of regional and sectoral impacts of changing weather patterns through to economic models of the global effects—shows that climate change will have serious impacts on world output, on human life and on the environment.

All countries will be affected. The most vulnerable—the poorest countries and populations—will suffer earliest and most, even though they have contributed least to the causes of climate change. The costs of extreme weather, including floods, droughts and storms, are already rising, including for rich countries.

Adaptation to climate change—that is, taking steps to build resilience and minimise costs—is essential. It is no longer possible to prevent the climate change that will take place over the next two to three decades, but it is still possible to protect our societies and economies from its impacts to some extent—for example, by providing better information, improved planning and more climate-resilient crops and infrastructure. Adaptation will cost tens of billions of dollars a year in developing countries alone, and will put still further pressure on already scarce resources. Adaptation efforts, particularly in developing countries, should be accelerated.

The costs of stabilising the climate are significant but manageable; delay would be dangerous and much more costly. * * *

Ultimately, stabilisation—at whatever level—requires that annual emissions be brought down to more than 80% below current levels.

This is a major challenge, but sustained long-term action can achieve it at costs that are low in comparison to the risks of inaction. Central estimates of the annual costs of achieving stabilisation between 500 and 550 ppm CO_2e [CO_2 equivalent] are around 1% of global GDP, if we start to take strong action now.

Costs could be even lower than that if there are major gains in efficiency, or if the strong co-benefits, for example from reduced air pollution, are measured. Costs will be higher if innovation in low-carbon technologies is slower than expected, or if policy-makers fail to make the most of economic instruments that allow emissions to be reduced whenever, wherever and however it is cheapest to do so.

It would already be very difficult and costly to aim to stabilise at 450 ppm CO_2e. If we delay, the opportunity to stabilise at 500-550 ppmCO_2e may slip away.

Action on climate change is required across all countries, and it need not cap the aspirations for growth of rich or poor countries.

The costs of taking action are not evenly distributed across sectors or around the world. Even if the rich world takes on responsibility for absolute cuts in emissions of 60-80% by 2050, developing countries must take significant action too. But developing countries should not be required to bear the full costs of this action alone, and they will not have to. Carbon markets in rich countries are already beginning to deliver flows of finance to support low-carbon development, including through the Clean Development Mechanism. A transformation of these flows is now required to support action on the scale required.

Action on climate change will also create significant business opportunities, as new markets are created in low-carbon energy technologies and other low-carbon goods and services. These markets could grow to be worth hundreds of billions of dollars each year, and employment in these sectors will expand accordingly.

The world does not need to choose between averting climate change and promoting growth and development. Changes in energy technologies and in the structure of economies have created opportunities to decouple growth from greenhouse gas emissions. Indeed, ignoring climate change will eventually damage economic growth.

Tackling climate change is the pro-growth strategy for the longer term, and it can be done in a way that does not cap the aspirations for growth of rich or poor countries.

A range of options exists to cut emissions; strong, deliberate policy action is required to motivate their take-up. * * *

With strong, deliberate policy choices, it is possible to reduce emissions in both developed and developing economies on the scale necessary for stabilisation in the required range while continuing to grow.

Climate change is the greatest market failure the world has ever seen, and it interacts with other market imperfections. Three elements of policy are required for an effective global response. The first is the pricing of carbon, implemented through tax, trading or regulation. The second is policy to support innovation and the deployment of low-carbon technologies. And the third is action to remove barriers to energy efficiency, and to inform, educate and persuade individuals about what they can do to respond to climate change. * * *

Climate change demands an international response, based on a shared understanding of long-term goals and agreement on frameworks for action. * * *

Countries facing diverse circumstances will use different approaches to make their contribution to tackling climate change. But action by individual countries is not enough. Each country, however large, is just a part of the problem. It is essential to create a shared international vision of long-term goals, and to build the international frameworks that will help each country to play its part in meeting these common goals. * * *

SECTION 2.3 ETHICS, WELFARE AND ECONOMIC POLICY

* * * Generally, poor countries, and poor people in any given country, suffer the most, notwithstanding that the rich countries are responsible for the bulk of past emissions. These features of climate change, together with the fact that they have an impact on many dimensions of human well-being, force us to look carefully at the underlying ethical judgments and presumptions which underpin, often implicitly, the standard framework of policy analysis. Indeed, it is important to consider a broader range of ethical arguments and frameworks than is standard in economics, both because there are many ways of looking at the ethics of policy towards climate change, and, also, because in so doing we can learn something about how to apply the more standard economic approach. There is a growing literature on the ethics of climate change: analysis of policy cannot avoid grappling directly with the difficult issues that arise. * * *

Climate change is an externality that is global in both its causes and consequences. Both involve deep inequalities that are relevant for policy.

The incremental impact of a tonne of GHG is independent of where in the world it is emitted. But the volume of GHGs emitted globally is not uniform. Historically, rich countries have produced the majority of GHG emissions. Though all countries are affected by climate change, they are affected in different ways and to different extents. Developing countries will be particularly badly hit, for three reasons: their geography; their stronger dependence on agriculture; and because with their fewer resources comes greater vulnerability. There is therefore a double inequity in climate change: the rich countries have special responsibility for where the world is now, and thus for the consequences which flow from this difficult starting point, whereas poor countries will be particularly badly hit. * * *

SECTION 2.4 THE LONG-RUN IMPACTS OF CLIMATE CHANGE: EVALUATION OVER TIME AND DISCOUNTING

The effects of GHGs emitted today will be felt for a very long time. That makes some form of evaluation or aggregation across generations unavoidable. The ethical decisions on, and approaches to, this issue have major consequences for the assessment of policy. * * *

If little or no value were placed on prospects for the long-run future, then climate change would be seen as much less of a problem. If, however, one thinks about the ethics in terms of most standard ethical frameworks, there is every reason to take these prospects very seriously.

SECTION 2.5 RISK AND UNCERTAINTY

The risks and uncertainties around the costs and benefits of climate policy are large; hence the analytical framework should be able to handle risk and uncertainty explicitly.

For the moment, we do not make a distinction between risk and uncertainty, but the distinction is important and we return to it below. Uncertainty affects every link in the chain from emissions of GHGs through to their impacts. There are uncertainties associated, for example, with future rates of economic growth, with the volume of emissions that will follow, with the increases in temperature resulting from emissions, with the impacts of these temperature increases and so on. Similarly, there are uncertainties associated with the economic response to policy measures, and hence about how much it will cost to reduce GHG emissions. * * *

The standard expected-utility framework involves aversion to risk and, in this narrow sense, a 'precautionary principle'.

This approach to uncertainty, combined with the assumption that the social marginal utility of income declines as income rises, implies that society will be willing to pay a premium (insurance) to avoid a simple actuarially fair gamble where potential losses and gains are large. * * * Potential losses from climate change are large and the costs of avoidance (the insurance premium involved in mitigation), we argue, seem modest by comparison.

The analytical approach incorporates aspects of insurance, caution and precaution directly, and does not therefore require a separate 'precautionary principle' to be imposed as an extra ethical criterion.

More modern theories embodying a distinction between uncertainty and risk suggest an explicit 'precautionary principle' beyond that following from standard expected-utility theory.

The distinction between uncertainty and risk is an old one, going back at least to Knight (1921) and Keynes (1921). In their analysis, risk applied when one could make some assessment of probabilities and uncertainty when one does not have the ability to assess probabilities. In a fascinating paper, Claude Henry (2006) puts these ideas to work on problems in science and links them to modern theories of behaviour towards risk. He uses two important examples to illustrate the relevance of a precautionary principle in the presence of uncertainty. The first is the link between bovine spongiform encephalopathy (BSE) in cows and Creutzfeld-Jacob Disease (CJD) in humans and the second, the link between asbestos and lung disease.

For the first, UK scientists asserted for some time that there could be no link because of 'a barrier between species'. However in 1991 scientists in Bristol succeeded in inoculating a cat with BSE and the hypothesis of 'a barrier' was destroyed. Around the same time, a scientist, Stanley Prusiner, identified protein mutations that could form the basis of a link. These results did not establish probabilities but they destroyed 'certainty'. By introducing uncertainty, the finding opened up the possibility of applying a precautionary principle.

For the second, a possible link between asbestos and lung disease was suggested as early as 1898 by health inspectors in the UK, and in 1911 on a more scientific basis after experiments on rats. Again the work was not of a kind to establish probabilities but provided grounds for precaution. Unfortunately, industry lobbying prevented a ban on asbestos and the delay of fifty years led to considerable loss of life. Application of the precautionary principle could have saved lives. * * *

SECTION 2.6 NON-MARGINAL POLICY DECISIONS

There is a serious risk that, without action to prevent climate change, its impacts will be large relative to the global economy, much more so than for most other environmental problems.

The impacts of climate change on economies and societies worldwide could be large relative to the global economy. Specifically, it cannot be assumed that the global economy, net of the costs of climate change, will grow at a certain rate in the future, regardless of whether nations follow a 'business as usual' path or choose together to reduce GHG emissions. In this sense, the decision is not a marginal one.

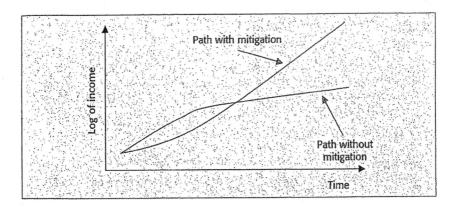

Figure 2.3 Conceptual approach to comparing divergent growth paths over the long term

The issues are represented schematically in Figure 2.3, which compares two paths, one with mitigation and one without. We should note that, in this diagram, there is uncertainty around each path, which should be analysed using the approaches of the preceding section. * * * Income on the 'path with mitigation' is below that on the path without ('business as usual') for the earlier time period, because costs of mitigation are incurred. Later, as the damages from climate change accumulate, growth on the 'path without mitigation' will slow and income will fall below the level on the other path. * * * The 'greener' path (with mitigation) allows growth to continue but, on the path without mitigation, income will suffer. * * *

SECTION 2.7 THE PUBLIC POLICY OF PROMOTING MITIGATION

* * * The basic theory of externalities identifies the source of the economic problem in untaxed or unpriced emissions of GHGs.

The externality requires a price for emissions: that is the first task of mitigation policy.

The first requirement is therefore to introduce taxes or prices for GHGs. * * * Faced with this tax, the emitters would choose the appropriate level of abatement.

However, the modern theory of risk indicates that long-term quantity targets may be the right direction for policy, with trading within those targets or regular revision of taxes to keep on course towards the long-run objective * * *. Given the long-run nature of many of the relevant decisions, whichever policies are chosen, credibility and predictability of policy will be crucial to effectiveness.

The second task of mitigation policy is to promote research, development and deployment.

However, the inevitable absence of total credibility for GHG pricing policy decades into the future may inhibit investment in emission reduction, particularly the development of new technologies. Action on climate change requires urgency, and there are generally obstacles, due to inadequate property rights, preventing investors reaping the full return to new ideas. Specifically, there are spillovers in learning (another externality), associated with the development and adoption of new low-emission technologies that can affect how much emissions are reduced. Thus the economics of mitigating climate change involves understanding the processes of innovation.

The spillovers occur in a number of ways. A firm is unlikely to be able to appropriate all the benefits, largely because knowledge has some characteristics of a public good. In particular, once new information has been created, it can be virtually costless to copy. This allows a competitor with access to the information to capture the benefits without undertaking the research and development (R&D). Patents are commonly used to reduce this problem. In addition, there are typically 'adoptive externalities' to other firms that arise from the processes whereby technology costs fall as a result of increasing adoption. These spillovers are likely to be particularly important in the case of low-emission technologies. * * *

Other interacting barriers or problems that are relevant include
   •   asymmetric and inadequate information—for example, about energy-efficiency measures
   •   policy-induced uncertainties—such as uncertainty about the implicit price of carbon in the future
   •   moral hazard or 'gaming'—for example firms might rush to make carbon-emitting investments to avoid the possibility of more stringent regulation in the future
   •   perverse regulatory incentives—such as the incentive to establish a high baseline of emissions in regimes where carbon quotas are 'grandfathered'
   •   the endogenous price dynamics of exhaustible natural resources—and the risk that fossil-fuel prices could fall in response to strong climate-change policy, threatening to undermine it.

These issues involve many of the most interesting theoretical questions studied by economists in recent years in industrial, regulatory and natural resource economics.

There are important challenges for public policy to promote mitigation beyond the two tasks just described. * * * These include regulation and standards and deepening public understanding of responsible behaviour.

Standards and regulation can provide powerful and effective policies to promote action on mitigation.

The learning process for new technologies is uncertain. There are probably important scale effects in this process due to experience or learning-by-doing and the externalities of learning-by-watching. In these circumstances, standards for emissions, for example, can provide a clear sense of direction and reduced uncertainty for investors, allowing these economies of scale to be realised.

In other circumstances, particularly concerning energy efficiency, there will be market imperfections, for example due to the nature of landlord-tenant relations in property, that may inhibit adaptation of beneficial investments or technologies. In these circumstances, regulation can produce results more efficient than those that are available from other instruments alone. * * *

Economists tend to put most of weight in public-policy analyses and rec-ommendations on market instruments to which firms and households re-spond. And there are excellent reasons for this—firms and households know more about their own circumstances and can respond strongly to incentives. But the standard 'sticks and carrots' of this line of argument do not constitute the whole story.

* * * Changing attitudes is indeed likely to be a crucial part of a policy package. But it raises ethical difficulties: who has the right or authority to attempt to change preferences or attitudes? We shall adopt the approach of John Stuart Mill and others who have emphasized 'government by discussion' as the way in which individuals can come to decisions individually and collec-tively as to the ethical and other justifications of different approaches to pol-icy.

SECTION 2.8 INTERNATIONAL ACTION FOR MITIGATION AND ADAPTATION

The principles of public policy for mitigation elaborated so far do not take very explicit account of the international nature of the challenge. This is a global problem and mitigation is a global public good. This means that it is, from some perspectives, 'an international game' and the theory of games does indeed provide powerful insights. The challenge is to promote and sustain international collective action in a context where 'free-riding' is a serious problem. Adaptation, like mitigation, raises strong and difficult interna-tional issues of responsibility and equity, and also has some elements of the problem of providing public goods.

Aspects of adaptation to climate change also have some of the character-istics of public goods and require public policy intervention.

Concerns about the provision of public goods affect policy to guide adap-tation to the adverse impacts of climate change. * * * Compared with efforts to reduce emissions, adaptation provides immediate, local benefits for which there is some degree of private return. Nevertheless, efficient adaptation to climate change is also hindered by market failures, notably inadequate in-formation on future climate change and positive externalities in the provision of adaptation (where the social return remains higher than the return that will be captured by private investors). These market failures may limit the amount of adaptation undertaken—even where it would be cost-effective. * * *

The poorest in society are likely to have the least capacity to adapt, partly because of resource constraints on upfront investment in adaptive capacity. Given that the greatest need for adaptation will be in low-income countries, overcoming financial constraints is also a key objective. This will involve transfers from rich countries to poor countries. The argument is strongly reinforced by the historical responsibility of rich countries for the bulk of accumulated stocks of GHGs. Poor countries are suffering and will suffer from climate change generated in the past by consumption and growth in rich countries.

Action on climate change that is up to the scale of the challenge requires countries to participate voluntarily in a sustained, coordinated, international effort.

Climate change shares some characteristics with other environmental challenges linked to the management of common international resources, including the protection of the ozone layer and the depletion of fisheries. Crucially, there is no global single authority with the legal, moral, practical or other capacity to manage the climate resource.

This is particularly challenging, because * * * no one country, region or sector alone can achieve the reductions in GHG emissions required to stabilise atmospheric concentrations of GHGs at the necessary level. In addition, there are significant gains to co-operating across borders, for example in undertaking emission reductions in the most cost-effective way. The economics and science point to the need for emitters to face a common price of emissions at the margin. And, although adaptation to climate change will often deliver some local reduction in its impact, those countries most vulnerable to climate change are particularly short of the resources to invest in adaptation. Hence international collective action on both mitigation and adaptation is required. * * *

Economic tools such as game theory, as well as insights from international relations, can aid the understanding of how different countries, with differing incentives, preferences and cost structures, can reach agreement. The problem of free-riding on the actions of others is severe. International collective action on any issue rests on the voluntary co-operation of sovereign states. Economic analysis suggests that multilateral regimes succeed when they are able to define the gain to co-operation, share it equitably and can sustain co-operation in ways that overcome incentives for free-riding.

Our response to climate change as a world is about the choices we make about development, growth, the kind of society we want to live in, and the opportunities it affords this and future generations. The challenge requires focusing on outcomes that promote wealth, consumption, health, reduced mortality and greater social justice. * * *

Notes and Questions

1. What does it mean to say that the costs of addressing climate change are a certain percentage of GDP? Assuming, for the moment that economic predictions have any credibility, most models indicate that the cost of mitigation or of the damages from unmitigated climate change will be in the range of +/- several per cent of GPD. "This sounds like a lot of money, and if it were heaped into a pile of bills in the middle of Central Park, it would certainly be a very large pile. But economies tend to grow. Let's say that the cost of developing and using only clean energy amounts to 3% of GDP every year. Let's also say that the economy is growing at a rate of 3% per year. Wait a year, and the GDP will grow to the size of the dirty-energy economy, just one year later. If the rate of growth were 1.5% per year, the clean economy would lag two years behind the dirty one." D. Archer, Carbon Economics and Ethics, The Long Thaw: How Humans Are Changing the Next 100,000 Years of Earth's Climate (2008). So, applying this to climate economic projections, instead of reaching a certain GDP in 20 years, that level of GPD might be reached in 21 years.

2. Economic analysis is dependent on what society declares to be property that is subject to the free market. In the United States human beings were once treated by the law as items of property. See Dred Scott v. Sanford, 60 U.S. (19 How.) 393 (1857). Slavery is now illegal and human beings cannot be treated as property. Climate change economics raises similarly large challenges to current assumptions, such as our consideration of intergenerational equity. David Archer, supra, describes "the awesome potential energy impacts of a gallon of gasoline on Earth. When it is burned, it yields about 2500 kilocalories of energy * * * Its carbon is released as CO_2 to the atmosphere, trapping Earth's radiant energy * * *. About three-quarters of the CO_2 will go away in a few centuries, but the rest will remain in the atmosphere for thousands of years. If we add up the total amount of energy trapped by the CO_2 from the gallon of gas over its atmospheric lifetime, we find that our gallon of gasoline ultimately traps one hundred billion (100,000,000,000) kilocalories of useless and unwanted greenhouse heat. The bad energy from burning that gallon ultimately outweighs the good energy by a factor of about 40 million."

3. Individual behavior can be significant in mitigating and adapting to climate change. However, as the tragedy of the commons and the prisoners' dilemma teach, it is hard to align individual choices with public benefit. One approach might be to design legislation that will lower transaction costs and provide incentives of various kinds to make it easier for individuals to make daily decisions that will advance climate change goals. See, e.g., J. Dernbach, Harnessing Individual Behavior to Address Climate Change Options for Congress, 26 Va. Envtl. L.J. 107 (2008). Well-designed "choice architecture" that structures the context within individual decisions are made can "nudge" us towards socially beneficial decisions without restricting freedom of choice. R.

Thaler & C. Sunstein, Nudge: Improving Decisions About Health, Wealth and Happiness (2008). How might this concept be used to address climate change?

4. For an evaluation of the adaptation cost estimates in the Stern Report (2006) and assessments made by the UNFCCC (2007), the World Bank (2006), UNDP (2007) and Oxfam (2007) see M. Perry, et al, Assessing the Costs of Adaptation to Climate Change: A review of the UNFCC and other recent estimates (2009) http://www.iied.org/pubs/display.php?o=11501iied. They conclude that the benefits of adaptation are "very worthwhile" when compared to the costs of mitigation or the cost of not taking any adaptation measures.

PROBLEM EXERCISE

Lord Stern's evaluation is in the context of a mature service sector and post-industrial modern economy, that of the United Kingdom, in which domestic wealth generated by natural resources exploitation plays are more modest role. Should his analysis be extended to economies that are growing by mining and timbering and exploiting nature? Or to the "economies" of multinational companies that mine and sell coal and oil, whose budgets often are larger than most nations' gross domestic product? Why is Canada allowing exploitation of its oil shale, with the resultant vast environmental externalities? Why did the Obama Administration approve in 2009 a transfrontier pipeline to bring the oil shale product to the USA for sale and consumption? Should the Canadian federal or provincial governments have paid to keep the oil shale lands, and their ecosystems, intact? Should the USA use its regulatory power to make Canada's oil shale exports profitably without doing more rigorous environmental impact assessments?

The Stern Report does not address how different nations should adapt their national or regional energy regimes from functioning to destroy Earth's climate to stabilizing and sustaining it. For instance, should nations make financial payments to those who own forests to keep their photosynthesis and ecosystem services intact, rather than harvesting timber? Should nations pay those with coal or oil deposits to keep this ancient fossilized solar energy in the ground, rather than mining it to release its already sequestered carbon dioxide?

Consider the comparative advantage of paying to sequester carbon dioxide after it is burned with the cost of keeping the coal in the ground. When coal or oil burns, the carbon atom combines with two oxygen atoms, producing a gas that occupies significantly greater space than did hard rock or fugacious fossil minerals themselves. Hans-Werner Shinn, president of Germany's Ifo Institute of Economic Research, drawing on IPPC reports, observes that "Carbon captured from anthracite coal would occupy five times as much space underground as the coal itself; in the case of crude oil three times the volume would be needed." He argues that governments need to act to reduce extraction rates of fossil fuels, which should be left underground where natural forces originally sequestered them. This will be a challenge, since the reverse is happen; as Sinn notes, European climate change laws "have not even caused a tiny dip in the rising emissions curve." With continuing economic growth and scarcity of fossil fuels, prices increase and there is no economic incentive to diminish extraction; indeed, faced with the prospect of future curbs on extraction, the pace of coal and oil mining is accelerating, to secure short-term profits. Sinn explains that "Some like to pin their hopes on a different effect: that green policies will eventually push the price of fossil fuels in the world market below the extraction costs, making extraction unprofitable. This hope is baseless, however, because, as with old Rembrandts, resources prices are driven by scarcity and have always been much higher than extraction costs. That is the case even now, in the midst of the dramatic fall in prices triggered by the current economic crisis. With oil prices at around $70 a barrel, extraction costs in the Arabian Gulf, including exploration, amount o between $1 and $1.50 a barrel. Even the extraction of Canadian tar sands cost no more than $15 a barrel. * * * An environmental policy based on pushing prices below production costs would need a very big hammer indeed." See Hans-Werner Sinn, How To Resolve the Green Paradox, Financial Times, p. 7 col. 1 (August 27, 2009).

Do you agree with Sinn's assessment that the laws will need to be adopted based on one of two alternatives? "To be effective, environmental policy has two options: either it uses the tax system to make it unattractive for resource owners to convert their fossil fuel wealth into financial investments, or it creates a seamless consumer cartel through the establishment of a global emissions trading system. The emissions trading system would effectively put a cap on world-wide fossil fuel consumption, thereby achieving the desired slowdown in extraction rates. Furthermore, part of the proceeds would be diverted from resources owners' pockets to the national treasuries of the countries selling emission certificates."

Why not tax fossil fuels and use the income to pay forest owners to maintain their photosynthesis services. Why not simply ban the extraction of further coal and oil, and use tax revenues to compensate owners only for their past acquisition costs. If there is no likelihood that a global cap on emissions will be agreed quickly, because of the bias for continuing business as usual, what steps should governments take to ban GHG releases? Should the largest greenhouse gas emitting nations institute steep emission reductions domestically? Should the production and use of all manufactured greenhouse gases be banned, as was done with Chlorofluorocarbons, without the need to compensate the "property owners" who manufacture these gases? Since there is no demonstrated technology for carbon capture and storage, and inadequate storage space for the carbon dioxide in any event, should governments take direct action to phase out mining. Will income from emissions trading be sufficient to finance the shift to a carbon neutral economy? Will not tax revenues be needed to pay the "property owners" of living solar biological photosynthesis realms to keep their plants intact, and to pay the "property owners" of the dead solar fossilized fuels to keep their carbon in the ground? Can you propose alternatives to these options?

B. QUESTIONING ECONOMIC FUNDAMENTALS

The challenges posed by the Bali Action Plan's climate change mitigation and adaptation goals are unique in world history. To be sure, the erosion of the stratospheric ozone layer required creation of a global natural resource management regime requiring all nations and all economic systems to reform to protect the ozone layer. This is being done even though scientists cannot tell if the stratospheric ozone layer will regenerate once the Ozone Depleting Substances (ODS) have been fully eliminated. In like vein, Part XII of the UN Convention on the Law of Sea requires all State Parties to "protect" the marine environment, but very few do so and the United States Congress has yet to ratify this global treaty. Scientific reports show that the ambient environmental quality of the marine environment is deteriorating. The oceans and their phytoplankton and the capacity for absorbing calcium are important in the model of managing the atmosphere, just as the ODS are all potent greenhouse gases whose elimination is critical to mitigating climate change. Yet these two global regimes address only two of the many global natural systems that are part of Earth's atmospheric natural systems and cycles.

Kenneth Boulding in The Economics of the Coming Spaceship Earth outlines the global scope of environmental issues on the eve of the 1972 United Nations Conference on the Human Environment held in Stockholm, Sweden. Boulding called upon economists, lawyers, governments and the public to regard the economy of the Earth as finite, a closed economic system based on the flow of energy from the sun. His fundamental model of the world's economy is very different than that of the sovereign nations who work through the International Financial Institutions (IFIs), like the World Bank, or who cultivate classical liberal economic models of "free trade" among the nations, facilitated by treaty bodies such as the World Trade Organization (WTO). Boulding's analysis has been intellectually of great importance, but it has not triggered a change in "business as usual."

Boulding wrote that:

The closed earth of the future requires economic principles which are somewhat different from those of the open earth of the past. For the sake of picturesqueness, I am tempted to call the open economy the 'cowboy economy,' the cowboy being symbolic of the illimitable plains and also associated with reckless, exploitative, romantic, and violent behavior, which is characteristic of open societies. The closed economy of the future might similarly be called the 'spacemen' economy, in which the earth has become a single spaceship, without unlimited reservoirs of anything, either for extraction or for pollution, and in which therefore, man must find his place in a cyclical ecological system which is capable of continuous reproduction of materials form even though it cannot escape having inputs of energy. The difference between the two types of economy becomes most apparent in the attitude toward consumption.

In the cowboy economy, consumption is regarded as a good thing and production likewise; and the success of the economy is measured by the amount of the throughput from the 'factors of production,' a part of which, at any rate, is extracted from the reservoirs of raw materials and non-economic objects, and another part of which is output into the reservoirs of pollution. If there are infinite reservoirs from which the effluvia can be deposited, then the throughput is at least a plausible measure of the success of the economy. The gross national product is a rough measures of this total throughput. It should possible, however to distinguish that part of the GNP [gross national product] which is derived from exhaustible and that which is derived from reproducible resources, as well as that part of consumption which represents effluvia and that which represents input into the productive system again. * * *

By contrast, in the spaceman economy, the throughput is by no means a desideratum, and is indeed to be regarded as something to be minimized rather than maximized. The essential measure of the success of the economy is not production and consumption at all, but the nature, extent, quality, and complexity of the total capital stock, including in this the state of the human bodies and minds included in the system. In the spaceman economy, what we are primarily concerned with is the stock maintenance and any technological change which results in the maintenance of a given total stock with a lessened throughput (this is, less production and consumption) is clearly a gain.

The idea that both production and consumption are bad things rather than good things is very strange to economists, who have been obsessed with the income-flow concepts to the exclusion, almost, of capital-stock concepts. ... It may be said, of course, why worry about all this when the spaceman economy is still a good way off (at least beyond the lifetimes of any now living), so let us eat, drink, spend, extract and pollute,, and be as merry as we can, and let posterity worry about the spaceship earth. It is always a little hard to find a convincing answer to the man who says, 'What has posterity ever done for me?' and the conservationist has always had to fall back on rather vague ethical principles postulating identify of the individual with some human community or society which extends not only back into the past but forward into the future...Why should we not maximized the welfare of this generation at the cost of posterity? 'Apres nous, le deluge' has been the motto of not insignificant numbers of human societies.

The only answer to this, as far as I can see, is to point out that the welfare of the individual depends on the extent to which he can identify himself with others* * *, and the most satisfactory individual identify is that which identifies not only with a community in space but also with a community extending over time from the past into the future. * * * The whole problem is lined up with the much larger one of the determinants of the morale, legitimacy, and 'nerve' of a society, and there is a great deal of historical evidence to suggest that a society which loses its identity with posterity and which loses its positive image of the future loses also its capacity to deal with present problems, and soon falls apart.

http://www.eoearth.org/article/The_Economics_of_the_Coming_Spaceship_Earth_(historical)#.

The IPCC reports excerpted in Chapter 2 describe the spaceship Earth reality that Boulding envisioned. Boulding's vision now is found in alternative measures of Earth's capital stock and how our economy is depleting this stock, and yet Gross National Product still measures output and ignores the depletion of natural resource. Boulding's views have not yet been accommodated by economic markets and the governments that manage those markets. The IPCC reports about the limited capacity of the atmosphere to receive any more GHG emissions without triggering significant climate change effects, makes Boulding's point. Since nations have pledged not to cause irreversible damage to the climate in the UN Framework Convention on Climate Change excerpted in Chapter 3 the question becomes how will law and legal institutions bring about adaptation to a "spaceship earth" economy?

The importance of the rule of law cannot be over-emphasized. Across the globe there is a deficit in law. Too many nations, perhaps a majority, do not have stable legal systems around the world that can implement climate change reforms. The United Nations General Assembly made advancing the rule of Law a new priority in 2008, See UNGA Resolution 63/128 (Nov. 12, 2008) on the report of the UNGA Sixth Committee (Legal), A/63/443. A new unit in the office of the Secretary-General has been established to promote the rule of law at the international and national levels.

John Boyd challenges the existing perspective of the World Bank and other international financial institutions which assume that free markets should be encouraged primarily through economics, rather than through what Adam Smith also emphasized was equally important: the administration of a sound regulatory system to sustain fair markets, or enhancing the rule of law and good governance systems. J. Boyd, Inadequate International Financial Institution Assistance for Adam Smith's Second Duty of the Sovereign: Protecting Against Injustice, 17 Kansas J. of L. & Pub. Policy 233 (2008). Speth takes this analysis one step further: if the markets are biased toward the self-aggrandizement of the individual or the corporation, not the community, how can markets be reformed?

THE BRIDGE AT THE EDGE OF THE WORLD: CAPITALISM, THE ENVRIONMENT, AND CROSSING FROM CRISIS TO SUSTAINABILITY
James Gustave Speth (2008)

We live in Market World—in supermarkets, stock markets, labor markets, housing markets, to mention a few. Competitive markets are central to capitalism. They are the arena where buyers and sellers exchange goods and services at a price determined by supply and demand. For many, many purposes the market and the price mechanism work well, for example, in manufacturing, retail sales, and other areas. No better system of allocating scarce resources has yet been invented, nor is it likely to be in the foreseeable future.

Democratic government has been and remains the principal counterbalance to the market. All but the most ideological advocates of laissez-faire recognize the necessity of government intervention in the market on many fronts for many purposes. In Washington today, business and finance are protected by the Securities and Exchange Commission and the Justice Department; consumers are protected by the Food and Drug Administration and the Consumer Products Safety Commission; the environment by the Environmental Protection Agency and the Department of the Interior; and on and on through the capital's alphabet soup.

Market forces are enormously powerful today, prices are potent signals, and businesses are constantly seeking to expand markets to new products and new geographic areas. It follows that if the market does not work for the environment, the stage is set for huge and hugely negative environmental consequences, and that is what the world has seen. It is vital to understand why this has happened and what can be done about it. The goal in this regard should be twofold: first, to transform the market into a powerful instrument for environmental protection and restoration, and second, to limit what Robert Kuttner has called the imperialism of the market. "Even in a capitalist economy," he reminds us in *Everything for Sale*, "the marketplace is only one of several means by which society makes decisions, determines worth, allocates resources, maintains a social fabric, and conducts human relations." As economist Arthur Okun has noted, "The market needs a place, but the market needs to be kept in its place." Paul Hawken, Amory Lovins, and Hunter Lovins put it well in *Natural Capitalism* when they write, "Markets are only tools. They make a good servant but a bad master and a worse religion."

Environmental economics is the modern-day economist's answer to the failure of the market to care for the environment. Primarily, it is today's neoclassical microeconomics applied to environment. It has a strong foothold in academia. Of all the avenues explored in this book, it is the most taught and the most theoretically rigorous. And it is the most consistent with our market-based economy. Wallace Oates and other environmental economists contend that environmental economics makes three major contributions. First, it makes a compelling, persuasive case for public intervention in the free market in order to correct market failure.

Second, it provides guidance on how far this government intervention should go in prescribing environmental goals and standards. Typically, as one moves from lax to tough controls, the first steps are the cheapest, and the costs of compliance rise as the proposed controls get tighter. Meanwhile, the extra social benefits of tougher intervention will decline, for example, as pollution is reduced to more tolerable levels. Environmental economics teaches that government should mandate investment in environmental protection up to the point that the (rising) cost of compliance equals the (declining) social benefits. To invest more would be wasteful because the marginal costs would exceed the marginal benefits.

And third, Oates and others point out that once one sets a goal or standard, by whatever means, environmental economics can guide us to the least-cost, most efficient way of achieving that goal. Let's take up each of these three contributions. * * *

Economists make a compelling case for the right kind of government intervention. * * * governments often intervene in the wrong way, creating perverse subsidies that further distort prices that are already environmentally misleading. They are misleading because they fail to reflect the true, full costs of production, namely, the environmental costs that are external to the firm—the so-called negative externalities. And subsidies created by governments can make this situation worse. * * *

In *Markets and the Environment*, environmental economists Nathaniel Keohane and Sheila Olmstead call attention to three distinct types of market failure where the environment is concerned. First, there are the negative externalities noted above, for example, all the indirect costs of the environmental damage imposed on those downstream of polluters and on the public at large, costs that the unaided market does not require the polluter to pay. The other two categories of market failure are public goods and the tragedy of the commons: Some environmental amenities, such as biodiversity, are enjoyed by lots of people, whether or not those people help pay for them. Economists call such goods public goods. A market failure arises because some individuals will end up being free riders: Rather than helping to provide the public good themselves, they merely enjoy what others provide for them. A third class of environmental problems is known as the tragedy of the commons. When a natural resource—such as a fishery or an underground aquifer—is made available to all, individuals will tend to exploit the resource far beyond the optimal level. This problem arises because the incentives of individuals diverge from the common good. We call it a tragedy because everyone would be better off if they could all commit themselves to act less selfishly. Thus individually rational actions add up to a socially undesirable outcome"

Environmental economists have indeed made a powerful case for government intervention to correct market failure and perverse subsidies. But unfortunately, that is not to say that environmental economists are powerful. Market failures and pro-business subsidies persist in abundance.

Below, I take up the environmental economists' second contribution, which addresses how standards should be set. At this point we will consider the third contribution-using market incentives and market mechanisms to achieve efficient, least-cost results, regardless of how the standard of protection is set. Here is where environmental economics has truly taken off and come into its own. It was not always thus. * * * Most environmentalists thirty years ago did not like the approach advocated by *Environmental Improvement Through Economic Incentives,* written by Fred Anderson and economists at Resources for the Future. Throughout the 1970s, when our major antipollution laws were being written, an intellectual war of sorts was under way. On one side were we lawyers and our allies in the scientific community, and we had the upper hand. We favored what are now somewhat pejoratively called "command and control" regulations. These regulations were often based on the best available antipollution technology. The idea was to set mandatory emission and effluent standards—performance standards—that would compel companies to adopt the best pollution control technology that was available and affordable. Because new sources of pollution had more flexibility—for example, they could easily make changes in their production processes—higher technology-based standards were applied to them. EPA elaborated discharge and emission limits based on available technology for each industry, and these limits were written into permits enforced against individual polluters. Occasionally, as under key provisions of the Clean Air Act, standard-setting was based not on best technology but on what was required to protect health and the environment.

On the other side of this little war were the economists, arguing instead for using market-based mechanisms and economic incentives. * * *

Effluent charges and other environmental charges have been furthest developed in Europe. In the United States, we have seen the rise of "cap and trade" schemes under which an overall ceiling is placed, say, on sulfur emissions in a particular region, and polluters in the region are allowed to trade emission rights or allowances among themselves in order to achieve the overall least-cost response to the cap. The caps are quantitative limits on the volume of pollutants that can be released.

The grand experiment with cap and trade in the United States was launched in the 1990 amendments to the Clean Air Act with the cap on sulfur emissions from power plants, designed to address the acid rain threat. Documented economic savings from cap and trade approaches, including in the U.S. acid rain program, have been real and substantial. The source of these savings is the ability of economic instruments to take advantage of the wide variation across firms in compliance costs. Deeper cuts are made where it is cheaper to do so. Virtually all of the climate protection bills before the Congress in 2007 seek to regulate carbon dioxide emissions with cap and trade. It seems likely that tradable permits and other market-based mechanisms for addressing environmental ills will continue to make inroads. So score another one for the economists.

The push to introduce economic incentives and market mechanisms has come about primarily to improve the efficiency and effectiveness of environmental programs. Environmental economists have been highly inventive in identifying a variety of market instruments to achieve these goals: establishing property rights to overcome the tragedy of the commons, creating markets where emission and effluent quantities can be traded, imposing pollution taxes and charges, designing "feebate" and rebate systems where charges are imposed on environmental harms but returned for good behavior, and so on. A "feebate" scheme, for example, might charge polluters a fee depending on the volume of pollution and then rebate the proceeds to the polluters in proportion to their output. Good performers therefore get their money back and more. * * * Environmental economists have thus been successful in making the intellectual case for government intervention and the practical case for using economic incentives. But there has been much less progress on the second contribution in Oates's framework, setting the environmental standard by equating marginal costs and benefits. Recall that the idea here is to move to a system whereby the marginal environmental cost of an activity is incorporated into the price of the product being produced. These environmental costs are normally external to the company—externalities, not paid by the company—and thus not incorporated in price. One way to overcome this market failure is to impose a tax or fee on the damaging activity, with the tax set equal to the value of the damage. For air pollutants, for example, the charge would be set equal to the value of the damages from an additional unit of emissions. Economists call this "getting the prices right," and it can be done equally well by capping emissions at the optimum level and allowing emissions trading rather than taxes to determine the price.

If there does not seem to be a groundswell of U.S. support for the key idea of environmental economics on how to set environmental standards, we should ask why. One reason, certainly, has been the lack of an informed political constituency for it. But political difficulties are not the only problem. Bigger and more fundamental is what is called the valuation problem. "Getting the prices right" involves putting a dollar value on environmental damages, and here there are many problems.

At the top of this list has got to be the sheer technical and analytical difficulty of applying this approach. Tom Tietenberg, in his leading environmental economics text, first explains how the pollution tax should be set to equalize marginal costs and benefits, and then has this to say: "Although the efficient levels of these policy instruments can be easily defined in principle, they are very difficult to implement in practice. To implement [them], it is necessary to know the level of pollution at which the two marginal cost curves cross for every emitter. That is a tall order, one that imposes an unrealistically high information burden on control authorities. Control authorities typically have very poor information [the polluter's] control costs and little reliable information on [environmental] damage functions. * * *

Some of the difficulties inherent in putting a dollar value on environmental assets and human life and health can be seen in the growing field of cost-benefit analysis, where economists have been more determined and inventive, and more controversial. Cost-benefit analysis can be applied to assess projects such as new dams or to evaluate policies and programs, such as the Clean Air Act. It requires that both costs and benefits be expressed in comparable terms, that is, dollars. That is, cost-benefit analysis requires valuation.

In *Priceless*, Frank Ackerman and Lisa Heinzerling are severely critical of the cost-benefit approach: "The basic problem with narrow economic analysis of health and environmental protection is that human life, health, and nature cannot be described meaningfully in monetary terms; they are priceless. When the question is whether to allow one person to hurt another, or to destroy a natural resource; when a life or a landscape cannot be replaced; when harms stretch out over decades or even generations; when outcomes are uncertain; when risks are shared or resources are used in common; when the people 'buying' harms have no relationship with the people actually harmed—then we are in the realm of the priceless, where market values tell us little about the social values at stake. * * *

The Ackerman-Heinzerling critique goes beyond the issue of how difficult the valuation issue is to the ethical and political issues it raises. Developmental disorders in pregnancy, the loss of Adirondack lakes, the extinction of a species, the drying out of the American Southwest or the Amazon—it is easy to see why many people find it ethically offensive to place a dollar value on these things for the purpose of weighing whether losing them is acceptable. That said, environmental economists are quick to point out that environmental regulations, willy-nilly, do place a price on even the value of a statistical life, as long as we are willing to figure out how much the regulation costs and how many lives are saved.

The valuation controversy is only one of several that swirl about in the effort to bring the reigning paradigm of neoclassical economics into sync with environmental realities and needs. Is a model based at its core on egoistic, anthropocentric, rationalistic calculation appropriate for making environmental choices? How should one set the discount rate used in evaluating costs and benefits that can stretch far into the future? And will "getting the prices right" in the economist's sense guarantee that the natural patrimony passes undiminished to future generations? These are all important issues, but my goal here is not to catalog the challenges faced by environmental economics. Rather, it is to describe some core concepts that if implemented could transform the market into a benign and restorative force.

A NEW MARKET

What are those key concepts? First, we live in a market economy where prices guide decisions and where environmental assets are increasingly scarce and threatened. We are not running out of economically relevant natural resources; we are running out of environment. In such a world it should be very expensive to do environmental harm and relatively inexpensive to do things that are environmentally harmless or restorative. It has been noted that the planned Soviet economy failed because prices did not reflect economic realities. Today we live in a market economy that risks failing because prices do not reflect environmental realities. Two initial steps are needed to move prices in this direction: governments must undo the damage they have done in creating environmentally perverse subsidies, and they must intervene in the economy to implement the "polluter pays" principle, broadly conceived.

As an initial platform for the move to sustainability, there must be a serious attack on that very juicy target, subsidies. In their 2001 book *Perverse Subsidies*, Norman Myers and Jennifer Kent analyzed the hundreds of studies that quantify subsidies in agriculture, energy, transportation, water, fisheries, and forestry. They classified as "perverse" those subsidies that had demonstrable negative effects both economically and environmentally. Their conclusion was that, at the behest of powerful interests, the world's governments have intervened in the marketplace to create perverse subsidies that now total about $850 billion annually. Admittedly a rough estimate, these subsidies come to about 2.5 percent of the global economy, creating a huge economic incentive for environmental destruction." The Congressional Research Service estimates that U.S. energy subsidies alone were between thirty-seven billion and sixty-four billion dollars in 2003 and were increased by two to three billion dollars annually by the provisions of the Energy Policy Act of 2005.

The polluter pays principle, writ large, says that polluters— indeed, any environmental consumer or despoiler—should be required to bear the full costs of all environmental damage caused to humans or nature, of all cleanup and remediation, and of all expenses required to reduce impacts to sustainable levels. Basically, there are three philosophies of environmental regulation. Each has a place, and each moves the polluter pays principle forward.

Getting the technology right. Regulatory standards can be based on what can be achieved with available technology or management practices. Here the gold standard is what can be done by applying the very best technology available.

Getting the prices right. Standards can be based on requiring despoilers to pay for their damages. Victim compensation schemes do this, as do requirements for environmental cleanup and restoration. Using taxes, charges, or tradable allowances to require despoilers to internalize their external costs also falls into this category. Here the gold standard is "getting the prices right" by internalizing all environmental costs.

Getting the environment right. Standards can also be based on what is needed to achieve a prescribed quality of the ambient environment. Here the gold standard is full protection of human health, no harvesting of resources beyond long-term sustainable yields, no release of waste products beyond assimilative capacities, and full protection of ecosystem structure and function.

Economic incentives and market mechanisms can be used in each of these three approaches to make them more cost-effective, and each approach has the result of driving up the market prices of environmentally destructive goods and services. In each case, the gold standard may mean no discharge or no impact or no product, for example where a particularly impressive technology is available or where phasing out a particularly harmful product is involved (for example, lead in gasoline, CFCs, or DDT).

Of the three approaches to regulation, the last, "getting the environment right" should be the preferred approach for most cases. It will likely drive prices futher in the right directions than other approaches, will best engage the talents of both scientist and economists, will force more technological innovation, and will be most protective of the environment and best understood by the public.

Environmental economists have developed an extensive literature on matching problems with the right "choice of instrument" to achieve an efficient and effective result. Under a cap and trade system, for example, the amount of the pollutant is fixed, and that is sometimes very important, but there is uncertainty about where the emissions will occur. For pollutants where there is little concern about location (sulfur dioxide, CFCs, carbon dioxide), cap and trade can be a good choice. Pollution fees and other economic incentive programs are not desirable, though, where metering of releases is difficult, where changes in ambient conditions can shift quickly for example stream flows can decline or atmospheric inversions can occur), where particularly hazardous substances or activities are involved, or where cap and trade or emission taxes can result in "hot spots" of concentrated pollutants. In such cases direct regulation is best.

Whatever philosophy of standard setting is used, and whatever economic instrument or other approach is chosen, the goal in all cases must be to ensure that the price on destruction of the environment of all types is discouragingly, forbiddingly high. One place to begin this project would be to identify those goods and services, both intermediate and final, that have the greatest environmental impacts. Industrial ecologists in Europe have made an excellent start at this. One could then work back through the production chain, imposing emission and effluent taxes, user fees, and other requirements on the most damaging activities. These charges could be steadily increased in an effort to close the gap between the private and public costs of production.

A second set of core concepts for market transformation is those put forward by Paul Hawken, Amory Lovins, and Hunter Lovins in *Natural Capitalism*. * * * They advocate a national investment strategy promoted by businesses and government that stresses radically increased resource productivity and large-scale regeneration of natural capital. Changes in the federal tax code could spur action in these areas, as could virgin materials extraction charges, appropriate governmental and private research and development programs, and major government support for environmental restoration initiatives.

A third area for market transformation stems from the work of economists Richard Norgaard and Richard Howarth. They show that "getting the prices right" for the current generation will not ensure sustainability, which is a matter of intergenerational equity. Sustainability requires that each generation consciously decide to redistribute sufficient resources to future generations, a process akin to redistributing resources within the current generations. To that end, they urge consideration of such measures as applying resource use taxes, building futures markets, holding mineral and other resources in public trust for future use, and subsidizing resource owners to slow the rate of extraction and depletion. A further measure in this context would be to require that a portion of the earnings from nonrenewable resource development (the portion above normal profits) be reinvested in developing renewable substitutes.

A fourth area for government action in market transformation stems from the fact that prices do not always work as well in practice as they do in theory. At one level, some factors mute price signals—a phenomenon of which economists are well aware. For example a 2006 study of energy markets by McKinsey and Company found that the global potential for energy productivity gains was huge, but realizing them would require more than high energy prices. The reasons? Some sectors have low price elasticity, so that higher prices do not generate big responses. Consumers lack the information and capital to improve energy productivity, and their price response is further muted by the priority given to convenience, comfort, style, or safety. * * *

A final area for government action to promote market transformation is the need to fix another misleading or, at least; misused and overused economic signal—Gross Domestic Product, or GDP. As currently constructed, GDP is widely recognized as a poor measure of national economic welfare, whatever its value as a measure of national output. Societies need a true measure of economic welfare to gauge how successfully market economies are providing for their populations. * * *

These changes and others should make the market work for the environment, reversing the historical pattern. But there is also the complementary need to recognize limits to and boundaries on market penetration. Commodification occurs when a nonmarketed good or service moves onto the market and is sold for a price. As natural assets become commodified, the human perspective on nature as something subservient to humans, existing for our use and benefit, to be bought and sold, intensifies.

Advocates for the poor are seeking to have access to drinking water declared a fundamental human right that must be recognized by governments and others. But water has in fact become a huge international commodity, with major business lines in wastewater services, drinking water supply, and bottled water. It is perfectly appropriate to demand that water be priced at its full costs to large consumers but inappropriate not to provide a drinking water lifeline affordable by and available to all. * * *

In his *Economy of the Earth*, Mark Sagoff has noted that while markets can and do fail, society does not intervene to correct market failure. "Social regulation of safety in consumer products, the workplace, and the environment historically responds to a need to make markets more humane, not necessarily to make them more efficient. * * * [S]ocial regulation expresses what we believe, what we are, what we stand for as a nation. * * * And there is no methodology for making 'hard decisions' and 'trade-offs.' We have to rely on the virtues of deliberation–open-mindedness, attention to detail, humor, and good sense." Sagoff expresses well the reality that transforming the market is about politics, not economics. It will require extremely difficult political decisions—uprooting subsidies, pushing up prices of gasoline and food flown in from halfway around the world, setting aside resources for future generations, restricting the reach of the market itself. Yet bringing about the transformation of the market is bedrock: in a market economy, there is simply no substitute for environmentally honest prices and other initiatives that can make the market as a whole work for the environment rather than against it. A serious if partial effort has begun in this direction. The further and faster market transformation is pursued, the better off our children and grandchildren will be.

PROBLEM EXERCISE ON CLIMATE ECONOMICS

Rising sea levels will "take" coastal lands from nations, indigenous peoples, private property owners and myriad species of flora and fauna. How does the human economy address these "losses"? In the case of a marina or property owner, should insurance reimburse them? If so, who will insure the intertidal ecosystems that erode and are displaced? How will local governments cope with the loss of real property tax revenues, when the property is gone? Do the rich coastal waters and lands have economic value beyond the real estate market? In the case of coastal erosion, do nations lose a part of their 200 mile exclusive economic zone because these are measured from the coastline?

Herman E. Daly questions economic assumptions that assume natural resources can be exploited and taxed for development, without having to address as yet unseen externalities. H. Daly, Beyond Growth (1996). How can our economic accounts, for gross domestic production, take into account the increasing losses of coastal lands and their ecosystems? How do we value ecosystem services? Do we value "thin air" and its capacity to absorb carbon dioxide?

William Nordhaus chaired a U.S. National Academy of Sciences panel that dealt with this question: "The intuitive idea behind the desire to broaden the U.S. national accounts is straightforward. Natural resources such as petroleum, minerals, clean water, and fertile soils are assets of the economy in much the same way as are computers, homes, and trucks. An important part of the economic picture is therefore missing if natural assets are omitted in creating the national balance sheet. * * * The panel concludes that developing a set of comprehensive non-market economic accounts is a high priority for the nation. Developing nonmarket accounts to address such concerns as envi ronmental impacts [and] the value of nonmarket natural resources * * * would illuminate a wide variety of issues concerning the economic state of the nation." National Academy of Sciences, Nature's Numbers: Expanding the National Income Accounts to Include the Environment 19-20 (1999).

What arguments would he need to persuade President Obama's Council of Economic Advisors, or his Treasury Secretary, or the White Economics Advisor, Lawrence Summers, that such accounts should be established? Should the U.S. support a UN program to establish and measure a global carbon account (the total carbon emissions that the atmosphere and biosphere can absorb before an agreed level [e.g. 400 or 450 ppm] of saturation would be reached, in order to avert a "tipping" point that irrevocably alters the climate of Earth? If we do not have accounts for how we deplete Earth's natural resources, how can we hope to measure mitigation goals or cope with adaptation demands? Or must we "fly blind?"

* * * * *

Carbon Neutral Law Schools: Most university climate change programs define their baseline carbon footprint, and then compute the economics of alternative strategies and tactics to reduce and eliminate those impacts. "Most of these measures involve one on of our types of action: (1) increased efficiency, (2) increased use of alternative fuels or green power, (3) fuel switching, or (4) reduced demand through changed behavior and expectations. Technology, policy mandates, social marketing, and incentives are all tools that can be used to achieve these results. Carbon trading or offsets are options for action; however, these will not necessarily reduce a college or university's emissions. Along similar lines, actions to adapt to climate change are important, but many adaptations will not reduce emissions." Chapter 5, p. 75, "Strategy and Tactics for Climate Action," in A. Rappaport & S. Creighton, Degrees That Matter—Climate Change and the University (2007). Has your university adopted the U.S. Green Building Council's "Leadership in Energy & Environmental Design" (LEED) standards for all its new construction and repair or replacement of existing buildings? As you conceive your carbon neutral law school, how can these for actions build on your law school's existing programs for recycling, and health and safety and its cost-cutting measures to cope with the current economic recession? What is the "pay-back" period for installing solar panels or a wind turbine on your campus, especially if your base-line costs are computed using full cost accounting, with the externalities also included? Should your baseline include offsetting all your law school's emissions since 1990?

CHAPTER 5. SUSTAINABLE ENERGY LAW

Climatescape: **Can energy efficiency and renewable energy innovation = Carbon-free Energy?**

Globally, burning fossil fuels releases more than 26 billion tons of CO_2 into the atmosphere. Most of these fuels produce electricity or move vehicles. The UN World Energy Assessment in 2004 launched a global analysis of the energy alternatives to consuming fossil fuels. Governments began to take seriously reducing waste in fuel consumption and ramping up renewable energy sources to meet energy demand. The energy efficiency approach seeks to make the use of all energy maximally efficient reduce CO_2 emissions and avert the need for existing and new fossil fuel use and power generation facilities. Energy-efficient buildings, non-polluting mass transit and low-carbon land use patterns, and appliances that use little to no energy are required, along with utility rates that discourage wasteful consumption, more efficient vehicles, and fossil fuel prices that include the cost of climate change externalities are needed. Supply-side approaches require substituting renewables for fossil fuels, and progressively retiring the use of fossil fuels. The legal regimes for these approaches are as yet few, and exist primarily within nations. There are virtually no treaties for sustainable energy. Energy efficiency provides emissions mitigation for the least cost. With upgraded grids for distributing electricity, and with renewable energy systems distributed off-grid for rural electrification, progress can be made toward the carbon neutral, sustainable development that is essential for climate adaptation. Energy efficiency improvements and renewable energy investments are directly dependent on the laws and policies a jurisdiction enacts and implements. Broad changes in energy use require fundamental reforms of the energy laws, which up until now have generally promoted increasing supplies of fossil fuels. More solar energy hits the earth in one hour than humanity uses in a year. This renewable energy can be used directly or indirectly by capturing the energy in wind, flowing water, and the oceans (which also get a daily surge of energy—tides—from the gravitational force of the moon). Chapter 6 will explore whether our laws are adequate to support rapidly deploying marine, wind, or solar technologies, and Chapter 9 will examine how the State of Delaware has reconceived its energy regime to transition to a carbon-neutral economy, and how China is approaching the same challenge. Subsidies enjoyed by fossil fuel suppliers have great inertia resists change. How can law best promote low- or no-carbon technology and innovation, and global implementation of these technologies, as the Bali Action Plan contemplates?

A. INTRODUCTION

Energy is central to society's well being. The availability of high quality energy is necessary to maintain and expand technology, to grow, distribute and cook food, to provide potable water, to prevent wastes from polluting our environment, to heat, cool and light our living spaces and to both maintain and expand economic prosperity.

Sadly, about 1.6 billion people in the world lack access to electricity; most living in South Asia (930 million) and Africa (554 million). International Energy Agency, World Energy Outlook 2006 (2007). About 2.5 billion people use, at an unsustainable rate, traditional inefficient biomass fuels (such as wood, charcoal, agricultural waste and animal dung) for cooking and heating, harming their health, the environment and their economic prospects. The health impacts can be severe: "About 1.3 million people–mostly women and children–die prematurely every year because of exposure to indoor air pollution from biomass." Id. In some African nations, for example, an inadequate supply of reliable, high quality energy has reduced economic growth by 2 percent. But, if energy needs are supplied from fossil fuels (coal, petroleum, natural gas), global emissions of greenhouse gases will soar, as will the adverse effects of pollution from mining, drilling, and transporting fuels, and the emission of sulphur dioxide, nitrogen dioxide, particulates, mercury and other air pollutants.

According to the International Energy Agency:

The world is facing twin energy-related threats: that of not having adequate and secure supplies of energy at affordable prices and that of environmental harm caused by consuming too much of it. ... Yet the current pattern of energy supply carries the threat of severe and irreversible environmental damage – including changes in global climate. Reconciling the goals of energy security and environmental protection requires strong and coordinated government action and public support. The need to curb the growth in fossil-energy demand, to increase geographic and fuel-supply diversity and to mitigate climate-destabilizing emissions is more urgent than ever.

Fossil fuels are reservoirs of high quality energy assembled by natural systems over long stretches of geologic time. These fuels, petroleum, coal and natural gas, have been the foundation of the industrial revolution and continue to be the essential support of modern society. However, the use of these fuels poses significant economic, environmental and social challenges. With respect to climate change, fossil fuels are the single largest source of greenhouse gas emissions.

Globally, fossil fuels burning releases over 26 billion tons of CO_2 into the atmosphere–almost 75% of global GHG emissions.* Most of those fuels are burned to make electricity or move vehicles. In the United States, fossil fuel burning accounts for virtually all of its CO_2 emissions. Electricity accounts for about half of that and transportation for another 30%. See Climate Analysis Indicators Tool (CAIT) version 6.0. (World Resources Institute, 2009) at http://cait.wri.org. In the U.S., coal–fired power plants account for about 2 billion tons of CO_2—about 1/3 of all U.S. GHG emissions, and nearly 40% of all CO_2 emissions, natural gas about 1.19 billion tons, and petroleum, another 2,581 million tons of CO_2. In 2006, China emitted 4.95 billion tons of CO_2 from burning coal, but just 0.1 billions tons from natural gas, and 0.96 billion tons from oil. U.S.E.I.A., Energy-Related Emissions Data, http://www.eia.doe.gov/environment.html. Globally, 41% of the world's electricity comes from coal and 42% of all CO_2 emissions are from coal. International Energy Agency, Key World Energy Statistics (2008). If historic trends continue, and if more nations decide to increase electricity use by adding coal-fired power plants, emissions and atmospheric concentrations will soar. The chart on the historic growth in energy use tells the story.

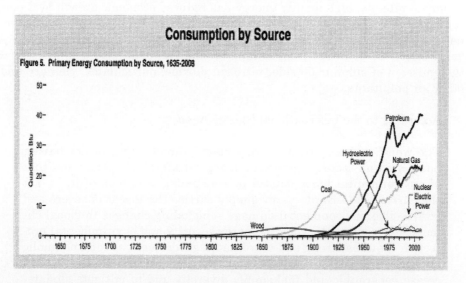

Consumption by Source

Figure 5. Primary Energy Consumption by Source, 1635-2008

Source: U.S.E.I.A., Annual Review of Energy (2008) (Energy use in the United States.)

Energy for sustainable development or sustainable energy presents a framework for addressing these urgent challenges. "Sustainable energy" is defined, in contrast to traditional fossil fuels as follows:

---

* This calculation does not include GHG emissions due to land use changes, deforestation, and the like. These issues are discussed in detail in the photosynthesis material in Chapter 6. WRI estimated that in 2000, GHG emissions from land use changes were about 7.6 billion tons. See www.cait.wri.org.

energy systems, technologies, and resources that are not only capable of supporting long-term economic and human development needs, but do so in a manner compatible with (1) preserving the underlying integrity of essential natural systems, including averting catastrophic climate change; (2) extending basic energy services to the more than 2 billion people worldwide who currently lack access to modern forms of energy; and (3) reducing the security risks and potential for geopolitical conflict that could otherwise arise from an escalating competition for unevenly distributed oil and natural gas resources. InterAgency Council, Lighting the Way: Toward a Sustainable Energy Future (2007).

At an economic development level, the gap between global demand and supply of petroleum is razor thin. As the Chinese and Indian economies grow, demand for petroleum to fuel cars, trucks, airplanes, boilers, and electric generators will grow rapidly. The price of oil will soar, hobbling economic development in developing nations. Moreover, our energy system will be ever more vulnerable to storms in the Gulf of Mexico and the North Sea, and political and labor unrest in oil-producing countries around the world. Even very modest supply disruptions can dramatically raise the price of petroleum.

The urgency is also environmentally driven. Global warming is rapidly approaching dangerous levels. Recent studies have indicated that sea levels are rising more rapidly than the tempered IPCC 2007 assessment predicted they would. See, *e.g.* DOE/Lawrence Livermore National Laboratory. "Ocean Temperatures And Sea Level Increases 50 Percent Higher Than Previously Estimated," (18 June 2008) https://publicaffairs.llnl.gov/news/news_releases/2008/NR-08-06-7.html. Warming may be accelerating–displaying levels at the upper range of IPCC estimates and suggesting rapid movement towards dangerous anthropogenic climate change.

There is also a social, equitable urgency. Nearly 1.6 billion people have no access to electricity and must use traditional biomass in inefficient stoves to cook, living with terrible indoor pollution from the smoke and soot as a result. So, the world faces a great sustainable development challenge–it must simultaneously provide billions of more people with access to high quality energy and also investigate and adapt to the effects of global warming.

The International Energy Agency blunted stated the dangers we face:

The world's energy system is at a crossroads. Current global trends in energy supply and consumption are patently unsustainable — environmentally, economically, socially. But that can — and must — be altered; *there's still time to change the road we're on*. It is not an exaggeration to claim that the future of human prosperity depends on how successfully we tackle the two central energy challenges facing us today: securing the supply of reliable and affordable energy; and effecting a rapid transformation to a low-carbon, efficient and environmentally benign system of energy supply. What is needed is nothing short of an energy revolution. * * *

Preventing catastrophic and irreversible damage to the global climate ultimately requires a major decarbonization of the world energy sources.

International Energy Agency, World Energy Outlook 2008 (2008) 3.

Meeting the capital requirements to maintain and expand the world's energy system will also be a staggering challenge. The I.E.A. estimates that to follow a business-as-usual path will require capital investment between 2007 and 2030 of $26 trillion dollars; nearly half of that money will be needed just to maintain existing energy supplies and infrastructure. Id. However, changing the way we use energy by improving how efficiently we use it and reducing waste is the fastest and most cost-effective strategy for meeting our energy and greenhouse gas reduction imperatives. E.I.A., an institution with the primary mission of ensuring adequate supplies of fossil fuels, estimates that energy efficiency investments could lower "fossil-fuel consumption by a cumulative amount of 22 billion tons of oil equivalent over 2010-2030, yielding cumulative savings of over $7 trillion." (22 billion ton s of oil is equivalent to about 163 billion barrels of oil. See American Phys. Soc., Energy Units, http://www.aps.org/policy/reports/popa-reports/energy/units.cfm.

The E.I.A.'s conclusions, Id. at 16, are stark and sobering, unlike any past annual assessment:

The energy future will be very different. * * * The world energy system will be transformed, but not necessarily in the way we would like to see. We can be confident of some of the trends highlighted in this report: the growing weight of China, India, the Middle East and other non-OECD regions in energy markets and in CO_2 emissions; the rapidly increasing dominance of national oil companies; and the emergence of low-carbon energy technologies. * * * [I]t is becoming increasingly apparent that the era of cheap oil is over. But many of the key policy drivers (not to mention other, external factors) remain in doubt. It is within the power of all governments, of producing and consuming countries alike, acting alone or together, to steer the world towards a cleaner, cleverer and more competitive energy system. Time is running out and the time to act is now.

WORLD ENERGY ASSESSMENT OVERVIEW: 2004 UPDATE

José Goldemberg and Thomas B. Johansson, eds.

BASIC ENERGY FACTS

An energy system is made up of an energy supply sector and energy end-use technologies. The objective of an energy system is to deliver to consumers the benefits that energy use offers. The term energy services is used to describe these benefits, which for households include illumination, cooked food, comfortable indoor temperatures, refrigeration, telecommunications, education, and transportation. Energy services are also required for virtually every commercial and industrial activity. For instance, heating and cooling are needed for many industrial processes, motive power is needed for agriculture and industry, and electricity is needed for telecommunications and electronics. It is the availability of and access to energy services, not merely energy supply, that is crucial.

The energy chain that delivers these services begins with the collection or extraction of primary energy that, in one or several steps, may be converted into energy carriers, or final energy such as electricity or diesel oil that are suitable for end uses. Energy end-use equipment—stoves, light bulbs, vehicles, machinery, etc.—converts the final energy into useful energy, which (with the help of additional technologies) provides the desired benefits: the energy services. * * *

Energy services result from a combination of various technologies, infrastructure (capital), labour (know how), materials, and primary energy. Each of these inputs carries a price tag, and they are partly substitutable for one another. From the consumer's perspective, the important issues are the economic value or utility derived from the services. Consumers are often unaware of the upstream activities required to produce energy services. * * *

Per capita use of primary energy in North America was 280 gigajoules in 2000, more than eleven times as much as used by an average sub-Saharan African (who used 25 gigajoules that year when both commercial and non-commercial energy are included).[7] In OECD Europe and OECD Pacific—developed countries in those regions—per capita energy use was about 142

---

[7] * * * [T]he term commercial energy refers to fossil fuels (oil, coal, and natural gas), nuclear energy, and large-scale hydropower. The term traditional energy is used to denote locally collected and often in processed biomass-based fuels, such as crop residues, wood, and animal dung. Most traditional energy is used non-commercially (i.e., non-commercial energy). Although traditional energy sources can be used renewably, the term new renewables refers to modern biofuels, wind, solar, small-scale hydropower, marine, and geothermal energy.

and 180 GJ, respectively. * * * Fossil fuels (oil, natural gas, and coal) represent nearly 80 percent of the total [energy used]. Nuclear power contributes approximately 7 percent; however, because nuclear power plants have only one third of thermal efficiency, the final electricity generated for consumption is basically the same as that generated by large hydropower. Large hydropower and "new" renewables (which includes modern uses of biomass and small hydropower, geothermal, wind, solar, and marine energy) each contribute slightly more than 2 percent; the percentage contribution of "new renewable energy sources" has changed little in recent years. * * *

Energy and Social Issues

The relationship between energy and social issues is two-way. The ability to pay for energy services and knowledge of what is available and how best to apply it will affect the level of demand and type of energy services used. Conversely, the quality (cleanliness, reliability, and convenience) and level of access (availability, affordability, and variety) of energy services have an effect on social issues. Lack of access to energy services is closely linked to a range of social concerns, including poverty, lack of opportunities, urbanisation, poor health, and a lack of education for women in particular. * * *

Poverty is the overriding social consideration for developing countries. Some 1.3 billion people in the developing world live on less than $1 per day. Income measurement alone, however, does not fully capture the misery and the absence of choice that poverty represents. The energy available to poor people—especially their reliance on traditional fuels in rural areas—is not supportive of the development and income generation needed to alleviate poverty.

World-wide, two billion people rely on traditional biomass fuels for cooking and/or have no access to modern energy services. For these people, cooking indoors with poorly vented stoves has significant health impacts. Hundreds of millions of people—mainly women and children—spend several hours per day in the drudgery of gathering firewood and water, often from considerable distances, for household needs. Because of these demands on their time and physical energy, women and children often have no opportunities for education and other productive activities, while their health suffers.

The two billion people lacking access to electricity have inadequate lighting and few labour-saving devices, as well as limited telecommunications and possibilities for commercial enterprise. Greater access to electricity, modern fuels, and clean, efficient technologies such as improved stoves for cooking can enable people to benefit from both short- and long-term advances in their quality of life. * * *

Low-income households in developing countries typically use traditional fuels and inefficient technologies. * * * [H]igher income segments of the population increasingly rely on modern fuels as income grows.

For low-income households, firewood is the dominant fuel. At higher incomes, commercial fuels and electricity replace wood, offering greater convenience, energy efficiency, and cleanliness. Because convenient, affordable energy can contribute to a household's productivity and income generating potential, its availability can help families and communities break out of the cycle of poverty. * * *

Energy technology choices in developing countries have important equity implications. Investments in centralised, capital-intensive conventional energy enterprises such as coal-fired power-generation and large dams largely benefit high- and middle-income urban communities, commercial establishments, and industries through electricity distributed through power grids. Poor, dispersed rural communities that are often far from the grid rarely benefit from such investments. Even in urban areas, low-income neighbourhoods and shantytowns are often not connected to the grid. A growing number of studies find that renewable and other decentralised small-scale energy technologies (such as diesel motors and hybrids) are important options for poverty alleviation, particularly technologies that are locally made and that operate using locally available fuels (e.g., hydro power, wind power, solar power, and modern biomass resources). These decentralized energy technologies can be a source of jobs, employment, and enterprise creation for both the rural and urban poor in developing countries, and can be competitive and affordable in isolated areas or other niche markets.

The increasing concentration of people in urban centers is another key development issue linked to energy. Although the general trend towards urbanisation has many components and may be inevitable, providing more options to rural residents through energy interventions could potentially slow migration and reduce pressure on rapidly growing cities. Energy inputs can improve agricultural productivity, generating better rural incomes and higher value added in this sector. Productive uses of energy provide employment opportunities and reduce the necessity to migrate to urban areas for employment. Productive uses allow income-generating opportunities that can help pay for the energy services, thus making them more affordable and sustainable. There is a clear need for mechanisms to cut the transaction costs between a large number of invisible potential consumers and a discrete number of suppliers of energy services, thereby promoting investment in local productive chains.

In developing countries, addressing the energy needs of the poor, who represent a large majority, will require major structural changes. In industrialized countries, on the other hand, adequate access to affordable energy is problematic only for a minority, and thus is more amenable to social policy solutions. Throughout the world, however, poor households pay a larger frac-tion of their incomes for energy than do the rich, and so are vulnerable to the effects of rapid increases in the price of energy. * * * In addition to paying a larger fraction of their income on energy services, poor households often pay more per unit of energy than rich households do. They have few energy serv-ices available to them and have little choice but to use inefficient fuels and technologies. The role of energy efficiency in improving this situation should not be overlooked. * * *

Energy and Economic Issues

If the global growth rate of about 1.5 percent per year in primary energy use continues, total energy use will double between 2000 and 2040, and triple by 2060. In the past thirty years, developing countries' commercial energy use has increased three and a half times as fast as that of OECD countries; energy use has increased even faster in China. This is partly the result of lifestyle changes made possible by rising personal incomes, coupled with higher population growth rates and a shift from traditional to commercial energy in developing countries. It is also partly the result of a shift towards less energy-intensive production and consumption patterns in the OECD countries. On a per capita basis, however, the increase in total primary en-ergy use has not resulted in notably more equitable access to energy services between industrialized and developing countries. Clearly, more energy will be needed to fuel global economic growth and to help deliver opportunities to the billions of people in developing countries who do not have access to ade-quate energy services and who live on less than $2 a day. The wide gap in per capita consumption of energy services between industrialized and devel-oping countries will not last indefinitely, and there will be considerable pres-sure on the available physical and human energy resources.

However, the amount of additional energy required to provide the energy services needed in the future, will depend on the efficiency with which the energy is produced, delivered, and used. Energy efficiency improvements could help reduce financial investments in new energy supply systems, as they have over the past two hundred years. The degree of interdependence between economic activity and energy use is neither static nor uniform across regions. Energy intensity (the ratio of energy use to GDP) often depends on a country's stage of development. In OECD countries, which enjoy abundant energy services, growth in energy demand is less tightly linked to economic production than it was in the past.

A detailed, long-term analysis of energy intensity for a number of coun-tries reveals a common pattern of energy use driven by the following factors:

- The shift from traditional to commercial forms of energy, indus-trialization, and motorization initially increases the commercial energy/GDP ratio.

■   As industrialization proceeds and incomes rise, saturation effects, as well as an expansion of the service sector (which is less energy intensive), decrease the ratio of commercial energy to GDP after it reaches a peak. Many countries have passed this point of maximum energy intensity, but low-income developing countries have not.

■   Given worldwide technology transfer and diffusion, energy efficiency improvements can be the main limiting factor in the growth of energy demand arising from increasing populations and growing production and incomes.

■   The more efficient use of materials in better-quality, well-designed, miniaturized products, the recycling of energy-intensive materials, and the saturation of bulk markets for basic materials in industrialized countries contribute to additional decreases in energy intensity.

■   In developing countries, technological leapfrogging (i.e., bypassing some of the steps followed in the past in industrialized countries and jumping directly to modern technologies) to the use of highly efficient appliances, machinery, processes, vehicles and transportation systems, and other energy technologies, offers considerable potential for energy efficiency improvements.

■   In transition economy countries, the decoupling of energy costs and prices, the promotion of energy rather than energy services, and the fact that energy use was often not even metered (and thus not paid for in relation to consumption levels) resulted in low energy efficiency and high-energy intensity for the level of GDP.

* * * While initial costs for more energy efficient technologies are often higher than for less energy efficient ones, a life cycle cost analysis, incorporating the savings from using less energy, shows lower costs. Therefore, in many countries, there are good reasons to adopt–early in the process of development–highly efficient appliances, machinery, industrial processes, vehicles, and transportation systems, thus "leapfrogging" some stages in the development process. * * *

[F]inancing is inadequate for energy projects in developing countries. Until the economic risks to foreign investors can be managed (for example, through clear and stable rules for energy and financial markets, steady revenue generation through bill collection, and profit transfers), most developing countries may have to continue to finance their energy development from domestic savings. In countries without such investment, energy will become a constraint on economic growth, particularly if they are oil and gas importers. In many developing countries, energy imports represent more than half of all imports, imposing a heavy burden on foreign exchange and contributing to indebtedness. * * *

Energy, the Environment, and Health

The environmental impacts of energy use are not new. For centuries, wood burning has contributed to the deforestation of many areas. Even in the early stages of industrialization, local air, water, and land pollution reached high levels. What is relatively new is acknowledgement of energy linkages to regional and global environmental problems and the implications of those linkages. Although energy's potential for enhancing human well-being is unquestionable, conventional energy production and consumption are closely linked to environmental degradation that threatens human health and quality of life and affects ecological balances and biological diversity.* * *

Energy Security

Energy security is a term that applies to the availability of energy at all times in various forms, in sufficient quantities, and at affordable prices, without unacceptable or irreversible impact on the environment. These conditions must prevail over the long term if energy is to contribute to sustainable development. Energy security has both a producer and a consumer side to it. In terms of energy resources worldwide to meet energy demand for the foreseeable future there is no energy security problem. However, whether these resources will be available in the marketplace at affordable prices depends on how markets perform, on government taxation and regulation, and on the role of policies such as electrification or subsidies. * * *

The potential for conflict, sabotage, disruption of production and trade, and reduction in strategic reserves cannot be dismissed. These potential threats lead to sudden transient price increases (price spikes) that cause economic disruptions in many countries and disrupt global economic growth.* * *

A range of actions can be taken to improve energy security. One important measure is to avoid excessive dependence on fossil fuel imports. This involves diversifying supply–both geographically and among various primary energy sources–as well as increasing end-use efficiency and encouraging greater reliance on local, including renewable, resources. Promoting renewable energy will have other positive externalities such as job creation and pollution reduction, provided that these do not have disproportionate costs or waste scarce resources. * * *

There is an absolute link between meeting the needs of economic growth, creating the conditions for an acceptable quality of life, and ensuring sustainable development while protecting the environment. Energy security is a delicate balance among these diverse requirements and there is no question that a least-cost mix of efficient use with more diverse, dispersed resources can make the energy system more resilient and sustainable.

ENERGY LAW AND SUSTAINABLE DEVELOPMENT
Nicholas A. Robinson
Foreword to A. Bradbrook and R. Ottinger, Energy Law and
Sustainable Development (2003)

The [2002] World Summit on Sustainable Development (WSSD) recommends that nations-undertake the reform of their energy regimes. This is a matter of great urgency, since most national systems for generating electrical energy, or otherwise consuming fossil fuels, are the primary sources of greenhouse gases contributing to climate change. Forthcoming debates about how most effectively to implement the Kyoto Protocol will lend urgency to these WSSD recommendations. The expert authors of this book provide us with important guidance on how nations may respond to the WSSD's recommendations on a worldwide basis.

Given the fundamental challenges posed by the reports of the Intergovernmental Panel on Climate Change (IPCC), affiliations inevitably will find themselves undertaking a far more fundamental assessment of their energy regimes than has ever been the case. The recommendations of the WSSD carry implications, which extend well beyond even the scope of the essays provided in the chapters of this book. By way of this foreword, one may speculate on some of these implications.

One principal analytic tool of ecosystem management is measuring the flow of energy through living and inanimate systems. Since climate change functions within Earth's biosphere, energy flow measurement should be assessed at this level, as well as within individual ecosystems. Solar energy fuels life in the biosphere, and is recycled over centuries in fossil fuels and over decades in trees. The process of photosynthesis channels solar energy into resources that sustain all life on earth. These natural laws are only dimly perceived, however, by the utilitarian human laws that govern how short-term energy is supplied to our human economy.

As contemporary energy law has developed over the past century in each nation, it has rarely had occasion to integrate such ecological assessment into its fundamental norms or legal framework. The challenge of the coming generations is to accomplish this integration. Without integration of energy law and environmental law, human society cannot meet the goals for sustainable development envisioned at the 1992 UN Conference on Environment and Development in Rio de Janeiro. Reformation of energy laws will be an essential element of the transition to attain sustainability within national and global economies. Energy law has developed through a disjointed body of statutes and treaties.

Energy law is most often considered to be merely a variant of public administrative law. However, rather than being a refined and integrated legal field of law, the laws of this sector are characterized by a lack of basic principles or integrative systems. Its costs are underwritten by application of public finance laws. It has evolved incrementally over time, in an essentially instrumental manner, reactive to perceived needs to find sources of energy to consume. Energy law facilitates the development of whatever energy system is possible in light of available technology. Its short-term goal is always to supply electricity or such other basic fuels as each society requires.

Energy law's emphasis has been on ensuring an adequate supply of energy, rather than providing energy systems with an emphasis on maximizing efficiency, respecting ecology or ensuring equity in use among all users. As a result, energy law has developed without much regard for the negative environmental impacts of energy generation. Prices for energy services for decades have ignored environmental externalities, and most often disregarded whether the poor can access such services. Most nations have been obliged to compensate for these shortcomings by enacting statutes, and negotiating several treaties to cope with the economic "externalities" generated by the energy sector. Principal among the environmental externalities are the following: air pollution including "acid rain," waste water pollution, significant solid and hazardous waste products from mining or combustion of coal or use of enriched uranium, disregard for the reclamation of mined lands and their ecosystems, discharge of waste heat from cooling systems into aquatic ecosystems, loss of habitat and soil salting in the wake of hydroelectric dam development, and impacts associated with constructing high tension electric power lines or natural gas pipelines.

Environmental laws currently only partially, and imperfectly, regulate these impacts of the energy sector. The continuing accumulation of such problems bodes ill for how energy law will handle the new challenges that the energy sector faces as it contemplates reduction of carbon dioxide emissions. * * * Because practically every nation has favored systems that supply energy exclusively through economic sector preferences, energy law today only superficially addresses how energy suppliers could better take economic, social or ecological responsibility for the adverse effects of their processes and services. In most places, since the utility services that supply energy are a near monopoly, those societies that decide to require energy suppliers to consider social or environmental issues have chosen to establish regulatory systems and to ensure that the pricing of energy is balanced between (a) generating fees sufficient to pay for the investment in building and operating the energy systems, (b) providing a "reasonable" profit to the governmental, parastatal, or private enterprises that build and operate the energy systems, and (c) ensuring that the public can afford to pay the fees and showing that the fees appear fair to the users.

Historically, the regulatory systems established to meet these energy objectives have operated as a distinct and relatively independent sector of government and the economy. For instance, regulations often establish exclusive service areas with enough customers to permit the enterprise generating and transmitting electricity to recover its costs associated with supplying electricity, and make a reasonable profit. Little attention has been devoted to how the energy sector relates to the broader environmental context in which it is embedded. Hydroelectric systems, and their dams, have been obliged to consider alternative uses of rivers and lakes, because these resources serve navigation and fishing interests also. For instance, during the Progressive era in the United States of America Congress enacted Section 10 of the Federal Power Act of 1920 requiring that the federal regulatory agency balance the competing demands of water before it could decide whether or not to authorize a new hydroelectric power facility which might interfere with other water uses. This has been held to require a study of alternative sources of energy that might obviate the need for the proposed hydroelectric facility. Out of specific licensing proceedings in the USA, for instance, experience was gained that helped Congress to enact a generic administrative procedure for weighing these sorts of alternatives. In consequence Congress enacted the National Environmental Policy Act of 1969, which first established environmental impact assessment procedures.

Environmental impact assessment is now widely used by many nations to determine what sort of new energy systems should be licensed. Unfortunately, far too often the EIA process is treated as a routine exercise, without requiring a thorough study of environmental effects or a valid consultation with potentially affected stakeholders. Even where EIA is well established in national law, EIA is not yet used to measure the ways to avoid greenhouse gas emissions, or to sequester any carbon dioxide that may be emitted. EIA procedures also are rarely, if ever, applied to existing energy development regimes, such as the refining, distribution and use of petrol.

Indeed, so effective are society's vested economic interests in the use of petroleum as a preferred energy source that the nations producing oil and gas prevented any sustainable use energy recommendations from being included in the action plan adopted at the UN Conference on Environment and Development in 1992 in Rio de Janeiro. Rio's Earth Summit recommended that EIA "shall" be used in national environmental decision-making, but EIA was not mentioned in the action plan adopted at the Rio Earth Summit, known as Agenda 21. The only references in Agenda 21 were to the need to use energy sources more efficiently and environmentally in the context of the transportation sector.

This does not mean that Agenda 21 was irrelevant to energy and climate issues. It also had a chapter on "safe and environmentally sound management of radioactive wastes," recognizing that this one fuel cycle had long-term and dangerous consequences for human health and the environment. In addition, a number of the chapters of Agenda 21 implicitly address an energy law agenda. For instance, between the 1972 United Nations Conference on the Human Environment in Stockholm and the 1992 UN Conference on Environment and Development in Rio de Janeiro, environmental law had emerged as the fastest growing field of law at both national and international levels (it still is today). The success that environmental regulation has had in abating pollution and enhancing environmental quality throughout States such as Singapore, the UK, the USA, Canada, Australia, or The Netherlands stands in stark relief against the acute and still growing threats to public health from air, soil, and water pollution in urban centers such as Bangkok, New Delhi, Mexico City, or Beijing. To combat the environmental degradation trends, Agenda 21 called for rapid development of further environmental law.

Experience with environmental laws illustrates how appropriate legal systems can foster progressively wider uses of clean energy and transportation systems. * * * For instance, air pollution control legislation commonly establishes health standards, monitors where those standards have not been attained, and then requires concrete and measurable steps to curb air emissions. Conversion to clean fuels and rigorous use of energy efficiency technology readily emerges as a cost-saving and immediately available means to comply with the strict air pollution laws. Laws requiring the public disclosure of all air emissions, and the media coverage of those emissions, have further stimulated companies and governmental authorities alike to seek to cut emissions, rather than receive the censure of the public.

In addition to air pollution issues, environmental impact assessments (EIAs) feature in environmental laws and are now a mature legal system established in all regions. EIA techniques have been used to promote the study of alternative means for supplying energy and meeting transportation needs. Since the legal framework for EIA is in place, EIA can and should be more conscientiously used for requiring the study of clean energy options. The retarding factor in EIA is often the lack of government will to use it toward these ends, coupled with the failure to permit public oversight or enforcement of the EIA process in many States. The success of public participation in the implementation of the National Environmental Policy Act (NEPA) in the USA demonstrates the value of such oversight in promoting sound energy practices. Agenda 21 was silent on how to implement EIA, but implicit in Principle 17 of the Rio Declaration on Environment and Development is that EIA's examination of "alternatives" to propose government actions must entail examining alternative means to promote energy efficiency and avoid exacerbating green house gas emissions.

Many experts in energy and environmental law recognized that these energy recommendations implicit in Agenda 21 would not by themselves be strong enough to reverse current unsustainable patterns of energy use. The UN Development Programme * * * undertook preparation of the World Energy Assessment. Released in September of 2000, this comprehensive report

assessed the fuel cycles used to generate energy supplied, and their competing values and problems. * * * Ironically, the UNDP discontinued its work to
promote an understanding of the World Energy Assessment in the same year
that the World Summit on Sustainable Development convened in Johannesburg. * * *

Ultimately, however, energy law reform is the quintessential national issue. Parliaments around the world need to address how to reshape national
energy laws. * * * [R]eshaping energy law will be a common challenge met by
each human community within Earth's biosphere.

B. THE SCALE AND SCOPE OF THE ENERGY CHALLENGE

Determinations about how efficiently energy is used and how much of
that energy comes from renewable sources are made, even required, by the
energy laws and policies of a state or province, nation, or inter-governmental
regime internationally. Intuitively, this should not be a surprise because in a
competitive market place a purveyor of power cannot make money by selling
less of its product. Without legislation for internalizing environmental externalities of power generation, the atmosphere—a global commons—will be used
as a free disposal ground for the by-products of burning fossil fuel. Fossil fuels represent millions of years of collection and concentration of solar power
(in the form of biomass) and the conversion of that collected material into a
fossil fuel. Nature does not charge us for the ecosystem services of manufacturing coal or oil. All we need do to use it is to dig it or pump it out of the
ground. In contrast, when we seek to use renewable energy we must pay for
the collection and conversion of solar energy into useable form of power.

What are the sources of energy that are available to meet the scale of the
world's needs? Energy efficiency represents a huge storehouse of energy-by
using the energy we otherwise waste, we can do more with less raw energy. It
is also the most cost-effective and rapidly obtainable source of new energy.
Two thirds of the energy used to generate electricity is lost before the electricity reaches the final consumer. So, for every kwh of energy we can save by
being more efficient, 3 kwh of electricity need not be generated, and associated greenhouse gases need not be emitted. Renewable energy, such as solar
power, wind power, biomass, represents is our largest source of energy. Consider carefully, Nathan Lewis' assessment of our energy choices. Does the
Report on the Climate Change bill passed by the House of Representatives
(H.R. 2454) accurately reflect the science?

POWERING THE PLANET
Nathan S. Lewis
11 Engineering & Science 2 (2007)

The Scale of Energy

Energy is *the* single most important technological challenge facing humanity today. Nothing else in science or technology comes close in comparison. If we don't invent the next nano-widget, if we don't cure cancer in 20 years, like it or not the world will stay the same. But with energy, we are in the middle of doing the biggest experiment that humans will have ever done, and we get to do that experiment exactly once. And there is no tomorrow, because in 20 years that experiment will be cast in stone. * * *

The currency of the world is not the dollar, it's the joule. * * *

Humanity's current energy consumption rate is 13 trillion thermal watts, or 13 terawatts. If you took the heat content of all the energy we consume in whatever form—kilowatt-hours of electricity, barrels of oil, cubic feet of natural gas—in a year, and divide it by the number of seconds in a year, you get thermal watts, which I will use as my standard unit, for ease of comparison. * * * [A] watt is a joule per second. * * * 13 terawatts that the whole globe consumes, on average. This is the scale of energy.

The United States consumes a quarter of the world's energy, at a rate of about 3.3 terawatts, but I won't say anything more about the United States. To physicists, it's not important. I care more about the 13 terawatts. Of the global consumption, about 85 percent comes from fossil fuel—coal, natural gas, and oil. These are primary fuels, that is, direct energy sources. And about 4.5 terawatts of that is used to make electricity—a form of secondary energy—resulting in the generation of about 1.5 terawatts of electricity.

I need to dissuade you up front from one important notion, that some low-cost process is magically going to take us away from fossil energy within the next 20 or 30 years. That's simply false. The Stone Age did not end because we ran out of stones, and the fossil-energy age is not going to end any time soon because we've run out of cheap fossil energy. * * * Any new energy-creating process is going to be a substitution product. * * *

Selling a substitution product requires fostering a marketplace where the technology can come to scale and compete. You can't wait for the cost of a mature, competing technology that is already at scale to rise fast enough, soon enough, to make the new technology affordable. There is no way to compete with technology that consists of just taking concentrated energy sources, like coal and oil, pulling them out of the ground, and burning them. We can discuss the true costs of putting carbon into the atmosphere, but on the current economic basis, if we wait for price signals to drive us away from fossil energy, we'll be waiting a very long time. * * *

In the Year 2050

"It's hard to make predictions, especially about the future."   * * *

I'm going to focus on the year 2050, which is not [41] years from now, it's five to 10 years from now.   Our energy infrastructure has a capital-investment sunk cost that lasts for 40 years, so when you think about 2050, you think about that *now*.   In addition, most of us—either our kids or ourselves—are going to be alive in 2050, so it's a good year to look at.

Obviously, people use energy.   The world population is projected to be nine to 10 billion people by 2050 (we're at about six billion now), so I'll pick 10 as a round number.   And I'll assume a gross domestic product, or GDP, growth of 1.6 percent per year per capita, which the IPCC calls the "business as usual" scenario, based on the average global GDP growth over the last century.   The IPCC did not foresee, 15 years ago, 10 percent growth annually in China, and 7 to 10 percent in India. And the developed countries now believe that 4 to 5 percent growth is sustainable.   But this doesn't matter, as the numbers just get worse as it gets higher.   And no country that I'm aware of has a policy *against* economic growth.

With population and GDP growth conspiring together, we would then obtain a tripling of energy demand by 2050.   This is partly mitigated, however, by the fact that we're using energy more efficiently per unit of GDP.   The ratio of energy consumption to GDP has been declining at about 1 percent, globally averaged, per year.   The United States actually saves energy at a faster rate, about 2 percent per year.   Because we have such a high per-capita energy baseline consumption, it is easier for us to save over that base, whereas the developing countries save less.   The "business as usual" scenario assumes that this will continue, and if we project that down, we will achieve an average energy consumption of two kilowatts per person within our lifetimes.   (The United States now uses 10 kilowatts per person.)   But factor in population growth and conservative economic growth, and we'll still need twice as much energy as we need now.   In terms of average thermal load, a person on a 2,000-calorie-per-day diet is basically a hundred-watt light bulb.   And in our highly mechanized western agricultural system, the energy embedded in food—to run the farm and grow the food and transport it to the supermarket and put it in the refrigerator—is 10 to 20 times the energy content of the food itself.   And the farther you live from the food source, the more embedded energy you consume.   If we are 100-watt light bulbs, this means that just keeping us fed requires one to two kilowatts.

The other thing we need to consider is the amount of carbon emitted per unit of energy produced, or the so-called carbon intensity of our energy mix on average. Back in the Stone Age, the carbon-to-energy, or C/E, ratio was quite high, as we were burning wood in caves. That's very inefficient. Most of the energy escapes into the air. We then moved to coal, and coal is not bad engineering, it's bad chemistry. We know how to burn coal efficiently, and when we burn all the carbon we get all carbon dioxide. When we burn natural gas, that's CH_4, we get one molecule of CO_2 but two H_2Os. So relatively more of the heat content 4 in joules is delivered by making H_2O rather than forming CO_2. Natural gas is thus more energy-efficient on a carbon-emitted basis. And oil is in between, having a chemical formula of CH_2, on average. These figures are constants you can do nothing about. They are simply the products of the chemical formulas and the heats of combustion of coal, oil, and natural gas.

If we follow the "business as usual" C/E projection, which is hardly business as usual except for drawing straight lines into the future, it predicts by 2050 an average carbon intensity of 0.45, which is lower than that of the least-carbon-intensive fossil fuel, natural gas. And the only way you can do that is with a significant infusion of carbon-free or carbon-neutral power, to bring the overall average lower than the least of its carbon-based components. Furthermore, if * * * we continue to burn oil and coal, because they are cheap, we'll need even more carbon-neutral energy to bring us down there. * * *

So we've magically, somehow, added enough carbon-free power that we can stay on this decarbonization curve. And I'll further assume that we've implemented highly aggressive energy efficiency to reduce our total demand per person down to two kilowatts. This assumes that we can get the energy embedded in our food down to one kilowatt as part of that aggressive conservation program, and that leaves us with one kilowatt per person to heat our houses, get to work, play video games, and do everything else we do. And under those assumptions, if we relate the amount of carbon emitted to the amount of energy consumed, it is simple arithmetic to calculate the amount of carbon that we will release into our atmosphere. That set of calculations brings us * * * to the "business as usual" scenario.

However, this is *still* insufficient to stabilize the atmospheric levels of CO_2 at any reasonably acceptable levels. Ice cores taken near Vostok Station, Antarctica, show that the CO_2 level has been in a narrow band between 200 and 300 parts per million by volume (ppmv) for the last 425,000 years; data from other cores have extended this back to 670,000 years. Current CO_2 levels are about 380 ppmv. "Business as usual" will require 10 trillion watts, 10 terawatts, of carbon-free power, and it never stabilizes CO_2 levels—they just keep going up. So even on that track, we are betting against data that goes back for almost a million straight years, and hoping that this time, we get lucky.

* * * [U]nfortunately, there is no natural destruction mechanism for carbon dioxide in our atmosphere. Unlike ozone depletion, it will not heal by itself through chemical processes. In our highly oxidizing atmosphere, CO_2 is an end product. The lifetimes of CO_2 in the atmosphere are well known, and the time for 500 to 600 ppmv of CO_2 to decay back to 300 ppmv is between 500 and 5,000 years. Which means that the CO_2 we produce over the next 40 years, and its associated effects, will last for a timescale comparable to modern human history. This is why, within the next 20 years, we either solve this problem or the world will never be the same. How different that world will be, we won't know until we get there. * * *

If we want to hold CO_2 even to 550 ppmv, even with aggressive energy efficiency we will need as much clean, carbon-free energy within the next 40 years, online, as the entire oil, natural gas, coal, and nuclear industries today combined—10 to 15 terawatts. * * * Furthermore, if we wait 30 years, the amount of carbon-free energy we'll need will be even greater, and needed even faster, because in the meantime we will have put out 30 years of accumulated CO_2 emissions that will not go away for centuries to millennia. So stabilizing at 550 ppm will then require about 15 to 20 terawatts of carbon-free power in 2050.

Kicking the Carbon Habit

We absolutely have to have universal, government-based policies to drive this transformation if we are going to make such a transition on this rapid a timescale. * * * It's a question of scale, as well as cost, not solely technology.

Let's talk first about energy efficiency. It's much cheaper to save a joule of energy than it is to make it, because the losses all along the supply chain are such that saving a joule at the end means you save making, say, five joules at the source. So lowering demand with energy-efficient LED lighting, fuel cells, "green" buildings, and so on is going to pay off much sooner than clean energy supplies. On the other hand, if we save as much energy as we currently use, combined, we will still need to make at least as much carbon-neutral energy by 2050 as we currently use, combined, merely to hold CO_2 levels to double where they are now. That's the scale of the challenge.

So let's look at carbon-neutral energy sources. We could go nuclear, which is the only proven technology that we have that could scale to these numbers. We have about 400 nuclear power plants in the world today. To get the 10 terawatts we need to stay on the "business-as-usual" curve, we'd need 10,000 of our current one-gigawatt reactors, and that means we'd have to build one every other day somewhere in the world for the next 50 straight years. I've been giving this talk in one version or another for five years—we should have already built on the order of 1,000 new reactors, or double what's ever been built, just to stay on track. So we're really behind.

There isn't enough terrestrial uranium on the planet to build them as once-through reactors. We could get enough uranium from seawater, if we processed the equivalent of 3,000 Niagara Falls 24/7 to do the extraction. Which means that the only credible nuclear-energy source today involves plutonium. * * * We'd need about 10,000 fast-breeder reactors and, by the way, their commissioned lifetime is only 50 years. That means that after we choose this route, we're building one of them every other day, or more rapidly, forever.

We don't have time for the physicists to figure out how to make nuclear fusion reactors * * * [A] multinational demonstration fusion reactor being built in the south of France, will demonstrate break even—that is, it will put out as much energy as it takes to run it—in 35 years, and it will run for all of one week before the entire machine will, by design, disintegrate in the presence of that high-neutron radiation and temperature flux. And in the meantime we would have to build a commercial fission reactor every day for the next 30 years. It's not going to happen.

We could get there by sequestering the carbon. We have plenty of cheap coal, globally. China is building two gigawatts' worth of coal-fired electric power plants every week now. We could pipe the CO_2 out to the deep ocean, but CO_2 dissolved in water becomes carbonic acid, and estimates are that in some places the local pH change would be about 0.1 pH units. That's probably not a good idea. We could pump the CO_2 into deep oil and natural gas wells, but there aren't enough of them to hold all the CO_2 we will make during the next 50 years. We could put it in deep aquifers, where there's about 100 to 200 years' worth of total capacity, which would give us enough time to bridge to something else—*if it works technically.* You should not assume that it works yet. The decay time of CO_2 in the atmosphere is, as I said before, between 500 and 5,000 years. That means that if one percent of the CO_2 in the reservoirs leaks, in 100 years the flux to the atmosphere would be identical to what you intended to mitigate in the first place. We know that CO_2 migrates underground. It bubbled up in Lake Nyos, Cameroon, on August 26, 1986, and killed some 1,700 people. So we're going to have to demonstrate within the next 10 years that it will leak less than 0.1 percent, globally averaged, for the next millennium in thousands of different aquifers around the world.

Every site is geologically different. So even if you validate sequestration at one site, that doesn't mean that it will work at the other thousands of sites we'll need. (Of which, by the way, nobody knows whether China has basically any.) And be careful what you wish for, because you might actually get it. *If it works,* a quick calculation based on the density of supercritical CO_2 at 1,000 meters' burial depth indicates that there will be enough buried CO_2

emissions from the United States that within 100 years, if uniformly distributed, it would cause a rise in the elevation of the lower 48 states by about five centimeters. Which will be good if the sea level rises; otherwise not so good.
* * *

Renewable Energy

Which brings us last to renewable resources—biomass, hydroelectric, geothermal, wind, and solar.

Hydroelectric power is a model renewable resource, but all the kinetic energy in all the rivers, lakes, and streams on our planet combined adds up to a rate of 4.6 terawatts. And we can't tap all of that, because we can't dam up the Okeefenokee Swamp and get much energy. So as a practical matter, there's 1.5 or so terawatts available, but that includes places like the Hudson River * * *. Similar economic considerations leave us 0.9 terawatts, and we've already built 0.6. So forget about hydroelectricity. It's cheap, it's abundant, and we've pretty much maxed it out.

You'll hear a lot about geothermal energy. The sustainable geothermal heat flux works out to 0.057 watts per square meter. That's from the temperature at the center of the earth, the thermal conductance of the earth, and the diameter of the earth. So from the entire continental surface of our planet, if you captured all of the heat flux at 100 percent efficiency (a small second-law problem!), you might get 11 terawatts. The heat of the earth isn't close to satisfying our thirst for energy. And such deep geothermal wells in hot dry rock tend to "run out of steam" in about five years.

Wind is the cheapest renewable-energy source now, because we cherry-pick the high-wind-velocity sites. As a bonus, the wind's potential energy goes up as the cube of the wind speed—1/2 mv^2 times the mass of air per unit time, which introduces another factor of v. And wind energy is relatively economic, about five cents per kilowatt hour in *very* high-wind-speed areas, but even adding in the lower-wind-speed areas, when you calculate the total kinetic energy that we can get at the surface of the earth, there is to be had in practical terms about two to four terawatts.

If we assume that the net energy return from biomass equals the gross energy production—that is, that it takes negligible energy input to run the farm and harvest the crop—generating 20 terawatts would require 31 percent of the total land area of the planet—4 x 10^{13} square meters. The problem is that photosynthesis is fundamentally inefficient. Leaves should be black instead of green. They have the wrong band gap, and they convert less than 1 percent of the total energy they receive from sunlight into stored energy on an annual basis.

And, by the way, the fastest-growing plants known are a mere factor of two or so under their ultimate CO_2 fixation rate. CO_2 is dilute in the atmosphere, so unless there's a transport system sucking carbon dioxide down from above, the natural mass-transport rates limit plant growth to a factor of two or so over the fastest that we already have. So if someone shows you pictures of little tomatoes and big tomatoes, and extrapolates from tall switchgrass to 20-times-taller switchgrass, that's defying the laws of physics.

You hear a lot about schools of management. I believe in the Willie Sutton school of energy management. The Willie Sutton principle is simple. Willie Sutton was a famous bank robber, and when they finally caught him someone asked, "Why do you rob banks, Mr. Sutton?" He said, "Because that's where the money is." I believe in that, too.

One hundred twenty thousand terawatts of solar power hits the earth, so Willie Sutton would say go to the sun because that's where the energy is. It is the *only* natural energy resource that can keep up with human consumption. Everything else will run up against the stops, soon. In fact, more solar energy hits the earth in one hour than all the energy the world consumes in a year.

For a 10-percent-efficient photovoltaic system, and the latest systems are 15 percent or better, we could supply all the United States' energy needs with a square of land some 400 kilometers on a side. * * *[T]his would cover the Texas and Oklahoma panhandles, part of Kansas, and a wee slice of Colorado. The good news is that this area is pretty lightly populated, and the residents of even a few counties there would make enough energy to become full-fledged members of OPEC. And six of these boxes would power the globe. Unfortunately, solar is also far and away the most expensive way we have of making electricity today, with costs ranging from 25 to 50 cents per kilowatt-hour for photovoltaic systems, that is to say solar panels. Solar thermal systems, which I'll talk more about in a moment, run 10 to 15 cents per kilowatt-hour, which is still too expensive. * * *

And, by the way, if we succeed and make really cheap solar cells, that alone will not solve much in the big picture of energy. Because as Johnny Cochran might have said, "If it does not store, you'll have no power after four." Solar cells convert sunlight into electricity. And there's no good way to bottle up and store vast quantities of electricity. If you have one, go buy electricity off the grid at five cents a kilowatt-hour at night, outside of peak load hours, and then sell it back to the grid at 25 cents per kilowatt-hour in the daytime to balance the load, and laugh all the way to the bank.

I believe that the best way to store massive quantities of electricity is to convert it into chemical fuel. The best technology for that purpose that we have now uses a solar thermal system that collects and concentrates solar energy to electrolyze water. You get H_2 for fuel, which you can distribute through pipelines and store in tanks. And then you can pump it out of the tank whenever you like and run it through a fuel cell, which converts it back into electricity and water. The problem is, the existing technology is not scalable. * * *

So, in summary, we're going to need more energy in order to lift people out of poverty and have economic growth. Even if we keep demand flat, it doesn't help us very much because CO_2 emissions are cumulative. And the globe has *never* had a year in which it has used less energy in a year than it did the year before.

No rational energy program would start without promoting energy efficiency. We should do all we can there. But no amount of saving energy ever turned on a lightbulb. No amount of saving energy actually put food on somebody's table. Energy efficiency is simply not enough to bridge the demand gap. On the supply side, there are only three big cards to play, in some combination: coal sequestration, if we dare; nuclear fission involving plutonium, if we double dare; or finding a way to make cheap, storable energy from the other big card that we have, which is the sun. But solar has to be *really* cheap, and scalable, *and* we've got to find a way to store it.

I haven't talked much about economics, but I will say that it's easy to prove, thinking 100 years out, on a risk-adjusted net-present-value basis, that the earth is simply not worth saving. It's a fully depreciated, four-billion-year-old asset. Unless you have policy incentives that reflect the true cost of doing this experiment, the economically efficient thing to do is just what we are doing now. On the other hand, with the appropriate policy incentives, the financial opportunities are commensurate with 50 Exxon Mobils on the supply side, and, in devising ways to lower our energy consumption from triple to double by 2050, 50 more Exxon Mobils on the demand side. This is both the challenge and the opportunity.

I leave it to you to decide whether this is something that we cannot afford to do, or something at which we simply cannot afford to fail. Remember, we get to do this experiment exactly once. And that time, like it or not, is now.

AN OCEAN OF ENERGY THERE FOR THE TAKING
Tundi Agarty, Ph.D. (2008)

Introduction

Some look to the ocean and take in seascapes that calm the mind and soothe the senses, while others see a bounty of living resources and biodiversity. The oceans have supported great societies and civilizations, and have been the setting for innumerable historical events. But more and more, people are looking to the sea for something the land is increasingly unable to provide at the levels we demand: energy. Oceans offer a vast array of energy options, whether conventional sources of oil and gas, renewable energy such as wind, wave and tidal, or radical new forms of energy such as algal-based biofuels. As our energy demands continue to grow and our conventional sources dwindle or become inaccessible, the oceans will be looked to more and more to meet our energy needs. * * *

Non-Renewables: Offshore Oil & Gas

* * * The United States and the countries of Northern Europe have a strong dependence on oceanic fossil fuels. In recent years, offshore (or OCS, standing for Outer Continental Shelf) oil and gas accounted for about a quarter of U.S. domestic supply; it is estimated that 30% of undiscovered oil and gas reserves in the U.S. exist as offshore fields. Some areas, like the Gulf of Mexico and the North Sea, are dotted with fixed oil rigs able to pump massive amounts of oil and gas to shore-based processing facilities. Floating rigs are also used in offshore areas. * * *

Many countries have recognized the potential of offshore reserves but have curbed oil exploration and extraction activities in sensitive coastal areas. A moratorium has been in place in the Canadian eastern seaboard for decades, and in 1990, President George H. Bush established an OCS moratorium in parts of Aleutian Islands, Pacific Coast, Eastern Gulf of Mexico, and the North Atlantic within U.S. jurisdictions. The latter restriction was renewed by President Clinton and remained in effect until this year [2007]. Increasingly, local jurisdictions have tried to limit offshore oil and gas activity. In the U.S., coastal states have exerted their jurisdictional authority, hoping to reduce risks of environmental catastrophe and reduce environmental effects within state waters (from 0-3 miles offshore).

Recent research has highlighted the potential for seabed-based methane hydrates to meet some energy demands. Methane hydrates are ice-like deposits found in the top few hundred meters of sediment in certain deep ocean areas of the continental margins. The methane gas is actually trapped in ice cages, and can be easily extracted from it, but removing the hydrates from the seabed has proved problematic. Russian energy experts have tried using antifreeze to remove the methane from hydrates, and recent research has focused on trying to pipe warm surface water down to melt the hydrates and then piping the gas to the surface using a parallel set of pipes. However, melting the hydrates to release methane may cause the seafloor to become unstable, and could have untold ecological impacts as well. In addition, if methane is lost to the atmosphere during the process, it could add to the global warming phenomenon, since methane is a potent greenhouse gas.

Nevertheless, methane hydrates have caused excitement in the energy field. Some researchers also believe that there is free-flowing methane gas beneath the several hundred meters deep hydrate layers. The National Energy Education Project (US) suggests that methane hydrates may contain over 30 times the existing natural gas resources and reserves worldwide.

Ocean-Based Renewable Energy

Fossil fuels like petroleum or other hydrocarbon resources are considered nonrenewable, since it takes millions of years to convert organic matter into these energy resources. As oil and gas becomes increasingly difficult to recover, as geopolitics complicate the access to both the resources and the markets for such energy products, and as existing supplies diminish and the world approaches peak oil production, interest in renewables has increased. Additionally, recent attention on carbon emissions from hydrocarbon use and their role in global warming and other climate changes means that renewable energy resources are fast becoming a preferred alternative. However, renewable energy resources are still at this point in time generally more expensive than conventional non-renewables, and production tends to be small scale.

There are four major classes of renewable energy available at sea: 1) kinetic energy unique to the ocean, such as energy provided by surface waves and tides, 2) renewable energy not unique to the ocean, such as wind and solar energy, 3) thermal energy, such as that produced by the temperature differential of surface and deep ocean waters, and 4) marine biofuels, such as those derived from algae.

Kinetic

Attempts have been made to harness the enormous energy potential of moving ocean water for decades. As far back as the middle of the 11th century, people were making the logical extension from exploiting energy in running rivers, streams, and canals (an ancient technology that probably predates even waterwheels for grinding flour) to trying to harness that same mechanical energy contained in waves and tides. The first commercial scale wave energy plant was commissioned for the Isle of Islay (Scotland) in 2000; at about the same time, the Japan Marine Science and Technology Center created a large scale experimental wave energy platform.

Early attempts to harness the kinetic energy contained in moving seawater were focused on estuaries, where both river hydrology and tides influence the movement of seawater or brackish water. But wave energy can be harnessed, in theory, anywhere where there are predictable waves, including in offshore areas. The first commercial scale wave power station was established in Scotland at the beginning of the century.

Oceanlinx, a company formerly known as Energetech, has developed wave energy projects in three areas of Australia (New South Wales, Victoria, and Tasmania), in two sites in the U.S. (Rhode Island and Hawaii), in South Africa, in Mexico, and in the United Kingdom. * * *

Tidal energy also has great potential as a renewable energy source, and has the advantage over waves of high predictability. Tides are caused by the gravitational pull of the moon and sun and their effects on the rotating Earth. In near shore areas, the differential between low and high tide (both of which occur twice a day) can approach 15 meters. However, there are a limited number of areas around the world where tidal range is high and topographic conditions would allow the utilization of tidal energy. According to the U.S. Department of Energy, only about 20 locations have good inlets and a large enough tidal range–(at least 3 meters)–to produce energy economically. * * *

Wind and Solar

Wind and solar energy generation are of course not unique to oceans. Yet oceans provide not only vast amounts of space and sufficient sunlight and wind—but also provide these as a commons property that can in theory be more easily accessed than private property to meet the public good.

Offshore windfarms are common in some parts of the world, such as Northern Europe. Oceanic wind is a preferred alternative to other forms of energy generation in areas where land is in short supply, and where coastal winds are sustained and strong. Denmark has led the effort in harnessing sea wind, and constructed the first offshore wind farm in 1991 off the Port of Vineby. According to the Financial Times, wind farms are expected to supply 8% of Denmark's electricity by 2008. The UK opened its first offshore wind farm in 2000 in Northumberland, and is following Denmark's lead with expanded wind farms and feasibility studies for siting in new areas.

The oceans are also the world's largest solar collector: one square mile contains more energy potential than 7,000 barrels of oil. Solar arrays with unfettered access to sunlight can be installed in virtually any coastal area sheltered from excessive wind or waves. Currently most offshore solar plants are used to power oil platforms and in situ research equipment.

Thermal

The oceans can also be harnessed for energy by using the temperature differential of surface and deep waters to drive energy generation The differential exists because the sun warms the surface layers of the ocean, especially in the tropics, while deep waters stay cool. In order for the technology to be able to capture the thermal energy, this temperature differential must be more than 25 degrees Celsius. * * *

Three types of systems are used to convert ocean thermal energy to electrical energy. Closed cycle systems use the warm surface water to vaporize a low-boiling point fluid such as ammonia. As the vapor boils and expands, it drives a turbine, which then activates a generator to produce electricity. Open cycle systems operate at low pressure and actually boil the seawater, which produces steam to drive the turbine/generator. Hybrid systems use elements of each, in an attempt to improve conversion efficiencies.

Although the temperature differential between surface waters and the deep ocean is significant in almost all parts of the globe, there are constraints to being able to harness this potential energy. Main among them is having deep cold water in close proximity to warm surface waters. Tropical island nations in the Pacific Ocean that have narrow continental shelves are particularly suited. According to NASA, some 98 tropical countries could benefit from the technology.

OTEC also has spin-off benefits, including air conditioning, chilled-soil agriculture, aquaculture, and desalination. And OTEC also may one day provide a means to mine ocean water for 57 trace elements, many of which are very valuable.

Thermal energy conversion has great potential, but enormous challenges remain. The technology is still very inefficient and piping large volumes across great depths of ocean (a kilometer or more) is a major engineering feat. Yet some energy experts believe OTEC could produce billions of watts of electrical power if it could be made cost-competitive with conventional power technologies.

Marine Biofuels

At the moment there is a flurry of interest in alternative fuels, especially biofuels. Biofuels can be derived from agricultural and forestry residues, energy crops, landfill gas, and the biodegradable components of municipal and industrial wastes. Such fuels can be used for transportation fuel, to provide heat, or to generate electricity. Biomass residues have been burned to create power since at least the middle of the 19th Century, but inefficiencies tended to be extremely high until R&D became focused on making biofuels economically viable.

Corn and switchgrass have received most of the attention as biofuel sources, but there is no reason why marine plants cannot provide the same cellulose for fuel conversion. This emerging technology is being tested in various venues.

Potential Downsides of Ocean Energy

According to a 2001 article in the Financial Times, ocean energy systems are becoming both more efficient and more economically viable. But these energy systems are not without cost.

First, there are the prospective ecological impacts. Constructing and operating facilities will undoubtedly have environmental costs, as will diverting, moving, or variously treating large volumes of seawater. Facilities will be generating their own pollution and wastes, including light pollution. Wind turbines and underwater turbines generate noise, which is a newfound concern of marine conservationists (see Exporting Pollution in the June issue of the World Ocean Observer). And removal of nonrenewable resources such as methane hydrates and renewable ones like algae may alter both the geology or oceanography and the ecology of some marine areas.

Underlying all of these ecological unknowns is the primary, unassailable fact that surveillance, monitoring, and protection of offshore facilities are infinitely more difficult than on land. This also means that security is more challenging, and energy plants may be more vulnerable to sabotage.

Converting the energy the oceans harbor is a technological puzzle that has been largely solved by enterprising engineers and scientists equipped with ever more sophisticated tools. But supplying that energy to users remains a daunting challenge. Energy is lost as it is brought from offshore onshore, and most large scale facilities are put as far offshore as possible to minimize conflicts with other ocean users.

Entrepreneurs face huge hurdles as well, which has resulted in constrained ocean energy development. In most developed countries the regulatory burden is immense, and the complexity of jurisdictions is reflected in a corollary complexity in obtaining the necessary permits for even demonstration projects. Recognizing these disincentives, the U.S. Federal Energy Regulatory Commission (FERC) announced a proposal to shorten the permitting process for pilot ocean energy projects to as little as six months.

Finally, an inadequately informed public has sometimes resisted (and in some cases even blocked) the development of new sustainable energy technologies at sea, despite the fact that the alternative—i.e. continued reliance on conventional energy sources—is likely to have far greater impacts on the environment of the oceans. * * *

C. AN OVERVIEW OF U.S. ENERGY POLICY AND LAW

REPORT, AMERICAN CLEAN ENERGY AND SECURITY ACT OF 2009 [H.R. 2454]
Committee on Energy and Commerce, U.S. House of Representatives, 111TH Cong. Rept. No. 111–137 (June 5, 2009)

BACKGROUND AND NEED FOR LEGISLATION

This may prove to be a watershed moment in the history of energy production and consumption. Between now and 2030, an estimated $1.5 trillion will be invested in energy infrastructure in the United States and more than $26 trillion will be invested worldwide. How these investments are made will have dramatic and consequential effects on the national security and economic future of the United States. How these investments are made may also determine the fate of our planet's climate. * * *

ENERGY

The United States is facing a deepening energy crisis. The most critical aspect of that crisis is our growing dependence on foreign oil, coupled with the volatility of oil and gasoline prices. But in a range of other key areas, including natural gas and electricity generation and transmission, the United States is facing challenges arising from growing demand, limits on supply, and rising global prices. At the same time, we find ourselves on the cusp of an unprecedented wave of investment in infrastructure and technology, which will benefit those workers and companies positioned to answer the challenge. Between now and 2030, more than $26 trillion will be invested in energy infrastructure worldwide, and an estimated $1.5 trillion will be invested in the United States power sector alone. This places us at a critical decision point in the development of the United States and global energy economies.

DEPENDENCE ON OIL

The single greatest energy security challenge facing the United States in the 21st century is our growing dependence on foreign oil. The United States imported more than 4 billion barrels of oil in 2008, or 57 percent of its total oil consumption. This represents an increase in imports compared to 2000, when the U.S. imported 53 percent of the oil it consumed and 1990, when imports stood at 42 percent. Our dependence on oil makes us vulnerable to price spikes and market manipulation. Because oil accounts for nearly a third of domestic global warming pollution, oil dependence is also a cause of significant environmental harm. * * *

Oil dependence imposes a significant cost on the United States economy. Oil imports cost the United States a staggering $342 billion in 2008. * * * Oak Ridge National Laboratory [study] estimates that the full cost of dependence on foreign oil to the United States economy is much higher—$750 billion in 2008, including a loss of potential GDP of $352 billion (about 2 percent of total GDP). [Oak Ridge National Laboratory, *Costs of Oil Dependence Update 2008: Summary* (Aug. 8, 2008).]

This growing dependence on foreign oil has dire implications for United States national security and economic stability. Dependence on imported oil makes the United States increasingly vulnerable to foreign governments' manipulation of supply and prices. Although Canada and Mexico supply a substantial proportion of United States imports, OPEC countries control virtually all of the world's marginal production capacity and therefore have the ability to set the global price for this commodity.

While many are calling for increased domestic production as the solution, the facts make clear that we cannot drill our way out of this problem. More drilling will have minimal impact on prices consumers pay for oil or gasoline and will not substantially reduce U.S. dependence on foreign oil. While nearly 83 percent of technically recoverable offshore oil reserves in the United States are located in areas *already* available for leasing and drilling prior to the October 1, 2008 expiration of the Congressional moratoria, the Department of Energy's Energy Information Administration (EIA) estimates that, even if drilling were permitted in the OCS of the entire continental United States, this would increase cumulative U.S. oil production by only 1.6 percent by 2030 and would have an "insignificant" impact on prices. EIA estimates that if the Arctic National Wildlife Refuge were opened for drilling, production would likely peak in 2027 at just 0.78 million barrels per day—reducing world oil prices by 75 cents per barrel in EIA's average price and resource case. In addition, EIA notes that "the Organization of Petroleum Exporting Countries (OPEC) could neutralize any potential price impact of ANWR oil production by reducing its oil exports by an equal amount."

Finally, regardless of U.S. oil production trends there are serious questions about whether increasing global demand can be met. * * * However, "proven reserves," those that have already been discovered and are expected to be economically producible are only estimated to produce between 1.1 trillion and 1.4 trillion barrels worldwide. At the same time, generating new oil supply is proving increasingly difficult. New oil fields are generally in expensive and hard-to-reach places like deep water areas in the Gulf of Mexico. Even with advances in technology, the average size of discoveries per exploratory well is around 10 million barrels, which is half the output of wells dug between 1965 and 1979.

The shrinking margin between stagnant supply and soaring demand provides yet another reason that the United States and the world need to begin to look beyond oil to meet our growing energy needs.

SOLUTIONS TO THE OIL DEPENDENCE

Addressing our dependence on oil is primarily a transportation challenge. The U.S. transportation sector produces roughly a third of total U.S. greenhouse gas emissions, accounts for approximately 69 percent of total U.S. oil consumption, and is 95 percent dependent upon petroleum. Reducing both oil consumption and global warming pollution in the transportation sector will require the United States to address three interrelated issues—the efficiency of our vehicles, the fuels that power them, and how much we drive them.

VEHICLES AND FUEL—INCREASE FUEL ECONOMY AND TRANSITION TO ELECTRIC DRIVE

Implementing higher fuel economy standards is one of the most important means to increase energy independence of the United States. The Energy Independence and Security Act of 2007 (EISA) mandated that fuel economy standards increase by at least 40 percent, to 35 mpg, by 2020. On May 19, 2009, President Obama announced his Administration's intent to harmonize fuel economy standards set by the U.S. Department of Transportation, tailpipe standards set by the Environmental Protection Agency and California's clean car regulations, such that the automotive fleet would achieve the equivalent of 35.5 miles per gallon by 2016. * * *

The development of plug-in hybrid electric vehicles (PHEVs) and all-electric vehicles holds great potential to enhance America's energy independence and reduce greenhouse gas emissions. Electric motors are three to four times more efficient at turning their fuel into useful work than either gasoline or diesel engines. They also consume no energy while idling and utilize regenerative braking to recharge the vehicle's battery. * * *

The electric grid is an important and readily available piece of infrastructure that could power the transport sector in the United States. The electricity infrastructure is currently designed to meet the highest expected demand for power, which only occurs for a few hundred hours a year. During the night more than 50 percent of generating capacity lies idle. By utilizing this idle generating capacity, * * * up to 84 percent of U.S. cars, pickup trucks, and sport utility vehicles can be transitioned to electricity without building a single new power plant. An 84 percent level of electric vehicle penetration is estimated to eliminate the consumption of 6.5 million barrels of oil equivalent per day, more than all the oil currently imported from OPEC countries. With the national average cost of electricity of 8.5 cents per kilowatt hour, an electric vehicle runs on an equivalent of around 75 cents per gallon.

PHEVs slash greenhouse gas emissions, even with our current electricity fuel mix. Even given the current U.S. electricity generation profile, almost half of which is comprised of carbon-intensive coal combustion, the nationwide deployment of battery-powered electric vehicles would still reduce greenhouse gas emissions by as much as 27 percent as compared to equivalent gasoline-powered vehicles. Greenhouse gas benefits will improve in the future as renewable and other low- or no-carbon electricity generation increases. * * *

REDUCE VEHICLE MILES TRAVELED WHILE IMPROVING

QUALITY OF LIFE

To meet our energy security and global warming pollution reduction goals, we must provide options for individuals who wish to get from place to place without driving. Americans drive much more than individuals in other advanced industrial countries—5,700 miles a year compared with 2,368 in Japan and 3,961 in Germany as of 1997. The number of vehicle miles traveled (VMT) nearly quadrupled between 1960 and 2000 43 and is projected to increase another 60 percent by 2030. If left unchecked, this projected VMT growth will substantially reduce the oil consumption and global warming pollution benefits of increased fuel economy and cleaner fuels.

A broad array of policies can help communities to "grow smarter," while reducing VMT. Increasing public transit and creating more pedestrian and bicycle-friendly infrastructure can encourage people to travel without using a car. Planning roads and pathways to create shorter, direct links to destinations can limit car distances. Communities that implement such improvements reduce global warming pollution, balance local budgets by avoiding infrastructure costs, and reduce family gasoline bills. Although most of these policies are implemented at the local, State, or regional level, federal policy can play a substantial role in supporting them.

THE ELECTRICITY CHALLENGE

The overall fuel mix for power generation in the United States has remained relatively stable over the past decade. In 2007, coal remained the leading fuel source, accounting for 49 percent of generation, followed by natural gas with 21 percent, and nuclear with 19 percent. Hydroelectric power accounted for 6 percent, and non-hydro renewables provided 3 percent. New capacity is shifting from reliance on coal to natural gas and wind energy. In 2008, natural gas accounted for 48 percent of all new generating capacity, wind accounted for 42 percent, and coal accounted for less than 6 percent— with solar, biomass, and geothermal making up most of the balance.

COAL

Coal is a key fuel for the electric power sector, both for the United States and the rest of the world. The United States has the largest coal reserves in the world (28% of global reserves) and produces more than a billion short tons of coal annually. More than 90% of U.S. coal consumption is used for electricity generation, and coal powers nearly 50% of all U.S. electricity generation. China and India, two of the largest, fastest growing economies in the world, both have large coal reserves and rely on coal for the majority of their electricity generation (78% for China and 69% for India).

Greenhouse gas emissions from coal use present a serious challenge in addressing global climate change. Because of coal's high carbon content, coal-fired power plants emit roughly twice as much carbon dioxide (CO_2) per unit of electricity as natural gas-fired plants. Existing coal-fired plants account for almost a third of U.S. CO_2 emissions. Globally, CO_2 emissions from coal have grown from 39% in 1990 to 41% in 2005, and are projected to reach 44% by 2030 absent an international agreement to limit emissions. * * *

A central element in discussions concerning federal climate change policy is how to reconcile the continued use of coal with the objective of achieving significant reductions in greenhouse gas emissions. While multiple strategies exist to reduce coal-related greenhouse gas emissions, a consensus has emerged that carbon capture and storage (CCS) technologies, involving physical capture of CO_2 at power plants and other major point sources and compression and injection of CO_2 into deep geological reservoirs, provide a likely path forward.

CARBON CAPTURE AND SEQUESTRATION

There are three principal technology options for capturing CO_2 emissions at coal-based power plants: (1) pre-combustion capture using integrated gasification combined cycle ("IGCC") technology; (2) pre-combustion capture using oxy-fuel combustion; and (3) post-combustion capture using solvents or membranes.

In an IGCC plant, coal is processed in a reactor with steam and oxygen before combustion to produce a mixture consisting mainly of carbon monoxide and hydrogen known as "synthesis gas" or "syngas." The carbon monoxide is then mixed with steam to produce CO_2 and more hydrogen. The hydrogen becomes a carbon-free fuel to power the plant, while the CO2 can be compressed for transport and ultimate storage. There are four IGCC plants in operation worldwide, including two in the United States.

Oxy-fuel combustion eliminates nitrogen from exhaust gases by burning the fuel in pure oxygen or a mixture of pure oxygen and CO_2-rich recycled flue gas. The main emissions from this process are CO_2 and water. Once compressed, dried, and purified, the CO_2 is ready for transport and storage. Although the key elements of oxy-fuel combustion technology are currently in commercial use, it has not yet been deployed for CO_2 capture on a commercial scale.

Post-combustion capture systems use a solvent or a membrane to separate CO_2 from the power plant's flue gases. Post-combustion capture technologies are already commercially available and are used to capture CO_2 from coal- and gas-fired plants in the food and beverage and chemical-production industries. They would have to be significantly scaled up from current applications to be used in large commercial power plants.

After CO2 is captured, it is compressed into a dense fluid (supercritical) state for transport via pipeline to an injection site. Three types of geologic formations are well-suited to long-term storage of injected CO_2: depleted oil and gas fields, saline formations, and deep coal seams. Surveys indicate that both global and U.S. storage capacity is potentially vast. The Department of Energy projects that U.S. domestic geologic formations "have at least enough capacity to store several centuries' worth of point source emissions" from the United States. There appears to be a good correlation between emissions sources and geological basins suitable for long-term storage, and preliminary assessments suggest that risks to human health and the environment from large-scale injection of CO_2 are limited. Underground injection of naturally produced CO_2 has been used since the early 1970s as part of enhanced oil recovery projects, and there are several major commercial projects around the world that inject captured CO_2 for underground storage. A variety of new projects are now under development.

Although most of the technologies on which CCS is based are already demonstrated, they have not yet been integrated or implemented at the scale needed to mitigate power plant emissions. Applying CCS to a single 500 megawatt coal-fired plant, for example, could involve capture and injection of 2–3 million metric tons of CO_2 annually.

In addition to technical concerns, there are economic obstacles to widespread deployment of CCS. For example, carbon capture technologies typically require significant amounts of power to operate; the energy penalty imposed and consequent requirement for "makeup" power carry a cost. The overall capital and operating costs to capture and sequester carbon are also substantial, though such costs are expected to decrease over time as technologies mature.

Such costs, in the absence of appropriate regulatory drivers, will impede commercial-scale deployment of CCS technologies. While current cost estimates for CCS are highly uncertain, they provide some sense of the point at which CCS will become a feasible mitigation strategy for coal-fired plants and other industrial emitters. A 2008 McKinsey study estimated between $38–57 per ton of CO_2 abated for its reference plants, though it put the cost for early demonstration projects at $77–115 per ton. Other studies estimate that CO_2 allowance prices would have to range anywhere from $30–60 per ton in order to make CCS economically viable. Because State utility regulation would likely prevent recovery of this cost differential between controlled and uncontrolled plants, utilities are unlikely to invest in CCS in the absence of a regulatory requirement to do so.

Large-scale underground injection and storage of CO_2 also presents a series of legal and regulatory questions. EPA has issued a proposed rulemaking addressing the subsurface aspects of sequestration under the Safe Drinking Water Act's Underground Injection Control program, but as yet there is no comprehensive regulatory regime for commercial-scale injection either at the federal or State level. Some of these questions—such as those related to subsurface property rights—will likely be answered at the State level. * * *

NATURAL GAS

The United States accounts for more than 22 percent of global consumption of natural gas, but has only 3.4 percent of global reserves. Domestic production satisfies 80 percent of U.S. demand—and more than 80 percent of U.S. imports come from Canada.

Natural gas has become the fuel of choice for new power plants in the United States. Natural gas accounted for nearly half of new generating capacity built in the United States in 2008. In addition, natural gas is a critical feedstock and fuel for U.S. manufacturing, accounting for 29 percent of U.S. natural gas use. Natural gas prices have been highly volatile in recent years, with large swings driven by high demand in some years, and more recently, downward pressure on prices due to reduced demand and increased domestic production.

NUCLEAR POWER

Electric utilities have recently filed 17 applications with the Nuclear Regulatory Commission for 26 new reactor operating licenses. In recent years, the projected cost of a new 1,000 megawatt reactor has increased from approximately $2 billion to $6–8 billion. In light of these costs and risks, it is unclear whether private financing would be available for new nuclear facilities without the assurance of federal government loan guarantees. * * *

Nuclear power faces a challenge in remaining competitive in electricity markets where low cost generation has priority dispatch to the grid. While the operating costs of nuclear power are comparatively low, it continues to be an expensive investment for electricity ratepayers due to large up-front capital costs.

RENEWABLE ENERGY

Renewable electricity currently generates 8.4 percent of the country's electricity, with non-hydroelectric renewables responsible for just 2.5 percent. Reaching 20 percent of total generation by 2020 is an ambitious, but achievable, target for renewable electricity.

The Committee believes that adoption of a national renewable electricity standard (RES) should be a centerpiece of our national energy strategy. State-level RES requirements have been a key driver of renewable energy growth in the U.S. Seventy-one percent of the population now lives in one of the 28 states with these mandatory policies in place. More than half of the non-hydroelectric renewable electricity capacity added in the U.S. over the last decade has occurred in States with RES programs, with little or no impact on consumer electricity rates. * * *

The renewable resources outlined below are among the most likely to contribute significantly to the U.S. and global electricity supply over the next two to three decades.

WIND

More than 27,000 megawatts of new wind capacity was installed worldwide in 2008, nearly a quarter of which was installed in the United States. Department of Energy research suggests generating 20 percent of electricity from wind in the United States is an ambitious yet feasible scenario if certain challenges are overcome. With policy support, the United States is projected to have more than 60,000 megawatts of wind installed by 2012 and by 2016 it could reach 112,000 megawatts, surpassing nuclear capacity in the United States.

As wind technology continues to improve, prices are falling and capacity factors are increasing. The cost of wind energy over the past 20 years has dropped from 40 cents per kWh to 4 to 6 cents per kWh at good sites. * * * Increases in the capacity factor of the turbines or the percentage of time in which they are producing at their full capacity—have grown 11 percent over the past two years and will continue to increase as the technology improves.

SOLAR

With more energy in the form of solar radiation striking the Earth's surface in an hour than humanity uses in an entire year, the available solar energy resource is enormous. Capturing this energy and converting it into electricity is primarily done through photovoltaic cells that convert sunlight into direct electrical current and concentrating solar power, which concentrates the sun's energy using huge mirrors or lenses and then uses this heat to run a conventional turbine.

Solar photovoltaics (PV) have experienced explosive growth over the last several years. World capacity grew 62 percent in 2007 alone 69 and solar PV installations in the United States grew by more than 80 percent in 2007. Over the next two decades, solar PV will become a major source of power—

both here in the United States and globally. Solar PV is projected to grow from a $20 billion industry in 2007 to a $74 billion industry within a decade. A study from the National Renewable Energy Laboratory found that installed capacity in the United States could climb to 10,000 megawatts by 2015, 26,000 megawatts by 2020, and ultimately more than 100,000 megawatts by 2030 with the passage of the critical 8-year extension of the investment tax credits included in the financial rescue package enacted in October, 2008.

Concentrating solar power (CSP) systems deliver large-scale, centralized electricity generation from solar energy. CSP systems are generally utility-scale projects with many acres of mirrors and lenses that can produce dozens to hundreds of megawatts of electrical power. The National Renewable Energy Laboratory has identified the potential for nearly 7,000,000 megawatts of solar thermal power generation in the southwestern United States, roughly seven times current U.S. electric generating capacity. More than 4,000 megawatts of solar thermal projects are currently in development nation-wide, and Environment America has projected 80,000 megawatts could be built by 2030 with investment tax credit support. The cost of energy from solar thermal power plants is estimated to be approximately 14 to 16 cents/kWh.

GEOTHERMAL

The United States has about 35 percent of the world's installed capacity of geothermal energy, with about 2,500 megawatts connected to the grid across six States. While several new facilities are in construction around the country, the amount of electricity produced from geothermal energy has essentially been flat for the past two decades. New facilities are estimated to be able to produce base load electricity for 5 to 7 cents/kWh.

The United States has massive, untapped geothermal energy resources. Scientists with the U.S. Geological Survey (USGS) recently found that the electric generation potential from currently identified geothermal systems distributed over 13 U.S. states is more than 9,000 megawatts. Their estimated power production potential from yet to be discovered geothermal resources is more than 30,000 megawatts. An additional 500,000 megawatts may be available by harnessing geothermal reservoirs characterized by high temperature, but low permeability, rock formations. * * *

BIOMASS

Biomass currently supplies more electricity in the United States than wind, solar, and geothermal power combined, and the potential for additional generation from this energy source is vast. Biomass available for electricity generation includes residues from forests, primary mills, and agriculture, as well as dedicated energy crops and urban wood wastes. Biomass can be used as the sole fuel source for power plants, or it can be used in conventional power plants to substitute for a portion of the traditional fuel, typically coal, in a process called co-firing. While most co-firing plants use biomass for between 1 and 8 percent of heat input, biomass can effectively substitute for up to 20 percent of the coal used in the boiler. Certain biomass can have important greenhouse gas benefits, and co-firing with biomass also lowers fuel costs, avoids landfilling, and reduces emissions of sulfur oxide and nitrogen oxide.

An EIA analysis of the impacts of a 15 percent national renewable electricity requirement found that electricity production from biomass could grow by a factor of eight between 2005 and 2030. Most of this generation would come in the southeastern United States, where nearly a third of the country's biomass feedstock potential exists. The EIA found that the Southeast region could meet nearly its entire 15 percent renewable requirement through 2020 with indigenous biomass resources.

TRANSMISSION PLANNING

Lack of adequate transmission capacity is a barrier to the wide-scale deployment of renewable electricity. Transmission lines must be constructed to move renewable electricity from rural areas and offshore, where it is most abundant and most reliably generated, to population centers where it can be used. Federal leadership will be critical in helping to ensure that efficient transmission is built.

BOOSTING EFFICIENCY

* * *

Market barriers prevent optimal adoption of energy efficiency measures. For example, the buildings and appliances sectors are characterized by split incentives. While home buyers or users of appliances would achieve lifecycle cost savings from more efficient homes or appliances, builders and manufacturers avoid energy efficiency improvements that would increase up-front costs. In addition, consumers generally lack adequate information to distinguish among buildings and products on the basis of efficiency. In addition, consumers may apply irrationally high discount rates in making purchasing decisions—requiring that a more efficient home or product "pay back" the increased cost within a very short time frame, even though the consumer would be financially better off in the medium- to long-term with the more efficient home or product. In the power sector, electric utilities often are the actor best positioned to increase demand-side efficiency, but have a disincentive to do so because revenues are based on the volume of electricity sold. Because a price on global warming pollution does not address these and other market barriers, additional policies are necessary to achieve the full cost-saving benefits of efficiency measures.

INCREASING EFFICIENCY OF BUILDINGS AND APPLIANCES

Buildings and appliances represent the areas of greatest emission abatement and energy- and cost-saving potential. Efficiency improvements in this category include lighting retrofits, higher performance for appliances, improvements in heating, ventilation and air conditioning systems, as well as better building envelopes and building control systems. Over the next 30 years, the built environment in the United States is expected to increase by an amount roughly equal to 70 percent of today's existing building stock—providing a crucial opportunity for energy savings and emission reductions.

Buildings contribute up to 48 percent of U.S. global warming pollution, the single largest source of emissions. In 2007 more than three-quarters of the electricity generated by U.S. power plants was used in commercial, residential, and industrial buildings, and roughly one-third of the natural gas consumed was used for residential and commercial use. Most of this energy consumption, and resulting emissions, stem from the energy used to operate lighting, heating, and cooling in buildings, and could be considerably decreased.

Building codes are critically important in driving energy efficiency. * * *
SMART GRID

Modernization of the electricity transmission and distribution system—particularly through Smart Grid investments—promises substantial benefits in increased system efficiency, reliability, and flexibility, and reduced peak loads and electricity prices. Smart Grid technologies pair digital communications and information technology with a variety of grid functions, including monitoring, measuring, and responding to electricity demand and congestion; sensing and locating system disruptions or security threats and deploying automated protective responses; implementing "smart" meters in homes and businesses that allow consumers to receive time-of-use pricing information and to communicate consumer preferences to the grid; and installing "smart" appliances that can be programmed to respond to communications from the grid regarding pricing or load. Collectively, these technologies can substantially increase the efficiency of the grid and can reduce peak load demand, both of which reduce the need for construction of new generation. In addition, an array of other grid modernization technologies—such as the deployment of high-efficiency superconductor power distribution cables—can further enhance grid efficiency and reliability.

Notes and Questions

1.   If you were a member of Congress, how would you prioritize these energy issues? Consider a recent analysis of the comparative costs in cents

per kwh of different energy technologies:

Alternatives:

- Solar PV (crystalline): 10.9 - 15.4 (cents/kwh)
- Fuel cell: 11.5 - 12.5
- Solar PV (thin film): 9.6 - 12.4
- Solar thermal: 9.0 - 14.5 (low end is solar tower; high end is solar trough)
- Biomass direct: 5.0 - 9.4
- Landfill gas: 5.0 - 8.1
- Wind: 4.4 - 9.1
- Geothermal: 4.2 - 6.9
- Biomass co-firing: 0.3 - 3.7
- Energy efficiency: 0.0 - 5.0

Coal/Nuclear/Gas:

- Gas peaking: 22.1 - 33.4
- IGCC: 10.4 - 13.4
- Nuclear: 9.8 - 12.6
- Advanced supercritical coal: 7.4 - 13.5 (high end includes 90% carbon capture and storage)
- Gas combined cycle: 7.3 - 10.0

Lazard Ltd, Levelized Cost of Energy Analysis ver. 2.0 (June 2008) http://www.narucmeetings.org/Presentations/2008%20EMP%20Levelized%20 Cost%20of%20Energy%20-%20Master%20June%202008%20(2).pdf.

In considering these comparative costs note that the analysis omits combined heat and power systems (which are discussed later in this chapter in connection with fossil fuels). According to Amory Lovins, one of the leading thinkers in the field of energy, the analysis arguably overstates wind costs, and understates nuclear costs. See A. Lovins et al., Nuclear Power: Climate Fix or Folly? (Rocky Mountain Institute Dec. 2008), www.rmi.org.

2. **Note on Nuclear Power.** In the article referenced above in Note 1, Lovins argues, based on a review of current data and past studies, that electricity from a new nuclear power plant will cost consumers of electricity 15–21¢/kWh, making it the most expensive low-carbon alternative. For a review of new nuclear technologies, including thorium-based plants, and small modular designs, see A. Lovins, New Nuclear Reactors, Same Old Story, RMI Solutions J. (Spring 2009), www.rmi.org/sitepages/pid592.php. For a thoughtful, informative web-based debate over the costs and benefits of new nuclear power, see P. Bradford, S. Berry, and A. Lovins, Nuclear Power and Climate Change http://thebulletin.org/roundtable/nuclear-power-climate-change (8/27/07).

In any event, despite substantial federal subsidies, the private capital market has shunned the nuclear power industry. Almost all new plants built over the past few decades have been built in government planned economies. A proposal for a new two-unit nuclear power station estimated the cost at $12 – 24 billion dollars. P. Russell, "FPL says cost of new reactors at Turkey Point could top $24 billion," Nucleonics Week, 3 (21 Feb 2008). According to Richard Meyers, vice president of policy development at the Nuclear Energy Institute (whose members include virtually all owners, operators, nuclear engineering firms, and fuel cycle companies), "[e]ven the largest U.S. electric company, with a market cap in the $40-billion range, would be hard-pressed to finance a $5–6-billion nuclear plant on balance sheet" without very large federal loan subsidies, and major banks have announced that they would not finance any new project without federal loan guarantees. He concluded, "NEI estimates that the U.S. electric industry must built [sic] at least 50,000 megawatts of new nuclear capacity by 2030 in order to maintain nuclear energy at 20 percent of U.S. electric supply," which would require a "heroic effort." Transcript of Loan Guarantee Program Public Meeting, Office of the Chief Financial Officer, U.S. Dept. of Energy (June 15, 2007) 82-84, www.lgprogram.energy.gov/061507-TPH.pdf. The effort will be especially heroic for the few remaining nuclear engineers, since universities in the U.S. either ended or drastically reduced their programs years ago.

Nuclear power also raises issues about long-term storage of nuclear wastes, vulnerability to terrorism, and nuclear proliferation. Climate change may also reduce the output of nuclear plants if cooling water supplies become scarce due to drought, or too hot due to heat waves. See Heatwaves can crimp power output across Europe, Reuters (June 30, 2009) (Reporting that the 2006 heat wave forced France to import 2,000 MW of power, and in 2009, depending on weather, France may need to import up to 8,000 MW of power to replace power lost due to reduced nuclear plant output.)

3.　　Are these issues for the federal government, state governments, or some combination? What policy tools could Congress use to address these energy issues? Does each issue require its own separate analysis and solution? Or, should the approaches be coordinated? What aspects of energy policy should be left to the market; which aspects are more appropriate for government to address?

PROBLEM EXERCISE ON RURAL ELECTRIFICATION

"As late as the mid-1930s, nine out of ten rural homes were without electric service. The farmer milked his cows by hand in the dim light of a kerosene lantern. His wife was a slave to the wood range and washboard. The unavailability of electricity in rural areas kept their economies entirely and exclusively to agriculture. Factories and businesses, of course, preferred to locate in cities where electric power was easily acquired. Even as late as July 1935, a group of utility company executives wrote a report in which they claimed that, in light of their earlier extensive research work, "there are very few farms requiring electricity for major farm operations that are not now served." National Rural Electric Cooperative Association, http://www.nreca.org/AboutUs/Co-op101/CoopHistory.htm

Private utility companies, who supplied electric power to most of the nation's consumers, argued that it was too expensive to string electric lines to isolated rural farmsteads and that most farmers, were too poor to be able to afford electricity. In 1933 Congress established the Tennessee Valley Act (TVA) to bring electricity to "farms and small villages that are not otherwise supplied with electricity at reasonable rates." To further advance rural electrification, President Franklin Delano Roosevelt signed in 1935 an executive order establishing the Rural Electrification Administration (REA) to provide loans and other assistance so that rural cooperatives—basically, groups of farmers—could build and run their own electrical distribution systems.

"Many groups opposed the federal government's involvement in developing and distributing electric power, especially utility companies, who believed that the government was unfairly competing with private enterprise. Some members of Congress who didn't think the government should interfere with the economy, believed that TVA was a dangerous program that would bring the nation a step closer to socialism. Other people thought that farmers simply did not have the skills needed to manage local electric companies." New Deal Network, http://newdeal.feri.org/tva/tva10.htm.

Within 2 years the REA electrified 1.5 million farms in 45 of the 48 states. By 1939 the cost of a mile of rural line had dropped from $2,000 to $600. Almost half of all farms were wired by 1942 and virtually all of them by the 1950s. REA's success encouraged private utilities to electrify the countryside as well. See National Academy of Engineering, Greatest Engineering Achievements of the Twentieth Century, http://www.greatachievements.org/?id=2990.

Over 99 percent of the nation's farms are now part of the nation's electrical grid. "Most rural electrification is the product of locally owned rural electric cooperatives that got their start by borrowing funds from REA to build lines and provide service on a nonprofit basis. An important part of the history of electric cooperatives has been the development of power marketing agencies (PMAs). In 1937, the federal government established the first PMA, the Bonneville Power Administration. The government then went on to form four more PMAs to market the power generated at 133 federal dams across the country. Today there are three PMAs in addition to Bonneville: Southeastern Power Administration; Southwestern Power Administration; and Western Area Power Administration. The federal law that governs PMAs gives preference in the sale of power at-cost to public bodies and electric cooperatives. The availability of low-cost power to electric cooperatives has promoted economic development and has offset the cost of serving sparsely populated areas." National Rural Electric Cooperative Association, http://www.nreca.org/AboutUs/Co-op101/CoopHistory.htm

1.   Today, some 1.5 billion people in developing countries lack electricity. What are the legal and policy barriers that impair electrification? Why did the U.S. engage in an aggressive effort to bring electricity to rural America? Do these reasons apply to the global rural poor who lack electricity? What institutions, policies, laws and regulations, and investments are needed to bring electricity to the world's rural poor? Do the rural poor have a human right to a water pump, an electric bulb, a refrigerator, a computer, a telephone? What about the additional GHG emissions that would result from generating electricity using fossil fuel? See, S. Ferry, Why Electricity Matters, Developing Nations Matter, and Asia Matters Most of All, 15 N.Y.U. Envtl. L.J. 113 (2007).

2.   Was America's return on its investment in rural electrification positive or negative? Should public investment seek private market-based rates of return or should they be based on a lower social rate of return? What difference does the expected rate of return make in deciding where and how to invest? Or should rate of return not be considered when evaluating public investments? For the past century or so, the government investments have tended to seek a real rate of return of 3%. See, R. Ottinger et. Al., eds., Environmental Costs of Electricity 85-87 (1990). What should be rate of return or social discount rate used in evaluating investments to mitigate climate change, to adapt to climate change? What is the value of avoidance of future human misery and death? How far into the future should we look?

D.   ENERGY EFFICIENCY

The U.S. Energy Information Agency reports that only about 34% of the energy used to generate electricity actually reaches the end user. Thus, for every unit of electricity that can be saved by efficiency or demand reduction, 3 units of energy is not burned. Basic physics dictates that energy efficiency is the single largest source of GHG emission reductions in the electricity sector. It is for this reason that it now widely recognized that mining additional energy from energy efficiency is the most cost effective and quickest method of increasing the available energy supply in the U.S. and elsewhere. Thus, by reducing demand for electricity from coal- and natural gas-fired power plants, it is possible to meet future needs without increasing GHG emissions. Moreover, with sufficient efficiency improvements, total emissions could drop as unnecessary fossil fuel plants would close.

IMAGINING THE UNIMAGINABLE: REDUCING U.S. GREENHOUSE

GAS EMISSIONS BY FORTY PERCENT
David R. Hodas
26 Virginia Environmental Law Journal 271 (2008)

The perception that reducing GHG emissions is impossible without seriously damaging the national economy is premised on a fundamentally incorrect underlying assumption about the cost of reducing GHG emissions. Most economic models predicting future environmental compliance costs seriously overestimate such costs. These models reflect a mistrust of the market's ability to innovate and invent solutions not imagined before the relevant environmental controls are in place. This is a serious flaw because until the market is required to innovate to meet a mandate, there is little economic incentive for businesses to invest in technology to meet that mandate. On the other hand, once a mandate is in place, competition to meet that new demand becomes fierce, innovation is rapid, and costs often plummet. Removing lead from gasoline, controlling benzene in the workplace, eliminating CFCs use to protect stratospheric ozone, and reducing sulfur emissions to mitigate acid precipitation are a few examples of seemingly unimaginable reductions achieved at remarkably low costs.

Predictions should be based on how markets actually respond, rather than on models that ignore these realities. If California's method of GHG reductions is used as an example, then not only is a thirty percent reduction possible, but forty percent would be relatively easy. If the nation's average annual per capita GHG emissions of twenty tons CO_2 per person, using 2001 data, were at the level of California's level of 11.4 tons per person, we would emit roughly forty-three percent fewer GHGs than we do now. California trusts this experience and is attempting to reduce emissions an additional twenty-five percent below its current levels. California emitted over 211 million tons of CO_2 from transportation alone in 2001–more than the total CO_2 emissions of all but six states. If the average annual U.S. per capita emissions were twelve tons, however, the United States would emit forty-percent less than it currently does; this would still leave it with the fourteenth highest per-capita emissions in the world.

Looking at the national and state CO_2 emission data maintained by World Resources Institute, some individual states would rank high on the world list of GHG emissions by country. For example, Texas would rank seventh in the world, between Germany and the United Kingdom; California would be twelfth, slightly below Mexico and above France. In fact, the top thirty-five states would rank within the top fifty CO_2 emitters in the world. Even Vermont, the lowest CO_2 emitting state in the United States, would rank 105th in the world. * * *

These numbers suggest that states face significant opportunities to become more efficient. Remarkably, if U.S. average emissions per capita were the same as that of California, total annual U.S. CO_2 emissions would be reduced forty percent—a 2.6 billion ton annual reduction. On average, a resident of Wyoming, North Dakota, Alaska, or West Virginia emits more than four times the CO_2 of the average person in California, a large state with a profound love affair with driving. At the same time, California's economy has grown nicely over the last three decades, from 229 billion dollars in 1977 to about 1.73 trillion dollars in 2006.

California achieves its commendable reductions by steadily taking small measures, both voluntary and forced, to improve energy efficiency and promote renewable energy. Each step is the result of innovative laws and regulations designed to implement energy efficiency policy. As a result, energy efficiency savings are enormous, achieved at a cost fifty to seventy-five percent lower than the cost of building new generation supplies. Most importantly, energy efficiency remains a huge energy resource. * * *

Preliminary results of recent analysis of the role of law and policy in advancing energy efficiency indicate that essentially all the energy efficiency savings are attributable to well-designed and implemented state laws and policies. In particular, building codes and appliance standards are the most cost-effective and durable means of achieving significant and durable energy efficiency. The range of effective legal tools also includes energy efficiency portfolio standards, energy efficiency utilities, and economic policies that link utility profit with energy efficiency, such as removing disincentives, decoupling rates from profits, bonus rates of return, and efficiency performance incentives.

As a result of implementing many of the above policies in its laws, California enjoyed a net savings in electricity and natural gas of over thirty-six billion dollars by 2003. Continuing along this track will yield even greater reductions: it is projected that the state's efforts will yield seventy-nine billion dollars in net savings by 2013. As of 2000, the cumulative savings from California's energy efficiency programs and energy efficiency standards were over 10,000 megawatts and 35,000 gigawatt hours of electricity—the equivalent of the output of 25 400 megawatt power plants. Similar success stories could be told about GHG emissions reductions in New York and several New England states whose per capita CO_2 emissions are similar to California's.

The path towards economically sensible GHG reductions is visible. While not every state must achieve the lower average, the United States as a whole must reduce its emissions to twelve tons per person. By setting a national per capita goal, market mechanisms can be adopted to meet the average, further reducing costs. At twelve tons per person, the U.S. average will still be more than twenty percent higher than the E.U. average of 8.7 tons per person.

Moreover, the twelve ton per person average does not take into account the potential impact of higher gasoline costs and more stringent motor vehicle efficiency standards needed to reduce demand and encourage adoption of efficiency technologies. The lesson here is that small, steady steps can produce significant results—and those results produce significant net economic benefits.

Moreover, the potential for future efficiency savings once the market signals a demand for efficiency innovation remains enormous. Given the correct policies and market signals to overcome market failures, potential new energy efficiency technologies may enable the United States to cut energy use drastically without diminishing the energy services most Americans want. The same phenomenon will occur in the renewable energy sector. * * *

Moreover, maintaining the current approach to energy use will entail huge additional investments in the United States' frail energy infrastructure. For instance, there have been no new oil refinery constructions in the United States since the late 1970s. Almost all of the nation's refineries are located in coastal areas or along rivers, and nearly half of the U.S. refining capacity is located in the Gulf of Mexico. Without new refining capacity, the United States is currently importing more refined gasoline than ever—roughly four million barrels per day and growing. As Hurricanes Katrina and Rita proved in 2005, the Gulf Coast refineries and pipelines that transport their product to much of United States are extremely vulnerable. In southeastern Florida, Hurricane Wilma disrupted electric service for about six million people; it took weeks to restore service in many places. Without electricity, gasoline stations could not pump gas, residences could not be air conditioned, street lights could not operate, and schools and businesses were closed. Sea level rise and more intense storms associated with global warming will only put more stress on the U.S. energy infrastructure. Climate change policies that reduce demand for fossil fuel-based energy will reduce the capital and human costs of maintaining and expanding the nation's energy infrastructure, will help reduce the rate of warming, and will enable the economy to be more resilient in responding to the effects of global warming.

Reduced gasoline consumption will lessen U.S. dependence on foreign sources of oil, thereby enhancing energy security and reducing the balance of trade deficits attributable to the purchase of foreign oil. Climate change initiatives by states alone will not solve any of these problems. States nevertheless can help alleviate the problem by providing ideas, leadership, and symbolic statements that advance their ethical, moral, political, and policy concerns.

[C]limate change initiatives aimed at reducing CO_2 emissions from fossil fuel combustion can also produce important secondary benefits. CO_2 emissions, for example, could be reduced by policies shifting transportation towards mass transit, walking, bicycling, or vehicles propelled by low or net-zero GHG sources, such as electricity produced from wind or photovoltaic solar power. One immediate by-product of these policies would be a reduction in pollution from motor vehicles. Reduced nitrogen dioxide (NO_2), volatile organic compounds (VOCs), and carbon monoxide (CO) from cars will improve urban air quality directly by reducing ground-level ozone (O_3) and associated smog. * * *

Notes and Questions

1. Failure to consider efficiency when making capital investment decisions can be very costly. Initial savings gained by employing inexpensive older technology that is less efficient than the current state of the art may be far more expensive on a system-wide least-cost basis. For example:

> In 1980, China decided to distribute refrigerators throughout the capital city of Beijing. It did so with resounding success, supplying refrigerators to over 60% of Beijing households by 1990, where only 6% had them in 1980. The reconditioned refrigerators from Japanese factories were thought to be cheap. They were not cheap, however, when the costs of the electric power supply necessary to run these very inefficient machines became apparent. In fact, the purchase and supply of inefficient equipment cost more than three times what would have been the cost of supplying the most efficient refrigerators on the world market [in 1991]. * * *

> Another example is the $150 million refurbishment * * * of thirteen * * * incandescent bulb factories in Hungary in 1990. * * * The $150 million [investment] could have been used to finance more than twenty new compact fluorescent lamp factories. The construction of fluorescent lamp factories could have avoided the construction of 12,000 megawatt (MW) power plants resulting in savings of $20 billion and minimizing air pollution in a country already suffocating in smog.

R. Ottinger, Energy and Environmental Challenges for Developed and Developing Countries, 9 Pace L. Rev. 55, 59-60 (1991).

2. The cumulative savings from efficiency improvements are substantial. For instance, by 2002 the average refrigerator in the U.S. used 450 kwh per year, down from 1,800 kwh per year in 1977. Yet the average useable space in refrigerators increased by 20% and prices declined by 60%. U.S. energy savings from the 150,000,000 refrigerators and freezers is about $17 billion annually. InterAcademy Council, Lighting the Way: Toward a Sustainable Energy Future (2007). However, their energy efficiency must overcome many "formidable barriers." These include high transaction costs, lack of information and analytical capacity, uncertain risk, institutional barriers, split-

incentives, lack of clear market signals, limited access to capital, the "difficulty of integrating complex systems," and "entrenched habits and cultural and institutional inertia." Id.

3. Efficiency improvements can help mitigate climate change while we work on moving to new renewable energy technologies. It has been argued, for this reason, that energy efficiency should be a central requirement in any new climate change treaty. John Dernbach argues that because "long-term greenhouse gas emissions [reductions] are virtually impossible without short-term reductions" any post-Kyoto agreement must "require early and substantial action," in Achieving Early and Substantial Greenhouse Gas Reductions Under a Post-Kyoto Agreement, 20 Geo. Int'l Envtl. L. Rev. 573, 575 (2008).

4. According to the McKinsey Global Institute, using only existing technology with an internal rate of return of 10% per year or more could reduce global energy growth to less than 1% annually; these efficiency investments would provide about 50% of the CO_2 emission reductions needed to cap atmospheric concentrations between 450 to 550 ppm. D. Farrell et al., Curbing Global Energy Demand Growth: The Energy Productivity Opportunity 12 (2007).

5. The House of Representatives' Report on The American Clean Energy & Security Act of 2009 (HR 2454) is also excerpted in Chapter 7, Section A, setting forth the impacts that require adaptation.

TRANSFORMING UTILITY AND RATEPAYER SUPPORT FOR ELECTRICAL ENERGY EFFICIENCY NATIONWIDE
David Hoppock, Jonas Monast, and Eric Williams
Climate Change Policy Partnership, Duke University (2008)
http://www.nicholas.duke.edu/ccpp/ccpp_pdfs/ee%20web.pdf

Concerns about climate change, energy security, and rising energy costs are increasing focus on low-carbon electricity generation. Greater investment in energy efficiency represents the most cost-effective, near-term solution for increasing energy security and significantly reducing U.S. greenhouse gas (GHG) emissions. * * *

Energy efficiency is a proven, low-cost method for consumers to save money and reduce their energy use, but without the proper policies and utility support, society cannot realize the full potential. * * * To achieve large-scale investment in energy efficiency, utilities and state utility regulators must view energy efficiency as equivalent to supply resources and invest in energy efficiency at levels similar to other generation sources. Utility regulations can be structured to allow investor-owned utilities to profit from increased efficiency, not just cover the costs of regulator-mandated efficiency programs. * * *

There are three primary models for regional and state electricity markets: traditional regulated utilities, restructured markets, and municipally/cooperatively owned utilities. In restructured markets, customers can choose an energy provider but transmission and distribution is conducted by a separate, regulated utility. Traditional regulated utilities are investor-owned, vertically integrated, regulator-sanctioned monopoly electricity providers. Municipal and cooperatively-owned utilities are controlled by local governments or local populations and regulate themselves. States generally play a minimal role in regulating municipal and cooperative utilities. Many states have a combination of one or more of the listed utility structures within their borders.

States and public utility commissions conduct most utility regulation and electricity market oversight. Regulations and regulator goals vary considerably between states. The Federal Energy Regulatory Commission regulates interstate electricity transmission and transactions and has rules to ensure interstate transmission reliability.

1. Traditional utility regulation

In a traditional utility regulation system, the utility presents a "rate case," with a proposed retail electricity rate, to the regulator. The utility forecasts all costs, including all operational costs, debt servicing, approved planned investments, and a reasonable rate of return on the utility's investments. The utility also forecasts the amount of electricity it expects to sell to retail customers. Electricity rates are found by dividing expected costs by expected kWh sales. This rate is the price of electricity that the utility needs to charge so that it can recover all of its expected costs, assuming it sells exactly the number of kWh in its forecast. Once the electricity rate is approved by the state regulator, the rate is generally fixed until the next rate case. During this time between rate cases, a utility has a strong incentive to sell more electricity than forecasted because every additional kWh sold results in additional profit above and beyond the allowable rate of return. * * * Conversely, if the utility sells less electricity than is projected in the rate case, the utility may not have sufficient revenues to cover its expenses, providing a strong disincentive to invest in energy efficiency. Traditional utility regulatory systems do not provide a guaranteed rate of return on energy efficiency investments and generally ignore energy efficiency as a resource. This means that a utility cannot profit from increased efficiency or recover costs if electricity sales are less than projected because retail rates are fixed. Traditional utility regulation creates no incentives for utilities to invest in energy efficiency and in effect encourages utilities to increase sales as much as possible within their given generation and distribution capacity, thereby increasing GHG emissions.

Wholesale electricity markets place no value on energy efficiency. Wholesale generators can only collect revenues from electricity they sell, not from electricity they do not sell. In restructured markets, transmission and distribution utilities are regulated much the same way traditional regulated utilities are while generators compete to sell electricity to customers. In restructured electricity markets, transmission and distribution utilities generally earn revenue through a wires charge on each kWh of electricity sold, discouraging transmission and distribution utilities from making investments in energy efficiency. Nevertheless, energy efficiency can help transmission and distribution utilities avoid costly capital improvements through reduced demand growth that eases the burden on congested transmission and distribution systems. * * *

Policy Options to Address Barriers to Investments in Energy Efficiency

A. Innovative state policies to increase energy efficiency investment

Multiple states have successfully adopted innovative policies to encourage large-scale energy efficiency investment. All of these policies to increase efficiency investment can be used in combination and many states and utilities have successfully implemented two or more of the following policies. Generators in restructured markets still face some regulation. These regulations vary from state to state.

1. Decoupling

Decoupling removes the connection between electricity sales and utility profits, eliminating the throughput incentive. Decoupling also allows utilities to recover costs if total sales are less than projected. Under decoupling, regulators set efficiency and performance goals that utilities must meet in order to earn a profit. Utilities typically place revenues in a regulator-controlled account. The account pays for the utility's operating costs and pays the utility a profit if it meets its efficiency and performance goals. Regulators periodically adjust electricity rates to ensure the account has sufficient funds to cover operating costs and utility profits. Decoupling rate adjustments are typically very minor (0 to less than 3%) and many states cap decoupling rate adjustments at 2% or 3% per year. * * *

Regulators can further encourage efficiency investment by structuring decoupling so that utilities are guaranteed a return on energy efficiency investment or guaranteed a higher rate of return on energy efficiency investments than on traditional generation and distribution investments. Regulators can also create annual lump-sum rewards for utilities that reduce total or per capita electricity demand by a specified amount.

The best-known decoupling example is California's decoupling of sales from profits for investor-owned utilities. California originally adopted decoupling for regulated, investor-owned utilities in 1982. In 1996, California restructured its electricity market and introduced competition in electricity generation, ending decoupling. The 2001 California energy crisis convinced the California government to abandon restructuring and reintroduce electricity generation regulation and decoupling. During the 2001 crisis, the California government directed a massive, statewide energy efficiency initiative that helped to end the crisis by reducing peak summer demand over 8% in one year. Since reintroducing decoupling in 2001 and re-emphasizing energy efficiency, investment in energy efficiency has increased significantly. Many other states, including Maryland, Oregon, New Jersey, Idaho, New York, Minnesota, Massachusetts, and Vermont, have also adopted some form of decoupling.

2. Energy efficiency resource standards

Energy efficiency resource standards use market-based mechanisms to encourage cost-effective energy savings, similar to the federal sulfur dioxide cap-and-trade program and state-based renewable portfolio standards (RPS). Under an energy efficiency resource standard, utilities receive energy savings targets for their service areas. Utilities document their energy savings using predetermined certification methods and receive energy efficiency certificates.[15] Each utility must have enough certificates at the end of the year to meet its energy savings target. Utilities can buy and sell energy efficiency certificates to meet their requirements, allowing the market to find the lowest-cost energy efficiency opportunities. Many states with energy efficiency resource standards allow utilities to buy efficiency certificates from the state at some predetermined rate, typically half the cost of retail electricity rates, to create a cap on certificate prices. The proceeds from these sales fund state-sponsored energy efficiency programs. Some states, such as Hawaii for example, allow utilities to meet a portion of their RPS obligation through energy efficiency, in effect combining an RPS and an energy efficiency resource standard.

Seventeen states now have energy efficiency resource standards or renewable portfolio standards that include energy efficiency. * * * Energy efficiency resource standards programs have also proven effective internationally. The United Kingdom and the Flemish Region of Belgium have exceeded their program goals with the UK spending less than 1.5 cents per kWh of energy saved on the program. Italy and France also recently adopted national energy efficiency resource standards. * * *

---

[15] Utility A offers rebates on high-efficiency dishwashers, which use 30% less electricity than conventional dishwashers. 1,000 customers utilize the rebates and purchase high-efficiency dishwashers. The state regulator then awards Utility A energy efficiency certificates for these energy savings.

3. Ratepayer-funded energy efficiency programs

Ratepayer-funded energy efficiency programs use charges paid by utility customers to pay for state energy efficiency programs. Many states adopted efficiency charges in the 1990s to ensure a source of funding for state energy efficiency programs in restructured markets. As of September 2007, twenty-seven states had ratepayer-funded energy efficiency programs. Two of the more successful and well-known programs include Efficiency Vermont and the Energy Trust of Oregon. Efficiency Vermont is a statewide energy efficiency utility that offers technical and financial assistance to individuals and businesses and is funded by statewide energy efficiency charges. The Energy Trust of Oregon uses a three percent public purpose charge to pay for residential and commercial efficiency programs as well as other renewable energy and research programs.

4. Declare energy efficiency as a priority resource

Multiple states have created rules or passed laws requiring utilities and utility regulators to make energy efficiency the priority supply in resource planning. California's Energy Action Plan II, released in 2005, placed energy efficiency as the first resource in the utility loading order, meaning California investor-owned utilities must invest in cost-effective energy efficiency before investing in additional renewable or fossil fuel energy sources. Another example is the recent law passed by New Mexico requiring the New Mexico Regulatory Commission, which regulates the utility industry in the state, to remove all disincentives to energy efficiency investment. Through this law, the New Mexico Regulatory Commission has the authority and is required to create regulatory incentives for utilities to invest in energy efficiency and achieve the state's goal of developing all cost-effective energy efficiency opportunities in the state.

B. Federal policy options to encourage large-scale nationwide investment in energy efficiency

The federal government currently plays a minimal role in electricity markets and does not regulate retail electricity sales. Federal policymakers considering legislation to improve efficiency should note that energy efficiency programs also take time to plan and implement, especially programs that encourage changes in customer behavior. Additionally, when considering any electricity policy, policymakers should focus on how much customers pay for electricity (i.e., their total electricity bill), not just electricity rates. Many efficiency programs raise rates slightly in the short term but create significant, long-term benefits for customers on their future energy bills. The following policy options would require little or no action from states that already have significant energy efficiency programs and are designed to encourage all states to make a minimum investment in energy efficiency.

1. Provide incentives to states that adopt utility decoupling

This policy would create federal incentives for states that adopt decoupling mechanisms for investor-owned regulated utilities and distribution and transmission utilities in restructured markets. If the goal of the policy is to maximize energy efficiency investment, the incentive should require that states provide utilities with an additional rate of return on investments in energy efficiency (compared to other capital investments). Potential incentives include offering states a percentage of revenues from GHG emissions cap-and-trade auctions, * * * increasing funding for mass transit, and increasing Federal Transportation Administration New Starts funding for transit capital investments such as light rail and bus rapid transit systems. * * *

These incentives would encourage states to remove the barriers to energy efficiency investment inherent in traditional utility regulation. Under decoupling, utilities can invest in energy efficiency as if it were an energy resource, like any other type of electricity generation. Nationwide, utilities are already spending billions of dollars per year on capital investment. With this policy, a portion of this capital investment could be invested in improving energy efficiency. * * *

4. National energy efficiency resource standard

A national energy efficiency resource standard would require all utilities to meet an annual energy savings target based upon each utility's annual sales, or buy energy efficiency certificates from other utilities that surpass their savings target.

ENERGY EFFICIENCY IN REGULATED AND DEREGULATED MARKETS
Edan Rotenberg
24 UCLA J. Envtl. L & Pol'y 259 (2006)

The possible efficiencies of the electricity system can be divided into generation efficiency, transmission efficiency, and end-use efficiency. Generation efficiency means economically and efficiently extracting energy from resources to power turbines or fuel cells and create an electric current. Transmission efficiency is the reduction of line losses to the most economically efficient level possible. This includes minimizing transmission distances through the planning and siting of energy generation near human settlements. Generation and transmission efficiency are often referred to as supply side efficiency. * * * A key goal is to ensure that electricity is used at a rate consistent with the true marginal social cost of providing it. * * * [E]nd-use efficiency is often referred to as demand side management (DSM).

* * * Integrated Resource Planning (IRP), a central component of energy efficiency planning under our former regulatory regime, is essentially a combination of DSM and supply side investment efficiency that tries to optimize resource use across all three aspects of the electric system. Essentially, IRP attempts to include an economically efficient role for reductions of end-use electricity consumption in the planning of generation and transmission capital investments. Infrastructure investments that are more expensive than measures reducing electricity consumption or growth of the electric load can be avoided. Instead, the funds that would have been used to expand transmission and generation are invested in DSM. * * *

Peak load reduction measures, such as load shifting and interruptible power, are conducted by utilities or private actors. Load shifting means convincing users to engage in energy intensive activities at non-peak hours. Interruptible power means contracting with customers to allow the utility to stop providing power or reduce the power level provided under certain conditions, for example at peak periods. It is unclear that load shifting or interrupting power reduce overall power use for a customer; they simply smooth the variability of customer demand. In recent variable pricing experiments in California, peak prices eight times greater than normal prices led overwhelmingly to load shifting, a cut in peak demand of 15% on average, and to a negligible reduction in overall load for the monitored periods. * * *

Decentralized and Renewable Energy as Energy Efficiency Measures

One aspect of renewable energy is decentralized generation with net metering. From the grid-centric point of view, this is a type of efficiency measure because a typical consumer of energy actually becomes a generator of electricity who may sell net electricity back to the grid. A consumer might decide that this is desirable for fiscal or other reasons including security of supply, personal or political desire to be "green," or to receive tax incentives. * * * If the source of the onsite electricity is a low-pollution source, then it is a net environmental benefit. * * *

Defining Regulation and Deregulation

Until the close of the 1980s, American electricity markets were all regulated monopolies. Both entry and price were regulated by state and federal government law. Several important changes occurred in sequence that led to less regulation. First, in the 1980s the Federal Energy Regulatory Commission (FERC) changed their policies to favor competition. Congress subsequently passed the Energy Policy Act of 1992, which lowered entry barriers for new generation technologies. Two years later the California Public Utilities Commission began to restructure the electricity sector in California. In 1996, the FERC took another step to encourage competition in the generation sector by ordering all utilities to provide full access to their grids.

The Regulated Market

A regulated electricity market is characterized by the existence of a vertically integrated electricity monopolist. That monopolist owns the generating capacity, the high voltage transmission grid, and the lower voltage distribution network going to individual consumers. The monopolist also contracts directly with those consumers to provide electricity. In this market, a utility's rate is set by a regulator, who endeavors through cost-based ratemaking, to set a "fair" price for electricity. In a monopolized market, the electric utility faces a downward sloping demand curve, and its marginal revenue is less than the price. Like any rational monopolist in this situation, the utility should restrict quantity to increase price and maximize total revenue by underproducing relative to market demand. A regulator tries to prevent this from happening by providing a rate of compensation that approximates the average cost of the utility.

Cost-based ratemaking tries to ascertain the costs incurred by the utility, tack on a reasonable profit, and then divide this cost amongst the utility's customers in some fashion. Under this basic system, a utility essentially has no incentive to reduce the electricity consumption of its users. It is incentivized to include every possible allowable cost and encourage demand growth to justify increased capacity investment. * * * [E]ncouraging energy efficiency in a regulated market often involves manipulating the utility's compensation formula to avoid this problem.

The "Deregulated" Market

A deregulated market is characterized primarily by the dismemberment of vertically integrated utilities in an attempt to create competitive generation markets. The Independent System Operator (ISO) is put in charge of the transmission grid and opens access to the grid equally to all qualified generators. The generation arm of the business is either spun off or forced to sell assets, and out-of-state generators are allowed to "wheel in" power to allow for generation competition. Transmission remains a regulated monopoly because to date no one has been convinced that it makes sense to have competing power lines to the same customers.

The retail end of the market is a far murkier story. Retail competition * * * has not occurred in most jurisdictions. Although 24 states passed retail competition laws, eight repealed or suspended them since the California Energy Crisis in June 2000. Every other state that had been considering retail competition dropped the issue by 2004. In those states that allow retail competition, it seems to be unsuccessful. * * *

An "economic theory of regulation" explanation for the rise and fall of the retail competition movement suggests that the push for deregulation occurred in large part because of the potential to get lower cost electricity * * * in a competitive market. This push for greater retail competition was initially supported by politicians seeking to pass on the benefits of lower prices to voters. This rationale began to fade because the price gaps between regulated and deregulated prices were not sufficiently large to stimulate political entrepreneurs. Utility companies continued the push for retail competition because they wanted the ability to recover stranded debt from consumers. In exchange for allowing retail competition, the utilities were allowed to charge all of the "stranded" liabilities of their generating assets to whoever purchased power in the market because regulators established a debt charge that was competitively neutral. When the energy crisis in California came, it drove a stake into the political future of retail competition. * * *

Competitive generation presents an interesting dilemma for energy efficiency. On the one hand, the first deregulatory experiment in California showed disastrous markets plagued by highly inelastic supply and demand. Energy efficiency can be attractive in such an environment. Just as electricity retailers can choose to lock into long term contracts to control price volatility, they can also choose to pay for efficiency measures or load shifting to help them avoid paying high spot prices for electricity. Consumers are also incentivized to use less electricity when it has a high price. On the other hand, if competition eventually leads to lower prices, it renders energy efficiency less attractive. In a market without adjustments for uncompensated environmental externalities, the price of power can be expected to stay far below social cost. Consequently, many socially desirable efficiency measures will not be performed.

    * * * [I]t is very important to distinguish between marginal cost pricing in a competitive retail market and Real Time Pricing (RTP). The two are independent: one can have RTP without competitive pricing or a competitive retail market without RTP. Currently, almost all homes and buildings have meters that record aggregate electricity use over [time]. The end-user is not aware of how many kilowatt-hours of power are used at any given time or date except over the [billing] * * * period. * * *

In contrast to the aggregate nature of retail electricity prices, the marginal cost in the spot markets depends essentially on hourly demand and the production decisions of generators. The spot price changes with the daily and seasonal peaks in demand. The highly variable wholesale spot price drives home the fact that the "marginal" cost in the retail market is a very strange thing. Typically, we think of marginal cost pricing not only as the price derived in a perfectly competitive market, but also as a price signal that accurately conveys the cost of an additional unit of a good produced to the purchaser. A marginal cost signal would tell the consumer who demands kilowatts at a peak period that the kilowatts she is asking for are very expensive. However, most consumers are completely unaware of the current price of electricity when they flip a switch. They know only how much they are billed during their total use over the * * * billing period. Similarly, suppliers do not know when each kilowatt-hour was demanded, only how much electricity each customer demanded over the entire period.

The lack of RTP is important because it means that consumers cannot react to daily or weekly high prices by curtailing demand. * * * Competition in generation allows generators to behave strategically and collectively withhold power to drive up the price. Enabling consumers to avoid rigid consumption and instead respond to higher prices is therefore an important counterbalance. * * *

The Wrong Price–Environmental Externalities & Perverse Subsidies

The existence of environmental externalities is one very strong reason to engage in energy efficiency. There is widespread agreement that environmental externalities exist in electricity generation. Environmental concerns are therefore a critical consideration in any electricity sector policy. * * *

The absence of environmental externalities in cost leads to price distortions. The price of fossil fuels seems cheap relative to their social cost because part of their social cost is not included in the purchase price. * * *Environmental externalities can be divided into three categories. First, there are those externalities that we are aware of and can quantify with a reasonably certain margin of error. Examples of this would be the negative health effects of nitrogen and sulfur oxides; ozone; * * * particulate matter from fossil fuel combustion; or the injury, loss of life, and increased occurrence of lung disease in coal miners.

A second category of externalities is those we are aware of but whose costs we cannot quantify completely. They cannot be quantified completely because we either lack information about the chain of causality or lack market prices for the impacted goods. Attempts to develop hedonic prices have not clearly led to an accepted market price. Examples of this second category include the costs of carbon dioxide related to global warming; the impact of mercury from coal burning on mental retardation in fetuses and small children; and the extinction of species and loss of habitat caused by water and air pollution.

The third category of externalities are those whose existence we are only now discovering or have yet to discover. Until recently, most of the effects of releasing carbon dioxide into the atmosphere fell into this category. * * * [G]iven the human experience of industrialization and environmental degradation over the last 200 years, some recognition that there might be other undiscovered externalities is not paranoid but simply a realistic, safe, and conservative assumption. * * *

All forms of electricity generation, including renewable ones, are associated with externalities over the life cycle of the generation process. This life cycle includes the construction of generation equipment, use, and disposal. Unfortunately, electricity generation from centralized fossil fuel burning power plants is both the dominant form of electricity generation and has the highest known and quantified externalities. * * *

[Typical estimates of the costs of externalities in terms of cents per kwh] * * * account for only a limited number of externalities. * * * Nonetheless, the external costs of oil, coal, and waste-to-energy add considerably to their costs. Even natural gas displays a significant external cost relative to the price of the gas itself. * * *

Proponents of energy efficiency measures argue that a reduction in electricity consumption also reduces pollution, and that the cost of efficiency measures should be compared to the marginal price of electricity plus the costs of calculated externalities. This is one of the bases of the environmental argument that the cost in "cost-based ratemaking" requires adjustments.

However, the externalities that cannot be internalized are of relevance too. * * * [O]ne could add the costs of global warming if they were known, the value of lost species were it calculable, and the costs of mercury loading if we understood more about how it enters into our food supplies. Even without considering the issue of appropriate discount rates and the calculation of prices in the absence of liquid markets, it is clear that externalities create a difficult consideration for electricity policy that is hard to reduce to dollars. * * *

The discussion to this point has been theoretical, particularly of the currently uninternalized externalities. Thus, I wish to present one example to underline the seriousness of the distortion caused by neglect of environmental impacts. It will also explain why there is room for energy efficiency measures to help fill the gap between the savings achieved in the current market and those that would be achieved in a market where electricity was used at a rate commensurate with its marginal social cost. The example is climate change, a currently uninternalized externality of fossil fuel combustion. * * *

Environmental externalities exist and are real. They prompt serious discussions about the appropriate cost of electricity that in turn affects the determination of which energy efficiency policies make economic sense and which do not. Externalities also create an incentive for market based pollution control policies that includes a necessary role for energy efficiency.

Nevertheless, environmental externalities are not the only price distortion. There are also large public subsidies for the use of fossil fuels: budgetary transfers, tax incentives, R&D, liability insurance provision, public leases, rights of way, waste disposal, and project financing or fuel risk guarantees. The World Bank and International Energy Agency estimate that annual public subsidies for fossil fuels range between $100 and $200 billion worldwide, with a high level of uncertainty. This is relative to the global expenditure of approximately $1 trillion on fossil fuels in 2004. This results in a massive distortion of the price of fossil fuels and consequently in the social cost of electricity generated from fossil fuels.

The basic theoretical conclusion is that the true social cost of electricity needs to account for environmental externalities and public subsidies. Given that this is impossible in practice, energy efficiency measures aimed at counteracting this distortion are justifiable. * * *

The "Wrong" Reaction–Barriers Created by Transaction and Information Costs

Even if it were possible, internalizing all environmental externalities into the price of electricity would not eliminate the case for energy efficiency. For this to be the case, our markets must be perfect markets with full information and no transaction costs. * * *

The empirical reality is that information and transaction costs can and should be reduced at a net social benefit. Whether utilities or the government should do this is an interesting question. * * *

* * * [M]any market barriers are not regulatory. Those barriers are structural problems of electricity production and consumption. * * *

One of the barriers most often listed by environmentalists is cross subsidies. A cross subsidy is a traditional cost-based ratemaking tool that solves the problem created by a natural monopoly by setting the price the utility charges at the utility's average cost (thereby subsidizing some consumers at the expense of others). Without marginal cost pricing, consumers are not actually aware what their electricity really costs society. This could still be a problem even with full internalization of externalities. Assuming that there is some cross-subsidization amongst consumers, the subsidized customers are incentivized to use too much electricity. * * *

Split incentives are another barrier cited by environmentalists. A split incentive results when decisions about electricity investments in end-use efficiency are made by people who do not pay the electric bills, such as landlords, architects and builders. * * *

Transaction costs and information costs are the * * * cost[s] to individuals, particularly residential consumers, in time and effort to develop the expertise necessary to implement energy efficiency measures which are large relative to the potential benefits they will see. However, the needed expertise and proprietary knowledge are actually in the hands of the utility. Thus, much regulation is designed to deal with the paradox that the party with the least incentive to engage in energy conservation, and the least incentive to reduce generation capacity investment, is also the most efficient saver of electricity. * * *

Consumers face substantial transaction and information costs. * * * [A]lthough manufacturers make claims about energy efficiency that are available to consumers, the information is often incomplete and inconsistent. This leaves residential consumers to sort between products ranging from small appliances to houses. These products come with a large range of up-front costs and potential energy savings, including some contingent upon certain installation and design details that are largely beyond the consumer's understanding. In the commercial sector, a key issue is often corporate commitment because high-level financial decision makers do not see electricity as a key business issue or a controllable category of costs. However, efficiency gains clearly exist to be captured. * * *

The difference between the information and transaction costs faced by utilities and consumers creates a phenomenon known as the payback gap. As a function of the market barriers they face, individuals and businesses have a higher expected return than utilities. Surveys show that consumers want to see a payback on their investment at an annual rate of 30% or greater when they install energy efficient technologies. * * * "[C]onsiderable empirical evidence indicates that consumers and business managers routinely forego efficiency opportunities with payback times as short as 6 months to three years - effectively demanding annual rates of return on efficiency investments in excess of 40-100%." Without quantifying the figure, the economist Paul Joskow has also concluded that "there is fairly compelling evidence that consumers use what appear to be very high implicit discount rates when they evaluate energy-efficiency investments." * * *

By contrast, utilities do not expect a return over 15% on their investments in generation capacity. Thus, many efficiency improvements that could be done by the homeowner will instead be replaced by new generation capacity built by the utility. Since under cost-based ratemaking a utility has no incentive to reduce its rate base and is incentivized to over-invest in capital (the Averch-Johnson effect), it will not voluntarily choose to substitute its investment into new capacity with reductions in energy consumption that would obviate the need for such investment. * * *

Energy Efficiency Under Regulation

* * * The fundamental problem of energy efficiency under regulation is that all the incentives are in the wrong places. Homeowners are limited * * * to finding only a very small number of energy efficiency improvements to be cost effective. Transactions costs also make it difficult for outside third parties with more knowledge than homeowners to make improvements. Though these third parties lower costs and thereby make a greater number of efficiency measures possible, there are still barriers. By far the actor best suited to engage in efficiency measures is the utility. The utility has the technical expertise of a third party expert combined with the savings of a distributor. Reduced demand means that less investment in infrastructure capacity is needed, adding a new type of savings that is unavailable to every other actor. However, under traditional cost-based ratemaking, it is against the interests of utilities to engage in the pursuit of electricity use savings. * * *

Planning

Planning requirements are generally called Integrated Resource Planning (IRP). IRP is a requirement that some party, typically either the local electricity commission or the vertically integrated utility, forecast demand. Then the regulator, the utility, or an outside consultant develops a plan to meet projected demand based on reaching the least cost outcome, drawing on both supply side (new generation) and demand side measures. Most regulations required the combination of supply and demand side measures to achieve the least-cost outcome. DSM measures were pursued to the extent that the regulator believed, or the party charged with planning argued, they were cheaper than developing new capacity or generation on existing equipment. IRP is a technique used commonly around the United States and internationally. It has remained in use in some states that have not restructured while other non-restructured states have allowed IRP legislation to lapse.

More inventively, some jurisdictions also adjusted the "least cost outcome" to account for environmental externalities. * * *

Rate Structure

The second area where regulators can promote energy efficiency is in the calculation of retail rates. * * *[R]etail rates under traditional cost-based ratemaking do not reflect marginal costs. Commentators have suggested modifying regulated prices by time of use rates, also known as peak load pricing, and inclining blocks. Time of use rates refer to rates that increase in blocks when demand for electricity is highest and are in common use. In their purest form, time of use rates go from being a fixed, two or three stage type of pricing to real-time retail rates for industrial, commercial, and perhaps some day even for residential consumers. These customers would actually pay the marginal cost of power. Inclining blocks are the inverse of bulk purchase discounts. Rather than rewarding customers for consuming more electricity, an escalating rate is charged such that the more power consumed, the more expensive the next kWh becomes. California began to use this method after the electricity crisis.

While inclining blocks are an uncomplicated energy efficiency tool, real time pricing (RTP) is more complicated. * * *RTP is used to decrease peak loads. While that is doubtless an economically efficient move on its face, the net electricity savings and environmental impact of shaving peak demand depends on several factors. It could be that shaving peak demand has a negative environmental impact by decreasing the use of peaking assets with a low environmental impact and increasing the use of non-peak assets with higher environmental impact.

Subsidy

The last important area to discuss in a regulated electricity sector is the creation of subsidies for energy efficiency. This includes the creation of incentives for electric utilities to implement energy efficiency measures. In order to overcome the previously discussed shortcomings of cost-based ratemaking, regulators use revenue adjustment mechanisms. Some mechanisms fix the utility's profits based on past experience to assure them their normal rate of return. Then regulators often add incentives for achieving efficiency targets. In other jurisdictions, utility expenditures on energy efficiency are considered part of the rate base, so they earn a return on them. The utilities may be further rewarded for meeting certain savings targets. * * *

Energy Efficiency Under Deregulation

To understand how energy efficiency measures work in a deregulated market, it is important first to understand what deregulation means while bearing in mind that energy efficiency will not disappear in a competitive market. * * * The issue is the price and amount of savings achieved. In a fully deregulated market, one that is competitive and does not require any actor to meet efficiency standards, the amount of energy conserved depends entirely on the price of electricity. This price determines the energy saving measures worth implementing. To the extent that the cost of electricity still does not reflect its true social cost in the deregulated market, we face the same problem as was faced in a regulated market. * * *

Competitive Generation

* * * This has several impacts on energy efficiency. First, there is an end to Integrated Resource Planning (IRP) of the type that requires utilities to avoid new plant investments by providing energy efficiency gains. * * * In the

past IRP requirements forced vertically integrated utilities to avoid investment in plants if lower cost investments in DSM could obviate the need for new plants. Now that utilities no longer own significant generating assets, the demand not to invest in new plants is less relevant. Most utilities still own some generating assets, so theoretically IRP rules may still have some effect. However, the critical question is not whether a utility owns its own plant but whether there is a monopolist utility at all. * * *

[T]he structural rigidity of electricity markets creates a strong incentive for generators in a competitive market to behave strategically. Generators can withhold supply to generate far higher prices without fear that demand will drop because demand is highly inelastic under conventional metering and pricing systems.

In the long term, the effect of RTP is to lower average electricity costs. This should discourage investment in energy efficiency through, for example, performance contracting. In addition, the increased use of efficiency measures achievable through decreased transaction costs could be cancelled out by decreased electricity costs. * * * [I]n a market where the price of electricity does not reflect externalized costs or hidden subsidies, the net environmental effect of RTP could be negative.

Retail Competition

Beyond the widespread transition to a competitive generation market, the impact of the deregulatory movement is more varied. It is by no means clear that deregulation leads to competitive retail markets. * * * [M]ost jurisdictions do not have retail competition and even those jurisdictions that have it do not have robust competition. * * *

Retail Monopoly

There is little new to say about energy efficiency with regard to a noncompetitive retail sector. * * * [A] regulated utility can still pursue IRP without owning substantial generation assets. The issue is whether the price of kilowatt-hours purchased from generators is greater than the price of energy savings achievable. The same manipulations of cost-based ratemaking that were practiced in the past can still be practiced. * * *

[I]n a competitive retail market, information and transaction costs may even increase as the array of choices and claims made by sellers grows. * * * [I]nformation about energy savings and choices are often incomplete and inconsistent. There are fewer actors trying to provide such information in a regulated market. Therefore, in theory, one benefit of regulation should be fewer inconsistencies and a lesser number of purported authorities seeking to profit from a confused customer. * * *

Price regulation, by definition, largely disappears in a competitive market. A competitive market does not have a regulator who sets a price and can demand that utilities work with customers to achieve all energy savings below that price. Every retail provider sets their own price and earns money solely through sales, not some regulated subsidy that compensates them for earnings lost to efficiency investments. If efficiency gains are to be made, they must be made directly by end-users or by third parties that provide energy management services to end-users. This means that price is even more important to the achievement of energy efficiency in a deregulated market than it is in a regulated market. To the extent that prices do not reflect social cost or that information and transaction costs impede the functioning of markets, energy efficiency will be even harder to achieve in a competitive market than in a monopolized market however. In a competitive retail market, a regulator can encourage private sector conservation measures, but the achievement of performance contracting will depend critically on the cost of electricity.

Retail competition, therefore, certainly does not mean that the need for planning disappears. A competitive market will still suffer from market failures such as environmental externalities, fossil fuel subsidies, lack of RTP, and information and transaction costs. The role of a regulator in the deregulated market will still be to take a macro perspective and optimize the system from a social point of view. * * * It is blatantly obvious but bears repeating: in a price-based system of electricity consumption, regulators will continually need to make efforts to bring the price of electricity close to its true social cost. Where this is not possible, they will need to take other steps to bring consumption down to the level they believe is efficient.

* * * [I]f the market price does not track the social cost of electricity because of environmental externalities, some intervention into retail rates is warranted. Regulation internalizes some of the environmental externalities through pollution control measures but does not account for all of them. For instance, American markets do not adequately account for mercury and carbon where they account for them at all. Thus, regulators will still need to exercise their power to structure the electricity sector. The remaining issue is what tools regulators ought to use.

Environmental Regulation

* * * Empirically it is difficult to determine the true social cost of pollution. While most agree that electricity costs do not reflect externalities, the size of those externalities is contested. Briefly, the problems involved in determining the size of an externality include (1) the uncertainty surrounding the net environmental, non-monetary, impacts of different electricity generating methods and (2) the uncertainties and assumptions needed to monetize

those impacts. The fundamental problem of ecology is that you cannot change just one thing. Ecosystems are interconnected and complex systems that we still do not fully understand. The dynamic feedbacks in natural systems, coupled with our uncertainty about the size and nature of material flows between the electricity industry and the environment, mean that we are not sure of the electricity generation's environmental impact. There is a different set of problems when trying to monetize those impacts. One must decide the proper standard to use for hedonic pricing, or the willingness of parties to pay and accept those costs. One must also decide on the appropriate discount rates and develop accurate shadow prices without adequate data about marginal choices. Thus, any attempt to use pollution taxes will require simplifying assumptions and conservative value judgments. * * *

Portfolio standards are the new market based tool directly related to the electricity sector. The idea was originally to create a Renewable Portfolio Standard (RPS). An RPS is a state level policy requiring a certain percentage of a utility's overall, or new, generating capacity or energy sales be derived from renewable resources. Twenty to twenty-one American states have an RPS. The idea has been adapted to create an Energy Efficiency Portfolio Standard (EEPS). * * *

* * * Although an EEPS is directly related to energy efficiency, neither RPS measures or emissions trading are. * * * In a market where pollution reductions have value, someone will try to claim the credit for the achievements of energy efficiency. If multiple parties claim the credit, a problem called "double counting," the integrity of the market is called into question - you get a market full of lemons. * * * Proponents of tradable pollution rights and renewable energy credits are concerned with the impact that energy efficiency measures will have on the value and integrity of these new commodities if energy efficiency proponents succeed in funding energy efficiency through the integration of energy savings from efficiency into other clean energy markets.

Notes and Questions

1.   An ingenious plan was devised by an organization called PAYS (pay as you save), www.pays.org. Under this plan the utility puts up all the front money to install efficiency measures, does the installation, and the customer pays through his utility bill – but PAYS guarantees that the savings from the efficiency measures will at least cover the bill expenses. One great feature of this plan is that it works for renters or people who sell their houses. The obligation goes with the utility contract, so the seller is relieved of any payment obligations and the buyer automatically picks up the billing costs and efficiency savings.

2.   What is the legal and policy structure where you live for promoting en-

ergy efficient investments? Is it effective? Innovative? Who pays for it?

REDUCING THE COST OF ADDRESSING CLIMATE CHANGE THROUGH ENERGY EFFICIENCY

Alliance to Save Energy, American Council for an Energy-Efficient Economy, American Institute of Architects, Environmental and Energy Study Institute, Environment Northeast, Johnson Controls, Inc., National Association of Energy Service Companies, Natural Resources Defense Council, Sierra Club, and Real Estate Roundtable

(February 2009)

//aceee.org/energy/climate/Reducing%20the%20Cost%20of%20Addressing%20 Climate%20Change.pdf

Energy Efficiency–The Cornerstone of a U.S. Carbon Cap-and-Trade Program

National climate change legislation faces the challenge of achieving deep reductions in GHG emissions while limiting both national economic costs and consumer costs from the program. A carbon cap-and-trade program, most frequently discussed, would provide a much needed market price for carbon. However, since one of the principal aims of cap-and-trade programs is to lower the overall societal cost of greenhouse gas emissions reductions, it is crucial to design the national cap-and-trade system so that it inherently taps the lowest-cost emission reductions available to the economy. Efficient end-use technologies in buildings, industry, and transportation systems will provide the lowest-cost resources available to lower GHG emissions – *thus a central aim of cap-and-trade design must be to deliver end-use efficiency in diverse applications across buildings and industry, and in transportation systems nationwide.*

This document focuses on how a cap-and-trade system can be designed to accelerate investments in energy efficiency, which would permit more rapid carbon reductions at a lower cost to consumers and the American economy. The * * * key points:

(1) Energy efficiency is the low-cost equivalent of a "carbon scrubber" for homes and commercial buildings and for the electric power sector. Improved vehicle efficiency is also the lowest-cost means of reducing emissions from the transportation sector. It is the most important resource to look to as the bridge fuel to the low-carbon economy we need in coming decades;

(2) Energy efficiency is the *key to cost containment* in a GHG cap-and-trade program. Although adding a carbon price signal to the cost of electricity and heating fuels is necessary and will have some energy-efficiency benefits, cap-and-trade programs that try to reduce emissions through price alone will be much more costly per ton reduced than a cap-and-trade program that includes proven techniques to deliver low-cost efficiency resources. At the con-

sumer level, there are a number of well-documented and very serious market barriers to the cost-effective deployment of efficiency investments across the economy. For this reason, many low-cost savings opportunities remain untapped and higher power and fuel prices alone will not reduce demand nearly enough to meet our carbon goals. At the generator level, only a very high carbon price would make a meaningful change in the dispatch of the existing generation fleet. At the level of consumer demand and generation high prices required in the absence of efficiency programs to produce the deep reductions now called for by climate scientists would impose unnecessarily high costs on consumers and the economy;

(3) Careful cap-and-trade designs can contain the cost of GHG reductions by allocating allowances for consumer benefit and investing allowance values in programmatic efficiency measures. Congress should build on this state and regional experience by (a) auctioning allowances and investing auction revenues to improve the energy fitness of homes and businesses across the nation; (b) creating an "efficiency allocation" of carbon credits to the states and utilities, a portion of which is performance based; and (c) enacting complementary policies to promote cost-effective energy efficiency investments.

The Efficiency Reservoir is Large and Can be Tapped at Low Cost

National climate legislation will necessarily cover power and fuel use in buildings as major components of the move to a lower-emissions economy. Energy consumption in buildings, including direct consumption of electricity and fossil fuels, accounts for nearly half of all of the nation's GHG emissions.

The *emissions reduction potential from efficiency* in these sectors is also significant. * * * [T]he buildings sector provides one of the largest sources of GHG emission reductions occurring through efficiency actions. * * *[B]y 2030 energy efficiency from buildings, transportation and industry could account for 40% of the U.S. carbon dioxide emissions reduced by that year. There are now many studies documenting that with policy commitments, aggressive efficiency investments can meet most of the expected growth in U.S. energy demand. Accelerated energy efficiency technology development and deployment can arrest the growth in GHG emissions that would otherwise occur with continuing demand growth, especially in the power sector.

In addition to being quite large, the efficiency reservoir *can be tapped at low cost*. In electricity markets, the efficiency savings potential has been shown to be on the order of 25% of total electricity usage at a levelized cost of about three cents per kilowatt-hour (kWh). Using efficiency efforts with levelized costs above three cents per kWh but below the average cost of supply would yield additional savings. This is much less than the average national retail price of electricity, currently more than 8 cents per kWh. This is also less than the marginal generation cost of new power plants, estimated, depending on the technology, to cost 5 to 10 cents per kWh or more. Energy efficiency reduces the cost of cap-and-trade as less new energy facilities are needed and a smaller portion of existing facilities need to be upgraded to meet emissions ceilings. Energy efficiency is thus the equivalent of a low-cost "carbon scrubber" for the power sector.

And the efficiency resource grows with time, as new technologies become feasible in the market due to programs that overcome market barriers. These new technologies go beyond the potentials documented in the studies mentioned here.

Investing Carbon Credits in Efficiency–A GHG Cost-Containment Strategy

Recapturing and recycling generator and fuel price increases to consumers will lower the consumer cost of a carbon capture program. But in what form should those benefits be returned to consumers? Some consumer advocates propose that revenues from the sale of carbon credits should be returned to consumers in the form of rate rebates. For low-income households in particular, some form of direct transfer payments to offset increased costs may be a necessary component of the climate program. However, overall, direct consumer payments alone will not produce the best long-term results for consumers.

The best outcome for consumers as a whole, and the best way to lower the societal cost of carbon reduction, is *to invest substantial carbon credit revenues in low-carbon resources*—especially low-cost energy efficiency measures. There is solid evidence for this conclusion. As a general matter, well-designed efficiency programs can deliver five to seven times more GHG savings for a given rate increase, than the rate increase alone would have delivered.[20] At the same time, it reduces the burden on consumers of higher costs by lowering bills. * * *

[E]nergy efficiency and renewable energy investments could reduce the wholesale price of electricity under a greenhouse gas cap-and-trade system, since these investments, reduce demand for conventional resources, allowing

---

[20] Richard Cowart, *Carbon Caps and Energy Efficient Resources: How Climate Legislation Can Mobilize Efficiency and Lower the Cost of Greenhouse Gas Emission Reduction*, 33 Vt. L. Rev. 201, 212-15. (2008). This is a dramatic difference, but the explanation is straightforward. Demand for electricity is relatively inelastic, and market barriers to end-use efficiency block investments by building owners, tenants, and even industrial customers. On the other hand, efficiency standards and programs by utilities, governments, and industry consortia can deliver significant savings at costs well below the marginal cost of new power sources. Thus, consumer response to a given carbon price premium is relatively weak compared to reductions from codes, standards, and efficiency programs.

more expensive projects to be deferred or canceled. Moreover, efficiency as a zero-carbon resource also lowers the *demand for carbon permits*, lowering both the direct and indirect costs of carbon allowances on the power system.

In sum, cap-and-trade (and the price signal this will generate) addresses a market failure called externality costs, but other barriers to energy efficiency will cause underinvestment in energy efficiency. Additional market interventions will still be necessary to address other market barriers, such as split incentives and lack of information. Since energy efficiency is a low cost carbon abatement resource, the overall cost of abatement will be much lower if market barriers that lead to underinvestment in energy efficiency are addressed.

Notes and Questions

1. What would an energy efficiency resource standard look like? Would this be implemented by the traditional state public service commissions or the federal government? Can the federal government mandate that states use their own resources, laws, and administrative structures to implement an energy efficiency resource standard? Does this raise 10th Amendment issues? If it does, what alternative approaches are available to the federal government to institute an energy efficiency resource standard? Compare, Federal Energy Regulatory Comm. v. Mississippi, 456 U.S. 742 (1982) (holding constitutional a federal law that required state utility regulators to "consider" whether utilities subject to their jurisdiction should be required to adopt energy efficiency programs.) Although the state commissions were not obligated to impose any energy efficiency requirement, they were under a federal mandate to consider, formally, whether to do so) with New York v. United States, 505 U.S. 144 (1992) (holding unconstitutional under the 10th amendment a federal law that mandated that any state that fails to arrange for proper disposal of the low level radioactive wastes generated within the state to take ownership of those wastes.)

2. Does Congress have the power to impose energy efficiency building codes on new residential, commercial, or industrial buildings? What about on any modification of existing buildings? How would such a requirement be enforced? Could Congress make the code requirements a mandatory minimum condition to be included in every state or local building permit? Who would oversee and enforce this mandate? Could Congress authorize citizens to sue as private attorney generals to supplement federal enforcement?

3. If the federal government were to provide financial incentives to make new buildings more energy efficient, would the owners of these new buildings be in a better position financially, than an owner of a recently constructed building who voluntarily made that building as energy efficient, but without

the governmental subsidy? How do we avoid the problem of making no good deed go unpunished?

4.　What is the ultimate goal the law is seeking to achieve? What policy approaches does this proposal use and what legal tools and institutions does it anticipate using to get the job done? What other approaches are possible? What are the advantages and disadvantages of the different approaches? What is more important, the theoretical economic efficiency of the underlying policy or the practical considerations of implementation, verification and enforcement? Is there an inherent tension between these two concerns? This has been a long-standing debate in the environmental law arena. One view is that an inflexible system does maximize economic efficiency and may result in more expensive measures than is necessary to achieve the environmental goal. See, e.g., B. Ackerman & R. Stewart, Reforming Environmental Law: The Democratic Case for Market Incentives, 13 Colum. J. Envtl. L. 171 (1988). Others reject "excessive preoccupation with theoretical efficiency" in favor of the pragmatic effectiveness of uniform standards that can realistically be enforced to create a functioning legal system. See, e.g., H. Latin, Ideal Versus Real Regulatory Efficiency: Implementation of Uniform Standards and 'Fine Tuning' Regulatory Reforms, 37 Stan. L. Rev. 1267, 1270 (1985).

5.　According to the National Research Council, Energy Research at DOE: Was it Worth It? Energy Efficiency and Fossil Energy Research 1978 to 2000, the $1.6 billion of DOE investment in energy efficiency RD&D resulted in $30 billion in economic benefits; energy efficiency RD&D had a benefit to cost ratio of 19 to 1.

LAYING THE FOUNDATION FOR IMPLEMENTING A FEDERAL ENERGY EFFICIENCY RESOURCE STANDARD
Laura Furrey, Steven Nadel, and John Laitner
ACEEE Report Number E091, http://aceee.org (March 2009)

* * * The Cost of Energy

Electricity prices are usually expressed as cents per kilowatt-hour (kWh) on electricity bills, with prices varying by location. For example, in 2007, Idaho had the lowest residential electricity prices, at $0.0635/kWh, while Hawaii had the highest at over $0.24/kWh, with American residents, on average, paying about $0.11/kWh. These numbers may sound small, but the average American household uses 11,000 kWh in electricity every year, which brings energy costs to almost $1,200 every year ($100 per month). Even a small manufacturing plant with 50 employees may pay $250,000 or more each year for electricity. And our demand for energy continues to grow as our population and our use of electronic appliances and devices increases.

About ninety percent of electricity in the United States is generated by coal, natural gas, and nuclear power. If new demand for energy were to be met by new power plants, at a cost between 7.3 cents per kWh and 13.5 cents per kWh, energy prices would rise accordingly. And these values do not even take into account the cost of additional infrastructure (i.e., transmission and distribution lines) that will be required to get this electricity to consumers. * * *

Cheaper

At a cost of between 0 and 5 cents per kWh, with an average cost of about 3 cents per kWh, energy efficiency measures are a more cost-effective option. From the day they are installed, energy efficiency measures will reduce how much energy is used. Similar to the additional cost of new power plants discussed above, the cost of energy efficiency measures are added to your electricity rate, but, unlike new power plants, because you're using less energy overall, your monthly bills will be lower.

Faster

Energy efficiency is available immediately. New compact fluorescent light (CFL) bulbs or a new air conditioner can be installed in less than a day and adding new or extra insulation to a home may take about a week. By contrast, in addition to being more expensive, new coal-fired and nuclear power plants take much longer to permit and construct. The Energy Information Administration (EIA) estimates that lead times for these plants are 4–6 years. This time frame most likely does not include the years of delay often associated with construction of such power plants due to community opposition and regulatory uncertainty.

Cleaner

Energy efficiency measures reduce the amount of energy consumed and, as a result of less energy being consumed, less fossil fuels (such as coal and natural gas) are burned. As we decrease the amount of fossil fuels we burn for energy, we also decrease the harmful pollutants and greenhouse gas emissions that are emitted into our air. Additionally, conventional power plants have the added problem of community opposition—nobody wants a coal-fired power plant, let alone a nuclear power plant, in their backyard. Few people, however, are opposed to saving money and energy. * * *

Why Isn't Everybody Doing It?

Even though energy efficiency is the cheapest, fastest, and cleanest energy resource, there are a variety of reasons why it is not being implemented as widely as it could be.

Split Incentives

The term "split incentives" is often used to describe the situation where decisions about efficiency levels are made by people who will not be paying the electricity bills, such as landlords or developers of commercial office space. When the tenant, for example, is responsible for paying energy bills, there is little or no incentive for the landlord to increase his or her own expense to acquire efficient equipment (e.g., refrigerators, heaters, and light bulbs) because the landlord does not pay operating costs and will not reap the benefits of reducing those costs.

Upfront Costs and Financing

When the decisions about energy efficiency are made by those paying the bills, a common problem is lack of upfront capital. Even though a highly efficient refrigerator, for example, or replacing all of the inefficient light bulbs in your home, would save money in reduced energy costs, paying for these measures all at once may be beyond the reach for some consumers. Additionally, borrowing the money is beyond the reach for some consumers, such as low-income individuals and small business owners. These classes of customers are frequently unable to borrow at any price as the result of their economic status or credit-worthiness.

In the commercial/industrial sector, accounting procedures often carefully review capital costs, favoring the purchase of inexpensive equipment. Long term operating and maintenance costs, however, are generally less scrutinized. Furthermore, when operating costs are reduced, the savings typically show up in a corporate-level account and are rarely passed on to the department that made the decision and the investment. This diversion of benefits discourages energy-saving investments.

Lack of Awareness

Many customers, in all customer classes, tend to underestimate their energy consumption and, consequently, the associated environmental impacts of operating the equipment. Very often, they are not even aware that different models can consume significantly different amounts of energy and that buying more efficient products can lead to energy and utility bill savings. In the commercial/industrial sector, many purchasing decisions are made by purchasing or maintenance staff who are often unfamiliar with the relative efficiencies and operating costs of the equipment they purchase.

Emergency Decisions

Even when the purchaser is aware of variations in energy efficiency, often he or she is too busy or rushed to research the cost-effectiveness of a decision, or information on high-efficiency products is not readily available. This is most often seen in emergency purchases, as the consumer rushes to replace a broken water heater, furnace or refrigerator.

Limited Stocking of Efficient Products

Equipment distributors generally have limited storage space and tend to only stock equipment that is in high demand. This creates a "Catch-22" situation: when users purchase inefficient equipment distributors only stock inefficient equipment. Purchasing efficient equipment thus may require a special order, taking more time. As stated earlier, most equipment that fails needs to be replaced immediately. Thus, if efficient equipment is not in stock, even customers who want efficient equipment are often stuck purchasing standard equipment.

Efficiency Bundled into Premium Products Only

Manufacturers will often produce two versions of the same product line: one commodity-grade and the other value-added. The commodity-grade line is the basic model and, typically, meets the minimum efficiency standards. The value-added line includes improved efficiency and other extra, non-energy features at a significantly higher cost than the basic model. A portion of the extra cost is for the improved efficiency but a majority of the extra cost is for the added "bells and whistles." Consumers desiring improved efficiency without the extra features usually purchase the commodity-grade model to save costs.

Manufacturer Price Competition

Since manufacturers are competing to have more of their company's products in the market, if a manufacturer voluntarily increases efficiency in the basic (commodity-grade) product line, they may find it impossible to pass on even small product cost increases to consumers without risking loss of market share. This is because all of the other manufacturers' basic product lines will be available at a lower cost and most customers only look at the initial, upfront cost of the product. In contrast, mandatory standards ensure a level playing field for all manufacturers.

Regulatory Barriers

There are also a variety of regulatory barriers that further limit * * * energy efficiency products. Utility practices, which vary not only by state but also by individual utility, often employ backup tariffs, which are charges to ensure available power should the customers' system fail, excessive liability insurance, and restrictions on connecting distributed energy sources to the grid. These challenges limit combined heat and power (CHP) installations and distributed generation investments and continue to limit the viability of such projects.

Moving Beyond the Barriers with a Federal Standard

At the state level, there has been continual progress in pushing energy efficiency past these well-known market barriers and increasing the amount of energy "acquired" through energy efficiency. * * * In recent years, one of the most effective and widely used policies has been state-based Energy Efficiency Resource Standards (EERS).

What Is an EERS?

An EERS is a law requiring the use of energy efficiency, usually specifying how much energy needs to be saved per year. An EERS is similar in concept to a renewable electricity standard (RES). An RES requires utilities to obtain a certain amount of energy from renewable resources (wind, solar, biomass, etc.) while an EERS requires electric utilities and natural gas distributors to attain a required level of efficiency savings. The savings are "required" because, at the state level, the state legislature approves the standard which becomes state law once it is signed by the governor. Failure to comply with the law typically results in penalties, generally specified in the legislation. At the federal level, Congress would need to pass the EERS which would then be signed into law by the President. * * *

How Does an EERS Work?

An EERS typically specifies how much energy the state or utilities need to save, either on an annual basis or on a cumulative basis, or both. Savings targets are usually expressed as a percent of energy sales (the baseline) and slowly increase over time. The most current federal proposals for an EERS state the cumulative energy savings targets and implies the annual incremental values * * *. It is useful to express the standard in cumulative terms, 15% electricity savings and 10% natural gas savings by 2020, to provide an incentive for long-lived and well maintained energy-saving measures. Most efficiency measures installed in early years will continue to save energy throughout the compliance period.

How Are Savings Targets Set?

The proposed savings targets build on various studies that demonstrate significant available cost effective savings at the state level and on actual savings targets being achieved in states with experience implementing an EERS. Various analyses conducted by ACEEE suggest that, at the state level, efficiency gains on the order of 20%-30% are achievable by 2025. These studies recommend a broad suite of energy policies and programs, which if implemented, could lead to cost-effective reductions in projected future use of electricity from conventional sources. These recommendations typically include adoption of an EERS, expanded Demand Response initiatives, policies supporting CHP, manufacturing initiatives, state and local government facilities initiatives, more stringent appliance and equipment efficiency standards and building codes, enhanced research, development and deployment strategies, consumer outreach and education, and low-income efficiency programs.

The EERS represents the core of these policies, providing a foundation upon which the other polices may be layered to achieve the greatest savings. Implementing these types of policies and programs could, for example, lead to energy savings of 29% in Florida, 22% in Texas, 19% in Virginia, and 29% in Maryland. As [ACEEE] reports document, there are plenty of cost-effective energy efficiency and demand response opportunities throughout the states. However, these opportunities will not be realized without changes in policies and programs in each state.

The federal EERS will enhance these states' efforts, calling for national policy and program changes. * * *

Although the "low-hanging fruit" may be reached in earlier years, greater investments in energy efficiency can lead to greater energy savings such that continually meeting higher incremental targets is achievable. For example, Efficiency Vermont achieved approximately 20,000 megawatt-hours (MWh) in energy savings in 2000, the first year of implementation. Energy savings grew steadily over time, reaching 55,000 MWh in 2006. In that year, Efficiency Vermont received an increase in funding from the Vermont Public Service Board. As a result of that increased investment, energy savings jumped from about 55,000 MWh in 2006 to 103,000 MWh saved in 2007, completely offsetting the underlying electric load growth rate in Vermont. Additionally, these later savings generated the most cost effective returns to date. The yield was 53 MWh saved per $10,000 invested in 2007 compared to a yield of about 40 MWh saved per $10,000 invested in 2006.

The proposed ramp-up in energy savings is, therefore, a valid model to use at the national level as increasing energy savings are achievable at decreasing costs. This is even more true as new, breakthrough energy-efficient technologies make their way to the market and heightened building codes and equipment standards are taken into account. * * *

How Are Savings Actually Achieved?

At the state level, the state Public Utilities Commission (PUC) or other designated state authority, which oversees electric utilities and natural gas distributors, crafts rules clarifying how the EERS will be implemented and administered and how savings will be measured. Typically, electric utilities and natural gas distributors file plans with the PUC describing the proposed energy efficiency programs and how such programs are designed to achieve the required savings. At the federal level, the Department of Energy would retain oversight for implementation of the standard. The federal bill [would] leave administration to states that are willing and able and it is anticipated that most states will choose to do so.

In practice, utilities, and, in some cases, non-utility state programs, implement and administer energy efficiency programs which help consumers reduce energy use. Many energy efficiency programs utilize energy audits, which help identify where energy efficiency measures will have the biggest impact in homes and businesses, and rebates, which can help customers pay for energy efficiency measures. Rebates are usually offered for highly energy-efficient appliances such as air conditioners, water heaters, furnaces, and lighting. Incentives are also available for home retrofits, such as improving home insulation to increase energy savings. Low-interest loans may also be incorporated to help end-users afford high efficiency appliances and home retrofits. Marketing, education, technical assistance and working with trade allies are also important aspects of end-user efficiency programs. Some utilities also provide incentives to distributors and suppliers for stocking high-efficiency products, negotiate purchase price buy-downs for efficient equipment with suppliers and retailers.

Sometimes, combined heat and power (CHP) systems and other high-efficiency distributed generation systems savings may be used to meet the savings targets. CHP systems produce power (e.g., electricity) and usable thermal energy (e.g., steam) from a single fuel source to meet energy needs at or near the location of the CHP system. The thermal energy displaces locally produced energy from a separate system (e.g., a boiler) and the power usually displaces electricity delivered by the utility. By combining the two systems and utilizing one fuel source, inherent inefficiencies in power generation and transmission can be substantially reduced, improving the overall fuel conversion efficiency. Savings from CHP systems are credited to the extent energy is saved relative to conventional power generation of power and steam.

Distribution system efficiency improvements can also count toward the savings target goal. * * * [P]ossible improvements include improved transformers and voltage controls or new conductors and wires that lower energy losses.

At the state level, savings from state and local building codes and state and federal equipment efficiency standards is generally not included in the state's energy savings targets. Some states with very aggressive savings targets include savings from codes and standards. At the federal level credit is given for savings from state and local building codes and state and federal equipment efficiency standards. ACEEE estimates that, of the total 15% electricity and 10% natural gas savings targets, approximately 5% electricity and 3% natural gas savings can be met through codes and standards by 2020. For an electric utility or a natural gas distributor to claim savings from building codes and equipment efficiency standards, the utility must have played a significant role in achieving the savings. Generally, the more energy efficiency measures eligible for savings, the higher the targets should be. * * *

What if a Utility Cannot Achieve the Prescribed Savings?

If a retail electric utility or natural gas distributor cannot achieve the required energy savings, there [could be] various flexibility mechanisms incorporated in the federal EERS. A utility that is unable to meet the standard may enter into a bilateral contract with a nearby over-achieving utility to purchase or transfer savings. A utility may also contract with an energy service company (companies that provide financing and/or installation of energy efficient equipment and processes) or with the state to meet the performance standard. Such transfers may occur in-state or to nearby states in the same power pool with state regulator permission. * * *

[A] retail electric utility or natural gas distributor also [would] ha[ve] the option of paying for the savings under the alternative compliance payment provision. If the federal EERS is being implemented by the state, a utility that cannot achieve the prescribed savings targets can pay the state $0.05 per kWh of electricity savings or $5 per million Btu of natural gas savings needed to make up any deficit with regard to the savings target. Any payments received by the state must be used to administer cost-effective energy efficiency programs in an attempt to make up for the lost savings on the part of the utility.

A penalty may be assessed against a retail electric utility or a natural gas distributor that fails to either achieve the specified savings target or make an alternative compliance payment. The proposed federal penalties are set at $0.10 per kWh of electricity savings shortfall and $10 per million Btu of missing natural gas savings. Penalties are higher than alternative compliance payments to encourage utilities to proactively use energy efficiency programs or the alternative compliance payment and minimize penalty situations. * * *

States Leading By Example

* * * Texas became the first state to establish an EERS in 1999, requiring electric utilities to offset 10% of load growth through end-use energy efficiency. After several years of meeting this goal at low costs, in 2007 the legislature increased the standard to 15% of load growth by 2009, 20% of load growth by 2010. A recent report commissioned by the Public Utilities Commission of Texas found that raising the goal to 50% of load growth is feasible.

As of 2000, Efficiency Vermont, an independent "efficiency utility" that delivers efficiency programs for the state, is contractually required to achieve energy and demand goals. Efficiency Vermont cumulatively met over 7% of Vermont's electricity requirements by the end of 2007 with 2007 programs alone met 1.7% of the state's electricity needs. The state's goals were recently updated to 2.0% per year through 2011.

In 2004, California set energy savings goals for investor-owned utilities for 2004 through 2013, which were expected to save more than 1% of total forecast electricity sales per year. In the early years, savings were less than 1% per year, but in 2007, measures installed that year met more than 1.5% of the state's electricity needs. In July 2008, the California PUC established new targets for energy savings for the years 2012 through 2020 for its regulated utilities. The new goals are expected to provide approximately 5% energy savings over that period. * * *

[Other states that have adopted laws setting energy savings standards are Hawaii, Pennsylvania, Connecticut, Nevada, Washington, Colorado, Minnesota, Virginia, Illinois, North Carolina, New York, New Mexico, Maryland, Ohio, Michigan, Iowa. Several other states, including Massachusetts, New Jersey, and Rhode Island are now actively considering similar policies.]

Electricity and Natural Gas Savings

A national EERS at these levels would produce electricity savings of 364 billion kWh and natural gas savings of 794 trillion Btu. This level of savings would offset currently projected electricity and natural gas load growth over the 2011–2020 period (EIA 2009). * * * The energy saved through the proposed federal EERS could power over 48 million households in 2020, accounting for about 36% of the households in the United States. Alternatively, this is more than enough energy to provide power to California and all of New England for that year.

One of the more compelling illustrations of an energy efficiency analysis is the number of power plants that can be avoided by achieving energy savings. This estimate utilizes peak demand savings to determine the number of power plants avoided. Power plants are needed to meet peak demand, and as such, peak demand is used as a prime rationale for constructing new power plants. To find the number of power plants prevented, the value of peak demand savings is divided by the capacity of an average, medium sized power plant—300 MW. It is estimated that peak demand will be reduced by approximately 117,000 MW by implementing the proposed federal EERS. This is roughly the equivalent of 390 power plants that will not be built.

Costs and Savings

By 2020, under the proposed federal EERS, customers will have invested approximately $78.5 billion in energy efficiency measures. This level of investment will yield almost $170 billion in net benefits as a result of energy efficiency measures installed in 2020.26 "Net benefits" are the total savings gained from energy efficiency measures minus the program costs and investments associated with the measures.

These benefits average about $1,280 in savings per household from efficiency measures installed by 2020. * * *

Avoided Carbon Dioxide Emissions

Another important metric is the amount of carbon dioxide emissions that have been prevented by energy savings. In 2020, carbon dioxide emissions will be reduced by 262 MMT—the equivalent of taking almost 48 million automobiles off the road for that year. [The estimate assumes that the average is driven] 2,000 vehicle miles are traveled per year, that average vehicle fuel economy is 20 miles per gallon, and that 20 lbs of carbon dioxide are emitted per gallon of fuel in the U.S. There are 2,204.6 pounds per metric ton. With these assumptions each car emits about 5.44 metric tons of carbon dioxide equivalent. * * *

Almost fifty percent of electricity comes from coal. As electricity use drops, so does the amount of coal being burned at the power plant. The need for additional power plants is also reduced. In addition to reduced carbon dioxide emissions discussed above, an EERS can help reduce sulfur oxides (SOx) and nitrogen oxides (NOx) which have also been found harmful to our environment. Additional environmental harms associated with coal combustion include mercury, asthma, tuberculosis, and other problems associated with lung diseases. In fact, the major source of mercury in the air is the combustion of coal at power plants. * * *

Notes and Questions

1. Why should the states who have already adopted energy efficiency standards and policies, and especially those states that have already made substantial investments in energy efficiency be interested in a federal standard? Would it make a difference if the standard were voluntary or mandatory?

2. Should the federal government set a minimum energy efficiency standard or target that each state must reach? If so, how should the Congress design the legislation? Can a federal statute order states to adopt or meet such targets or standards? Can it use the spending clause of Article 1, Sec. 8 of the Constitution? Should Congress use a federal agency to implement and enforce the requirement? If so, what agency? Will it need to create a new agency or modify the powers of an existing agency? Would EPA be a better

choice than the Federal Energy Regulatory Commission ("FERC")?

3. "Based on 2007 economic accounts for the U.S., electric and natural gas utilities support approximately 7 direct and indirect jobs per million dollars of revenue. All other sectors of the economy support about 17 direct and indirect jobs per million dollars of revenue. Subsequently, as a result of energy savings, every $1 million in lost revenue in the electric and natural gas industry supports, on average, 7 fewer jobs in the economy. But if businesses and consumers have a savings of $1 million, an average of 17 jobs is gained. In this case the economy is better off by 10 net jobs on the positive side of the ledger." L. Furrey, S. Nadel, & J. Laitner, Laying the Foundation for Implementing Federal Energy Efficiency Standard, ACEEE Report Number E091, (March 2009) http://aceee.org

E. FEDERALISM AND RELATED CONSTITUTIONAL ISSUES

Many state governments are already actively pursuing climate change policies designed to reduce GHG emissions. California has been an aggressive leader both in setting ambitious goals and in developing concrete actions to meet those goals. By 2004 it had already inventoried all its GHG sources and sinks and had proposed GHG standards for motor vehicles, has proposed a broad range of climate change related regulations (see Ch. 6 for coverage of the motor vehicle standards and Clean Air Act), and even published a list of many hundreds of actions that could be taken immediately. For information on California, see its Climate Change Portal, http://www.climatechange.ca.gov/.

In the east, 10 states, after extensive, complex and difficult negotiations instituted the Regional Greenhouse Gas Initiative, the first mandatory, market based CO_2 trading program; its aim is to cap and then reduce CO_2 emissions from the power sector 10% by 2018. It has been in operation since the fall of 2008 and has already conducted a number of auctions of emission allowances. Although the price of each allowance (good for one ton of CO_2) has been low at a little over $3 per ton, it has generated millions of dollars for each of the states to use for renewable energy and energy efficiency investments. See http://www.rggi.org/home. In H.R. 2454, Congress would prohibit these regional trading regimes, which would eliminate this revenue stream that early acting states had created. How should the relationship between the federal government and states be organized to best address climate change?

STATE LAW RESPONSES TO GLOBAL WARMING: IS IT
CONSTITUTIONAL TO THINK GLOBALLY AND ACT LOCALLY?
David R. Hodas
21 Pace Environmental Law Review 53 (2003)

* * * Defining the scope of federal legislative power, and prohibitions on
the use of that power, of the United States and the several states is only the
beginning of our analysis of whether state laws affecting GHG emissions are
constitutional. Where valid federal law and state law conflict, the Constitution declares the rule, which shall be obeyed by all judges, that the federal
law is the "supreme law of the land" despite any state law to the contrary.
Thus, absent a conflict between federal and state law, or a state law that violates one of the limited set of constitutional prohibitions, states faced no other
explicit federal constitutional constraint.

However, state power has also been constrained by judicially articulated
federalism doctrines derived from the structure of the Constitution, not its
explicit language. From the Supremacy Clause comes the preemption doctrine, which preempts state laws that Congress expressly preempts, when
federal law occupies the field, or where the law, generally or as applied, ob-
structs a federal law from achieving its purpose. Another judicially announced federalism limitation on state power has been derived from the
Commerce Clause. Known as the dormant commerce clause, this doctrine
bars any otherwise valid state laws that discriminate against interstate
commerce or unduly burden interstate commerce. * * *

A third federalism limit on state power is the foreign affairs power, which
resides in the President's fundamental executive powers, as well as in certain
powers granted to Congress, such as the power to regulate commerce with
foreign nations, to declare war, raise and maintain military forces, ratify
treaties and approve international agreements, establish rules for immigration and naturalization, fund foreign aid programs, and to participate in international institutions such as the United Nations, the World Bank, the International Monetary Fund, and the North American Treaty Organization
(NATO). * * * In the context of GHG regulations to stem global warming,
where states are thinking globally, but acting locally, we must consider
whether federal law preempts these efforts, violates the dormant commerce
clause, or unconstitutionally limits the foreign affairs power of the President.
* * *

[T]he Court originally developed the dormant commerce clause to restrict
states from interfering with or discriminating against interstate commerce,
even where Congress was silent. Thus, even when Congress had not regulated or addressed a particular interstate commerce concern, states were restricted in the scope of their activities. This long-standing doctrine is consistent with the nationalist concerns of the framers, who abandoned the Articles

of Confederation in large part because of state restrictions on the free flow of commerce. * * *

[F]ederalism limits on state GHG statutes might emerge from the dormant commerce clause. Dormant commerce clause concerns might be acute when states are regulating electric utilities by favoring in-state resources over out-of-state fuels, or by discriminating against out-of-state electricity generators over in-state suppliers. However, states may legitimately use their traditional power to regulate natural electricity monopolies without violating the dormant commerce clause, even if out-of-state suppliers of electricity may incidentally be adversely affected. Thus, a state may impose an externality valuation in regulating utilities, so long as the valuation does not discriminate against interstate commerce or out-of-state interests. Nor may state regulatory control of electric utilities be used to impair trading of SO_2 emissions allowances under the Clean Air Act, even if a downwind state believes that trades by in-state utilities to utilities in up-wind states will have a direct, adverse impact on air quality in the down-wind state. Thus, unless state statutes, regulations, or administrative orders that require consideration of GHG emissions effects (which may occur outside the states borders) in integrated resource planning and rate-making are designed to discriminate against interstate commerce or unduly burden interstate commerce they would not appear to raise dormant commerce clause questions. * * *

The dormant commerce clause, derived from the Commerce Clause and historic federalism imperatives when the nation was founded, is sufficiently developed and detailed to be considered its own doctrine. It could also be viewed, at least at a conceptual level, to be a category of constitutional law that might be called "federalism preemption;" i.e., the Supremacy Clause operates on the dormant commerce clause to invalidate (preempt) state laws that offend the dormant commerce clause. The Supremacy Clause is the essential federalism dictate of the Constitution of 1787. It announces the general rule that federal law is the supreme law of the land. It is the Supremacy Clause which has always provided the rule of decision, now generally located in the preemption doctrine, when state law and federal statutory or regulatory law collide.

As a working rule, the preemption doctrine is straightforward:

> Preemption may be either expressed or implied and "is compelled whether Congress' command is explicitly stated in the statute's language or implicitly contained in its structure and purpose." Absent explicit preemptive language, we have recognized at least two types of implied pre-emption: field preemption, where the scheme of federal regulation is "so pervasive as to make reasonable the inference that Congress left no room for the States to supplement it," and conflict pre-emption, where "compliance with both federal and state regula-

tions is a physical impossibility," or where state law "stands as an obstacle to the accomplishment and execution of the full purposes and objectives of Congress."

* * * This leads us to the question of whether state and local legislative initiatives to address global warming are valid within our constitutional system. The question can be analyzed at several levels. The first is whether any of the specific state laws are preempted by federal statutes. Clearly, if a state statute conflicts with federal statute, the state statute is preempted. So, for instance, a Massachusetts law (the so-called Burma Law) enacted to support human rights and democracy in Burma by barring state agencies from purchasing goods and services from Burma was unconstitutional because it conflicted with a subsequent federal statute which imposed sanctions on Burma, and authorized the President to impose further sanctions. The Massachusetts law, more stringent and rigid than Congress' enactment, was "an obstacle to the accomplishment of Congress's [sic] full objectives under the federal Act." * * *

We turn now to consider whether state and local laws addressing global warming and greenhouse gases offend the Constitution by intruding on the foreign affairs power of the federal government. Certainly, duly ratified treaties and the federal statutes that implement them are the supreme law of the land. As such, they preempt conflicting state laws.

Nor does the Tenth Amendment provide refuge for a state. For instance, in Missouri v. Holland, [252 U.S. 416 (1920)] a Missouri game warden sued the United States to enjoin enforcement of the federal Bird Treaty Act of 1918, which had to be enacted into law to meet the United States promises under the Migratory Bird Treaty of 1918. Missouri argued that the "statute is an unconstitutional interference with the rights reserved to the States under the Tenth Amendment," namely Missouri's traditional police power to regulate hunting of wild animals in the state. Justice Holmes presented the federalism questions and how to decide it:

> [W]hen we are dealing with words that are also a constituent act, like the Constitution ... we must realize that they have called into life a being the development of which could not have been foreseen completely by the most gifted of its begetters. It was enough for them to realize and hope that they had created an organism; it has taken a century and has cost their successors much sweat and blood to prove that they created a nation. The case before us must be considered in light of our whole experience and not merely in that of what was said a hundred years ago. The treaty in question does not contravene any prohibitory words to be found in the Constitution. The only question is whether it is forbidden by some invisible radiation from the general terms of the Tenth Amendment. We must consider what that nation

has become in deciding what that Amendment has reserved.

Justice Holmes then held that the treaty and statute preempt the state's police power to regulate hunting within the state. As to the Tenth Amendment, the Court dismissed Missouri's claim that it owned these wild, migratory birds (at least while they were in Missouri) or that the Tenth Amendment protected its putative ownership.

Holmes articulated the relationship between national and state interests:

> We see nothing in the Constitution that compels the Government to sit by while a food supply is cut off and the protectors of our forests and our crops are destroyed. It is not sufficient to rely on the States. The reliance is in vain, and were it otherwise, the question is whether the United States is forbidden to act. We are of the opinion that the treaty and statute must be upheld.

Thus, the Tenth Amendment provides no federalism limit on the treaty power, even though, "no agreement with a foreign nation can confer power on the Congress, or on any other branch of Government, which is free from the restraints of the Constitution." Presumably, the Court was here referring to protections of individual rights guaranteed by the Constitution. Justice Black later explicitly confirmed Justice Holmes' view that the Tenth Amendment provides no such constraints:

> [In Missouri v. Holland] the Court carefully noted that the treaty involved was not inconsistent with any specific provision of the Constitution. The Court was concerned with the Tenth Amendment which reserves to the States or the people all power not delegated to the National Government. To the extent that the United States can validly make treaties, the people and the States have delegated their power to the National Government and the Tenth Amendment is no barrier. [*Reid v. Covert*, 354 U.S. 1, 16 (1957)] * * *

The final question to examine is whether the various state GHG laws and initiatives offend the Foreign Affairs powers of the President or Congress under the Constitution because they reflect a state response to an international problem that offends the federalism balance of powers that the Framers' built into the Constitution. Although the Court has had the opportunity to answer this question, it has declined to do so. Instead, it appears to be developing a doctrine of foreign affairs preemption, although the specifics of the doctrine, the boundaries of its coverage, and even its existence are uncertain. This issue has not been directly addressed by the Supreme Court in the few foreign affairs federalism cases it has considered. Most foreign affairs cases considered the issues through the lens of separation of powers among the three branches of the federal government. Even then, the Court has tended to not resolve the constitutional issue by deeming it to be a political question, better resolved by Congress and the President.

Notes and Questions

1. For a more detailed analysis of the dormant commerce clause and federalism in the electricity context, see K. Engel, The Dormant Commerce Clause Threat to Market-Based Environmental Regulation: The Case of Electricity Deregulation, 26 Ecology L.Q. 243 (1999). See generally W. Andreen, Federal Climate Change Legislation and Preemption, 3 Envtl. & Energy L. & Policy J. 26 (2008); K. Engel, Whither Subnational Climate Change Initiatives in the Wake of Federal Climate Legislation, Publius: The Journal of Federalism (2009); S. Ferrey, Goblets of Fire: Potential Constitutional Impediments to the Regulation of Global Warming, 35 Ecology L.Q. 835 (2008); A. Klass, State Innovation and Preemption: Lessons from State Climate Change Efforts, 41 Loy. L.A. L. Rev. 1653 (2008); L. McAllister, Regional Climate Regulation: From State Competition to State Collaboration, 1 San Diego J. of Climate & En. L. (No. 1 2009).

2. Dormant foreign affairs preemption of state laws is, at best, an unclear doctrine. The Supreme Court remains conflicted. For instance, now retired Justice Souter, writing for the majority in Am. Ins. Ass'n v. Garamendi, 539 U.S. 396, 419 (2003), noted "it is a fair question whether respect for the executive foreign relations power requires a categorical choice between the contrasting theories of field and conflict preemption ... but the question requires no answer here." In contrast, Justice Ginsburg, dissenting, was of the view that "we would reserve foreign affairs preemption for circumstances where the President, acting under statutory or constitutional authority, has spoken clearly to the issue at hand. '[T]he Framers did not make the judiciary the overseer of our government.' And judges should not be the expositors of the Nation's foreign policy, which is the role they play by acting when the President himself has not taken a clear stand. As I see it, courts step out of their proper role when they rely on no legislative or even executive text, but only on inference and implication, to preempt state laws on foreign affairs grounds." Id. at 442-43. For more analysis of the confusion in this area, see The Supreme Court, 2002 Term: Leading Cases, 117 Harv. L. Rev. 226, 235 (2003) (arguing that the dormant foreign affairs preemption concept is incoherent and deserves "burial").

3. The Supreme Court has a long history of ruling that matters related to foreign affairs are non-justiciable political questions, e.g., Oetjen v. Central Leather Co., 246 U.S. 297 (1918), although the Court has ruled on the merits with respect to whether the President has the power to enter into executive agreements instead of treaties. See also Dames & Moore v. Regan, 453 U.S. 654 (1981). As to whether the subject matter of a treaty is constitutional, see

Missouri v. Holland, 252 U.S. 416 (1920). On the other hand, the Supreme Court has held to the political questions disputes about: a) when a "war" begins or ends, a power vested exclusively in Congress in Commercial Trust Co. v. Miller, 262 U.S. 51, 57 (1923); b) recognition of foreign governments or Indian tribes in United States v. Blemont, 301 U.S. 324 (1937), and United States v. Sandoval, 231 U.S. 28, 45-46 (1913); and c) the validity, ratification, and interpretation of treaties in Goldwater v. Carter, 444 U.S. 996 (1979).

Although the Supreme Court has not addressed the issue, federal courts have applied the reasoning behind these rulings to find that disputes over the President's exercise of war powers are political questions. See Holtzman v. Schlesinger, 484 F.2d 1307, 1309 (2d Cir. 1973), cert. denied, 416 U.S. 936 (1974) (challenge to Vietnam War); Crockett v. Reagan, 720 F.2d 1355 (D.C. Cir. 1983), cert. denied, 467 U.S. 1251 (1984) (challenge to President's use of the military in El Salvador); Ange v. Bush, 752 F. Supp. 509 (D.D.C. 1990) (challenge to the first Iraq war). The application of the political question doctrine has been the subject of vigorous scholarly debate. See, e.g., M. Redish, Judicial Review and the Political Question, 79 Nw. U.L. Rev. 1031 (1985); L. Henkin, Vietnam in the Courts of the United States: Political Questions, 63 Am. J. Int'l L. 284 (1969).

4.   For a 50-state survey of state climate change responses, go to http://www.abanet.org/abapubs/globalclimate/.

F. FOSSIL FUELS

Fossil fuels remain the dominant source of energy for both electricity and transportation in the U.S. As the chart below indicates, the choice of which fossil fuel to use has significant climate change implications. For example, to get the same energy from natural gas as from coal will lower CO_2 emissions by 84%. Petroleum is also lower in carbon per unit of energy than coal.

As a result, one approach to mitigating climate change might be to switch from coal to natural gas for generating electricity. Is there sufficient natural gas to make a difference? How expensive would natural gas be if it is used extensively to generate electricity? Natural gas is a valuable fuel for heating homes, which it can do efficiently and cleanly. It is also an important raw material for the plastics industry and for other uses. Some people have said that it is too valuable to waste on making electricity. Others see it as an important transitional fuel to employ as with making the transition to a low-carbon economy. Combined cycle gas generators are about double the efficiency of typical coal-fired power plants. There may also be considerable quantities of natural gas under the United States, although the U.S. imports large quantities. A formation, Marcellus shale, in western Pennsylvania and New York is believed to have enormous amounts of gas trapped within. See http://www.eia.doe.gov/oil_gas/natural_gas/info_glance/natural_gas.html.

However, drilling in the formation is exceedingly difficult; the rock is so hard that only very high-pressure water in very large quantities can cut into it. N.Y. State Dept. of Environmental Conservation, Gas Well Drilling in the Marcellus Shale. http://www.dec.ny.gov/energy/46288.html.

CARBON DIOXIDE EMISSION FACTORS

(Million metric tons CO_2 per quadrillion Btu)

<u>EMISSIONS COEFFICIENTS</u>

PETROLEUM	
Crude Oil	74.54
Motor Gasoline(A)	70.88
Jet Fuel	70.88
Kerosene	72.31
COAL	
Coal Electric Power	94.70
NATURAL GAS	53.06
BIOFUELS	
Wood	0.00
Waste Energy	0.00
Alcohol Fuels	65.95

For every unit of energy obtained from natural gas, coal produces 84% more CO_2, gasoline 34% more, and alcohol fuels 24% more. Thus, just by switching fuels to get the same heat output, GHG emissions can be substantially changed.

Source: U.S. E.I.A., www.eia.doe.gov/environment.html

One of the central questions in the arena of climate change mitigation is what do we do about existing and future coal-fired power plants. We consider this question here; in Chapter 6 we address coal again in the context of geologic sequestration.

A BRIEF HISTORY OF COAL USE
United States Department of Energy (2009)
http://www.fossil.energy.gov/education/energylssons/coal/coal_
history.html

Coal is the most plentiful fuel in the fossil family and it has the longest and, perhaps, the most varied history. Coal has been used for heating since the cave man. Archeologists have also found evidence that the Romans in England used it in the second and third centuries (100-200 AD).

In the 1700s, the English found that coal could produce a fuel that burned cleaner and hotter than wood charcoal. However, it was the over-whelming need for energy to run the new technologies invented during the Industrial Revolution that provided the real opportunity for coal to fill Its first role as a dominant worldwide supplier of energy.

In North American, the Hopi Indians during the 1300s in what is now the U.S. Southwest used coal for cooking, heating and to bake the pottery they made from clay. Coal was later rediscovered in the United States by explorers in 1673. However, commercial coal mines did not start operation until the 1740s in Virginia.

The Industrial Revolution played a major role in expanding the use of coal. A man named James Watt invented the steam engine which made it possible for machines to do work previously done by humans and animals. Mr. Watt used coal to make the steam to run his engine.

During the first half of the 1800s, the Industrial Revolution spread to the United States. Steamships and steam-powered railroads were becoming the chief forms of transportation, and they used coal to fuel their boilers.

In the second half of the 1800s, more uses for coal were found.

During the Civil War, weapons factories were beginning to use coal. By 1875, coke (which is made from coal) replaced charcoal as the primary fuel for iron blast furnaces to make steel.

The burning of coal to generate electricity is a relative newcomer in the long history of this fossil fuel. It was in the 1880s when coal was first used to generate electricity for homes and factories.

Long after homes were being lighted by electricity produced by coal, many of them continued to have furnaces for heating and some had stoves for cooking that were fueled by coal. * * *

Notes and Questions

1. As of 2006, electric utilities consumed 92 percent of the coal mined in the United States. See also Appalachian Voices v. State Corp. Comm'n, 30 ELR 20092 (Va. April 17, 2009) (upholding the Virginia statutory requirement that Virginia coal-fired power plants use Virginia coal).

2. Coal-fired power plants use coal combustion to produce steam, which then drives a turbine to produce electricity. The combustion process is a major source of air pollutants, including 67 percent of the sulfur dioxide (SO_2), 23 percent of the nitrogen oxides (NO_X), 33 percent of the mercury, and 38 percent of the carbon dioxide from energy related sources. In addition, power

plants are responsible for about half of the fine particulate matter in many parts of the U.S., a major source for respiratory problems, heart and lung disease, and haze. Coal-fired power plants are also the largest U.S. source of developmental and neurological air toxics, ranking 5 out of 87 in sources of air toxins based on a 1998 Toxins Release Inventory data.

COAL-FIRED POWER PLANT REGULATION

In light of climate change and due to the lack of development of CO_2 standards by the EPA for coal fired power plants, some state legislatures have decided to take control of CO_2 emissions on their own. For example, in November 2007, Washington State's Energy Facility Siting Council rejected the proposed Kalama coal-fired power plant for failing to include carbon sequestration as required by a new Washington state law. Plans for the plant were subsequently abandoned in favor of a possible gas-fired plant at the same location.

A full year later on November 13, 2008, the EPA'S Environmental Appeals Board (EAB) in response to a petition from the Sierra Club issued a formal decision calling into question whether a best available control technology (BACT) analysis was required for CO_2 during a major new source review. In its petition, the Sierra Club argued that acid rain provisions require CO_2 monitoring, thus CO_2 is already subject to CAA regulation and should be protected against in new source reviews. The EPA response that CO_2 is not a pollutant subject to regulation under CAA, unless substantive emission control requirements applied and that the acid rain provision requiring CO_2 monitoring, while proposed, was never actually incorporated into implemented CAA standards. The EAB remanded the case to the EPA to document their reasoning behind not requiring BACT for CO_2.

On December 18, 2008, EPA Administrator Stephen Johnson responded to this remand repeating EPA's conclusion that CO_2 is not subject to regulation under the CAA. Mr. Johnson found that a pollutant is not a regulated New Source Review (NSR) pollutant unless there is a standard in place requiring actual emissions control of that pollutant. Furthermore, Title IV power plants are already required to monitor and report CO_2 to EPA quarterly. However, simply monitoring or reporting a pollutant does not make it a NSR pollutant. In addition, an endangerment finding does not constitute regulation under CAA; until control standard is issued, CO_2 is not a regulated NSR pollutant. However, despite this rejection of CO_2's regulation under the CAA, EPA's response opened the door that major source status could be determined in the future for CO_2. If applied to its full implication, facilities with moderate sized commercial water heaters would even be considered major sources for CO_2 thus requiring major new source review. The entire official response can be found at: //www.epa.gov/nsr/documents/psd_interpretive_memo_12.18.08.pdf.

The story continued when on January 12, 2009, EPA issued a rule to revamp the NSR, which states when coal-fired power plants expand or modernize and calculate their emissions, plants need not add in emissions from unrelated activities at the same plant. In a supporting statement, Robert Meyeres, EPA's deputy assistant administrator, said it did not make sense to count distinct projects together if there is no substantial economic and technical relationship between the projects. Critics argued that this ruling would allow for facility expansion without limitations on additional emissions resulting from the expansion.

During that same month on January 20, 2009, but under the guidance of the Obama Administration which took office that very same day, President Obama's Chief of Staff Rahm Emanuel issued a memorandum directing all agencies to cease any new regulations signed by Johnson but not yet published in the Federal Register. Environmentalists hoped this was a sign that new coal-fired power plants would be subjected to CO_2 regulations and that the earlier EPA rulings finding otherwise would be reversed. In an even more exciting development, on February 5, 2009, the United States Department of Justice announced its decision to launch a campaign to "stop illegal pollution" from coal-fired power plants. As the first step under this new campaign, the Department of Justice filed suit against Westar Energy's 1500MW coal-fired Jeffrey Energy Center in Kansas, which had made major modifications without installing required controls. The plant had been announced as one of the dirtiest in the nation in 2004, but no lawsuit was filed until 2009.

Continuing on this trend, on February 17, 2009, EPA Administrator Lisa Jackson announced that the EPA was considering whether to regulate greenhouse gas emissions, including CO_2, from coal-fired power plants. In addition, the EPA granted Sierra Club's petition to reconsider their December decision described above. The very next day, the EAB ordered Michigan regulators to reconsider air pollution permits issued to a proposed coal-fired power plant in the Upper Peninsula for failing to consider CO_2 emissions.

While all of these announcements may translate into big changes for coal-fired power plants' greenhouse gas emissions regulations, it may be a long time before these regulations are implemented. This wait may be too long; as of February 2009, one hundred new coal-fired power plants are currently in the permitting process without limits on greenhouse gas emissions, including CO_2.

Notes and Questions

1. In a separate case requesting the installation of expensive, but more effective pollution control technology, the Sierra Club petitioned the Environmental Appeals Board (EAB) to review a Clean Air Act prevention of signifi-

cant deterioration (PSD) permit issued by EPA to Deseret Power to allow the construction of a new waste-coal-fired utility generating unit at its existing Bonanza Power Plant in Utah. In the appeal, the Sierra Club alleged that the permit violated the CAA since it did not require the installation of the best available control technology (BACT). In response to the Sierra Club petition and EPA's reply, in November 2008, the EAB rejected EPA's reasons for excluding CO_2 limits from PSD and urged EPA to establish a national rule rather than use permit-by-permit determinations to ensure notice and uniformity across the states. See also Arizona Public Service Co. v. EPA, 39 ELR 20082 (10th Cir. April 14, 2009); Hempstead County Hunting Club v. Southwestern Electric Power Co., 39 ELR 20060 (8th Cir. March 12, 2009); Sierra Club v. EPA, 39 ELR 20043 (6th Cir. Feb. 26, 2009).

2. In a similar case, Longleaf Energy v. Friends of the Chattahoochee, environmental groups challenged Georgia's decision to avoid a BACT analysis for a PSD permit issued to Dynegy Energy's proposed 1200 MW Longleaf Energy Station. In June 2008, the trial court held that Georgia was required to conduct a BACT analysis to determine adequate controls for CO_2, finding CO_2 was already subject to CAA regulations. All plans for the Longleaf Energy Station were immediately put on hold pending an appeal. As the economy down-turned in January 2009, Dynegy formally announced that it was pulling out of agreements to build four coal-fired power plants, including the Longleaf Energy Station. The company has decided to await the determination of "technologically feasible and cost effective" controls for greenhouse gas emissions, including carbon dioxide.

3. The House of Representatives on June 26, 2009, passed H.R. 2454, the American Clean Energy and Security Act of 2009, following intense debate, and concessions to states whose economies depend upon coal mining. Most states' electricity depends on coal–fired electrical power generating plants. Some concessions to a transition from coal to "clean coal" to no coal appealed to members of the House of Representatives to be politically inevitable. The House bill included no provisions for performance standards to curb carbon dioxide emissions from existing power plants. The House bill provided that new plants after 2009 would be required to reduce emissions by 50% or more. This repeats, and may be deemed to constrain, what the Clean Air Act already covers through best available control technology standards (BACT), as at least one court has held. Friends of the Chattahoochie, Inc. v. Counch, Georgia Superior Court, 2008 CV 146398 (2008). If the EPA determines that BACT can reduce more than 50% of emissions, should it be authorized to make the administrative decision, or should Congress fix a limit by statute? EPA has not always made BACT decisions to advance use of best available technologies. See Sierra Club v. EPA, 499 F. 3d 653 (7th Cir. 2007). Coal fired power plants have gone to great lengths to avoid upgrading the air pollution controls on existing plants and plants modified to extend their useful "life." Wisconsin Electric Power Co. v. Reilly, 853 F. 2d 901 (7th Cir., 1990).

Courts have often sanctioned the power plants conduct. United States v. Duke Energy Corp. 411 F. 3d 539 (4th Cir. 2005). In light of the US EPA Endangerment Finding, should EPA reconsider its regulation framework for existing plants or new sources that continue to avoid installing new emission controls or burning fuels other than coal? Is there any justification to grandfathering existing emissions sources in an era when it is essential to mitigate all greenhouse gas emissions expeditiously?

4. Beyond the carbon dioxide emissions, existing plants and new plants also produce mercury emissions and contribute to acid rain. Should the EPA commence new rule-making under 33 USC 7411 (standards for performance for new stationary sources) and 33 USC 7412 (hazardous air pollutants) to design a new framework that maximizes reduction of all pollutants in light of current technological capabilities? Should EPA begin rule-making to establish a maximum achievable control technology (MACT) standard for mercury under Clean Air Act Section §112(d)(2), 42 USC 7412 (d)(2)? Such a standard would require choices between using coal as fuel vs. other fuels, cleaning coal before combustion, or cleaning emissions. The externality of "free" mercury emissions would be contained. Would it not be likely that coincident with controls of hazardous pollutant emissions or emissions of precursors of acid rain, emission sources would have an opportunity to reduce carbon dioxide emissions? Should EPA promulgate a more holistic and mutually reinforcing set of air pollutant controls, rather than a disaggregated approach?

REGULATORY AND COMMON LAW CONTROLS ON COAL-FIRED POWER PLANTS

The administrative process of deciding whether to implement stronger emissions controls on coal-fired power plants is a lengthy one. In addition, emissions from coal-fired power plants don't remain directly above the power plants that emit them. Instead these emissions flow across county, state lines, and national boundaries affecting people that may be hundreds or thousands of miles away from the source. And there are times when interested parties may feel that the administrative process does not provide adequate relief. For these and other reasons, resort may be had to public nuisance theories.

For example, the state of North Carolina brought a suit under nuisance theory against the Tennessee Valley Authority (TVA), listing eleven coal-fired power plants owned and operated by TVA in other states, alleging that airborne particles from TVA's coal fired power plants threatened the health and financial viability of North Carolina citizens and the beauty and purity of North Carolina ecosystems. District Judge Thornburg of the Western District of North Carolina held that whether coal-fired power plants located out of state were a public nuisance within North Carolina is a matter of state law to be determined by the state where the power plant is located. Looking through case law state-by-state, Judge Thornburg further held that the two listed Alabama coal-fired power plants were public nuisances and ordered the prompt installation and year-round usage of appropriate pollution control technologies at the Alabama coal-fired power plants. Moving to the two Kentucky coal-fired power plants listed in the Complaint, Judge Thornburg held, based on Kentucky state law, that the plants were located in areas too remote to be deemed a public nuisance to the citizens of North Carolina. In regards to the seven listed Tennessee power plants, Judge Thornburg found these plants to be public nuisances and again ordered the immediate installation of readily available pollution control technology. North Carolina v. Tennessee Valley Authority, 593 F.Supp.2d 812 (W.D.N.C. 2009).

One of the readily available pollution control technologies specifically mandated for the TVA to install is the "scrubber," or flue gas desulfurizer, which captures sulfur dioxide. As the court describes, "[s]crubbers, which use chemical processes to remove SO_2 from the flue gas, come in two varieties: wet and dry. Dry scrubbers can be expected to remove over 90% of SO_2 from the flue gas; wet scrubbers remove as much as 98% or more. Scrubbers are typically very large; one witness stated, you can think of [a scrubber] as almost adding a chemical plant to a coal-fired power plant. They're multiple buildings. They're several stories. They have very large footprints * * * oftentimes even larger than the original plant itself." Id. at 821. For nitrous oxide emissions, the court described "selective catalytic reduction (SCRs) and selective non-catalytic reduction (SNCRs). SCRs work by converting NO_x in the flue gas into molecular nitrogen and water, which have no air pollution impact. Like scrubbers, they are typically very large and often require custom engineering when they are retrofit onto aging EGUs. SCRs can remove about 90% of the NO_x in the flue gas." Id. Both SCRs and scrubbers also act to remove 85-90% of mercury emissions from smokestacks when installed together.

North Carolina achieved a significant victory against out-of-state coal-fired power plants through the court's injunction requiring pollution controls to be installed and regularly maintained within some of the listed power plants. In addition, the court ordered semi-annual accounting of TVA's progress in installing these pollution control mechanisms and their effectiveness. Id. at 833. It now seems that both the judiciary, through public nuisance cases like the one described above, and the executive branch, through the EPA, are beginning to require that these pollution control technologies be installed.

COAL-FIRED POWER PLANTS, GREENHOUSE GASES, AND STATE STATUTORY SUBSTANTIAL ENDANGERMENT PROVISIONS: CLIMATE CHANGE COMES TO KANSAS
Robert L. Glicksman
56 U. Kansas L. Rev. 517 (2008)

Despite (or because of) the federal government's failure to impose mandatory controls on GHG emissions from stationary sources, many states have taken steps to limit GHG emissions by electric generating facilities. State regulation has taken various forms. These include renewable portfolio standards requiring that power be produced from alternative energy sources that generate relatively low levels of GHG emissions. They also include regional or state-by-state limits on GHG emissions from stationary sources generally or from power plants in particular. These limits are often accompanied by emissions trading programs similar to the CAA's federal acid deposition control program. Recently, the tools used by the states to reduce emissions that contribute to climate change have expanded to include the denial of permits or licenses to coal-fired plants or the issuance of permits conditioned on actions to reduce the applicants' impact on climate change.

More than twenty states (although not Kansas) have enacted renewable portfolio standards ("RPS") as a means of minimizing reliance on traditional, carbon-laden fossil fuels to generate electricity. These standards are designed to increase the percentage of energy supplied by renewable resources. The standards typically require that a minimum percentage (which varies widely from state to state) of a utility's power plant capacity or generation come from renewable sources such as solar, wind, or biomass. RPS programs can increase the role of renewable energy by increasing the required percentage over time. RPS programs often include a credit trading mechanism whose function is to provide flexibility in compliance options for utilities and to reward the efficient use of renewable energy technologies. * * *

Probably the most prominent state program for controlling GHG emissions from the electricity sector is the Regional Greenhouse Gas Initiative ("RGGI") in which several northeastern and mid-Atlantic states are participating. That program mandates reductions in CO_2 emissions from power plants, but it includes a cap-and-trade program that permits regulated utilities to comply with their reduction obligations by purchasing emissions credits from other regulated entities that exceed their mandated emissions cuts. The states participating in RGGI agreed to cap global warming emissions from the region's power plants at current levels and reduce them by 10% by 2019. * * *

Individual states also have adopted GHG emission reduction requirements for stationary sources, including electric utilities. The California legislature adopted the path-breaking statute of this type, the Global Warming Solutions Act of 2006. The Act requires a reduction in GHG emissions statewide to 1990 levels by 2020, and authorizes the California Air Resources Board to adopt technology-based emissions reduction regulations applicable to categories of sources, which are anticipated to include electric utilities. The statute also authorizes the Board to develop an emissions trading program, under which sources emitting fewer GHGs than their permits allow may sell emissions credits to sources exceeding their individual GHG caps.

Some states have adopted specific statutory or regulatory GHG emissions caps for new power plants. Oregon's regulations offer new power plants various options for meeting their reduction requirements, including the operation of certified cogeneration projects, the implementation of approved offset projects, or the payment of per ton offset fees. Washington state legislation mandates that new, large fossil fuel-fired electric generating facilities be subject to an approved CO_2 mitigation plan that involves some combination of payments to third parties to provide mitigation, direct purchase of permanent carbon credits, and investment in applicant-controlled carbon dioxide mitigation projects, including cogeneration. Facility approval is subject to the requirement that 20% of the total CO_2 emissions produced by the facility be mitigated. Even in states in which regulators have refused thus far to impose CO_2 emission controls on proposed new coal-fired power plants, such as Montana, the need for and the inevitability of such controls in the future has been noted.

In addition, some states, such as Massachusetts and New Hampshire, have established emissions caps for existing power plants. New Hampshire's Clean Power Act imposes annual limits through 2010 on emissions of CO_2, as well as some criteria pollutants. Regulated plants may comply either by reducing their own emissions or purchasing emissions credits through a trading program approved by state regulators. The state environmental agency may approve off-site reduction measures such as carbon sequestration, shutdown of CO_2-emitting sources, and electricity generation through renewable sources. * * *

Another development in state efforts to reduce the contribution of power plants to climate change is the denial by state regulators of permission to construct or operate such plants. The refusal of state legislative and regulatory bodies to allow certain kinds of electricity producing facilities is not unprecedented. * * *

To date, no state has gone that far in restricting the development of coal-fired electric facilities. In 2007, however, three states denied permits for coal-fired plants and in another state, plans to construct eleven new coal-fired plants were dramatically curtailed in light of the public outcry spurred by the original proposal. The regulatory climate for coal-fired power is clearly becoming more hostile at the state level. * * *

The Florida Public Service Commission ("FPSC") in 2007 denied permission to construct a coal-fired power plant. Florida Power & Light Company ("FPL") filed the petition for a determination of need for two electric power plants in Glades County. FPL proposed to put into service by 2013 and 2014 two ultra-supercritical pulverized coal ("USCPC") generating units with a combined net capacity of 1960 megawatts. The Florida Electrical Power Plant Siting Act ("Siting Act") is designed to balance increased demand for electric power with the broad interests of the public, including use of the state's natural resources. The Siting Act lists a series of factors that the FPSC must consider in deciding whether to approve a proposed new electric generating facility, without specifying the weight to be afforded each. The FPSC must take into account the need for electric system reliability and integrity, the need for adequate electricity at a reasonable cost, the need for fuel diversity and supply reliability, and whether the proposed plant is the most cost-effective alternative available. In addition, the agency must consider the "conservation measures taken by or reasonably available to the applicant . . . which might mitigate the need for the proposed plant." Finally, the Siting Act authorizes the FPSC to consider "other matters within its jurisdiction which it deems relevant."

The FPSC concluded that it was "in the public interest to deny FPL's petition for determination of need." It found that the applicant failed to demonstrate that the proposed plants were the most cost-effective alternative available, taking into account the uncertainty associated with future natural gas and coal prices and with emerging energy policy decisions at both the state and federal level. In addition, the Commission relied on a 2005 amendment to the Siting Act which authorized the Commission to consider fuel diversity as a factor in determining need. The FPSC recognized the need for additional generation to meet current and future growth and declared that:

> uncertainty about cost-effectiveness alone will not necessarily control the outcome of every need determination decision. We find in this case, however, that the potential benefits regarding fuel diversity offered by FPL in support of the [proposed plants] fail to mitigate the additional costs and risks of the project, given the uncertainty of present fuel prices, capital costs, and current market and regulatory factors. * * *

The decision did not mention climate change or GHG emissions. Instead, it was couched vaguely in terms of uncertainty over fuel prices, capital costs, and unidentified "regulatory factors." Nevertheless, environmental concerns contributed to the outcome. * * * Climate change * * * played a role. FPSC members indicated that they were concerned that the price of coal could become unstable if Congress decides to regulate GHGs. They also indicated that they regarded CO_2 as well as mercury emissions as risks if the plant were approved. * * * Governor Charlie Crist had previously made it clear that he preferred that no new coal-fired power plants be licensed, and had issued an executive order requiring the adoption of standards to reduce greenhouse gas emissions from power plants to 2000 levels by 2017 and to 1990 levels by 2025. * * *

Several months after the FPSC's decision, the State of Washington's Energy Facility Site Evaluation Council ("EFSEC") also refused to endorse a proposal to construct a coal-fired power plant. This time, the decision was based more explicitly on climate change-related concerns. Energy Northwest ("ENW") proposed to construct the Pacific Mountain Energy Center, a combined cycle 793-megawatt electrical generating facility which would operate on synthetic gas produced from petroleum coke, a byproduct of refining, or coal. According to the EFSEC, ENW's proposal was the first to involve an Integrated Gasification Combined Cycle ("IGCC") project with carbon sequestration. The agency described the project as involving "environmental technology that seeks to minimize carbon emissions, to recapture byproducts such as sulfur, and to utilize as its fuel, products such as petroleum coke, a refinery waste product that might otherwise not be recycled, and coal."

State legislation gave EFSEC the authority to recommend to the governor whether the state should enter into a site certification agreement that would authorize a power plant applicant to construct and operate the facility. About seven months after ENW filed its application, the legislature amended the statute to * * * require new facilities generating more than 1100 pounds of GHGs per megawatt hour of electricity to sequester GHGs to that level or below. * * *

ENW * * * took the position that it was impossible to prepare a plan as contemplated by the statute due to the technological and economical infeasibility of geological sequestration. Instead, ENW proposed:

To prepare a specific plan in the future, perhaps as late as 2020, when geological sequestration becomes a proven technology for use by power plants and a number of asserted technological, engineering, and legal questions have been answered. In the interim, ENW proposed to consider offsets. * * *

The issue before EFSEC was whether ENW's submission complied with the statute. It concluded unanimously that it did not * * *.

EFSEC interpreted the statute as requiring an applicant to make "specific plans for specific actions to accomplish a specific goal," sequestration of GHGs, and receive a Site Certification Agreement from the Governor. These requirements must be met "before [the applicant] can ask for relief by the purchase of offsets." * * * EFSEC rejected ENW's claims that compliance was futile, that it made a good faith effort to comply, and that the doctrine of impossibility should apply. ENW argued that its approach was a legitimate effort to engage in "adaptive management" by "allow[ing] details of compliance to be developed through different measures, over time, allowing learning from and improving upon compliance measures." EFSEC responded that the statute does not allow "adaptive management" to substitute for the *545 specific statutory requirements. Further, it disagreed that ENW's GGRP qualified as adaptive management, a decisionmaking process which pursues specific goals through clearly identified means. Instead, the GGRP was "a proposal to develop goals and measures later." * * *

The ENW decision, like the FPL decision, rejected a utility's plans to put into service a new coal-fired power plant. The FPL decision rested primarily on matters traditionally considered by state utility commissions—the cost of service to be supplied by the plant if approved—although a recent statutory amendment relating to fuel diversity played a part. The FPSC rested its decision on the uncertainty attributable to the impact of unspecified "regulatory factors," a veiled reference to the cost of compliance with future federal or state climate change regulation. The ENW decision was based squarely on the potential environmental impact of unsequestered CO_2 emissions. EF-SEC's decision responded to a set of statutory requirements enacted to deal specifically with ENW's proposed plant. Although it provides another example of the increasing regulatory obstacles facing proposed new coal-fired power plants, it is likely to have little value as precedent in licensing decisions in a state (such as Kansas) lacking the kind of statutory sequestration requirements in effect in Washington. * * *

North Carolina energy regulators in 2007 took a less absolute approach than the refusals to license new coal-fired power plants reflected in the Florida and Washington decisions. In 2005, Duke Energy sought a certificate of public convenience and necessity allowing it to construct two new 800-megawatt coal-fired electric generating facilities, along with related transmission facilities. * * * The commission concluded that the public convenience and necessity supported the construction of only one plant. The certificate was conditioned, however, on the retirement by Duke of four existing units at the site of the new plant. In addition, the commission required Duke to invest 1% of its annual retail electricity revenues in energy efficiency and demand reduction programs. Finally, the agency required Duke to retire older coal-fired units (in addition to the four existing units at the proposed new plant site) on a megawatt-by-megawatt basis, after considering the impact on reliability. The utilities commission explained that its decision would "allow Duke to increase its baseload generating capacity without significantly increasing its environmental footprint." * * *

[E]ven though the commission acknowledged that the abundance of domestic supplies of coal as compared to natural gas makes "coal a more attractive choice for baseload generation," it took a go-slow approach due to the contribution of coal-fired power to the problems associated with climate change. The commission did so even though the factors relevant to the issuance of a certificate of convenience and necessity, at least as described by the commission, do not explicitly include environmental impact, no less impact on climate change. * * *

The North Carolina decision is noteworthy for at least two reasons. First, like EFSEC's decision, the state agencies relied explicitly on their desire to minimize the contribution of electricity generation to climate change, notwithstanding the fact that GHGs were not being regulated under state law. Second, unlike the FPSC and EFSEC decisions, the disposition of the North Carolina permit application did not rest on recent legislation designed, explicitly or otherwise, to deal with climate change. The state utilities commission instead rested its decision on more general legislative criteria not adopted with climate change in mind.

In a fourth situation that came to a head in 2007, ambitious plans for the construction of a series of coal-fired power plants were severely curtailed before they ever got off the drawing board, in part because of the CO_2 emissions that the plants would have generated. In April 2006, the TXU Corporation announced that it would build eleven new coal-fired power plants. Texas Governor Rick Perry tried to fast-track issuance of permits for the eleven plants. The project quickly generated opposition, however. TXU's chief executive neglected to curry favor with consumers, community groups, or state legislators, who either doubted the need for the additional generating capacity or feared that the plants would result in increased electricity prices. Environmental groups objected not only because of the plants' impact on local pollution, but also because of their contribution to climate change. The eleven new plants would have generated seventy-eight million tons of CO_2 annually, adding to the carbon emissions that already made Texas the nation's largest CO_2 emitter. When some of TXU's shareholders complained about the carbon footprint the plants would create, the chief executive reacted dismissively. * * *

By the summer of 2006, "TXU had become a national symbol of a carbon dioxide emitter." * * * In November 2006, Texas Pacific Group, Kohlberg Kravis Roberts & Co., and Goldman Sachs approached TXU about buying the company for $45 billion and taking it private. The prospective buyers asked William Reilly, the Administrator of the federal EPA during the first Bush presidency and a vice president of Texas Pacific Group, to help negotiate the deal.

Reilly negotiated an agreement with two major environmental groups—Environmental Defense and the Natural Resources Defense Council—under which the groups agreed to drop pending lawsuits to block construction of the plants and support the buyout. In return, the TXU buyers agreed to build only three of the eleven coal plants originally proposed, to cut electricity prices, to reduce emissions of regulated air pollutants by 20%, to reduce CO_2 emissions to 1990 levels by 2020, and to support legislation restricting GHG emissions. In addition, the buyers promised to consider the use of coal gasification technology for future plants, which would allow the capture and storage of CO_2 when sequestration technology is more fully developed. TXU's chief executive admitted that public opposition to the plant was one reason he made the deal. The buyers also would pursue more wind power and double the amount spent on energy efficiency programs to $80 million for the next five years. In February 2007, TXU's Board of Directors agreed to sell the company. The company agreed not to propose building any traditional, pulverized coal plants outside of Texas, despite plans to do so in the Northeast. It subsequently announced plans to more than double its current purchase of wind power and to invest $400 million in conservation programs and incentives for consumers to lower use during peak hours. TXU also indicated that it would reopen several natural gas plants. * * *

Subsequent to the TXU deal, utilities in several other states cancelled plans for new coal-fired electric facilities, and coal-fired plants in other jurisdictions were opposed on the basis of the impact they would have on climate change. The hostile reception generated by plans to build new coal-fired plants increased investors' interest in natural gas, renewable, and nuclear energy sources.

Recent proposals to build coal-fired power plants in other states also have foundered. Although the decisions in these states restricting the ability of utilities to rely on coal-fired power have been based primarily on need rather than environmental factors, regulators have also expressed concern over the GHGs emitted by coal-fired electricity generation. The Oregon Public Utility Commission ("OPUC") rejected a bid by PacifiCorp to build two new coal-fired power plants on the ground that the utility failed to justify the need for that much baseload capacity. In addition, the agency concluded that the proposal to build a combined 1109 megawatts of new coal-fired generation was inconsistent with the utility's own OPUC-approved plan to focus on conservation, renewable resources, and demand-side measures to meet electricity demand. * * * In addition, regulators viewed skeptically PacifiCorp's plan to sell surplus power to customers in other states in light of the aversion to coal-fired generation in those states. OPUC noted, for example, that California had recently limited imports of coal-fired power from other states to plants whose emissions are comparable to natural gas-fired plants.

State regulators have also wounded proposed coal-fired projects more indirectly. In late 2007, the Minnesota Public Utilities Commission ("MPUC") refused to require Xcel Energy to buy power from a 600-megawatt coal-fired power plant proposed by Excelsior Energy. * * * It cited growing disillusionment with coal, assurances from Xcel that it did not need the additional power, and the high cost to Xcel's customers of the proposed plant's output as reasons for refusing to compel Xcel to purchase power from the proposed plant.

The Chairman of the MPUC described the regulatory environment for coal-fired power plants as having undergone a "paradigm shift," noting the delay or cancellation of coal-gasification projects in several other states. * * *

Despite the absence of federal regulation restricting GHG emissions from stationary sources, many states, individually or collectively, have taken steps to minimize the contribution to global climate change of coal-fired electric generating facilities, one of the largest sources of CO_2 emissions. These efforts have included renewable portfolio standards designed to increase the slice of electric power derived from renewable or low-carbon fuels, emissions reduction requirements applicable to broad categories of stationary sources or to power plants in particular, cap-and-trade programs, and carbon sequestration requirements. Each of these approaches has the potential to make it difficult if not impossible for utilities to pursue plans to enhance generating capacity by operating facilities that burn coal to produce electricity.

Kansas has resorted to none of these regulatory devices. Yet, the KDHE's October 2007 decision on the Sunflower Electric Power Corporation's bid to build two new coal-fired generators places Kansas among the states that have denied permission to construct coal-fired power plants on the basis of the CO_2 emissions these plants generate. KDHE either could not or chose not to base its denial of the Sunflower applications on the grounds that formed the basis of the decisions by Florida and Washington regulators to reject coal-fired power plant applications. KDHE might have relied on the uncertainty of the cost of coal-fired power resulting from emerging federal and state energy and environmental policies that the FPSC cited in denying FPL's application. KDHE could not have cast its decision along the lines of EFSEC's denial of ENW's application because Kansas lacks a statute mandating the formulation and implementation of carbon sequestration plans. Instead, KDHE based its denial of the Sunflower application directly on the adverse impacts on public health and the environment that construction of the Holcomb generators would cause by virtue of their CO_2 emissions. * * *

Sunflower sought permission in February 2006 to build coal-fired generators in Holcomb, Kansas, adjacent to its existing Holcomb coal-fired generator. * * * Each new unit would have been a super-critical 700 megawatt, pulverized coal-fired boiler. * * *

The plants were designed by Sunflower to be part of a "bio-energy center" that would include an ethanol plant and a facility to use an experimental algae process to capture CO_2 emissions from the generating units. The two units had the potential to emit eleven million tons of CO_2 annually. According to Sunflower, however, the bioenergy center would have cut the plants' CO_2 emissions to 3.6 million tons a year. * * *

According to Governor Sebelius, only 15% of the proposed plants' electric output would have been consumed by Kansans; the rest would have been exported to users in Texas and Colorado. These facts fueled concern that most of the adverse effects resulting from the plant's operation would be borne by Kansans, while the new generating capacity would largely benefit consumers in other states.

Environmental groups claimed that the technology envisioned for use at the bioenergy center was too experimental to be a reliable means for minimizing the plants' CO_2 emissions. The attorneys general of eight eastern states reacted to the Holcomb application in similar fashion. They requested that KDHE not issue the permit "unless Sunflower designs the plant in a way that minimizes the generation of (CO_2) emissions and/or allows the capture of such emissions." All eight states had made reduction of CO_2 emissions a priority, but, according to the attorneys general,

> the annual emissions from the Holcomb plant extension would cancel out all the emissions reductions resulting from the RGGI. With a lifetime of more than 60 years, the Holcomb units, if built as proposed, might well emit more than one billion tons of CO_2 in total, thus significantly contributing to the public health and environmental damage associated with global warming.

The letter also argued that state and federal laws required issuance of a CAA permit by KDHE to Sunflower before construction on Holcomb could begin. Because the plants would be located in an area in compliance with the CAA's national ambient air quality standards, Sunflower had to show, before KDHE could issue a permit to it, that the units would use the best available control technology ("BACT"). The attorneys general asserted that the CAA required the use of "'innovative fuel combustion techniques' to achieve the 'maximum degree of reduction for each pollutant subject to regulation' under the [CAA]." They claimed that the CAA's legislative history indicates that Congress intended that BACT analysis include "the full range of production methodologies," including IGCC, which they characterized as "an established and available production process." The attorneys general also charged that KDHE "must consider the energy, environmental, and economic impacts of each unit as part of its BACT analysis." They added that, even if the increased CO_2 emissions resulting from the proposed Holcomb units might not require their own BACT analysis as "regulated pollutants" under EPA's interpretation of the CAA, the "detrimental environmental effects of these emissions" had to be considered under the "environmental impacts prong of BACT."

Recognizing that a rejection of the Sunflower application based on its effect on climate change would be without precedent in Kansas, KDHE solicited an opinion from the state's Attorney General on the legality of a denial of the application on those grounds. * * *

The Attorney General interpreted * * * the statute to "contemplate" preventive as well as remedial actions on the part of the secretary in order to protect persons and the environment in situations where the secretary receives information that emission of air pollution presents substantial endangerment to either." The Opinion pointed out that both the terms "air pollution" and "air contaminant" are broadly defined. The Attorney General reasoned, based on these provisions, that the Secretary need not wait to take action * * * to prevent air pollution "until there are federal or state regulations establishing limitations on a particular pollutant," as long as he makes the findings required by [the statute.] * * *

Several weeks after issuance of the Attorney General's Opinion, KDHE's staff recommended issuance of an air quality construction permit to Sunflower to allow it to build the two new 700-megawatt coal-fired steam generating units at its Holcomb generating station. Its recommendation identified plant operating conditions, including enforceable limitations on emissions of various air pollutants, not including CO_2, as well as emissions testing and monitoring and recordkeeping and reporting requirements. The staff made only two brief references to GHGs. It noted that one of the public comments filed with KDHE had argued that the agency should address CO_2 issues. The staff responded that "[t]here are no provisions to regulate carbon dioxide in PSD permits. * * * Similarly, the Sierra Club had argued that KDHE was required to deny the permit because the proposed plant would emit GHGs and mercury at rates that pose a substantial endangerment to the public health and the environment. * * *

[KDHE Secretary] Bremby interpreted the Act and KDHE's implementing regulations as vesting in the Secretary broad authority to protect health and the environment, including the denial of an air quality permit * * * Bremby noted the Supreme Court's decision in April 2007 in Massachusetts v. EPA, in which the Court held that CO_2 qualifies as an air pollutant under the federal CAA. He reasoned that "[t]he Kansas air quality act similarly has a broad definition of what constitutes air pollution." The Secretary also referred to the Supreme Court's recognition of the "deleterious impact of greenhouse gases on the environment in which we live." Similarly, Bremby concluded that the information gathered during the Sunflower permit proceeding "provides support for the position that emission of air pollution from the proposed coal fired plant, specifically carbon dioxide emissions, presents a substantial endangerment to the health of persons or to the environment." Based on that information, Secretary Bremby denied the permit. * * *

Governor Sebelius backed the decision. In an "open letter to the people of Kansas" she applauded the denial as a decision that would improve the health of Kansas residents, "improve prospects for 'sustainable economic growth,' and uphold a 'moral obligation to be good stewards of this beautiful land.'" The governor expressed support for the pursuit of "'other, more promising energy and economic development alternatives.'"

Opposition to the decision from other quarters, however, was immediate and pointed. Criticism of the decision reflected two main arguments, one based on the alleged absence of legal authority and the other on the alleged adverse public policy implications of the permit denial. The first contention rested on the premise that KDHE acted outside the scope of its statutory and regulatory authority in denying an air quality permit for the Holcomb units. * * *

The thrust of the policy-based criticism was that the permit denials would have a devastating economic impact on the state to avoid a nonexistent or insignificant environmental problem. The State Senate President and House Speaker asserted that * * * that efforts to mandate carbon reductions "below market levels will increase energy costs for Kansas consumers and businesses [and] companies considering locating or expanding in Kansas may reconsider if a reliable source of reasonably priced energy is not available." * * *

Concurrently with the filing of administrative and judicial appeals of KDHE's decision, the supporters of the plant sought to reverse the decision by statute. The 2008 session of the Kansas legislature was consumed almost entirely by a pitched battle over the fate of the Holcomb units. The legislature passed three bills that would have required KDHE to approve Sunflower's application and stripped KDHE of its authority to regulate GHG emissions in the absence of federal regulation. * * * Governor Sebelius vetoed the first two bills. The state Senate voted to override the two vetoes, but the Kansas House fell just short of the votes needed to override. In addition, on what was supposed to be the last day of the wrap-up session of the 2008 legislative term, the Holcomb plant's supporters inserted into several economic development proposals provisions similar to those in the two bills successfully vetoed by the Governor. The Governor promptly vetoed the third bill, and the legislature adjourned without mustering an effort to override it.

Notes and Questions

1. President Obama appointed Gov. Sibelius to be Secretary of Health and Human Services. Lt. Gov. Mark Parkinson became the new Kansas governor. Within days, Gov. Mark Parkinson reached an agreement on a plan that would allow Sunflower to build the plant. However, at the end of June, EPA announced that because of changes in the project, Sunflower Electric Power Corp. must reapply for a Clean Air Act permit for the its planned 895-megawatt coal plant. William Rice, Acting Admin., EPA Region 7, Letter to Roderick Bremby, Sec. Kan. Dept. of Health and Education (July 1, 2009)

www.epa.gov/region7/programs/artd/air/nsr/archives/2009/r7comments/sunflo
wer_holcomb_2009_project_comments.pdf.

2. Under current law in the United States, who decides whether a coal-fired
power plant should be built? The impacts are local, regional, national, and
global. Should the nature of the impacts affect who decides?

3. The Federal Energy Regulatory Commission (FERC) has exclusive jurisdiction over interstate transmission and interstate wholesale sales of electricity. Any wholesale transaction on a wire on an electric grid that is connected
to another state is within FERC's exclusive jurisdiction. Before electricity
deregulation the vast majority of all generating assets were owned by a vertically integrated utility that were regulated by state public utility commissions as natural monopolies. As part of that regulation, states would set retail rates and determine whether new power plants should be built. FERC
now allows the market to set wholesale rates. Since deregulation, utilities
own almost none of the electricity generating plants that provide electricity to
customers. Instead local utilities are just distributors of electricity bought
from others (wholesale) to the ultimate users. Local utilities buy electricity
from others either on the grid's spot market or via long-term contracts with
regulators.

4. How does Congress address this issue in its climate change legislation?
Who will decide on whether new coal-fired power plants will be built? What
criteria will be used? Are these criteria consistent with the nation's and the
world's climate change mandates?

5. Can Congress prohibit the construction of new coal-fired power plants?
Can it mandate that coal-fired power plants reduce their CO_2 emissions by
50%?

6. Are new coal-fired power plants needed? Can the energy be mined at
lower cost from efficiency improvements?   Let us return again to the legal
question: who decides and on what criteria? A recent review of 26 new national appliance standards found that, if adopted, total U.S. electricity use
would be reduced by over 1,900 terawatt-hours (1.9 trillion kilowatt-hours—
"roughly enough power to meet the total electricity needs of every American
household for 18 months") cumulatively by 2030 while saving consumers and
businesses over $123 billion; 65,000 MW of peak demand would be saved.
These new standards could cut CO_2 emissions 158 million tons per year by
2030, roughly the amount emitted by 63 large conventional coal-fired power
plants. According to the report, the average payback for the 26 reviewed
products is 3.1 years, and over each product's lifetime the average benefit-
cost ratio of 4 to 1. Appliance Standards Awareness Project, Ka-BOOM! Appliance　Standards　Make　a　Big　Bang　(July　22,　2009),
http://www.standardsasap.org/news/press34.html. The full report is available

at http://www.aceee.org/pubs/a091.htm.

7. Note on Combined Heat and Power: Modern cogeneration facilities using improved microturbines are a low cost, efficient way to provide electricity and use the waste heat remaining after the electricity is generated. EPA explains:

> Combined heat and power (CHP), also known as cogeneration, is an efficient, clean, and reliable approach to generating power and thermal energy from a single fuel source. By installing a CHP system designed to meet the thermal and electrical base loads of a facility, CHP can greatly increase the facility's operational efficiency and decrease energy costs. At the same time, CHP reduces the emission of greenhouse gases, which contribute to global climate change. CHP can be powered by biomass (plant material, vegetation, or agricultural waste) or biogas (methane produced by the aerobic or anaerobic digestion of biomass). * * *

> Electric utilities and others have used large-and medium-scale gas-fired turbines to generate electricity since the 1950s, but recent developments have enabled the introduction of much smaller turbines, known as microturbines. * * * By generating electricity at the point of use, microturbines reduce the need to generate electricity from sources such as large electric utility plants. When coupled with heat recovery systems that capture excess thermal energy to heat water and/or spaces, microturbines also reduce the need to use conventional heating technologies such as boilers and furnaces, which emit significant quantities of CO_2 * * * When well-matched to building or facility needs in a properly designed CHP application, microturbines can increase operational efficiency and avoid power transmission losses, thereby reducing overall emissions and net fuel consumption. Microturbines also can be designed to operate using biogas from sources including animal waste, wastewater treatment plants, and landfills. Biogas is a renewable resource that otherwise goes unused because it is typically flared or vented to the atmosphere. * * *

> For systems that both generate electricity and use the waste heat, total system efficiencies ranged from 33.4% to 71.8%. * * * Microturbine/CHP systems can be used at residential, commercial, institutional, and industrial facilities to provide electricity at the point of use and reduce the need to use conventional heating technologies.

U.S. E.P.A., Combined Heat and Power Partnership, Basics http://www.epa.gov/chp/basic/index.html. The U.S. Department of Energy describes the basic microturbine technology:

> Microturbines are small combustion turbines, approximately the size of a refrigerator, with outputs of 25-500 kW. They evolved from

automotive and truck turbochargers, auxiliary power units for airplanes, and small jet engines and are composed of a compressor, a
combustor, a turbine, an alternator, a recuperator, and a generator.

Microturbines offer a number of potential advantages over other
technologies for small-scale power generation. These include their
small number of moving parts, compact size, light weight, greater efficiency, lower emissions, lower electricity costs, and ability to use
waste fuels. They can be located on sites with space limitations for
the production of power, and waste heat recovery can be used to
achieve efficiencies of more than 80%. * * *

Because of their compact size, relatively low capital costs, low operations and maintenance costs, and automatic electronic control, microturbines are expected to capture a significant share of the distributed generation market.

U.S.   Dept.   of   Energy   Distributed   Energy   Program
http://www.eere.energy.gov/de/microturbines/tech_basics.html.

G. RENEWABLE ENERGY

In this book we will use the definition of renewable energy that is the
basis for the new international agency, International Renewable Energy
Agency (IRENA). The 135 nations that established this agency, including the
United States, charged IRENA "to become the main driving force for promoting a rapid transition towards the widespread and sustainable use of renewable energy on a global scale." See http://irena.org/. The Statute of the International Renewable Energy Agency defines "renewable energy" as "all forms
of energy produced from renewable sources in a sustainable manner, which
include, inter alia: bioenergy, geothermal energy; hydro energy; ocean, including inter alia tidal, wave, and ocean thermal energy; solar energy; and
wind energy." IRENA/FC/Statute (26 Jan 2009).

Hydropower includes large and small dams and kinetic technology, solar
power includes photovoltaic technology and solar thermal facilities, wind
power is available both on land and off-shore, biomass generally is used as a
fuel, ocean energy includes waves, thermal (temperature differences of water
at different depths, tidal, and osmotic, and geothermal uses heat from below
ground. For a comprehensive review of renewable energy around the world
see the reports of the Renewable Energy Policy Network for the 21st Century
(REN21), http://www.ren21.net/.

In this section we will address legal and policy questions associated with
biofuels and wind energy. Solar voltaic technology is advancing rapidly. The

efficiency of photovoltaic material in converting sunlight to electricity has improved markedly to over 15%, and the cost of manufacture has dropped. The major challenges facing photovoltaics are the need to drive costs down to make them competitive on the grid and to increase the variety and supply of products and manufacturing capacity See John M. Lushetsky, U.S. Dept of Energy, Office of Energy Efficiency and Renewable Energy, The State of Solar: Technology and Markets (Feb. 16, 2009) www.narucmeetings.org/Presentations/Lushetsky_NARUCPresentation_Final.pdf

We will cover some solar legal issues in connection with renewable portfolio standards, solar carve-outs and other legal innovations later in this chapter. The effect of property and zoning laws on a property owner's ability to install solar panels is covered along with other legal questions in Chapter 7. Innovative financing methods are discussed in chapter 9 in the coverage of the Delaware Energy Plan. The National Renewable Energy Laboratory has extensive information on the wide range of solar voltaic technologies

Large-scale solar thermal plants can generate significant amounts of energy. They are generally sited in desert or arid areas; Spain and California are the leaders. These plants come in a wide range of designs and technologies, which are under constant development. The basics of solar thermal technologies are straight-forward:

> Concentrating solar power (CSP) offers a utility-scale, firm, dispatchable renewable energy option that can help meet our nation's demand for electricity. CSP plants produce power by first using mirrors to focus sunlight to heat a working fluid. Ultimately, this high-temperature fluid is used to spin a turbine or power an engine that drives a generator. And the final product is electricity.

> Smaller CSP systems can be located directly where the power is needed. Single dish/engine systems can produce 3 to 25 kilowatts of power and are well suited for such distributed applications. Larger, utility-scale CSP applications provide hundreds of megawatts of electricity for the power grid. Both linear concentrator and power tower systems can be easily integrated with thermal storage, helping to generate electricity during cloudy periods or at night. Alternatively, these systems can be combined with natural gas, and the resulting hybrid power plants can provide high-value, dispatchable power throughout the day.

U.S. Dept. of Energy, Solar Energy Technologies Program http://www1.eere.energy.gov/solar/printable_versions/csp_basics.html. For a more information about solar thermal power see, National Renewable Energy Laboratory, Concentrating Power Solar Research, http://www.nrel.gov/csp/.

Advances in solar thermal installation will depend on further cost reductions, efficiency improvements, and the identification of the appropriate land areas for construction with minimal environmental impacts. The primary legal concerns that are raised with these facilities are local siting issues, such as fragile ecosystems and biodiversity, potential release of high temperature or molten salts or other heat sinks, and the need for high-voltage transmission lines to be built to connect these remote plants to the electricity grid. These issues are no different than many of the transmission issues discussed later in this chapter and environmental concerns, such as the Endangered Species Act and environmental impact statements, addressed later in the book.

Geothermal energy is also renewable but is location specific; it presents limited potential to replace fossil fuels at a large scale. In the United States, California is the leader in geothermal energy. For information about the various geothermal technologies see National Renewable Energy Laboratory, Geothermal Technologies, http://www.nrel.gov/geothermal/.

1. Biofuels

BIOFUELS AND SUSTAINABLE DEVELOPMENT: REPORT OF AN EXECUTIVE SESSION ON THE GRAND CHALLENGES OF A SUSTAINABILITY TRANSITION
Henry Lee, William C. Clark and Charan Devereaux (San Servolo Island, Venice, Italy: May 19-20, 2008)
http://belfercenter.ksg.harvard.edu/files/biofuels%20and%20sustainable%20d evelopment.pdf.

Liquid biofuels can provide a much needed substitute for fossil fuels used in the transport sector. They can contribute to climate and other environmental goals, energy security, economic development, and offer opportunities for private companies to profit. If not implemented with care, however, biofuel production can put upward pressure on food prices, increase greenhouse gas (GHG) emissions, exacerbate degradation of land, forests, water sources, and ecosystems, and jeopardize the livelihood security of individuals immediately dependent on the natural resource base. Guiding biofuel development to realize its multiple potential benefits while guarding against its multiple risks requires the application of a similarly diverse set of tailored policy interventions. Most session participants agreed that any single rule–such as production subsidies, a simple ban on biofuel production, or the immediate revocation of existing mandates for biofuel use–is too blunt an instrument, and will almost certainly do more harm than good.

Biofuels and Sustainable Development

Biofuels have emerged as a centerpiece of the international public policy debate. All of the G8+5 countries, with the exception of Russia, have created transport biofuel targets. Some countries have mandated the use of these fuels. For example, in January of 2008 the European Union reaffirmed a goal that 10% of vehicle fuel be derived from renewable sources by 2020. And the U.S. Energy Security and Independence Act requires that 36 billion gallons of renewable fuels be blended into gasoline by 2022. Recently, however, increased food prices triggered in part by converting food crops such as maize to fuel have raised public concerns about such goals. These concerns have been reinforced by several studies which indicate that biofuels may aggravate the net emissions of greenhouse gases rather than reduce them. While the potential benefits of biofuels have induced some governments to embrace their potential, many leaders are now concerned about the costs–particularly those that impact food prices and the environment.

Biomass can be used to provide energy in many forms including electricity, heat, solid, gaseous, and liquid fuels. These bioenergy options have been actively pursued in both the developed and developing world. Further, approximately two billion of the world's poorest people use biomass directly for cooking and heating, often seriously endangering their health and their environment.

This Session focused exclusively on one part of the bioenergy menu: liquid biofuels for transportation. The Session asked three principal questions. Why should countries care about biofuels? Why should they be concerned about the negative spillover effects of biofuel production? What can be done to mitigate these negative effects, while promoting the development of a sustainable biofuel industry?

1. WHY BIOFUELS?

Policymakers, business representatives, academics, and members of civil society are pushing development of biofuels for different reasons. Some see biofuels as a substitute for high priced petroleum, either to ease the burden on consumers, to diversify the sources of energy supplies, or to reduce escalating trade deficits. Some have focused on biofuels as a way to extend available energy in the context of increasing world demand for transportation fuels. Others target biofuels as a substitute for more carbon intensive energy. Still others see biofuels as an economic opportunity. This latter group can be divided into two sectors: those who see biofuels as an economic development opportunity, and companies who see biofuels as a potential market in which to invest.

1.1. Energy: The world currently uses 86 million barrels of oil per day,1 with forecasts that demand for liquid fuels will increase to 118 million barrels by 2030. Most of the incremental fuel will come from OPEC and specifically from the Middle East. In the last two years the world's supply of oil has had difficulty keeping up with demand, and prices have skyrocketed to $140 per barrel and more. This has triggered economic hardship, especially among the poorest importing countries. As more and more funds are required to pay for oil products, importing countries find their current account balances eroding and the costs of producing and transporting goods and services increasing. Today, many forecasters predict that while prices will fluctuate, the era of low-cost oil is over and countries must adjust by seeking alternative energy options and strategies.

More than 60% of the oil consumed in the OECD countries is used for transportation. While there are many substitutes for oil in the heating and power sectors, this is not the case in the transportation sector. Fossil fuel based alternatives, such as oil shale and coal liquefaction, could potentially provide additional transportation fuels, but their production will have large impacts on greenhouse gas emissions and water resources.

In the short term, producing liquid fuels from biomass is one of the only alternatives to petroleum-based transportation fuels. As a result, countries are looking at a menu of biofuel options to reduce their future reliance on petroleum. Since biofuels are likely to be produced in countries outside of OPEC, they may also allow oil-consuming nations to diversify the sources of their transport fuels, and hence provide energy security benefits. While some debate the significance of the energy security advantages, until alternative transportation fuels (such as hydrogen and electricity) can be produced and consumed at a competitive price, biofuels are one of the few short-term options available to national governments worried about dependence on imported oil.

1.2. Climate: Growing concern over global climate change has motivated growing interest in all manner of renewable energy sources, biofuels among them. With transport contributing around 25% of global carbon dioxide (CO_2) emissions and with very few viable alternative fuels available, biofuels have been presented as a potentially significant contributor to strategies for reducing net greenhouse gas emissions from the transportation sector. There is little question that when produced and used appropriately, biofuels can deliver substantially lower net greenhouse gas emissions than fuels derived from fossil sources. This is particularly true when considering the greenhouse gas intensive synthetic fuels produced from coal or oil shale that are one of the principal alternatives for liquid transport fuels. But the net greenhouse gas emissions of biofuels vary significantly depending on the feedstocks and technologies used in their production and consumption. And the overall impact of biofuel development on climate is more complex still, tied up with differences in carbon stocks and solar reflectance between the biomass crops and the vegetation they replace. It seems virtually certain that biofuels will (and should) have a role in national and global strategies to address the dangers of climate change. What is the most appropriate nature, scale, and location of that role remains an open question.

1.3. Economic Development: Biofuels and their feedstocks could be an important source of export income for developing nations. History has shown that participating in the global economy through export activity is a crucial part of the economic development process. In some tropical countries, biofuel production can bring with it "stepping stone" effects such as the extension of transportation networks, as well as job creation.

In addition to, or in some cases in lieu of, growing biofuels for export, countries can substitute domestically-produced biofuels for imported oil products, reducing the micro and macro impacts of the sharp escalation in oil prices. In addition, biofuels present an opportunity for new entrepreneurial companies and small holders to emerge while simultaneously increasing economic activity in both developed and developing countries.

2. WHAT ARE THE CONCERNS ABOUT BIOFUELS?

Just as there are multiple goals that many seek to achieve through appropriate biofuel production and use, there are also multiple concerns. Many have blamed biofuels for higher food prices.

Critics have also questioned the carbon mitigation claims surrounding biofuels. Others have pointed out that some kinds of increased biofuel production may dramatically increase nitrogen flows into lakes, streams, and coastal waters. Intensive use of land to produce biofuels – just like intensive use of land to produce food and fiber – can have serious impacts on conservation and ecosystem services, and on the livelihood security of poor land users. There are economic challenges as well. Many of the poorer tropical countries identified as potential targets for future investments currently lack the transportation and agricultural infrastructure to fully realize the potential of biofuels. Furthermore, trade barriers continue to block the development of a global biofuels market. More generally, critics argue that without appropriate public policy, the potential benefits of increased biofuel production may be outweighed by the costs.

It is important to carefully characterize the concerns raised about biofuels in order to tailor effective policy. Any single policy that attempts to address every challenge simultaneously is almost certain to be ineffective and would likely foreclose the opportunity to realize the potential benefits outlined above. In fact, it is well established that good policy generally needs as many different instruments or interventions as it has targets or objectives. To address the four or five concerns noted above, good biofuel policy should generally expect to need four or five instruments, each tailored to the particular challenge at hand. Of course reality is more complex, and it will also be important to consider the interactions among such instruments, and to pick ones that are mutually supportive. The broader point remains, however, that by being specific and clear about goals and constraints on the one hand, and specific interventions to address each of them on the other, an analytical rather than ideological approach to biofuels can become possible. In this way, policymaking can isolate problems about biofuels and start down the path toward mitigating those problems so as to secure in a responsible manner the potential benefits that biofuels can almost certainly offer to society.

2.1. Food versus Fuel: According to the Food and Agriculture Organization of the United Nations (FAO), global food prices have increased dramatically, rising by nearly 40% in 2007 and continuing to increase at the time of this session. Nearly all agricultural commodities have been affected, including major grains such as maize, wheat and rice. The causes of the price hikes include adverse weather in key production areas, higher agricultural input prices (especially oil and oil-derived products such as fertilizers), and limited elasticity in agricultural production capability. Demand for food has also grown, especially in Asia and sub-Saharan Africa. While experts differ as to the extent of its role, increased biofuel production has also clearly played a part in higher food prices, shifting land away from food production and triggering increased competition for land use.

Another major underlying factor in the increase in food prices is that agricultural practices have not kept up with changing challenges and demands. Agricultural research and development has been underfunded for several decades, as have investments in rural infrastructure such as modern irrigation technologies and roads. In addition, energy and environmental policies that have pushed biofuel development have had little interaction or coordination with agricultural policies. Thus, biofuels production has not been fully integrated or embedded in strategic agriculture policy.

2.2. Greenhouse Gases: When measured over the entire production chain, the production of some biofuels, such as sugarcane-based ethanol, results in significant reductions in carbon dioxide emissions compared to conventional gasoline. The production of some biofuels can lead to smaller reductions, or even increases, in net carbon emissions. In particular, Session participants identified the clearing of forests to grow energy crops as a major concern as this practice can release large amounts of carbon dioxide to the atmosphere. Other sources of greenhouse gases emissions were also a cause for concern, such as the oxidation of peat that has resulted from the clearing of swamp forests for oil palm plantations in Indonesia. Several participants pointed out that the significance of N_2O as a greenhouse gas should not be neglected as its impacts can be exacerbated by biofuel production and use.

Biofuel development that results in an increase in greenhouse gas emissions, rather than a reduction, erodes climate goals. Polices are needed to ensure forest protection and to encourage changes in agricultural practices to reduce net greenhouse gas. There is presently a lack of consistent methodologies for carbon emissions accounting that would allow society to precisely assess the impact of different agricultural and forestry practices. The absence of an agreed methodology is a major barrier to the development and implementation of a sustainable biofuels industry and associated policies. This barrier is being addressed by several international organizations including the Global Bioenergy Partnership.

2.3. Ecosystems: * * * Air pollution, water pollution (especially nitrogen run-off), deforestation, loss of biodiversity, and overuse of water for irrigation in countries that are likely to face increased water shortages over the next several decades are all issues that require close attention in the development of agriculture for both increased food and biofuel production. The extent to which mixed-model development, including production from small holders, might balance ecosystem protection with economic development should be examined more closely.

2.4. Market Concerns: A free and open market for biofuels in which products, technologies, and producers can freely compete on relevant terms will encourage product improvement, capacity growth, and cost reductions. But clearly the environmental land use and economic costs will require regulatory intervention to set minimum standards and create a level playing field. Concerns about the market can be grouped into three areas: trade, incentives, and infrastructure.

2.4.1. Trade: Currently, a world market for biofuels does not exist. Import tariffs and non-tariff trade barriers erected by potential biofuel-consuming nations constrain the emergence of a functioning global market and eliminate economic opportunities for a number of developing countries. Such policies also reduce access to lower-priced biofuels in consuming countries. However, direct competition should be avoided where possible between western farmers intent on protecting their domestic markets and food and fuel suppliers from developing regions intent on identifying and accessing new markets.

2.4.2. Incentives: Session participants raised concerns about the inadequate design of existing incentives and mandates for biofuel production. Many were uncomfortable with mandates, arguing that they often target the wrong goals, and therefore serve as an ineffective instrument for achieving the full potential benefit from biofuels. However, as a recent UNCTAD study pointed out, no country has ever established a biofuels market without the use of mandates and subsidies. Prematurely removing existing mandates would have a chilling effect on the nascent biofuel industry, as investors who have committed funds in response to these mandates might walk away, stranding established production capacity. Uncertainty about policy and programmatic consistency was identified as a major constraint on future investment.

Several participants argued that if a second generation of biofuels is to emerge, financial rewards should be linked to reductions in greenhouse gas emissions at all stages of the production chain. Simply relying on prohibitions and other negative incentives to achieve these ends would not be sufficient.

Much discussion centered on biofuel certification processes, and on how to design them to ensure that environmental and developmental goals were addressed. The common sentiment was that these processes, if poorly designed, could severely restrain the market without appreciably improving sustainability or reducing greenhouse gas emissions. Several participants suggested that the principles embodied in the Roundtable on Sustainable Biofuels should be generally supported.

2.4.3. Infrastructure: An additional market challenge is that many of the poorer potential biofuel-producing nations lack the transportation, institutional, regulatory, and service infrastructures to support a biofuel industry.

It is unlikely that investments in this infrastructure will precede investments in biofuel production since development banks will not provide financing unless the demand for the product is clearly identifiable. For example, if the World Bank is to finance a road in the Congo to support a burgeoning biofuels industry, it must have assurances that there will be an industry present to use the road or it will not take on the demand risk. However, unless there is a reasonable probability that adequate infrastructure will exist to transport their products, investors will not put up their money. Significant investments in infrastructure are required, but they must be sequenced in a manner that is reasonable both for the investors and the banks.

Many poorer developing countries lack the regulatory, institutional, and legal systems necessary to induce investors to take the financial risks inherent in building a nascent industry. Their governments are struggling to develop and implement such systems and need technical, and in some instances financial, assistance to design appropriate governance frameworks.

2.4.4. Land Use: The biofuel debate is about how countries use their land. As food and fuel prices increase, competition for the world's land, especially for forests–will become more fierce. Many countries, including those in the developed world, lack the institutional capacity to tailor policies and programs that integrate agriculture, energy and environmental policies into a coherent land use policy. Governments will be under increased pressures to play the role of facilitator between local communities, businesses, and interest groups.

They presently lack a coherent menu of institutions and policies to fill this new responsibility. For many governments, this would be a particularly challenging and unfamiliar task for which technical assistance and external policy advice may be required.

3. WHAT'S TO BE DONE?

What are the most important actions that could be taken to overcome the barriers impeding the use of biofuels for sustainable development? Who should be responsible for those actions?

As noted in earlier sections, many at the Session agreed that a necessary though insufficient step to realize the potential of a sustainable biofuel industry in developing countries is the emergence of an international market to couple supply, demand, and the incentives for investment and innovation at the largest possible scale. Ideally, such an international market would encourage the production of biofuels in locations where they can be grown most efficiently and where undesirable impacts are the smallest, and the consumption of biofuels in locations where the need for them is greatest. There was a strong feeling among the participants that the potential benefits of an international market in biofuels could be outweighed by risks of damage to food and environment systems unless adequate protective measures were simultaneously introduced.

These protective measures will likely include the explicit recognition that sustainable production of biofuels cannot be expanded indefinitely. There are intrinsic limits on the productive capacity of ecosystems, constraining yields per unit of available area, and the amount of area that can be dedicated to sustainable biofuels production.

3.1. Industry Development: Support for infrastructure and vastly expanded R&D are essential for the development of any global biofuel industry. If that industry is to be sustainable, governments must also put into place a portfolio of incentives aimed at minimizing the collateral impacts, including environmental damage, increased food prices, and additional greenhouse gas emissions. *Responsibility for action in this arena lies largely with national governments and multi-national firms.*

3.2. Infrastructure Development: Biofuel production is infrastructure intensive. At the national level, many poorer countries will find it difficult, especially in the early years, to develop the physical and institutional infrastructure needed to exploit their potential for sustainable production of biofuels unless provided with substantial outside support. Without the means to transport and store both the feedstock and the final product, biofuel companies in poorer developing countries will not be able to attract significant investment.

3.2.1. Public Good Infrastructure: Much of the needed support is of a public good variety that can generally be provided only by international, bilateral, and private aid programs. Such assistance should be directed to traditional development infrastructure projects such as roads to connect production areas with refining facilities and markets. (Such projects, wherever possible, should be "dual use," providing infrastructure needed for biofuel development that can also support agricultural and other development.)

Additional assistance for public good infrastructure is also needed to support the development of biofuel-related public goods such as research (see below) and production processes that help to reduce environmental impacts that would otherwise be externalized (e.g., highly efficient irrigation and fertilization; low-impact harvest). *Responsibility for action in this arena lies primarily with development banks; international, bilateral, and private aid programs; and developing country governments.*

3.2.2. Private Good Infrastructure: Some of the infrastructure support needed for biofuel development can generate returns to investors and is thus a potential opportunity for loans or direct foreign investment. Examples include investments in production, refinery/processing, and product distribution facilities. *Responsibility for action in this arena lies with banks and multi-national firms seeking to develop operations in the producing countries.*

3.3. Standards and Certification: Session participants expressed broad agreement with the view that creation of appropriate standards and certification protocols is essential for the sustainable development of biofuels. Certification or standards should be treated as means to advancing sustainable development of biofuels, not as an end in themselves.

They need to balance the complexity desired to cover all concerns with the simplicity needed to promote practical and timely development and implementation. Actions are needed to stimulate the development of an efficient market for biofuels while simultaneously guiding that development in sustainable directions. There was support at the Session for the idea that while standards or certification protocols may be needed to realize many of the major goals for the sustainable development of biofuels, efforts to control or regulate biofuels through any single global certification process or standard are likely to fail. Instead certification processes should be targeted towards specific, clearly defined problems that are not, or cannot be, addressed by other regulatory or policy mechanism. A "one measure for all problems" approach relies on an overly blunt instrument and is not likely to succeed.

3.3.1. Basic Product Standards: "Plain vanilla" product standards are needed to facilitate the emergence of a biofuel market by helping buyers and sellers to share an understanding of just what they are bargaining about. (For example, oil traders can specify an interest in "Arabian light crude oil" with the reasonable expectation that the kind of product the buyer expects to get will be the kind of product that the seller actually provides.) To encourage competition and improvements, biofuel product standards should be developed for categories of fuels (such as fuel for spark-ignition engines) rather than particular products (such as ethanol). Such product standards are generally most useful if developed and promulgated under international auspices with engagement of both producers and consumers in their design. *Responsibility for action in this arena lies with multi-national, multi-stakeholder partnerships.*

3.3.2. Greenhouse Gas Standards or Certification: Depending upon the methods used to produce them, biofuels may have net impacts on the global carbon cycle and on emissions of other critical greenhouse gases that are either positive (releasing less carbon dioxide and other greenhouse gases than fossil fuel alternatives), or negative (releasing more carbon dioxide and other greenhouse gases than fossil fuel alternatives). Several Session participants pointed out that in this respect, biofuels are similar to other uses of land resources, such as food production. They argued that it could unduly constrain realization of the potential benefits of biofuel development to impose different certification requirements for specific emissions on land used to produce fuel than on land used to produce food and fiber. The direct and indirect impacts on land resources from increased demand for biofuels are intrinsically no different than the impacts from increased demand for food.

If, however, biofuel development projects claim that they should receive special treatment or financing because of their supposed contribution to solving the climate problem, then they need to be able to document that contribution for buyers, investors, and regulators. Similar needs exist if land-use interventions generally (e.g. forestry, food, and fiber production) are called upon under future climate agreements to account for their net contribution to greenhouse gas emissions. To provide such documentation, it seemed essential to most Session participants that reliable and standardized life-cycle-accounting (LCA) methods be developed to assess the net carbon budgets associated with particular biofuel and other land use projects. More generally, assessment frameworks need to be developed and applied that will allow us to address the impacts of alternative biofuel strategies not only on greenhouse gas emissions, but also on other determinants of climate change (e.g. surface reflectivity). *Responsibility for this area of work lies most appropriately in cooperative action involving the international science community and the countries/firms involved in biofuel production.*

3.3.3. Standards or Certification Relevant to Food and Ecosystem Service Concerns: Should standards or certification similar to those discussed for greenhouse gases be developed to trace the impact of biofuel development on food production or other ecosystem services? For example, some participants argued that biofuels ought to be grown only on soils that do not support forests, are degraded, or are otherwise unable to support food crops. Those who shared this view were primarily motivated by concerns about the impact of biofuel development on greenhouse gas emissions, the loss of biodiversity, and a host of other environmental consequences, and thus focused their attention on designing a carbon certification process. Still others argued for feedstock-based standards, designed to document which biofuels are produced from non-food feedstocks. There were also concerns that any substantial additions of fertilizer use due to biofuel development could further exacerbate existing problems of eutrophication and "dead zones" in coastal seas.

Others made a case for not stifling biofuel development with requirements that would not be made for other land use projects, e.g. those taking land out of food crop production and into use for fiber crops or for lumber used in building homes. The Session did not come to closure on this issue. There was, however, a general consensus that the best way to handle concerns about the impacts of biofuels beyond greenhouse gases was to build comprehensive plans for assuring food security and the conservation of ecosystem services, and to hold biofuel projects accountable to standards comparable to those imposed on other proposals for land use change (see later section on Governance). Such standards should be developed in a transparent, independent, and participatory manner. Work on such standards has begun in a number of forums, including the Roundtable on Sustainable Biofuels.

3.4. Mandates and Incentives: Targets for biofuel use and incentives for biofuel production have had a major impact on the rate and pattern of biofuel development. Few would argue that these impacts have been optimal. Unintended consequences have emerged because mandates and incentives have often targeted the means (i.e. specific technologies or volumes of use) rather than the ultimate goals of biofuel development.

For example, volume mandates have almost certainly pushed producers to use crop feedstocks, since crops tend to have the best developed production technologies and are therefore usually the cheapest way to produce volume. The resulting competition between fuel and food has been a major source of tension. Better incentives should target goals, such as focusing biofuel development on non-food biomass, low net carbon life cycles, or approaches that protect ecosystem services. At the enterprise level, second generation biofuel production is often more expensive than fossil fuel production. Hence companies will seek greater financial rewards and subsidies for developing these fuels. Any such rewards or subsidies should be clearly linked to greenhouse gas reductions and the attainment of sustainability goals.

The shortcomings of many existing mandates and incentives notwithstanding, there was a belief among many Session participants that precipitous roll-backs or moratoria on existing mandates or incentives should be avoided. As mentioned in section 2.4, such actions may have serious impacts on biofuel investment, undermining confidence, stranding assets, and generally setting back the development of sustainable biofuels.

Needed instead is careful analysis of the mandates, with targeted adjustments only where necessary for sustainability. This should include a limit to extensions of existing mandates or incentives that are not carefully targeted on the ultimate goals of biofuel development discussed in section 1. In addition, governments should begin an orderly, innovation-sustaining transition toward incentives that are targeted on such multi-dimensional goals such as reduction of net GHG emissions, increasing utilization of non-food feedstocks, the attainment of sustainability targets, the conservation of biodiversity, etc. *Responsibility for this action arena lies primarily with national and regional governments in the United States, European Union, and other powerful markets. Important assistance could come, however, from the international community of scholars and policy experts who should help develop "model incentives" for nations to consider when designing incentive packages appropriate for their own particular contexts.*

3.5. Research and Development: Advancing a strategy for sustainable development of biofuels that meets concerns for availability, cost effectiveness, greenhouse gas reductions, food competition, and ecosystem protection will be a knowledge-intensive activity. A great deal of R&D is currently focused on the engineering and molecular biology of biofuel production. Some R&D resources are directed towards the relevant aspects of the global carbon cycle and some into biofuel production processes. Very little is going into research on the agricultural and natural resource systems needed to sustainably "scale up" a significant biofuel production system, into the limits of sustainable expansion, or into the ways that biofuel production interacts with the environment at global, regional, and local scales. Indeed, for years, the international system has neglected research and development in the agriculture and natural resource sectors. Even the most basic food and fiber crops have suffered from underinvestment.

For the complex, multi-use landscapes that will almost certainly be an essential component of a strategy for sustainable development of biofuels, only the very beginnings of the necessary knowledge base exist. Along with a lack of investment in biotechnology, irrigation, and roads, this underinvestment in knowledge has resulted in a long-term decline in land productivity. Food, fiber, and fuel production could be stimulated by increasing investment in research and supporting reforms targeted at increased production of multiple crops to serve multiple uses. The interactions among agriculture, energy, and the environment require that more of the research should be interdisciplinary in nature and should focus on the boundaries between these three fields. Some Session participants recommended doubling the public agriculture budget to revitalize the system, including support to the relevant research centers of the Consultative Group on International Agricultural Research (CGIAR). Such a reinvigoration of the CGIAR system, and its collaboration with other public and private sector experts in engineering and molecular biology, could begin to grow the necessary research capacity for sustainable development of biofuels. *Responsibility for action in this area resides jointly with the international scientific community (which needs to develop a strategic science plan on sustainable biofuels), the national and international funders of the CGIAR, related public goods research institutions, and large private-sector actors active in the biofuels arena.*

3.6. Governance: The increased demand for food and the emerging interest in biofuels has created a new challenge for governments at all levels. Biofuels are not only an energy issue, but also have major land use implications and thus must be approached from energy, agriculture, and conservation perspectives; all of which come together in land use. Most national governments separate agricultural, energy and environmental policy and natural resources planning into separate agencies. Too often the decision processes are stove piped with each agency focusing primarily on its own mandate and embracing the needs and demands of its own constituencies. In addition, the coordination between national governments and local and regional governance institutions where most of the land use decisions are made, is poor, or in some cases, non-existent.

Participants felt that it was important that biofuels not be the primary driver of land use policy. National governments should embrace the principles of integrated planning, but to do this they must be able to tap into and coordinate the interests of the many diverse stakeholders. This coordination can best be achieved at the local or regional level, which means that the role of the national governments becomes more that of a facilitator, providing guidance, financial assistance, and technical support to local and regional institutions. Local governments will often not have the technical capacity to design and develop the matrices to measure the impacts of land use changes. Thus national governments should provide technical guidelines and implementation training to sub-national governments. It also means that the relevant national agencies must develop coordinating mechanism, both among each other and with local entities.

Responsibility for this action arena should lie primarily with national governments, but guidance and information should be supplied by international institutions including the multilateral development banks. The best way to develop such internationally recognized guidance and information is almost certainly through multi-stakeholder mechanisms such as the Roundtable on Sustainable Biofuels and the Global Bioenergy Partnership.

2. RENEWABLE ENERGY - WIND

WIND POWER: BARRIERS AND POLICY SOLUTIONS
Chi-Jen Yang, Eric Williams, and Jonas Monast
Duke University Climate Change Policy Partnership (Nov. 2008)
www.nicholas.duke.edu/ccpp

II. Introduction

Wind power is increasingly recognized by the utilities as a mainstream power-generating technology. While wind generators currently provide less than 1% of electricity in the United States, the share of wind in the nation's power system is increasing faster than any other source of energy. Interest in wind will likely continue to grow as policymakers seek low-carbon energy sources to reduce the nation's greenhouse gas emissions. * * *

The DOE 20% Wind report provides a vision with detailed discussion of various issues that need to be addressed. However, the report did not propose specific actions for addressing those issues. The issues fall into a wide range of jurisdictions. Many federal and state agencies are involved. For example, the Department of Interior's Minerals Management Services (MMS) is in charge of approving offshore wind projects. The MMS is conducting a wide range of studies on the environmental impacts of offshore wind farms. Siting land-based wind projects is mainly within the jurisdiction of state governments, while the U.S. Fish and Wildlife Service provide guidance regarding wildlife impacts. The Federal Energy Regulatory Commission (FERC) is in charge of interstate transmission policies and is revising transmission rules to accommodate the expansion of wind power. The DOE is supporting a great deal of research and development on wind technologies. The provision of a Production Tax Credit (PTC) has been authorized by Congress. The Emergency Economic Stabilization Act of 2008 has recently extended the PTC for wind power until the end of 2009. It will require efforts from legislators, federal and local government agencies, and industries, as well as the public, to fully exploit the potential of wind energy.

Wind power is already a commercially competitive power-generating technology for utilities. Currently, the size of a typical wind turbine is around 1–3 MW. A large wind farm, with an array of hundreds of turbines, may have a capacity in the range of a few hundred MW. Because wind does not blow all the time, the capacity factor (actual power output over theoretical full capacity output) is significantly lower than coal-fired and nuclear power plants. The average U.S. wind power capacity factor is 27% in 2007 (compared to 73.6% for coal-fired and 91.5% for nuclear in the same year) (DOE/EIA, 2008). Because wind is intermittent and operators have no control over when it blows, a power system may become unstable once wind energy reaches a certain proportion of total power output.[1] A simultaneous stoppage of many wind farms may cause a blackout, unless the system is

---

[1] The percentage depends on the system's capacity in managing intermittence, which depends on many factors such the capacity of standby dispatchable power, the transmission capacity, the accuracy of wind forecasts, the availability of storage facilities, etc. The upper limits to wind power penetration would vary from place to place.

coupled with a dispatchable backup source or an energy storage system.

Wind resources are not evenly distributed. In the United States, the richest wind energy resources exist in the Midwestern region from Texas to North Dakota and in offshore regions along the east and west coasts. Current estimates of U.S. land-based and offshore wind resources suggest that the resource base is many times more than enough to supply the electrical energy needs of the entire country. Challenges remain in developing the required physical and institutional infrastructure (wind farms, transmission, regulations, financial incentives, etc.) to utilize the resource.

Currently, wind power is the most competitive source of renewable electricity. In 2007, the total installed wind power capacity in the US was 16.9 GW and annual growth rates during the past decade hovered around 20%. To grow to 305 GW by 2030 (DOE 20% target), annual wind power installation must maintain an average growth rate of 14% for the next 22 years. While possible, it is undoubtedly challenging to maintain such high growth rate over decades. This policy brief outlines barriers that will likely interfere with the expansion of domestic wind energy and suggests policy options for addressing the barriers if policymakers wish to maintain or accelerate the industry's growth.

III. Benefits of Wind Power Generation

Wind power generation does not emit greenhouse gases, though, as with any technology, wind power does have a small carbon footprint due to the energy consumed and carbon emitted in manufacturing, transporting, and installing wind turbines. The lifecycle carbon emissions for wind power are among the lowest of all energy technologies. A study by the International Energy Agency (IEA) estimated lifecycle carbon dioxide emissions for wind power at 7–9 grams of carbon dioxide per kilowatt-hour (kWh). By comparison, coal- and natural gas-fired plants released 955 and 430 grams per kWh, respectively.

The cost of electricity generated from wind power is largely competitive with fossil-fueled power, thanks in part to the Production Tax Credit (PTC) scheduled to expire in December 2009. The costs of wind power vary with the quality of the wind sites, size of the turbines, and scale of wind farms. In 2007, the amortized costs range from approximately 3–6.5 cents/kWh with the PTC or 5–8.5 cents/kWh without PTC. By comparison, the levelized electricity production cost at new coal-fired power plants is estimated at about 4.7–7.0 cents per kWh with varied assumptions on future coal prices.

Wind turbines are commercially available and can be quickly deployed on a moderate scale. The environmental impacts (excluding visual impact) of wind turbines are minimal or manageable. Wildlife collisions, in particular those involving birds and bats, with wind turbines are a real concern, but no significant impacts on bird or bat populations have been documented to date. A wind turbine causes almost no irreversible damage to a site. If a wind turbine is determined undesirable after it is installed, it is usually possible to remove it and restore the site to its original state.

The growth of the wind power industry can contribute to job creation. The logistical difficulty involved in transporting large blades from factory to wind farm will dictate that factories be located close to demand. Due to the rapid growth in the past few years, several major turbine makers are opening or expanding their blade production capacity in the United States (Vestas in Colorado, Suzlon in Minnesota, GE Wind in Iowa, and Gamesa in Pennsylvania). The manufacturing of wind turbine blades is a labor-intensive process which therefore creates new job opportunities.

The current economic environment (uncertain economic outlook, high fuel cost, and impending carbon regulation) is favorable to investment in wind power. When the outlook is uncertain, there is a value in postponing costly investments such as new nuclear or coal-fired power plants. The small-scale nature of wind power allows investments in small increments and thus reduces the magnitude of risks involved. Construction of wind energy projects generally completes in 5 to 12 months. By comparison, it takes 3 to 5 years to build coal-fired power plants and 5 to 10 year for nuclear plants. Only gas-fired power plants can be completed in a similar timeframe as wind projects and with similarly small upfront capital investment. In addition, wind turbines require no fuel and emit no carbon. It seems very likely that wind power will play an increasing role in the electric power system both in the United States and worldwide. Nevertheless, there are many barriers that, if not addressed, may slow down or even stop the expansion of wind power.

IV. Near-Term Bottlenecks

Although there are many political and business leaders advocating for faster expansion of wind power, many bottlenecks remain. Some of these bottlenecks are already being addressed. It requires a certain amount of resources, deliberation, and time to remove the bottlenecks. In some cases, faster near-term growth is not necessarily beneficial to the long-term health of the wind power industry. For example, the wind farm rush in California in the 1980s led to the wind industry's poor quality control and eventually the bankruptcy of nearly the entire U.S. wind turbine industry in the 1990s. It requires carefully designed policies to mitigate these constraints. * * *

A. Uncertain financial outlook

1. Policy-induced incentive uncertainty

The U.S. Government's provision of a production tax credit (PTC) for renewable energy has been on-again off-again. The most recent PTC provision is scheduled to expire at the end of 2009. Historically, the on-and-off provision of a PTC has created a boom-and-bust cycle of wind turbine installations. Even for projects that could be profitable without a PTC, there is still a strong incentive to postpone the projects until the PTC becomes available again. The policy-induced boom-and-bust cycle creates artificial market volatility and uncertainty and has widespread impacts on the industry. For example, the uncertain market outlook discourages wind turbine manufacturers and component suppliers from expanding aggressively. Volatile demand imposes serious risk to suppliers. From a manufacturer's perspective, it is generally safer to have a large backlog of unfilled orders than to build excessive capacity (often funded with loans). If the PTC is not provided on a long-term basis, the expansion of wind power is likely to slow down significantly. A long-term (through 2030, for example), stable provision of the PTC or a sufficiently high carbon price pursuant to a national cap-and-trade system is likely necessary to ensure a transparent incentive outlook, which is in turn essential for stable and rapid growth.

2. Market-driven price uncertainty

Its small-scale nature provides wind power with a competitive edge over coal-fired power and nuclear, but not over gas-fired power, which is equally small-scale. In fact, gas-fired power enjoys a very important advantage because it is dispatchable. High natural gas prices in the past few years have contributed to the rapid growth of wind power. If natural gas prices drop in the coming years, wind power's competitiveness might decline significantly, putting its potential carbon saving at risk. Without policies to maintain the competitiveness of wind power, it would be optimistic to assume that the high growth rate of wind power will sustain over decades.

B. Transmission bottlenecks

A large number of excellent wind sites are located in remote areas currently without either access to the power grid or, if they do have access, are without sufficient capacity to transmit the power output to population centers. A wind farm is impractical if it cannot sell electricity through the power grid. The transmission problems are widely recognized by the utilities and regulators. * * * Texas has started the Competitive Renewable Energy Zones (CREZs) process. CREZ designation is designed to solve the "chicken-or-the-egg" transmission dilemma: wind project developers are reluctant to build in areas without transmission, while transmission developers would not build lines to such areas without any generation facilities. In July, 2005, the Texas State Legislature authorized the Public Utility Commission of Texas to designate CREZs and develop a plan to construct transmission lines to deliver electricity from the CREZs to customers. The CREZ transmission lines are paid for by all utilities consumers. The Texas CREZ is a pioneering model for resolving the transmission bottlenecks for wind power. California is also assessing CREZs both within the state and possibly in neighboring states.

However, on the national level, the transmission issues are far more complicated. The U.S. power grid is an extremely complex system. Seven Regional Transmission Organizations (RTOs) and Independent System Operators (ISOs) operate the sections with deregulated power markets, where transmission and generation are managed by separate entities. Vertically integrated utilities operate the parts of power grid known as non-RTO areas. The power grid is divided into about 500 owners. As a result, a vast number of stakeholders (owners, operators, generators, consumers, regulators, etc.) with different interests are involved in the system. Different rules are followed at different parts of the interconnected grid. It is extremely difficult to obtain a permit to build an interstate transmission line. The fragmented governance has hindered the development of transmission system. For the past 15 years, investment in transmission lagged behind the growth of power demand and generation. There are already many bottlenecks and congestion problems in the system. The responsible institutions can barely keep up with the daily transmission demand, much less expand it to meet the future requirements of wind power. The balkanized institutional structure cannot be changed without a great deal of legal, regulatory, and institutional overhauls.

Many people are advocating for a national power transmission system to accommodate greater expansion of wind power. For example, the American Wind Energy Association (AWEA) has recommended several transmission corridors for wind power–American Electric Power (AEP) proposed an interstate transmission backbone system for wind resources integration. A consulting firm Anbaric Holding LLC also advocates a national electric superhighway. However, it remains unclear how to overcome the institutional and regulatory barriers to carry out any of these proposals.

Because many existing transmission policies were developed with conventional power generators in mind, they place wind power at a disadvantage. For example, transmission users are often required to schedule their use of the transmission system in advance. Transmission operators historically would charge severe penalties on deviations to the schedule. The rationale for imposing such penalties was to motivate generators to follow their schedule. This turned out to be unfair to wind power generators, however, because they have no control over the schedule of wind. The FERC issued a Notice of Proposed Rulemaking on imbalance penalties for intermittent resources in April 2005 and adopted a final rulemaking that exempts intermittent generators (such as wind power) from higher imbalance penalties in February 2007. This particular case exemplifies a trend: as wind power becomes increasingly recognized as a mainstream power technology, transmission policies are gradually modified to accommodate the special features of wind power.

Cost responsibility for transmission upgrades represents another aspect of the transmission bottleneck. Currently, the standard approach is the first-mover-pays rule. A proposed generation project is responsible for the reliability effects and costs of all transmission upgrades associated with its particular interconnection. However, due to the relatively small size of wind projects compared to typical power plants, the cost of transmission upgrades often amount to a substantial burden. A wind developer often abandons a project at the last moment only to reenter the queue later to take advantage of a later developer's upgrades. In order to break the logjams, some transmission operators are in the process of changing the rules to spread transmission upgrade costs among multiple developers, utilities, or end-users. For example, the California Independent System Operator (ISO) has established a new category of transmission asset called Multi-User Resource Trunkline. The California ISO would invest in grid expansion in anticipation of new wind power projects and recover the cost through ISO-wide transmission access charges. As wind power gains importance in the power system, we may expect regulators to gradually adopt this type of rule change more broadly.

C. Intermittency

A major disadvantage of wind power is its intermittency.[4] The capability of managing fluctuant output is a default feature of every power system, however, simply because the demand for electricity is fluctuant. The consumption of electricity varies with the time of day and season of the year. Any electric power system would require a certain amount of dispatchable capacity with or without an intermittent source like wind. It is commonly quoted that as long as wind power constitutes a certain proportion of the electricity mix (about 20%), the intermittency of its contribution would have a very limited and manageable impact on the stability of the system. However, since no country in the world has ever operated a power system predominantly supplied with intermittent sources, rapid escalation of wind power to a dominant power source in the near-term would be risky.

Globally, Denmark has the highest percentage (nearly 20%) of wind power in its total power mix. The Danish grid manages the intermittency by interconnecting with the hydropower-dominated Norwegian grid. Hydropower is highly dispatchable and can therefore compensate for the intermittency of wind power. Rapid expansion of wind power in Texas has already had an impact on the power grid. On February 26, 2008, a sudden drop in wind power output triggered an electric emergency and forced the Texas grid operator to cut service to some large customers.

---

[4] Some argue that the term "variability" represent the problem better than "intermittency", because even when wind is blowing, the strength of wind is not stable and the power output is variable.

Intermittency may be mitigated by connecting an array of geographically-dispersed wind farms. The peak and trough of power outputs from different locations can cancel each other out and provide a relatively stable output. However, the transmission system in this country must be significantly improved to take advantage of the geographically-dispersed and interconnected wind systems.

Transmission capacity has a direct impact on wind power's profitability. When wind farms generate excess electricity that cannot reach demand due to constraints on the transmission grid, they are forced to pay the transmission operator to accept their electricity. Wind power generators are increasingly forced to accept negative prices[5] in the western part of Texas as wind projects have expanded in this area. * * *

The grid system must deal with wind power intermittency as a part of its load management. There are many options to enhance grid operators' capacity in managing load fluctuation. For example, instead of paying a power producer to supply more output, a grid operator may pay the customer to shut down some of his/her electric appliances, which is known as demand side response or dispatchable load. Switching off some wind turbines for operational reserve or running them at reduced output (known as curtailment) can also be an option to ensure system stability. Although curtailment may be an effective method to ensure grid stability, it should used only as the last resort because this approach renders wind resources wasted. Better wind forecasting would enhance wind power's integration into the grid.

Although wind power is now exempted from imbalance penalties, the aberrations to schedule still incur grid-wise costs. If wind forecasting becomes more accurate, the magnitude of aberration will reduce and wind power will become more competitive. Smart grids[6] may also improve load management and prevent system failures. In the long term, the problem with intermittency might be resolved if utility-scale electricity storage technologies become commercially competitive and widely deployed.

D. Wind turbine supply constraints: Quality and reliability

Since 2005, the demand for wind turbines has been outgrowing supply. * * * Although manufacturers are already expanding their capacity to produce more gearboxes and bearings, the supply is unlikely to catch up with the fast

---

[5] Although the prices fall below zero, a wind plant may continue operating if the negative electricity price does not entirely negate the value of the 2 cents/kWh federal renewable electricity production tax credit plus the value of other state incentives.

[6] Smart grids are advanced power transmission systems equipped with intelligent, distributed, and highly-adaptive control systems to improve the efficiency, reliability, and safety of power transmission.

growing demand in the next few years. This supply constraint allows manufacturers to raise their prices as well as profit margins. Although wind turbines remain generally available, the prices have increased significantly. * * * [T]he price of land-based wind turbines has risen 74% in the past three years.

There are two rationales behind suppliers' reluctance to expand faster. First, rapidly ramping up production has historically led to difficulties in quality control. Rapid expansion would inevitably bring in inexperienced managers and workers. The risks of mismanagement, lower productivity, and quality deterioration increase with the speed of expansion. In situations where certain components are highly sensitive to malfunctions—bearings and gearboxes are the wind turbine components most likely to malfunction—the suppliers' reputations are highly valuable assets. Quality control problems could ruin a company's reputation and jeopardize its long-term survival. Second, profit margins have historically been low, and the market growth rates have been volatile. The intermittent U.S. PTC policy certainly adds to this reluctance. Ditlev Engel, president and chief executive officer of Vestas, commented: 'Over the last 10 years, the U.S. production tax credit for wind generation has been extended repeatedly for brief periods. If you would have instead said in 1999, "Let's make a ten-year PTC," I can tell you we would already by now have seen many more industries being built and developed in the United States, including ourselves.'

On the global level, the wind turbine market is oligopolistic. Less than ten turbine manufacturers, including Vestas (Denmark), Suzlon (India), GE Wind (United States), Gamesa (Spain), and Siemens (Germany), dominate the wind turbine markets in most countries except China, where the market is split by over 40 small domestic turbine suppliers plus the international manufacturers. Among major turbine producers, Suzlon has been relatively aggressive in expansion. Unfortunately, there have been news reports that Suzlon is having quality problems, which forced the recall of almost all the wind turbine blades it sold in the United States.

Many wind turbine components require labor-intensive manufacturing processes. Manufacturers may want to shift some of their production activities to countries with low wages. Although the difficulties in the transportation of large turbine blades push for local production, many other components may be outsourced. It is also possible to import blades of small turbines. Unlike major international turbine manufacturers that are conservative in expansion, Chinese wind turbine producers are expanding aggressively. * * * [M]ore than 40 wind turbine newcomers eager to capture a piece of this booming market. * * *

Few Chinese turbine manufacturers operate internationally. They are mostly small startups without sufficient testing facilities and quality assurance systems. These companies are usually unable to provide warranty and maintenance service overseas. * * * Due to lower efficiency and more frequent technical failures, Chinese wind turbines operate at an average capacity factor of about 20%, which is significantly below global rates (~25–30%). Another disadvantage of Chinese wind turbine manufacturers is that they generally lack state-of-the-art technology and mainly focus on producing small turbines. (Although small turbines are easier to transport, they are less efficient.) * * *

E. Workforce constraint

Due to rapid growth in recent years, the wind power industry is currently facing a workforce shortage. The wind power industry needs specialized technicians with knowledge of mechanics, hydraulics, computers, and meteorology. The maintenance technicians must be willing to climb over 200–300 feet in all kinds of weather. In the long term, as long as wind power remains profitable, more personnel will be trained and drawn into this industry. In the near term, however, if expansion accelerates beyond the rate of workforce buildup, the quality of construction, maintenance, and worker safety may suffer. * * *

VI. Policy Options to Address Barriers to Wind Energy

The ongoing wave of enthusiasm for faster expansion of wind power is facilitating the removal of many near-term bottlenecks. However, technological exuberance is likely a two-sided blade. Hasty expansion could eventually be counterproductive if policymakers and industry executives do not address the barriers described above. The following policy recommendations are aimed both at relieving near-term bottlenecks as well as addressing long-term social desirability.

A. Long-term investment certainty

1. Provide long-term price certainty with PTC and/or carbon price

The extension of PTC is unlikely to provide any further boost to wind power since the industry has already built it into their assumptions for the next 4–5 years. However, it will be serious blow if the PTC expires at the end of 2009. Unless the provision of PTC becomes permanent or at least long-term, the political uncertainty will likely continue to constrain suppliers' willingness to expand aggressively.

An alternative/addition to PTC is to impose a price on carbon emissions. Depending on the level and scope of the carbon price, it could provide wind power with a competitive advantage over fossil-fueled power. The incentive would be even stronger if the carbon price were coupled with the provision of a PTC.

2. Federal Renewable Portfolio Standard (RPS)

A renewable portfolio standard mandates utilities and other power providers to supply a specified minimum percentage of their power output with renewable energy sources. Wind power is usually the primary beneficiary of a RPS. Currently, twenty four states and the District of Columbia have a RPS. RPS mechanisms tend to be most successful when the federal PTC is in place. During the hiatuses of the federal PTC, the RPS mechanisms alone were not able to sustain the growth of wind power. A federal RPS would provide a stable demand for wind power. It could also provide a long-term visibility of wind turbine market growth and encourage manufacturers to expand accordingly.

Renewable energy potential varies significantly among the states, however. If a federal RPS set a uniform standard without a mechanism to harmonize the unequal cost burdens due to divergent resources, it may not be fair to all the states. Several RPS proposals have been introduced in the Congress, but none has passed. The Edison Electric Institute, for example, has opposed a nationwide RPS. An important rationale for the opposition is that a federal RPS would "create inequities among states." It is possible to address the inequalities with proper design. For example, if the federal RPS scheme allows tradable credits, utilities in states without renewable resources may purchase renewable credits from resource-abundant areas and transfer the credits back to their home state to fulfill the RPS obligations. Market mechanisms would equalize the cost burdens among states.

B. Transmission

1. Federal funding for power transmission grid expansion

Although many stakeholders recognize the need to expand and upgrade the transmission infrastructure to accommodate wind power, they spend a great deal of time on allocating costs. Transmission operators tend to be reluctant to invest in grid expansion in anticipation of wind power projects because such investments tend to be risky. If the wind project is not completed as planned, their investment will be wasted. Wind project developers are also generally unwilling to pay for transmission expansions because it would amount to substantial financial burdens. Federal funding for new and upgraded transmission would accelerate the expansion of wind generation by removing concerns over who will pay.

2. Accelerate FERC rulemaking on transmission policies

The Federal Energy Regulatory Commission (FERC) routinely reviews transmission policies and makes or changes federal standards. As exemplified in the case of imbalance penalties for intermittent resources, the rulemaking process usually takes a year or two. A concerted effort to review transmissions rules and streamline the rule-development process may be necessary to facilitate the continued rapid expansion of the domestic wind industry. It is important to note, however, that changing transmission rules often involves complicated deliberations and numerous stakeholders. Whether the rulemaking process could be reasonably expedited without abridging stakeholders' rights needs to be assessed.

3. Federal Competitive Renewable Energy Zones (CREZ) process

The boom in wind energy in Texas is no coincidence. Texas is in a unique position to pioneer innovative policy like CREZ because Texas Interconnect is an independent power grid located entirely within the state of Texas. Unlike other parts of the United States, the Texas state government enjoys plenary authority over its power grid.

The Energy Policy Act of 2005 authorized the DOE to designate "National Interest Electric Transmission Corridors." For the first time in U.S. history, the FERC was granted limited authority over transmission permit. The FERC has developed a permit process for the designated corridors. These corridors are designed to relieve existing transmission congestion rather than to support new deployment of renewable energy. If the purposes of the national interest corridors would be expanded to support renewable energy, they could be developed into the federal version of CREZ.

In order to replicate the Texas CREZ model nationally, the expansion and strengthening of federal authority over transmission would be necessary. * * * [One idea is to] require the President to designate national renewable energy zones and the FERC to promulgate regulations for cost recovery for transmission providers that build and operate facilities for the national renewable energy zones.

* * * [Another proposal] would require the President to designate national renewable energy zones and direct the FERC to pass regulations to ensure that investors of transmission capacity for renewable energy zones can recover their costs and a reasonable return through transmission service rates. It also directs the FERC to permit a renewable energy trunkline. In addition, the act would establish a Federal Transmitting Utility and a Transmission Fund that finances, owns, and operates electric transmission facilities of renewable energy trunklines.

4. Streamlining transmission permit process

The transmission permit process is highly complicated and uncertain. Permit difficulties have hindered investment in transmission capacity. Since the 1990s, utilities have added transmission capacity at a much lower rate than loads have grown. The regulatory authority over proposed transmission facilities is fragmented. Interstate transmission siting approvals are particularly complex and lengthy. Every state has its own transmission siting process, and the siting process is often contentious. Many communities along the transmission line may require local approvals. If the line crosses any federal lands or waterways, it will require additional approvals from respective federal agencies. The permitting process may take up to 10 years. In the case of Cross Sound Cable (connecting Long Island and Connecticut), legal disputes delayed the commercial operation even after the construction was completed. * * *

5. Creation of a national power grid

An underlying cause of the difficulties in revamping the national power grid is rooted in its balkanized institutional structure. The U.S. electric grid was not originally designed as a nationally integrated system. It is a collection of numerous small grids that were initially built by individual utilities to meet customer needs with locally generated electricity. The regulatory oversight was set up mainly at the state level. The FERC has only limited authority restricted to interstate issues. State public utility commissions (PUCs) generally allow cost recovery for only the projects with direct benefits to the state's rate-payers. It is difficult to gain approval for the financing of interstate transmission. Siting approvals are similarly confined by state boundaries. Siting a proposed transmission line is a localized process. Those seeking to construct new interstate transmission lines have to comply with the varying and potentially inconsistent requirements of several jurisdictions. Local oppositions often block projects that are in the broader public interest. The United States lacks a national system of long-range transmission backbones and has no institutional arrangement that can construct and maintain such a system. There are proposals on the physical design of interstate electric superhighway, but the institutional and legal arrangements for implementing these plans are lacking.

If an institution is established and authorized to build, own, and operate a national power grid, the decision-making, rulemaking, and financing might be greatly simplified and accelerated. Certainly, it would be a daunting political challenge to nationalize the grid. * * *

It has been recognized that the U.S. power grid is outdated and that revamping the power grid is an urgent task. The need to revamp the antiquated and fragmented institutional structure should be as important as revamping the physical infrastructure.

6. Deploying smart grid technologies

Smart grids use automated systems (such as remote sensing equipment and automated switches) to improve the management of fluctuant loads. The system will be designed to anticipate and automatically respond to system disturbances (a feature known as "self-healing"). Smart grids are supposed to help prevent power outages, limit their spread, and restore power more quickly; they would therefore improve the power grid's capacity to accommodate intermittent power sources such as wind. Title XIII of the Energy Independence and Security Act of 2007 established the Federal Smart Grid Task Force to coordinate smart grid activities across the Federal government and the DOE has developed plans to develop and deploy the smart grid. Supporting the deployment of the smart grid would facilitate the integration of wind energy into the power grid over the long-term.

The DOE wants state regulators to require utilities to at least consider smart grid technologies before they propose power plants or transmission lines. However, although the remote sensing and automatic response devices could enhance the reliability, efficiency, and security of the power grid, they may not qualify as a transmission capacity upgrade, transmission expansion, or power generation. Under current pricing rules (which differ from place to place), investors of smart grid devices may not be able to recover their costs. Smart grid technology may benefit a wide range of free-riders, but the incentives to stimulate smart grid investments are lacking. In order to facilitate the deployment of smart grids, it is important that the regulations are modified such that investment becomes profitable.

C. Wind turbine supply quality and reliability

1. Testing facilities and quality certification system

Rapid expansion of the wind power industry may cause deterioration of quality control. The continued shortage of wind turbines may also force project developers to accept inexperienced suppliers. Although major established wind turbine manufacturers have in-house testing facilities, new and small entrants often lack of such capacity. Ensuring quality may become challenging with accelerated wind power deployment. The federal government could help mitigate this risk by providing testing facilities and quality certification services to domestic wind project developers. Historically, the lack of authoritative product information and the absence of institutional mechanisms to provide such information contributed to the massive failure of American wind turbine industry in the 1970s and 1980s. In order to ensure safety and reliability, the federal government may need to establish a trustworthy certification system and provide transparent information on wind turbine quality and reliability. * * *

F. Siting/landscape issues

1. Streamlining siting processes

Wind power siting processes are developing rapidly with legislative or regulatory changes occurring regularly across the country. The process differs from state to state, and not every state has siting guidelines. Potential offshore wind sites are largely within the jurisdiction of the federal government, which has not yet developed a streamlined licensing process for offshore wind projects. The first offshore wind power project [an offshore wind in Nantucket Sound off Cape Cod, Massachusetts] in the United States filed an application in November 2001 and has not yet been approved. This process is even lengthier than the siting schedule of a nuclear power plant. For example, Exelon applied for an early site permit for a nuclear power plant at Clinton, Illinois in September 2003 and received approval in March 2007. In order to facilitate the siting process, the federal government may need to develop a consistent methodology to review and approve projects. * * *

2. Guidelines on landscape preservation

There is a general consensus that the most valued landscapes (such as national parks, national historical monuments) should be preserved and not be made available for installing wind turbines. However, there will always be gray areas where people disagree on the tradeoff between the values of landscape aesthetic and clean energy. The Nantucket Sound offshore wind power project is a salient example. Currently, there is a lack of guidance on landscape preservation. Local communities are often unpleasantly surprised by the imposition of wind power projects, triggering outrage and causing the stakeholders to perceive wind turbines in negative ways. Any proposal that involves significant landscape transformation should require early engagement of stakeholders. However, if the engagement process is designed in a way that allows local communities to veto or delay projects, it might increase the hurdle for wind developers. It requires a carefully designed policy with clear guidelines on landscape preservation to clarify the gray areas, reduce conflicts, and facilitate the siting of wind projects. While it may be more appropriate for plan development and implementation to occur at the state and local levels, federal policymakers may consider providing guidance and resources to assist with the efforts.

3. Indemnification of visual impact liability

Some landowners who lease lands to wind project developers are requesting compensation for losses in property value that might occur as a result of the wind turbines. Due to the subjective and intangible nature of visual impacts, the loss of property value is difficult to measure. Landowners are not the only ones who could claim to be victims. If wind power companies bear the burden of all possible losses of property values in the viewshed of its turbines, the liability might become an unbearable risk. Although studies in the past indicate that wind turbines had no significant impacts on property values, the experience from the past is not a sufficient warranty for the future.

A possible way to reduce the risk of wind power projects is for the government to indemnify the liability of visual impacts. While wind turbines have other impacts (noise, wildlife, gear oil pollution, etc.), visual impacts are the most intangible and therefore the associated financial risks are the least predictable. If Congress preempts with an indemnification, the possible liability may be contained. However, it is also possible that an indemnification law may be interpreted as an official recognition of wind power's detrimental effect on property value and trigger more opposition.

Notes and Questions

1. For litigation by neighboring landowners seeking to enjoin a Virginia wind project as a private nuisance, see Burch v. NedPower Mount Storm, LLC, 647 S.E. 2d 879 (W.Va. 2007). Regarding bird kill from onshore wind turbines, see Center for Biological Diversity v. FPL Group, 166 Cal. App. 4th 1349 (2008). See also E. Burleson, Wind Power, National Security, and Sound Energy Policy, 17 Penn. St. Envtl. L. Rev. 137 (2009); B. Luciano, Is Vermont Ready to Embrace the Winds of Change or are There Gale Force Winds of Controversy Still Surrounding Wind Power, 10 Vt. J. Envtl. L. 337 (2009); D. Merriam, Regulating Backyard Wind Turbines, 10 Vt. J. Envtl. L. 291 (2009); T. Rule, A Downwind View of the Cathedral: Using Rule Four to Allocate Wind Rights, 46 San Diego L. Rev. 207 (2009).

2. The intermittency problem is a serious financial and technical impediment to wind and solar power. The wind may not blow hard enough or the sun may be blocked by clouds during times when the electricity could be used. At these times, the generator has nothing to sell and is not helping to meet the electricity demand. At other times, the wind may be strong and steady, or the sun shining brightly, but the demand for electricity may be low, so the excess power must go to waste. The answer to both problems is to store the energy when it is not needed and release it when the demand requires. However, storage technology is expensive and limited in capacity. A promising approach would be to deploy a large fleet of vehicle-to-grid (V2G) cars which could store and discharge electricity on command when the vehicle is not parked. Since the battery would be paid for by the vehicle owner when buying the car, that storage capacity would be essentially free (other than installing the electrical plugs in parking facilities, garages and homes.) The successful integration of the existing technologies with appropriate software is described in W. Kempton et al., A Test of Vehicle-to-Grid (V2G) for Energy Storage and Frequency Regulation in the PJM System, www.magicconsortium.org. (Jan. 2009).

See generally D. MacKay, Sustainable Energy (2009); D. Miller, Selling Solar: The Diffusion of Renewable Energy in Emerging Markets (2009); A. Nowamooz, Inadequacy of Transmission Lines: A Major Barrier to the Development of Renewable Energy, 3 Envtl. & Energy L. & Policy 176 (2008); F.

Sissine, L. Cunningham, & M. Gurevitz, Energy Efficiency and Renewable Energy Legislation (2008); B. Sovacool & C. Cooper, Congress Got It Wrong: The Case for a National Renewable Portfolio Standard and Implications for Policy, 3 Envtl. & Energy L. & Policy J. 85 (2008); J. Tomain & R. Cudahy, Energy Law in a Nutshell (2004).

What roles if any should nuclear energy play in reducing GHG emissions? In 2009 the Polish government adopted an action plan for nuclear power plant instruction starting in 2016 despite strong opposition from the Polish coalmining industry. See J Gray, Choosing the Nuclear Option: The Case for a Strong Regulatory Response to Encourage Nuclear Development, 41 Ariz. St. L.J. 315 (2009).

3. Proposed comprehensive federal climate change legislation (H.R. 2454, 111th Cong., June 26, 2009) would require federal agencies to purchase increasing percents of their electricity needs from renewable sources and authorize states to require electric utilities serving the state to purchase renewable energy at specified rates under what are known as "feed in tariffs". In contrast to renewable energy portfolio standards discussed above, under the feed in tariffs used in several nations, all renewable energy offered to the utility at the specified rates must be purchased, in lieu of requiring the utility to achieve any particular renewable portfolio percentage.

4. For more on ocean wind, wave, and tidal energy, see Chapter 6 Section E.

ACCOMMODATING HIGH LEVELS OF VARIABLE GENERATION TO ENSURE THE RELIABILITY OF THE BULK POWER SYSTEM
Integration of Variable Generation Task Force, North American Electric Reliability Corporation (April 2009), www.nerc.com

Reliably integrating high levels of variable resources—wind, solar, ocean, and some forms of hydro—into the North American bulk power system will require significant changes to traditional methods used for system planning and operation. * * *

Today, the bulk power system is designed to meet customer demand in real time—meaning that supply and demand must be constantly and precisely balanced. As electricity itself cannot presently be stored on a large scale, changes in customer demand throughout the day and over the seasons are met by controlling conventional generation, using stored fuels to fire generation plants when needed.

Variable resources differ from conventional and fossil-fired resources in a fundamental way: their fuel source (wind, sunlight, and moving water) cannot presently be controlled or stored. Unlike coal or natural gas, which can be extracted from the earth, delivered to plants thousands of miles away, and stockpiled for use when needed, variable fuels must be used when and where they are available. * * *

2.3. Variable Generation Technologies

* * * [V]ariable generation technologies generally refer to generating technologies whose primary energy source varies over time and cannot reasonably be stored to address such variation. Variable generation sources which include wind, solar, ocean and some hydro generation resources are all renewable based.[22] There are two major attributes of a variable generator that distinguish it from conventional forms of generation and may impact the bulk power system planning and operations: variability and uncertainty.

* * *The major underlying technologies include:

Wind Generation: Wind power systems convert the movement of air into electricity by means of a rotating turbine and a generator. Wind power has been among the fastest growing energy sources over the last decade, with around 30 percent annual growth in worldwide installed capacity over the last five years. On- and off-shore wind energy projects are now being built worldwide, with the commercial development of very large wind turbines (up to 5 MW) and very large wind plant sizes (up to several GW).

Solar generation consists of two broad technologies, Solar Thermal and Photovoltaic:

Solar Thermal Generation: Solar thermal plants consist of two major subsystems: a collector system that collects solar energy and converts it to heat, and a power block that converts heat energy to electricity. Concentrating solar power (CSP) generators are the most common of the solar thermal systems. A CSP generator produces electric power by collecting the sun's energy to generate heat using various mirror or lens configurations. Other solar thermal systems, like the solar chimney and solar ponds, which collect solar heat without the aid of concentrators, are in development.

Solar Photovoltaic Generation: Solar photovoltaic (PV) converts sunlight directly into electricity. The power produced depends on the material involved and the intensity of the solar radiation incident on the cell.

Hydrokinetic Generation: * * * Hydroelectric power harnesses the poten-

---

[22] Note the reverse is not necessarily true i.e. not every renewable energy source is variable. For example biomass is renewable and can be stored and used to fuel a thermal power plant and is therefore not variable. Another example is hydroelectric power with a large storage reservoir, to the extent it is not diminished due to drought.

tial energy of fresh water on land. Those with reservoirs are normally not variable, but run-of-river hydroelectric plants are. Wave power harnesses the energy in ocean waves—to date there are no commercial devices in operation. Tidal power harnesses the gravitational energy in ocean water movements. There are a number of pre-commercial devices in existence. Tidal energy has a unique characteristic amongst the variable generation resources as its generation pattern corresponds to easily predictable tides. * * *

3.3. Transmission Planning

* * * Transmission system expansion is also vital to unlock the capacity available from variable generation. Further, in those regions with a competitive generation marketplace, regulatory targets such as Renewable Portfolio Standards heavily influence the location and timing of renewable generation investments and their development. Furthermore, government policy and any associated cost allocations (i.e. who pays for transmission, additional ancillary services and ramping capability) will be a key driver for variable generation capacity expansion. Therefore, an iterative approach between transmission and generating resource planning is required to cost-effectively and reliably integrate all resources. * * *

3.4. Voltage Stability and Regulation Considerations

There are many large metropolitan and populate regions of the South and South Western states of the U.S. where the transmission system has become voltage stability limited due to growing residential load (particularly residential air-conditioning) and economic and environmental concerns pushing generation to be remote from the load centers. * * * Locating conventional fossil-fired generation closer to the load centers can potentially mitigate the problem (due to the inherent reactive capability of synchronous generators), however many factors, such as emission constraints, economic reasons (cheaper power can be bought from remote generation if the transmission system is supported by smoothly control reactive support), etc., may preclude the viability of this option.

Wind and solar (CSP) resources are typically located remote from load centers. This condition further heightens the need to pay careful attention to the issues of voltage stability and regulation. The key conclusion here is, whether due to the advent of larger penetration of variable renewable generation resources (which are typically remote from load centers) or the fact that new conventional generation facilities of any kind, are being located more remotely from load centers, issues related to voltage control, regulation and stability must be carefully considered and the power system must have sufficient reactive power resources (both dynamic and static) to maintain reliability. * * *

3.6. Flexibility in the Resource Portfolio

* * * There are many different sources of system flexibility including; 1) ramping of the variable generation (modern wind plants can limit up- and down-ramps), 2) regulating and contingency reserves, 3) reactive power reserves, 4) quick start capability, 5) low minimum generating levels and 6) the ability to frequently cycle the resources' output. Additional sources of system flexibility include the operation of structured markets, shorter scheduling intervals, demand-side management, reservoir hydro systems, gas storage and energy storage. System planners must ensure that suitable system flexibility is included in future bulk power system designs, as this system flexibility is needed to deal with, among many conditions, the additional variability and uncertainty introduced into power system operations by large scale integration of variable generation. This increased variability/uncertainty occurs on all time scales, particularly in the longer timeframes, (i.e. ramping needs). In fact, some power systems have already experienced significant ramping events across a large geographic area creating significant operating challenges. * * *

Notes and Questions

1. For renewable energy generation to be expanded, especially in rural areas where the required large amount of space is often more available, there will first need to be a more robust and sophisticated transmission and distribution system built. Siting and permitting of transmission lines to accomplish this purpose is generally a state function.

2. Fights over proposed transmission lines have often been contentious and hard-fought as citizens declare "Not in my backyard" (NIMBY). One facet of the famous Storm King Mountain dispute in the 1960s was the need for new transmission lines. See, Scenic Hudson Preservation Conference v. Federal Power Comm'n, 354 F.2d 608 (2d Cir. 1965). In that case, a utility sought a permit to carve out the top of a mountain on the Hudson River to create a reservoir for water that would be pumped up at night-using excess power from a nearby nuclear power plant—and discharge the water back to the river during the day when extra power was needed. It would take 3 kilowatts of power to get 2 kilowatts from the water discharge. The facility design allowed for the potential of 3,000 megawatts. In addition to the enormous facility itself, the project also entailed building a 25 mile high-voltage transmission line to New York City.

3. Should transmission and facility siting decision remain primarily under the authority of state and local governments?

4. *Carbon Neutral Law Schools*: Many universities already have sought to "mine" their expenditures for energy by adopting sustainable energy reforms,

such as employing lighting efficiency practices in buildings (see EPA's Green Lights and other energy efficiency programs, www.energystar.gov/index.), replacing inefficient hot water systems, adding new insulation, switching from heating with #1 oil to a mix of biofuels and diesel, or to all bio-fuels, beginning to install photovoltaic panels for solar energy or installing geothermal systems for air cooled or heated buildings. Ultimately, your law school's mix of sustainable energy reforms will require an integrated and phased approach. What sort of campus governance system is best suited to rapidly convert from business as usual to a carbon neutral sustainable energy system in your law school? Traditionally these decisions were removed from students and teachers and housed in a business office or building and grounds department. Is this a sustainable governance system? Do your tuition payments support unsustainable energy systems on your campus? See Value at Risk: Climate Change and the Future of Governance (June 2003) at http://www.ceres.org/Page.aspx?pid=596.

Emerging Areas of Law Practice. Former Dean and Congressmen R. Ottinger believes that "the most urgent issues for environmental lawyers to work on are those related to climate change mitigation and adaptation" such as:

- Laws to promote energy efficiency -- decoupling utility profits from sales; pay as you save (see www.pays.org; standards and incentives for efficient buildings, appliances, vehicles; government efficiency requirements, allowing agencies to retain at least a part of the savings; military procurement efficiency requirements.

- Laws to promote use of renewable energy: feed-in tariffs as pioneered in Germany; renewable energy portfolio standards; incentives.

- Subsidy reform -- remove subsidies for fossil fuels and devote the funds to renewable energy R&D and incentives.

- Tax reform: Revenue-neutral carbon taxes; auto taxes and license fees calculated on auto efficiency; taxes on sales of appliances calculated on efficiency; appliance and vehicle efficiency labeling.

- Agricultural reforms: Incentives for use of organic fertilizers and pesticides; requirements or incentives for use of drip irrigation; promotion of organic foods and farmers' markets; promotion of locally grown foods over imports; standards for GHG emissions from biofuels.

- Preservation of forests and reforestation.

PROBLEM EXERCISE ON RETHINKING THE ROLE OF SOLAR AND

WIND POWER IN ELECTRICITY AND TRANSPORTATION

We face a dual challenge in addressing climate change, in making our energy system sustainable, and in addressing the 2.4 billion people who rely in poor-quality, highly polluting traditional fuels, such as firewood, charcoal and dung, as their source of cooking energy; and the 1.6 billion people in the world who live without any access to electricity.[7] From an economic, environmental and equity perspectives, the scope of our sustainable energy challenge is daunting. A brief historic analysis demonstrates the scale of our challenges. Over the past hundred years or so, human being increased from about 1.6 billion to over 6 billion people, global per capita income rose about 900%, and primary energy use increased 10 times, with fossil fuel use growing some 20 times. By 2050 population may well be 9 billion people, income may quadruple, and energy use, if we stay on a business as usual trajectory will soar.

As we have seen, energy efficiency can substantially reduce the growth in energy use, but unless we switch to renewable energy, we will not be able to stabilize greenhouse gases in the atmosphere at a level that will prevent dangerous increases in global temperature. In 2006, about 2/3 of global electricity was generated by burning fossil fuels, mostly coal, and nearly 99% all of transportation was fueled by petroleum or natural gas and fossil fuels accounted for about 28 billion tons of CO_2.[8] So we will need to make our electricity from renewable energy and drive our cars without burning gasoline. In the United States, 98% of the energy used in transportation comes from fossil fuels.[9]

In the United States our use of electricity continues to rise rapidly. Electricity demand from computers and flat screen televisions is projected to grow 3.5% per year, and already electricity use from electronic telecommunications and media devices are rivaling the amount of electricity used by traditional household appliances, such as refrigerators,[10] and summer demand for electricity to run air conditioners grows (and will grow further as the climate gets warmer). Even with aggressive energy efficiency efforts, we must to find ways to make our electricity from renewable energy.

The scale of the challenge is enormous. Is it possible to power our transportation and generate our electricity with renewable energy without burning fossil fuels? When considering what sources of energy are available to power

---

[7] InterAcademy Council, Lighting the Way (2007) www.interacademycouncil.net.
[8] International Energy Agency, Key World Statistics, 24, 37, 44 (2008).
[9] United States Energy Information Agency (U.S.E.I.A.), Annual Energy Review, Table 2.1e, http://www.eia.doe.gov/emeu/aer/pdf/pages/sec2_8.pdf
[10] E. Comer, Transforming the Role of Energy Efficiency, 23 Nat. Res. & Env. 34,35 (Summer 2008).

our society (and the world), other than fossil fuels, solar energy is the only source large enough to meet our needs. Yet in the United States of our total 2007 energy consumption 101.6 quadrillion Btus (Quads), wind supplied just over 0.3% (0.32 quads) and solar 0.08% (.08 quads).[11]

A huge wind resource sits off the mid-Atlantic coast in the Mid-Atlantic Bight that runs from North Carolina to Cape Cod–more than four times present electricity demand of the adjacent states. With 5 interconnected wind farms distributed across the area, based on historic wind records, power would be produced 99.3% of the time.[12]

There are many reasons why wind and solar energy comprise such a small portion of our national energy portfolio. But one of the central obstacle to using wind of solar power to generate electricity is that the power is intermittent. When the sun does not shine, solar power cannot be generated. Everyday the sun sets for the evening, and photovoltaic cells also go to sleep. Less predictable, but also significant, is the loss of generation due to cloud cover. Similarly, wind turbines require the wind to blow with adequate force to generate electricity. However, electricity must be used the moment it is generated or it is lost. Conversely, it must be generated the moment it is needed. So, if the wind does not blow, no electricity is generated and if the electricity is not needed the moment it is generated, it is lost.

Storing electricity is very difficult – and expensive. Because of this intermittency problem, renewable electricity generators can only sell a small portion of the electricity the equipment is rated to make. Additionally, to the extent that the power availability is unpredictable, utilities will not consider the electricity to be sufficiently reliable to include as part of the baseload capacity of the system. or may only allow the wind generator to have a small percentage of its total generating capacity included in the baseload supply of the utility, or be used to satisfy the utility's requirement to hold a certain amount of electricity generating capacity in reserve. The financial consequences of these realities is that the renewable electricity is expensive–large facilities are needed so that when the wind blows or sun shines, that renewable energy can be converted into electricity, but at other times this generation capacity sits idle, producing no income. And sometimes it produces more electricity than can be used.

On the motor vehicle side of the ledger, electricity is difficult to use because it is very hard to connect an electric wire to a car that is being driven. Liquid fuels that a vehicle can carry in its tank are far more practical and

---

[11]U.S.E.I.A., Energy Flow 2007, www.eia.doe.gov/emeu/aer/pdf/pages/sec1_3.pdf.

[12] R. W. Garvine and W. Kempton, Assessing the wind field over the continental shelf as a resource for electric power, 66 J. of Marine Research 751-773 (2008).

inexpensive. Battery-powered electric cars can carry their own electricity. However, given current battery technology, cars can only drive limited distances before they must be recharged.

If cars, when not in use, could be recharged with renewable electricity (wind or solar) and the car batteries could be available to discharge electricity back to the grid when the power was needed, it is possible to imagine an integrated system that could overcome the problem of electricity storage for the generators, and enable vehicle owners to drive their cars with only renewable generated electricity powering the vehicles. If electric cars could become a major, instantly accessible source of electricity, then renewable power would have a place to store the electricity generated when it would otherwise not be needed, and then the vehicles would be powered solely be renewable electricity.[13]

In 2007 Americans burned about 400 million gallons of gasoline each day (about 9.1 million barrels; a barrel is 44 gallons)–that's about 278,000 gallons of gasoline every single minute, 24 hours per day, seven days week.[14] We added over 2400 metric tons of CO_2 into the atmosphere every minute burning the gasoline.[15] Every year we add more gasoline powered vehicles to our fleet, we drive more miles each year per person, and that the fuel economy of our fleet of gasoline vehicles has only improved marginally over the last two decades.[16] Since 2004 the average weight of the overall fleet has remained relatively constant, however, average horsepower has steadily increased. By 2008 the average light vehicle will have increased more than 900 pounds and average horsepower will have doubled since the early 1980s. EPA also reports the that since 1975 there has been a dramatic reduction in the time it takes cars to go from 0 to 60 mph.

Put somewhat differently, car and light truck engines have become more efficient, but the engine improvements have been dedicated to increasing the weight and acceleration of our cars, SUVs and light trucks, while keeping average fuel economy per vehicle flat. Light vehicles can carry more pounds with each gallon of gasoline, but that capability was used to make the vehicles heavier and faster. If the improvements in engine efficiency had been

---

[13] Gasoline electric hybrid vehicles can also work as V2G vehicles; the gasoline engine would only be used on long trips that exceeded the battery capacity. In that case, the vehicle would be emitting CO_2, but only when the electric battery range was exceeded.

[14] U.S. E.I.A., Annual Energy Review, Table 5.13c Estimated Petroleum Consumption: Transportation Sector, Selected Years, 1949-2007, www.eia.doe.gov/emeu/aer/pdf/pages/sec5_32.pdf

[15] Every gallon of gasoline burned emits 19.564 pounds of CO_2. EIA, Table of fuel energy coefficients. www.eia.doe.gov/oiaf/1605/coefficients.html.

[16] U.S. E.P.A., Light-Duty Automotive Technology and Fuel Economy Trends: 1975 Through 2008, EPA Doc. EPA420-R-08-015 (September 2008) 5 - 6

used to improve fuel economy, average miles per gallon would have improved by 20%.[17]

Technical capability has not held down our fuel economy. Market and public policy choices simply directed innovation towards increased weight and speed. Could our existing technical capability be used to reduce CO_2 emissions from both electricity generation and transportation? This can happen only if we shift to renewable sources of electricity, which itself can only occur if we meet the challenge of how to store electricity for when it is needed. Perhaps a new breed of vehicles, two-way vehicle to grid cars can help meet the challenge.

Vehicle to Grid (V2G) technology is built into electric-gasoline hybrids or fully-electric vehicles so that the vehicles can both receive power from and send power back to the electricity grid.[18] A recent study of V2G role within a national grid found that "V2G, will improve the efficiency of the electric power system, lower CO_2 emissions and improve the ability to integrate wind power. In a less detailed, final analysis, V2G was combined with other measures such as heat pumps and active regulation of CHP plants, showing that end use integration, combining building and transportation end-uses, can form a coherent solution to the integration of wind power into sustainable energy systems, and that very high levels of wind power are possible, even without centralized storage or regional electric entities."[19]

According to the Mid-Atlantic Grid Interactive Car Consortium (MAGICC) "a fully electric car can draw or produce up to 19 kW, the average power need of 13 US houses." A car with that capability could be useful and economically valuable if can meet the typical driving requirements expected of cars and if the aggregated power in a dispersed fleet of cars can be called on to "meet the time-critical "dispatch" needed by the electric distribution system." If so, then the cost of storing energy can be shared between the vehicle transportation sector and the electricity sector, thereby reducing the cost of storage and recapture of electricity. Since the average car is driven one hour per day, the car could be available to the electricity grid 23 hours each day. When the car is not being driven, the grid operator, using internet or radio communications could "'talk' to plugged-in cars, buying electricity from car owners when it is needed, and selling it back when demand is lower."

---

[17] American Phys. Soc., How America Can Look Within to Achieve Energy Security and Reduce Global Warming (Sept. 2008) 31, www.aps.org/energyefficiencyreport/.

[18] Mid-Atlantic Grid Interactive Car Consortium, What is V2G, www.magicconsortium.org.

[19] H. Lund and W. Kempton, Integration of renewable energy into the transport and electricity sectors through V2G, 36 Energy Policy 3578 (2008) doi:10.1016/j.enpol.2008.06.007.

Such a system would improve electric grid reliability and efficiency: "V2G cars can take load off over-loaded distribution feeders when energy demands are high. They can supplement or replace spinning reserves and provide regulation up and down as demand fluctuates, and do so a much faster ramp rates than any existing generation." Also, and of enormous importance, this technology would allow a fleet of cars to store electricity generated by wind or solar power and overcome much of the intermittency challenge solar and wind power face. To substitute wind and solar power for significant amounts of fossil fuel electricity generation, the grid will need to store large amounts of renewable electricity generated at times when it was not needed. MAGICC proposes that "[f]leets of V2G-capable vehicles [could] constitute such a system, capable of holding MWs of electricity for later use."

To understand how this would work, and could be economically valuable, we need to understand some fundamental facets as to how our electricity system works. Our electric power system is "a complex and critical infrastructural system, yet it lacks energy storage capacity, so electricity must be simultaneously produced and consumed. Automobiles contain distributed energy storage; today, that storage is in the form of liquid fuel but we, and much of the industry, anticipate a shift to electricity. Both the power system and automobiles are designed to meet peak demands—peak electric use for the power system and the power to accelerate to full speed for the automobile. The actual level of utilization of both assets is far less than 100% most of the time, especially for local commute vehicles for individual urban families."[20]

Large-scale inexpensive storage would improve today's grid, by increasing reliability and reducing power system costs. As the power system develops more renewable generation, the need for electrical storage is likely to increase. Electric vehicles have the ability to store energy and control loads across the grid. An electric vehicle can be used as both a load and a generating source to balance the system frequency by charging the battery when there is too much generation in the grid and acting as a generator by discharging the battery when there is too much load in the system. In addition to regulation, vehicles can provide other services including: spinning reserve to provide power during unplanned outages of base load generators; back-up service, where one or more vehicles can be connected together to serve as a micro-grid during power outage in a given neighborhood; and peak management, when there are a significant number of V2G cars parked and connected to help reduce system peak. Millions of V2G-capable electric vehicles could provide the large, dispersed storage renewable energy needs.

According to EIA, the U.S. electricity generation capacity is 978 GW and

---

[20] W. Kempton, et al., A Test of Vehicle-to-Grid (V2G) for Energy Storage and Frequency Regulation in the PJM System (January 2009), www.magicconsortium.org/_Media/test-v2g-in-pjm-jan09.pdf.

the average load is 436 GW. If a V2G electric car connected to the grid could store 15 kw then the U.S. fleet of about 241 million cars would have a storage capacity of 3,615 GW–the power stored in our fleet of cars would be three ties the total generation capacity of the U.S. and eight times the average load! That fleet of cars could store (and release back to the grid) more than all the renewable electricity the nation needs. Such a system could displace our entire inventory of coal-fired power plants.

MAGICC has demonstrated that an electric car can be connected to the grid and can be controlled to be charged and to discharge back to the grid on command. Thus far the V2G test car has worked on each distribution system on which it was test and no grid problems were identified in the testing.[21] However, to increase the scale of the project distribution and transmission systems must have sufficient capacity to supply and accept power in and out of the car.

This would require huge investments in renewable electricity, particularly wind (on the middle and north Atlantic coasts, in the Midwest, Texas, and other locations with good, steady wind) and solar (particularly in the southwest and west, and southeast U.S.) to power the cars. But the storage capacity of the cars would enable enormous amounts of otherwise intermittent wind and solar energy to be installed, replacing coal-fired power. We could reduce our imports of petroleum, easing our nation security threats from our oil dependence, reduce urban smog, SO_2, NO_x, mercury and particulate pollution, and reduce greenhouse gas emissions from burning coal and gasoline. We would create demand for a new generation of motor vehicles. We would upgrade our electricity infrastructure. We would get an electricity grid that is far more widely distributed, so far more reliable and less subject to attack. We would have an energy system that no longer is subject to fuel price increases. And car owners would be paid for storing and releasing the renewable energy. All of this from integrating existing technology, thinking innovatively, and adopting appropriate laws and policies to support the efforts and to remove obstacles.

We will need to shift our investment strategy in a deregulated electric system to support renewable electricity linked to V2G. We will need to upgrade our infrastructure and develop legal policies and instruments that will enable homeowners, parking lots, business, and the deregulated electric industry to invest in the smart meters, necessary local and grid upgrades. This may require new or modified federal and state legislation and regulatory instruments. We will need laws for smart meters and to support new business models for entities to be V2G aggregators. There will be energy law, tax, property, contract, and liability issues. The program will need to be designed in a way to fit in with any national cap and trade system for greenhouse gases. V2G is a big idea, and will require innovative, timely and well-

---

[21] Id.

designed legal policies to midwife its birth.

PROBLEM: Conceptualize a legal system that would allow every owner of a V2G vehicle to become a market participant in this new, integrated energy system. How would CO_2 emission reduction credits be calculated? Who would get them? How would a V2G integrated system fit within the existing energy law system in the United States? What existing laws and agencies at the federal, state and local level should be considered? What legal problems do you anticipate?

CHAPTER 6. MITIGATING CLIMATE CHANGE

Climatescape: **Reducing Greenhouse Gas Emissions into the Air and Removing Greenhouse Gases from the Air**

The diverse human acts forcing change on Earth's atmosphere can be addressed by either removing the emission of carbon dioxide and other greenhouse gases, or by system that cause "sinks" to absorb carbon dioxide. How will the law of mitigation be enacted and integrated? Chapter 3 illustrated how the Montreal Protocol created a successful regulatory regime to remove one set of manufactured greenhouse gases. The U.S. Supreme Court's landmark decision in *Massachusetts v. EPA* in 2007 sustains the regulatory approach within the USA through application of the Clean Air Act. Regulatory tools exist at state and local levels of government, often together with the adaptation regulations discussed in Chapter 7. Requiring energy efficient building codes can reduce energy consumption, which guiding design of structures that better withstand weather impacts. While both taxation and cap-and-trade regimes require enactment of the regulatory laws to establish and provide the legal framework for their administration, these regimes seek to adapt private-sector economic decisions to internalize the climate externalities introduced in Chapter 4. The European Union has in place an Emission Trading System, as well as taxation and regulatory systems. How realistic is the "either/or" debate in the U.S. Congress about climate taxes vs. cap-and-trade in terms of achieving the quantum of greenhouse gas mitigation that the scientific reports excerpted in Chapter 2 suggest required to stabilize the climate before experiencing extreme disruption? What cap will the USA, nationally, or as a member of the UN FCCC accept? Additionally, what law reforms are needed to maximize the use of "sinks," in environmentally sustainable ways? Can biologic sequestration be ramped up to a global scale (only China has massive afforestation regimes)? Why is so little done globally for biologic sequestration? Can geologic sequestration be sustained in time, over time, or be achieved without unacceptable collateral environmental damage? What legal reforms will be needed to facilitate the rapid deployment of renewable sources of energy so that reliance on carbon-fuels can be eliminated? How can government deploy existing laws, such as the environmental impact assessment regimes of the National Environmental Policy Act (NEPA) for climate change mitigation?

A. WHAT IS MITIGATION?

Mitigation as Defined in Climate Change 2007: Impacts, Adaptation and Vulnerability, Contribution of Working Group II to the Fourth

Assessment Report of the Intergovernmental Panel on Climate Change

Mitigation: An *anthropogenic* intervention to reduce the anthropogenic forcing of the *climate system*; it includes strategies to reduce *greenhouse gas sources* and emissions and enhancing *greenhouse gas sinks*.

B. USING THE CLEAN AIR ACT TO REDUCE U.S. GREENHOUSE GAS EMISSIONS

MASSACHUSETTS v. EPA
549 U.S. 497 (2007)

Justice STEVENS delivered the opinion of the Court.

A well-documented rise in global temperatures has coincided with a significant increase in the concentration of carbon dioxide in the atmosphere. Respected scientists believe the two trends are related. For when carbon dioxide is released into the atmosphere, it acts like the ceiling of a greenhouse, trapping solar energy and retarding the escape of reflected heat. It is therefore a species—the most important species—of a "greenhouse gas."

Calling global warming "the most pressing environmental challenge of our time," a group of States, local governments, and private organizations, alleged in a petition for certiorari that the Environmental Protection Agency (EPA) has abdicated its responsibility under the Clean Air Act to regulate the emissions of four greenhouse gases, including carbon dioxide. Specifically, petitioners asked us to answer two questions concerning the meaning of § 202(a)(1) of the Act: whether EPA has the statutory authority to regulate greenhouse gas emissions from new motor vehicles; and if so, whether its stated reasons for refusing to do so are consistent with the statute.

In response, EPA, supported by 10 intervening States and six trade associations, correctly argued that we may not address those two questions unless at least one petitioner has standing to invoke our jurisdiction under Article III of the Constitution. * * *

I

Section 202(a)(1) of the Clean Air Act * * * provides:

The [EPA] Administrator shall by regulation prescribe (and from time to time revise) in accordance with the provisions of this section, standards applicable to the emission of any air pollutant from any class or classes of new motor vehicles or new motor vehicle engines, which in his judgment cause, or contribute to, air pollution which may reasonably be anticipated to endanger public health or welfare.[22] * * *

The Act defines "air pollutant" to include "any air pollution agent or combination of such agents, including any physical, chemical, biological, radioactive ... substance or matter which is emitted into or otherwise enters the ambient air." § 7602(g). "Welfare" is also defined broadly: among other things, it includes "effects on ... weather ... and climate." § 7602(h). * * *

In 1990, the Intergovernmental Panel on Climate Change (IPCC), a multinational scientific body organized under the auspices of the United Nations, published its first comprehensive report on the topic. Drawing on expert opinions from across the globe, the IPCC concluded that "emissions resulting from human activities are substantially increasing the atmospheric concentrations of * * * greenhouse gases [which] will enhance the greenhouse effect, resulting on average in an additional warming of the Earth's surface."

Responding to the IPCC report, the United Nations convened the "Earth Summit" in 1992 in Rio de Janeiro. The first President Bush attended and signed the United Nations Framework Convention on Climate Change (UNFCCC), a nonbinding agreement among 154 nations to reduce atmospheric concentrations of carbon dioxide and other greenhouse gases for the purpose of "prevent[ing] dangerous anthropogenic [i.e., human-induced] interference with the [Earth's] climate system." S. Treaty Doc. No. 102-38, Art. 2, p. 5 (1992). The Senate unanimously ratified the treaty.

Some five years later—after the IPCC issued a second comprehensive report in 1995 concluding that "[t]he balance of evidence suggests there is a discernible human influence on global climate"—the UNFCCC signatories met in Kyoto, Japan, and adopted a protocol that assigned mandatory targets for industrialized nations to reduce greenhouse gas emissions. Because those targets did not apply to developing and heavily polluting nations such as China and India, the Senate unanimously passed a resolution expressing its sense that the United States should not enter into the Kyoto Protocol. See S. Res. 98, 105th Cong., 1st Sess. (July 25, 1997) (as passed). President Clinton did not submit the protocol to the Senate for ratification.

II

---

[22] The 1970 version of § 202(a)(1) used the phrase "which endangers the public health or welfare" rather than the more-protective "which may reasonably be anticipated to endanger public health or welfare." Congress amended § 202(a)(1) in 1977 to give its approval to the decision in Ethyl Corp. v. EPA, 541 F.2d 1, 25 (C.A.D.C.1976) (en banc), which held that the Clean Air Act "and common sense ... demand regulatory action to prevent harm, even if the regulator is less than certain that harm is otherwise inevitable."

On October 20, 1999, a group of 19 private organizations filed a rulemaking petition asking EPA to regulate "greenhouse gas emissions from new motor vehicles under § 202 of the Clean Air Act." Petitioners maintained that 1998 was the "warmest year on record"; that carbon dioxide, methane, nitrous oxide, and hydrofluorocarbons are "heat trapping greenhouse gases"; that greenhouse gas emissions have significantly accelerated climate change; and that the IPCC's 1995 report warned that "carbon dioxide remains the most important contributor to [man-made] forcing of climate change." The petition further alleged that climate change will have serious adverse effects on human health and the environment. As to EPA's statutory authority, the petition observed that the agency itself had already confirmed that it had the power to regulate carbon dioxide. In 1998, Jonathan Z. Cannon, then EPA's General Counsel, prepared a legal opinion concluding that "CO_2 emissions are within the scope of EPA's authority to regulate," even as he recognized that EPA had so far declined to exercise that authority. (memorandum to Carol M. Browner, Administrator (Apr. 10, 1998) (hereinafter Cannon memorandum)). Cannon's successor, Gary S. Guzy, reiterated that opinion before a congressional committee just two weeks before the rulemaking petition was filed. See id. at 61. * * *

On September 8, 2003, EPA entered an order denying the rulemaking petition. The agency gave two reasons for its decision: (1) that contrary to the opinions of its former general counsels, the Clean Air Act does not authorize EPA to issue mandatory regulations to address global climate change, and (2) that even if the agency had the authority to set greenhouse gas emission standards, it would be unwise to do so at this time. * * *

EPA reasoned that climate change had its own "political history": Congress designed the original Clean Air Act to address local air pollutants rather than a substance that "is fairly consistent in its concentration throughout the world's atmosphere"; declined in 1990 to enact proposed amendments to force EPA to set carbon dioxide emission standards for motor vehicles, ibid; and addressed global climate change in other legislation. Because of this political history, and because imposing emission limitations on greenhouse gases would have even greater economic and political repercussions than regulating tobacco, EPA was persuaded that it lacked the power to do so. In essence, EPA concluded that climate change was so important that unless Congress spoke with exacting specificity, it could not have meant the agency to address it.

Having reached that conclusion, EPA believed it followed that greenhouse gases cannot be "air pollutants" within the meaning of the Act. ("It follows from this conclusion, that [greenhouse gases], as such, are not air pollutants under the [Clean Air Act's] regulatory provisions ..."). The agency bolstered this conclusion by explaining that if carbon dioxide were an air pollutant, the only feasible method of reducing tailpipe emissions would be to improve fuel economy. But because Congress has already created detailed mandatory fuel economy standards subject to Department of Transportation (DOT) administration, the agency concluded that EPA regulation would either conflict with those standards or be superfluous.

Even assuming that it had authority over greenhouse gases, EPA explained in detail why it would refuse to exercise that authority. The agency began by recognizing that the concentration of greenhouse gases has dramatically increased as a result of human activities, and acknowledged the attendant increase in global surface air temperatures. EPA nevertheless gave controlling importance to the NRC Report's statement that a causal link between the two "cannot be unequivocally established." Given that residual uncertainty, EPA concluded that regulating greenhouse gas emissions would be unwise. * * *

III

Petitioners, now joined by intervenor States and local governments, sought review of EPA's order in the United States Court of Appeals for the District of Columbia Circuit. Although each of the three judges on the panel wrote a separate opinion, two judges agreed "that the EPA Administrator properly exercised his discretion under § 202(a)(1) in denying the petition for rule making." 415 F.3d 50, 58 (2005). The court therefore denied the petition for review. * * *

Only one of the petitioners needs to have standing to permit us to consider the petition for review. We stress here, as did Judge Tatel below, the special position and interest of Massachusetts. It is of considerable relevance that the party seeking review here is a sovereign State and not, as it was in Lujan, a private individual. * * *

With that in mind, it is clear that petitioners' submissions as they pertain to Massachusetts have satisfied the most demanding standards of the adversarial process. EPA's steadfast refusal to regulate greenhouse gas emissions presents a risk of harm to Massachusetts that is both "actual" and "imminent." There is, moreover, a "substantial likelihood that the judicial relief requested" will prompt EPA to take steps to reduce that risk. Duke Power Co. v. Carolina Environmental Study Group, Inc., 438 U.S. 59, 79 (1978).

The Injury

The harms associated with climate change are serious and well recognized. Indeed, the NRC Report itself-which EPA regards as an "objective and independent assessment of the relevant science,"—identifies a number of environmental changes that have already inflicted significant harms, including "the global retreat of mountain glaciers, reduction in snow-cover extent, the earlier spring melting of rivers and lakes, [and] the accelerated rate of rise of sea levels during the 20th century relative to the past few thousand years. * * *"

Petitioners allege that this only hints at the environmental damage yet to come. According to the climate scientist Michael MacCracken, "qualified scientific experts involved in climate change research" have reached a "strong consensus" that global warming threatens (among other things) a precipitate rise in sea levels by the end of the century, "severe and irreversible changes to natural ecosystems," a "significant reduction in water storage in winter snowpack in mountainous regions with direct and important economic consequences," and an increase in the spread of disease, id. He also observes that rising ocean temperatures may contribute to the ferocity of hurricanes.[23]

That these climate-change risks are "widely shared" does not minimize Massachusetts' interest in the outcome of this litigation. See Federal Election Comm'n v. Akins, 524 U.S. 11, 24 (1998) ("[W]here a harm is concrete, though widely shared, the Court has found 'injury in fact'"). According to petitioners' unchallenged affidavits, global sea levels rose somewhere between 10 and 20 centimeters over the 20th century as a result of global warming. These rising seas have already begun to swallow Massachusetts' coastal land. Because the Commonwealth "owns a substantial portion of the state's coastal property," it has alleged a particularized injury in its capacity as a landowner. The severity of that injury will only increase over the course of the next century: If sea levels continue to rise as predicted, one Massachusetts official believes that a significant fraction of coastal property will be "either permanently lost through inundation or temporarily lost through periodic storm surge and flooding events." Remediation costs alone, petitioners allege, could run well into the hundreds of millions of dollars.

Causation

EPA does not dispute the existence of a causal connection between manmade greenhouse gas emissions and global warming. At a minimum, therefore, EPA's refusal to regulate such emissions "contributes" to Massachusetts' injuries.

EPA nevertheless maintains that its decision not to regulate greenhouse

---

[23] In this regard, MacCracken's 2004 affidavit—drafted more than a year in advance of Hurricane Katrina—was eerily prescient. Immediately after discussing the "particular concern" that climate change might cause an "increase in the wind speed and peak rate of precipitation of major tropical cyclones (i.e., hurricanes and typhoons)," MacCracken noted that "[s]oil compaction, sea level rise and recurrent storms are destroying approximately 20-30 square miles of Louisiana wetlands each year. These wetlands serve as a 'shock absorber' for storm surges that could inundate New Orleans, significantly enhancing the risk to a major urban population."

gas emissions from new motor vehicles contributes so insignificantly to petitioners' injuries that the agency cannot be haled into federal court to answer for them. For the same reason, EPA does not believe that any realistic possibility exists that the relief petitioners seek would mitigate global climate change and remedy their injuries. That is especially so because predicted increases in greenhouse gas emissions from developing nations, particularly China and India, are likely to offset any marginal domestic decrease. * * *

And reducing domestic automobile emissions is hardly a tentative step. Even leaving aside the other greenhouse gases, the United States transportation sector emits an enormous quantity of carbon dioxide into the atmosphere—according to the MacCracken affidavit, more than 1.7 billion metric tons in 1999 alone. That accounts for more than 6% of worldwide carbon dioxide emissions. To put this in perspective: Considering just emissions from the transportation sector, which represent less than one-third of this country's total carbon dioxide emissions, the United States would still rank as the third-largest emitter of carbon dioxide in the world, outpaced only by the European Union and China. Judged by any standard, U.S. motor-vehicle emissions make a meaningful contribution to greenhouse gas concentrations and hence, according to petitioners, to global warming.

The Remedy

While it may be true that regulating motor-vehicle emissions will not by itself reverse global warming, it by no means follows that we lack jurisdiction to decide whether EPA has a duty to take steps to slow or reduce it. See also Larson v. Valente, 456 U.S. 228 (1982) ("[A] plaintiff satisfies the redressability requirement when he shows that a favorable decision will relieve a discrete injury to himself. He need not show that a favorable decision will relieve his every injury"). Because of the enormity of the potential consequences associated with man-made climate change, the fact that the effectiveness of a remedy might be delayed during the (relatively short) time it takes for a new motor-vehicle fleet to replace an older one is essentially irrelevant. Nor is it dispositive that developing countries such as China and India are poised to increase greenhouse gas emissions substantially over the next century: A reduction in domestic emissions would slow the pace of global emissions increases, no matter what happens elsewhere.

We moreover attach considerable significance to EPA's "agree[ment] with the President that 'we must address the issue of global climate change,'" and to EPA's ardent support for various voluntary emission-reduction programs. As Judge Tatel observed in dissent below, "EPA would presumably not bother with such efforts if it thought emissions reductions would have no discernable impact on future global warming." 415 F.3d, at 66.

In sum-at least according to petitioners' uncontested affidavits-the rise in sea levels associated with global warming has already harmed and will continue to harm Massachusetts. The risk of catastrophic harm, though remote, is nevertheless real. That risk would be reduced to some extent if petitioners received the relief they seek. We therefore hold that petitioners have standing to challenge the EPA's denial of their rulemaking petition. * * *

VI

On the merits, the first question is whether § 202(a)(1) of the Clean Air Act authorizes EPA to regulate greenhouse gas emissions from new motor vehicles in the event that it forms a "judgment" that such emissions contribute to climate change. We have little trouble concluding that it does. In relevant part, § 202(a)(1) provides that EPA "shall by regulation prescribe * * * standards applicable to the emission of any air pollutant from any class or classes of new motor vehicles or new motor vehicle engines, which in [the Administrator's] judgment cause, or contribute to, air pollution which may reasonably be anticipated to endanger public health or welfare." 42 U.S.C. § 7521(a)(1). Because EPA believes that Congress did not intend it to regulate substances that contribute to climate change, the agency maintains that carbon dioxide is not an "air pollutant" within the meaning of the provision.

The statutory text forecloses EPA's reading. The Clean Air Act's sweeping definition of "air pollutant" includes "any air pollution agent or combination of such agents, including any physical, chemical ... substance or matter which is emitted into or otherwise enters the ambient air." § 7602(g) * * *. On its face, the definition embraces all airborne compounds of whatever stripe, and underscores that intent through the repeated use of the word "any." Carbon dioxide, methane, nitrous oxide, and hydrofluorocarbons are without a doubt "physical [and] chemical ... substance [s] which [are] emitted into * * * the ambient air." The statute is unambiguous.[24] * * *

---

[24] In dissent, Justice SCALIA maintains that because greenhouse gases permeate the world's atmosphere rather than a limited area near the earth's surface, EPA's exclusion of greenhouse gases from the category of air pollution "agent[s]" is entitled to deference under Chevron U.S.A. Inc. v. Natural Resources Defense Council, Inc. 467 U.S. 837, 104 S.Ct. 2778, 81 L.Ed.2d 694 (1984). * * * EPA's distinction, however, finds no support in the text of the statute, which uses the phrase "the ambient air" without distinguishing between atmospheric layers. Moreover, it is a plainly unreasonable reading of a sweeping statutory provision designed to capture "any physical, chemical ... substance or matter which is emitted into or otherwise enters the ambient air." 42 U.S.C. § 7602(g). Justice SCALIA does not (and cannot) explain why Congress would define "air pollutant" so carefully and so broadly, yet confer on EPA the authority to narrow that definition whenever expedient by asserting that a particular substance is not an "agent." At any rate, no party to this dispute contests that greenhouse gases both "ente[r] the ambient air" and tend to warm the atmosphere. They are therefore unquestionably "agent[s]" of air pollution.

EPA finally argues that it cannot regulate carbon dioxide emissions from motor vehicles because doing so would require it to tighten mileage standards, a job (according to EPA) that Congress has assigned to DOT. But that DOT sets mileage standards in no way licenses EPA to shirk its environmental responsibilities. EPA has been charged with protecting the public's "health" and "welfare," 42 U.S.C. § 7521(a)(1), a statutory obligation wholly independent of DOT's mandate to promote energy efficiency. See Energy Policy and Conservation Act, § 2(5), 89 Stat. 874, 42 U.S.C. § 6201(5). The two obligations may overlap, but there is no reason to think the two agencies cannot both administer their obligations and yet avoid inconsistency.

While the Congresses that drafted § 202(a)(1) might not have appreciated the possibility that burning fossil fuels could lead to global warming, they did understand that without regulatory flexibility, changing circumstances and scientific developments would soon render the Clean Air Act obsolete. The broad language of § 202(a)(1) reflects an intentional effort to confer the flexibility necessary to forestall such obsolescence. See Pennsylvania Dept. of Corrections v. Yeskey, 524 U.S. 206 (1998) ("[T]he fact that a statute can be applied in situations not expressly anticipated by Congress does not demonstrate ambiguity. It demonstrates breadth" (internal quotation marks omitted)). Because greenhouse gases fit well within the Clean Air Act's capacious definition of "air pollutant," we hold that EPA has the statutory authority to regulate the emission of such gases from new motor vehicles.

VII

The alternative basis for EPA's decision—that even if it does have statutory authority to regulate greenhouse gases, it would be unwise to do so at this time-rests on reasoning divorced from the statutory text. While the statute does condition the exercise of EPA's authority on its formation of a "judgment," 42 U.S.C. § 7521(a)(1), that judgment must relate to whether an air pollutant "cause[s], or contribute[s] to, air pollution which may reasonably be anticipated to endanger public health or welfare,"ibid. Put another way, the use of the word "judgment" is not a roving license to ignore the statutory text. It is but a direction to exercise discretion within defined statutory limits.

If EPA makes a finding of endangerment, the Clean Air Act requires the agency to regulate emissions of the deleterious pollutant from new motor vehicles. Ibid. (stating that "[EPA] shall by regulation prescribe * * * standards applicable to the emission of any air pollutant from any class of new motor vehicles"). EPA no doubt has significant latitude as to the manner, timing, content, and coordination of its regulations with those of other agencies. But once EPA has responded to a petition for rulemaking, its reasons for action or inaction must conform to the authorizing statute. Under the clear terms of the Clean Air Act, EPA can avoid taking further action only if it determines that greenhouse gases do not contribute to climate change or if it provides some reasonable explanation as to why it cannot or will not exercise its discretion to determine whether they do. Ibid. To the extent that this constrains agency discretion to pursue other priorities of the Administrator or the President, this is the congressional design.

EPA has refused to comply with this clear statutory command. Instead, it has offered a laundry list of reasons not to regulate. For example, EPA said that a number of voluntary executive branch programs already provide an effective response to the threat of global warming, that regulating greenhouse gases might impair the President's ability to negotiate with "key developing nations" to reduce emissions, and that curtailing motor-vehicle emissions would reflect "an inefficient, piecemeal approach to address the climate change issue."

Although we have neither the expertise nor the authority to evaluate these policy judgments, it is evident they have nothing to do with whether greenhouse gas emissions contribute to climate change. Still less do they amount to a reasoned justification for declining to form a scientific judgment. In particular, while the President has broad authority in foreign affairs, that authority does not extend to the refusal to execute domestic laws. In the Global Climate Protection Act of 1987, Congress authorized the State Department—not EPA—to formulate United States foreign policy with reference to environmental matters relating to climate. EPA has made no showing that it issued the ruling in question here after consultation with the State Department. Congress did direct EPA to consult with other agencies in the formulation of its policies and rules, but the State Department is absent from that list. * * *

In short, EPA has offered no reasoned explanation for its refusal to decide whether greenhouse gases cause or contribute to climate change. Its action was therefore "arbitrary, capricious, ... or otherwise not in accordance with law." 42 U.S.C. § 7607(d)(9)(A). We need not and do not reach the question whether on remand EPA must make an endangerment finding, or whether policy concerns can inform EPA's actions in the event that it makes such a finding. Cf. Chevron U.S.A. Inc. v. Natural Resources Defense Council, Inc., 467 U.S. 837, 843-844 (1984). We hold only that EPA must ground its reasons for action or inaction in the statute.

VIII

The judgment of the Court of Appeals is reversed, and the case is remanded for further proceedings consistent with this opinion. * * *

Justice SCALIA, with whom THE CHIEF JUSTICE, Justice THOMAS, and Justice ALITO join, dissenting.

    * * * The provision of law at the heart of this case is § 202(a)(1) of the

Clean Air Act (CAA), which provides that the Administrator of the Environmental Protection Agency (EPA) "shall by regulation prescribe ... standards applicable to the emission of any air pollutant from any class or classes of new motor vehicles or new motor vehicle engines, which in his judgment cause, or contribute to, air pollution which may reasonably be anticipated to endanger public health or welfare." As the Court recognizes, the statute "condition[s] the exercise of EPA's authority on its formation of a 'judgment.'" There is no dispute that the Administrator has made no such judgment in this case. * * *

The question thus arises: Does anything require the Administrator to make a "judgment" whenever a petition for rulemaking is filed? Without citation of the statute or any other authority, the Court says yes. * * *

[T]he Court invents a multiple-choice question that the EPA Administrator must answer when a petition for rulemaking is filed. The Administrator must exercise his judgment in one of three ways: (a) by concluding that the pollutant does cause, or contribute to, air pollution that endangers public welfare (in which case EPA is required to regulate); (b) by concluding that the pollutant does not cause, or contribute to, air pollution that endangers public welfare (in which case EPA is not required to regulate); or (c) by "provid[ing] some reasonable explanation as to why it cannot or will not exercise its discretion to determine whether" greenhouse gases endanger public welfare, (in which case EPA is not required to regulate). * * * But the statute says nothing at all about the reasons for which the Administrator may defer making a judgment-the permissible reasons for deciding not to grapple with the issue at the present time. * * *

EPA's interpretation of the discretion conferred by the statutory reference to "its judgment" is not only reasonable, it is the most natural reading of the text. The Court nowhere explains why this interpretation is incorrect, let alone why it is not entitled to deference under Chevron U.S.A. Inc. v. Natural Resources Defense Council, Inc., 467 U.S. 837 (1984). As the Administrator acted within the law in declining to make a "judgment" for the policy reasons above set forth, I would uphold the decision to deny the rulemaking petition on that ground alone. * * *

Even before reaching its discussion of the word "judgment," the Court makes another significant error when it concludes that "§ 202(a)(1) of the Clean Air Act authorizes EPA to regulate greenhouse gas emissions from new motor vehicles in the event that it forms a 'judgment' that such emissions contribute to climate change." For such authorization, the Court relies on what it calls "the Clean Air Act's capacious definition of 'air pollutant.'"

"Air pollutant" is defined by the Act as "any air pollution agent or combination of such agents, including any physical, chemical, ... substance or matter which is emitted into or otherwise enters the ambient air." 42 U.S.C. § 7602(g). The Court is correct that "[c]arbon dioxide, methane, nitrous oxide, and hydrofluorocarbons," fit within the second half of that definition: They are "physical, chemical, ... substance[s] or matter which [are] emitted into or otherwise ente[r] the ambient air." But the Court mistakenly believes this to be the end of the analysis. In order to be an "air pollutant" under the Act's definition, the "substance or matter [being] emitted into ... the ambient air" must also meet the first half of the definition-namely, it must be an "air pollution agent or combination of such agents." The Court simply pretends this half of the definition does not exist.

The Court's analysis faithfully follows the argument advanced by petitioners, which focuses on the word "including" in the statutory definition of "air pollutant." As that argument goes, anything that follows the word "including" must necessarily be a subset of whatever precedes it. Thus, if greenhouse gases qualify under the phrase following the word "including," they must qualify under the phrase preceding it. Since greenhouse gases come within the capacious phrase "any physical, chemical, ... substance or matter which is emitted into or otherwise enters the ambient air," they must also be "air pollution agent[s] or combination[s] of such agents," and therefore meet the definition of "air pollutant[s]." * * *

In short, the word "including" does not require the Court's (or the petitioners') result. It is perfectly reasonable to view the definition of "air pollutant" in its entirety: An air pollutant can be "any physical, chemical, ... substance or matter which is emitted into or otherwise enters the ambient air," but only if it retains the general characteristic of being an "air pollution agent or combination of such agents." This is precisely the conclusion EPA reached: "[A] substance does not meet the CAA definition of 'air pollutant' simply because it is a 'physical, chemical, ... substance or matter which is emitted into or otherwise enters the ambient air.' It must also be an 'air pollution agent.'" ("The root of the definition indicates that for a substance to be an 'air pollutant,' it must be an 'agent' of 'air pollution'"). Once again, in the face of textual ambiguity, the Court's application of Chevron deference to EPA's interpretation of the word " including" is nowhere to be found. Evidently, the Court defers only to those reasonable interpretations that it favors. * * *

Using (as we ought to) EPA's interpretation of the definition of "air pollutant," we must next determine whether greenhouse gases are "agent[s]" of "air pollution." If so, the statute would authorize regulation; if not, EPA would lack authority.

Unlike "air pollutants," the term "air pollution" is not itself defined by the CAA; thus, once again we must accept EPA's interpretation of that ambiguous term, provided its interpretation is a "permissible construction of the statute." Chevron, 467 U.S., at 843. In this case, the petition for rulemaking asked EPA for "regulation of [greenhouse gas] emissions from motor vehicles to reduce the risk of global climate change." Thus, in deciding whether it had authority to regulate, EPA had to determine whether the concentration of greenhouse gases assertedly responsible for "global climate change" qualifies as "air pollution." EPA began with the commonsense observation that the "[p]roblems associated with atmospheric concentrations of CO_2," bear little resemblance to what would naturally be termed "air pollution":

"EPA's prior use of the CAA's general regulatory provisions provides an important context. Since the inception of the Act, EPA has used these provisions to address air pollution problems that occur primarily at ground level or near the surface of the earth. For example, national ambient air quality standards (NAAQS) established under CAA section 109 address concentrations of substances in the ambient air and the related public health and welfare problems. This has meant setting NAAQS for concentrations of ozone, carbon monoxide, particulate matter and other substances in the air near the surface of the earth, not higher in the atmosphere .... CO_2, by contrast, is fairly consistent in concentration throughout the world's atmosphere up to approximately the lower stratosphere."

In other words, regulating the buildup of CO_2 and other greenhouse gases in the upper reaches of the atmosphere, which is alleged to be causing global climate change, is not akin to regulating the concentration of some substance that is polluting the air.

We need look no further than the dictionary for confirmation that this interpretation of "air pollution" is eminently reasonable. The definition of "pollute," of course, is "[t]o make or render impure or unclean." Webster's New International Dictionary 1910 (2d ed.1949). And the first three definitions of "air" are as follows: (1) "[t]he invisible, odorless, and tasteless mixture of gases which surrounds the earth"; (2) "[t]he body of the earth's atmosphere; esp., the part of it near the earth, as distinguished from the upper rarefied part"; (3) "[a] portion of air or of the air considered with respect to physical characteristics or as affecting the senses." EPA's conception of "air pollution"-focusing on impurities in the "ambient air" "at ground level or near the surface of the earth"-is perfectly consistent with the natural meaning of that term.

In the end, EPA concluded that since "CAA authorization to regulate is generally based on a finding that an air pollutant causes or contributes to air pollution," the concentrations of CO_2 and other greenhouse gases allegedly affecting the global climate are beyond the scope of CAA's authorization to regulate. "[T]he term 'air pollution' as used in the regulatory provisions cannot be interpreted to encompass global climate change." Once again, the Court utterly fails to explain why this interpretation is incorrect, let alone so unreasonable as to be unworthy of Chevron deference.

* * *

The Court's alarm over global warming may or may not be justified, but it ought not distort the outcome of this litigation. This is a straightforward administrative-law case, in which Congress has passed a malleable statute giving broad discretion, not to us but to an executive agency. No matter how important the underlying policy issues at stake, this Court has no business substituting its own desired outcome for the reasoned judgment of the responsible agency.

Justice ROBERTS dissent omitted.

Notes and Questions

1. The Court's holdings in Massachusetts v. EPA have been summarized as follows:

> (1) that the harm projected from global warming and climate change gives Massachusetts standing to sue even if the harm is widely shared and EPA can do little to alleviate most of it, (2) that the Clean Air Act gives EPA the authority to regulate greenhouse gas emissions, and (3) that EPA is required to regulate such emissions unless it determines that they do not contribute to climate change or the agency provides a reasonable explanation of why it cannot or will not determine whether they do.

R. Percival, Massachusetts v. EPA: Escaping the Common Law's Growing Shadow, 2007 The Supreme Court Review 111, 127 (2008). What is the significance of each of these rulings for U.S. efforts to combat global climate change? Consider that U.S. motor vehicle emissions constitute 6% of global CO_2 emissions and 4% of global greenhouse gas emissions. Id. at 136.

2. Massachusetts v. EPA is interpreted as significant win for environmental advocates. Focusing on how Massachusetts successfully gained judicial review can help create a roadmap for future climate change plaintiffs. See A. Torbitt, Judicial Review Obstacles Facing Climate change Plaintiffs and How They Were Overcome in Massachusetts v. EPA (U. of Oregon Western Environmental Law Update 2009). The first element of judicial review, jurisdiction, was claimed in the federal district court under the Clean Air Act's section 307(b)(1) due to EPA's denial of Massachusetts' petition for rulemaking. Establishing the second element, violation of a legally enforceable duty by the defendant, was not as straightforward. While aesthetic interests in witnessing and enjoying "scenery, natural and historic objects and wildlife" was recognized as a legally protected interest in Sierra Club v. Morton, 405 U.S. 727

(1972), the courtroom door was all but closed to environmental advocates in Lujan v. Defenders of Wildlife, 504 U.S. 555 (1992), a case challenging a federal rule limiting the Endangered Species Act's jurisdiction to actions within the United States or on the high seas. In Lujan, Justice Scalia emphasized that for a non-regulated plaintiff, for example an environmental advocacy group, in contrast to a regulated automobile manufacturer, who "is not himself the object of the government action or inaction he challenges, standing is not precluded, but is ordinarily 'substantially more difficult' to establish." In Massachusetts v. EPA, the non-regulated Commonwealth of Massachusetts submitted a petition for rulemaking to the EPA requesting greenhouse gas emission regulations and had been denied. As mentioned above, the Supreme Court held that the EPA does indeed have a duty under the Clean Air Act to protect the public "health" and "welfare" and was violating that duty by refusing to regulate greenhouse gases. Thus, even though Lujan made standing substantially more difficult for non-regulated plaintiffs, Massachusetts was successful in showing that, even as a non-regulated plaintiff, the EPA owed the state a legally enforceable duty, which was violated by the EPA's denial to regulate greenhouse gas emissions. See also Center for Biological Diversity v. U.S. Dept. of Interior 2009 U.S. App. LEXIS 8097 (D.C. cir. April 17, 2009) (Massachusetts v. EPA distinguished in NGO and native village challenge to offshore oil and gas leasing program).

Success in Massachusetts v. EPA on the redressability prong of standing represents a groundbreaking achievement for environmental litigants. As an illustration, in Lujan, the plurality cited to a case where the agency at issue supplied only 10% of the funding for a project when explaining why the plaintiffs also failed the redressability prong of standing. Focusing on this minimal amount of harm the agency could control, the court found it "entirely conjectural" whether the desired court order would have any noticeable effect. Yet in Massachusetts v. EPA, the majority found the EPA's violation of the Clean Air Act, resulting in only a projected 4% increase in greenhouse gas emissions, was enough to satisfy redressability.

3. With respect to the Court's third ruling summarized in Note 1 above, J. Dernbach & S. Kakade, Climate Change Law: An Introduction, 29 Energy L.J. 1, 25 (2007), suggested that EPA had three choices:

> It can find that greenhouse gases may reasonably be anticipated to endanger public health or welfare (an endangerment finding) and regulate greenhouse gases from motor vehicles; it can find no endangerment and refuse to regulate greenhouse gases, an option that may not be possible because of the state of climate change science; or it can refuse to regulate based on another reason that is not inconsistent with the statute.

On April 2, 2008, one year after the Court's decision, many of the plaintiffs and amici petitioned the D.C. Circuit Court of Appeals for a writ of mandamus ordering EPA to end its delay in complying with the Court's decision. Massachusetts v. EPA, D.C. Cir. No. 03-1361 (April 2, 2008). The circuit court denied the petition June 27, 2008.

On July 11, 2008, EPA issued an Advance Notice of Proposed Rulemaking (ANPR) soliciting public input within 120 days on the effects of climate change and potential application of the CAA to those effects. 73 Fed. Reg. 44,354 (July 30, 2008). In a preface to the APNR, EPA's administrator expressed the view that the CAA is "ill-suited for the task of regulating global greenhouse gasses." This view was supported by accompanying letters from several high-level executive branch officials including four cabinet secretaries, and the chairs of the Council on Environmental Quality and the Council of Economic Advisors. However, after the change in administrations following the November 2008 election of President Obama, EPA issued a proposed endangerment finding under CAA section 202(a) which is excerpted following these notes and in Chapter 2.

4.　Shortly after the Court's decision President Bush directed EPA to cooperate with the departments of Energy and Transportation in addressing vehicle greenhouse gas emissions. Executive Order 13,342, 72 Fed. Reg. 27, 717 (May 14, 2007). See C. Openchowski, The Next Greenhouse Gas Executive Order?, 38 Envtl. L. Rep. 10077 (2008). In December 2007 the President signed H.R.6, the Energy Independence and Security Act of 2007, Pub. L. No. 110-140, requiring new vehicles sold in the United States to average 30 mpg by 2020, a 40% improvement over current standards. Shortly after taking office President Obama requested final rulemaking from the agencies for model year 2011. 74 Fed. Reg. 4907 (Jan. 28, 2009).

On the same day that President Bush signed H.R.6, EPA rejected California's petition submitted pursuant to 42 U.S.C. § 7521(b) to allow it to impose state controls on four greenhouse gases beginning in model year 2009 pursuant to Cal. Health & Safety Code § 43018.5 and Cal. Code Regs Tit. 13, § 1961. See 73 Fed. Reg. 12156 (March 6, 2008). Since the 1970s, EPA had approved all previous California requests to adopt air pollution standards more stringent than federal ones and several other states had then adopted California's standards pursuant to 42 U.S.C. § 7507. Several other states have adopted California's 2009 vehicle greenhouse gas emission standards as well. Senate Bill 2555, introduced in the 110th Congress, would have overturned EPA's denial of California's waiver request for more stringent greenhouse gas emission standards. California also filed suit in the Ninth Circuit Court of Appeals, challenging the denial as well. California v. EPA, No. 08-70011 (9th Cir. April 10, 2008). See A. Haughey, California Sues EPA After "Unconscionable" Waiver Denial, Sustainable Development L. & Policy Winter 2008 at 14. The Ninth Circuit rejected California's challenge. 38 ELR 20219 (9th Cir. July 25, 2008).

Through the Court's second ruling, the majority rejected EPA's argument that the 1975 Energy Policy and Conservation Act's (EPCA), 49 U.S.C. §§ 32901-19, mandate for national vehicle fuel economy standards established by the Transportation Department represented Congressional intent that EPA did not have authority to regulate vehicle greenhouse emissions under the CAA. Thus the Court's decision also supported state arguments that Congress did not intend to preempt state vehicle greenhouse gas emission standards when it enacted EPCA. See Central Valley Chrysler-Jeep, Inc. v. Goldstone, 38 ELR 20150 (E.D. Cal. June 24, 2008); Green Mountain Chrysler Plymouth Dodge Jeep v. Crombie, 508 F. Supp. 2d 295 (D.Vt. 2007), appeal pending. Shortly after taking office President Obama requested that EPA reconsider its denial of California's petition. 74 Fed. Reg. 4905 (Jan. 28, 2009), and EPA announced it would reconsider California's waiver request. 74 Fed. Reg. 7040 (Feb. 12, 2009).

On May 19, 2009 a settlement of all the California related litigation was announced the essence of which was that the California vehicle GHG emission standards already adopted by 13 states and the District of Columbia would become national standards through 2016, at which time California could seek EPA approval of even stricter standards. Letter from Arnold Schwarzenegger, Governor of California, to Lisa Jackson, Administrator, U.S. Environmental Protection Agency, and Raymond H. LaHood, Secretary of Transportation (May 18, 2009). To implement the settlement, EPA and the Department of Transportation announced a joint rulemaking under the CAA and EPCA, 74 Fed. Reg. 24007 (May 22, 2009), and EPA approved California's waiver request a few weeks later. 74 Fed. Reg. 32744 (July 8, 2009).

Proposed H.R. 2454 (111th Cong. June 26, 2009), the comprehensive climate change bill approved by the U.S. House of Representatives, would allow this motor vehicles emissions settlement to be implemented while adjusting the provisions governing other mobile sources. Provisions of this bill are discussed throughout this book.

5. The CAA also authorizes EPA to establish air pollutant emission standards for new and modified stationary sources such as fossil fuel power plants pursuant to 42 U.S.C. § 7411. Prior to the Court's decision in Massachusetts v. EPA, environmental and state and local government plaintiffs had challenged EPA's claim in proposed stationary source regulations (71 Fed. Reg. 9866, 9869, (Feb. 27, 2006) that it had no authority to regulate greenhouse gases, New York v. EPA, D.C. Cir. No. 06-1322 (Sept. 13, 2006), contrary to the Court's second ruling in Massachusetts v. EPA. See also Environmental Defense v. Duke Energy, 127 S. Ct. 1423 (2007); CleanCOALition v. TXU Power, 38 ELR 20182 (5th Cir. July 21, 2008); In re Otter Tail

Power Co., 744 N.W. 2d 594 (S.D. 2008). On November 13, 2008, the EPA's Environmental Appeals Board ruled that the best available control technology (BACT) must be used to control CO_2 emissions from new coal-fired power plants such as Deseret Power's proposed second Bonanza plant in Utah. Other CAA sections identified by Professor John Bonine affected by the Court's ruling and EPA's April 2009 proposed section 202(a) [42 U.S.C. §7521(a)] endangerment finding regarding motor vehicle emissions excerpted below include §§7408(a)(1)(A) (new and existing sources), 7415(a) (international air pollution), 7547 (off-road vehicles), 7571(a)(2)(A) (aircraft engine emissions), and 7671n (stratospheric ozone). The applicability of many of these and several other CAA sections to GHG emissions would be replaced by new CAA GHG provisions included in proposed H.R. 2454 (111th Cong. June 26, 2009) discussed above in connection with vehicle emissions and below in connection CAA § 108.

In March 2009, EPA proposed mandatory reporting of GHG emissions from large sources pursuant to the FY 2008 Consolidated Appropriations Act (H.R. 2764; P.L. 110-161), 74 Fed. Reg. 16448 (April 10, 2009) and announced the availability of its draft. Inventory of U.S. Greenhouse Gas Emissions and Sinks: 1990-2007, 74 Fed. Reg. 10249 (March 10, 2009).

7. A useful starting point for EPA responses, recommended in R. McKinstry, J. Dernbach, & T. Peterson, Federal Climate Change Legislation As if the States Matter, 22 Natural Resources & Envirnonment 3 (Winter 2008), is establishing a national ambient air quality standard (NAAQS) pursuant to CAA § 109, 42 U.S.C. § 7409, sufficient to prevent "dangerous anthropogenic" climate change parallel with the goal of the United Nations Framework Convention on Climate Change discussed in Chapter 3 to which the United States is a party. They further note that: (1) states have considerable flexibility in achieving such NAAQS through their EPA-approved State Implementation Plans (SIPs), and that (2) Congress should amend the CAA to authorize SIPs, based on tons of greenhouse gases emitted as achieved through state energy efficiency standards and other measures such as carbon taxes and cap-and-trade programs. These concepts are discussed further in the article excerpted below by L. Peterson, R. McKinstry, & J. Dernbach, Developing a Comprehensive Approach to Climate Change Policy in the United States That Fully Integrates Levels of Government and Economic Sectors, 26 Va. Envtl. L.J. 227 (2008). See also H. Doremus & W. Hanneman, Of Babies and Bathwater: Why the Clean Air Act's Cooperative Federalism Framework Is Useful in Addressing Global Warming, 50 Ariz. L. Rev. 799 (2008).

8. On a lighter note regarding climate change science, Justice Scalia provided a humorous moment during the oral arguments in Massachusetts v. EPA:

JUSTICE SCALIA: . . . your assertion is that after the pollutant leaves the air and goes up into the stratosphere it is contributing to global warming.

MR. MILKEY: Respectfully, Your Honor, it is not the stratosphere. It's the troposphere.

JUSTICE SCALIA: Troposphere, whatever, I told you before I'm not a scientist.

(Laughter.)

JUSTICE SCALIA: That's why I don't want to have to deal with global warming, to tell you the truth.

Transcript of Oral Argument at 22-23, Massachusetts v. EPA, 127 S.Ct. 1438 (No. 05-1120), 2006 WL 3431932.

9. The Court's ruling that Massachusetts had standing to challenge EPA's administrative inaction due to injuries already suffered from sea-level rise has been much noted. L. Heinzerling, Climate Change in the Supreme Court, 38 Envtl. L. 1 (2008); L. Heinzerling, Supreme Court Reviews: Massachusetts v. EPA, 22 J. Envtl. L. & Litigation 301 (2007); O. Houck, Standing on the Wrong Foot: A Case for Equal Protection, 58 Syracuse L. Rev. 1 (2007); H. Osofsky, The Geography of Climate Change Litigation Part II: Narratives of Massachusetts v. EPA, 8 Chicago J. of Intl. L. 573 (2008); J. Pleune, Is Scalian Standing the Latest Sighting of the Lochner-ess Monster?: Using Global Warming to Explore the Myth of the Corporate Person, 28 Envtl. L. 273 (2008). The focus here is on the climate change litigation implications of the Court's standing ruling.

Massachusetts v. EPA involved a suit against the EPA, an agency of the federal government. How would a suit against a private party be different? Does a private corporation have a legally enforceable duty to prevent climate change? Prior to the Massachusetts v. EPA ruling, federal district courts had dismissed on political question grounds public nuisance actions brought by 8 states and New York City against 6 utilities emitting 10% of U.S. CO_2, Connecticut v. American Electric Power Co., 406 F. Supp. 2d 265 (S.D.N.Y. 2005), appeal pending Second Circuit, by California against the 6 largest auto makers alleging that they are responsible for 9% of global and over 30% of California CO_2 emissions, California v. General Motors, 2007 WL 2726871 (N.D. Cal. 2007), appeal pending, and tort actions brought by homeowners damaged during Hurricane Katrina against oil, chemical, and coal companies whose CO_2 emissions were alleged to have caused their damages. Comer v. Murphy Oil USA, Inc. No. 05-CU-436LG (S.D. Miss., Aug. 30, 2007), appeal pending. The Comer case also was dismissed due to the plaintiff's lack of standing to raise defendants' greenhouse gas emissions as a cause of the damages they suffered. In addition, a public nuisance suit was filed in February 2008 by the Alaska Arctic coastal village of Kivalina against 5 oil companies, 14 electric utilities, and the largest U.S. coal company because of coastal flooding caused by a warming Arctic climate. See Native Village of Kivalina v. Exxon Mobil Corp. No. 08-CV-1138 (N.D. Cal. Feb. 26, 2008) (see Chapter 7 for more detail). According to Percival, 2007 The Supreme Court Review at 159.

> While the Court's decision may help plaintiffs establish standing premised on the harms caused by climate change, it is still unlikely that nuisance litigation directed at this problem will be successful. Unlike the harm caused by the copper smelters in Georgia v. Tennessee Copper, the century-old precedent on which the Massachusetts v. EPA Court relied for its standing analysis, the causes and consequences of climate change are truly global in scope. Massachusetts v. EPA confirms that it is not necessary to tackle the entire problem at once in order to seek judicial redress. Its "every little bit helps" approach is consistent with what the plaintiffs in Connecticut v. American Electric Power are seeking—modest reductions in emissions of greenhouse gases from the defendant utilities. Indeed, this is essentially what the Supreme Court ultimately mandated in Tennessee Copper—modest emissions reductions that did not threaten the economic viability of the enterprises, but which helped spur the development of new pollution control technology. Although the U.S. Supreme Court's decision in Tennessee Copper ultimately resulted in an injunction that limited emissions from a copper smelter, the initial emissions limits were set at a level that did not threaten the economic viability of the company. But the threat of future liability and particularly the uncertainty concerning the ultimate remedy to be applied by courts in abating nuisances helped encourage the companies to develop new technology.

10. If nuisance actions still have many obstacles, what other litigation strategies can be used to combat climate change? Clean Water Act citizen suits on increased evaporation leading to accumulation of pollution in already limited water sources? Resource Conservation and Recovery Act (RCRA) or Comprehensive Environmental Response, Compensation, and Liability Act (CERCLA) violations if greenhouse gases can be defined as hazardous substances? Humanitarian or civil rights approaches? Constitutional violations? In a Nigerian federal high court case, Gbemre v. Shell Petroleum Development Company of Nigeria, the claimant argued successfully that the flaring of gases in Nigeria, which contributes more greenhouse gases than all other sub-Saharan sources combined, was a "gross violation" to the Nigerian constitutional right of life and dignity. See http://www.climatelaw.org for current information on climate change litigation strategies on an international front.

11. The Court's second ruling that the EPA can regulate greenhouse gas emissions raises the question whether federal common law nuisance claims against greenhouse gas emitters are now preempted by the CAA pursuant to

Illinois v. Milwaukee, 451 U.S. 304 (1981), where the Court held interstate water pollution nuisance claims preempted by the federal Clean Water Act. See S. Olinger, Filling the Void in an Otherwise Occupied Field: Using Federal Common Law to Regulate Carbon Dioxide in the Absence of a Preemptive Statute, 24 Pace Envtl. L. Rev. 237 (2007). Even if the Court were to so hold, the Court's subsequent decision in International Paper Co. v. Ouelette, 479 U.S. 481 (1987), might allow nuisance suits based on the emissions sources state's nuisance law rather than the neighboring state's law. Such actions could be supported by the CAA's provision (42 U.S.C. § 7416) allowing state and local governments to adopt more stringent emissions standards than federal standards. And where the emitters are federal facilities such as the Tennessee Valley Authority's coal-fired power plants, neighboring states such as North Carolina may be able to enforce their nuisance laws through the CAA's provision requiring federal facilities to comply with "all federal, state, interstate, and local" air pollution requirements. 42 U.S.C. § 7418; see North Carolina v. TVA, 39 ELR 20037 (4th Cir. Jan. 31, 2008) (denial of TVA's motion to dismiss North Carolina's complaint affirmed); K. Murchison, Waivers of Immunity in Federal Environmental Statutes of the Twenty-First Century: Correcting a Confusing Mess, 32 Envtl L. & Policy Rev. 359 (2008).

12. The Court's state standing holding in Massachusetts v. EPA involved plaintiffs litigating about EPA's CAA greenhouse gas rulemaking authority and process. Northwest Environmental Defense Center v. Owens Corning, 434 F. Supp. 2d 957 (D.Or. 2006), decided prior to Massachusetts v. EPA, upheld NGO standing under the CAA's citizen suit provision (42 U.S.C. § 7204) to challenge state approval of a polystyrene foam insulation manufacturing plant which would emit large amounts of the ozone depleting greenhouse gas HCFC-142b. In denying defendant's motion to dismiss due to lack of standing, the court stated:

> [t]he challenged emissions source is local, not halfway around the globe. Members of the plaintiff organizations reside, work, and recreate near the partially-completed Gresham facility. Assuming the truth of the allegations in the Complaint, as I must on a motion to dismiss, those individuals would suffer some direct impact from emissions entering into the atmosphere from Defendant's facility, as would the local ecosystem with which these individuals constantly interact.
>
> Other forecasted impacts from these emissions would operate less directly. For instance, ozone-depleting emissions from Defendant's facility must ascend to the stratosphere before impacting persons on the ground in Oregon. Global warming likewise operates indirectly. Higher sea levels in Oregon will supposedly result from melting ice in the earth's polar regions. Changes in weather patterns, winds, ocean currents, and rainfall do not occur in isolation. Nevertheless, the adverse effects alleged in Plaintiffs' Complaint would be felt by them

here in Oregon, and the source of Defendant's emissions would be in Oregon. * * * issues such as global warming and ozone depletion may be of 'wide public significance' but they are neither 'abstract questions' nor mere 'generalized grievances.' An injury is not beyond the reach of the courts simply because it is widespread.

Under a court approved settlement agreement, Owens Corning agreed to never use HCFC-142b or similar substances in Oregon, to spend $300,000 on local renewable energy projects, and to pay the plaintiffs' attorney fees. M. Gerrard, ed., Global Climate Change and U.S. Law 196 (2007). Regarding federal enforcement of the CAA's restrictions on ozone depleting substances, many of which are also greenhouse gases, see United States v. Custom Climate Control, Inc., No. 8:07-cv-2295-T-24TGW (M.D. Fla. Dec. 18, 2007)(CAA defendant involved with the improper maintenance and disposal of ozone-depleting substances through its servicing and selling air conditioning units must pay a $5,000 civil penalty and must carry out specific injunctive relief to comply with the act and its implementing regulations), 73 Fed. Reg. 1231 (Jan. 7, 2008). See also A. Altman & J. Lewis, Recent Clean Air Act Developments 2007, 38 Envtl. L. Rep. 10357 (2008); A. Gillespie, Climate Change, Ozone Depletion and Air Pollution: Legal Commentaries with Policy and Science Considerations (2005); J. Martel, Polarization and Dialogue in Clean Air Law, 38 Envtl. L. Rep. 10418 (2008); E. Schaffer, A Fresh Start for EPA Enforcement, 38 Envtl. L. Rep. 10385 (2008); M. Squillace & D. Wooley, Air Pollution (3d ed. 1999).

PROPOSED ENDANGERMENT AND CAUSE OR CONTRIBUTE FINDINGS FOR GREENHOUSE GASES UNDER SECTION 202(a) OF THE CLEAN AIR ACT
U.S. Environmental Protection Agency
74 Fed. Reg. 18,886 (April 24, 2009)

I. Introduction

A. Summary

Pursuant to section 202(a) of the Clean Air Act (CAA or Act), the Administrator proposes to find that the mix of six key greenhouse gases in the atmosphere may reasonably be anticipated to endanger public health and welfare. Specifically, the Administrator is proposing to define the "air pollution" referred to in section 202(a) of the CAA to be the mix of six key directly emitted and long-lived greenhouse gases: carbon dioxide (CO_2), methane (CH_4), nitrous oxide (N_2O), hydrofluorocarbons (HFCs), perfluorocarbons (PFCs), and sulfur hexafluoride (SF_6). It is the Administrator's judgment that the total body of scientific evidence compellingly supports a positive endangerment finding for both public health and welfare. The Administrator reached this judgment by considering both observed and projected future effects, and by considering the full range of risks and impacts to public health and welfare occurring within the U.S., which by itself warrants this judgment. In addition, the scientific evidence concerning risks and impacts occurring outside the U.S., including risks and impacts that can affect people in the U.S., provides further support for this finding. Under section 202(a) of the CAA, the Administrator is to determine whether emissions of any air pollutant from new motor vehicles and their engines cause or contribute to air pollution which may reasonably be anticipated to endanger public health or welfare. The Administrator further proposes to find that combined emissions from new motor vehicles and new motor vehicle engines of four of these greenhouse gases – carbon dioxide, methane, nitrous oxide, and hydrofluorocarbons – contribute to this air pollution. The other greenhouse gases that are the subject of this proposal (perfluorocarbons and sulfur hexafluoride) are not emitted by motor vehicles.

The Administrator's proposed findings come in response to the Supreme Court's decision in *Massachusetts v. EPA*, 549 U.S. 497 (2007). That case involved a petition submitted by the International Center for Technology Assessment and 18 other environmental and renewable energy industry organizations requesting that EPA issue standards under section 202(a) of the Act for the emissions of carbon dioxide, methane, nitrous oxide, and hydrofluorocarbons from new motor vehicles and engines. The proposed findings are in response to this petition and are for purposes of section 202(a). EPA is not proposing or taking action under any other provision of the Clean Air Act. * * *

2. Statutory Basis for This Proposal

Section 202 (a) (1) of the CAA states that: The Administrator shall by regulation prescribe (and from time to time revise)...standards applicable to the emission of any air pollutant from any class or classes of new motor vehicles or new motor vehicle engines, which in [her] judgment cause, or contribute to, air pollution which may reasonably be anticipated to endanger public health or welfare. Before the Administrator may issue standards addressing emissions of greenhouse gases from new motor vehicles or engines under section 202(a), the Administrator must satisfy a two-step test. First, the Administrator must decide whether, in her judgment, the air pollution under consideration may reasonably be anticipated to endanger public health or welfare. Second, the Administrator must decide whether, in her judgment, emissions of an air pollutant from new motor vehicles or engines cause or contribute to this air pollution.[3] If the Administrator answers both questions in the

---

[3] To clarify the distinction between air pollution and air pollutant, the air pollution is the atmospheric concentrations and can be thought of as the total, cumulative stock problem of greenhouse gases in the atmosphere. The air pollutants, on the other hand, are the emissions of greenhouse gases and can be thought of as the flow that changes the size of the total stock.

affirmative, she must issue standards under section 202(a). *Massachusetts v. EPA*, 549 U.S. at 533.

Typically, the endangerment and cause or contribute findings have been proposed concurrently with proposed standards under various sections of the CAA, including section 202(a). * * * However, there is no requirement that the Administrator propose the endangerment and cause or contribute findings with proposed standards. The Administrator is moving forward with this proposed endangerment finding and a cause or contribute determination while developing proposed standards under section 202(a).

The Administrator is applying the rulemaking provisions of CAA section 307(d) to this action. Thus, these proposed findings will be subject to the same rulemaking requirements that would apply if the proposed findings were part of the standard-setting rulemaking. Any standard setting rulemaking under section 202(a) will also be subject to these notice and comment rulemaking procedures. * * *

II. Legal Framework for This Action

* * *

A. Section 202(a) - Endangerment and Cause or Contribute

* * * [S]ection 202(a) of the CAA calls for the Administrator to exercise her judgment and make two separate determinations: first, whether air pollution may reasonably be anticipated to endanger public health or welfare, and second whether emissions of any air pollutant from new motor vehicles or engines cause or contribute to this air pollution.

Based on the text of this provision and its legislative history, the Administrator interprets the two-part test as follows. First, the Administrator is required to protect public health and welfare. She is not asked to wait until harm has occurred but instead must be ready to take regulatory action to prevent harm before it occurs. The Administrator is thus to consider both current and future risks. Second, the Administrator is to exercise judgment by weighing risks, assessing potential harms, and making reasonable projections of future trends and possibilities. It follows that when exercising her judgment the Administrator balances the likelihood and severity of effects. This balance involves a sliding scale; on one end the severity of the effects may be significant, but the likelihood low, while on the other end the severity may be less significant, but the likelihood high. Under either scenario, the Administrator is permitted to find endangerment. If the harm would be catastrophic, the Administrator is permitted to find endangerment even if the likelihood is small. In the context of climate change, for example, the Administrator should take account of the most catastrophic scenarios and their probabilities. As explained below, however, it is not necessary to rely on low-probability outcomes in order to find endangerment here.[5]

Because scientific knowledge is constantly evolving, the Administrator may be called upon to make decisions while recognizing the uncertainties and limitations of the data or information available, as risks to public health or welfare may involve the frontiers of scientific or medical knowledge. At the same time, the Administrator must exercise reasoned decision making, and avoid speculative or crystal ball inquiries. Third, the Administrator is to consider the cumulative impact of sources of a pollutant in assessing the risks from air pollution, and is not to look only at the risks attributable to a single source or class of sources. Fourth, the Administrator is to consider the risks to all parts of our population, including those who are at greater risk for reasons such as increased susceptibility to adverse health effects. If vulnerable subpopulations are especially at risk, the Administrator is entitled to take that point into account in deciding the question of endangerment. Here too, both likelihood and severity of adverse effects are relevant, and here too, catastrophic scenarios and their probabilities should be considered. * * * [V]ulnerable subpopulations face serious health risks as a result of climate change.

This framework recognizes that regulatory agencies such as EPA must be able to deal with the reality that "[m]an's ability to alter his environment has developed far more rapidly than his ability to foresee with certainty the effects of his alterations." *See Ethyl Corp v. EPA*, 541 F.2d 1, 6 (D.C. Cir.), *cert. denied* 426 U.S. 941 (1976). Both "the Clean Air Act 'and common sense . . . demand regulatory action to prevent harm, even if the regulator is less than certain that harm is otherwise inevitable.'" *See Massachusetts v. EPA*, 549 U.S. at 506, n.7 (citing *Ethyl Corp.*). To be sure, the concept of "expected value" has its limitations in this context, but it is useful insofar as it suggests that when severe risks to the public health and welfare are involved, the Administrator need not wait as evidence continues to accumulate. * * *

3. Additional Considerations for the Cause or Contribute Analysis

By instructing the Administrator to consider whether emissions of an air pollutant cause *or contribute* to air pollution, the statute is clear that she need not find that emissions from any one sector or group of sources are the sole or even the major part of an air pollution problem. The use of the term

---

[5] *Cf. Massachusetts v. EPA*, 549 U.S. at 525 n.23, citing *Mountain States Legal Foundation v. Glickman*, 92 F.3d 1228, 1234 (D.C. Cir. 1996) ("The more drastic the injury that government action makes more likely, the lesser the increment in probability to establish standing"); *Village of Elk Grove Village v. Evans*, 997 F.2d 328, 329 (7th Cir. 1993) ("[E]ven a small probability of injury is sufficient to create a case or controversy—to take a suit out of the category of the hypothetical—provided of course that the relief sought would, if granted, reduce the probability.").

contribute clearly indicates a lower threshold than the sole or major cause. Moreover, the statutory language in section 202(a) does not contain a modifier on its use of the term contribute. Unlike other CAA provisions, it does not require "significant" contribution. *See, e.g.,* CAA §§ 111(b); 213(a)(2), (4). Congress made it clear that the Administrator is to exercise her judgment in determining contribution, and authorized regulatory controls to address air pollution even if the air pollution problem results from a wide variety of sources. While the endangerment test looks at the entire air pollution problem and the risks it poses, the cause or contribute test is designed to authorize EPA to identify and then address what may well be many different sectors or groups of sources that are each part of the problem. * * *

B. Air Pollutant, Public Health and Welfare

The CAA defines both "air pollutant" and "welfare." Air pollutant is defined as:

> Any air pollution agent or combination of such agents, including any physical, chemical, biological, radioactive (including source material, special nuclear material, and byproduct material) substance or matter which is emitted into or otherwise enters the ambient air. Such term includes any precursors to the formation of any air pollutant, to the extent the Administrator has identified such precursor or precursors for the particular purpose for which the term "air pollutant" is used. CAA § 302(g).

Greenhouse gases fit well within this capacious definition. *See Massachusetts v. EPA*, 549 U.S. at 532. They are "without a doubt" physical chemical substances emitted into the ambient air. * * *

Regarding "welfare", the CAA states that

> [a]ll language referring to effects on welfare includes, but is not limited to, effects on soils, water, crops, vegetation, man-made materials, animals, wildlife, weather, visibility, and climate, damage to and deterioration of property, and hazards to transportation, as well as effects on economic values and on personal comfort and well-being, whether caused by transformation, conversion, or combination with other air pollutants. CAA § 302(h)

This definition is quite broad. Importantly, it is not an exclusive list due to the use of the term "includes, but is not limited to, ..." Effects other than those listed here may also be considered effects on welfare.

Moreover, the terms contained within the definition are themselves expansive. For example, deterioration to property could include damage caused by extreme weather events. Effects on vegetation can include impacts from changes in temperature and precipitation as well as from the spreading of invasive species or insects. Prior welfare effects evaluated by EPA include impacts on vegetation generally, and changes in crop and forestry specifically, as well as reduced visibility, changes in nutrient balance and acidity of the environment, soiling of buildings and statues, and erosion of building materials. * * *

There is no definition of public health in the Clean Air Act. The Supreme Court has discussed the concept in the context of whether costs can be considered when setting National Ambient Air Quality Standards. *Whitman v. American Trucking Ass'n*, 531 U.S. 457 (2001). In *Whitman*, the Court imbued the term with its most natural meaning: "the health of the public."

When considering public health, EPA has looked at morbidity, such as impairment of lung function, aggravation of respiratory and cardiovascular disease, and other acute and chronic health effects, as well as mortality. *See, e.g.*, Final National Ambient Air Quality Standard for Ozone, 73 FR 16436 (2007). * * *

7. Summary

The Administrator concludes that, in the circumstances presented here, the case for finding that greenhouse gases in the atmosphere endanger public health and welfare is compelling and, indeed, overwhelming. The scientific evidence described here is the product of decades of research by thousands of scientists from the U.S. and around the world. The evidence points ineluctably to the conclusion that climate change is upon us as a result of greenhouse gas emissions, that climatic changes are already occurring that harm our health and welfare, and that the effects will only worsen over time in the absence of regulatory action. The effects of climate change on public health include sickness and death. It is hard to imagine any understanding of public health that would exclude these consequences. The effects on welfare embrace every category of effect described in the Clean Air Act's definition of "welfare" and, more broadly, virtually every facet of the living world around us. And, according to the scientific evidence relied upon in making this finding, the probability of the consequences is shown to range from likely to virtually certain to occur. This is not a close case in which the magnitude of the harm is small and the probability great, or the magnitude large and the probability small. In both magnitude and probability, climate change is an enormous problem. The greenhouse gases that are responsible for it endanger public health and welfare within the meaning of the Clean Air Act.

IV. The Administrator's Cause or Contribute Finding

* * *

1. Proposed Definition of Air Pollutant

When making a cause or contribute finding under section 202(a), the Administrator must first look at the emissions from the source category and decide how to define the air pollutant being evaluated. In this case, the source category emits four gases, which share common physical properties relevant to climate change: all are long-lived in the atmosphere; all become globally well mixed in the atmosphere; all trap outgoing heat that would otherwise escape to space; and all are directly emitted as greenhouse gases rather than forming as a greenhouse gas in the atmosphere after emission of a pre-cursor gas. There are other gases which share these common properties which are not emitted by the section 202(a) source categories. Nonetheless, it is entirely appropriate for the Administrator to define the air pollutant in a manner that recognizes the shared relevant properties of all of these six gases, even though they are not all emitted from the source category before her.

The Administrator is proposing to define a single air pollutant that is the collective class of the six greenhouse gases. It is the Administrator's judgment that this collective approach for the contribution test is most consistent with the treatment of greenhouse gases by those studying climate change science and policy, where it has become common practice to evaluate greenhouse gases on a collective CO_2-equivalent basis. For example, under the UNFCCC, the U.S. and other Parties report their annual emissions of the six greenhouse gases in CO_2-equivalent units. This facilitates comparisons of the multiple greenhouse gases from different sources and from different countries, and provides a measure of the collective warming potential of multiple greenhouse gases. There are also several federal and state climate programs, such as EPA's Climate Leaders program and California's Climate Action Registry that encourage firms to report (and reduce) emissions of all six greenhouse gases. Furthermore, the Administrator recently signed (March 10, 2009) the Proposed Greenhouse Gas Mandatory Reporting Rule, which proposes the reporting of greenhouse gas emissions on a CO_2-equivalent basis above certain CO_2-equivalent thresholds, thereby also recognizing the common and collective treatment of the six greenhouse gases. * * *

The Administrator recognizes that only four of the six greenhouse gases covered in the definition of air pollution are emitted by section 202(a) source categories. It is not unusual for a particular source category to emit only a subset of a class of substances that constitute a single air pollutant. For example, a source may emit only 20 of the possible 200 plus chemicals that meet the definition of volatile organic compound (VOC) in the regulations, but that source is evaluated based on its emissions of "VOCs," and not its emissions of the 20 chemicals by name.

Nonetheless, the Administrator recognizes that each greenhouse gas could be considered a separate air pollutant. Thus, although proposing to define air pollutant as the class of six greenhouse gases, and basing the proposed contribution finding on that air pollutant, the Administrator also considered each greenhouse gas individually * * *.

B. Proposed Cause or Contribute Finding

* * *

1. Overview of Section 202(a) Source Categories and Cause or Contribute Analysis

The relevant mobile sources under section 202 (a)(1) of the Clean Air Act are *"any class or classes of new motor vehicles or new motor vehicle engines, ..."* CAA §202(a)(1) (emphasis added). The motor vehicles and motor vehicle engines (hereinafter "Section 202(a) source categories") addressed are:

- Passenger cars
- Light-duty trucks
- Motorcycles
- Buses
- Medium/heavy-duty trucks

As noted earlier, in the past the requisite contribution findings have been proposed concurrently with proposing emission standards for the relevant mobile source category. Thus, the prior contribution findings often focused on a subset of the section 202(a) (or other section) source categories. Today's proposed cause or contribute finding, however, is for all of the section 202(a) source categories and the Administrator is considering emissions from all of these source categories in the proposed determination.

Sources covered by section 202(a) of the Act emit four of the six greenhouse gases that in combination comprise the air pollutant being considered in the cause or contribute analysis: carbon dioxide, methane, nitrous oxide, and hydrofluorocarbons.[32] To support the Administrator's assessment, EPA has analyzed historical data of these greenhouse gases for motor vehicles and motor vehicle engines in the U.S. from 1990 to 2006. * * *

There are a number of possible ways of assessing "cause or contribute" and no single approach is required or has been used exclusively in previous determinations under the Act. Because the air pollution against which the contribution is being evaluated is the mix of six greenhouse gas concentra-

---

[32] Emissions of hydrofluorocarbons result from the use of HFCs in cooling systems designed for passenger comfort, as well as auxiliary systems for refrigeration.

tions, the logical starting point for any contribution analysis is a comparison of the emissions of the air pollutant from the section 202(a) category to the total, global emissions of the six greenhouse gases. The Administrator recognizes that there are other valid comparisons that can and should be considered in evaluating whether emissions of the air pollutant cause or contribute to the combined concentration of the six greenhouse gases. To inform the Administrator's assessment, the following types of comparisons for both the collective and individual emissions of greenhouse gases from section 202(a) source categories are provided:

- As a share of total current global aggregate emissions of the six greenhouse gases included in the proposed definition of air pollution;
- As a share of total current U.S. aggregate emissions of the six greenhouse gases; and
- As a share of the total current global transportation emissions of the six greenhouse gases.

In addition, when reviewing each greenhouse gas as an individual pollutant, the Administrator also considered the following comparisons:

- As a share of current global emissions of that individual greenhouse gas;
- As a share of total section 202(a) source category emissions of the six greenhouse gases; and
- As a share of current U.S. emissions of that individual greenhouse gas, including comparisons to the magnitude of emissions of that greenhouse gas from other non-transport related source categories. * * *

3. Proposed Finding That Emissions of the Collective Group of Six Greenhouse Gases Contributes to Air Pollution Which May Reasonably Be Anticipated to Endanger Public Health and Welfare

a. Total Greenhouse Gas Emissions From Section 202(a) Source Categories

As discussed above, the Administrator is proposing to define air pollutant for purposes of the contribution finding as the collective group of six greenhouse gases. Section 202(a) source categories emit four of the greenhouse gases (CO_2, CH_4, N_2O, and HFCs), therefore the emissions of the single air pollutant are the collective emissions of these four greenhouse gases. * * *

b. Proposed Contribution Finding for the Single Air Pollutant Comprised of the Collective Group of Six Greenhouse Gases

* * *

It is the Administrator's judgment that the collective greenhouse gas emissions from section 202(a) source categories are significant, whether the comparison is global (over 4 percent of total greenhouse gas emissions) or domestic (24 percent of total greenhouse gas emissions). The Administrator believes that consideration of the global context is important for the cause or contribute test but that the analysis should not solely consider the global context. Greenhouse gas emissions from section 202(a) source categories, or from any other U.S. source, will become globally mixed in the atmosphere, and thus will have an effect not only on the U.S. regional climate but on the global climate as a whole, and indeed for years and decades to come. The Administrator believes that these unique, global aspects of the climate change problem tend to support a finding that lower levels of emissions should be considered to contribute to the air pollution than might otherwise be considered appropriate when considering contribution to a local or regional air pollution problem.

Importantly, because no single greenhouse gas source category dominates on the global scale, many (if not all) individual greenhouse gas source categories could appear too small to matter, when, in fact, they could be very significant contributors in terms of both absolute emissions or in comparison to other similar source categories within the U.S. If the U.S. and the rest of the world are to combat the risks associated with global climate change, contributors must do their part even if their contributions to the global problem, measured in terms of percentage, are smaller than typically encountered when tackling solely regional or local environmental issues. Total U.S. greenhouse gas emissions make up about 18 percent of the world's greenhouse gas emissions, and individual sources within the U.S. will be subsets of that 18 percent. The Administrator is placing significant weight on the fact that section 202(a) source categories contribute to 24 percent of total U.S. greenhouse gas emissions for the proposed contribution finding. * * *

Notes and Questions

1. What implications does the EPA Endangerment Finding hold for the promulgation of new regulations under all of the clean air act's regulatory authorities? Can EPA rule-making reduce greenhouse gas emissions from CO_2 by as much as 20% from a 1990 baseline year?

2. The EPA Endangerment Finding is also excerpted in Chapter 2 Section D.

STATE IMPLEMENTATION PLANS

The Clean Air Act requires each State to adopt a State Implementation Plan for national primary and secondary ambient air quality controls. Does not the EPA endangerment finding, in the wake of the Massachusetts v. EPA ruling, make it necessary for the EPA to propose regulations for carbon dioxide under Clean Air Act §108, 42 U.S.C. §7408? Should emissions of carbon dioxide be limited in order to achieve a level capable of sustaining both public health and public welfare, at a level that can be justified based upon a rulemaking for arriving at an ambient air quality control standard? If EPA were to establish a level of atmospheric concentration requisite to protect the public health and welfare (e.g. a past level to be restored, of 350 ppm, or maintaining a current level of 387 ppm, or the likely level within a decade of 400 ppm), EPA could then engage the states in planning to attain and sustain this level since most states already have enacted provisions to reduce or cap GHG emissions in their states, D. Hodas, The State Response to Climate Change: 50 State Survey, in M. Gerrard, ed., Global Climate Change and U.S. Law (2007), updated at http://www.abanet.org/bapubs/globalclimate/, could not also the EPA require the states to revise their State Implementation Plans (SIPs) to demonstrate how each state will attain the new carbon dioxide pollutant standard?

CAA §110(a)(2)(A) is broad enough to cover most of the climate change laws that states already have been promulgating: "include enforceable emission limitations and other control measures, means, or techniques (including economic incentives such as fees, marketable permits, and auctions of emission rights), as well as schedules and timetables for compliance * * *." §110(a)(2)(B) requites states to provide monitoring and compilation of data and to share this data with the EPA. §110(a)(2)(C) requires states to have enforcement systems in place, and (E) requires that states have the personnel in place to implement the standard. States are familiar with SIPs and all have a framework in place for SIP compliance, so adding they have the statutory and administrative law systems in place to respond at once to a SIP revision. Moreover, the public hearings associated with such proceedings would permit states to engage their citizens and the public in evaluating how most effectively and efficiently to curb carbon dioxide and other GHG emissions.

Mr. Justice Marshall noted in Union Electric v. EPA, 427 U.S. 246 (1976) that the "State has virtually absolute power in allocating emissions limitations so long as the national standards are met * * * Congress plainly left to the States, so long as the national standards were met, the power to determine which sources would be burdened by regulation and to what extent." Since each State has a unique socio-economic context, should EPA not engage each State to use its CAA authority under §119 and promulgation a SIP that can turn the nation to carbon-neutral energy production?

DEVELOPING A COMPREHENSIVE APPROACH TO CLIMATE CHANGE POLICY IN THE UNITED STATES THAT FULLY

INTEGRATES LEVELS OF GOVERNMENT AND ECONOMIC SECTORS

Thomas D. Peterson, Robert B. McKinstry, Jr., and John C. Dernbach 26 U. Virginia Envtl. L. Rev. 227 (2008)

With the Supreme Court's landmark decision in Massachusetts v. Environmental Protection Agency, the release of the Fourth Assessment Report of the Intergovernmental Panel on Climate Change, the announcement of new state greenhouse gas (GHG) mitigation plans, and the success of Al Gore's documentary, An Inconvenient Truth, many believe that a mandatory and comprehensive federal response to climate change is inevitable.

The Supreme Court's decision in Massachusetts v. EPA makes possible a national program to address climate change under the Clean Air Act (CAA). Reversing the Administration's denial of a petition to regulate mobile source emissions under section 202 of the CAA, the Court held that (1) the Act gives the U.S. Environmental Protection Agency (EPA) the authority to regulate emissions of carbon dioxide and other GHGs as "pollutants," and (2) the EPA improperly failed to articulate reasons for its refusal to regulate GHG emissions pursuant to the statutory requirement that the EPA Administrator regulate emissions that "in his judgment, cause, or contribute to, air pollution which may reasonably be anticipated to endanger public health or welfare." The Court remanded the matter to the EPA to make a finding consistent with the statutory standard.

Given the state of the science and the relevant statutory standard, the EPA cannot reasonably refuse to regulate mobile source emissions of GHGs. Because sections 108 and 111 of the CAA contain language identical to that construed by the Court in Massachusetts v. EPA, the establishment of National Ambient Air Quality Standards (NAAQS), state implementation plans (SIPs), new source performance standards, and the full panoply of regulatory mechanisms of the CAA should be applied to GHGs. * * *

Fortunately, existing state and federal laws provide a workable template for full integration of governmental and economic needs with respect to climate change. By adapting and enhancing the existing framework of national standards, state programs, and market-based systems found in the CAA, the United States could create a highly tested and widely approved method to address climate change. At the same time, the United States could begin to take swift action on critical near-term policy opportunities while building towards longer-term policy strategies needed to support major shifts in emissions. In the process, the United States could regain global leadership and provide a template for national action by other nations. * * *

Most notably, while the acid deposition cap-and-trade program established by Subchapter IV-A of the CAA succeeded in achieving very significant reductions of acid rain precursors at a minimal cost, its success was due to a number of unique circumstances. While a number of the characteristics of GHG emissions suggest that a trading system may be an effective tool to address climate change, there are important limitations that militate towards limiting the use of such a system to particular circumstances. An effective trading program requires design constraints as well as careful consideration of where such a program can be effective. These design constraints will inform where the trading mechanism fits in a larger portfolio approach—in other words, where a trading mechanism will work most effectively, where other measures will be required to make the trading mechanism work effectively, and where other tools will work more effectively. In particular, the acid deposition cap and trade system's success is the result of the following specific factors:

- The program built upon and complemented an array of regulatory tools already incorporated into the CAA to control sulfur dioxide and nitrogen oxide emissions (the principal acid rain precursors). The program built upon requirements for permits, monitoring, and enforcement already required by the CAA. More importantly, for controls of acid deposition precursors emitted from sources not subject to the cap and trade program, it relied upon controls established pursuant to other sections of the CAA related to SIPs and technology-based standards for automobile emissions and new and modified stationary sources.

- The acid deposition program was limited to the utility sector, which was already highly regulated in 1990. Allowances could be allocated to the utility sector with minimal concerns about equity and impacts on competition, since costs and benefits could be apportioned equitably among the shareholders and the users of electricity, who were protected by rate regulation. Other sources of acid rain precursor emissions were permitted to opt-in voluntarily.

- The acid deposition cap-and-trade program also worked well because market imperfections were minimized. Market allocations work best where costs are imposed upon those who have the requisite knowledge and control to minimize costs. Limitations on acid rain emissions required choices about types of generation technology, air pollution control technology and fuels that could best be made by the utilities which controlled emissions.

- The program was limited to two pollutants, sulfur dioxide and nitrogen oxides, which are controlled through installation of pollution control equipment, fuels, and generation technology switching.

- There was no concern about "hot spots"—areas where high concentrations can cause local adverse impacts on health or the environment.

Local concentrations were limited under the existing provisions of the CAA.

Applying the above considerations, trading can undoubtedly be a powerful tool for control of GHG emissions. GHG hotspots are not of concern because there is sufficient mixing of carbon dioxide, the principal GHG constituent. The various GHGs can be traded at ratios that can be readily established. A trading program involving GHGs can build upon the tools already incorporated in the CAA, which can readily be applied to GHG emissions. But many of the other conditions that made the acid deposition cap and trade program so successful do not apply to GHG emissions.

* * * In the case of acid deposition control, the utility market was highly regulated, which provided assurance that allocations of emissions rights would not cause unjust enrichment. But many of the markets involved in potential GHG regulation are not regulated, so distributional considerations come into play. Moreover, since the creation of the acid deposition program, even the electric generation sector of the utility industry has been deregulated.

The distribution and initial allocation of GHG emissions allowances raises significant ethical issues that were of less significance with respect to the acid deposition program. An allocation of allowances for GHG emissions involves an allocation of a global commons that has significant distributional considerations.

Market imperfections will make the use of market mechanisms more problematic for reduction of GHG emissions in many sectors. While the trading provisions in the 1990 CAA amendments aimed to encourage energy conservation, there is little evidence that they had that effect. GHG emissions reductions require decreases in energy demand through mechanisms such as green buildings and smart growth. Unlike the utility sector, those making the decisions in these sectors are not the same entities that will incur the costs. For example, housing location and character will often be determined by builders rather than the homeowners. Those buying homes will be more motivated by the price of the home and may not have the knowledge or sophistication to make comparisons based on the present value of future energy consumption arising from the home's heating system and insulation or its location. Additionally, the persisting state regulation of the utility industry may limit utilities' ability to pass through the costs of emissions controls in a way that matches market incentives to demand.

These concerns suggest that a broader and somewhat different approach will be required for control of GHG emissions. To be effective, a tax or cap-and-trade mechanism, or both, should be a part of the mix, but other measures will be also required and must be integrated with the cap-and-trade program and with each other. Most importantly, careful thought must be given to the question of which tool to use where. Such thinking is not fully evident in current legislation. * * *

With the Supreme Court's holding in Massachusetts v. EPA, there is little doubt that the regulatory construct for addressing climate change at the federal level will build upon the CAA. Because it is very unlikely that Congress will amend the law to remove environmental protections, the focus has necessarily shifted from the question of whether there will be a federal response under the CAA to the question of how that response should best be managed and what amendments will be required to make the federal response appropriately integrated with international, state, and local efforts. * * *

To avoid these delays and uncertainties, Congress could require the EPA to implement a national climate change program through amendments to the CAA. Alternatively, the states could voluntarily coordinate their efforts to allow continued progress in emissions reduction while providing a model that Congress or the EPA could copy in ways that support a full range of emissions reduction actions proven effective and politically acceptable at the state and local level. This approach would consist of the following elements:

- The establishment of NAAQS at a level sufficient to prevent dangerous anthropogenic climate change;

- The establishment of short, intermediate and long term emissions reduction goals necessary to maintain the NAAQS with corresponding sectoral and state elements;

- National and regional performance or technology-based limits and cap and trade programs for some sectors;

- SIPs designating additional measures necessary to achieve emissions reduction goals;

- Provisions to effectively engage individuals in implementation; and

- Establishment of United States as a serious actor in the international community.

Equally importantly, provisions are needed to integrate these measures and require specific EPA action. The CAA provides adequate authority for the EPA to implement most of the measures described below, and the EPA could promulgate regulations that would provide for such implementation and the integration suggested below. * * *

Even if the EPA were inclined to take rapid action, numerous barriers are present. The EPA would be required to gather information, formulate several series of draft regulations, and provide an opportunity for public notice and comment. Even after the rulemaking process ends, regulations are subject to judicial review. This could result in remand and additional delays.

Because delay will increase the ultimate cost of achieving necessary reductions and make achieving climate stabilization more difficult, some mechanism to reduce delays is desirable. Amending the CAA to incorporate specific directives and deadlines with the specificity normally found in regulations would be one mechanism to minimize delays and uncertainty. That approach was adopted by Congress in the mid-1980s when it was faced with an EPA unwilling to respond to environmental issues under more general statutory authority. States could also contribute by adopting consistent deadlines and plans that could serve as SIPs if and when a federal system is in place. Cooperative ventures, already underway by several states, could also provide Congress with a model for action.

A. National Ambient Air Quality Standards for GHGs

The first step towards a coordinated federal approach under the CAA would be the establishment of NAAQS. After listing an air pollutant under section 108, the EPA Administrator is required by section 109 of the CAA to establish primary NAAQS which, "allowing an adequate margin of safety, are requisite to protect the public health," as well as secondary NAAQS "requisite to protect the public welfare from any known or anticipated adverse effects associated with the presence of such air pollutant in the ambient air." The requirements applicable to these standards mesh neatly with the requirements of the UNFCCC, which establishes the goal of preventing "dangerous anthropogenic" climate change and directs that the parties adopt a "precautionary" approach that aims to anticipate and to prevent harm. In light of these requirements, it would appear appropriate to set the primary and secondary NAAQS for GHGs at an atmospheric level equal to that needed to prevent "dangerous anthropogenic" climate change."

Although significant scientific uncertainties make the establishment of NAAQS for GHGs difficult, scientists are currently addressing the issue by determining what level of GHGs will prevent "dangerous anthropogenic" climate change. Information currently suggests that the threshold should be established at a level that would seek to keep atmospheric concentrations of carbon dioxide below 450 ppmv and concentrations of total GHGs below 500 ppmv in carbon dioxide equivalents. Because there are a variety of GHGs with different warming potentials, both emissions and concentrations are typically established in terms of carbon dioxide equivalents. Consequently, NAAQS will likewise need to be established for total GHGs in terms of carbon dioxide equivalents at the 500 ppmv level.

There are uncertainties concerning the establishment of NAAQS for GHGs that may be resolved with better scientific information. Similar uncertainties arise with respect to most NAAQS, however, and the standards for existing criteria pollutants are often modified as better information becomes available. Indeed, the CAA specifically contemplates this process by requiring that the EPA review air quality criteria and standards every five years and make revisions as warranted.

Leaving it to the EPA to establish NAAQS administratively will entail substantial delays, even assuming that the Agency would take action initially.[98] Progress is better assured if Congress specifies a 500 ppmv GHG NAAQS, allowing this figure to be reevaluated and revised consistent with evolving science and international accords, as already provided for in the CAA. This approach is already taken by the many states that establish ambitious long term reduction goals.

B.   Short, Intermediate, and Long-Term Emissions Reduction Goals

The CAA requires the adoption and implementation of SIPs to achieve and maintain the NAAQS. The statute gives states considerable flexibility in

---

[98] In the case of lead, where the EPA voluntarily initiated action to regulate the lead content of gasoline, litigation was brought to compel the Agency to establish a broader listing, which would then require a NAAQS. Natural Res. Def. Council, Inc. v. Train, 545 F.2d 320, 324-25 (2d Cir. 1976). The timeline for the adoption of lead regulations is instructive. The EPA began evaluating controls on leaded gasoline shortly after the 1970 enactment of the Clean Air Act. See Regulation of Fuel Additives, 36 Fed. Reg. 1486 (proposed Jan. 30, 1971) (to be codified at 42 C.F.R. pt. 479). It then twice proposed a schedule to reduce the maximum amount of lead allowed in gasoline pursuant to its "endangerment" authority in section 211(c)(1)(A) over the objections of industry. Regulation of Fuels and Fuel Additives, 37 Fed. Reg. 3882 (proposed Feb. 23, 1972) (to be codified at 40 C.F.R. pt. 80); Regulation of Fuels and Fuel Additives, 38 Fed. Reg. 1258 (proposed Jan. 10, 1973) (to be codified at 40 C.F.R. pt. 80). It finally adopted lead phase down regulations almost three years after voluntarily initiating this process. Control of Lead Additives in Gasoline, 38 Fed. Reg. 33,734 (final rule Dec. 6, 1973) (to be codified at 40 C.F.R. pt. 80). Three years later, the Court of Appeals affirmed a district court decision requiring the EPA to adopt an NAAQS, NRDC v. Train, 545 F.2d at 328. Finally, four years after that, the Court of Appeals for the District of Columbia affirmed the EPA's establishment of a NAAQS for lead, the culmination of a decade-long process. Lead Indus. Ass'n v. Envtl. Prot. Agency, 647 F.2d 1130, 1184 (D.C. Cir. 1980). Assuming a similar administrative process for GHGs would project a 2017 date before a NAAQS for GHGs would be settled—three years before the initial 2020 goals for most state climate change action plans. Although states that have already taken action will continue to pursue these goals and more can be expected to join them, many of the largest emitters of GHGs, including Texas, the second highest emitter, and many mid-western coal states, have not yet taken action and if their emissions continue to grow under a "business as usual" scenario, it will be very difficult to achieve the economy-wide reductions necessary to prevent "dangerous anthropogenic" climate change.

the choice of regulated sources as well as legal and policy tools, so long as the SIP is capable of achieving and maintaining the NAAQS.

Some suggest that SIPs are not an appropriate legal tool for regulating GHGs. The reasoning underlying this distinction is flawed insofar as it is based on the nature of pollutants regulated under the SIP mechanism in the past, all of which tend to have localized effects. Other criteria pollutants do not mix uniformly, they vary in their concentrations from airshed-to-airshed, they have a relatively short residence time in the atmosphere, and their local concentrations can be affected relatively quickly by changes in control strategy. For that reason, SIPs have focused on regulation aimed at achieving or maintaining local air pollutant concentrations. This focus requires extensive modeling and monitoring of local air movements and concentrations to bring out-of-compliance areas into compliance with the NAAQS, and to maintain those local areas that are already in compliance with the NAAQS. GHGs, by contrast, have a relatively uniform concentration throughout the atmosphere. Most areas will be in compliance with the NAAQS for GHGs when and if they are promulgated. GHGs mix rapidly in the atmosphere, and their health and welfare impacts arise from average concentrations. GHGs reside in the atmosphere for long periods of time. Consequently, in order to maintain levels below the NAAQS, emissions levels will need to be dramatically reduced well before they even approach the NAAQS.

Consequently, establishment of NAAQS for GHGs will require somewhat different SIP implementation mechanisms than those used for other criteria pollutants. NAAQS could be implemented either under the existing CAA through the promulgation of regulations calling for regulation of GHGs, or through a statutory amendment mandating such an approach. Because of the nature of GHG emissions, it would be appropriate for the EPA to establish specific numeric emissions reduction goals on a national basis that are phased in over time and that are horizontally and vertically differentiated among states, sectors, and policy implementation mechanisms.

Maintenance of the NAAQS would therefore require the establishment of total emissions reduction goals with corresponding emissions caps. Such an emissions-based approach to SIPs could be accommodated within the current structure of the CAA. The Act calls for the establishment of air quality control criteria simultaneously with the promulgation of a new NAAQS and calls for promulgation of regulations defining criteria for SIPs. Such criteria and regulations could establish a cap-based approach aimed at emissions reductions.

While an emissions cap approach appears appropriate for GHGs, what the reduction goals and caps will look like raises a number of questions. These relate to what the ultimate goals and caps should be, how a cap for the United States relates to international emissions, whether and how the reductions should be phased in, and how reduction goals and caps should be allocated among the states. Again, the experience of the states is instructive.

Any approach to determining an emissions reduction goal must start with what is necessary to stabilize worldwide emissions to maintain the NAAQS. Most sources concur that worldwide emissions must be reduced fifty to eighty-five percent by 2050, and many states set long term emissions goals based on that number. The United States, which only contains five percent of the world's population, emits twenty-two percent of the world's emissions. Consequently, the emissions reductions goal, if based upon the assumption that each person in the world is entitled to emit an equal increment of GHGs, would be in the range of ninety-four to ninety-six percent.

Neither the seventy-five percent nor the ninety-six percent emissions reduction goal can be achieved without realistic intermediate benchmarks and immediate reduction incentives to guide the market. Intermediate reduction goals are particularly important. Because carbon dioxide accumulates, less radical reductions will be required later on if there are earlier reductions. For this reason, many states are facing the difficult question of what degree of reduction will ultimately be required for the United States and adopt intermediate goals appropriate for any of the most significant national reduction goals. This approach is taken by California, which sets the goal of eighty percent reductions from 1990 levels by 2050. Intermediate national goals could also be based upon those set forth in the NEG/ECP Climate Action Plan. Alternatively, goals could be derived by scaling up the various intermediate goals originating from the state planning processes. This latter approach would make it possible for states to coordinate their actions by specifying common goals, even before Congress acts. * * *

Long term goals and planning are not only necessary to achieve the emissions reductions required, but also to assist industry. Many capital investment decisions require a long term horizon. Many capital goods and buildings have minimum life spans of twenty years, and some have life spans ranging up to fifty years. Capital investment decisions also require long lead times. The establishment of long term goals, with opportunities to adjust in light of emerging science and actual experience, will enable capital investment decisions to be based on a long term horizon.

After long-term and intermediate national emissions reductions goals are established, it is necessary to allocate those emissions reductions among states and sectors of the economy. This requires consideration of (1) the emissions reductions that will be achieved through national technology-based standards under the CAA, (2) emissions reductions that will be required under sectoral cap-and-trade systems, and (3) characteristics of the states that will govern the establishment of emissions reduction goals for state implementation plans. Finally, mechanisms must be established to modify these goals in light of actual experience. These mechanisms will be described below.

C. National Technology-Based Limits and Cap-and-Trade Programs for Some Sectors

Under the CAA, uniform national or multi-state performance or technology-based limitations or sectoral cap-and-trade programs will be established as primary tools for emissions reductions in industrial and mobile source sectors, where feasible and appropriate. Factors to consider in establishing uniform national or multi-state performance or technology-based limits include the economic importance of national or multi-state standards, the potential emissions reductions to be achieved through uniform performance or technology-based standards, the extent to which the creation of such standards would augment or disrupt existing state efforts to control emissions from the same class of sources, and the extent to which there are already performance or technology-based standards for other pollutants from the same sources under the CAA. The last factor would include technology-based standards for mobile sources and some stationary sources under sections 202 and 111 of the CAA and electric power sector cap and trade programs. Some of the bills before Congress would force the adoption of such standards for GHGs.

Massachusetts v. EPA makes the promulgation of mobile source emissions standards under section 202 of the CAA appear likely at some point. Technology-based standards are particularly appropriate for mobile sources, for which cap and trade programs are difficult to administer.[116] California already has emissions standards, and at least twelve states have adopted the California standards. But on December 21, 2007, the EPA announced its intention to deny California's application for an exemption from preemption under the CAA; this was the first time that the EPA ever denied such a request. In light of the EPA's intransigence, amendments to the CAA could require the adoption of standards at least as stringent as California's, or require that the EPA adopt new federal standards on par with other major industrialized nations every five years. * * * Congress could also consider repealing preemption of state mobile source standards, or broadening the California exemption from preemption to allow any state or group of states to establish more stringent mobile source standards if they exceed a certain population threshold.[121]

---

[116] A cap-and-trade system for mobile sources would necessarily require regulation "upstream" with allowances provided for the sale of gasoline. Robert B. McKinstry, Jr., Adam Rose & Coreen Ripp, Incentive-Based Approaches to Greenhouse Gas Mitigation in Pennsylvania: Protection the Environment and Promoting Fiscal Reform, 14 Widener L. J. 205 (2004).

[121] Mobile sources represent an exception to the general rule against federal preemption of more protective state standards under the CAA. 42 U.S.C. § 7416 (2006).

In lieu of technology-based standards, sectoral cap-and-trade programs similar to the acid deposition cap-and-trade program could be established for the utility sector and most major industrial sectors. For GHG emissions, it makes most sense for caps to be established representing the emissions reductions needed to achieve climate stability through 2100, dropping in predictable amounts consistent with nationwide emissions reductions. Although the caps could initially be specified through 2100, provisions would need to be included for reassessment in light of new science and actual experience. The caps could also provide for adjustments that will be warranted because of emissions reductions and reductions in demand for electricity through SIP implementation, as described below. In the establishment of caps and the allocation of credits, it would be important to include assurances that early reducers be given full credit for their reductions. This could be accomplished by treating their early reductions as "banked." * * *

Changes in the law would remove any question regarding authority and could more precisely guide the EPA in implementation. Designation of longterm goals might be more readily achieved through statutory amendment. California and the states participating in the Regional Greenhouse Gas Initiative (RGGI) already initiated efforts to establish similar sectoral programs. Although state cap-and-trade programs deal solely with initial caps and do not include long term reduction requirements, the existing model could be employed to establish long term caps.

For some industrial sources, a cap-and-trade program may not be desirable. Such a program may be cumbersome for industries with many small emissions sources because of its needs for effective monitoring and reporting. For these sources, performance or technology-based standards could be established. While such standards might be established for new or modified sources under section 111 of the CAA, a different model establishing standards applicable to new and existing sources, similar to that employed in some cases by the Clean Water Act, may be more appropriate. While this approach might be employed by the EPA under section 110 of the CAA * * * statutory amendments requiring such an approach and requiring periodic adjustments of these limitations could be included in CAA amendments.

Any amendments to the CAA should necessarily address the problems created by NSR requirements and the need to integrate GHG emissions reductions with those for other pollutants. By abandoning its original "four-pollutant strategy" and focusing on conventional pollutants without consideration of GHGs, for example, the Bush Administration might be encouraging industries to develop control technology that increases GHG emissions rather than promoting a switch to inherently low emissions technologies. Delaying the requirements for conventional pollutants or otherwise authorizing states and the EPA to relax the requirements of NSR for projects replacing high emission technologies with low emission technologies would enhance efficiency and pollution reduction.[128]

All remaining emissions reductions could be achieved through SIPs. Much as state climate plans do today, SIPs could address crucial demand reduction measures for utilities, other stationary sources, and mobile sources. SIPs could also independently address other sectors not directly addressed by the cap-and-trade and technology-based standards, such as commercial and residential heating, cooling, and hot water.[129] The use of SIPs provides a higher level of certainty that legal and policy measures would be vertically integrated at federal, state, and local levels in an effective manner.

Establishment of the emissions reductions goals for SIPs requires calculations of (1) demand reductions for the utility sector, (2) reductions required to achieve the necessary national emissions reductions after consideration of reductions that will be achieved after application of technology-based standards and sectoral cap and trade programs, and (3) allocation of emissions reductions among the various states. Some of these calculations will follow from the measures employed and others will best be informed from state experience. Current state climate action plans provide an excellent starting point for these allocation decisions by providing estimates of emissions reductions from specific, sector based actions agreed upon through rigorous stakeholder negotiation.

It would be useful for Congress to require that GHG SIPs draw, at least initially, from the same menu of legal and policy tools. State actions to date tend to be based on energy efficiency and conservation, clean and renewable energy, transportation and land use efficiency, agriculture and forestry conservation, waste management, and industrial processes. Within each category is a standard set of legal and policy tools. Many of these tools, in turn, are specific to particular economic sectors like electricity generation and transportation. For example, two tools within the category of "clean and renewable energy" for the electricity generation sector are renewable energy portfolio standards and tax credits. This menu would put in front of any state the most comprehensive list of available choices that is available anywhere. It would thus help states choose the most appropriate and cost-effective options needed to meet emissions reductions targets. The "other" category is intended to include legal and policy choices that are not specifically identified

---

[128] For example, coal-fired utilities may spend hundreds of millions of dollars installing scrubbers to remove sulfur dioxide and nitrogen oxides, while increasing energy consumption and thus increasing GHG emissions. Abandoning a conventional coal-fired plant to a combined cycle coal gasification plant would increase efficiency while reducing emissions of all pollutants.

[129] It may be possible to create federal technology standards for some of these sectors, but a statutory amendment would likely be required, similar to the "area source" mechanism for hazardous air pollutants under section 112 of the CAA. 42 U.S.C. § 7412(k) (2006).

on the menu but can nonetheless contribute to reduction of the state's GHG emissions. The menu should, in turn, be periodically revised to specifically identify new legal and policy tools and otherwise reflect new experience and learning.

The "efficiency and conservation" category will necessarily include the calculation of electricity demand reduction measures. The electric utility sector will not achieve the proportional reductions required to stabilize carbon dioxide levels without reduction in demand, which continues to grow. Many of the measures that can be employed to reduce demand from the electric utility industry are best employed at the state and local level. These include measures such as green building, replacement of traffic lights and indoor lighting with LED bulbs and compact fluorescents, and other measures traditionally managed by state and local governments. Scaling up the demand reduction measures developed by state plans could be used to calculate emissions reductions in the utility sector that can be achieved through demand reduction. This scaling up could then be used to generate both the demand reduction goals for SIPs and the percentage of the emissions reductions necessary to meet utility caps.

The relationship between state and local demand reduction measures and attempts to eliminate barriers to emissions reductions in utility caps is one of the most notable issues not well addressed by various legislative proposals. Utilities require long term planning to meet demand and emissions reduction requirements. The two are interrelated, and the applicable requirements of the two must be integrated. If, for example, a state does not formulate an adequate demand reduction program as part of its SIP, it would not be fair to punish the utility for emissions associated with furnishing necessary electricity service to that state. Accordingly, if states do not meet their emissions reduction goals, the caps of utilities serving the state will need to be adjusted upwards and appropriate sanctions placed on the offending states. Similarly, if states exceed their demand reduction goals, caps will need to be reduced downward. Thus, provisions will need to be made for reassessment of progress towards demand reduction and adjustment of caps at regular intervals. If the cap for the power industry were initially established for 2015 at ninety percent of 2000 levels and SIPs called for demand management techniques (such as appliance and building codes) to reduce demand by two percent by 2015, the cap needed to achieve the same ten percent reduction for that sector would be eighty-eight percent. Credits would need to be provided if the demand adjustment were not actually achieved.

Integration of demand reduction requirements into SIPs and integration of utility emissions reductions requirements with demand requirements could theoretically be accomplished through the promulgation of regulations under existing authority provided by the CAA. But statutory amendments specifying these procedures would better facilitate implementation. Amendments would also be required to provide a more appropriate sanctioning mechanism for states failing to meet their demand reduction requirements. The elimination of transportation funding or the promulgation of a federal implementation plan as provided by the current version of the CAA are not appropriately targeted sanctions. A measure such as a standby federal tax on the sale of electricity sold within non-complying states would be a more effective sanction and would help to remedy non-complying states' failures.

Before establishing emissions reductions goals for SIPs, it is necessary to calculate the emissions reductions that will be required. This will require calculation of the emissions reductions that will be achieved through emissions caps and technology-based standards, and then subtracting that number from the overall emissions reductions required across the United States. For example, if the initial goal requires a ten percent reduction and half of those reductions can be achieved through the application of uniform federal standards, the SIPs will need to develop measures that account for the remaining half or five percent reduction.

The final calculation would involve allocation of the nationwide emissions reduction goals among the states. This will undoubtedly become the subject of much negotiation. Here, state experience can also provide instruction. The states with completed plans have varying economic growth rates. The business-as-usual extrapolation of emissions growth and the emissions reductions identified for 2020 and 2040 provide realistic individual goals for other states. Allocations must consider factors such as population and projected growth rates. The results of the state planning efforts described above, however, suggest that very similar results can be achieved in states with dramatically different growth rates, so that this task will be less difficult than it might seem, whether the allocation is made via rulemaking or by Congressional action.

The phasing of reductions will also be necessary. Overall reductions and appropriate caps should be phased to achieve reductions needed through 2100. These reductions could be paralleled by reductions in caps, with demand reduction measures allocated pro rata. It will likely be feasible to project technology-based emissions through 2020, so that the SIPs would be required to plan for necessary reductions to meet a 2020 goal with a roadmap to achieve the ultimate 2100 goal. Plan revisions and reallocation of goals by the EPA could be required periodically (five or ten years), so that a plan required in 2010 would need to achieve the reductions for 2025, one required in 2020 would need to achieve the reductions for 2035, and so forth.

Regardless of whether Congress mandates these changes or the EPA acts independently to create the system described above, additional measures would be desirable to assure that some of the problems with existing SIP implementation do not arise. For example, a measure for approval by third party certifiers might be provided.[131]

---

[131] These SIPs may be simpler to implement than existing SIPs because they will be based on emissions reductions rather than local air quality and would consequently

E. Provisions to Effectively Engage Individuals in Implementation

Any comprehensive effort must fully engage citizens and consumers in its implementation. The CAA contains a variety of provisions for citizen participation in its enforcement and implementation, including citizen suits. Beyond the availability of these mechanisms, the precision with which Congress directs agency and nongovernmental activities will have considerable bearing on the speed with which any legislation is implemented, and on the effectiveness of citizens in influencing its implementation. Fully engaging individuals also means fully engaging consumers by providing them with information, incentives, and the means necessary to make energy conservation and renewable energy both attractive and available. * * *

Notes and Questions

1. North Carolina v. EPA, 2008 WL 2698180 (D.C. Cir. July 11, 2008), illustrates some of the issues that would be raised by EPA implementation of CO_2 cap-and-trade programs under CAA section 110. The court invalidated as arbitrary and capricious key parts of EPA's Clean Air Interstate Rule, 70 Fed. Reg. 25,162 (May 12, 2005), including provisions establishing cap-and-trade programs for SO_2 and NO_x covering the eastern half of the U.S. The global and national significance of U.S. CO_2 emission regulation under the CAA would eliminate some but not all of these issues.

For commentary on the Peterson article suggesting the CAA NAAQS process is so ill-suited for global pollutants that it should not be used for GHGs, see 39 ELR 10723, 10727, 10730, 10732 (Aug. 2009). See also Duke/Harvard conference on regulating climate under the CAA, http://www.niicholas.duke.edu/institute/clean.air.2009.html.

2. Is it wise for Congress to legislate a concentration of CO_2 in the atmosphere within the U.S.? If a 500 ppm level were set, even as a default, scientific models indicate it would sanction irreversible impacts. Should "sound science" or governmental convenience determine this standard? Review the scientific analysis in Chapter 2.

3. H.R. 2454 (111th Cong. June 26, 2009), the comprehensive climate change legislation passed by the House of Representatives, would establish a national cap and trade program in lieu of EPA regulation of GHG emissions under CAA § 108 as described in the Peterson article or as a "hazardous" air pollutant as discussed in D. Brian, Regulating Carbon Dioxide Under the Clean Air Act as a Hazardous Air Pollutant, 33 Colum. J. Envtl. L. 369 (2008). All sources emitting over 10,000 metric tons per year would report

---

not require considerations such as air dispersion modeling. Although consideration of demand changes from other states would be necessary, interference resulting from GHG emissions from other states would not create the same difficulties present under the current SIP process.

and those emitting over 25,000 tons would be subject to the cap and trade program. Goals of the program are to reduce 2020 emissions by 17% from 2005 levels, and 2050 emissions by 83% from 2005 levels, the same goal as that of the U.S. Climate Action Partnership, which includes General Electric, Shell, and General Motors. 15% of the initial emission allowances would be auctioned and the proceeds used to reduce energy costs for lower-income individuals and families. An extensive program of emissions offsets from U. S. agriculture and forestry would be administered primarily by the Agriculture Department under the supervision of EPA and a new Offsets Integrity Advisory Board.

4. Carbon taxes are another market-based tool for reducing emissions. The next materials explore their legal and policy implications in comparison to cap- and- trade programs like those that would be created by H.R. 2454 and are already operating in the European Union and in the U.S. Northeast under the state-created Regional Greenhouse Gas Initiative (RGGI), and for SO₂ emissions in the Northeast as described in the Peterson article above. Critical to all market-based approaches is the concept of carbon accounting which is discussed in the next excerpt. For a comprehensive assessment of the E.U. trading regime, see M. Fauve and M. Peeters, eds., Climate Change and European Emissions Trading Lessons for Theory and Practice (2008).

CARBON ACCOUNTING: A PRACTICAL GUIDE FOR LAWYERS
Peter L. Gray and Geraldine E. Edens
ABA Natural Resources and Environment 41 (2008)

If Congress enacts a cap-and-trade scheme, as many observers predict it will, a massive new market in carbon emission credits will be created overnight. * * * The stakes obviously will be enormous, and there will be significant financial pressure on companies to reduce their carbon footprints. Environmental lawyers, both in-house and outside, will need to understand the basics of carbon accounting to advise clients confronting a carbon-constrained economy: how to determine the baseline emissions of an entity (also known as the carbon footprint), how to identify the options for reducing the carbon footprint, and how to calculate and certify the carbon emission reductions associated with each of those options. Without a basic understanding of these methods and the assumptions upon which they rely, it is not possible to assess short- and long-term project benefits, determine whether project investments are justified, or effectively negotiate transactions or otherwise advise clients in this field. * * *

Basics of Carbon Accounting

Because carbon offsets are intangible commodities, GHG accounting standards are necessary to ensure that GHG reductions are transparent, representative of actual emissions reductions, verifiable, permanent, and enforceable. In other words, accounting standards must ensure that "a ton of carbon is always a ton of carbon." * * *

The WRI/WBSCD GHG Project Protocol brings together in one place the key concepts, principles, and methods to account for GHG emission reductions from any type of GHG project, e.g., wind, energy efficiency, afforestation, switching fuel sources, forest management, and carbon capture. The Project Protocol provides detailed instructions for developing a GHG emission "baseline" from which to measure projectbased GHG reductions. It also explains how to account for the unintended changes in GHG emissions a project might cause and how to report GHG emission reductions for maximum transparency. It is compatible with the UN's Clean Development Mechanism (CDM), which certifies emissions reductions generated by specific projects toward targets agreed to by industrialized countries under the Kyoto Protocol.

The basic accounting steps for a GHG project under the Project Protocol are (1) identify the project activities, (2) identify the primary effects, (3) consider all secondary effects and evaluate their significance, (4) develop a baseline scenario, (5) estimate baseline emissions, (6) monitor project activity emissions, and (7) quantify GHG reductions.

A GHG project consists of a specific activity or set of activities intended to reduce GHG emissions, increase carbon storage, or enhance GHG removals from the atmosphere. Project activities may include modifications to existing processes or services or the introduction of new services that reduce GHGs. * * *

Emissions reductions achieved through implementing a GHG project are measured against baseline emissions scenarios and are calculated by taking into account both the primary and secondary effects of a project. A primary effect is the intended change in emissions caused by a project activity. For example, installing equipment to capture methane gas emitted from a landfill has the primary effect of reducing emissions of a potent GHG. If the captured methane is then used to generate electricity, the primary effect would also include a reduction in combustion emissions from electricity generation to the extent the methane displaces higher GHG emitting fossil-fuel-powered electric generators.

A secondary effect is the unintended change in emissions caused by a project activity. Secondary effects are sometimes referred to as "leakage." Secondary effects may be additional emissions reductions (a positive effect) or emissions increases (a negative effect). For example, if a company intends to replace its coal-based fuels with biofuels, a possible secondary effect is increased combustion emissions associated with the transportation of the biofuels (a negative effect). Secondary effects generally are small in comparison to primary effects, but they should nevertheless be evaluated before proceeding with a GHG project.

Because GHG reductions are measured against baseline emissions scenarios, developing a baseline scenario and addressing the concept of "additionality" are critical to quantifying GHG emission reductions. The baseline scenario is a hypothetical description of what would have most likely occurred in the absence of any considerations about climate change mitigation. A baseline scenario may be the continuation of current practices (the "business as usual" approach), the use of same technologies or practices used in the GHG project, or the use of alternative technologies or practices that could provide the same product or service as the GHG project activity.

The Project Protocol provides two methods for developing baseline scenarios from which to calculate baseline emissions: the project-specific procedure and the performance standard procedure. Under the project-specific procedure, a baseline scenario is developed through a structured analysis of the project activity and its alternatives. Baseline emissions are valid only for the project activity considered. The performance standard procedure estimates baseline emissions using a GHG emission rate derived from GHG emission rates of all alternative technologies and practices that could provide the same product or service as the project activity. A performance standard is sometimes referred to as a multiproject baseline because it can be used to estimate emissions for multiple project activities with common characteristics.

It is generally presumed that emissions from a GHG project activity will differ from its baseline GHG emissions scenario. However, in some cases a project activity, or the same technologies or practices it employs, may have been implemented anyway, and thus represent the baseline scenario. In these cases, the project activities are not "additional" to what otherwise would have occurred. While the concept of "additionality" seems relatively straightforward, in practice there is no precise way to determine if a project is in fact additional. A number of tests for additionality have been developed that try to isolate the reasons for implementing a GHG project, e.g., the legal and regulatory test, the financial test, and the common practice test. (Illustrations of each of these tests follow in the forest carbon sequestration discussion below.) The Project Protocol does not incorporate these additionality tests; rather, it takes the view that additionality is implicit in the procedure of developing a baseline scenario. Nevertheless, the Protocol acknowledges that there is some degree of subjectivity in developing a baseline scenario and, therefore, project developers may want to evaluate the additionality requirements imposed by specific GHG programs and those mandated by GHG legislation and regulations. In general, it should be possible to estimate a baseline GHG emission rate for the technologies or practices employed. For example, if the GHG project is to retrofit a piece of equipment to reduce GHG emissions and the baseline scenario is business as usual, baseline emissions can be estimated as the historical emission rate for the equipment that is being retrofitted.

Monitoring GHG emissions from the project activity can be achieved by directly measuring GHG emissions or by calculation methods (e.g., calculating GHG emissions from fuel consumption data). Both approaches have some degree of scientific or estimation uncertainty. Data uncertainties should be described and explained. The Protocol recommends that where uncertainties exist, project developers should use conservative estimates that will tend to underestimate GHG reductions.

The final step in GHG project accounting is to quantify GHG reductions. GHG reductions can be quantified by *ex ante* estimation or *ex post* quantification using the same basic procedures. An *ex ante* estimate involves making predictions about the project activity's performance over time. *Ex post* quantification uses actual monitoring data once the GHG project has been implemented. There are a number of formulas available to calculate GHG reductions, depending upon the type of GHG project. In general, the formulas calculate the difference in emissions under the baseline scenarios and the GHG project. However, emerging international trading rules and domestic law will probably require some form of independent postproject verification of GHG emission reductions for the credits to be tradable.

As noted above, the carbon accounting principles set forth in the WRI/WBCSD Project Protocol are found in most of the other carbon accounting standards. How the various standards apply these principles differs because the goals of the various programs differ. Thus, a single, harmonized accounting standard for carbon accounting may not be possible. Reconciling these differences remains one of the fundamental challenges of this emerging field.

Carbon Sequestration: The Forestry Model

There are two ways for a party to reduce its carbon footprint: (1) reduce its own GHG emissions, or (2) offset its GHG emissions by either acquiring emission reduction credits greater than its emissions or by sequestering (permanently removing carbon from the atmosphere) or buying sequestration credits for more carbon than it emits. In this section, we will discuss carbon sequestration through forest-related activities.

Any discussion of carbon sequestration must begin with the basics. Carbon sequestration is the process of incorporating atmospheric carbon into plants, soil, and water. Those resources or processes that absorb atmospheric carbon are commonly referred to as "carbon sinks" because of their ability to absorb, rather than emit, CO_2. Some typical practices and processes that sequester CO2 from the atmosphere include conservation of riparian buffers;

conservation tillage on croplands; grazing land management; afforestation, reforestation, forest preservation, and forest management; underground geologic suppositories; and oceanic uptake.

Carbon is sequestered in trees primarily through the natural process of photosynthesis in which plants convert CO_2 and water to glucose and oxygen. CO2 in the atmosphere thus is incorporated as fixed carbon into the roots, trunks, branches, and leaves of trees. According to the U.S. Environmental Protection Agency (EPA), approximately 50 percent of carbon storage in trees occurs in the woody biomass. (*See* EPA, Carbon Sequestration in Agriculture and Forestry: Representative Rates, www.epa.gov/sequestration/rates/html). The shedding of leaves does not significantly diminish the amount of carbon stored in a tree, as only 3 percent of tree carbon is fixed in the foliage. Moreover, most of the carbon in decaying leaves will be absorbed by soil. Several factors affect how much CO_2 can be absorbed by trees, including tree size, age, and species. According to forestry experts, a mature tree can absorb up to 48 pounds of CO_2 a year. * * *

Planting trees and enhancing forest management techniques will be a key strategy for many GHG emitters to reduce their carbon footprints. For some, the cost of reducing their GHG emissions will simply be cost prohibitive, and they will be forced to consider credits and offsets such as carbon sequestration projects. A recent study by the Pew Center on Global Climate Change concludes that climate change policies adopted by the United States should encourage activities that increase carbon sequestration in our forests: "Climate change is the major global environmental challenge of our time and in order to deal with it in the most cost-effective way, we need to consider the full range of solutions—and that includes carbon storage and forests." Eileen Claussen, President of the Pew Center on Global Climate Change, further notes, "If we ignore the potential for forest-based sequestration, any projection of the cost and feasibility of addressing climate change is going to be overly pessimistic and wrong." * * *

According to EPA estimates, growing a Douglas fir forest for a century is 25–50 percent more efficient at reducing CO_2 buildup than using an equivalent amount of land to grow biofuels. For example, if you were to grow switch grass hay to produce ethanol-based power, you will allow roughly 25–50 percent more CO_2 to remain in the atmosphere than if you had planted a fir forest on the same amount of acreage and used coal to supply that power instead. This highlights the crucial importance of forestry in the GHG reduction equation. As discussed below, however, accounting issues present a significant obstacle to the viability of forestry-based carbon sequestration.

There are numerous accounting standards for calculating the amount of carbon sequestered in forest projects, including (1) the Inter-Governmental Panel on Climate Change (IPCC) Good Practice Guidance for Land Use, Land Use Change, and Forestry (LULUCF), published in 2003; (2) the World Resources Institute (WRI) LULUCF Guidance for Greenhouse Gas Project Accounting, published in 2006; (3) DOE's Voluntary Greenhouse Gas Reporting Program, published in 2005 (56 Fed. Reg. 15,176); (4) the California Climate Registry (www.climateregistry.org); and (5) the Chicago Climate Exchange (CCX), which has published technical and reporting guidelines on forestry projects (www.chicagoclimatex.com). Parsing the differences between these programs is an exercise we would prefer to leave to economists and agronomists. For present purposes, a more useful exercise is to articulate the common principles found in most, if not all, of these standards and the issues they present.

Conceptually, to determine how much a forest-based carbon sequestration project will reduce CO_2 buildup in the atmosphere, one must begin with the identification of a credible baseline, i.e., the amount if carbon sequestered in the project area over time if the project were not undertaken. With forestry projects—whether they involve afforestation, reforestation, preventing deforestation, or forest management—one must first establish a starting point (time zero) from which changes in carbon content of the project area will be compared. Carbon content must be determined for both the vegetation on-site and the soil. This may be done using either site-specific calculations or regional average data to show how similar situations change over time. This analysis establishes a "without project" baseline that can be projected over the planned life of the project.

Next, one must determine how much carbon is actually being sequestered in the project area. The difference between the baseline and the project estimate is the additional carbon that is sequestered as a result of the project. That is not the end of the analysis, however. The product satisfies the "additionality" requirement. If other legal obligations would require the planned forestry management activities, then the project is not "additional." For example, a landowner may be required by law to plant trees on certain lands. California, which heavily regulates forest practices under its Forest Practices Act, is a prime example. These GHG-independent tree-planting obligations are central in determining whether a forest project meets the additionality requirement: if the projectvactivities are required by law, then they do not satisfy the "additionality" criterion. Similarly, some carbon sequestration accounting standards require that an economic analysis be performed to determine if an economically rational owner of the project area would have undertaken the project without the project generating any carbon offsets credits. If the owner would have done so, then the project does not satisfy the additionality requirement.

A forestry project's secondary effects on carbon consumption, referred to as "leakage," must also be considered in evaluating the amount of carbon sequestered. Often these secondary effects are negligible by comparison to the amount of carbon sequestered as a result of project management. For example, the effect of emissions associated with the use of fertilizer in an afforestation project is a secondary effect, even though, when compared to the carbon sequestered by the project, the secondary effect may be a relatively small reduction in project carbon sequestration. On the other hand, some secondary effects of forestry projects may not be so insignificant, specifically, "activity shifting leakage." For example, if the forestry project prohibits tree harvesting in a large swath of forest, logging firms may simply shift their activities to adjacent areas outside the project zone, thus zeroing out any net carbon sequestration. By contrast, afforestation projects are unlikely to pose this leakage problem. A farmer's decision to plant trees on his or her land is unlikely to cause a forest elsewhere to be removed.

Finally, evaluation of any forest management project requires assessment of the reversibility or permanence of the project. This is one of the more vexing of the carbon accounting issues associated with valuing a forestry-based carbon sequestration project. Forests can be destroyed by fire or disease, illegal logging, or farmers, or even squatters seeking land, releasing back to the atmosphere the carbon that had been sequestered in a project area. More fundamentally, trees will eventually die, and most of the carbon sequestered in a dead tree—if left to decay—will return to the atmosphere. Even if tree carbon is converted to forest products, such as lumber used for housing or furniture, the carbon will only be stored while the lumber or furniture remains intact. Moreover, large quantities of carbon in the trunks, root system, and debris that remains after logging will decay, releasing carbon into the atmosphere. Unless dying trees are systematically replaced within a project area, the carbon offset will eventually be completely reversed. The cost of preventive measures to reduce the risk of loss and to replace trees and maintain "carbon equilibrium" within the project area in perpetuity must be factored into the cost of a project. The economics of this analysis are quite complex and have been the subject of many studies. *See, e.g.,* R. Stavins & K. Richards, The Cost of U.S. Forest-Based Sequestration (Pew Center on Global Climate Change, January 2005).

We are not suggesting that attorneys counseling clients on carbon sequestration projects must become experts on the economic and ecological esoterica that permeates this field. Rather, we recommend that attorneys operating in this field acquire sufficient familiarity—as they would in representing clients in any other transactional setting— with the issues to be able ask the right questions (to be capable of "issue spotting" as we used to call it in law school). Which accounting standards will apply to the project and does the project meet those standards? What happens if the forestry project is destroyed by fire or disease? Who pays to replace the trees? Is there an insurance vehicle to cover such liability? Attorneys operating in this field must be prepared to ask these types of questions and sufficiently sophisticated to be able to understand the answers. Make no mistake: there is no substitute for having expert consultants to assist. But the lawyer on such deals cannot cede all authority to consultants.

C. TAXATION VS. CAP AND TRADE

Economic markets are the engines that drive contemporary socio-economic development locally and globally. Left without appropriate supervision, markets destabilize, and market failures result. H. Minsky, Finance and Stability: The Limits of Capitalism (1993). In the wake of the market recession that emerged in 2007, a frantic effort has emerged to restore stability to the financial sector, and to the wider economy. Efforts to restore markets have not yet addressed the new regulatory reforms that will be fashioned by legislatures and administrative agencies to build buffers against future market meltdowns. The immediate concern is to cope with the collapse of the market system. New reforms will emerge. President Obama has emphasized that he is committed to making sure that our financial system is stable.

As economic markets are being redesigned for the 21st century, the most pervasive challenge will be to rapidly design and attain an economic model that addresses climate change. The range of economic instruments available to cope with environmental externalities is well understood. For example, a government can use a tax or give a tax exemption, grant a subsidy, establish a fee for an action or require a permit to reflect costs associated with its compliance standards, acquire or own and manage an enterprise. See the seven volumes of papers from the annual conferences on "Critical Issues In Environmental Taxation." Given the severity of the climate change impacts, modest adjustments to market regulations will not suffice. To stabilize environmental conditions within which economic markets function, it is likely that all those emitting greenhouse gases will need to off-set their emissions and perform in a carbon-neutral way, and for some period of time also operate to remove legacy CO_2 and other GHGs from the atmosphere.

If we characterize GHGs as classic economic externalities, we can use several economic instruments to re-incorporate these values into the market. The legal systems design and establish these economic instruments. Two of the approaches most immediately available are 1) to assess a tax on GHG emissions, or 2) to establish limits on the total amount of GHG emissions permitted into the atmosphere, and establish a new market for trading emission allowances. Taxes have the advantage of setting a price that is certain, but do not cap emissions. A cap sets a limit on emissions but is uncertain as to what the price of emission allowances will be. In other words, taxes seek to reduce demand by raising prices whereas caps reduce supply. Other regulatory approaches are also available: energy efficiency standards, renewable portfolio requirements, building codes, automobile mileage standards, land use law changes, and examples.

The use of either a taxation or a cap and trade system, or both, is further complicated by the reality that Earth's atmosphere and the accumulating GHG concentrations are global, while the GHG emissions from the territory of a taxing authority or trading region are local and finite. Moreover, much of the trade in coal, oil, and natural gas is international, while the governmental capacity to tax, or limit extraction and condition sequestration of any quantum of CO_2 equivalents, exists within national borders. Finally, there is a wide range of efficiencies of taxing authorities around the world. Some are efficient, and some barely function, depending on the capacity of the government to observe the rule of law. In a global context, it may be necessary to focus on the nations with the largest concentrations of GHG emissions, and harmonize a set of taxation and cap-and-trade systems for these markets as an initial step, and build the integrity of the tax and regulatory systems to ensure that these larger markets become carbon neutral. Once this phase is in place, international cooperation could address the other governments in countries whose capacity does not meet an international standard of performance. See J. Burniaux, et. al, The Economics of Climate Change Mitigation: How to Build the Necessary Global Action in a Cost-Effective Manner, OECD Economics Dept. Working Paper #701, ECO/WKP(2009)42 (05 June 2009) www.oecd.org/eco/working_papers.

Lord Nicholas Stern reflects the current consensus that a cap and trade system is needed to harmonize market forces and array them behind attaining deep reductions in GHG emissions. He observes that "carbon taxes have their role to play but they too have their problems: finding international coordination on taxes is never easy; taxes do not give the same degree of confidence in quantity reductions; national governments may not be convincing in their continuity over time, given that they may become a domestic political football; and taxes may not guarantee a flow of finances from rich to poor countries." Nicholas Stern, A Blueprint for a Safer Planet, 193-4 (2009). At the same time, while economic markets are in meltdown, and banks are not engaged in extending credit for new economic development, is it hubris to think a new market in GHG emissions can be created with integrity?

The global atmosphere is a commons, but nations do not agree on a global models of how much GHG emissions it can absorb without causing irretrievable anthropogenic adverse impacts on the climate. If James Hansen is correct, as discussed in Chapter 2, this level has been exceeded, and we need to scrub the atmosphere and remove GHGs. If a cap is set somewhat arbitrarily, the volume of emissions can be known as a political decision, but its efficacy from a scientific perspective may be questioned. Thus, it is not so easy to apply welfare economic models to arrive at the marginal social costs. Classical economics seeks a point of equilibrium where no individual actor in the market can improve her or his satisfaction without lowering the satisfaction of another, and thereby aggregate value is maximized for the economy. This efficiency is called "Pareto Optimality," after the 19th century Italian economist, Vilifredo Pareto, who first put forth this analytic framework.

For this model to work, resource economists posit that markets must (a) be fair and competitive ("no particular firm can affect any market price significantly by decreasing or increasing the supply of goods and services offered"), (b) all market participants are fully informed "as to the quantitative and qualitative characteristics of goods and services and the terms of exchange"; and (c) the valuable assets, emission rights, can be individually owned and managed without violating the competitive assumption." A. Kneese, Economics and the Environment 18-19 (1977). How can all three conditions be ensured in a cap and trade regime? Can a tax approximate the marginal social cost and remove the perverse subsidy that an a firm enjoys benefits from exploiting an externality? The social costs of climate change have been recognized now for many years, see e.g. J. Hansen, et al., Climate Impact of Increasing Atmospheric Carbon Dioxide, 213 Science 957 (1981). Why have governments not acted, or have acted only slowly and tentatively, to establish laws to correct the market failure that this GHGs represent?

In a democracy, where vested interests lobby to defend the benefits that each receives from exploiting the externality, will legislators favor the business as usual model? Where costs are passed onto consumers, as in the case of electricity bills when electrical utilities pay fees to capture the GHG emissions from their burning of coal or oil or natural gas, will legislators vote to increase the costs for their constituents? In creating tradable emission allowances, as a part of a cap and trade program, should they be granted to companies without cost, as the European Emission Trading System (ETS) has begun, or be allocated by auction, as the North East US Regional Greenhouse gas Initiative (RGGI) has provided. If Congress were to give some allowances away and set prices on others, how would it fairly distinguish different classes of emitters. Could a narrow market for emissions be constructed with such clear "property" rights to emit GHGs that it would satisfy the expectations of Ronald Coase in his seminal article, The Problem of Social Cost, 3 J. Law & Economics 1 (1960)? Coase suggested the theoretical model of abating pollution through voluntary transactions between the affected parties, with the government allocating rights and enforcing the contracts, rather than relying on a regulatory model. The "Coase Therorem" assumes that (a) ownership rights to an emission allowance or right are clear, (b) transaction costs are zero (or so negligible to be closed to zero), and (c) parties have a capacity and opportunity to negotiate.

Does the fact that since the emission of GHGs to the atmosphere is a global phenomenon, no ownership right to an emission allowance can be created unless it is an equivalent property right in every nation? Most developing nations still do not have land title and real property ownership rights; how will they build capacity to manage an ownership interest in CO_2 emissions? With "free riders" is it even "fair" to all to create an ownership interest in GHG emission allowances? Even within ETS or RGGI, transaction costs are not negligible. Governments spend substantial money to design, create and manage the cap and trade market. Moreover, as the initial auctions and trades for GHG allowances indicate, the price for this new entitlement is relatively low. Economic parties are willing to pay only a relatively small price to obtain this new allowance. This is the "endowment effect," described by C. Sunstein, Endogenous Preferences, Environmental Law, 22 J. Legal Studies 217 (1993).

If governments quantify the amount of GHG emissions each will allow, and sets a fee for that activity, could governments adjust this fee to accommodate discoveries in climate science and the need to more intensively mitigate greenhouse gas emissions, or raise funds for adaptation? Would a cap and trade system lock in GHG emission levels (as has happened to the acid rain emissions in the USA under the Clean Air Act), and impede governments capacity to use economic valuations to control the GHG externality? Is a GHG abatement challenge different from other forms of pollution? Consider the fee system discussed in R. Stewart, Economics, Environment, and the Limits of Legal Control, 9 Harvard Envtl. L. Rev. 1 (1985).

Finally, as you read these excepts, how will the design of a taxation or a cap and trade system be evaluation from an ethical perspective? Ultimately, does a regulatory system that can set a fee on all emissions and control the emissions through a permit or license have advantages over the use of an economic instrument?

Notes and Questions

1. Since a significant volume of atmospheric carbon dioxide is related to land use, forestry practices, and photosynthesis, how should taxes, or regulations, or "trading" regimes be structured to best effect reforms that stabilize climate conditions? Is this decision one to be guided by science, or by accommodating short-term economic and social impacts of the legal tools enacted? In August 2009, The United Nations launched a service to monitor international cooperation designed for Reducing Emissions from Deforestation and Degradation" or REDD, to enhance understanding about this sector. See Chapter 3.D above, available at un-redd@un-redd.org . What kinds of global consensus about REDD be enough to permit agreement on treaties, or national legislation, to effectively provide climate mitigation from this sector?

2. Recall the readings on Chapter 1, above. What is the strong motivation among political leaders to favor an emission trading system ahead of other legal forms climate mitigation? The UNFCCC obligates States to consider many different ways to mitigate greenhouse gas emissions. Why does the European Union chose to favor an Emission Trading System, or why the US House of Representatives in its American Clean Energy and Security Act, HR

2454, assign importance to a cap and trade regime ahead of other legal measures?

COMBATING GLOBAL CLIMATE CHANGE: WHY A CARBON TAX IS A BETTER RESPONSE TO GLOBAL WARMING THAN CAP AND TRADE
Reuven S. Avi-Yonah and David M. Uhlmann
28 Stanford Envtl. L. J. 3 (2009)

The leading proposal in the United States and abroad for addressing global climate change is some form of market-based cap and trade system. * * *

The popularity of a cap and trade system may reflect the fact that cap and trade offers something for everyone. For environmentalists, cap and trade promises a declining cap on the carbon dioxide emissions that are the principal cause of global warming. For industry groups, cap and trade offers the possibility of a new market in carbon allowances and therefore the potential for significant income for companies who can inexpensively reduce their carbon dioxide emissions. For economists, cap and trade allows the market to take into account externalities as it determines the price of carbon. For politicians, cap and trade offers the opportunity to take action to combat global warming without implementation of a complex regulatory permitting scheme or imposition of a tax on fossil fuels. * * *

The popular and intellectual appeal of a cap and trade system, however, obscures a number of practical considerations that, at a minimum, counsel against cap and trade as the leading edge of domestic efforts to combat climate change. First, * * * it would be years before a cap and trade system would become operational, because of the inherent delays of the rulemaking process (including the likelihood of litigation over whatever regulatory system is adopted). Second, the effectiveness of a cap and trade system could be undermined by the challenges of setting baselines for emission reduction targets, the free distribution of allowances, and the use of offsets in lieu of meaningful emission reduction measures. Third, while a cap and trade system promises fixed reductions in carbon dioxide emissions, the tradeoff is uncertainty about the price of those reductions. If the price of carbon rises too high, there will be political pressure to relax the carbon cap, thus removing the primary benefit of a cap and trade system.

Moreover, an international environmental crisis is not the best time to experiment with a largely untested emissions control system on a global scale. It is far from clear that a cap and trade system for carbon dioxide emissions will work on a national and international level. While the United States utilized a cap and trade system to reduce acid rain in the 1990s, we have never used cap and trade to address an emissions problem that involves such a wide variety of sources, nor do we have experience with a global cap and trade system.

A more efficient and effective market-based approach to reduce carbon dioxide emissions would be a carbon tax imposed on all coal, natural gas, and oil produced domestically or imported into the United States. A carbon tax would enable the market to account for the societal costs of carbon dioxide emissions and thereby promote emission reductions, just like a cap and trade system. A carbon tax would be easier to implement and enforce, however, and simpler to adjust if the resulting market-based changes were either too weak or too strong. A carbon tax also would produce revenue that could be used to fund research and development of alternative energy and tax credits to offset any regressive effects of the carbon tax. Because a carbon tax could be implemented and become effective almost immediately, it would be a much quicker method of reducing greenhouse gas emissions than a cap and trade system. In addition, because a carbon tax could be effective in advance of any international treaty regarding greenhouse gas emissions, a carbon tax would provide the United States much needed credibility in the negotiations over international carbon dioxide limits. A carbon tax could then supplement an international cap and trade system, combine with emission caps in an international hybrid "cap and tax" approach, or become the focal point for the next international treaty to address global climate change.

A carbon tax carries its own practical limitations, perhaps the most significant of which is the challenge of enacting tax legislation in the United States. Those political considerations may be compounded by instability in energy prices (which peaked at over $140 per barrel during the summer of 2008, only to fall below $50 per barrel by November 2008) and economic concerns created by the global credit crisis during the fall of 2008. A cap and trade system may be more viable politically, because it is not labeled a tax nor is it as transparent about its effect on energy prices. The political advantages of cap and trade may be more illusory than real, however, since opponents of climate change legislation will argue that either approach would increase energy costs and further damage an already weakened economy. * * *

B. Market-Based Limits on Carbon Dioxide Emissions

While regulatory tools are available to reduce carbon dioxide emissions, and their use may be desirable as part of a broad-based approach to climate change mitigation, most of the debate among policymakers and scholars has focused on market-based approaches to limit carbon dioxide emissions. The emphasis on market-based approaches may reflect in part the inherent complexity of the Clean Air Act and the delays that would face any regulatory system to reduce carbon dioxide emissions. Indeed, if past experience under the Clean Air Act is any guide, litigation would ensue once a new regulatory regime was established, leading to even greater delays in carbon dioxide reductions.

1. The benefits of market-based limits

The major driving force behind market-based approaches is the belief that harnessing market forces is critical to developing the operational changes and alternative technologies needed to reduce carbon dioxide emissions. Theoretically, reliance on market-based forces would allow development of the most innovative and cost-effective form of carbon dioxide reductions, which may be less likely to occur if the government mandates particular types of emission controls under the Clean Air Act or a comparable statutory scheme focusing on carbon dioxide emission controls.[105] * * *

2. Upstream versus downstream market-based limits

Both a carbon tax and a cap and trade system could be imposed either "upstream" or "downstream." * * * [A]n upstream carbon tax or cap and trade system would focus on fossil fuel production (oil, coal, and natural gas), since together energy use accounts for approximately eighty percent of carbon dioxide emissions in the United States. An upstream market-based approach would have the greatest ability to ensure that all sources of carbon dioxide emissions are affected, because it focuses on carbon at the point that it enters the economy.

Alternatively, either a carbon tax or a cap and trade system could be imposed downstream on the facilities that are the major sources of carbon dioxide emissions. A downstream approach would focus on the same facilities that would likely be regulated under state implementation plans (if carbon dioxide

---

[105] Many academics assume that market-based approaches will produce more innovation than traditional regulatory approaches. * * * David Driesen challenges the assumption of market advocates, particularly their argument that emissions trading programs promote greater innovation. See David M. Driesen, "Does Emissions Trading Encourage Innovation?," 33 Envtl. L. Rep. (Envtl. Law Inst.) 10094 (2003). Driesen claims that cap and trade systems only promote innovation by companies that are selling credits and asserts that traditional regulation can promote innovation more effectively than emissions trading programs. David M. Driesen, "Sustainable Development and Market Liberalism's Shotgun Wedding: Emissions Trading Under the Kyoto Protocol," 83 Ind. L.J. 21, 51-58 (2008). We agree with Driesen that cap and trade may limit innovation to sellers of credits and that technology-forcing performance standards can promote innovation effectively. We do not interpret Driesen's arguments to undermine our view that a carbon tax would provide incentives for innovation, however, particularly when combined with tax credits for alternative energy and carbon sequestration. Indeed, Driesen acknowledges that a carbon tax would promote more innovation than a cap and trade system. David M. Driesen, Economic Instruments for Sustainable Development in Environmental Law For Sustainability: A Critical Reader 303 (Stepan Wood & Benjamin J. Richardson eds., 2005).

became a criteria pollutant) or under Title V permits. A well-designed downstream approach could also reach all sectors of the economy, enabling costs to be distributed as evenly as an upstream approach.

The challenge under a downstream approach is the number and kinds of facilities that would be monitored and the inherent difficulty in reaching all forms of energy use, most notably motor vehicle use and electricity, which contribute significantly to carbon dioxide emissions. The broader range of facilities to be monitored would heighten the administrative complexity; the increased number of facilities would require greater resources for compliance assurance and enforcement. In addition, it is not clear how energy use by individuals would be addressed, despite their significant contribution to the carbon dioxide emissions problem. For these reasons, either a carbon tax or a cap and trade system would be easier to implement under an upstream approach, with a more targeted approach to polluting facilities and motor vehicles perhaps coming over time through regulation under the Clean Air Act.

3. Key features of a carbon tax and cap and trade

An upstream carbon tax arguably is the most straightforward approach to the global climate change problem. A carbon tax would be imposed on all oil, coal, and natural gas production in the United States, as well as all imports. The tax rate would be based on the marginal cost of carbon dioxide emissions (also referred to as the "social cost of carbon") and would be increased annually to reflect the increase in the harmful effects of carbon dioxide emissions. A carbon tax thereby would provide a price signal that captures what is now an externality, namely the harmful effects of carbon dioxide emissions. Tax credits would be provided for carbon sequestration programs, which eliminate or reduce carbon dioxide emissions (and, in some circumstances, could be used to generate energy). Tax revenues would be used to expand tax credits for development of alternative energy and to address any regressive effects of the carbon tax.

If the carbon tax did not produce the desired reduction in carbon dioxide emissions, the tax would be increased; if the tax "overcorrected" and produced greater than anticipated reductions, it could be decreased. Implementation and enforcement of a carbon tax would occur through existing programs within the Internal Revenue Service and the Energy Department. Moreover, by establishing a carbon tax in advance of any international agreement on global carbon dioxide emissions, the United States would meet its obligation to begin reducing its carbon dioxide emissions and establish much-needed credibility in the ensuing international negotiations.

An upstream cap and trade system would establish a cap on the carbon content of fuels in much the same way that an upstream carbon tax would impose a tax on those fuels. The cap would decline over time to achieve the desired level of carbon dioxide emission reductions. Where a cap and trade system becomes more complicated and * * * potentially unwieldy, is in the setting of baselines for the distribution of allowances and in the monitoring and enforcement of a complex allowance system.

Under an upstream cap and trade system, all producers and importers of fossil fuels would be required to have allowances to "cover" the carbon content of the fuels they produce. The number of those allowances would be limited by the overall "cap" imposed by the system. Allowances could be distributed either for free, through an auction system, or some combination. * * * Absent an auction, no revenue would be generated by cap and trade to support the development of alternative energy or carbon sequestration technologies. But, theoretically, market forces would provide a substitute for government subsidies: companies that developed alternative energy and otherwise found ways to limit their carbon dioxide emissions would have "surplus" allowances that they could sell to companies that needed more allowances.

The best example of a cap and trade system on a national level in the United States is the cap and trade program under Title IV of the Clean Air Act, which was implemented under the Clean Air Act Amendments of 1990 to curtail acid rain. The acid rain program is widely viewed as an overwhelming success, both in terms of the environmental protection it provided and the degree to which change occurred without significant economic dislocation. Because the acid rain problem focused on 111 facilities in the Midwest (the so-called "Big Dirties"), however, we do not have experience in the United States--or the rest of the world--with an economy-wide cap and trade system.

In contrast to the limited experience in the U.S. with cap and trade, carbon taxes have been successfully implemented in a growing number of countries. Carbon taxes have been implemented in Quebec and British Columbia as part of Canadian efforts to meet the requirements of the Kyoto Protocol. In addition, Denmark, Finland, Italy, the Netherlands, Norway, and Sweden have introduced carbon taxes in combination with energy taxes. The existing carbon taxes are too new to draw meaningful conclusions about their long-term benefits, but many economists believe that a carbon tax would be the most effective method of reducing carbon dioxide emissions. Cap and trade systems for carbon dioxide emissions have been implemented by the European Union and on a regional basis in New England; in addition, seven Western states and four Canadian provinces have taken steps to develop a cap and trade system. * * * [T]he European Union system has not been particularly successful to date, but that has not diminished enthusiasm in the United States and abroad for relying on cap and trade systems as the principal method of reducing carbon dioxide emissions.

III. The Case for a Carbon Tax

* * * Why is cap and trade so much more complicated than the carbon tax? A carbon tax is inherently simple: a tax is imposed at X dollars per ton of

carbon content on the main sources of carbon dioxide emissions in the economy, namely coal, oil, and natural gas. (Other greenhouse gas sources, such as methane, are not included because energy accounts for nearly eighty-five percent of the 7147 million metric tons of greenhouse gases in the U.S. economy.) The tax is imposed "upstream," i.e., at the point of extraction or importation, which means than it can be imposed on only about 2000 taxpayers (500 coal miners and importers, 750 oil producers and importers, and 750 natural gas producers and importers). Credits can be given to carbon sequestration projects and to other projects that reduce greenhouse gas emissions (although this would need to be addressed in a way that does not dilute the price signal or create undue complexity), and exports are exempted. Beyond that, the main question is what to do with the revenue, which will be discussed below.

Cap and trade, on the other hand, is inherently more complicated. While the cap can also be imposed "upstream," it has several features that require complexity. First, baselines need to be set for purposes of establishing the emissions cap. Second, the proposal needs to determine how allowances will be created and distributed, either for free or by auction. Free distribution requires deciding which industries receive allowances, while an auction requires a complex monitoring system to prevent cheating. Third, the trading in allowances needs to be set up and monitored: a system needs to be devised to prevent the same allowance from being used twice, and penalties need to be established for polluters who exceed their allowances. Fourth, if allowances are to be traded with other countries, the international trading of allowances would need to be monitored as well. Fifth, to prevent Cost Uncertainty, cap and trade proposals typically have complex provisions for banking and borrowing allowances, and some of them provide for safety valves. Sixth, offsets are needed for carbon sequestration and similar projects, and those are more complicated than credits against a carbon tax liability. Finally, most cap and trade proposals involve provisions for coordinating with the cap and trade policies of other countries, and for punishing countries that do not have a greenhouse gas emissions control policy.

It is important to note that this difference in complexity is inherent in the two policies as initially proposed, before any legislative amendments and before any implementation and enforcement issues. A pure cap and trade system is inevitably more complex than any carbon tax.

Cap and trade is also relatively untried: we have never had an economy-wide cap and trade system, while we have extensive experience with economy-wide excise taxes on a wide variety of products, including gasoline. * * *

In addition to its inherent complexity, cap and trade also is more difficult to enforce. Under cap and trade, an elaborate mechanism would need to be set up to distribute and collect allowances and to ensure that allowances are real (a difficult task, especially if allowances from non-United States programs are permitted) and that polluters are penalized if they emit greenhouses gases without an allowance. A new administrative body would need to be set up for this purpose, or at least a new office within EPA, and new employees with the relevant expertise would need to be hired. A carbon tax, on the other hand, could be enforced by the IRS with its existing staff, which has the relevant expertise in enforcing other excise taxes.

Cap and trade also raises collateral issues that are not present in a carbon tax, such as the need for the Securities and Exchange Commission to enforce rules regarding futures trading in allowances. A good example is the tax implications of both policies. A carbon tax, as a federal tax, has no tax implications: it is simply collected and is not deductible. Allowances under cap and trade, on the other hand, raise a multitude of tax issues: What are the tax implications of distributing allowances for free? What are the tax implications of trading in allowances? Should allowance exchanges be permitted to avoid the tax on selling allowances? What amount of the purchase price of a business should be allocated to its allowances? If borrowing and banking occur, what are the tax consequences? Can allowances be amortized? None of these issues arise under a carbon tax.

2. Revenue

A carbon tax by definition generates revenue. A relatively modest tax of $10 per ton of carbon content is estimated to generate $50 billion per year; the America's Energy Security Trust Fund Act envisages a tax of $16.50 per ton and generates correspondingly more revenue. While the current federal budget deficit and even larger actuarial deficit may justify revenue raising measures in general, revenues from a carbon tax should be segregated and devoted to addressing any regressive effects of the tax and reducing greenhouse gas emissions. Some carbon tax proposals promise "revenue neutrality" and focus on eliminating regressive effects. We agree that regressive effects must be addressed but otherwise would use revenues from the carbon tax to provide tax credits for alternative energy development and more energy-efficient motor vehicles, since the positive externalities that result from such research and development means that funding is likely to be undersupplied by the private sector even with a carbon tax in place. Revenues could also be used to support carbon sequestration projects and other projects that reduce greenhouse gas emissions, like mass transit and green building.

Segregating the revenue from a carbon tax and using the proceeds to support further greenhouse gas reductions is justified because it reduces Benefit Uncertainty, which is the most serious drawback of a carbon tax compared to cap and trade. In addition, segregating the revenue is likely to reduce some political opposition to raising taxes in general, at least to the extent that such opposition is based on the perception that government is wasteful.

In theory, cap and trade can be used to generate the same amount of revenue as a carbon tax, if all the allowances are auctioned. In practice, however, all cap and trade proposals introduced in Congress, as well as most academic proposals and existing cap and trade programs in the United States and abroad, include some free distribution of allowances. For example, the EU cap and trade regime distributed ninety-five percent of the allowances for free, and most Congressional proposals distribute over half of the allowances for free. The reason is obvious: for politicians, a significant attraction of cap and trade is that it creates from nothing a new, scarce resource that they can use to reward their constituents and donors. But if allowances are distributed for free, cap and trade generates less revenue than a carbon tax, and this means less potential to support research and development, carbon sequestration, and other greenhouse-gas-reducing efforts.

Moreover, it seems unlikely that free allocation of allowances would produce the optimal reduction in greenhouse gas emissions. Some polluting industries are likely to get too many allowances, and that would affect the trading price of allowances. At the extreme, the result would be what occurred in Europe, where politicians created so many free allowances that no reduction from business as usual was required at all, the price of allowances collapsed, and the EU failed to meet its goals under the Kyoto Protocol.

A similar risk to free distribution of allowances under a carbon tax would be pressure from affected industries for tax exemptions. The process of enacting tax exemptions is more visible than the process of distributing free allowances, however, and any exemption to one of the three industries affected (coal, natural gas, and oil) would be met by resistance from the other two, hopefully resulting in no exemptions at all.

3. Cost certainty

A carbon tax ensures Cost Certainty: the cost is the amount of the tax, and whatever the incidence of the tax (i.e., whether it can be passed on to consumers or not), the cost cannot rise above the tax rate. This enables businesses to plan ahead, secure in the knowledge that raising the tax rate beyond any automatic adjustment, which can be planned for, requires another vote in Congress that they can hope to influence.

A cap and trade regime, on the other hand, suffers from inherent Cost Uncertainty. While allowances may be initially distributed for free, the key question for polluting businesses that need to acquire allowances to address a reduction in the cap is what would be the future price of allowances. Existing cap and trade programs like the Southern California RECLAIM system for nitrogen oxide emissions, in which the allowance prices spiked in 2000 to more than twenty times their historical level, and the EU Emission Trading

Scheme (ETS), in which the price of allowances collapsed when it became clear that too many allowances had been distributed, illustrate the problem of Cost Uncertainty in cap and trade programs. Cost Uncertainty makes it inherently difficult for businesses to plan ahead. The fundamental problem is that the reduction in the cap that is built into cap and trade would necessarily make allowances more expensive. How much more expensive depends on the development of future technologies, which cannot be predicted with any accuracy over the longer time period (fifty years or more) required for a cap and trade program to achieve its environmental goals.

Cap and trade proponents argue that Cost Uncertainty can be mitigated by provisions for banking extra allowances for use in future years, and borrowing allowances from future years to use in the present. These provisions add complexity, and it is unclear whether they will be effective: in the early years of the program, there are few allowances to bank, while borrowing risks leaving the business with insufficient allowances in the future when the cap is lower.

Ultimately, the only sure way of preventing Cost Uncertainty in a cap and trade regime is to build in a "safety valve," which would permit businesses to receive or purchase at a fixed price additional allowances if the market price of allowances becomes too high. Several of the current proposals in Congress have such built-in safety valves. However, the problem with safety valves is that they sacrifice Benefit Certainty, which is the main advantage of cap and trade: by definition, providing extra allowances when the cap is lowered means raising the cap.

Even if a cap and trade program has no safety valve built into it from the start, the commitment to Benefit Certainty may be misleading. If the lowered cap begins to seriously hurt businesses and the price of allowances spikes, one should expect strong pressure on politicians to stop lowering the cap. Benefit Certainty under cap and trade as implemented may therefore be an illusion, while Cost Uncertainty is very real.

4. Signaling

A carbon tax sends a clear signal to polluters: pollution imposes a negative externality on others, and you should be forced to internalize that cost by paying the tax. There is no ambiguity about the message that is intended to be conveyed. Greenhouse gas emissions are costly, and even if people are willing to pay the price, they should be aware of the societal cost they are imposing.

A cap and trade system, however, sends a different and more ambiguous message. On the one hand, its goal is to reduce greenhouse gas emissions. On the other hand, it achieves that goal by either allowing polluters to purchase the right to pollute (from the government or from each other), or to receive permits to pollute for free. The underlying message is that the government permits you to pollute as long as you are willing to pay. Of course, the message (and the cost imposed) may be the same, regardless of whether a tax is paid or whether an allowance is purchased, although it is not the same if allowances are distributed for free. Labels are important, however, and calling the cost a tax sends a different signal than calling it the purchase price for a right to pollute. * * *

C. Disadvantages of a Carbon Tax

1. Political resistance

A primary reason that both presidential candidates supported cap and trade during the 2008 election, and that other political leaders and many academics support cap and trade, rather than a carbon tax, reflects concern that a carbon tax cannot get enacted because it is a tax. Politicians vividly remember the fate of the Clinton-Gore BTU tax proposal in 1993, and "to be BTU'd" has become the shorthand among Clinton Administration veterans for what happens to supporters of politically unpopular proposals. * * *

Moreover, opponents of cap and trade inevitably liken it to a carbon tax. If allowances are auctioned, or even if they have to be purchased from private parties, the resulting cost is likely to be passed on to consumers. Thus, cap and trade is not just more complicated, it is also subject to the same criticism as a carbon tax: it will "increase gas prices at the pump"--an argument every voter understands. If we are to mitigate greenhouse gas emissions, politicians will need to face down inevitable resistance whether they propose a carbon tax or cap and trade. * * *

2. Benefit uncertainty

The main substantive disadvantage of a carbon tax compared to cap and trade is Benefit Uncertainty. There can be no assurance that any given tax level will result in the desired reduction in greenhouse gas emissions. If the desired benefit is not achieved, the tax may have to be raised, resulting in renewed political opposition, which could defeat the tax increase and thereby limit the environmental benefits of the tax.

However, there are several reasons not to reject the carbon tax because of Benefit Uncertainty. First, as pointed out above, cap and trade may in fact be subject to similar Benefit Uncertainty, because if costs rise too high one can expect pressure to adjust the cap, even if there is no built-in safety valve.

Second, the tax rate can in fact be adjusted. General experience with other taxes has shown that once a tax is in place, it is usually not as hard to raise its rate despite political opposition to tax hikes; this is why people say that "an old tax is a good tax." The United States income tax began in 1913 with a rate of one percent, and has been raised (and lowered) many times since then (although Americans have become increasingly unwilling to accept tax increases). The Value Added Tax (VAT), which is now the most important tax in the world, was typically introduced in over 100 countries at a much lower rate than the current one. If it becomes clear that the carbon tax rate needs to be raised to achieve the necessary reduction in emissions, and if voters remain convinced of the need to reduce emissions, historical experience suggests that the rate could be raised, notwithstanding the political challenges.

Finally, neither cap and trade (without a safety valve) nor a carbon tax can truly achieve Benefit Certainty, because the desired level of emissions (450 ppm) is based on worldwide emissions, not United States emissions. We can have the strictest cap and trade regime and suffer the full cost, but if China and India do nothing, we will not have Benefit Certainty.

From this perspective, in addition to reducing greenhouse gas emissions in the United States, both a carbon tax and a cap and trade system serve the essential function of persuading the rest of the world that we are serious, and therefore that they should cooperate in a global policy to curb greenhouse gas emissions. Both cap and trade and a carbon tax are equally useful from that perspective, but for the reasons explained above, a carbon tax can be implemented much faster than cap and trade and, therefore, is preferable from the standpoint of international leadership. Stated differently, Benefit Certainty requires bringing large developing countries to the bargaining table, and a carbon tax is better and faster in doing so than cap and trade.

3. Tax exemptions

Proponents of cap and trade argue that it is better than a carbon tax because the political bargain over which industries will get relief from its cost has to be reached up front as part of the decision of how to allocate allowances. They also argue that a carbon tax will be subject to pressure to enact permanent exemptions for affected industries, which will permanently weaken its effect and exacerbate its Benefit Uncertainty. * * *

The choice between free allocation of allowances under cap and trade and exemptions under a carbon tax is similar to the familiar debate in the tax literature over whether direct subsidies or tax expenditures are superior. Tax expenditures are indirect subsidies delivered through tax reductions or exemptions. While the traditional view has favored direct subsidies because they are arguably more transparent and easier to administer, recently the consensus has shifted to view both types of programs as equally transparent, and so the choice between them comes down to administrative considerations, which generally favor tax expenditures that can be administered by the IRS.

In the cap and trade versus carbon tax debate, the choice between free allowances and tax exemptions is simpler. Tax exemptions are not necessary at all, but if they are enacted they will be quite transparent and subject to criticism as giveaways to unpopular industries. They will also be relatively easy to administer by the IRS. Free allowances, on the other hand, are inherently more complicated to distribute and monitor, for the reasons given above. This debate therefore favors the carbon tax.

4. Coordination

Another alleged advantage of cap and trade and disadvantage of the carbon tax is that it is easier to coordinate with the regimes implemented by other countries, and especially the EU ETS. Proponents of cap and trade envisage direct transfers of allowances between the United States cap and trade and the EU ETS, as well as other potential cap and trade regimes in, for example, Canada.

Coordination issues may become more significant over time, if cap and trade emerges as the dominant global approach to climate change mitigation. * * *

Moreover, exchanging allowances with foreign cap and trade regimes exponentially increases the enforcement difficulties inherent in cap and trade. Foreign allowances would have to be carefully monitored and verified to prevent widespread cheating. This problem is exacerbated under the EU ETS because allowances are distributed "downstream" to many different polluters. A carbon tax, on the other hand, can easily be collected on imports and rebated on exports, and as long as it is also imposed on domestic production, it does not pose significant World Trade Organization compliance issues.

Notes and Questions

1. In the Canadian province of British Columbia, recent climate change legislation imposes a carbon tax, as well as industry GHG emission reductions, carbon neutral requirements applicable to provincial and local government operations, and a Green Building Code. See also D. Farber, Adapting to Climate Change: Who Should Pay, 23 J. of Land Use & Envtl. L. 1 (2007); R. Mann, The Case for the Carbon Tax: How to Overcome Politics and Find Our Green Destiny, 39 ELR 10118 (2009); R. Mann, To Tax or Not to Tax Carbon, ABA Nat. Res. & Envt. (Summer 2009) (excerpted in Chapter 4); J. Milne, Carbon Taxes in the United States: The Context for the Future, 10 Vermont J. of Envtl. L. No. 1 (2008); J. Volkman, Making Change in a New Economy: Incentives and the Carbon Economy, 29 Public Land & Resources L. Rev. 1

(2008); M. Waggoner, How and Why to Tax Carbon, 20 Colo. J. of Intl. L. & Policy 1 (2009).

2. Carbon taxes were examined at the 9th Global Conference on Environmental Taxation convened at the National University of Singapore in November of 2008. See L. Lye et al., eds., Critical Issues in Environmental Taxation (2009).

A MEANINGFUL U.S. CAP-AND-TRADE SYSTEM TO ADDRESS CLIMATE CHANGE
Robert N. Stavins
32 Harvard Envtl. L. Rev. 293 (2008)

While there are tradeoffs between two alternative market-based instruments—a cap-and-trade system and a carbon tax—the best approach for the short- to medium-term in the United States is a cap-and-trade system. * * *

The environmental integrity of a domestic cap-and-trade system for climate change can be maximized and its costs and risks minimized by: targeting all fossil fuel-related CO_2 emissions through an upstream, economy-wide cap; setting a trajectory of caps over time that begins modestly and gradually becomes more stringent; establishing a long-run price signal to encourage investment; adopting mechanisms to protect against cost uncertainty; and including linkages with the climate policy actions of other countries. Importantly, by providing the option to mitigate economic impacts through the distribution of emission allowances, this approach can establish consensus for a policy that achieves meaningful emission reductions. It is for these reasons and others that cap-and-trade systems have been used increasingly in the United States to address an array of environmental problems.

A cap-and-trade system should not be confused with emission reduction credit or credit-based programs, in which those reporting emission reductions generate credits that others may or must buy to offset obligations under some other policy. A credit-based program could be used as a means of encouraging emission reductions from activities outside the scope of a cap-and-trade system, emissions tax, or standards-based policy. But they typically require measurement--or, more likely, estimation--of emission reductions, which, unlike emissions themselves, cannot be observed directly. Hence, these programs generally face difficulties establishing that reported reductions would not have occurred absent the credit-based program. This is the baseline or "additionality" problem: making a comparison with an unobserved and fundamentally unobservable hypothetical (what would have happened had the credit not been generated). This problem reduces environmental effectiveness if credits generated by activities that would have occurred even without the credit program are used to satisfy real emission reduction obligations. Despite these obstacles, cost savings still may be achieved through selective use of credit-based programs targeting certain activities, * * * such as various types of carbon-saving land management that otherwise would be too costly or infeasible to integrate into a cap-and-trade system.

Another major alternative to a cap-and-trade system is the use of command-and-control standards, such as energy efficiency or emission performance standards, which require firms and consumers to take particular actions that directly or indirectly reduce emissions. The costs of standards often are largely invisible except to those directly affected by them, but standards would impose significantly greater economic impacts than market-based policies. Standards would offer firms and consumers far less flexibility regarding how emission reductions are achieved and could not target many low-cost emission reduction opportunities. Moreover, the effectiveness of standards in achieving nationwide emission targets is highly uncertain, in part because they could only cover a fraction of nationwide emissions, leaving many sources unregulated. In contrast, market-based policies can cover all sources of fossil fuel-related CO_2 emissions, and, unlike other alternatives, a cap-and-trade system can essentially guarantee achievement of emission targets for sources under the cap. * * *

Even a credible long-run cap-and-trade system may provide insufficient incentives for investment in technology development because it would not address certain well-known factors (market failures) that discourage such investment, such as those stemming from the public good nature of knowledge that comes from research and development efforts. Thus, a cap-and-trade system alone will not encourage the socially desirable level of investment in research, development, and deployment of new technologies that could reduce future emission reduction costs. To achieve this desired level of investment, additional policies may be necessary to provide additional government funding or increase incentives for private funding of such research activities.

1.3 Applications of Cap-and-Trade Mechanisms

Over the past two decades, tradable permit systems have been adopted for pollution control with increasing frequency in the U.S. and other parts of the world. As explained above, tradable permit programs are of two basic types, credit programs and cap-and-trade systems. The focus of this brief review of other programs is on the applications of the cap-and-trade approach. * * *

1.3.1 Previous Use of Cap-and-Trade Systems for Local and Regional Air Pollution

The first important example of a trading program in the United States was the leaded gasoline phasedown that occurred in the 1980s. Although not strictly a cap-and-trade system, the phasedown included features, such as trading and banking of environmental credits, which brought it closer than other credit programs to the cap-and-trade model and resulted in significant cost savings. The lead program was successful in meeting its environmental targets, and the system was cost-effective, with estimated savings of about $250 million per year. Also, the program provided measurable incentives for cost-saving technology diffusion.

A cap-and-trade system was also used in the United States to help comply with the Montreal Protocol, an international agreement aimed at slowing the rate of stratospheric ozone depletion. The Protocol called for reductions in the use of CFCs and halons, the primary chemical groups thought to lead to depletion. The timetable for the phaseout of CFCs was accelerated, and the system appears to have been relatively cost-effective.

The most important domestic application of a market-based instrument for environmental protection arguably is the cap-and-trade system regulating sulfur dioxide ("SO_2") emissions, the primary precursor of acid rain. This program was established under the U.S. Clean Air Act Amendments of 1990. The program is intended to reduce SO_2 and nitrogen oxide ("NO_x") emissions by 10 million tons and 2 million tons, respectively, from 1980 levels. A robust market of SO_2 allowance trading emerged from the program, resulting in cost savings on the order of $1 billion annually, as compared with the costs under some command-and-control regulatory alternatives. The program has also had a significant environmental impact: SO_2 emissions from the power sector decreased from 15.7 million tons in 1990 to 10.2 million tons in 2005.

In 1994, California's South Coast Air Quality Management District launched a cap-and-trade program to reduce NO_x and SO_2 emissions in the Los Angeles area. This Regional Clean Air Incentives Market ("RECLAIM") program set an aggregate cap on NO_x and SO_2 emissions for all significant sources, with an ambitious goal of reducing aggregate emissions by 70% by 2003. Trading under the RECLAIM program was restricted in several ways, with positive and negative consequences. Despite problems, RECLAIM has generated environmental benefits, with NO_x emissions in the regulated area falling by 60% and SO_2 emissions by 50%. Furthermore, the program has reduced compliance costs for regulated facilities, with the best available analysis suggesting 42% cost savings, amounting to $58 million annually.

Finally, in 1999, under EPA guidance, twelve northeastern states and the District of Columbia implemented a regional NO_x cap-and-trade system to reduce compliance costs associated with the Ozone Transport Commission regulations of the 1990 Amendments to the Clean Air Act. Emissions caps for two geographic regions regulated from 1999-2003 were 35% and 45% of 1990 emissions, respectively. Compliance cost savings of 40% to 47% have been estimated for the period 1999-2003, compared to a base case of continued command-and-control regulation without trading or banking.

1.3.2 CO_2 and Greenhouse Gas Cap-and-Trade Systems

Although cap-and-trade has proven to be a cost-effective means to control conventional air pollutants, it has a very limited history as a method of reducing CO_2 emissions. Several ambitious programs are in the planning stages or have been launched.

First, the Kyoto Protocol, the international agreement that was signed in Japan in 1997, includes a provision for an international cap-and-trade system among countries, as well as two systems of project-level offsets. The Protocol's provisions have set the stage for the member states of the European Union to address their commitments using a regional cap-and-trade system.

By far the largest existing active cap-and-trade program in the world is the European Union Emissions Trading Scheme ("EU ETS") for CO_2 allowances, which has operated for the past two years with considerable success, despite some initial--and predictable--problems. The 11,500 emitters regulated by the downstream program include large sources such as oil refineries, combustion installations, coke ovens, cement factories, ferrous metal production, glass and ceramics production, and pulp and paper production, but the program does not cover sources in the transportation, commercial, or residential sectors. Although the first phase, a pilot program from 2005-2007, allowed trading only in CO_2, the second phase, 2008-2012, potentially broadens the program to include other GHGs. In its first two years of operation, the EU ETS produced a functioning CO_2 market, with weekly trading volumes ranging between 5 and 15 million tons, with spikes in trading activity occurring along with major price changes. There have been some problems with the program's design and early implementation, but it is much too soon to provide a definitive assessment of the system's performance. * * *

Finally, California's Greenhouse Gas Solutions Act of 2006 ("Assembly Bill 32" or "AB 32") is intended to begin in 2012 to reduce emissions to 1990 state levels by 2020 and may employ a cap-and-trade approach. Although the Global Warming Solutions Act does not require the use of market-based instruments, it does allow for their use, albeit with restrictions that they must not result in increased emissions of criteria air pollutants or toxins; must maximize environmental and economic benefits in California; and must account for localized economic and environmental justice concerns. This mixed set of objectives potentially interferes with the development of a sound policy mechanism. The Governor's Market Advisory Committee has recommended the implementation of a cap-and-trade program with a gradual phase-in of caps covering most sectors of the economy. Allowances will be freely distributed or auctioned, with a shift toward more auctions in later years.

1.4 Criteria for Policy Assessment

Three criteria stand out as particularly important for the assessment of a domestic climate change policy: environmental effectiveness, cost effectiveness, and distributional equity.

Environmental effectiveness addresses whether it is feasible to achieve given targets with a specific policy instrument. This will include the technical ability of policymakers to design and the administrative ability of governments to implement technology standards that are sufficiently diverse and numerous to address all of the sources of CO_2 emissions in a modern economy. It will also involve the ability of political systems to put in place costs that are sufficiently severe to achieve meaningful emission reductions (or limits on global greenhouse gas concentrations, or limits on temperature changes).

In addition, the environmental-effectiveness criterion considers the certainty with which a policy will achieve emission or other targets. Although alternative policy designs may aim to achieve identical targets, design choices affect the certainty with which those targets are achieved. For example, a cap-and-trade system can achieve emission targets with high certainty because emission guarantees are built into the policy. On the other hand, with policies such as carbon taxes or technology standards, actual emissions are difficult to predict because of current and future uncertainties. Consequently, while such policies can aim to achieve particular emission targets, actual emissions may exceed or fall below those targets depending on factors beyond policymakers' control.

Moreover, the tendency of taxes and standards to grant exemptions to address distributional issues weakens the environmental effectiveness of these instruments. By contrast, distributional battles over the allowance allocation in a cap-and-trade system do not raise the overall cost of the program or affect its climate impacts. * * *

The cost-effectiveness criterion considers a policy's relative cost of achieving emission targets as compared with alternative policy designs. One policy is considered more cost-effective than another if it achieves a given reduction at a lower cost. Many categories of economic costs are relevant to the evaluation of alternative policy designs. * * *

While a climate policy will adversely affect many firms, some may experience "windfall" profits. For example, less carbon-intensive firms may enjoy windfall profits if a climate policy increases market prices for their products more than it increases their costs. Thus, evaluation of a climate policy's distributional implications requires identifying its ultimate burdens and reflecting all adjustments in market prices, rather than just its initial impacts on costs.

While discussion often focuses on the impact of climate policies on firms, all economic impacts are ultimately borne by households in their roles as consumers, investors, and/or workers. As producers pass through increased costs, consumers experience increased prices of energy and non-energy goods, as well as reduced consumption. As a policy positively or negatively affects the profitability of firms, investors experience changes in the value of investments in those firms. Finally, workers experience changes in employment and wages.

2. Proposal for a Meaningful Cap-and-Trade System

The U.S. can launch a scientifically sound, economically rational, and politically feasible approach to reducing its contributions to the increase in atmospheric concentrations of greenhouse gases by adopting an upstream, economy-wide CO_2 cap-and-trade system that implements a gradual trajectory of emission reductions and includes mechanisms to reduce cost uncertainty. These mechanisms might include multi-year compliance periods, provisions for banking and borrowing, and possibly a cost containment mechanism to protect against any extreme price volatility.

The permits in the system should be allocated through a combination of free distribution and open auction. This mix balances legitimate concerns by some sectors and individuals who will be particularly burdened by this (or any) climate policy with the opportunity to achieve important public purposes with generated funds. The share of allowances freely allocated should decrease over time, as the private sector is able to adjust to the carbon constraints, with all allowances being auctioned after 25 years.

In addition, it is important that offsets be made available both for underground and biological carbon sequestration to provide for short-term cost-effectiveness and long-term incentives for appropriate technological change. The federal cap-and-trade system can provide for supremacy over U.S. regional, state, and local programs to avoid duplication, double counting, and conflicting requirements. At the same time, it is important to provide for harmonization with selective emission reduction credit and cap-and-trade systems in other nations, as well as related international systems.

2.1 Major, Though Not Exclusive, Focus on CO_2

This proposal focuses on reductions of fossil fuel-related CO_2 emissions, which accounted for nearly 85% of the 7,147 million metric tons of U.S. GHG emissions in 2005, where tons are measured in CO_2-equivalent. Carbon dioxide emissions arise from a broad range of activities involving the use of different fuels in many economic sectors. In addition, biological sequestration and reductions in non-CO_2 GHG emissions can contribute substantially to minimizing the cost of limiting GHG concentrations. Some non-CO_2 GHG emissions might be addressed under the same framework as CO_2 in a multigas cap-and-trade system. But challenges associated with measuring and monitoring other non-CO_2 emissions and biological sequestration may necessitate separate programs tailored to their specific characteristics * * *.

2.2 A Gradually Increasing Trajectory of Emission Reductions Over Time

The long-term nature of the climate problem offers significant temporal flexibility regarding emission reductions. Policies taking advantage of this "when flexibility" by setting annual emission targets that gradually increase in stringency can avoid many costs associated with taking action too quickly without sacrificing environmental benefits. Such policies can also prevent premature retirement of existing capital stock and production and siting bottlenecks that may arise in the context of rapid capital stock transitions. In addition, gradually phased-in targets provide time to incorporate advanced technologies into long-lived investments. Thus, for any given cumulative emission target or associated atmospheric GHG concentration objective, a climate policy's cost can be reduced by gradually phasing in efforts to reduce emissions.

Because of the long-term nature of the climate problem and because of the need for technological change to bring about lower-cost emission reductions, it is essential that the caps constitute a long-term trajectory. The development and eventual adoption of new low-carbon and other relevant technologies will depend on the predictability of future carbon prices, themselves brought about by the cap's constraints. Therefore, the cap-and-trade program should incorporate medium- to long-term targets, not just short-term ones.

While cost savings can be achieved by setting targets that gradually become more stringent, it is a mistake to conclude that " flexibility" is a reason to delay enacting a mandatory policy. On the contrary, the earlier a mandatory policy is established, the more flexibility there is to set emission targets that gradually depart from BAU emission levels while still achieving a long-run atmospheric GHG concentration objective. The longer it takes to establish a mandatory policy, the more strict near-term emission targets will be needed to achieve a given long-run objective.

Gradually increasing the stringency of emission targets may also reduce the near-term burdens of a climate policy and, therefore, decrease the costs and significant challenges associated with gaining consensus. On the other hand, a policy that shifts reduction efforts too far into the future may not be credible, thus reducing incentives for investment in advanced technologies.

Several types of policy-target trajectories are possible, including emission caps, emission reduction targets, global concentration targets, and allowance price trajectories. Given the long-term nature of the climate problem described above, the best measure of policy stringency may be the sum of national emissions permitted over some extended period of time. * * * [I]f banking and borrowing of allowances is allowed, then only the sum is consequential, not the specific trajectory of legislated caps, because market activity will generate the cost-minimizing trajectory.

How should the sum of capped national emissions be identified? The classical economic approach would be to choose targets that would maximize the difference between expected benefits and expected costs. Such an approach is simply not feasible in the current context. First of all, reliable information about anticipated damages—even in biophysical terms, let alone economic terms—is insufficient. And such a calculation could be made only at the global (not the national) level due to the global-commons nature of the problem. Furthermore, it is increasingly clear that it is insufficient to carry out such an analysis with expected benefits and expected costs, since it is the small risks of catastrophic damages that are at the heart of the problem. * * *

2.3 Upstream Point of Regulation and Economy-Wide Scope of Coverage

* * *

Although the point of regulation determines which entities are ultimately required to hold allowances, this decision can be made independently of decisions regarding how allowances are initially allocated. The point of regulation does not dictate or in any way limit who could receive allowances if allowances are freely distributed. Furthermore, the point of regulation decision also has no direct effect on either the magnitude of emission reduction costs or the distribution of the resulting economic burdens. A cap has the same impact on the effective cost of fuel for downstream firms regardless of the point of regulation. With upstream regulation, the allowance cost is included in the fuel price. Since all suppliers face the same additional allowance cost, they all include it in the prices they set for downstream customers. With downstream regulation, the downstream customer pays for the allowances and fuel separately. In either case, the downstream customer ultimately faces the same additional cost associated with emissions from its fuel use.

This has two important implications. First, the distribution of costs between upstream and downstream firms is unaffected by the point of regulation decision. Second, firms and consumers will undertake the same emission reduction efforts—and thereby incur the same emission reduction costs—in either case because they face the same carbon price signal.

An upstream program will not dilute the carbon price signal, because allowance costs will be passed through to downstream emitters. In particular, higher fuel prices will reduce demand. This, in turn, will lead producers to moderate their price increases, thereby absorbing some of the allowance costs themselves. This argument is valid, but it is not unique to upstream systems. With a downstream point of regulation, fossil fuel would become more expensive because emitters would be required to surrender allowances. This would reduce their demand, and lead to the same offsetting effect on fuel prices. In a similar way, some may find an upstream point of regulation counterintuitive, since it does not control emissions per se. However, an upstream approach gets at the problem more directly: it caps the amount of carbon coming into the system.

2.3.1 Environmental-Effectiveness of the Upstream Point of Regulation

An economy-wide cap, which is enabled by an upstream point of regulation, provides the greatest certainty that national emission targets will be achieved. Limiting the scope of coverage to a subset of emission sources leads to emissions uncertainty through two channels. First, changes in emissions from unregulated sources can cause national emissions to deviate from expected levels. Second, a limited scope of coverage can cause "leakage," in which market adjustments resulting from a regulation lead to increased emissions from unregulated sources outside the cap that partially offset reductions under the cap. For example, a cap that includes electricity-sector emissions (and thereby affects electricity prices) but excludes emissions from natural gas or heating oil use in commercial and residential buildings may encourage increased use of unregulated natural gas or oil heating (instead of electric heating) in new buildings. As a result, increased emissions from greater natural gas and oil heating will offset some of the reductions achieved in the electricity sector. More generally, any cap-and-trade system that is not economy-wide in scope will encourage entities that are covered by the cap to exploit this incomplete coverage by seeking ways to avoid regulation. * * *

2.3.2 Cost-Effectiveness of the Upstream Point of Regulation

An upstream point of regulation makes economy-wide scope of coverage feasible. The aggregate cost of emission reductions undertaken to meet a cap is directly affected by the scope of coverage, with costs declining more than proportionately with increases in the program's scope. While the point of regulation decision does not directly affect emission reduction costs, it does affect a cap's administrative cost.

An emission cap with broad coverage of emission sources reduces the cost of achieving a particular national emissions target. Three factors contribute to lower costs. First, a broader cap expands the pool of low-cost emission reduction opportunities that can contribute to meeting a national target. Even if a sector may contribute only a small portion of reductions, including that sector under the cap can yield significant cost savings by displacing the highest-cost reductions that would otherwise be necessary in other sectors. For example, the cost of achieving a five percent reduction in U.S. CO_2 emissions could be cut in half under an economy-wide cap compared with a cap limited to the electricity sector.

Second, an economy-wide cap provides important flexibility to achieve emission targets given uncertainties in emission reduction costs across sectors. By drawing from a broader, more diverse set of emission reduction opportunities, an economy-wide cap reduces the risk of unexpectedly high emission reduction costs much like a mutual fund reduces investment risk through diversification.

Third, an economy-wide cap creates incentives for innovation in all sectors of the economy. Such innovation increases each sector's potential to contribute cost-effective emission reductions in future years, and the resulting long-run cost savings from starting with a broad scope of coverage may far exceed any short-term gains. * * *

The point of regulation decision is a primary determinant of a cap-and-trade system's administrative costs through its effect on the number of sources that must be regulated. As the number of regulated sources increases, the administrative costs to regulators and firms rise. The point of regulation should be chosen to facilitate and minimize the administrative costs of a desired scope of coverage.

The upstream point of regulation makes an economy-wide cap-and-trade system administratively feasible, making it possible to cap nearly all U.S. CO_2 emissions through regulation of just 2,000 upstream entities. A key advantage of an upstream program is that it eliminates the regulatory need for facility-level GHG emissions inventories, which would be essential for monitoring and enforcing a cap-and-trade system that is implemented downstream at the point of emissions. The fossil fuel sales of the 2,000 entities to be regulated under the upstream cap-and-trade system are already monitored and reported to the government for tax and other purposes. Monitoring is of little use without enforcement, so meaningful and credible penalties are important. These penalties might include fees set at up to ten times marginal abatement costs, plus the requirement for firms to make up the difference. Such a scheme has resulted in virtually 100% compliance in the case of the SO_2 allowance trading program.

2.3.3 Distributional Consequences of Upstream Point of Regulation

An economy-wide emissions cap spreads the cost burden of emission reductions across all sectors of the economy. In contrast, limiting the scope of coverage both increases the overall cost and shifts burdens across sectors, regions, and income groups. Sectors remaining under the cap experience a greater economic burden as the cost of achieving emission reductions is both increased and spread over fewer sources.

Limiting the scope of coverage may have unintended consequences as well. For example, limiting a cap's coverage to the electricity sector would lead to greater electricity rate impacts and more regional variation in those impacts than would be anticipated under an economy-wide cap. In addition, excluding direct emissions from residential and commercial buildings would alter regional variation in household impacts because of regional differences in household use of electricity, heating oil, and natural gas.

2.4 Elements of a Cap-and-Trade System that Reduce Cost Uncertainty

While a cap-and-trade system can minimize the cost of meeting an emissions target, a poorly designed system can lead to emission reduction costs that are greater than anticipated. This risk arises because, barring mechanisms described below that control costs, regulated sources will meet an emissions cap regardless of the cost. This cost uncertainty is one factor that favors a carbon tax, which largely eliminates cost uncertainty (but introduces emissions reduction uncertainty) by setting the carbon price at a predetermined level. But policymakers can protect against cost uncertainty under a cap-and-trade system through the adoption of a few key design elements: provision for banking and borrowing of allowances and possible inclusion of a cost containment mechanism. These cap-and-trade provisions can reduce cost uncertainty while largely maintaining certainty over emissions.

2.4.1 The Nature of Cost Uncertainty

Cost uncertainties arise from numerous factors: many advanced technologies expected to contribute significantly to achieving emission reductions have highly uncertain costs and/or have not yet been commercially demonstrated; people's willingness to adopt less emissions-intensive and energy-intensive technologies is not well understood; and unanticipated events could significantly affect the cost of meeting particular emission targets, including future exogenous changes in energy prices or GDP growth, as well as future political decisions.

Concern about cost uncertainty in the context of cap-and-trade systems derives from the possibility of unexpected, significant cost increases. The experience with the southern California RECLAIM cap-and-trade system for NO_x emissions is a frequently cited example. RECLAIM had no automatic mechanism to relax emission caps in the face of unexpectedly high costs, and, in 2000, allowance prices spiked to more than 20 times their historical levels. Cost uncertainty may increase the long-run cost of emission caps because uncertainty about future allowance prices may deter firms from undertaking socially desirable, capital-intensive emission reduction investments, forcing greater reliance on costlier measures that are less capital-intensive. Furthermore, although price spikes in allowance markets may be of interest to relatively limited populations, such price spikes pass through to affect the prices of goods and services that are more broadly consumed, such as electricity prices in the case of RECLAIM or gasoline prices in the case of an economy-wide cap on CO_2 emissions.

2.4.2 Include Provision for Allowance Banking and Borrowing

Allowance banking and borrowing can mitigate some of the undesirable consequences of cost uncertainty by giving firms the flexibility to shift the timing of emission reductions in the face of unexpectedly high or low costs. If the cost of achieving targets is unexpectedly and temporarily high, firms can use banked or borrowed allowances instead of undertaking costly reductions. Thus, banking and borrowing mitigate undesirable year-to-year variation in costs. Banking of allowances—undertaking extra emission reductions earlier, so that more allowances are available for later use—has added greatly to the cost-effectiveness of previous cap-and-trade systems. However, banking provides little protection when costs remain high over extended periods, which could eventually lead to exhaustion of banked allowances. This problem may be particularly acute in a cap's early years, when relatively few allowances have been banked. Therefore, borrowing of allowances from future years' allocations can be a particularly useful form of cost protection in these early years.

Banking offers cost protection while guaranteeing achievement of long-run cumulative emission targets. While banking may shift some emissions from earlier to later years (from when allowances are banked to when they are used), cumulative emissions at any point during the cap's implementation can never exceed the number of allowances issued up to that point in time. Credible mechanisms need to be established to ensure that the use of borrowed allowances is offset through future emission reductions. One possible mechanism would be a provision that firms can borrow from their own future supplies, while entering into a contractual—possibly bonded—agreement with the government that the borrowed emissions will be repaid at a subsequent date. Another possible mechanism would be for the government to allocate a future year's permits that can be used in the current year, thereby decreasing a firm's future allocation by the same amount.

2.4.3 Include Provision for a Sensible Cost-Containment Mechanism

Ultimately, the most robust cost control feature of a cap-and-trade program is a broad and fluid market. In this sense, offsets can play a very important role in keeping costs down. Another issue is cost uncertainty linked with short-term allowance price volatility. Banking and borrowing can be exceptionally important in reducing long-term cost uncertainty, but the possibility of dramatic short-term allowance price volatility may call for the inclusion of a sensible cost containment mechanism. Such a mechanism could allow capped sources to purchase additional allowances at a predetermined price. This price would be set sufficiently high that it would be unlikely to have any effect unless allowance prices exhibited truly drastic spikes, and the revenues from the fee would be dedicated exclusively to finance emissions reductions by uncapped sources like non-CO_2 greenhouse gases, or to buy back allowances in future years. This is very different from standard proposals for a "safety valve," both because environmental integrity (the cap) is maintained by using the fees exclusively to finance additional emissions reductions or buy back allowances in future years, and because the predetermined price is set at a high level so that it has no effect unless there are drastic price spikes.

The pre-determined fee places a ceiling on allowance prices and hence on abatement costs because no firms would undertake emission reductions more costly than the trigger price. To be used as an insurance mechanism, the fee should be set at the maximum incremental emission reduction cost that society is willing to bear. At this level, the mechanism would be triggered only when costs are unexpectedly and unacceptably high. Of course, a cost containment mechanism that was set too high would provide no insurance against excessive costs.

Importantly, because revenues from the fee would be used to finance emissions reductions by uncapped sources or to buy back allowances in future years, the cost containment mechanism would reduce cost uncertainty and increase cost effectiveness, while simultaneously maintaining environmental effectiveness.

2.5 Allocation of Allowances

The cap-and-trade system will create a new commodity, a CO_2 allowance, which has value because of its scarcity (fostered by the cap on allowable emissions). The government can distribute allowances freely or auction them. This proposal recommends an allowance allocation mechanism that combines the two, with auctions becoming more important over time.

The aggregate value of allowances will be substantial. Indeed, if all allowances are auctioned, annual auction revenues would be significant even compared with annual federal tax receipts. From the perspective of firms that would need to buy auctioned allowances, total allowance costs would significantly exceed the cost of emission reductions that would be undertaken to meet a modest cap. Under an economy-wide emissions cap that reduces nationwide emissions by 5%, for example, while regulated firms would incur costs associated with reducing those emissions, they would have to purchase allowances for the remaining 95% of their emissions.

The fact that allowance requirements can contribute substantially to firm-level costs indicates that there are important distributional implications associated with the choice of allocation method (auctioning versus free distribution) and with decisions about how to distribute free allowances or how to use auction revenues. By contrast, the allocation choice does not affect achievement of emission targets, and--as emphasized above--the allocation issue is independent of the point of regulation. Indeed, since alternative points of regulation lead to the same ultimate distribution of economic burdens, there is no economic rationale for tying allocation choices to the point of regulation. For example, under an upstream cap, it is possible to freely distribute allowances to downstream energy-intensive industries that are affected by the cap even though they are not directly regulated by it. This is one approach to compensating those entities for the impact of a climate policy, since they can then sell the allowances to those firms that are directly regulated under the cap.

2.5.1 The Choice Between Auction and Free Distribution: Overall Cost Concerns

While all allocation decisions have significant distributional consequences, whether allowances are auctioned or freely distributed can also affect the program's overall cost. Generally speaking, the choice between auctioning and freely allocating allowances does not influence firms' production and emission reduction decisions. Firms face the same emission costs regardless of the allocation method. Even when using an allowance that was received for free, a firm loses the opportunity to sell that allowance. Thus, the firm takes this "opportunity cost" into account when deciding whether to use an allowance. Consequently, in many respects, this allocation choice will not influence a cap's overall costs. But there are two ways that the choice to freely distribute allowances can affect a cap's cost.

First, auction revenue may be used in ways that reduce the costs of the existing tax system or fund other socially beneficial policies. Free allocations forego such opportunities. Second, free allocations may affect electricity prices in regulated cost-of-service electricity markets and thereby affect the extent to which reduced electricity demand contributes to limiting emissions cost-effectively.

In discussions about whether to auction or freely distribute allowances, much attention has been given to the opportunity to use auction revenue to reduce existing "distortionary" taxes. Taxes on personal and corporate income discourage desirable economic activity by reducing after-tax income from work and investment. Use of auction revenue to reduce these taxes in a fiscally neutral fashion can stimulate additional economic activity, offsetting some of a cap's costs. The magnitude of potential auction revenue, compared with existing tax receipts, suggests that auction revenue could allow for significant tax reductions. Studies indicate that "recycling" auction revenue by reducing personal income tax rates could offset 40 to 50% of the economy-wide social costs that a cap would impose if allowances were freely distributed.

Achieving such gains may be difficult in practice, because climate policy would need to be tied to particular types of tax reform. The estimated cost reductions in these studies are for policies in which auction revenue is used to reduce marginal tax rates that diminish incentives to work and invest. If, instead, auction revenue funded deductions or fixed tax credits, such tax reform would have a lesser effect (and perhaps no effect) on incentives to work and invest. On the other hand, auction revenue could yield economic gains without tax reform by reducing fiscal imbalances and, therefore, reducing the need for future tax increases.

In general, auctioning generates revenue that can be put to innumerable uses. While all uses have distributional implications, some create greater economic gains than others. Reducing tax rates is just one example of a use that creates larger overall economic gains than would result from free distribution of allowances. Other socially valuable uses of revenue include reduction of the federal debt (including offsetting a cap's potentially adverse fiscal impacts) or funding desirable spending programs (for example, research and development). On the other hand, some government uses of auction revenue may generate less economic value than could be realized by private sector use of those funds. Thus, the opportunity to reduce the aggregate cost of a climate policy through auctioning, rather than freely distributing allowances, depends fundamentally on the ultimate use of auction revenues.

2.5.2 The Choice Between Auction and Free Distribution: Distributional Concerns

Auctioning has the potential to reduce a climate policy's economy-wide costs. On the other hand, depending on how auction revenues are used, free distribution of allowances provides an opportunity to address the distribution of a climate policy's economic impacts. Free distribution of allowances can be used to redistribute a cap's economic burdens in ways that mitigate impacts on the most affected entities, and a sensible principle for allocation is to try to compensate the most burdened sectors and individuals. Such redistribution of impacts may help establish consensus on a climate policy that achieves meaningful emission reductions. Thus, the choice between auctioning and free allocations introduces a potential tradeoff between a cap's aggregate cost and achievement of distributional objectives.

While there are some important exceptions, in competitive markets, the benefits of free allowances generally accrue only to their recipients. While free allocations will increase recipients' profitability or wealth, free allocations generally will not benefit consumers, suppliers, or employees of those recipients. Hence, while the cost of allowance requirements can be expected to ripple through the economy, the benefits of free allocations will not do so. Therefore, in competitive markets (including deregulated electricity markets), when used for purposes of compensation, free distribution of allowances should be directly targeted at those industries, consumers, and other entities that policymakers wish to benefit. Having said this, it is important to keep in mind that firms per se are not the final recipients of these benefits. After a portion of increased profits are turned over to the government through tax payments, the remainder accrues to shareholders, a subset of the general population.

Because free allocations may increase a cap's overall cost, it is important to consider what share of allowances need to be freely distributed to meet specific compensation objectives. A permanent allocation of all allowances to affected firms would, in aggregate, significantly overcompensate them for their financial losses. This is the case because much of the cost that a cap-and-trade system initially imposes on firms will be passed on to consumers in the form of higher prices. In effect, before any free allocation, firms are already partially compensated by changes in prices that result from the cap. Thus, freely allocating all allowances in perpetuity to affected firms would both overcompensate them in aggregate and use up resources that could otherwise be put toward other uses, including compensating consumers that bear much of the ultimate burden.

2.5.3 Proposal for a Mixed System of Auction and Free Distribution

Faced with important differences in the implications of free allocation and an auction, the best alternative is to begin with a hybrid approach wherein half of the allowances are initially auctioned and half are freely distributed to entities that are burdened by the policy, including suppliers of primary fuels, electric power producers, energy-intensive manufacturers, and particularly trade-sensitive sectors. The share of allowances that are freely distributed should decline over time, until there is no free allocation 25 years into the program. Over time, the private sector will have an opportunity to adjust to the carbon constraints, including industries with long-lived capital assets. Thus, the justification for free distribution diminishes over time.

In the short term, however, free distribution provides flexibility to address distributional concerns that might otherwise impede initial agreement on a policy. The half that are initially auctioned will generate revenue that can be used for public purposes, including compensation for program impacts on low-income consumers, public spending for related research and development, reduction of the federal deficit, and reduction of distortionary taxes.

The time path of the proportional division between the share of allowances that is freely allocated and the share that is auctioned (beginning with a 50–50 auction-free allocation, moving to 100% auction over 25 years) is consistent with analyses which have been carried out of the share of allowances that would need to be distributed freely to compensate firms for equity losses.
* * *

The time-path recommended here for an economy-wide program—50% of allowances initially distributed freely, with this share declining steadily (linearly) to zero after 25 years—is equivalent in terms of present discounted value to perpetual allocations (as those previously analyzed) of 15%, 19%, and 22%, at real interest rates of 3%, 4%, and 5%, respectively. Hence, the recommended allocation is consistent with the principal of targeting free allocations to burdened sectors in proportion to their relative burdens. It is also pragmatic to be more generous with the allocation in the early years of the program.

2.6 Credits for Specified Activities

It is important to provide credits to those who report specific activities or emission reductions. Covered firms may buy these credits to offset their obligations under the cap. This is a potentially advantageous means of lowering costs and encouraging emission reductions from activities outside the scope of the cap-and-trade system. An important concern, however, is the additionality problem, or the challenge of identifying whether a credit is really warranted, which requires making a comparison with an unobservable hypothetical (what would have happened had the credit not been generated). Despite this problem, significant cost savings can be achieved through selective use of credit-based programs targeting certain activities that otherwise would be too costly or infeasible to integrate into the cap-and-trade system.

The proposed upstream program should include selective use of the credit mechanism to address the small portion of fossil fuels that are not combusted and the use of downstream emission reduction technologies, such as carbon capture and storage ("CCS"). First, credits should be issued for major non-combustion uses of fossil fuels, such as in some petrochemical feedstocks, as well as fuel exports.

Second, credits should be issued for CCS. Emission reductions from CCS technologies can be readily measured, and because there is no incentive to install CCS equipment absent a climate policy, emission reductions achieved by CCS are clearly additional. As CCS technologies may play a significant role in achieving long-run emission reduction goals, this credit mechanism is an essential component of the upstream cap. Indeed, it might even be desirable to intentionally over-compensate CCS activities with credits to provide a stronger incentive for research and development.

Third, a program of credits for selected cases of biological sequestration through land use changes should be included. A cost-effective portfolio of climate technologies in the United States would include a substantial amount of biological carbon sequestration through afforestation and retarded deforestation. Translating this into practical policy will be a considerable challenge, however, because of concerns about monitoring and enforcement, additionality, and permanence. In principle, monitoring and enforcement is technologically feasible via third-party verification through remote sensing, but its cost may be high. Additionality is an even greater challenge, although it is likely to be less of a problem with afforestation than with avoided deforestation. The issue of permanence can be addressed, in principle through renewal of contracts to keep carbon stored, but someone must bear the risk of default. Despite these challenges, it would be important to begin to develop at least a limited system of credits for biological sequestration, partly because otherwise there may be significant leakage due to policies that affect biofuel production.

Fourth, provision should be made to provide coverage over time of non-CO_2 greenhouse gases. Although CO_2 is by far the most important anthropogenic greenhouse gas (84% of radiative forcing linked with emissions in 2005), it is by no means the only greenhouse gas of concern. Carbon dioxide, methane ("CH_4"), nitrous oxide ("N_2O"), and three groups of fluorinated gases—sulfur hexafluoride ("SF_6"), HFCs, and PFCs—are the major greenhouse gases and the focus of the Kyoto Protocol. The non-CO_2 GHGs are significant in terms of their cumulative impact on climate change, representing about 16% of radiative forcing in 2005. Because some emission reductions could be achieved at relatively low cost, their inclusion in a program would be attractive in principle.

The sources of some of these gases are many in number and highly dispersed, making their inclusion in a cap-and-trade program problematic. The answer may be to phase in regulation selectively over time with credit (offset) mechanisms, being careful to grant credits in CO_2-equivalent terms only for well-documented reductions. Over time, such approaches could be developed for industrial emissions of methane and NO_2 and for the manufacture of key industrial gases in the case of refrigerants (HFCs), circuits (PFCs), and transformers (SF_6). Thus, cap-and-trade of non-CO_2 GHGs would likely combine upstream and downstream points of regulation.

More broadly, because of concerns about additionality and related perverse incentives, the role of project-based offsets should be defined carefully. In particular, it is important that offsets be real, additional, verifiable, and permanent. Constraints should not be created in quantitative or geographic terms, however. Allowing even a small number of bad offsets does not make sense, nor does it make sense to deny high-quality offsets. Instead, strict criteria should be developed for allowing the generation of approved offsets, but without reference to quantity or location.

2.7 Linkage with Other Cap-and-Trade Systems and Other Nations' Policies

Three distinct linkage issues are important. These are: the relationship of the proposed national cap-and-trade system with any existing state or regional systems in the United States; the linkage of the proposed cap-and-trade system with other such systems in other parts of the world; and, more broadly, the relationship between the proposed cap-and-trade system and other nations' climate policies.

2.7.1 Linkage with Other Domestic Cap-and-Trade Systems

In the absence of a national climate policy, ten northeast states have * * * [implemented] a downstream cap-and-trade program among electricity generators in their RGGI, and California is considering implementing a cap-and-trade program at the state level. The proposed economy-wide, national, upstream cap-and-trade system could take the place of any regional, state, and local systems to avoid duplication, double counting, and conflicting requirements. It is likely that a decision will be reached on a national cap-and-trade system before any of the regional or state programs have actually been implemented.

2.7.2 Linkage with Cap-and-Trade and Emission Reduction Credit Systems Outside of the United States

In the long run, linking the U.S. cap-and-trade system to cap-and-trade systems in other countries or regions, such as the EU ETS, will clearly be desirable to reduce the overall cost of reducing GHG emissions and achieving any global GHG concentration targets. But there is a question of what level and type of linkage is desirable in the early years of the development of a U.S. cap-and-trade system. In the short term, it may be best for the United States to focus on linkage with emission reduction credit ("ERC") programs, such as the Kyoto Protocol's Clean Development Mechanism ("CDM").

First, by tapping low-cost emission reduction opportunities in developing countries, linkage of the U.S. system with CDM has a greater potential to achieve significant cost savings for the United States than does linkage with cap-and-trade systems in other industrialized countries (where abatement costs are similar to those in the United States).

Second, linkage with an ERC system such as CDM can only have the effect of decreasing domestic allowance prices, since transactions are unidirectional (i.e., U.S. purchases of low-cost CDM credits). In contrast, bidirectional linkage of the U.S. system with another cap-and-trade system can either increase or decrease the domestic allowance price, depending upon whether marginal abatement costs (and hence allowance prices) are lower or higher in the other cap-and-trade system. Similarly, other countries contemplating linking their cap-and-trade systems with a U.S. system may object to buying allowances from the U.S. system if the U.S. cap is less stringent (and hence has a lower allowance price).

Third, the U.S. may have to choose between adopting a cost-containment mechanism and linking with cap-and-trade systems in other countries. It appears unlikely that the European Union would agree to linking its Emissions Trading Scheme with a U.S. system that employed a safety valve or other such cost-containment measure. On the other hand, the U.S. could link with ERC systems, such as CDM, even with a cost-containment measure in place. In summary, compared with linking with other cap-and-trade systems, linking with CDM would give the United States greater autonomy over the allowance price that emerges from its system and over efforts to control cost uncertainty.

Fourth, given that other cap-and-trade systems likely will be linked with CDM, linking the U.S. system with CDM will have the effect of indirectly linking it with those other cap-and-trade systems in a way that avoids the short-term problems identified above. For example, to the extent that the U.S. system bids CDM credits away from Europe, the offsetting emission reductions associated with resulting increased emissions in the United States would come from Europe, not from the countries that originally supply the CDM credits.

Fifth, this indirect linkage should reduce concerns about additionality normally associated with linking with CDM. If another country or region (for example, the European Union) has already linked with CDM, the effect of U.S. linkage with CDM will differ significantly from the effect if the United States were the only country linking with CDM. While there may indeed be significant additionality concerns associated with CDM credits, many of the credits that the U.S. system would ultimately purchase would be used by other linked cap-and-trade systems if the United States did not link with CDM. Hence, for these credits, there is no incremental additionality concern regarding the U.S. decision to link with CDM. Any U.S. use of these credits would result in emission reductions in the other linked cap-and-trade system that would otherwise have used the credits.

Sixth and finally, the indirect linkage created by a U.S. link with CDM can achieve some and perhaps much of the cost savings that would arise from direct linkage with other cap-and-trade systems. CDM credits can be sold on the secondary market and ultimately will go to the linked cap-and-trade system with the highest allowance price, thereby pushing the allowance prices of the various cap-and-trade systems toward the convergence that would be achieved by direct linkage among cap-and-trade systems. If there is a sufficient supply of low-cost CDM credits, linkage between the various cap-and-trade systems and CDM would achieve the same outcome as direct linkage among cap-and-trade systems. Therefore, at least in the short term, bilateral linkage between the various national and regional cap-and-trade systems and CDM will achieve significant cost savings.

For these reasons, linkage of the U.S. cap-and-trade system with CDM may be a sensible first step as cap-and-trade systems begin to develop around the world, with the expectation that the United States will explore direct linkage with these other systems over time.

5. Common Objections and Responses

In the past, a variety of objections have been raised to the use of cap-and-trade systems in general or to the specific application of the cap-and-trade mechanism to CO_2 and other GHG reduction. In this section, these objections are briefly described, and brief responses are provided.

5.1 "Cap-and-Trade is Unethical—It Allows Firms to Buy and Sell the Right to Pollute"

Over the 25 years in which market-based instruments have become an accepted part of the portfolio of environmental regulation, there has been a considerable decline in the frequency of claims that cap-and-trade systems are morally flawed because they allow firms to "buy and sell the right to pollute." But the argument has been made as recently as the late 1990s, in the context of global climate change policy, that the cap-and-trade approach is unethical because it eliminates the moral stigma which should exist for polluting. However, few would agree that people are behaving immorally by cooking dinner, heating their homes, turning on a light, or using a computer, despite the fact that all of these activities result in CO_2 emissions. Under conventional regulatory approaches, the "right to pollute" is not sold by government. Rather, it is given away for free.

5.2 "Cap-and-Trade Creates Hot Spots of Pollution"

Because GHG emissions uniformly mix in the atmosphere, there are no hot spots of GHG emissions themselves. The question is whether localized pollutants whose emissions are correlated with the emissions of a GHG might become excessively concentrated in particular areas as a result of allowance trading activity. This concern has frequently been expressed in California's debates regarding a potential cap-and-trade system to implement AB 32.

The answer to this concern is simple: a cap-and-trade system for GHG emissions would not supplant existing local air quality regulations. If a firm's actions in engaging in an emission trade would violate local air quality regulations for NO_x emissions, for example, then such actions would be illegal and disallowed no matter how many GHG emission allowances were obtained. Thus, a cap-and-trade system for GHG emissions would not interfere with local air quality regulations--only legal trades would be allowed.

5.3 "Upstream Cap-and-Trade Will Have Minimal Effects on the Trans-

portation Sector"

Approximately one-third of U.S. CO_2 emissions from energy consumption are from the transportation sector. An upstream cap-and-trade system that provides a uniform price signal for cost-effective, economy-wide emission reductions will lead to the achievement of those emission reductions wherever they are least costly. This almost certainly will not mean proportionate reductions in emissions from each type of source or each economic sector. And it is quite true that the greatest percentage of emission reductions would be in the electric power sector, followed by the industrial sector, with much smaller percentage reductions in the commercial, transportation, and residential sectors. From an economic perspective (that is, cost-effectiveness), this is both appropriate and desirable if the reason for the policy is climate change. If there are other, non-climate related reasons for concerns about the use of transportation fuels, such as oil dependence, then those concerns should be addressed through other, appropriate policies.

5.4 "It Would Be Better to Begin with Narrow Coverage Across a Few Sectors"

It has been argued that, for political expediency, it would be better to initiate a cap-and-trade system with narrow coverage of only a few sectors and to broaden that coverage over time, rather than employing an economy-wide system such as that proposed here. There are several problems with beginning with narrow coverage. First, narrow coverage is inevitably more costly for whatever environmental gains are achieved, because some of low-cost emission reduction opportunities are unavailable. Second, in terms of the political forces that are at the heart of the recommendation for narrow coverage, it makes much more sense to begin broadly and then go deep. Resistance from uncovered sectors will only increase with the stringency of policy and its associated economic burdens. This lesson can be observed in the debates surrounding proposals to expand the sectoral coverage of the European Union's downstream cap-and-trade program.

5.5 "A Cap-and-Trade System Will Create Barriers to Entry and Reduce Competition"

It is true--in principle--that emission allowances have considerable value and could be used strategically by incumbent firms to keep new entrants from competing in respective product markets. It is for this reason that the SO_2 allowance trading program provides an annual allowance auction so that the government can be a source of last resort. There has been no evidence in any implemented cap-and-trade system, however, that allowances have been withheld from the market by incumbent firms for strategic purposes. Furthermore, the CO_2 cap-and-trade system proposed here includes a large auction of allowances from the very beginning.

5.6 "The Price Spike in RECLAIM and the Price Drop in the EU ETS Demonstrate that Extreme Price Volatility is an Inherent Part of Cap-and-Trade Systems"

It is unquestionably true that a cap-and-trade system fixes the quantity of aggregate emissions and allows the price of CO_2 emissions to adjust to ensure that the emissions cap is met. A cap-and-trade system (at least one that establishes rigid annual caps) therefore offers less certainty about costs because it provides greater certainty about emissions. But the significant price volatilities that were observed in the RECLAIM program and the EU ETS were associated with particular, problematic design features, as well as special circumstances.

The price spike observed for NO_x allowances during the California electricity crisis was partly a consequence of design flaws in the RECLAIM program and partly a consequence of the electricity crisis itself. RECLAIM does not allow banking from one period to the next. Therefore, it did not provide incentives for facilities to install pollution control equipment that would have allowed them to reduce their current emissions and bank allowances for the future. The result was that, during the 2000-01 electricity crisis, some units facing high demand levels were unable to purchase allowances for their emissions. When emissions essentially exceeded allowances, an allowance price spike occurred. Even in the context of the electricity crisis and the absence of an allowance bank, the price spike would still not have occurred had a safety valve or other cost-containment mechanism been available in the RECLAIM market.

The allowance price collapse observed in the spring of 2006 during the pilot phase of the EU ETS was a consequence of a combination of the design of the system, generous allowance allocations, data problems, and modeling mistakes. In the spring of 2006, when it became clear that the allocation of allowances had exceeded emissions, a dramatic fall in allowance prices occurred.

Another claim has been that as it now appears that the EU may not meet its aggregate target under Kyoto, the fault is with the EU ETS. The real reason is that the downstream system covers only 45% of European CO_2 emissions. The failures to reduce emissions are concentrated in the sectors not covered by the program.

Likewise, observations of windfall profits among electric power producers have been used as evidence of an inherent problem with cap-and-trade. Here too, the evidence is otherwise. As explained above, the ETS guidelines called for at least 95% of allowances to be freely distributed in the first compliance period, and most countries freely distributed 100% of their allowances. This is in contrast with the cap-and-trade system proposed here, which provides for 50% of the allowances to be auctioned initially, with this share rising to 100% over 25 years.

Notes and Questions

1. The EU's Emissions Trading Scheme comprises only 45% of the EU's GHG emissions. CO_2 emissions from the transporttion sector are not part of the trading scheme. See European Env't Agency, Greenhouse Gas Emission Trends and Projections in Europe 2006 (2006), available at http://www.eea.europaeu/eea_report_2007_5/en. Even so, ETS administrative cost are relatively high because there are about 11,000 sources in the EU ETS, 90% of which account for less than 10% of total emissions. D. Ellerman, B. Buchner & C. Carraro eds., Allocation in the European Emissions Trading Scheme: Rights, Rents and Fairness (2007).

2. Stavins notes that "[I]f permits are freely allocated, the allocation should be on the basis of some historical measures, not on the basis of measures that firms can affect." He also observes that an allowance trading scheme must also address "whether to freely allocate allowances to new facilities and whether to strip closing facilities of their allocations. * * * [R]ewarding new investments with free allowances or penalizing closures by stripping firms of their free allocations can encourage excessive entry and undesirable, continued operation of old facilities, leading to significant inefficiencies, as has apparently happened with the European Union's Emissions Trading Scheme. Denny Ellerman, New Entrant and Closure Provisions: How Do They Distort? 10-11 (MIT Center for Energy and Envtl. Policy Research, Working Paper No. 06-013, 2006)." Stavins supra at 96. For commentary on Stavins, see 39 ELR 10767, 10770 (Aug. 2009).

3. Compare the criteria that Stavins outlines to the cap-an-trade provisions of the American Clean Energy and Security Act of 2009 (H.R. 2454) summarized in the notes following the Peterson excerpt. What would Stavins make of this legislation?

4.   Standards, such as building codes or appliance efficiency standards are generally better policy choices when it is too costly to measure and monitoring   actual emissions or fuel use. In those circumstances, well designed standards are better than allowances. For instance, the benefits from U.S. appliance standards are more than 2,000 to 2,500 times greater than the programs' administrative costs, and have yielded a net societal benefit of about $3 for ever $1 spent after the appliance was purchased. T. Kubo et al., Opportunities for New Appliance and Efficiency Standards: Energy and Economic Savings Beyond Current Programs (2001). Other standard setting examples are described in R. Ottinger & A. Bradbrook, eds., UNEP Handbook for Drafting Laws on Energy Efficiency and Renewable Energy Resources (2007).

ECONOMIC ISSUES IN DESIGNING A GLOBAL AGREEMENT ON GLOBAL WARMING
William D. Nordhaus, Keynote Address at Climate Change: Global Risks, Challenges, and Decisions
Copenhagen, Denmark, (March 10-12, 2009)
http://climatecongress.ku.dk/speakers/professorwilliamnordhaus-plenaryspeaker-11march2009.pdf/

Introduction

Climate change involves a tale of two cultures. The natural sciences are doing an admirable job of describing the geophysical aspects of climate change. The science behind global warming is well established. While the exact trajectory of climate change is imprecisely known because of cascading uncertainties from economic activity through emissions, the carbon cycle, and earth-ocean systems, economic analysis should take the scientific findings as inputs.

But designing an effective political and economic strategy to control climate change will require the second culture—the social sciences—to analyze how to harness our economic and political systems to achieve our climate goals effectively and at low cost. This second task involves a very different set of issues from the natural-science questions. It requires examining questions such as the impacts on the economy and on non-market activities, the costs of slowing or mitigating climate change, the strength and timing of emissions reductions with an eye to the costs and benefits of slowing climate change, the risks of asymmetric and irreversible damages, and the policy instruments for implementing such emissions reductions. * * *

For this discussion, I focus on carbon dioxide (CO_2) as the most important greenhouse gas (GHG). The economics of climate change is straightforward. Virtually every human activity directly or indirectly involves the combustion of fossil fuels, producing emissions of carbon dioxide into the atmosphere. Emissions of carbon dioxide are externalities, i.e., social consequences that are not accounted for in the market place. They are market failures because people do not pay for the current and future costs of their emissions.

If economics provides a single bottom line for policy, it is that we need to correct this market failure by ensuring that all people, everywhere, and for the indefinite future face a market price for the use of carbon that reflects the social costs of their activities. Economic participants—thousands of governments, millions of firms, billions of people, all making trillions of decisions each year—need to face realistic prices for the use of carbon if their decisions about consumption, investment, and innovation are to be appropriate.

I will unpack this idea succinctly. Raising the market price of carbon provides strong incentives to reduce carbon emissions through four mechanisms. First, it provides signals to consumers about what goods and services produce high carbon emissions and should therefore be used more sparingly. Second, it provides signals to producers about which inputs (such as electricity from coal) use more carbon, and which inputs (such as electricity from wind) use less or none. It thereby induces producers to move to low-carbon technologies. Third, high carbon prices provide market signals and financial incentives to inventors and innovators to develop and introduce low-carbon products and processes which can eventually replace the current generation of carbon-intensive technologies. Finally, and most subtle of all, the use of carbon pricing economizes on the information requirements that market participants need to undertake each of these three tasks. Of course, placing a market price will not work magic. There remain many further externalities and market imperfections in energy and other markets. But without a strong price signal, there is simply no hope for making the vast number of decisions in a remotely efficient manner.

This is the inconvenient truth from economics: Raising the price of carbon is a necessary condition for implementing carbon policies in a way that will reach the multitude of decisions and decision makers over space, time, nations, and sectors.

The High Cost of Non-Participation

Economics leads to a second important truth about climate-change policies. The analytical basis for an efficient global-warming policy is extremely simple. Because global warming is a global public good, everyone, everywhere must face the same price. The rub arises because for global public goods like global warming, there are widely disparate incentives to participate in measures to mitigate the damages. The differences reflect different perceptions of damages, income levels, political structures, environmental attitudes, and country sizes. For example, Russia may believe that it will benefit from limited warming, while low-lying countries may believe they will be devastated. Within the United States, some regions are energy exporters and resist measures to tax carbon fuels, while others are environmentally oriented and have already enacted local legislation to limit carbon emissions.

Current international agreements differentiate among countries in their responsibilities to undertake measures to limit emissions. Under the Kyoto Protocol, Annex I countries must limit their emissions, while non-Annex I countries have a variety of non-binding commitments as well as the ability to participate in the "clean development mechanism." Moreover, while some countries have implemented strong internal mechanisms to control emissions, these often cover only a limited part of national emissions. For example, the European Trading Scheme covers only about half of EU emissions.

A centrally important question is the extent of inefficiency inherent in the patchwork nature and incomplete participation that characterizes the current international control regime. New evidence from economic studies suggests that the costs of non-participation are much higher than was earlier thought.

We can simplify the discussion by considering a "participation function." The participation function is a mathematical representation of the cost of partial participation. This approach assumes that a subset of countries has harmonized emissions reductions, while the balance of countries undertakes no emissions reductions. This assumption is approximately the structure of the current Kyoto model. Using this stylized assumption, we can estimate the costs of incomplete participation.

The results are very sobering. Annex I countries including the United States constituted about 66 percent of global CO_2 emissions in 1990. With a 66-percent participation rate, the cost of incomplete participation is 2.1 times the cost with complete participation (all countries). However, by 2010, the participation rate (with the U.S. withdrawal and the increasing share of developing countries) is estimated to be about 33 percent. The cost with incomplete participation is estimated to be 7.4 times the cost of the same global emissions reduction with complete international participation.

We have also estimated the required participation to attain ambitious targets, such as the 2 °C target proposed by some European countries. Our work indicates that it will be necessary to attain close to universal participation by the middle of the 21st century to make this target.

One response to the criticism about non-participation is that the cap-and-trade system actually extends participation through the clean development mechanism (CDM). I fear that the emissions reductions from CDM will prove to be minimal. There is no way of verifying that the projects in fact reduced emissions in the host countries, yet CDM has been a major source of accounting emissions reductions. By one reckoning, most of the emissions reductions in EU-ETS have come from CDM. According to a World Bank staff report, the CDM has produced 280 million tons of offsets of CO_2 for the EU whereas emissions reductions for the first budget period are only 130 million tons of CO_2. We see many firms springing up to provide CDM credits. We may be heading down the road to another set of opaque instruments that are the environmental equivalent of mortgage-backed securities.

It is clear that non-participation will be an issue under any international agreement on climate change, whether the agreement follows the Kyoto model or one based on carbon taxes. The unfortunate feature of the Kyoto model is that it pretends to solve the problem of bringing developing countries into the regime, whereas in fact we have no idea of the actual emissions reductions that have been achieved in developing countries under the CDM. There is no future to this illusion.

The second bottom line from economics is this: Universal participation at a harmonized level is a critical part of an efficient global warming regime. There are extremely high costs of non-participation. A rough estimate is that the penalty from exempting half the global emissions from an agreement is a cost increase of around 250 percent.

Harmonized Carbon Taxes

Perhaps the most controversial policy question in the design of economic systems to control global warming involves the decision whether to rely primarily on quantity-based or price-based constraints. More specifically, the question concerns the relative advantage of a cap-and-trade system (such as is embodied in the Kyoto model), or a carbon tax system (such as is used for limiting gasoline or cigarette consumption).

The quantity-type system of the Kyoto model is well-known. I will describe briefly that carbon tax approach. This more precisely defined as a *system of harmonized domestic taxes on carbon emissions*. Under this approach, countries would agree to penalize carbon emissions at an internationally harmonized "carbon price" or "carbon tax." Conceptually, the carbon tax is a dynamically efficient Pigovian tax that balances the marginal social costs and marginal social benefits of additional emissions. The carbon price might be determined by estimates of the price necessary to limit GHG concentrations or temperature changes below some level thought to be "dangerous interference." From a conceptual point of view, the tax (or price on carbon) should be equal in all countries and sectors. In reality, as with any system, reality will depart from the ideal, but it is useful to keep the conceptual ideal in mind when designing the system.

An important feature of the system I envision is that the revenues would be collected and retained domestically. It would naturally fit into the domestic fiscal system and should be seen as an alternative mechanism for collecting the revenues needed by all countries. They are not (in my view) an attempt to provide revenues for other worthy causes. They are primarily designed to raise the price of carbon, with countries retaining the right to use the revenues according to domestic priorities.

All this leaves the appropriate carbon tax as an open question. The major point to note, robust across almost all models and vintages, is that the social cost of carbon and the appropriate carbon tax will rise sharply in the years ahead – at a rate of about 4 percent per year over inflation.

The Advantage of Carbon Taxes over a Cap-and-Trade Approach

The debate about the relative merits of cap-and-trade versus carbon taxes has moved from the academic journals to legislatures and scientific congresses. It is not a simple matter, but I believe that the difficulties of the Kyoto model approach are insufficiently appreciated. I will outline why I think price-type approaches such as a harmonized carbon tax are a more promising policy approach.

To begin with, tax systems are mature and universally applied instruments of policy. Countries have used taxes for centuries, and their properties are well understood. Every country uses taxes, has an administrative tax system, has tax collectors, and needs revenues. By contrast, there is no experience—zero—with international cap-and-trade systems. Just as it would be irresponsible for military planners to use a completely untested weapon to defend against grave threats, it would be similarly perilous for the international community to rely on an untested system like international cap-and-trade to prevent dangerous climate change.

A related point is that quantitative limits have proven to produce severe volatility in the market price of carbon under an emissions-targeting approach. The volatility arises because of the inelasticity of both supply and demand of permits. I have reviewed the history of the market prices of tradable permits for both the SO_2 trading system in the U.S. and for the CO_2 system in the EU. These prices show an extremely high level of volatility. I found that the prices of U.S. SO_2 emissions allowances have been approximately as volatile as oil prices. The volatility of CO_2 allowances in the EU ETS is similarly large: in the period from October 2008 to February 2009 alone, ETS carbon prices varied between €9 and €24 per ton of CO_2. It should be emphasized that the volatility of allowances is not due to policy errors. It is inherent in this kind of instrument. The high level of volatility is economically costly and provides inconsistent signals to private-sector decision makers. Clearly, a carbon tax would provide consistent signals and would not vary so widely from year to year, or even day to day.

In addition, a tax approach can capture the revenues more easily than quantitative approaches can, and a price-type approach will therefore cause fewer additional tax distortions. The tax approach also provides less opportunity for corruption and financial finagling than do quantitative limits, because the tax approach creates no artificial scarcities to encourage rent-seeking behavior.

Carbon taxes have the apparent disadvantage that they do not steer the world economy toward a particular climatic target, such as a CO_2-concentration limit or a global temperature limit. This suggests that a carbon tax cannot ensure that the globe remains on the safe side of "dangerous anthropogenic interferences" with the climate system. This advantage of quantitative limits is in my mind largely illusory. We do not currently know what emissions would actually lead to the "dangerous interferences"–or if there are "dangerous interferences"—or even what global climate change will be implied by a system such as the Kyoto model. We might make a huge mistake–either on the high or the low side–and impose much too rigid and expensive, or much too lax, quantitative limits. In other words, whatever initial target we set is almost sure to prove incorrect for either taxes or quantities. More important, the current system, or even the modifications that have been proposed, does not come close to being efficient or attaining the strict environmental goals because of the high levels of non-participation.

This leads to a final point about the two systems. A carbon-tax model provides a friendly way for countries to join a climate treaty. Currently, countries joining the Kyoto limitations would need to enter into highly politicized and uncertain negotiations on the extent of their emissions reductions. Under the carbon-tax model, by contrast, countries would need only to guarantee that their domestic carbon price would be at least the level of the international norm. If I were a small country—worried about climate change, eager to join the effort, but wary of the heavy pressures that big countries can apply—I would find the carbon-tax approach most attractive.

The Perils of the Current Cap-and-Trade System

The international community is making a huge wager on the Kyoto model. The wager is that the cap-and-trade structure contained in the Kyoto model will do the job of slowing global warming. The new United States administration advocated that the U.S. adopt this system as its contribution to solving the global problem, and the primary legislation in the U.S. Congress is firmly a cap-and-trade proposal.

But, as I have suggested above, the cap-and-trade approach is a poor choice of mechanism. It is untested in the international context; it has been unable to attain anything close to universal participation; and it has the inherent flaws just described. It is unlikely that the Kyoto model, even if strengthened, can achieve its climate objectives in an efficient and effective manner. To bet the world's climate system and global environment on an untested approach with such clear structural flaws would appear a reckless gamble.

Given the advantages of tax-type systems, as well as the problems inherent in the Kyoto model, an important question is how to modify the Kyoto Protocol to include tax-type models. Some have suggested a hybrid approach that could combine the strengths of both quantity and price approaches. An example of a hybrid plan would be a traditional cap-and-trade system combined with a floor carbon tax and a safety-valve price. For example, the initial carbon tax might be $30 per ton of carbon with safety-valve purchases of additional permits available at a 50 percent premium. These would be an improvement on a pure cap-and-trade system, but we would be wary that a faint-hearted cap-and tax would have low or non-existent floors and high caps, in which case it would be little better than a cap-and-trade system.

An even better approach would be to broaden the Kyoto treaty to allow countries to fulfill their treaty obligations if they have a domestic regime with a minimum carbon price attached to all emissions. This would require international negotiations about that minimum price and its trajectory, but such an approach would allow a much broader set of policy regimes. * * *

So, if the Kyoto model turns out to be another failed model, it has lots of company. But it would be better to recognize and change it now, rather than in one or two more decades of ineffective and inefficient efforts to slow emissions. The international community should move quickly to replace the current cap-and-trade structure by one in which the central economic mechanism is a tax on greenhouse-gas emissions.

NORDHAUS' CARBON TAX: AN EXCUSE TO DO NOTHING?
Clive Hamilton, (May 2009)
http://www.clivehamilton.net.au/cms/media/critique_of_nordhaus.pdf

Discarding fairness

The carbon tax proposal put forward by Professor Nordhaus is both unfair and unworkable. * * * Nordhaus appears to assume that all of the thorny problems of how to divide up responsibility for emission reductions would somehow vanish with his proposed carbon tax. "Under this approach", he writes, "countries would agree to penalize carbon emissions at an internationally harmonized 'carbon price' or 'carbon tax'". Just like that.

The idea of a harmonized tax rate contradicts the universally endorsed ethical basis of the UN Framework Convention on Climate Change, which commits all parties to protect the climate system "on the basis of equality and in accordance with their common but differentiated responsibilities and respective capabilities." A uniform carbon tax would be as unfair as a flat rate income tax.

The principle of common but differentiated responsibilities led to the division between Annex I (rich) and Annex II (poor) countries and the initial obligation on the former to cut their emissions first. So how would Bangladeshis or Ugandans react to the idea that they should from the outset pay the same rate of tax on fossil fuels as people in the United States and Australia, the ones who created the global warming problem? There is no principle of justice that Nordhaus could invoke to defend a system that penalises the innocent and subsidises the guilty. * * *

In his scheme, every nation must set the same rate at the outset. In the tradition of neoclassical economics, the distribution of income, and by extension the distribution of the burden of abatement costs, is taken as a given. Indeed, in his recent book Professor Nordhaus compares the prevailing distribution of incomes with "the eating habits of marine organisms," suggesting the level of inequality in any society follows from some biological law rather than government policies and social structures, a view common in economics but rejected by most other social scientists.

Discounting the future

If Nordhaus' advice prevailed, any carbon tax would almost certainly be set at a rate much lower than the one science indicates is needed to avert dangerous climate change. That would undoubtedly be so if the rate were taken from Nordhaus' economic modelling, because the model reflects his own philosophical position, one that breeds caution. The Stern Review urged more rapid carbon abatement by arguing that climate policy should be based on a low discount rate because we should treat the welfare of future generations on a par with our own and to do otherwise is "ethically indefensible." In reply, Nordhaus accused Stern of abandoning accepted economic principles, writing a "political" document, making "extreme assumptions" and reaching "extreme findings", even suggesting that in commissioning the report the Blair Government was "perhaps stoking the dying embers of the British Empire".

While carried out as a dispute over where to set the discount rate, the underlying argument between Stern and Nordhaus is over the ethical status of private markets. Like most neoclassical economists, Nordhaus believes implicitly that our private behaviour in the marketplace always represents our true preferences so that whatever the market generates is value-free and sacrosanct. Thus in considering the long-term impacts of policy we must use the discount rate determined by our behaviour in private markets, even if that means the interests of future generations disappear from the analysis. Any discount rate other than that thrown up by the market is regarded as "normative," a code-word in economics meaning biased and invalid. Yet the belief that the market is value free has been comprehensively debunked.

Whatever the future might hold, Nordhaus argues, it is not legitimate to try to second-guess the market, going so far as to propose that people may "come to love the altered landscape of the warmer world", which suggests a disregard for those who will be driven from their lands by rising seas and famine. It reflects a kind of market absolutism: what people do in private markets today is the only valid evidence of what they value. In such a world, if people were really concerned about losing their homelands it would be reflected now in their market behaviour. It may indeed be rational for the people of Tuvalu to begin planning to evacuate their island home, but that does not make it right that they must do so nor absolve rich countries of the duty to try to prevent it.

Of course, accepting a discount rate generated by private market behaviour means endorsing as somehow natural and therefore unchallengeable the prevailing distribution of income and wealth. This is a moral judgment, yet by comparing the prevailing distribution of incomes with a biological law Nordhaus commits two well-known philosophical mistakes—the "is-ought" error (shifting imperceptibly from describing what is to deeming what ought to be) and the "naturalistic fallacy" (the assumption that what is natural is good and right).

In a philosophical move with no justification, neoclassical economists unthinkingly convert ethical arguments into potential changes in money incomes. They cannot imagine another realm of decision-making in which people act as citizens concerned with collective interests and long-term effects, rather than consumers and investors determined to maximise short-term private gain. If we recognise this non-market realm, we have to accept that we may not always prefer what we choose because we may have "second-order preferences", preference for certain preferences that describe the world we would prefer to occupy even though we succumb to various impulses and temptations in practice. This explains why we may do nothing to reduce our own greenhouse gas emissions yet vote for governments that promise strong measures to require us all to cut emissions. Reducing ballot box behaviour to supermarket behaviour deprives us of our citizenship. In the end, Nordhaus' policy prescriptions based on cost-benefit analysis and discount rates set in private markets allow us to be consumers only and never citizens. If there are no citizens there is no democracy.

Inviting more delay

The process of negotiating an international treaty under which all nations agree on how to resolve something as politically fraught as climate change is long and arduous. Every gain is precious. The process under the Framework Convention drawing all nations into an agreement to constrain carbon emissions now has great momentum, even if progress has been intermittent and slow. * * *

[F]or some of those who want no action, arguing for a carbon tax has become the tactic *du jour*. They know that if a carbon tax emerged as a serious proposal in global negotiations, every contentious question of fairness would be reopened and nations would have to spend, quite literally, years working through the implications. Imagine the arguments about the rate at which the carbon tax should be set, and the inevitable process of bidding it down. It would be no easier than the horse-trading that led to the emissions targets at Kyoto. And every difficulty that has weakened the effectiveness of cap-and-trade systems, both in the Protocol and in national schemes, would apply to a carbon tax.

If a harmonized carbon tax were adopted globally and the US Congress had to legislate to enact it, it is unlikely the 2,340 energy lobbyists in Washington would sit back and declare "Our hands are tied by an international treaty". There would be enormous pressure for exemptions, tax holidays, special deals, compensation and so on. The gasoline price increase alone would probably see domestic legislation sink, thereby wrecking the international agreement. The choice is not, as Professor Nordhaus presents it, between a flawed cap-and-trade system and a perfect carbon tax; it's between a flawed cap-and-trade system now and a flawed carbon tax at some point in the future.

Who bears the risk?

In addition, the carbon tax rate would need to be renegotiated regularly and, with the science of climate change becoming more exact and more worrying, the rate would in all likelihood have to escalate rapidly. Here we get to the most important advantage of a legislated limit on emissions over a tax on emissions. Although governments are always pressured to insert loopholes, a cap sets a binding limit on the quantity of emissions, so that the price of carbon fluctuates in response to market conditions. The carbon tax alternative raises the price of fossil fuels by a fixed amount and allows the quantity of emissions to fluctuate. Those more concerned about global warming want certainty for the atmosphere so that the fluctuations are absorbed by the economy.

Those who put a premium on business certainty and want the environment to absorb the risks are less concerned about global warming. * * * The commitment to put the interests of the atmosphere first is the greatest advantage of a quantitative limit over a carbon tax.

* * * Nordhaus exaggerates the risks to business of carbon price volatility. His own figures suggest that volatility in carbon permit prices would be a

little less than volatility in oil prices. He says this is a bad thing, but in fact it is good news. Businesses around the world are accustomed to dealing with oil price volatility, and good managers of affected businesses would manage carbon price volatility in the same way.

Nordhaus rejects the argument that a carbon tax is inferior to a quantitative target because a tax cannot ensure the world reaches a particular climate goal. He claims that this alleged advantage of quantitative limits is "largely illusory" because the climate science is so uncertain we do not know what goal to set. * * *

Moreover, the claim that we do not know enough to set a quantitative target is an explicit rejection of the precautionary principle, a foundational principle of the Framework Convention. Article 3.3 of the UNFCCC states: Where there are threats of serious or irreversible damage, lack of full scientific certainty should not be used as a reason for postponing such measures, taking into account that policies and measures to deal with climate change should be cost-effective so as to ensure global benefits at the lowest possible cost. * * *

Nordhaus' basic fear is encapsulated in his belief that "We might make a huge mistake". While others are worried that we might make a huge mistake by failing to respond adequately to the climate crisis, Nordhaus is concerned with the economy, insisting that anything but a cautious carbon tax approach would be a "reckless gamble". This is despite the fact that his own modelling confirms that the impact on income growth of even radical emission cuts would be disappearingly small. He estimates that implementing the Stern Review's proposals—which he judges to be "extremely expensive"—would in fact reduce the discounted value of future global income by less than one per cent.

This paralysing cautiousness is reflected in Nordhaus' criticisms of the Stern Review, whose results he describes as "extreme". He uses the results of his DICE model to conclude that adopting the path recommended by Stern would be worse than doing nothing at all to prevent global warming. * * * While more serious measures may be needed in some decades, he urges "modest" measures now.

In sum, the Nordhaus carbon tax proposal contravenes globally agreed principles. * * * To suggest that a carbon tax system would obviate the need for "highly politicized and uncertain negotiations" and that, by contrast, "a carbon-tax model provides a friendly way for countries to join a climate treaty" indicates that Nordhaus' carbon tax sits comfortably in a text book but has little relevance to the real world of climate policy.

D. SEQUESTRATION STRATEGIES

1. Introduction

Emissions of carbon dioxide can be prevented by different mitigation strategies, or if emissions cannot be avoided, the gas can be removed from the atmosphere by different techniques. Capturing of carbon dioxide during combustion and then pumping it into deep geologic formations n the earth, including former oil and natural gas cavities, or coal mines, and then sealing the deposits, is one technique. It is relatively expensive (each plant costs an estimated $1.5 billion) and while it has been done on a small scale, it is still an experimental methodology on the vastness of a global or national scale. Another is using photosynthesis, to permit plants and bacteria to absorb the carbon dioxide as they grow and fix it in the fibers. This is relatively inexpensive but requires a vast amount of planting of trees, known as afforestation or reforestation, on land, or of cultivating algae in water. Both systems require investment in training personnel and establishing regimes for long-term maintenance and monitoring of the gases so sequestered.

Lord Rees, president of the Royal Society in the United Kingdom, and Nick Butler of the Cambridge University Judge Business School, envision that even with rapid deployment of new energy efficient technologies and demand side management methods, carbon fuels will be used and thus rapid deployment of carbon sequestration is a necessity. "Today, oil, coal and natural gas provide more than 80% of world demand. On business as usual projections that percentage will be unchanged in 2030. That mean volumes will increase by about 50% with a comparable growth in emissions. * * * There seems no way to curtain the serious risk of long-term global warming unless–well before 2050–we capture much of the carbon emitted when fuels are burnt." M. Rees & N. Butler, Carbon Capture Stations Must Not Be Delayed, Financial Times, p. 9, col.6 (September 15, 2008).

According to P. Glaser et al., Global Warming Solutions Regulatory Challenges and Common Law Liabilities Associated with the Geologic Sequestration of Carbon Dioxide, 6 Geo. J. L. & Pub. Policy 429, 430-431 (2008):

> The fundamental goal of [geologic sequestration] GS is to return CO_2 generated from the use of a fossil fuel to where it came from—underground. CO_2 can be injected into any porous formation that lies deep underground beneath an impermeable cap. These formations can often be found in oil and gas fields, coal seams, and deep saline formations. To maximize storage capacity of these formations, CO_2 must be injected in a supercritical state; i.e., at certain temperatures and pressures such that the CO_2 exhibits properties of both a liquid and a gas. In order to maintain the supercritical state of CO_2, it must be injected at least 800 meters below the surface. * * *

Unlike most substances currently being injected into the ground for either disposal or for enhanced oil recovery, CO_2 will be more buoyant than the natural underground brines that it will be injected into, causing the CO_2 to migrate upward upon injection and pool beneath any confining layer. Any penetration of that layer will allow CO_2 to ascend to the surface and be released into the ambient air, reducing the effectiveness of the GS project. The longer the CO_2 remains underground, the more secure its storage will become, because much of the CO_2 will either dissolve in the brine waters or be transformed into calcium carbonate or other carbonate minerals over centuries or millennia that follow the initial injection.

Injection of waste into deep underground formations is not new—the first deep injection projects began as early as 1930 as a way of disposing of brines produced from oil and gas wells. Currently, CO_2 is being injected into oil and gas wells for the purpose of conducting enhanced oil recovery (EOR), a process that uses injected substances to liberate residual oil deposits that can not otherwise be extracted economically. Other injection experience has also been gained from storage of natural gas in abandoned oil and gas wells.

Although there are a number of small, pilot GS projects underway, there are only a handful of commercial-scale projects currently in operation. No commercial-scale GS project yet exists within the United States * * *.

Carbon sequestration also can take the form of ocean sequestration in which CO_2 is sequestered under the seabed or in ocean waters overhead. "Although offshore storage provides the benefit of minimizing any risk of harm to humans or underground drinking water sources, offshore injection will be more expensive and will involve even less regulatory certainty and legal issues given the intersection with maritime and international law." Glaser supra at 430 n. 6. Legal issues surrounding all 3 types of carbon sequestration are discussed in the balance of this section.

2. Biologic Sequestration

a. Legal Recognition of Photosynthesis as a Global Ecosystem Service

Perhaps as much as 50% of greenhouse gas emissions do not come from industrial burning of fossil fuels. They are the result of biomass burning. Cleansing the atmosphere of levels of carbon dioxide that accelerate climate change and restoring a stable "balance" to Earth's atmosphere necessitates assigning a priority to enhancing photosynthesis.

Plants are one of the Earth's primary natural forces, fueled by solar energy to convert carbon dioxide to oxygen while sequestering carbon in their wood and pulp. To undertake this process, plants require nutrition, water and nitrogen and other minerals derived principally through their root systems in soils. In order to sustain photosynthesis, it is necessary to maintain each habitat which sustains the plant life found within it. Because photosynthesis is essential to the climate on Earth, governments must rigorously sustain the ecosystems of which plant life is an essential component, in order to effectively address their obligations under the UNFCCC to stabilize the Earth's climate.

In terms of greenhouse gas emissions, intergovernmental focus has given priority to emissions from industrial and electrical generating enterprises. Relatively little attention has been given to greenhouse gases from biomass burning, such as forest fires, either wild or set deliberately for clearing lands for conversion to agricultural uses, and biomass burning associated with agricultural productions (e.g. burning sugar cane fields in Brazil as part of harvesting). Even less attention has been given to sustaining the preventative role that photosynthesis plays in removing carbon dioxide from the atmosphere, or scrubbing the CO_2 from the ambient air.

Under Article 4 of the UNFCCC, states have an obligation to address these issues.

Article 3.3 of the Kyoto protocol allowed states to include changes in "afforestation, reforestation, and deforestation" in measuring net changes to these greenhouse gas emissions since 1990. Since forestry entails timber and economic use of forests, these provisions have generated controversy as to their application. Rather than regarding photosynthesis as the *process* to be enhanced, states focus on the commodity of timber as a *product*. The states focus on measuring their activities involving forests for meeting Kyoto Protocol obligations, not as a matter of promoting more sequestration.

States currently approach the loss of forests as the problem to address, rather than afforestation, rebuilding bio-diverse forest systems, and enhancing photosynthesis world-wide. In this regard, states view their obligations in ways reminiscent of the approach of the Convention to Combat Desertification. The recommendations on REDD, Reducing Emissions from Deforestation and Degradation, address steps to contain unsustainable land use practices, as do the recommendations on LULUCF, Land Use, Land Use Change, and Forestry. UNFCC, Bonn Agreement part VII: Land-Use, Land–Use Change and Forestry (July 2001).

Moreover, these recommendations do not appear to be grounded upon the considerable experience that governments have with regulating environmentally important lands and resources. There is a considerable body of international experience on management of international water resources e.g. Canada and U.S. Boundary Waters Treaty of 1909 and International Joint Commission and Water quality Agreement of 1972 and The Convention for the Protection of The Marine Environment and Coastal Region of the Mediterranean (1976, Barcelona); and on management of wetlands (e.g. Ramsar Convention on Wetlands of International Importance (1971)), and some with international river systems (see, e.g. the 1997 UN Convention on Nonnavigational Uses of Watercourses, 36 I.L.M. 700) What is missing from all these agreements is a climate change focus, and the States Parties to each need to elaborate this. Conversely, UNFCC negotiations need to make this link also.

However, there has been little attention devoted to how the obligations of the 1992 UN Convention on Biological Diversity can serve to both sustain biodiversity and facilitate the plant photosynthesis so needed for stabilizing the climate. One further legal innovation can be found in the Great Lakes Compact, which entered into force in 2008. This Compact, between all states in the Great Lakes Basin, with a companion agreement including all Provinces of Canada in the Basin, provides now for a rolling 5-year incremental impact assessment process to guide its planning and joint conservation measures, which will necessarily include analysis of the effects of climate change, and identifying ways to protect the Great Lakes Basin. At national and local levels of government, there is considerable experience with regulatory measures than can promote photosynthesis. This is a common responsibility of all states and, regardless of the levels of socio-economic development, there are measures that each state can take to address their duties. Most have enacted national environmental legislation, and the challenge now is to implement it and strategically align it in support of enhancing photosynthesis.

How on-going climate negotiations will integrate the overlapping programs and obligations of the Biodiversity and Climate Change conventions, both launched at the 1992 Rio Earth Summit, and to link these to the mission of the Convention to Combat Desertification remains to be seen. Each convention has a shared mission to address issues related to climate change.

The contributions each convention could make to the problem of GHG emissions is illustrated by the issues of biomass burning. The UN Food and Agricultural Organization estimates that more than 40% of biomass lost to wild fires occurs in Africa, FAO "Fire In The Agriculture-forestry Interface" (Report for the 24th Regional Conference For Africa, Bamako, Mali, 2006). Africa is also experiencing desertification, often at crisis proportions. This burning releases about 3,431 million tones of CO_2, as well as significant quantities of other emissions, and where fire adapted or fire dependent ecosystems can regrow and then resequester some of this carbon through photosynthesis, degraded and eroded systems can dexperience little or no re-growth, with no resequestration.

In order to promote photosynthesis as a means to scrub CO_2 out of the atmosphere, it is also necessary to address the role of forest management to enhance forest photosynthesis, and move beyond the preoccupation of the UN Forum on Forests on timber as a commodity. Through combining the over-lapping treaty obligations of the CBD and UNFCCC, as for instance in a new protocol providing for new afforestation and enhanced stewardship of photo-synthesis, governments can make advances in meeting the UNFCCC target of reducing greenhouse gas concentrations in the atmosphere to levels that do not cause grave disruptions to the Earth's climate systems.

Studies at the Max Planck Institute for Chemistry in Germany have evaluated the diverse scientific and technical reports and data bases on bio-mass burning. "Biomass burning releases about two-thirds as much CO_2 as fossil fuel burning. It can be argued that a substantial fraction of CO_2 re-leased from vegetation burning is taken up into the biosphere again after a short time. This only applies, however, as long as burning is done in a sus-tainable manner, which is not the case for deforestation fires and much do-mestic biofuel use. For two other greenhouse gases, methane and nitrous oxide, pyrogenic emissions are very significant as well. In the case of meth-ane, fires emit about one one-third as much as fossil fuel activities, (including pipeline losses, etc). For N_2O, pyrogenic sources rival the sum of all industrial emissions." M. Andreae, Assessment of Global Emissions From Vegetation Fires, 31 International Wildfire News 112 (July-December 2004). This study concludes that "Given the magnitude of the emissions from biomass burning, one must expect significant impacts in air quality, human health, climate and the water cycle."

Recent experience with uncontrolled fires suggests that nations are wholly ill equipped to prevent or combat them. In all regions, the FAO re-ports that people are the cause of 90% of the wild fires experienced. People also suffer immediate and visible consequences from fires, while atmospheric accumulations of greenhouse gases are longer-terms from fires and less evi-dent impact. In 1997-98, fires destroyed vast areas in North and South America, South East Asia, Africa and Eurasia, in both temperate and tropical forest areas. Weather conditions associated with the oscillations of the El Niño phenomena made conditions for such fires favorable, but defaults in government capacity is what allowed the fires to burn out of control. In the heat waves of 2003, a new record was set in the extent and number of wild fires in Europe. No region is immune from this phenomena. How can capac-ity be built quickly to deal with this phenomena? Would the use of mutual aid agreements provide a valuable first step? See N. Robinson, Forest Fires as a Common International Concern: Precedents for the Progressive Development of International Environmental Law, 18 Pace Envtl. L. Rev. 459 (2001):

> Transnational air pollution from forest fires, for the first time, became a tragic reality on a worldwide basis during 1997 and 1998. The scope of these fires was unprecedented. In May of 1998, state environmental protection officials in Texas declared the air unfit to breathe from the coast of the Gulf of Mexico for over 100 miles inland, and the entire state went on an air pollution alert. Hazy skies were reported as far north as Colorado and South Dakota. The smoke caused health problems and cut visibility. The fires were burning in Mexico, which was experiencing its worst drought in seventy years. The number of forest fires reached 11,000 from an average of 7,000. Over 1,500 square miles burned. Meanwhile, during the same year, forest fires in Central America consumed 2,150 square miles of forests, primarily in Guatemala, Honduras and Nicaragua. During the same period, forest fires in Africa burned around Mt. Kilimanjaro in Tanzania, as well as in Kenya, Rwanda, Congo, and Senegal, all exacerbated by the drought accompanying El Niño weather patterns in Africa. In South America, fires in Brazil consumed some 20,000 square miles, or an area half the size of New York State. The journal Nature called the Brazilian patterns of unmanaged logging that led to new surface fires and a cycle of forest impoverishment that contributed to further fires, a kind of "cryptic deforestation." In Siberia, 15,000 forest fires in 1997 and over 19,000 in 1999 burned with little effective means of extinguishing them. Some fire fighting forces and equipment reached the peat forest fires in Belarus and European Russia, but substantial burning elsewhere was not controlled. Perhaps the most extensive and acute forest fire phenomena were found in South East Asia. The fires of 1997 in Kalimantan and Sumatra, Indonesia, and in parts of Malaysia and Papua New Guinea, produced plumes of smoke that blanketed Singapore and Malaysia and reached the Philippines and Thailand. The loss of photosynthesis and release of carbon dioxide and other gases in these fires constitute a significant climate impact. No convention addresses this issue currently.

Photosynthesis, combined with active responses to wild forest-fires and limits to deforestation, could become an essential element of a global strategy under the UNFCCC. Since humans know how to plant trees and manage biomass burning, no new technological innovations are required. Often no new or large financial services are needed. Rather, governments must do what they know how to do, but do not now do. What legal measures can be deployed to bring this about? There are two dimensions to this obligation.

b. Afforestation

Governments, and indeed all social and economic agencies and enterprises, and also individuals, will need to restore the forest and plant cover to the Earth. Humans have been denuding the Earth of its plant cover, leaving behind the scourge of desertification. The UN Convention to Combat Desertification can play a major role in this effort by stabilizing soils at risk to erosion and desiccation, but that remedial task needs to be complemented by the more comprehensive global mission of restoring the forest cover to the planet. Afforestation efforts may benefit from the elevated levels of CO_2 in the atmosphere, but drought and adequate soil conditions and other factors will affect the planting of new trees. J. Huang et. al., Response of Forest Trees to Increased Atmospheric CO_2,, 26 Critical Reviews in Plant Sciences 265 (2007).

China has rigorously promoted afforestation for decades, although under the period of rapid economic growth efforts at afforestation took a secondary role to other social objectives. To enhance photosynthesis, nations need to enact legislation such as the Chinese afforestation laws. This is a much neglected area, although it should seem self-evident that massive planting of trees is relatively easily accomplished. There must be environmental assessments made to determine the kind of trees to plant in order to enhance biological diversity, and to avoid creating monocultures that are vulnerable to disease. There is an urgent need for legal measures to begin the afforestation policy analysis and action. M. Boyland, The Economics of Using Forests to Increase Carbon Storage, 36 Canadian Journal of Forest Research 36 (2006) reports that "Unfortunately, there are no forest-management analyses that approach the level of modeling detail required to project the economics of carbon forest-management actions nor project the amount of carbon that would likely be sequestered. ...[D]efinitive analysis of forest-management options for carbon sequestration have yet to be completed, and it is premature to declare that existing forest cannot be included to increase carbon sequestration."

Restoring deforested areas may be a permanent phenomenon, or may be temporary, as when timbered areas are replanted. Assuming a commercial fir tree matures in 30-40 years and each tree sequesters about a ton of carbon, a photosynthesis budget for permanent or temporary sequestration could be formulated. Commercial replanting that is on-going would need to be audited and sustained over time. It has been estimated that commercial replanting in the U.S. since 1990 will reach 800 million tons of carbon by 2010, or 16% of U.S. 1990 GHG emissions. How this CO_2 should be managed once these trees are cut remains to be determined.

Given the magnitude of the need to scrub the atmosphere of carbon, tree planting on a rapid pace is a readily available technique. Why is it so little promoted?

c. Ecosystem Stewardship

This requires a fundamental revisiting of the laws and policies that govern the biomes where photosynthesis resides: (a) forests, (b) wetlands, (c) grasslands, (d) tundra, and (e) phytoplankton in the oceans.

Forests: Climate stabilization will necessitate measures to protect forests that already exist, and assigning a high priority to monitoring their health and taking affirmative measures to encourage forest health. The UN Food & Agricultural Organization reported that in 2000, satellite analysis revealed that 350 million hectares world-wide experienced vegetation fires. Fire Management—Global Assessment 2006 (FAO Forestry Paper 151, Rome 2007).

In tropical forests, measures are needed to manage the use of fire to clear land for agriculture, and manufacturing charcoal as a fuel, or burning wood and dung as a fuel, needs to be evaluated and quantified and addressed. Agreed measures remain to be taken to eliminate the unlawful timber operations and set to regulate parameters for sustainable forestry practices, including provision of enforceable rules for international trade in forest products. Tropical forests are Earth's largest biomass carbon reservoir, and some CO_2 enrichment of the atmosphere actually encourages more plant growth with an uptake in carbon sequestration through photosynthesis. However, increased economic development and conversion of forests to non-forest agricultural and other uses advances more rapidly than the perceived benefits from this sequestration phenomena.

In temperate forests, this will require also preventing or containing wild fires, and allowing ecologically essential fires in forest management that do not jeopardize wide photosynthesis services or damage other essential ecological and human conditions. Forest fires bring a double impact to the climate, because they release vast amounts of carbon dioxide into the atmosphere while eliminating or reducing markedly the on-going sequestration of atmospheric carbon dioxide through photosynthesis. All temperate forests of course are not the same, and governmental management systems will need to address the characteristics of each forest region. For example, forests in mountain ranges, regions require management rules appropriate for the mountainous environment. For instance, mountain areas also provide important sources of freshwater, and need to be sustained as catchment areas and watersheds, capable of retaining and storing and gradually releasing waters needed by human societies lower in the watersheds. The preservation of the Forest Preserve in the Adirondack and Catskill Mountains of New York in 1894, through adoption of a provision to preserve the areas a "forever wild" in Article XIV of the state's Constitution, has provided the basis for stewardship of such a valuable forest region for more than a century. The Convention for the Protection of the Alps (1991) and the Framework Convention on the Protection and Sustainable Development of the Carpathians (2003) provide examples of treaty systems to provide this stewardship across forest habitats shared by several nations.

Unfortunately, forest fire management and unsustainable timber operations have left existing forests vulnerable to destruction, with the attendant loss of forest photosynthesis. The fires that swept through Europe in 2003, Australia in 2006-9, across Greece in 2007, or in the recurrent "plague" of global forest fires in 1997-98 that afflicted all regions of the world during dry periods, have provided ample notice of the need for governments to address forest wildfire management as a high priority. Few have done so.

There is scientific debate, and varying experiments with computer models, as to how much the particulate matter and aerosols from burning biomass can provide smog and clouds of air pollution whose albedo effect reflects solar radiation back into space and helps cool the planet. These debates, while important, do not address the question of how to maximize photosynthesis as a tool that needs to be deployed in order to scrub carbon from the atmosphere. The technology exists to deploy this tool, but the legal means to do so remain to be elaborated.

(b) *Wetlands*: Both saltwater estuarine wetlands and mangroves and freshwater wetlands provide an enormously rich abundance of ecosystems services. Their hydrological absorption capacity is essential to containing flood surges and protecting upland areas from such adverse effects of climate change. As such, wetlands are essential for adaptation. Since for the past several hundred years, vast areas of wetlands have been drained and converted for development as "dry" land, their ecosystem services have been lost. If the myriad ecosystem services of wetlands are to be sustained, including their photosynthesis services, then governments will need to preserve all remaining wetlands systems, and begin the process of restoring coastal and estuarine wetlands and mangroves in order to allow migration of these regions inland as sea levels rise. In addition, freshwater wetlands will need to be restored to assist with absorption of flood waters in upland areas.

Thus, wetlands law serves two climate concerns: mitigation of the concentration of carbon dioxide in the atmosphere through photosynthesis, and adaptation to the effects of climate change through absorption of flood waters. Wetland mapping and regulation is well developed in many nations. Wetlands legislation needs to be come universal and compliance and enforcement measures need to be developed.

(c) *Grasslands*: Grasslands and savannahs extend over large portions of the planet, and are subject to rapid loss by over-grazing or other misuse leading to erosion and desertification. Savannah fires contribute significantly to greenhouse gas emissions. For instance, in 2001 Bolivia's savannah forest and grassland fires produced 82.6 million tons of CO_2 into the atmosphere. I.

Martinez and W. Cordero, Fire Situation in Bolivia, 28 International Forest Fiore News 41 (2003). FAO reports that, from 2000-2004, 9 million acres of steppe vegetation burned in Mongolia, most as a result of negligence accompanying new economic development, and that uncontrolled forest fires in the boreal forests of Russia "are a major threat to the global carbon budget." FAO "Fire Management Global Assessment 2006," (FAO Forestry Paper 151, Rome 2007). Past losses of grasslands diminish this biotic resource; in the United States, most of the prairies have been destroyed, leading to the "Dust Bowl" phenomena in the 20th century. Their soils are important in the exchange of carbon dioxide. Alpine meadows are also at risk of degradation by developmental activities and excessive pastoral uses. Soil conservation measures need to be sustained over time; the elimination of the U.S. Soil Conservation Service during the Clinton Administration illustrates that governments can forget why they need to affirmatively maintain services to sustain soil health. Relatively few nations have effective soil conservation laws. IUCN's Commission on Environmental Law, in cooperation with the European Soils Bureau, has prepared a proposed Protocol on Soil Conservation. National legislation is needed in this sector.

(d) *Tundra*: Tundra, the vegetation and ecosystems of the closed boreal forest is essential to averting further releases of greenhouse gases to the atmosphere. The grasses and plants that live in the tundra regions provide a living blanket on the frozen soils beneath, insulating them, as they provide habitat for many species and contribute modestly through photosynthesis to the climate. Boreal forests grow very slowly and once disturbed, as by a forest fire in Siberia, may not recover the carbon released. Nonetheless, in this capacity, they prevent what could be a massive release of methane to the atmosphere with catastrophic climate change consequences. As the climate warms, polar regions are warming especially rapidly. The tundra is at risk of melting as the climate warms and coastal tundra is affected by the rise of sea levels rise. Arctic and Antarctic tundra are doubly important to averting further anthropogenic harm to atmosphere; buried under the surface tundra are large amounts of methane, a potent greenhouse gas, which could be released to the atmosphere if the tundra melted. Exploration and development of the Arctic for oil and gas extraction poses a double threat to the climate, first by producing more fossil fuels for combustion and second by jeopardizing the frozen conditions. The melting of the North Polar ice cap has accelerated economic interest in exploitation of the region. The pollution associated with the development of Alaska's Prudhoe Bay and the construction of the Alaska Pipeline suggests that the nations in the polar regions should make through use of Environmental Impact Assessment before allowing any measures that would jeopardize the frozen tundra. From a climate perspective, further development of tundra lands should be deferred and then any development pursued only on a regional basis, thorough the cooperative management guidance of the Arctic Council.

(e) *Phytoplankton*: As discussed ocean phytoplankton are the basis for the marine food web and important for photosynthesis. Ocean uptake of CO_2 from the increasing CO_2 in the atmosphere, contributed to the reduction of pH (acidification) and that can reduce phytoplankton productivity. Mostly outside national jurisdiction, marine phytoplankton provide a vast but little quantified photosynthesis service. The health of the oceans is a primary national obligation under the UN Convention on the Law of Sea, which provides that parties shall "protect and preserve the marine environment."

However, UNCLOS environmental provisions in Part XII are silent on the role of the oceans as a habitat for phytoplankton, although it is clear that pollution of the seas that could adversely affect marine life is to be controlled. Nations should negotiate a UNCLOS protocol or separate agreement to provide monitoring and conservation of phytoplankton as a renewable natural resource service provider of photosynthesis.

Consider next how governments, individually at all levels, and through regional cooperation or international agreements, can address or strengthen these dimensions of managing the environment to enhance photosynthesis.

d. Legal Instruments

i) China's Afforestation Law

Afforestation is the replanting of trees in areas where they once existed. So important is this in China that the re-enactment of the law on afforestation was one of the first three laws to be repromulgated after the "Cultural Revolution." In 1985, the provisions on afforestation were codified in the Forestry Law of the People's Republic of China. China currently is in the sixth year of a 10-year program to plant 170,000 square miles of trees, an area roughly the size of California. (Xinhua News Agency, May 15, 2002). As a result of its sustained afforestation programs, China manages today some 46.7 million hectares of reforested lands. Zhou Shengxian, Director of the PRC State Forest Administration, has noted: "In contrast to the forest coverage rate of 8.6 percent in the early 1950s, 16.55 percent of China's territory is currently covered with 158.7 million hectares of forest." China's Afforestation Reported, People's Daily (January 23, 2002), accessed at www.china.cn/english/2002/Jan/25708.htm

In the late 1800s, afforestation programs were widespread in the northeast United States. New York State, for example, still maintains a state nursery at Saratoga Springs within the Department of Environmental Conservation. Secondary growth forest has returned to extensive areas of North America. The extraction of timber as a commodity produced substantial revenues around the world, but little to none of this is invested in afforestation. China's 10-year program is estimated to cost $2.4 billion, paid from the central budget. What are the obligations of the agricultural sector in each country to assist with afforestation, since 90% of areas such as Brazil's Atlantic Forest were cleared for agricultural and other non-forest uses? Should some of the revenues from a carbon cap and trade program be invested in afforestation? How much?

Should each government enact a provision similar to the following articles of the Forestry Law of the People's Republic of China?

* * * * *

Chapter IV Tree Planting and Afforestation

[www.china.org.cn/environment/2007-08/27/content_1207457.htm]

Article 26 People's governments at all levels should work out planning for tree planting and afforestation and determine the goals to be striven for in raising forest coverage of the respective areas in the light of local conditions.

People's governments at all levels should organize all trades and professions and rural and urban inhabitants in the fulfillment of tasks set in the planning for tree planting and afforestation.

On barren hills and waste lands suitable for afforestation that belong to the state, afforestation shall be organized by the competent departments of forestry and other competent departments; on those belonging to collectives, afforestation shall be organized by collective economic organizations.

Afforestation shall be organized by the competent departments concerned in the light of local conditions on either side of railways, highways, on either banks of rivers and on the rim of lakes and reservoirs; on land under use by industrial and mining areas, organs and schools, armed forces barracks as well as areas managed by farms, cattle farms and fish farms, afforestation shall be the responsibility of the said units.

State-owned and collective-owned barren hills and waste lands suitable for afforestation may be contracted out to collectives or individuals for afforestation.

Article 27 Woods planted by state-owned enterprises and institutions, organs, societies and armed forces shall be managed by the units that have planted them and gains from the woods shall be budgeted pursuant to state provisions.

Woods planted by a unit of collective ownership shall belong to the said unit.

Trees planted by rural inhabitants at the front and back of their farm houses, on plots of land for personal needs and plots on hills for personal needs belong to the said individuals. Trees planted by urban and township inhabitants, workers and staff members in the courtyards of their own houses belong to the said individuals.

For state-owned and collective-owned barren hills and waste lands suitable for afforestation contracted out to collectives or individuals for afforestation, the trees planted after contracting belong to the contracting collectives or individuals; provisions of the contract shall be adhered to in case of separate provisions in the contract.

Article 28 Local people's governments shall organize closure of mountains and hills for afforestation in newly-planted young forest lands and other places that necessitate the closure of mountains and hills for afforestation.

* * * * *

ii) Mutual Aid Agreements

There is a basis for international cooperation on fire monitoring and management in the Global Wildland Fire Network which works with the U.N. Food and Agricultural Organization. Recognizing that nations need to meet their common responsibility to contain greenhouse gases released from wildfire biomass burning, what immediate legal measures can they initiate? To provide a cooperative framework for monitoring (early warning), training and community capacity building (preparedness), combating fires (suppression), and post-fire soil conservation and ecological restoration, governments can enter mutual aid agreements at the regional and local levels as well as at the international level. In addition they can use air force and army personnel to serve some fire surveillance and fire fighting objectives.

Community Organizing

Community organization to fight fires is the first step in self-sufficiency. Examples of organizing in this way can be found in developing nations. For instance, the first volunteer fire-fighting corps in Chile was organized in 1850 in Valparaiso. The model took hold there much as it did in New York State. There are now some 35,000 volunteers in 1,100 fire companies in Chile. Even in rural areas there are usually one or two volunteer fire companies. These are organized under 276 fire departments, or corps, and they raise funds locally for a barracks, a fire truck, communications equipment, and fire fighting tools. The corps are essentially private nongovernmental corporations. In 1970, the Junta Nacional de Cuerpos de Bomberos de Chile was founded to provide national integration of the system. There is a National Fire Fighters Academy (Academia Nacional de Bomberos) which coordinates the training for all the volunteers, and the national budget allocates some $11 million to the network.

Intergovernmental Fire Compacts

Next consider the example of the 1949 Northeastern Interstate Forest Fire Protection Compact, codified at New York Environmental Conservation Law § 9-1123:

ARTICLE I

The purpose of this compact is to promote effective prevention and control of forest fires in the northeastern region of the United States and adjacent areas in Canada by the development of integrated forest fire plans, by the maintenance of adequate forest fire fighting services by the member states, by providing for mutual aid in fighting forest fires among the states of the region and for procedures that will facilitate such aid, and by the establishment of a central agency to coordinate the services of member states and perform such common services as member states may deem desirable.

ARTICLE II

This agreement shall become operative immediately as to those states ratifying it whenever any two or more of the states of Maine, New Hampshire, Vermont, Rhode Island, Connecticut, New York and the Commonwealth of Massachusetts have ratified it and the congress has given its consent. Any state not mentioned in this article which is contiguous with any member state may become a party to this compact. Subject to the consent of the congress of the United States, any province of the Dominion of Canada which is contiguous with any member state may become a party to this compact by taking such action as its laws and the laws of the Dominion of Canada may prescribe for ratification. In this event, the term "state" in this compact shall include within its meaning the term "province" and the procedures prescribed shall be applied in the instance of such provinces, in accordance with the forms and practices of the Canadian government.

ARTICLE III

Each state joining herein shall appoint three representatives to a commission hereby designated as the Northeastern Forest Fire Protection Commission. One shall be the state forester or officer holding an equivalent position in such state who is responsible for forest fire control. The second shall be a member of the legislature of such state designated by the commission or committee on interstate cooperation of such state, or if there be none, or if said commission on interstate cooperation cannot constitutionally designate the said member, such legislator shall be designated by the governor thereof;

provided that if it is constitutionally impossible to appoint a legislator as a commissioner from such state, the second member shall be appointed by the governor of said state in his discretion. The third member shall be a person designated by the governor as the responsible representative of the governor. In the event that any province of the Dominion of Canada shall become a member of this commission, it shall designate three members who will approximate this pattern of representation to the extent possible under the law and practices of such province. This commission shall be a body corporate with the powers and duties set forth herein.

ARTICLE IV

It shall be the duty of the commission to make inquiry and ascertain from time to time such methods, practices, circumstances and conditions as may be disclosed for bringing about the prevention and control of forest in the area comprising the member states, to coordinate the forest fire plans and the work of the appropriate agencies of the member states and to facilitate the rendering of aid by the member states to each other in fighting forest fires. * * *

ARTICLE V

Any two or more member states may designate the Northeastern Forest Fire Protection Commission as a joint agency to maintain such common services as those states deem desirable for the prevention and control of forest fires. Except in those cases where all member states join in such designation for common services, the representatives of any group of such designating states in the Northeastern Forest Fire Protection Commission shall constitute a separate section of such commission for the performance of the common service or services so designated provided that, if any additional expense is involved, the states so acting shall appropriate the necessary funds for this purpose. The creation of such a section as a joint agency shall not affect the privileges, powers, responsibilities or duties of the states participating therein as embodied in the other articles of this compact.

ARTICE VI

The commission may request the United States forest service to act as the primary research and coordinating agency of the Northeastern Forest Fire Protection Commission, in cooperation with the appropriate agencies in each state and the United States forest service may accept the initial responsibility in preparing and presenting to the commission its recommendations with respect to the regional fire plan. Representatives of the United States forest service may attend meetings of the commission and of groups of member states.

* * *

ARTICE VIII

It shall be the duty of each member state to formulate and put in effect a forest fire plan for that state and to take such measures as may be recommended by the commission to integrate such forest fire plan with the regional forest fire plan.

Whenever the state forest fire control agency of a member state requests aid from the state forest fire control agency of any other member state in combating, controlling or preventing forest fires, it shall be the duty of the state forest fire control agency of that state to render all possible aid to the requesting agency which is consonant with the maintenance of protection at home.

Each signatory state agrees to render aid to the forest service or other agencies of the government of the United States in combating, controlling or preventing forest fires in areas under their jurisdiction located within the member state or a contiguous member state.

ARTICLE IX

Whenever the forces of any member state are rendering outside aid pursuant to the request of another member state under this compact, the employees of such state shall, under the direction of the officers of the state to which they are rendering aid, have the same powers (except the power of arrest), duties, rights, privileges and immunities as comparable employees of the state to which there are rendering aid. * * *

Each member state shall provide for the payment of compensation and death benefits to injured employees and the representatives of deceased employees in case employees sustain injuries or are killed while rendering outside aid pursuant to this compact, in the same manner and on the same terms as if the injury or death were sustained within such state.

For the purposes of this compact the term employee shall include any volunteer or auxiliary legally included within the forest fire fighting forces of the aiding state under the laws thereof.

e. Biochar

**BIOCHAR: AN EXAMINATION OF AN EMERGING CONCEPT TO
MITIGATE CLIMATE CHANGE**
Kelsi S. Bracmort, Congressional Research Service (Feb. 3, 2009)
http://assets.opencrs.com/rpts/R40186_20090203.pdf

* * *

Biochar is a charcoal similar in appearance to potting soil. It is produced under high temperatures using crop residues, animal manure, or any type of organic waste material. Biochar is regarded by some as a product that can meet pressing environmental demands by sequestering large amounts of carbon in soil. However, little is known about how the adaptation of biochar production could successfully be implemented and what the effect would be on long-term operations in the U.S. agriculture and forestry sectors. Studies underway at federal government research institutions and in academia are focused on ensuring that biochar production systems are a practical and reliable technology for producers to adopt. The utilization of biochar is of interest to those seeking to sell or purchase carbon offsets, increase soil conservation efforts, improve crop yield, and produce alternative energy. Some contend that it will be a considerable amount of time before this technology reaches its full potential.

Biochar has the capability to both curtail greenhouse gas emissions and other environmental hazards in the near term and benefit agricultural producers as a soil amendment and source of alternative energy. Thus far, biochar use in the United States has been limited to small-scale applications reflective of the limited but growing number of researchers in this area over the last few years.

Biochar is a soil supplement that may have the potential to help mitigate global climate change through carbon sequestration in the soil. As a charcoal containing high levels of organic matter, biochar is formed from plant and crop residues or animal manure under pyrolysis conditions. Pyrolysis is the chemical breakdown of a substance under extremely high temperatures in absence of oxygen. The quantity and quality of biochar production depends on the feedstock, pyrolysis temperature, and pyrolysis processing time. A "fast" pyrolysis (~500°C) produces biochar in a matter of seconds, while a "slow" pyrolysis produces considerably more biochar but in a matter of hours.

The three main outputs of a biochar production system are syngas, bio-oil, and biochar. The biochar production system is operated using energy produced by the system. Biochar production via pyrolysis is considered a carbon-negative process because the biochar sequesters carbon while simultaneously enhancing the fertility of the soil on which the feedstock used to produce the bioenergy grows.

Whether applied to the soil as a fertilizer or burned as an energy source (e.g., for cooking and heating), biochar provides numerous potential environmental benefits, some of which are not quantifiable. The three primary potential benefits are carbon sequestration, greenhouse gas emission reduction, and soil fertility.

Carbon sequestration is the capture and storage of carbon to prevent it from being released to the atmosphere. Studies suggest that biochar sequesters approximately 50% of the carbon available within the biomass feedstock being pyrolyzed, depending upon the feedstock type. The remaining percentage of carbon is released during pyrolysis and may be captured for energy production. Large amounts of carbon may be sequestered in the soil for long time periods (hundreds to thousands of years at an estimate), but precise estimates of carbon amounts sequestered as a result of biochar application are scarce. One scientist suggests that a 250-hectare farm could sequester 1,900 tons of CO_2 a year.

Biochar retains nutrients for plant uptake and soil fertility. The infiltration of harmful quantities of nutrients and pesticides into ground water and soil erosion runoff into surface waters can be limited with the use of biochar. If used for soil fertility, biochar may have a positive impact on those in developing countries. Impoverished tropical and subtropical locales with abundant plant material feedstock, inexpensive cooking fuel needs, and agricultural soil replenishment needs could see an increase in crop yields.

Recognizing that biochar technology is in its early stages of development, there are many concerns about the applicability of the technology in the United States. Three issues paramount to technology adoption are feedstock availability, biochar handling, and biochar system deployment. Successful implementation of biochar technology is rooted in the ability of the agricultural community to afford and operate a system that is complementary to current farming practices.

The availability of a plentiful feed supply for biochar production is an area for further study. To date, feedstock for biochar has consisted of mostly plant and crop residues, a primary domain of the agricultural community. There may be a role for the forestry community to be involved as woody biomass is deemed a cost-effective, readily available, feasible feedstock. Little is known about the advantages of using manure as a biomass feedstock. Some researchers have stated that manure-based biochar "has advantages over typically used plant-derived material because it is a by-product of another industry and in some regions is considered a waste material with little or no value. It can therefore provide a lower cost base and alleviate sustainability concerns related to using purpose-grown biomass for the process."

The spreading of biochar onto soil as a fertilizer is ripe for further exploration. Specifically, the ideal time to apply biochar and ensure that it remains in place once applied and does not cause a risk to human health or degrade air quality are concerns. Particulate matter, in the form of dust that is hard for the human body to filter, may be distributed in abnormal quantities if the biochar is mishandled. Additionally, there are potential public safety concerns for the handling of biochar as it is a flammable substance.

Biochar systems are designed based on the feedstock to be decomposed and the energy needs of an operation. It would be ambitious to expect a "one size fits all" standard biochar system. According to proponents, a series of mass-produced biochar systems designed for the needs of a segment of the agriculture or forestry communities might prove to be feasible (e.g., forestry community in the southeastern region, corn grower community in the mid-western region, poultry producer community in the mid-Atlantic region). Extensive deployment of biochar systems would be dependent upon system costs, operation time, collaboration with utility providers for the sale of bio-oil, and availability of information about technology reliability. * * *

In 2006, 6% of total U.S. greenhouse gas emissions were attributed to the agricultural sector. While not as large as the amounts produced by some other sectors, agricultural emissions come from a large number of decentralized sources, leading many to conclude that controlling such emissions would be difficult. On the other hand, some argue that soil carbon sequestered as a result of biochar application is easily quantifiable and transparent, which may be ideal for carbon trading requirements. Others contend that ancillary benefits could include additional revenue earned by agricultural producers through the sale of carbon credits earned from biochar application or the sale of biochar as a fertilizer. Energy costs for a producer's operation may be reduced by using the alternative energy generated from the biochar production system. Additionally, some assert that the use of biochar results in higher crop yields. This could be a criterion to consider within the larger land use debate. * * *

Biochar's fate as a viable component of the long-term solution to mitigate climate change by way of carbon sequestration depends upon further development by the scientific and technology transfer communities; in particular, biochar's practical application at various locations and scales using multiple feedstocks throughout the United States is an area for additional study. A policy vehicle to communicate the status of biochar technology to decision-makers and interested communities has not been identified. Natural resources conservation policy, alternative energy policy, or climate change policy are a few examples of possible policy areas. Policy that encourages academia and other institutions to conduct in-depth research and development could quicken the pace of technology deployment.

* * * Biochar's success rate as a potential clean development mechanism (CDM) mitigation technology may provide insight on its use for U.S. carbon trading purposes. * * *

U.S. Department of Agriculture (USDA) Agricultural Research Service (ARS) * * * ARS estimates that the United States could use biochar to sequester 139 Tg of carbon on an annual basis if it were to harvest and pyrolyze 1.3 billion tons of biomass. * * *

Notes and Questions

1.   The International Biochar Initiative, an international NGO, currently has a range of projects in progress in developing countries to analyze cost-effective alternatives for the introduction and adoption of biochar, including an environmental, economic, and social assessment of introducing biochar technology at the household level, studies on how to promote the use of biochar to stabilize and buffer soil salinity and increase water retention, efforts to develop a sustainable pyrolysis cook-stove and biochar system for rural agricultural households. see http://www.biochar-international.org/

2.   Although biochar (also known as *terra preta*) may present the opportunity to sequester up to 6 billion tons of Of CO_2 each year, many questions remain. According to Olive Heffernan, Best practice for biochar, Nature Reports Climate   Change,   doi:10.1038/climate.2009.53   (2   June   2009) http://www.nature.com/climate/2009/0906/full/climate.2009.53.html:

> * * * [D]espite its astounding potential, caution is warranted in implementing biochar on any sizeable scale. Though re-creating *terra preta* sounds simple, recent research suggests that modern-day soils may respond less well to the treatment and that the carbon may escape sooner than anticipated. On these questions alone, all of the evidence is not in. Yet we clearly don't have the luxury of time to answer them definitively.

> The recent exuberance over biochar is reminiscent of the earlier fervour over biofuels, as critics have been eager to highlight. But both face some of the same problems—most controversially, the need for land should carbon credits command a high enough price—suggesting there is scope here to learn from previous errors.

> What's now needed is an international code of best practice for biochar that evolves as knowledge comes in. For a start, this would clearly define acceptable land-use policy for plantations, as well as a lower limit on carbon sequestered from those claiming certification. Inclusion in a global climate deal will certainly speed the adoption of biochar, but it can also help ensure that this solution is applied responsibly.

* * * * *

3. Geologic Sequestration

Regarding the U.S. property law, water rights, applicability of the Safe Drinking Water Act, 42 U.S.C. 300 ("SDWA"), and tort liability issues raised by underground geologic sequestration (GS) of CO_2, consider the following excerpt.

GLOBAL WARMING SOLUTIONS: REGULATORY CHALLENGES AND COMMON LAW LIABILITIES ASSOCIATED WITH THE GEOLOGIC SEQUESTRATION OF CARBON DIOXIDE
P. Glaser et al.
6 Geo. J.L. & Pub. Policy 429 (2008)

PROPERTY RIGHTS ISSUES ASSOCIATED WITH GEOLOGIC SEQUESTRATION

Even if all regulatory hurdles are overcome, common law tort and property issues will still arise with the development and operation of commercial-scale GS projects. Absent statutory clarification, these issues likely will be resolved through litigation in the several states. The two main property law issues involve the questions of (1) ownership of the storage formation and (2) ownership of the CO_2 once injected. Resolution of the first issue determines, among other things, who profits by charging for storage, which property rights a prospective injector must acquire or, where permissible, condemn, and who may bring a tort action against a GS project. Resolution of the second issue may determine most of the liability issues—that is, who may be held responsible for CO_2 leakage, and who maintains liability for trespass associated with migrating CO_2 or for damage caused by associated seismic activity or catastrophic release. * * *

A third issue will be the method for acquiring the necessary interests. Likely, prospective injectors will negotiate the purchase or lease of the necessary rights. Should this fail, a prospective injector might condemn the geologic formation. To do so requires state or federally granted condemnation powers specific to the purpose of GS. Strain v. Cities Serv. Gas Co. 83 P.2d 124, 126 (Kan. 1938) (holding general condemnation statute insufficient for purposes of condemning geologic formation for storage of natural gas because condemnation should not be "enlarged by implication"). * * *

A. Ownership of the Storage Formation

Ownership of the storage formation is likely to be determined by state mineral law or state groundwater law depending on which type of formation is used. Ownership of oil and gas formations or unmineable coal seams will likely be determined based on state mineral law, in accordance with case law developed in the context of natural gas injection. Ownership of deep saline formations is likely to be determined based on state groundwater law.

There are two significant property interests relevant to ownership of the geologic formation—the surface interest and the mineral interest. Often these interests are severed and owned independently.   Historically, the valuable component of a mineral interest was the minerals themselves, and ownership of the minerals and the right to extract them were clearly a part of the mineral interest. With GS, however, the value is in the geologic formation's capacity for long-term, stable storage. In the GS context, the key issue will be ownership of the formation, not the minerals.

Ownership of the formation will depend on whether the state in which the formation lies follows the English Rule or the American Rule for subsurface property rights. Under the English Rule, the mineral interest holder owns the geologic formation.   The English Rule is the minority rule in the United States and, even where it remains the law, it has been limited in circumstances involving storage.   In contrast, under the American Rule, the surface interest owner will own the geologic formation.   In practice, however, prospective injectors will have to deal with both interests. Even in English Rule states, GS will require surface activities, *e.g.*, injection facilities, wells, and pipelines, which will necessitate dealing with the surface interest holder. Similarly, in American Rule states, prospective injectors may not interfere with the mineral interest holder's right to explore for and extract any minerals remaining in the formation.   Accordingly, under most circumstances, a prospective injector will have to negotiate with both the surface and the mineral interest holders in nearly every case.

A more difficult ownership issue arises when the geologic formation is a deep saline aquifer rather than an existing or former oil or gas well. In this case, formation ownership will likely be determined by state groundwater law, which varies greatly from state to state. Moreover, state groundwater law has generally arisen in the context of withdrawals from valuable freshwater aquifers rather than injections into the largely valueless saline aquifers.

There are five different varieties of state groundwater law:

- The Absolute Dominion Rule holds that the land owner owns from the heavens to the center of the earth. Under this rule, a land owner may use the fresh water beneath its land as it wishes and to the detriment of its neighbors (where the groundwater beneath neighboring properties is depleted). In the context of GS, however, injected carbon would migrate from the injector's land to neighboring property, which might permit a trespass action.

- The Reasonable Use Rule limits the Absolute Dominion Rule in that it limits a landowner to reasonable use of the groundwater. This doctrine prohibits, among other things, waste and off-site water use.

- The Correlative Rights Rule further limits the Reasonable Use Rule and holds that a land owner may use groundwater in proportion to its surface ownership.

- The Restatement of Torts Rule permits a landowner to use ground water to the extent that it does not cause substantial harm to a neighbor's water use, including loss of aquifer pressure.

- The Prior Appropriations Rule holds that a landowner's right to withdraw and use groundwater is based on when the withdrawal was established—the so called first-in-time-is-first-in-right rule.

Under each of these rules a landowner has some right to use the groundwater. Presumably, this means that each overlying landowner has some right to use the underlying storage potential of the formation. Accordingly, a prospective GS project would have to acquire permission to impact the aquifer or risk committing a trespass. Even so, the existence of so many variants of state law in this area poses an added layer of complexity to GS projects.

B. Ownership of the CO_2

Ownership of the injected CO_2 will be an issue of first impression in virtually all states. However, case law has developed in the context of determining ownership of injected natural gas. Those cases developed based on the rule of capture and the doctrines of ownership or non-ownership in place and will likely be instructive to courts determining ownership of injected CO_2.

The rule of capture essentially treats injected gas like *ferae naturae,* or wild animals. As such, the gas is not owned until brought into personal possession by capture. Based on this principal, the doctrine of "non-ownership in place" holds that the title to the gas is lost upon injection. In the few states where this theory still applies, however, it has been limited and does not apply where the reservoir is capable of being defined with certainty and the integrity of the reservoir is capable of being maintained. This aptly describes formations suitable for GS and thus, the non-ownership doctrine is not likely to apply to GS projects even in states that follow it. The doctrine of ownership of injected gas holds that title to injected gas is not lost upon injection. As such, injected CO_2 will likely be owned by the injector in all states.

C. IOGCC Approach

The Interstate Oil and Gas Compact Commission (IOGCC) CO_2 Geologic Sequestration Task Force addressed these property law issues in a **2005** report on GS. In its report the task force proposes a conceptual framework for states to implement. Under this framework, GS operators would have condemnation powers, permitting them to condemn the necessary property rights for a GS project. As a prerequisite to exercising this power, the GS operator would have to demonstrate that the formation is suitable for GS and the value of any remaining minerals (for purposes of determining just compensation). Under the framework set out by the IOGCC, the GS operator would own the injected CO_2 and would be liable for injury associated with it. The IOGCC leaves open the concern that different states could make different interpretations with regard to what liability and property laws apply to commercial-scale GS projects.

TORT LIABILITY ISSUES ASSOCIATED WITH GEOLOGIC SEQUESTRATION

Even if all necessary property rights have been acquired, and even if all existing regulatory requirements have been met, significant liability concerns with commercial-scale GS projects still exist, given the risks noted above. Generally, the liability risks associated with GS will be governed by state common law, which will vary between jurisdictions. In addition, the property rights issues previously discussed will also necessarily intersect the liability issues—trespass and nuisance actions will depend on whether sufficient property rights have been obtained by the GS operator, and ownership of CO_2 itself may suggest responsibility for any harm resulting from release or migration of the CO_2.

If operation of a GS project results in harm to person or property, common law claims will likely arise, including trespass, nuisance, negligence, abnormally dangerous activities, and potentially other tort law claims. Breach of contract claims may also be available to the extent the GS project operator has agreed to provide CO_2 storage service to a stationary source.

Trespass claims could potentially arise in one of two possible scenarios—trespass to surface property or trespass to subsurface property. Trespass to surface property will most likely be associated with exploratory activities or well construction sites; if property rights are not obtained to authorize those activities, trespass claims may result. Even if exploration activities determine that a particular site is unsuitable for GS, the landowner could potentially claim the trespass resulted in a lost opportunity to lease the land for the exploration rights. A significant release of CO_2 from the storage formation to the surface or shallow subsurface could also give rise to a claim for trespass.

Trespass to subsurface property is less straightforward because property rights for underground geologic formations are often uncertain. Although subsurface property rights may be fairly well-defined in oil and gas rich states, the majority of states have not specifically addressed the specific property rights or liability issues associated with subsurface geologic formations, and those that have addressed the issue are not all consistent. Early cases relied on "negative rule of capture," which suggested that releasing a material underground would not result in a trespass even if the material migrated beneath another's property. But more recent cases have rejected application of the rule of capture to the disposal of materials through underground injection, suggesting that perhaps migration of injected CO_2 could result in an actionable trespass.

Even assuming the migration of injected CO_2 could give rise to an actionable trespass, there are significant hurdles to a recovery under a trespass theory. First, potential plaintiffs will likely find it difficult to prove that the materials have migrated into the subsurface beneath their property. The fact that current regulations rarely, if ever, require monitoring makes it difficult to prove migration of injectates. As a result, most cases will have to either rely on a battle of computational models, which some courts have questioned, or on more direct monitoring, which would likely be cost-prohibitive. Second, future plaintiffs may also have difficulty proving that the trespass resulted in compensable damages. At least one court has even found that some interference with reasonable and foreseeable uses of the subsurface is a necessary element of an actionable subsurface trespass. Proving any compensable diminution in property value resulting from deep underground storage of CO_2 will also prove challenging for future plaintiffs.

Although similar to trespass, nuisance claims involve the interference with the use and enjoyment of property rather than simply the physical invasion of it. Typically, nuisance claims are some of the most amorphous in all the common law, and they depend on the specific facts and circumstances of each claim. If a plaintiff can show that the injection of CO_2 is interfering with the right to enjoy its property, a court may find that the GS constitutes a common law nuisance. Plaintiffs may be able to show interference by either proving an impact to a drinking water well, diminished production from mineral or oil/gas wells, or any impact to the surface that damages the human population or the natural environment.

As with nearly any other enterprise, GS projects will also be exposed to negligence claims if a plaintiff believes that he or she has been harmed by the negligent operation of a CO_2 injection well. The GS operator will have a duty to take precautions against the reasonable risks of harm the project may pose to others. If the operator fails to conduct proper monitoring, or constructs a well in an improper fashion, and harm results, a plaintiff could potentially recover for that harm. A plaintiff could also argue that negligence should be presumed if any of the operator's practices failed to comply with existing statutory or regulatory requirements. Potential plaintiffs will also be faced with other hurdles as well, namely proving that the CO_2 injected by the operator was the cause of the harm. As with other common law actions, proof of actual damages may also be difficult without resort to theoretical models that could be subject to attack.

A final tort theory that could arise in the context of GS is the common law principle of strict liability for abnormally dangerous activities. Generally, the common law will allow a plaintiff to recover for damage resulting from the defendant's engagement in an abnormally dangerous activity without requiring the plaintiff to prove that the defendant was negligent. Essentially, the law presumes that certain activities are so dangerous that any party engaging in such activities should be responsible for any damage that results, regardless of fault.

The activity most often associated with this form of strict liability, and quite possibly the only clear case of an abnormally dangerous activity, is blasting. In fact, almost every court that has accepted the principle of strict liability for abnormally dangerous activities has begun with a case involving blasting, leading many defendants to argue that the doctrine should only apply to blasting cases. On the other hand, plaintiffs, emboldened by the potential prize of escaping the difficult task of proving negligence, have brought abnormally dangerous activity claims in a wide variety of cases, including many activities not usually considered to be abnormally dangerous.

It is unlikely that injection of CO_2 will be considered an abnormally dangerous activity. Courts faced with such claims in the future will likely analyze a number of case-specific factors to determine whether the injection of CO_2 at a particular location should be considered abnormally dangerous. Even if CO_2 injection is determined to be abnormally dangerous in a specific case, the plaintiff must still prove that the activity caused actual damage in order to recover.

A GS project is unlikely to qualify as an abnormally dangerous activity unless the project is conducted in a heavily populated area, significant harm is extremely likely to occur, and no amount of care could eliminate that risk. The issue of whether the benefits of GS outweigh its risks could also arise in the context of attempts to characterize GS as an abnormally dangerous activity. Because of the case-by-case nature of the analysis, and the lack of experience with use of GS for long-term storage of CO_2, it is possible that a court may find a GS project to be abnormally dangerous in certain contexts.

Outside of the tort context, GS operators could also be liable for releases of CO_2 to the extent such releases violate a contract that the operator has with the source of the CO_2. If future climate change legislation or regulation sets up a command-and-control system for addressing CO_2 emissions, sources could be vulnerable to enforcement if its chosen GS operator fails to sequester the CO_2 provided to it. Likewise, in any future cap-and-trade system, sources may fall short on emissions credits if its GS operator allows some of the CO_2 to leak and therefore cannot provide a sufficient number of credits to meet regulatory requirements. Sources of CO_2 are therefore likely to demand from their GS operators contractual protection for the operator's promise to sequester the CO_2 delivered. To the extent GS operators accept such responsibility significant leakage could render GS operators liable for breach of contract.

On the other hand, if the program for regulating GS places the responsibility for regulatory compliance on the operators of the GS project instead of the original source of the CO_2, other issues may arise. For instance, GS operators may demand contract provisions allowing the refusal of any CO_2 in the event the reservoir shows signs of failure. Sources that agree to cease delivery of CO_2, if a failure is detected, could face significant consequences if an alternative storage location is not readily available. Also, a program that releases a source of CO_2 from any compliance duties once the CO_2 is delivered to a GS operator is likely to draw criticism based on the lack of any incentive for sources to choose their GS operators carefully.

A final issue of concern with respect to liability implications of GS projects is the application of statutes of limitation or statutes of repose to common law claims for damage resulting from GS projects. Because of the long-term nature of the storage projects, harm may not result until hundreds of years after the CO_2 is injected into the ground. This may raise a number of potential timing issues for courts to resolve.

FUTURE REMEDIES

Given the legal uncertainty, an appropriate regulatory framework is essential to ensure the risks associated with GS are managed appropriately. While no regulatory program could possibly eliminate all risk, a number of approaches are available to manage the remaining risks and liability associated with GS projects. Private insurance, risk-spreading or risk-allocating contracts, government insurance, compensation funds, and liability caps and exemptions are all possible solutions capable of ensuring that the public is adequately protected from the risks of GS and ensuing potential liability issues do not prevent development of a viable GS industry.

In practice, a combination of these solutions would likely prove most effective. By way of example, the Price-Anderson Act uses a liability cap in combination with mandatory private insurance to spread the risks associated with nuclear power plants. Under this system, nuclear power plant operators must meet certain government set operational safety standards to minimize the likelihood of a catastrophic event. In addition to meeting these regulatory safety standards, operators must purchase insurance for the maximum amount available. If damages exceed this primary insurance amount, each plant must purchase secondary insurance in proscribed amounts. The plants must demonstrate the financial ability to purchase this secondary insurance should it be necessary. The third level of liability limitation is a liability cap, above which the operators will not be liable. A similar combination may prove useful in encouraging GS projects and in ensuring the public is protected from the risks of the industry.

Another solution worthy of some discussion is the use of compensation funds. Compensation funds have been used in a number of different contexts to allocate certain types of risks, most often in the context of personal injury. For example, Congress established the Vaccine Injury Compensation Trust Fund in 1986 to prevent vaccine manufacturers from leaving the market due to perceived liability risks. The fund is financed by an excise tax on the vaccines, and claimants receive compensation by showing either that they have one of the injuries listed on an injury table or by demonstrating that the vaccine caused their injury. The key issues in establishing an appropriate fund are the proper allocations and payment levels, as well as establishment of eligibility and amounts for compensating injured parties from the fund.

Under an administrative GS compensation fund, GS operators or CO_2 producers would periodically make payments into a fund and injured parties could be compensated from that fund through an administrative proceeding. Currently, the uncertainty of risks associated with GS have not risen to the level where Congress is likely to act to create a compensation fund.

CONCLUSION

GS faces many significant technical and legal hurdles, and neither existing regulations nor existing common law fully address these challenges. The absence of legal clarity will have significant consequences. First, deployment of GS technology could be delayed as those seeking to engage in GS struggle with the uncertain legal and regulatory implications of constructing a GS project. Second, a lack of proper regulatory oversight could result in a failure to sufficiently address the unique risks associated with GS. On the other hand, overly burdensome regulations could impede GS projects. Finally, without some clarification as to how common law principles should apply in disputes arising in the GS context, lengthy litigation could result. If different jurisdictions treat GS differently, the legal background may affect siting decisions that should otherwise be made on the basis of technical feasibility alone.

Filling the gaps left by existing law could require the adoption of novel approaches to property rights (such as the framework proposed by the IOGCC) and to liability issues (such as the federal program for nuclear power plants under the Price-Anderson Act) that will likely arise in the context of GS. Regardless of the approach taken, establishing regulatory and legal certainty will be necessary to advance GS and foster a viable GS industry. Failure to develop a comprehensive legal framework for GS prior to establishing actual emissions reduction requirements would be unfortunate.

Notes and Questions

1. Regarding liability issues, Glaser et al. in their article excerpted above also note that:

> To the extent GS projects are not co-located with the stationary sources capturing the CO_2 that will be injected, there will also be risks associated with transportation of the CO_2 from the source to the storage reservoir. Generally, such transportation will occur via pipeline and is currently regulated under the Hazardous Liquids Pipeline Safety Act. 49 U.S.C § 60102 (2000); 49 C.F.R. § 195. Large volumes of CO_2 are already being moved safely under that program as part of enhanced oil recovery projects, but common law liability concerns will nevertheless continue to exist * * * [because] compliance with regulatory requirements does not provide immunity from common law liability. See Action Marine v. Cont'l Carbon, Inc., 481 F.3d 1302, 1320 (11th Cir. 2007) (noting that an air quality permit does not empower a company to damage property) * * * [and that] CO_2 does not qualify as a "natural gas" [exempted from] the SDWA. Arco v. EPA, 14 F.3d 1431, 1436-37 (10th Cir. 1993). Glaser et al. supra nn. 36, 56, 80.

Separate SDWA regulations for GS were proposed by EPA and are codified at 40 C.F.R. Parts 144 and 146. See also O. Anderson, Geologic CO_2 Sequestration: Who Owns the Pore Space?, 9 Wyo. L. Rev. 97 (2009); A. Andrews, Picking Up on What's Going Underground: Australia Should Exempt Carbon Capture and Geo-Sequestration from Part III A of the Trade Practices Act, 17 Pacific Rim L. & Policy J. 407 (2008); D. Attanasio, Surveying the Risks of Carbon Dioxide: Geological Sequestration and Storage Projects in the United States, 39 Envtl. L. Rep. 10376 (2009); L. Baugh & W. Troutman, Assessing the Challenges of Geologic Carbon Capture and Sequestration: A California Guide to the Cost of Reducing CO_2 Emissions, IX Sustainable Dev. L. & Policy Winter 2009 at 16; S. Bryant, Geologic CO_2 Storage–Can the Oil and Gas Industry Help Save the Planet, 2008 Mineral Law Institute at 2-11 J. Fish & J. Wood, Geologic Carbon Sequestration: Property Rights and Regulation, 54 Rocky Mtn. Min. L. Inst. 2-1 (2008); 54 Rocky Mtn. L. Inst. 3-1 (2008); D. Hayano, Guarding the Viability of Coal and Coal-Fired Power Plants: A Road Map for Wyoming's Cradle to Grave Regulation of Geologic CO_2 Sequestration, 9 Wyo. L. Rev. 139 (2009); D. Hayes & J. Beauvais, Carbon Sequestration in M. Gerrard, ed., Global Climate Change and U.S. Law (2007); A. Klass & E. Wilson, Climate Change and Carbon Sequestration: Assessing a Liability Regime for Long-Term Storage of Carbon Dioxides 58 Emory L.J. 103 (2008).

2. Regarding the link between CO_2 emissions regulation and GS projects, consider the following from D. Hunter et al., International Environmental Law and Policy 658 (3d ed. 2007):

In addition to questions over the long–term viability of underground sequestration and serious public health issues, one of the main barriers to deploying * * * [GS] technology is cost. Generally speaking, it would have to be cheaper for power plants to sequester CO_2 emissions underground than emit them into the atmosphere in order for the technology to be viable. In December 2005, the U.S. Department of Energy estimated that it costs about $150/tonne to sequester carbon with current technologies, noting that at that time the price of a carbon allowance under the European Union's Emissions Trading System was around $25 per tonne. But BP and other companies interested in * * * [GS] predict that at some point, as emissions regulations grow more stringent, it will eventually be cheaper to store carbon underground than to emit it into the atmosphere.

PROBLEM EXERCISE ON LEGAL ASPECTS OF BIOLOGIC AND GEOLOGIC SEQUESTRATION

H.R. 2454 (111th Cong. June 26, 2009) would mandate a studies of legal and regulatory barriers to biologic and geologic sequestration as part of its comprehensive climate change provisions. Based on the above excerpts, which legal issues would you recommend be highlighted in the study? Can sequestration risks be adequately managed under current federal and state environmental laws? That issue would also be studied under H.R. 2454. H.R. 2454 also would establish a national tree planting program and recognize emission offset credits from U.S. agriculture and forestry sources.

4. Ocean Sequestration

a. Ocean Fertilization

Ocean "fertilization" to stimulate CO_2 absorption in the marine environment has been attempted. According to D. Hunter at al., International Environmental Law and Policy 659 (3d ed. 2007): "In 1999, an international research team dumped over 8600 kilograms of iron into the ocean off the coast of Tasmania. One month later, the algae bloom could be seen from satellites and an estimated 3000 tons of carbon were removed from the atmosphere to the sea. Margaret Munro, Ironing out Global Warming, The National Post, A18 (Oct. 17, 2000); Phillip Boyd, et al., A Mesoscale Phytoplankton Bloom in the Polar Southern Ocean Stimulated by Iron Fertilization, Nature 695-702 (Oct. 12, 2000)." What authority determines if such conduct conforms to the international law of the sea?

In November 2007 U.S. based Planktos, Inc. withdrew its proposal to dump hundreds of tons of iron into the ocean near the Galapagos Islands to stimulate a CO_2 absorbing phytoplankton bloom. The following article examines ocean fertilization in Southern Ocean waters surrounding Antarctica as a sequestration technique. See also D. Freestone & R. Rayfuse, Ocean Iron Fertilization and International Law, 364 Marine Ecology Progress Series 227 (2008); R. Rayfuse, M. Lawrence, & K. Gjerde, Ocean Fertilisation and Climate Change: The Need to Regulate Emerging High Seas Use, 23 Intl. J. of Marine & Coastal L. 297 (2008). Are these examples of geo-engineering, that is irreversible, beyond "mere" sequestration?

THE DAY AFTER TOMORROW: OCEAN CO₂ SEQUESTRATION AND THE FUTURE OF CLIMATE CHANGE

Karen N. Scott
18 Georgetown Intl. Envtl. L. Rev. 57 (2005)

IV. Ocean Fertilization Techniques

The * * * technique of oceanic CO_2 sequestration seeks to increase CO_2 uptake by enhancing the ocean's biological pump or, more euphemistically, its invisible forest. In many ways this is the most controversial proposed climate change mitigation measure, partly because of the potential impact it may have on the vulnerable Antarctic ecosystem and partly because there is a growing body of research which disputes its effectiveness in actually increasing long-term oceanic CO_2 uptake. It is well known that parts of the oceans, such as the North and Equatorial Pacific and Southern Ocean, are relatively "infertile," meaning that although nutrients are high, plankton biomass is low. As early as 1934 it was suggested that the relative scarcity of iron (Fe) in the Southern Ocean may be the cause of low phytoplankton density in the region. In the late 1980s, extrapolating from evidence discovered in the Vostok ice core, which suggested that concentrations of CO_2 were low when atmospheric iron dust was abundant, John H. Martin concluded that iron was a limiting factor in phytoplankton productivity and, consequently, in the biological uptake of CO_2. This led to his famous conclusion, "Give me half a tanker of iron and I will give you an ice-age." Martin advocated the addition of iron dust to infertile regions so as to stimulate algal blooms, which would result in the uptake of substantial quantities of CO_2, transporting it into the deep ocean and sequestering it from the atmosphere for many hundreds of years.

In any case, even if Martin's original hypothesis is proved correct, there is growing consensus among scientists that, contrary to earlier estimates, an area larger than the Southern Ocean would have to be fertilized in order to draw down just thirty percent of annual anthropogenic CO_2 emissions. This raises doubts over the efficacy of fertilization induced sequestration. In contrast to geological and even direct ocean injection storage strategies, substantial short term leakage of CO_2 from the ocean into the atmosphere is predicted under this approach, which could only be prevented if fertilization were sustained over fifty or even one hundred years. Moreover, scientists have suggested that because the Southern Ocean is a deep-water source for the tropics, an increase in biological activity in the former zone may cause a decrease in biological activity and, accordingly, a decrease in the draw down of CO_2 in the latter. Tropical productivity may actually exceed the increase in Southern Ocean capacity. * * *

Notwithstanding the predicted impacts and scientific uncertainty that surround this method of sequestration, four fertilization experiments have been carried out to date within the Pacific and, more recently, the Southern Ocean. There have also been a number of applications filed for U.S. commercial patents with respect to fertilization processes. Although these activities have been largely ignored by international lawyers, it is axiomatic that fertilization experimentation should be carried out in a manner which is consistent with the environmental provisions of UNCLOS. More particularly, given that the focus of the most recent experiments has been on the Southern Ocean, the 1959 Antarctic Treaty and 1991 Protocol to the Antarctic Treaty on Environmental Protection are of regulatory relevance in this context.

A.   Ocean Fertilization within the Framework of UNCLOS

States' broad rights and duties to explore and exploit the oceans as set out above in relation to geological and, particularly, direct injection sequestration strategies are equally applicable to ocean fertilization with iron or other nutrients. In particular, the freedoms of the high seas are pertinent as fertilization takes place on the surface of the sea and the region where success is most likely is the Southern Ocean, which, in general, comprises high seas.

To date, ocean fertilization has taken place in the context of scientific experimentation as opposed to large-scale sequestration projects. All states have the right to conduct scientific research in or on the oceans subject to a number of general principles. Research must be compatible with UNCLOS, avoid unjustifiable interference with other users, including those with fishing interests, and comply with all relevant regulations, including those enacted for the protection and preservation of the marine environment. Within the territorial sea it is the coastal state which has the exclusive right to authorize research. Within the Exclusive Economic Zone (EEZ) or on the continental shelf, on the other hand, although the consent of the coastal state must be obtained prior to carrying out research, such consent must not normally be withheld where it is designed to benefit mankind. It can be argued that research into all sequestration strategies is for the benefit of mankind if it assists in the mitigation of climate change; nevertheless, the consent of the coastal state can be withheld where the research involves the "introduction of a harmful substance into the environment," such as CO_2 or even iron dust, drilling onto the continental shelf, or the construction of an artificial installation. Finally, it should be noted that states and relevant international organizations are responsible and liable for damage caused by pollution of the marine environment arising out of marine scientific research activities.

Ocean fertilization activities will be subject to the general duties of UNCLOS to prevent pollution and to protect and preserve the marine environment. In contrast to geological and direct injection strategies, ocean fertilization activities do not involve the direct introduction of CO_2 into the marine environment. It is not clear whether the introduction of iron dust into the marine environment constitutes pollution as defined in Article 1(1)(4) of UNCLOS. Indeed, rather than harm local biodiversity, its addition is designed to stimulate biological growth. The predicted negative consequences of fertilization lie in the impacts an enhanced phytoplankton biomass will have on the wider ecosystem and food chain. Nevertheless, iron dust introduced into the ocean to stimulate phytoplankton productivity *should* be classed as "pollution," as there is a direct causal link between the substance introduced and the consequential harm to the marine environment. It is, however, unlikely that the increased CO_2 uptake can be described as "pollution," notwithstanding that the definition of pollution includes *indirect* introduction of substances into the marine environment. Unlike geological or direct injection sequestration strategies, the draw down of CO_2 into the marine environment is a natural process. Moreover, not only is it difficult to realistically assess how much CO_2 is sequestered via the biological pump, as opposed to the solubility pump, it would be almost impossible to determine whether CO_2 sequestration has occurred as a result of fertilized or unfertilized phytoplankton and indeed whether sequestered CO_2 is anthropogenic in origin.

Parties are obligated to take all measures to reduce pollution from *any source*. Moreover, Article 196(1) stipulates that states shall take all measures necessary to prevent, reduce and control pollution of the marine environment resulting from the use of technologies under their jurisdiction or control, or the intentional or accidental introduction of species, alien or new, to a particular part of the marine environment, which may cause significant and harmful changes thereto.

A potential negative consequence of iron fertilization is the stimulation of toxic algae and non-indigenous phytoplankton, which may alter the local ecology or impact fragile food chains, such as those in the Antarctic region. However, as discussed above in the context of pollution, fertilization projects do not involve the addition, intentionally or even accidentally, of alien species. This is an indirect consequence of fertilization strategies and therefore, arguably, such strategies are not regulated by Article 196 of UNCLOS.

Beyond these general obligations, UNCLOS provides a limited scope for the regulation of ocean fertilization activities. The process whereby iron dust is deliberately released from vessels into the marine environment bears much in common with the practice of dumping. However, the definition of dumping refers to the deliberate *disposal* of wastes and excludes the "placement of matter for a purpose other then mere disposal, provided that such placement is not contrary to the aims of" UNCLOS. Even if iron dust is categorized as "waste," its release into the marine environment is clearly for a purpose other than disposal, namely, that of stimulating phytoplankton growth in order to draw down CO_2 from the atmosphere. Notwithstanding that the term "placement" is more appropriate to the toppling of platforms and the sinking of vessels to form artificial reefs, the provision when taken as a whole is likely to exclude the release of iron dust for the purpose of fertilization from the definition of dumping. Nevertheless, all placement activities must be reported to the International Maritime Organization. While iron dust originates from land, the fact that it is released from a vessel means that it cannot be categorized as a land-based source of pollution. Nor, however, is it technically vessel-source pollution, as Article 211 of UNCLOS applies the global standards of MARPOL 73/78, which regulates operational and accidental vessel-source pollution only. However, the general environmental provisions of UNCLOS, most notably those relating to environmental impact assessment, monitoring, and the controls on marine scientific research are clearly applicable to fertilization experiments and projects.

B.   Regional Controls of Ocean Fertilization: The Southern Ocean

While a number of fertilization experiments have taken place in the North Pacific, research suggests that the most promising region for enhanced biological sequestration of CO_2 is the Southern Ocean. Parts of this region benefit from the relatively stringent environmental protection provided in the 1991 Protocol to the Antarctic Treaty on Environmental Protection (Madrid Protocol) and the 1980 Convention on the Conservation of Antarctic Marine Living Resources (CCAMLR). * * *

The Madrid Protocol ambitiously aims to protect "the Antarctic environment and dependent and associated ecosystems and the intrinsic value of Antarctica, including its wilderness and aesthetic values and its value as an area for the conduct of scientific research." The emphasis of the Madrid Protocol on ecosystem protection, notwithstanding its evident geographical limitation, is important in the context of ocean fertilization activities. Fertilization of the ocean may lead to undesirable impacts on the ecosystem and food chain that may be detrimental to the wider Antarctic environment.

In contrast to the instruments discussed above in the context of geological and direct injection sequestration of CO_2 the controls on marine pollution within the Southern Ocean are unlikely to be suitable for the regulation of iron fertilization activities. Annex IV of the Madrid Protocol is primarily concerned with the control of pollution from vessels and essentially implements the provisions of MARPOL 73/78 on a regional basis. Rather, it is the general provisions of the Madrid Protocol that address planning activities and, to a lesser extent, seek to protect Antarctic flora and fauna that are likely to prove significant.

The facilitation of scientific research within the region is a fundamental aim not only of the Madrid Protocol but also of the 1959 Antarctic Treaty itself. In particular, scientific research that is necessary for the better understanding of the global environment is to be accorded priority when carried out within the ATA. These provisions may well benefit the conduct of fertilization experimentation, as opposed to commercial projects, particularly where the experiments further scientific understanding of the ocean carbon cycle. Nevertheless, the stringent planning regulations provided for under the Madrid Protocol are as applicable to research projects as they are to tourism or plans to establish a scientific base. All activities must be planned and conducted so as to limit adverse effects on the Antarctic environment and dependent and associated ecosystems, as well as to avoid adverse effects on climate and weather patterns. More relevantly, activities must also avoid significant adverse effects on water quality, significant changes in marine environments, and detrimental changes in the distribution, abundance, or productivity of species or populations of species of flora and fauna. Research suggests that iron fertilization may well lead to adverse effects on water quality such as, in a worst case scenario, the deprivation of oxygen within areas of the Southern Ocean, creating so-called dead zones. Such activities are also likely to lead to other significant changes in the marine environment that may fall outside of the text of Article 3(2)(b)(iii) of the Madrid Protocol, which does not appear to require a *detrimental* change. Irregardless, the whole process of iron fertilization is designed to cause an alteration in the abundance and productivity of phytoplankton. In contrast to Article 3(2)(b)(iii), Article 3(2)(b)(iv) seeks to prevent a *detrimental* change and while this is a possible consequence of fertilization, it is not necessarily inevitable.

All activities which have more than a minor or transitory impact on the environment are subject to either an initial environmental evaluation (IEE) or a comprehensive environmental evaluation (CEE) pursuant to Article 8 and Annex I of the Madrid Protocol. Where the activity has less than a minor or a transitory impact, it may proceed without an environmental impact assessment, but must comply with other relevant provisions of the Madrid Protocol. Fertilization for the purpose of scientific experimentation would likely be regarded as having a transitory impact only. Notwithstanding concerns that algal blooms induced by iron fertilization last for longer than natural blooms, the extent of the impact seems to be confined to less than a month and takes place over a relatively small patch of ocean. However, commercial projects that would need to be carried out over a number of years within a vast geographical region would undoubtedly be subject to the CEE provisions.

Theoretically, of course, a CEE can legitimately be confined to the ATA. However, where such projects extend beyond this area, a CEE arguably should consider the area of potential impact as a whole, in order to maintain consistency with the Madrid Protocol's objective to protect Antarctica and its dependant and associated ecosystems. Where the project takes place wholly outside the ATA there does not appear to be an obligation to carry out a CEE under the Madrid Protocol, although the environmental impact assessment provisions under UNCLOS will apply. * * *

The Madrid Protocol also provides for specific obligations with respect to the protection of native flora and fauna. In particular, the taking of, or harmful interference with, native flora and fauna is prohibited, except where authorized by a permit. It is unclear as to whether phytoplankton is included within the remit of Annex II given that native plants are defined as including terrestrial and freshwater algae only. However, more broadly, "harmful interference" is defined as including "any activity that results in the significant adverse *modification of habitats* of any species or populations of native mammal, bird, plant, or invertebrate." Iron fertilization, as noted above, is clearly designed to modify the marine habitat in confined areas and such modification may be significantly adverse if oxygen levels are reduced in the seawater or toxic algae are introduced. Harmful interference may be authorized by means of a permit "to provide for unavoidable consequences of scientific activities," but the issuance of permits must be limited in order to ensure that "the diversity of species, as well as the habitats essential to their existence, and the *balance of the ecological systems* existing within the [ATA] are maintained."

The introduction of non-native species into the Antarctic ecosystem that may occur as a consequence of iron fertilization is prohibited. More relevantly, parties to the Madrid Protocol must take precautions in order to prevent the introduction of micro-organisms, including viruses, bacteria, parasites, yeasts, and fungi, not present in native flora and fauna in the region. This would include those micro-organisms introduced as a result of fertilization activities. Finally, areas designated Antarctic Specially Protected Areas and Antarctic Specially Managed Areas under Annex V of the Madrid Protocol benefit from more stringent regulation, or even prohibition, of activities which take place therein. It would be most unlikely that fertilization experiments could take place within these areas and, indeed, areas of the marine environment could be specially designated in order to prevent such activities from taking place therein.

In contrast to the Madrid Protocol, the CCAMLR applies to the whole Antarctic ecosystem, meaning, to all species, which is broadly defined as including fin fish, mollusks, crustaceans, birds, and *all other species of living organisms* found south of the Antarctic Convergence. However, CCAMLR regulates only harvesting and associated activities. Accordingly, CCAMLR will be relevant in the context of fertilization experiments only if the experiments can be categorized as "activities associated with harvesting." At first sight this would appear to be unlikely. However, a predicted byproduct of fertilization programs is an increase in fish biomass and, indeed, some early fertilization experiments had this rather than climate change mitigation as their aim. * * *

In conclusion, while the Madrid Protocol does not prevent either scientific experimentation or commercial fertilization projects *per se*, the impacts on the Antarctic ecosystem of all activities within the ATA must be considered, particularly in relation to habitat alteration. Undoubtedly any commercial project designed to fertilize large areas of the Southern Ocean, within the ATA, over a substantial period of time must seek authorization by means of carrying out a CEE. It is possible that the Madrid Protocol's environmental impact provisions do not apply to small-scale experimental activities where the impacts are likely to be transitory. Nevertheless, if numerous small-scale fertilization experiments are carried out over a similar time scale, their cumulative impact may be substantial and therefore require an impact assessment. Where fertilization experiments and projects intend to mitigate climate change, it is unlikely that CCAMLR will be applicable, even where an increase in fish biomass is a byproduct of the activity. * * *

[Scott concludes as follows with respect to use of the oceans for direct injection of CO_2 into ocean waters, seabed carbon sequestration, and fertilization:]

An examination of the current legal framework suggests that the direct injection of CO_2 into the water column or beneath the seabed from a vessel or platform is prohibited under UNCLOS and its associated instruments, unless such activities constitute scientific experimentation or take place as part of an enhanced oil and gas recovery procedure. This analysis also appears to be consistent with the tenor of the conclusions reached by the OSPAR Group of Jurists and Linguists with respect to the placement of CO_2 in the OSPAR region. Unless the parties to both the OSPAR Convention and the London regime dissent from this interpretation, it will be necessary to amend all three instruments in order to permit such sequestration activities. In the past, these instruments generally have been amended in order to prohibit *existing* dumping practices. Nevertheless, a convention amendment designed to permit the release of a *new* substance into the marine environment might be regarded as a novel, but not necessarily an improbable, development. Any amendment must of course be consistent with the object and purpose of each instrument, and implement a precautionary approach to ocean ecosystem management.

By comparison, CO_2 disposed of from land onto or under the seabed is permissible, subject to minimal and largely hortatory regulation. Accordingly, this is an issue which ought to feature on the agendas of relevant global and regional organizations, such as the United Nations Open-Ended Informal Consultative Process on Oceans and the Law of the Sea, the OSPAR Commission, and UNEP, with a view to their developing regulation with respect to sequestration processes effected from land. Moreover, these organizations also provide appropriate forums for the formulation of detailed and rigorous guidelines to govern the execution of scientific research on, in, and under the oceans, which would complement the general principles as provided in Part XIII of UNCLOS. Where CO_2 sequestration related activities take place beyond national jurisdictions, such as within the Area of the Southern Ocean, they should be managed by the appropriate international organization. Within the Area, activities such as direct ocean injection of CO_2 must be conducted so as to avoid harmful effects to the marine environment and to contribute to the benefit of mankind. * * *

Inevitably the ultimate decision to engage in, or not to engage in, oceanic CO_2 sequestration will be made on the basis of policy and politics as opposed to treaty interpretation. UNCLOS is sufficiently ambiguous to admit an interpretation of its obligations under Part XII as *either* permitting *or* prohibiting oceanic sequestration activities. Instruments such as the 1996 London Protocol and the OSPAR Convention are amenable to amendment in the event of an interpretation of their obligations that is regarded as unfavorable to an appropriate quorum of parties. Consequently, the ultimate question is not whether oceanic CO_2 sequestration is *lawful*, but whether it is *legitimate*.

The decision to engage in, or not to engage in, oceanic CO_2 sequestration must be underpinned by the fundamental values of sustainable development, precaution, and concern for the interests of future generations. These values or principles represent the quiddity of the law of the sea as it relates to environmental protection, the climate change regime, and modern international environmental law generally. While not inevitably incompatible with sustainable development, excessive reliance on oceanic CO_2 sequestration to mitigate the impacts of climate change, as opposed to reducing emissions at the source, is unlikely to be sustainable in the long run. Moreover, the scientific uncertainty surrounding the nature of the ocean carbon cycle and the impact that increased CO_2 concentrations will have on the marine environment suggests that in the interests of precaution, direct injection of CO_2 and ocean fertilization with iron ought not to be permitted at this point in time. Finally, it must also be assessed whether an increased oceanic CO_2 concentration, combined with the risk that CO_2 may be unexpectedly released from the oceans into the atmosphere (thus making climate change much worse in the medium term), is in the interests of future generations. Conversely, it may be contended that the potential impacts of climate change are so great that oceanic CO_2 sequestration represents a sustainable mitigation measure. Risks associated with geological sequestration, as well as direct injection and fertilization techniques, might be deemed acceptable when assessed in the context of a catastrophic climate change event, and consequently, oceanic CO_2 storage is arguably in the interests of future generations. It is ineluctable that notwithstanding the work already undertaken, and due to be executed by a number of marine-related organizations, oceanic CO_2 sequestration as a climate change mitigation measure must ultimately be examined by the parties to the UNFCCC within the broader context of a global climate change mitigation strategy.

Notes and Questions

1. For analysis of the application of the London Convention and its 1996 Protocol to undersea carbon sequestration by nations party to those treaties, see R. Purdy, The Legal Implications of Carbon Capture and Storage Under the Sea, VII Sustainable Development Law & Policy Fall 2006 at 22. See also A. Weeks, Subsea Carbon Dioxide Sequestration as a Climate Mitigation Option for the Eastern United States: A Preliminary Assessment of Technology and Law, 12 Ocean & Coastal L. J. 245 (2007).

2. Underground injection of CO_2 has been used since the early 1970s to enhance recovery of oil and gas. For oil and gas fields leased from the federal government on the U.S. Outer Continental Shelf (OCS), section 354(a)(2)(B) of the 2005 Energy Policy Act, P.L. 109-58 (July 27, 2005), authorizes reductions in the royalties charged oil companies who increase their production by injecting CO_2 into their OCS wells. See 71 Fed. Reg. 11577 (March 8, 2006).

3. For domestic ocean carbon sequestration legislation, a possible model for the U.S. is Australia's federal and parallel state legislation which is described in J. Fahey & R. Lyster, Geosequestration in Australia: Existing and Proposed Regulatory Mechanisms, 4 J. Eur. Envtl. Plan. L. 378 (2007). Australia ratified the Kyoto Protocol in 2008, established a cabinet-level Minister for Climate Change, and is proceeding more quickly than the U.S. with climate change mitigation and adaptation measures in several sectors. See http://www.climatechange.gov.au/emissionstrading/legislation/index.html.
See also L. Godden, Law in the Schism: Its Role in Moving Beyond the Carbon Economy in Australia, in D. Zillman et al., eds, Beyond the Carbon Economy: Energy Law in Transition 459-280 (2008); R. Lyster, Chasing Down the Climate Change Footprint of the Public and Private Sectors: Forces Converge–Part I, 24 Envtl. & Planning L. J. 281 (2007), Part II, id. at 450; J. Stephens, A Slow Burn: The Emergence of Climate Change Law in Australia, in G. Burch ed., Water, Wind, Art and Debate: How Environmental Concerns Impact on Disciplinary Research (2007); S. Scott & R. Refuse, Special Issue: Australia's Climate Change Law and Diplomacy, 11 Asia Pac. J. of Envtl. L. 1 (2008).

Regarding climate change litigation in Australia, see J. Boch & J. Brown, Recent Developments in Australian Climate Change Litigation: Forward Momentum from Down Under, VIII Sustainable Devel. L. & Policy Winter 2008 at 39; L. McAllister Litigating Climate Change at the Coal Mine, 45 San Diego L. Rev. No. 2 (2008); J. Peel, The Role of Climate Change Litigation in

Australia's Response to Global Warming, 24 Envtl. & Planning L. J. 90 (2007; J. Peel & L. Godden, IX Sustainable Devel. L. & Policy Winter 2009 at 37; J. Smith & D. Shearman, Climate Change Litigation: Analysing the Law, Scientific Evidence & Impacts on the Environment, Health & Property (2006). For an early unsuccessful challenge to a coal-fired power plant in New South Wales, Australia, see Greenpeace Australia v. Redbank Power Co., 86 LGERA 143 (1994).

E. DEPLOYING OCEAN RENEWABLES

CONFLICT RESOLUTION FOR ADDRESSING CLIMATE CHANGE WITH OCEAN-ALTERING PROJECTS
Mark J. Spalding and Charlotte de Fontaubert
37 Environmental Law Reporter 10740 (2007)

* * * [M]any new emerging technologies designed to address climate change through the development of alternative sources of energy are increasingly being deployed in marine ecosystems. The most promising of these technologies are also the most threatening to marine ecosystems: offshore wind farms; carbon sequestration; tidal and wave energy; and ocean thermal energy conversion (OTEC). While the impact of these new technologies is often localized, the benefits expected from their development are global in scale, leading to the question of how to know whether 'a few places shall be sacrificed for the good of the whole.'

Table 1. Examples of Problems With Wind and
Wave Energy Projects

Issues With Wind Energy	Issues With Wave Energy
Damage to natural sea floor at placement and under cables	Disturbance or indirect destruction of marine life
Fragmentation of habitat	Site closed to fishing
Relatively low return of energy per built acre	Turbine blade mortality to marine life
Noise pollution from construction and operational vibrations	Threat to navigation accident/spills
Seabird kills from turbine blade collisions	Vulnerable to sea-level rise, changes in current patterns, and storms
Threat to navigation	
Vulnerable to climate pattern shifts and intense storms	

* * *

One of the problems with addressing climate change is that some of the sources of clean energy that can help reduce the severity of climate change may require placing structures on the sea floor, in the water column, or on the coast—solutions involving structures that the ocean conservation community normally views as threats to coastal and benthic habitats, waves, or various marine species. Unfortunately, it is becoming more accepted that climate change cannot be slowed without the development of clean energy, which, paradoxically, may be detrimental to the health of local oceans. There is an increasingly vocal interest in tapping the oceans for alternative energy sources such as wind and tidal/wave power.

At the very least, then, the costs of clean energy projects in the ocean must be compared against those that would result from likely offshore oil and gas developments. Great untapped oil resources likely lie in offshore reserves, as recently evidenced by the large reserves found in the Gulf of Mexico by Chevron. Likewise, proposals for new oil and gas rigs and pipelines, as well as facilities for liquefied natural gas, have appeared mostly along the coasts, particularly in the United States. There are increased risks and impacts from seismic surveys on the continental shelf, particularly for marine mammals, and the exploitation of seabed methane is being considered.

Table 2. Environmental Accounting (Cost-Benefit Analysis) of Clean Energy Projects and Offshore Drilling in Marine Ecosystems

"Clean" Energy Projects in Marine Ecosystems	Offshore Oil and Gas Drilling
Short-term destruction of local coastal and marine ecosystem	Short-term destruction of local coastal and marine ecosystem
Potential permanent long-term benefits of new structures as artificial reefs	Potential mid-term, but ultimately ephemeral benefits of new structures as artificial reefs
No risks of discharge due to the absence of hydrocarbons	Long-term destruction risk due to operational discharges (ultimately unavoidable)
No increased risks of discharge due to absence of hydrocarbons	Increased short and long-term risks due to accidental discharges (risks linked to collisions, explosions, etc.)
Sustainability of the projects, which do not call for the development of new sites, particularly if sufficient conservation measures are undertaken in parallel	Long-term exhaustion of resources and need for further sites, even if sufficient conservation measures are undertaken in parallel

As shown in Table 2, the question is not one of knowing whether there will be potentially destructive projects in coastal and marine areas, but rather, whether these projects will be devoted to clean energy or the further exploitation of hydrocarbon resources known to contribute greatly to climate change. In both cases, local communities are often vocal in their opposition to such developments. States like California have succeeded in opposing federally mandated off-shore oil exploration, while others, such as Alabama, Louisiana, Mississippi, and Texas, have been more welcoming, anticipating economic benefits from such developments, especially in the wake of a new law returning a greater portion of the revenue to states' coffers.

Perhaps the best-known example of local opposition to coastal energy development is playing out in the near-shore waters off Cape Cod in Massachusetts, where eight energy generation wind farms have been proposed. The wind farms are expected to provide alternative sources of energy to supplement other more conventional sources to meet prospective energy demand, and to thus improve air quality and contribute to a reduction in GHG emissions. There has, however, been strong and vocal opposition from local communities and environmental groups who are opposed to the projects on aesthetic and habitat disruption grounds. The Cape Wind project includes a proposal for a 130-turbine wind farm in Nantucket Sound and is the first off-shore wind energy project to go through the federal permitting process. Opponents believe that the project will have negative impacts on navigation, fishing, boating, birds, and commercial recreation and tourism. In this location, some groups seek responsible project implementation, while others seek ocean protection, aesthetic protection, and no project alternatives. * * *

To build anything in the oceans will induce change, which is a major reason why marine and coastal conservation groups have worked so hard to get restrictions on construction of everything from piers to drilling platforms. Clearly, the Cape Wind opposition has to decide whether a Cape Wind project is worth the sacrifice of the benthic community and seabirds, as well as disturbance of other marine plants and animals. Some groups will continue to answer no, often on not-in-my-backyard grounds, while others are clearly arguing that the local sacrifice is justified in the face of the larger global threat of climate change. On the other side of the equation, many scientists argue that climate change could be the single biggest threat to the oceans, now and in the future, making reductions in the emission of GHGs one of several priorities. Tapping alternative energy in the ocean could replace fuels that are far more dangerous from a climate change perspective, and thus, may be worth the immediate environmental risk. Wind farms can cause local disruption to marine ecosystems and coastal communities, but they may also bring regional improvements in air quality and reductions in airborne nitrogen deposition into watersheds if they replace "dirtier" sources of electric power. A deep skepticism of all energy development has affected views on an energy policy for the ocean. The poor environmental track record of oil production and the shipping industry reinforces this skepticism. However, the complex intersection with the climate change issue and the promise of cleaner fuels argues for a careful, thoughtful, and to the extent possible, unemotional reassessment of the U.S. attitude toward coastal energy development. A positive environmental agenda with regard to energy may help leverage progress on marine-protected areas, ecosystem-based planning, and vital reforms to ocean governance, as all of these issues are interconnected and will relate to efforts on ocean zoning and use designations.

* * * * *

Legal processes for resolving the conflicts identified by Spalding and de Fontaubert include those administered by the Interior Department's Minerals Management Service (MMS) under the Outer Continental Shelf Lands Act (OCSLA), see Center for Biological Diversity v. U.S. Dept. of Interior, 2009 U.S. App. LEXIS 8097 (D.C. Cir. April 17, 2009) (oil and gas consumption's climate change impacts not required to be considered in issuing offshore oil and gas leasing program), and by the Federal Energy Regulatory Commission (FERC) under the Federal Power Act (FPA).

For renewable ocean energy facilities located on the OCS beyond coastal state boundaries 3 nautical miles offshore, OCSLA § 8(p), 43 U.S. § 1337(p), requires MMS to:

(1) consult with state and local governments;
(2) collect a 'fair return' and distribute 27% of the revenues from 3-6 miles offshore to coast states within 15 miles of the facility;
(3) get surety bonds or other security from the OCS lessee operating the facility;
(4) reject facilities located in offshore national parks, monuments, wildlife refuges, and marine sanctuaries.

Section 8(p) also preserves the jurisdiction of other federal and state agencies rather than preempting them, and in April 2009 the Interior Secretary and FERC's Acting Chairman agreed that FERC would be the primary siting authority for OCS wave energy projects which would also require OCS leases from MMS. Under the Memorandum of Understanding, MMS retains exclusive jurisdiction over OCS wind and solar projects. See Memorandum of Understanding between the U.S. Department of the Interior and the Federal Energy Regulatory Commission (Apr. 9, 2009), http://www.ferc.gov/legal/majord-reg/mou/mou-doi.pdf. Regulations implementing section 8(p) are in 30 C.F.R. pts 250, 285, 290 and are summarized in the excerpt below. Using those regulations, the Interior Department issued five exploratory OCS wind energy leases off New Jersey and Delaware in June 2009. See also 74 Fed. Reg. 35204 (July 20, 2009) (MMS offshore renewables application procedures); MMS, Alternative Energy Programmatic EIS (Oct. 2007); MMS, Worldwide Synthesis and Analysis of Existing Information Regarding Environmental Effects of Alternative Energy Uses on The Outer Continental Shelf (OCS Study MMS 2007-038 July 2007).

Regarding the Cape Wind project discussed by Spalding and de Fontaubert, federal approval of a data gathering tower for the project was upheld in Ten Taxpayer Citizens Group v. Cape Wind Associates, 373 F.3d 183 (1st Cir. 2004) and Alliance to Protect Nantucket Sound v. U.S. Army, 98 F.3d 105 (1st Cir. 2005); see B. Brown & B. Escobar, Wind Power: Generating Electricity and Lawsuits, 28 Energy L.J. 489 (2007); J. Firestone & W. Kempton, Public Opinion About Large Offshore Wind Power: Underlying Factors , 35 Energy Policy 1584 (2007); J. Hadam, The Latest Development in the Debate over Nantucket Sound: Alliance to Protect Nantucket Sound, Inc. v. Energy Facilities Siting Board, 13 Ocean & Coastal L.J. 121 (2007); M. Koehler, Developing Wind Power Projects in Massachusetts: Anticipating and Avoiding Litigation in the Quest to Harness the Wind, 12 Suffolk J. Trial & App. Advoc. 69 (2007); T. Hayden, Reception on Nantucket Sound? A Summary of Current Offshore Wind Farm Litigation and a Federal Legislative Proposal Taking Cues from Cellular Tower Legislation, 13 Penn St. Envtl. L. Rev. 217 (2005); R. Kennedy, Jr., An Ill Wind Off Cape Cod, The New York Times, Dec. 16, 2006.

In Texas' Gulf of Mexico waters an offshore wind developer has leased 11,355 acres from the state and installed a data gathering tower. Offshore Wind Energy: Texas and Massachusetts Rush to be First, NOAA Coastal Services, May/June 2007 at 4. A proposed wind project off the northwest coast of British Columbia has drawn opposition from local crab fishermen and environmentalists. Pacific Fishing July 2008 at 18. See also Center for Biological Diversity v. FPL Group, 146 Cal. App. 4th 1349 (2008). See generally J. Firestone et al., Regulating Offshore Wind Power and Aquaculture: Messages from Land and Sea, 14 Cornell J. of L. & Public Policy 71 (2004), reprinted in 35 Envtl. L. Rep. 10289 (2005); J. Ladenburg & A. Dubgaard, Preferences of Coastal Zone User Groups Regarding the Siting of Offshore Wind Farms, 52 Ocean & Coastal Mgmt. 233 (2009); R. McGraw, It's for the Birds: Criminal Prosecution of Wind Energy Producers, Oregon State Bar Environmental & Natural Resources Outlook 12 (Spring 2009). M. Portman, Involving the Public in the Impact Assessment of Offshore Renewable Energy Facilities, 33 Marine Policy 332 (2008), and consider the following excerpt on tidal energy.

Offshore wind turbines tend to be located on the OCS while wave and tide projects tend to be located in state waters within 3 nautical miles of the shore where they are subject to FERC regulation under the FPA. Most types of offshore energy facilities also need federal and state approval of their seabed cables bringing the power generated ashore.

For wave and tide projects, FERC has adapted its procedures previously applied to non-federal hydroelectric projects in rivers which are discussed in the next excerpt. Policy Statement on Conditioned Licenses for Hydrokinetic Projects, 121 FERC 61, 221 (2007); see M. Walsh, A Rising Tide in Renewable Energy: The Future of Tidal In-Stream Energy Conversion, 19 Vill. Envtl. L. J. 193 (2008); E. Anderson et al, Siting and Permitting Ocean and Tidal Power Projects in The Law of Ocean and Tidal Energy: A Guide to Business and Legal Issues, chapter 3 (Stoel Rives LLP 2007). Other 2007 publications on alternative energy sources by the Portland, Oregon Stoel Rives LLP law firm include Lava Law: Legal Issues in Geothermal Energy Development, The Law of Biofuels, Lex Heluis: The Law of Solar Energy, and the Law of Wind focused on onshore wind projects. See http://www.lawofrenewableenergy.com/.

ENVIRONMENTAL LAW IN A CLIMATE CHANGE AGE
David R. Hodas
21 ABA Natural Resources and Environment 46 (2007)

A current effort to promote the use of tidal flows to generate electricity illustrates the tensions between existing environmental laws and the imperative of reducing GHG emissions. Because water is about 800 times denser than air, moving water, even slowly moving water, contains enormous force with which to turn an electric turbine. To capture this kinetic power, small turbines with propellers have been developed that can be placed underwater to capture the energy in tidal or steadily flowing water. The 21 kilowatt turbine generators, which would be firmly attached to the water's bed, have 16-foot blades that turn slowly (about 35 revolutions per minute) to generate electricity. In a free-flowing river or stream, the blades would spin 100 percent of the time. By contrast, in a tidal setting, the turbine will only run about 30 percent of the time—when the tide is coming in or leaving, but not when the tide is slack. In either case, the turbines will generate reliable, predictable, pollution-free electricity. The turbines would be entirely underwater and invisible from the surface, would be quiet, and would not require any dams or water impoundments. A pilot project is underway in the East River of New York to determine the turbines' efficacy to generate electricity and effect on the river's aquatic life, particularly fish.

Under the Federal Power Act (FPA), the Federal Energy Regulatory Commission (FERC) has exclusive jurisdiction to license hydroelectric projects, and any activity "for the purpose of developing electric power" is unlawful without a license from FERC. 16 U.S.C. § 817(b). Thus, FERC is the lead decision-making agency for the turbine project. However, the Clean Water Act, Endangered Species Act, Rivers and Harbors Act, Coastal Zone Management Act, National Historic Preservation Act, Marine Mammal Protection Act, Migratory Bird Protection Act, the Magnuson-Stevenson Fisheries Act, the National Environmental Policy Act, and applicable state water-quality and related laws and regulations also apply. * * *

Once it determined the project was feasible, Verdant Power wanted to install six units into the river to evaluate over an eighteen-month testing period the potential impacts of the technology on fish, navigation, and other resources and to obtain operational-performance data on the experimental kinetic hydroelectric technology. If the turbines proved to be effective electric generators and environmentally benign, a permanent operating license would be sought for the project. Unfortunately Verdant Power faced a potential "Catch 22": the FPA prohibits all hydroelectric generation unless FERC grants a license, 16 U.S.C. § 817(b); but without the operational data and experience from installing and operating the kinetic hydroelectric technology, Verdant Power would not have the information necessary to successfully prosecute a FERC license application. Verdant Power thus petitioned FERC for "licensing relief" in the form of a rule that a license would not be necessary under the FPA for feasibility testing. In response, FERC granted the licensing relief on the condition that "(1) the technology in question is experimental, (2) the proposed facilities are to be utilized for a short period for the purpose of conducting studies necessary to prepare a license permit, and (3) power generated from the test project will not be transmitted into, or displace power from, the national electric grid." * * *

The environmental data gathering requirements before any turbines could be permanently installed in the river were extensive, and the project must gather data for another eighteen months after the six turbines are installed under the terms of the test license from FERC. Data were first gathered from a barge-mounted turbine beginning in January 2003, but all six turbines in the river bed were not installed until April 2007 after Verdant Power was granted the licensing relief by FERC. A further condition of the demonstration permit was that studies be made examining the ecological, navigational, recreational, hydrodynamic, and historic preservation impacts of the project. To do this, the applicant must conduct many studies, including benthic habitat characterization; a water-quality assessment; an East River hydrodynamic survey; a mobile hydroacoustic survey; a fixed hydroacoustic survey; an assessment of impacts on any rare, threatened, or endangered species; a biological survey of the East River; a recreational resources assessment; a navigational and security assessment; and an historical resources assessment. In about two years after the studies are completed (2009), Verdant Power can return to FERC with an application for a license to build and operate a commercial-scale project in the East River, which will proceed according to FERC regulations.

From an environmental perspective, these studies are important and prudent requirements, particularly since a new technology is involved. As a society, we need this information so we do not plunge into the deep water of committing to a new technology without understanding its potential impacts. However, if this same decade-long process were to apply to a second project, kinetic water turbine technology will be drowned. Quite simply, Verdant, which is willing to do all of these studies for the East River project, at great cost, will abandon the field if it must repeat the process every time.

Instead of deploying a valuable, new renewable-energy technology, we will be left with existing sources of electricity—particularly coal-fired power plants, many of which still claim the Clean Air Act grandfather exemption for major sources in existence prior to 1970. Clearly, we cannot approve permits blindly and must evaluate the environmental and human impacts of new projects before they are installed; however, we must be able to balance the need for new renewable energy technology against the laudable policies and values embedded in our environmental laws. To meaningfully address GHG emissions, we must balance the prudence our environmental laws urge with the imperative to mitigate global warming. We must rethink all of our environmental laws from a global-warming perspective so that environmental law does not stifle our response to a larger environmental problem. * * *

Notes and Questions

1. FERC has issued 55 permits for pilot turbine generating projects in the Mississippi River downriver from St. Louis. See http://blog.nola.com/tpmoney/2009/05/energy_upstarts_dive_in_to_gen.html. Regarding the role of ocean zoning in the siting of renewable ocean energy facilities offshore, R. Hildreth, Keynote Address: Ocean Zoning Implications for Wave Energy Development (WED), Proceedings of Ecological Effects of Wave Energy Development in the Pacific Northwest: A Scientific Workshop (Oct. 11, 2007). The July 2009 draft ocean plan prepared under see the 2008 Massachusetts Ocean Act, Mass. Gen. Laws ch. 21A §4C, ch. 132A grants refusal rights to coastal communities that directly abut proposed wind farms and requires that facilities proposed for sensitive areas prove that there is no better alternative location.

Regarding wave energy development off California and Oregon, see L. Koch, The Promise of Wave Energy, 2 Golden Gate U. Envtl. L. J. 162 (2008). Regarding wave energy development off Florida, see L. Kelley, The Power of the Sea: Using Ocean Energy to Meet Florida's Need for Power, 37 Envtl. L. Rep. 489 (2007). Regarding wave energy development off Oregon, see D. Dubson & P. Mostow, Oregon & Ocean Renewable Ocean Energy, Oregon Insider No. 399 at 4-6 (Sept. 2006); D. Henkels, M. Langlas, & L. Maffei, Coastal Law in Oregon, Oregon Insider Nos. 422 & 423 at 5-10 (Sept. 2007).

H.R. 2148 (111th Congress) would promote the development of marine renewable energy technologies. H.R. 1690 (111th Congress) would amend the federal Coastal Zone Management Act (CZMA) to authorize grants to coastal states to initiate and complete surveys of coastal state waters and adjacent federal waters to identify potential areas suitable or unsuitable for the exploration, development, and production of renewable energy.

2. The ocean is also used as a source of drinking water produced by coastal desalination plants and off Hawaii, by pumping deep ocean water to the surface for desalination and bottling. As discussed in the hydrology section of this chapter, brackish inland waters are being desalinated for drinking water in Texas from the Rio Grande and to meet U.S. treaty commitments to Mexico on the Colorado River. As reported in H. Doremus & M. Hanemann, The Challenges of Dynamic Water Management in the American West, 26 UCLA J. Envtl. L. & Pol'y 55, 60 n.11 (2008):

> For the first time, desalination projects look like they might make economic sense in many parts of the West. As of March 2004, some two dozen desalination projects had been proposed along the California coast. California Coastal Commission, Seawater Desalination and the California Coastal Act 5 (Mar. 2004), available at http://www.coast-al.ca.gov/energy/14a-3-2004-desalination.pdf. Two years later, the Pacific Institute found twenty proposed projects which, cumulatively, would represent a 70-fold increase in desalination capacity but still would supply only 6% of California's year 2000 water demand. Heather Cooley, Peter H. Gleick & Gary Wolff, Desalination with a Grain of Salt: A California Perspective 29 (Ian Hart ed., Pacific Inst. 2006), available at http://www.pacinst.org/reports/desalination/desalination_report.pdf.

A San Diego County project could be producing 10 percent of the county's needs by 2012. See also R. Craig, Water Supply, Desalination, Climate Change, and Energy Policy (2009) available at http://ssrn.com/abstract=1418675; J. Huffman et al., Desalination in California: Should Ocean Waters Be Utilized to Produce Freshwater, 57 Hastings L.J. 1343 (2006).

3. The greenhouse gas emissions of ocean-going vessels are a significant contribution to climate change and are much less stringently regulated than land-based sources. See International Council on Clean Transportation, Air Pollution and Greenhouse Gas Emissions from Ocean-going Ships: Inpacts, Mitigation Options and Opportunities for Managing Growth, Maritime Studies March-April 2007 at 3. The MARPOL Convention administered by the International Maritime Organization (IMO) controls accidental and operational discharges from ships. MARPOL Annex VI controlling air pollution from ships entered into force May 19, 2005. Annex VI does not address CO_2 emissions, but does reduce emissions of powerful GHG nitrogen oxides (NOx) from certain large new marine diesel engines up to 30 percent from 1990 levels. Annex VI also prohibits the deliberate emission of ozone-depleting substances. The U.S. is a party to Annex VI (see S. Treaty Doc. No. 108-7 (2003); 152 Cong. Rec. S 3400, April 7, 2006) which is implemented by P.L. 110-280 (110th Cong. July 21, 2008).

The climate change legislation enacted by the House of Representatives (H.R. 2454, June 26, 2009), would amend the Clean Air Act to require new marine vessels to reduce their emissions to the greatest degree achievable taking into account cost, energy and safety factors. See also Pacific Merchant Shipping Association v. Goldstene, 517 F.3d 1108 (9th Cir. 2008) (California regulation of emissions from ships' auxiliary diesel engines used to generate onboard power preempted by Clean Air Act). The agendas for the international climate change negotiations discussed in Chapter 3 include reducing ship GHG emissions through actions of the IMO. What is the likelihood of rules being adopted by legislatures that would be inconsistent with the international rules under consideration?

4. For further analysis of U.S. ocean and coastal laws relevant to climate change adaptation, see D. Bauer, T. Eichenberg, & M. Sutton, Ocean and Coastal Law and Policy (2008); D. Christie & R. Hildreth, Coastal and Ocean Management Law in a Nutshell (3d ed. 2007); J. Kalo et al., Coastal and Ocean Management Law (3d ed. 2007); T. Street, Domestic Ocean and Coastal Resource Law and Policy and Climate Change, Sustainable Development L. & Policy Winter 2008 at 61.

RENEWABLE ENERGY AND ALTERNATE USES OF EXISITING FACILITIES ON THE OUTER CONTINENTAL SHELF
30 CFR PARTS 250, 285, AND 290
Minerals Management Service (MMS), U.S. Dept. of the Interior
74 Fed. Reg. 19,638 (April 29, 2009)

SUMMARY: The MMS is publishing final regulations to establish a program to grant leases, easements, and rights-of-way (ROW) for renewable energy project activities on the Outer Continental Shelf (OCS), as well as certain previously unauthorized activities that involve the alternate use of existing facilities located on the OCS; and to establish the methods for sharing revenues generated by this program with nearby coastal States. These regulations will also ensure the orderly, safe, and environmentally responsible development of renewable energy sources on the OCS. * * *
Mandate of Energy Policy Act of 2005 (EPAct)

* * * Under this authority, MMS will regulate the generation of electricity or other forms of energy from sources other than oil and natural gas on OCS facilities and the transmission on project easements and ROWs issued under this part. The MMS will not regulate sales of electricity or other forms of energy. The MMS will not regulate the transmission of electricity or other forms of energy on State lands.

In addition, the EPAct requires the Secretary to share with nearby coastal States a portion of the revenues received by the Federal Government from authorized renewable energy and alternate use projects on certain areas of the OCS. * * *

While the MMS is the lead agency for authorizing OCS renewable energy and alternate use activities, we recognize that other Federal agencies have regulatory responsibility in such activities. The new authority does not expressly supersede or modify existing Federal laws, and all activities must comply fully with such laws. For instance, FERC has exclusive jurisdiction to issue licenses for hydrokinetic projects under Part I of the Federal Power Act and issue exemptions from licensing under Section 405 and 408 of the Public Utility Regulatory Policies Act of 1978 for the construction and operation of hydrokinetic projects on the OCS. However no FERC license or exemption for a hydrokinetic project on the OCS shall be issued before MMS issues a lease, easement, or right-of-way. The MMS possesses the exclusive authority to issue leases, easements, and rights-of-way for renewable energy projects on the OCS. * * *

MMS and Federal Energy Regulatory Commission (FERC) MOU

      * * *

Under this new agreement, those entities interested in operating a hydrokinetic project on the OCS must first obtain a lease from MMS. The MMS will issue a public notice to determine whether competitive interest exists in the area, and will proceed with either the competitive or noncompetitive lease issuance process depending on responses received to this public notice. The MMS will conduct the NEPA analysis necessary for the lease issuance and any site assessment activities that will occur on the lease. After an applicant acquires a lease from MMS, FERC may issue a license or exemption for the hydrokinetic project, and conduct any necessary NEPA analysis. After a license is issued, construction and operations of the project may begin as per the terms of the license. To facilitate efficient processing of the lease and license applications, it may be helpful for potential lessees to apprise both MMS and FERC of their interest in hydrokinetic development at the start of the process. * * *

Importantly, the agreement addresses the issue of potential site-banking by developers on the OCS by eliminating redundant regulatory processes for acquiring use of OCS lands. In addition, by eliminating dual regulatory processes, the agreement addresses the potential for granting conflicting awards of OCS sites to developers by the two agencies. Specifically, FERC has agreed not to issue preliminary permits for hydrokinetic activities on the OCS, and MMS has agreed that FERC will have the primary responsibility to issue licenses for these activities. The Federal Government has effectively eliminated the opportunity for abuse by entities seeking to reserve, block, or acquire for speculative purposes large portions of the OCS. These concerns were raised by many commenters on the REAU rulemaking. The DOI/FERC MOU creates a unified, coherent process for the authorization of hydrokinetic activities on the OCS, ensuring that U.S. resources on the OCS will not be subject to a "land rush," and will be developed in the most efficient manner possible. * * *

The most common topics addressed by commenters included: aquaculture, State and local consultation, bonding, confidentiality, alternate-use liability transference, jurisdiction, revenue sharing, and environmental review processes. * * *

Section 388 of EPAct 2005 requires that any activity permitted under this authority be carried out in a manner that provides for, among other things, protection of the environment, conservation of the natural resources of the outer continental shelf; coordination with relevant Federal agencies; protection of national security interests of the United States, prevention of interference with reasonable uses and functions of the exclusive economic zone, the high seas, and the territorial seas, and consideration of any other use of the sea or seabed, including, but not limited to fisheries, protection of biodiversity and ecosystem function, sealanes, potential siting of deepwater ports, or navigation. Consistent with this statutory direction, MMS understands that this rule will be applied in conjunction with interagency-led planning activities that are undertaken to avoid conflicts among users and maximize the economic and ecological benefits of the OCS. These activities will include multifaceted spatial planning effort that will incorporate ecosystem based science and stewardship along with socioeconomics, research, and modeling in the context for demands for other ocean uses and functions. It is anticipated that the Council on Environmental Quality will help coordinate this intergancy effort, with the National Oceanic and Atmospheric Administration (NOAA) playing a key role, along with MMS. Through this type of coordination and advance planning, we expect to be able to speed the process of developing renewable energy projects in the OCS. * * *

The MMS expects that renewable energy projects in the near term will involve the production of electricity from wind, wave, and ocean current. In the future, other types of renewable energy projects may be pursued on the OCS, including solar energy and hydrogen production projects. These regulations were developed to allow for a broad spectrum of renewable energy development, without specific requirements for each type of energy production. * * *

Commercial and Limited Leases

The MMS will issue two types of leases: (1) commercial or (2) limited. A commercial lease would convey the access and operational rights necessary to produce, sell, and deliver power through spot market transactions or a long-term power purchase agreement. A commercial lease provides the lessee full rights to apply for and receive the authorizations needed to assess, test, and produce renewable energy on a commercial scale over the long term (approximately 30 years). A commercial lease will include the right to a project easement, which will be issued to allow the lessee to install gathering, transmission, and distribution cables to transmit electricity; pipelines to transport other energy products (i.e., hydrogen); and appurtenances on the OCS, as necessary, for the full enjoyment of the lease. The project easement will be issued upon approval of the COP (for commercial leases) or GAP (for limited leases).

A limited lease will convey access and operational rights for activities on the OCS that support the production of energy, but do not result in the production of electricity or other energy product for sale, distribution, or other commercial use exceeding a limit specified in the lease. In a change from the proposed rule, MMS has decided to permit
limited leases that generate power during technology testing to sell that power within limits set in the lease instrument. For example, a limited lease could include in its terms and conditions the authorization to sell electricity produced during the testing of experimental ocean current turbine generators of up to 5 megawatts (MW) total installed
capacity, thereby allowing the lessee to recoup some of the expenses entailed in its limited lease activities. Limited leases may be issued for site-assessment purposes only or for site assessment and development and testing of new or experimental renewable energy technology. Limited leases will be issued for a short term, 5 years. Under the provisions of these regulations, limited leases may be renewed, but they cannot be converted to commercial leases. If the holder of a limited lease wished to pursue commercial development on the OCS, the leaseholder will need to obtain a new commercial lease through the leasing process, as defined in these regulations.

RUE grants and ROW grants

The MMS will issue RUE grants authorizing the use of a designated portion of the OCS to support renewable energy activities on a lease or other approval not issued under this part (e.g., on a State-issued lease).

The MMS will issue ROW grants to allow for the construction and use of a cable or pipeline for the purpose of gathering, transmitting, distributing, or otherwise transporting electricity or other energy product generated or produced from renewable energy not generated on a lease issued under this part. An ROW grant could be used to transport electricity from a State lease to shore or from one State to another State through a transmission line that must cross the Federal OCS. An ROW is not the same as a project easement issued with a renewable energy lease under this part.

Alternate Use RUEs

The MMS will issue an alternate use RUE for the energy- or marine-related use of an existing OCS facility for activities not otherwise authorized by this subchapter or other applicable law. * * *

Federal Compliance for the Leasing Process

All activities permitted under this part must comply with all relevant Federal laws, regulations, and statutes, including, but not limited to, the following:

Responsible Federal Agency/Agencies	Statute/Executive Order (E.O.)	Summary of Pertinent Provisions
Council on Environmental Quality	National Environmental Policy Act of 1969, as amended (NEPA) (42 U.S.C. 4321 et seq.)	Requires Federal agencies to prepare an EIS to evaluate the potential environmental impacts of any proposed major Federal action that would significantly affect the quality of the human environment, and to consider alternatives to such proposed actions.
U.S. Fish and Wildlife Service (FWS); National Oceanic and Atmospheric Administration (NOAA) National Marine Fisheries Service (NMFS)	Endangered Species Act of 1973, as amended (16 U.S.C. 1531 et seq.)	Requires Federal agencies to consult with the FWS and the NMFS to ensure that proposed Federal actions are not likely to jeopardize the continued existence of any species listed at the Federal level as endangered or threatened, or result in the destruction or adverse modification of critical habitat designated for such species.
FWS (walruses, sea and marine otters, polar bears, manatees and dugongs); NMFS (seals, sea lions, whales, dolphins, and porpoises)	Marine Mammal Protection Act of 1972, as amended (16 U.S.C. 1361-1407)	Prohibits, with certain exceptions, the take of marine mammals in U.S. waters and by U.S. citizens on the high seas, and the importation of marine mammals and marine mammal products into the United States.
NMFS	Magnuson-Stevens Fishery Conservation and Management Act (also known as the Fishery Conservation and Management Act of 1976, as amended by the Sustainable Fisheries Act) (16 U.S.C. 1801 et seq.)	Requires Federal agencies to consult with the NMFS on proposed Federal actions that may adversely affect Essential Fish Habitats that are necessary for spawning, breeding, feeding, or growth to maturity of federally managed fisheries.
U.S. Environ-	Marine Protection,	Prohibits, with certain exceptions,

mental Protection Agency (EPA); U.S. Army Corps of Engineers (ACOE); NOAA	Research, and Sanctuaries Act of 1972, as amended (33 U.S.C. 1401 et seq.)	the dumping or transportation for dumping of materials including, but not limited to, dredged material, solid waste, garbage, sewage, sewage sludge, chemicals, biological and laboratory waste, wrecked or discarded equipment, rock, sand, excavation debris, and other waste into ocean waters without a permit from the EPA. In the case of ocean dumping of dredged material, the ACOE is given permitting authority.
NOAA	National Marine Sanctuaries Act (16 U.S.C. 1431 et seq.)	Prohibits the destruction, loss of, or injury to, any sanctuary resource managed under the law or permit, and requires Federal agency consultation on Federal agency actions, internal or external to national marine sanctuaries, that are likely to destroy, injure, or cause the loss of any sanctuary resource.
FWS	E.O. 13186, "Responsibilities of Federal Agencies to Protect Migratory Birds" (January 10, 2001)	Requires that Federal agencies taking actions likely to negatively affect migratory bird populations enter into Memoranda of Understanding with the FWS, which, among other things, ensure that environmental reviews mandated by NEPA evaluate the effects of agency actions on migratory birds, with emphasis on species of concern.
NOAA's Office of Ocean and Coastal Resource Management (NOAA OCRM)	CZMA of 1972, as amended (16 U.S.C. 1451 et seq.)	Specifies that coastal States may protect coastal resources and manage coastal development. A State with a coastal zone management program approved by NOAA OCRM can deny or restrict development off its coast if the reasonably foreseeable effects of such development would be inconsistent with the State's coastal zone management program.
EPA; MMS	Clean Air Act, as amended (CAA) (42 U.S.C. 7401 et seq.)	Prohibits Federal agencies from providing financial assistance for, or issuing a license or other approval to, any activity that does not conform to an applicable, approved implementation plan for achieving and maintaining the National Ambient Air Quality Standards

		(NAAQS). Requires EPA (or an authorized State agency) to issue a permit before construction of any new major stationary source or major modification of a stationary source of air pollution. The permit—called a Prevention of Significant Deterioration (PSD) Permit for stationary sources located in areas that comply with the NAAQS, and a Nonattainment Area Permit in areas that do not comply with the NAAQS—must control emissions in the manner prescribed by EPA regulations to either prevent significant deterioration of air quality (in attainment areas), or contribute to reducing ambient air pollution in accordance with an approved implementation plan (in nonattainment areas). Requires the owner or operator of a stationary source that has more than a threshold quantity of a regulated substance in a process to submit a Risk Management Plan to EPA. In the western portion of the Gulf of Mexico, MMS has authority pursuant to the OCS Lands Act for clean air regulations.
EPA; U.S. Coast Guard (USCG); MMS	Clean Water Act (CWA), Section 311, as amended (33 U.S.C. 1321); E.O. 12777, "Implementation of Section 311 of the Federal Water Pollution Control Act of October 18, 1972, as Amended, and the Oil Pollution Act of 1990"	Prohibits discharges of oil or hazardous substances into or upon the navigable waters of the United States, adjoining shorelines, or into or upon the waters of the contiguous zone, or in connection with activities under the OCS Lands Act, or which may affect natural resources belonging to the United States. Authorizes EPA and the USCG to establish programs for preventing and containing discharges of oil and hazardous substances from nontransportation-related facilities and transportation-related facilities, respectively. Directs the Secretary of the Interior (MMS) to establish requirements for preventing and containing discharges of oil and hazardous substances from offshore facilities, including associated pipelines, other

		than deepwater ports.
USCG	Marking of Obstructions (14 U.S.C. 86)	The Coast Guard may mark for the protection of navigation any sunken vessel or other obstruction existing on the navigable waters or waters above the continental shelf of the U.S. in such manner and for so long as, in his judgment, the needs of maritime navigation require.
EPA	CWA, Sections 402 and 403, as amended (33 U.S.C. 1342 and 1343)	Requires a National Pollutant Discharge Elimination System (NPDES) Permit from EPA (or an authorized State) before discharging any pollutant into territorial waters, the contiguous zone, or the ocean from an industrial point source, a publicly owned treatment works, or a point source composed entirely of storm water.
ACOE; EPA	CWA, Section 404, as amended (33 U.S.C. 1344)	Requires a permit from the ACOE before discharging dredged or fill material into waters of the United States, including wetlands.
USCG	Ports and Waterways Safety Act, as amended (33 U.S.C. 1221 et seq.)	Authorizes the USCG to implement, in waters subject to the jurisdiction of the United States, measures for controlling or supervising vessel traffic or for protecting navigation and the marine environment. Such measures may include but are not limited to: reporting and operating requirements, surveillance and communications systems, routing systems, and fairways.
ACOE	Rivers and Harbors Appropriation Act of 1899 (33 U.S.C. 401 et seq.) Section 10 (33 U.S.C. 403) delegates to the ACOE the authority to review and regulate certain structures and work that are located in or that affect navigable waters of the United States. The OCS Lands Act extends the jurisdiction	Requires waste generators to determine whether they generate hazardous waste and, if so, to determine how much hazardous waste they generate and notify the responsible regulatory agency. Requires hazardous waste treatment, storage, and disposal facilities (TSDFs) to demonstrate in their permit applications that design and operating standards established by the EPA (or an authorized State) will be met. Requires hazardous waste TSDFs to obtain permits.

	of the ACOE, under Section 10, to the seaward limit of Federal jurisdiction. EPA Resource Conservation and Recovery Act, as amended by the Hazardous and Solid Waste Amendments of 1984 (42 U.S.C. 6901 et seq.)	
National Park Service (NPS); Advisory Council on Historic Preservation; State or Tribal Historic Preservation Officer	National Historic Preservation Act of 1966, as amended (16 U.S.C. 470-470t); Archaeological and Historical Preservation Act of 1974 (16 U.S.C. 469-469c-2)	Requires each Federal agency to consult with the Advisory Council on Historic Preservation and the State or Tribal Historic Preservation Officer before allowing a federally licensed activity to proceed in an area where cultural or historic resources might be located; authorizes the Interior Secretary to undertake the salvage of archaeological data that may be lost due to a Federal project.
NPS; Advisory Council on Historic Preservation; State or Tribal Historic Preservation Office	American Indian Religious Freedom Act of 1978 (42 U.S.C. 1996); E.O. 13007, "Indian Sacred Sites" (May 24, 1996)	Requires Federal agencies to facilitate Native American access to and ceremonial use of sacred sites on Federal lands, to promote greater protection for the physical integrity of such sites, and to maintain the confidentiality of such sites, where appropriate.
Federal Aviation Administration (FAA)	Federal Aviation Act of 1958 (49 U.S.C. 44718); 14 CFR part 77	Requires that, when construction, alteration, establishment, or expansion of a structure is proposed, adequate public notice be given to the FAA as necessary to promote safety in air commerce and the efficient use and preservation of the navigable airspace.

* * *

We received several comments recommending that we provide for accepting the results of competitive processes conducted by States and utilities to select developers of offshore wind generation projects. Notably, during the time that MMS has been promulgating this rule, the States of Delaware, New Jersey, and Rhode Island have conducted competitive processes and have selected companies to develop wind resources on the OCS. We believe that the pre-existing State processes are relevant to the competitive processes that

MMS is required to conduct following approval of this rule. We intend to do so by using a competitive process that considers, among other things, whether a prospective lessee has a power purchase agreement or is the certified winner of
a competitive process conducted by an adjacent State. We also may consider a similar approach to recognize the winners of competitions held by States in the future. * * *

CZMA Compliance

For purposes of Federal consistency, MMS will treat ROW grants and RUE grants issued through a competitive process as direct Federal agency activities and follow the subsection 307(c)(1) procedures of the CZMA. The MMS will determine if the ROW grant or RUE grant is reasonably likely to affect any land or water use or natural resource of a State's coastal zone and comply with the appropriate Federal consistency regulations under 15 CFR part 930 subpart C.

The MMS will treat ROW grants and RUE grants issued noncompetitively as Federal licenses or permits, which will follow requirements of CZMA subsection 307(c)(3)(A) and 15 CFR part 930 subpart D. For ROW grants and RUE grants issued noncompetitively, MMS requires the applicant to submit a proposed GAP simultaneously with the application for the ROW or RUE grant. The GAP is a Federal license or permit under current CZMA regulations since it will describe activities and operations proposed to be undertaken in areas of the OCS that are not under a lease; and therefore, does not qualify as an OCS plan (as defined by 15 CFR 930.73). * * *

PROBLEM EXERCISE ON OFFSHORE WIND ENERGY

Assume the following facts with respect to the conservation and development of coastal and ocean resources in and adjacent to the state of Massachusetts, USA:

1.　130 wind turbines would be installed offshore and linked together by an electric power transmission cable 12 inches in diameter crossing the bottom of Nantucket Sound to the mainland at Cape Cod, Massachusetts.

2.　Massachusetts' federally approved coastal management program (Mass. CMP) includes the Massachusetts renewable energy statutory and draft ocean plan provisions cited above.

3.　Nantucket Sound waters are visited by endangered Northern Right whales.

Consider in your analysis the following:

(A) U.S. Minerals Management Service (MMS) authority over the proposed 130 wind turbines based on OCSLA § 8(p)(10) and its implementing regulations summarized above.

(B) The potential impact on MMS decisionmaking of the Northern Right whale's status as an endangered marine mammal.

(C) Massachusetts' regulatory authority (if any) over the 130 wind turbines and their connecting electric power transmission cables, including any potential roles of the Mass. CMP in the MMS decisionmaking process.

(D) The potential relevance (if any) to the proposed 130 wind turbines and their connecting electric power transmission cable of (i) the public trust doctrine, (ii) federal navigation servitude, and (iii) the littoral rights of Cape Cod shoreline property owners discussed in the sea level rise sections of this chapter.

H.R. 2454 (111th Cong. May 21, 2009), as part of its comprehensive climate change provisions would have supported marine spatial planning for renewable ocean energy facilities based on ecosystem-based management principles. Based on the foregoing wind energy problem and other section materials, what provisions would you recommend for inclusion in the national and regional plans called for by that legislation?

F. ENVIRONMENTAL IMPACT ASSESSMENT

Mitigation of greenhouse gases, or their sequestration, on a national or global scale cannot be achieved by a single agency or authority. Every human action has the potential to either emit GHGs or avoid or contain them. Virtually no act is carbon neutral by itself. It must be evaluated and designed to that end. There is one decision-making technique that is already enacted in federal law, and in nearly half the States, that already requires this type of decision-making: environmental impact assessment. EIA requires that all agencies examine, to the fullest extent possible, the environmental impacts of their proposed action, weight alternatives to the actions, and identify ways to mitigate all adverse effects, and take public comment on such assessment before finalizing it and selecting a preferred action. The process is both a full disclosure information rule and a rule to restore, maintain and enhance environmental quality.

Two symposia examine the role of the National Environmental Policy Act of 1969, 42 U.S.C. §4321 et seq. in addressing climate change and other aspects of environmental quality: The Environmental Law Institute's Environmental Law Reporter "NEPA at 40" Symposium, 39 ELR 10674 (July 2009) and the ABA Natural Resources & Environment issue devoted to NEPA, volume 23, Spring 2009.

The NEPA regulations at 40 CFR Part 1500 are models for the federal agencies own NEPA rules, as well as for the "Little" NEPAs" enacted in states such as California and New York. They are also models for environmental impact assessment (EIA) procedures adopted in many nations around the world.

Read closely the CEQ's NEPA regulations. Do they adequately already require an assessment of climate change and GHG emissions? If so, why have so few assessment been undertaken? The environmental assessment (1508.9) and the scope of an EIA (1508.25) includes analysis of the cumulative impact (1508.7) and both direct and indirect effects (1508.8), as well as all possible "mitigation" measures (1508.20). The President's Council on Environmental Quality (CEQ) has the authority to amend the NEPA regulations to provide an express provision for assessing the climate change impacts of any action, and defining the significance (1508.27) of the impacts. State agencies similarly issues guidance for their state EIA regulations. Review the CEQ regulations in light of the EPA Endangerment Finding, and determine how they should be interpreted in light of that Finding. Should CEQ issues a policy guidance on how to do so, or move at once to amending the CEQ regulations to mandate all federal agencies to make climate change assessments?

Do NEPA decisions in the courts suggest that a need for clearer regulatory mandates? In Center for Biological Diversity v. NHTSA, 538 F. 3d 1172 (9th Cir. 2008), court of appeals held that the National Highway Traffic Administration had failed, in establishing a 2006 rule for the Corporate Average Fuel Economy (CAFÉ) standards for "light trucks," to evaluate the cumulative and incremental impacts of the carbon dioxide emissions. The court observed that "The impact of greenhouse gas emissions on climate change is precisely the kind of cumulative impacts analysis that NEPA requires agencies to conduct. Any given rule setting a CAFÉ standard might have an 'individually minor' effect on the environment, but these rules are 'collectively significant actions taking place over a period of time.'" Id. at 1217. The court also found that the agency had failed to look at alternatives to the action that might have mitigated the adverse effects.

A petition filed in February of 2008 by the International Center for Technology Assessment, the Sierra Club and the Natural Resources Defense Council, requests CEQ to promulgate new climate change rules under NEPA. Does the tepid judicial support for applying NEPA to indirect climate change effects, as in North Slope Borough v. Minerals Management Service, 2008 WL 110889 (D. Alaska, 2008), suggest that CEQ will need to promulgate regulations in order to secure a consistent pattern of climate change impact assessment across all federal agencies? See P. Lehner & J. Dean, SEQRA's Alarm Rings for Climate-Impact Considerations, 238 N.Y. L. J. 4 (Aug. 28, 2007); N. Dupont, NEPA and Climate Change: Are We at the 'Tipping Point'?" 23 ABA Nat. Res. & Envt. 18 (2009). Even if NEPA's regulations do apply to climate change, there are those who argue it should not mandate a strong GHG mitigation approach, but rather let agencies have flexibility and leave to avoid discussing climate change if the links to tenuous. C. Moore, L. Allen, & M. Forman, Indirect Impacts and Climate Change: Assessing NEPA's Reach, 23 ABA Nat. Res. & Envt. (2009). If you were advising the Chair of President Obama's CEQ about revising the NEPA regulations to address climate change mitigation, what would you recommend?

On NEPA and adaptation, see Chapter 7, Section G.

PROBLEM EXERCISE ON NEPA

The CEQ NEPA regulations were codified in the Carter Administration. They have been amended very infrequently. Those who have attached EIA in the past have been unable to weaken NEPA in the Congress, or through CEQ. When the Stimulus Bill was being enacted in the Congress, to deal with the Recession that began in 2907, some lobbies attacked NEPA as requiring slow and dilatory environmental assessments that would delay the spending of economic stimulus funds. Congress decline to exempt the economic recovery projects from the normal NEPA reviews. §1609(a) of the 2009 economic stimulus law found that NEPA "helps to provide an orderly process for considering federal actions and funding decisions and prevents litigation and delay that would otherwise be inevitable and existed prior to the establishment of NEPA" and "adequate resources within this bill must be devoted to ensuring that applicable environmental reviews under NEPA are completed on an expeditious basis and that the shortest existing applicable process under NEPA shall be followed." 115 Cong. Rec. S1617-02 (Senator Barbara Boxer on amendment No. 363).

In preparing a revision to NEPA to expedite analysis of climate change, should a new technique be developed that goes beyond the tried and true EIA procedures of §102(2(C)? What unused authority does CEQ presently have to fashion a world-wide tool that can address climate change more effectively than in an impact statement. See §102(2) (A), (B), (F), and (G); N. Robinson, NEPA at 40: International Dimensions, 39 ELR 10674 (2009).

Notes and Questions

1. Regarding the type of analysis required under NEPA, the 9th Circuit Court noted in Center for Biological Diversity v. NHTSA that "Without some analysis, it would be 'impossible for NHTSA to know...whether a change in GHG emissions of 0.2% or 1% or 5% or 10%...will be a significant step toward averting the tipping point and irreversible adverse climate change." 508 F.3d at 554. Considering that judicial review is largely based on arbitrary/capricious and sufficient evidence tests, how much is "some analysis"? Do we expect courts to require IPCC-caliber research for each EIS, especially

from agencies that may not be equipped to do such analyses? Is this where CEQ guidance on what to consider and what to analyze would come in most handily? If the NHTSA had found a significant impact, had done an EIS that determined that the GHG release would impact the global and U.S. environment, does that necessarily mean that they would have chosen other alternatives? Economic, industrial, and regulatory considerations beyond climate change went into the development of the standards. Also, the decision as to what standards to set is ultimately one within the discretion of the agency. Does development of climate change analyses like emissions sources, mitigation options, and adaptation alternatives really point to agency consideration of its actions on the global climate? If CEQ developed regulations that outlined exactly how to conduct an EIS inquiry into GHG sources, would that necessarily translate into GHG reductions?

2. *Carbon Neutral Law Schools*: What greenhouse gas emissions can be cut almost immediately at your law school? Thermostat levels for air conditioning and heating can be reset, lights turned off, new light bulbs installed outdoors and in hallways (see Federal Trade Commission, Energy Efficient Light Bulbs: A Bright Idea, www.ftc.gov/bcp/online/pubs/productions/ffclight.htm), existing vehicles replaced with hybrid and electric vehicles, or on-going maintenance reviewed to ensure that it is roots out GHG emissions just like mold, dust, grime or litter. More pervasively, law school and university procurement contracts can be revised; do you know what is in the contracts that your law school has for constructions and facilities maintenance, for dining services, for vending machines, for transit service providers, for copiers, and for computer equipment? Does your law school have programs to buy green power, recycled products, and locally produced food for cafeterias. The Green-e Renewable Electricity Certification Program (www.green-e.org) will help identify efficient and effective renewable products. See also W. Toor & S. Havlick, Transportation and Sustainable Campus Communities: Issues, Examples, Solutions (2004). Your law school's transportation carbon footprint is a part of the significant 27% of total US greenhouse gas emissions. What mitigation can you leverage to reduce that impact? What opportunities does your campus present for planting new trees, reducing lawns and dependencies on fertilizers and irrigation, and promoting photosynthesis and sequestering greenhouse gas emissions. Can your law school guide the municipality where you are situated to revise its local laws and practices to adopt comparable mitigation regimes?

CHAPTER 7. ADAPTING TO CLIMATE CHANGE

Climatescape: **Laws Adjusting Human and Natural Systems**

Whether or not the mitigation examined in Chapter 6 is fully effective, sea level rise and alternation of flooding and drought conditions require significant adaptation in all Earth's regions. The impacts to coastal and marine environments necessitate a retreat from the coast, and a reshaping of coastal natural resources to retain their ecological and hydrologic benefits. Property law regimes require adjustments, as do state and municipal laws providing infrastructure. In polar regions, the impacts are forcing adaptation. Are the laws for nature conservation and sustaining environmental quality adequate to guide adaptive coastal redesigns of wetlands for species habitats and flood surge absorption? Many local authorities have taken the leadership in designing adaptation regimes, and amending local laws accordingly. John Nolon's analysis indicates local governments can achieve substantial mitigation benefits, while adapting. The financial resources for doing come from both public and private sectors, and as discussed in Chapter 8, a new global market in climate risk insurance is emerging, and is a part of the UNFCCC negotiations since much of the world lacks any insurance regime. How can implementation of existing environmental laws, such as the environmental impact assessment laws enacted at national of federal or state governments across most of Earth's regions, be applied to guide climate change adaptation?

A. WHAT IS ADAPTATION?

Adaptation as Defined in Climate Change 2007: Impacts, Adaptation and Vulnerability, Contribution of Working Group II to the Fourth Assessment Report of the Intergovernmental Panel on Climate Change

Adaptation: Adjustment in natural or *human systems* in response to actual or expected climate stimuli or their effects, which moderates harm or exploits beneficial opportunities. Various types of adaptation can be distinguished, including anticipatory, autonomous and planned adaptation:

> **Anticipatory adaptation**-Adaptation that takes place before impacts of climate change are observed. Also referred to as proactive adaptation.
> **Autonomous adaptation**-Adaptation that does not constitute a conscious response to climate stimuli but is triggered by ecological changes in natural systems and by market or *welfare* changes in *human systems*. Also referred to as spontaneous adaptation.
> **Planned adaptation**-Adaptation that is the result of a deliberate policy decision, based on an awareness that conditions have changed

or are about to change and that action is required to return to, maintain, or achieve a desired state.

B. ADAPTING TO SEA LEVEL RISE

1. Introduction

Climate related sea level rise comes from thermal expansion of the ocean and glaciers and ice caps melting on land. As the U.S. Supreme Court recognized in Massachusetts v. EPA:

> [T]he rise in sea levels associated with global warming has already harmed and will continue to harm Massachusetts. The risk of catastrophic harms, though remote, is nevertheless real. 127 S. Ct. at 1458.

Thus, adapting to sea level rise is a key component of national climate change policies. Responses included armoring the coast, restoring coastal wetlands and eroded beaches, and retreat from the coast. The regulations of the Rhode Island Coastal Resources Management Program addressing these issues are excerpted below. In assessing legal issues raised by their implementation, please bear in mind that in the United States most coastal wetlands and beaches are privately owned if they are located inland of the mean high tide line (MHT), defined as the intersection with the current shore of the average of all the high-tide elevations measured over the 18.6 year lunar cycle. See D. Christie & R. Hildreth, Coastal and Ocean Management Law in a Nutshell 11-14 (3rd ed. 2007); J. Kalo, et al., Coastal and Ocean Management Law 1-3 (3d ed. 2007).

RHODE ISLAND REGULATION TEXT
RI ADC 04 000 010
February 22, 2008
Coastal Resources Management Council

To address the issues of climate change and sea level rise by creating a programmatic section for the [Rhode Island coastal] management plan. * * *

Section 140. Setbacks.

A. Definition: a setback is the minimum distance from the inland boundary of a coastal feature at which an approved activity or alteration may take place.

B. Setbacks shall be maintained in areas contiguous to coastal beaches, coastal wetlands, coastal cliffs and banks, rocky shores, and existing manmade shorelines, and apply to the following categories of activities and alterations:

1) Filling, removal, or grading, except when part of an approved alteration involving a water-dependent activity or structure (Section 300.2);

2) Residential buildings and garages excluding associated structures (Section 110.4);

3) New individual sewage disposal systems, sewage treatment plants, and associated sewer facilities excluding outfalls (Section 300.6). Repairs and replacements of existing (permitted) individual sewage disposal systems shall be exempt from the Council's setback requirements;

4) Industrial structures, commercial structures, and public recreation structures that are not water-dependent (Section 300.3); and

5) Transportation facilities that are not water-dependent (Section 300.13).

C. Setbacks will be determined using the rates of change as found on the accompanying Shoreline Change Maps for Watch Hill to the Easternmost Point of Quicksand Beach (Little Compton) abutting Massachusetts. The minimum distance of a setback shall be not less than 30 times the calculated average annual erosion rate for less than four dwelling units and not less than 60 times the calculated average annual erosion rate for commercial, industrial or dwellings of more than 4 units. At a minimum however, setbacks shall extend either fifty (50) feet from the inland boundary of the coastal feature or twenty-five (25) feet inland of the edge of a Coastal Buffer Zone, whichever is further landward. Due to site conditions over time, field verification of a coastal feature or coastal buffer zone may result in a setback determination different than that calculated using a shoreline change rate.

D. Applicants for alterations and activities who cannot meet the minimum setback standards may apply to the Council for a variance (Section 120).

E. The setback provisions do not apply to minor modifications or restoration of structures that conform with all other policies and standards of this program.

Section 145. Climate Change and Sea Level Rise.

A. Definitions

1. Climate is the long-term weather average observed within a geographic region, and climate change refers to fluctuations in the Earth's climate system as a result of both natural and anthropogenic causes. Currently the long term climate change trend is evidenced by rising global temperatures; increasing extremes within the hydrologic cycle resulting in more frequent floods and droughts; and rising sea level.

2. Sea level rise refers to the change in mean sea level over time in response to global climate and local tectonic changes. Sea level is the height of the sea with respect to a horizontal control point, or benchmark (e.g., The National Geodetic Vertical Datum of 1929 or NGVD 29; The North American Vertical Datum of 1988 or NAVD 88). * * *

Conversions between the datums can be made at www.tidesandcurrents.noaa.gov or calculated through the US Army Corps of Engineers CORPSCON, http://crunch.tec.army.mil/soft-ware/corpscon/corpscon.html.

4. Sea level rise includes eustatic contributions—global changes responsible for worldwide variations in sea level (e.g., thermal expansion of seawater, melting glacial ice sheets), and isostatic effects—regional changes in land surface elevations that are related to the tectonic response to ice or sediment loading, and land subsidence due to extraction of water or oil. The combination of eustatic and isostatic effects at a particular location is known as relative sea level rise.

B. Findings * * *

20. Pursuant to R.I.G.L. § 46-23-6, the Council is authorized to develop and adopt policies and regulations necessary to manage the coastal resources of the state and protect life and property from coastal hazards resulting from projected sea level rise and probable increased frequency and intensity of coastal storms due to climate change. The Council is also authorized to collaborate with the State Building Commissioner and adopt freeboard calculations (a factor of added safety above the anticipated flood level), in accordance with R.I.G.L. § 23-27.3-100.1.5.5.

C. Policies

1. The Council will review its policies, plans and regulations to proactively plan for and adapt to climate change and sea level rise. The Council will integrate climate change and sea level rise scenarios into its operations to prepare Rhode Island for these new, evolving conditions and make our coastal areas more resilient.

2. The Council's sea level rise policies are based upon the CRMC's legislative mandate to preserve, protect, and where possible, restore the coastal resources of the state through comprehensive and coordinated long-range planning.

3. The Council recognizes that sea level rise is ongoing and its foremost concern is the accelerated rate of rise and the associated risks to Rhode Island coastal areas today and in the future. Accordingly, for planning and management purposes, it is the Council's policy to accommodate a base rate of expected 3 to 5 foot rise in sea level by 2100 in the siting, design, and implementation of public and private coastal activities and to insure proactive stewardship of coastal ecosystems under these changing conditions.

It should be noted that the 3-5 ft. rate of sea level rise assumption embedded in this policy is relatively narrow and low. The Council recognizes that the lower the sea level rise estimate used, the greater the risk that policies and efforts to adapt sea level rise and climate change will prove to be inadequate. Therefore, the policies of the Council may take into account different risk tolerances for differing types of public and private coastal activities. In addition, this long term sea level change base rate will be revisited by the Council periodically to address new scientific evidence. * * *

Many of the state's barriers have been mapped and assigned by the Coastal Resources Management Council to three categories. * * * The barriers or portions thereof are designated by the federal government as undeveloped pursuant to their criteria, under the Coastal Barrier Resources Act of 1982 (Public Law 97-348). * * * In these federally designated areas, flood insurance for most forms of construction is not available.

2. Undeveloped barriers are essentially free of commercial/industrial buildings, (excluding public utility lines) houses, surfaced roads, and structural shoreline protection facilities.

3. Moderately developed barriers are those that are essentially free of houses, commercial/industrial buildings and/or facilities (excluding utility lines) that contain surfaced roads, recreational structures, and/or structural shoreline protection facilities.

4. Developed barriers contain houses and/or commercial/industrial structures; they may also contain surfaced roads and structural shoreline protection facilities. * * *

C. Policies

1. On barriers classified as undeveloped * * *, the Council's goal is to preserve, protect, and where possible, restore these features as conservation areas and as buffers that protect salt ponds and the mainland from storms and hurricanes.

2. On barriers classified as developed * * *, the Council's goal is to ensure that the risks of storm damage and erosion for the people inhabiting these features are minimized, that activities that may reduce the effectiveness of the barrier as a storm buffer are avoided, and that associated wetlands and ponds are protected.

3. On barriers classified as moderately developed * * *, the following policies shall apply:

(a) New development is prohibited on moderately developed barriers except where the primary purpose of the project is restoration, protection or improvement of the feature as a natural habitat for plants and wildlife or as allowed under paragraph (c) of this section;

(b) Existing roads, bridges, utilities and shoreline protection facilities may be maintained only, in accordance with the requirements of Section 300.14;

(c) Existing recreational structures may be altered, rehabili-tated, expanded or developed (as defined in the glossary of the RICRMP) according to the following standards:

(i) Any expansion of or development activities associated with existing recreational structures shall not occur within or extend into any flood zone designated as V on the most current Federal Insurance Rate Maps, or as established by the Federal Emergency Management Agency;

(ii) All activity shall be confined to the existing footprint of disturbance; for the purposes of this section, the footprint of disturbance shall be defined as that area encompassed by the perimeter of the structural foundation and/or areas determined by the CRMC to be substantially altered due to associated structures, excluding dunes, wetlands and areas encompassed within pertinent setback and buffer zone requirements of this program;

(iii) Any proposed expansion of existing recreational structures shall be limited to an area equal to 25% of the square footage of the ground floor area encompassed by the structural foundation of the existing building as of June 23, 1983; associated structures shall not be used in calculating existing area;

(iv) The activity shall meet or exceed all relevant standards for the appropriate flood zone designation;

(v) All activities shall be subject to relevant setback and buffer zone requirements of this program, including accessory structures such as decks, porches, walls, boardwalks, swimming pools, roads driveways, parking lots and other structures integral to or ancillary to the existing recreational structure.

4. Alterations to undeveloped barriers are prohibited except where the primary purpose of the project is protection, maintenance, restoration or improvement of the feature as a natural habitat for native plants and wildlife. In no case shall structural shoreline protection facilities be used to preserve or enhance these areas as a natural habitat or to protect the shoreline feature.

5. The Council recognizes the highly dynamic nature of barriers and that storms may cause sudden and significant changes to the geomorphic form of these coastal features. Accordingly, large scale public infrastructure improvements and dense development is inappropriate. Therefore, the construction or expansion of new infrastructure or utilities shall be prohibited on all barriers including water, gas and sewer lines. It is not the intention of these policies to apply to individual, on-site water supply systems or individual sewage disposal systems, or gas lines. The use of plastic snow-fencing on all barriers is prohibited. * * *

7. With the exception of boardwalks and snow fencing utilized to trap sand, all residential and non-water-dependent recreational, commercial, and industrial structures on undeveloped barriers physically destroyed 50 percent or more by storm-induced flooding, wave or wind damage may not be reconstructed regardless of the insurance coverage carried.

8. Persons utilizing undeveloped beaches are required to observe the following rules:

(a) Destruction or removal of signs, snow fencing, or other sand-stabilizing devices is prohibited; camping is prohibited unless in vehicles equipped with a self-contained toilet.

(b) Vehicles are permitted only on marked roads or trails and on the beach. Vehicles that drive on the beach and designated unstabilized trails on undeveloped barriers shall abide by the policies found in Section 210.1.

(c) Persons shall be at all times subject to applicable town ordinances and regulations restricting the use of private, state, or federal properties.

9. Existing recreational structures, such as beach pavilions, located on undeveloped and moderately-developed barriers that enhance the public's access to the water and generate tourism revenue for the State of Rhode Island may be permitted to be

reestablished in the event that they are physically destroyed 50% or more as a result of storm induced flooding, wave, or wind damage, provided that: (a) applicable policies and standards of the RICRMP are met; and, (b) public access to the shore is enhanced. Where possible, the reconstruction of these structures shall be behind the foredune zone as defined in Section 210.1.

Notes and Questions

1.   The Rhode Island Coastal Resources Management Program excerpted above is federally funded under the Coastal Zone Management Act (CZMA) 16 U.S.C. §§ 1451-64. One of the Act's goals is:

> the management of coastal development to minimize the loss of life and property caused by improper development in flood-prone, storm-surge, geological hazard, and erosion-prone areas and in areas likely to be affected by or vulnerable to sea level rise, land subsidence, salt-water intrusion, and by the destruction of natural protective features such as beaches, dunes, wetlands, and barrier islands.   16 U.S.C. §1452 (2)(B).

State responses to this goal are summarized in Coastal States Organization, The Pole of Coastal Zone Management Programs in Adaptation to Climate Change (Sept. 2008); P. Rubinoff, N. Vinhateiro, & C. Piecuch, Summary of Coastal Program Initiatives that Address Sea Level Rise as a Result of Global Climate Change (Rhode Island Sea Grant Feb. 2008). See, e.g., Mass. Gen. Laws, ch. 21A, § 4C(i). H.R. 1905, 111th Congress, 155 Cong. Rec. H 4520 (daily ed. April 2, 2009) would amend the CZMA to authorize state additions to their coastal management programs for climate change mitigation and adaptation like the Rhode Island regulations excerpted above. Not dealt with in the Rhode Island regulations but recommended for priority attention in R. Craig, A Public Health Perspective on Sea Level Rise: Starting Points for Climate Change Adaptation, 15 Widener L. Rev. No. 2 (2009) are saltwater intrusion into drinking water supplies, changes in disease exposure, and toxic contamination of seawater due to sea level rise. Regarding hazardous chemical releases during coastal storm events, see T. Malloy, Of Natmats, Terrorists, and Toxics: Regulatory Adaptation in a Changing World, 26 U.C.L.A. J. Envtl. L. & Pol'y 93, 102-106 (2008). For management responses to sea level rise in the United Kingdom, see R. Few, Climate Change and Coastal Management Decisions, Governance for Sustainable Coastal Futures, 35 Coastal Mgmt. 499 (2007).

2.   Given the mix of public (below MHT) and private (above MHT) property rights in coastal resources, the U.S. Constitution's Fifth Amendment "takings" clause plays an important role as illustrated in a challenge to Rhode Island statutes and regulations protecting undeveloped coastal wetlands, which can serve as a natural buffer against sea level rise and storm events and are an important carbon sink.

See Palazollo v. State, 2005 WL 1645974 (R.I. Super. 2005), where the court on remand from the U.S. Supreme Court denied compensation based on Palazzollo's lack of reasonable investment-backed expectations that he could fill and develop private wetlands, a significant factor in takings analysis under the Court's Penn Central opinion (438 U.S. 104) as emphasized in Justice O'Connor's concurring opinion in Palazollo v. Rhode Island, 533 U.S. 606 (2001). See also Graham v. Estuary Properties, 399 So. 2d 1374 (Fla. 1981), cert. denied Taylor v. Graham, 454 U.S. 1083 (1981), where the Florida Supreme Court found that the denial of a state permit to dredge and fill 1800 acres of mangrove wetlands was not a taking because the owner could not have had reasonable expectations to develop the property in a manner that would seriously affect the environment.

3. Coastal wetlands also are protected to some extent under two federal laws administered by the U.S. Army Corps of Engineers (Corps) and the federal Environmental Protection Agency (EPA), River and Harbors Act § 10, 33 U.S.C. § 403, and Clean Water Act § 404, 33 U.S.C. § 1344, requiring Corps permits to alter navigable waters and their connected wetlands. See Christie & Hildreth, supra at 106-114, 125-126. Thus Fifth Amendment compensation is sometimes but not always required for the regulatory decisions of those agencies affecting privately owned wetlands. Compare Kaiser-Aetna v. U.S., 444 U.S. 164 (1979), with Palm Beach Isle Associates v. U.S., 58 Fed. Cl. 657 (2003).

PROBLEM EXERCISE ON COASTAL ZONE MANAGEMENT

The Coast Zone Management Act of 1972, 16 USC 1451-1465, enjoyed a remarkably successful history of cooperative federalism in the USA. The Congress provided planning grants to the States, and a promise that federal agencies would act in accordance with any State Coastal Zone Plan that was approved by the Administrator of National Oceanic and Atmospheric Administration (NOAA). CZMA §307(c), the federal consistency clause. The States developed quite varied coastal zone plans, according to their needs and policies. However, in light of climate change effects, the assumptions underlying the CZMA will need to be revisited. States assumed that coast lines and zone were largely static, and made no provision for a retreat from the coasts as sea levels rise. States also tended to zone their coastal uses, as a static form of coastal use allocations. Some designed coastal zones, e.g. in Connecticut, are as wide as the coastal watershed, while others, e.g. New York, are only the distance from the coast to the first road or pipeline or railway. This has led to inconsistent coastal planning and contributed to the deterioration of environmental quality in shared resources such as Long Island Sound. Congress assigned to the CZMA the task of examining harmful algal blooms in many coast regions, from Hawaii and Alaska to Texas and Florida and Puerto Rico, and New York. Harmful Algal Bloom and Hypoxia Research & Control Act, P.L. 105-383, 112 Stat. 3447 (1998). In light of the impacts of climate change on the coastal areas, what new Congressional Findings should be adopted for §303 of the CZMA, 42 USC 1452? Should Congress amend the CZMA to require that al States update and revise that coastal zone plan in accordance with any new climate change findings and policies that Congress might adopt? Even before Congress may act, should the Administrator of NOAA convene all the state CZM agencies to scope out an agreed new planning procedure under 306(d) (2) (H), for the "planning process for energy facilities likely to be located in or which may significantly affect the coastal zone" and (I) the "planning process for assessing the effects of, and studying and evaluating ways to control or lessen the impact of shoreline erosion, and to restore areas adversely affected by such erosion"? Draft recommendations for the NOAA Administrator with respect to how you would wish her to respond to these questions.

2. Retreat from the Coast

In addition to Rhode Island's regulations excerpted above, another leading example of a retreat strategy is the South Carolina Beachfront Management Act, S.C. Code § 48-39-250 et seq. Its implementation led to the Court's best known takings decision Lucas v. South Carolina Coastal Council, 505 U.S. 1003 (1992), decision on remand, 424 S.E. 2d 484 (1992), requiring compensation to an investor in two erosion prone lots on which housing was subsequently prohibited by amendments to the Act which rendered the lots "valueless" according to the record on appeal. In such circumstances the Court held that the state owed Mr. Lucas Fifth Amendment compensation unless the state's regulatory restrictions coincided with restrictions on the land derived from background principles of the state's property and nuisance law. Background principles supporting implementation of a coastal retreat strategy without compensation identified in subsequent court opinions include the public trust doctrine protecting state-owned tidelands below the MHT as in McQueen v. South Carolina Coastal Council, 58 S.E. 2d 116 (S.C. 2003), cert. denied, 540 U.S. 982 (2003), public and private nuisance law, Monks v. City of Rancho Palos Verdes, 2008 WL 4416188 (Cal. App. Oct. 1, 2008), and customary public beach access rights in Severance v Patterson, 485 F, Supp. 2d 793 (S.D. Tex, 2007) and Stevens v. City of Cannon Beach, 854 P. 2d 449 (Ore. 1993), cert. denied with dissenting opinion, 510 U.S. 1207 (1994). Such background principles can also support compensation denials under state property owner compensation rights statutes. See C. Klein, The New Nuisance: An Antidote to Wetland Loss, Sprawl, and Gobal Warming, 48 Boston College L. Rev. 1155 (2007); J. Ruhl, The "Background Principles" of Natural Capital and Ecosystem Service—Did Lucas Open Pandora's Box?, 22 J. of Land Use & Envtl. L. 525 (2007); Symposium, Balancing Public and Private Rights in the Coastal Zone in the Era of Climate Change: The Fifteenth Anniversary of Lucas v. South Carolina Coastal Council, 16 Southeastern Envtl. L. J. 1 (2007).

Where coastal private property has not been rendered valueless by a regulation implementing a retreat strategy, courts have applied Penn Central to deny compensation as in Esposito v. South Carolina Coastal Council, 939 F. 2d 165 (4th Cir. 1991), cert. denied, 505 U.S. 1219 (1992), where owners of existing residences on Hilton Head Island challenged the S.C. Beachfront Management Act's prohibitions on rebuilding houses located on erosion-prone land if they were destroyed. The court upheld the statute because it did not interfere with plaintiff's existing uses and any value diminution it caused was insufficient to establish a taking. See also Gove v. Zoning Board of Appeals of Chatham, 831 N.E. 2d 865 (Mass. 2005) (building prohibition on vacant coastal lot subject to flooding which had value for private recreational uses held not a taking based on Penn Central); Esplanade Properties v. Settle, 307 F. 3d 978 (9th Cir. 2002), cert. denied 539 U.S. 926 (2003) (facts similar to Gove); Virginia Beach v. Bell, 498 S.E. 2d 414 (Va. 1998) (no compensation owed to owner who purchased after Coastal Primary Sand Dune Protection Act's enactment).

State and local moratoriums on further coastal development imposed to allow research and planning in support of a retreat strategy probably do not require compensation in most circumstances under the Court's ruling in Tahoe-Sierra Preservation Council v. Tahoe Regional Planning Agency, 535 U.S. 302 (2002), upholding a development moratorium lasting several years without compensation. See also L. Simons, Building Moratorium, Proposed Flood Zoning and Expropriation After Katrina, 9 Loy. J. Pub. Int. L. 39 (2007).

As in Rhode Island and South Carolina, coastal setbacks are a primary tool in coastal construction regulation. Approximately half of the coastal states have implemented a retreat policy of some degree by creating zones at the ocean's edge where development is prohibited or strictly regulated. See F. Gable and S. Edwards, Optimal Development Setbacks for the U.S. Coastal Zone, in E. Borgese et al. eds, Ocean Yearbook 15 (2001); J. Houlahan, Comparison of State Construction Setbacks to Manage Development in Coastal Hazard Areas, 17 Coastal Mgmt. 219 (1989). Early setback lines generally prohibited or limited construction in areas within a prescribed distance from a baseline, usually the mean high water line, the vegetation line, or a line associated with the primary dune. The distances were relatively arbitrary and generally ranged from 40 to 100 feet. As understanding of beach and dune processes increased and as coastal engineering became more sophisticated, delineation of setback lines also began to become more sophisticated and highly technical. Many states now have a second type of regulatory setback line based on complicated calculations of seasonal shoreline fluctuations, vulnerability to storms surges, and the rate of shoreline erosion. See, e.g., Island Harbor Beach Club, Ltd. v. Department of Natural Resources, 495 So. 2d 209 (Fla. App. 1986) (finding that because of the complexity of the technical and scientific issues and the high degree of scientific uncertainty involved, agency determinations of coastal construction control lines should be given great deference). Although this second type of setback line has more scientific validity, the complexity is confusing to landowners who can more readily understand the impact of a fixed setback distance in conceiving their uses of the land.

Hawaii uses the first type of setback line for controlling coastal development. Construction must be located a minimum of forty feet inland from the shoreline, which is defined as the debris or vegetation line, whichever is further inland. See Haw. Rev. Stat. § 205A.

South Carolina's Beachfront Management Act (BMA), S.C. Code §§ 48-39-270–48-39-360, discussed above is one of the country's most comprehensive coastal construction laws. Under the state's coastal management program, the South Carolina Coastal Council has jurisdiction to regulate beachfront construction. The BMA required the Coastal Council to establish a baseline on the Atlantic coast at the "crest of an ideal primary oceanfront sand dune." From this baseline, a setback line was calculated at a distance of forty times the average annual erosion rate, but at a minimum distance of twenty feet landward of the baseline. The area within twenty feet landward of the baseline was a "dead zone" in which major structures were not permitted. In the remaining area between the baseline and the setback line, construction is limited to habitable structures not larger than 5000 square feet, located as far landward on a lot as possible, and meeting other demanding conditions. In the wake of Hurricane Hugo and a host of legal challenges, the BMA was amended in 1990 to eliminate the twenty-foot dead zone, making all construction between the baseline and setback line subject to the same standards. In addition to the Lucas, Esposito cases discussed above, see Beard v. S.C. Coastal Council, 403 S.E. 2d 620 (S.C. 2000); South Carolina Coastal Conservation League v. S.C. Dept. of Health, 582 S.E. 2d 410 (S.C. 2003); see also D. Kendall, Preserving South Carolina's Beaches: The Role of Local Planning in Managing Growth in Coastal South Carolina, 9 South Carolina Envtl. L.J. 61 (2000); Smith, Analysis of the Regulation of Beachfront Development in South Carolina, 42 S.C. L. Rev. 717 (1991).

Florida has similar legislation with two beachfront regulatory lines. See the Coastal Zone Protection Act of 1985, Fla. Stat. §§ 161.52-.58. The coastal construction control line (CCCL), based generally on the 100-year storm surge, creates a zone in which construction is subject to state permitting and strictly regulated. The second zone of jurisdiction is created by projecting, on a case-by-case basis, the seasonal high water line, as it will exist thirty years after the construction permit application. In this zone, all major construction is prohibited, except for certain single-family dwellings that can be constructed landward of the frontal dune structure. See generally D. Christie, Growth Management in Florida: Focus on the Coast, 3 J. Land Use & Envtl. L. 33 (1987); K. Jancaitis, Florida on the Coast of Climate Change: Responding to Rising Seas, 31-SPG Environs Envtl. L. & Policy J. 157 (2008). Note that Florida's "retreat" policy is not as rigorous as South Caroline's policy; it allows some habitable development in areas that are projected to be in the water in thirty years and provides for no future buffer zone. See, Fla. Stat. § 161.053(5)(b) (creating a variance from some CCCL permitting requirements where existing adjacent structures form a "reasonably continuous and uniform construction line" seaward of the CCCL and the existing structures have not been "unduly affected by erosion." Retreat strategies generally apply only to undeveloped beachfront property. Existing development is usually "grandfathered in."

A problem concerning existing structures is when do they become subject to the new regulatory scheme. South Carolina's Beachfront Management Act prohibits rebuilding structures that are "destroyed beyond repair" and originally banned their reconstruction within the dead zone or seaward of the baseline. Destroyed beyond repair means "more than sixty six and two-third percent of the replacement value of the habitable structure * * * has been destroyed." See S.C. Code Ann. § 49-39-270. In the wake of Hurricane Hugo, the South Carolina legislature amended the BMA in 1990 to give the Coastal Council the authority to issue special permits to allow reconstruction of habitable structures under certain conditions, even if they were located seaward of the baseline. The Florida Coastal Zone Protection Act provides that CCCL and thirty-year erosion zone requirements will apply to all new construction except "modification, maintenance, or repair to any existing structure within the limits of the existing foundation which does not require . . . any additions to, or repair or modification of, the existing foundation." See Fla. Stat. § 161.053(12).

Hurricanes Hugo, Andrew, Katrina, Rita, and Ike all highlighted the need for strict building codes for coastal construction. Substandard housing is not only subject to greater damage in a storm, but also creates a hazard for other nearby properties. The creation of the National Flood Insurance Program (NFIP) by the National Flood Insurance Act of 1968, 42 U.S.C.A. §§ 4001-4128, has led to widespread adoption of minimum federal building standards for flood prone areas, including beaches. The NFIP is intended to reduce federal flood disaster relief by supplying guaranteed flood insurance coverage to communities that adopt building standards and land use controls that minimize flood damages and property losses. State and local regulation may be stricter than federally imposed safety and building standards, and governments are encouraged to adopt land use regulations that guide development away from flood hazard areas. See, e.g., Fla. Stat. § 161.55(1)(d) (requiring major coastal structures to withstand wind velocities of 110 miles per hour and structures in the Florida Keys to withstand 115 mile per hour winds).

In addition to guaranteeing flood insurance for communities participating in the NFIP, the program also imposes penalties for nonparticipation. If a community with areas susceptible to flooding does not join the program, federal agencies like the Small Business Administration and the Veterans Administration are prohibited from providing federal assistance for development in flood-prone areas. See 42 U.S.C. § 4106(a). The NFIP has been upheld as a constitutional imposition of strict federal building standards on the states that does not constitute a taking of private property as a result of diminished property values in nonparticipating communities. See Adolph v. Federal Emergency Management Agency, 854 F.2d 732 (5th Cir. 1988); Texas Landowners Rights Ass'n v. Harris 453 F. Supp. 1025 (D.D.C. 1978). Furthermore, administration of the NFIP must be carried out in compliance with the federal Endangered Species Act's federal agency consultation requirements discussed in the polar and hydrology sections. Florida Key Deer v. Paulison, 522 F. 3d 1133 (11th Cir. 2008).

Unregulated coastal construction can also interfere with the habitat values of a beach. For example, beaches from North Carolina to Texas are nesting sites for endangered sea turtles. Many states strictly regulate the construction of sea walls and the placement of riprap on the beaches of turtle nesting areas and limit other coastal construction during nesting season. In addition, because hatchling turtles gravitate toward light, public safety needs must be balanced against protection of the young turtles in regulating light for coastal buildings and highways. See Trepanier v. County of Velusia, No. 5 DO5-3802 (Fla. App. Sept. 14, 2007); M. Fish et al, Construction Setback Regulations and Sea-Level Rise: Mitigating Sea Turtle Nesting Beach Loss, 51 Ocean & Coastal Management 51 (2008). On the west coast, old growth forests and the endangered snowy plover bird also depend on beaches for breeding; coastal old growth forests are critical habitat for the threatened marbled murrelet bird. See Coos County Board of County Commissioners v. Kempthorne, 2008 WL 2522202 (9th Cir. June 26, 2008); American Forest Resource Council v. Hall, 2008 WL 2549040 (D.D.C. June 26, 2008).

Much of the development on the nation's coasts could not take place without federal and state assistance and subsidies. Federal and state programs, including flood insurance, highway programs, sewage treatment facility funding, and disaster relief, have tended to subsidize and encourage growth on barrier islands. Such development also involves tremendous costs: average annual storm damage to coastal property amounts to billions of dollars. See C. Klein & S. Zellner, Mississippi River Stories: Lessons from a Century of Unnatural Disasters, 60 SMU L. Rev. 1471 (2007).

The 1982 Coastal Barrier Resources Act (CBRA), 16 U.S.C.A. §§3501-3510, coordinates environmental protection with federal fiscal policy. CBRA's purposes include preserving the natural resources of coastal barrier islands, minimizing loss of human life from hazardous coastal development, and restricting federal support for such development. Within undeveloped coastal barrier areas Congressionally designated as the Coastal Barrier Resources System (CBRS), the Act restricts federal assistance or expenditures for new development. This includes federal flood insurance coverage, government loans, non-emergency disaster relief, new bridges, roads and other infrastructure, and other forms of federal assistance and subsidies. The Act does not restrict the rights of private or non-federal public owners to develop barrier islands, but the intent is that the expense and the risks of new development must be borne by the developer and subsequent purchasers of coastal barrier island property. See E. Jones, The Coastal Barrier Resources Act: A Common Cents Approach to Coastal Protection, 21 Envtl. L. 1015 (1991).

In Bostic v. United States 753 F.2d 1292 (4th Cir. 1985), developers and landowners of property of Topsail Island, North Carolina, asserted that CBRA had wrongly designated their land as part of an undeveloped coastal barrier, making them ineligible for federal flood insurance. The Bostic court held, however, that since the map adopted by Congress specifically designated the island as an undeveloped coastal barrier, Congress unquestionably intended to include it in the CBRS, and the designation was not a reviewable agency action. The court also found that inclusion of the property in the CBRS was substantially related to the purposes of CBRA.

Under the CBRA, the states' roles are essentially limited to formally commenting on and informally influencing the federal Interior Department's designation recommendation to Congress. Some states have followed the lead of the federal government. For example, the coastal infrastructure policy of Florida's Coastal Zone Protection Act of 1985 reinforced the expenditure limitation approach originally imposed by an executive order. Fla. Stat. § 380.27(1) mandates that no state funds be used for constructing bridges or causeways to coastal barrier islands that are not currently accessible by bridge or causeway. The coastal infrastructure policy also emphasizes state-local cooperation by allowing state allocation of funds to expand infrastructure only if the construction is consistent with the approved coastal management element of local government comprehensive plans. The state's local government planning legislation provides that it is the intent of the legislature that local governments also cooperate in developing funding policies. Local governments are instructed to design their comprehensive plans to "limit public expenditures in areas that are subject to destruction in natural disaster." Fla. Stat. § 163.3178(1).

3. Coastal Restoration, Ambulatory Boundary Rules, and Property Owner Littoral Rights

Gradual sea level rise, dramatic coastal events such as hurricanes and tsunamis, and responses to them all involve the state and federal common law regarding: (1) changes in the exact location of the line dividing private uplands from public tidelands and (2) the upland owner's littoral rights to use the immediately adjacent public tidelands and the waters overhead. See B. Flushman, Water Boundaries: Demystifying Level Boundaries Adjacent to Tidal or Navigable Waters (2002); R. Hildreth, Coastal Natural Hazards Management, 59 Ore. L. Rev. 201 (1980).

The rules regarding the public-private boundary's location distinguish between gradual and sudden ("avulsive") changes in the shoreline: the public-private line follows gradual shoreline changes such as erosion but remains in its previous location if the shoreline changes suddenly due to storm events or construction of seawalls, dikes, and rip rap to armor the coast, and piers and jetties to support navigation. The public-private dividing line then follows gradual shoreline changes subsequent to these sudden alterations except that many states deny the shoreline owner gradual shoreline additions ("accretions") caused by the owner's own activities such as constructing groins perpendicular to the shoreline to trap sediments. See also 33 C.F.R. § 329.13. Sea level rise due to human CO_2 emissions since the industrial revolution would seem to be gradual enough that courts will move the public-private boundary inland accordingly. See also 33 C.F.R. § 328.5. Research continues on those emissions' impacts on the frequency and intensity of coastal storm events to which the rules about sudden shoreline changes will continue to be applied for the foreseeable future.

Different from most other states, Washington state claims ownership of all accretions along the shore, whether natural or artificial, Hughes v. Washington, 389 U.S. 290 (1967), and California law denies the shoreline owner all artificial accretions, not just those caused by the shoreline owner. See California v. United States, 457 U.S. 273, reh'g denied, 458 U.S. 1131 (1982). In applying that rule, the California Supreme Court had to decide whether downstream accretions caused by hydraulic gold mining far upstream were artificial or natural. The court's decision treating them as natural and thus belonging to the downstream shoreline owners rather than the state suggests that court would treat any accretion caused by human-induced climate change as natural as well, and thus move the public-private boundary seaward due to that accretion. The court stated:

> We thus hold that accretion is artificial if directly caused by human activities that occurred in the immediate vicinity of the accreted land. Accretion is not artificial merely because human activities far away contributed to it. The dividing line between what is and is not in the immediate vicinity will be decided on a case-by-case basis, keeping in mind that the artificial activity must have been the direct cause of the accretion before it can be deemed artificial. The larger the structure or the scope of human activity, the farther away it can be and still be a direct cause of the accretion, although it must always be in the gen-

eral location of the accreted property to come within the [California] artificial accretion rule.

State Lands Commission v. Superior Court, 90 P. 2d 648 (Cal. Sup. Ct. 1995).

But the more likely climate change scenario is gradual erosion due to sea level rise. Different from accretion, no U.S. courts so far have distinguished between artificial and natural erosion. See State v. Bishop, 359 N.Y.S 2d 817 (1974). Thus the likely outcome would be that the public-private boundary would move inland due to erosion caused by climate change. Pending litigation noted in the polar and U.S. Clean Air Act sections seek to impose liability for coastal flooding in the Arctic on major sources of U.S. CO_2 emissions. See Kivalina v. Exxon Mobil Corp. supra. Such liability would be an extension of the rules discussed below in the armoring section under which public and private sector actors causing coastal erosion are sometimes held responsible.

Legislative changes to these rules favorable to private upland owners must comply with public trust doctrine protections of public rights in state-owned tidelands; the Fifth Amendment constrains changes unfavorable to upland owners. See Hildreth supra at 208-10; M. Hiatt, Come Hell or High Water: Reexamining the Takings Clause in a Climate Changed Future, 18 Duke Envtl. L. & Policy Forum 371 (2008).

The rule awarding shoreline owners gradual accretions not caused by their own shoreline construction activities also is one of their common law littoral rights to use adjacent public tidelands and waters. Under this rule the owner's land increases and remains immediately adjacent to the water when gradual additions occur. This and other littoral rights such as the right to an unobstructed view of the adjacent waters recognized in some states are relevant to private and publicly funded beach restoration projects that are favored in some locations over an armoring or retreat response. Compare Ocean City v. Maffuci, 740 A. 2d 630 (N.J. 1999) (Fifth Amendment compensation awarded for view lost to dune restoration project) with Slavin v. Town of Oak Island, 584 S. E. 2d 100 (N.C. 2003) (littoral right of water access can be restricted to specific corridors through restored dunes without compensation).

Beach restoration projects also present the question of who owns the beach created by the project, the adjacent inland owners who want to maintain their status as littoral owners with direct waterfront access while excluding the public, or a public entity, e.g., the government agency which funded the project or the local government within whose boundaries the project is located. Compare City of Long Beach v. Liu, 833 9. 2d 106 (N.J. 2003) (avulsion rule applied resulting in public ownership of federally financed beach nourishment project) with Michaelson v. Silver Beach Improvement Assn, 173 N.E. 2d 273 (1961) (accretion rule applied resulting in private ownership of beach created by government project). A Florida statute eliminating littoral rights in restored beaches was held not to be a facial taking of beachfront owner property rights in Walton County v. Stop the Beach Renourishment, Inc., 38 ELR 20254 (Fla. Sup. Ct. Sept. 29, 2008). See P. King, Financing Beach Restoration in California, 76 Shore & Beach No. 2 at 44 (2008).

Courts in Texas have dealt with public beach access and other issues raised when private structures end up closer to the water due to storm events, failed armoring and restoration projects, and retreat responses to sea level rise and erosion. Compare Hirtz v. Texas, 773 F. Supp 6 (S.D. Texas 1991) vacated on other grounds, 974 F. 2d 663 (5th Cir. 1992) (repairs allowed) with Matcha v. Mattox, 711 S.W. 2d 95 (Tex. App. 1986), cert. denied, 481 U.S. (1987) (repairs not allowed) and Mikoslpa v. Galveston, 328 F. Supp. 2d 671 (S.D. Texas 2004), remanded, 419 F. 3d 431 (5th Ctr. 2005). See also Smiley v. S.C. Dept. of Health, 2007 S.C. LEXIS 292 (S.C. Sup. Ct. July 30, 2007) (beach user had standing to challenge state-approved sand excavation project). See generally M. Caldwell & C. Segall, No Day at the Beach: Sea Level Rise, Ecosystem Loss, and Public Access Along the California Coast, 34 Ecology L. Q. 553 (2007); J. Kalo, North Carolina Oceanfront Property and Public Waters: The Rights of Littoral Owners in the Twenty-first Century, 83 N.C. L. Rev. 1427 (2005).

Under international and U.S. ocean law, some important federal and state jurisdictional boundary lines offshore would move landward due to sea level rise. See G. Mangone, Marine Boundaries: States and the United States, 21 Intl. J. of Marine & Coastal L. 121 (2006); C. Di Leva, Maritime Rights of Coastal States and Climate Change: Should States Adapt to Submerged Boundaries? (2008).

4. Armoring the Coast: Regulation and Liability

Most non-federal armoring projects above and below the MHT require Corps approval under the Rivers and Harbors Act § 10, 33 U.S.C. § 403, and Clean Water Act, § 404, 33 U.S.C. § 1344; private armoring projects above and below the MHT also require state and local government approval. See Ocean Harbor House Homeowners Assn. v. California Coastal Comm., 2008 Cal. App. LEXIS 770 (2008); South Carolina Coastal Conservation League v. S.C. Department of Health, 582 S.E. 2d 410 (S.C. 2003); Stevens v. City of Cannon Beach, 854 P. 2d 449 (Ore. 1993), cert. denied with dissenting opinion, 510 U.S. 1207 (1994). See also Scott v. City of Del Mar., 68 Cal. Rptr 2d 317 (1997) (removal of seawalls and rip rap as public nuisances). Under the older "common enemy" doctrine neighbors injured by a private armoring project's interference with previous accretion cycles have no recourse. See Grundy v. Brock Family Trust, 67 P. 3d 500 (Wash. App. 2003). More states now apply a reasonableness standard in determining the armorer's liability for injuries to neighbors. Lummis v. Lilly, 429 N.E. 2d 1146 (Mass. 1982). A "natural flow" rule would protect neighbors from any interference from private armoring projects. See Hildreth supra at 211; M. Corfield, Sand Rights: Using California's Public Trust Doctrine to Protect Against Coastal Erosion, 24 San Diego L. Rev. 727 (1987); N. Jacobsen, Sand or Concrete at the Beach? Private Property Rights on Eroding Oceanfront Land, 31 Environs Envtl. L. & Policy J. 217 (2008); M. Reed, Seawalls and the Public Trust: Navigating the Tension Between Private Property and Public Beach Use in the Face of Shoreline Erosion, 20 Fordham Envtl. L. Rev. 305 (2009). See also Symposium, Extreme Re-engineering of the Coast, 76 Shore & Beach No. 4 (Fall 2008).

Most disruptions of previous accretion cycles attributed to public navigation projects are shielded by federal and state navigation servitude law. See Applegate v. U.S., 1996 WL 208458 (Fed. Cl. 1996); Miramar Co. v. Santa Barbara, 143 P. 2d 1 (Cal. 1943). However, those servitudes generally do not extend inland above the public-private dividing line along the shore. See Banks v. U.S., 78 Fed. Cl. 603 (2007).

Some of the litigation over private damages suffered due to Hurricane Katrina in 2005 involved federal liability for failed Corps armoring and flood control projects along the Gulf Coast. See In re Katrina Canal Beaches Consolidated Litigation, 39 ELR 20071 (E.D. La. March 20, 2009) See also Barasiach v. Columbia Gulf Transmission Co., 467 F. Supp. 2d 676 (E.D. La. 2006) (defendants not liable for Louisiana coastal wetlands loss); Blanco v. Burton, 2006 WL 2366046 (E.D. La. Oct. 24, 2006) (post-Katrina offshore oil and gas development challenged for failure to account for hurricane's damage to facilities and wetlands); Lee Brothers v. Crowley Liner Services, 2007 Wl 1858744 (S.D. Miss. June 26, 2007) (shipping company not liable for inland damages caused by its shipping containers during Hurricane Katrina); Northrop Grumman v. Factory Mutual Ins. Co., 2008 U.S. App. LEXIS 17270 (9th cir. Aug. 14, 2008) (Hurricane Katrina storm surge damage excluded from coverage by insurance policy's flood damage exclusion provision); Paul v. Landsafe Flood Determination, Inc., 2008 U.S. App. LEXIS 25297. (5th Cir. Dec. 5, 2008) (cause of action stated for negligent flood zone determination); Six Flags Inc. v. Westchester Surplus Lines Ins. Co., 2009 U.S. App. LEXIS 8273 (5th Cir. April 21, 2009) (insurance policy flood damage exclusions); D. Farber & J. Chen, Disasters and the Law (2006), G. Guzy, Insurance and Climate Change in Gerrard, Global Climate Change and U.S. Law 541, 546-550 (2007) (insurance industry responses to Hurricane Katrina); J. Nolan & D. Rodriguez, Losing Ground: A Nation on the Edge (2007).

The Pew Ocean Commission's 2003 report and the United States Commission on Ocean Policy's 2004 report both noted the increased hurricane vulnerability of the Louisiana coast due to the extensive loss of buffering wetlands, but neither dealt with the consequences of sea level rise due to climate change. The NGO Joint Ocean Commission Initiative formed to follow up on both reports includes climate change impacts on the oceans among its priority concerns. The 2007 Water Resources Development Act, enacted through Congress' first override of a veto by President Bush, included several billion dollars for restoring the Louisiana coast. Also enacted in 2007 as part of Pub. L. 109-479 (110th Cong.) was the Tsunami Warning and Education Act intended to reduce losses of people and property due to a tsunami striking the U. S. coast. No legislation enacted to date has sought either to immunize coastal armorers from liability or provide compensation to shoreline owners injured by either gradual erosion or sudden shoreline losses caused by armoring activities.

C. ADAPTING IN POLAR AREAS

Polar bears in the Arctic are being adversely affected by declining sea ice. In May 2008 they were listed as threatened under the U.S. Endangered Species Act, 16 U.S.C. § 1531 et. seq. See 50 C.F.R. § 17.11(h). The reasons for and climate change implications of that listing are discussed in the following excerpts from the U.S. Fish and Wildlife Service's (FWS) listing decision and their responses to public comments, as required by Section 4 of the Endangered Species Act.

DETERMINATION OF THREATENED STATUS FOR THE POLAR BEAR (URSUS MARITIMUS) THROUGHOUT ITS RANGE

Department of the Interior
Fish and Wildlife Service
50 CFR Part 17
(73 Fed. Reg. 28212 (May 15, 2008))

We, the U.S. Fish and Wildlife Service (Service), determine threatened status for the polar bear (Ursus maritimus) under the Endangered Species Act of 1973, as amended (Act) (16 U.S.C. 1531 et seq.). Polar bears evolved to utilize the Arctic sea ice niche and are distributed throughout most ice-covered seas of the Northern Hemisphere. We find, based upon the best available scientific and commercial information, that polar bear habitat—principally sea ice—is declining throughout the species' range, that this decline is expected to continue for the foreseeable future, and that this loss threatens the species throughout all of its range. Therefore, we find that the polar bear is likely to become an endangered species within the foreseeable future throughout all of its range. This final rule activates the consultation provisions of section 7 of the Act for the polar bear. The special rule for the polar bear, also published in today's edition of the Federal Register, sets out the prohibitions and exceptions that apply to this threatened species. * * *

On April 28, 2008, the United States District Court for the Northern District of California [in Center for Biological Diversity v. Kempthorne, [2008 WL 1902703 (N.D. Cal.)] ordered us to publish the final determination on whether the polar bear should be listed as an endangered or threatened species by May 15, 2008. * * *

International Agreements and Oversight
International Agreement on the Conservation of Polar Bears

Canada, Denmark (on behalf of Greenland), Norway, the Russian Federation, and the United States are parties to the Agreement on the Conservation of Polar Bears (1973 Polar Bear Agreement) signed in 1973; by 1976, the Agreement was ratified by all parties. The 1973 Polar Bear Agreement requires the parties to take appropriate action to protect the ecosystem of which polar bears are a part, with special attention to habitat components such as denning and feeding sites and migration patterns, and to manage polar bear populations in accordance with sound conservation practices based on the best available scientific data. The 1973 Polar Bear Agreement relies on the efforts of each party to implement conservation programs and does not preclude a party from establishing additional controls. * * *

Convention on International Trade in Endangered Species of Wild Fauna and Flora (CITES)

The Convention on International Trade in Endangered Species of Wild Fauna and Flora (CITES) is a treaty aimed at protecting species at risk from international trade. The CITES regulates international trade in animals and plants by listing species in one of its three appendices. The level of monitoring and regulation to which an animal or plant species is subject depends on the appendix in which the species is listed. Appendix I includes species threatened with extinction that are or may be affected by trade; trade of Appendix I species is only allowed in exceptional circumstances. Appendix II includes species not necessarily now threatened with extinction, but for which trade must be regulated in order to avoid utilization incompatible with their survival. Appendix III includes species that are subject to regulation in at least one country, and for which that country has asked other CITES Party countries for assistance in controlling and monitoring international trade in that species.

Polar bears were listed in Appendix II of CITES on July 7, 1975. As such, CITES parties must determine, among other things, that any polar bear, polar bear part, or product made from polar bear was legally obtained and that the export will not be detrimental to the survival of the species, prior to issuing a permit authorizing the export of the animal, part, or product. The CITES does not itself regulate take or domestic trade of polar bears; however, through its process of monitoring trade in wildlife species and requisite findings prior to allowing international movement of listed species and monitoring programs, the CITES is effective in ensuring that the international movement of listed species does not contribute to the detriment of wildlife populations. All polar bear range states are members to the CITES and have in place the CITES-required Scientific and Management Authorities. The Service therefore has determined that the CITES is effective in regulating the international trade in polar bear, or polar bear parts or products, and provides conservation measures to minimize those potential threats to the species.

Domestic Regulatory Mechanisms
United States

Marine Mammal Protection Act of 1972, as amended

The Marine Mammal Protection Act of 1972, as amended (16 U.S.C. 1361 et seq.) (MMPA) was enacted to protect and conserve marine mammals so that they continue to be significant functioning elements of the ecosystem of which they are a part. The MMPA set forth a national policy to prevent marine mammal species or population stocks from diminishing to the point where they are no longer a significant functioning element of the ecosystems. * * *

Outer Continental Shelf Lands Act

The Outer Continental Shelf Lands Act (43 U.S.C. 1331 et seq.) (OCSLA) established Federal jurisdiction over submerged lands on the Outer Continental Shelf (OCS) seaward of the State boundaries (3-mile limit) in order to expedite exploration and development of oil/gas resources on the OCS in a manner that minimizes impact to the living natural resources within the OCS. Implementation of OCSLA is delegated to the Minerals Management Service (MMS) of the Department of the Interior. The OCS projects that could adversely impact the Coastal Zone are subject to Federal consistency requirements under terms of the Coastal Zone Management Act, as noted below. The OCSLA also mandates that orderly development of OCS energy resources be balanced with protection of human, marine, and coastal environments. The OCSLA does not itself regulate the take of polar bears, although through consistency determinations it helps to ensure that OCS projects do not adversely impact polar bears or their habitats.

Oil Pollution Act of 1990

The Oil Pollution Act of 1990 (33 U.S.C. 2701) established new requirements and extensively amended the Federal Water Pollution Control Act (33 U.S.C. 1301 et. seq.) to provide enhanced capabilities for oil spill response and natural resource damage assessment by the Service. It requires us to consult on developing a fish and wildlife response plan for the National Contingency Plan, input to Area Contingency Plans, review of Facility and Tank Vessel Contingency Plans, and to conduct damage assessments associated with oil spills.

Coastal Zone Management Act

The Coastal Zone Management Act of 1972 (16 U.S.C. 1451 et seq.) (CZMA) was enacted to "preserve, protect, develop, and where possible, to restore or enhance the resources of the Nation's coastal zone." The CZMA provides for the submission of a State program subject to Federal approval. The CZMA requires that Federal actions be conducted in a manner consistent with the State's CZM plan to the maximum extent practicable. Federal agencies planning or authorizing an activity that affects any land or water use or natural resource of the coastal zone must provide a consistency determination to the appropriate State agency. The CZMA applies to polar bear habitats of northern and western Alaska. The North Slope Borough and Alaska Coastal Management Programs assist in protection of polar bear habitat through the project review process. The CZMA does not itself regulate the take of polar bears, and, overall, is not determined to be effective at this time in addressing the threats identified in the five factor analysis.

Alaska National Interest Lands Conservation Act

The Alaska National Interest Lands Conservation Act of 1980 (16 U.S.C. 3101 et seq.) (ANILCA) created or expanded National Parks and National Wildlife Refuges in Alaska, including the expansion of the Arctic National Wildlife Refuge (NWR). One of the establishing purposes of the Arctic NWR is to conserve polar bears. Section 1003 of ANILCA prohibits production of oil and gas in the Arctic NWR, and no leasing or other development leading to production of oil and gas may take place unless authorized by an Act of Congress. Most of the Arctic NWR is a federally designated Wilderness, but the coastal plain of Arctic NWR, which provides important polar bear denning habitat, does not have Wilderness status. The ANILCA does not itself regulate the take of polar bears, although through its designations it has provided recognition of, and various levels of protection for, polar bear habitat. In the case of polar bear habitat, the Bureau of Land Management (BLM) is responsible for vast land areas on the North Slope, including the National Petroleum Reserve, Alaska (NPRA). Habitat suitable for polar bear denning and den sites have been identified within NPRA. The BLM considers fish and wildlife values under its multiple use mission in evaluating land use authorizations and prospective oil and gas leasing actions. Provisions of the MMPA regarding the incidental take of polar bears on land areas and waters within the jurisdiction of the United States continue to apply to activities conducted by the oil and gas industry on BLM lands.

Marine Protection, Research and Sanctuaries Act

The Marine Protection, Research and Sanctuaries Act (33 U.S.C. 1401 et seq.) (MPRSA) was enacted in part to "prevent or strictly limit the dumping into ocean waters of any material that would adversely affect human health, welfare, or amenities, or the marine environment, ecological systems, or economic potentialities." The MPRSA does not itself regulate the take of polar bears. There are no designated marine sanctuaries within the range of the polar bear. * * *

Conclusions

Therefore, * * * we find that the polar bear populations of Western Hudson Bay, Southern Beaufort Sea, and Baffin Bay are not currently in danger of extinction, but are likely to become so in the foreseeable future. * * *

Critical Habitat

Critical habitat is defined in section 3(5) of the [Endangered Species] Act as: (i) the specific areas within the geographical area occupied by a species, at the time it is listed in accordance with the Act, on which are found those physical or biological features (I) essential to the conservation of the species and (II) that may require special management considerations or protection; and (ii) specific areas outside the geographical area occupied by a species at the time it is listed, upon a determination that such areas are essential for the conservation of the species. "Conservation" is defined in section 3(3) of the Act as meaning the use of all methods and procedures needed to bring the species to the point at which listing under the Act is no longer necessary. The primary regulatory effect of critical habitat is the requirement, under section 7(a)(2) of the Act, that Federal agencies shall ensure that any action they authorize, fund, or carry out is not likely to result in the destruction or adverse modification of designated critical habitat. * * *

A careful assessment of the designation of marine areas as critical habitat will require additional time to fully evaluate physical and biological features essential to the conservation of the polar bear and how those features are likely to change over the foreseeable future. In addition, near-shore and terrestrial habitats that may qualify for designation as critical habitat will require a similar thorough assessment and evaluation in light of projected climate change and other threats. Additionally, we have not gathered sufficient economic and other data on the impacts of a critical habitat designation. These factors must be considered as part of the designation procedure. Thus, we find that critical habitat is not determinable at this time. * * *

With the world community acting in concert, we are confident the future of the polar bear can be secured. * * *

* * * * *

For threatened species like the polar bear, ESA § 4(d), 16 U.S.C. § 1534(d), requires the Interior Secretary to issue any regulations deemed necessary to conserve the species. For the polar bear, these section 4(d) regulations consist of the pre-existing protections of the Marine Mammal Protection Act, 16 U.S.C. §1361 et. seq., the United States-Russia Polar Bear Conservation and Management Act of 2006, P.L. 109-479, title IX (Jan. 12, 2007), the Convention on International Trade in Endangered Species of Wild Fauna and Flora to which the U.S. is a party and the ESA regulations applicable to all threatened species. See 50 C.F.R. §§ 17.31, 17.32, 17.40(q). The decision not to attempt to protect polar bears more directly from climate change impacts is also explained by the U.S. Fish and Wildlife Service at 73 Fed. Reg. 28306 (May 15, 2008). This approach to a polar bear Special Rule was reconfirmed by the Service in December 2008. *See* 73 Fed. Reg. 76,249 (Dec. 16, 2008). Also, the exclusion of greenhouse gas emissions from ESA Section 7 consultations regarding the polar bear was extended to all Section 7 consultations by amendments to 50 C.F.R. part 402, adopted in December 2008. *See* 73 Fed. Reg. 76,272 (Dec. 16, 2008). These rules were immediately challenged by the State of California and three environmental groups in separate lawsuits, and the Congress authorized the Obama Administration to immediately withdraw them, Omnibus Appropriations Act, 2009, Pub. L. No. 111-8, div. E, tit. IV, sec. 429, which it did in May 2009, see 74 Fed. Reg. 20421 (May 4, 2009), while leaving the above Special Rule approach in place.

Compare with the above polar bear listing excerpts the climate change roles envisioned for the ESA in J. Ruhl, Climate and the Endangered Species Act: Building Bridges to the No-Analog Future, 88 Boston U. L. Rev. 1 (2008), and J. Kostyack & D. Rohlf, Conserving Endangered Species in an Era of Global Warming, 38 Envtl. L. Rep. 10203, 10210-10213 (2008), including the following excerpt from the latter:

CONSERVING ENDANGERED SPECIES IN AN ERA OF GLOBAL WARMING
John Kostyack and Dan Rohlf
38 Environmental Law Reporter 10203 (2008)

VI. Conserving Wildlife in a Changing Climate: Policy Recommendations

We have already begun to see the initial effects of climate change, and we must now act quickly to put in place new legal mechanisms to deal with its pervasive threats to biodiversity. At a broad level, it is crucial that Congress include within any climate change legislation specific provisions—and specific funding—to conserve biodiversity in a warming world. At the same time, policymakers must reaffirm the ESA's role as a primary legal tool for protecting the nation's at-risk species and their habitats. As noted above, the statute's comprehensive provisions and inherent flexibility enable it to deal with climate-based threats without major modifications to the law itself. However, within the framework of the existing statute, we recommend new policies and implementation schemes to ensure that agencies meaningfully confront threats to biodiversity posed by climate change. A key premise underlying these recommendations is that lawmakers, agencies, and the American public must reaffirm the nation's commitment to protecting other species and the ecosystems upon which they depend. Myriad reasons exist for doing so, but one should suffice—given the tremendous value of wildlife and ecosystem services to humans, our economies, and our very survival, we cannot afford not to.

A. Addressing Endangered Species in Federal Climate Change Legislation

While lawmakers do not appear poised to make fundamental changes to the ESA itself anytime in the near future, it seems likely that Congress will soon enact legislation with consequences for endangered species that are much more far-reaching than any ESA overhaul. * * *

Congress can take no more important step to help wildlife and ecosystems than to legislate substantial, economy-wide reductions in global warming pollution. It is also crucial that auctions of emissions credits be used to generate billions of dollars of dedicated funding annually to enable federal and state natural resource agencies to confront inevitable global warming. Although some may consider dedicating a substantial sum of such new annual funding for wildlife (say, $5 billion) a steep price to pay for biodiversity protection given the other urgent priorities for addressing global warming, it is in fact a necessary investment to maintain and restore the natural systems that serve as the foundation of our economy and quality of life.

Rather than trying to create new wildlife programs, Congress should direct natural resource agencies to spend these new dollars on updating their implementation of the ESA and other conservation programs so that they fully integrate global warming science. One historically underused provision of the ESA could play a key role in this process. Section 7(a)(1) directs all federal agencies to carry out, in consultation with the FWS and the NMFS, programs to conserve threatened and endangered species; unfortunately, most agencies often ignore this affirmative mandate. Lawmakers should breathe new life into this provision by directing federal agencies to craft comprehensive programs for conserving wildlife and ecosystems threatened by global warming. To facilitate this process, Congress should create one or more global warming and wildlife science centers within the federal agencies. Such centers, coupled with the consultation mandate of §7(a)(1), would enhance all agencies' scientific capacities to conserve listed species in the face of threats posed by climate change.

B. Making Adaptive Management a Central Focus of the ESA

Although each year scientists are able to identify and project the ecosystem changes attributable to global warming with increasing degrees of precision, the exact consequences of global warming will always defy prediction. The average surface temperatures around the globe already exceed levels ever experienced since modern wildlife management began roughly a century ago, and they will soon exceed levels experienced since the beginning of human civilization approximately 13,000 years ago. This means that careful observation and the flexibility to change course in response to new information will be especially important components of ESA implementation in the coming years.

The concept of adaptive management is not new. In recent years, natural resource agencies have often touted the use of adaptive management in implementing the ESA and other wildlife programs. Unfortunately, however, agencies' use of this term has often proven to be more in the way of lip service than actual implementation. In order to practice adaptive management, the Services should enact regulations that insist upon a high degree of rigor in carrying out adaptive management programs. Key elements of any adaptive management program promulgated by the Services would be:

- Systematic observations of the impacts of global warming on wildlife and wildlife habitats;
- Projections and conservation planning based on these observations and on models of future climate conditions;
- Conservation actions pursuant to such projections and plans;
- Monitoring and evaluation; and
- Adjustments to projections, plans, and conservation actions based on monitoring and evaluation.

The Services must incorporate these adaptive strategies into day-to-day implementation of the ESA, as we discuss more specifically below. To make such a rigorous program feasible, Congress must provide the needed funding. Ideally, as discussed above, this funding would not be subject to the vagaries of the annual appropriations cycle, but instead would be a dedicated stream provided through climate change legislation.

The ESA, with its mandate to conserve all species listed as threatened and endangered and to incorporate the best available science in all management decisions, is well suited to help our nation meet the challenge of addressing global warming's impacts on wildlife. However, defining what constitutes the best available science will be a major challenge. Given the rapid pace of ecological change brought about by global warming, agencies cannot simply assume that data collection and studies produced on an ad hoc basis will be adequate to answer top-priority management questions. As we proceed into a warming century, providing answers to these questions requires integrating into ESA implementation a new and rigorous adaptive management program.

C. Other Important ESA Updates

1. Ecosystem-Based Approaches

Given the overwhelming numbers of individual species likely to be put at risk due to climate change, it will be vital for the Services to develop methods of identifying species at risk and planning for the conservation of listed species that are more efficient than the current species-by-species approach to listing and recovery planning. Though largely ignored for the past few years, the FWS in 1994 adopted a policy statement calling for an ecosystem approach to implementing the ESA; the policy specifically mentions making listing decisions and developing recovery plans on an ecosystem basis when possible. The Services should update this policy statement to address how ecosystems will be defined and managed in light of changes in species distribution, disassembly of ecological communities, and other disruptions caused by global warming. Regardless of how these difficult definitional issues are resolved, it will remain essential to pursue ecosystem-based listing and recovery planning strategies. In places where climate change affects a large number of species—in Arctic and coral reef ecosystems, for example—such strategies would advance conservation with much less cost and much greater speed than carrying out listing and recovery planning actions on an individual species basis.

In addition to updating and giving life to its ecosystem policy, the FWS should revise its current schemes for prioritizing listing and recovery planning decisions to explicitly afford greater priority to ecosystem-based actions. Such action would substantially accelerate legal protections and conservation actions for groups of species imperiled by climate change.

Congress could support such ecosystem-oriented strategies by authorizing and funding programs to conserve ecosystems particularly hard-hit by climate change (drawing lessons learned from the Chesapeake Bay, Everglades, and Great Lakes programs). River basins, estuaries, and other aquatic systems deserve particularly urgent attention in light of the prolonged droughts and other major disruptions of hydrological cycles currently underway due to global warming. Such programs will need to go well beyond the confines of federal natural resource managers and elicit the participation of state, tribal, and local governments.

2. Recovery Planning and Implementation

Historically, implementation has been a key shortcoming of the recovery planning process; plans often occupy shelf space rather than substantially influence real-world activities. With much less room for error in an era when climate change greatly exacerbates threats to biodiversity, science-based blueprints for stabilizing and conserving listed species and their habitat must drive management decisions affecting listed species. While additional resources are necessary to carry out more affirmative measures in recovery plans, the Services could also improve plan implementation by explicitly linking recovery plans to the §7(a)(2) consultation process. The Services often pay little attention to recovery plans in determining whether proposed federal agency actions—including approvals of HCPs and incidental take permits (ITPs)—jeopardize the continued existence of listed species or destroy or adversely modify designated critical habitat. The Services likewise do not necessarily look to recovery plans in designing reasonable and prudent measures and associated terms and conditions to minimize incidental take by federal agencies. The Services could change this by requiring that recovery plans serve as the yardsticks for assessing jeopardy and critical habitat modification, as well as the templates for designing measures to minimize incidental take. Directly linking actions and prohibitions set forth in recovery plans to these §7 determinations would provide a powerful mechanism to ensure that day-to-day decisions of federal agencies are consistent with maintaining and even recovering listed species. Such an action would also be consistent with recent court decisions holding that consideration of impacts to species' recovery is relevant to assessing jeopardy and adverse modification of critical habitat, and that the Services should consider recovery plans in deciding whether to approve HCPs and ITPs.

* * * [I]t is crucial that recovery plans incorporate adaptation actions. These plans should explicitly address the key adaptation challenges and opportunities facing the species, including: (1) corridors for species movement that allow transitions to more hospitable areas; (2) measures particularly aimed at managing and protecting vulnerable resources such as water availability and specialized habitat needs; (3) better use of population and habitat availability projections; (4) stronger adaptive management programs for long-term operations such as dams; (5) protection and acquisition of northerly or higher elevation portions of species' ranges; and (6) targeted population supplementation and reintroductions.

Finally, the Services should ensure that their actions to implement recovery plans are integrated with broader public and nongovernmental initiatives to adapt to climate change. This means participating in the numerous stakeholder planning processes that have been launched to respond and adapt to the inevitable impacts of global warming on current and future infrastructure, human health, natural resources, and natural resource-based industries.

3. Applying the ESA to the Causes of Global Warming Pollution

As noted in the previous section, the ESA will increasingly intersect with a broad array of activities whose only connection to risks to listed species is emissions of GHGs. The trigger for application of §7's substantive and procedural obligations is a federal action that may affect listed species. Rather than denying the impact of global warming pollution on listed species, the Services should construe any action that results in non-trivial net increases of GHGs as meeting this threshold. Similarly, the Services should interpret §9's prohibition against take of protected species as covering the actions of nonfederal GHG emitters.

While it is important to acknowledge the vast array of actions that threaten biodiversity by contributing to climate change, casting such a broad net also poses a danger of overwhelming the Services' §7 and take enforcement programs. Indeed, going through the consultation process at the individual project level for all federal actions that may affect listed species as a result of GHG emissions would pose a virtually insurmountable obstacle for federal agencies. Even assuming that substantial additional resources will be made available for ESA implementation in the coming years, such resources should not be directed toward projects with no connection to listed species or their habitats beyond their GHG emissions. The Services are simply unqualified to address technical questions about how projects can reduce their GHG emissions. The Services and other agencies should use any additional ESA implementation funds to acquire, restore, and manage habitats and otherwise improve the ability of listed species to survive global warming.

For projects with no impacts on listed species apart from GHG emissions, the Services should develop a streamlined programmatic method for ensuring ESA compliance with §§7 and 9. The ideal—and most simple—method would be development of a form in which the emitter simply certifies compliance with the applicable national program capping GHG emissions.

This solution has three potential weaknesses. Most glaringly, no national GHG cap currently exists to which the Services can tie ESA compliance. This absence will hopefully prove temporary; current momentum in Congress appears to present a strong likelihood that lawmakers will enact a national GHG cap in the near term. While the nation awaits this crucial legislative action, there remains the possibility of an effort at ESA enforcement against agencies or other entities based solely on their GHG emissions. This scenario holds the potential to create a legal "train wreck" between ESA requirements and the practical difficulties of implementing the statute in a warming world. While no agency or environmental group has yet sought to combat such global warming pollution through ESA enforcement—elkhorn and staghorn coral have been listed for nearly two years without ESA claims against GHG-emitting projects—such a showdown will become increasingly likely if Congress does not directly mandate reductions in carbon emissions. To date, conservation groups have focused their efforts to reduce global warming pollution on energy and transportation policy and carbon sequestration, but impatience with continued inaction in Washington, D.C., could cause some environmental groups to turn to the ESA.

Second, currently available scientific data cannot predict how much additional GHG pollution—if any—can be emitted without jeopardizing the existence of listed species or otherwise violating the ESA. If a species is already declining due to the impacts of global warming, any project that is not carbon neutral or better could potentially jeopardize that species. Ideally, when Congress enacts national caps on GHG pollution, it will do so with full recognition of the need to avoid or minimize further disruption of ecosystems. A prudent cap would enable the Services to initially tie federal agencies' compliance with §7's prohibitions against jeopardy and critical habitat destruction to adherence to the national GHG emissions standard. To deal with uncertainties surrounding the impacts of climate change, lawmakers should provide substantial dedicated funding for scientific research to explore further the topic of what is needed for native species to survive global warming. Once the scientific community reaches a firmer understanding of what atmospheric GHG concentrations, surface temperatures, and other targets are needed to maximize the chances for species survival, Congress may need to revisit the ESA to ensure that its programs and strategies play a significant role in achieving these targets.

Finally, under this proposed solution, it would be virtually impossible for the Services to identify a reasonable and prudent alternative if a proposed project were to exceed its allocated share of the national cap on GHG emissions and thereby jeopardize listed species affected by climate change. Presumably, therefore, any failure of a project to comply with that project's allocation under the national cap would be subject to EPA enforcement action pursuant to whatever global warming legislation is enacted as well as enforcement or citizen suit under the ESA. The availability of an ESA action for injunctive relief to protect wildlife at risk of extinction would serve as an additional deterrent against violations of GHG emissions limits.

4. Habitat Conservation Planning

The Services should take more modest steps under §10 to more effectively regulate nonfederal projects that directly affect the habitat of species threatened by climate change. Current regulations require HCPs to include provisions for "changed circumstances," but to date, the Services have not required consideration of climate change impacts to be considered changed circumstances. The agencies should reverse this policy and require that long-term HCPs contain adaptive management provisions to deal with climate change-related impacts as a condition of HCP approval and issuance of ITPs. The

Services should grant regulatory assurances only for limited time periods and only for applicants that include climate change-oriented adaptive management provisions in their HCPs. * * *

5. Private Landowner Incentives

Climate change produces an array of threats to imperiled species that require affirmative conservation measures and are not well suited for remedying through traditional regulatory prohibitions. For example, experts already point to ways that global warming exacerbates the spread of invasive species and wildlife disease, which often require aggressive prevention and control measures. When such problems arise on private land, private landowner incentives such as technical and financial assistance provide perhaps the best strategy for confronting them. Existing programs already provide such incentives to a limited extent * * *. However, a major expansion will be needed as the climate changes. These incentives provide yet another example of the funding gap that a federal cap-and-trade climate change program would need to address. * * *

Notes and Questions

1. The Center for Biological Diversity which had petitioned and litigated for the polar bear's listing filed suit one day after the listing and ESA § 4(d) protective regulations were issued. See Center for Biological Diversity v. Kempthorne, N.D. Cal., No. 08-1339 (May 16, 2008). Under the circumstances, what possible additional protections are possible? Compare the FWS regulations approving incidental, unintentional takes of small numbers of polar bears and Pacific walruses as part of oil and gas exploration activities in the Chukchi Sea and adjacent western coast of Alaska (50 C.F.R. § 18.27, 50 C.F.R. 18, Subpart I (73 Fed. Reg. 33212, 33225 (June 11, 2008)).

For litigation challenging oil and gas development in the Chukchi Sea on climate change grounds, see Native Village of Point Hope v. Kempthorne, (No. 1:2008cv00004) (D. Alaska 2008). Regarding the FWS's obligation to include climate change impacts on listed species in ESA §7 consultations with other federal agencies such as MMS, see Natural Resources Defense Council v. Kempthorne, 506 F. Supp. 2d 322 (E.D. Cal. 2007) noted in the hydrology section of this chapter. But see 73 Fed. Reg. 47868, 47872 (Aug. 15, 2008) expessing FWS's "view that there is no requirement to consult on greenhouse gas (GHG) emissions' contribution to global warming and its associated impacts on listed species (e.g., polar bears)," and S. 3071, 110th Cong., 154 Cong. Rec. S4793 (daily ed. May 22, 2008) which would have prohibited the Interior Secretary from considering climate change in deciding whether to list a species under the ESA. The delisting of the grizzly bear has been challenged on the grounds that climate change is causing a rapid decline in its essential food sources in Western Watersheds Project v. Servheen, No. 4: 2007 cv 00243

(D. Ida. June 4, 2007). See also J. Joly & N. Fuller Advising Noah: A Legal Analysis of Assisted Migration, 39 ELR 10413 (2009).

2. Given the changes to habitats in the wake of sea level rise and global warming, combined with the on-going world-wide extinction of species, is the approach of the Endangered Species Act an adequate tool in the adaptation of climate change? Are not methods and programs needed not just to save species on the brink of extinction, but also for stewardship of habitats and ecosystems experiencing climate change effects. The pace of once exotic, or alien species, moving in to new habitats is accelerating. The loss of coastal estuarine areas means that either species will decline, or to provide for replacement habitats humans will help create the conditions for such areas by removing human infrastructure for the coasts and restoring or establishing conditions for wetlands or mangroves and intertidal wild life. A new kind of biological service will need to be conceived, to complement the existing nature conservation agencies. The standards for such a proactive service for sustaining biological diversity and ecosystem, services is emerging. The tools of ecosystem management will need to incorporate active adaptive management and human governance of resilience conditions to adapt to climate change effects. See C. Folke et al., Regime Shift, Resilience and Biodiversity in Ecosystem Management, 35 Ann. Rev. Ecol. Evol. Syst. 557 (2004). Does the methodology for sustaining scope for natural resilience in climate adaptation require enactment as statutory duty of all governmental activity that affects ecosystems services and biodiversity? See B. Walker & D. Salt, Resilience Thinking—Sustaining Ecosystems and People in a Changing World (2006).

3. Should other laws that govern species and biodiversity in different natural areas take on a climate change adaptation responsibility? The US Army Corps of Engineers is charged with conducting a "public interest review" before granting a Section 404 wetlands permit under the Clean Water Act, §404, 33 USC 1344, and 33 CFR §320.1(a)(1) (2009). This review requires the Corps to balance "favorable impacts [of the proposed activity] against the detrimental impacts." Id. Specifically, the Corps is to consider "conservation, economics, aesthetics, general environmental concerns, wetlands, historic properties, fish and wildlife values, flood hazards, floodplain values, land use, navigation, shore erosion and accretion, recreation, water supply and conservation, water quality, energy needs, safety, food and fiber production, mineral needs, consideration of property ownership and, in general, the needs and welfare of the people. 33 CFR §320.4(a)(1) (2009). Compare: Alliance to Protect Nantucket Sound, Inc., v U.S. Army, 398 F. 3d 105 (1st Cir., 2005); U.S. v. Alaska, 503 US 569 (1992); Zabel v. Tabb, 430 F. 2d 199 (5th Cir., 1970). In light of the scientific findings on the effects of climate change, should the Corps use its public interest review to identify ways to expand the adaptive roles of wetlands, for example as hydrologic absorbers of flood water, as habitat for species, as buffers for storm-driven wind and wave impacts. Should the national policy of "no-net loss of wetlands" be replaced by a policy to pro-

hibit any loss of wetlands and require the design and expansion of wetlands? Since more than 50% of the nations wetlands have been converted to non-wetland uses, there is room to restore and expand many coastal wetlands. Will adapting to climate change require statutory expansion of the Army Corps roles from wetlands regulator to wetlands cultivator?

4. In addition to the 1973 Polar Bear Agreement with other Arctic nations, the U.S. has entered a bilateral agreement with Russia and a Memorandum of Understanding with Canada. As discussed in the FWS polar bear rule-making decisions excerpted above, hunting polar bear for subsistence and cultural purposes is allowed under the U.S. ESA and MMPA, the laws of other Arctic countries, and relevant international laws.

*　*　*　*　*

Extinction of the polar bear is just one climate-change related threat to native peoples' traditional way of life in their traditional Arctic locations. Coastal peoples especially are threatened by melting ice and rising seas flooding their villages. See R. Abate, Climate Change, the United States, and the Impacts of Artic Melting: A Case Study in the Need for Enforceable International Environmental Human Rights, 26A Stanford Envtl. L.J. 3 (2007); M. Burkett, Just Solutions to Climate Change: A Climate Justice Proposal for a Domestic Clean Development Mechanism, 56 Buffalo L. Rev. 169 (2008); J. Hand, Global Climate Change: A Serious Threat to Native American Lands and Culture, 38 Envtl. L. Rep. 10329 (2008); S. Kravchenko, Right to Carbon or Right to Life: Human Rights Approaches to Climate Change, 9 Vt. J. Envtl. L. 513 (2008); H. Osofsky, The Inuit Petition as a Bridge? Beyond Dialectics of Climate Change and Indigenous Peoples' Rights, 31 American Indian L. Rev. 675 (2007); R. Jacobs, Treading Deep Waters: Substantive Law Issues in Tuvalu's Threat to Sue the United States in the International Court of Justice, 14 Pac. Rim. L. & Policy J. 103 (2005).

In February 2008, the flooded Arctic Village of Kivalina sued 10 oil companies, 14 utilities, and 1 coal company as public nuisances for their contributions to climate change. See Complaint, Kivalina v. Exxon Mobil Corp., (N.D. Cal. Feb. 26, 2008), available at http://www.adn.com/static/adn-/pdfs/Kivalina%20Com-plaint%20-%20Final.pdf (last visited Apr. 6, 2008); which is excerpted next.

KIVALINA V. EXXON MOBIL CORP.
U.S.D.C., N.D. Cal. 2008

As climate change warms the Arctic, there has been a corresponding loss in sea ice, especially in the Chukchi Sea, upon which Kivalina sits. With less coastal sea ice in the fall, winter, and spring, Kivalina loses shoreline stability in the face of storms. Coastal erosion has taken its toll on the village, causing losses of homes, school buildings, fuel storage tanks, airport runway, and regular flooding of the village streets. From 2001 to 2004, numerous stabilization projects were undertaken, none with any positive results. In September 2006, a seawall was built at tremendous cost; on October 12, a storm destroyed the entire structure and Kivalina was forced to endure another storm season of erosion without coastal protection.

In the lawsuit, the villagers claim damages from climate change impacts sourced in the polluting activities by the defendants. Damages are claimed under the theories of public nuisance and conspiracy to mislead the public:

Global warming is destroying Kivalina and the village thus must be relocated soon or be abandoned and cease to exist. Relocating will cost hundreds of millions of dollars and is an urgent matter. The U.S. Army Corps of Engineers and the U.S. Government Accountability Office have both concluded that Kivalina must be relocated due to global warming and have estimated the cost to be from $95 million to $400 million as stated in the complaint:

> Kivalina brings this action against defendants under federal common law and, in the alternative, state law, to seek damages for defendants' contributions to global warming, a nuisance that is causing severe harms to Kivalina. Kivalina further asserts claims for civil conspiracy and concert of action for certain defendants' participation in conspiratorial and other actions intended to further the defendants' abilities to contribute to global warming.

> Defendants contribute to global warming through their emissions of large quantities of greenhouse gases. Defendants in this action include many of the largest emitters of greenhouse gases in the United States. All Defendants directly emit large quantities of greenhouse gases and have done so for many years. Defendants are responsible for a substantial portion of the greenhouse gases in the atmosphere that have caused global warming and Kivalina's special injuries. * * *

> Each of the defendants knew or should have known of the impacts of their emissions on global warming and on particularly vulnerable communities such as coastal Alaskan villages. Despite this knowledge, defendants continued their substantial contributions to global warming. Additionally, some of the defendants, as described below, conspired to create a false scientific debate about global warming in order to deceive the public. Further, each defendant has failed promptly and adequately to mitigate the impact of these emissions, placing immediate profit above the need to protect against the harms from global warming.

Kivalina seeks monetary damages for defendants' past and ongoing contributions to global warming, a public nuisance, and damages caused by certain defendants' acts in furthering a conspiracy to suppress the awareness of the link between these emissions and global warming. * * *

While the global warming to which defendants contribute injures the public at large, Kivalina suffers special injuries, different in degree and kind from injuries to the general public. Rising temperatures caused by global warming have affected the thickness, extent, and duration of sea ice that forms along Kivalina's coast. Loss of sea ice, particularly land-fast sea ice, leaves Kivalina's coast more vulnerable to waves, storm surges and erosion. Storms now routinely batter Kivalina and are destroying its property to the point that Kivalina must relocate or face extermination.

The U.S. Army Corps of Engineers, Alaska District, in an April 2006 report on erosion suffered by Alaska Native Villages, concluded that global warming has affected the extent of sea ice adjacent to Kivalina: "[W]ith global climate change the period of open water is increasing and the Chukchi Sea is less likely to be frozen when damaging winter storms occur. Winter storms occurring in October and November of 2004 and 2005 have resulted in significant erosion that is now threatening both the school and the Alaska Village Electric Cooperative (AVEC) tank farm." The United States Government Accountability Office, in a December, 2003 report also addressing erosion in Alaska Native Villages, reached similar conclusions regarding Kivalina: "[I]t is believed that the right combination of storm events could flood the entire village at any time." The GAO concluded that "[r]emaining on the island . . . is no longer a viable option for the community." * * *

Civil Conspiracy Allegations

There has been a long campaign by power, coal, and oil companies to mislead the public about the science of global warming. Defendants ExxonMobil, AEP, BP America Inc., Chevron Corporation, ConocoPhillips Company, Duke Energy, Peabody, and Southern ("Conspiracy Defendants") participated in this campaign. Initially, the campaign attempted to show that global warming was not occurring. Later, and continuing to the present, it attempts to demonstrate that global warming is good for the planet and its inhabitants or that even if there may be ill effects, there is not enough scientific certainty to warrant action. The purpose of this campaign has been to enable the electric power, coal, oil and other industries to continue their conduct contributing to the public nuisance of global warming by convincing the public at-large and the victims of global warming that the process is not man-made when in fact it is. * * *

Notes and Questions

1. Do you notice the similarities in this complaint, namely in the civil conspiracy sections, to the historic tobacco litigation of the 1990s? If so, this is not a coincidence as two of the plaintiff attorneys in the Kivalina case met from opposite sides of the courtroom during the tobacco litigation.

2. How effective a response to climate change is nuisance litigation like the Kivalina case? In answering, consider the discussion of nuisance litigation in the notes following *Massachusetts v. EPA.*

3. Changes occurring in the Arctic and Antarctic are strong evidence of polar warming due to global climate change. The Arctic is divided among several nations who continue to work out the exact boundaries of their national claims as discussed in Chapter 3. See B. Carpenter, Warm is the New Cold: Global Warming, Oil, UNCLOS article 76, and How an Artic Treaty Might Stop a New Cold War, 39 Envtl. L. 215 (2009); M. Nordquist, J. Moore, & A. Skaridov, eds., International Energy Policy, the Arctic and the Law of the Sea (2005); B. Patterson, The Growing Importance of the Polar Regions to Australian and Canadian Strategic Thinking, Maritime Studies March-April 2007 at 11; 2008 Symposium on Climate Change Conflicts and Cooperation in the Artic, 24 Intl. J. of Marine & Coastal L. 347 (2009).

National claims to Antarctica have been suspended in favor of the international treaty regime discussed in Chapter 3. The U.S. has important interests in both polar areas. See Symposium, Environmental Change in Polar Regions, VIII Sustainable Development Law & Policy No. 3 (Spring 2008). While there are no indigenous peoples or polar bears in Antarctica, whales, seals, fish, penguins, and other birds, some already protected by the U.S. MMPA and ESA, inhabit the area and several nations including the U.S. have research stations there. Since biodiversity has changed very little in the last 100 years in south polar islands such as the South Orkney Islands, biodiversity there can serve as an important benchmark for measuring the future impacts of climate change. For example, one projection shows a 75% decrease in Antarctic penguin colonies with a two degree Celsius increase in global temperature. The U.S. National Environmental Policy Act's (NEPA) environmental impact assessment (EIA) requirements have been held applicable to federal food waste incineration activities in Antarctica. Environmental Defense Fund v. Massey, 986 F. 2d 528 (D.C. Cir. 1993).

The treaty regime for Antarctica in which the U.S. is a major participant includes the 1959 Antarctic Treaty, 19 I.L.M. 860, its 1991 Protocol on Environmental Protection, 30 I.L.M. 1461, excerpted in chapter 3, and the 1980

Convention on the Conservation of Antarctic Marine Living Resources, 19 I.L.M. 837 (1980), none designed as a mechanism for dealing with the Antarctic impacts of global scale challenges such as climate change. As discussed in the preceding chapter, the regime can be applied to climate change mitigation responses such as fertilizing the Southern Ocean surrounding Antarctica. See K. Scott, The Day After Tomorrow: Ocean CO_2 Sequestration and the Future of Climate Change, 18 Georgetown Intl. Envtl. L. Rev. 57, 93-104 (2005) excerpted in Chapter 6.

Both polar regions have benefited significantly from global actions taken in response to atmospheric ozone depletion under the 1985 Vienna Convention for the Protection of the Ozone Layer, 26 I.L.M. 1529, and its 1987 Protocol, 26 I.L.M. 1550 also discussed in Chapter 3.

PROBLEM EXERCISE ON NUISANCE REMEDIES

How effective are judicial remedies in addressing climate change losses? The injury is often concrete and quantifiable. The victims exist. But who is the proper defendant, and for what action? What class of carbon dioxide emitters has the capacity to abate the greenhouse gas emissions and avert further climate change related damage?

Most common law remedies involve actions between two, or more, distinct interests. Thus trespass is an unauthorized intrusion on land that you own, or negligence involves an injury proximately caused to you by another in a violation of a duty of care owed to you. Private nuisance involves individuals also. More widespread injuries, shared by you and others, are subject to abatement through invoking public nuisance and citing your particularized and special injury to justify your standing to assert the claims of all who are harmed.

The coal industry has refused to accept responsibility for its carbon dioxide emissions, and declines to phase out its emissions. How would you frame a public nuisance action designed to avoid the limitations of *Kivalina v. Exxon Mobil Corp.*? Does there remain a cause of action under federal common law for public nuisance after Illinois v. Milwaukee, 451 U.S. 304 (1981)? Could the State of Alaska, or the Inuit in either Alaska or Canada, bring a claim against utilities that coal to produce electricity, now that their carbon dioxide contributions to cause global warming and sea level rise have been acknowledged by the U.S. Supreme Court in Massachusetts v. EPA? Is injured plaintiffs could bring such a public nuisance action, how might the rule of indivisible harm, as articulated in Landes v. East Texas Salt Water Disp. Co. 151 Tex. 251, 248 S.W. 73 (1982) be applied? 75 law schools mooted these issues in the 19th Annual Pace National Environmental Law Moot Court Competition. See the winning students bench briefs at 24 Pace Envtl. L. Rev. (2007) and the bench brief outlining competing legal arguments at M.

Schoonmaker & J. Simpson, 2007 Judge's Bench Memorandum, 24 Pace Envtl. L. Rev. 479 (2007), accessible at http://digitalcommons.pace/envlaw/532. Would the outcome be different if the claim was transnational, with harmful emissions from the U.S. contributing to injuries in the Canadian Province of Nunavut?

D. OCEAN IMPACTS OF CLIMATE CHANGE

1. Introduction

TESTIMONY OF JANE LUBCHENCO
Professor, Oregon State University, and Former President, American Association for the Advancement of Science (AAAS)
(Appointed Administrator, National Oceanic and Atmospheric Administration in 2009)

To the U.S. House of Representatives Select Committee on Energy Dependence and Global Warming
April 29, 2008
Washington, DC

IMPACTS

Predicted Impacts: Warmer water, rising sea level, more acidic seawater. I begin by summarizing three key impacts of climate change on oceans, all of which were predicted, based on scientific understanding of the climate system, then focus on another possible impact that has taken us by surprise. In each case, I'll describe the physical change first, then the biological and ecological consequences of the physical change. The three predicted impacts are: (1) increases in ocean temperatures, (2) increases in sea level, and (3) increases in the acidity of seawater.

(1) Warmer waters: There is unequivocal evidence that the ocean are warming. The temperature of every ocean basin around the world increased over the second half of the 20th century. Taken as a whole, the ocean is now significantly warmer than it was in the middle of the 1900s.

Warmer waters have numerous consequences for life in the oceans:

(a) Corals, when stressed by warmer temperatures, respond by expelling the microscopic plants they harbor—a phenomenon known as 'coral bleaching.' Although bleached corals do not always die, they often do. The incidence of bleaching events is increasing globally. Because coral reefs provide the three-dimensional habitat for millions of other species in tropical waters, their demise would have dire consequences for these rich oases of biodiversity. People who depend upon coral reef ecosystems for food, recreation and many associated livelihoods are already experiencing the consequences of disrupted and degraded coral reef ecosystems.

(b) Numerous species are shifting their geographic ranges, in response to changing ocean temperatures. In the north Atlantic, for example, herring, cod, capelin and mackerel are shifting poleward. In some cases, predators and prey shift differentially, with consequent disruptions to their ecosystems.

(c) Other species such as polar bears and other Arctic ice-dependent species face likely extinction as warmer waters melt the ice upon which they depend for food or shelter.

(2) <u>Rising Sea Level</u>: Sea level has risen steadily over the last century, on average about 6 inches, due to both thermal expansion and the melting of glaciers, ice caps and ice sheets on land. Sea level is expected to continue to rise, although the exact amount depends on a number of factors for which current information is insufficient for precise predictions. The consequences of rising sea level may be significant for people living on or near the shore, and significant for already-stressed coastal estuaries, salt marshes and mangrove ecosystems. On balance, however, the consequences of sea level rise are minimal for most marine species.

(3) <u>Increasing acidity</u>: Between 1/3 and 1/2 of the carbon dioxide that humans have released into the atmosphere has been taken up by oceans. When absorbed by oceans, CO_2 is converted into carbonic acid, making seawater more acidic. Measurements indicate that the oceans are becoming more acidic. Experiments in the laboratory suggest that this increasing acidity is likely to be problematic for any marine species that makes a shell or skeleton from calcium carbonate. The rate at which a new shell or skeleton is made depends on temperature and acidity. Likewise, the rate at which a shell or skeleton is dissolved depends on temperature acidity. Hence a wide variety of life in oceans—ranging from corals to microscopic plants to snails, clams, mussels, oysters, sea stars, sea urchins, lobsters and crabs—is likely to be negatively impacted by an increasingly acid ocean.

I've summarized three major ways in which climate change is impacting life in the oceans: warmer waters, rising sea level and increasing acidity. Warming and acidification pose very serious threats to marine life and to many of the benefits that ocean ecosystems provide to people. It is important to note that although each of the three impacts was predicted, the <u>rate</u> of change for each has been faster than initially predicted. Most climate predictions have been conservative. In addition, these changes may interact with one another. A PISCO researcher, Dr. Gretchen Hofmann and her team at the University of California at Santa Barbara are finding that some species may be able to cope with changes in acidity alone or changes in temperature alone, but not the combination of the two.

A possible unexpected impact: Changes in coastal winds and circulation. I will next describe a recently discovered perturbation of the ocean ecosystem off the west coast of the U.S., specifically along the coasts of Washington and Oregon. Beginning in 2002, our PISCO team has documented a new 'dead zone' that appears each summer. This dead zone is an area of the ocean where the levels of oxygen are too low to support most marine life. Fish and invertebrates suffocate if they cannot swim or scuttle away as the oxygen levels plummet.

This dead zone is unlike most of the other dead zones around the world, for example, the one in the Gulf of Mexico, that are driven by nutrient pollution coming from the land. The dead zone off the Pacific Northwest appears to be caused by changes in atmospheric and oceanic conditions, both of which are suspected of being related to climate change.

To understand how this dead zone develops, a little background information about normal upwelling dynamics is helpful. Around the world, on the western sides of continents, winds (driven by the differences in atmospheric pressure over the land and over the ocean) blow along the coast toward the equator. Because the earth is rotating, surface waters are pushed away from the coast and nutrient-rich but low-oxygen water from the dark, deeper portions of the ocean are pulled to the surface. This 'upwelling' of deep water brings nutrients to the surface and fuels the rich ecosystems typically found off these coasts. 'Coastal upwelling ecosystems' collectively represent about 1% of the surface area of oceans but they have historically provided about 20% of global fisheries, in large part due to this infusion of nutrients into sunlit, coastal waters. Other coastal upwelling ecosystems occur off the coasts of Chile and Peru, South Africa and Namibia, and Morocco.

In the Pacific Northwest, beginning in 2002, however, this normal pattern shifted slightly, but the slight shifts brought dire consequences. Suddenly fishermen were hauling up Dungeness crab pots only to find them full of dead crabs. Coastal residents and tourists reported mass numbers of dead fishes and crabs washed up on beaches. Recreational divers reported seeing huge schools of rockfish in unusual places. Scientists documented dead fish on the ocean floor and biological 'erratics': deep-dwelling fishes stranded in intertidal tide pools. Researchers with Oregon State University's Partnership for Interdisciplinary Studies of Coastal Oceans (PISCO) team figured out the cause of these anomalies: there was not enough oxygen in some of the water for most crabs and fishes to live, so they escaped or suffocated.

Since 2002, this dead zone has reappeared each summer: we've documented six dead zone events in six years. In a paper published in *Science* in

February, we reported that these recent events are highly unusual compared to the last 60 years (as far back as reliable dissolved oxygen measurements go.) Hypoxia ('low oxygen') appears to have become the 'new normal' for summertime off our coasts. * * *

We cannot say definitively that these dead zones are caused by climate change, but we can say that they are consistent with our understanding of climate change dynamics. Moreover, there is no other obvious explanation for the appearance of dead zones off an open coast such as ours. This dead zone is a consequence of changes in oceanic and atmospheric conditions, not runoff of nutrients from the land. * * *

* * * * *

Additional facts regarding climate change and oceans include:

- Oceans cover 71 percent of the Earth's surface and average over 12,200 feet in depth.

- Water holds approximately 1,000 times the amount of heat as air, and the interaction between ocean circulation and the global distribution of heat is the primary driver of climatic patterns.

- The oceans are warming, particularly since 1950s, with global mean sea surface temperature having increased roughly one degree Fahrenheit in the 20th century.

- Sea levels rose 7 inches during the 20th century and nearly 1.5 inches between 1993 and 2003.

- Oceans are a major carbon sink and have absorbed fully half of all fossil carbon released to the atmosphere since the beginning of the Industrial Revolution.

Joint Ocean Commission Initiative, Addressing Oceans and Climate Change in Federal Legislation 2 (July 2007). See also C. Nelleman, S. Hain, & J. Alder, In Dead Water: Merging of Climate Change with Pollution, Overharvest and Infestations in the World's Fishing Grounds (2008).

2. International Ocean Law

International law regarding the oceans derives mainly from the 1982 United Nations Convention on the Law of the Sea (UNCLOS), 1833 U.N.T.S. 397, also discussed in Chapter 3 and in Chapter 6. While the U.S. has not ratified UNCLOS, many of its provisions reflect customary international law binding on all nations including the U.S., with the primary exception being its extensive dispute resolution provisions summarized in the next excerpt. They bind nations ratifying the convention, although the U.S. Department of State has determined that much of UNCLOS is customary international laws which the U.S. is bound to observe. The following excerpt opens with important questions about UNCLOS's climate change roles.

CLIMATE CHANGE AND THE USE OF THE DISPUTE SETTLEMENT REGIME OF THE LAW OF THE SEA CONVENTION
Meinhard Doelle
37 Ocean Devel. & Intl. L. 319 (2006)

Do the provisions of UNCLOS designed to protect and preserve the marine environment provide any legal avenues to motivate states to take action to mitigate climate change so as to reduce its impacts on the marine environment? More specifically, does UNCLOS provide a mechanism for states to seek recourse against other states that have not taken or are not taking adequate action to reduce their contributions to climate change? * * *

There is little indication from either the text of UNCLOS or historical accounts of the negotiations that climate change per se was on the minds of negotiators at the time the Convention was developed. The protection and preservation of the marine environment, however, has a prominent place among the objectives of UNCLOS. In this section, the extent to which the objectives of protecting and preserving marine ecosystems were translated into firm obligations and commitments will be considered. Next, the link between these obligations and responsibilities and climate change mitigation will be explored.

General Provisions of UNCLOS

In the Preamble of UNCLOS, the importance of establishing a legal order for the oceans that promotes, among other things, the protection and preservation of the marine environment is recognized. At the same time, the Preamble recognizes the tension that exists between these and other objectives designed to protect the common interest in the oceans on the one hand, and state sovereignty on the other. The Preamble urges parties to adopt a holistic approach to ocean issues.

UNCLOS, Article 1 includes the following definition of "pollution of the marine environment": the introduction by man, directly or indirectly, of substances or energy into the marine environment, including estuaries, which results or is likely to result in such deleterious effects as harm to living resources and marine life, hazards to human health, hindrance of marine activities, including fishing and other legitimate uses of the sea, impairment of quality for use of sea water and reduction of amenities.

A traditional interpretation of UNCLOS wording, including the definition of pollution, would tend to focus on what the parties contemplated at the time UNCLOS was negotiated. Using this approach, it could be argued that climate change was not on the minds of negotiators and, therefore, the term *energy* in the definition of pollution of the marine environment was not intended by the parties to include increases in ocean temperature resulting from GHG emissions.

It is suggested that such an interpretation is inappropriate for a number of reasons. First, this approach would be an unduly restrictive interpretation of the intention of the parties at the time. It seems clear from the plain wording that the overriding objective of the definition of pollution was to capture a full range of possible threats to the marine environment. There is no indication that the parties were intending to limit the definition to only those specific threats that were clearly identified at the time it was negotiated. Such an approach to general treaty interpretation would relegate many international treaties to irrelevance soon after they are negotiated. For international treaties to serve a constructive role over time, they should be interpreted in light of changing circumstances.

Furthermore, while the specific case of temperature increase from climate change may not have been on the minds of negotiators, it is clear from the work of the Joint Group of Experts on the Scientific Aspects of Marine Pollution (GESAMP) that the potential impact of temperature changes to marine ecosystems was within the contemplation of negotiators. The sources of energy under consideration at the time may have been more local, such as land-based effluent from industrial facilities, and likely did not include climate change. The threat of temperature change to the marine environment, however, was clearly identified. The inclusion of "energy" in the definition of pollution can be read as an indication that negotiators were aware of this threat.

Finally, Article 293 of UNCLOS specifically opens the door to progressive interpretation of UNCLOS obligations by bringing in other sources of international law not inconsistent with UNCLOS. Taking this into account, it is suggested that a broader interpretation of pollution is more consistent with the plain wording of Article 1 and its purpose at the time it was negotiated. It is also one that commentators have advocated in the context of Part XII. Crylle de Klemm, for example, suggested even before the completion of UNCLOS that the general provisions on the marine environment in UNCLOS had to be read to include an obligation to protect threatened species and ecosystems. At the same time, others argued that these provisions include an obligation to protect the fauna and flora of the seafloor from harm. * * *

Assuming the science is convincing, there is a strong basis for the position that GHG emissions cause marine pollution due to the increase in energy in the oceans resulting from GHG emissions. An alternative approach is to take an "effects-based" view of marine pollution, to include within marine pollution the release of any substance that causes harm to the marine environment. Either approach can lead to the conclusion that GHG emissions result in marine pollution as defined in Article 1 of UNCLOS.

Part XII of UNCLOS, Marine Environmental Protection

Part XII of UNCLOS deals generally with state obligations with respect to the marine environment. As early as 1991, Part XII was characterized by academics as constitutional in character, reflecting in part existing customary international law, but at the same time providing the first comprehensive statement on the protection of the marine environment in international law.

The starting point for Part XII is the general obligation under Article 192 to "protect and preserve the marine environment," balanced with a reaffirmation of the right of states to exploit their natural resources "in accordance with their duty to protect and preserve the marine environment." Pursuant to Article 194, states are obligated to take all measures consistent with the Convention necessary "to prevent, reduce and control pollution of the marine environment *from any source*, using the best practical means." Article 194 is central to any analysis of state obligations under UNCLOS to mitigate climate change as it provides the foundation for the following specific obligations that provide some further guidance on what a state may be expected to do to protect and preserve the marine environment:

- an obligation for states to act individually or jointly as appropriate;
- an obligation to take all measures necessary to prevent, reduce, and control pollution of the marine environment;
- an obligation for states to use best practical means at their disposal;
- an obligation for states to act in accordance with their capabilities;
- an obligation to endeavor to harmonize policies with other states;
- an obligation for states to control activities under their control or jurisdiction so as to not cause damage by pollution to other states and their environment;
- an obligation to prevent pollution from spreading to areas outside of a state's jurisdiction of control; and
- a specific obligation for the preservation and protection of rare or fragile ecosystems and the habitats of species at risk.

Article 195 directs states in taking measures to prevent, reduce, and control pollution of the marine environment, to prevent the transfer of harm from one type of area to another. While the exact scope of this provision is not clear, it does at a minimum introduce the concept that mitigation measures must be designed so as to not result in other environmental damage, an issue that has been the subject of considerable controversy in the context of climate change. In so doing, UNCLOS may have been ahead of its time by providing a simple, yet potentially very effective, tool to require states to take a holistic approach to addressing environmental issues.

Article 212 is another provision of UNCLOS that, while not drafted with climate change in mind, can now be reasonably interpreted to apply to the issue. Article 212 obligates states to adopt laws and regulations and take other necessary measures "to prevent, reduce and control pollution of the marine environment from or through the atmosphere." It essentially obligates states to prevent or control pollution from or through any air space over which a state has jurisdiction.

Similarly, Article 207, dealing with pollution from land-based sources, is sufficiently broad to cover GHG emissions. It requires states to endeavor to establish regional and global rules to prevent, reduce, and control marine pollution from land-based sources. In determining a party's contribution to such efforts, economic capacity and need for economic development are to be taken into account. Article 213 requires states to enforce domestic laws passed in accordance with Article 207 and any other international obligation to address land-based sources of marine pollution. Overall, these provisions appear to be weaker than Articles 192 and 195 in that they require states only to endeavor to control pollution, and therefore are less likely to play a significant role in determining state obligations to mitigate climate change.

Part XII and the Duty to Mitigate Against Climate Change

On their face, the provisions of UNCLOS, particularly Part XII, are sufficiently broad to allow for a state to claim that a failure by another state to mitigate climate change violates its obligations to preserve and protect the marine environment. Particularly relevant in this regard, as noted earlier, is the definition of marine pollution to include energy. Obligations under Article 194 to preserve and protect the marine environment through the prevention reduction, and control of pollution, and the obligation to use the best practical means in accordance with a state's capabilities may also be important provisions. Finally, the obligation to prevent pollution from spreading outside a state's jurisdiction may also prove to be significant. * * *

One issue that will be interesting to follow when the Part XII provisions are interpreted by international tribunals is the connection made, if any, to other international agreements. In particular, for UNCLOS parties that are also parties to the Convention on Biological Diversity (CBD), the CBD may provide a new context for understanding marine pollution and the effort required to meet the obligations under UNCLOS to protect and preserve the marine environment. Given the wide acceptance of both Conventions, the influence of the CBD on the interpretation of the marine environment provisions of UNCLOS may turn out to be substantial. In the context of the interpretation of parties' obligations under UNCLOS, an interesting connection is the general recognition that climate change is a significant threat to biological diversity, and the further recognition that biological diversity is crucial to good ecosystem health. By providing this context to the connection between climate change and obligations to protect and preserve the marine environment under UNCLOS, the CBD may play a significant role in interpreting obligations of parties to mitigate climate change. As indicated above, UNCLOS Article 293 invites the application of the CBD as an interpretative tool to the extent that it is not incompatible with UNCLOS. The application of the CBD as an interpretive tool is, of course, limited to disputes involving parties who are bound by both treaties.

* * * * *

Besides UNCLOS, what other treaties and conventions might be invoked to help protect the oceans from climate change? See, e.g., W. Burns, A Voice for the Fish? Climate Change Litigation and Potential Causes of Action for Impacts Under the United Nations Fish Stocks Agreement, 48 Santa Clara L. Rev. 605 (2008). Two other possibilities, the 1975 World Heritage Convention, 1037 U.N.T.S. 151, and the 1992 Convention on Biological Diversity, 31 I.L.M. 818 excerpted in Chapter 3, are discussed next.

EXISTING LEGAL MECHANISMS TO ADDRESS OCEANIC IMPACTS FROM CLIMATE CHANGE
Lucy Wiggins
VII Sustainable Development Law & Policy 22 (March 2007)

The World Heritage Convention

The World Heritage Convention requires a state to 'do all it can,' within its capabilities to 'ensur[e] the identification, protection, conservation, presentation and transmission to future generations' of areas of outstanding natural beauty or cultural heritage. Once recognized as a World Heritage Site, protection of the site becomes the combined responsibility of the international community as a whole; states cannot deliberately take measures that would damage these sites, 'directly or indirectly' and must adopt internal policies to protect and rehabilitate its own heritage sites. It does not stretch the imagination to interpret these provisions to include cuts in GHG emissions among the many measures a state should take to 'do all it can.' * * *

When listing alone does not halt the decline of a heritage site, the Convention provides that sites threatened 'by serious and specific dangers,' can be designated as being 'in danger.' In danger status increases the amount of funding and international attention given to a site. If successfully listed as in danger, the member state must develop a 'programme for corrective measures' to abate the causes of the site's deterioration. Consequently, in danger status requires affirmative steps to repair damaged areas, in effect reversing the causes of the destruction in the first place, on top of the general obligation against taking deliberate measures that could harm a site.

In November 2004, a NGO in Belize tested the power of these provisions to force member states to take steps mitigating the impacts to oceans from climate change by filing a petition with the World Heritage Committee requesting that it list the Belize Barrier Reef as an in danger site. * * * The Committee ordered a policy paper from the World Heritage Centre on the impacts of climate change to sites. It then took a decision recognizing that climate change was impacting at least 125 heritage sites and indicated that it would continue to review petitions to grant in danger status to sites threatened by climate change on a 'case by case basis' [In 2009 the Belize Barrier Reef was listed as "in danger".] * * *.

The Convention on Biological Diversity

The CBD is a conservation-oriented convention providing for the protection of biological diversity, the promotion of sustainable development and the equitable sharing of benefits derived from natural resources. In similar fashion to the World Heritage Convention, the CBD only covers areas existing within the control of individual states.

Under the CBD, states develop strategies for the conservation of their biodiversity and create 'as far as possible and appropriate . . . a system of protected areas or areas where special measures need to be taken to conserve biological diversity.' In doing so, states should also '[p]romote the protection of ecosystems, natural habitats and the maintenance of viable populations of species in natural surroundings.' The CBD specifically includes 'marine and other aquatic ecosystems and the ecological complexes of which they are part,' as part of the definition of biological diversity, while mandating implementation 'with respect to the marine environment consistently with the rights and obligations of states under the law of the sea.'

Broadly interpreted then, the Convention obligates member states to establish protected marine areas and to take steps to shelter these areas from the impacts of climate change. Additionally, because the ocean is one of the least understood and least studied areas, the CBD could require states to increase their funding for scientific studies into the predicted aquatic impact form climate change. It might also require member states to consider potential ocean impacts when conducting environmental assessments or deciding whether to grant certain permits, such as those for factories intending to emit GHGs.

Under the CBD, states have been successful in establishing protected areas, but the Secretariat acknowledges that marine protected areas remain 'under represented.' The CBD also recognizes the establishment of marine protected areas outside the areas of national jurisdiction as a priority. Conceding that the impacts from climate change will not simply disappear, even if GHG emissions are cut, the CBD recommends the development of 'biological corridors' to facilitate the unhampered migration of species to more suitable habitats. * * *

Notes and Questions

1. M. Jaen, Protecting the Oceans from Climate Change: An Analysis of the Role of Selected International Instruments on Resources and Environmental Protection in the Context of UNCLOS in Ocean Yearbook 21 at 91, 122-123 (2007), summarizes the CBD's limitations:

> The CBD aims to preserve and protect marine biodiversity, although global climate change and its effects are not specifically mentioned; the Jakarta Mandate, which stemmed from the CBD's COP 2, urges States to take timely action to further these aims. As well, the work program recommended by COP 4 specifies the impending need for action with regards to coral reefs and 'small islands,' actions which would deal largely with the effects of global warming. Thus, it can be seen that the issue of global climate change is becoming more and more recognized as a relevant problem with regards to biodiversity. Unlike the Kyoto Protocol, there is no provision in the Convention for enforcement; no international inspection or observer system has been established. Such is not possible for this type of Convention, whose function is to provide a framework for observing 'soft' obligations. The efficacy of its mandates requires that a great deal of national legislation be enacted. Nevertheless, the Convention is unique in that it provides a high degree of inducement for participation and compliance.

2. For the Belize Reef World Heritage petition mentioned in the Doelle excerpt above, see Belize Institute of Environmental Law and Policy, Petition to the World Heritage Committee Requesting Inclusion of Belize Barrier Reef Reserve System in the List of World Heritage in Danger as a Result of Climate and for Protective Measures & Actions (Nov. 15, 2004), available at http://www.climatelaw.org/media/UNE-SCO.petitions.release/belize.barrier.reef.doc (last visited Feb. 15, 2007). Law students at the University of Florida (Gainseville) program in Costa Rica provided the legal services for this initiative.

See also The Sydney Centre for International and Global Law, University of Sydney, Australia, Global Climate Change and The Great Barrier Reef: Australia's Obligations Under the World Heritage Convention 3 (2004), available   at   http://www.law.us-yd.edu.au/scig/SCIGLFinalReport21_09_04.pdf (arguing that Aus-tralia's [initial] decision not to ratify the Kyoto Protocol constituted a breach of the World Heritage Convention). Australia ratified the Kyoto Protocol in 2008.

In February 2006, a petition was filed with the World Heritage Committee to also list the Waterton-Glacier International Peace Park spanning the border between Alberta, Canada and northwestern Montana as a "World Heritage Site in Danger" due to climate change. The Bush Administration filed a memorandum arguing that under the convention the Committee's role is limited to research and advice rather than policy prescriptions, and that even if all human greenhouse gas emissions ceased, it is not clear that glacial retreat due to climate change would stop. M. Gerrard, Climate Change and U.S. Law 223-24 (2007).

3.   Regarding the ocean acidification problem identified by Lubchenco, a National Research Council study of how this affects the U.S. was authorized by H.R. 5946 § 701, P.L. 109-479 (Jan. 12, 2007), enacted to amend and reauthorize the Magnuson-Stevens Fishery Conservation and Management Act. The roles of the U.S. environmental laws in responding to ocean acidification are at issue in Center for Biolgoical Diversity v. EPA (W.D. Wash., complaint filed May 14, 2009) and Center for Biological Diversity v Locke (N.D. Cal. Complaint filed May 28, 2009). Ocean acidification would be specifically recognized as an impact of climate change to which the U.S. should adapt by H.R. 2454 (111th Cong. June 26, 2009). For more on climate change's ocean impacts, see E. Laws, Climate Change, Oceans, and Human Health in Ocean Yearbook 21 at 129 (2007).

3. Coral Reef Degradation

As Lubchenco testified to Congress, ocean warming and acidification are damaging coral reefs like the Belize Barrier Reef. The coral bleaching problem due to warming is discussed further in M. Jaen supra Note 1 at 96-99:

There is scientific concern about the correlation between the increase in the ocean temperature and coral bleaching and mortality. Coral bleaching is a direct result of an increase in the temperature of surface water in the ocean. Coral reefs generally have enormous adaptability to changes in water temperature and conditions, although the estimated future increase is a cause of unease for specialists in the area. * * *

Of the 110 countries whose waters host coral reefs, 93 have already experienced some type of environmental destruction. About 27 percent of the world's coral reefs are considered at high risk for damage; for those reefs in populous areas, this figure is 80 percent. The GCRMN report informs that an estimated 20 percent of the coral reefs globally have already been irreparably damaged and show little sign of recuperation. The major conclusions regarding 'reefs status and the future threats posed by climate change' are described in the GCRMN report as follows:

(1) coral reefs are affected in terms of health and sustainability by stresses stemming from both climate and local non-climate sources, frequently in a synergistic manner;

(2) loss, degradation and alteration will continue in coral reefs, especially where these effects are already evident;

(3) there will be regional variation in the net effects on coral reef ecosystems from global climate change;

(4) organisms and communities inhabiting the coral reefs may not necessarily becomes extinct, even though climate change will result in net negative effects on the reefs;

(5) Further research into adaptation processes and recovery mechanisms, along with improved monitoring in coral reef ecosystems, will assist us in learning from the changes observed, so that we may influence the course of events rather than merely witnessing the decline. * * *

Unfortunately, for coral reefs and their ecosystems, the reduction in greenhouse gas emissions is 'the ultimate solution' to all the threats imposed by climate change, concurrent with a maximum effort in the conservation of reefs found to be particularly resistant to bleaching and those which appear to recover quickly from its effects. A focus on tourist reefs and those associated with large-scale fish spawning is important from an economic standpoint. The idea is to assist those responsible for managing reefs in preparing for and dealing with extensive bleaching events, while States discuss and try to implement a long-term plan to reduce GHG emissions. For coral reefs, however, the time required for planning strategies and implementing policies may be too long. * * *

Notes and Questions

1. Because most coral reefs lie within national jurisdiction extending 200 nautical miles offshore, national laws such as Australia's 1975 Great Barrier Reef Marine Park Act are very important to their protection. See M. Gray, Protecting Coral Reefs: The Principal National and International Legal Instruments, 26 Harvard Envtl. L. Rev. 499 (2002). The full range of potentially useful U.S. laws is reviewed in R. Hildreth, Place-Based Ocean Management: Emerging U.S. Law and Practice, 51 Ocean & Coastal Management 659 (2008); M. Masry, Coral Reef Protection under the United States Federal Law: An Overview of the Primary Federal Legislative Means by Which Coral Ecosystems and Their Associated Habitat May Be Protected, 14 U. Balt. J. Envtl. L. 1 (2006).

2. The 2000 Coral Reef Conservation Act, 16, U.S.C. § 6401 et seq., established an interagency coral reef conservation program. Two 2008 National Oceanic and Atmospheric Administration reports on deep sea corals recently discovered in U.S. waters identified "climate change and ocean acidification" as "threats requiring further research." See National Oceanic & Atmospheric Administration, Implementation of the Deep Sea Coral Research and Technology Program (March 2008), and The State of Deep Coral Ecosystems of the United States (Feb. 2008). In addition, during 2007-09, the U.S. co-hosted the Secretariat for the International Coral Reef Initiative (ICRI) which then designated 2008 as the International Year of the Reef. The ICRI is the primary international coordinating mechanism for scientific, governmental, and NGO efforts to protect coral reef ecosystems. H.R. 560 (111th Congress, July 9, 2009) would reauthorize the act and amend the act's purposes to include "developing sound scientific information on * * * large-scale threats related to climate change, such as ocean acidification."

3. The first U.S. coral reef management action taken in response to climate change was the 2006 Endangered Species Act listing of two North American coral species, the elkhorn and the staghorn, 71 Fed. Reg. 26852 (May 9, 2006). The NGO Center for Biological Diversity believes that the designation of the coral's critical habitat as a follow up to their listing "moves the entire Endangered Species Act onto a firm legal foundation for challenging global-warming pollution." J. Ruhl, Climate Change and the Endangered Species Act: Building Bridges to the No-Analog Future, 88 Boston U. L. Rev. 1, 30 n. 116 (2008). See 73 Fed. Reg. 72209 (Nov 26, 2008). Other ESA listed marine species explicitly connected to climate change include the polar bear as discussed in the polar section of this chapter and the Stellar sea lion. See Greenpeace v. National Marine Fisheries Service, 237 F. Supp. 1181, 1188 (W.D. Wash. 2002).

E. ADAPTING TO HYDROLOGICAL CHANGE

As noted in Chapter 2, a warmer atmosphere holds more water vapor and changing global wind patters shift patterns of precipitation. Drought and flood conditions emerge in new ways. National water law throughout the world was enacted by legislatures or determined by courts without anticipating the effects of dynamic climate change. See A. Foerster, Progress on Environmental Flows in Southeastern Australia in Light of Climate Change, 39 Envtl. L. Rep. 10426 (2009). According to J. Miller, Remedying Our Fragmented Governmental Structure to Deal With Our Nation-on-Edge Problems, 38 Entl. L. Rep. 10187, 10188 (2008): "Both the world and the United States are on edge with water as well as with climate. The two are intimately intertwined. Much of the world and much of the United States has either too much water or too little water. Too much water causes flooding in Bangladesh, just as too much water causes flooding in our own backyards. Too little water causes desertification in Saharan and sub-Saharan Africa and not enough water to go around in the U.S. Southwest. Climate change warms the polar ice caps, adding to water in the sea, causing coastal flooding. Climate change alters rainfall, transposing some of the areas getting too much or too little water. Water pollution adds to the too little water problem making some of the already too little water unusable."

As you read the following excerpts, what modifications do you consider will be required to reform water law?

ADAPTING TO CLIMATE CHANGE: ENVIRONMENTAL LAW IN A WARMER CLIMATE
Matthew D. Zinn
34 Ecology L. Q. 61 (2007)

In the western United States, one of the most important expected effects of climate change is that of rising temperatures on precipitation. Changes in precipitation patterns promise a host of challenges, including problems for water supply, energy production, and flood control. * * *

Recent studies have shown that climate change is likely to significantly affect western hydrology. As temperatures increase, some winter and early spring precipitation that currently falls as snow will begin to fall increasingly as rain. Moreover, precipitation that does continue to fall as snow will have a shorter life in the snowpack as the snowpack melts even earlier. Indeed, by some accounts, the snowpack may almost disappear from some western mountain ranges, such as California's Sierra Nevada, by century's end.

The combination of earlier snowmelt and an increasing proportion of precipitation falling as rain means that runoff will increase in the winter and early spring months and decrease in the late spring and summer. Streams will run dry ealier in the season as more water is released during winter and early spring. Late spring and summer runoff may be further reduced by climate-induced increases in evapotranspiration, the process by which plants take up water from the soil through their roots and release it to the atmosphere through their leaves, though the extent of potential increases remains unclear. Direct evaporation from soil and water bodies, including reservoirs, also increases with temperature, further reducing the water available in warmer months.

1. Water Supply

Water supply systems in the West were designed around the existing hydrologic regime. Because precipitation falls mostly during the winter and early spring, water must be stored for use throughout the rest of the year. These systems rely heavily on the snowpack to provide natural in situ storage of water over the winter and spring and to gradually release it over the late spring and summer. Engineered reservoirs then catch and retain runoff from snowmelt, which allows water deliveries to downstream users to be further extended into the dry summer and early fall months. Reservoirs release water into rivers for diversion through a complex of canals and further reservoirs, such as the Bureau of Reclamation's massive Central Valley Project in California, for eventual delivery to end users.

It is hard to overstate the significance of climate change's implications for western water supply. More winter rain and earlier snowmelt undermines the crucial assumption that snowpack is available to augment engineered storage. As it stands, the system does not include sufficient engineered storage to compensate for the loss of the snowpack. Reservoirs that reach capacity with winter and early spring runoff will be forced to release some of that runoff before the summer and fall months, when it is most needed. Thus, even assuming that climate change does not affect the total volume of precipitation, the change in its timing and form will mean that more water must be released to flow to the ocean. The problem is compounded by increased evaporative losses in warmer months and increases in summer and early fall water demand caused by increasing summer temperatures. In California, for example, assuming median estimates of warming, '[b]y the end of [the] century, increasing temperatures are expected to increase the crop demand for water [by] 13 percent.' A warmer climate would also stimulate increased urban water demand, an effect likely to be exacerbated by the significant population growth expected in the West in coming decades.

What kinds of adaptations and secondary impacts might these changes encourage? To adapt to declining water storage in snowpack, we might expand engineered storage by building new dams and reservoirs or raising existing dams to increase the capacity of exiting reservoirs. Dams and reservoirs have a number of adverse environmental effects. They fundamentally alter upstream aquatic habitat, replacing riparian areas with flat water, and inundate and destroy terrestrial ecosystems. Dams also block fish access to former spawning grounds and may impair downstream water conditions by, for example, raising water temperatures or reducing or eliminating flow.

Alternative responses are of course available, with a range of potential environmental effects. In lieu of on-stream storage in reservoirs, runoff could be released from reservoirs early in the season, but captured downstream and pumped into groundwater aquifers for later withdrawal. Seawater desalination may also become economically feasible for high-value urban water uses. These adaptations may not involve the severe ecological costs associated with the expansion of engineered on-stream storage, but they will have their own adverse effects. Large-scale aquifer recharge is energy intensive, as water must be pumped twice: into the aquifer for storage and then out again for use. Desalination also uses a great deal of energy in pumping saline water through a filter membrane at very high pressure. Power generation to satisfy these energy demands could have significant pollution impacts. Desalination has potential adverse effects as well in impinging and entraining aquatic species in influent water and releasing highly concentrated brine as a byproduct of treatment.

Other potential adaptations include the establishment of more robust water markets to reallocate increasingly scarce water and mandatory agricultural or urban water conservation or recycling. Water markets have potential distributional impacts on in-stream water uses by shifting flows among basins and water bodies without regard to ecosystem needs. Water conservation and recycling appear to have the least severe environmental consequence of the available adaptations. The challenge * * * comes in seeing that such least-environmental-cost alternatives can compete in the political arena with more costly alternatives.

2. Hydropower

Beyond its effects on water supply, acceleration of runoff could also disturb the western energy grid. Western states rely heavily on hydropower, particularly to meet summer energy demand. Storage of water in mountain reservoirs allows a steady flow of hydropower as water is released during the spring and summer; reservoirs effectively store power by storing water. As runoff accelerates, water released during the winter and spring months to prevent dam overflows will be unavailable to generate hydropower during the critical summer months, when electricity demand peaks to run air conditioners. Moreover, as summer temperatures rise with a warming climate, electricity demand would increase inversely with the decline in hydropower production.

Of the potential water supply adaptations discussed previously, only construction or expansion of engineered on-stream reservoirs, with the attendant severe environmental impacts discussed previously, could avert the loss of hydropower. Beyond adding new storage capacity, another foreseeable adaptation to the loss of hydropower is expanding reliance on other energy sources, most likely coal or natural gas. While hydropower generation causes impingement or entrainment of fish and changes the timing of flows in downstream rivers, fossil fuel-fired electricity generation has a broader array of impacts to ecosystems and human health. Fossil fuel combustion produces a raft of harmful air pollutants including oxides of nitrogen (NOx), sulfur dioxide, and mercury, as well as climate-forcing carbon dioxide. The extraction of fossil fuels imposes enormous ecological and health costs as well.

Alternatively, the energy deficit left by the loss of hydropower might be made up with nuclear power or renewable energy sources such as wind and solar or as-yet-untapped sources such as tidal power. Of course, nuclear power entails a variety of infamous environmental and health risks, concern for which has prevented development of new nuclear generating capacity in the United States. Renewable sources would avoid most of the human health and ecological impacts that nuclear and fossil fuel produce, but are not without environmental effects. In any event, in a world of climate adaptation rather than mitigation, the greenhouse gas regulation and attendant price signals that could have encouraged the development of such alternatives to fossil-fueled energy sources would be absent.

3. Flood Control

By storing and gradually releasing water from precipitation, the mountain snowpack also provides flood control benefits. With unmitigated change, higher winter and early spring runoff would deliver more water to overtaxed reservoirs. Reservoirs management involves a tradeoff between storage of runoff for use in the dry season and short-term storage of winter and early spring storm runoff to prevent downstream flooding. Filling reservoirs earlier in the year to ensure water supply for the dry season renders them unable to accommodate late season storm events, but reserving capacity in the reservoir for late season storms risks leaving the reservoir below capacity heading into the dry season if late precipitation does not materialize. Higher early-season runoff caused by climate change increases the risk of early-season floods, as runoff from storm events made more severe by climate change, potentially causing flooding in communities downstream. In California, for instance, the low-lying Sacramento urban area in the floodplains of the American and Sacramento Rivers already faces a flood risk greater than that of recently and catastrophically flooded New Orleans, and that risk will be exacerbated by climate induced changes in precipitation and runoff. Some early flooding might be avoided by keeping reservoirs low to absorb early runoff, but at the cost of aggravating water supply shortfalls in the dry months.

The greater flood risks under unmitigated climate change invite a range of adaptations. Potential engineered adaptations include construction or expansion of reservoirs to store storm runoff (discussed above), construction of new levees, or raising of existing levees. Non-engineered adaptations include redirection of new development away from floodplains and relocation of existing floodplain development. Buildings may be designed to withstand a flood, such as by raising the ground floor of the structure above the elevation of the projected flood. The environmental effects of these adaptations range in severity from plainly severe (reservoir construction or relocation of entire communities away from floodplains) to likely minor (building design). Given this range of impacts, the question again is whether we will be able to make a choice that minimizes or moderates those impacts. * * *

Further, rising sea levels threaten coastal estuaries such as Chesapeake Bay, the Mississippi Delta, and the San Francisco Delta. One commentator 'estimates that a 1 meter rise in sea level could easily inundate the entire Delta and triple the areal extent of the San Francisco Bay.' The Delta ecosystem is already under severe pressure from California's water supply infrastructure, which uses it as a conduit for delivery of freshwater to agricultural users in the San Joaquin Valley and eventually to urban users in Southern California. The freshwater diversions change salinity levels and the pattern of flows through the Delta contributing to the decline of some species. Rising sea levels will further increase the salinity of Delta waters. Furthermore, rising sea levels would threaten the water supply system itself and thus require adaptations on a grand scale. If saltwater were to intrude far enough into the Delta, it would reach the pumps and headgates of the massive canals that divert freshwater south, rendering the canals useless.

To adapt to rising sea levels in the San Francisco Bay Delta and prevent saltwater from reaching the canals, freshwater might need to be diverted further upstream by building a 'peripheral canal' that would bypass the Delta entirely. The canal would have adverse environmental effects in the construction of massive canals and diversion structures, such as habitat loss and fragmentation. Whether it would help or harm the Delta ecosystem as a whole, however, is subject to debate. Some have argued that it would damage the ecosystem by preventing freshwater from reaching the Delta and thus encouraging further saltwater intrusion from the Bay. By contrast, others note that the canal would eliminate the massive pumping of water from the southern Delta thought to harm Delta species.

Finally, rising sea levels will also cause or increase saltwater intrusion in to coastal aquifers presently used for drinking water or irrigation. The loss of water supply in turn would require development of new water supplies or further abandonment of coastal areas and concomitant inland development. As previously discussed, water supply adaptations in coastal areas such as desalination and groundwater recharge have high energy demands, and inland development often occurs on undeveloped open space and destroys or fragments habitat. * * *

CLIMATE CHANGE, REGULATORY FRAGMENTATION, AND WATER TRIAGE
Robin Kundis Craig
79 University of Colorado Law Review 825 (2008)

* * * [A]s the effects of climate change begin to be felt in the United States, conflicts between claims for consumptive water use for human populations, agriculture, and development and other in situ demands for water, including ecosystem demands, are only likely to escalate.

Within these conflicts, moreover, [Endangered Species Act] ESA litigation over water use is especially likely to increase. First, climate change is likely to increase the number of species that qualify for protection under the ESA as a result of climate-related loss of habitat and other effects.[268] According to the U.S. Global Climate Change Research Program ("USGCCRP"), "The natural ecosystems of the Arctic, Great Lakes, Great Basin, Southeast, and the prairie potholes of the Great Plains appear highly vulnerable to the projected changes in climate," suggesting that their species may become ESA candidates with increasing frequency. Indeed, NMFS has listed the Acropora corals as threatened species in part because of climate change effects, and the USFWS has * * * [listed] the polar bear almost entirely because of the effects climate change is having on the polar bear's habitat.

> Second, climate change is likely to place additional stress on species already listed, including and perhaps especially water-dependent species. As the USGCCRP has noted, "Surface water temperature fluctuates more rapidly with reduced volumes of water, likely affecting vital habitats," and "[w]ater quality is also likely to be affected by climate change in a variety of ways. * * * Groundwater supplies are less susceptible than surface water to short-term climate variability; they are more affected by long-term trends. Groundwater serves as the base flow for many streams and rivers. In many areas, groundwater levels are very likely to fall, thus reducing seasonal streamflows." * * *

Finally, changes in water supply may call into question the continued utility of existing water law rules and water consumption patterns in many

---

[268] See, e.g., American Lands Alliance v. Norton, 242 F. Supp. 2d 1, 6 (D.D.C. 2003) (noting that ecologists had identified climate change and global warming as factors that warranted listing of the Gunnison sage grouse under the ESA); Greenpeace v. National Marine Fisheries Service, 237 F. Supp. 2d 1181, 1188 (W.D. Wash. 2002) (noting that NMFS's Biological Opinion indicated that climate change was a factor in the population reduction of the Stellar sea lion); Friends of the Wild Swan, Inc. v. U.S. Fish & Wildlife Service, 12 F. Supp. 2d 1121, 1128 (D. Or. 1997) (noting that the Jarbridge River population segment of the bull trout would be most susceptible to global warming).

areas of the country, unsettling rights and expectations long considered sacrosanct. On the one hand, to the extent state water law allows courts or legislatures to act, climate change may well prompt changes in that law. As noted above, water law is already more sensitive than many other kinds of law to the ecological conditions that dominate in an area—hence the divide in the United States between riparian and prior appropriation doctrine states. If water-stressed areas begin to receive greatly increased overall supplies of water, or if previously water-rich areas begin to experience continual shortages, their systems of water law may also begin to evolve, unsettling what were considered "settled" rights in water. * * *

Climate change only underscores the need for a comprehensive regulatory approach to protect marine ecosystems. Excess carbon dioxide levels are already acidifying the oceans, and some of the more confidently predicted effects of climate change are increases in ocean temperatures and sea level rise. All of these effects can distress marine-especially coastal-ecosystems and hence already threaten a large sector of the United States' economic productivity. Considering the effects of upstream water resources decisions on coastal and marine ecosystems thus makes economic as well as ecological sense. * * *

The regulatory fragmentation that characterizes water resource management in the United States in effect presumes that aquatic resources are abundant enough that the nation can tolerate their inefficient management and the incidental effects of upstream management on downstream resources. The evidence is increasingly all to the contrary—litigation indicates that conflicts among the fragmented regulatory regimes governing water are becoming more frequent, requiring the piecemeal prioritization of uses and goals. * * *

In coming decades, and especially in combination with population growth and other existing stressors, climate change is likely to underscore the problems of water's regulatory fragmentation by creating or worsening water stress in many parts of the country. Specifically, climate change is likely to increase water shortages and the number of conflicts that such shortages generate. In many areas of the country, as has already been seen in the Colorado River, the likely result will be some form of *de facto* water triage—the unconscious sacrificing of some uses and some ecosystems, especially downstream marine ecosystems, in pursuit of "more pressing'" local needs. * * *

As the country enters the regulatory chaos that climate change may bring, it should also ensure that no water-dependent resources remain unattended regulatory orphans. Two commissions have concluded that significant legal reforms, both structural and substantive, are needed to protect the nation's valuable marine resources, including the incorporation of upstream effects. Nevertheless, examples across the country demonstrate that coastal marine ecosystems often suffer from decisions made under the current reality of water's regulatory fragmentation, in terms of both reductions in flow and increased pollution. These saltwater ecosystems are the regulatory orphans of freshwater management regimes, and increasing water shortages and water conflict are an unpromising context in which to generate spontaneous improvements in watershed-wide cooperation and marine-inclusive management. * * *

One of the most basic regulatory aspects of water-and arguably, the aspect with the most ability to influence downstream ecological outputs, particularly in areas experiencing freshwater shortages-is the law governing who has the right to remove fresh water from its natural watercourse and to use that water for some consumptive purpose, such as irrigation, drinking water, or industrial manufacturing. From this perspective, freshwater resources, both surface water and groundwater, are generally considered the states' regulatory domain, and state water law dominates in regulating the removal and use of fresh water. As a result, regulatory authority over water diversions in interstate watersheds is necessarily fragmented among the relevant states.

Nor do the states agree in their regulatory priorities. Indeed, the exact principles and requirements governing the withdrawal and consumptive use of water can vary considerably from location to location. However, in broad-brush strokes, the eastern states inherited from England the doctrine of riparianism, which ties the right to use water to ownership of the land adjoining the water source-i.e., the riparian landowners. Common law riparian doctrine emphasizes domestic use, water sharing, correlative and adjustable rights to water, and a limit on withdrawals from the natural watercourse. Riparianism works adequately in areas with plenty of water, and it is fairly supportive of aquatic ecosystems. However, the legal connection of consumptive use rights to riparian land ownership limits non-riparian development, and most eastern states have transitioned to "regulated riparianism" and administrative permitting, which allow for increased consumptive and off-site use of water and concomitant adverse effects on aquatic ecosystems.

In contrast, the perpetually water-limited and drought-threatened western states generally rejected riparianism in favor of the prior appropriation doctrine. Prior appropriation operates on a principle of "first in time, first in right"—the first user to apply water to a beneficial use, without waste or abandonment, acquires a continued right to a water supply superior to that of later users drawing water from the same source. Moreover, given its origin in western mining on federal public lands, prior appropriation doctrine has never linked water use to riparian land ownership, removing legal obstacles to transporting water from its source to distant farms or other uses. However, the prior appropriation doctrine has also traditionally lacked any impetus to leave water in situ, promoting (especially in conjunction with natural conditions where drought is already common) far more destruction of and stress upon aquatic ecosystems than eastern riparianism. Legal mechanisms that allow for the protection of ecological values, such as the recognition of instream rights, expansion of the state public trust doctrine, and incorporation of public interest review into permitting regimes, are relatively recent innovations in prior appropriation states.

In addition to these variations within state law, three federal law doctrines are relevant to the implementation of state water law, especially when viewing water in a large ecosystem context. As a result, federal agencies and courts also play a role in assigning water rights, further fragmenting authority over water diversions.

First, the federal common law doctrine of equitable apportionment controls—absent interstate compact or direct congressional action—the division of interstate water resources among the relevant states. As applied by the U.S. Supreme Court, equitable apportionment generally follows the legal regime of the relevant states (prior appropriation in the West, riparianism in the East) and strives to preserve existing uses. As such, states with interstate waterways have strong incentives to develop that water quickly and extensively. Indeed, fears about downstream California's rapid development helped to drive interstate and congressional apportionment of the Colorado River.

Second, the federal public trust doctrine limits the states' ability to abdicate title to and especially regulatory authority over the beds and banks of waters that are navigable-in-fact or influenced by the tides. This doctrine seeks to preserve the public's right to use these waters for, at minimum, navigation, commerce, and fishing and hence provides some impetus for leaving water in its natural location.

Finally, and most importantly in the western states, the doctrine of federal reserved rights recognizes that, in some circumstances, the federal government will be deemed to have reserved water rights for federal purposes that trump state water rights. Federal reserved rights are particularly important for tribes and federal parks, involving those tribes and the relevant federal agencies in water diversions and management. While many such reserved rights have yet to be fully litigated, when these rights are finally acknowledged in prior appropriation states they tend to have early priority dates and hence can significantly alter the implementation of other water rights. In addition, the federal presence is often dominant in the variety of federal reclamation and irrigation projects that exist in the United States, especially in the West. * * *

Finally, aquatic ecosystems are just that-ecosystems that provide habitat and life support to numerous species. Nevertheless, no single federal or state statute addresses all of the considerations relevant to water's status as habitat, especially not at the ecosystem level. Instead, a variety of laws confers partial regulatory authority on a variety of entities.

The Clean Water Act encourages states, the EPA, and the Army Corps to think about water's status as habitat. As noted, one of the Act's overall goals is to restore and maintain the fishability of rivers. The EPA must establish guidance water quality criteria that reflect "the latest scientific knowledge" regarding "plankton, fish, shellfish, wildlife, plant life, shorelines, beaches, esthetics, and recreation" and regarding "the effects of pollutants on biological community diversity, productivity, and stability. . . ." States, in turn, use these criteria in setting their water quality standards, subject to EPA approval. States must also consider their waters' uses for "propagation of fish and wildlife" when establishing the water quality standards. Permit standards for discharges into the oceans must consider the effects of the pollutants on "plankton, fish, shellfish, wildlife, shorelines, and beaches" and on marine life generally, including "changes in marine ecosystem diversity, productivity, and stability" and "species and community population changes." Similar considerations govern when the Army Corps issues permits for discharges of dredged or fill material. In addition, the USFWS must be given the opportunity to comment on all such "dredge and fill" permits. Thus, three federal agencies and fifty state water quality agencies, as well as agencies in U.S. territories, are all partially empowered to regulate water as an ecosystem.

Nevertheless, the Clean Water Act's regulatory focus remains pollution prevention and mitigation, not habitat preservation *per se*. Direct considerations of aquatic habitat impairments are far more likely to come about as a result of the federal Endangered Species Act of 1973 ("ESA") or similar requirements of state law.

The USFWS implements the federal ESA for terrestrial species, including most freshwater species, while NMFS implements the Act for marine and anadromous species. The ESA states explicitly that one of its purposes is "to provide a means whereby the ecosystems upon which endangered species and threatened species depend may be conserved," and "the present or threatened destruction, modification, or curtailment of [a species'] habitat or range" is the first reason given for listing a species for protection. * * *

Finally, state endangered species protections and state water permitting requirements can serve to acknowledge and to protect aquatic ecosystems and the habitat they provide. State endangered species protections vary, but many states protect species not already protected under the federal ESA. In addition, many states have incorporated ecosystem and habitat considerations into their water law and consumptive use permitting. Most often, these considerations are incorporated into permitting decisions through a public interest review. For example, under Oregon statutes, the state Water Resources Department may deny a reservoir owner's water right permit application if the reservoir "[w]ould pose a significant detrimental impact to existing fishery resources." Other states have found other ways to incorporate such considerations. California and Hawaii, for example, use their public trust doctrines to harmonize water law and species protections. * * *

As noted, the health of coastal marine ecosystems depends, at least in part, on the quantity and quality of fresh water that reaches those ecosystems. In addition, as the Pew Center on Global Climate Change has pointed out, "[c]limate change may decrease or increase precipitation, thereby altering coastal . . . ecosystems.'" These facts explain why coastal and ocean regulators must look upstream if they want to ensure that the United States' marine ecosystems can continue to provide the wealth inherent in sustainable marine biodiversity.

Nevertheless * * * marine ecosystems also suggest relevant output measures that could provide regulatory focus and coherence for upstream freshwater resource management. For example, asking what water quality goals in the Mississippi River watershed "should" be is close to a meaningless question when asked in the context of the current Clean Water Act. Because of the Clean Water Act's cooperative federalism, states set water quality goals for particular water segments, a state-local focus that almost never takes account of cumulative watershed effects or large aquatic ecosystems. In other words, applying the Act's requirements for ambient water quality goals to the Mississippi River quickly devolves into an uncoordinated promotion of state and local priorities rather than a comprehensive evaluation of the River (let alone the watershed) as a whole.

However, if instead one asks how water resources in the Mississippi River should be managed both to promote state and local priorities and to restore the Gulf of Mexico by reducing or eliminating the Gulfs hypoxic zone, priority regulatory issues come immediately into focus-namely, controlling nutrient pollution, which in turn requires a focus on agriculture. As such, focusing on marine outputs in this watershed immediately underscores two of the Clean Water Act's gaping regulatory "holes": agriculture and nonpoint source pollution. Such a marine output focus also reveals that water quantity regulation is not a particularly important issue for the Mississippi.

In stark contrast, in the Colorado River both water quality and water quantity issues are relevant, while in the Apalachicola River water quantity and water flow regimes are most important. The Gulf of California suffers from both lack of incoming water and water pollution, while the Apalachicola Bay oysters suffer almost entirely as a result of reduced water flows and altered flow regimes. Water quality issues are at least subject to the minimum federal requirements in the Clean Water Act; in contrast, water quantity issues are almost entirely state-local in focus. As Reed Benson has comprehensively discussed, several federal doctrines and statutes do limit the deference accorded to state water allocations and states' power to make such allocations. Nevertheless, no federal law creates a comprehensive water resource management regime. Instead federal claims and laws provide one basis for locus-specific water resource disputes, disputes that pit the state-local interest at stake against federal claims of priority *for that particular water or river segment*, whether for navigation, Tribes, reclamation projects, hydropower, or endangered fish. Universal application of ecologically motivated minimum flow regimes does not yet exist, to the detriment of the Gulf of California, Apalachicola Bay, and several other coastal ecosystems.

Thus, the first reality that a marine output-based focus reveals is that the regulatory issues for marine and aquatic ecosystems can vary considerably from watershed to watershed. "Protecting the oceans" is thus not a univalent regulatory goal, and incorporation of marine ecosystem goals into freshwater management is as likely to reveal differences in watershed management choices and priorities as it is to reveal similarities.

This recognition of difference, in turn, is important for at least two reasons. First, and most basically, the types of sources that need to be addressed and the types of regulatory refinements that need to be made in order to protect marine ecosystems will vary. Second, in times of decreased water supply and water shortage, regulating to protect marine resources will be far more politically and economically viable in some watersheds than in others. As a result, incorporating marine ecosystem considerations into freshwater management would make it less likely that marine ecosystems will be "unwittingly destroyed" through unconscious triage in those watersheds where, if marine ecosystems were in fact consciously considered, economics, cultural values, and/or the availability of relatively minor regulatory accommodations would accord marine ecosystem protection higher regulatory priority than it currently receives.

Finally, an output-based, marine-inclusive approach to water management would certainly be better for the oceans, but incorporation of marine ecosystem goals is also likely to better protect upstream ecosystems and many upstream uses. For example, reductions in atmospheric deposition of mercury sufficient to prevent contamination of marine fish would also address mercury bioaccumulation in freshwater fish, adverse effects on protected species such as the Florida panther, and potential human health impairments. Similarly, reductions in other types of land-based water pollution to protect ocean water quality would almost certainly simultaneously better protect freshwater quality. Ensuring that enough water flows through waterways to support the estuaries and other coastal ecosystems at the end of the line would simultaneously help to ensure that sufficient water remained in those waterways to support the freshwater ecosystems and protected species within them, would support efforts to improve water quality, could improve navigation and recreation when low flows threaten passage, and would support hydropower generation. * * *

As in medical triage, water triage accepts the reality (however lamentable) that not all aquatic ecosystems are likely to survive current and projected future levels of human use. More specifically, water triage would identify three categories of aquatic and marine ecosystems: (1) those that are likely to survive as functional ecosystems regardless, or with only minimal additional regulatory intrusion over current regulatory practice; (2) those that can be saved as functional ecosystems, but only with significant additional regulatory intervention; and (3) those that are likely to die, or become significantly impaired ecosystems, regardless of what regulatory authorities might do.

To be sure, given the value of marine—and indeed all aquatic—ecosystems, one would hope that waters placed into the third category, or ignored despite being in the second category, would be kept to a minimum through better regulatory coordination, interstate cooperation, and water conservation measures. * * *

Ideally, therefore, a new system of water resources management would pursue several goals simultaneously: (1) reduction of the current regulatory fragmentation while acknowledging the varying levels of governmental, public, and private interests in water resources; (2) maintenance of instrumental regulatory flexibility, in acknowledgement that aquatic ecosystems and the demands upon them differ in important ways; (3) establishment of concrete priorities for specific aquatic ecosystems in the face of water stresses and shortages; (4) deliberative decisionmaking; and (5) public accountability. The most rational restructuring of water resources management to achieve these goals would use a watershed approach, acknowledging that the relevant "watershed" includes the marine ecosystems at the end of the line. This much should be relatively uncontroversial. * * *

Note and Questions

1. For analysis of how the proposed Great Lakes interstate compact would support climate change adaptation with respect to water resources in that region, see N. Hall & B. Stuntz, Climate Change and the Great Lakes Water. Resources: Avoiding Future Conflicts with Conservation, Hamline L. Rev. (2008). For the role of interstate compacts in achieving regional marine ecosystem-based management as advocated by Craig in the excerpt above, see R. Hildreth, Regional Ocean Resources Management, 3 Coastal Zone '91 at 2583. In this connection, P. Mulroy, Climate and the Law of the River—A Southern Nevada Perspective, 14 Hastings West-Northwest 1603 (2008), reviews the

positive roles the 1922 Colorado River Compact has and can play as the southwest adapts to the even greater aridity projected for that region due to climate change. Possible state water law and policy adjustments in California as a key Colorado River Compact state are reviewed in J. Andrew, J. Pearson & J. Woodling, California Water Management: Subject to Change, 14 Hastings West-Northwest 1463 (2008); B. Gray, Global Climate Change: Water Supply Risks and Water Management Opportunities, 14 Hastings West-Northwest 1453 (2008). Climate change adaptation challenges in the arid Rio Grande basin are discussed in M. Padilla, The Thirsty Rio Grande: Sustainable Water Planning Along the Rio Grande in the Age of Global Warming, Sustainable Development L. & Policy, Winter 2008 at 71. There brackish groundwater is being desalinated by a federally funded project that is the largest inland desalination plant in the world. Desalination of ocean water is discussed in the oceans section of this chapter.

For the possible roles water rights general adjudications could play in climate change adaptation, see S. Odem, The General Adjudication of the Yakima River Tributaries for the Twenty-First Century and a Changing Climate, 23 J. Envtl. L. & Litigation 275 (2008).

2. As noted by Craig in the excerpt above, in addition to water supply laws, federal and state water pollution laws have important roles to play in climate change adaptation and mitigation processes. For more on those roles, see Miller's article quoted briefly above and Craig's article The Clean Water Act on the Cutting Edge: Climate Change and Water Quality Regulation, 24 ABA Natural Resources and Environment No. 2 (Fall 2009). For example, underground drinking water supplies would be protected by the federal Safe Drinking Water Act from the possible adverse impacts of carbon sequestration through underground storage of CO_2. See D. Hayes & J. Beauvais, Carbon Sequestration in M. Gerrard ed., Global Climate Change and U.S. Law 691, 716-719 (2007); P. Glaser et al., Global Warming Solutions: Regulatory Challenges and Common Law Liabilities Associated with the Geologic Sequestration of Carbon Dioxide, 6 Geo. J.L. & Pub. Policy 429 (2008).

Judicial precedents supporting an integrated state management approach to water supply and water pollution concerns include In re Water Use Permit Applications, 9 P.3d 409 (2000), remanded in part, 93 P.3d 643 (2004) (Hawaii public trust doctrine); National Audubon Society v. Superior Court, 658 P.2d 709 (1983) (California public trust doctrine); U.S. v. Gila Valley Irrig. Dist., 920 F. Supp 1444 (D. Ariz. 1996) (Arizona prior appropriation law); U.S. v. State Water Resources Control Board, 227 Cal. Rptr. 161 (Cal. Ct. App. 1986) (California water law).

The hydrological adaptation roles of California's and other western states' "assured supply" laws focused on the water needs of new development in the region are reviewed in L. Davies, Just a Big "Hot Fuss"? Assessing the Value of Connecting Suburban Sprawl, Land Use, and Water Rights through Assured Supply Laws, 34 Ecology L. Q. 1217 (2007). See also C. Roos, From H2O to CO2: Lessons of Water Rights for Carbon Trading, 50 Ariz. L. Rev. 91 (2008).

3. Within California, hydrological adaptation responsibilities are scattered among several agencies as noted by Zinn supra at 86:

> Like most if not all states, California has no coordinated approval process to select and implement a comprehensive water supply strategy for the state. While the state Department of Water Resources (DWR), State Water Resources Control Board (SWRCB), and federal Bureau of Reclamation play important roles in approving major surface water projects such as dam construction, they would play a lesser role, if any, in approving development of alternative water sources, such as groundwater recharge and desalination, and less role still in adaptations that do not involve new supply, such as mandatory conservation or water recycling. Moreover, in California, no agency regulates withdrawals from groundwater, though groundwater injection (which would be required for aquifer storage) is regulated by the Department of Toxic Substances Control, an agency with no water supply planning authority or expertise. Likewise, local governments and the California Coastal Commission make siting decisions for desalination plants, though neither has much interest in or authority to do comprehensive water supply planning.

4. As noted by Craig, the federal Endangered Species Act's protection of threatened and endangered aquatic and marine species (including polar bears as discussed in the polar section of this chapter) supports management of water resources on a coordinated ecosystem basis as exemplified by NRDC v. Kempthorne, 506 F. Supp. 2d 322 (E.D. Cal. 2007). There the court ordered federal agencies such as the Fish and Wildlife Service (FWS) to consider climate change impacts on water including the listed delta smelt fish and its habitat in California's Central Valley. The case's potential significance is noted in J. Ruhl, Climate Change and the Endangered Species Act: Building Bridges to the No-Analog Future, 88 Boston U. L. Rev. 1, 45-46 (2008):

> Indeed, one recent judicial opinion makes it clear that the FWS must at least address the effects of climate change in jeopardy consultations. In Natural Resources Defense Council v. Kempthorne, the FWS had prepared its consultation report, known as a biological opinion (BiOp), regarding the effects of the Central Valley Project-State Water Project (CVP-SWP) in California on a small fish, the Delta smelt. The BiOp's conclusions were based in part on the assumption that the hydrology of the water bodies affected by the project would follow historical patterns for the next 20 years. Undercutting this as-

sumption, a number of environmental groups directed FWS's attention to several studies on the potential effects of climate change on water supply reliability, urging that the issue be considered in the BiOp. Reminiscent of the EPA's position in Massachusetts v. EPA, the FWS attempted to defend its failure to consider climate change at all, as the court summarized:

> Defendants and Defendant-Intervenors respond by arguing (1) that the evidence before FWS at the time the BiOp was issued was inconclusive about the impacts of climate change; and (2) that, far from ignoring climate change, the issue is built into the BiOp's analysis through the use of [saline water condition data] as a proxy for the location and distribution of Delta smelt.

But the court evidenced little tolerance for the agency's failure to address these issues in the consultation documents:

> [T]he climate change issue was not meaningfully discussed in the biological opinion, making it impossible to determine whether the information was rationally discounted because of its inconclusive nature, or arbitrarily ignored. . . .

> The BiOp does not gauge the potential effect of various climate change scenarios on Delta hydrology. Assuming, arguendo, a lawful adaptive management approach, there is no discussion about when and how climate change impacts will be addressed, whether existing take limits will remain and the probable impacts on CVP-SWP operations.

> FWS acted arbitrarily and capriciously by failing to address the issue of climate change in BiOp. * * *

The FWS does not have the pollution control expertise of the EPA, nor does any provision of the ESA explicitly provide authority to engage in emissions regulation. Given that all emission sources contribute to warming effects, the threat of jeopardy findings would have to be applied universally to all sources. This, in turn, might induce emission sources to engage in emission offsets (e.g., by purchasing forestation credits) or technological and operational emission reductions. But is the FWS equipped to assume the role of nationwide regulator of farms, industrial facilities, auto emissions, and everything else? In short, the idea that all emission sources present jeopardy conditions to each and every climate-threatened species would prove too much, and likely render the ESA and the FWS political targets in the first degree.

On the other hand, the climate change issue in Kempthorne did not involve analysis of the indirect effects of a project's greenhouse gas emissions, but rather focused on how the cumulative effects of climate change will influence the effects of a project on a protected species. The FWS evaluated the effects of the project on the smelt assuming no change in hydrology relevant to the smelt, but there was evidence that climate change could adversely affect hydrological conditions for the smelt in a way that could have altered the consultation effects analysis. The effect of Kempthorne is to require that where downscale modeling and filed observations indicate it is 'reasonably certain' that climate change will lead to changes in ecological conditions to the detriment of a protected species, the FWS must engage in a consultation to determine whether the project, taking those changes into account as cumulative effects, is 'reasonably expected' to jeopardize the species. The FWS may in many cases point to the difficulty of downscaling climate change effects to support a no-jeopardy finding, but that does not absolve it of the duty to conduct the analysis. * * *

The Kempthorne court then ordered federal officials to produce a new biological opinion by September 2008 and mandated enhanced monitoring for Delta smelt and reductions in pumping to ensure favorable flows at key times. Interim Remedial Order Following Summary Judgment and Evidentiary Hearing, NRDC v. Kempthorne, No. 1:05-cv-1207 OWW GSA (Dec. 14, 2007), available at http://www.earthjustice.org/library/legal_docs/delta-smelt-final-remedy-order.pdf. The California Department of Water Resources estimated that compliance with the order would cut water deliveries anywhere from 7 to 30%. Department of Water Resources, Advisory (Dec. 25, 2007), http://www.water.ca.gov/news/newsreleases/122407wan-ger.pdf. See H. Doremus & M. Hanemann, The Challenges of Dynamic Water Management in the American West, 26 UCLA J. Envtl. L. & Pol'y 55, 73n.40 (2008). See also Pacific Coast Federation of Fisherman's Ass'ns v. Gutierrez, 2008 WL 2223070 (E.D. Cal. May 20, 2008).

5. The Bureau of Reclamation's failure to evaluate climate change impacts on the Columbia River Basin in an Environmental Impact Statement (EIS) prepared under the National Environmental Policy Act was challenged in litigation filed in December 2008 by the Center for Environmental Law & Policy and the Columbia Riverkeeper. The Bureau proposed increased water withdrawals from Lake Roosevelt behind Grand Coulee Dam without preparing an EIS.

6. For navigable freshwater lakes and rivers, most physical shoreline changes also change the boundary between their publicly-owned beds and privately-owned riparian uplands adjacent to them. The relevant rules are discussed more fully in this chapter's sea level rise section and in B. Flush-

man, Water Boundaries: Demystifying Land Boundaries Adjacent to Tidal or Navigable Waters (2002); D. Pensley, The Legalities of Stream Interventions: Accretive Changes to New York State's Riparian Doctrine Ahead?, 25 Pace Envtl. L. Rev. 105 (2008); S. Warner, Down to the Waterline: Boundaries, Nature, and the Law in Florida (2005).

7. The U.S. shares the Colorado and Rio Grande Rivers with Mexico, and the Great Lakes and the Columbia River with Canada. Unfortunately, the global and multinational implications of hydrological change noted in the brief quotes from Hunter and Miller above are not yet reflected in the international laws governing freshwater lakes and rivers and their downstream marine waters shared by more than one nation. See O. McIntyre, Environmental Protection of International Watercourses under International Law (2007); O. McIntyre, The Role of Customary Rules and Principles of International Environmental Law in the Protection of Shared International Freshwater Resources, 46 Nat. Resources J. 157 (2006); S. Vinogradov, Marine Pollution via Transboundary Watercourses—An Interface of the "Shoreline" and "River-Basin" Regimes in the Wider Black Sea Region, Intl. J. of Marine & Coastal L. 585 (2007). On the marine side, Chapter 17 of the non-binding Agenda 21 adopted at the 1992 U.N. Conference on Environment and Development, U.N. Doc. A/CONF. 151/26 (vols. I, II, & III) (1992), does recommend "addressing critical uncertainties for the management of the marine environment and climate change" as one of seven international marine program areas including "contingency plans for human induced and natural disasters, including likely effects of potential climate change and sea level rise."

Fortunately, the U.S., Mexico, and Canada have in place longstanding bilateral treaty regimes which may provide an adequate framework for hydrological adaptation in their shared lake and river basins. See D. Hunter, J. Salzman, & D. Zaelke, International Environmental Law and Policy 885-889 (3d ed. 2007).

* * * * *

Consider the following integrated approach for Oregon developed by the staff of Governor Ted Kulongoski:

HEADWATERS TO OCEAN (H₂O)
A Strategy for Meeting Oregon's Water Needs in the
Face of Climate Change
(draft May 2008)

Making a Case For Water

Oregon's waters are an integral part of a healthy state economy and one of the foundations of its quality of life. The demand for water continues to grow for a wide variety of beneficial uses from irrigation, municipal, and industrial, to fisheries, aquatic health, recreation, and aesthetics. Oregonians are guided by the need to protect the unique environmental resources of this state and we need to protect the unique environmental resources of this state and we need to manage our waters in a way that recognizes the importance and validity of all of these uses.

However, water resource management in Oregon is facing a number of significant challenges. Surface water is nearly fully allocated during the summer months and ground water is showing declines in both quantity and quality in many areas. More than 1,100 water bodies are impaired for at least one pollutant. Twenty-four fish species have been identified as Threatened or Endangered under the Federal Endangered Species Act, while another 31 are listed as state sensitive species.

These challenges are heightened by two relatively new and increasing pressures: climate change and rapid population growth. Climate change will greatly influence how we collect, store, and use water in Oregon. Rapid population growth will radically affect demand for water. Climate change and rapid population growth are bringing a new sense of urgency to water resources management in Oregon.

Fortunately, we have good models for innovation and partnership when it comes to water resources, as demonstrated by the "Healthy Streams Partnership" and its successor, "The Oregon Plan for Salmon and Watersheds." Additionally, Oregon is renowned for its approach to natural resource planning. This "Headwaters to Ocean (H2O) Initiative," therefore, will continue a long tradition of partnership and planning.

Primary Water Resources Goal: Achieve sustainable water supplies and quality to benefit Oregon's people, communities, economy, environment and ecosystems, and fish and wildlife.

Geographic Focus: From the top of watersheds to the territorial sea including all the lakes, rivers, streams, wetlands, underground aquifers, and manmade storage reservoirs along the way.

Water Resource Management Challenges: This section catalogues the primary challenges Oregon faces in terms of water supply, water quality, water for ecosystem benefits and administrative needs.

Ground water:
- Protect and manage critical ground water areas to prevent further depletion and intrusion of pollutants.
- Recharge depleted aquifers to sustain existing agriculture and community use.

- Limit impacts of ground water withdrawals on other ground water and surface water supplies.

Surface water, including lakes, rivers, streams, estuaries, and coastal waters:
- Secure adequate in-stream flows for fish, wildlife and recreation.
- Ensure water quality and quantity for beneficial uses.
- Monitor and reduce pollutants from point and non-point sources.
- Address persistent bio-accumulative toxins and fish consumption levels.
- Restore and protect watershed functions.
- Use natural systems, where feasible, to improve water quality

Stored water:
- Develop and capture available winter water.
- Encourage feasibility studies and identify potential storage opportunities.
- Construct necessary infrastructure, including aquifer storage and recovery sites and off-stream surface storage reservoirs with adequate environmental protections.
- Minimize the effects of loss of snowpack, related to climate change.

Source water protections:
- Use conservation, efficiency, and re-use to develop additional supply and preserve water in-stream.
- Prevent toxics from reaching water supplies in the first place.
- Protect and restore solutions to store water using natural systems like wetlands.
- Remediation of polluted sites using both engineered and biological solutions.

Administrative:
- Restore core capacity for statutorily-mandated functions lost in previous years, due to budget reductions.
- Increase measurement and monitoring, including monitoring programs, data gathering and processing, and equipment.
- Secure additional staff and resources to implement this H_2O Initiative, without creating new institutions.
- Assist local jurisdictions in developing and maintaining critical water infrastructure.
- Address limited funding, by considering partnerships, technical assistance, and other sources.
- Ensure existing protections, while emphasizing voluntary programs and economic incentives.
- Prioritize basins for state funding. Prioritize our development and use of tools/approaches.

Guiding Principles for Water Resources Management:

Planning and managing Oregon's water resources represents long-term commitment and long-term investment. It should also be a thoughtful and inclusive process. We have a shared responsibility in this regard. The fundamental aim is to follow a state-wide strategy that fosters involvement and innovation at the basin level. Partners at the basin level should engage in cooperative planning efforts to which the state can bring tools—including economic incentives and technical assistance.

As such, this strategic document is designed to serve as guidance for the water-related initiatives, programs, and investments that will follow in the ensuing months and years. Although water-related needs in the state of Oregon are many, our resources are finite. Therefore, any water-related initiatives that receive state monies should clearly relate to the needs and principles spelled out in this document. * * *

The Strategy represents a guaranteed investment, for a minimum of ten years, using a dedicated source of funding supported by the legislature and ratified by the voters of Oregon. * * * [the total cost of the program is estimated at $100,350,000].

* * * * *

What laws discussed above will be most helpful to the state in implementing the governor's strategy? See also A. Amos, Freshwater Conservation in the Context of Energy and Climate Policy: Assessing Progress and Identifying Challenges in Oregon and the Western United States, 12 Denver Water L. Rev. 1 (2008).

F. LOCAL MITIGATION AND ADAPTATION

SHIFTING GROUND TO ADDRESS CLIMATE CHANGE: THE LAND USE LAW SOLUTION
John R. Nolon
10 Gov't., L. and Policy J. 23 (2008)

Robert Socolow, a professor of engineering at Princeton, set an action agenda for mitigating climate change by identifying 15 strategic "stabilization wedges," each one capable of preventing the emission of at least a billion metric tons of carbon annually using existing technologies. The genius of Socolow's strategy is that it divides the daunting and discouraging task of climate change mitigation into categories that enable us to order our response efficiently. It makes a formidable challenge seem more doable and allows us to identify the actors who are capable of effective adaptation within each wedge and to formulate strategies that enable and empower those actors to succeed. One of Socolow's wedges focuses on reduced use of vehicles (vehicle miles traveled), which lowers the use of fossil fuels consumed by vehicles. A second aims at creating energy efficient buildings and appliances. A third fosters wind energy and a fourth energy produced through solar power. A fifth aims at preserving forests and vegetated soils to capture and sequester carbon.

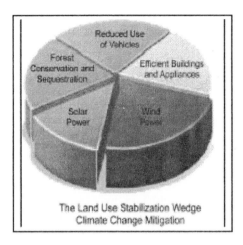

The Land Use Stabilization Wedge
Climate Change Mitigation

This article conceives and describes a Land Use Stabilization Wedge: a strategy that aggregates these five wedges and further organizes strategic energies. * * * This builds on Socolow's optimistic assertion that "an excuse for inaction based on the world's lack of technological readiness does not exist." I assert that the existing legal authority of state and local governments to regulate and guide land use and building is a powerful "technology already deployed somewhere in the world." The Land Use Stabilization Wedge aggregates several of Socolow's initiatives and employs multiple mitigation techniques available to citizens in every locality in the country. * * *

The Land Use Stabilization Wedge comprises all the ways the device of land use control can reduce CO_2 and other greenhouse gas emissions. These include:

1. shifting development patterns so that less driving occurs,

2. reducing the size of housing units,

3. creating more compact and thermally efficient buildings,

4. reducing the materials consumed in building construction,

5. creating more energy efficient buildings,

6. utilizing more efficient equipment and appliances,

7. permitting and encouraging the use of wind energy generation facilities,

8. permitting and encouraging the use of solar energy generation facilities,

9. preserving undisturbed vegetated areas that sequester carbon, and

10. retaining agricultural lands and the production of farm products close to urban centers, further reducing transportation costs.

This article touches on corollary benefits that result from the implementation of the Land Use Stabilization Wedge. These include reduced use of drinking water, reduced impervious coverage and flooding, prevention of water pollution, and others. (See Chart 2).

These objectives can be achieved by local governments in most states through the legal authority already delegated to them to regulate land use and building construction. The Land Use Stabilization Wedge targets local governments as key actors in climate change mitigation, understanding that considerable support and assistance from state and federal agencies and the cooperation and guidance of the private sector are essential to their success.

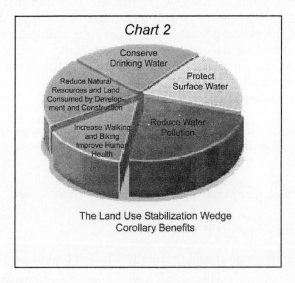

Potential Effects of Mitigation Through Land Use and Building Control—Shifting Ground

   * * *

The new paradigm for development, one consistent with the Land Use Stabilization Wedge strategic approach, is a more compact, dense and mixed-use human settlement pattern, one capable of being implemented through coordinated local land use law. This envisions a shift in the dominant pattern of development from single-family, single-use neighborhoods to neighborhoods characterized by smaller homes, clustered and stacked, mixed with service and retail uses reachable by foot or on bicycle, with nearby schools and recreation, served by transit stops, now or in the future. * * *

Reducing Use of Vehicles

How can the Land Use Stabilization Wedge reduce the number of trips taken and the vehicle miles traveled in the U.S.? Comprehensive plans and zoning laws adopted by local governments, when aggregated, create the blueprint for the development of land and buildings for their region. Through changes in plans and zoning laws, communities can create transit-oriented development and transportation efficient development that shift development patterns from a single-family dominant pattern to one that fosters compact, mixed-use development. This new pattern greatly reduces automobile dependency, vehicle trips, and vehicle miles traveled: a method of implementing Socolow's Vehicle Travel Reduction Wedge.

Central cities and their older and developing suburbs constitute the relevant region for transportation planning purposes. In these regions, Metropolitan Planning Organizations (MPOs) prepare capital plans for all types of transportation infrastructure, including transit services. Developing mechanisms to coordinate state and MPO transportation planning with local land use planning is key to the success of connecting higher density urban developments and compact developments to transit services now or in the future and is arguably required under federal law.

Whether legally mandated or not, for practical reasons, land use planning among localities in a transportation region must be coordinated with transportation infrastructure planning and development. Local land use plans and zoning determine how much population can increase over time, and this, in turn, determines demand for various types of transportation services. Transit lines for rail and Bus Rapid Transit (BRT) services cannot be planned in isolation, station by station. The economics of transit station development and rail and bus lines are dependent upon land use densities; there must be a sufficient number of commuters in a relevant group of adjacent communities to provide a minimal level of ridership throughout the area served by the transit system. Where transit service is not feasible because of insufficient land uses and densities, other modes of transportation must be planned.

Transportation Efficient Development (Compact Development)

Compact developments may not be intense enough to support ridership at various locations in a transportation region. In the near term, they may have to be developed as "transportation efficient" communities that are ready to receive transit services in the future as the region grows. Compact developments not near existing transit services can incorporate a variety of land use and transportation features that reduce vehicle miles and trips. Land use plans can allow for mixed uses, a variety of housing types and sizes, parking and bicycle facilities, and transportation related improvements. These can be coordinated with planned capital improvements such as interconnected sidewalks and trails, bike paths, and jitney service from moderate density hamlets to regional transit stations. Together these initiatives can reduce congestion and car dependency, and provide for transit stops in the future. * * *

Transit-Oriented Development (Higher Density Urban Development)

In many urban areas served by transit stations, densities of housing at 15–40 dwelling units per acre can be achieved. Around transit stops, particularly, higher urban density development can be planned for and supported by zoning and infrastructure planning. These types of developments, as demonstrated above, significantly reduce per-capita carbon emissions and yield numerous other climate change and environmental benefits. * * *

Efficient Building Location, Construction, and Operation

Suburban and urban communities can mitigate carbon emissions and promote energy efficiency by adopting building design and location standards, such as those promoted by the Leadership in Energy and Environmental Design (LEED) criteria promulgated by the U.S. Green Building Council. They can do this in at least three ways: by committing themselves to meeting LEED and other energy standards in newly built or renovated municipal buildings, or in those funded by the municipality; by requiring new privately built or renovated buildings to meet such standards; and by adopting zoning standards for appropriate districts similar to those contained in the Council's evolving Neighborhood Development Rating System.

There are four levels of LEED certification for individual buildings which can be attained by accumulating points for implementing design standards in the categories of sustainable site development, water savings, energy efficiency, materials selected, and indoor environmental quality. The LEED standards can serve as a model for incorporating energy efficient design standards into local building codes and requirements. LEED standards also contain design features normally associated with land use planning and zoning. For example in a LEED for Homes Certification, a new home receives 10 points, one-third of the required number of points for certification, just for being smaller than the national average. A project can also earn points toward certification by developing at higher densities, by being located near public transportation, or by using energy efficient appliances.

Building Code Adaptation

New York is one of 22 states that have adopted a set of building codes that must be enforced at the local level but that allow local legislatures to add more restrictive standards. These codes create the standards that local building inspectors must enforce when asked for a building permit by a private contractor or developer prior to undertaking a building project. Under section 379 of the New York Executive Law, the legislative body of a local government may adopt local ordinances imposing more restrictive standards for construction to ensure energy efficiency and minimize carbon loading. * * *

Zoning Law Reform

The Boston Zoning Code Green Building Amendments were adopted in 2007 to "ensure that major building projects—buildings over 50,000 square feet—are planned, designed, constructed, and managed to minimize adverse environmental impacts; to conserve natural resources; to promote sustainable development; and to enhance the quality of life in Boston." The Boston legislation incorporates by reference the U.S. Green Building Council's LEED rating system. The LEED building certification standards do not impose requirements but rather allow developers to choose among a variety of criteria to obtain sufficient points for the project to become a certified LEED building. Compliance with the local law is required but developers are allowed to choose voluntarily which LEED standards to meet.

The U.S. Green Building Council is providing additional guidance to municipalities interested in promoting energy efficiency at the neighborhood development level. Under its LEED for Neighborhood Development [LEED-ND] rating system, it integrates smart growth, new urbanism, and green building standards into a system for designing and rating neighborhood development. Under this system, both the location and the design of buildings can be certified as meeting the Council's standards for environmentally responsible and sustainable development.

The U.S. Green Building Council adopted the LEED-ND program as a pilot. At the end of 2008, the early results will be evaluated and a revised rating system will be instituted. Among the standards contained at the pilot stage are reduced automobile dependence, creation of a bicycle network, compact development, diversity of uses and housing types, affordability of housing, the proximity of housing and job sites, reduction of parking footprints, proximity to transit facilities, and transportation demand management. These are matters that go to the heart of traditional local land use regulation and are at the forefront of integrating transportation and land use planning.

Communities can incorporate the lessons of the LEED-ND program in their land use plans, regulatory standards, and development approval processes.

Regulation and Use of Public Buildings and Property

The City Council of Scottsdale, Arizona, adopted a formal Green Building Policy for municipal buildings in March 2005. The mandatory policy for municipal buildings requires that "all . . . city buildings of any size will be designed, contracted and built to LEED Gold Certification levels or higher." The Township of Cranford, New Jersey, passed a local ordinance in 2005 adopting a policy that township owned and funded projects will meet LEED Silver ratings.

There are 40,000 localities in the U.S. Many of them are recycling solid waste, planting trees, greening public buildings, using biodiesel fuel in vehicles and machinery, developing methane recovery systems in landfills, using solar energy to power municipal buildings, installing geothermal pump systems to heat and cool public facilities, replacing incandescent traffic signals with light-emitting diode signals, mounting police on bicycles, adopting anti-idling protocols for municipal vehicles, and exhibiting extraordinary creativity along the way.

Wind Power

Although wind-generated power constitutes a small fraction of the nation's power needs (around 1%), it is growing quickly and could eventually meet over 20% of the nation's demand for energy. General Electric, whose Renewable Energy Global Headquarters are in Schenectady, NY, is in the process of building nearly 900 1.5 megawatt wind turbines, many in upstate New York. A 1.5 megawatt turbine can supply the power needs of over 400 single-family homes. This trend is encouraged by New York State's adoption of a state policy establishing a goal that 25% of energy consumed by 2013 will be produced by renewable sources such as wind, solar, biofuels, tidal energy, and other mechanisms.

One way that municipalities may encourage wind power use is to purchase electricity from wind farms to run locally owned utilities or to heat and cool town buildings. Lisle, a village in Illinois, purchases 4,500 megawatt-hours a year of electricity from a nearby wind farm to provide power to its water utility, saving nearly five million pounds of carbon dioxide emissions annually.

Localities may also amend zoning to permit and encourage homeowners to install individual wind generation systems. Individuals are beginning to install backyard wind turbines on towers 50-70 feet high that generate enough power for their household use. In some cases, excess power is created that can be directed back to the local power company grid, sometimes for credit or cash. Some claim that a single wind turbine of this size can produce enough electricity for two average sized homes in an area with moderate wind speeds, raising a host of regulatory and real estate law issues. These types of "distributed generation systems" are supported by the American Planning Association's Energy Policy Guide. Under the New York State Real Property Tax Law, local tax assessors are permitted to offer property owners who construct small wind energy systems an exemption or partial exemption from local real property taxes for the increased value of the property due to the addition of the facility to the land.

Local governments are adopting comprehensive plan components that contain local energy goals and policies, moratoriums that prevent the construction of wind-generation facilities until they can be properly regulated, and a number of zoning, subdivision, site plan, special use, and environmental review mechanisms to balance the benefits of wind-generated power and the detrimental effects such facilities can have on the community. While these laws can be used to limit and discourage wind generation facilities, they can also become part of the Land Use Stabilization Wedge by encouraging the construction and use of wind-generation projects both large and small through zoning and site plan provisions, tax abatement, and other initiatives.

Solar Power

Local governments can mitigate climate change in at least two ways that employ solar energy generation: equip public buildings with solar facilities and adopt land use regulations that encourage their use by homeowners and businesses. * * *

An impressive number of state and federal initiatives are available to local governments as well as private property owners that lower the capital costs of solar installations.

In 1979, the [New York] state legislature granted express power to local governments to add provisions to their zoning regulations to permit and encourage solar energy systems and equipment, including access to sunlight. The legislature declared that access to solar energy is a valid public purpose and left it to each local government to adopt regulations suitable to its local environment and circumstances. This authority, which probably existed as an implied power prior to the act, makes the power of local governments to permit solar power facilities explicit. Local governments may amend their zoning to permit solar energy systems in all zoning districts, to provide waivers of any height, area, or bulk requirements that obstruct solar facilities, or to create zoning overlay districts within which solar access is particularly appropriate.

Carbon Capture Through Sequestration

In developing suburban areas, there are often significant land areas that have been undeveloped for some time that contain undisturbed vegetated areas. As noted earlier, suburban communities can mitigate climate change by zoning to accommodate the bulk of population growth in compact developments * * *. By so doing, they may find it easier politically to adopt strong environmental protection ordinances applicable to the land outside these higher density zones. Density bonuses can be provided to developers of compact developments and cash contributions can be received in exchange for such bonuses, which can be used to purchase the development rights of valuable open space areas that contain critical natural resources.

The preservation of such resources will provide valuable environmental benefits such as carbon sequestration, food production, wetlands and habitat preservation, storm water management and flood prevention, watershed protection, and the prevention of erosion and sedimentation. Soil organic carbon accumulates in undisturbed naturally vegetated areas. Further carbon stabilization occurs when developing communities preserve existing farmland where food products can be produced closer to population centers, thereby reducing transportation costs. Wetlands preservation, seen through the lens of climate change mitigation, offers the additional benefit of carbon sequestration since most wetlands have been undisturbed by previous development.

In local zoning and subdivision regulations, standards that prevent the disturbance of soils and vegetation on development sites have similar effects. The emerging field of "low impact development" experiments with pervious alleys and green roofs in urban projects and, in compact developments, vegetated swales that replace curbs and gutters for storm water control, cluster development, tree retention, and retaining permeable topsoil on site during and after construction. * * *

Notes and Questions

1. As of April 2008, the U.S. Mayors Climate Protection Agreement had been signed by 831 mayors. See H. Osofsky & J. Levit, The Scale of Networks: Local Climate Change Coalitions, 8 Chicago J. of Int'l L. 409 (2008); H. Osofsky, Transporting Climate Change: The Environmental Rights Implications of Local Choices in the Next American City (May 2006). See also Cooper-Walsh Colloquium, Cities and Climate Change, 36 Fordham Urb. L.J. 159 (2009); R. Ewing, et. Al., Growing Cooler: Evidence on Urban Development and Climate Change (2008); N. Grimm, Global Change and the Ecology of Cities, 319 Science 756 (2008); J. Kushner, Global Climate Change and the Road to Extinction: The Legal and Planning Responses (2009); D. Tarlock, Fat and Fried: Linking Land Use Law, the Risks of Obesity and Climate Change, 3 Pitt. J. Envtl. L. & Pub. Health L. 31 (2009).

In addition, a number of county and municipal governments are planning or taking action to reduce their vulnerabilities to climate change damages. ICLEI–Local Governments for Sustainability is an organization that has been playing a leading role in developing and sharing information about these activities through its Climate Resilient Communities Initiative. See www.iclei.org. R. Repetto, The Climate Crisis and Adaptation Myth (2008). However, "at the state level, most community climate change action plans focus on mitigation options, not adaptation, or seek to identify adaptation measures that could be taken in the future. An exception to this future orientation is found in Boston, Massachusetts, where the Deer Island Sewage Treatment Plant in the middle of Boston Harbor was built at a higher elevation than originally planned to prevent flooding."

For the law surrounding local government use of impact fees to discourage urban sprawl and encourage climate friendly development, see B. Kingsley, Making it Easy to be Green: Using Impact Fees to Encourage Green Building, 83 N.Y. U. L. Rev. 532 (2008).

2. Regarding local, regional, and state transportation and state transportation initiatives and land use policies, consider California Senate Bill 375 enacted into law on Aug. 22, 2008:

SECTION 1. The Legislature finds and declares all of the following:

(a) The transportation sector contributes over 40 percent of the greenhouse gas emissions in the State of California; automobiles and light trucks alone contribute almost 30 percent. The transportation sector is the single largest contributor of greenhouse gases of any sector.

(b) In 2006, the Legislature passed and the Governor signed Assembly Bill 32 (Chapter 488 of the Statutes of 2006; hereafter AB 32), which requires the State of California to reduce its greenhouse gas emissions to 1990 levels no later than 2020. According to the State Air Resources Board, in 1990 greenhouse gas emissions from automobiles and light trucks were 108 million metric tons, but by 2004 these emissions had increased to 135 million metric tons.

(c) Greenhouse gas emissions from automobiles and light trucks can be substantially reduced by new vehicle technology and by the increased use of low carbon fuel. However, even taking these measures into account, it will be necessary to achieve significant additional greenhouse gas reductions from changed land use patterns and improved transportation. Without improved land use and transportation policy, California will not be able to achieve the goals of AB 32.

(d)   In addition, automobiles and light trucks account for 50 percent of air pollution in California and 70 percent of its consumption of petroleum.   Changes in land use and transportation policy, based upon established modeling methodology, will provide significant assistance to California's goals to implement the federal and state Clean Air Acts and to reduce its dependence on petroleum.

(e)   Current federal law requires regional transportation planning agencies to include a land use allocation in the regional transportation plan. Some regions have engaged in a regional "blueprint" process to prepare the land use allocation. This process has been open and transparent. The Legislature intends, by this act, to build upon that successful process by requiring metropolitan planning organizations to develop and incorporate a sustainable communities strategy which will be the land use allocation in the regional transportation plan.

(f)   The California Environmental Quality Act (CEQA) is California's premier environmental statute. New provisions of CEQA should be enacted so that the statute encourages developers to submit applications and local governments to make land use decisions that will help the state achieve its climate goals under AB 32, assist in the achievement of state and federal air quality standards, and increase petroleum conservation.

(g)   Current planning models and analytical techniques used for making transportation infrastructure decisions and for air quality planning should be able to assess the effects of policy choices such as residential development patterns, expanded transit service and accessibility, the walkability of communities, and the use of economic incentives and disincentives.

(h)   The California Transportation Commission has developed guidelines for travel demand models used in the development of regional transportation plans. This act assures the commission's continued oversight of the guidelines, as the commission may update them as needed from time to time.

(i)   California local governments need a sustainable source of funding to be able to accommodate patterns of growth consistent with the state's climate, air quality, and energy conservation goals.

* * * * *

See J. Malaczynski & T. Duane, Reducing Greenhouse Gas Emissions from Vehicle Miles Traveled: Integrating the California Environmental Quality Act with the California Global Warming Solutions Act, 36 Ecology L.J. 71 (2009); H. Stern, A Necessary Collision: Climate Change, Land Use, and the Limits of A.B. 32, 35 Ecology L. J. 611 (2008); See also American Trucking Ass'ns v. Los Angeles, 38 ELR 20238 (C.D. Cal. Sept. 9, 2008), reversed, 559 F.3d 1046 (9th Cir. 2009) (reducing emissions from trucks servicing ports); Nat'l Ass'n of Homebuilders v. San Joaquin Valley Unified Air Pollution Control District, 38 ELR 20253 (E.D. Cal. Sept. 18, 2008) (developers required to reduce emissions from their projects or pay offset fees).

* * * * *

Local and state solar legislation includes the following examples:

LEX HELIUS: THE LAW OF SOLAR ENERGY: A GUIDE TO BUSINESS AND LEGAL ISSUES
Stoel Rives LLP 2008

A total of approximately 34 states have presently passed laws or taken measures to promote the installation and use of a solar energy system. The states have two primary mechanisms for ensuring that the "green" property owner can access sunlight to operate the system:

• Allowing neighboring property owners to voluntarily enter into solar easement contracts that, like any other property right, must be documented in writing and recorded in accordance with local requirements. Be sure to check for state-specific recordation procedures.

• Prohibiting the imposition of an outright embargo on the placement of a system in a community, or of unreasonable restrictions on the placement of devices such that their installation, operation, or functionality is adversely impacted.

Any contract creating a property right must contain certain universal legal elements no matter where the property is situated. Most states require the contract to describe the dimensions of the easement, the estimated amount of sunlight directed to the system, any shading provided by vegetation and other plantings, the corresponding reduction in access to sunlight, and any proposed compensation to the grantor of the easement. Any terms or conditions for revising or terminating the easement should be included as well. The contracting parties may include their own remedies for breach of the easement, or default to state law, allowing a court to order any interference with the system to stop and awarding damages for the capital cost of the system, any additional energy charges caused by the breach, and attorney's fees and costs.

However, to be enforceable, a contract creating a solar easement must also contain any state-specific requirements. A state's focus may be affected by weather, terrain, or the character of the area. Some states and/or local governing bodies can be height- or design-sensitive (California, Colorado) or locale-sensitive (Hawaii), or may focus on visibility and placement (North Carolina), orientation (Wisconsin), zoning (Rhode Island), or setback issues (Oregon).

Some states pay special attention to subdivisions. Subdivision developers should be aware that homeowners associations' rules may include covenants that prohibit the installation of solar energy systems or unreasonably restrict their placement to a location that impairs function or increases cost. Other states will not provide state grant funding for solar energy projects to a public entity that has restricted the installation of solar devices. In California, public entities are required to certify that they are not engaging in such behavior, and anyone working on such a project may wish to review the certification as part of due diligence.

SMART GROWTH AND THE GREENING OF COMPREHENSIVE PLANS AND LAND USE REGULATIONS
Pat Salkin
Available at: http://ssrn.com.abstract=1162-499 (July 17, 2008)

Solar energy captured through photovoltaic panels is becoming a more viable option for power production on a smaller scale, often affixed on residences and commercial buildings. However, many localities have ordinances that have the effect of inhibiting solar panel placement. Former Vice-President Al Gore encountered such an ordinance when he attempted to install solar panels on his Belle Meade home, and he petitioned the town board to have the ordinance altered. Some states have enacted laws that preserve the right to install and use solar panels, some localities have taken action to promote it. For example, the Solar Rights Acts in Florida and Arizona provide the right to install solar panels, regardless of any local ordinances or community covenants that would otherwise prohibit the installation. Maryland's solar Protection laws require that restrictions not impose an "unreasonable limitation" on the installation of solar collection systems.

Pursuant to recent legislation, Berkeley's Financing Initiative for Renewable and Solar Technology (FIRST) initiative, slated to begin in June 2008, provides financing for people who want to install solar collection systems on their homes. The city will levy a tax against such individuals to pay for the cost of installation over a 20 year period, and such tax will be equal to or lower than the cost that the building's owner would save on utilities. The financing mechanism is based on the "underground utility district" concept, whereby a city would finance to have a community's utility wires placed underground, with that community then paying the principal back in the form of a tax. Boulder, Colorado has enacted an ordinance that protects solar access, providing different levels of protection for different areas of the city. It defines a hypothetical "solar fence" around the property, that insures that neighboring properties do not intrude on sunlight available to appropriately placed solar panels.

Although some municipalities have not yet specifically enacted zoning regulations to protect solar implementation, they have relaxed parts of their codes that normally would have prohibited its use, through modifying historic preservation laws and providing exemptions from maximum building height requirements. For example, Northampton, MA specifically exempts the installation of solar panels from review by the Historic District Commission. Orleans, MA, takes a more moderate approach to the issue allowing the installation of skylights, wind generators and solar panels in their Historic District only insofar as such installation does not compromise the historical integrity of the buildings or the district itself, per guidelines specified in the ordinance. Berlin, NJ does not count the height of solar panels as contributing to the overall maximum height requirement of the building, except that it can't be 10 feet or 10% above the maximum height.

Notes and Questions

1. What legal issues are raised by municipal ordinances and state statutes which protect land owners from solar shading by their neighbors? Cf. Bormann v. Kossuth County Bd. of Supervisors, 548 N.W. 2d 309 (Iowa Sup. Ct. 1998), cert. denied, 525 U.S. 1172 (1999); Loretto v. Teleprompter Manhattan CATV, 458 U.S. 419 (1982), on remand, 446 N.E. 2d 4-28 (N.Y. 1983). For state legislation supporting the voluntary creation of solar and wind access easements between neighbors and voiding anti-solar covenants, see Ore. Rev. Stat. §§ 105.880-.914. In the absence of such express easements, a landowner's previous reliance on solar or wind access is at best protected only against subsequent unreasonable interference by a neighbor. Compare Prah v. Maretti, 321 N.W. 2d 182 (Wis. Sup. Ct. 1982) with Fontainebleau Hotel Corp. v. Forty-five Twenty-five, Inc., 114 So. 2d 357 (Fla. App. 1959) and Bryant v. Lefever, 4 C.P. Div. 172, 48 L.J. 380, C.P., (Ct. Apps. 1879). See T. Rule, A Downwind View of the Cathedral: Using Rule Four to Allocate Wind Rights, 46 San Diego L. Rev. 207 (2009). See also Ore. Rev. Stat. §§ 215.044, 215.047.

To further encourage their installation, solar facilities could be exempted from the property taxes that would normally be assessed against the value they added to the property. See G. Sergienko, Property Law and Climate Change, ABA Natural Resources & Envmt. 25 (Winter 2008). See also R. Delay, Solar Power and NYC Schools: Good Government and Electric Sparkplug, 19 Fordham Envtl. L. Rev. 161 (2009).

In April 2009 the European Parliament mandated that starting in 2019, all new buildings in the European Union will have to produce more energy on-site than the energy they consume.

2.   To reduce summer temperatures in urban areas, cities such as Chicago are implementing "green roof" grant programs to encourage roof top gardens. A. Carlson, Heat Waves Global Warming, and Mitigation, 26 UCLA J. Envtl. L. & Policy 169, 213-214 n. 186 (2008). See also J Colburn, Solidarity and Subsidiarity in a Changing Climate: Green Building as Legal and Moral Obligations, 5 U. St. Thomas L.J. 232 (2008); J. Abair, Green Buildings: What It Means to Be "Green" and the Evolution of Green Building Laws, 40 Urban Lawyer 623 (2008); J. Ruhl, Cities, Green Construction, and the Endangered Species Act, 27 Va. Envtl. L.J. 147 (2009).

3.   Local governments also have key regulatory and planning roles to play in adapting to sea level rise. See J. Nolon & D Rodriquez, eds, Losing Ground: A Nation on Edge (2007); A. Christoff, House of the Setting Sun: New Orleans, Katrina, and the Role of Historic Preservation Law in Emergency Circumstances, 95 Geo. L.J. 78 (2007).

PROBLEM EXERCISE ON CLOTHESLINES

In 2008, almost 60 million people lived residences governed by community associations. A large number of these associations prohibit the use of clotheslines to dry clothes. Many local zoning laws also prohibit clotheslines, and many homes are built in developments subject to restrictive covenants that prohibit outside clothes drying. This is true even in desert-like regions of the country such as southern California. Nationally, over 67 million electric clothes dryers account for 5.8% residential electricity use and for the CO_2 emitted in generating that electricity. Another 20.3 million dryers use natural gas, propane or LPG. See U.S. E.I.A., 2005 Residential Buildings Energy Consumption Survey.

Why have clotheslines been so widely banned in the U.S.? What could Congress do to deban clotheslines. Should the legally, long-established esthetic concerns of property owners trump national and state energy policies and climate change mitigation efforts? What are the competing interests at stake? Design a law that a state might enact to enable homeowners and apartment dwellers to dry their clothes outside? For background see, G. Sergienko, Property Law and Climate Change, ABA Nat. Res. & Env. (Winter 2008) and K. Hughes, To Fight Global Warming, Hang a Clothesline, The New York Times (April 12, 2007) www.NYTimes.com.

PROBLEM EXERCISE ON URBAN HEAT ISLANDS

"Urban heat islands" are urban areas where on warm summer days, the air is hotter than its surrounding areas. For instance, central Los Angeles summer temperatures are typically 5°F higher than the surrounding suburban and rural areas. Heat islands are caused by dark roofs, dark pavement, and lack of tress and other vegetation. Higher temperatures in urban heat islands bring with them increased energy use, mostly due to a greater demand for air conditioning. As power plants burn more fossil fuels, they increase both the pollution level and energy costs. "On warm afternoons in Los Angeles, for example, the demand for electric power rises nearly 2% for every degree Fahrenheit the daily maximum temperature rises. In total, we estimate that about 1-1.5 gigawatts of power are used to compensate the impact of the heat island. This increased power costs the Los Angeles ratepayers about $100,000 per hour, about $100 million per year." Heat Island Group, Environmental Energy Technologies Division, E.O. Lawrence Berkeley National Laboratory, http://eetd.lbl.gov/HeatIsland/EnergyUse/.

Two families, the Browns' and the Greens', live adjacent to each other in Los Angeles. The Browns' plan to replace the old roof on their home with a new roof with black asphalt shingles. Their next door neighbors, the Greens, who have a white roof, want to enjoin them from installing any color but white. The Greens claim that the black roof will raise the air temperature in the summer, causing them to either suffer with a higher inside temperature, or run their air conditioner more than they would otherwise need to if the roof were white. What legal recourse is available?

Does the owner or operator of a building in an urban heat island have any legal responsibility to neighbors for increasing the area's ambient temperature by having a dark roof, running the building's air conditioner excessively either by setting the temperature low, using heat generating equipment indoors that requires more cooling or both (thereby discharging additional heat into the area)? Is the property owner's heat discharge creating a private or public nuisance? If the extra electricity needed for the added air conditioning due to heat islands results in increased CO_2 emissions, is any one legally responsible to neighbors, residents of the metropolitan area, the state, region, nation, world? What about home owner association rules that mandate dark roofs?

White roofs, "green" roofs and enough appropriately located trees and vegetation can reduce heat island effects significantly. Should law mandate roof color and design? Should laws mandate cooling landscaping? How does existing property law address this? How would one design such a law? Should it be federal, state or local? How would it be enforced?

How might U.S. efforts (or lack thereof) to reduce GHG emissions attributable to urban heat islands affect the U.S. position in negotiating a post-Kyoto climate change agreement?

* * * * *

As discussed in the following excerpt, local governments in several states have climate change assessment responsibilities under state environmental impact assessment legislation. See also D. Gold & M. Imwalle, Accounting for Climate Change in Environmental Review Documents, TRENDS (ABA Jan./Feb. 2008); D. Owen, Climate Change and Environmental Assessment Law, 33 Col. J. Envtl. L. 57 (2008).

THINKING GLOBALLY, ACTING LOCALLY: THE ROLE OF LOCAL GOVERNMENT IN MINIMIZING GREENHOUSE GAS EMISSIONS FROM NEW DEVELOPMENT
Judi Brawer and Matthew Vespa
44 Idaho L. Rev. 589 (2008)

V. LEVERAGING STATE ENVIRONMENTAL POLICY ACTS TO COMPEL CONSIDERATION OF IMPACTS TO GLOBAL WARMING FROM LOCAL PROJECT APPROVALS

In addition to localities voluntarily addressing greenhouse gas emissions through green building requirements and smart growth based planning, states are leveraging their environmental statutes to compel the comprehensive analysis and mitigation of the emissions generated by new development projects and long range planning documents. Three states, California, Massachusetts, and Washington, incorporate the consideration of greenhouse gas impacts to varying degrees into the environmental review process required by their existing environmental review statutes, also referred to as "little-NEPAs."[141] While local ordinances may target specific aspects of a project's

---

[141] Fifteen states, the District of Columbia, and Puerto Rico have environmental policy acts modeled to varying degrees after the National Environmental Policy Act (NEPA). ARK. CODE ANN. §§ 8-1-101 to -107 (2007); CAL. PUB. RES. CODE §§ 21000 to 21006 (West 2007); CONN. GEN. STAT. ANN. §§ 22a-14 to -20 (West 2006); D.C. CODE §§ 8109.01 to .11 (2001); HAW. REV. STAT. ANN. §§ 343-1 to -8 (LexisNexis 2004); IND. CODE ANN. §§ 13-12-4-1 to -10 (LexisNexis 2005); MD. CODE ANN., NAT. RES. §§ 1-301 to -305 (LexisNexis 2005); MASS. ANN. LAWS ch. 30, §§ 61 to 62H (LexisNexis 2007); MINN. STAT. ANN. §§ 116D.01 to 116D.11 (West 2005 & Supp. 2008); MONT. CODE ANN. §§ 75-1-101 to -234 (1998); N.Y. Envtl. Conserv. Law §§ 8-0101 to -0117 (McKinney 2005 & Supp. 2008); N.C. GEN. STAT. §§ 113A-1 to -13 (2007); P.R. LAWS ANN. tit. 12, §§ 1121-1127 (2007); S.D. CODIFIED LAWS §§ 34A-9-1 to -13 (1999); VA. CODE ANN. §§ 10.1-1188 to -1192 (2006 & Supp. 2007); WASH. REV. CODE §§ 43.21C.010 to .914 (2006); WASH. ADMIN. CODE § 197-11 (2007); WIS. STAT. ANN. §§ 1.11 to .13 (West 2004); WIS. ADMIN. CODE NR §§ 150.01 to .40 (2007).

carbon footprint, such as energy efficiency, environmental review under a NEPA state corollary provides the opportunity to examine all of a project's greenhouse gas impacts and implement a wide range of mitigation measures and/or alternatives to reduce these impacts. In California, the environmental review statute also compels consideration of greenhouse gas emissions within the broader context of city and county land use and transportation planning documents.

Even in states that do not have an environmental review statute, the experiences of California, Massachusetts, and Washington are instructive. Especially in the case of California, where guidance on the evaluation and mitigation of all aspects of a project's greenhouse gas emissions is becoming increasingly detailed, the review process for greenhouse gas emissions from project approvals is transferable to any state or local government inclined to adopt its own greenhouse gas review process.

A. The California Environmental Quality Act

The California Environmental Quality Act (CEQA) requires all state and local agencies to analyze and disclose all significant environmental impacts of their discretionary project approvals. CEQA provides for varying levels of review based on the nature of the project's impacts. Where there is a "fair argument" that the project would have one or more significant environmental impacts, an Environmental Impact Report (EIR) must be prepared. Like NEPA, a project has a significant effect on the environment where the project's environmental effects are "individually limited but cumulatively considerable." Even *de minimis* contributions to an existing problem are considered significant. Once an impact is identified as "significant," the lead agency must develop alternatives to the project and indicate the manner in which the significant effects can be mitigated or avoided. Unlike NEPA, which does not require federal agencies to choose the least environmentally harmful alternative, CEQA mandates that an agency cannot lawfully approve a project "if there are feasible alternatives or feasible mitigation measures available which would substantially lessen the significant environmental effects" of the project.

Review of a project's greenhouse gas emissions under CEQA has rapidly evolved since its origins in late 2006 and continues to be an area of some uncertainty. CEQA's application to the analysis and mitigation of greenhouse gas emissions was raised on September 8, 2006, in public comments from the Center for Biological Diversity to the City of Banning on a draft EIR for a proposed 1,400 home development located in an isolated area of Riverside County, California." The comments argued that, like any other potential environmental impact, CEQA requires the analysis of greenhouse gas emissions. The comments provided evidence that anthropogenic greenhouse gas emissions are responsible for profound environmental effects, included protocols by which the City of Banning could measure project emissions, and asked the city to analyze and mitigate the project's cumulative greenhouse gas impacts. The city asserted that CEQA does not require the analysis of greenhouse gas emissions and approved the draft EIR. The Center for Biological Diversity subsequently filed litigation challenging the city's approval of the EIR.

Continuing to assert that CEQA encompasses the environmental impacts of greenhouse gas emissions, conservation groups and the California Attorney General challenged San Bernardino County's General Plan Update EIR for failing to account for impacts from the plan's greenhouse gas emissions. In August 2007, after the lawsuit was filed, the Attorney General and the county reached a settlement whereby the county would adopt a greenhouse gas emissions reduction plan to include: (1) an inventory of all known sources of emissions within the county, (2) an estimate of 1990 emissions, (3) a projected inventory for 2020, (4) an emissions target for those sources of emission reasonably attributable to the county's discretionary land use decisions, and (5) the adoption of feasible reduction measures to meet the emissions reduction target. In addition, the Attorney General informed numerous other counties and cities that the failure to evaluate greenhouse gases in their respective general plan updates would constitute a violation under CEQA.

Shortly thereafter, the Attorney General entered into a settlement with ConocoPhillips over a proposed refinery expansion that required ConocoPhillips to pay $7 million to a carbon offset fund created by the local air district. The fund provided grants for local projects undertaken to achieve quantifiable greenhouse gas reductions and also gave $2.8 million to California Wildfire ReLeaf for reforestation and conservation projects.

The aggressive use of CEQA to address greenhouse gas emissions caused considerable consternation among the building, manufacturing and oil industries, who, in a letter to California Governor Schwarzenegger, "asked for 'urgent legislative action' to counter what [was] described as 'premature and unwarranted' environmental lawsuits." In addition, during budget negotiations in the summer of 2007, Republicans in the California legislature sought to exempt greenhouse gas emissions impacts from CEQA analyses. Ironically, Republican efforts to derail CEQA resulted in Senate Bill 97, which provided a narrow and temporary exemption of greenhouse gas analysis for a small set of infrastructure projects but also recognized that an analysis of the environmental impacts of greenhouse gas emissions is required under CEQA.[158]

---

[158] Senate Bill 97 requires the Office of Planning and Research to prepare guidelines "for the mitigation of greenhouse gas emissions or the effects of greenhouse gas emissions as required by [CEQA], including, but not limited to, effects associated with transportation or energy consumption." S.B. 97, 2007 Reg. Session (Cal. 2007), codified as CAL. PUB. RES. CODE § 21083.05 (West Supp. 2008) (emphasis added). The California Bill analysis for Senate Bill 97 states that Senate Bill 97 "confirm[s] that

Until this point, the evaluation of greenhouse gas impacts under CEQA was a legal theory advanced by the Attorney General and environmental groups which had yet to be legislatively or judicially recognized. Senate Bill 97 further requires the adoption of guidelines for the mitigation of greenhouse gas emissions for projects approved under CEQA.

While consideration of the impacts of greenhouse gas emissions in EIRs has risen dramatically, treatment has varied just as dramatically. Some agencies recognize the cumulatively significant impacts and have adopted mitigation measures to address them, while other agencies, citing a lack of guidance and significance thresholds from regional air districts, declare the issue too speculative for evaluation. As guidance becomes available, however, these arguments lose credibility. In January 2008, the California Air Pollution Control Officers Association (CAPCOA) issued a white paper, entitled "CEQA & Climate Change: Evaluating and Addressing Greenhouse Gas Emissions from Projects Subject to the California Environmental Quality Act."[161] The CAPCOA white paper provides methodologies for quantifying the direct and indirect emissions from various project types (residential development, general plans, landfills, etc.) as well as ways to evaluate the significance of a project's greenhouse gas emissions.[162] Potential approaches to determine significance, which triggers the mandatory adoption of all feasible mitigation measures and alternatives, include: (1) a zero-emissions threshold, (2) a uniform percentage decrease from reduction from business as usual emissions (for example 50%), and (3) compliance with a general plan that demonstrates that emissions levels projected for 2020 are mitigated to a level less than or equal to 1990 emissions. While CEQA vests the approving agency with discretion to determine whether a particular impact is significant, the determination must be supported by "substantial evidence in light of the whole record." Using the CAPCOA white paper as a starting point for discussions, the South Coast Air Quality Management District-the air district with jurisdiction over Orange County and the urban portions of Los Angeles, Riverside and San Bernardino counties-has convened a working group to develop a threshold of significance for greenhouse gas emissions. * * *

GHG emissions are a significant adverse effect under" CEQA. S.B. 97, 2007 Reg. Sess. (Ca. 2007).

[161] Greg Tholen et al, CEQA & Climate Change, Evaluating and Addressing Greenhouse Gas Emissions from Projects Subject to the California Environmental Quality Act (2007), available at http://www.capcoa.org/index.php. Because CEQA requires that an approving agency must "do the necessary work to educate itself about the different methodologies that are available" to analyze an impact under CEQA, an EIR that ignores methods of evaluating greenhouse gas emissions may be deemed inadequate under CEQA. Berkeley Keep Jets Over the Bay Comm. v. Bd. of Port Comm'rs, 111 Cal. Rptr. 2d 598, 618 (Ct. App. 2001).

[162] See also Cal. Climate Action General Reporting Protocol 2.2 (2007) (explaining the methodologies to quantify components of a projects's total greenhouse gas emissions).

Because CEQA applies to virtually all new development in the State of California as well as long-range land use and transportation plans, its application to the review of greenhouse gas emissions has the potential to significantly slow the growth rate of emissions from new sources. While the limits of CEQA's use to reduce greenhouse gas emissions from new projects is still being defined, its requirement that all feasible measures be adopted to reduce significant environmental effects could prod planners and developers to implement design features, such as on-site renewable power generation, or incorporate smart growth measures for planning documents that might not otherwise have been considered. For example, the Attorney General and environmental groups have submitted CEQA comments on the environmental review process for regional transportation plans requesting consideration of alternatives that increases emphasis on urban transit rather than freeway expansion to reduce greenhouse gas emissions. Similarly, it could also be credibly argued that energy conservation measures, currently voluntarily adopted, must be incorporated into every county or city general plan in order to mitigate the greenhouse gas emissions resulting from planned new development. With regard to offsets, feasible mitigation suggested by CAPCOA include payment to a greenhouse gas retrofit fund which could be used to provide incentives to upgrade older buildings and make them more energy efficient. As mitigation funds are put in place, future development in California could move toward carbon neutrality.

B. Washington

Like California, the Washington State Environmental Policy Act (SEPA) requires all state and local agencies to review the potential environmental impact of their discretionary project approvals. Following the completion of an initial environmental checklist, the agency issues a determination of nonsignificance if it determines that the proposed project is unlikely to have a significant adverse environmental impact or prepares an EIS if information from the checklist indicates the proposal is likely to have a significant environmental impact. Under SEPA, the "environment" is specifically defined to include "climate."' In addition, SEPA's statutory purpose includes the promotion of "efforts which will prevent or eliminate damage to the environment and biosphere."

On June 27, 2007, King County, Washington issued an executive order requiring that the County departments "evaluate the climate change impacts of those actions being evaluated under the authority of the State Environmental Policy Act." To assist project applicants in evaluating project emissions when completing the environmental review, the County developed a worksheet that includes the calculation of emissions associated with obtaining construction material, fuel used during construction, energy consumed during building operation, and transportation used by building occupants. The King County Executive Order only requires that adverse climate change impacts be described. Regulatory requirements that may be imposed to mitigate a project's adverse climate impacts will occur in 2008 as part of the four-year update to the King County Comprehensive Plan.

C. The Massachusetts Environmental Policy Act

The Massachusetts Environmental Policy Act (MEPA) requires state agencies or state permit applicants to prepare an EIR for certain types of actions. Like CEQA, MEPA requires agencies to make a finding that all feasible measures have been taken to avoid or minimize "damage to the environment." However, its reach is significantly more limited as environmental review is only triggered for state projects, projects requiring a state permit, and projects receiving state financial assistance, and only if these projects exceed certain thresholds (for example, direct alteration of more than twenty-five acres of land or the creation of more than five acres of impervious surface).

Unlike California, where litigation was the catalyst for consideration of greenhouse gases under the state environmental quality act, Massachusetts addressed the consideration of greenhouse gas emissions in its environmental policy act through regulation. In April 2007, Massachusetts issued a MEPA Greenhouse Gas Emissions Policy and Protocol that determined that "'damage to the environment' as used in [MEPA] includes the emission of greenhouse gases caused by Projects subject to MEPA review."[183] The Policy applies to projects where the state is the proponent or providing financial assistance, or to private projects that require an air quality or vehicular access permit.

In considering greenhouse gas emissions from a proposed project, applicants must quantify "direct emissions" from on-site stationary sources and indirect emissions from the project's energy consumption and traffic generation. The project proponent is then required to compare the greenhouse gas emission from the project as proposed with an alternative that adopts mitigation to the "maximum extent feasible." The Policy includes a list of suggested mitigation measures related to site design, building design and operation, and transportation. While "direct mitigation should be prioritized over off-site measures," the Policy also recognizes the use of offsets, with a preference toward verifiable offsets that have local or regional benefits.

Notes and Questions

1. Does the Massachusetts MEPA discussed above require that climate change mitigation measures identified in an EIA be taken? Could the EIA's listing of mitigation and adaptation alternatives help the public to comment in a more informed manner? Regarding the analogous application of New

---

[183] MEPA Greenhouse Gas Emissions Policy and Protocol 1 (2007) * * * available at http://www.mass.gov/envir/mepa/pdffiles/misc/ghg-emissionspolicy.pdf.

York's SEQRA to climate change, see K. Kendall, SEQRA and Climate Change (2008); P. Lehmer & J. Dean, SEQRA's Alarm Rings for Climate-Impact Considerations, 238 New York Law Journal 4 (2007).

Other state legislative constraints on local government land use approvals relevant to climate change mitigation include "assured water supply" laws. See L. Davies, Just a Big "Hot Fuss?" Assessing the Value of Connecting Suburban Sprawl, Land Use, and Water Rights Through Assured Supply Laws, 34 Ecology L.Q. 1217 (2007).

2. On federal environmental impact assessment issues in adaptation see Section G, *infra*. On February 28, 2008, the International Center for Technology Assessment, the Sierra Club, and the Natural Resources Defense Council submitted a petition to the Council on Environmental Quality requesting that the CEQ amend its NEPA regulations to clarify that climate change analyses be included in federal environmental documents. Specifically, the groups requested that the CEQ issue guidance documents to instruct agencies "on how, where, and when to best integrate climate change analyses into their respective NEPA processes." Petition at 3. Federal courts have applied NEPA's requirements to federal activities with climate change implications both outside, Border Power Plant Working Group v. DOE, 260 F. Supp. 2d 997 (S.D. Cal. 2003); Friends of the Earth v. Mosbacher, 488 F. Supp. 2d 889 (N.D. Cal. 2007), and inside the U.S., Center for Biological Diversity v. U.S. Dept. of Interior, 2009 U.S App. LEXIS 8097 (D.C. Cir. April 17, 2009); Los Angeles v. NHTSA, 912 F. 2d 478 (D.C. Cir. 1990); Mayo v. Surface Transportation Board, 472 F. 3d 545 (8th Cir. 2006); Center for Biological Diversity v. NHTSA, 508 F.3d 508 (9th Cir. 2007); Mont. Envtl. Info. Center v. Johanns, No. 07-1311 (filed July 23, 2007, D.D.C.) See C. Christopher, Success by a Thousand Cuts: The Use of Environmental Impact Assessment in Addressing Climate Change, 9 Vermont J. of Envtl. L. 549 (2008); D. Farber, Adaptation Planning and Climate Impact Assessments: Learning from NEPA's Flaws, 39 Envtl. L. Rep. 10605 (2009); J. Ferrell & S. Jones, Project Development in the Shadow of Climate Change, 2008 Mineral Law Institute at 8-1; M. Gerrard, Climate Change and the Environmental Impact Review Process, 22 Nat. Res. & Envt. 20 (2008).

However, a prior Congress was not disposed to extend NEPA's scope to cover fossil fuel and climate impacts. The Energy Policy Act of 2005 contained 5 new categorical exclusions from NEPA's EIA requirement for federal oil and gas activities. See S. Klopf, N. Culver, & P. Morton, A Road Map to a Better NEPA: Why Environmental Risk Assessments Should be Used to Analyze the Environmental Consequences of Complex Federal Actions, 7 Sustainable Development Law & Policy No. 4 at 38 (Fall 2007). Regarding the roles of scientific uncertainty under NEPA see The Lands Council v. McNair, 2008 WL 2640001 (9th Cir. July 2, 2008).

On NEPA and mitigation, see Chapter 6 Section F.

3. Not all federal actions will have the same impact on climate change. Moreover, with such a global phenomenon as climate change, many, if not most, federal actions may be fairly described as not significantly impacting, on its own, the global climate. In part, this problem is addressed by the 9th Circuit in its discussion of the need for adequate cumulative impact analyses, but consider the following recommendation:

> Because disclosure and mitigation of greenhouse gas emissions should be an important concern for all projects, those actions that do not meet or surpass the project type and size thresholds should conduct a qualitative analysis of climate change impacts in order to create more agency and public awareness of an action's contribution to climate change.

> As a general guide, there should therefore be three categories of EIS actions: (1) actions that require a quantitative analysis of greenhouse gas emissions, such as major construction projects, power plants, major re-zonings, and projects generating a large increase in traffic; (2) actions that do not warrant any substantive analysis of climate change impacts, like certain rule-making actions; and (3) all remaining actions subject to an EIS that likely only require a qualitative analysis of the action's climate change impacts.

K. Kendall, SEQRA and Climate Change (2008).

Should EIA procedures incorporate these categories to deal with climate change effects?

4. *Carbon Neutral Law Schools*: Adaptation to the effects of climate change can be dramatic, as in the case of law schools in New Orleans or law schools in Houston in the midst of the 2007 historic drought without sufficient water. Adaptation can be mundane, as in deciding to phase out all non-recycled products used in a law school. Legislation and new regulations will force adaptation on law schools along with all other commercial enterprises and non-profit institutions. Should your law school seek to minimize expenditures and invest in adaptation now, rather than having costs forced upon it later? See "Planning and Policies for Climate Change," Chapter 9, in A. Rappaport & S. Creighton, Degrees That Matter—Climate Change and the University (2007). What drives your planning? What will drive your planning to adapt? Can you set a target of reducing GHG emissions by 20% from 1990 levels by 2020?Compare some of the conservative existing targets of universities such as the Massachusetts Institute of Technology www.mit.edu/environment/commitment/env_goals.html or the Ivy League

universities,   or   www.ivycouncil.org/pdf/ivycoirpos_resolutuion_11-15-
2003.pdf. At some schools, students have elected to pay additional fees to pay
for reducing their GHG emissions. The University of Oregon students pay an
energy   surcharge.   See
www.uoregon.edu/~ecostudy/slpenergy/Energyuse.html. What obstacles can
you see to such actions? A court in Washington state enjoined such a fee on
the grounds that it was a tuition increase, which only that State's legislature
could enact. B. Gose, Students in Washington Win Energy-Fee Dispute,
Chronicle of Higher Education, p. 21 (November 30, 2001).

PROBLEM EXERCISE ON U.S. ADAPTATION PLANNING

Proposed H.R. 2454 (111th Cong., June 26, 2009) would provide federal
support for state, tribal and local adaptation programs through the sale of
emission allowances. What modifications in support of climate change mitigation and adaptation would you recommend to your state's legislation
authorizing local governments to engage in land use planning and zoning?
And what legal responses would be available to local governments to follow
up on your state-level recommendations? Based on the materials covered to
date, what issues would you recommend be covered in the State Climate Adaptation Plans required by that bill? In the federal Natural Resource Agency
Adaptation Plans also required by the bill?

H.R. 2454 would also create the following climate change mitigation and
adaptation programs for state and local implementation: community building code administration grants conditioned on solar energy friendly building
permit requirements; resources and other federal support for energy efficient
building retrofits, neighborhoods, low-income communities, multifamily housing projects; property appraisals, mortgage loans, transportation strategies;
and urban, rural, and tribal renewable energy development and facility leasing.   Under the bill, federal regulations prohibiting restrictions on solar energy systems in deed covenants, lease provisions, homeowners association
rules and other documents for single-family dwellings would be issued by the
federal Department of Housing and Urban Development.

G. ENVIRONMENTAL IMPACT ASSESSMENT FOR ADAPTATION

No single program can imagine and address off the possible adverse impacts from climate change. In order to build resilience into existing infrastructure and land uses, whether for agriculture, transportation, human settlements and housing, natural parks and recreation areas, manufacturing, or
a myriad of other uses, it will be necessary to both retrofit existing structures
and designs, and adaptively redesign proposals for new development. There
is one law governing decision-making that is already well designed to require
such adaptations: environmental impact assessment (EIA) under the National Environmental Policy Act of 1969, 42 USC 4321, and the "Little

NEPAs" enacted in the states, as discussed above in Section F.2. As discussed in Chapter 3, many other nations have enacted EIA laws, and so this tool is available world-wide, and can be harnessed to guide adaptation to climate change across all kinds of human activities affected the environment. EIA is likely to be more important for adaptation than for mitigation. To be sure, it can find ways to minimize GHG emissions or build capacity to off-set carbon dioxide in the atmosphere, be since it may take a score of years to restore the atmosphere to a kind of balance in the carbon cycle, it will be necessary to make adaptation in every sector of human endeavors. No other legal process is as well suited top ensuring adaptation measures are implemented that is EIA.

Nicholas C. Yost, the principal draftsman of the NEPA regulations at 40 CFR Part 1500, has stressed the utility and versatility of CEQ's interpretation of its regulations in the "40 Most Asked Questions Concerning CEQ's NEPA Regulations, " 46 Fed. Reg. 18,026 (March 16, 1981), at http://ceq.hss.doe.gov/nepa/regs/40/40p3.htm. The NEPA regulations will require examination of alternatives that can build in resilience to possible climate change impacts and avoid actions that exacerbate those impacts or shift them to others. See N. Yost, CEQ's "Forty Questions:" The Key to Understanding NEPA, 23 ABA Nat. Res. & Envt. 8 (2009).

While the existing CEQ regulations can be so employed, the US Supreme Court has been reluctant to find in NEPA any directive that obliges a federal agency, or applicant for a major federal action significantly protecting the quality of the human environment under NEPA §102(2)(C), to undertake substantive measures to protect the environment. Robertson v. Methow Valley Citizens Council, 490 US 332 (1989). It is probable therefore, that once the CEQ has fashioned analytic tools to enable federal agencies to cope with climate change impacts, Congress will need to amend NEPA to clarify the law and make it plain that all agencies have a duty to study and select the means to adapt to climate change whenever a major federal action is under consideration and decision.

NEPA essentially incorporates the simple rule of "look before you leap." EIA is a methodology that puts the precautionary principle into practice. Since climate change will bring some major new impacts, quite apart from a proposed federal action, EIA will have to identify the probable adverse climate impacts as a background foundation for assessing proposed actions, and not assume that the environmental conditions of today are the context for assessing the impacts. The EIA process needs a rolling and regularly revisited and revised database for environmental assessments. Moreover, it will be necessary routinely to require post-project monitoring and perhaps post-project actions when climate conditions turn out to be other than predicted in an EIA. Some nations require that the EIA be up[dated every five years, not unlike the NPDES Permits under the Clean Water Act. The EIA approval is provisional, and subject to constant review. How could EIA be coordinated with data gathering and a re-iterative, adaptive management approach be built into the NEPA procedures?

The Great Lakes Compact of 2008, Pub. L. 110-342, 122 Stat. 3739, provides for a rolling cumulative impact assessment of the entire Great Lakes basin, to provide this sort of on-going database. This review is to function across all the Great Lakes Provinces, States and indigenous nations within the watershed. Should not other regions adopt a similarly comprehensive approach to framing the baseline data that can be used by all authorities and interests in the watershed in order to know and respond to climate change conditions as they emerge?

For 25 years, Dinah Bear served as the General Counsel to the President's Council on Environmental Quality. Despite the lack of adequate staff resources, she efficiently and effectively shepherded federal agencies, and successive White House Administrations, through complying with NEPA. Revising the CEQ regulations to take on climate change will not require a vast bureaucracy. By all accounts, NEPA's procedures for full disclosure of information and public participation has had a salutory effect of governmental decision-making. But more could be done with NEPA. There is a need to integrate the policies of §101 into the procedures of §103(2)(C): As Bear has noted, "The NEPA process, of course, was actually intended to implement the policies of NEPA * * * we, as a country, have really lost sight of the importance of the policies that the process is supposed to implement." M. Mason, Snapshot Interview of Dinah Bear, 23 Nat. Res. & Env. 44 (Spring 2009). Bear considers that "NEPA covers climate change. I think that the regulations, fairly read, also already cover climate change * * *. So I don't want to get into that mode of [thinking that] every time there's another impact, we need to have a regulation specific[ally] on it. I do think what is needed and is long overdue from CEQ, is the publication of guidance that affirms the fact that * * * climate change is an environmental impact covered under NEPA that gives the agency some useful guidance about doing that, some tools to use, some parameters to think about, some guidance that can be deferred to by the courts." Id. at 63.

A CEQ guidance memorandum on how to apply the NEPA process to climate change is akin to the 40 Most asked Questions. It is an interpretation of the law by the administrative agency charged with overseeing the NEPA process. The Supreme Court gives deference to CEQ, Andrus v. Sierra Club, 442 US 347 (1979). Is Bear right that using the NEPA EIA process as it is today is an adequate response to the needs of climate change adaptation? Consider the more urgent arguments set forth in L. Heinzerling, Climate Change, Human Health, and the Post-Cautionary Principle, 96 Georgetown L. J. 445 (2008).

PROBLEM EXERCISE ON INTERNATIONAL ADAPTATION
STRATEGIES

Based on the polar, sea level rise, ocean, hydrological, and local adaptation materials presented in this chapter, what specific adaptation measures would you emphasize in the international adaptation efforts discussed in Chapter 3? What roles could the U.S. International Climate Change Adaptation Program created by proposed H.R. 2454 (111th Cong., June 26, 2009) play in these efforts? See also C. Crawford, Our Bandit Future? Cities, Shantytowns and Climate Change Governance, 36 Fordham Urb. L.J. 211 (2009); M. Mani, A Markandya, & V. Ipe, Climate Change—Adaptation and Mitigation in Development Programs: A Practical Guide (2008).

CHAPTER 8. BUSINESS LAW AND CLIMATE CHANGE

Climatescape: **The Corporate and Commercial Implications of Climate Change**

Climate change law is becoming the basis for new legal practices in law firms, and new legal divisions or units in governmental agencies world-wide. The "melt-down" of the global economy in the Great Recession of 2007 coincides with the perceptions about the literal melting of the world-wide cryosphere because of climate change. How will climate cap-and-trade regimes, as discussed in Chapter 6, become a part of the commercial law of climate change? The UNFCCC provides for integrating regional cap-and-trade systems, as noted in Chapter 3. Will the regulatory enhancements to restore rigor to the financial disclosures for investment markets require reporting on company climate change adaptation and risk management? Should these tools be restricted to what is a material impact on the investment, or should companies be required to report how they attain benchmarks in climate change mitigation and adaptation. What are governments to make of the record that companies world-wide have produced most of the greenhouse gases and mined the fossil fuels, without regard for their destructive impacts on the biosphere and climate? Are corporate social responsibilities tools sufficiently robust to convert companies from greenhouse gas emitters to climate stewards, or must the corporate laws chartering companies be amended to make climate stewardship a legal condition of doing business?

A. INTRODUCTION

Since its roots in the 1970s, environmental law has become a staple practice of law. Law firms maintain environmental law specialists to ensure compliance with environmental requirements in real most real estate transactions, in mergers and acquisitions, in corporate environment, health and safety (EHS) compliance, and a host of other matters. Local governments must both comply with environmental laws and enforce their municipal ordinances. International law firms and corporate in house lawyers routinely conduct due diligence to ensure that firms with operations in different countries are in compliance with environmental laws. The elements of such practices are well established. See e.g., F. Friedman, Practical Guide to Environmental Management (8th ed.).

These practices are expanding to serve clients with respect to for both climate change mitigation and adaptation. As local authorities reform that land use laws to require energy efficient building code standards, to retreat from eroding coasts and to provide enhance protection from flooding, real estate practices will change. As financial institutions insure property for climate changed risks, new insurance products and regimes will be incorporated into corporate and real estate agreements. There is already a growing body of lawsuits from those who seek to press climate change reforms, or from those whose interests are adversely affected by climate change reforms. Citizen suits to compel reductions in greenhouse gases, and enforcement actions by government agencies, are increasing. M. Gerrard & J. Howe, Climate Change Litigation in the U.S., www.climatecasechart.com excerpted in Chapter 1. Like environmental cases, such suits often engage a multitude of parties, including government entities, public interest citizen non-governmental organizations, and a mix of economic parties in interest.

The elements of the expanding climate change law practices emerge from the new regulations of the U.S. Environmental Protection Agency, and state environmental agencies in the wake of the Supreme Court's ruling in Massachusetts v. EPA. See, for example, Pennsylvania Governor Rendell's approval on October 15, 2008 of the State's extensive "Energy Efficiency and Demand Response" legislation, Act 129 of 2008, requiring replacement of all electrical meters in the State in the next 15 years with "smart meters" capable of hourly price adjustments. It also sets the stage for requiring geological carbon sequestration measures. Other states are enacting comparable reforms. See D. Hodas, State Responses to Climate Change: 50-State Survey, in M. Gerrard ed., Global Climate Change and U.S. Law (2007), updated annually by Pace Law students for the ABA Section on Environment, Energy and Resources, at http://www.abanet.org/abapubs/globalclimate/.

In the wake of EPA's proposed endangerment finding under § 202(a) of the Clean Air Act excerpted in Chapters 2 and 6, EPA's regulatory programs will expand. EPA's launch of rules for mandatory annual reporting of greenhouse gas emissions, 74 Fed. Reg. 16448 (April 10, 2009), is needed for both a cap and trade program and for enforcement actions to require GHG mitigation. This rule results from a Congressional mandate in the Consolidated Appropriation Act of 2008, P.L. 110-161, 121 Stat. 1844, 2128 (2008) that directed EPA to use its authority under CAA §§ 114(a)1) and 208. Regulated facilities will turn to their house counsel and law firms to advise on how to report their GHG emissions. Facilities that fail to accurately report are subject to enforcement under CAA §§ 113, 203-05. As these regulations are refined and applied, their impact will be complicated by the enactment of new federal statutes such as The American Clean Energy and Security Act (H.R. 2454), adopted by the House of Representatives on June 26, 2009, and noted throughout this book.

Practices in sustainable energy law will seek to use the incentive for investments in renewables. The American Recovery and Reinvestment Act of 2009 ("AARA", also known as the "Stimulus Bill,") signed into law on February 17, 2009, contains significant provisions for funding, tax incentives, and grants for renewable energy and energy efficiency, as well as carbon capture and storage. The AARA includes demonstration grids as a prelude for developing a new national "smart grid," which is intended eventually to redesign the entire national transmissions system and build distributed energy storage capacity into every one linked to the grid. Solar investment tax credits are enhanced and allocations for New Clean Renewable Energy Bonds and Qualified Energy Conservation Bonds increased. Abroad, similar economic incentives are being enacted. For example, on July 21, 2009, China enacted a subsidy program to pay 50% of the costs of new solar energy systems, and the costs of linking them to the grid (or 7% of new solar systems that cannot link to the grid). J. Bai & L. Walet, "China Offers Big Solar Subsidies, Shares Up," Reuters News Service at: (www.reuters.com/article/rbssTechMediaTelecomNews/idUSPEK1257092009 0721).

Keeping up with the detail of these new financing and regulatory initiatives requires dedication and expertise. How would you counsel a firm to build a new climate change practice department? Should it be an extension of the existing energy law or environmental law department, adapting the due diligence for environmental law compliance to a wider set of questions? Should the firm's corporate finance and tax departments take the lead? Many such practices currently seek to advise clients on recent changes in the law that might affect them, or to help them measure and curb or off-set their carbon emissions in order to get ready for dealing with new climate change laws. While this is a useful way to build a practice, is it enough?

Do the scientific reports excerpted in Chapter 2 require more of the lawyer? Given that the tools exist to transition to a low carbon, or carbon neutral economy, see McKinsey & Company, Pathways to a Low Carbon Economy (2009), is it in the public interest for the bar to support clients whose vest economic interests would perpetuate dependence upon carbon fuels and continuing the emission of GHGs? How would you apply the Code of Professional Responsibility to respond to such a question? Is your response under the edict of legal ethics at variance norms of with environmental ethics? Compare the code of professional responsibility applicable in your jurisdiction with the injunctions of the Earth Charter (www.earthcharter.org).

Will the emerging practice of climate change law be sufficient to facilitate attaining the remedial ends of climate change mitigation and adaptation? Did the past four decades of environmental law, since the early origins in the 1970s through to the enactments of multilateral environmental agreements world-wide, stem the spread of pollution and preserve biodiversity? What more needs to be done for climate change mitigation and adaptation?

As you read the following excerpts, can you envision the scope of the emerging world-wide practice of climate change law? In many cases, such as investing in renewable sources of energy or in expanding the protection of climate insurance to all regions of the world, the emerging legal practices will do well by doing good. In other contexts, the practice may be a more routine extension of existing legal services provided to clients. Are the commercial legal practices being framed to help client's cope with climate change merely an extension of "business as usual," uninformed by the concerns that Robert Repetto outlined in the first chapter of this book? Or is the new law practice a reflection of a fundamental shift in how governments regulate carbon fuels and phase out the use of carbon fuels, and cut GHG emissions? Are disclosure rules and economic flexibility systems enough to ease the global economy into carbon neutrality, or is more fundamental law reform required as Gus Speth's concluding excerpt in this chapter contends?

B. CORPORATE AND SECURITIES LAW

The existence of the corporation, both within nations and internationally through the model of the multinational company, is perhaps the most important contemporary influence on international economics. Joint stock companies are chartered within a nation, but can operate across borders and achieve efficiencies on a transnational level. The major multinational companies have larger economic characteristics than do more than half of the Member States. Companies have created enormous benefits for human societies, as in the research for and creation and distribution of important new medicines or in manufacturing foods efficiently and disseminating them with quality and low prices across the world. At the same time, it was the multinational investment banks that created and sold derivatives and collateralized debt obligations so recklessly that they caused market collapse, harming the multinational manufacturing enterprises and socio-economic life world-wide.

Companies have developed internal compliance assurance systems to obey environmental and other laws in every jurisdiction in which they operation. Best management practices that ensure such compliance are well developed, if not always applied. See e.g., EPA, "Environmental Auditing Policy Statement," 51 Fed. Reg. 25004 (July 9, 1986), or the International Standards Organization, ISO 14000 Environmental Management System, J. Cascio, The ISO 14000 Handbook (1996). The European Union and the U.S. Environmental Protection Agency have adopted Environmental Management Systems (EMS) to help companies anticipate how to ensure compliance with applicable environmental laws. The International Standards Organization has developed the ISO 14,000 Environmental Audit certification procedures, whereby companies can have third-party inspections to demonstrate their compliance with applicable environmental laws.

Many companies have gone beyond these basic standards of operation to design and implement Corporate Social Responsibility (CSR), through internal rules and programs. Companies set benchmarks and seek to attain sustainable management objectives, and issue CSR reports. The best corporate practices reflect decisions to incorporate sustainable development goals into a company's business plan. S. Schmidheiny, Changing Course: A Global Business Perspective on Development and Environment (1992), prepared on the eve of the UN Conference on Environment and Development in Rio de Janeiro (The "Earth Summit") with the Business Council for Sustainable Development.

However, EMS and CSR practices are hardly universal. Leading national and multinational public stock companies, with their corporate headquarters in developed nations, have developed such practices and shared them through the work of the Business Council for Sustainable Development (www.bcsd.org) or the World Environment Center (www.wec.org). The vast majority of privately held companies and companies headquartered in other regions than North American, the EU or Japan and Australia, are not ISO 14,000 certified and lack EMS or CSR programs. Moreover, many CSR programs do not yet embrace climate change as an issue; companies do not measure their carbon footprint and lack proactive efforts to eliminate their hydrocarbon emissions.

The governance model of the corporation has produced autonomous economic enterprises that are largely autonomous of the control of their shareholders. Corporate law restricts the capacity of shareholders in electing directors, and company boards of directors are largely self-perpetuating bodies. The collapse of the financial sector has resulted in forced revisions of the boards of some major banks, such as Citigroup, but even in the financial sector most boards remain in place even after the economic recession began in 2007. Inertia favors a "business as usual" model in corporate governance around the world.

Most of the trends in natural resources depletion and over-exploitation, in the extinction of species and losses of habitats and in growing pollution levels around the world reflect behavior by people organized into companies. An emphasis in sustaining corporate profits, a focus on building the value of a company's stock traded on the stock markets, and an emphasis on minimizing operating costs, leave little corporate attention or resources on identifying or addressing a company's externalities. Many environmental externalities benefit the company's bottom line. The leading companies have developed management systems to anticipate and avoid reliance on externalities, and many find that by eliminating "waste," they actually save money and enhance profitability. D. Esty & A. Winston, Green to Gold (2007). However, so long as the laws allow economic enterprises to exploit natural resources and take advantage of externalities, companies do so. CSR has not penetrated the business model deeply enough to change this.

The fact that companies are responsible for degradation of the environment, and defend their use of coal and oil, or make little provision for the care of public goods and community resources, has prompted public interest advocates to contend that the time has come for governments to question their right to unbridled economic growth at the expense of the environment. Just as laws prevent companies from exploiting child labor or underpaying women or tolerating "wage slave" conditions, and just as laws regulate the handling of toxic waste and hazardous substances, so regulatory regimes will need to address a company's carbon footprint. Can companies reform their practices to achieve a carbon-neutral operating model?

If you find that Kenneth Boulding's vision of an economy for spaceship Earth quoted in Chapter 4 is becoming the current reality, then as a consequence must laws other than energy and environmental laws change to reflect the new reality? Do the statutes that authorize the organization of corporations also need reform? The quasi-governmental mercantile enterprises of the colonial era have been eliminated, and just as slave-holding enterprises were eliminated; is the regime that sanctions economic enterprises that extracts unsustainable profits from Earth's natural systems, including the atmosphere, in need of comparable reform. Susan Smith advocates enacting laws to charter all multinational companies as "sustainable corporations." As a privilege of operating transnational, such companies should be required to incorporate environmental and social responsibility in to their corporate charters, and be observed as a prerequisite to all operations before taking profits. S. Smith, Chartering Sustainable Transnational Corporations (2009).

At the end of this chapter, Gus Speth examines the factors that militate in favor of reforming the laws that governing the incorporation and governance of companies, to enable them to move to a sustainable business model. The fact that the chief executive offices and boards of most economic enterprises act, and doubtless sincerely believe, that they are entitled to exploit externalities and have not duty to abandon their reliance on fossil fuels, means that legislation or treaties will be required to compel companies to adapt.

Multinational companies are the only entities, other than the military and the university, that operate on a proven "business model" around the world transferring technology and knowledge. Companies have many positive attributes. A multinational company can become the agent of change in mitigating and adapting to climate change. Companies will develop the new technologies and tools for coping with the effects of climate change. Companies can provide the new patterns of food production and distribution, and can assist in developing new urban centers and mass transit systems, to accommodate migrating populations. Rather than bemoan the companies for their excesses, should not legislators seek to design laws that will harness the talents of companies to help with the transformation from a fossil fuel dependent society to a carbon free society? What should the governance model be for the companies in an era of climate change?

At the same time, where legislation allows certain economic sectors, such as the banks and finance companies, to make excessive, speculative investments that systemically undermine the global economy, it is arguable that significant reform of the law governing the financial institutions is needed. Investment banking has neither supported sustainable development nor provided investment loans to help with climate change mitigation and adaptation. R. Posner, A Failure of Capitalism (2009). The reform of the banking sector will be critical to the success of new global cap and trade systems. N. Robinson, Hedging Against Wider Collapse: Lessons from the Meltdowns, in K.   Dekeleter, L. Lye et al., eds. Critical Issues In Environmental Taxation (Vo. VII, 2009). Robinson concludes that until governments require transparency and accountability in the investment banking sectors, efforts to launch trading in greenhouse gases are likely to fall short of their intended goals. The world's financial system established in the Bretton Woods negotiations at the end of World War II, and little reformed since the 1940s, is undergoing its first major reconsideration in the Group of 20 nations; at the same time a wholly new commodity system in GHG trading is being fashioned. Is it possible that nations can address both the reforms of the Earth's human economy and nature's economy at the same time, without coordinating their efforts?

As Robinson observed, "When Nicholas Stern outlined the economic implications for the United Kingdom of coping with the effects of climate change, rather than responding with decisions to invest in cost-effective adaptation to changing climatic conditions, economists and finance ministries debated whether the correct discount rates were employed. There was little concern to assign funds to avert possible near term, or longer term, economic implications associated with the literal meltdown of Earth's Cryosphere. * * *

"The human economy is the product of human constructs. We set the rules of the game, and enter the market place to trade and produce. Classic economic theory treats nature as a given, assuming that natural resources plus human labor provide a source of economic wealth. Classical philosophers share this bias, for they begin their elegant theories by assuming a stable "state of nature." Economists ask how to do so most efficiently. Philosophers ask how to do so ethically, with distributive justice. Yet both these liberal, classical traditions are ecologically illiterate. They assume a static concept of nature, as a constant presence. * * *

"Human society evidences a deep seated preference to business as usual, and to assuming the continuity of known conditions. * * * In order for nations to fashion a set of regional markets for trading GHGs and sequestering carbon dioxide into plants through photosynthesis, or other sequestration methods, they must accomplish something unique in our human history. States need to marry the expertise of Wall Street and the Bronx Botanical Garden, of Kew Gardens and the City of London. They need to integrate the conferences of the parties of the 1992 Convention on Biological Diversity with that of the 1992 UNFCCC, and all other multilateral environmental agreements.

"The mandates of the narrowly circumscribed and now obsolete Bretton Woods Institutions need to be combined with the tepid and manifestly weak 1972 mandate of the UN Environment Programme. The financial and environmental regimes have each evolved apart from the other. * * * There are few interlocutors between these world of economics and nature. * * *

* * * Can economic markets be shaped to accommodate an environmental climate regime? Doing so goes far beyond attempts to use economic instruments for marginal environmental protection objectives, such as adopting modest taxes on pollutants or removing subsidies for certain natural resource exploitation. A deeper critique of economic components will be required, and it must begin with an assessment of how natural systems in the biosphere function.

* * * What if this does not happen, and finance ministers narrowly address the human economy ignoring the climate negotiators? The short-term, immediate economic crisis is serious; as the *Financial Times* has editorialized, 'Only if every significant country acts in parallel, with measures that are mutually supportive, will they be able to halt the crisis.' The same is true of mitigating and adapting to climate change, although Finance Ministers may either be ignorant of this reality or lack the mandate to address it. It is likely that those coping with the economic meltdown will again ignore the environmental meltdown."

C. CLIMATE DISCLOSURES

Can the merging legal practice of climate change law for corporate clients, real estate clients and other commercial interests enable the economy to adapt to new climatic conditions and mitigate climate change? The scope of this practice appears in M. Gerrard, ed., Global Climate Change and U.S. Law (2007), compiled by the American Bar Association's Section on Environment, Energy and Resources. This book complements and extends the many texts on the practical aspects of counseling client son how to comply with environmental laws and thereby contribute to solving society's environmental problems.

Environmental lawyers today counsel clients with respect to many legal procedures for ensuring corporate compliance with environmental laws. This practice, which embraces local land use laws, state and federal pollution laws, laws for remediation of contaminated sites, laws on natural resource conservation and stewardship, and a host of other subject from public and occupational health to the emerging management of nanotechnology. This environmental law practice is now becoming also a "Climate Change Practice." Law firms have established climate change practice groups for their clients, counseling them on how to identify and measure that GHG emissions and evaluate their areas of risk from the anticipated effects of climate change.

As regulatory agencies such as the US, such as the US Environmental Protection Agency, address the implications of Massachusetts v. EPA, they will elaborate existing environmental laws and apply them to the emission of GHGs and the use of fossil fuels and the loss of forest cover that provides photosynthesis to remove CO_2 from the atmosphere. Some of these laws such as California's Proposition 65 require public disclosure of environmental risks. They require disclosure of potential health risks or the presence of and potential exposure to hazardous substances in the sale and transfer of parcels of real property or interests in property. Given these disclosure obligations, companies have found it profitably to reduce their dependence on hazardous materials by reformulating manufacturing and eliminated wastes, and company lawyers advise them on each step in these processes.

Climate change disclosures are becoming a part of all these environmental law practices. The new obligations for climate change disclosures affect corporate governance at the level of the Board of Directors, or for lawyers in the office of corporate counsel assigned to advise on environmental compliance.

The same reforms will come for governmental agencies. Generally, federal, state, and local governments must comply with those same environmental laws and have their own Environmental Management Systems. As the methodologies for mitigating and adapting to climate change become clearer, EIA laws will require assessment of climate change issues whenever government acts.

How will lawyers advise companies about their climate change disclosures? Consider the following commentaries.

BOARDROOM CLIMATE CHANGE
Jeffrey Smith and Matthew Morreale
New York Law Journal (July 16, 2007)

Recent Corporate accounting scandals and the ongoing controversy over executive compensation have refocused the courts, investors and the public on basic principles of fiduciary duty law. In most of the recent high-profile cases, the business judgment rule (BJR) has protected directors and officers from liability despite decision-making that often has raised eyebrows and sometimes lowered stock prices. * * *

It has long been recognized that directors and officers manage the business and affairs of a corporation. This managerial power carries with it fiduciary obligations to the corporation and its shareholders: the duties of due care and loyalty.[2]

The traditional view of these fiduciary duties gives management broad latitude to make judgments that may not be acute or forward-looking. Similarly, the BJR generally dictates deference to informed decision-making by the board, creating a legal defense for most board action and encouraging reasonable entrepreneurial risk.[3]

The importance of knowledge and nimbleness in the boardroom on climate change issues has already been heightened by questions of science, the uncertainty of the regulatory framework, the unpredictable nature of the way commercial and financial marketplaces will respond, and, of course, the potential ecological consequences of global warming itself.

Expectations flowing from the board's duty of care, including its obligations to inquire, to be informed and to employ adequate internal monitoring mechanisms may create new consequences for boards and new norms by which their conduct is judged.

In particular, any failure by a board to engage in a thorough inquiry is a natural point of attack for shareholders, who can allege that impending business risks (or opportunities) presented by climate change would have been obvious if more thorough processes for gathering and evaluating information had been used. * * *

An instructive example of how the courts might judge failed technical and commercial analyses and inadequate internal monitoring was handed down in 2002 by the District Court for the Eastern District of Michigan. In Salsitz v. Nasser, shareholders tried, and failed, to impose liability for three areas of director oversight that damaged Ford Motor Company's financial results and arguably contributed to deaths and injuries around the world.[4]

Shareholders alleged mismanagement of an internal investigation of a technical matter relating to defective ignition switches and ill-conceived handling of an external concern—a problematic tire supplier. Shareholders also alleged a "sustained or systematic failure of the board to exercise oversight," claiming that management had relied on under-qualified employees to execute a sophisticated metals trading strategy, resulting in huge write-offs.

---

[2] Aronson v. Lewis, 473 A.2d 805, 811 (Del. 1984), overruled on other grounds by Brehm v. Eisner, 746 A.2d 244 (Del. 2000); Smith v. Van Gorkom, 488 A.2d 858 (Del. 1985).

[3] In re Disney Shareholder Litig., 2005 Del. Ch. LEXIS, *153 (Del. Ch 2005) citing Gagliardi v. TriFoods Int'l. Inc, 683 A.2d 717, 720 (Del. 1971).

[4] Salsitz v. Nasser, 208 F.R.D. 589 (E.D. Mich. 2002)

Without forcing the parallels, because climate change is in many respects sui generis, a similar suite of allegations could readily be brought against a company for its responses to this new challenge.

A utility might be challenged for the way it conducted a technical investigation to determine its greenhouse gas (GHG) emission reduction strategies.

A company might be faulted for its dealings with significant external forces, such as non-uniform and volatile state and regional regulations, or the rapidly evolving science related to management of its carbon footprint, such as the cost and feasibility of carbon sequestration technology. A company might also ill-advisedly entrust the technical assessment of its carbon emission position to employees who lack necessary skills or market sophistication.

The court in Salsitz found the board and management blameless under well-settled principles of Delaware law, reinforcing the strong presumption that traditional protections for directors will prevail even in the face of failures that seem calamitous through a layman's lens.

Despite the resilience of these protections, however, five new phenomena, occurring simultaneously and in a charged public atmosphere, pose new challenges for directors overseeing climate change decision-making:

1) uncertain and fragmented environmental legislation and regulations;
2) the reactions of capital and insurance markets to emerging business opportunities (and matching risks) posed by climate change;
3) the increasing financial significance of stakeholder activism;
4) pending litigation with potentially significant direct and indirect effects; and
5) the rapidly evolving scientific debate over proper responses to climate change. * * *

Officers and directors evaluating the implications of climate change are faced with an unpredictable regulatory landscape.

In the United States, instead of comprehensive federal legislation, a variety of competing proposals, as well as local, state-specific and regional initiatives, obstruct cohesive corporate planning. Companies in GHG emission-intensive industries are faced with huge potential swings in expenditures that are dependent almost exclusively on regulatory outcomes. Multinational operations may be faced with even more complex decisions.

The unsettled regulatory picture also poses risks when long-term decisions are necessary to meet future market demands, such as the significant capital commitments and many years necessary to site, permit and build a new power plant.

While regulatory and economic uncertainties alone may not excuse inaction, taken together they may allow management to make the case that doing nothing is the prudent course, at least for the short term. A board must probe the facts and rationale behind management's decision to stand pat in response to climate change with particular care, however, because ignorant inaction arguably is the least protected course of conduct.

A far-sighted company may choose inaction, but at the same time develop carefully considered contingency plans for all possible regulatory outcomes and be poised to move into compliance as soon as one outcome is certain and binding. Companies also can advocate for a particular outcome. * * *

The risk of missing commercial opportunities related to climate change may be particularly damaging for some companies.

Being able to predict accurately the availability of government subsidies and to prepare for regulatory mandates in emerging markets could create substantial advantage for first-movers. For instance, Toyota's Prius has arguably seized market share with leading technology, and the competition faces high costs to buy it back. * * *

At the top of the supply chain, General Electric has already made a widely-publicized and thus far commercially successful move into "green power" through its "Ecomagination" initiative, announced in May 2005. With GE as a major mover in the wind turbine industry, the makers of components ranging from rotor blades to batteries in theory should be readying their production capacity to meet new demand.

Given some of the drawn-out and spectacular public failures in garnering the necessary approvals for siting wind farms, however, and the ongoing uncertainty about the tax status of such projects, a board should scrutinize any business plan that rests principally on successful completion of such projects.

In the traditional fiduciary duty framework, a board would be protected both for failing to make the most of the opportunities and for allowing management to rely too heavily on the possibility that they would generate substantial profits. Nevertheless, an informed decision-making process remains important.

Further down the wind turbine supply chain, a well-established maker of high strength, lightweight resins, which had previously marketed exclusively to the aerospace industry, might find an application for its products as a replacement for metals in the frames or blades of wind farm infrastructure. While this might one day prove to be a lucrative market, the board ordinarily would be protected from a breach of fiduciary duty lawsuit for the lost opportunity if the company merely continued in its traditional business lines and ignored the climate change opportunity.

Change a few elements of this equation, however, and the dynamic by which the board's conduct might be judged could shift. If, for example, the composites company only achieved growth and profit through new applications, and the board was systematically ignorant of the increasingly robust wind-farm market, then, as the company's profits and stock price declined, shareholders might mount a more credible case.

Financial markets also have become sensitized to climate change, and prudent boards should track them closely. For example, the management of companies with access to GHG credit markets, such as the EU Emission Trading System (EU ETS), or those who are evaluating the GHG emission cap and trade constructs which are gaining favor in the United States, must decide how to establish a cost effective program for meeting emissions limits, utilizing allocations and buying emission credits. * * *

The marketplace demanding this information is increasingly sophisticated and financially significant. Ten years ago, environmental issues were often framed, or ignored, in boardrooms as an appeasement of fringe interest groups. Today, response to climate change is a mainstream movement, enforced by daily headlines and the backing of the substantial assets of public pension funds. * * *

Management must not only ask, "Is our company in the right place on this issue?"; it must also assure itself that the appropriate stakeholders understand the direction the company is taking. * * *

Although most companies are not named parties in such cases, corporate boards should track major climate change litigation, because it will shape the future regulatory environment; early decisions are likely to have profound precedential consequences across industry groups; and these decisions may lead more generally to increased judicial scrutiny of corporate conduct, notwithstanding the BJR. * * *

Climate change decision-making is rapidly evolving to encompass factual, scientific, political and economic considerations that are far removed from tightly focused, short-term business scenarios. Thus, while it has become critical to ask whether a board has fully informed itself before acting, or failing to act, it is harder to answer the question definitively.

Reliance on "experts" has an obvious role in the climate change context. In most instances, directors will not possess sufficient scientific expertise on which to base their views or to question management meaningfully on the company's strategy. Under Delaware law, a director is "fully protected in relying in good faith upon...information, opinions, reports or statements presented...by any other person as to matters [the director] reasonably believes are within such other person's professional or expert competence and who has been selected with reasonable care by or on behalf of the corporation."

Uncertainties surrounding the science of climate change, however, are a constant reminder that unquestioning reliance on "expert" opinions may not be an automatic shield against liability. The related questions of what constitutes "professional or expert competence" in this area and whether, in light of underlying uncertainties, it is reasonable or rational to rely on any one such opinion, have yet to be raised directly in the courts and therefore dictate caution. * * *

WARMING UP TO CLIMATE CHANGE RISK DISCLOSURE
Jeffrey M. McFarland
14 Fordham J. of Corp. & Fin. L. 281 (2009)

Public companies in the United States do a poor job of disclosing to investors how climate change affects their businesses. Despite repeated requests from investor groups for more disclosure, and despite increasing public interest in the effects of global warming, poor disclosure persists. * * *

In 2007, a study by a group of institutional investors found that "disclosure practices among the nation's 500 largest companies are severely lacking." * * * In September 2007, a separate group of institutional investors, environmental organizations and governmental officers petitioned the United States Securities and Exchange Commission (SEC) to release guidance for reporting climate change issues under existing mandatory disclosure rules and regulations. And, at the company level, shareholders frequently submit proposals relating to climate change disclosure for inclusion in annual proxy statements. * * *

Part I. Securities Disclosure Framework

A. Disclosure Required in Public Company Reports

Section 13(a) of the Exchange Act requires all issuers of registered securities to file periodic reports with the SEC, and grants the SEC rulemaking authority to prescribe the form and content of those reports. The periodic reports required to be filed by issuers under Section 13(a) and the associated rules include the annual report on Form 10-K, and quarterly reports on Form 10-Q, among others.

Forms 10-Q and 10-K are scarcely forms at all, at least not as the term is commonly understood. While they provide a framework for the required disclosure, they explicitly state in their instructions that they are not blank forms, but rather "guide cop[ies]" to be used in preparing the periodic reports. Instead, Forms 10-Q and 10-K refer to Regulation S-K, adopted by the SEC in connection with the filing of forms under the Exchange Act and the Securities Act of 1933 (the "Securities Act"). Regulation S-K provides a more detailed set of guidelines for disclosure in the quarterly and annual reports, but is broad enough to maintain flexibility across a wide range of business activities.

Both the quarterly and annual reports require the issuer to disclose information about the company's financial condition, results of operations and legal proceedings, and risks to which the company is subject. The annual report further requires a discussion of the business developments at the company. Those matters implicate Items 101, 103, 303 and 503(c) of Regulation S-K, and the company's audited financial statements. * * *

2. Legal Proceedings (Item 103)

Item 103 of Regulation S-K is designed for the company to disclose "any material pending legal proceedings, other than ordinary routine litigation incidental to the business." However, the instructions to Item 103 state that an issuer need not provide information with respect to a litigation proceeding seeking damages if the damages would not exceed 10% of the consolidated assets of the company and its subsidiaries. Companies involved in climate change-related litigation must therefore disclose that litigation under Item 103 only if the 10% threshold is reached. Thus, at present, climate change disclosure is likely to appear under Item 103 only if the company has run afoul of an environmental regulation that carries significant monetary penalties or civil liability. Liability of this magnitude is relatively scarce and would likely grab headlines irrespective of the disclosure required by Item 103.

3. MD&A: Management's Discussion and Analysis (Item 303)

Item 303 of Regulation S-K is designed to allow management to disclose its own explanation for the financial condition and results of operations for the time period covered by the form. Although Item 303 contains significant detail about what the issuer must disclose, such as trends and commitments related to the company's liquidity and capital resources, the issuer also must provide all information it believes is "necessary to an understanding of its financial condition, changes in financial condition and results of operations," even if the information is not specifically itemized in Item 303 of the regulation. Thus, management might describe climate change risks under Item 303, particularly if they have a significant financial impact. If, however, management has not yet evaluated the financial impact of climate change, there would be nothing to disclose in the MD&A regarding climate change risk.

4. Risk Factors (Item 503(c))

Item 503(c) of Regulation S-K requires the company to disclose the most significant factors that make ownership of the company's securities risky. The risk factors are included in the company's prospectus, which is delivered at the time the securities are first issued, and also appear in the annual reports on Form 10-K. In addition, Form 10-Q requires quarterly reports to include any material changes in the risk factors that were reported in the last annual report.

Risk factors are taken seriously enough by the SEC that Item 503(c) explicitly requires a concise and logically organized presentation. The risk factors may not be hidden amongst the rest of the often lengthy and technical reports. Item 503(c) does not attempt to itemize the entire range of risks that may require disclosure, instead providing only a generic list of risks, including lack of operating history, lack of recent profitable operations, and lack of a market for the common stock of the company. Actual risk factor disclosure normally goes far beyond these generic categories. Thus, details about climate change risks are a natural fit in the risk factors section of the periodic reports - assuming management is aware of and knowledgeable about climate change risks. At present, companies are not, in any widespread sense, using the 503(c) risk factors section to disclose climate change risks.

5. Financial Statements

Each annual report on Form 10-K must include audited financial statements of the company for the most recently completed fiscal year, with comparative information for prior years. Audited financial statements include in the footnotes a section on contingent liabilities. The contingent liability rules apply when there is "an existing condition, situation, or set of circumstances involving uncertainty as to possible . . . loss . . . to an enterprise that will ultimately be resolved when one or more future events occur or fail to occur." Examples include "[p]ending or threatened litigation . . . [a]ctual or possible claims and assessments . . . [and] [r]isk of loss from catastrophes assumed by property and casualty insurance companies including reinsurance companies."

Disclosure of asserted claims is required if the loss is probable and can be reasonably estimated, or if there is at least a reasonable possibility that a loss may have occurred (regardless of whether it can be reasonably estimated). Under the FASB rules, a loss is "probable" if it is "likely to occur." A "reasonable possibility" of loss means the chance of the loss occurring is more than slight, but less than likely. If a claim is unasserted, disclosure is required only if the loss is probable and there is a reasonable possibility that the outcome will be negative.

It is possible for plaintiffs to assert claims associated with climate change risk and other environmental matters now, particularly if they relate to a violation of governmental laws or regulations. In that event, such contingent liabilities must be disclosed if the potential negative financial consequences meet the FASB standards. These requirements for the audited financial statements, however, cover much the same ground as the Item 103 disclosures relating to litigation, although the triggers for disclosure are stated differently. Still, this captures only a small piece of the climate change risk puzzle: the portion that results in litigation with potential financial consequences exceeding the FASB thresholds. Many contingent liabilities associated with climate change may be in the unasserted category at this stage of climate change science, meaning disclosure will only be triggered in the financial statements only if the loss is probable and there is a reasonable possibility that the outcome will be negative.

B. Materiality

Even under these SEC rules and regulations, information must be disclosed in quarterly and annual reports only if it is material. The United States Supreme Court has formulated the materiality standard as information a reasonable investor would consider important in making an investment decision. With respect to future events, the probability of the event occurring must be evaluated in light of the magnitude of the event. Public corporations must consider this materiality standard in determining whether to disclose information about how climate change is affecting, or may affect, their businesses. Judging from the issuers' responses, many corporations do not consider climate change risk material to their businesses, contrary to what investors are saying is important to them.

The SEC has at times viewed materiality primarily through an economic lens, leaving so-called "social disclosure" out of the process. For example, in the early 1970s, the Natural Resources Defense Council proposed mandatory disclosure of environmental and civil rights matters. The SEC, however, decided that such matters were not material to investors, in part because they were not economically focused. Clearly, the tide has shifted with respect to global warming and other environmental matters, which are no longer considered mere social issues. At the time of the NRDC petition, only a small segment of the investing public was interested in better environmental disclosure. Today, the Social Investment Forum suggests that socially responsible investing accounts for approximately 11% of the investment market, compared to a very small fraction cited at the time of the SEC's decisions on the NRDC petition.

Harvard Professor Cynthia Williams disagrees with the premise that materiality is primarily an economic consideration, both from the standpoint of the legislative authority given to the SEC, and the SEC's determinations of materiality on other issues of corporate accountability. Yet it certainly is arguable that climate change risk disclosure fits the materiality standard if evaluated solely by its economic effects. Even without a direct economic tie-in, climate change risk disclosure also serves the purpose of "providing investors with full and fair information necessary to make informed investment decisions and to cast well-informed votes to continue with the present management of a company, to pressure management to adopt new strategies, or to vote for new management." Moreover, there is justification for taking into account the underlying moral issue when determining materiality to investors. Corporations are given the status of legal persons by state law, and should have as much responsibility - arguably more - for the health of the planet and its inhabitants as any natural person.

Part II. Current State of Climate Change Risk Disclosure

A. Company Participation in Existing Disclosure Systems

Researchers have decried the lack of meaningful public reporting on climate change risks. Several coalitions have engaged in efforts to improve climate change risk disclosure. * * *

CERES reports that fewer than half of the companies in the S&P 500 responded to a questionnaire about climate change risks, opportunities and strategies, a much lower figure than the FT Global 500, a worldwide analog to the S&P 500. Among those companies that responded, nearly one-third refused to make their responses public. Overall, responding companies provided approximately 25% of the information investors are seeking. * * *

The Carbon Disclosure Project (CDP) also maintains a reporting system for climate change data, and its findings are no more encouraging. The CDP, whose work in 2006 is relied upon in the CERES Report, is a non-profit organization designed to foster the relationship between investors and corporations on issues relating to climate change. * * *

According to the CDP, there are over 1,550 responding companies around the world. The 2007 results of the CDP questionnaire show 64% of the companies in the S&P 500 Index respond to the questionnaire, but only 49% of the S&P 500 companies publish their disclosures on the CDP's website. * * *

The poor state of climate change disclosure was recently echoed more directly by investors. In a 2007 petition to the SEC, a group of investors, environmental organizations and governmental constituencies pointed out variations in the quality of disclosure among SEC filings of members of the auto, insurance, energy, petrochemical and utilities industries from 2001-2006, calling it an "inconsistent patchwork of disclosure."

B. Why Is Climate Change Disclosure So Scarce?

   * * * There are intuitive, non-mechanical reasons for reluctance to disclose climate change risks. First, the scope of the evaluation of climate
change risk within an organization may be enormous, depending on the nature of the business. Daniel Esty and Andrew Winston postulate that the
evaluation of climate change risk involves more than the normal risk analysis, because it involves the upstream and downstream supply chain.   * * * A
large investigative scope would normally associate with significant cost factors. Research and development costs may be large at the outset, and may
continue into the foreseeable future, particularly because the exact effects of
climate change are still being studied - and will be for some time. While there
are profit opportunities in the environmental arena, they tend to have a long
horizon, given the initial cost outlay. A long horizon of profitability does not
fit well with the current Wall Street culture that judges companies on a quarterly earnings basis.

   * * * Even those companies that have evaluated the risk may not fully
appreciate its significance, or may have a distorted view of the risk. If the
current corporate norm is averse to disclosing climate change risk, it may
obscure the true nature of that risk. Some managers may even believe the
SEC's relative silence on climate change disclosure is indicative that disclosure is not yet ripe.

   There is also evidence that managers do not make decisions that are ultimately rational. The field of behavioralism seeks to explain the psychology
of decision making, including decisions made within an organizational structure. To the extent a corporation is a reflection of its upper management,
these behavioral factors may significantly influence a company's decision
about whether a particular issue is material and thus ripe for disclosure, or
immaterial and exempt from disclosure requirements. * * *

   It is easy to see that these biases could become more pronounced where
the managers are incentivized to maximize short-term profits, because climate change risk evaluation and disclosure may threaten those incentives.
Management may be reluctant to discover new problems, particularly those
with a long horizon, costly resolution and, in some cases, the shame of public
attention those problems might receive. * * * In addition, the fact that some
companies are willing to file sustainability reports with the Carbon Disclosure Project, but not make them publicly available or include them in securities filings, indicates that management fears the potential liability associated
with securities law disclosure.

   Part III. Evaluating Current Climate Change Disclosure Systems and Pro-
                                   posals

* * *

In a recent symposium at the University of Virginia School of Law, Cornell law student Andrew Schatz argued for a scheme of mandatory disclosure of GHG emissions through the creation of a Greenhouse Gas Release Inventory (GGRI).[114] This proposed GGRI would exist outside the securities regulation framework. Schatz identified five underlying principles of the GGRI proposal: "1) mandatory disclosure, 2) standardized information, 3) identification of companies, 4) reporting at regular intervals and 5) a primary purpose of reducing risks."

Schatz's proposed GGRI is an interesting idea, particularly because it incorporates the elements of an effective disclosure system. However, because the GGRI is not part of the periodic reporting system required by the securities laws, it would not be a sufficient means of getting information to securities investors. By Schatz's own admission, investors may not have the time and energy to find the GGRI information. Moreover, the GGRI would rely on The Greenhouse Gas Protocol adopted by the World Resources Institute, a data-based reporting system calling for reporting of "scope 1 and scope 2 emissions," "emissions data for all six GHG's separately (CO_2, CH_4, N_2O, HFCs, PFCs, SF_6)" and "direct CO_2 emissions from biologically sequestered carbon," among other things. This information would be appropriately standardized, but even if an investor could find the GGRI, the level and kind of raw detail in a GGRI is still unlikely to be understood by even the most sophisticated investor. The GGRI is geared towards technical information to accomplish risk reduction. Investors need a version of the risks posed by GHG emissions that they can understand.

The sheer number of registries and reporting systems presents an inefficient solution for investors, particularly when considering the kind of technical data that these reporting systems require. If companies were more willing to make disclosures, and investors were able to find them, there are still too many reporting systems for companies to use all of them. Such fractured reporting would only confuse investors, even if they were able to find the different reports and interpret them accurately.

B. CERES Requests for Improved Securities Disclosure

The CERES report in March 2007 (the "CERES Report") encouraged companies to "elevate climate change as a corporate priority and communicate openly with investors about their strategies and responses." The CERES Report contains specific recommendations for climate change reporting under the securities laws, relying heavily on the Global Framework for Climate Risk Disclosure. The Global Framework for Climate Risk Disclosure was developed by fourteen institutional investors in October 2006 to standardize

---

[114] Andrew Schatz, "Regulating Greenhouse Gases by Mandatory Information Disclosure," 26 Va. Envtl. L.J. 335 (2008).

climate risk disclosure. Specifically, the four elements of disclosure are: (1) disclosing historical, current and projected greenhouse gas emissions; (2) analyzing climate risk and emissions management; (3) assessing physical risks; and (4) analyzing regulatory risks relating to greenhouse gases.

The CERES recommendations are well thought out and clear, but they do not represent the first requests from investors for more climate change risk disclosure. Requests have been coming from institutional investors for twenty years. These repeated requests have resulted in more disclosure in periodic securities filings, but progress has been slow * * *. While the CERES recommendations are laudable, they have not gained sufficient traction in their present form. * * *

C. Climate Risk Petition to SEC

A collection of institutional investors, governmental officers, attorneys general, environmental organizations and non-profit groups is addressing the disclosure issue more directly under the securities law framework. In the aforementioned Climate Risk Petition, these groups are asking the SEC to issue interpretive guidance for reporting climate change issues under existing mandatory disclosure rules and regulations, including Items 101, 103 and 303 of Regulation S-K. The petition also discusses financial disclosures of climate change risks under FASB No. 5. Specifically, the petition requests prompt "clarification" from the SEC that registrants must review relevant information about climate change risks and disclose material information associated with climate change physical risks and legal proceedings, as well as financial risks and opportunities associated with CO_2 emissions.

The core concept underlying the Climate Risk Petition is that climate change is now material for many, if not most, companies. * * * The Climate Risk Petition recognizes that the securities regulatory scheme already has in place a mandatory disclosure system based on rules in Regulation S-K and the concept of materiality. However, the current disclosure system is not tailored to global warming risks, and the SEC has been unclear about its policies relating to climate risk disclosure under the securities laws. This explains the petition's request for "clarification" from the SEC regarding climate change disclosure under the securities disclosure system, as well as its plea for the SEC to act promptly. * * *

Part IV. Proposed Elements of Mandatory Climate Change Disclosure in Securities Filings

* * * Because the CERES report seeks voluntary disclosure, however, it requests some information that would not be proper for mandatory disclosure under the securities laws. For one, the CERES requests include items that are generally inconsistent with other aspects of the securities regulation scheme, as detailed further below. Moreover, some of the requested informa-

tion runs the risk of being overly complex or too voluminous. In fact, too much disclosure and overly-complex disclosure actually hinder good decision making by investors. The "raw" reporting systems of GRI, the Carbon Disclosure Project, and the proposed Greenhouse Gas Release Inventory suffer significantly from this problem; the CERES recommendations less so. Nevertheless, an effective disclosure system needs to be reasonably concise. * * *

* * * The SEC does not require companies to make forecasts or projections. Therefore, requiring companies to make forecasts in connection with mandatory disclosure of climate change risks would likely be enough to prevent any mandatory disclosure rules from passing muster. The same can be claimed of the CERES-recommended "scenario planning."

A more appropriate approach in the mandatory disclosure context would be for the SEC to highlight in its guidance or rules the potential materiality of government regulations associated with climate change issues. Like the disclosure of physical risks, the specific mention of climate change regulation in SEC guidance or rules ought to cause companies to improve upon their current disclosure of these regulatory risks. Whether a company chooses to forecast emissions reductions or the effects of various scenarios ought to be voluntary, and subject to forward-looking statement safe harbors. * * *

* * * Some will no doubt object that climate change risk disclosure is merely a system to effect regulation on issues of climate change, and an inefficient one. Whether mandatory securities law disclosure ought to have substantive regulatory goals is the subject of debate. On the topic of climate change risk disclosure, however, it should be enough that investors are clamoring for information as part of their decision-making processes. Mandatory disclosure need not be based solely on financial impact, but also can be geared towards providing investors with more information by which to make decisions about company management.

Notes and Questions

1. The Securities and Exchange Commission (SEC) is considering revisions to its corporate environmental disclosure rules. How would you anticipate the SEC might revise SEC Regulation S-K, 17 C.F.R. 229 in light of the new climate of regulation and litigation involving a company's carbon footprint? In light of the state of rapidly evolving knowledge about the causes and effects of climate change, as illustrated in the reports of the Intergovernmental Panel on Climate Change, or in the US EPA Endangerment Finding, how would you advise a client company to be in compliance with SEC Rule 10b-5. How should knowledge about climate change affect what is considered materials for Rule 10b-5? TSC Industries Inc. v. Northway, Inc., 426 U.S. 438 at 449 (1976). Consider the enforcement action by New York State Attorney General Andrew Cuomo against 5 energy companies in 2007, who were al-

leged to be "selectively revealing favorable facts or intentionally concealing unfavorable information about climate change" and thus "misleading investors." "Cuomo Reaches Landmark Agreement with Major Energy Company, Xcel Energy, To Require Disclosure of Financial Risks of Climate Change to Investors," NYS Dept. of Law, www.oag.state.ny.us/media_cenbter/2008/ayg.aug27a_08.html.

2. Proposed legislation in Oregon would have established corporate climate change responsibilities as part of a company's charter to do business. See A. Torbit, Implementing Corporate Climate Change Responsibility, 88 Oregon L. Rev. (2009). The law would have extended House Bill 2826, codified as ORS 60.047(2)(e), which authorizes a company in Oregon to conduct the business of the corporation in a manner that is environmentally and socially responsible. It would mandate explicit disclosures on climate change mitigation and adaptation. Does amending corporate charters by legislation offer advantages that regulations or even criminal law enforcement cannot?

3. Some financial companies are contemplating offering securitized derivatives in carbon credits and carbon trades even before disclosure rules are in place. Is this speculative investing prudent? This is the sort of collateralized debt obligation contributed to the deep recession that began in 2007. Should such secondary trading be banned? If allowed, what sort of safeguards should be required. Finance sector lobbyists helped draft the provisions in H.R. 2454 that would create a carbon derivatives market. Is this legislative mandate transparent and consistent with the goals of climate change mitigation and adaptation?

D. INSURANCE

Adverse effects of climate change, such as floods or droughts, can be ameliorated through the use of insurance. Most of the developing world, and the vast majority of the Earth's cities and other human settlements and their inhabitants, lack any insurance at all. How can governments extend the insurance system that is enjoyed in the USA or in the European Union globally. Can micro-finance tools be used to create insurance pools for poor people in places like Bangladesh or India or China? Should insurance only be available to affluent communities? Should insurance be available to restore essential infrastructure and ecosystem services that are damaged during climate change events? How should governments assist the insurance industry as it examines these questions: Is not the insurance sector essential to climate change adaptation? How important was it to include insurance in the December 2009 Copenhagen Conference of the Parties for the UNFCCC?

FROM RISK TO OPPORTUNITY: INSURER RESPONSES TO CLIMATE CHANGE 2008
Evan Mills (Ceres April 2009)
http://insurance.lbl.gov/opportunities/risk-to-opportunity-2008.pdf

The insurance sector finds itself on the front lines of climate change, and its response to the challenge has varied enormously. Insurers are, by definition, selective and cannot be expected to insure all risks. At a minimum, insurers are messengers of climate risks through their pricing, terms, and conditions, and help society diversify the costs of losses. Insurers are intrinsically vulnerable and, in some cases, hampered by insufficient data. * * *

Progress in the scientific understanding is no doubt driving the growing engagement of insurers. * * * In the words of an associate editor at "National Underwriter": "Given the stakes for insurers covering catastrophic losses, waiting for proof instead of taking action now would amount to just plain foolish behavior."

The economic analysis has shifted as well, as reports such as the UK government's "Stern Review" turn on its head the conventional wisdom that taking action on climate change will harm the economy. Companies and investors now increasingly realize that, in fact, it is the lack of action to combat climate change that is the true threat to the economy, while engaging with the problem and mounting solutions represents not only a duty to shareholders but also a boon for economic growth. * * *

Insurers' own analyses have provided a sobering outlook for insured economic risks, and one that is increasingly consistent with what scientists predict for the physical world. Modeling studies conducted by The Association of British Insurers find that losses in typical and extreme future years will exceed today's by a factor of two or three. * * *

The initial reaction of many insurers—particularly in the United States—has been to focus on financial means for limiting their exposure to losses, e.g. by limiting availability, tightening terms, and raising prices. The availability-affordability issue places a bright light on the respective roles of the public sector and insurers, and the likelihood that government will have to assume more climate risks if the private sector recedes. This comes as the existing subsidy-based model for public flood insurance in the United States, the FEMA-managed National Flood Insurance Program, was rendered insolvent in 2005 by Hurricane Katrina and likely again in 2008 by Hurricane Ike, with a combined deficit approaching $30 billion. * * *

* * * [I]n addition to existing risks, the very technological and behavioral responses to climate change will usher in new risks. Examples include safety issues associated with a resurgence of nuclear power or the introduction of carbon capture and storage technology. Even some "green" strategies will bring new risks, while mitigating old ones. As such, climate change is a textbook example of Enterprise Risk Management (ERM), a modality that has resonated very strongly with the insurance community in recent years by integrating an otherwise fragmented risk-management process. ERM recog-

nizes the combined influence of internal and external pressures and how they interact across a broad portfolio of activities, including underwriting and asset management operations. * * *

Meanwhile, many insurers perceive massive opportunities in responding to climate change. Green-building construction investment is expected to exceed $12 billion in 2008, while hybrid car sales grew by 38% to 350,000 vehicles (almost 50% year-over-year growth). The electric power industry foresees large investments in renewable technologies and end-use energy efficiency.

Another indicator of this changing business environment is shareholder resolutions regarding climate change. The number of such resolutions hit an all-time record of 57 in 2008, as well as an all-time high of 25% of shareholders voting for the resolutions. The number of subsequent withdrawals provides an indication that shareholders obtained their desired outcomes. * * *

As the world's largest industry—generating more than $4 trillion in premium revenue in 2007, plus another trillion or so in investment income—with core competencies in risk management and finance, the insurance industry is uniquely positioned to further society's understanding of climate change and advance creative solutions to minimize its impacts. * * *

Integrating Climate Change into Traditional Catastrophe Modeling

A leading modeler recently drew considerable attention by stating that the industry has become overly dependent on these models, to the point of complacency, and has "stopped thinking about risks independently". While accused of allowing models to "dumb down the underwriting process", insurers are endeavoring to become more cautious and skilled in using these models.

* * * A major obstacle to insurers taking action on climate change has been that the models the industry uses to manage and price risk have been backward-looking and thus, by definition, unable to take climate change into account. The modeling industry has, to its credit, focused significant effort in recent years on finding ways to reconcile its risk models with the forward-looking models used by climate scientists. * * *

The catastrophe (CAT) models used by the insurance industry to understand its exposure to large weather-related events have been focused almost exclusively on windstorm risk. Efforts have been made recently to broaden their application to other hazards (e.g. wildfire, storm surge, and sinkholes). * * *

Promoting Loss Prevention

Managing risks and controlling losses is central to the insurance business, and is evident in the industry's history as founders of fire departments and advocates for building codes. Insurers are increasingly engaging in the process of adapting to climate change. While their primary focus has been on financially managing risks (through exclusions, price increases, derivatives, etc.), physical risk management is receiving renewed attention, and could play a large role in preserving the insurability of coastal and other high-risk areas.

Improved building codes and land-use management are important starting points, but insurers and others face many barriers. Insurers are increasingly finding value in a whole genre of energy-efficient and renewable-energy technologies that also make infrastructure less vulnerable to insured losses, and in improved management of forests, agriculture, and wetlands. Insurers are gradually finding a role in helping to understand the risk profiles of "green" technologies and practices. The scale and breadth of insurer efforts in all of these areas remain extremely modest in the context of their overall business operations.

Traditional Risk Management

The climate-policy community has concluded that the only effective response to climate change requires a combination of loss prevention (adaptation) coupled with emissions reductions (mitigation). Most of the examples from the insurance sector documented in this report pertain to the latter, but insurers have long been involved in loss prevention as well, which traditionally often takes place at the individual customer level (improved storm shutters, fire suppression, etc.) Climate change certainly calls for more of this, but also for prevention at much larger scales, especially for regional defensive infrastructure. * * *

Improving Land-Use Planning

Supporting the integration of climate change considerations into land-use planning is another natural role for insurers, although the public sector clearly has lead responsibility. * * * [P]ost-Katrina analysis revealed that per-capita economic losses were three times lower in areas where building codes and comprehensive land-use planning were in use. Allianz reviewed examples from many countries that supported the same conclusion. * * *

Better Management of Forestry, Agriculture, and Wetlands

* * * Wetlands and mangrove protection also offers win-win benefits. Hurricane Katrina would have been less damaging had it not been preceded by decades of wetlands destruction. A recent study indicates that coastal wetlands offer $23.2 billion per year in storm-protection value in the United States alone. A few insurance companies have pursued sustainable land-

management practices as part of their carbon-offset programs. As an example, well aware of cyclone-related risks, the Japanese insurer Tokio Marine Nichido has been active in mangrove protection. Since 1999, it has reforested 5,395 hectares (13,331 acres) of mangroves in Indonesia, Fiji, Thailand, Philippines, Myanmar, and Vietnam, and its work continues. The company states that the tsunami of 2005 did less damage to areas behind these reforested areas, though the company does not underwrite in these areas. * * * [N]o insurers have yet offered products for insuring forestry-related carbon offsets. * * *

'Rebuilding Right' Following Losses

Insurers can promote risk-prevention strategies in the context of rebuilding after losses. "Rebuilding Right" in the aftermath of Hurricane Katrina * * * could involve everything from wetlands restoration to energy-efficient and disaster-resistant housing to renewably-based distributed energy supplies that are less vulnerable to disruption from future extreme weather events. * * *

The concept is beginning to spread to transportation. In 2008, Fireman's Fund introduced the first commercial-fleet hybrid vehicle upgrade endorsement in the event of loss, which includes significant additional incentives by covering full-replacement value (no depreciation) and no deductible for the first three years. * * *

Assigning Directors & Officers Liability

In 2007, the three leading U.S. insurance trade journals devoted cover stories to the looming implications of climate change for insurance liability claims. The Wall Street Journal echoed the concern. Insurers providing Directors and Officers policies might face claims against their customers from shareholders. Business Insurance noted that D&O insurers have not given the issue nearly as much scrutiny as have shareholders. Conversely, insurers themselves could be found liable for not disclosing climate risks—both from their insurance business and their investments—to their shareholders. * * *

The world's largest insurance broker, Marsh, has articulated the following questions with respect to assessing climate change and D&O risk:
- Management accountability/responsibility: Does a company allocate responsibility for the management of climate-related risks? If so, how?
- Corporate governance: Is there a committee of independent board members addressing the issues?
- Emissions management and reporting: What progress, if any, has a company made in quantifying, disclosing, and/or reporting its emissions profile?

•   Regulatory anticipation: How well has a company planned for future regulatory scenarios?

* * * In 2008, Zurich added D&O coverage extensions to incorporate climate change. Liberty Mutual introduced what it referred to as liability coverage for "global warming litigation," including directors and officers, employment practices liability, fiduciary responsibility, pollution defense and standard ISO crime fidelity.

Recognizing and Rewarding Correlations Between Sustainable Practices and a Low-Risk Profile

A growing number of insurers perceive a "halo effect" in which adopters of climate-change mitigation technologies are viewed as low-risk customers. This acknowledges an overlap between behaviors that are risk-averse with those that are environmentally responsive. For example, Travelers has stated that: "* * * commercial property owners who embrace 'green' technologies are likely to be more risk management-minded, practicing greater care in building maintenance and operation." * * *

Auto insurers also have recognized the "halo effect." A Japanese trade association asserted a positive correlation between safe driving, fuel-economy, and environmental protection. A number of vehicle insurers are offering discounts for policyholders of fuel-economic vehicles. For example, Sompo Japan Insurance has provided a 1.5% premium credit for low-emission and fuel-efficient vehicles, reaching 3.25 million policyholders as of 2005, and Tokio Marine Nichido reached 6.23 million customers (48% market penetration) as of 2006. Farmers Insurance introduced a 5% premium credit for hybrid vehicles in California in 2005, expanding it to 37 states in by mid-2008. Farmers' parent, Zurich, also offers the product in Japan and Germany. In 2006, Travelers announced 10% premium credits for drivers of hybrid vehicles, citing the "preferred" characteristics of these drivers as well as a desire within the company to develop business associated with this "innovative" trend in technology and to play a part in accelerating the transition to more efficient vehicles. * * *

Crafting Innovative Insurance Products & Services

* * * Microinsurance is being introduced at large scale for those in the developing world currently lacking access to insurance, and innovative pilot projects are pioneering techniques through which insurers can collaborate with international aid organizations to improve disaster resilience. Renewable energy has seen a flurry of activity, but most appears to be little more than bundling/repackaging of existing offerings, rather than pure innovation to fill coverage gaps or carefully tailor coverage to the unique features of these technologies. More fundamental opportunities could be tapped through

new business lines in energy auditing, retrofit evaluation, installation and management, as well as a host of quality-assurance services (e.g. commissioning) that manage the performance risks of energy-saving and carbon-offset projects. Warranty and service contracts represent an emerging area with few examples, but considerable potential. * * *

Energy-Savings Insurance

* * * Energy-savings insurance (ESI) is an innovative product in which policies protect the installer or owner of an energy-efficiency project from under-achievement of predicted energy-savings. ESI differs in fundamental ways from surety bonds that might be associated with energy-savings projects. Surety bonds are designed strictly to guarantee the installation-of-measures portion of a project. The surety will specifically exclude from coverage of operational energy savings or any savings guarantee.

A prior study identified 12 past and present providers, and a potential $1 billion market for ESI in the United States alone. There are some market drivers for ESI. For example, some state statutes require a contractor to obtain a performance and payment bond relating to the installation of energy-efficiency measures in an amount equal to the predicted savings. * * *

Demand is low. This is no doubt partly because of the ways in which performance-based financial products have fallen out of favor more generally, combined with a profound lack of recognition on the part of customers that predicted energy savings cannot be taken for granted. In many cases, energy-efficiency projects suffer from lack of quality control, and underperform as a result. * * *

Renewable-Energy Project Insurance

The global market for renewable-energy is projected to grow from $55 billion in 2006 to more than $225 billion in 2016. Insurers have for decades offered varying degrees of coverage for renewable-energy projects, and we do not attempt to catalog those here. Our focus is on innovative products or endorsements that fill coverage gaps or otherwise improve on the standard coverages.

A survey conducted by Marsh found that many insurers offered at least one of eight forms of insurance for renewable energy projects, but numerous risks and barriers also were noted. * * *

One insurance-related obstacle for the renewable-energy sector has been the fragmented nature of insurance and the need to assemble multiple forms of coverage in order to manage risk across the full project cycle. [A number of companies have created products] which combine insurance with engineering and finance consultation. * * *

The ambiguity around many of these efforts is the degree to which the companies are simply integrating and "repackaging" existing capacity as opposed to creating new products and services. A good example is the case of off-shore wind systems, which some insurers exclude (citing higher risks and repair costs) while others cover.

* * *

Wind Power: One example is wind power derivatives, in which payments are made to the producer if revenues fall below a predetermined level, and, conversely, payments made to the derivative provider if performance exceeds expectations. * * * [One insurer] offers renewable-production insurance derivatives for both wind and solar-electric systems. Emblematic of the expansion of traditional energy insurers into alternatives is Navigators Group's new focus on wind energy. The company's Offshore Wind Turbine segment will include insurance for project cargo, contractor's all risks, start-up delays, operational material damage, business interruption and third party liability. Swiss Re is reported to cover wind-resource risks under its carbon-offset delivery insurance program.

Solar Photovoltaics: In 2008, Munich Re introduced a product for insuring income shortfalls from solar photovoltaic plants and wind farms resulting from fluctuations in solar resource availability. AXA offers coverage for production shortfalls for wind and solar photovoltaic projects above 150 kilowatt-peak (kWp).

Geothermal Energy: Munich Re has successfully piloted exploration-risk insurance for geothermal energy companies, AXA's unit in Germany also offers cover for geothermal "drilling productivity losses." With funding from the Global Environmental Facility (GEF), The World Bank has created a $3.7-million "Geothermal Risk Insurance" exploration-risk product in conjunction with investment and consultancy services for the first geothermal energy plant to be constructed in Hungary.

Biofuels: Aon created a new agri-fuels group to offer risk-management services for the emerging biofuels industry. * * *

Green-Buildings & Equipment Insurance

* * * [A]s localities increasingly incorporate green features into existing building codes and standards, "green" practices are becoming the new norm and will be automatically covered under some insurance contracts (e.g. those with code-upgrade clauses). In either case, there is a complex array of risks for a variety of parties around the construction and operation of the green buildings, any of which could result in insurance claims. Aon characterizes

these risks as follows:

For owners: (1) not being able to get the building certified or not achieving the expected level of certification (2) being unable to qualify for a tax credit that is contingent upon certification (3) not meeting requirements to qualify for a loan or green-building incentive (4) increased soft costs because of delays in completion or the requirement for additional documentation

For design professionals: (1) a higher standard of care due to the requirement that LEED certified individuals participate in the process (2) design defects that result in the failure to achieve certification or the level of certification promised (3) liability arising out of the operating phase due to systems or components that do not perform as intended over the life cycle of the structure

For contractors: (1) failure to deliver features or performance promised in the construction contract (2) construction defects (3) failure of the completed structure and systems to perform as intended over the lifecycle of the building.

* * * While any of these risks might compel an injured party to seek a remedy through litigation and insurance, current policies might or might not provide the desired coverage. Insurance policies have begun to respond to these issues. Although emerging products have focused initially on reconstruction after a loss to replace pre-existing green features or upgrade to meet a higher green standard of performance, their scope is gradually increasing. * * *

Microinsurance and Other Initiatives for the Developing World

Most of the world's population cannot afford conventional insurance for health, life, crops, or property. The practice of microinsurance dates back at least to the 1950s, although the entry of commercial insurers is relatively recent. Microinsurance for property is much less common than that for life and health. A comprehensive study found that only 3% of the poor (albeit 78 million people) in the world's 100 poorest countries have access to insurance products. A separate study identified 122 microinsurance products for agriculture, about two-thirds of which were in Latin America, followed by Asia and then Africa. Total premiums for 2005 were estimated at more than $1 billion. Risks tend to be borne by a mix of public and private players. * * *

In 2007, Swiss Re created the Climate Change Adaptation Program, a high-tech microinsurance product for drought. Swiss Re's original weather-risk products for developing countries had been sold to 320,000 small farmers in India. * * *

In 2008, AXA Re introduced the first-ever insurance for humanitarian emergencies, an innovative approach that reduces human suffering and drastically reduces the overall cost of responding to humanitarian crises by mobilizing aid faster than is possible using traditional approaches. * * *

Innovative Insurance for Faster and Less Costly Humanitarian Relief

Beginning with catastrophic crop-loss risk faced by farmers in Ethiopia, AXA crafted a rainfall derivative product purchased by the United Nations World Food Programme (WFP). Pooling data from 26 weather stations across Ethiopia, rainfall amounts and patterns are tracked and used to develop an index. If the trigger is surpassed, claims are paid well in advance of when post-event relief would be distributed. Participants in the program estimate that $7 million of insurance claims paid before the catastrophe avert $1 billion in conventional aid that would otherwise be required. As a result, the ultimate costs of the event are lower and the amount of human suffering much reduced. The WFP estimates that the new mechanism speeds up the process of delivering relief by four to six months.

In September 2007, Swiss Re launched its Climate Adaptation Development Programme (CADP) at the Clinton Global Initiative 2007 meeting. The program is designed to develop a financial risk transfer market for the effects of adverse weather in emerging countries. In a first phase, it will aim at providing financial protection against severe drought conditions for up to 400,000 people in several villages in Kenya, Mali, and Ethiopia. The contracts protect smallholder farmers against drought-related livelihood shocks such as food shortages and famines. Satellite-based sensing is used to determine when the loss trigger is passed.

Offering Carbon Risk-Management and Carbon-Reduction Services

* * * A small but increasing number of insurers has spurred the burgeoning market for carbon trading while securing additional business by providing mechanisms for participants to better manage carbon risk. There has been a recent burst of activity involving bundling carbon offsets with insurance products, particularly automobile and travel insurance. Insurers are becoming involved in providing property and liability insurance for carbon-reduction capital projects, as well as consultative services in designing and managing such projects so as to maximize their technical and financial upside. Lack of a mandatory trading system in the United States is often cited by insurers as their reason for hesitating to enter the market. Insurers also have begun to pay attention to the quality of carbon-offset approaches. * * *

The market response to the emergence of carbon markets is exemplified by a new intermediary—Carbon Re—that specializes in the area. Working closely with Munich Re, Carbon Re offers a series of insurance products and risk assessment/management services. HSB Solomon Associates offers an integrated set of engineering, benchmarking, project development, and risk-management services for developing and executing energy- and emissions-reduction projects, particularly in industrial facilities, such as oil refineries. * * *

The world's carbon markets are projected to be valued at more than $166 billion by the end of 2008, growing to $550 billion by 2012 and $3 trillion by 2020. Many risks are associated with carbon trading, and new insurance products and services are being developed to manage them. Under the European Union Emissions Trading System, more than 6,000 companies face mandatory emissions-reduction targets and stringent penalties for noncompliance. * * * In the United States, regional trading systems are being put in place and the Obama administration will no doubt institute a national mandatory cap-and-trade program in the near future. * * *

The value proposition for carbon-credit insurance is quite real. For instance, the Regional Greenhouse Gas Initiative (an agreement by a group of states in the northeastern United States to jointly cap power plant greenhouse gas emissions) imposes a 10% "discount rate" on any offsets obtained from carbon-sequestration projects because of uncertainties with that technology. Insurers of carbon-offset projects have the opportunity as well to reward better practices that reduce risk through higher-quality project design. * * *

RNK Capital LLC and Swiss Re jointly implemented the carbon markets' first insurance product for managing Kyoto Protocol-related risk in carbon credit transactions. The insurance provides coverage for risks related to Clean Development Mechanism (CDM) project registration and the issuance of Certified Emission Reductions (CERs) to RNK under the Kyoto Protocol. These risks include failure or delay in the approval, certification, and/or issuance of CERs from CDM projects by the United Nations Framework Convention on Climate Change (UNFCCC). Notably, the Swiss Re program can pay claims either in monetary units or by providing replacement offsets. * * *

Munich Re offers a "Kyoto Multi Risk Cover" that insures an agreed value per carbon credit and compensates entities that invest in CDM and JI (Joint Implementation) projects if losses arise from failure to deliver the agreed number of emission rights. Standard risks (property, engineering, surety, and credit) are included. * * *

Financing Climate-Protection Improvements

Insurers, especially those associated with banking operations, are in a position to engage in financing customer-side projects that either improve resilience to the impacts of climate change or contribute to reducing emissions. In some cases this takes the form of secondary credit support * * * such as preferential credit terms for energy-efficient appliances and home upgrades. * * * AXA MPS (Italy) offers an all-risk insurance product for photovoltaic systems linked with loans. The main guarantees are: damages caused by natural events, photovoltaic system's damages, fire, civil responsibility, and loss of revenue in case of low production. * * *

Climate Change Liability: Emerging Risks, Emerging Opportunities

While much has been said on the issue of property losses from climate change, it is becoming increasingly clear that losses arising from the causes/impacts of climate change as well as the emerging responses also will pierce the liability lines. The numerous potential triggers include:

- Abrupt impacts of extreme events linked to climate change
- Gradual impacts such as increased mold losses from warmer and wetter climates and flooding
- Secondary consequences of climate-linked events (e.g. waste spills)
- Failure to adapt quickly or adequately to climate change impacts
- Demands for compensation for prudent adaptation costs
- Political risks
- Poor corporate governance and failure to fulfill fiduciary duties in light of climate change risks and opportunities
- Professional liability associated with implementation of new technologies
- Contract performance in carbon-offset or energy production/saving projects; carbon credit nondelivery
- False advertising (greenwashing)
- Disinformation/fraud (Figure 20)
- Inadequate fiduciary responsibility (investment choices)
- Worsening roadway risks affecting vehicle liability losses

Insurers have been assuming certain risks in this domain (e.g. under pollution liability covers) for which they are neither collecting adequate underwriting information or premiums, or having adequate surplus. Meanwhile, professionals working in this sphere need to be attentive to changing standards of care, as new data, methodologies, and technologies become the norm. * * *

Carbon Capture and Storage: The Billion-ton Coverage Gap

Carbon capture and storage (CCS) is one of the most heralded—and unproven—techniques for responding to climate change. The intriguing process involves capturing carbon dioxide at the point of combustion (currently conceived only for large stationary combustion locations) and injecting the material into geological formations beneath the surface of the Earth, where it is hoped to remain indefinitely. The somewhat Orwellian term "clean coal" often has been offered in the context of the prospective use of CCS with coal-fired electric power plants. In reality, non-CO_2 emissions are still released along greenhouse gas emissions such as methane associated with the precombustion phase of the fuel-cycle. This, combined with postcombustion toxic fly ash (such as that contained in an accidental release of 1 billion gallons of slurry in Tennessee—100-times the size of the notorious Exxon Valdez disaster—in the closing days of 2008), contributes to what some refer to as "The Myth of Clean Coal." CCS is thus not a panacea for the environmental impacts of energy use, but does promise to manage one of the key greenhouse gas pollutants.

The technological enthusiasm for this approach—and the societal imperative to better manage greenhouse gas emissions—has thus far eclipsed the effort spent on technical and financial risk assessment. One insurer noted that "the public dialogue to date has focused on the technology and has not yet focused on the business risk models in a disciplined way because not all the correct stakeholders are at the table" and expressed concern that subsidies and public indemnity of CCS projects could mask or even magnify CCS risks, while creating complacency and moral hazard.

An executive from Duke Energy recently stated that "utilities would be foolish to build large CCS facilities without having assurance that they would not be liable for damages if the CO_2 leaks out". The insurance risks of CCS range from generic considerations pertaining to any technological system (construction, property, machinery breakdown, business interruption, general liability, credit risk, etc.) to a host of risks specific to the technology. These include unintended environmental impacts such as the contamination of drinking water or injury or death to humans or animals if the captured gas leaks in sufficient quantities, as well as engineering risks such as vapor cloud explosion (VCE) or catastrophic failure of the cryogenic air separation unit (ASU). CCS projects would have a particularly complex lifecycle, including political, financial and regulatory risks before project start-up; site identification/development; at the point of capture; during carbon transport; during the siting and sequestration process; during closure of injection points; and during the stewardship period.

Containment will have to span centuries, which presents long-term risks that private insurers would presumably prefer to defer to governments (similar to the insurance provided by governments for nuclear power plants). As part of the business proposition of CCS is to capture "carbon credits" for CO_2 not released to the atmosphere, the same performance and liability risks apply to CCS as discussed elsewhere in this report for other strategies for trimming emissions. * * *

The Intrinsic Role of Regulators

Insurance regulators have two overarching and interrelated goals: to maintain the availability and affordability of insurance for customers, and to guard against insurer insolvency. While there are many appropriate roles for regulators in climate change vulnerability assessment, we focus here on their role in enabling the types of traditional and innovative responses described in this report.

Regulators have a responsibility to see that rates are adequate and that state-operated insurance pools have sufficient capacity to pay losses. In a changing climate this will, among other things, require consideration of the ability of catastrophe models to account for climate change. Where insurers desire to provide differentiated premiums or financial incentives to encourage risk-reducing behavior, it is often necessary to demonstrate to regulators that there will be an offsetting reduction in losses. * * *

It is thus important that concerned insurance regulators review existing rules and policies, identifying potential barriers and providing more flexibility for "doing the right thing." Similarly, they should play an active role in ensuring the validity of insurer climate initiatives. One example would be to review the quality of carbon offsets offered to customers, or purchased for in-house use. The quality and completeness of carbon accounting by insurers (and most other industries) is very uneven; regulators might play a role in improving the procedures used.

Requests or requirements to undertake the sorts of innovative strategies outlined in this report could originate from the insurance regulators. For example, regulators could call for separate rating of hybrid vehicles, keep track of loss experience, and ultimately utilize the results to propose differential treatment of customers owning these cars. Regulators also can call for more complete disclosure of climate risks, both in the core business of insurance underwriting as well as in the selection of weather-sensitive investments that could affect their solvency. * * *

PROBLEM EXERCISE ON CLIMATE RISK

Assume that ski resorts in Colorado can no longer operate on their normal schedule because there is no longer enough snow falling on their slopes and there is insufficient water to make snow. What claims might they bring against others for the harms? Must insurers provide a legal defense? Are they liable for any damages? What about claims by fishers against industrialized nations because species they harvested are no longer present due to warmer ocean temperatures, or claims by Alaskan natives filing against automobile manufacturers and energy companies alleging that global warming due to CO_2 emissions have reduced ice floes making hunting more dangerous, and is melting permafrost rendering their villages uninhabitable?

INDEX INSURANCE AND CLIMATE RISK: PROSPECTS FOR DEVELOPMENT AND DISASTER MANAGEMENT

Molly E. Hellmuth, Daniel E. Osgood, Ulrich Hess, Anne Moorhead and Haresh Bhojwani, eds., Policy Brief Climate and Society No. 2. International Research Institute for Climate and Society (IRI) (2009)
http://iri.columbia.edu/csp/issue2

The climate has always presented a challenge to those whose livelihoods depend on it. Moving away from such dependence is usually an early step in economic development, but many millions have not yet succeeded in taking that step. As climate variability and uncertainty increase with climate change, human development reversals are a distinct possibility. Climate has thus become an urgent issue on the development agenda.

For poor people, a variable and unpredictable climate presents a risk that can critically restrict options and so limit development. The risk materializes at two levels: the direct effects of a weather shock, and the indirect effects due to the threat of a weather shock (whether it occurs or not). When a weather shock occurs, poor people are vulnerable. Local coping strategies often break down. Poor people have few assets to fall back on, and may be forced to sell these in order to survive so that when the crisis is over they are in a much worse position than before. These impacts can last for years in the form of diminished productive capacity and weakened livelihoods. And climate change threatens both more frequent and more severe extreme events.

Under the threat of a possible weather shock, poor people avoid taking risks. They shun innovations that could increase productivity, since these innovations may increase their vulnerability, for example by exhausting the assets they would need to survive a crisis or by requiring them to spend money without being sure of a return. Creditors are unlikely to lend to farmers if drought (for example) might result in widespread defaults, even if loans can be paid back easily in most years. This lack of access to credit critically restricts access to agricultural inputs and technologies, such as improved seeds and fertilizers. Even though a drought (or a flood, or a hurricane) may happen only one year in five or six, the threat of the disaster is enough to block economic vitality, growth and wealth generation in all years—good or bad.

Poverty limits the capacity of people to manage weather risks, while these same risks contribute to keeping people poor. Climate change will greatly exacerbate this situation; and developing countries, which are least responsible for climate change, face its greatest impacts. New tools are urgently needed to help vulnerable people deal with climate change, and the uncertainty that accompanies this.

It is not only the poor who need such tools. After a climate-related disaster, governments struggle to finance relief and recovery efforts and maintain essential government services. Disaster response can be delayed for several months as humanitarian aid trickles in, which results in even higher human and economic costs.

Risk transfer approaches such as insurance have played a role in mitigating climate risk in many parts of the world. However, they have generally not been available in developing countries, where insurance markets are limited if they exist at all, and are not oriented towards the poor. A new type of insurance–index insurance–offers new opportunities for managing climate risk in developing countries. If designed and introduced carefully, it has the potential to contribute significantly to sustainable development, by addressing a gap in the existing climate risk management portfolio. However, this potential has yet to be proven; and there are some significant challenges that must first be addressed.

Index insurance can be applied across a diverse range of weather-related risk problems, from loss of crops due to drought, to loss of livestock in harsh winter conditions, to losses resulting from hurricanes. It can be purchased at different levels of society – at 'micro-level' by small-scale farmers, at 'meso-level' by input suppliers or banks, or at 'macro-level' by governments, for example. It is not a 'cure-all' and will be inappropriate in many situations; but it may be a useful option in many others. As awareness and knowledge of this new tool increase, and if the challenges described in this publication can be overcome, index insurance could become widely available as an additional option for those facing a weather risk.

The introduction of index insurance can bring together a new set of actors and new resources to address some of the more persistent problems associated with poverty. It also reflects a growing interest in, and a move towards, market-driven solutions to these problems. Shifting responsibilities from public agencies, which 'provide' interventions to 'beneficiaries', to market-based mechanisms where people choose the services and technologies they prefer, may offer the poor a more sustainable development model. Public–private partnerships and private-sector development are key to this approach, which must ultimately deliver what customers demand. * * *

A brief introduction to index insurance. Index insurance is insurance that is linked to an index, such as rainfall, temperature, humidity or crop yields, rather than actual loss. This approach solves some of the problems that limit the application of traditional crop insurance in rural parts of developing countries. One key advantage is that the transaction costs are lower. In theory at least, this makes index insurance financially viable for private-sector insurers and affordable to small farmers. Another important advantage is that index insurance is subject to less adverse selection and moral hazard than traditional insurance.[1]

An example of index insurance, and the most common application in developing countries so far, is the use of an index of rainfall totals to insure against drought-related crop loss. Payouts occur when rainfall totals over an agreed period are below an agreed threshold that can be expected to result in crop loss. Unlike with traditional crop insurance, the insurance company does not need to visit farmers' fields to assess losses and determine payouts. Instead, it uses data from rain gauges near the farmer's field. If these data show the rainfall amount is below the threshold, the insurance pays out.

As well as reducing costs, this means that payouts can be made quickly—a feature that reduces or avoids distress sales of assets. * * *

Rapid payouts are the major advantage of index insurance when this is used as a disaster management tool. Again, time-consuming loss assessments are not needed, as payouts are based on objective data. With index insurance in place, governments and relief agencies can plan ahead of crises, knowing that funds will be available when they need them. Planning is also facilitated because governments and relief agencies can track the index and prepare an early response.

But several critical components need careful attention if index insurance is to be workable. Index insurance is new, and can be difficult for stakeholders to understand—time and resources must be invested in explaining how it works. It depends on the availability and reliability of quality data, which is a significant challenge in most developing countries. But perhaps most importantly, index insurance is vulnerable to basis risk. Simply put, basis risk is when insurance payouts do not match actual losses—either there are losses but no payout, or a payout is triggered even though there are no losses. Obviously, if either of these situations occurs too frequently, the insurance scheme will not be viable, and may even damage livelihoods. The contract design, and in particular the selection of an appropriate index, is crucially important in minimizing basis risk. Other factors that have implications for basis risk are proximity Index insurance, development and disaster management of the insured crop to a weather station, and availability of climate data.

---

[1] Adverse selection occurs when potential borrowers or insurees have hidden information about their risk exposure that is not available to the lender or insurer, who then becomes more likely to erroneously assess the risk of the borrower or insuree. Moral hazard occurs when individuals engage in hidden activities that increase their exposure to risk as a result of borrowing or purchasing insurance. These hidden activities can leave the lender or insurer exposed to higher levels of risk than had been anticipated when interest or premium rates were established. uses objective, publicly available data, so individuals are unable to distort a situation to their benefit.

The potential of index insurance has been demonstrated by a number of projects in various developing countries. * * * Index insurance is just one of a number of related index-based financial risk transfer products that work on the same principles. * * * [T]he term index insurance is used loosely to include the range of products. * * *

Index insurance for disaster management. Several pilot projects have been exploring the use of index insurance as part of the disaster risk management portfolios of governments and relief agencies. Disaster risk reduction emphasizes preparedness ahead of disasters, in order to limit the lives, livelihoods and assets lost. Governments and relief agencies, which usually bear the costs of responding to large-scale disasters, have taken out insurance policies linked to weather indices that will pay out when extreme weather events precipitate a disaster. The key advantages are the speed of payout, which allows rapid response; and the ability to plan ahead of a disaster, in the knowledge that funds will be available when they are needed.

As in the case of index insurance products designed for development, integrating index insurance into disaster management strategies can help poor people whose livelihoods are closely linked to the weather and who are at risk of falling into poverty traps if a weather shock occurs. Such people have assets – animals or farming equipment, for example – but may be forced to sell them to survive a crisis, and then find themselves without the means to earn a living once the crisis is over. Here, insurance is designed to enable prompt disaster response, allowing people to hold on to their assets and quickly recover after the crisis. * * *

Climate change and index insurance. There is much debate about the implications of climate change for index insurance, centered around the following three questions. Can index insurance contribute to adaptation strategies in developing countries? Can it play a role in managing the uncertainty associated with climate change? And does climate change challenge the viability of index-based insurance products?

There are at least three ways in which index insurance might help build adaptive capacity: as a risk transfer mechanism within a comprehensive strategy for managing climate risk in the face of climate change; as a mechanism to help people access the resources needed to escape climate-related poverty; and as a mechanism to incentivize risk reduction.

A comprehensive strategy for adaptation in the agricultural sector, for example, could include adapted crop varieties, microirrigation, rainwater harvesting and improved soil conservation practices. However, a certain amount of risk would remain—and this remaining risk might be covered by index insurance.

The second way index insurance can contribute to adaptation is through building more resilient livelihoods by enabling access to increased credit, technology and inputs. Insured loans allow lenders to recuperate their money even in a year where the climate causes production losses. The loans allow people to invest in more intensive livelihood strategies which may help them to escape poverty traps. The increase in wealth and in economic resilience allows people to buffer themselves from the direct impacts of the climate.

Beyond this, a key challenge in designing insurance in the face of climate change is to incentivize risk reduction through price signals and risk management stipulations. For example, contracts could stipulate that certain risk reduction mechanisms, such as the adoption of wind-resistant cropping patterns or drought-tolerant crop varieties, must be in place if crops are to be covered. In Ethiopia, a pilot project is testing a scheme in which cash-constrained farmers pay for insurance premiums through their labor on community assets which reduce risk, such as water-harvesting structures. The cost of the premiums in this project contains a component that is a price signal to reflect long-term trends. * * *

The climate variations experienced over the next few decades will include variations due to increasing greenhouse gases, but also variations arising from natural processes within climate systems. With the world's climate scientists largely focusing on the former, the latter are currently little understood. Yet these internal components are likely to have at least as much impact on the climate over the coming decades as increased emissions. This realization is leading to increased efforts to understand these decadal processes. * * *

Next steps * * *. Most projects involving index insurance have so far been small-scale, with two notable exceptions in India and Mexico, which have successfully scaled up. The projects have tested the use of index insurance in a range of applications and for different groups, from supporting poor farmers in their efforts to protect and enhance their livelihoods to helping governments or relief agencies manage climate-related crises. It is still an open question whether index insurance can contribute significantly to sustainable development and to disaster management. If it is to do so, it will need to scale up to reach very many more people. * * *

Many are advocating scale-up as the next stage—but this must be accompanied by a caution. We do not yet fully understand the behavioral responses to index insurance, or the impacts it may ultimately have. * * *

There is also a danger that eagerness to see benefits from index insurance may cause pilots to be scaled up too rapidly, before appropriate methodologies have been developed or before supporting markets and systems can be strengthened. * * * [T]ime and resources must be invested in capacity building at the local level. It will be important to strengthen the innovation system as a whole, so that index insurance can play its part in a robust portfolio of responses to climate risk that include a range of management options. * * *

Identifying and quantifying the risk. At the core of contract design is determining what risks should be addressed and how these might be addressed through an index. The contract design question is not how to cover every risk, but which risks can best be covered using this financial tool, and when this tool is more cost-effective than other options for managing a particular risk.

The 'right' risk that index insurance can address is one that is an important livelihood constraint, is not adequately addressed through other options, and can be closely correlated with an index that can be reliably measured. It is important to remember that there are many risks that cannot be addressed through index insurance. Also, the insurance must respond to customer needs and demands.

Scaling up index insurance: Legal and regulatory issues

Often legal and regulatory frameworks must be developed or improved so that they address the new issues raised by the introduction of index insurance. The International Association of Insurance Supervisors (IAIS) has yet to produce guidance on how insurance laws, regulations and practices may need to be adapted to ensure that index-based insurance is regulated and supervised in accordance with international standards. However, a number of pilot projects have shown that index insurance can fit within existing national legal and regulatory frameworks while at the same time adhering to the basic principles underlying international standards. Regulators are generally supportive of efforts to develop index insurance once properly informed about its potential social benefits. * * *

One significant regulatory issue is whether index products should be classified as derivatives or insurance. Insurance contracts are intended to cover losses, whereas derivatives are purely finance market contracts. Derivatives are financial instruments whose values are derived from the value of something else (known as the underlying value). The underlying value can be an asset, an index (e.g. interest rates or exchange rates), weather conditions or other items. The option taken depends on the application.

For programs aiming at development, insurance is the preferred classification as it is simpler to regulate. This is because the regulatory framework for insurance is well suited to protect the interests of a large number of smaller clients, with regulations focused not only on honoring contracts, but also guaranteeing protection against losses. It is also a widely accepted financial instrument, often with existing delivery chains that currently reach intended clients.

Derivatives are more common as negotiated deals between two large entities, each with a substantial capacity for analysis. Because of this, disaster relief contracts are typically transacted as derivatives.

The laws of most countries require that, to be considered insurance, a risk transfer product must have certain key characteristics. The two characteristics that offer the greatest challenge for an index-based product are: (i) an insurance contract must indemnify or compensate the insured for loss sustained due to the occurrence of the insured risk; and (ii) the insured must have an insurable interest in the subject insured. If the index is a sufficiently good proxy for the loss, there is a clear link between loss and payout and the first condition can be satisfied. Although there may be some basis risk, this is also the case for traditional insurance products, even where the loss is assessed by a loss adjuster. In some cases, framing the index insurance product as a form of business interruption insurance also eases the regulator's concerns about basis risk, by allowing the insurance to target risks it can cover more transparently. The second condition is less of a challenge when products are developed with exposed users in mind as it is relatively easy to make the case that the insured has an insurable interest. In some cases, limits may be needed on the sum insured, so as to ease the regulator's concerns that users might take on larger financial commitments due to the availability of insurance and thereby increase their risk exposure rather than reduce it. The second condition can make it challenging to offer insurance to laborers or merchants who do not own cropland but who are impacted by the crop losses of others.

Regulators should be involved from the beginning of the product development process, as specific aspects of the contract design may determine whether or not it meets regulatory conditions. Likewise, if contingent capital is required, potential reinsurers should be involved in contract design to make sure that the risk can be transferred into reinsurance markets. * * *

Index insurance can help vulnerable populations better manage climate risk, and could be a useful strategy for climate change adaptation. Index insurance should be investigated as an adaptation strategy. Whether it targets development or disaster management, index insurance is designed to help vulnerable people, communities or governments manage climate risk. The scale-up seen in India and in Mexico shows that this tool can indeed play this role, alongside other risk management options.

As a climate change adaptation tool, index insurance has three potential uses. It can work as a risk transfer mechanism within a comprehensive strategy for managing climate risk in the face of climate change; as a mechanism to help people access the resources needed to escape climate-related poverty; and as a mechanism to incentivize risk reduction. However, the uncertainty linked to climate change threatens the affordability of premiums. The challenge is to accommodate the added uncertainty due to climate change while keeping premiums affordable. * * *

Strict regulation is an important element in avoiding abuses and building trust. As such, it is vital to have a robust regulatory system in place before scaling up is attempted. Regulators must be actively involved in developing the market for index insurance, making sure that products, and the ways in which they are managed, are fair to both buyers and sellers. Because payouts are not necessarily correlated with actual losses, a robust regulatory system is needed to mitigate the legal and other risks that can emerge with the introduction of index insurance. * * *

Capacity-building for regulators is a critical investment, needed at an early stage of a country's involvement in index insurance. Experiences in several projects – Malawi, Mongolia, Ukraine – showed that regulators need time to gain familiarity with index insurance before they are in a position to approve its promotion on the open market. Policies and regulations may need to be fine-tuned to accommodate this new kind of product and barriers to its introduction lifted. * * *

Insurance and the Climate Change Negotiations

Insurance is mentioned as a CRM tool in the 1992 UNFCCC (Article 3.14), the 1997 Kyoto Protocol (Article 4.8), and the 2007 Bali Action Plan (adopted at COP13). The Bali Action Plan calls for "consideration of risk sharing and transfer mechanisms, such as insurance" to address loss and damage in developing countries particularly vulnerable to climate change (Decision -/CP.13, Bali Action Plan). * * *

CLIMATE RISK MANAGEMENT MECHANISM
Munich Climate Insurance Initiative (MCII)
www.climate-insurance.org (2009)

Preventing or minimizing losses is the bedrock of effective risk management. Insurance activities must be viewed as part of a climate risk management strategy that includes, first and foremost, activities that prevent human and economic losses from climate variability and extremes. The proposed Prevention Pillar links carefully designed insurance instruments to risk reduction efforts. Progress in prevention helps countries qualify for participation in the Insurance Pillar. The estimated cost is 3 billion dollars per year, but does depend on the number of countries involved and the scope of prevention and risk reduction activities.

Insurance Pillar

In spite of best efforts to prevent and reduce risk, countries will face rising medium and high level climate-related risks. MCII proposes an Insurance Pillar with two tiers to deal with these. The figure below illustrates the two tiers of the proposed insurance pillar.

A two-tiered insurance pillar as part of a Climate Risk Management Mechanism

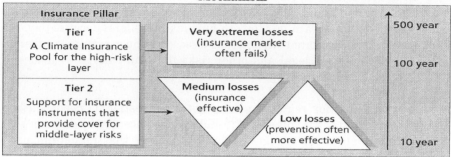

Climate Insurance Pool

Even with the best prevention and risk reduction activities, the increasing number and intensity of major weather catastrophes will affect countries. To address these, a Climate Insurance Pool will absorb a pre-defined proportion of high-level risks of disaster losses, particularly in vulnerable countries, at no cost to the beneficiary countries. The Climate Insurance Pool will be reinsured against extreme loss years in the global reinsurance market. The Climate Insurance Pool would require financial resources of approximately between USD 3.2 billion and USD 5.1 billion, in case of an assumption of a 30% attribution of global warming to weather related losses and depending on annual indemnification limits set at US$ 10 billion (15 year return period) or US$ 50 billion (100 year return period). The key features of the Climate Insurance Pool include:

- CIP Premium Paying Entities: The CIP receives a fixed annual allocation from a multilateral adaptation fund based on the expected climate change related losses. This fund will fully cover the premium payments (some recent proposals are based on criteria such as capability ("ability to pay") and responsibility ("polluter pays").
- Beneficiaries of CIP Coverage: Countries that participate in the insurance program that fall victim to rare but extreme climate-related disasters that go beyond their capacity to respond and recover;
- Risk Carrier: CIP operations will be managed by a dedicated professional insurance team that will be responsible for risk pricing, loss evaluation and indemnity payments, as well as placing reinsurance.

Negotiators considering the creation of a Climate Insurance Pool might ask: Why invest adaptation funds in a CIP when we could, instead, allocate these same funds to national adaptation programs that include an insurance mechanism? One answer: Disbursing a portion of climate adaptation funds to the CIP pools the risks of extraordinary losses, costing far less money or requiring far less reinsurance than if each country created its own fund or made individual insurance arrangements.

Climate Insurance Assistance Facility

At medium levels of risk—events such as a 1 in 50 year event—a Climate Insurance Assistance Facility, will incentivize the private sector to engage in insurance and public-private solutions. Tier Climate Insurance Assistance Facility addresses middle-layer risks to enable public/private insurance systems for vulnerable communities. Many examples of programs for these middle-layer risks exist: micro-insurance for agriculture (like in Malawi), reinsurance for aid agencies (as in Ethiopia), and pooled solutions for countries in certain regions (like the Caribbean). Each of these initiatives was made possible with outside technical and financial support. The Climate Insurance Assistance Facility could directly enable the poor to participate, if deemed appropriate, through targeted support and minimally- distorting subsidies that would not crowd out private incentives for wider market segments. Regional centers can help build the market capacity for different kind of safety nets as well as for new markets for climate related insurance including micro- insurance. The estimated cost for a Climate Insurance Assistance Facility is 2 billion dollars per year.

PROBLEM EXERCISES

1. Global Economic Reform. The New "Bretton Woods" Negotiations, The Group of 20, has begun a discussion about how to reform the international organizations that manage the world's economic relations. Some of these bodies, such as the International Bank for Settlements in Basle, Switzerland, are essentially private enterprises. Some are creations of the period immediately after the Second World War, before the colonies became independent nations. Some have a powerful, but narrowly focused mandate to promote and maintain free trade concepts, such as the World Trade Organization (WTO). Some, like the International Tropical Timber Organizations (ITTO) or Organization of Petroleum Exporting Countries (OPEC) are mandated to manage commodity stocks to maintain price stability and flow. The so-called International Energy Organizations was launched by the Organization of Economic Cooperation and Development (OECD) to ensure a stable flow of oil that was affordable to western economies.

Governments assign to International Financial Institutions, such as the World Bank or the Asian Development Bank, duties to help build economic growth. Under the United Nations, the regional economic commissions, have built cooperation among the governments in their respective regions.

Nations not included in the G-20 have taken to the United Nations General Assembly the issue of whether all nations should have a hand in the design of any new post-Bretton Woods institutions. Both these UN debates, and the G-20 discussions are outside of the Bali Action Plan and vice versa. How can the reform of the financial economy and its hydrocarbon foundation, take into account the economy of nature and the need to eliminate greenhouse gases and stabilize the Earth's carbon cycle?

2. Tax Reform. Should governments around the world agree on a standard carbon tax, to neutralize any competitive impact such a tax could have on its manufacturing and commercial trading sectors. Would a nation ever yield its power to tax to such an international agreement? Would a transfer tax for hydrocarbons shipped across borders be more palatable politically?

3. Corporate Law. Has the climate crisis gone to such an extreme that routine concepts of fiduciary duties or disclosure laws are too ineffective to change patterns of greenhouse gas releases. Should the basic corporation law in each jurisdiction be amended to require that companies eliminate their greenhouse gases as a condition of doing business.

4. Insurance Law. Munich Re, working with the German international aid agency GTZ, and an Indonesian insurer, Asurasi Wahana Tata, have developed a micro-insurance instruments for areas of Jakarta, Indonesia, that are subject to repeated flooding. J. Aglionby, "Munich Re Pilots Jakarta Flood Policy, " Financial Times, p. 15, col. 2 (May 4, 2009). With the exception of the developed nations, most of the world has no casualty insurance sector. With climate related risks growing, how can a global insurance system be developed, appropriate to each country's socio-economic conditions? What steps governments take to make climate change risk management insurance widely available?

5. Private Law Firm Climate Change Practice Groups. Lawyers representing companies and banks and real estate interests face new challenges and issues of professional responsibility in addressing their clients' client change needs. Do they also face ethical issues? Can a firm defend the continuation of major greenhouse gas emissions, consistent with the firm's professional responsibility obligations to the client and civic duties to the environment and society?

E. MORE FUNDAMENTAL CORPORATE LAW REFORM: UNREALISTIC OR ESSENTIAL?

Insurance is provided by limited liability companies, corporations. They are part of the financial sector. They are usually closely regulated. Are these companies a model for the sort of corporation that will be needed during an era of climate change?

How do we distinguish a company that is serves social and economic needs, and one that does not? Can we? Are the traditional tools for corporate and securities regulation, developed in the 1930s, adequate for the task of making the company everywhere a leader in climate change mitigation and adaptation? Cannot a company's CEO simply find that any "extra" work on mitigation or adaptation is *ultra vires* and would hurt shareholders' economic interests? Consider the issues that a legislature must consider in determining how much support to give to companies that resist becoming carbon neutral in their operations. As an attorney advising a corporate board of directors on their company's climate change responsibilities, how would you respond to the six reforms proposed by Gus Speth in the next excerpt?

THE BRIDGE AT THE EDGE OF THE WORLD: CAPITALISM, THE ENVIRONMENT, AND CROSSING FROM CRISIS TO SUSTAINABILITY

J. Gustave Speth (2008)

Corporations are the principal actors on capitalism's stage. They are capitalism's most important institutions, perhaps the most important institutions of our time. If capitalism is a growth machine, corporations are doing the growing. If growth is destroying the environment, then corporations are doing most of the destroying. In the United States, growth and capitalism have few critics. But corporations, in contrast, are fair game. They have been in the crosshairs of social critics for generations, and for good reason.

Of course, there is a positive side. Corporations also do tremendous good in the world. They made my TiVo; built my hybrid cars and the photovoltaic energy system I purchased, keep me more or less informed, do my banking, and make my blood pressure medication. I am grateful for all of these, and much more. And today there's a lot of genuine corporate greening going on. In 1970 I would not have recommended a career in business to students concerned about the environment; I do that often now. But still, in a world where the environment is in as much trouble as today's and corporations are such a dominant force, something major must be done.

THE MODERN CORPORATION

The modern corporation is a relatively recent invention, dating from the mid-nineteenth century, but its rise has been rapid. Corporations comprise only about 20 percent of U.S. firms; most businesses are proprietorships and partnerships. But the corporate sector accounts for 85 percent of U.S. business revenue. On a global scale, the thousand largest corporations produce about 80 percent of the world's output. The corporation has several defining characteristics that dramatically affect its behavior:

1. The separation of ownership from management. Shareholders own the corporation, but it is managed by the company's directors and the officers

they hire. Adam Smith warned long ago that the directors "being managers of other people's money...cannot well be expected [to] watch over it with the same anxious vigilance they would their own money."

2. Limited liability. Unlike proprietorships and partnerships, corporate owners can lose their investment, but that's all. Corporate owners, the shareholders, are not personally liable to the firm's creditors. Limited liability is one reason corporations must be chartered by some government authority—states in the United States—and the chartering authority has the right to supervise and regulate the corporations, though this is rarely done in practice.

3. Personhood. The story of how corporations became people enjoying the protection of constitutional provisions intended to guarantee rights to individuals is fascinating. In the 1886 Supreme Court case of *Santa Clara County v. Southern Pacific Railroad*, the chief justice merely said from the bench during oral argument that Southern Pacific was entitled to the protection of the Fourteenth Amendment. This comment, irrelevant to the Court's disposition of the case, made it into the clerk's notes on the case, not the decision itself, and the rest is history. And the history continues: In June 2007, the Supreme Court struck down a provision of the 2002 McCain-Feingold campaign finance law, one restricting political ads, on the ground that it violated a corporation's First Amendment rights. And in February 2007, the Supreme Court threw out a jury verdict against a cigarette manufacturer on the grounds that the punitive damages award violated the company's constitutional right to due process.

4. The "best interest of the corporation" principle. This principle, a key part of corporate law, states that directors and managers have a duty to act in the best interest of the corporation, which has been interpreted as a duty to maximize the wealth of shareholders. This principle—shareholder primacy—is a huge obstacle to corporate evolution toward a more socially responsible institution. Joel Bakan, in his book *The Corporation*, explains the result: "A corporation can do good only to help itself do well, a profound limit on just how much good it can do.... The people who run corporations are, for the most part, good people, moral people. They are mothers and fathers, lovers and friends, and upstanding citizens in their communities....Despite their personal qualities and ambitions...their duty as corporate executives is clear: they must always put their corporation's best interests first and not act out of concern for anyone or anything else (unless the expression of such concern can somehow be justified as advancing the corporation's own interests)."

5. Externalization of costs. We explored earlier the corporation's powerful drive to maximize profits in a capitalist system; a drive we now see has legal backing as well, in the principle just discussed. Bakan describes how this drive makes the corporation into an externalizing machine: "Nothing in its legal makeup limits what it can do to others in pursuit of its selfish ends, and it is compelled to cause harm when the benefits of doing so outweigh the costs. Only pragmatic concern for its own interests and the laws of the land constrain the corporation's predatory instincts, and often that is not enough

to stop it from destroying lives, damaging communities, and endangering the planet as a whole....All the bad things that happen to people and the environment as a result of corporations' relentless and legally compelled pursuit of self-interest are...neatly categorized by economists as externalities—literally, other people's problems....[I]t is no exaggeration to say that the corporation's built-in compulsion to externalize its costs is at the root of many of the world's social and environmental ills. That makes the corporation a profoundly dangerous institution."

Another prominent feature of corporate capitalism is the limits it places on democratic control. Everyone knows there is a tug of war between corporate power and citizen power, and in the day-to-day world of politics, it is generally not an equal match. First, business leaders can exert great power directly in the political process—through lobbying, campaign contributions, and in other ways. In 1968 there were fewer than a thousand lobbyists in Washington. Today there are about thirty-five thousand. Corporate political action committee (PAC) spending increased almost fifteenfold over the past three decades, from fifteen million dollars in 1974 to $222 million in 2005. Of the one hundred largest lobbying efforts in Washington between 1998 and 2004, ninety-two were corporations and their trade associations. The U.S. Chamber of Commerce was the largest.

Second, corporations can shape public opinion and the policy debate. Business owns the media, and even public broadcasting depends significantly on corporate donations. Expensive issue advertising, support for business-oriented think tanks, well-funded studies, and policy entrepreneurs are all tools of the trade. Business leaders sit on nonprofit boards and contribute to their fundraising efforts. Business supports university and other research. Its influence can be strong or subtle, but it is there.

Third, there is economic power. Labor can strike, but so can capital. It can leave an area or refuse to invest there if the "business climate" is not right. As long as regions and nations are hell-bent on attracting investment and growth, and competing with each other, corporate interests will be served.

Last, there is an asymmetry in access to information. It is often in the corporation's interest to hold back information that the government and the public can obtain only with difficulty, if at all.

As a result, corporations are not merely the dominant economic actors, they are the dominant political actors as well. William Domhoff is now into the fifth edition of his well-known and provocative book *Who Rules America?* His answer to his title's question: the corporate community. His analysis shows how "the owners and top-level managers in large companies work together to maintain themselves as the core of the dominant power group....[Despite] highly visible policy conflicts among rival corporate leaders...the corporate community is cohesive on the policy issues that affect its general welfare, which is often at stake when political challenges are made by organized workers, liberals, or strong environmentalists."

In Domhoff's view, "The corporate community's ability to transform its economic power into policy influence and political access, along with its capacity to enter into a coalition with middle-class social and religious conservatives, makes it the most important influence on the federal government." He notes that corporate leaders are regularly appointed to top positions in the executive branch and that the policy recommendations of corporate experts are listened to carefully in Congress. "This combination of economic power, policy expertise, and continuing political success makes the corporate owners and executives a dominant class, not in the sense of complete and absolute power, but in the sense that they have the power to shape the economic and political frameworks within which other groups and classes must operate." * * *

CORPORATIONS AND GLOBALIZATION

Many corporations have grown to become giants, and, increasingly, they bestride the narrow world. Of the hundred largest economies in the world, fifty-three are corporations. Exxon alone is larger than more than 180 nations. In 1970 there were seven thousand multinationals; by 2007 there were at least sixty-three thousand. These sixty-three thousand companies directly employ about ninety million people and contribute a quarter of gross world product. They are driving the processes of economic globalization. In 1975 world trade was less than a trillion dollars; by 2000 it was over five trillion dollars. The world stock of foreign direct investment in 1975 was two hundred billion dollars; by 2005 it was over six trillion dollars. In 2006, the thirty members of the OECD made foreign direct investments of more than a trillion dollars. Cross-border mergers and acquisitions have also skyrocketed, reaching over one trillion dollars in 2000. So the global corporation has flown the national coop and has replaced the transnational corporation, just as the global economy has replaced a network of trading national economies. And of course, these multinationals have a huge impact on the global environment, generating, for example, half the gases responsible for global warming. They also control half of the world's oil, gas, and coal mining and refining. Globalization is indeed occurring, but it is the globalization of market failure. Economic globalization and the rise of the global corporation have both increased corporate power and weakened the capacity to control it. One analysis concluded that "with their vast resources and technical capabilities and without the responsibilities of nationhood, the corporation can move quickly when challenge[d] or opportunity strikes. When unfettered by national or international laws, ecological understanding, or social responsibility, this freedom can lead to enormously destructive acts. At the same time, their agility and access to capital and resources allow them to innovate, produce goods and services, and influence the world on a scale and at a speed the world has never seen before."

Much of the recent criticism of corporations has been directed at the multinationals and the globalization process. John Cavanagh, Jerry Mander, and the other authors of *Alternatives to Economic Globalization: A Better World Is Possible* present a sustained critique of the ascendancy of what they call the "corporate globalists." These authors, brought together by the International Forum on Globalization, are the intellectual leaders of what is often called the antiglobalization movement. Agree with them or disagree, they offer a coherent perspective on what is wrong, why the environment is under such threat, and what should be done about it. The antiglobalization movement is thought by some to be confused, self-contradictory, and even anarchistic. My reading of their 2002 book and other writings suggests that they are none of these things. Although I agree with them on many points and disagree on others, I think what they actually are is idealistic, and that's not such a bad thing.

Their assault is aimed squarely at the dominant structures of the modern economy and polity: "Since World War II, the driving forces behind economic globalization have been several hundred global corporations and banks that have increasingly woven webs of production, consumption, finance, and culture across border. * * *

"These corporations have been aided by global bureaucracies that have emerged over the last half-century, with the overall result being a concentration of economic and political power that is increasingly unaccountable to governments, people, or the planet. * * *

"Together these instruments are bringing about the most fundamental redesign of the planet's social, economic, and political arrangements since the Industrial Revolution. They are engineering a power shift of stunning proportions, moving real economic and political power away from national, state, and local governments and communities toward unprecedented centralization of power for global corporations, bankers, and global bureaucracies. * * *

"The first tenet of the globalization design is to give primary importance to the achievement of ever-more rapid, never-ending corporate economic growth—hypergrowth—fueled by the constant search for access to new resources, new and cheaper labor sources, and new markets...To achieve hypergrowth, the emphasis is on the ideological heart of the model—free trade—accompanied by deregulation of corporate activity. The idea is to remove as many impediments as possible to expanded corporate activity."

Environmental deterioration is placed unambiguously at the doorstep of these forces: "Economic globalization is intrinsically harmful to the environment because it is based on ever-increasing consumption, exploitation of resources, and waste disposal problems. One of its primary features, export-oriented production, is especially damaging because it is responsible for increasing global transport activity...while requiring very costly and ecologically damaging new infrastructures such as ports, airports, dams, canals, and so on."

Placing themselves in the camp of the social greens, they argue that not much can be done about negative environmental trends absent far-reaching changes in the way economic and political power is distributed in modern society. The antiglobalization critique, then, is fundamentally political: "The current and future well-being of humanity depends on transforming the relationships of power within and between societies toward more democratic and mutually accountable modes of managing human affairs."

In response they offer a different vision: "The corporate globalists who meet in posh gatherings to chart the course of corporate globalization in the name of private profits, and the citizen movements that organize to thwart them in the name of democracy, are separated by deep differences in values, worldview, and definitions of progress. At times it seems that they must be living in wholly different worlds—which, in fact, in many respects they are. * * *

"Citizen movements see a very different reality. Focused on people and the environment, they see the world in a crisis of such magnitude that it threatens the fabric of civilization and the survival of the species—a world of rapidly growing inequality, erosion of relationships of trust and caring, and failing planetary life support systems. Where corporate globalists see the spread of democracy and vibrant market economies, citizen movements see the power to govern shifting away from people and communities to financial speculators and global corporations replacing democracies of people with democracies of money, replacing self-organizing markets with centrally planned corporate economies, and replacing diverse cultures with cultures of greed and materialism." To address these concerns, the authors of *Alternatives to Economic Globalization* and similar critics are clear that the corporation must be the main object of transformative change: "At the dawn of the twenty-first century, the global corporation stands as the dominant institutional force at the center of human activity and the planet itself. * * * We must dramatically change the publicly traded, limited liability global corporation, just as previous generations set out to eliminate or control the monarchy."

This is a powerful critique of corporate capitalism as we know it. Tone it down, and it is still a powerful critique. And there are many others. What, then, should be done to tame the corporation—to make it an instrument of environmental protection rather than a force for environmental destruction? And what are the prospects for such measures, given the power relationships just reviewed? * * *

CORPORATE GREENING

On the first, voluntary initiatives front, corporations are clearly taking steps to green their operations and products in ways not required by government. Some would say the level of activity is unprecedented, and environmental groups deserve much credit for moving these changes forward. The business press today is crammed with stories * * * The green trend is driven by many factors, but prominent among them is a clear-eyed focus on the bottom line. There are more green consumers today, and green is good for corporate image and brand-name products. The Financial Times reports, "A string of household names—including General Electric, Wal-Mart, and Unilever— have been lining up to show off their green credentials in an effort to woo customers, at least at the high end of the market....The UK's Institute of Grocery Distribution reports that sales of 'ethical' products are increasing by 7.5 percent a year, compared with 4.2 percent for conventional products." *Business Week* in 2007 carried a major story on companies that are "doing well by doing good."

Demand is also growing for new, solution-oriented technologies and products. GE's wind machine business is booming, as is its overall "Ecomagination" line. Daniel Esty and Andrew Winston's 2007 book *Green to Gold* analyzes these developments in detail. They report, "In a world of constrained natural resources and pollution pressures, the business case for environmental stewardship grows stronger every day. * * * Companies that successfully anticipate emerging new directions in public policy and regulatory risk will be ahead of the competition, securing early market share for new products and services and building the institutional know-how required in a changed setting. * * *

Another factor driving change is the emergence of what has been called the "new capitalists." In 1970, a relatively modest number of wealthy individuals controlled corporations. Today, a variety of funds—pension funds, mutual funds, and so on—own more than half of all U.S. stock, up from 19 percent in 1970. These institutional investors seek top returns to be sure, but they have also been increasingly assertive on responsible management and sustainability issues.

Reflecting the trend in business toward embracing the "sustainable enterprise" concept, with its triple bottom line of economy, environment, and society, "corporate social responsibility" has become a catchphrase and CSR an established acronym. CSR can refer to both not-for-profit and for-profit corporate initiatives, provided the for-profit initiatives seem to have a strong social or environmental component. Counted here are the rapidly mounting number of voluntary codes of conduct and product certification schemes operating at both the national and international levels: the Global Reporting Initiative's guidelines for corporate reporting on sustainability; the LEED certification of new green buildings; the Forest Stewardship Council and the Marine Stewardship Council programs for certifying and ecolabeling forest and fish products; the environmental performance principles adopted by major banks; the U.N. Global Compact aimed at promoting good corporate behavior on labor, environmental, and human rights issues; the ISO 14000 program; and numerous others. * * *

The threat of global warming is a key driving force important in all these processes of corporate greening and accounts for a large share of the change occurring. Corporations see the handwriting on the wall, foretelling a future of tough national and international regulation and a wave of new products to meet them. * * * And at least some corporate leaders are aware that a world of unchecked climate change will be very disruptive for their operations.

Corporate greening is thus driven by green consumerism; by lenders, investors, and insurers worried about risks both environmental and financial; by the blame and shame campaigns of NGOs; by existing government regulation and the prospect of future regulation at home and abroad; by sales opportunities opened up by new green products and technology; and by the general need to improve corporate standing as good citizens. In the old days, the model was simple: government regulated, corporations complied. Now there are multiple stakeholder pressures on the corporation. They open up a range of better outcomes beyond simple compliance, including fewer problems requiring regulation, new products for sustainability markets, and better corporate behavior in policy and political arenas.

Encouraging change is thus occurring in the corporate sector today, but how reliable and extensive will these changes be? Two studies of voluntary initiatives and CSR raise doubts regarding their potential. Berkeley business professor David Vogel reaches the following conclusions in his book *The Market for Virtue*: "There are important limits to the market for virtue. The main constraint on the market's ability to increase the supply of corporate virtue is the market itself. There is a business case for CSR, but it is much less important or influential than many proponents...believe. CSR is best understood as a niche rather than a generic strategy: it makes business sense for some firms in some areas under some circumstances * * *

In their recent book *Reality Check*, economists at Resources for the Future assess the results of a long series of voluntary environmental programs in the United States, Europe, and Japan. They conclude that "voluntary programs can affect behavior and offer environmental gains but in a limited way....[N]one of the case study authors found truly convincing evidence of dramatic environmental improvements. Therefore, we find it hard to argue for voluntary programs where there is a clear desire for major change in behavior."

RELIABLY GREEN

It would thus be a mistake to count too heavily on CSR and voluntary initiatives, as both Vogel and the RFF economists have warned, and they are not alone in their skepticism. Much depends on the continued strengthening of the drivers of corporate greening just mentioned. The big gorilla in the room—the main force driving corporate greening in the past and in the future—is government action, actual and anticipated, domestic and foreign. To change corporate dynamics, government action is needed across a wide front. * * * A reliably green company is one that is required to be green by law. Even the best-intentioned manager will avoid actions that are desirable but costly when faced by a competitor lacking a conscience. These environmental regulations and other controls must be promoted at the international level as well as at the national and state levels. * * *

The arena of needed government action also includes an array of worthwhile measures that are not strictly environmental:

1. Revoke corporate charters. Most corporate law statutes contain provisions allowing government to revoke charters if the corporation has grossly violated the public interest. Making this threat alive and real could have very salutary effects. One way to do this would be to require periodic public reviews and rechartering.
2. Exclude or expel unwanted corporations. This tactic has been used extensively in India, for example, by the farmers and consumers who organized the "Monsanto: Quit India" campaign. In the United States there have been campaigns to block Wal-Mart and other giant retailers from various sites.
3. Roll back limited liability. Corporate directors and top managers should be personally liable for gross negligence and other major failings. Eventually, personal liability should extend to shareholders in certain cases. That would make buying a company's stock a rather more serious affair and would make management far more circumspect on environmental, labor, and human rights issues.
4. Eliminate corporate personhood. There is a nascent movement in the United States to do just that. Spurred by local corporate abuses and corporate claims of due process and First Amendment rights, Porter Township, Pennsylvania, and Arcata, California, both passed (largely symbolic) measures aimed at stripping corporations of the legal fiction of personhood and thus their ability to claim constitutional rights intended for people. Short of outright reversal of a long string of Supreme Court decisions, modification of

Supreme Court rulings protecting corporate speech and advertising are over-due.

5. Get corporations out of politics. This can best be done by moving to pub-licly financed elections. The "clean elections" cause is gathering some sup-port. A further step would be to impose tighter restrictions on conflicts of interest by limiting the revolving door between government and corporations and by attending with great care to the process of confirming proposed politi-cal appointees.

6. Reform corporate lobbying. Environmental economist Robert Repetto has urged some important initial steps in this direction. "Should corporate man-agement lobby on public policy issues with broad societal implications, using shareholders' money, with no oversight by shareholders' representatives on the board of directors?" Repetto asks rhetorically in his paper. Repetto notes, "If lobbying on public policy issues is an intrinsic and important aspect of a company's business, then boards of directors, as part of their fiduciary 'duty of care,' have a responsibility to be informed about the company's lobbying activities and positions and to oversee them." He argues in favor of oversight of corporate policy positions and lobbying expenditures by a committee of the corporate board of directors, the majority of whom would be "outside directors with a broad view of the economy and political horizon." * * *

THE CORPORATION OF THE FUTURE

These six points comprise a far-reaching agenda. Others could be added, such as mandating the Securities and Exchange Commission to require a truly sophisticated array of financial and environmental disclosures. Some of the initiatives, like imposing personal liability in certain cases and abolishing corporate personhood, are sufficiently transformative that they could be con-sidered in the third and final category of actions—those that seek to change the nature of the corporation itself. But the major change in the nature of the corporation that is needed now, and that will be essential in the future, is to change the legal mandate that requires the corporation strictly to pursue its own self-interest and to give primacy to maximizing shareholder wealth. The corporation must be, in Bakan's words, "reconstituted to serve, promote, and be accountable to broader domains of society than just themselves and their shareholders."

Allen White of the Tellus Institute believes, correctly I think, that "shareholder primacy is the single greatest obstacle to corporate evolution toward a more equitable, humane and socially beneficial institution." He ar-gues for "fundamental changes to the current privilege accorded capital pro-viders and to the legal, regulatory, and financial market structures that en-able such privilege to persist. The 'gladiatorial culture' that deifies competi-tive advantage, efficiency and, above all, shareholder returns is not a corpo-rate culture that comports with [a sustainable economy and a humane soci-ety]. The behavior it induces and societal consequences it engenders lay at the heart of the low esteem and high distrust in which the public holds the business community."

The corporation of the future, as envisioned by White and others, must be built around the idea that the wealth produced by the corporation is the joint product of all resource providers—shareholders, employees, unions, future generations, government, customers, communities, and suppliers. Each provides resources for wealth creation over time, and each has a right to expect returns for its contribution: "Framing the corporation as the beneficiary of multiple resource providers opens up horizons for transformation that shareholder primacy stifles. In this [new] framework, the diverse parties that contribute their resources to create goods and services are not simply secondary and dispensable contributors to the production process. Instead, they hold rightful claims to both the surplus generated by the firm as well as to accountability from its board and management. They are, in short, equals, not subordinates to capital providers. This reinterpretation of the nature of the corporation has profound implications for governance, charters and securities laws, as well as the means of corporate wealth distribution.

"Whereas scale, growth and profit-maximization were previously viewed as intrinsic goods and core goals of the corporation, the new corporation marches to a whole different set of principles; namely, those serving the public interest, sustainability, equity, participation and respect for the rights of human beings. Corporate forms [should include] a rich pluralism conforming to global norms that [would] govern business conduct regardless of place, sector or scale." White envisions "a multi-tiered structure in the form of global, regional and local agents, norms, and powers that enables the exercise of citizen rights and democratic control over the corporation. The public purpose of the corporation [should ascend] to preeminence, supported by policies, procedures and instruments that bring democratic process to the forefront of corporate governance."

Is such a future realistic? * * * It is sometimes said that there are no good answers to today's challenges. The rich array of options for transformative change presented here and in other chapters indicates otherwise. With the distrust of corporations and the stirrings already visible, motivation for change is building. What we need are opportunities for transformative change. It seems highly likely that such opportunities will come along, given our crisis-prone world and the dynamics that now govern corporate behavior. And of course, that day can be hastened by citizen demand.

Notes and Questions

1. Is consumption a personal choice, beyond the law, or does the legal regime legitimize and sustain a market favorable to consumer consumption beyond what is needed or even affordable? See T. Kasser et al., Materialistic

Values: Their Causes and Consequences, in T. Kasser & A. Kanner, Psychology and Consumer Culture: The Struggle for a Good Life in a Materialistic World (2004). Recall that at the Rio Earth Summit 1992, Agenda 21 made specific recommendations in Chapter 4 on "Changing Consumption Patterns," but governments have largely ignored these proposals. Should they be enacted as law? What does it take to induce us as consumers to consume thoughtfully? Are advertising guidelines needed, along the lines of the curbs on pornography?

2.   If companies, and in particular the banks and other financial institutions, have caused the deep global recession that began in 2007, what reforms in corporate governance should be considered to make such activities less likely in the future? Are existing models of shareholder "democracy" in electing company directors and proposing shareholder policies sufficient for the often deep reforms needed for climate change mitigation and adaptation? Short of averting repeats of the bankruptcies and reorganizations of Chrysler and General Motors, what alternate variant of corporate governance may be needed? See A. White, Transforming the Corporation, Tellus Institute's Great Transformation Initiative (2006), www.gtinitiative.org. How would you revise the Corporations Law of the State where your law school is situated to ensure that corporate governance responds to the public interest in climate change mitigation and adaptation?

3.   *Carbon Neutral Law Schools*: Teach-ins or classes, even degree programs on climate change build knowledge. "Knowledge does not equal action." Chapter 10, p. 245, in A. Rappaport & S. Creighton, Degrees That Matter– Climate Change and the University (2007). Faculty and staff live in a law school for many years, students often for only six semesters. How can student choices and faculty preferences be reconciled? Should campuses invest in audio-video classrooms and use more distance learning tools, rather than move faculty and students to conferences or classrooms that are often far away from the law school? How can computers be powered-off more of the time in law libraries and dorm rooms? Ultimately, is the decision-making about such matters the choice of the company board of directors or the university board of trustees, or is the individual choice of each student and teacher? If your reply is a hybrid answer, is the governance system in companies and law schools up to the tasks ahead? Should student fees and faculty/staff pay be tied to their climate mitigation performance? Your law school's governance system sets these fees or pay scales. Does it consider climate change? Should it?

CHAPTER 9. THE EVOLVING CLIMATE CHANGE LAW PARADIGM

Climatescape: **Moving toward a carbon-neutral economy**

The preceding chapters scope out alternative visions of how law can be marshaled to address climate change mitigation and adaptation. Many governments, such as The Netherlands or Singapore, are quite advanced in retooling their administrative law and other regimes to address climate change. China has taken significant legal steps that promise to effect mitigation and adaptation reforms. The Administration of President Obama has taken significant initial steps, particularly through the initiatives of the "economic stimulus" legislation and spending to address the Great Recession of 2007, and the decisions of the Department of Energy and the U.S. Environmental Protection Agency. The State of Delaware has developed a comprehensive State Energy Plan, designed to make Delaware a carbon-neutral State. The UNFCCC negotiations under the Bali Action Plan call for capacity-building and a roll out of comparable measures among all nations, with national action plans for climate change mitigation and adaptation. In 2007, China launched its first national plan for coping with climate change. In 2008, India and other nations began to frame their first national plans. What common patterns are emerging from these parallel national plans? How do they differ? How can international and national law, and private sector initiatives, make the reforms needed to attain a carbon neutral economy world-wide? Should climate ministries take precedence over ministries of commerce, on a par with the military defense ministries? Or are adaptations with existing governmental systems sufficient?

A. INTRODUCTION

The first decade of this 21st century is a period of extraordinary innovation in governance about the climate. Historically, energy decision-making has been a product of *laissez-faire* markets, tempered by the role of state public service commissions in setting the rates companies may charge consumers of energy since the grids and pipelines constitute a "natural monopoly." As a consequence, releases of greenhouse gases associated from energy consumption are most often the result of local decisions. There has been only minimal governmental institutions and legislation. The regulatory vacuum, which characterized many aspects of the production and use of the energy resources that serve our post-modern economy around the world, meant that there has been no standard practice about managing the demand for energy.

While governments left most decisions about the supply of energy resources to market forces, gradually in the 20th century some regulatory regimes were established. When energy prices increased, public service commissions and other governmental agencies produced innovations in demand-side management and energy efficiency. Tools emerged for adapting such models from one nation to another. See, e.g., R. Ottinger, Drafting Laws on

Energy Efficiency and Renewable Energy Resources (UNEP 2007). Nonetheless, the absence of any traditional government regimes to manage the energy systems has meant that governments at all levels—from local to regional to state or federal and international—find less fertile ground for experimentation exploring how best to supply electricity without releasing greenhouse gases.

Most of the governmental programs relative to energy and the gathering and consumption of fuel and other energy resources were left to the private sector, or to cities and regional governmental authorities. The only international agency explicitly associated with energy was created by the developed nations, through the Organization for Economic Cooperation and Development (OECD) to ensure a supply of oil to market The International Energy Agency (IEA). Within countries, occasionally a nation regulated access to scarce energy sources, such as the siting of facilities for generating hydroelectric power, e.g. Federal Power Act of 1920 and Scenic Hudson Preservation Commission v. FPC, 354 F. 2d 608 (2d Cir. 1965), cert. denied, 384 U.S. 941 (1966), or the routes for natural gas pipelines (e.g. the current role of the Federal Energy Regulatory Commission), or regulated the price charged to link to a grid of wires supplying electricity, which constitute a natural monopoly that could subject consumers to unfair marketing (e.g., the role of public service commissions in the several states of the USA). Most often however, across North America and on other continents, no standard governmental regime for energy has existed. There are few, if any, energy ministries and very little planning to account for how energy would be supplied in future years. As demand for energy resources grew, the market place was left to expand supply to meet demand. Governments gave tax incentives and subsidies to facilitate the search of new energy resources, and made little effort to account for the economic externalities involved. Environmental degradation associated with coal mining has expanded.

The growing public awareness that greenhouse gas releases need to be measured and mitigated, if not entirely eliminated, has stimulated a range of new state and local innovations. Several nations have taken strong leadership positions. Among the fifty states of the United States of America, a rich array of new innovations has appeared, and every state has established laws and policies to address climate change. D. Hodas, State Initiatives, in M. Gerrard, ed., Global Climate Change and U.S. Law (2007). A survey of the "State Response to Climate Change," prepared and annually updated by the Pace University School of Law Center for Environmental Legal Studies, is available through the web site of the ABA Section of Environment, Energy and Resources at www. Abanet.org/abapubs/globalwarming/).

What is needed to move to a carbon-neutral legal system for energy? What combination of policies, laws and techniques provides an optimal energy system in a given jurisdiction? Given differing opinion about how to combat greenhouse gas emissions, and debate over appropriate adaptations toward a carbon-neutral supply of energy, it is rare that all these techniques can be enacted at once. Is it likely that eventually all these elements will be part of a standard model of climate change energy law in each jurisdiction? Is it possible for a jurisdiction to develop a comprehensive energy and climate plan, or are there too many variables and difficulties to do so?

Is it necessary to make quantum leaps forward in energy and climate law? In developing nations and newly booming economies that lack any comprehensive energy law, should the law that is adopted represent a new 21st century model that leap-frogs over old industrial policy, technology, policy, and legal rules and structure? If so, where will examples of new models come from? Conventional approaches, as in the United States, where law is built on the foundational premise that fossil fuels are plentiful and low-cost, support and encourage our carbon-intensive economies. The political scientist, Charles Lindblom, in his essay "The Science of Muddling Through", 19 Pub. Admin. Rev. 79 (1959), makes the analogy to a tree, and contrasts how a "root" method can be employed to make a comprehensive analysis of available options to reach defined objectives, and a "branch" approach makes incremental and gradual steps by small degrees toward objectives. Lindblom suggests that a comprehensive plan or root method may not be possible for complex policy questions. How can the national climate adaptation action plans contemplated under the UN Framework Convention on Climate Change be effective in light of such considerations? Is reform of the energy sector to meet climate objectives susceptible to comprehensive, rooted reforms, or should it best progress in incremental steps? Is "muddling through" the likely and pragmatic approach to climate change law reform? Or do we need a paradigm shift, a new way of thinking about our legal system?

One comprehensive approach toward fashioning a carbon-free state energy program is the 2009 plan prepared for Delaware excerpted next. What laws and policies are proposed in the plan? Why was governance the first recommendation? Does the plan establish a framework for moving to a new paradigm? Does the plan meet its stated goal of identifying what concrete action should be undertaken in the next 5 years so that the state can have a sustainable energy system in 20-30 years? Is sustainable energy the plan's goal? What goals would you set? What would you have done in the next five years to put your nation or state on a path to achieve that goal?

FRAMEWORK FOR ENERGY RESOURCE MANAGEMENT AND TWO ISSUES OF GENERAL APPLICATION
Richard L. Ottinger
UNEP Handbook on Drafting Laws on Energy Efficiency and Renewable Energy Resources (2007)

* * * There are a number of legislative requirements important for environmental management of the energy sector that apply to all energy media, and these are particularly important for promotion of energy efficiency and renewable energy. * * *

1. Disclosure and Public Participation

Consultation by the sponsor of an energy project or by the permitting government agency with the communities that will be affected often is required, as well as with all government agencies that may have responsibilities affecting the project. Community consultation is particularly important to assure that there will be public acceptance and cooperation with the project, especially important if the community will be expected to pay some or all of the costs of the project. Hearings on EAs provide a good vehicle for educating the public and eliciting community concerns.

Meaningful public participation requires access by the public to all information concerning the specifications, benefits and costs of a project. Many jurisdictions have legislative requirements for access to all pertinent information, often through petition to the permitting agency with judicial review of any information denial.

2. Enforcement

The best environmental and safety codes and standards are ineffective if a means of enforcement of them is not provided. Enforcement provisions may include the ability of the relevant agencies to grant, deny or specify conditions for granting permits for the project, to examine the project site during and after construction and to issue stop orders for projects found not to be complying with relevant laws. Provision for citizen suits to challenge allegedly illegal actions are particularly valuable because there often is political pressure to advance projects not meeting requirements that inhibits the relevant government agencies from taking enforcement actions. Allowance of attorney fees and court costs for meritorious citizen suit actions is helpful and can be legislatively provided.

3. Pricing

In jurisdictions where governments own and operate the energy facilities, energy prices are set by the relevant agency. In privatized systems, the relevant companies set their own prices in accordance with market conditions, but often subject to government regulation. In either case, it is important that, in making the decisions an selection of resources, accurate pricing systems be employed.

The pricing regulations discussed in the Handbook include most importantly the removal of subsidies. Subsidies distort the marketplace and make it impossible to make accurate price comparisons among resources. Legislative measures also have been adopted to require life-cycle costing (the cost of a resource over its useful lifetime), Use of life-cycle costing is particularly important for renewable resources like solar, wind and hydro where the initial capital cost tends to be large, but the lack of fuel costs and low maintenance costs make these resources more competitive over their useful life. Inclusion of externality costs (e.g. the costs to society of early deaths and of illnesses and the costs of environmental degradation) also can be mandated. These costs can be large, particularly for coal and oil, and ignoring them also distorts accurate cost comparisons. Some jurisdictions require what is known as "integrated resource planning (IRP)" where the appropriate government agency requires that before resources are acquired, competing resources be evaluated based on the costs and benefits of each, including life-cycle costs and externalities. Under privatization, measures need to be adopted to prevent fraud, collusion, corruption and monopolization.

4. Education and Training

In the introduction of new energy technologies and the regulation of all technologies, legislation providing for the education and training of personnel making energy decisions at all levels needs to be provided. Governments usually provide these services either themselves or by contract with private experts. Sometimes the technology providers ore required to provide education and training for operators and users.

5. Regulatory Frameworks

In some jurisdictions, national, state, government agencies own and operate energy facilities, production, transmission and distribution. In these situations, legislation will be needed to impose environmental, safety, performance and pricing requirements on the relevant agencies. In countries providing for private ownership and operation of energy facilities, there are two principal methodologies for regulation: 1) command and control and 2) market-based regulations. Often a combination of both methodologies is used.

Command and control regulations require that certain energy equipment, performance, safety and environmental conditions be met, subject to penalties for failure to meet them. Examples covered include requirements for EAs, environmental regulations (e.g. providing limits on power plant pollution emissions), miles per gallon specifications for all vehicles sold within a jurisdiction, appliance efficiency standards, lighting standards, motor standards and building efficiency codes.

Market-based provisions covered at the national level include taxes on pollution or carbon emissions (that can account for externalities of polluting fuels), incentives for renewable and efficiency resources, and emission trading "cap and trade" regulations under which a cap is placed on the level of emissions of specified pollutants and each polluting facility is allocated a specified emission allotment; then if a facility lowers its emission of the pollutant below its allocation, it can sell the resulting pollution allowances, or if its emissions exceed its allotment, it can purchase allowances from another facility that has available excess allotments. This cap and trade system permits pollution reductions at lower costs to the emitters.

Usually at the state or municipal level, regulation of electric energy is handled by a statutorily created Utility Regulatory Commission empowered to set rates where utilities are regulated and to set conditions for electricity sales where the utility system has been privatized. Some municipal governments have Energy Commissions that also set local energy policies.

6. Energy Efficiency

More efficient utilization of existing energy resources can save energy and money. The energy savings reduce pollution. Standards have been adopted to achieve significant savings in industrial processes, most significantly through requirements for use of more efficient electric motors and through combined heat and power or cogeneration, utilizing the heat emissions from power plants either to produce additional electricity or for industrial hot water uses and domestic heating purposes; home appliances such as refrigerators, heating boilers, cook stoves and computers; buildings through improved insulation, use of energy-efficient windows, and use of light-colored surfaces that reflect sunlight and heat; and in vehicles through requirements restricting vehicle sales to those achieving greater miles per gallon. Incentives also can be enacted to encourage sales of low-emission vehicles such hybrids propelled in part by electricity. Vehicle manufacturers can receive incentives to do research on new technologies such as hydrogen-propelled vehicles. Car-pooling incentives at factories and office buildings can save substantial energy, as can legislatively required subsidies for worker use of mass transportation and required payments for parking. Legislation to provide restricting specified highway lanes for use only by multi-occupant vehicles is another measure often adopted.

B. THE DELAWARE ENERGY PLAN

DELAWARE ENERGY PLAN 2009-2014
Governor's Energy Advisory Council (David R. Hodas, Chair)
March 26, 2009
http://www.dnrec.delaware.gov/energy/Documents/Energy%20Plan%20Counc il%20report%20-%20Final.pdf

Council Chair's Introduction

In 2003, the Delaware General Assembly recognized the need for a "comprehensive energy policy which will ensure an adequate, reliable and continuous supply of energy...which [protects] public health and the environment and which promotes our general welfare and economic well-being."[25] A little over a year later the General Assembly established the Governor's Energy Advisory Council and charged it, among other things, to update the Delaware Energy Plan every five years.[26] In the spring 2007, the Council began the extensive task of drafting a new plan, building on the 2003 Governor's Energy Task Force Report, *Bright Ideas for Delaware's Energy Future*. The range of issues that needed to be considered included energy costs associated with urban sprawl, the projected effects of climate change on Delaware, an analysis of energy trends in Delaware, the potential to increase energy efficiency and renewable sources of energy, the need for an improved and smarter electricity transmission system, the link between energy policy and economic development, the energy implications of our transportation system, the strengths and weaknesses of current Delaware laws, policies, and programs—and a comparison with the "best practices" developed in other states—and a review of the energy related governance structure in Delaware to identify the opportunities for improved effectiveness.

The goal for the energy plan was to identify where Delaware's energy system should be headed over the next 20 to 30 years, and to identify what can and ought to be done over the next five years to move Delaware in that direction. The process of developing the energy plan was governed by five Guiding Principles that the Council established at the outset:

  • Increasing energy end-use efficiency and conservation
  • Reducing the environmental impacts (footprint) of energy used and generated in Delaware
  • Reducing energy used for transportation
  • Maximizing clean energy economic development opportunities
  • Maintaining and improving the reliability and security of Delaware's energy systems
  • Minimizing energy-related costs and impacts on Delaware citizens

As an important first step, the Council surveyed Delawareans about their priorities in setting Delaware's energy future, with more than a thousand people responding. The results, reported in Appendix C, confirmed the General Assembly's findings in 2003 and guided the Council in setting up five work groups: 1) Reducing Energy Use, 2) Reducing the Environmental Footprint of Energy Used by Delawareans, 3) Reducing Transportation Energy

---

[25] 74 Del. Laws ch. 38 §1 (2003)

[26] 29 Del. C. § 8055.

Use, 4) Ensuring Efficient and Effective Energy Transmission and Distribution systems, and 5) Supporting and Growing Delaware's Clean Energy Businesses. Each work group was comprised of about 20 –30 volunteers and a chair. The groups met monthly, working diligently to evaluate a wide range of data and information, identify specific energy issues, needs, and goals, and finally to develop consensus-based recommendations for the Council to consider. The Council debated the recommendations, accepting some, rewriting others, rejecting some, and adding a number of its own. The final result is the set of Recommendations for the Governor. Each recommendation in this report represents the unanimous vote of the Governor's Energy Advisory Council.

* * * Implementation of the recommendations in the energy plan, by promoting energy efficiency and renewable energy, can expand Delaware's economic base, create many new, good, green jobs, and help Delaware prosper in both the short and the long run. The energy planning process revealed that a shift to a greener energy economy presents a remarkable opportunity to ensure a prosperous, healthy, vital Delaware in the 21st century.

This energy plan represents the emergence of a new generation of energy policy that will begin to move us from a fossil fuel dependent society to a sustainable energy future. Several energy storms are headed in our direction. First, global warming requires that we drastically reduce our greenhouse gas emissions from burning fossil fuels. Second, we need to worry about our dependence on foreign oil. The price of oil has dropped, due to a collapse of demand in response to the global recession, but as the world's economy picks up, demand will rapidly rise, and oil prices will soar again. We must face the fundamental fact that the global demand for petroleum in a healthy world economy will rapidly bump up against real limits on the total oil supply. While Delaware is far too small to affect global climate change or world energy markets, it can prepare itself to be more resilient and less dependent on fossil fuels.

Energy from the sun and wind, although currently more expensive to use than fossil fuels, does not go up in price. Investments today in energy efficiency and renewable energy will produce a secure, long-term yield. The yield will manifest itself in energy savings, in economic growth, in new businesses and jobs, in healthier air, in a better place to live, and in long-term capital savings that can be reinvested to strengthen Delaware's social fabric, and make Delaware ready to meet future challenges.

However, if Delaware were to proceed in its business-as-usual fashion, its future would be worrisome. Delaware and Delawareans spend much more money on energy today than we need to. According to the U.S. Energy Information Agency, in 2006, Delaware spent just over $3.6 billion on energy, ranking us as the 20th highest energy use per capita of all the states. Delaware ranks last in the nation in renewable energy production; overall, less than .05% of our energy in 2006 came from renewable sources. We are so low, that the next lowest state, Rhode Island, with a population slightly larger than Delaware's, generated more than 50 times the amount of electricity from renewable energy than did Delaware. Nor can we be proud of our efforts to use electricity efficiently; for many years, Delaware was tied for last in the nation with regard to money spent on energy efficient investments. We have improved slightly since then; we are now tied at 32ⁿᵈ with Virginia, but have a very long way to go to even become average. * * *

Considering that we, and the nation, now face daunting economic challenges and need to restructure our economy to create many good new jobs, we can no longer afford to needlessly burn our money. If we continue along our current path, the state's economic future will be held hostage to the global fossil fuel market and we will have little resilience to respond to energy price spikes or to future federal mandates to reduce our greenhouse gas emissions from burning fossil fuel. Instead, we will continue burning money that could be put to important, productive uses. On the other hand, the opportunities for improvement are dramatic if we make a full-fledged commitment to improve our energy efficiency and shift to renewable energy. The potential to create new green energy industries and reduce our energy waste is enormous. But these changes will not occur on their own. The reason some states are efficient and have more renewable energy is primarily the result of the laws, policies and institutional frameworks that a state adopts.

Our present energy use creates pollution, contributes to climate change, creates a risk to our national security, and is a drag on our economic well-being. Delaware's prosperity depends on having a reliable, adequate, safe, clean, continuous supply of energy at a reasonable, nonvolatile cost. Inefficient use of fossil fuels exposes us to the risks of price swings, especially in a world economy with so many emerging and rapidly growing economies. By using energy efficiently we can make our economy more productive, the air cleaner, reduce our emissions of greenhouse gases, and make the shift to renewable energy more affordable.

This Energy Plan for Delaware faces these challenges directly. It proposes major, innovative changes in the laws and policies that determine how we go about using energy. This plan is intended to put us on a new path. It is the start of a long journey, but contains the concrete first steps to start us on our way to a prosperous Delaware driven by green and clean energy. The plan's recommendations, if implemented, will propel our transition to a state powered by efficient use of renewable energy—a green energy future. The extent to which we achieve these goals, how much more efficient we can be, and how much money we save over time depends on how, and the extent to which, we implement this plan. The choice is ours. * * *

Delaware's Energy Challenges and Issues

The energy challenges facing Delaware in 2009 can be grouped into three main areas:

Increasing Energy Demand
Although population growth is slower than at the time of the last energy plan, Delaware's growth is still higher than the national average, resulting in increased demand for energy services. Although many new homes are being built more energy efficiently, average house size has increased, and the number of electricity-based products in homes is increasing.

Increased and Variable Energy Cost
Removal of the electricity price caps, oil that recently topped $130/barrel, and fluctuating natural gas prices have significantly increased average home and business energy costs in Delaware since the initial energy plan in 2003.
* * *

Environmental Issues & Climate Change
Energy generation and use is the single largest contributor to pollution, smog and greenhouse gases. Public awareness of the link between energy generation and consumption and climate change has grown considerably over the past 5 years.

Energy Issues

The Governor's Energy Advisory Council began the energy planning process with an internal exercise to identify the key energy issues in Delaware over the next 5 to 10 year timeframe. There were 18 issues identified by the Council:

Energy Efficiency - Energy efficiency includes using energy efficient appliances, lighting, heating and cooling systems, and building design in homes, commercial and public buildings

Land Use Issue/Sprawl - The impacts of sprawl on energy use through increased driving/commuting and on the energy infrastructure; i.e. the ability to get the electricity and heating fuels out to the homes

Residential Energy Costs - Impact on residents of the cost of electricity, heating fuels, and means to mitigate cost increases

Climate Change - Evaluating and preparing for impacts on Delaware and Delawareans of changing temperatures, weather and sea level rise

Greenhouse Gas Emissions - Reducing releases of greenhouse gases, such as carbon dioxide and methane, from people, transportation, and businesses

Industrial and Commercial Energy Use and Costs - Impacts of energy costs on costs of goods produced, industrial energy efficiency, prices relative to neighboring states, etc.

Transportation Energy Costs - Impact on residents and businesses of the cost of transportation fuels

Transportation-Related Energy Use - Mass transit (buses, light rail), vehicle fuel efficiency, alternatives for reducing overall energy consumption in the transportation sector, and transportation-related pollution in urban areas

Transportation Fuels - Availability of fuels, cost of alternative fuels v. gasoline and diesel, production of bio-diesel, ethanol or other bio-based fuels, alternative fuel vehicles

Agricultural Energy Use - Impact of cost of fuel and energy on food prices, crops for food or fuel, impact of corn being grown for fuel on Delaware's poultry industry

Electricity Generation - Developing and maintaining capacity to meet future electricity needs in Delaware, including reliability, price stability and cost effectiveness

Environmental Impact of Electricity Generation - Types of fuels used to generate electricity (coal, natural gas, oil, wind, biomass, solar) and their resultant environmental impacts

Localized Heating and Electricity Generation (i.e. Distributed Generation) - Increasing the use of solar electricity generation, solar hot water, fuel cells, geothermal, small wind, etc

Electricity Transmission and Distribution - New/expanded transmission through Delaware, right-of-way issues, and developing system capacity infrastructure to serve all areas of the State

Natural Gas Availability - Increasing areas of the state where natural gas is available for residential, commercial and industrial use, where economically feasible

Energy Technology-Based Economic Development - Encouraging the location and growth of businesses researching, developing, and producing advanced and alternative energy technologies

Energy Education - Educating students, residents and businesses about energy issues and response options

Recycling- Developing feasible alternatives for residents and providing convenient recycling infrastructure * * *

Sustainable Energy Utility

The Sustainable Energy Utility (SEU) was created by the Legislature in 2007. The SEU is a pioneering effort by the State of Delaware to create an institution to comprehensively plan, develop and implement energy efficiency, energy conservation and distributed renewable energy programs in a self-sustaining manner. * * * [T]he SEU model is an alternative to the conventional approach to energy efficiency, which has treated various aspects of the energy system as distinct "silos" with limited overlap and coordination between them.

Energy Use in Delaware

Annual world energy consumption is approximately 400 Quads,[27] with the US representing about one-quarter of that at approximately 100 Quads per year. Annual energy consumption in Delaware is approximately 0.3% of total US energy consumption.

Total energy use across all sectors of Delaware's economy was 301 trillion BTUs in 2006, with a per capita use of 353 million BTUs. The US average 2006 per capita energy use was 333 million BTUs; Delaware ranked as the 20th highest per capita user of energy. Delaware also ranks poorly when compared to neighboring Mid-Atlantic States. * * *

Rhode Island, New York and Massachusetts, have 2006 per capita energy consumption of 204, 204, and 230 million BTUs, respectively. Per capita energy use in each of these states is less than two-thirds of that in Delaware. * * *

Gasoline purchases in Delaware increased 19% (by 73 million gallons) from 2000 to 2007, an average annual increase of 2.6%. The Division of Motor Vehicles projects a steady 2% annual increase in fuel sales. Even at that conservative estimate, by 2012, over 512 million gallons of gasoline will be purchased annually in Delaware.

The increase in gasoline purchases reflects the steady growth in vehicle miles travelled (VMT). Travel on Delaware's major highways increased by 45% from 1990 to 2005 (from 6.5 billion VMT to 9.5 billion VMT). As shown

---

[27] One Quad = One quadrillion BTU.

in Figure 7, vehicle travel is expected to increase by another 35 percent by 2020, reaching 12.8 billion VMT. * * *

Air Pollution Emissions from Transportation in Delaware

* * * The DNREC Air Quality Management Section estimates the annual mobile emissions per household (based on projected car trips) for new developments:

- 153.5 lbs of Volatile Organic Compounds (VOC)
- 127.1 lbs of NO_x
- 93.8 lbs of SO_2
- 8.3 lbs of Fine Particulate Matter (PM2.5)
- 12,839.2 lbs of CO_2

The location of the development affects the estimated vehicle emissions; emissions are higher for developments located in areas of the state designated as level 4 (the areas where growth is not desired, typically farther from towns and other communities). For example, a typical development of 100 units located 10 miles outside the growth zone will produce an additional 59 tons per year of VOC emissions, 77 tons per year of NO_x emissions and 1 ton per year of PM emissions, compared to the exact same development built within the growth zone.

RECOMMENDATIONS TO THE GOVERNOR

Energy Planning Governance Recommendation

Recommendation G-1: Energy Planning Governance

* * *

While the Delaware Code establishes responsibility for development of an energy plan, it does not appear to clearly establish responsibility for looking at the whole picture of energy in Delaware and developing policy. An integrated perspective from a body that looks at all the players and sets a consistent policy could strengthen Delaware Energy Policy. Currently many parties and agencies in Delaware have responsibility for and impact on Delaware Energy Policy, including the Governor's Office, the General Assembly, Department of Natural Resources and Environmental Control (DNREC (including the State Energy Office), Public Service Commission, Division of the Public Advocate, Governor's Energy Advisory Council, municipalities, utilities, generators, the regional electric grid operator, PJM, the Federal Energy Regulatory Commission, and a number of non-governmental organizations (NGOs). * * *

Recommendations to Reduce Energy Use through Energy Efficiency and Conservation

Recommendation EE-1. Energy Reduction Goal & Vision

The Governor should adopt the following goal and vision for reducing Delaware's energy use:

Goal: *Halt the growth in Delaware's energy use, and begin to reduce Delaware's energy consumption through energy efficiency, conservation, and distributed renewable energy resources. Achieve energy self-sufficiency and carbon neutrality[28] in Delaware's built environment by 2030.*

Vision: *Sustained actions, starting immediately and pursued consistently over the next 20-30 years to achieve this goal will help create an ecologically viable and economically strong Delaware in which:*
-   *Residential and commercial buildings are energy and carbon neutral, from their construction through their useful lifespan;*
-   *Delawareans practice conservation and utilize energy efficient equipment, appliances and techniques as standard practice;*
-   *Commercial and industrial buildings are as efficient as feasible;*
-   *Industrial and commercial processes are state of the art in energy efficiency;*
-   *State government demonstrates leadership in energy conservation and efficiency.*

Energy Codes are a subset of a broader group of codes known as building codes. Building codes are written legal requirements governing the design and construction of buildings. Most of the codes adopted by state and local governments set minimum standards for safe occupancy and to protect individuals from substandard living and working conditions. All building codes generally reflect a consensus of current design and construction practice. They are intended to lock in safe current practice as a minimum standard for design and construction of residential and commercial structures. * * *

The International Energy Conservation Code (IECC) is the benchmark residential energy code by which the US Department of Energy makes its determinations for the purposes of fulfilling the mandate set forth in federal law. Many states reference these standards in their state building or energy conservation codes, although a number of states have also developed their own energy codes. * * * The IECC is generally promulgated once every three years, with amendments and supplements made available in between editions.

---

[28] Carbon neutrality, as used by the American Institute of Architects in their 2030 Challenge, is that a carbon neutral building uses no fossil fuel energy.

Building Codes for Energy Efficiency

Recommendation EE-2: Residential Energy Code

Delaware's Residential Building Energy Code should be updated to reflect the adoption of the most current edition of the International Energy Conservation Code (IECC). Additionally, the Delaware Energy Office should be given the authority through legislation to administratively require an update of the State Building Energy Code to most current IECC every three years based on current code promulgation cycles. Training needs to be provided to all building code officials upon adoption of each update to the code. * * *

Energy Codes are a subset of a broader group of codes known as building codes. Building codes are written legal requirements governing the design and construction of buildings. Most of the codes adopted by state and local governments set minimum standards for safe occupancy and to protect individuals from substandard living and working conditions. All building codes generally reflect a consensus of current design and construction practice. They are intended to lock in safe current practice as a minimum standard for design and construction of residential and commercial structures. * * *

The International Energy Conservation Code (IECC) is the benchmark residential energy code by which the US Department of Energy makes its determinations for the purposes of fulfilling the mandate set forth in federal law. Many states reference these standards in their state building or energy conservation codes, although a number of states have also developed their own energy codes. * * * The IECC is generally promulgated once every three years, with amendments and supplements made available in between editions.

The 2003 Energy Plan recommended that the State adopt updated building energy codes in both the residential and commercial sectors. As a result, Senate Bill 306 was introduced and passed in 2004 updating the State's Energy Code to the IECC 2000 edition on the residential side and ASHRAE Standard 90.1 -1999 on the commercial side. Attempts in 2007 and 2008 to update these codes to the most current editions failed in the General Assembly. * * * The 2009 edition is expected in the Spring. * * *

Energy codes capture what would otherwise be lost opportunities. Current energy standards provide energy efficiency provisions that are relatively easy and inexpensive to address in new construction, and that are far more expensive, or even impossible, after the fact. Building energy codes are one of the easiest and most cost efficient ways for states and local jurisdictions to implement energy management policies. * * *

Residential Energy Use Reduction

Recommendation EE-4: Enhanced Energy Efficient Construction of New Homes

The State should supplement the Federal tax credit by extending a home-builder a tax credit for building a home that uses 50% less energy than the most recent IECC code.

It is easier to incorporate energy efficiency measures into a home under construction than it is to change these items later. To that end, builders of new homes must be encouraged to build to a higher standard. * * *

Recommendation EE-5: Expand the Weatherization Assistance Program

Significantly increase the budget of the Weatherization Assistance Program to enable the program to provide substantially more weatherization services to low-income owner-occupied and rental households as rapidly as possible. * * *

* * * Delaware households that receive weatherization save on average 16%-18% of their annual household energy usage, or $227 annually. * * * Delaware's Weatherization Assistance Program benefits not only low-income households, but the entire State, achieving a societal benefit-cost ratio of [over 3 to 1]. Even so, Delaware has not significantly invested in low-income weatherization programs. Delaware currently augments federal funding for its Weatherization Assistance Program by a weatherization surcharge on electricity rates of Delmarva Power customers of $0.000095 per kWh * * *.

Recommendation EE-6: Geothermal in New Home Construction

Delaware, through regulatory adoption or state legislation, should require a percentage, the specific amount to be determined, of all new homes constructed in Delaware to utilize ground water source heat pumps as their primary HVAC source, where spatially and geologically feasible. The State Energy Office should conduct the necessary research to determine the appropriate percentage and should increase its marketing efforts for geothermal heat pump systems in the existing home market. * * *

State Government Energy Use Reduction

Recommendation EE-7: State Energy Efficiency Policy

The Office of Management and Budget should create and implement a State Energy Efficiency Policy which would establish a standard for the de-

sign, construction, renovation, and operation of all State funded facilities, including schools, to optimize energy efficiency and minimize overall energy consumption. * * *

Recommendation EE-8: Public Buildings and Facilities Renewable Energy Policy

The Office of Management and Budget should develop and implement a policy that sets standards and requires cost effective renewable energy systems to be incorporated in new construction and renovations of public facilities. * * *

Recommendations under the purview of the Sustainable Energy Utility

The following are the recommendations to reduce energy use for which the Sustainable Energy Utility (SEU) is envisioned as the primary vehicle for delivery of the services detailed in the recommendations. The Governor and the Council should closely monitor progress on the recommendations and, if necessary, assess how best to move forward on achieving the objectives of the recommendations, should alternative approaches be required.

Recommendation SEU-1: Distributed Renewable Energy

The SEU should defray the cost of installing customer-sited renewable energy as a mechanism to reduce electric transmission and distribution energy losses, dependence on the electricity grid, peak electric demand, and Delaware's carbon footprint. * * *

Recommendation SEU-2: Retrofitting of Existing Homes for Energy Efficiency

The SEU should defray energy efficiency investments of existing homes, both rental units and owner-occupied. * * *

Recommendation SEU-3: Energy Efficiency Financing of New and Existing Homes

The Energy Office should explore, in coordination with the SEU, new energy efficiency financing models of new and existing homes. * * *

Recommendation SEU-4: Enhanced Energy Efficient Construction of New Homes

The SEU should defray the incremental investments required for meeting the EPA Energy Star Program requirements.

It is easier to incorporate energy efficiency measures into a home under construction than it is to change these items later. To that end, builders of new homes must be encouraged to build to a higher standard. * * *

Recommendations to Reduce Delaware's Transportation Energy Use

* * *

Recommendation TE-1: Goal to Reduce Vehicle Miles Travelled

The Governor should adopt a goal that by 2030, the total vehicle miles travelled in Delaware will not exceed the levels in 2009.

Vehicle miles travelled (VMT) is one of three core factors in transportation energy use. National trend data indicates that not only has VMT grown substantially (outpacing population growth and vehicle registration), growth will continue, regardless of new federal proposed standards. Indeed, the Department of Energy projects that by 2030, the number of VMT will be two times the 1990 level. * * *

Any effort to reduce the energy associated with transportation use must therefore include controlling VMT while also leveraging the use of new vehicle and fuel technologies to reduce transportation-related energy use. * * *

The expected benefit is better land use and related decisions that will result in fewer vehicle miles travelled, and reduced associated energy use and emissions. * * *

Recommendation TE-2: Employer Trip Reduction Programs

The Governor, through the Secretaries of Natural Resources & Environmental Control and Transportation should convene a committee, including representatives of Delaware employers such as the State Chamber of Commerce, to develop standards and incentives for employer participation in commute alternatives programs. * * *

Recommendation TE-5: Transit Investment

DelDOT should raise fixed-route transit capital spending to at least 20% of total transportation spending in the region and create a dedicated funding stream for the system. * * *

Recommendation TE-6: Bus Rapid Transit Feasibility

The Delaware Department of Transportation should explore the feasibility of creating a phased bus rapid transit system throughout the Mid-Atlantic Area (Delaware, Maryland, Pennsylvania, New Jersey). * * *

* * * [A] bus rapid transit system (BRT) would * * * provide the following benefits: a more efficient land-use pattern, reduced traffic congestion, increase economic competitiveness of the region in today's global marketplace, and provide an environmental friendly solution to traffic management. * * *

[A] typical heavy rail system in the US can cost $200 million or more per mile to construct, and a typical light rail system can cost $70 million per mile or more. By contrast, the most expensive BRTs cost around $25 million per mile. * * *

Recommendation TE-7: Bicycle and Pedestrian Transportation

TE-7A. DelDOT and other state agencies and cooperators should encourage bicycling and walking as alternative transportation.

TE-7B. The Governor or the Legislature should implement a "Complete Streets" requirement statewide by statute or Executive Order.

TE-7C. DelDOT and other appropriate agencies should increase funding for pedestrian and bicycle transportation.

The US Census estimates that about 11,000 Delaware workers (2.7% of State mode split) utilized walking as their primary means of travel to work in 2007—making it the fourth most popular mode choice just behind transit. Walking is most utilized in the State's urban north with its greater density; nearly 8,100 (3.1% of county mode split) of the estimated 11,000 dedicated walkers in the State are in New Castle County. According to the Census, less people bike to work. In 2000, the latest available year, less than 900 residents (0.2% of the State mode split) used the bicycle as a primary means to get to work. * * *

Increased use of bicycles and walking for transportation will reduce VMT. Delaware can take a number of steps to encourage more Delawareans to walk, including an increased focus on Safe Routes to Schools. The steps to encourage increased travel by bicycle include, among others, making roads safer for bicycles and enhancing education of riders and drivers on their respective responsibilities. * * *

Complete Streets Policy: A complete street is a road that is designed to be safe for drivers, bicyclists, transit vehicles and users, and pedestrians of all ages and abilities. "'Complete streets' focuses more on road users and is about making multimodal accommodation routine so that multimodal roads do not require extra funds or extra time to achieve. The intent is to change the everyday practice of transportation agencies so that every mode should be part of every stage of the design process in just about every road project-whether a minor traffic signal rehabilitation or a major road widening. The ultimate aim is to create a complete and safe transportation network for all modes." * * *

Increasing Vehicle Efficiency/Reducing Energy Use per Mile

Recommendation TE-8: Vehicle Fees &/or Fuel Taxes

The Delaware Department of Transportation should develop and propose vehicle-related fees and/or fuel taxes which encourage increased fuel efficiency and decrease miles travelled. * * *

Recommendation TE-9: Alternative Fuel/Fuel Efficient Vehicles

TE-9A. The Office of Management and Budget should establish high standards for fuel efficiency and environmental impacts for new fleet purchases by the State.

TE-9B. As new alternative fuel vehicle technologies become commercialized, the State Energy Office should conduct studies of options for making the support infrastructure available and convenient to the public in an economically feasible and environmentally safe manner.

* * * Adoption of new technologies often begins with fleet purchases. These purchases increase the demand for these new vehicles, allowing more to be built, driving down the costs of production. * * *

Reducing the Impact of Land Use on Energy Use

Recommendation LU-1: Smart Growth

The Governor, through the Office of State Planning, should strengthen Delaware's efforts to effectively direct growth into growth zones and require Smart Growth.

Fundamentally reversing trends in sprawling land use is the linchpin for achieving reductions in VMT. Greater density enables a more effective and efficient public transit system and non-motorized transportation network. Single-occupancy vehicle trips will drop as density increases. Smart Growth is characterized by interconnectivity; compact development; a mix of housing, commercial and retail; walkable neighborhoods; and a variety of transportation choices. * * *

The following are examples of successful Smart Growth approaches and techniques that could be utilized:

- Making well-planned Smart Growth a requirement.

• Consistent enforcement by State and County governments of restrictions on growth outside designated growth zones.

• Charging carbon impact fees on new development that create automobile-dependent neighborhoods.

• Prioritizing public funding for improvements to facilities within identified growth zones.

• Requiring that all city, county and state government buildings be built in growth zones.

• Requiring that new schools be built within growth zones, and as infill, where possible.

• Limiting transportation investments outside identified growth zones.

• Actively encouraging local governments to grant density bonuses and reduce or waive fees for building infill, for redeveloping in blighted areas, and for workforce housing which embodies Smart Growth characteristics, making certain that it is within designated growth zones and near transit.

• Utilizing Transfer of Development Rights (TDRs) regularly and effectively to save open space and provide for higher density in growth zones.

• Educating local governments on how they can utilize State Tax Increment Financing enabling legislation in growth zones, and particularly in redevelopment areas.[78]

Developing better methods of assessing the traffic impacts (including Level of Service) of mixed-use developments and the accurate capture of the benefits of this development type. * * *

Recommendation LU-2: Transit-Oriented Development

The Office of State Planning should work with local governments to promote Transit-Oriented Development as an innovative strategy and design tool to create livable healthy communities that are integrated with public transit, linked to a network of walkable, bikeable streets. * * *

Recommendation LU-3: Emissions Standards for Development

The Department of Natural Resources and Environmental Control, Air Quality Management Section should establish an "Emissions Standard and Mitigation Regulation" for land use development. * * *

Reducing the Environmental Footprint of Delaware's Energy Use
Recommendations

---

[78] With tax increment financing, money raised from a bond sale is given to a developer as reimbursement for infrastructure costs on a project. The additional property tax generated as the value of the site increases goes to pay off the bond.

The Need to Address Climate Change

Recommendation FP-1: Climate Change Commission

The Governor should establish a greenhouse gas reduction goal and a Climate Change Commission to develop a detailed Climate Change Action Plan for Delaware, including a trajectory for the reduction in greenhouse gas emissions and an adaptation plan, incorporating periodic review and evaluation of the plan. * * *

Increasing Renewable Energy Use

Recommendation FP-2: Green Energy Program

The Green Energy Program should be examined and aligned to complement other state and federal programs, including the Sustainable Energy Utility and federal tax credits, to help achieve Delaware's renewable energy goals * * *.

Recommendation FP-3: Net Metering

Legislation should eliminate forfeiture provisions from the Net Metering Law

In Delaware, as required by the Renewable Portfolio Standards (RPS), a certain percentage of electricity sold in the state must come from renewable generation sources, and a certain portion of that must be from solar photovoltaic generation, reaching 2% by 2019. Utilities may satisfy their solar requirements by purchasing Solar RECs from the owners of photovoltaic systems.

Delaware has a net metering law which allows electric customers to get a credit against their electricity bills for electricity they generate using renewable resources. This electricity generated creates Renewable Energy Credits (RECs). RECs are an attribute separate from the energy itself and are tradable commodities.

The Delaware Code provides that any excess generation in a billing period may be carried forward as a credit to the customer's bill until the end of a 12 month period. At that point, the excess credits are forfeited to the Green Energy Fund. * * *

The Code further provides that SRECs [Solar Renewable Energy Credits] associated with the forfeited energy costs are given to the electric supplier. Thus, if a customer has used less than he/she generated, SRECs associated with the excess are conveyed to the customer's electric supplier. * * * [T]he customer, who paid for the generating facility, should retain ownership of all his/her SRECs. This treatment would be comparable to the way other generators are treated.

Delaware law limits the net metering provisions to systems that are sized to meet the needs of the customer. Eliminating the forfeiture provisions and allowing a reasonable limitation for customer sizing which addresses cost and reliability issues would support increased installation of photovoltaic systems. The current forfeiture arrangement means that customers have a financial incentive to install less solar power than they think they will need in order to provide a cushion from forfeiture, whereas, as public policy, we want to encourage the installation of more solar power. There are additional anti-energy conservation and anti-efficiency consequences of the forfeitures provisions:

Solar owners who have installed enough solar power to meet or almost meet their power requirements have no financial incentive to reduce further their electric use because they will forfeit the value of their energy savings.

Solar owners who have generated more electricity than they have used will lose SRECs associated with the excess power. Currently SRECs are trading in excess of $200/SREC. Thus, a customer with excess solar generation would lose greater than $200 for each megawatt-hour of excess generation. This customer has a significant financial incentive to increase his power use to be sure he does not forfeit his SRECs. * * *

Recommendation FP-4: Solar/Renewable Energy Access
Solar and renewable energy rights should be available to the citizens of Delaware. Barriers, and methods to relieve those barriers, need to be identified and examined and addressed. The Governor and Legislature should enact legislation addressing deed restrictions and/or covenants that unduly prohibit the use of renewable energy sources.

Presently, deed restrictions exist in many communities that do not allow solar hot water or solar electricity systems, creating a substantial roadblock to new business opportunities in solar energy conversion. * * * [H]omeowner associations have prevented individuals from installing renewable energy systems. The reasons have varied from fear of the impact on home values to aesthetics. * * *

[Legislation is needed to] prohibit restrictive covenants on roof mount solar and wind turbine systems. * * *

Recommendation FP-5: Renewable Energy Portfolio Standards

The Governor should examine and, if necessary, propose revisions to the Renewable Energy Portfolio Standard (RPS) to achieve Delaware's renewable energy goals and to determine whether or not to increase the RPS requirement to be greater than the current specification of 20% by 2019.

[Current law requires that] * * * an increasing percentage of electricity sold in the state to Delmarva customers to come from renewable energy sources. The percentage started at 2% in 2007 and increases each year to 20% in 2019. The legislation also created a "solar carve-out", increasing to 2% per year in 2019.

Currently, twenty-four states and the District of Columbia have RPS policies in place; four others have nonbinding goals for adoption of renewable energy. The more aggressive requirements are California, which has a requirement of 20% by 2010, and Oregon and Illinois, which both have requirements of 25% by 2025.

Electricity production in Delaware and the rest of the nation is a significant source of CO_2 and other pollutants with more direct and immediate health impacts such as fine particulates, SO_x, NO_x and mercury. While major reductions in Delaware's greenhouse gas (GHG) emissions will already occur from the generation sector, additional reductions may be desired [by] a * * * transition from energy sources for electricity from fossil fuels to renewable energy sources.

Delaware has a potential supply of clean renewable energy in the form of off-shore wind and contract arrangements for out-of-state on-shore wind energy. Additional development of the off-shore wind resource (excluding shipping lanes, migratory bird flyways, etc.) to a depth of 50m could provide potential power of 6200 MW if fully developed—over 4 times the state's total electrical power consumption (1300 MW by all users.) While the off-shore wind generating resource potential is vast, the development of such resources will require considerable investment, transmission upgrades and a means of overcoming reliability concerns due to intermittency. In addition, the success of further development of off-shore wind will be dependent upon market forces and financial incentives. * * *Electricity production in Delaware and the rest of the nation is a significant source of CO_2 and other pollutants with more direct and immediate health impacts such as fine particulates, SO_x, NO_x and mercury. While major reductions in Delaware's greenhouse gas (GHG) emissions will already occur from the generation sector, additional reductions may be desired [by] a * * * transition from energy sources for electricity from fossil fuels to renewable energy sources.

Delaware has a potential supply of clean renewable energy in the form of off-shore wind and contract arrangements for out-of-state on-shore wind energy. Additional development of the off-shore wind resource (excluding shipping lanes, migratory bird flyways, etc.) to a depth of 50m could provide potential power of 6200 MW if fully developed—over 4 times the state's total electrical power consumption (1300 MW by all users.) While the off-shore wind generating resource potential is vast, the development of such resources will require considerable investment, transmission upgrades and a means of overcoming reliability concerns due to intermittency. In addition, the success of further development of off-shore wind will be dependent upon market forces and financial incentives.

Nationally, recommendations for reducing GHG emissions have included a reduction in global carbon dioxide emissions by 80% by 2050 * * *; increasing the percentage of electricity from renewable energy sources is integral to most climate change mitigation proposals. * * *

Clean Energy Economic Development Recommendations

Recommendation CE-1: Clean Energy Business Development Initiative

The Delaware Economic Development Office should develop, implement and fund a comprehensive Clean Energy Business Development Initiative. * * *

Wind: Delaware has an opportunity to develop a significant wind energy industry. The state has jumpstarted the US industry with its historic power purchase agreement (PPA) between Bluewater Wind and Delmarva Power, garnering national and international attention and stimulating other states to solicit projects. This happened because the state took an active role in requiring a new, in-state power plant with a long-term contract for stable-priced power. As a result, Delaware has already been emulated by New Jersey and Rhode Island, with others, including Maryland, considering * * * off-shore wind. * * *

Beyond the next 10 years, additional off-shore wind capacity could be added for the purpose of exporting power to neighboring inland states. This consideration would require the Mid-Atlantic Power Pathway (MAPP) project to be designed to include options for transmission interconnection and storage devices to accommodate the variability of wind power production. * * *

Solar: Sunlight can be used for generating electricity, heating and cooling of buildings, domestic and process water heating, and pool heating. These approaches have been aggressively implemented in Europe over the past decade and, in many ways, the US is still a developing country with respect to solar energy. Delaware is in an excellent position to benefit from the expected growth in the solar energy field. It has several key players in research, manufacturing, and education, such as GE Energy, DuPont, the University of Delaware, and Delaware State University. In addition, the creation of the Sustainable Energy Utility (SEU) has the potential to significantly increase the deployment of solar technologies as distributed energy sources throughout Delaware. * * *

Recommendation CE-5: Vehicle to Grid Development

The Governor, through his policy office, should convene an advisory group to determine the infrastructure, incentives and rules needed to facilitate Vehicle-to-Grid (V2G) development and implementation.

Vehicle-to-grid (V2G) interconnects the automotive industry and the electric industry. The batteries in plug-in cars, whether all-electric or plug-in hybrid, are used for services of value to the electric system. These include balancing fluctuations in power (called "regulation") for the large grid operators - in our region, PJM Interconnect. As solar and wind power increase on the grid, electrical storage in batteries will also become valuable to smooth out mismatches between renewable power output and the need for electricity ('load'). * * *

Recommendation TD-1: Permitting, Siting & Right-of-Way Coordination

*The Governor, through the Executive Office of Energy Policy or other agency as determined by the Governor, should convene a stakeholder group to discuss and ascertain the best means of increasing coordination between all stakeholders to simplify the permitting, siting and right-of-way acquisition process for electric and natural gas transmission and distribution projects. * * ***

Increasing electric transmission capacity in Delaware * * * [is] a major issue, not just for serving existing and future load but also for transporting energy from new generation facilities, including renewable energy facilities that will be sited in the State. * * * While [Delmarva Power] has been successful in making use of its existing rights-of-way to add new transmission lines, those existing rights-of-way are quickly being utilized and soon it will be necessary to obtain additional corridors to continue expanding the transmission system to meet future load growth and accommodate new generation. Problems facing the increased need for transmission capacity include siting transmission facilities and right-of-way acquisition.

Siting of transmission facilities - There are sixty local governments in Delaware: three counties and fifty-seven municipalities. Land use decisions, for the most part, are made by the local governments. * * * Local governments control land use through the adoption and implementation of Comprehensive Plans, and enforcement of their associated ordinances, including zoning ordinances. * * *

Several state agencies are also involved in the siting of public utility generation, transmission, and/or distribution facilities. The Department of Natural Resources and Environmental Control (DNREC) issues permits relating to air emissions, wetlands or sub-aqueous lands. The Department of Transportation (DelDOT) has control over street rights-of-way, which has been discussed in terms of co-locating transmission and distribution facilities in existing rights-of-way. The Office of State Planning Coordination (OSPC) also has a role to play, albeit not a regulatory role. To date, the OSPC has been effective in addressing and coordinating land use issues and activities between state and local governments, as well as between state agencies. * * *

Obtaining Right-of-Way - Obtaining right-of-way for new electric transmission facilities is becoming increasingly difficult. Right-of-way that can be permitted and is suitable for building transmission facilities is becoming more scarce and valuable, and there are aesthetic concerns from the general public around electrical transmission facilities. A utility can be successful in negotiations for a majority of a proposed route, but one or two landowners can stop the entire project by refusing to negotiate. It is possible for a landowner to delay construction of transmission facilities for extended periods by virtue of withholding land rights. With the current rate of load growth, a delay or cancellation in a project can lead to supply and reliability concerns. There is also the concern for the "Not in My Back Yard" mentality which is almost always present at public hearings; a transmission line is may benefit the entire state or region, but nobody wants it in their backyard. These problems are anticipated to increase as population increases.

Delaware does not grant condemnation rights to electric utilities nor is there a state siting process that can ultimately resolve these issues. The possibility of a condemnation alternative can assist with negotiations and preclude one land owner from unreasonably withholding the granting of an easement or demanding unjust compensation for such easement. This right of condemnation is a critical issue for energy utilities: without it, projects, including capacity additions, can be delayed, canceled, or may experience significant cost increases. Because of these concerns, the federal government identified certain areas of the country as 'national electric corridors'. In areas with this designation—which includes all three counties in Delaware—the federal government can exercise eminent domain authority if a state fails to provide siting within a one-year timeframe. * * *

Transmission line redesigns, made necessary by reluctant landowners, can also create other problems for utilities. Some rerouting leaves only wetlands or other environmentally sensitive areas as a plausible route, requiring careful planning, environmental permitting and mitigation efforts.

MARKELL SIGNS LANDMARK ENERGY LEGISLATION INTO LAW

Office of Governor Jack Markell, Press Release (July 29, 2009)
http://governor.delaware.gov/news/2009/07july/20090729-
energy.shtml#TopOfPage

Requirement for utilities to reduce consumption 15% by 2015 is one of the most aggressive in the country

NEWARK – Gov. Jack Markell signed two pieces of his administration's energy agenda into law * * * that is helping to put Delaware on the leading edge of the Green Economy.

"Placing environmental sustainability at the forefront of our public policy debate creates jobs and opportunities for Delaware residents and companies," Markell said * * * "We must boldly move forward because efficiency produces real cost savings, environmental benefits, and economic opportunity. By reducing our energy use, we will have more money to save and spend in our local communities, generating well-paying jobs and greater prosperity for us all."

Senate Bill 59 updates Delaware's building codes to increase energy efficiency requirements for new buildings and promotes the construction of "zero net energy" homes and office buildings. A "zero net energy" building does not consume more energy than it generates.

Senate Bill 106, the centerpiece of the administration's energy agenda, requires Delaware's utilities to reduce their energy consumption 15 percent by 2015, one of the most aggressive targets in the country. The Energy Conservation and Efficiency Act of 2009 also establishes a "loading order" for new energy supplies that requires energy efficiency to be considered before new supply-side resources are obtained (cost-effective renewable before traditional fossil fuels) and identifies energy efficiency as the least expensive way to meet Delaware's growing energy demands.

Earlier this month, the Governor signed a package of bills that remove obstacles that prevented homeowners from taking advantage of solar and wind power. The legislative package also rewards homeowners and farmers who make that investment by allowing them to sell excess power they generate but do not use.

"My administration's energy agenda is moving Delaware toward achieving the promise of a green economy — green jobs and careers, opportunities for companies, and savings for residents and businesses — by seizing the opportunities presented by our nation's commitment to energy independence and the growing concern over climate change," Markell said. * * *

Notes and Questions

1. Delaware's "Energy Conservation and Efficiency Act of 2009" is now codified as 26 Del C. Chapter 15. The energy efficiency first "loading order" is at 26 Del. C § 1020. The requirement is that all building codes be regularly adjusted to meet the most current version of the International Code Council, International Energy Conservation Code is 16 Del. C. § 7602. The law prohibits all zoning laws, deed restrictions, homeowner association rules and the like that restrict a homeowner from installing wind energy is 29 Del. C. § 8060. The law allows a minimum set back of one times the turbine height, sets noise level limits, and allows further restrictions in historic districts. The Delaware general Assembly also passed a law prohibiting future deed restrictions and other legal instruments, and enabling amendment of existing limitations, that unreasonably limit the ability of a homeowner to install solar panels on the home's roof. 25 Del. C § 318. Finally, the legislature amended the state's net-metering law to remove the provision that forfeited the value of all renewable energy generated by a farmer or a homeowner that exceeded on-site use of electricity. 26 Del. C § 1014(d)(1) and 1014(e). The effect of this forfeiture rule was to discourage farms and homeowners from installing solar and renewable energy equipment that would produce more energy that the owner actually used, thereby keeping new supplies of renewable energy from being added to the grid.

An additional element of the energy plan was implemented at the Delaware Public Service Commission. It adopted, based on a request initiated by the Department of Nature Resources and Environment, a new IRP regulation that mandates that integrated resource plans include the value of environmental externalities, including human and environmental harm, from fossil fuel emissions in the evaluation of its sources of power. Integrated Resource Planning Regulation, Delaware Public Service Commission (Aug. 18, 2009) http://depsc.delaware.gov/orders/7628.pdf.

The energy plan and the new laws and regulations is widely viewed as raising "nearly insurmountable obstacles to building new fossil-fuel power plants to supply utilities in Delaware or even importing a bigger share of fossil power, putting the state on the brink of a new energy era. * * * Local and national officials say the changes rank Delaware's energy program among the most ambitious in the country, at least on paper." Jeff Montgomery, New era may end need for fossil fuel, Sunday News J., 1 (Aug. 9, 2009). Governor Markell also changed the energy governance structure within the state government by giving the Secretary of the Dept. of Nature Resources and Environment (where the state energy office is located) overall responsibility for implementing the new energy plan. Secretary Colin O'Mara believes that the new energy policy "begins to fundamentally change the way we think about energy in the state, and moves us beyond cost being the sole determinant of supply." Id.

2. The Delaware Energy Plan addresses how that State's energy needs could be met efficiently and in a cost-effective way, while minimizing adverse environmental impacts and striving to become carbon neutral. How these ends can be balanced in other jurisdictions will vary depending on the local circumstances, but in each case some universal objectives need to be met if the Plan is to be a component of an international vision for sustaining climatic conditions on Earth. What metrics and reporting will be needed to permit evaluation of whether the plan does so?

3. Delaware's Plan required extensive public participation. Its drafts and reports of its meetings were all posted on-line and available to everyone. Its meetings were noticed and open to the public. Such measures are time consuming and delay issuance of a plan. What benefits does such a commitment to transparency and inclusiveness bring to the plan? Does the Delaware Energy Plan address the key issues outlined by Richard Ottinger? How? Where does the plan miss the mark?

4. Given that Delaware's economic life is wholly integrated into that of the United States and the global economy as well, how does Delaware address the pricing of energy within its jurisdiction?

5. Should plans such the Delaware Energy Plan have been required to undergo a programmatic environmental impact assessment before being completed? What is the "value added" that a strategic or generic environmental impact statement can provide to such a planning process?

6. Is the regulatory framework in Delaware adequate to implement the Delaware Energy Plan? How can this be determined? Should "law reform commissions" be constituted to deal with the development of whatever new governmental agencies may be needed to administer the components of the Delaware Energy Plan?

7. The Delaware planning process was open to all interested parties and studies and deliberations all made available through the Internet. How can such transparency and inclusiveness be continued during implementation of the plan's recommendations?

7. As laboratories for innovation, the state governments are engaged in enacting new energy laws to contribute to mitigating the releases of greenhouse gases and adapting to the effects of climate change. Should Congress defer to these diverse measures, or seek to impose a national regime that might supplant all or part of programs such as the Delaware Energy Plan? What level of government, federal, regional, state, or local, is the appropriate level to address each of the component parts of the Delaware Energy Plan? For example, the proposed 2010-30 five-state Regional Energy Plan prepared by the Northwest Power Planning and Conservation Council created by federal

statute in 1970 relies 85% on conservation and 15% on wind and natural gas to meet new power needs in the region.

8. Does the Delaware Plan cover the same elements that a developing nation would need to cover in its national climate change action plan? What would be different? Does Delaware have the trained human resources to implement its plan, or will training be needed? What educational components should be added? If Delaware will rely on the private sector to supply necessary technology and services to implement its Plan, how will a developing country secure comparable technology and services?

PROBLEM EXERCISE ON STATE ENERGY PLANNING

The state or local authority where you are located has assembled some, but not all of the elements of a comprehensive energy plan to address climate change objectives. Both the legislature and the governor have indicated that law reform to combat climate change is needed, and each branch of the government signals its intention to take action. What legal and administrative law measures is each branch best equipped to address? What is the likelihood that each branch will act in complementary, rather than in competitive, ways? What is the likelihood that state action might interfere with innovative programs adopted by local governments?

Should your state climate change plan make use of the planning authority that exists under Section 110 of the Clean Air Act, amending your State Implementation Plan? What advantages would there be for your state to follow the national climate implementation plan formats being developed under the UN Framework Convention on Climate Change and the Bali Action Plan? Does your state have a proactive program for Reducing Emissions from Deforestation and Degradation (REDD)? Should your plan make use of environmental impact assessment procedures? What form of public participation and disclosure of information is needed?

For instance, how could the provision of information, and public education, actually motivate each branch of government to take effective action, and in turn motivate the public and private sectors affected also toward effective action? Consider the life-cycle cost analysis authority enacted in Maine. Maine Statutes, Title 5, Section 1764. What effect on public decision-making could result from a state requirement for "energy related life-cycle cost analysis of alternative architectural or engineering designs, or both, and * * * the efficiency of energy utilization for designs in the construction and lease of public improvements and public school facilities"? In such analyses, life-cycle costs are to include "the reasonably expected energy costs over the life of the building, as determined by the designer, that are required to maintain illumination, power, temperature, humidity and ventilation and all other energy consuming equipment in a locality."

C. ENERGY AND CLIMATE PLANNING ON A LARGE SCALE

Since the 1960's China has increased its use of coal more than ten-fold and its fossil-fuel CO_2 emissions have grown nearly 80% in 2000 alone. In 2006, China emitted over 6 billion metric tons of CO_2, surpassing the United States as the world's largest emitter of CO_2 due to fossil-fuel use and cement production. From 1950 to 2005 China emitted 91 billion tons of CO_2. China's emissions growth is dominated by it use of coal, which accounted for 98.7% of the emissions total in 1950 and 72.9% in 2006. China is the world's largest coal producer. With the introduction of cars and the use of diesel fuel to run generators at many factories in China, oil-based fuels now contribute 15.7% of emissions and are growing. China is not only the world's largest coal producer, it is by far the world's largest hydraulic cement producer. To support its explosive building boom, China produced over 1.2 billion metric tons of hydraulic cement in 2006, nearly half of all global production. Emissions from cement production account for 9.8% of China's 2006 total industrial CO_2 emissions. China's population has doubled over the past four decades and now exceeds 1.3 billion people. Per capita emissions increased considerably over this period and 2006 marks the first year China's per capita emission rate (4.66 metric tons of CO_2 exceeded the global average (4.6 metric tons of CO_2). See T.A. Boden, et al, Global, U.S. Department of Energy Regional, and National Fossil-Fuel CO_2 Emissions (Carbon Dioxide Information Analysis Center, Oak Ridge National Laboratory 2009) doi 10.3334/CDIAC/00001.

How is China addressing its energy challenges and GHG emissions? What legal models is it trying to use? Does their approach have merit? What are the strengths and weakness of China's laws? Do they contain ideas that might work in the United States, with its enormous energy use and GHG emissions? What lessons do we learn that might apply to other emerging economies such as India, Brazil, Mexico, and Indonesia? Go to the CAIT date base maintained by World Resources Institute (cait.wri.org) to find the emissions profile and growth trends of those nations.

CHINA: CLIMATE CHANGE SUPERPOWER AND THE CLEAN TECHNOLOGY REVOLUTION
Margret J. Kim and Robert E. Jones
ABA Natural Resources & Environment 9 (Winter 2008)

Move over America. China has sprinted to the front of the pack in carbon dioxide (CO_2) emissions.

Lost in the euphoria of skyrocketing stock markets and the debate over trade imbalances, poisoned pets, and toxic toothpaste and toys was the announcement that China now has the dubious distinction of being the largest producer of CO_2 in the world. Following closely on the heels of the International Energy Agency's prediction that China was expected to overtake the

United States as early as the end of 2007, the Netherlands Environmental Assessment Agency announced that this milestone had already been reached. According to the Dutch report, "[t]he surging power demand from China's rapidly expanding economy caused CO_2 emissions to rise by 9% in 2006 . . . that increase, coupled with a slight United States decline, meant that China's emissions for the year surpassed those of the US by 8%." Despite a knee-jerk response by a high-ranking Chinese official disagreeing with the report and criticizing its measurement criteria, an official at China's Energy Research Institute remarked in a less bellicose fashion that Chinese researchers would study the report but that their estimates indicated that China would in any event surpass the United States by the end of 2007.

This revelation puts China front and center in the climate change debate. The sleeping giant has truly emerged from its century-long slumber to become not only the workshop of the world but the climate change superpower. The speed with which China has overtaken the United States is particularly worrisome. In 2005, China's CO_2 emissions were 2 percent lower than those of the United States; in 2006, they were about 8 percent higher at 6.2 billion tons compared with U.S. emissions of 5.8 billion tons. In fact, recent research from University of California Berkeley indicates that the Kyoto Protocol underestimated the magnitude of the projected increase of CO_2 emissions in China, and with her plan to quadruple gross domestic product (GDP) by 2020, greenhouse gas (GHG) emissions will skyrocket—possibly double—thus negating any attempt at reduction by the rest of the globe.

The Energy Information Agency predicts that China will experience the largest growth in CO_2 emissions between now and the year 2030. While current emissions per capita are only about one-fifth of U.S. per capita emissions, China's economy continues its meteoric rise * * * and a recent overtaking of Germany as the third-largest economy. The rise is fuelled largely by inexpensive, dirty coal-fired power with installation at the rate of two large 500 megawatt (MW) coal-fired units per week. As the world's largest producer and user of coal, China continues to depend on CO_2-heavy coal for nearly 70 percent of her primary energy consumption, and this will not change anytime soon. In addition, with the exponential growth in car ownership in China expected to reach 140 million by 2020 and the importance of the automobile industry as an engine of economic growth, vehicle carbon emissions are also expected to surge.

With the fast-approaching expiry of the Kyoto Protocol in 2012 and the absence of any successor framework, there is a new urgency to mount global efforts to combat climate change. Indeed, how China handles this new responsibility will have far-reaching repercussions for the world * * *

It's Not Fuzzy Science

Just four years ago, nobody talked about *quan qiu bian nuan* (climate change) and certainly not about the effects of climate change in China. The subject of climate change at that time involved no more than a handful of officials trying to determine how Clean Development Mechanism (CDM) investment could serve as a means to gaining much-needed technology. All that has changed. * * * The 400-page *First National Climate Change Assessment*, drafted over a four year period by scientists and officials from dozens of Chinese ministries and agencies, clearly shows consensus among a broad range of officials that global warming poses a clear and present danger to China's development. For example, rising sea levels threaten low-lying megacities such as Shanghai, the jewel in China's financial crown.

With extreme weather and other classic global warming manifestations occurring across the country, China sees climate change as a grave threat. Western glaciers will have largely melted by century's end, drying up large portions of the rivers that they feed. Other predictions are direr, indicating that 80 percent of Tibet's glaciers could be lost by 2035. In far northwest China, Number One Glacier in Xinjiang's Tian Shan Mountain has already lost 20 million cubic meters of ice in just four decades and actually split in half in 1993, with the eastern and western sections receding by 3.5 and 5.9 meters annually. The total glacier area has shrunk by 20 percent.

The changing climate threatens not only China's dwindling and heavily polluted water resources but possibly her food security. The northeastern province of Liaoning, a leading corn-producing area, is suffering its worst drought in more than thirty years, limiting drinking water for more than 1 million people. Shortly before the drought's onset, Liaoning suffered its worst snow storm in half a century. A recent study also found that 17.5 percent of the lakes at the source of the Yangtze have completely disappeared. Coupled with an increasing rise in annual mean temperatures (expected to exceed 3.3° Celsius (C) by 2050), the absence of a viable water supply (in the absence of adaptive changes) could result in grain production declines of up to 10 percent by 2030 and a staggering 37 percent by mid-century. Clearly, this latter scenario especially cannot be permitted to play out, not only for China's sake, but for the stability of world grain markets.

Climate Change: The View from Behind the Great Wall

In a June 4, 2007, press conference, Ma Kai, Minister of the National Development Reform Commission, said that "China is committed to pursuing a more sustainable, lower carbon future, but not at the expense of economic development . . . it is too early, too abrupt and too blunt for the international community to impose emission caps on China." Despite the growing number of predictions of a grand environmental disaster, climate change remains to

China more about politics and economics than about global environmental health. Her interest in climate change is driven primarily by (1) energy security, (2) the opportunity for technology transfer, and (3) the need to build her credentials as a global power.

So what does China propose to do in the face of mounting pressure from the international community to cap her emissions? The simple answer is very little, at least in the near term. In June 2007, just two days before President Hu Jintao attended a meeting of the G8 in Germany, China unveiled her first national plan on climate change (the Plan), setting out broad policy goals for tackling the effects of global warming and for cutting GHG pollution. See National Development and Reform Commission, China's National Climate Change Programme (2007), http://en.ndrc.gov.cn/newsrelease/P020070604561191006823.pdf

In reality, the Plan simply rehashed China's official stance: China is very aware of the global warming conundrum but has no intention of sacrificing her economic growth to mitigate global warming. Moreover, in China's view, as most of the GHG emissions were released by the developed nations, those nations should bear the brunt of mitigation responsibility, not China. Even the modest "carbon intensity goal" of reducing intensity (CO_2 per unit of gross national product) by 40 percent from 2000 levels by 2020, as suggested in an early draft report, was absent in the final Plan.

Despite China's ranking highest in annual CO_2 emissions, the Plan defends China's low per capita emissions and states that its climate change policy will be guided by the principle of "common but differentiated responsibilities." Under this doctrine, developed countries, such as the United States, should take the lead in reducing GHG emissions, rather than developing countries, such as China, that are not responsible for the present climate predicament. Developed countries likewise should provide financial and technical support to developing countries, as they continue to enjoy unfettered economic growth born mostly on the backs of developing countries. The Plan acknowledges that China lacks the best technology in virtually all areas of energy production and use. For China, the issue is one of environmental justice—the outsourcing of both production and CO_2 pollution from the developed to the developing world.

Beyond broader policy statements, however, the Plan articulates several goals and initiatives that, on their face, suggest intent to take action. For example, the Plan elevates the issue of climate change (at least in the political hierarchy) to a whole new level through its establishment of the National Leading Group to Address Climate Change with Premier Wen as its head. In addition, the Plan calls for the establishment of a regional administration system for coordinating climate change work and mandates local government leadership to formulate and implement local climate change programs.

The Plan also generally discusses a broad array of policies that China already has and will implement to mitigate and adapt to climate change, including the existing "one child family planning" policy. The most significant part of the Plan deals with the reduction of energy intensity to 20 percent below 2005 levels by 2010 (although this is a reiteration of existing policies) and increasing renewables in the primary energy supply, such as hydroelectric energy, by 10 percent by 2010.

In addition, the Plan calls for an expansion of nuclear power, as well as the promotion of clean coal technology and biofuels. In the area of energy efficiency, the Plan prohibits the production, importation, and sale of products that fail to meet energy efficiency standards; encourages consumers to purchase energy-saving products; and devises incentives to encourage energy saving in buildings, vehicles, iron and steel manufacture, and other high-energy-use sectors. The Plan also states that industrially produced nitrous oxide will be held at 2005 levels, the growth rate of methane emissions will be controlled, and the percentage of forest-covered land will be increased from 18.2 to 20 percent, in an effort to soak up ever-increasing emissions of carbon dioxide.

In addition to the Plan, China enacted other domestic policies and programs designed to alleviate the side effects of climate change. The "Top 1000 Enterprises" program of 2006 sought to ramp up energy efficiency of the one thousand largest consumers of primary energy in China. During the last few years, the National Institute of Standardization issued new appliance efficiency standards for consumer appliances, such as air conditioners, washing machines, refrigerators, televisions, and lamps, with the purpose of reducing electricity use by 10 percent in 2010. The last year also has seen several developments in the area of energy conservation, with new national conservation standards for public and residential buildings seeking to reduce energy consumption by 65 percent in Beijing, Chongqing, Shanghai, and Tianjin and by 50 percent in smaller cities. By 2020, China plans to renovate 25 percent of public and residential buildings in large cities, 15 percent in medium-sized cities, and 10 percent in small cities. To improve compliance and enforcement in energy and environmental standards, the central government is setting up an "accountability system" under which officials' promotion will be tied to their performance in environmental protection and energy efficiency. In fact, China's Communist Party elite abandoned their business suits and ties for white, short-sleeved shirts at the recent Central Committee meeting at the Central Party School in Beijing. The sudden change in attire by China's top officials proved very welcome as temperatures approached triple digits and as China literally begins to "warm" to the idea of being more energy efficient.

In June 2007, the State Council decreed that public buildings could not set their thermostats below 26°C (79 degrees Fahrenheit (F)) during the summer and above 20°C (68°F) in the winter. The latest weapon in China's energy efficiency arsenal is a team of twenty-two highly trained officials, whose job is to roam the streets of Beijing to make spot-checks on offices, hotels, malls, and other large buildings to ensure that the "no cooler than 26°C rule" is followed. At a macroeconomic level, investment, fiscal, and trade policies are being transformed to promote a series of green policies. For example, taxes on energy intensive industries are being increased, while tariffs on environmental goods and services will be lowered in order to attract cleaner technology. Additionally, a new "green credit system" is being developed, under which enterprises with poor environmental records are identified and then provided to financial institutions in order to dry up their funding sources. Sun Xiaohua, Blacklist of Polluters Distributed—New System Aims to Cut Credit Availability to Non-Green Firms, China Daily (July 31, 2007).

Finally, on the automobile front, new passenger vehicle fuel-efficiency standards took effect in July 2005 that call for more stringent standards than those in the United States, with average fuel economy of new vehicles rising to an impressive 36.7 miles per gallon in 2008. As for public transport, China already has one of the largest bus fleets in the world using cleaner-burning compressed natural gas (CNG) and plans to convert 90 percent of buses to CNG by 2008. There is also a move afoot to introduce hybrid-electric buses, which can be converted to use fuel cells.

From Red to Green: A Different Kind of Revolution

Will China be able to successfully meet her long list of climate mitigation goals, including the 20 percent energy intensity reduction by 2010 and the boosting of renewable energy use to 10 percent by 2010? China is well known for announcing lofty goals and launching old-style campaigns together with the appropriate slogans and rhetoric. However, when looking at her compliance track record and woefully inadequate enforcement of environmental laws, one can be excused for being a little skeptical about future success. Or will it be different where energy goals are concerned, given China's current fixation with energy security and the opportunity to acquire much-needed technology transfer?

In a country with a strong disconnect between the more progressive central and the development-at-any-cost local governments, a chronic lack of capacity at the implementation level, institutionalized corruption (30,000 officials were prosecuted in 2006 alone, Broken China, Business Week (July 23, 2007)), little sense of civic responsibility, a lack of transparency and accountability, as well as the general absence of the rule of law, the challenges presented by climate change seem almost insurmountable. Notably, China lacks a credible monitoring system to measure carbon, and even if she had one, she probably would not be very eager to share the information publicly, as witnessed in a recent World Bank report where "sensitive information" regarding critical health impacts from pollution was taken out at the government's insistence.

While market-based mechanisms are part of the answer, significant help is needed at a very fundamental level to build sound legal and governance capacity and to create a new sustainable growth paradigm. Moreover, laws need to be enforced through an independent judicial system not subject to the whims of local government, even when it comes to prosecuting important members of the local corporate community and the Party. This transformation, however, can only be expected to occur from within and incrementally over the longer term. Where the West can help now and be a part of a short- to medium-term solution is in the area of clean technology transfer, an essential part of the aforementioned new sustainable growth paradigm.

Given China's poor track record and apparently tough international stance on climate change, pessimism is to be expected. Yet the ascension of China to climate change superpower status may not be the harbinger of gloom and doom that some might expect. In fact, China will benefit enormously from much-needed clean technology transfer, helping not only to alleviate energy security concerns, but precipitating a clean technology revolution by creating unimagined economies of scale to address global climate change. In other words, the country that poses the greatest threat could actually provide the solution. Clean technology venture capital investment in China will reach $580 million in 2007, rise to $720 million in 2008, and is expected to approach $1 billion by the end of this decade.

In 2002, China ratified the Kyoto Protocol, but as a non-Annex I developing country, she is exempt from the current phase (2008–12) of GHG emission cuts. One of the most significant aspects of the Kyoto Protocol is the CDM, which allows developed countries (Annex I Party) to invest in cost effective projects aimed at reducing or sequestrating GHG emissions in developing countries (non-Annex I Party) such as China. The resulting certified emission reductions (CERs) can then be used by the developed country to meet its own emission reduction targets, thus reducing its cost of compliance. For information on China's CDM process, visit http://cdm.ccchina.gov.cn/english/.

Although the CDM got off to a slower start in China than in other large developing countries, such as India and Brazil, China is rapidly catching up and is expected to host upwards of 60 percent of the world's CDM projects. As of mid-July 2007, China had more than 13 percent of the world's CDM projects (ninety-nine registered and more than six hundred approved by China's Designated National Authority and now on the way to the CDM Executive Board for review) and roughly 44.26 percent of expected annual CERs. France, Japan, Canada, and Italy have entered into bilateral agreements with China to establish local CDM centers (sometimes called environmental service centers) at provincial and city levels to help build CDM capacity and pave the way for developing projects with their respective corporate interests.

As China grows as a "clean tech" consumer, domestic innovation and manufacture will be further bolstered with the investment of a significant portion of taxes collected by the $2 billion CDM Fund launched in February. Taxation rates of CERs have been structured in such a way as to incentivize the priority development of renewables, methane, and energy efficiency CDM projects, with a whopping 65 percent rate for the least desirable industrial hydrofluorocarbon (HFC) projects (China produces most of the world's HFC-23) to only 2 percent for high-priority renewables and energy efficiency. According to the Plan, the CDM Fund will also support climate-change-related science and technology research, raising national adaptation and mitigation capacity. Methane capture is poised to become one of the hottest CDM project areas in the next few years as China strives to alleviate water pollution problems caused by manure from the world's largest herds of pigs and flocks of poultry; remove the dangerous gases that make China's mining industry the deadliest in the world; and use ever-mounting landfill waste.

The Renewable Energy Law (http://china.lbl.gov/publications/re-law-english.pdf), which took effect in January 2006, provides for government support in the form of tax breaks, targeted loan subsidies, and special funding for wind, solar, water, and biomass, with the lion's share going to wind. According to a recent report, China intends to spend around $200 billion on renewables in the next fifteen years. The past five years have seen the investment of more than $1 billion in wind turbines in a dozen provinces, with a goal of increasing capacity tenfold by 2020 (from 3.5 gigawatts (GW) to 30 GW). By offering significant financial incentives, China has set ambitious targets for biomass power generation (20 GW by 2020). Although most of China's biomass power is in the bagasse (fiber remaining after extracting sugar from sugarcane) sector, there is significant untapped biomass potential, especially in agricultural and forest residues. However, China lacks mature conversion technologies to harness this energy.

The United States has a very significant role to play in providing funding, technology, and know-how. Companies from China are already tapping American equity markets, creating frenzy over Chinese solar stocks, reflecting the confluence of two major trends: growing interest in clean technology stocks and demand from investors for more plays on China's booming economy. Given China's size, even modest adoption rates of solar, wind, biofuels, and other renewables, could result in significant cost reductions globally. Last year China overtook the United States as the world's third-largest producer of solar panels (mostly for export), coming in after Germany and Japan. China is already the largest producer of solar water heaters in the world with nearly one in ten households owning one, accounting for approximately 60 percent of the world total installed capacity. Wind turbine manufacture is also rapidly growing as the Chinese government is determined to build her domestic industry, demanding that 70 percent of wind turbine equipment purchased for wind farm projects be made with local components. In addition, China is the third-largest biofuels and ethanol producer in the world; she also manufactures 80 percent of the world's energy-saving lights (although local use remains low).

Climate change is also creating other opportunities for China's agricultural sector, raising farmers' incomes by attracting international investment for voluntary emission reduction projects through forest and soil sequestration and biogas from manure and agricultural waste. In addition there are programs supported by the United Nations focusing on provinces that are most susceptible to climate change and fossil-fuel intensive areas in order to analyze the effects of climate change and identify opportunities for mitigation. * * *

The initial trickle of investment in clean technology is becoming a veritable flood, with some describing it as a "clean tech gold rush." China's already voracious appetite for clean tech will likely create one of the most lucrative market opportunities in the next two decades for cleaning up the almost three decades of environmental degradation affecting not only China but neighboring countries and now even the West Coast of the United States. In fact, California is already feeling the effects of Chinese pollution via the jet stream. According to Dr. Steven Cliff, an atmospheric scientist at University of California Davis, "it's apparent that there is a lot of pollution coming from Asia (mostly China), and that pollution is increasing. A persistent Asian plume is evident in the air over California." * * * Fellow researcher, Tony VanCuren at the California Air Resources Board similarly observed that "much of the year, Asian pollution, including soot, ash and dust from farms, motor vehicles, factories and coal-fired power plants hovers high over the Golden State and is on average equal to a quarter of the State's legally allowed concentrations of these particles." And this, of course, is only the pollution that we can see, unlike insidious and invisible climate warming GHGs.

Chinese government officials and environmentalists alike are saying that the only hope to head off environmental catastrophe is through the use of the kind of technology the Silicon Valley offers. Thus, perhaps there is a certain poetic justice to the application of innovative technology and expertise as the "clean tech capital of the world," Silicon Valley, is poised to take advantage of this great opportunity. * * *

With China sprinting past the United States as the largest CO_2 emitter, the pressure is on for some sort of deal after 2012, when the Kyoto Protocol expires. But are we asking too much of China too soon, given the fact that her per capita emissions are only about one fifth of those in the United States? China has coined a new phrase, "Climate Terrorism," to refer to what she sees as the latest weapon in the West's arsenal to hold back China's growth—

the endeavor to impose a cap on GHG emissions. To China, climate change is very much a "fairness" issue. Why should China accept caps on GHGs and slow down her growth when the West has already enjoyed unfettered economic development? Ironically, China's fairness argument provides the United States with a good cover as it continues to spew GHG into the atmosphere while arguing that it will not accept caps without China doing the same. This global game of "chicken" is a game that the world cannot afford to play. While the United States continues to drag its feet, knowing full well that China will not "blink first," China's emissions continue to grow at an alarming rate. Although it will be impossible for China to make absolute reductions, she must make an international commitment to reducing her carbon intensity as the first step. As for the United States, she needs to take leadership in the face of a real WMD (weapon of meteorological destruction), global climate change.

Notes and Questions

1.   Prof. Tseming Yang worries that even if China puts effective climate policies in place, it lacks the regulatory and enforcement structure to see that the policies are implemented. He notes that although China's existing environmental laws and regulations are "fairly extensive and modern," they are "poorly implemented and enforced." T. Yang, The Implementation Challenge of Mitigating China's Greenhouse Gas Emissions, 20 Geo. Int'l. Envtl. L. Rev. 681, 693 (2008). China's legal implementation and enforcement challenges start with "'local protectionism' * * * the tendency of government leaders to shield local businesses from the burdens of environmental regulatory requirements, including enforcement actions." Id. at 694. Other barriers, according to Prof Yang, are national officials' limited ability to control local government action, "China's deficit of democratic governance," the "weakness of the rule of law and supporting institutions" in China, corruption and conflicts of interest. Id. at 695-699.

2.   What are the common climate change interests of the U.S. and China? How should the two nations work together to mitigate climate change? What about the E.U., India, Brazil, Indonesia, Mexico, lesser and least-developed nations?

EDITORIAL: WHO'S AFRAID OF 2°C?
Sunita Narain
Down to Earth (Centre for Science and Environment, India 2009)
www.downtoearth.org/in/cover_nl.asp?mode=1

The latest fuss about the 2°C global temperature target India apparently acceded to at the Major Economies Forum in L'Aquila, Italy, is important to unravel. The declaration by the world's 20 biggest and most powerful countries recognized the scientific view that the increase in global average temperature above pre-industrial levels should not exceed 2°C. The statement was widely criticized in India as a sign we had 'given in' to pressure to take commitments, to cap our emissions. But it was not quite clear why something as obtuse as 2°C equaled a target, so confusion followed. It seemed we were against capping temperature increase at 2°C; we wanted emissions to grow; that temperature increase was bad for us and for the world. The Western media tom-tommed it as another proof India was the renegade in climate negotiations.

Let's sort this issue. It is widely accepted keeping global temperature rise below 2°C, measured from pre-industrial levels (1850), is the threshold that will leash climate change from being 'dangerous' to becoming 'catastrophic'. To put this number into context, consider current average global temperature increase is 0.8°C; add on the fact that another 0.8°C is inevitable, because of the amount of greenhouse gases (GHGs) already pumped into the atmosphere. So, we are already close to the threshold.

Now, let's understand the politics. Once the world accepts the need to cap temperature, it also accepts the need to cap emissions. The 2°C target is possible only if the world limits GHG concentration at 450 ppm CO_{2-e}, taking together the stock and current emissions. It gets complicated here. Think of the atmosphere as a cup of water, filled to the brim. More water can only be filled if the cup is emptied to create space. But since there are many claimants on the water that needs to be filled in the cup, the space will have to be apportioned - budgeted - so that the earlier occupiers vacate and the new claimants fill in, in some proportion of equity.

In other words, the emission budget of 450 ppm CO_{2-e} has to be apportioned, based on equity, between nations. The problem with the L'Aquila declaration is not that it caps the increase in temperature, but that it does not make explicit this limit will require sharing the budget equally between nations who have already used up their common atmospheric space and new entrants to economic growth. Without budget-sharing the temperature cap becomes a virtual cap on the emissions of the developing world, for we are told we will also have to peak in the midterm and take meaningful deviations from our carbon-growth trajectory.

Let us be clear: the space is very limited. We know concentration of all GHG emissions is already close to 430 ppm. But with some 'cooling' allowance, because of aerosols, it comes to 390 - 400 ppm. In sum, not much space remains to be distributed and shared in our intensely unequal world.

But this is not all that confounds the science. The fact is greenhouse gases have a very long life in the atmosphere. Gases released, say, since the late 1800s when the Western world was beginning to industrialize, are still up there. This is the natural debt that needs to be repaid, like the financial debt of nations.

It was for this reason the Kyoto Protocol, agreed in 1997, set emission limits on industrialized countries - they had to reduce so that the developing world could increase. It is a matter of record the emissions of these countries continued to rise. As a result, today there is even less atmospheric space for the developing world to occupy. It is also evident the industrial world did nothing; it knew it needed to fill the space as quickly as possible. Now we have just crumbs to fight over.

It is also no surprise, then, that Western academics are now calling upon the developing world to take on emission reduction targets: there is no space left for them to grow. The logic is simple, though twisted and ingenious. No space left to grow. Ergo, "you cannot ask for the right to pollute," they tell the developing world.

This is unacceptable. We know emissions of carbon dioxide are linked to economic growth, therefore, capping emissions without equal apportionment will mean freezing inequity in this world.

Unacceptable.

We know also that this apportionment is an intensely political decision, for it will determine the way the world will share both the common space and economic growth. It is only when we agree on the formula for sharing that we can agree on how much the already - industrialized countries have to cut and by when, and how much the rest (India included) have to cut and by when.

Instead, what we have is a pincer movement. The already - industrialized do not want to set interim targets to reduce their emissions drastically. They want to change the base - year from when emission reduction will be counted - 2005 or 2007, instead of 1990. This means two things. One, they want to continue to grow (occupy space) in the coming years.

Two, the space they have already occupied - as their emissions vastly increased between 1990 and 2007 - should be forgiven. All this when we know meeting the 450 ppm target requires space to be vacated fast - they must peak within the next few years and then reduce drastically by at least 40 per cent by 2020 over 1990 levels. But why do this, when you can muscle your way into space?

So how will the world share the carbon budget? The only answer is it will have to be based on equity. We will discuss these issues, even as the climate clock ticks.

Notes and Questions

1.   India is the world's fourth largest emitter of CO_2; it emitted 1,511 million metric tons of CO_2 in 2005. Its CO_2 emissions more than doubled from 1990 to 2005. From 1950 to 2005 India emitted about 23.8 billion metric tons of CO_2. Its trajectory is one of increased growth in use of coal for electricity and oil for its rapidly growing fleet of cars. However, if it is unwilling to reduce its energy, GHG emissions will grow without significant equitable concessions from the industrialized world.

India's National Action Plan on Climate (Jan 2008) confirms this approach to equity officially: "We are convinced that the principle of equity that must underlie the global approach must all each inhabitant of the earth an equal entitlement to the global atmospheric source. In this connection, India is determined that its per capita greenhouse gas emissions will at no point exceed that of developed countries even as we pursue our development goals." http://www.indiaenvironmentportal.org.in/files/napcc.pdf. Developments in policy and law in India regarding climate change can be studied through "Indepth: The   Climate   Change   on   India   Environment   Portal,"   at www.indiaenvironmentportal.org.in/indepth/term/1937.

2.   If China and India stay on their present business as usual path, their emissions will grow so large that even if the United State and Europe went to zero, GHG concentration will continue to rise well past any safe level. China and India have a stake in the outcome of global negotiations—their coastal cities will flood and their major fresh water sources in glaciers and the Himalayas will diminish. Is the argument over cumulative emissions resolvable?

3.   India's universities and schools are adopting innovative practices to manage their own natural resources and environmental impacts. The Center for Science and Environment in India has established the *Gobar Times Green Schools Award,* to acknowledge leading academic institutions. See www.cseindia.org/programme/eeu/html/awards.asp?id=5 . Should comparable academic recognition programs be established for countries like China or the USA? The Sierra Club ranks U.S. universities for their environmental sustainability   programs.   Where   does   your   university   rank?   See http://www.sierraclub.org/sierra/200909/coolschools/default.aspx.

D. THE LAW THAT MUST BE MADE: A NEW INTERNATIONAL CLIMATE CHANGE PARADIGM

Human civilization has entered the Anthropocene era, a time in which human activities constitute the overarching force that alters the Earth. To focus on "climate" alone is to neglect the damage being done to the food chains and ecosystems upon which humans depend. To focus on "cap and trade" as a business-like way to curb greenhouse gas emissions is to neglect the depletion of forests and extinction of species. Humans put themselves at risk to disease and other perils when they destroy the Earth's biological diversity. Negotiating a climate agreement without linking it to the other multilateral environmental agreements is to continue tinkering with the web of life, one strand at a time. The web is measurably weaker.

The message of the Intergovernmental Panel on Climate Change is clear, but little heeded by governments or corporations or the public. The atmosphere has a maximum level of carbon dioxide that it can absorb without irrevocably altering all life on Earth. M. Allen, et al., The Exit Strategy, Nature Reports (30 April 2009), www.nature.com/reports/climatechantge. Internationally a cumulative carbon budget can be framed, but the reluctance to do so among governments precludes doing so. How close to irreversibility can civilization risk approaching? S. Solomon, et al., Irreversible Climate Change Due to Carbon Dioxide Emissions, 106 Proceedings of the National Academy of Science 1704-1709 (2009) www.pnas.org/cgi/doi/10.1073/pnas.o812721106 (February 10, 2009).

If we were to limit our cumulative emissions from 2000 to 2050 to 1,000 Gt CO_2 (one trillion tons) there is a 75% chance that the global will not warm more that 2°C. A limit of 1,440 Gt CO_2 would mean a 50% chance that the earth would warm more than 2°C. Between 2000 and 2006 234 Gt CO_2 were emitted, leaving 766 Gts to go. To achieve that goal we must limit ourselves to using less than half of the world's presently proven economically recoverable oil, gas and coal reserves. M. Meinshausen, et al., Greenhouse-gas emission Targets for Limiting Global Warming to 2°C, 458 Nature 1158 (2009). Setting emission limits based on limiting cumulative emissions of carbon dioxide is "more robust to scientific uncertainty than emission-rate or concentration targets." M. Allen et al., Warming Caused by Cumulative Carbon Emissions Towards the Trillionth Tonne, 458 Nature 1163 (2009).

The world in 2005 emitted about 37.8 billion tons CO_{2eq} (27.5 billion tons of CO_2). World Resources Institute Climate Analysis Indicators Tool (CAIT) Version 6.0. (2009) http://cait.wri.org. At the present rate we will reach maximum emissions in about 20 years.

How should the 766 billion tons be allocated? Consider the following proposal.

DESIGNING A GLOBAL POST-KYOTO CLIMATE CHANGE PROTOCOL THAT ADVANCES HUMAN DEVELOPMENT
Albert Mumma and David Hodas
20 Geo. Int'l Envtl. L. Rev. 619 (2008)

A GLOBAL CAP ON GHG CONCENTRATIONS AS A DRIVER FOR ENERGY EFFICIENCY

At a philosophical level we trust that the free market will again do its innovation magic once the cap is established, the proper price signals are given to the marketplace, policy barriers are removed, and the private sector recognizes the profit opportunities presented. The consistent history of environmental law has been that before legal mandates are imposed, there is often no technology to achieve a given goal, or at a minimum, in a cost-effective fashion. This should come as no surprise to anyone familiar with welfare economics—if no firm seeks to buy pollution control technology then no firm will invest in developing it. However, once the mandate is firmly in place, the opportunity for profit appears and the market responds with remarkable innovation, and the costs of meeting the mandate drop precipitously from the sky-high estimates businesses suggest when there is no market. Examples are legion: elimination of lead from gasoline, elimination of CFCs, the Clean Air Act SO_2 allowance program to reduce acid precipitation. We believe that a combination of energy efficiency investments and renewable energy will go a long way, and relatively quickly, towards meeting both the cap on GHG concentrations in the atmosphere and the sustainable development of even the poorest nations.

Clearly, fossil fuels and nuclear power will be needed, but they are too costly financially and environmentally to be the centerpiece of the world's energy supply. The fact that most people cannot imagine how the world could survive in a low-carbon economy does not change the reality that the free market always responds to the demands and limitations a society chooses, so long as the market is given the freedom to innovate. In 1961 the world understood the physics required to put a person on the moon but had no idea how to do it. In 1969 it was done, and along the way the world developed whole new technologies, dreamed of only by science fiction writers.

Clearly, developing nation economies need to grow. Some 1.5 to 2 billion people in the world have no access to electricity. They have no light at night (unless they burn kerosene or candles), no refrigeration, no radio. They have no cars or trucks. They burn (unsustainably) biomass to cook. Providing the poor access to modern energy sources would increase fossil fuel consumption. Even under the most efficient scenario, sustainable development in the developing world will require that a GHG emissions cap be imposed on developing nations and the poorest nations that will allow their economies to grow. As we discussed above, that is the meaning of common but differentiated responsibilities.

However, the international community also can expect (demand) that the cap must reflect an economy that uses energy very efficiently and maximizes the use of low carbon energy. Many developing countries have a low per capita energy use, and a low CO_2 per capita emission rate, but those rates may well be much higher than need be because the energy is used so inefficiently.

Unfortunately, in many developing countries, energy use has become less efficient over time, that is, energy intensity, and energy consumed per unit of output is increasing. Thus, in setting caps, the international community must insist that efficient per capita GHG emissions are required. On the other hand, "[a] number of technical studies have shown that if developing countries were to use the best practices and technology now available, dramatic declines in new energy requirements would theoretically be possible."

The world simply cannot let any energy go to waste. Critical social and economic progress is at risk. It may well be that the electricity shortage crisis in South Africa could have been averted or drastically mitigated, for example, if sound energy efficiency policies had been in place—instead it was "an energy-profligate nation." Moreover, the cost of making additional electric power available by using it more efficiently is far less than the cost of constructing new coal-fired power plants, and does not increase GHG emissions. That saved capital could have been available for education, infrastructure, health care, and other high priority social needs. What is important for all economies is not its energy use per capita, but whether the society efficiently obtains the energy services it needs to prosper—light, heat, cooling, transportation, electric power for motors and computers, etc.

So, what is the contribution that energy efficiency can make in a world with ever increasing demand for energy services? It is enormous. One major study estimates that improving the productive use of energy could reduce global growth in energy demand to less than 1 percent annually, inexpensively, using "existing technologies with an [internal rate of return] of 10% or more. This would free up resources to increase consumption or investment elsewhere." Additionally, this energy productivity improvement would "contribute up to a half of the GHG emission abatement required to cap the long-term concentration at 450 to 550 parts per million." The economic potential may be much higher since the McKinsey study eliminates all investments with an internal rate of return of less than 10 percent, and does not factor in the emergence of new technologies; also it was predicated on the price of oil being US$70 a barrel. Thus the actual technical potential improvement in energy productivity is much larger. Another recent study found remarkable efficiency improvement potential in residential and commercial buildings, appliances, industry, and transportation.

THE NEED FOR POLICY REFORMS

However, market forces alone are insufficient to capture the energy efficiency opportunities available. It is now well established that to achieve the technical potential of energy, efficiency policies must be put into place that make it possible for firms to profit by supply energy services through energy efficiency investments. Policies must be adopted that remove fossil fuel subsidies, a serious problem in developing countries. Also, policies must be adopted that help remove the many barriers that efficiency investments must overcome. These include, informational, institutional, behavioral, financial, and legal barriers, large and small, that make the transactional costs of becoming more energy efficient too high to overcome the inertia inherent in business as usual. Principle-agent or split incentives such as those between landlord and tenant or builder and buyer, lack of adequate information, lack of access to capital and a variety of other problems deter investments in energy efficiency even though those investments are the least-cost means of increasing usable energy for the economy and society. Policy approaches to eliminate these barriers are well known but must be discussed more concretely another time.

On the other hand, if good legal policies are adopted, many of these barriers can be removed. Preliminary results of a recent study of eight states indicate that between 95.7 and 99.5 percent of a state's energy efficiency profile is determined by the kind of laws and policies the jurisdiction has implemented. For example, by adopting ambitious energy efficiency standards for refrigerators, in California (and now the whole U.S. nation) the average refrigerator now uses about 75 percent less electricity than it did in 1977, while average refrigerator size increased more than 20 percent and the cost of a refrigerator dropped more than 60 percent.

In developing countries, where light is provided either by candle or kerosene, or, if electricity is available, by an inexpensive incandescent bulb, new LED light technology could provide light using only 1 watt of power, which could be generated by a small solar panel and backed up by ordinary rechargeable batteries; total costs: US$25. These are examples of the astounding efficiency opportunities, that can be remotely powered without having to construct power plants or transmission lines, and that will provide light where none was before, or will eliminate GHG from burning fossil fuels or biomass. These LEDs are 1000 times more efficient at generating light than fuel based light (candles or kerosene), produce no indoor pollution, and have the potential, if they replaced fuel-based lighting, to save the equivalent of about 1.3 million barrels of oil per day. That would be a savings, at US$100 per barrel oil, of about US$130 million per day—over US$47 billion per year—mostly in the poorest nations in the world, and virtually all of this money would be used to import the fuel. Reinvesting these savings in other energy efficient technologies could multiply the savings, while simultaneously improving the lives of over a billion people. And, as an added benefit, it would eliminate the 190 million tons of CO_2 released annually when the fuel is burned.

So, in our view, placing a GHG emissions cap—or an emissions entitlement—-on developing countries need not compromise their opportunities for sustainable development: what matters is the level at which the cap is placed. * * * [I]n determining the appropriate level of GHG emissions entitlement for each country account must be taken not only of the overall global GHG concentrations cap, but also of the present stage of economic development of the particular country as well as the level of efficiency of its energy use.

VI. PROPOSALS FOR A POST KYOTO PROTOCOL CLIMATE CHANGE REGIME

For the system we propose to operate equitably and without leakage, *all* countries must be allocated emission entitlements or rights to emit GHGs as a slice of the overall global cap. This is on account of the fact that the GHG emissions allocations are in essence entitlements to emit a defined volume of GHG in the course of productive and consumptive activities. This is because when a cap on the overall volumes that may be emitted globally without causing dangerous anthropogenic global warming is established, GHG emissions will become an exhaustible global resource. This limited stock of GHG emissions must therefore be shared equitably among all the nations.

A. EQUITY AS THE BASIS FOR ALLOCATING GHG EMISSION ENTITLEMENTS

The poor countries' position at negotiations for a post Kyoto protocol should be that the allocation of emission entitlements should be based on the sustainable development principle of intra-generational equity, i.e., equity among the present generations. Intra-generational equity requires that the world's resources—in this case GHGs emission rights—be allocated equitably among all nations since the emission entitlements, in effect, are a proxy for the right to develop and meet the needs of one's nation and the well-being of its people.

Poor countries' position at the post Kyoto regime negotiations must be that the basis of equitable allocation should be the Human Development Index developed by the U.N. Development Program (UNDP) combined with historic GHG emissions, energy use increases needed to improve low HDI and associated Human Poverty indices, and the efficiency with which energy is used. The Human Development Index is more nuanced than the principle of per capita emissions, which currently dominates the discussions regarding the formula for assigning responsibility for mitigating climate change.

It is easy for the developing nations to argue on the basis of per capita emissions of the developed world is primarily responsible for historic GHG emissions: collectively, the United States, Russia, Germany, United Kingdom, France, Japan, Canada and Poland account for about 70 percent of all the CO_2 that has been emitted since 1840.[82] On a per capita basis, the historic emissions of the United States (about 1,100 tons per person) are more than an order of magnitude greater than those of China (about 66 tons per person) and India (about 23 tons per person). Moreover, this disparity continues in terms of current GHG emissions. The United States (20.4 tons per person) emits far more per person than China (3.8) or India (1.2). However, the gross national carbon footprint of some developing nations, such as China and India, are large and growing rapidly. These historic emissions created today's climate change problem and have consumed much of the atmosphere's absorption capacity—"[i]n effect, the ecological 'space' available for future emissions is determined by past action."

The sole use of per capita emissions is inappropriate on two grounds. First, the UNFCCC defines the relations and obligations of nation states, not individuals within those nation states. Under international law, rights are held by nation states, not individuals within the state. Therefore the allocations must be aggregated and assigned to the state. Since each nation has the "sovereign right to exploit their own resources pursuant to their own environmental and development policies," the international community has no way of ensuring the equitable per capita allocation of the emission entitlements to the population within the nation state. Additionally, as we have argued, the concept of per capita emissions must be qualified by the introduction of considerations arising from the efficiency of the use of the energy allocated. Given that sustainable development is all about inter- and intra-generational equity, the principle of per capita emissions on its own does not form a sufficient basis for determining emission entitlements to the nation state.

B. A WORLD OF THREE GROUPS

The following two factors comprise our proposed formula for equitably allocating a global GHG cap:

a. The present per capita emissions of each country: the higher a country's present per capita emissions the less the volume of GHG emissions to which the country is entitled for future emissions.

b. The potential capacity of a country for future per capita emissions: the higher a country's potential capacity for future per capita emissions the lower the volume of GHGs to which the country is entitled for future emissions.

The volume allocated would be the average of these two factors. Consequently, countries with historically low responsibility and low potential for future GHG emissions would be entitled to the highest allocations of emissions rights under a post Kyoto Protocol climate change mitigation regime. Into this category fall predominantly African countries, but also other small economies in Asia, as well as many of the small island states. Conversely, countries with historically high responsibility for emissions and a high potential for future emissions would be allocated the lowest emissions entitlements. Into this category fall predominantly Annex I countries. The third category of countries is countries with historically low responsibility for GHG emissions but high potential for future GHG emissions. Into this category fall the large newly industrializing countries of China, India, Brazil, Mexico, South Africa, and other rapidly industrializing economies. This category of countries would be allocated moderate emission entitlements.

As can be seen, resort to this Equitable Emissions Index as the basis for determining emission entitlements gives rise to three, and not two, categories of countries. It provides a way out of the impasse that has bogged down discussions on climate change mitigation since its inception and provides a win-win formula based on equity.

An allocation based on this principle would mean that countries with low emission allocations would be forced to utilize the flexible mechanisms by carrying out development projects/activities in countries with high emission entitlements, in which most benefit is to be derived in emissions avoidance. Poor—low carbon emitting—countries which currently have limited attraction for those investing in projects under the Clean Development Mechanism, would derive economic development benefits through "clean development" options (energy efficient development activities that avoid high GHG emissions).

Middle nations, such as China, would still have the ability to grow, and could use that cap to attract significant capital investment from developed countries. Such investments could finance improving the efficiency of China's coal fired power plants from 30 to 45 percent by 2030, which would reduce China's emissions about 1.8 gigatons of CO_2 less than projected—a reduction equivalent to about one-half of the European Union's current CO_2 emissions. Energy efficiency investments will lower GHG emissions, lower the emissions of other pollutants, and reduce a nation's energy costs. The existing low levels of energy efficiency in developing nations impair mitigation of GHG emissions. Investments that raise energy efficiency levels could transform that serious challenge to mitigation "into an opportunity, generating large gains for human development in the process." Although developing countries will benefit from energy efficiency through reduced energy costs and reduced pollution generally, and the world will benefit from the low cost reductions in CO_2 emissions, "unfortunately, the world lacks a credible mechanism for unlocking this win-win scenario."

Our proposal could help provide a key to unlocking this potential. This design leads to a number of features, which makes it a win-win solution to the climate change mitigation dilemma.

(i) It recognizes that allocation of emission rights represent a right to utilize Earth's resources for development.

(ii) It gives effect to the sustainable development principle of intragenerational equity, allocating the largest development rights (represented by emission entitlements) to the poorest countries.

(iii) It places all countries under reduction/avoidance obligations and therefore eliminates the key objection, which led the U.S. not to ratify the Kyoto Protocol, that potentially future large emitters have no reduction/avoidance obligations under Kyoto Protocol.

(iv) It ensures that the risk of leakage arising from CDM projects, jeopardizing the chances of achieving the ultimate objective of UNFCCC, is minimized.

(v) It eliminates the marginalization of poor countries, in particular countries in Africa, in the implementation of the market based flexible mechanisms, since these poor but GHG resource-rich countries would be the automatic choice for CDM projects. Currently the lion's share of the CDM projects are being undertaken in the countries with the largest potential for future emissions, mainly China and India, and Africa has a negligible proportion of projects.

(vi) It facilitates the flow of funds through private sector driven market based projects (rather than development aid) from industrialized to nonindustrialized countries.

THE PROBLEM THAT MUST BE SOLVED

Critique the Mumma/Hodas proposal. How many tons should each nation get? What does a paradigm shift look like? Does it seek to rethink assumptions? To integrate previously isolated ideas into a new whole? Is the proposal a good or bad idea? Why? How could it be improved? What alternatives might be preferable? What needs to be done to move this idea into concrete law? Is it technology forcing? Would it promote developing nations to follow the rule of law? Does it address the leakage problems that make forestry offsets and CDM projects so problematic?

Is it so widely off-target that it should not even be considered? If so, what different approach would be better?

Based on everything you have studied thus far, develop and justify a method of allocating among the nations and people of the world the remaining 766 billion tons of CO_{2e} that can be emitted over the next 50 years so that the global temperature increase might be limited to 2° C. What factors should be considered? How much weight should each factor be given? Go to the CAIT database, www.cait.wri.org. Pick three different countries in different regions of the world and at different stages of development. Assess each country across the social, economic, environmental, and energy factors you would use as valid, reliable measures of equity that should be included in an allocation scheme? Why should all the nations of the world agree to this formula? What else might be needed to achieve consensus? Draft language that should be in a climate treaty to make this allocation a legally binding obligation.

Notes and Questions

Carbon Neutral Law Schools: Law schools are always "becoming," adapting to new challenges and teaching lawyers to cope with ever changing legal conditions. Law schools are places that need to be continuously re-inventing their curriculum and their tools. Rapid changes in technology have permitted law schools to remake legal research and communications and refine practice skills. As law schools respond to climate change mitigation and adaptation, many questions will emerge beyond those presented in this book. Climate change means that the USA or EU or Chinese or Brazilian legal systems cannot protect themselves from adverse effects unless all nations harmonize their behavior. Yet, half the governments around the Earth lack effective rule of law. More than half the nations could not develop such a plan like the Delaware Plan without international assistance, and even with a plan the weakness of executive and judicial branches mean that aspects of the plan could be corrupted.

For the protection of the Stratospheric Ozone Layer, the Montreal Protocol built up a legal system to contain and curb Ozone Depleting Substances (ODS) that were also greenhouse gases. The ODS program is world-wide but very focused and narrow in scope, and reasonably well resourced nations created a special implementation and compliance regime for one class of gas. Climate change mitigation is far more extensive and this in turn requires a robust rule of law. Yet few share a recognition that the rule of law is a climate change priority. In 2008 the ABA House of Delegates adopted a formal position on climate change:

> **RESOLVED**, that the American Bar Association urges the United States government to take a leadership role in addressing the issue of climate change through legal, policy, financial, and educational mechanisms.
>
> **FURTHER RESOLVED**, that the American Bar Association urges Congress to enact and the President to sign legislation that would:
> * Cap and reduce United States greenhouse gas emissions to help prevent the rise of worldwide atmospheric greenhouse gas concentrations to dangerous levels;
> * Utilize market mechanisms designed to minimize compliance costs, such as cap and trade, carbon taxation, or emissions trading;
> * Recognize and incorporate sustainable development principles;
> * Increase fuel economy and energy efficiency standards, promote greater use of renewable energy, promote fuel diversity through the use of carbon neutral or low carbon technologies that reduce, eliminate, or sequester emissions of greenhouse gases and minimize costs of controls or mitigation measures;
> * Provide for broad coverage of various sectors of the economy
> *

responsible for greenhouse gas emissions;

- Enable the United States to adapt to existing and projected climate changes in a way that minimizes individual hardship, damage to its natural resources, and economic cost;
- Coordinate and integrate state and local actions into a federal program; and
- Require the United States government to encourage all other countries to take steps to limit their greenhouse gas emissions so that world levels of emissions will be reduced to prevent dangerous anthropogenic climate change.

FURTHER RESOLVED, that the American Bar Association urges the United States government to engage in active international discussions and to negotiate and ratify treaties or other agreements to address and reduce climate change.

The American Bar Association's rule of law programs has had virtually no support from the federal or state governments, and very modest support from governments abroad. In late 2007, the UN General Assembly has created a rule of law unit reporting directly to the UN Secretary General, to help countries build the rule of law both nationally and internationally. These programs are not well financed and admit that they are insufficient to build the rule of law? No world-wide intergovernmental agency provides capacity-building for judicial integrity.

Will the deep and diverse challenges of climate change mitigation and adaptation require law schools around the world to do more to make the rule of law a reality? What can your law school do? Since most law schools in developing nations lack adequate resources to meet ABA accreditation standards for legal education, what steps should your law school do to build the capacity of law schools in other lands to provide the legal education needed for designing and building climate change mitigation and adaptation laws?

E. CONCLUDING THOUGHTS

What will be required to make the paradigm shift from a human economy that destroys the strands of life in the Biosphere to one that sustains the biodiversity? The Delaware Plan illustrates that the change can be begun. Agents of this paradigm shift include scientists, engineers, lawyers, manufacturers, and others. Many different visions of a new regime of global cooperation exist. See, e.g., P. Brown et al., Right Relationship: Building A Whole Earth Economy (2009). Science has presented a new image of Earth and how we humans live with it. For many, the findings of the IPCC constitute a revolutionary new way of understanding the previously unthinkable abandonment of tried and true fossil fuels and society's long-standing investment in them. In the past the acceptance of comparable scientific revolutions has been slow. Will the Internet, nearly instantaneous global communications, unprecedented monitoring from space and all regions of the planet, tremendous computer modeling capacity, and the capacity to induce revolutionary technological innovations be deployed to allow humans to stabilize the climate? In short, will decision-makers recognize that the Anthropocene era is a revolutionary new reality? Will the Anthropocene era's scientific revolution take hold in time to restabilize the Earth's carbon cycle?

INDEX